Teacher's Edition

by
Siegfried Haenisch

AGS Publishing
Circle Pines, Minnesota 55014-1796
800-328-2560
www.agsnet.com

About the Author

Siegfried Haenisch, Ed.D., holds a master's degree in mathematics and has taught mathematics at every level, from elementary to graduate school, most recently as Professor in the Department of Mathematics and Statistics at the College of New Jersey. The Mathematical Association of America granted him the 1995 Award for Distinguished Teaching of Mathematics. Dr. Haenisch was the site director for the training of teachers in the New Jersey Algebra Project. He was a member of the National Science Foundation Institutes in Mathematics at Rutgers University, Oberlin College, and Princeton University. At Yale University, he was a member of the Seminar in the History of Mathematics, sponsored by the National Endowment in the Humanities. Dr. Haenisch currently serves as a mathematics curriculum consultant to school districts.

Photo credits for this textbook can be found on page 524.

The publisher wishes to thank the following educators for their helpful comments during the review process for *Mathematics: Pathways*. Their assistance has been invaluable.

Laura L. Duff, Teacher Consultant Mathematics, Northside Independent School District, San Antonio, Texas; **Merilyn Fox,** Teacher, Henry Kelsey Sr. P. S., Scarborough, Ontario, Canada; **Karen Jackman,** Math Teacher, Newburg Middle School, Louisville, Kentucky; **Toby Ann Nitardy,** EBD Resource Teacher, Campbell County Middle School, Alexandria, Kentucky; **Bethanne Pearce,** Scientific Learning Disabilities Math Teacher, Tomlin Middle School, Plant City, Florida; **Peter Saarimaki,** Educational Consultant—Mathematics, Psycan Corporation, Scarborough, Ontario, Canada; **Märit C. Sheffield,** Teacher, Jamacha Middle Community School, Spring Valley, California; **Larry Stott,** District Mathematics Coordinator, West High School, Salt Lake City, Utah; **Wade T. Williford,** Teacher, Carlsbad Village Academy, Carlsbad, California

Publisher's Project Staff

Vice President, Product Development: Kathleen T. Williams, Ph.D., NCSP; Associate Director, Product Development: Teri Mathews; Assistant Editors: Karen Anderson and Sarah Brandel; Development Assistant: Bev Johnson; Creative Services Manager: Nancy Condon; Senior Designers: Daren Hastings and Diane McCarty; Desktop Production Artists: Jack Ross and Peggy Vlahos; Purchasing Agent: Mary Kaye Kuzma; Senior Marketing Manager/Secondary Curriculum: Brian Holl

Editorial and production services provided by The Mazer Corporation

© 2004 AGS Publishing
4201 Woodland Road
Circle Pines, MN 55014-1796
800-328-2560 • www.agsnet.com

AGS Publishing is a trademark and trade name of American Guidance Service, Inc.

Printed in the United States of America

ISBN 0-7854-3605-7

Product Number 93872

A 0 9 8 7 6 5 4 3 2

Contents

Mathematics: Pathways will prepare your students for the next level of math learning. The text uses a step-by-step approach to teach basic mathematic concepts and introduce algebra. The text meets the standards set by most states and the National Council of Teachers of Mathematics (NCTM). Because students learn in many different ways, emphasis is placed on instruction that uses a variety of modalities to promote concept mastery.

The text is organized into 13 discrete chapters. Chapters open with a photograph and description of an application of the chapter content. These real-life applications help students see the relevance of what they are studying. Goals for Learning introduce students to key objectives in each chapter.

Problem-solving strategies are presented in the How to Use This Book section of the student text. A four-step method of solving problems encourages students to think about how they approach word problems. To extend this concept, problem-solving examples are presented throughout the book to help students apply their new math skills. To encourage the use of calculators, exercises are included with suggested problems when applicable.

Short lessons with lots of examples illustrate and teach each new skill. Rules are highlighted for quick reference. Math terms are defined in the side column and in the glossary. The curriculum includes hands-on manipulative activities and exercises that have students construct models and demonstrate selected lesson concepts. Frequent sets of activities let students practice their newly acquired skills. Sample solutions are provided in the back of the text for the first activity in each exercise set, along with the answers to all odd-numbered problems. In addition to the many opportunities for practice within a lesson, supplemental problems in the back of the student text offer extra reinforcement.

As recommended by NCTM, students are encouraged to write about mathematics. To promote understanding and motivation, problem-solving exercises are integrated throughout the lessons. These exercises present real-life situations that require mathematical thinking and analysis. To extend this concept, an Application Activity is included with each chapter. These activities help students relate concepts to everyday situations and allow them to connect math instruction with the real world.

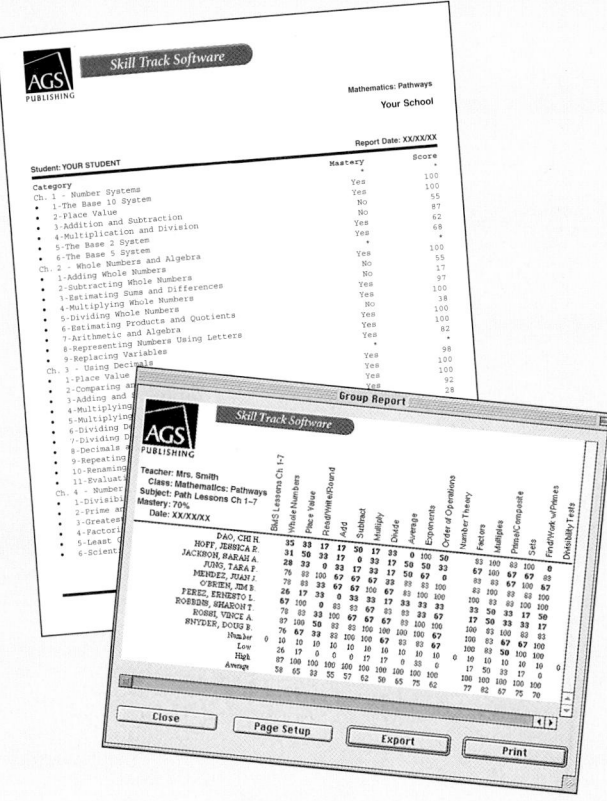

Skill Track Software The Skill Track Software program allows students using AGS Publishing textbooks to be assessed for mastery of each chapter and lesson of the textbook. Students access the software on an individual basis and are assessed with multiple choice items.

Students can enter the program through two paths:

Lesson

Six items assess mastery of each lesson.

Chapter

Two parallel forms of chapter assessments are provided to determine chapter mastery. The two forms are equal in length and cover the same concepts with different items. The number of items in each chapter assessment varies by chapter, as the items are drawn from content of each lesson in the textbook.

The program includes high-interest graphics to accompany the items. Students are allowed to retake the chapter or lesson assessments over again at the instructor's discretion. The instructor has the ability to run and print out a variety of reports to track students' progress.

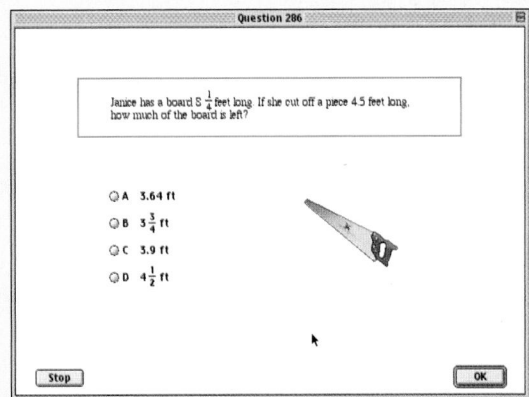

Interest Level: Grades 6–12

Focus your math lessons with Teaching Strategies in Math Transparencies.

This transparency set contains graphic organizers that present concepts in a meaningful, visual way. They stimulate learning and discussion, while teaching students how to manage information.

Types of graphic organizers include:

◆ Number Line
◆ Venn Diagram
◆ Concept Web
◆ Spider Map
◆ Circle Organizer
◆ Network Tree
◆ Three-Column Chart
◆ Problem-Solving Strategy

This transparency set provides teachers with clear objectives and teaching strategies. You're shown how to introduce each transparency to your students, followed by ways to practice, apply, check-up, and extend the use of each graphic organizer.

For more information on AGS Publishing worktexts and textbooks:
call 800-328-2560, visit our Web site at www.agsnet.com, or e-mail AGS Publishing at agsmail@agsnet.com.

Enhance your math program with AGS Publishing textbooks—an easy, effective way to teach students the practical skills they need. Each AGS Publishing textbook meets your math curriculum needs. These exciting, full-color books use student-friendly text and real-world examples to show students the relevance of math in their daily lives. Each presents a comprehensive coverage of skills and concepts. The short, concise lessons will motivate even your most reluctant students. With readabilities of all the texts below fourth grade reading level, your students can concentrate on learning the content. AGS Publishing is committed to making learning accessible to all students.

Guidelines for Using Manipulatives

The manipulative activities in the *Mathematics: Pathways* Teacher's Edition are intended to develop students' mathematical understanding at a concrete level. Manipulatives are used to build visual representations, or models, of algebraic concepts and relationships and their symbols. Students who are introduced to algebraic concepts through the use of manipulatives will develop an understanding of symbolic representations and algorithms more quickly and in a deeper, more internalized manner. For this reason, the manipulative activities are presented along with *Teaching the Lesson* in the three-step lesson plan.

To successfully include manipulatives into your mathematics program, here are some general guidelines:

◆ When an activity or concept is first introduced, spend as much time as necessary on guided practice in order for students to understand the use of the manipulatives before they begin using them independently.

◆ Students should have manipulatives available at their desks during group instruction so they can practice the activity along with your explanation.

◆ Present the activities in order. Students will develop their understanding of the use of the manipulatives in small, incremental steps.

◆ Repetition is important. The suggested exercises represent the minimum amount of practice necessary for most students. For students who require more practice, additional exercises are available in the Student Workbook.

◆ The term *symbolic equivalent* is used to refer to the mathematical symbols and terms that represent algebraic concepts and relationships. Students need to recognize the connection between the manipulative models and the symbols used to represent them. For this reason, students should sketch each model they build and write the corresponding symbolic equivalent.

◆ Help students develop the habit of using the manipulatives to check their work. Reviewing and evaluating one's own work is a metacognitive skill that improves problem-solving ability.

Manipulatives Used with Mathematics: Pathways

All of the ETA/Cuisenaire® manipulatives used with *Mathematics: Pathways* are available for purchase from AGS Publishing. Call 800-328-2560 and request product number 93885. For your information and planning, the chart below shows the manipulatives used throughout program. In addition, the Teacher's Resource Library (TRL) includes Manipulatives Masters 1–5 (shown below).

Basics for Using Algebra Tiles™

Algebra Tiles are a set of colorful plastic pieces used to represent positive and negative variables. Instructions for their use follow.

Identifying the Algebra Tiles Pieces The edge of the Algebra Tiles shape represents a variable or a number. A long edge represents x and a short edge represents 1. The large square represents x^2, the rectangle represents $1x$, and the small square represents 1. Shapes that are the same are congruent and represent like terms. Congruency is not affected by color.

Type of ETA/Cuisenaire® Manipulative	Chapter Reference												
	1	2	3	4	5	6	7	8	9	10	11	12	13
Base Ten Blocks	✔	✔	✔										
Base Ten Mat		✔											
Pattern Blocks		✔							✔		✔		
Cuisenaire Rods		✔		✔	✔		✔	✔	✔				
Algebra Tiles				✔		✔					✔		
Two-Color Counters	✔												✔
1-6 Number Cubes													✔
Other										✔		✔	

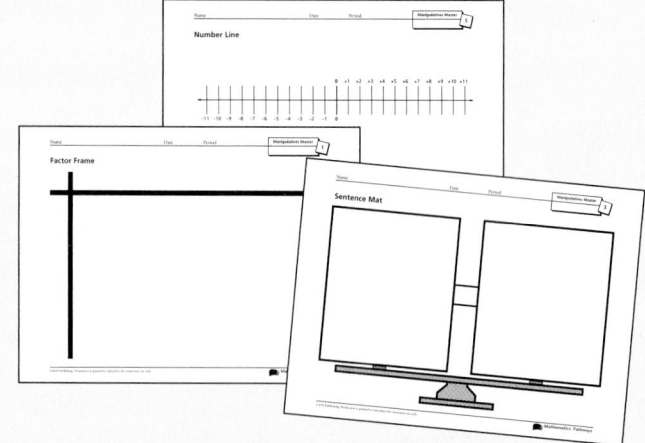

Modeling Expressions A variety of algebraic expressions can be modeled with the Algebra Tiles shapes.

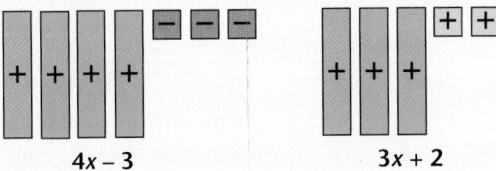

$4x - 3$ 　　　　 $3x + 2$

The Zero Rule When a value and its additive inverse are combined, the result is zero. The additive inverse of each Algebra Tiles shape is represented by the congruent piece of a different color. When you combine two pieces of the same shape but different color (and sign), the result is zero. When you combine terms or simplify expressions, you can add or remove pairs of additive inverses without changing the value of the expression. This is referred to as *applying the Zero Rule.*

Using the Factor Frame The Factor Frame (Manipulatives Master 1) is used with the Algebra Tiles and the Cuisenaire® Rods to model factoring.

Factoring and Finding the GCD: The greatest common divisor of two terms is found by building rectangles with the largest possible common dimension inside two Factor Frames. Each term is placed inside a Factor Frame. As shown below with Algebra Tiles, it is possible to find a common factor of two terms that is not, however, the *greatest* common factor.

$4x - 8$

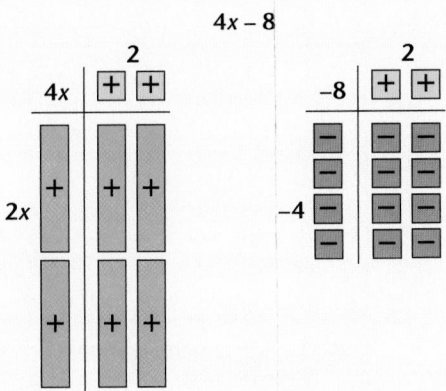

The largest common dimension (2) is written outside the parentheses: 2( ). The terms that remain are written inside the parentheses: $2(2x - 4)$. There is still another factor common to these terms. The following figure shows the arrangement of factors that identifies the GCD, which is 4.

$4x - 8$

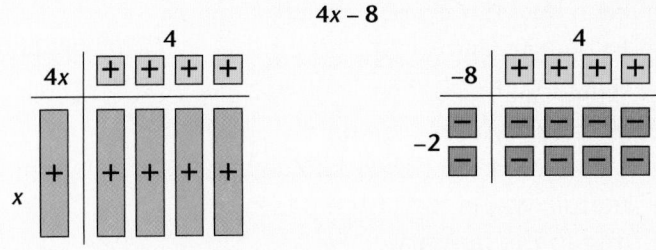

To write the symbolic equivalent, the GCD is written outside the parentheses, while the remaining factors replace the original terms inside the parentheses: $4(x - 2)$.

Finding Prime Factors: To find the prime factors of a number, use the Cuisenaire Rods to build a rectangular model of the number in the Factor Frame. Use any convenient dimensions. Identify which factors are prime and not prime. Continue to build rectangular models of factors that are not prime until only prime factors are left. The following example illustrates finding the prime factors of 48.

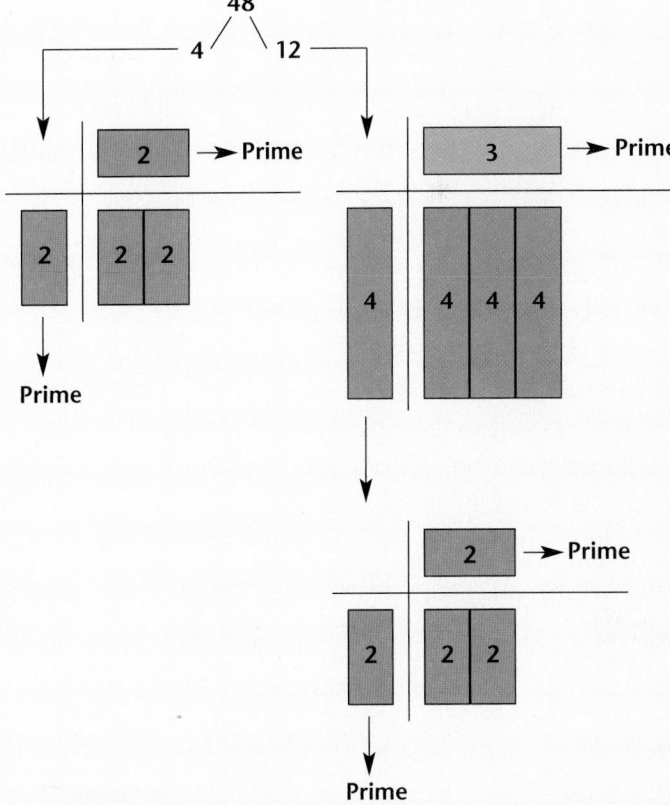

The prime factorization of 48 is $2 \cdot 2 \cdot 2 \cdot 2 \cdot 3$ or $2^4 \cdot 3$.

Student Text Highlights

◆ Each lesson is clearly labeled to help students focus on the skill or concept to be learned.

◆ Vocabulary terms are bold-faced and then defined in the margin at the top of the page and in the glossary.

◆ Reminder notes and tips help students recall and apply what they already know.

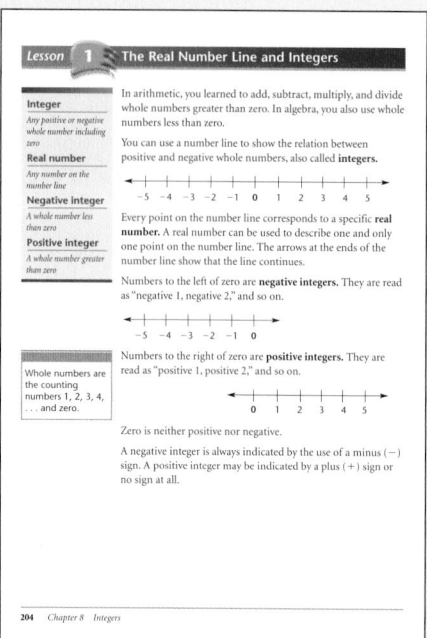

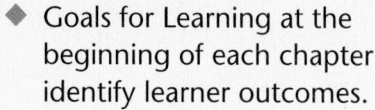

Real number

Any number on the number line

Whole numbers are the counting numbers 1, 2, 3, 4, . . . and zero.

◆ Goals for Learning at the beginning of each chapter identify learner outcomes.

Goals for Learning

◆ To identify the absolute value of integers

◆ To compare the values of negative and positive whole numbers

◆ To add and subtract integers

◆ To multiply and divide integers

◆ Problem-solving exercises give students opportunities to use skills they have learned to solve practical problems.

◆ Simple, step-by-step examples provide problem-solving strategies students need to complete problems within the lesson.

◆ Exercise sets parallel the instruction and examples in each lesson.

PROBLEM SOLVING

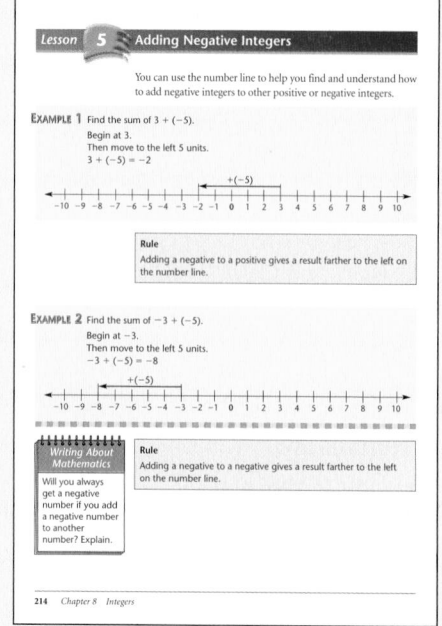

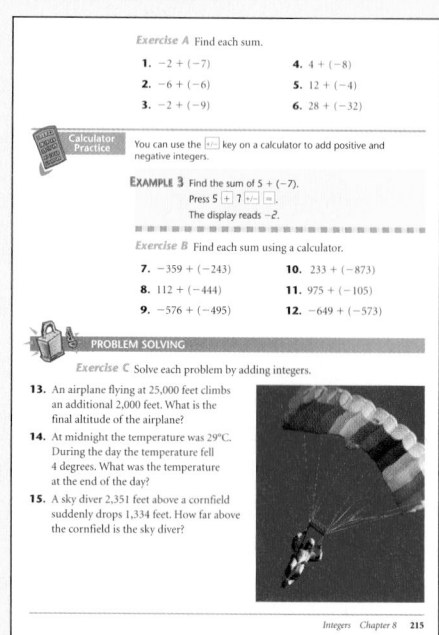

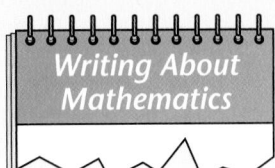

Writing About Mathematics

Technology Connection

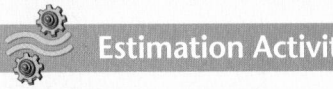

Estimation Activity

Calculator Practice

Math in Your Life

Try This

Build a Model

◆ Many features reinforce and extend student learning beyond the lesson content.

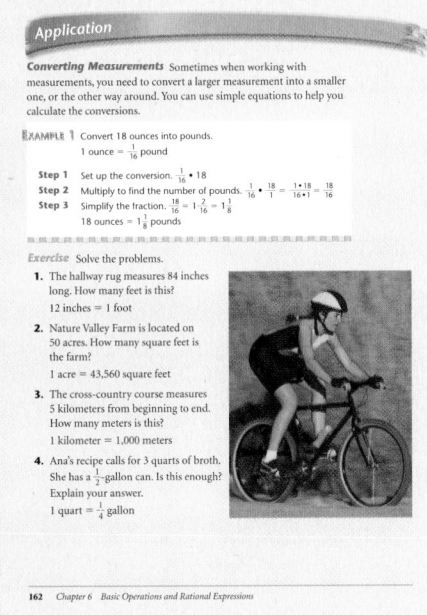

Application

Converting Measurements Sometimes when working with measurements, you need to convert a larger measurement into a smaller one, or the other way around. You can use simple equations to help you calculate the conversions.

EXAMPLE 1 Convert 18 ounces into pounds.

1 ounce = $\frac{1}{16}$ pound

Step 1 Set up the conversion. $\frac{1}{16} \cdot 18$

Step 2 Multiply to find the number of pounds. $\frac{1}{16} \cdot \frac{18}{1} = \frac{1 \cdot 18}{16 \cdot 1} = \frac{18}{16}$

Step 3 Simplify the fraction. $\frac{18}{16} = 1\frac{2}{16} = 1\frac{1}{8}$

18 ounces = $1\frac{1}{8}$ pounds

Exercise Solve the problems.

1. The hallway rug measures 84 inches long. How many feet is this?
   12 inches = 1 foot

2. Nature Valley Farm is located on 50 acres. How many square feet is the farm?
   1 acre = 43,560 square feet

3. The cross-country course measures 5 kilometers from beginning to end. How many meters is this?
   1 kilometer = 1,000 meters

4. Ana's recipe calls for 3 quarts of broth. She has a $\frac{1}{2}$-gallon can. Is this enough? Explain your answer.
   1 quart = $\frac{1}{4}$ gallon

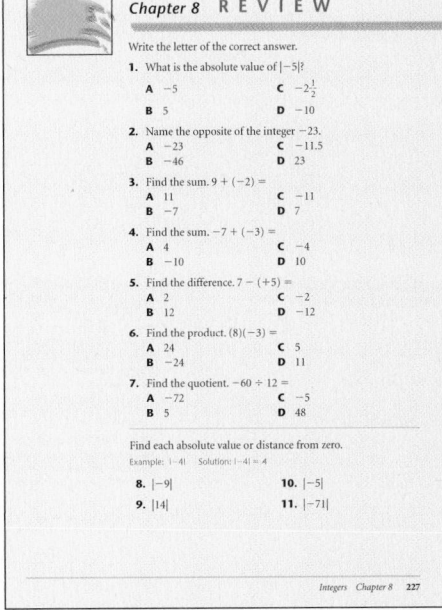

Chapter 8 REVIEW

Write the letter of the correct answer.

1. What is the absolute value of $|-5|$?
   A −5   C $-2\frac{1}{2}$
   B 5   D −10

2. Name the opposite of the integer −23.
   A −23   C −11.5
   B −46   D 23

3. Find the sum. 9 + (−2) =
   A 11   C −11
   B −7   D 7

4. Find the sum. −7 + (−3) =
   A 4   C −4
   B −10   D 10

5. Find the difference. 7 − (+5) =
   A 2   C −2
   B 12   D −12

6. Find the product. (8)(−3) =
   A 24   C 5
   B −24   D 11

7. Find the quotient. −60 ÷ 12 =
   A −72   C −5
   B 5   D 48

Find each absolute value or distance from zero.
Example: 1−41 Solution: 1−41 = 4

8. $|-9|$ 10. $|-5|$
9. $|14|$ 11. $|-71|$

◆ Application activities help students relate the chapter content to real-life situations.

◆ Chapter Reviews allow students and teachers to check for skill mastery. Multiple-choice items are provided for practice in taking standardized tests. Supplementary Problems at the back of the book provide additional practice.

Chapter 8 REVIEW - continued

Name the opposite of each integer.
Example: −5 Solution: 5 is the opposite of −5

12. 8   14. 7
13. −4   15. 43

Compare each pair. Use <, >, or =.
Example: 9 ■ −2 Solution: 9 > −2

16. 7 ■ −7   18. −4 ■ 0
17. 4 ■ 0   19. −2 ■ |−5|

Find each sum.
Example: −8 + 3 Solution: −8 + 3 = −5

20. 8 + 3   24. −9 + (−2)
21. 6 + 4   25. −7 + 4
22. −6 + (−6)   26. 8 + (−3)
23. 6 + (−6)   27. −9 + (−9)

Find each difference.
Example: −8 − (−5)   Solution: −8 − (−5) = −3

28. −9 − (−11)   31. −7 − (−4)
29. −6 − (−4)   32. 5 − (−4)
30. 10 − (−7)   33. −9 − (−2)

Find each product.
Example: (4)(−7) Solution: (4)(−7) = −28

34. (3)(5)   37. (−8)(−12)
35. (−6)(7)   38. (9)(5)
36. (−6)(−6)   39. (5)(−8)

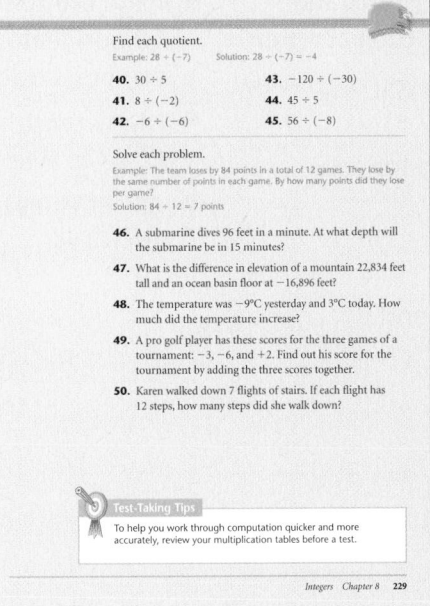

Find each quotient.
Example: 28 ÷ (−7)   Solution: 28 ÷ (−7) = −4

40. 30 ÷ 5   43. −120 ÷ (−30)
41. 8 ÷ (−2)   44. 45 ÷ 5
42. −6 ÷ (−6)   45. 56 ÷ (−8)

Solve each problem.
Example: The team loses by 84 points in a total of 12 games. They lose by the same number of points in each game. By how many points did they lose per game?
Solution: 84 ÷ 12 = 7 points

46. A submarine dives 96 feet in a minute. At what depth will the submarine be in 15 minutes?

47. What is the difference in elevation of a mountain 22,834 feet tall and an ocean basin floor at −16,896 feet?

48. The temperature was −9°C yesterday and 3°C today. How much did the temperature increase?

49. A pro golf player has these scores for the three games of a tournament: −3, −6, and +2. Find out his score for the tournament by adding the three scores together.

50. Karen walked down 7 flights of stairs. If each flight has 12 steps, how many steps did she walk down?

Test-Taking Tips
To help you work through computation quicker and more accurately, review your multiplication tables before a test.

◆ Test-Taking Tips at the end of each Chapter Review help reduce test anxiety and improve test scores.

The comprehensive, wraparound Teacher's Edition provides instructional strategies at point of use. Everything from preparation guidelines to teaching tips and strategies are included in an easy-to-use format. Activities are featured at point of use for teacher convenience.

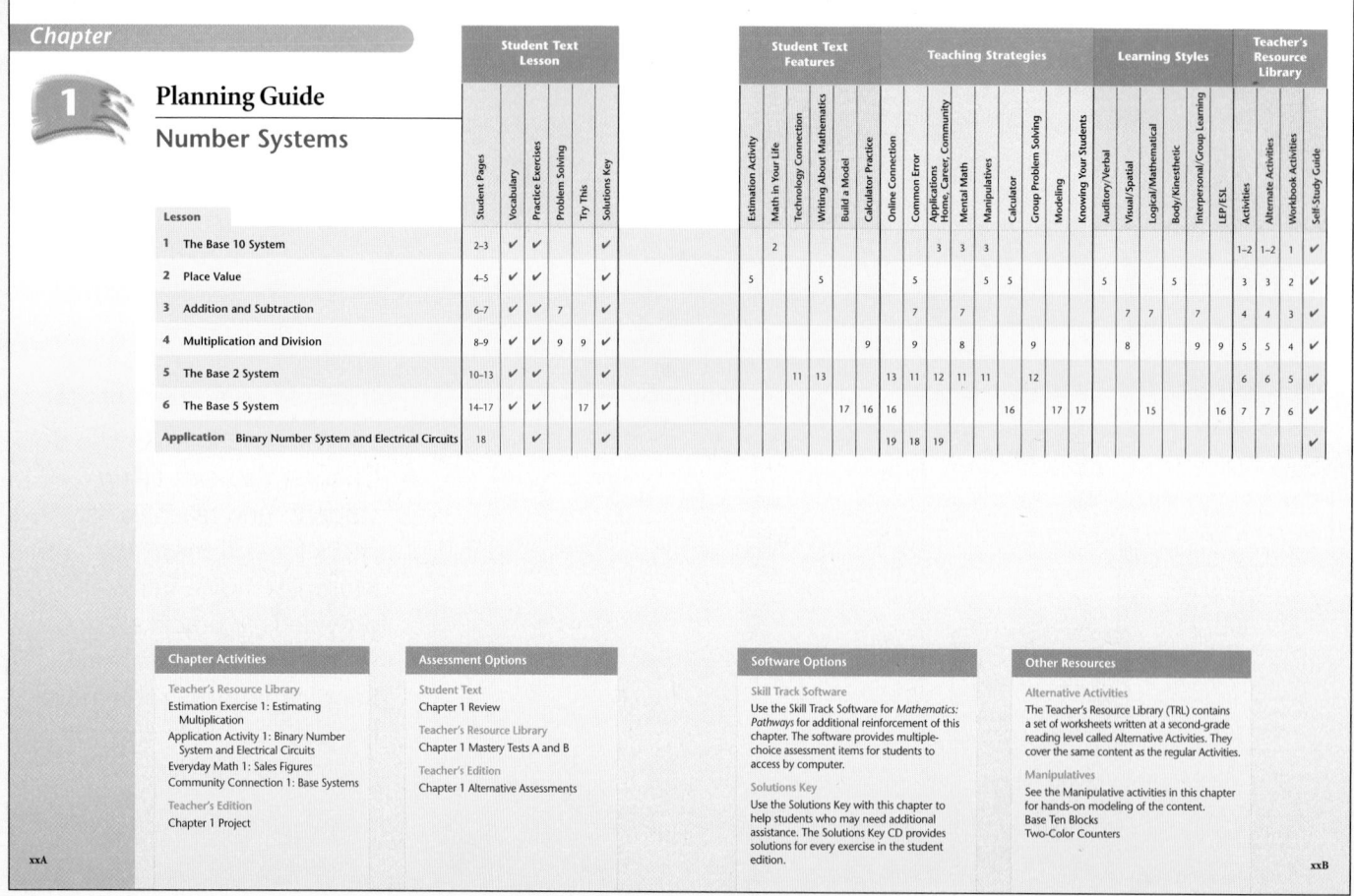

Chapter 1

Planning Guide
Number Systems

Lesson	Student Pages	Vocabulary	Practice Exercises	Problem Solving	Try This	Solutions Key	Estimation Activity	Math in Your Life	Technology Connection	Writing About Mathematics	Build a Model	Calculator Practice	Online Connection	Common Error	Applications Home, Career, Community	Mental Math	Manipulatives	Calculator	Group Problem Solving	Modeling	Knowing Your Students	Auditory/Verbal	Visual/Spatial	Logical/Mathematical	Body/Kinesthetic	Interpersonal/Group Learning	LEP/ESL	Activities	Alternate Activities	Workbook Activities	Self-Study Guide
1 The Base 10 System	2–3	✔	✔			✔		2							3	3	3											1–2	1–2	1	✔
2 Place Value	4–5	✔	✔			✔	5			5				5		5	5					5		5				3	3	2	✔
3 Addition and Subtraction	6–7	✔	✔	7		✔								7		7						7	7		7			4	4	3	✔
4 Multiplication and Division	8–9	✔	✔	9	9	✔						9		9		8			9			8			9	9		5	5	4	✔
5 The Base 2 System	10–13	✔	✔			✔			11	13			13	11	12	11	11		12									6	6	5	✔
6 The Base 5 System	14–17	✔	✔		17	✔				17	16	16					16		17	17			15				16	7	7	6	✔
Application Binary Number System and Electrical Circuits	18		✔			✔						19	18	19																	✔

Chapter Activities

Teacher's Resource Library
Estimation Exercise 1: Estimating Multiplication
Application Activity 1: Binary Number System and Electrical Circuits
Everyday Math 1: Sales Figures
Community Connection 1: Base Systems

Teacher's Edition
Chapter 1 Project

Assessment Options

Student Text
Chapter 1 Review

Teacher's Resource Library
Chapter 1 Mastery Tests A and B

Teacher's Edition
Chapter 1 Alternative Assessments

Software Options

Skill Track Software
Use the Skill Track Software for *Mathematics: Pathways* for additional reinforcement of this chapter. The software provides multiple-choice assessment items for students to access by computer.

Solutions Key
Use the Solutions Key with this chapter to help students who may need additional assistance. The Solutions Key CD provides solutions for every exercise in the student edition.

Other Resources

Alternative Activities
The Teacher's Resource Library (TRL) contains a set of worksheets written at a second-grade reading level called Alternative Activities. They cover the same content as the regular Activities.

Manipulatives
See the Manipulative activities in this chapter for hands-on modeling of the content.
Base Ten Blocks
Two-Color Counters

xxA

xxB

Chapter Planning Guides

◆ The Planning Guide saves valuable preparation time by organizing all materials for each chapter.

◆ A complete listing of lessons allows you to preview each chapter quickly.

◆ Assessment options are highlighted for easy reference. Options include:
Chapter Reviews
Chapter Alternative Assessments
Chapter Mastery Tests, Forms A and B
Midterm and Final Tests

◆ Page numbers of Student Text and Teacher's Edition features help customize lesson plans to your students.

◆ Many teaching strategies and learning styles are listed to help include students with diverse needs.

◆ All activities for the Teacher's Resource Library are listed.

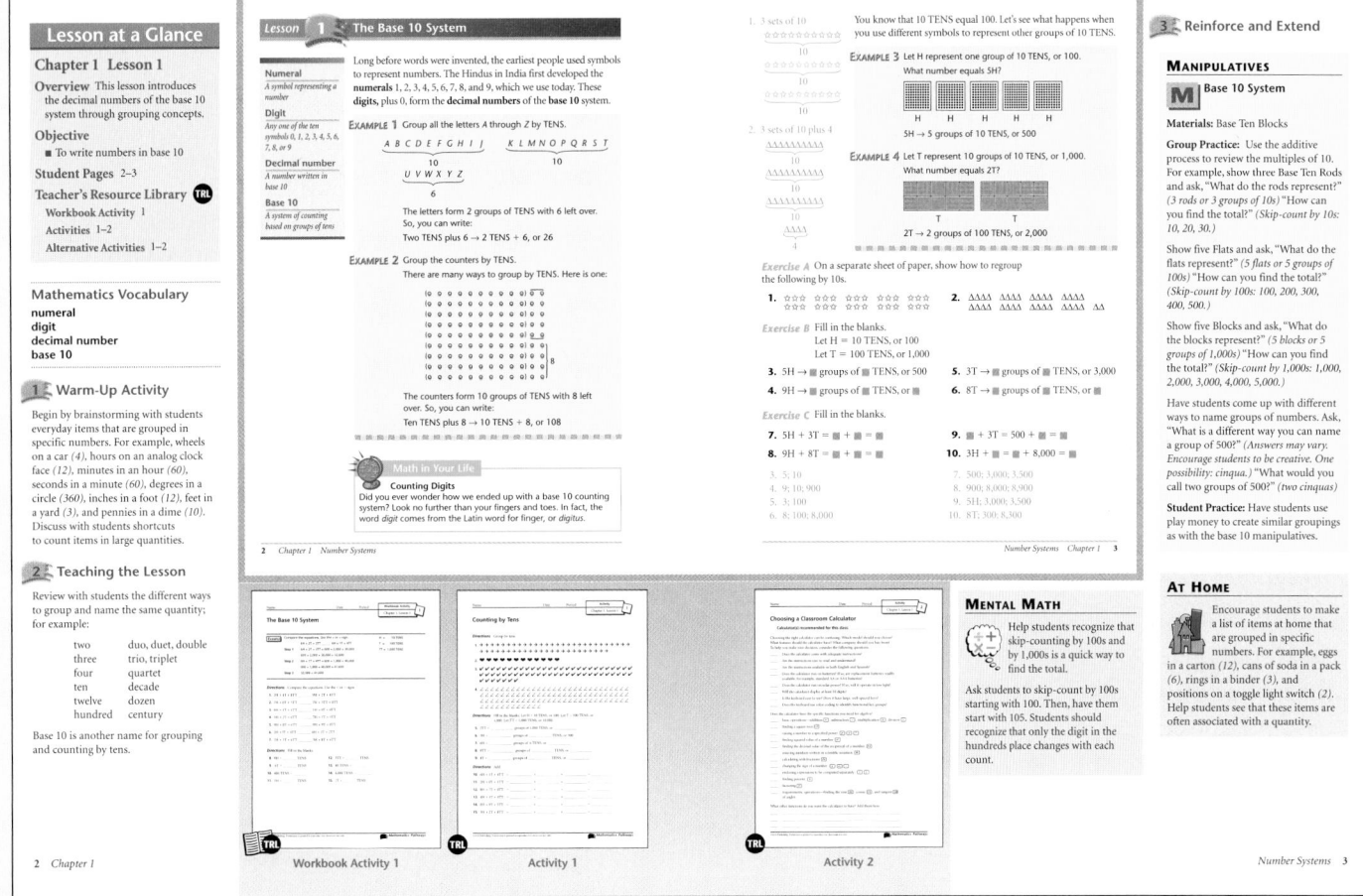

Lessons

- Quick overviews of chapters and lessons save planning time.

- Lesson objectives are listed for easy reference.

- Page references are provided for convenience.

- Easy-to-follow lesson plans in three steps save time: Warm-Up Activity, Teaching the Lesson, and Reinforce and Extend.

- Common Error alerts teachers to possible student errors before they are made.

- Mental Math activities encourage students to think independently.

- Manipulative and Modeling activities develop students' mathematical understanding at a concrete level.

- Calculator activities provide students with practice using a calculator.

- Applications: Three areas of application—Career Connection, In the Community, and At Home—help students relate math to the world outside the classroom. Applications motivate students and make learning relevant.

- Group Problem Solving provides group work for students.

- Relevant Web sites are listed in Online Connections.

- Knowing Your Students targets specific adolescent development information as it relates to mathematics understandings.

- Learning Styles provide teaching strategies to help meet the needs of students with diverse ways of learning. Modalities include Auditory/Verbal, Visual/Spatial, Body/Kinesthetic, Logical/Mathematical, and Interpersonal/Group Learning. Additional teaching activities are provided for LEP/ESL students.

- Answers are provided in the Teacher's Edition for all exercises in the Student Text. A separate Solutions Key for the student text is available on CD-ROM. Answers to the Teacher's Resource Library and Student Workbook are provided at the back of this Teacher's Edition and on the TRL CD-ROM.

- Workbook and Activity pages from the Teacher's Resource Library are shown at point of use in reduced form.

(TRL) All of the activities you'll need to reinforce and extend the text are conveniently located on the AGS Publishing Teacher's Resource Library (TRL) CD-ROM. These reproducible activities are ready to select, view, and print. Additionally, you can preview other materials by directly linking to the AGS Publishing Web site.

Workbook
Workbook Activities reinforce and extend skills from each lesson of the textbook. Also available in a bound workbook format.

Activities/Alternative Activities
Lesson activities for each lesson of the textbook give students additional skill practice. Alternative Activities cover the same content but are written at a second-grade reading level.

Application Activities
Everyday Math
Community Connections
Estimation Exercises
Relevant activities help students extend their knowledge to the real world and reinforce concepts covered in class.

Review of Basic Skills
These skill pages provide extra practice for basic math skills.

Self-Study Guide
An assignment guide provides the student with an outline for working through the text independently.

Mastery Tests
Chapter, Midterm, and Final Mastery Tests are convenient assessment options.

Answer Key
All answers to reproducible activities are included on the TRL and in the Teacher's Edition.

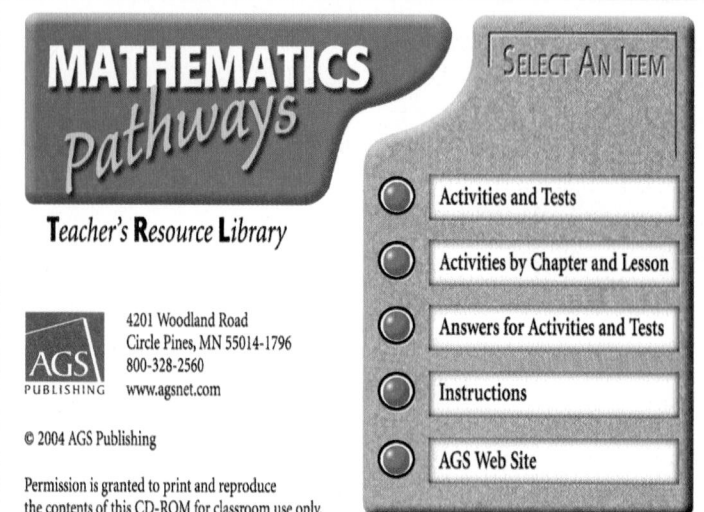

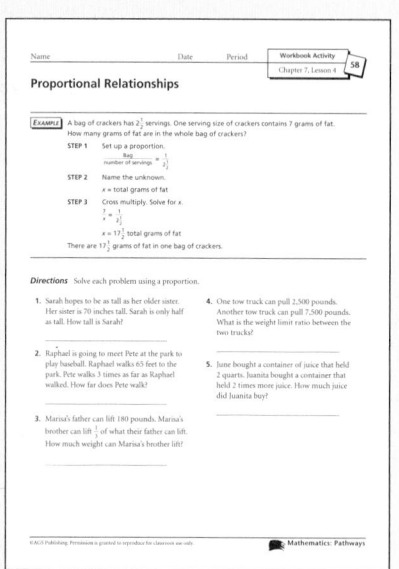

Workbook Activities

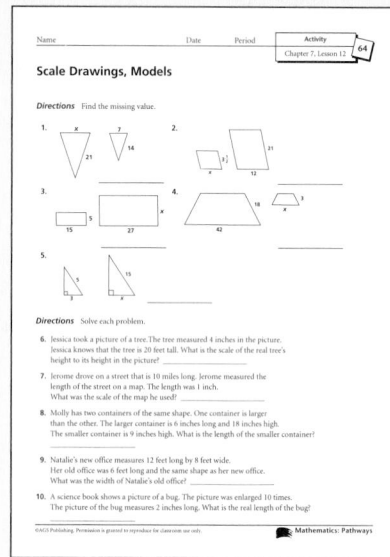

Activities

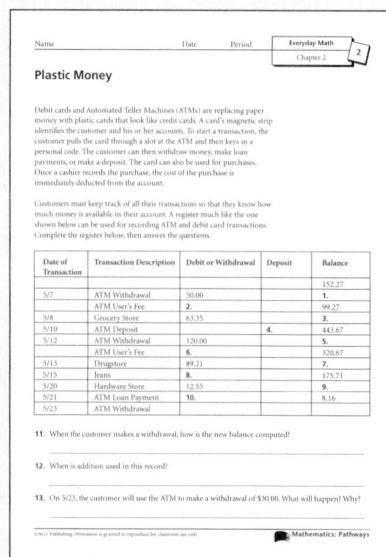

Everyday Math

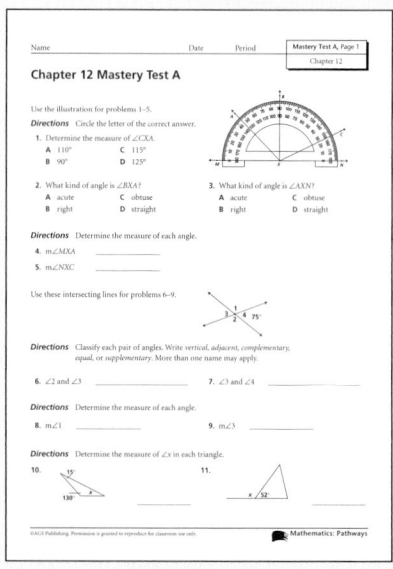

Mastery Tests

Correlation of Mathematics: Pathways to the NCTM Standards

STANDARD 1 Number and Operations

Instructional programs should enable all students to:

◆ understand numbers, ways of representing numbers, relationships among numbers, and number systems;

◆ understand meanings of operations and how they relate to one another;

◆ compute fluently and make reasonable estimates.

Mathematics: Pathways

Understand numbers: pages 1–18, 24–33, 48–67, 76–94, 100–132, 168–177, 204–225, 232–249.

Understand meanings: pages 6–9, 24–33, 54–61, 126–131, 138–141, 160–161, 220–226, 234–237, 426–427.

Compute fluently: pages 5–9, 16, 28–29, 34–35, 37, 41, 52–70, 77, 90, 109, 116–130, 140–141, 155, 187, 189, 193, 213, 215, 221, 233, 241, 244–245, 280, 291, 301, 305, 333, 341, 343, 346, 365, 379, 411, 413.

STANDARD 2 Algebra

Instructional programs should enable all students to:

◆ understand patterns, relations, and functions;

◆ represent and analyze mathematical situations and structures using algebraic symbols;

◆ use mathematical models to represent and understand quantitative relationships;

◆ analyze change in various contexts.

Mathematics: Pathways

Understand patterns: pages 320–321, 330–352, 400–401.

Represent and analyze: pages 40–41, 138–161, 186–193, 232–260, 320–351.

Use mathematical models: Application exercises help students to model mathematical situations. See pages 18, 42, 70, 94, 132, 162, 198, 226, 260, 308, 352, 394, 428. See also *Build a Model* features on pages 38, 147, 257, and 351.

Analyze change: pages 332–333, 344–347, 352.

STANDARD 3 Geometry

Instructional programs should enable all students to:

◆ analyze characteristics and properties of two- and three-dimensional geometric shapes and develop mathematical arguments about geometric relationships;

◆ specify locations and describe spatial relationships using coordinate geometry and other representational systems;

◆ apply transformations and use symmetry to analyze mathematical situations;

◆ use visualization, spatial reasoning, and geometric modeling to solve problems.

Mathematics: Pathways

Analyze characteristics: pages 254–260, 266–308, 357–381.

Specify locations: pages 324–333, 344–347, 382–385, 388–393.

Apply transformations: page 382–394.

Use visualization: pages 238–247, 254–260, 292–308, 366–369, 372–373, 387–393.

See *Build a Model* features on pages 38, 180, 257, 281, 351, and 393.

Refer to *Problem Solving* exercises on pages 269, 273, 281, 283, 297, 301, 305, 369, 377.

See also *Application* exercises on pages 308 and 394; and *Math In Your Life:* pages 287, 371.

STANDARD 4 Measurement

Instructional programs should enable all students to:

◆ understand measurable attributes of objects and the units, systems, and processes of measurement;

◆ apply appropriate techniques, tools, and formulas to determine measurements.

Mathematics: Pathways

Understand measurable attributes: pages 70, 162, 174–175

Apply appropriate techniques, tools, and formulas: pages 176–177, 238–245, 251–257, 260, 266-291, 294-308.

STANDARD 5 Data Analysis and Probability

Instructional programs should enable all students to:

◆ formulate questions that can be addressed with data and collect, organize, and display relevant data to answer them;

◆ select and use appropriate statistical methods to analyze data;

◆ develop and evaluate inferences and predictions that are based on data;

◆ understand and apply basic concepts of probability.

Mathematics: Pathways

Formulate questions: pages 399–428.

Select and use: pages 399–419.

Develop and evaluate: pages 408–411, 420–425.

Understand and apply: pages 408–411, 420–425.

STANDARD 6 Problem Solving

Instructional programs should enable all students to:

◆ build new mathematical knowledge through problem solving;

◆ solve problems that arise in mathematics and in other contexts;

◆ apply and adapt a variety of appropriate strategies to solve problems;

◆ monitor and reflect on the process of mathematical problem solving.

Mathematics: Pathways

Problem Solving exercises throughout provide students opportunities to apply *problem-solving strategies.* See examples on pages xviii–xix, 7, 9, 25, 27, 31, 33, 53, 57, 61, 63, 67, 79, 81, 87, 91, 101, 105, 111, 115, 125, 131, 145, 151, 159, 161, 169, 173, 175, 177, 185, 191, 197, 207, 209, 215, 219, 223, 225, 239, 241, 249, 252, 269, 273, 281, 283, 297, 301, 305, 321, 323, 327, 347, 369, 377, 411, 413, and 417.

In addition, see *Application* exercises on pages 18, 42, 70, 94, 132, 162, 198, 226, 260, 308, 352, 394, 428; *Estimation Activities* on pages 5, 37, 65, 77, 117, 141, 187, 221, 245, 291, 341, 365, 413; and *Math In Your Life* on pages 2, 33, 59, 90, 119, 149, 183, 206, 235, 287, 319, 371, and 420.

STANDARD 7 Reasoning and Proof

Instructional programs should enable all students to:

◆ recognize reasoning and proof as fundamental aspects of mathematics;

◆ make and investigate mathematical conjectures;

◆ develop and evaluate mathematical conjectures;

◆ develop and evaluate mathematical arguments and proofs;

◆ select and use various types of reasoning and methods of proof.

Mathematics: Pathways

Reasoning skills/processes, conjectures, and argumentation are applied throughout in exercises at the end of each lesson and in *Problem Solving* and *Application* exercises listed above, and in *Chapter Reviews.* Patterns can be found particularly on pages 320–321, and 330–352.

STANDARD 8 Communication

Instructional programs should enable all students to:

◆ organize and consolidate their mathematical thinking through communication;

◆ communicate their mathematical thinking coherently and clearly to peers, teachers, and others;

◆ analyze and evaluate the mathematical thinking and strategies of others;

◆ use the language of mathematics to express mathematical ideas precisely.

Mathematics: Pathways

Helps students develop *mathematical communication skills* in a number of ways:

— Oral explanation and discussion: *Problem Solving* exercises provide opportunity for oral language.

— *Learning Styles: Auditory/Verbal* sidebars in Teacher's Edition.

— Graphical representations: pages 6–7, 51, 102, 112–114, 204–206, 208–209, 212, 214, 216–217, 222, 224, 246–247, 314–352, 400–401, 404–409, 418–419, and 428.

— Definitions of topic-relevant terms are included in each lesson throughout, used in context and defined in glossary.

— Power, scientific notation, and exponents are addressed on pages 4, 10, 14, 54–55, 58–59, 92–93, and 232–243.

— *Writing About Mathematics* features on pages 5, 13, 26, 39, 41, 55, 79, 81, 89, 93, 105, 119, 127, 130, 141, 154, 157, 181, 184, 214, 223, 233, 257, 285, 332, 335, 351, 359, 364, 371, 381, 389, 393, 405, 412, 425.

Instructional programs should enable all students to:

- recognize and use connections among mathematical ideas;
- understand how mathematical ideas interconnect and build on one another to produce a coherent whole;
- recognize and apply mathematics in contexts outside of mathematics.

Mathematics: Pathways

Relationships among diverse mathematical concepts such as arithmetic, linear equations, percentages, exponents, polynomials, data, fractions, inequalities, irrational numbers, geometry, and quadratic equations are explored throughout, and principles are presented as an integrated whole. In addition, the *role of mathematics in other disciplines* is explored in chapter openers on pages 1, 23, 47, 75, 99, 137, 167, 203, 231, 265, 313, 357, and 399 as well as *Problem Solving* exercises on pages 7, 9, 25, 27, 31, 33, 53, 57, 61, 63, 67, 79, 81, 87, 91, 101, 105, 111, 115, 125, 131, 145, 151, 159, 161, 169, 173, 175, 177, 185, 191, 197, 207, 209, 215, 219, 223, 225, 239, 241, 249, 252, 269, 273, 281, 283, 297, 301, 305, 321, 323, 327, 347, 369, 377, 411, 413, and 417; *Application* exercises on pages 18, 42, 70, 94, 132, 162, 198, 226, 260, 308, 352, 394, and 428; in *Try This* activities on pages 9, 17, 27, 33, 49, 51, 80, 93, 109, 115, 141, 151, 181, 193, 211, 225, 235, 237, 247, 257, 269, 273, 341, 347, 365, 387, 407, 421, and 425; in *Writing About Mathematics* activities on pages 5, 13, 26, 39, 41, 55, 79, 81, 89, 93, 105, 119, 127, 130, 141, 154, 157, 181, 184, 214, 223, 233, 257, 285, 332, 335, 351, 359, 364, 371, 381, 389, 393, 405, 412, and 424; in *Technology Connections* on pages 11, 25, 55, 85, 123, 157, 171, 218, 253, 276, 325, 339, 367, and 403; *Math in Your Life* activities on pages 2, 33, 59, 90, 119, 149, 183, 206, 235, 287, 319, 371, and 420; and in *Estimation Activities* on pages 5, 28-29, 34-35, 37, 65, 77, 117, 141, 187, 221, 245, 291, 341, 365, and 413.

Instructional programs should enable all students to:

- create and use representations to organize, record, and communicate mathematical ideas;
- select, apply, and translate among mathematical representations to solve problems;
- use presentations to model and interpret physical, social, and mathematical phenomena.

Mathematics: Pathways

Many different types of *representations* are used throughout the text in order to maximize *student understanding of concepts and relationships.* See the following examples:

Build a Model: 17, 38, 51, 93, 130, 147, 180, 213, 257, 281, 351, 393, 425

Applications: 18, 42, 70, 94, 132, 162, 198, 226, 260, 308, 352, 394, 428

Drawings: pages 2, 3, 8, 17, 100–101, 106, 108, 113, 130, 132, 147, 174–175, 178–181, 194–197, 238–243, 245–247, 249, 251–260, 266–308, and 358–394.

Charts/Tables: pages 10–12, 14–16, 42, 48, 51, 81, 172, 259, 402–407, 413, and 415.

Graphs: pages 6–7, 51, 102, 112–114, 204–206, 208–209, 212, 214, 216–217, 222, 224, 246–247, 314–352, 400–401, 404–409, 418–419, and 428.

Manipulative exercises can be found throughout the Teacher's Edition.

Learning Styles

The learning style activities in the *Mathematics: Pathways* Teacher's Edition provide activities to help students with special needs understand the lesson. These activities focus on the following learning styles: Visual/Spatial, Auditory/Verbal, Body/Kinesthetic, Logical/Mathematical, Interpersonal/Group Learning, LEP/ESL. These styles reflect Howard Gardner's theory of multiple intelligences. The writing activities suggested in the Student Text are appropriate for students who fit Gardner's description of Verbal/Linguistic Intelligence.

The activities are designed to help teachers capitalize on students' individual strengths and dominant learning styles. The activities reinforce the lesson by teaching or expanding upon the content in a different way.

Following are examples of activities featured in the *Mathematics: Pathways* Teacher's Edition:

Visual/Spatial

Students benefit from seeing illustrations or demonstrations beyond what is in the text.

LEARNING STYLES

Visual/Spatial
Provide concrete examples of units of measure. A gallon jug, liter container, tape measure, and ruler will help students comprehend different measurements. Allow students to transfer a liquid between the containers or to measure something in the classroom in different units.

Body/Kinesthetic

Learners benefit from activities that include physical movement or tactile experiences.

LEARNING STYLES

Body/Kinesthetic
Have students work with paper cups and small identical objects such as paper clips to model algebraic expressions for different values. For example, for $3x + 5$, provide three paper cups, and explain that x will equal 3. Place three paper clips in each cup and 5 in a separate pile. Have students count clips and evaluate the expression for $x = 3$. *(14)* Then have a volunteer model the expression when $x = 4$. *(17)*

Interpersonal/Group Learning

Learners benefit from working with at least one other person on activities that involve a process and an end product.

LEARNING STYLES

Interpersonal/ Group Learning
Point out to students that they can represent 50¢ in several different ways using equivalent fractions. Have pairs of students write fractions representing several coin combinations that are equivalent to 50¢. If possible, have students work with play money to form different combinations. Caution them that all the parts (coins) must be the same size (worth).

LEP/ESL

Students benefit from activities that promote English language acquisition and interaction with English-speaking peers.

LEARNING STYLES

LEP/ESL
Students who have difficulty translating the exponential notation directly into a product can make a table like this:

Power of 10	10^1	10^2	10^3
Multiply	10	10×10	$10 \times 10 \times 10$
Product	10	100	1,000
# of zeros	1	2	3

Auditory/Verbal

Students benefit from having someone read the text aloud or listening to the text on audiocassette. Musical activities appropriate for the lesson may help auditory learners.

LEARNING STYLES

Auditory/Verbal
Have students work in pairs to develop number riddles modeled on the following: "I'm thinking of a number. The sum of its digits is divisible by 9. What other whole number(s) are divisors of the number?" *(3)* Pairs should share and solve other pairs' riddles, explaining how they found the answer.

Logical/Mathematical

Students learn by using logical/ mathematical thinking in relation to the lesson content.

LEARNING STYLES

Logical/Mathematical
Have students use folded paper to represent the fractions in Exercise B. Suggest that they put their models in two groups: those representing proper fractions and those representing improper fractions. Ask students to form a generalization about the number of sheets of paper needed to make proper and improper fractions.

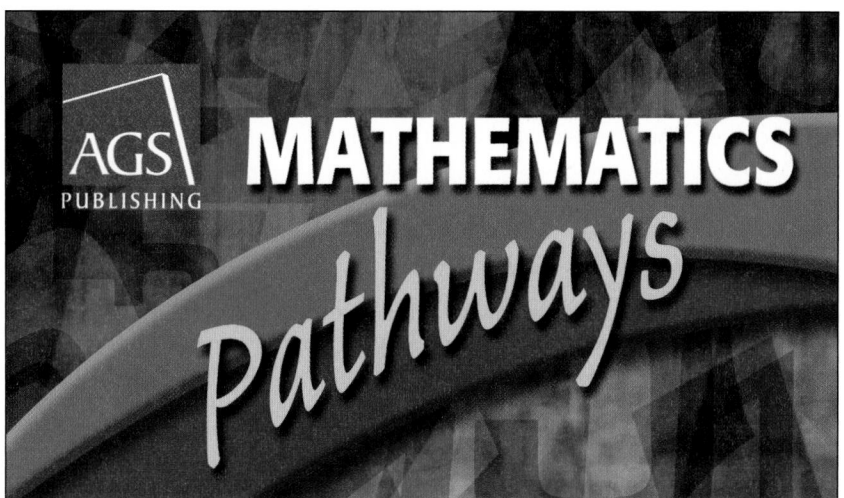

by
Siegfried Haenisch

AGS Publishing
Circle Pines, Minnesota 55014-1796
800-328-2560

About the Author

Siegfried Haenisch, Ed.D., has taught mathematics at every level, from elementary to graduate school, most recently as Professor in the Department of Mathematics and Statistics at the College of New Jersey. The Mathematical Association of America granted him the 1995 Award for Distinguished Teaching of Mathematics. Dr. Haenisch was the site director for the training of teachers in the New Jersey Algebra Project. He was a member of the National Science Foundation Institutes in Mathematics at Rutgers University, Oberlin College, and Princeton University. At Yale University, he was a member of the Seminar in the History of Mathematics, sponsored by the National Endowment in the Humanities. Dr. Haenisch currently serves as a mathematics curriculum consultant to school districts.

Photo credits for this textbook can be found on page 524.

The publisher wishes to thank the following educators for their helpful comments during the review process for *Mathematics: Pathways.* Their assistance has been invaluable.

Laura L. Duff, Teacher Consultant Mathematics, Northside Independent School District, San Antonio, Texas; **Merilyn Fox,** Teacher, Henry Kelsey Sr. P. S., Scarborough, Ontario, Canada; **Karen Jackman,** Math Teacher, Newburg Middle School, Louisville, Kentucky; **Toby Ann Nitardy,** EBD Resource Teacher, Campbell County Middle School, Alexandria, Kentucky; **Bethanne Pearce,** Scientific Learning Disabilities Math Teacher, Tomlin Middle School, Plant City, Florida; **Peter Saarimaki,** Educational Consultant—Mathematics, Psycan Corporation, Scarborough, Ontario, Canada; **Märit C. Sheffield,** Teacher, Jamacha Middle Community School, Spring Valley, California; **Larry Stott,** District Mathematics Coordinator, West High School, Salt Lake City, Utah; **Wade T. Williford,** Teacher, Carlsbad Village Academy, Carlsbad, California

Publisher's Project Staff

Vice President, Product Development: Kathleen T. Williams, Ph.D., NCSP; Associate Director, Product Development: Teri Mathews; Assistant Editors: Karen Anderson and Sarah Brandel; Development Assistant: Bev Johnson; Creative Services Manager: Nancy Condon; Senior Designers: Daren Hastings and Diane McCarty; Desktop Production Artists: Jack Ross and Peggy Vlahos; Purchasing Agent: Mary Kaye Kuzma; Senior Marketing Manager/Secondary Curriculum: Brian Holl

© 2004 AGS Publishing
4201 Woodland Road
Circle Pines, MN 55014-1796
800-328-2560 • www.agsnet.com

AGS Publishing is a trademark and trade name of American Guidance Service, Inc.

Printed in the United States of America

ISBN 0-7854-3604-9

Product Number 93870

A 0 9 8 7 6 5 4 3 2 1

Contents

Chapter 9

Exponents, Radicals, and the Pythagorean Theorem 230

How to Use This Book: A Study Guide

Overview

This section introduces *Mathematics: Pathways*, reviews study strategies, and identifies text features.

Objectives

- To introduce the structure and purpose of *Mathematics: Pathways*
- To review study skills
- To preview the student text

Student Pages xii–xix

Teacher's Resource Library

How to Use This Book 1–7

Introduction to the Book

As a class, read the first three paragraphs of the introduction. Ask students to briefly summarize each paragraph and its purpose. After they read the introductory paragraphs, encourage students to list on the board situations in which they or family members use mathematics. Help them conclude that people use mathematics daily.

How to Study

Ask a volunteer to read each bulleted study tip. Discuss how each suggestion can help students study more effectively.

Distribute copies of How to Use This Book 1, Study Habits Survey, pages 1 and 2. Students can complete the survey to assess their study and test-taking habits. Read the directions with students. Have them use the directions provided to score the completed survey. Encourage students to identify ways that they can improve their study and test-taking skills. Give them several weeks to improve their skills and then have them complete the survey again to assess their improvement. Advise students to review the survey occasionally to see whether they have improved their study and test-taking habits. Distribute How to Use This Book 2, Weekly Schedule, to show students one way to organize their time better.

How to Use This Book: A Study Guide

Welcome to *Mathematics: Pathways*. This book guides you on the path from basic concepts of mathematics to algebra concepts. Having these skills will help you on life's journey. There are many jobs that use mathematics and algebra. People who work in food service, banking, printing, electronics, surveying, and insurance all use these skills on the job. You will also use these skills at home and in school.

As you read this book, notice how each lesson is organized. Information will appear at the beginning of each lesson. Read this information carefully. A sample problem with step-by-step instructions will follow. Use the instructions to learn how to solve a certain kind of problem. Once you know how to solve this kind of problem, you will have the chance to solve similar problems on your own. If you have trouble with a lesson, try reading it again.

Before you start to read this book, it is important that you understand how to use it. It is also important to know how to be successful in this course. This first section of the book is here to help you achieve these things.

How to Study

These tips can help you study more effectively:

- Plan a regular time to study.
- Choose a quiet desk or table where you will not be distracted. Find a spot that has good lighting.
- Gather all the books, pencils, paper, and other equipment you will need to complete your assignments.
- Decide on a goal. For example: "I will finish reading and taking notes on Chapter 1, Lesson 1, by 8:00."
- Take a five- to ten-minute break every hour to keep alert.
- If you start to feel sleepy, take a break and get some fresh air.

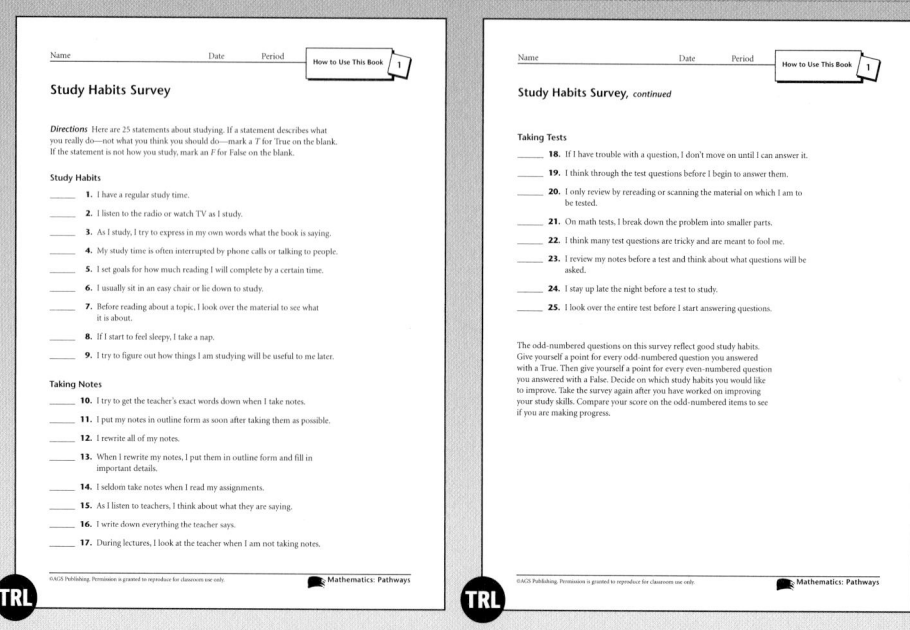

How to Use This Book 1, pages 1 and 2

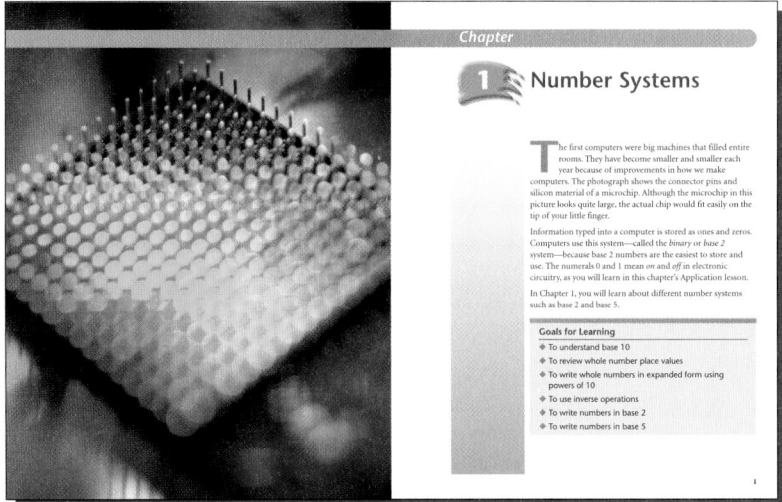

Before Beginning Each Chapter

◆ Read the chapter title and study the photograph. What does the photo tell you about the chapter title?

◆ Read the opening paragraphs.

◆ Study the Goals for Learning. The Chapter Review and tests will ask questions related to these goals.

◆ Look at the Chapter Review. The questions cover the most important information in the chapter.

Note the Chapter Features

Application

A look at how a topic in the chapter relates to real life

Notes

Hints or reminders that point out important information

> Look for this box for helpful tips!

The Chapter

Together with students, read Before Beginning Each Chapter and Note the Chapter Features on pages xiii and xiv. Tell students that you will preview a chapter to help them determine content and structure. On chart paper, write the heading Chapter Features. Then list the following features: chapter title, chapter-opening photographs, Goals for Learning, Notes, Technology Connection, Try This, Writing About Mathematics, Application, Calculator Practice, Math in Your Life, Build a Model, and Chapter Review. Ask small groups of students to examine one of the chapters in the text and identify each feature and its purpose. Write the purpose of each feature next to its name on the chart paper. Post the chart paper on a classroom wall for easy reference.

Ask students to turn to page 5 of Chapter 1. Have them read the Writing About Mathematics feature. Discuss what the activity asks students to do. (*Write a paragraph explaining the importance of zero in our counting system.*) Hand out copies of How to Use This Book 3, Writing About Mathematics. Explain that you will make copies of the page available for students to use for the writing activities in each chapter.

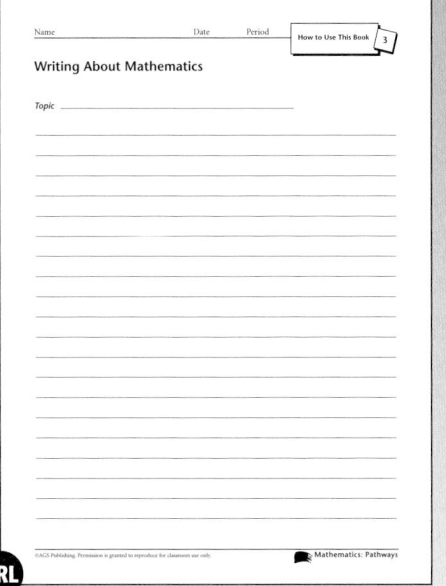

How to Use This Book 2

How to Use This Book 3

The Lesson

Read Before Beginning Each Lesson and As You Read the Lesson on pages xiv and xv together with students. On the board, draw a two-column chart, with one column labeled *Lesson Feature* and the other labeled *Purpose*. Help students complete the chart by identifying these features and their purposes: bold words, example boxes, practice exercises, and headings. Preview several lessons, helping students note the information given in paragraphs and the different kinds of practice exercises. Make sure students understand that the examples in the lessons provide models for performing basic operations and completing the practice exercises.

Technology Connection
Use technology to apply math skills

Writing About Mathematics
Opportunities to write about problems and alternate solutions

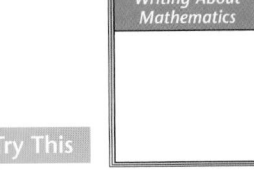

Try This
New ways to think about problems and solve them

Build a Model
Create a model of a math concept

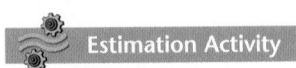

Estimation Activity
Use estimation as a way to check reasonableness of an answer

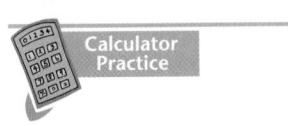

Calculator Practice
How to solve problems using a calculator

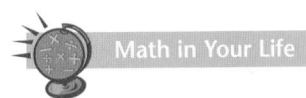

Math in Your Life
Relates math to the "real world"

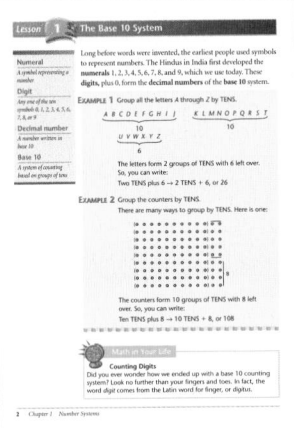

Before Beginning Each Lesson

Read the lesson title and restate it in the form of a question.

For example, write: *What is the base 10 system?*

Look over the entire lesson, noting the following:

◆ bold words

◆ text organization

◆ exercises

◆ notes in the margins

◆ photos

As You Read the Lesson

◆ Read the major headings.

◆ Read the subheads and paragraphs that follow.

◆ Read the content in the example boxes.

◆ Before moving on to the next lesson, see if you understand the concepts you read. If you do not, reread the lesson. If you are still unsure, ask for help.

◆ Practice what you have learned by doing the exercises in each lesson.

Using the Bold Words

Bold type

Words seen for the first time will appear in bold type

Glossary

Words listed in this column are also found in the glossary

Knowing the meaning of all the boxed words in the left column will help you understand what you read.

These words appear in **bold type** the first time they appear in the text and are often defined in the paragraph.

Proper and improper fractions are examples of **ratios.**

All of the words in the left column are also defined in the **glossary.**

Ratio (rā′ shē ō) A comparison of two like quantities using a fraction (p. 168)

What to Do with a Word You Do Not Know

When you come to a word you do not know, ask yourself:

◆ **Is the word a compound word?**
Can you find two words within the word? This could help you understand the meaning. For example: *rainfall.*

◆ **Does the word have a prefix at the beginning?**
For example: *improper.* The prefix *im-* means "not," so this word refers to something that is not proper.

◆ **Does the word have a suffix at the end?**
For example: *variable, -able.* This means "able to vary."

◆ **Can you identify the root word? Can you sound it out in parts?**
For example: *un known.*

◆ **Are there any clues in the sentence that will help you understand the word?**

Look for the word in the margin box, glossary, or dictionary. If you are still having trouble with a word, ask for help.

Vocabulary Strategy

Mathematics, like other curricula, has its own specialized vocabulary. It is essential that students know and understand the mathematics terms so that they can communicate in the discipline. *Mathematics: Pathways* highlights the important vocabulary by printing it in bold type and providing on-page definitions in the margins.

Have students read page xv, which identifies the treatment of important mathematics terminology in the text and also provides a strategy for decoding words in context. On the board, write this sentence: *Read the directions carefully so that you do not make a mistake.* Ask students to use the strategy to help them decode the word *carefully.* Students should note that the word is *care* with two suffixes: *-ful* meaning "full of" and *-ly* meaning "in the manner." *Carefully* then means "in a manner full of care."

Distribute copies of How to Use This Book 4, Word Study. Tell students that they can use the sheet to help them determine meaning of words they do not know. Encourage students to use and keep a copy of each completed sheet. They can keep the copies in a notebook to build their own personal glossaries.

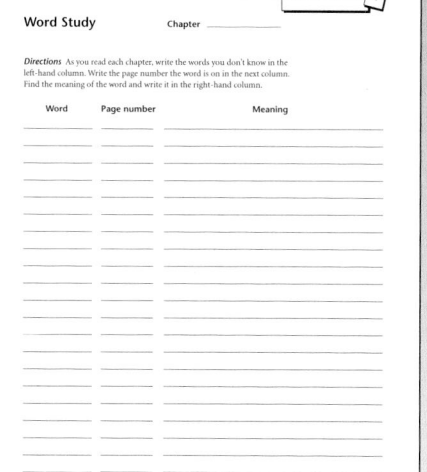

How to Use This Book 4

Using Tables to Solve Problems

Have students turn to the tables on pages 498–501. Discuss the addition and subtraction tables, pointing out that addition and subtraction are inverse operations as are multiplication and division. Discuss the meaning of *inverse operations* and how they can help students understand mathematics processes. Emphasize that when they know one fact, students know the inverse fact as well. For example, if they know $8 + 8 = 16$, then students know that $16 - 8 = 8$.

Review and Test

After they read Using the Chapter Reviews and Preparing for Tests, remind students that the review will help prepare them for taking the test. Refer them once again to the chapter's Goals for Learning. The review and test focus on these major objectives.

With the class, read the Test-Taking Tip for Chapter 1. Explain that every tip provides a suggestion for preparing for or taking tests. Ask students if the tip for Chapter 1 provides a suggestion for taking a test or preparing for a test.

Remind students to read directions and the complete test or review item before they try to solve a problem or answer a question. Provide strategies for helping students complete the different kinds of review and test questions. For example, on multiple choice questions, students can first eliminate items they know are incorrect. For problems requiring computation, suggest that students use scratch paper to do the computation and then neatly transfer their work to the test or review paper.

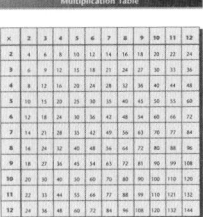

Using Tables to Solve Problems

Four tables can be found in the back of this book. There is one for each of the four main math operations: addition, subtraction, multiplication, and division. You are encouraged to memorize these tables or refer to them as needed. If you are allowed to use a calculator, you may choose to use one instead of these tables.

Using the Chapter Reviews

◆ For each Chapter Review, answer the multiple choice questions first.

◆ Answer the questions under the other parts of the Chapter Review.

◆ To help you take tests, read the Test-Taking Tips at the end of each Chapter Review.

Test-Taking Tip

Before you start, scan the entire test. Do the easier problems first so that you will have more time to spend on the harder ones.

Preparing for Tests

◆ Complete the exercises in each lesson. Make up similar problems to practice what you have learned. You may want to do this with a classmate and share your questions.

◆ Review your answers to lesson exercises and Chapter Reviews.

◆ Test yourself on vocabulary words and key ideas.

◆ Practice problem-solving strategies.

Using the Answer Key

Pages 458–491 of this book show answers and solutions to selected problems. The problems with black numbers show answers. The problems with red numbers also show step-by-step solutions. Use the answers and solutions to check your work.

Using a Calculator

An electronic calculator can help you with many math problems. There are many different kinds of calculators available. Some calculators have a few keys and perform only a few simple operations. Other calculators have many keys and do many advanced calculations. It is important to know what your calculator can do and how to use it. Here are some tips for using the keys on most calculators. To learn more about your own calculator, read the instructions that come with it.

The diagram shows an example of a scientific calculator. It describes the keys that you will most likely use in *Mathematics: Pathways*.

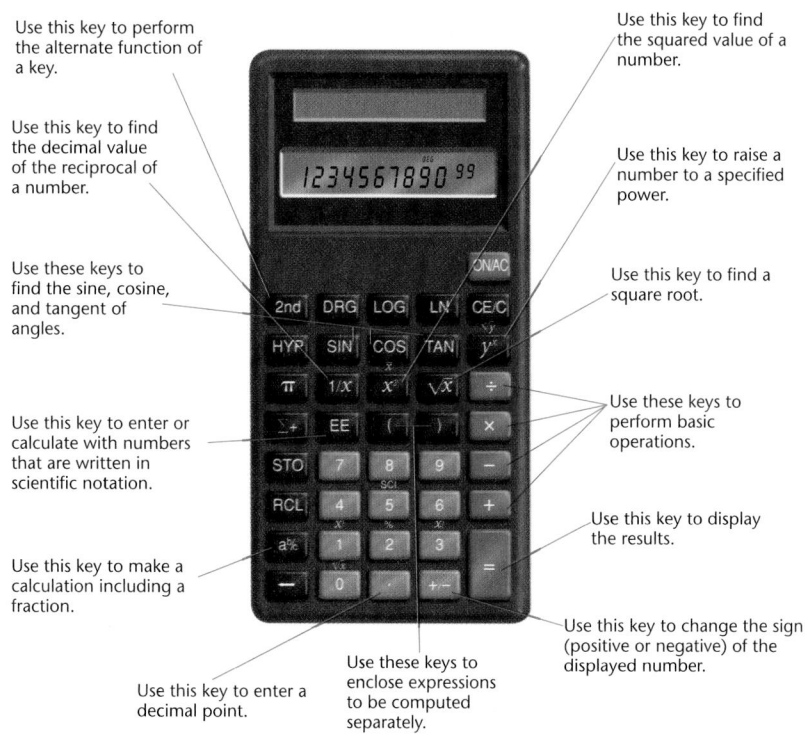

Use this key to perform the alternate function of a key.

Use this key to find the decimal value of the reciprocal of a number.

Use these keys to find the sine, cosine, and tangent of angles.

Use this key to enter or calculate with numbers that are written in scientific notation.

Use this key to make a calculation including a fraction.

Use this key to enter a decimal point.

Use these keys to enclose expressions to be computed separately.

Use this key to find the squared value of a number.

Use this key to raise a number to a specified power.

Use this key to find a square root.

Use these keys to perform basic operations.

Use this key to display the results.

Use this key to change the sign (positive or negative) of the displayed number.

Using a Calculator

Have students read the calculator paragraphs and call-out descriptions on page xvii. Demonstrate some of the calculator functions or ask student volunteers to show some of the calculator functions. Have students go to the Calculator Practice feature on page 9. Read the instructions out loud, then encourage students to complete Example 5.

Problem-Solving Strategies

Help students understand that a clear strategy for solving problems is one of the greatest math tools they can have. Emphasize that students will be better problem solvers if they follow strategic steps, such as Read, Plan, Solve, and Reflect.

After reading about the problem-solving strategy with students, write this sample problem on the board.

> Monday through Friday, Arturo works part-time at a card shop. This week he worked 18 hours. He worked 3 hours on both Monday and Wednesday. He worked 4 hours on both Tuesday and Thursday. How many hours did he work on Friday? (*4 hours*)

Distribute copies of How to Use This Book 5–6 to students. As a class, work through the questions on sheet 5 (Problem-Solving Strategies) and solve the problem. Help students note that different solution strategies will work on this problem. Tell students that their choice of a solution strategy may depend on the type of problem involved or on their personal preferences. Sheet 6, Problem Solving, can provide a visual for the problem-solving process. Encourage students to refer to and use these worksheets as they solve problems throughout the text. Students can also use How to Use This Book 7, Venn Diagram, to organize chapter concepts and to help solve problems.

Problem-Solving Strategies

The main reason for learning math skills is to help us use math to solve everyday problems. You will notice sets of problem-solving exercises throughout your text. When you learn a new math skill, you will have a chance to apply this skill to a real-life problem.

Following these steps will help you to solve the problems.

| 1 | Read |

Read the problem to discover what information you are to gather. Study the problem to decide if you have all the information you need or if you need more data. Also study the problem to decide if it includes information you do not need to solve the problem. Begin thinking about the steps needed to solve the problem.

Ask yourself:
◆ Am I looking for a part of a number?
◆ Am I looking for a larger number?
◆ Am I looking for more than one number?
◆ Will solving the problem require multiple steps?

For example, read this problem:

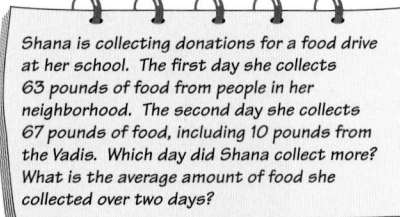

> Shana is collecting donations for a food drive at her school. The first day she collects 63 pounds of food from people in her neighborhood. The second day she collects 67 pounds of food, including 10 pounds from the Vadis. Which day did Shana collect more? What is the average amount of food she collected over two days?

This problem asks you to figure out which day Shana collected the most food and the average amount of food collected per day. It also gives unnecessary information about the family that donated the most food.

In order to answer the questions, you see that you need to compare the collected amounts on the two days, then calculate the average. You will solve for two numbers.

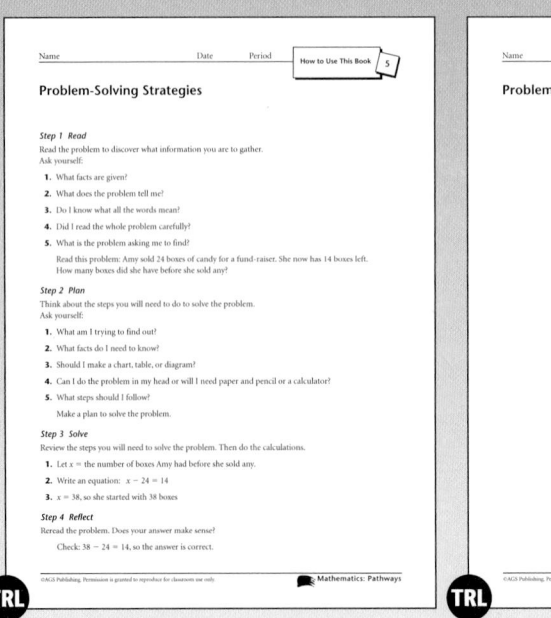

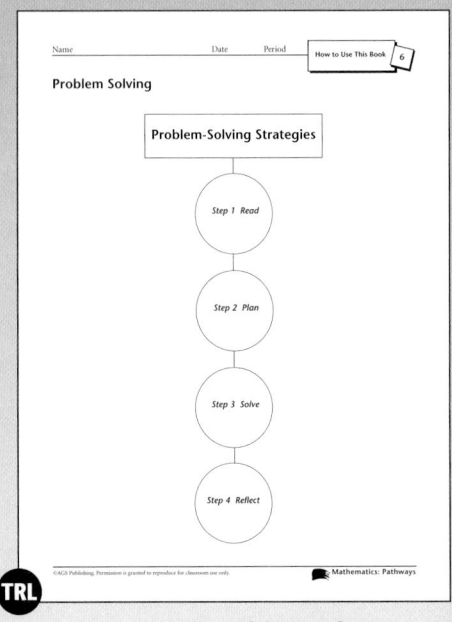

2	Plan

Think about the steps you will need to do to solve the problem. Decide if you are going to calculate this mentally, on paper, or with a calculator. Will you need to add, subtract, multiply, or divide? Will you need to do more than one step? If possible, estimate your answer.

These strategies may help you to find a solution:

- ◆ Simplify or reword the problem
- ◆ Divide the problem into smaller parts
- ◆ Draw a picture
- ◆ Look for a pattern
- ◆ Make a chart or graph to illustrate the problem
- ◆ Use a formula or write an equation

Divide the example problem into two parts.

- ◆ First, compare the two amounts to decide which day Shana collected more food.
- ◆ Second, find the average of the two numbers. Use the formula for finding the average or mean of a set of values.

3	Solve

Follow your plan and do the calculations. Check your work. Make sure to label your answer correctly.

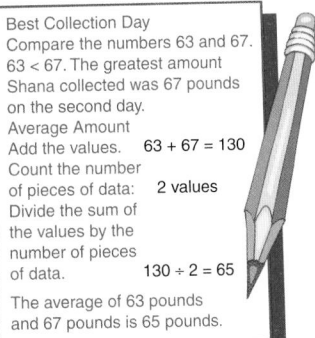

Best Collection Day
Compare the numbers 63 and 67.
63 < 67. The greatest amount Shana collected was 67 pounds on the second day.
Average Amount
Add the values.   63 + 67 = 130
Count the number of pieces of data: 2 values
Divide the sum of the values by the number of pieces of data.   130 ÷ 2 = 65

The average of 63 pounds and 67 pounds is 65 pounds.

4	Reflect

Reread the problem and ask yourself if your answer makes sense. Did you answer the questions? You can also check your work to see if your answers are correct.

Shana's best day was her second day, because she collected 67 pounds of food, and 67 is greater than 63. Her average amount collected was 65 pounds per day. The answer makes sense because 65 is halfway between 63 and 67.

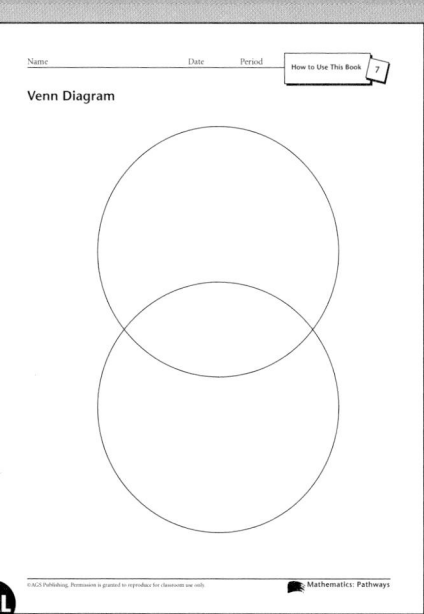

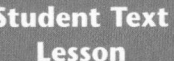

Planning Guide

Number Systems

Lesson	Student Pages	Vocabulary	Practice Exercises	Problem Solving	Try This	Solutions Key
1 The Base 10 System	2–3	✔	✔			✔
2 Place Value	4–5	✔	✔			✔
3 Addition and Subtraction	6–7	✔	✔	7		✔
4 Multiplication and Division	8–9	✔	✔	9	9	✔
5 The Base 2 System	10–13	✔	✔			✔
6 The Base 5 System	14–17	✔	✔		17	✔
Application Binary Number System and Electrical Circuits	18		✔			✔

Chapter Activities

Teacher's Resource Library
Estimation Exercise 1: Estimating Multiplication
Application Activity 1: Binary Number System and Electrical Circuits
Everyday Math 1: Sales Figures
Community Connection 1: Base Systems

Teacher's Edition
Chapter 1 Project

Assessment Options

Student Text
Chapter 1 Review

Teacher's Resource Library
Chapter 1 Mastery Tests A and B

Teacher's Edition
Chapter 1 Alternative Assessments

Student Text Features						Teaching Strategies									Learning Styles						Teacher's Resource Library			
Estimation Activity	Math in Your Life	Technology Connection	Writing About Mathematics	Build a Model	Calculator Practice	Online Connection	Common Error	Applications Home, Career, Community	Mental Math	Manipulatives	Calculator	Group Problem Solving	Modeling	Knowing Your Students	Auditory/Verbal	Visual/Spatial	Logical/Mathematical	Body/Kinesthetic	Interpersonal/Group Learning	LEP/ESL	Activities	Alternate Activities	Workbook Activities	Self-Study Guide
	2						3		3	3											1–2	1–2	1	✔
5			5				5			5	5				5				5		3	3	2	✔
							7		7							7	7		7		4	4	3	✔
					9		9		8			9				8			9	9	5	5	4	✔
		11	13			13	11	12	11	11		12									6	6	5	✔
				17	16	16					16		17	17			15			16	7	7	6	✔
						19	18	19																✔

Software Options

Skill Track Software

Use the Skill Track Software for *Mathematics: Pathways* for additional reinforcement of this chapter. The software provides multiple-choice assessment items for students to access by computer.

Solutions Key

Use the Solutions Key with this chapter to help students who may need additional assistance. The Solutions Key CD provides solutions for every exercise in the student edition.

Other Resources

Alternative Activities

The Teacher's Resource Library (TRL) contains a set of worksheets written at a second-grade reading level called Alternative Activities. They cover the same content as the regular Activities.

Manipulatives

See the Manipulative activities in this chapter for hands-on modeling of the content.
Base Ten Blocks
Two-Color Counters

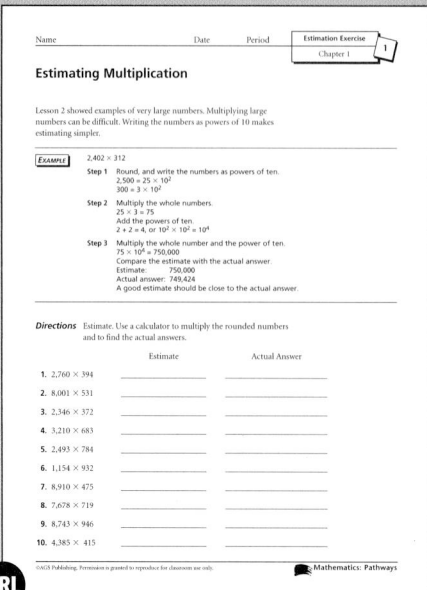

Estimation Exercise 1

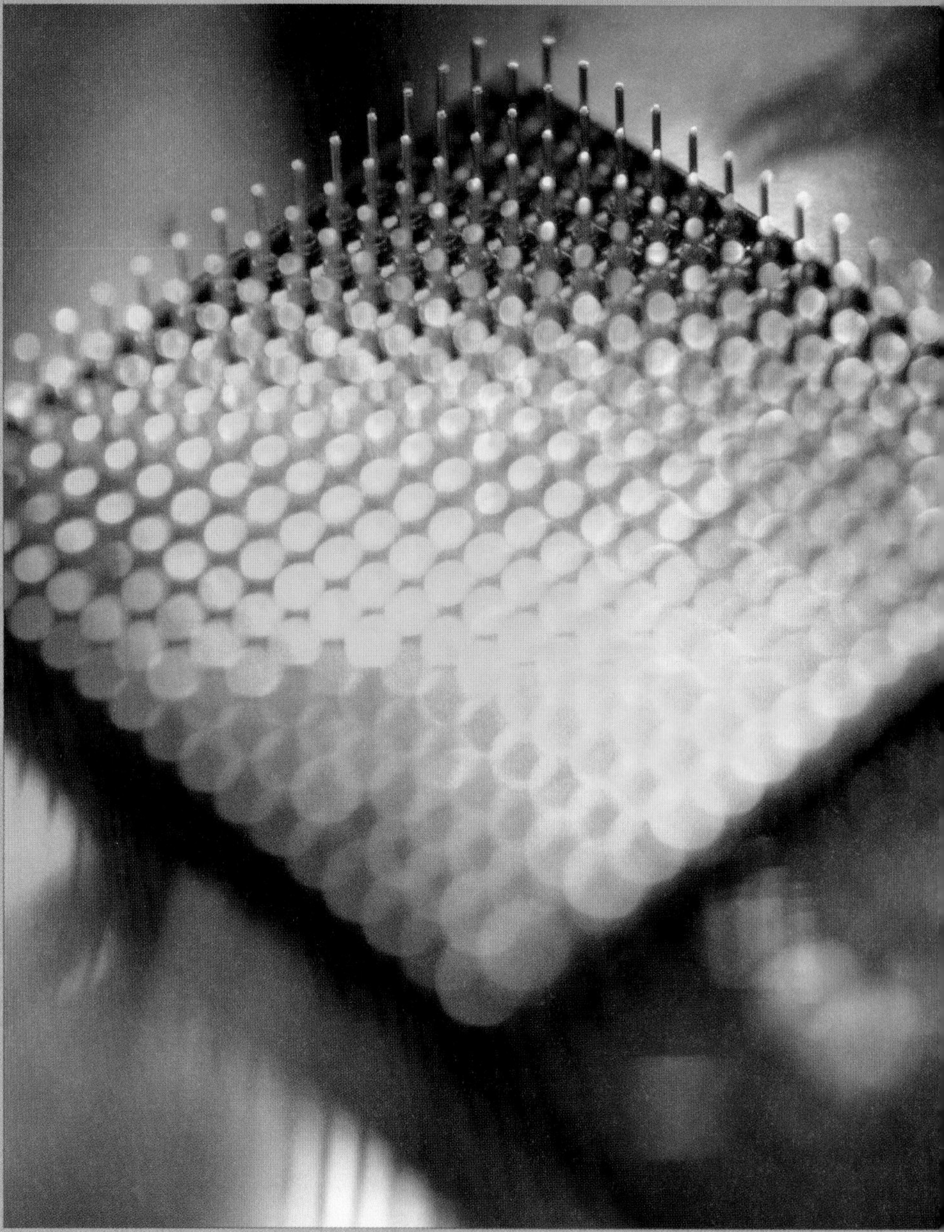

Community Connection 1

Number Systems

The first computers were big machines that filled entire rooms. They have become smaller and smaller each year because of improvements in how we make computers. The photograph shows the connector pins and material of a microchip. Although the microchip in this picture looks quite large, the actual chip would fit easily on the tip of your little finger.

Information typed into a computer is stored as ones and zeros. Computers use this system—called the *binary* or *base 2* system—because base 2 numbers are the easiest to store and use. The numbers 0 and 1 mean *on* and *off* to a computer. You will learn more about that in this chapter's Application lesson.

In Chapter 1, you will learn about different number systems such as base 2 and base 5.

Goals for Learning

- ◆ To understand base 10
- ◆ To review whole number place values
- ◆ To write whole numbers in expanded form using powers of 10
- ◆ To use inverse operations
- ◆ To write numbers in base 2
- ◆ To write numbers in base 5

1

Sorting and classifying is a basic human endeavor dating back to the Stone Age. Starting with stick figures painted on cave walls, mathematics has evolved over the centuries to include number systems that are fundamental to the way we live today. The base 10 system defines how we count. It is a universal language of symbols that can cross barriers between spoken languages. Point out to students that we use the four operations to manipulate the values represented by the numerals— from simple calculations to complex algebraic algorithms. Other number systems besides base 10 also define our world. Base 2 drives the binary functions fundamental to modern computer and calculator technology. Base 60 forms the system for telling time.

CHAPTER PROJECT

Organize the class into small groups to work on a five-minute class presentation. Each presentation should be a mathematics topic of the group's choice. For example, they can delve into ancient cultures and the development of counting, or they can research modern-day applications of number theory. Each group can present its topic using any format: displaying a computer presentation, using a trifold board, making a model, or acting out a play.

TEACHER'S RESOURCE

The AGS Publishing Teaching Strategies in Math Transparencies may be used with this chapter. They add an interactive dimension to expand and enhance the program content.

CAREER INTEREST INVENTORY

The AGS Publishing Harrington-O'Shea Career Decision-Making System-Revised (CDM) may be used with this chapter. Students can use the CDM to explore their interests and identify careers. The CDM defines career areas that are indicated by students' responses on the inventory.

Name _____ Date _____ Period _____ *SELF-STUDY GUIDE*

CHAPTER 1: Number Systems

Goal 1.1   To understand base 10

Date	Assignment	Score
_____	1: Read pages 1–3. Complete Exercises A–C on page 3.	_____
_____	2: Complete Workbook Activity 1.	_____

Comments:

Goals 1.2 and 1.3   To review whole number place values; to write whole numbers in expanded form using powers of 10

Date	Assignment	Score
_____	3: Read pages 4–5. Complete Exercises A–D on page 5.	_____
_____	4: Complete Workbook Activity 2.	_____

Comments:

Goal 1.4   To use inverse operations

Date	Assignment	Score
_____	5: Read pages 6–7. Complete Exercises A–D on page 7.	_____
_____	6: Complete Workbook Activity 3.	_____
_____	7: Read pages 8–9. Complete Exercises A–C on page 9.	_____
_____	8: Read and complete the Calculator Practice on page 9.	_____
_____	9: Complete Workbook Activity 4.	_____

Comments:

Mathematics: Pathways

Name _____ Date _____ Period _____ *SELF-STUDY GUIDE*

CHAPTER 1: Number Systems, continued

Goal 1.5   To write numbers in base 2

Date	Assignment	Score
_____	10: Read pages 10–12. Complete Exercises A–C on page 13.	_____
_____	11: Complete Workbook Activity 5.	_____

Comments:

Goal 1.6   To write numbers in base 5

Date	Assignment	Score
_____	12: Read pages 14–15. Complete Exercises A–B on page 16.	_____
_____	13: Read and complete the Calculator Practice on pages 16–17.	_____
_____	14: Complete Workbook Activity 6.	_____
_____	15: Read and complete the Application on page 18.	_____
_____	16: Complete the Chapter 1 Review on pages 19–21.	_____

Comments:

Student's Signature _____ Date _____
Instructor's Signature _____ Date _____

Mathematics: Pathways

Chapter 1 Self-Study Guide

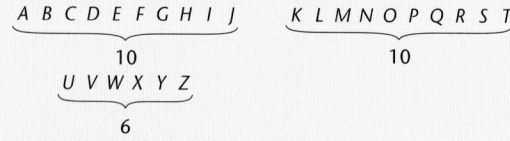

Lesson at a Glance

Chapter 1 Lesson 1

Overview This lesson introduces the decimal numbers of the base 10 system through grouping concepts.

Objective
- To write numbers in base 10

Student Pages 2–3

Teacher's Resource Library TRL

Workbook Activity 1

Activities 1–2

Alternative Activities 1–2

Mathematics Vocabulary

numeral
digit
decimal number
base 10

---

1 Warm-Up Activity

Begin by brainstorming with students everyday items that are grouped in specific numbers. For example, wheels on a car *(4)*, hours on an analog clock face *(12)*, minutes in an hour *(60)*, seconds in a minute *(60)*, degrees in a circle *(360)*, inches in a foot *(12)*, feet in a yard *(3)*, and pennies in a dime *(10)*. Discuss with students shortcuts to count items in large quantities.

2 Teaching the Lesson

Review with students the different ways to group and name the same quantity; for example:

two	duo, duet, double
three	trio, triplet
four	quartet
ten	decade
twelve	dozen
hundred	century

Base 10 is another name for grouping and counting by tens.

Lesson 1 The Base 10 System

Numeral
A symbol representing a number
Digit
Any one of the ten symbols 0, 1, 2, 3, 4, 5, 6, 7, 8, or 9
Decimal number
A number written in base 10
Base 10
A system of counting based on groups of tens

Long before words were invented, the earliest people used symbols to represent numbers. The Hindus in India first developed the **numerals** 1, 2, 3, 4, 5, 6, 7, 8, and 9, which we use today. These **digits**, plus 0, form the **decimal numbers** of the **base 10** system.

EXAMPLE 1 Group all the letters *A* through *Z* by TENS.

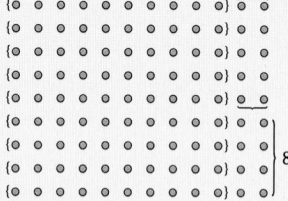

The letters form 2 groups of TENS with 6 left over. So, you can write:

Two TENS plus 6 → 2 TENS + 6, or 26

EXAMPLE 2 Group the counters by TENS.

There are many ways to group by TENS. Here is one:

The counters form 10 groups of TENS with 8 left over. So, you can write:

Ten TENS plus 8 → 10 TENS + 8, or 108

Math in Your Life

Counting Digits
Did you ever wonder how we ended up with a base 10 counting system? Look no further than your fingers and toes. In fact, the word *digit* comes from the Latin word for finger, or *digitus*.

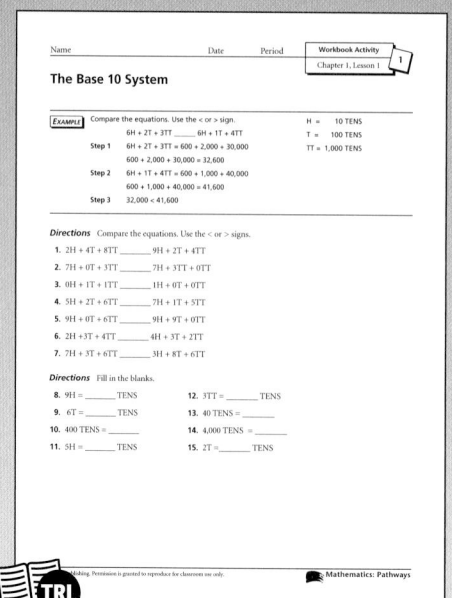

Workbook Activity 1

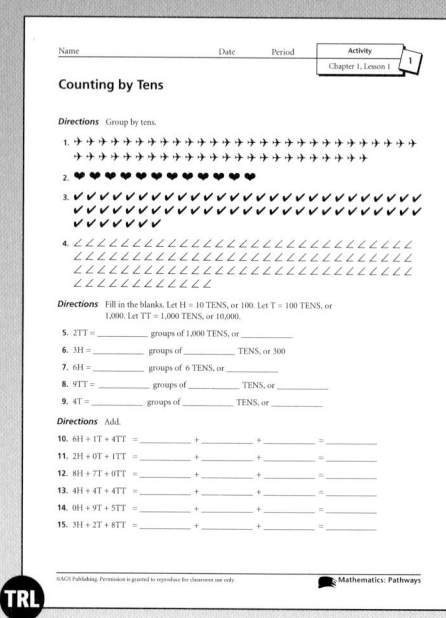

Activity 1

1. 3 sets of 10

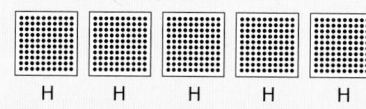

2. 3 sets of 10 plus 4

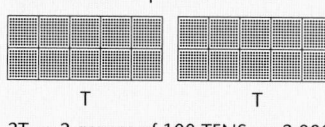

You know that 10 TENS equal 100. Let's see what happens when you use different symbols to represent other groups of 10 TENS.

EXAMPLE 3 Let H represent one group of 10 TENS, or 100.
What number equals 5H?

5H → 5 groups of 10 TENS, or 500

EXAMPLE 4 Let T represent 10 groups of 10 TENS, or 1,000.
What number equals 2T?

2T → 2 groups of 100 TENS, or 2,000

Exercise A On a separate sheet of paper, show how to regroup the following by 10s.

1. ☆☆☆ ☆☆☆ ☆☆☆ ☆☆☆ ☆☆☆
☆☆☆ ☆☆☆ ☆☆☆ ☆☆☆ ☆☆☆

2. ∆∆∆∆ ∆∆∆∆ ∆∆∆∆ ∆∆∆∆
∆∆∆∆ ∆∆∆∆ ∆∆∆∆ ∆∆∆∆ ∆∆

Exercise B Fill in the blanks.
Let H = 10 TENS, or 100
Let T = 100 TENS, or 1,000

3. 5H → ■ groups of ■ TENS, or 500

4. 9H → ■ groups of ■ TENS, or ■

5. 3T → ■ groups of ■ TENS, or 3,000

6. 8T → ■ groups of ■ TENS, or ■

Exercise C Fill in the blanks.

7. 5H + 3T = ■ + ■ = ■

8. 9H + 8T = ■ + ■ = ■

9. ■ + 3T = 500 + ■ = ■

10. 3H + ■ = ■ + 8,000 = ■

3. 5; 10
4. 9; 10; 900
5. 3; 100
6. 8; 100; 8,000

7. 500; 3,000; 3,500
8. 900; 8,000; 8,900
9. 5H; 3,000; 3,500
10. 8T; 300; 8,300

---

3 Reinforce and Extend

MANIPULATIVES

M Base 10 System

Materials: Base Ten Blocks

Group Practice: Use the additive process to review the multiples of 10. For example, show three Base Ten Rods and ask, "What do the rods represent?" *(3 rods or 3 groups of 10s)* "How can you find the total?" *(Skip-count by 10s: 10, 20, 30.)*

Show five Flats and ask, "What do the flats represent?" *(5 flats or 5 groups of 100s)* "How can you find the total?" *(Skip-count by 100s: 100, 200, 300, 400, 500.)*

Show five Blocks and ask, "What do the blocks represent?" *(5 blocks or 5 groups of 1,000s)* "How can you find the total?" *(Skip-count by 1,000s: 1,000, 2,000, 3,000, 4,000, 5,000.)*

Have students come up with different ways to name groups of numbers. Ask, "What is a different way you can name a group of 500?" *(Answers may vary. Encourage students to be creative. One possibility: cinqua.)* "What would you call two groups of 500?" *(two cinquas)*

Student Practice: Have students use play money to create similar groupings as with the base 10 manipulatives.

MENTAL MATH

Help students recognize that skip-counting by 100s and by 1,000s is a quick way to find the total.

Ask students to skip-count by 100s starting with 100. Then, have them start with 105. Students should recognize that only the digit in the hundreds place changes with each count.

AT HOME

Encourage students to make a list of items at home that are grouped in specific numbers. For example, eggs in a carton *(12)*, cans of soda in a pack *(6)*, rings in a binder *(3)*, and positions on a toggle light switch *(2)*. Help students see that these items are often associated with a quantity.

Lesson at a Glance

Chapter 1 Lesson 2

Overview This lesson reviews the place value of numbers up to millions.

Objectives

- To review whole number place value up to millions
- To name the place value and value of digits in a number
- To write numbers in expanded form using powers of 10

Student Pages 4–5

Teacher's Resource Library  **TRL**

Workbook Activity 2

Activity 3

Alternative Activity 3

....

Mathematics Vocabulary

place value
expanded form
power of 10
exponent

....

1 Warm-Up Activity

Review with students the names of the place-value chart. Show on the board or an overhead:

Millions	Hundred-Thousands	Ten-Thousands	Thousands	Hundreds	Tens	Ones

← increase   decrease →

Remind students that the value increases tenfold from right to left and decreases tenfold from left to right.

Place value
Worth of a digit based on its position in a number

Expanded form
Numbers written to show the place value of each digit

Power of 10
A product of 10 multiplied by itself one or more times

Exponent
Number that tells how many times another number is a factor

The digits 0, 1, 2, 3, 4, 5, 6, 7, 8, and 9 are symbols only. The worth of each symbol depends on its **place value** in a number.

EXAMPLE 1 Name the place value of each digit in the number 1,384,972.

$$1, 3\ 8\ 4,9\ 7\ 2$$
↑ ↑ ↑ ↑ ↑ ↑ ↑
Millions, Hundred-thousands, Ten-thousands, Thousands, Hundreds, Tens, Ones

EXAMPLE 2 Name the place value of the underlined digit.

2,394,750   6,028   41,007
↑   ↑   ↑
Millions   Hundreds   Ten-thousands

EXAMPLE 3 Name the value of the underlined digit.

2,394,750   6,028   41,007
↑   ↑   ↑
2 million   0 hundreds   4 ten-thousands or 40 thousands

Another way to show the place value of a number is to write it in **expanded form.**

EXAMPLE 4 Write the number 84,972 in expanded form.

$(8 \times 10{,}000) + (4 \times 1{,}000) + (9 \times 100) + (7 \times 10) + (2 \times 1)$

The **powers of 10** can also be used to write numbers in expanded form. Remember that:

$$1 = 1 = 10^0$$
$$10 = 10 = 10^1$$
$$10 \times 10 = 100 = 10^2$$
$$10 \times 10 \times 10 = 1{,}000 = 10^3$$
$$10 \times 10 \times 10 \times 10 = 10{,}000 = 10^4$$
$$10 \times 10 \times 10 \times 10 \times 10 = 100{,}000 = 10^5$$
$$10 \times 10 \times 10 \times 10 \times 10 \times 10 = 1{,}000{,}000 = 10^6 \text{ and so on.}$$

The **exponent** shows the number of times 10 is multiplied by 10. Here 2 is the exponent. So, $10^2 = 10 \times 10$.

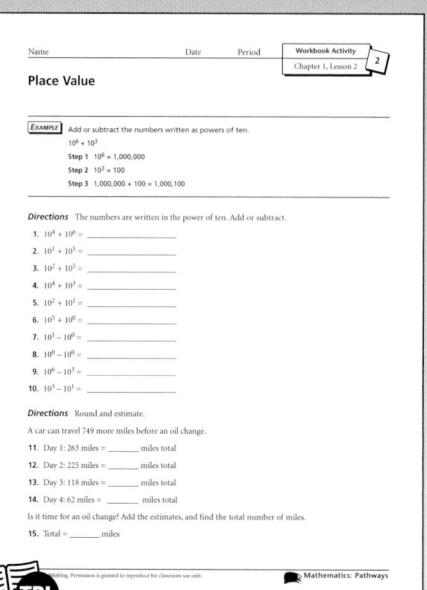

Workbook Activity 2

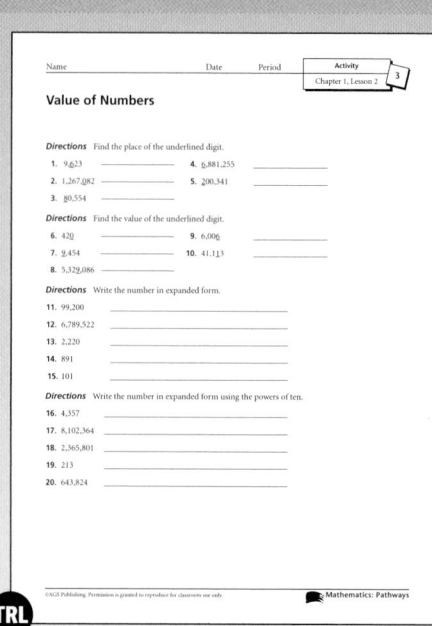

Activity 3

EXAMPLE 5 Write the number 2,905 in expanded form using the powers of 10.

$$2,905 = (2 \times 10^3) + (9 \times 10^2) + (0 \times 10^1) + (5 \times 10^0)$$

 Zero times any number equals zero.

Exercise A Name the place value of the underlined digit.

1. 34,285   hundreds
2. 546,812   thousands
3. 4,592,013   millions
4. 301,866   ten-thousands
5. 8,722,004   tens
6. 1,563,027   hundred-thousands

Exercise B Name the value of the underlined digit.

7. 648   4 tens
8. 5,375   5 thousands
9. 1,809   9 ones
10. 2,180   0 ones
11. 14,256   1 ten-thousand
12. 5,623,576   6 hundred-thousands

Exercise C Write the number in expanded form.

13. 162   14. 2,949   15. 413,078

Exercise D Write the number in expanded form using the powers of ten.

16. 3,158   18. 68,523   20. 2,279,823
17. 7,623   19. 12,568

Answers in left margin:

. $(1 \times 100) + (6 \times 10) + (2 \times 1)$
. $(2 \times 1,000) + (9 \times 100) + (4 \times 10) + (9 \times 1)$
. $(4 \times 100,000) + (1 \times 10,000) + (3 \times 1,000) + (0 \times 100) + (7 \times 10) + (8 \times 1)$
. $(3 \times 10^3) + (1 \times 10^2) + (5 \times 10^1) + (8 \times 10^0)$
. $(7 \times 10^3) + (6 \times 10^2) + (2 \times 10^1) + (3 \times 10^0)$
. $(6 \times 10^4) + (8 \times 10^3) + (5 \times 10^2) + (2 \times 10^1) + (3 \times 10^0)$
. $(1 \times 10^4) + (2 \times 10^3) + (5 \times 10^2) + (6 \times 10^1) + (8 \times 10^0)$
. $(2 \times 10^6) + (2 \times 10^5) + (7 \times 10^4) + (9 \times 10^3) + (8 \times 10^2) + (2 \times 10^1) + (3 \times 10^0)$

 Estimation Activity

Although mathematics is very precise, in real life we often rely on an *estimate,* or an approximate number.

Estimate: You have $15. Is this enough to buy a loaf of bread at $3.85, a quart of milk at $2.30, a dozen eggs at $1.99, and pasta at $3.45?

Solution: When making a purchase, it is best to round up the individual costs.

$3.85 → $4
$2.30 → $3   } 13 { $1.99 → $2
$3.45 → $4

Yes; $15 will cover the cost of the items purchased.

Number Systems   Chapter 1   5

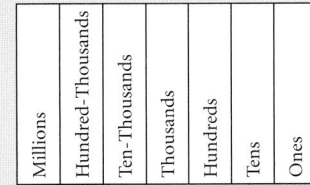

2 Teaching the Lesson

Place digits on a place-value chart, and ask students to read the number. Help them distinguish between *place* and *value*.

Millions	Hundred-Thousands	Ten-Thousands	Thousands	Hundreds	Tens	Ones
		5	2	0	7	8

For example, ask, "Where is the digit 5?" *(in the ten-thousands place)* "What is the value of the digit 5?" *(5 ten-thousands, or 50 thousand)*

3 Reinforce and Extend

Number Systems   5

Lesson at a Glance

Chapter 1 Lesson 3

Overview This lesson applies the concept of inverse operations to addition and subtraction.

Objectives

- To review addition and subtraction
- To use inverse operations to check sums and differences

Student Pages 6–7

Teacher's Resource Library (TRL)

Workbook Activity 3

Activity 4

Alternative Activity 4

Mathematics Vocabulary

addition
subtraction
inverse
operation

---

1 Warm-Up Activity

Review with students familiar words or ideas that convey opposites, specifically actions that cancel each other. For example:

> in and out
> to and from
> back and forth
> up and down
> income and expense
> shrink and expand
> deposit and withdrawal
> increase and decrease

2 Teaching the Lesson

Start the lesson by reminding students that addition and subtraction undo each other. As an example, show 5 counters. Add 4 counters. Ask, "What action is needed to return to 5 counters?" *(Remove 4 counters.)*

Use the number line to demonstrate adding on. Help students understand that the sum represents the total number of increments. Therefore, on the number line $7 + 4$ means 4 increments after 7. This concept is very important, especially when students work with negative numbers.

Addition and **subtraction** are **inverse operations.** Addition is the operation of combining two or more numbers, and subtraction is the operation of taking one number away from another. These two operations are the opposite of each other.

Addition
The arithmetic operation of combining two or more numbers to find a total

Subtraction
The arithmetic operation of taking one number away from another

Inverse
Opposite or reverse

Operation
Addition, subtraction, multiplication, and division

EXAMPLE 1 Use $7 + 4$ to show that addition and subtraction are inverse operations.

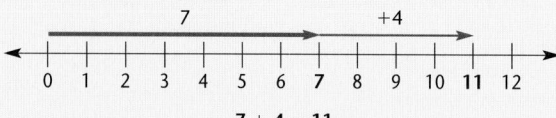

$$7 + 4 = 11$$

When you subtract 4 from 11, the result is 7.

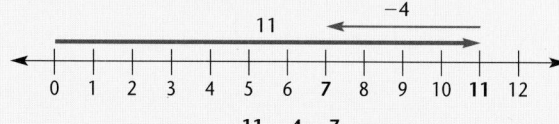

$$11 - 4 = 7$$

You can use inverse operations to check your work.

$$\begin{array}{r} 7 \\ + 4 \\ \hline 11 \end{array} \qquad \begin{array}{r} 11 \\ - 4 \\ \hline 7 \end{array}$$

After regrouping, you can subtract 9 ones from 13 ones

$$\begin{array}{r} 13 \\ - 9 \\ \hline 4 \end{array}$$

and subtract 1 ten from 6 tens.

$$\begin{array}{r} 60 \\ - 10 \\ \hline 50 \end{array}$$

EXAMPLE 2 Add $54 + 19$. Then subtract to check your answer.

$$\begin{array}{r} {\scriptstyle 1} \\ 54 \\ + 19 \\ \hline 73 \end{array} \qquad \begin{array}{r} {\scriptstyle 6\ 13} \\ 7\cancel{3} \\ - 19 \\ \hline 54 \end{array}$$

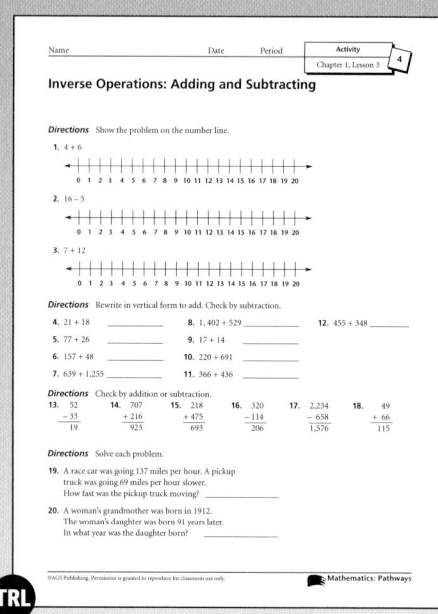

EXAMPLE 3 Find the difference of 937−518.

$$\begin{array}{r} {}^{2\,17}\\ 9\cancel{3}\cancel{7}\\ -\ 518\\ \hline 419 \end{array}$$

Then add to check your answer.

$$\begin{array}{r} {}^{1}\\ 419\\ +\ 518\\ \hline 937 \end{array}$$

Exercise A Use a number line like this one to show the computation.

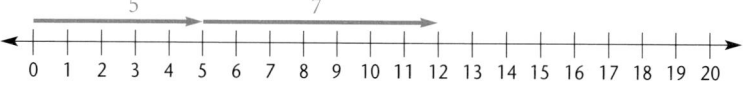

1. $5 + 7 = 12$

2. $9 - 4 = 5$

3. $11 + 4 = 15$

Exercise B Add, then check by subtraction.

4. $17 + 6 = 23$ **5.** $26 + 45 = 71$ **6.** $39 + 54 = 93$ **7.** $63 + 256 = 319$
$23 - 17 = 6$ $71 - 26 = 45$ $93 - 39 = 54$ $319 - 63 = 256$

Exercise C Use an inverse operation to check the answer.

8.
$$\begin{array}{r} 91\\ -\ 25\\ \hline 66 \end{array} \qquad \begin{array}{r} 66\\ +\ 25\\ \hline 91 \end{array}$$

9.
$$\begin{array}{r} 38\\ +\ 49\\ \hline 87 \end{array} \qquad \begin{array}{r} 87\\ -\ 49\\ \hline 38 \end{array}$$

10.
$$\begin{array}{r} 652\\ +\ 209\\ \hline 861 \end{array} \qquad \begin{array}{r} 861\\ -\ 209\\ \hline 652 \end{array}$$

11.
$$\begin{array}{r} 590\\ -\ 137\\ \hline 453 \end{array} \qquad \begin{array}{r} 453\\ +\ 137\\ \hline 590 \end{array}$$

12.
$$\begin{array}{r} 1{,}205\\ -\ 856\\ \hline 349 \end{array} \qquad \begin{array}{r} 349\\ +\ 856\\ \hline 1{,}205 \end{array}$$

13.
$$\begin{array}{r} 684\\ +\ 1{,}009\\ \hline 1{,}693 \end{array} \qquad \begin{array}{r} 1{,}693\\ -\ 1{,}009\\ \hline 684 \end{array}$$

 PROBLEM SOLVING

Exercise D Solve each problem.

14. Alex left home at 8:11 A.M. Her first class starts at 8:35 A.M. How much time does she have to get to school? 24 minutes

15. In 1964, volleyball became an official Olympic sport. Basketball originated 73 years earlier. In what year was basketball invented? 1891

 **3** **Reinforce and Extend**

COMMON ERROR

 Some students might have difficulties regrouping across zeros when adding or subtracting. Remind students that 0 is a placeholder and has value.

MENTAL MATH

 Use mental math to review addition facts for sums between 20 and 30. Write in vertical form addition problems such as:

$$\begin{array}{r} 17\\ +\ 4\\ \hline \end{array} \qquad \begin{array}{r} 17\\ +\ 5\\ \hline \end{array} \qquad \begin{array}{r} 17\\ +\ 6\\ \hline \end{array}$$

Have students name the sum without pencil and paper. Work with students until they are proficient, and then mix up the order of the problems before moving on to different addends.

LEARNING STYLES

Visual/Spatial
Some students will benefit from blocking out the increments to visualize moving left or right on the number line. For example, to show moving 3 spaces left in the subtraction $18 - 3$:

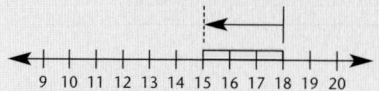

LEARNING STYLES

Logical/Mathematical
Have pairs of students play an Inverse Operation game in which the first student in the pair calls out the instruction, while the second student does the mental math. For example, the first student would say, "Name a number between 10 and 15. Now, add 7. Subtract 4. Add 4. Subtract 7."

Ask, "How is it that you end up with the same number?" Direct each pair to write a brief explanation.

LEARNING STYLES

Interpersonal/Group Learning
Organize students into small groups. To reinforce the concept of inverse operations, ask students why the following would NOT be correct:

stop and go
black and white
here and there
bits and pieces

Ask students to think of other such terms that do NOT represent one action canceling another.

Chapter 1 Lesson 4

Overview This lesson applies the concept of inverse operations to multiplication and division.

Objectives

- To review multiplication and division
- To use inverse operations to check products and quotients

Student Pages 8–9

Teacher's Resource Library TRL

Workbook Activities 4

Activity 5

Alternative Activity 5

Mathematics Vocabulary

multiplication
division

1 Warm-Up Activity

MENTAL MATH

Use mental math to review multiplication facts. Have students name, without using pencil and paper, the product of such problems as:

5	6	7
× 7	× 7	× 7

If students experience difficulties, use familiar factors to help them out. For example, if students stumble on 7 × 7, ask, "What is 7 × 5? 7 × 6?"

LEARNING STYLES

Visual/Spatial
Some students will benefit from visualizing multiplication on a number line. For example, use 5 × 7 to demonstrate the clustering of 5s seven times to reach a product of 35.

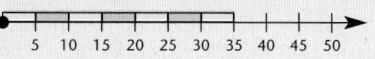

Multiplication
The arithmetic operation that adds a number a given amount of times

Division
The arithmetic operation of finding how many times a number goes into another number

Just as addition and subtraction are inverse operations, so are **multiplication** and **division**. Multiplication adds a number a given number of times, and division finds how many times a number goes into another number.

EXAMPLE 1 Use counters to show 4 × 8 = 32.

You can show 4 × 8 = 32 in two ways.

4 groups of 8 = 32   8 groups of 4 = 32

EXAMPLE 2 Use counters to show 32 ÷ 8 = 4.

Here is a way to show the division:

Instead of writing all the steps, here is a short cut:

```
  1
  42
×  7
 294
```

Carry the 10, and mark a 1 in the tens place.

Because multiplication and division are inverse operations, you can use one to check the calculation of the other.

EXAMPLE 3 Multiply 42 × 7. Then use division to check your answer.

```
    42                          42
  ×  7                      7 ) 294
    14  → 7 × 2 = 14        − 28  → 7 × 4 = 28
 + 280  → 7 × 40 = 280        14
  294  → 14 + 280 = 294     − 14  → 7 × 2 = 14
                               0
```

EXAMPLE 4 Divide 576 ÷ 8. Then use multiplication to check your answer.

```
     72                       72
 8 ) 576                    ×  8
                             576
```

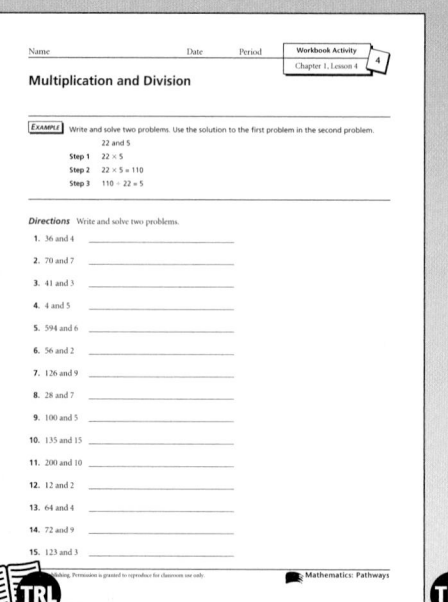

Workbook Activity 4   **Activity 5**

Exercise A Find the answer.

1. $5 \times 7 = 35$ **2.** $12 \times 8 = 96$ **3.** $21 \div 7 = 3$ **4.** $128 \div 4 = 32$

Exercise B Use an inverse operation to check the answer.

5. $9 \times 7 = 63$ **6.** $6 \times 8 = 48$ **7.** $69 \div 3 = 23$ **8.** $145 \div 5 = 29$
$63 \div 7 = 9$ $48 \div 6 = 8$ $23 \times 3 = 69$ $29 \times 5 = 145$

PROBLEM SOLVING

Exercise C Solve each problem.

9. Serina's height is about 10 times the length of her hand. If her hand measures about 6 inches long, about how many feet tall is Serina? 5 ft

10. When divided by 8, the answer is a 1-digit number. When divided by 2, the answer is a 2-digit number. The mystery number has an 8 in the ones place. Name the number. 48

 **Calculator Practice**   Which function key — $+$, $-$, $\times$, or $\div$?

EXAMPLE 5 Name the operation for the equation $56 \blacksquare 4 = 60$.
Think: The answer is greater than the other two numbers.
Try: Press 56×4. The display reads *224*.
Try Again: Press $56 + 4$. The display reads *60*.
Write: $56 + 4 = 60$

 **Try This**

Show that the two multiplications below are the same.

$\begin{array}{r} 34 \\ \times\ 5 \end{array}$ $\begin{array}{r} 5 \\ \times\ 34 \end{array}$

Exercise D Write the correct operation symbol in the $\blacksquare$. Then use your calculator to check your answer.

11. $39 \blacksquare 64 = 103$ $+$ **14.** $144 \blacksquare 12 = 12$ $\div$

12. $18 \blacksquare 5 = 90$ $\times$ **15.** $43 \blacksquare 29 = 72$ $+$

13. $75 \blacksquare 25 = 50$ $-$

GROUP PROBLEM SOLVING

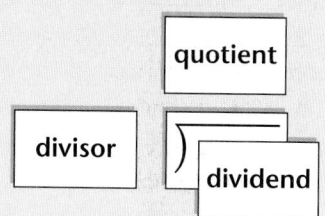

Work in small groups. Complete the Inverse Operations game. All four operations must be used. The students will start with 26, end with 26, and have 8 steps in between.

Ask, "Can you have fewer than 8 steps in this game? Explain your thinking." *(No; each operation must be canceled by its inverse; there must be 8 steps for four operations.)* "What do you notice about the numbers used in each step?" *(The same numbers must be used when applying an inverse. For example, add 3 can be canceled only by subtract 3.)*

LEARNING STYLES

 **LEP/ESL**
Ask students to write one word or symbol on each index card: divisor, dividend, quotient, factor, product, $\times$, $=$, and the long division symbol. Then ask students to show how they would position the index cards.

quotient

divisor

dividend

Start the lesson by reminding students that multiplication and division undo each other. As an example, give 3 volunteers 5 counters each. Ask, "What happens when you pool your counters together?" *(There are 15 counters.)* "What happens when you each take your own counters? (Each person will have only 5 counters.)*

Help students recognize that multiplication and division operate on the idea of grouping together and grouping apart.

COMMON ERROR

 Students often make place-value errors in the quotient when computing long division. Remind students to always check by multiplying the quotient and the divisor.

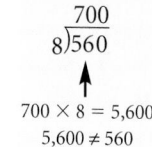

$\begin{array}{r} 700 \\ 8\overline{)560} \end{array}$ $\begin{array}{r} 70 \\ 8\overline{)560} \end{array}$ $\begin{array}{r} 7 \\ 8\overline{)560} \end{array}$

$700 \times 8 = 5{,}600$ $70 \times 8 = 560$ $7 \times 8 = 56$
$5{,}600 \neq 560$ YES $56 \neq 560$

 3 **Reinforce and Extend**

LEARNING STYLES

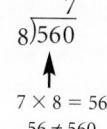 **Interpersonal/Group Learning**
Organize students into small groups. To reinforce the concept of inverse operations, ask students why the following would be correct:

lock and unlock
input and delete
push and pull
inhale and exhale

Ask students to think of other such terms that would represent one action canceling another.

Lesson at a Glance

Chapter 1 Lesson 5

Overview This lesson introduces the base 2 number system.

Objectives

- To learn about the base 2 number system
- To write base 10 numbers in base 2
- To write base 2 numbers in base 10

Student Pages 10–13

Teacher's Resource Library

Workbook Activity 5

Activity 6

Alternative Activity 6

....

Mathematics Vocabulary

base 2
binary system
power of 2

....

1 Warm-Up Activity

Help students recall that the product of a number multiplied by itself one or more times is called the *power of* that number. In other words, 7^4 means $7 \times 7 \times 7 \times 7$, and the product is 2,401.

Exponent, or the number of times a factor is multiplied

$7^4 = 7 \times 7 \times 7 \times 7 = 2,401$

Base, or the number being multiplied

In the base 2 number system, students will work with the powers of 2. For example:

$2^8 = 2 \times 2 \times 2 \times 2 \times 2 \times 2 \times 2 \times 2 = 256$

2 Teaching the Lesson

Explain to students that the base 2 number system is another way to count, but using only the numerals 0 and 1. In base 2, the periods are determined by the powers of 2. Instead of the base 10 periods 1, 10, 100, 1,000, and so on, in base 2 the periods are 1, 2, 4, 8, 16, 32, and so on.

Lesson 5 The Base 2 System

Base 2

A system of counting in powers of 2

Binary system

A system of counting that uses only the numerals 0 and 1

Power of 2

The product of 2 multiplied by itself 1 or more times

Base 10	Base 2
1	1
2	10
3	11
4	100
5	101
6	110
7	111
8	1000
9	1001

In base 10, the number 13 is written:

Base 10

Tens	Ones
1	3

1 ten + 3 ones = 13

Earlier you learned about the base 10 system and the numerals 0, 1, 2, 3, 4, 5, 6, 7, 8, and 9. Another way to count is to use only 2 numerals, 0 and 1. This system is called the **base 2** system or the **binary system.**

In the binary system, the value of each numeral 0 and 1 is based on the **power of 2.** Here are the powers of 2.

$$1 = 1 = 2^0$$
$$2 = 2 = 2^1$$
$$2 \times 2 = 4 = 2^2$$
$$2 \times 2 \times 2 = 8 = 2^3$$
$$2 \times 2 \times 2 \times 2 = 16 = 2^4$$
$$2 \times 2 \times 2 \times 2 \times 2 = 32 = 2^5$$
$$2 \times 2 \times 2 \times 2 \times 2 \times 2 = 64 = 2^6 \text{ and so on.}$$

The base 2 place value chart is similar to the base 10 chart. The values increase from right to left.

Base 2						
64 or 2^6	32 or 2^5	16 or 2^4	8 or 2^3	4 or 2^2	2 or 2^1	1 or 2^0

You can use only the numerals 0 and 1 to write a base 2 number.

To write any base 10 number in base 2, you need to find the highest power of 2 contained in the base 10 number.

EXAMPLE 1 Change 13 base 10 to a base 2 number.

Step 1 Use the base 2 place value chart to find the highest power of 2 contained in 13. The greatest power of 2 contained in 13 is 8. Write the numeral 1 in the 8 column.

Base 2						
64 or 2^6	32 or 2^5	16 or 2^4	8 or 2^3	4 or 2^2	2 or 2^1	1 or 2^0
			1			

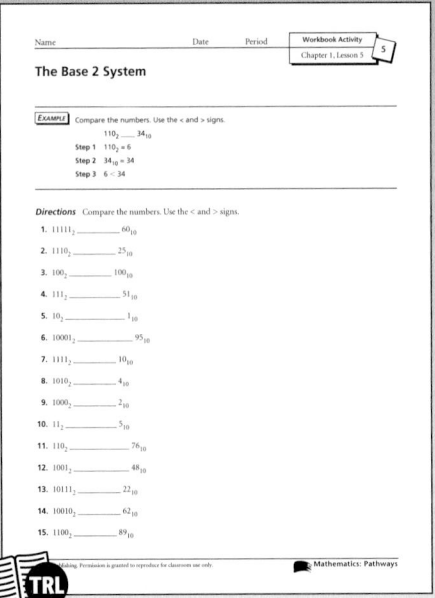

Workbook Activity 5　　　　**Activity 6**

EXAMPLE 1 *(continued)*

Step 2 Because you know that $13 - 8 = 5$, you need to find numbers that when added equal 5. $4 + 1 = 5$. Write the numeral 1 in the 4 and 1 columns.

Base 2						
64 or 2^6	32 or 2^5	16 or 2^4	8 or 2^3	4 or 2^2	2 or 2^1	1 or 2^0
			1	1		1

Step 3 Write the numeral 0 in the empty value between the marked columns. Base 2 numbers always begin with the numeral 1. The chart should look like this:

Base 2						
64 or 2^6	32 or 2^5	16 or 2^4	8 or 2^3	4 or 2^2	2 or 2^1	1 or 2^0
			1	1	0	1

$8 + 4 + 1 = 13$

In base 2, the base 10 number 13 is 1101.

EXAMPLE 2 Change 11011_2 to a base 10 number.

11011_2 ← Symbol to show that 11011 is a base 2 number. It is read: *one one zero one one base 2*

STEP 1 Place the numerals in the base 2 place value chart.

STEP 2 Add the values of each place.

Base 2						
64 or 2^6	32 or 2^5	16 or 2^4	8 or 2^3	4 or 2^2	2 or 2^1	1 or 2^0
		1	1	0	1	1

$(1 \times 16) + (1 \times 8) + (0 \times 4) + (1 \times 2) + 1 =$
$16 + 8 + 0 + 2 + 1 = 27$

The number 11011_2 is 27 in base 10, or 27_{10}.

7_{10} can also be written as 7_{ten}.

So, 10_2 can be written as 10_{two}.

Technology Connection

Binary means base 2. The numerals *0* and *1* are called *binary digits,* or *bits* for short. Historically, bits are grouped in eights, and each group of 8 bits is called a *byte.* Computer hard disk space is measured in megabytes (MB) or gigabytes (GB). In relation to binary units:

1 MB = 1,000,000 bytes or 8,000,000 bits
1 GB = 1,000,000,000 bytes or 8,000,000,000 bits

MENTAL MATH

Memorize the first few powers of 2. One quick method is to start with 2 and double to find the next power.

	2
$2 + 2 =$	4
$4 + 4 =$	8
$8 + 8 =$	16
$16 + 16 =$	32
$32 + 32 =$	64
$64 + 64 =$	128
$128 + 128 =$	256 and so on

MANIPULATIVES

 Base 2

Materials: Two-Color Counters

Use counters to demonstrate how to rewrite 13 from base 10 to base 2.

13 counters

Count out loud to find the highest power of 2 that is in 13.

$2, 4, 8, 16, \ldots$

Because there are 13 counters, the highest power of 2 in 13 is 8.

8 or 2^3   **5 counters left over**

Now regroup the 5 counters left over. Count out loud to find the highest power of 2 that is in 5. $(2, 4, 8, \ldots)$ The highest power of 2 in 5 is 4. One counter is left over.

4 or 2^2   **1 or 2^0**

Use a base 2 place-value chart to show how to write the numerals 0 and 1. For every power of 2 identified, write a 1 in the corresponding column. Where there was no value for 2, write a 0 in that column. For example, the number 13 rewritten in base 2 is 1101, read *one one zero one.* To double check, add the values.

COMMON ERROR

 Students often confuse the meaning of the exponent. Use the following quick check-up to assess student understanding. For example, show:

7^2

$7 \times 7 = 49$

$7 + 7 = 14$

Ask, "Which two cards name the same number?"

GROUP PROBLEM SOLVING

Present the following choice to small groups of students:

Suppose that you are offered two jobs. One job pays $1 a day for 30 days in a row. A second job pays 10¢ on the first day, double that on the second day, double the second day's pay on the third day, and so on. The doubling continues for 30 days.

Which job would you take and why? *(The second job; by the tenth day, the amount paid will have passed the total earned on the first job; the final payment on Day 30 is over $53 million.)*

CAREER CONNECTION

IT stands for *Information Technology*. Did you know that one out of every three jobs in the United States is an IT-related job with an IT firm or one that is dependent on IT skills? Experts predict that soon all jobs will require IT skills.

Help students start a log of news stories about an IT company. It could be one in your area or a national company like Apple, Hewlett-Packard, or Microsoft. Use the Internet and different media to find out about the company students pick. How many times did the company make the news? What can students notice about the stories? What types of career opportunities are available?

EXAMPLE 3 Write 35_{10} in base 2.

Step 1 Use the base 2 place value chart to find the highest power of 2 contained in 35.

Write the numeral 1 in the 32 column.

Step 2 Because you know that $35 - 32 = 3$, you need to find values that when added equal 3. $2 + 1 = 3$. Write the numeral 1 in the 2 and 1 columns.

Step 3 Write the numeral 0 in the empty values between the marked columns. The completed chart should look like this:

Base 2						
64 or 2^6	32 or 2^5	16 or 2^4	8 or 2^3	4 or 2^2	2 or 2^1	1 or 2^0
	1	0	0	0	1	1

$32 + 2 + 1 = 35$

In base 2, the number 35_{10} is 100011, or 100011_2.

EXAMPLE 4 Complete. $50_{10} = \blacksquare_2$

Step 1 Use the base 2 place value chart to find the highest power of 2 contained in 50.

Write the numeral 1 in the 32 column.

Step 2 Because you know that $50 - 32 = 18$, you need to find values that when added equal 18. $16 + 2 = 18$. Write the numeral 1 in the 16 and 2 columns.

Step 3 Write the numeral 0 in the empty values between the marked columns. The completed chart should look like this:

Base 2						
64 or 2^6	32 or 2^5	16 or 2^4	8 or 2^3	4 or 2^2	2 or 2^1	1 or 2^0
	1	1	0	0	1	0

$32 + 16 + 2 = 50$

$50_{10} = 110010_2$

Remember, binary numbers always begin with 1.

Writing About Mathematics

Just as numerals have evolved over time, so have the four operation symbols.

 Add

 Subtract

 Multiply

 Divide

Write a paragraph on the origins of the four operation symbols and how they have changed over the centuries.

Exercise A Change to a base 2 number.

1. 10_{10} 1010_2 **4.** 33_{10} 100001_2

2. 16_{10} 10000_2 **5.** 59_{10} 111011_2

3. 25_{10} 11001_2 **6.** 101_{10} 1100101_2

Exercise B Change to a base 10 number.

7. 10_2 2   **10.** 1000000_2 64

8. 101_2 5   **11.** 1110_2 14

9. 111_2 7   **12.** 1001_2 9

Exercise C Complete.

13. $7_{10} = \blacksquare_2$ 111_2 **17.** $\blacksquare_{10} = 100_2$ 4_{10}

14. $29_{10} = \blacksquare_2$ 11101_2 **18.** $\blacksquare_{10} = 1010_2$ 10_{10}

15. $40_{10} = \blacksquare_2$ 101000_2 **19.** $\blacksquare_{10} = 11001_2$ 25_{10}

16. $77_{10} = \blacksquare_2$ 1001101_2 **20.** $\blacksquare_{10} = 1011010_2$ 90_{10}

Computers use the binary system.

Online Connection

For a listing of computer-related options, direct students to visit www.computer.org or www.cybercareers.org. Students will find information at these sites about pre-college activities at the high school level, college course work guidelines, and computer career options.

Chapter 1 Lesson 6

Overview This lesson introduces the base 5 number system.

Objectives

- To learn about the base 5 number system
- To write base 10 numbers in base 5
- To write base 5 numbers in base 10

Student Pages 14–17

Teacher's Resource Library **TRL**

Workbook Activity 6

Activity 7

Alternative Activity 7

....

Mathematics Vocabulary

base 5
power of 5
quinary system

1 Warm-Up Activity

Review with students groupings of fives. Have them name some familiar items or groups that come in fives. *(Answers may include nickels, quintuplets, pentagons, Olympic rings, fingers, toes, points on a star, five senses, members of a basketball team.)*

Follow up by asking, "When you think of these items or groups, a certain quantity comes to mind. For example, when you think of 5 nickels, what is the quantity you are referring to?" *(5 nickels is the same as 25 pennies.)*

Help students recognize that when items are grouped, we often count by the grouping number. Instead of saying 25 pennies, we say 5 nickels, knowing that 5 nickels represent 25 pennies.

2 Teaching the Lesson

Start by reminding students that the powers of 5 are not the same as the multiples of 5. A power of 5 is the product of 5 multiplied by itself one or more times.

$$5 \times 5 \times 5 = 125 \qquad 5 \times 3 = 15$$

power of 5   multiple of 5

| Lesson | 6 | The Base 5 System |

Base 5

A system of counting in powers of 5

Power of 5

The product of 5 multiplied by itself 1 or more times

Quinary system

A system of counting that uses only the numerals 0, 1, 2, 3, and 4; also known as base 5

Using the numerals 0, 1, 2, 3, and 4, we can count by **powers of 5**. This is called the **base 5**, or **quinary,** system.

Here are the powers of 5:

$$1 = 1 = 5^0$$
$$5 = 5 = 5^1$$
$$5 \times 5 = 25 = 5^2$$
$$5 \times 5 \times 5 = 125 = 5^3$$
$$5 \times 5 \times 5 \times 5 = 625 = 5^4$$
$$5 \times 5 \times 5 \times 5 \times 5 = 3{,}125 = 5^5$$
$$5 \times 5 \times 5 \times 5 \times 5 \times 5 = 15{,}625 = 5^6 \quad \text{and so on.}$$

There is also a base 5 place value chart.

Base 5						
15,625 or 5^6	3,125 or 5^5	625 or 5^4	125 or 5^3	25 or 5^2	5 or 5^1	1 or 5^0

To write quinary numbers, think in powers of 5.

Base 10	Base 5
1	1
2	2
3	3
4	4
5	10
6	11
7	12
8	13
9	14
10	20

EXAMPLE 1 Change 39_{10} to a base 5 number.

Step 1 Use the base 5 place value chart to find the highest power of 5 contained in 39. 25 is the highest power of 5 contained in 39.

Place the numeral 1 in the 25 or 5^2 column.

Base 5						
15,625 or 5^6	3,125 or 5^5	625 or 5^4	125 or 5^3	25 or 5^2	5 or 5^1	1 or 5^0
				1		

Step 2 You know that $39 - 25 = 14$. Now find the highest power of 5 contained in 14. 2 groups of 5 or $5^1 = 10$.

Place the numeral 2 in the 5 or 5^1 column.

Base 5						
15,625 or 5^6	3,125 or 5^5	625 or 5^4	125 or 5^3	25 or 5^2	5 or 5^1	1 or 5^0
				1	2	

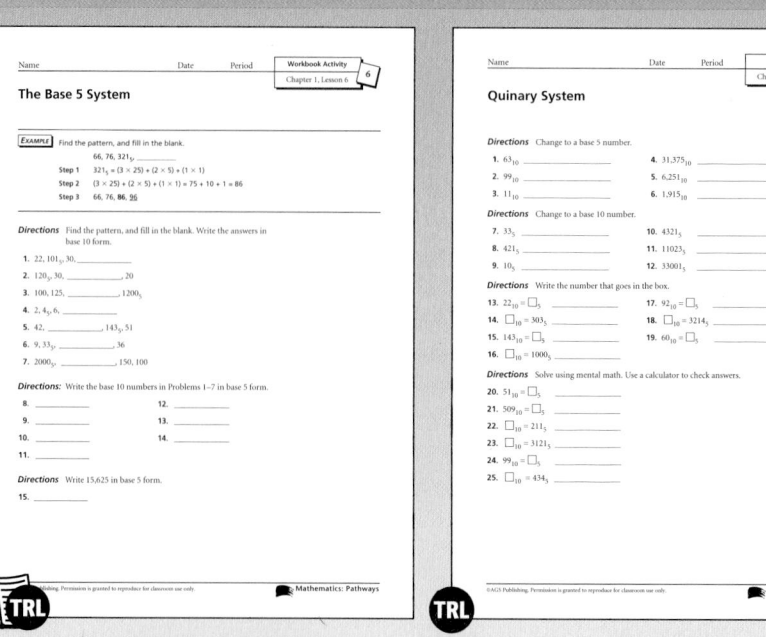

Workbook Activity 6   **Activity 7**

EXAMPLE 1 (continued)

Step 3 Because there are 4 ones remaining, place the numeral 4 in the 1 or 5^0 column. The completed chart should look like this.

Base 5						
15,625 or 5^6	3,125 or 5^5	625 or 5^4	125 or 5^3	25 or 5^2	5 or 5^1	1 or 5^0
				1	2	4

$25 + 2(5) + 4 = 25 + 10 + 4 = 39$

EXAMPLE 2 The number 39_{10} is 124 in base 5.

Change 2431_5 to a base 10 number.

Step 1 Position the numerals in the base 5 place value chart.

Base 5						
15,625 or 5^6	3,125 or 5^5	625 or 5^4	125 or 5^3	25 or 5^2	5 or 5^1	1 or 5^0
			2	4	3	1

Step 2 Add the values of each numeral.

$(2 \times 125) + (4 \times 25) + (3 \times 5) + 1 =$
$250 + 100 + 15 + 1 = 366$

EXAMPLE 3 The number 2431_5 is 366 in base 10 or 366_{10}.

Complete. $1042_5 = \blacksquare_{10}$

Step 1 Position the numerals in the base 5 place value chart.

Base 5						
15,625 or 5^6	3,125 or 5^5	625 or 5^4	125 or 5^3	25 or 5^2	5 or 5^1	1 or 5^0
			1	0	4	2

Step 2 Add the values of each numeral.

$(1 \times 125) + (0 \times 25) + (4 \times 5) + 2 =$
$125 + 0 + 20 + 2 = 147$

Zero times any number equals zero.
$1042_5 = 147_{10}$

Explain to students that as in base 2, the numeral 0 is again used to show *no value*. Like base 2, base 5 numbers never begin with 0. But unlike base 2, in base 5 there are 4 numerals to work with along with 0: 1, 2, 3, and 4. Each numeral is a multiplier of the power. So, a numeral 3 in the 25 or 5^2 column means

$$3 \times 5^2 = 3 \times 25 = 75$$

Direct students to Example 2. The numerals in the number 2431_5 (read *two four three one base 5*) represent multipliers of the powers. Use the place-value chart to highlight the individual products.

125 or 5^3	25 or 5^2	5 or 5^1	1 or 5^0
2	4	3	1

$2 \times 125 = 250$ $3 \times 5 = 15$
    $4 \times 25 = 100$ $1 \times 1 = 1$

Help students recognize that the base 10 number is the sum of all the individual products.

$$250 + 100 + 15 + 1 = 366$$

For Example 3, also use the place-value chart to highlight the individual products.

125 or 5^3	25 or 5^2	5 or 5^1	1 or 5^0
1	0	4	2

$1 \times 125 = 125$ $4 \times 5 = 20$
    $0 \times 25 = 0$ $2 \times 1 = 2$

The base 10 number is the sum of all the individual products.

$$125 + 0 + 20 + 2 = 147$$

 **3 Reinforce and Extend**

LEARNING STYLES

Logical/Mathematical
Have students explain why there are only 4 numerals that can be used in base 5 numbers. Suggest that they use manipulatives or the base 5 place-value chart to explain their thinking. *(Students should reach the conclusion that 5 numerals would generate the next product in the place value.)*

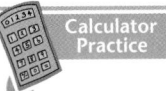

Base 5						
15,625 or 5^6	3,125 or 5^5	625 or 5^4	125 or 5^3	25 or 5^2	5 or 5^1	1 or 5^0

Exercise A Change to a base 5 number.

1. 40_{10} 130_5
2. 58_{10} 213_5
3. 78_{10} 303_5
4. 100_{10} 400_5
5. 107_{10} 412_5
6. 131_{10} 1011_5
7. $3{,}250_{10}$ 101000_5
8. $15{,}725_{10}$ 1000400_5

Exercise B Change to a base 10 number.

9. 13_5 8_{10}
10. 24_5 14_{10}
11. 111_5 31_{10}
12. 403_5 103_{10}
13. 1324_5 214_{10}
14. 10243_5 698_{10}
15. 100104_5 $3{,}154_{10}$
16. 1000111_5 $15{,}656_{10}$

Calculator Practice You can use a calculator to help you change a base 5 number to a base 10 number.

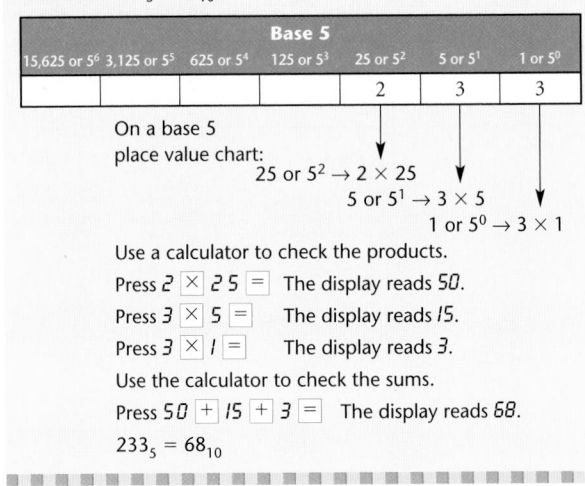

EXAMPLE 4 $233_5 = \blacksquare_{10}$

Base 5						
15,625 or 5^6	3,125 or 5^5	625 or 5^4	125 or 5^3	25 or 5^2	5 or 5^1	1 or 5^0
				2	3	3

On a base 5 place value chart:

25 or $5^2 \rightarrow 2 \times 25$

5 or $5^1 \rightarrow 3 \times 5$

1 or $5^0 \rightarrow 3 \times 1$

Use a calculator to check the products.

Press $2 \times 25 =$ The display reads 50.
Press $3 \times 5 =$ The display reads 15.
Press $3 \times 1 =$ The display reads 3.

Use the calculator to check the sums.

Press $50 + 15 + 3 =$ The display reads 68.

$233_5 = 68_{10}$

CALCULATOR

Solve problems using mental math. Use a calculator to check answers.

$10_{10} = \square_5$ *(20)* $\square_{10} = 100_5$ *(25)*
$49_{10} = \square_5$ *(144)* $\square_{10} = 1010_5$ *(130)*
$83_{10} = \square_5$ *(313)* $\square_{10} = 2020_5$ *(260)*
$102_{10} = \square_5$ *(402)* $\square_{10} = 1304_5$ *(204)*
$\square_{10} = 23_5$ *(13)*

After completing the problem, use the calculator to check mental math skills.

EXAMPLE $68_{10} = \square_5$

On a base 5 place-value chart, 68_{10} is shown this way:

5^2 5^2 5^1 5^1 5^1 5^0 5^0 5^0

$\downarrow$ $\downarrow$ $\downarrow$ $\downarrow$ $\downarrow$ $\downarrow$ $\downarrow$ $\downarrow$

$25 + 25 + 5 + 5 + 5 + 1 + 1 + 1$

Use the calculator to check the sum.

$5^2 \rightarrow 2$ $5^1 \rightarrow 3$ $5^0 \rightarrow 3$

$68_{10} = 233_5$

Exercise C Use a calculator to help find the answers.

17. $23_5 = \blacksquare_{10}$ 13_{10} **19.** $2020_5 = \blacksquare_{10}$ 260_{10}

18. $100_5 = \blacksquare_{10}$ 25_{10} **20.** $1304_5 = \blacksquare_{10}$ 204_{10}

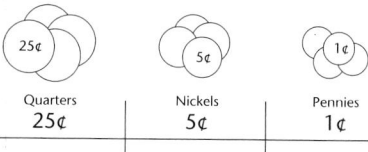

Try This

Is $10_{\text{any base}}$ = base (expressed in base 10)? Try 10_{10}, 10_2, and 10_5.

$10_{10} = 10$, $10_2 = 2$, $10_5 = 5$

Build a Model

Did you know that you can use coins to change some base 5 numbers into base 10 numbers? On a separate sheet of paper, draw the place value mat below. Above each column, place four of each coin as shown.

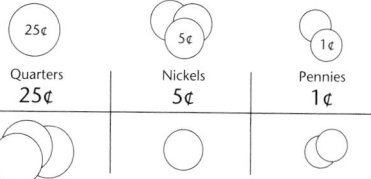

25¢	5¢	1¢
Quarters	Nickels	Pennies
25¢	5¢	1¢

Use the coins to change 312_5 to a base 10 number. Use 3 quarters to represent the 3, 1 nickel to represent the 1, and 2 pennies to represent the 2.

25¢	5¢	1¢
Quarters	Nickels	Pennies
25¢	5¢	1¢

Add the value of the coins in base 10.   75¢ + 5¢ + 2¢ = 82¢

Change from base 5 to base 10: 402_5 144_5 231_5 324_5

102_{10} 49_{10} 66_{10} 89_{10}

MODELING

Help students recognize that the values of the three coin types match the first three powers of 5. Before students begin, first familiarize them with the chart. Point out that the values start at the right and increase from one column to the next, moving toward the left.

Remind students that to rewrite any number in base 5, they need to add up the powers. For example, to write 15_{10} in base 5, look at the chart to find the highest power of 5 that is in 15. Then add up to complete the sum.

For each power of 5 that applies, write 1-4. For each power of 5 that does not apply, write 0. Remind students that quinary numbers never start with 0. So, zeros are only positioned *between* the numbers that apply.

Direct students to complete each column one at a time. They should start from the left and move toward the right.

Suggest that students who finish early work in pairs to make coins for the rest of the powers of 5 on the base 5 place value chart. They can use the coins to model the numbers in Exercise A and Exercise C.

The transition from elementary school to the secondary level affects students in many ways, emotionally and physically. Students experience a significant transition in their learning curve as well. This is the period during which they begin to cross the bridge between concrete and abstract thinking. They are fascinated by new and intriguing concepts. They want to learn by doing and to model the actions or behavior of adults and peers. As with all developmental stages, how long this period is and how easily each student manages this period of growth is unique. There is no typical pattern. However, what is special about adolescents is their inquisitiveness and eagerness to be challenged. Their desire to please is still foremost. Hence, parent/teacher approval and encouragement is key to success for many, if not all, youngsters. Given the appropriate tools and sufficient support, all students can achieve a positive learning experience in math class. Some students will make quantum leaps, and others might take smaller steps. All students will move forward.

Lesson at a Glance

Chapter 1 Application

Overview This lesson provides an application of using the binary system to operate electric circuits.

Objective

■ To evaluate an electric circuit on the basis of its binary code

Student Page 18

Teacher's Resource Library TRL

Application Activity 1

Everyday Math 1

 **1 Warm-Up Activity**

Tell students that many home security systems have codes that allow owners to open their doors and windows without setting off the alarm. If the correct code is not used, the doors and windows will not open and an alarm may go off. If the correct code is used, the owner can enter or leave his or her home as needed. Explain to the students that an electric circuit operates the same way. The proper binary number "code" must be present for the electricity to flow through the circuit.

2 Teaching the Lesson

Remind students that both switches in a parallel circuit do not need to be closed. Point out that the examples show a parallel circuit with a 1 and a 0, but not a 1 and a 1. As long as one switch is closed (shown by a 1), the electricity will flow.

COMMON ERROR

Students may see the word *open* and think that an open circuit allows electricity to pass through. An open circuit is similar to a raised bridge in that nothing can pass over it.

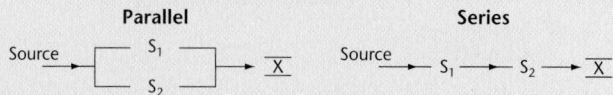

Binary Number System and Electrical Circuits There are two basic types of electric circuits, parallel and series.

S_1 and S_2 stand for Switch 1 and Switch 2.

$\underline{X}$ stands for the destination.

We can use the binary numerals to indicate the flow of electricity from source to destination.

0 means *open circuit* (no current flows)

1 means *closed circuit* (current flows)

In the parallel circuit, current will flow as long as one switch is closed. In the series circuit, *both* switches must be closed for the current to flow from the source to the destination.

EXAMPLE 1 Current will flow:

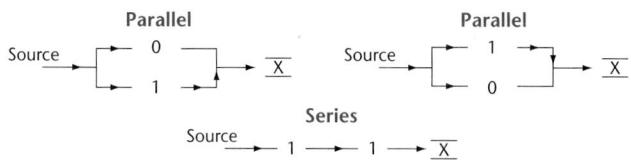

EXAMPLE 2 Current will *not* flow:

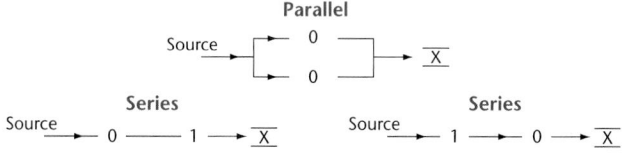

Exercise Look at the diagram to tell whether current will flow. Write *yes* or *no*.

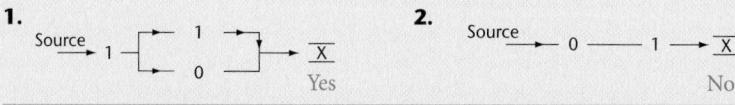

18 Chapter 1 Number Systems

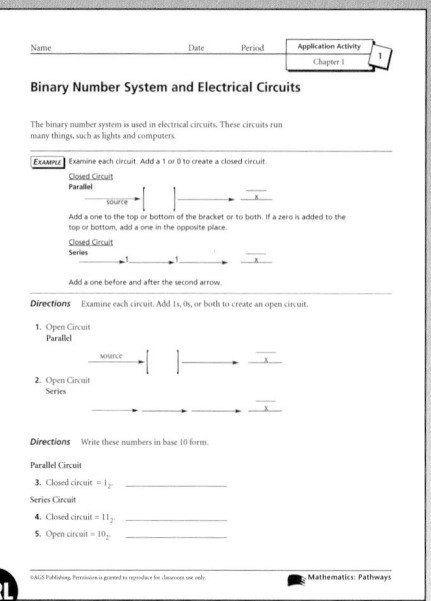

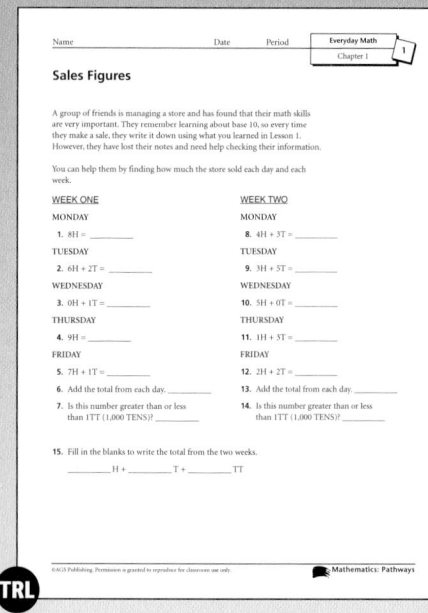

Chapter 1 REVIEW

Write the letter of the correct answer.

1. Name the place value of the underlined digit: 52,3<u>0</u>6 B
  A ones
  C hundreds
  B tens
  D thousands

2. Find the number that is 2,306 written in expanded form. B
  A $(2 \times 1,000) + (3 \times 100)$
  B $(2 \times 1,000) + (3 \times 100) + (0 \times 10) + (6 \times 1)$
  C $(2 \times 1,000) + 306$
  D 306

3. Find the number 3,496 written in expanded form using the powers of 10. A
  A $(3 \times 10^3) + (4 \times 10^2) + (9 \times 10^1) + (6 \times 10^0)$
  B $(3 \times 1,000) + (4 \times 100) + (9 \times 10) + (6 \times 1)$
  C $3,000 + 400 + 90 + 6$
  D $(3 \times 1,000) + (4 \times 100) + (9 \times 10) + 6$

4. Find the inverse of $894 + 677 = 1,571$. D
  A $1,571 = 894 + 677$
  C $1,571 \times 894 = 677$
  B $1,571 \div 894 = 677$
  D $1,571 - 894 = 677$

5. Find the inverse of $144 \div 12 = 12$. B
  A $12 = 144 \div 12$
  C $12 \div 12 = 144$
  B $12 \times 12 = 144$
  D $144 \times 12 = 12$

6. Find the powers of 2. B
  A $0, 1, 2, 3, 4, 5, \ldots$
  C $1, 10, 100, 1,000, 10,000, \ldots$
  B $1, 2, 4, 8, 16, 32, 64, \ldots$
  D $1, 2, 4, 6, 8, 10, \ldots$

7. Find the powers of 5. B
  A $0, 1, 2, 3, 4, \ldots$
  B $1, 5, 25, 125, 625, 3,125, 15,625, \ldots$
  C $1, 5, 10, 15, 20, 25, 30, \ldots$
  D $5, 15, 25, 35, 45, 55, \ldots$

3 Reinforce and Extend

AT HOME

Ask students to list five to ten objects in their homes that run on electricity. After the name of each object, have the students draw a closed circuit for objects that are off and an open circuit for objects that are on.

IN THE COMMUNITY

Your local utility provider, the Internet, or a computer technician at your school can be valuable resources. Direct students to use these and other community resources to further explore the relationship between the binary system and electric circuits.

Chapter 1 Review

Each set of problems in the Chapter Review includes an example and solution to illustrate the concept. Use the given examples for reteaching the materials in Chapter 1. For additional practice, refer to the Supplementary Problems for Chapter 1 (pages 432–433).

Chapter 1 Mastery Test

The Teacher's Resource Library includes parallel forms of the Chapter 1 Mastery Test. The difficulty level of the two forms is equivalent. You may wish to use one form as a pretest and the other form as a posttest.

ONLINE CONNECTION

The Physics and Astronomy Department at Georgia State University maintains a site with useful information on a variety of scientific subjects. At hyperphysics.phy-astr.gsu.edu/hbase/electronic/number4.html, students will find the department's number system conversion program. Here, students can enter a positive decimal number and the program will convert it automatically to its binary, hexadecimal, base 8 (octal), and BCD (binary coded decimal) equivalents. Assure students that they do not need to understand the BCD number at this time, except to know that both BCDs and hexadecimals are used by computers. Suggest to students that they enter integers such as today's date, their age, the number of their favorite sports figure, or their lucky number. Mention to students that, after entering a number, they need to click in any other field to activate the conversion.

ALTERNATIVE ASSESSMENT

■ To understand base 10

Hand out cards on which are printed various three- and four-digit base 10 numbers. Next, write a three- or four-digit number on the board. Ask each student to find another student whose number creates an addition equation equal to the number on the board. For example, suppose that you wrote 6,500. Students with the numbers 6,000 and 500 could hold up their cards, as could the students with 5,000 and 1,500, 3,000 and 3,500, and so on. You could also have students create equations that are less than or greater than the number on the board. Write a new number on the board, and repeat the process until every student has participated at least once.

■ To review whole number place values

Place ten cards numbered 0 through 9 in a bag. On the board, write a three- or four-digit base 10 number. Next to it, write place values in random order. Tell students that they are to pull cards from the bag in the same order that you have written the place values (not in the order that the digits appear as they read the number left to right). If a card is drawn that does not match the required place, it should be returned to the bag, but if it matches the place value, it is kept out and it is now the next student's turn. For example, suppose that you wrote 3,574 on the board and next to it you wrote *tens, hundreds, ones,* and *thousands.* The first student would need to understand the place value of each digit, realize that 7 is in the tens place, and then pull cards from the bag until he or she selected 7. The next student would need to do the same for the hundreds place and pull 5 from the bag. The student after that would be responsible for number 4, and the last student for number 3. Repeat this process with a new number and a new place-value order until every student has had the opportunity to select a number from the bag. It may be helpful for students to talk through the process as they try to determine which number they need to select because it is easy to

---

Chapter 1   R E V I E W - continued

Write the number in expanded form using the power of 10.

Example: 2,517,639
Solution:
$(2 \times 10^6) + (5 \times 10^5) + (1 \times 10^4) + (7 \times 10^3) + (6 \times 10^2) + (3 \times 10^1) + (9 \times 10^0)$

8. $(6 \times 10^2) + (7 \times 10^1) + (8 \times 10^0)$

9. $(3 \times 10^4) + (0 \times 10^3) + (8 \times 10^2) + (9 \times 10^1) + (4 \times 10^0)$

10. $(1 \times 10^5) + (2 \times 10^4) + (2 \times 10^3) + (5 \times 10^2) + (8 \times 10^1) + (5 \times 10^0)$

11. $(8 \times 10^6) + (1 \times 10^5) + (7 \times 10^4) + (1 \times 10^3) + (9 \times 10^2) + (8 \times 10^1) + (5 \times 10^0)$

8. 678

9. 30,894

10. 122,585

11. 8,171,985

Use an inverse operation to check the answer.

Example: 239
+ 403
642

Solution: 642
− 403
239

12. 2,871
+ 520
3,391

3,391
− 520
2,871

14. 3,562
+ 6,819
10,381

10,381
− 6,819
3,562

13. 73,902
− 19,785
54,117

54,117
+ 19,785
73,902

15. 1,492
− 642
850

850
+ 642
1,492

Use an inverse operation to check the answer.

Example: 12
× 3
36

Solution: 12
3)36

16. 17
4)68

17. 13
× 5
65

16. 17
× 4
68

17. 13
5)65

18. 34
× 9
306

19. 5
25)125

18. 34
9)306

19. 25
× 5
125

Change the base 2 number to a base 10 number.

Example: 101_2 Solution: $4 + 0 + 1 = 5$

Base 2						
64 or 2^6	32 or 2^5	16 or 2^4	8 or 2^3	4 or 2^2	2 or 2^1	1 or 2^0
				1	0	1

20. 10_{10} 21. 15_{10}

22. 18_{10} 23. 53_{10}

20. 1010_2 **21.** 1111_2 **22.** 10010_2 **23.** 110101_2

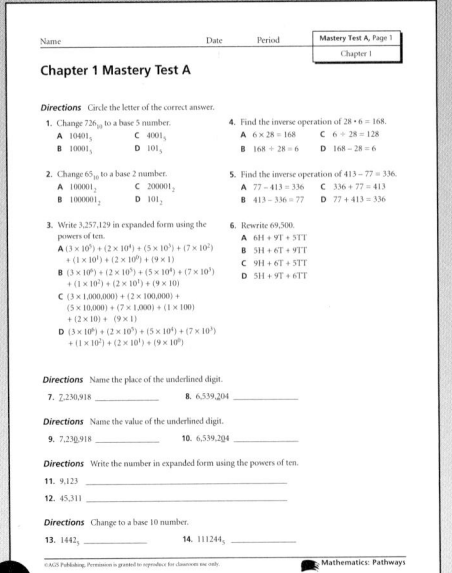

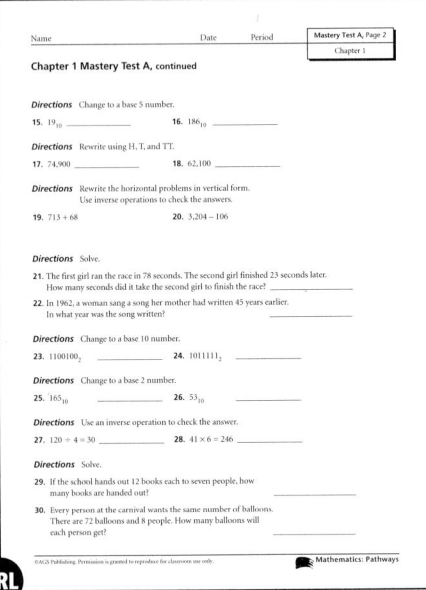

Chapter 1 Mastery Test A

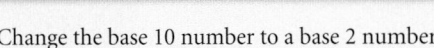

Change the base 10 number to a base 2 number.

Example: 75_{10} Solution: $64 + 0 + 0 + 8 + 0 + 2 + 1 = 75,$
so $75_{10} = 1001011_2$

Base 2						
64 or 2^6	32 or 2^5	16 or 2^4	8 or 2^3	4 or 2^2	2 or 2^1	1 or 2^0
1	0	0	1	0	1	1

24. 23_{10} **25.** 44_{10} **26.** 67_{10} **27.** 83_{10}

24. 10111_2

25. 101100_2

26. 1000011_2

27. 1010011_2

Change the base 10 number to a base 5 number.

Example: 897_{10} Solution: $(1 \times 625) + (2 \times 125) + (0 \times 25) + (4 \times 5) + (2 \times 1) = 625 + 250 + 0 + 20 + 2 = 897,$
so $897_{10} = 12042_5$

Base 5						
15,625 or 5^6	3,125 or 5^5	625 or 5^4	125 or 5^3	25 or 5^2	5 or 5^1	1 or 5^0
		1	2	0	4	2

28. 20_{10} **29.** 536_{10} **30.** 700_{10} **31.** $3,130_{10}$

28. 40_5

29. 4121_5

30. 10300_5

31. 100010_5

Change the base 5 number to a base 10 number.

Example: 10422_5 Solution: $(1 \times 625) + (0 \times 125) + (4 \times 25) + (2 \times 5) + (2 \times 1) = 625 + 0 + 100 + 10 + 2 = 737,$ so $10422_5 = 737_{10}$

Base 5						
15,625 or 5^6	3,125 or 5^5	625 or 5^4	125 or 5^3	25 or 5^2	5 or 5^1	1 or 5^0
		1	0	4	2	2

32. 12_5 **33.** 102_5 **34.** 10031_5 **35.** 1100_5

32. 7_{10}

33. 27_{10}

34. 641_{10}

35. 150_{10}

Test-Taking Tip

Before you start, scan the entire test. Do the easier problems first so that you will have more time to spend on the harder ones.

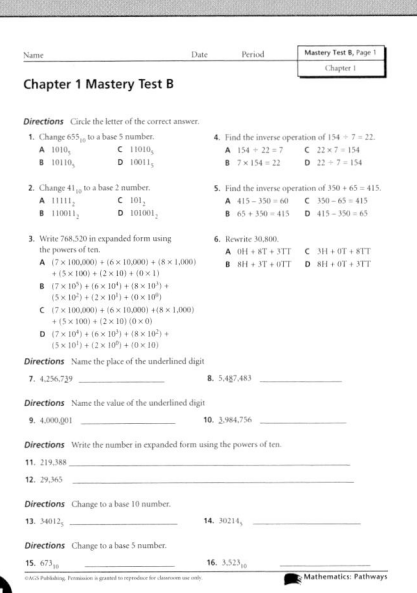

Chapter 1 Mastery Test B

confuse the place value and the next digit in order.

■ **To write whole numbers in expanded form using powers of 10**
Ask each student to work with a partner. One student from each pair should write a three- to six-digit number. The other will identify each digit's place value and show, using marbles, beans, rice, or other small objects, the number of zeros behind each one. Partners will write the number in expanded form using powers of 10 with each number multiplied by the correct power. Students will then change roles and repeat the process.

■ **To use inverse operations**
Create a board containing random numbers (each up to four digits). Play the game by calling out problems involving the basic operations ($+$, $-$, $\times$, $\div$). Students must solve the problem, find the matching solution on the board, and write an inverse of the original problem in the square. Students may mark off squares in any pattern, but the inverse operations must also be written correctly to win.

■ **To write numbers in base 2**
Give each student a paper containing a base 2 place-value chart, and organize students in groups. One student from each group will choose a number (up to three digits), one student will write the number in base 2 form on the chart, and the third student will check the answer. Calculators may be used if necessary. Students will then change roles and continue.

■ **To write numbers in base 5**
Provide a list of ten numbers in base 5 form (each up to seven digits). Ask students to identify those that are written correctly in base 5 and those that are not. Students should explain their choices and convert correctly written numbers to base 10.

For example, 12464_5 is not written correctly. The base 5 system uses only the digits 0, 1, 2, 3, and 4. However, 110021_5 is written correctly and should be rewritten as $3,761_{10}$.

2

Planning Guide

Whole Numbers and Algebra

Lesson		Student Pages	Vocabulary	Practice Exercises	Problem Solving	Try This	Solutions Key
					Student Text Lesson		
1	Adding Whole Numbers	24–25	✔	✔	25		✔
2	Subtracting Whole Numbers	26–27	✔	✔	27	27	✔
3	Estimating Sums and Differences	28–29	✔	✔			✔
4	Multiplying Whole Numbers	30–31	✔	✔	31		✔
5	Dividing Whole Numbers	32–33	✔	✔	33	33	✔
6	Estimating Products and Quotients	34–35	✔	✔		35	✔
7	Open Statements	36–37	✔	✔			✔
8	Using Letters to Represent Numbers	38–39	✔	✔			✔
9	Replacing Variables	40–41	✔	✔			✔
Application	Using Patterns	42		✔			✔

Chapter Activities

Teacher's Resource Library
Estimation Exercise 2: Estimating Addition
Application Activity 2: Using Patterns
Everyday Math 2: Plastic Money
Community Connection 2: Fund-Raiser

Teacher's Edition
Chapter 2 Project

Assessment Options

Student Text
Chapter 2 Review

Teacher's Resource Library
Chapter 2 Mastery Tests A and B

Teacher's Edition
Chapter 2 Alternative Assessments

Student Text Features						Teaching Strategies									Learning Styles						Teacher's Resource Library			
Estimation Activity	Math in Your Life	Technology Connection	Writing About Mathematics	Build a Model	Calculator Practice	Online Connection	Common Error	Applications Home, Career, Community	Mental Math	Manipulatives	Calculator	Group Problem Solving	Modeling	Knowing Your Students	Auditory/Verbal	Visual/Spatial	Logical/Mathematical	Body/Kinesthetic	Interpersonal/Group Learning	LEP/ESL	Activities	Alternate Activities	Workbook Activities	Self-Study Guide
		25				25				25											8	8	7	✔
			26				27			27		27									9	9	8	✔
														29	29				29	29	10	10	9	✔
							31		31			31					31				11	11	10	✔
	33						33		33			33			33						12	12	11–12	✔
																35				35	13	13	13	✔
37									37										37		14	14	14	✔
		39		38			39											39			15	15	15	✔
		41			41		41			41	41										16	16	16	✔
							42	43	42			43												✔

Software Options

Skill Track Software

Use the Skill Track Software for *Mathematics: Pathways* for additional reinforcement of this chapter. The software provides multiple-choice assessment items for students to access by computer.

Solutions Key

Use the Solutions Key with this chapter to help students who may need additional assistance. The Solutions Key CD provides solutions for every exercise in the student edition.

Other Resources

Alternative Activities

The Teacher's Resource Library (TRL) contains a set of worksheets written at a second-grade reading level called Alternative Activities. They cover the same content as the regular Activities.

Manipulatives

See the Manipulative activities in this chapter for hands-on modeling of the content.

Base Ten Blocks
Base Ten Mat
Pattern Blocks
Cuisenaire Rods

Chapter at a Glance

Chapter 2: Whole Numbers and Algebra
pages 22–45

Lessons

Skill Track for Mathematics: Pathways

Teacher's Resource Library TRL

- Workbook Activities 7–16
- Activities 8–16
- Alternative Activities 8–16
- Application Activity 2
- Estimation Exercise 2
- Everyday Math 2
- Community Connection 2
- Chapter 2 Self-Study Guide
- Chapter 2 Mastery Tests A and B

(Answer Keys for the Teacher's Resource Library begin on page 528 of this Teacher's Edition.)

Name Date Period — Estimation Exercise, Chapter 2

Estimating Addition

Clustering is an estimation strategy that works well with groups of numbers that cluster around a common value.

EXAMPLE Add 21, 22, 27, 34, 39, and 41.

Step 1 Choose a number in the middle of the cluster. It doesn't have to be one of the numbers given. A common or middle value would be 30.

Step 2 Multiply the common value by the number of values you must add. In the example, there are six numbers to add, so $30 \times 6 = 180$.

Step 3 Check the actual sum against the estimate. $21 + 22 + 27 + 34 + 39 + 41 = 184$

Directions Estimate each sum by clustering. Choose a common value, and find an estimate. Then, using a calculator, add the numbers to find the actual sum.

1. 30, 32, 33, 31, 38
   Common value: ______ Estimate: ______ Actual sum: ______
2. 42, 51, 53, 45, 40
   Common value: ______ Estimate: ______ Actual sum: ______
3. 129, 134, 135, 138
   Common value: ______ Estimate: ______ Actual sum: ______
4. Caitlin was collecting canned goods for a food drive at her community center. She collected cans for six days. Her totals for each day were 10, 12, 9, 15, 17, and 13. What is a good common value of these numbers? ______
   What is the best estimate? ______
   What is the actual number of cans of food Caitlin collected? ______
5. Julio is observing traffic on his street for a neighborhood project. In 10 different one-hour stretches, he counts 22, 31, 34, 40, 30, 20, 45, 38, 28, and 36 cars. What is a good common value of these numbers? ______
   What is the best estimate? ______
   How many cars did Julio actually count? ______

©AGS Publishing. Permission is granted to reproduce for classroom use only. Mathematics: Pathways

TRL

Estimation Exercise 2

Name Date Period — Community Connection, Chapter 2

Fund-Raiser

Plan an event to raise funds for your school. Choose a car wash, dog wash, used book sale, or other event. Make a plan for the event. Decide on a fund-raising goal. Find out how much your event will cost. Figure out how much you will charge for each item. Then determine how many cars you need to wash or books you need to sell to meet your goal.

Step 1 What plans do you have for the funds you raise? How much money will you need to make your planned purchase?

Step 2 How much will your fund-raiser cost? What is the cost of soap, cloths, hoses, and buckets for the car or dog wash? Where will you get tables for a book sale? How much will you spend on advertising your event?

Step 3 What is a reasonable price to charge? Is \$3.00 a car wash enough to help you meet your goal? Will you be able to sell hardcover books at \$2.00 each and paperbacks at 50¢ each?

Step 4 How many washes or books do you need to sell to cover your cost? How many more washes or books do you need to sell to meet your goal?

Step 5 Is your estimate of the number you need to sell reasonable based on the number of students in your school? Explain your reasoning.

©AGS Publishing. Permission is granted to reproduce for classroom use only. Mathematics: Pathways

TRL

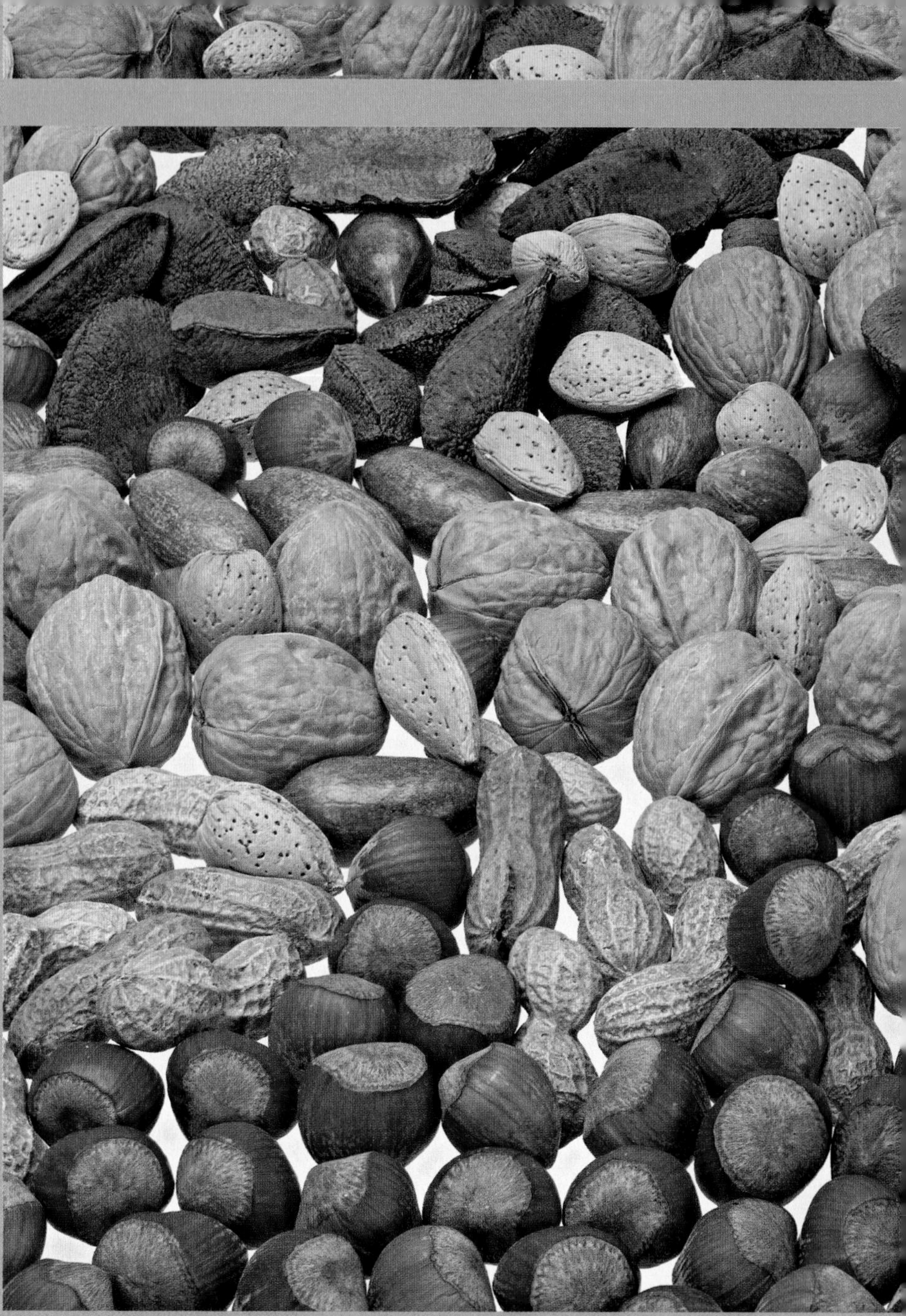

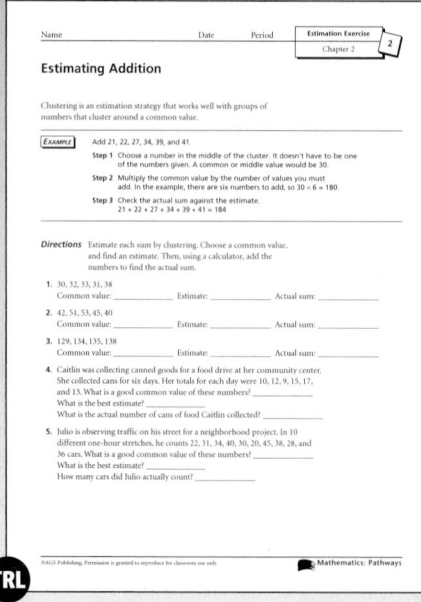

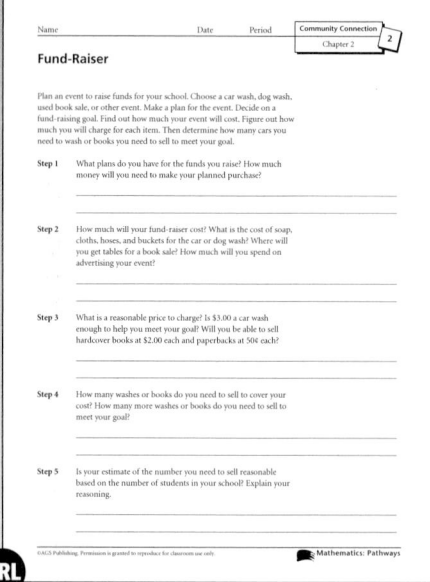

Community Connection 2

2 Whole Numbers and Algebra

The language of mathematics is "spoken" using the numbers 0, 1, 2, 3, 4, 5, 6, 7, 8, and 9. All over the world, people can talk about the ideas of quantity or value by using these numbers. For example, street vendors in open-air markets sell nuts to tourists by writing the price per pound. The idea gets across without a single word being spoken.

Long before any form of writing, people counted, sorted, and grouped. They used symbols to represent both amounts they knew and didn't know. As the problems became more difficult, mathematicians came up with *algebra* which uses letters to stand for unknown numbers.

In Chapter 2, you will review basic arithmetic operations and be introduced to simple algebraic expressions.

Goals for Learning

◆ To review addition and subtraction using whole numbers

◆ To learn to estimate sums and differences

◆ To review multiplication and division using whole numbers

◆ To learn to estimate products and quotients

◆ To recognize true, false, and open statements

◆ To recognize algebraic and numerical expressions

◆ To evaluate algebraic expressions

23

Introducing the Chapter

Have students identify the four basic math operations. Tell students that this chapter will help them improve their skills and will teach them new skills to better perform these tasks. Then model an algebraic expression, and identify the variable. Explain that using variables in operations is called *algebra*. Add that algebra will be introduced and practiced in this chapter.

CHAPTER PROJECT

Have students work in small groups to measure quantities or sizes within the class or the classroom (numbers of boys and girls, number of people who belong to at least one club, number of desks in classroom, width and length of classroom, and so on). The groups should then make the same measurements in another classroom. After students determine what questions they wish to answer using their data, have them manipulate their numbers using addition, subtraction, multiplication, and division to establish totals, differences, products, and quotients. Have the groups show the problems they solved and prepare a report for the sister classroom, explaining what was discovered and how it was discovered.

TEACHER'S RESOURCE

The AGS Publishing Teaching Strategies in Math Transparencies may be used with this chapter. They add an interactive dimension to expand and enhance the program content.

CAREER INTEREST INVENTORY

The AGS Publishing Harrington-O'Shea Career Decision-Making System-Revised (CDM) may be used with this chapter. Students can use the CDM to explore their interests and identify careers. The CDM defines career areas that are indicated by students' responses on the inventory.

Self-Study Guide (left sheet)

Name _____ Date _____ Period _____ *SELF-STUDY GUIDE*

CHAPTER 2: Whole Numbers and Algebra

| Goal 2.1 | To review addition and subtraction using whole numbers |

Date	Assignment	Score
_____	1: Read pages 23–24. Complete Exercises A–C on page 25.	_____
_____	2: Complete Workbook Activity 7.	_____
_____	3: Read page 26. Complete Exercises A–C on page 27.	_____
_____	4: Complete Workbook Activity 8.	_____

Comments:

| Goal 2.2 | To learn to estimate sums and differences |

Date	Assignment	Score
_____	5: Read page 28. Complete Exercises A–C on page 29.	_____
_____	6: Complete Workbook Activity 9.	_____

Comments:

| Goal 2.3 | To review multiplication and division using whole numbers |

Date	Assignment	Score
_____	7: Read pages 30–31. Complete Exercises A–C on page 31.	_____
_____	8: Complete Workbook Activity 10.	_____
_____	9: Read page 32. Complete Exercises A–D on page 33.	_____
_____	10: Complete Workbook Activities 11 and 12.	_____

Comments:

| Goal 2.4 | To learn to estimate products and quotients |

Date	Assignment	Score
_____	11: Read pages 34–35. Complete Exercises A–C on page 35.	_____
_____	12: Complete Workbook Activity 13.	_____

Comments:

©AGS Publishing. Permission is granted to reproduce for classroom use only. Mathematics: Pathways

Self-Study Guide (right sheet)

Name _____ Date _____ Period _____ *SELF-STUDY GUIDE*

CHAPTER 2: Whole Numbers and Algebra, *continued*

| Goal 2.5 | To recognize true, false, and open statements |

Date	Assignment	Score
_____	13: Read page 36. Complete Exercises A–C on page 37.	_____
_____	14: Complete Workbook Activity 14.	_____

Comments:

| Goal 2.6 | To recognize algebraic and numerical expressions |

Date	Assignment	Score
_____	15: Read page 38. Complete Exercises A–C on page 39.	_____
_____	16: Complete Workbook Activity 20.	_____

Comments:

| Goal 2.7 | To evaluate algebraic expressions |

Date	Assignment	Score
_____	17: Read page 40. Complete Exercises A–C on pages 40–41.	_____
_____	18: Read and complete the Calculator Practice on page 41.	_____
_____	19: Complete Workbook Activity 16.	_____
_____	20: Read and complete the Application on page 42.	_____
_____	21: Complete the Chapter 2 Review on pages 43–45.	_____

Comments:

Student's Signature _____ Date _____
Instructor's Signature _____ Date _____

©AGS Publishing. Permission is granted to reproduce for classroom use only. Mathematics: Pathways

Chapter 2 Self-Study Guide

Chapter 2 Lesson 1

Overview This lesson reviews addition of whole numbers and introduces the concept of algebra.

Objectives

- To add whole numbers, considering place values, to find a sum
- To add whole numbers and letters to find a sum

Student Pages 24–25

Teacher's Resource Library 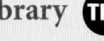 **TRL**

Workbook Activity 7

Activities 8

Alternative Activities 8

Mathematics Vocabulary

arithmetic
addend
sum
whole number
algebra

1 Warm-Up Activity

Group students in fives, and ask them to determine how much allowance the entire group receives in a week. When groups have their answers, have each group demonstrate to the class how the members found this amount. Ask, "What process did you use?" *(addition)*

2 Teaching the Lesson

Review the concept of place value with students. Assess their understanding by having them name the number of ones, tens, hundreds, and thousands in a series of numbers on the board:

59
(5 tens, 9 ones)

251
(2 hundreds, 5 tens, 1 one)

1,843
(1 thousand, 8 hundreds, 4 tens, 3 ones)

Lesson 1 Adding Whole Numbers

You know that addition is the **arithmetic** operation of combining two or more numbers, or **addends,** to find a total. The result of addition is a **sum.** Remember to combine like place values whenever you add.

The numbers 54 and 19 are **whole numbers.** In **algebra,** you use letters as placeholders for numbers, so you add letters.

Arithmetic

The study of the properties of numbers using four basic operations—addition, subtraction, multiplication, and division

Addend

Number to be added to another

Sum

The result of addition

Whole number

A number such as 0, 1, 2, 3, 4, 5, 6, . . .

Algebra

The branch of mathematics that uses both letters and numbers to show relations between quantities

EXAMPLE 1

$$\begin{array}{r} 54 \\ + 19 \end{array}$$

Add the ones first. $4 + 9 = 13$

Regroup 13 ones as 1 ten and 3 ones.
Write 3 in the ones column.
Write 1 in the tens column.

Add the tens. $1 + 5 + 1 = 7$

Check. $19 + 54 = 73$

$$\begin{array}{r} 1 \\ 54 \\ + 19 \\ \hline 3 \end{array} \Big\rangle \text{addends}$$

$$\begin{array}{r} 1 \\ 54 \\ + 19 \\ \hline 73 \leftarrow \text{sum} \end{array}$$

EXAMPLE 2

$$\begin{array}{ll} 2a & \text{or } a + a \\ + 3a & \text{or } a + a + a \\ \hline 5a & a + a + a + a + a \end{array}$$

Add the ones bring down the *a*.

Check. $2a + 3a = 5a$

EXAMPLE 3 Add $267 + 1{,}342 + 68$.

Write the problem in vertical form. Add the ones. Regroup 17 ones as 1 ten and 7 ones. Write 7 in the ones column. Write 1 in the tens column.

$$\begin{array}{r} 1 \\ 267 \\ 1{,}342 \\ + \ \ 68 \\ \hline 7 \end{array}$$

Add the tens. Regroup 17 tens as 1 hundred and 7 tens. Write 7 in the tens column. Write 1 in the hundreds column.

$$\begin{array}{r} 1 \\ 267 \\ 1{,}342 \\ + \ \ 68 \\ \hline 77 \end{array}$$

Add the hundreds. Write 6 in the hundreds column.

$$\begin{array}{r} 1 \\ 267 \\ 1{,}342 \\ + \ \ 68 \\ \hline 677 \end{array}$$

Add the thousands. Write 1 in the thousands column.

$$\begin{array}{r} 267 \\ 1{,}342 \\ + \ \ 68 \\ \hline 1{,}677 \end{array}$$

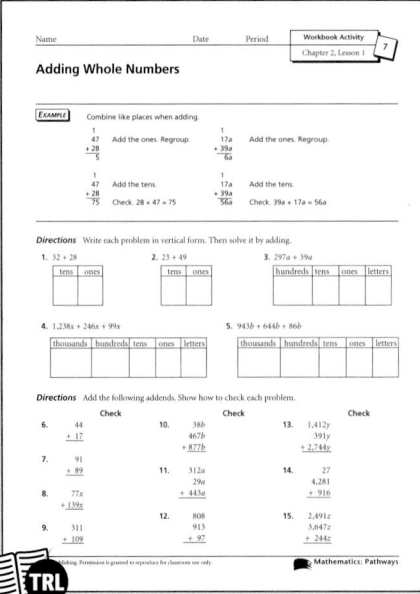

Workbook Activity 7

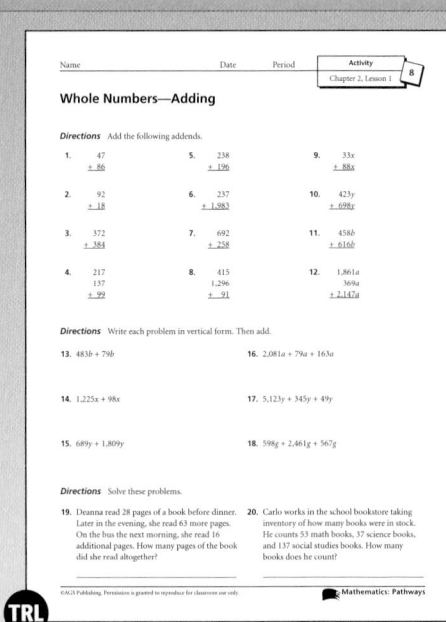

Activity 8

Exercise A Add the following addends.

1. 23
    + 9
    ―――
    32

2. 38
    + 13
    ―――
    51

3. 27
    + 54
    ―――
    81

4. 18
    + 45
    ―――
    63

5. $4a$
    $+ 8a$
    ―――
    $12a$

6. $92x$
    $+ 68x$
    ―――
    $160x$

Exercise B Write each problem in vertical form. Then add.

7. $158 + 64 + 352$ 574

8. $91 + 56 + 165$ 312

9. $1,269 + 789 + 56$ 2,114

10. $503a + 17a + 407a$ 927a

PROBLEM SOLVING

Exercise C Solve each problem.

11. Natawa has $85 in her savings account. She deposits $55 that she received for her birthday. How much money is in her account now? $140

12. Brett has 324 sports cards. His sister, Mariette, has 1,232 sports cards. How many cards do they have altogether? 1,556 sports cards

13. On Tuesday Leon drove 412 miles. On Wednesday he drove 463 miles. How many miles did he drive altogether? 875 miles

14. Ana has 32 CDs, Gina has 51 CDs, and Callie has 46 CDs. How many CDs do they have altogether? 129 CDs

15. Ann earned $121 the first week, $132 the second week, and $128 the third week at her cashier's job. How much money did she make in the three weeks? $381

Technology Connection

Using a Calculator to Budget Your Money
Calculators are so small that you can take them everywhere. They're handy tools. Carry one with you to a ball game or a shopping mall. You can use the calculator to help you make the most of your spending money. Think about the snacks and items you want to buy. Use the calculator to subtract their cost from the cash you have. You'll be able to see whether or not you can afford them all—before you actually spend your money.

ONLINE CONNECTION

www.aaamath.com is a student-friendly site where students can practice addition and algebraic operations through exercises, games, puzzles, and riddles. This site also offers a glossary, a list of resource books, and explanations for many topics. Encourage students to return to the site as needed to practice math skills in this chapter and throughout the book.

34,728
(3 ten thousands, 4 thousands, 7 hundreds, 2 tens, 8 ones)

Have students test for themselves the commutative property of addition. Give groups of three students a problem such as the following:

297
42
+ 713

Each member should add the numbers in a different order (top to bottom, middle first, bottom to top), and then the members should compare the three answers.

MANIPULATIVES

Adding Whole Numbers

Materials: Base Ten Blocks, Base Ten Mat

Group Practice: Use Example 1, 54 + 19. To model the first addend, place five 10-rods in the tens column on the mat and four unit cubes in the ones column. Model the second addend with one 10-rod and nine unit cubes. Combine the cubes in the ones column, replacing ten cubes with a 10-rod in the tens column. Repeat with the tens column to find the sum. Sketch each model, and write the symbolic equivalent (see pages T8–T9) for each step. Repeat with additional problems students generate. Regroup ten 10-rods for a 100-square, as necessary.

Student Practice: Have students use the blocks for Exercise A, problems 1–4; Exercise B, problems 7–8; and Exercise C, problems 11, 13–15.

Lesson at a Glance

Chapter 2 Lesson 2

Overview This lesson explains subtraction as the inverse operation of addition.

Objectives

- To compute the difference between two whole numbers
- To rename place values by borrowing

Student Pages 26–27

Teacher's Resource Library TRL

Workbook Activity 8

Activity 9

Alternative Activity 9

Mathematics Vocabulary

difference
rename

---

1 Warm-Up Activity

Give two students an identical envelope of coins (including, for example, a quarter, 2 dimes, 3 nickels, and 5 pennies). Have the class compute how much money each student has. *(65 cents)* Then ask the two students to role-play a transaction between them (repaying a debt, purchasing something), explain what they are doing, and complete the transaction. Ask, "Now how much does each have?" Discuss how students know this and why one student's amount increased by the amount the other's decreased. *(Subtraction is the opposite of addition.)*

2 Teaching the Lesson

Review the process of renaming with students. Using Example 3 on page 26, ask a volunteer to draw a diagram on the board or overhead proving that 5 tens and 3 ones are equal to 4 tens and 13 ones.

Ask students what advantage they gain by writing subtraction problems in vertical form. *(It is easier to see place values and rename vertically than horizontally.)*

Difference
The result of subtraction

Rename
To give a new form that is equal to the original

Just as you can check the answer to a subtraction problem by adding, you can check the answer to an addition problem by subtracting. For example,
610 + 22 = 632.
Check:
632 − 22 = 610.

Writing About Mathematics

Write a short paragraph expressing your opinion about whether using coupons is worthwhile. Be sure to give reasons to support your opinion.

You know that subtraction is the arithmetic operation of taking one number away from another. The result of subtraction is a **difference**.

In algebra, you use letters for numbers, so a subtraction problem could look like this.

EXAMPLE 1

$$
\begin{array}{r}
18 \\
-\ 6 \\
\hline
12 \leftarrow \text{Difference}
\end{array}
\qquad
\begin{array}{r}
\text{Check.}\quad 12 \\
+\ 6 \\
\hline
18
\end{array}
$$

EXAMPLE 2

$$
\begin{array}{lll}
4x & \text{or} & x + x + x + x \\
-\ 2x & \text{or} & -\ \underline{\ x + x} \\
\hline
2x & \text{or} & x + x
\end{array}
$$

Sometimes when you subtract, you need to **rename**.

EXAMPLE 3 $53 - 9 = \blacksquare$

You cannot subtract 9 from 3.

Rename 5 tens 3 ones as 4 tens 13 ones.

$$
\begin{array}{r}
53 \\
-\ 9
\end{array}
\qquad
\text{Rename:}\quad
\begin{array}{r}
4\ 13 \\
5\ \cancel{3} \\
-\ \ \ 9
\end{array}
$$

Then subtract.

$$
\begin{array}{r}
4\ 13 \\
5\ 3 \\
-\ \ \ 9 \\
\hline
4\ 4
\end{array}
\qquad \text{Check. } 44 + 9 = 53
$$

EXAMPLE 4 $4{,}321 - 586 = \blacksquare$

Write the problem in vertical form.

$$
\begin{array}{r}
4{,}321 \\
-\ \ 586
\end{array}
$$

You cannot subtract 6 from 1. Rename 2 tens 1 one as 1 ten 11 ones. Subtract. Then rename the hundreds and thousands and subtract.

$$
\begin{array}{r}
3\ 12\ 11\ 11 \\
4{,}3\ 2\ 1 \\
-\ \ 5\ 8\ 6 \\
\hline
3{,}7\ 3\ 5
\end{array}
$$

Check.
$$
\begin{array}{r}
3{,}735 \\
+\ \ 586 \\
\hline
4{,}321
\end{array}
$$

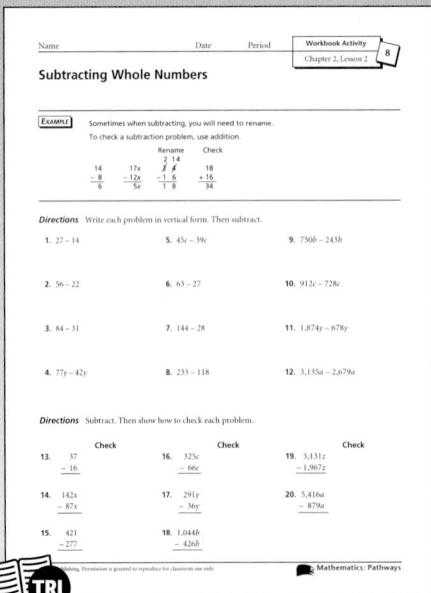

Workbook Activity 8

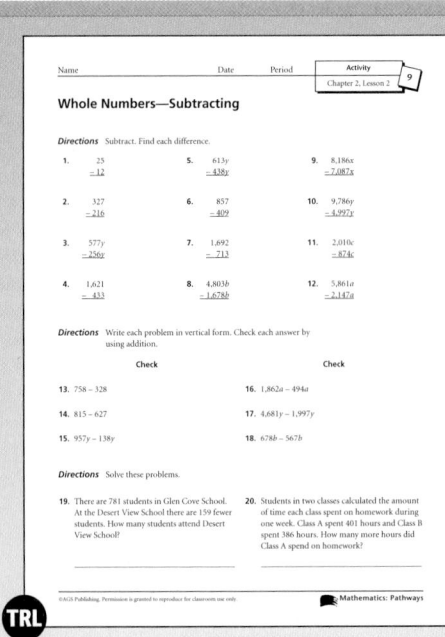

Activity 9

Exercise A Subtract. Find the difference.

1. 74
$- 68$
6

4. 41
$- 8$
33

7. $36a$
$- 7a$
$29a$

2. 90
$- 32$
58

5. 47
$- 18$
29

8. $54a$
$- 29a$
$25a$

3. 55
$- 6$
49

6. $62x$
$- 9x$
$53x$

9. $23x$
$- 5x$
$18x$

> Addition problems have *addends* and *sums*. Subtraction problems have *minuends, subtrahends,* and *differences.*
>
> 18 ← minuend
> −6 ← subtrahend
> 12 ← difference

Exercise B Write the problems in vertical form. Then subtract.

10. $1,400 - 379$ 1,021   **14.** $7,125x - 836x$ $6,289x$

11. $5,000 - 748$ 4,252   **15.** $152,647a - 36,458a$ $116,189a$

12. $24,115 - 4,246$ 19,869   **16.** $34,472k - 14,854k$ $19,618k$

13. $167,124y - 18,246y$ $148,878y$

 **PROBLEM SOLVING**

Exercise C Solve each problem.

17. Tasty Apple Orchard has 385 bushels of apples for sale. The orchard sells 223 bushels in one week. How many bushels are left? 162 bushels

18. At the local supermarket, a loaf of bread usually costs $2.15. This week, bread is on sale for $1.59. How much can you save by buying one loaf of bread this week? $0.56

19. The library has 2,530 children's books. If 335 children's books have been checked out, how many remain in the library? 2,195 books

20. The Lincoln High School team won the basketball game with 123 points. Washington High School's team scored 15 fewer points. What was the Washington team's final score? 108

Answers will vary. Students will use subtraction to find the answer. (Price of item) − (Amount on coupon) = Price paid

 **Try This**

Newspapers often have coupons for products. Cut out a coupon for one item. Find out how much the item costs without the coupon. How much will you pay if you redeem the coupon when you buy the item?

 *Whole Numbers and Algebra*   Chapter 2   **27**

GROUP PROBLEM SOLVING

 Have groups of three students play "Who's Gifted?" Give each group a page from a department store catalog (featuring items that are in an appropriate price range). Allow each group $100 to spend on gifts. Each person makes a selection, rounds it to the nearest dollar, and subtracts his or her amount from the group fund. The object of the game is to come as close to a zero balance as possible without overspending. If enough money remains after all members have purchased a gift, the group can spend a second round.

Try This

For more practice, bring to class a weekly supermarket insert and have students calculate savings or item cost with coupons. Have groups of students make up a short grocery list including three sale items and use both addition and subtraction to discover how much they will save in total.

MANIPULATIVES

M Subtracting Whole Numbers

Materials: Base Ten Blocks, Base Ten Mat

Group Practice: Use the first example, $18 - 6 = 12$. Model 18 on the mat by placing one 10-rod in the tens column and eight unit cubes in the ones column. To subtract, remove six unit cubes from the ones column. The 10-rod remains in the tens column, so the difference is 12. To model regrouping, use Example 3, $53 - 9$. Replace a 10-rod from the tens column with ten unit cubes in the ones column. Write the symbolic equivalent for this step. Next, subtract in the ones and tens columns by removing cubes and rods, obtaining the difference. Repeat with other 2- and 3-digit regrouping problems students generate. Sketch each model, and write the symbolic equivalent.

Student Practice: Have students use the blocks for Exercise A, problems 1–5 and Exercise C, problems 17–18, and 20. Provide students with additional 2- and 3-digit subtraction problems if they need more practice.

3   Reinforce and Extend

COMMON ERROR

 Aligning numbers and writing neatly in a subtraction problem are crucial because students quickly become lost if they cannot easily see the columns from which they must "borrow" ones, tens, and so on. As with addition, have students who have difficulty write problems on graph paper to make sure that they align places accurately.

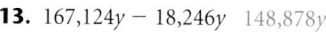

Whole Numbers and Algebra   **27**

Lesson at a Glance

Chapter 2 Lesson 3

Overview This lesson gives students a strategy for checking the sense of answers by estimating.

Objective

■ To estimate sums and differences by rounding

Student Pages 28–29

Teacher's Resource Library

Workbook Activity 9

Activity 10

Alternative Activity 10

....

Mathematics Vocabulary

estimate

....

1 Warm-Up Activity

On the board, write a sum that represents the treasury balance of a club, for example, $389.30. Have students suggest an amount they think the club will earn with its upcoming bake sale and write it on the board. Ask, "Will the club then have enough for its school garden planting project, which will cost about $500?" Encourage students to explain the strategy they used to answer without calculating on paper.

2 Teaching the Lesson

Provide extra practice in rounding for students. To make the process more flexible, do not always have students round to the greatest place value, but instead give specific directions:

- Round $429.99 to the nearest ten dollars. (*$430*)

- Round 372 viewers to the nearest hundred. (*400*)

- Round 7,544 flower bulbs to the nearest hundred. (*7,500*)

- Round 33,725 citizens to the nearest thousand. (*34,000*)

Point out to students that they can use their calculators to check their answers.

Lesson 3 Estimating Sums and Differences

Estimate
A careful guess; a close or nearly correct answer

When rounding a number to its greatest place value, look at the numeral next to the greatest place value. If the numeral is 5 or more, round up. If it is less than 5, round down. For example, round 591 up to 600 and 531 down to 500.

You can use **estimation** to check whether a sum or difference makes sense.

EXAMPLE 1 Estimate 3,243 + 262 + 1,894.

Round each number to its greatest place value.

$$3,243 \rightarrow 3,000$$
$$262 \rightarrow 300$$
$$1,894 \rightarrow 2,000$$

Add the rounded numbers.

```
  3,000
    300
+ 2,000
  5,300
```

An estimate of the sum
3,243 + 262 + 1,894 is 5,300.

EXAMPLE 2 Estimate 1,984 − 632.

Round each number to its greatest place value.

$$1,984 \rightarrow 2,000$$
$$632 \rightarrow 600$$

Subtract the rounded numbers.

```
  2,000
−   600
  1,400
```

An estimate of the difference
1,984 − 632 is 1,400.

Whenever you add or subtract to find exact sums and differences, estimate first. Then compare your exact answer to your estimate and decide whether your answer makes sense.

28 *Chapter 2 Whole Numbers and Algebra*

Name _____ Date _____ Period _____ **Workbook Activity 9**
Chapter 2, Lesson 3

Estimating Sums and Differences

EXAMPLE Use an estimate to check whether a sum or a difference makes sense. To estimate, look at the numeral next to the greatest place value.

```
Round up if the numeral is    59 ———→      60
5 or more.                   263 ———→     300
                          + 1,720 ———→  + 2,000
                                        2,360 estimate

Round down if the numeral  1,065 ———→   1,000
is less than 5.            − 237 ———→   − 200
                                         800 estimate
```

Directions Round each number to the greatest place value.

1. 67 _____   6. 362 _____   11. 8,125 _____
2. 136 _____   7. 5,187 _____ 12. 654 _____
3. 241 _____   8. 488 _____   13. 5,871 _____
4. 1,047 _____ 9. 237 _____   14. 453 _____
5. 2,668 _____ 10. 551 _____   15. 9,412 _____

Directions Estimate each sum. Use rounding. Then find the exact sum.

16. 64 + 87 =   18. 714 + 892 =   20. 3,821 + 451 =
17. 252 + 524 =   19. 1,561 + 243 =

Directions Estimate each difference. Use rounding. Then find the exact difference.

21. 65 − 42 =   23. 852 − 361 =   25. 1,961 − 457 =
22. 431 − 297 =   24. 631 − 288 =

©AGS Publishing. Permission is granted to reproduce for classroom use only. ▲ Mathematics: Pathways

Workbook Activity 9

Name _____ Date _____ Period _____ **Activity 10**
Chapter 2, Lesson 3

Sums and Differences—Estimation

Directions Estimate each sum. Round each number to its greatest place value.

1. 41 + 29   4. 684 + 2,789
   Rounded estimate: _____   Rounded estimate: _____

2. 67 + 42   5. 1,414 + 2,789
   Rounded estimate: _____   Rounded estimate: _____

3. 251 + 63   6. 3,129 + 1,543
   Rounded estimate: _____   Rounded estimate: _____

Directions Estimate each difference. Round each number to its greatest place value.

7. 62 − 27   10. 543 − 78
   Rounded estimate: _____   Rounded estimate: _____

8. 847 − 356   11. 982 − 723
   Rounded estimate: _____   Rounded estimate: _____

9. 731 − 422   12. 3,129 − 1,543
   Rounded estimate: _____   Rounded estimate: _____

Directions Estimate each difference. Round each number to its greatest place value.

13. There are 67 people waiting in line for one movie and 84 people waiting in line for another movie. About how many people are waiting in line?

14. Dan sold 57 boxes of oranges during the band's efforts to raise money. Keesha sold 35 boxes. About how many more boxes did Dan sell?

15. A store clerk counted 428 pairs of jeans before a big sale. After the sale, there were 78 pairs left. About how many pairs of jeans were sold?

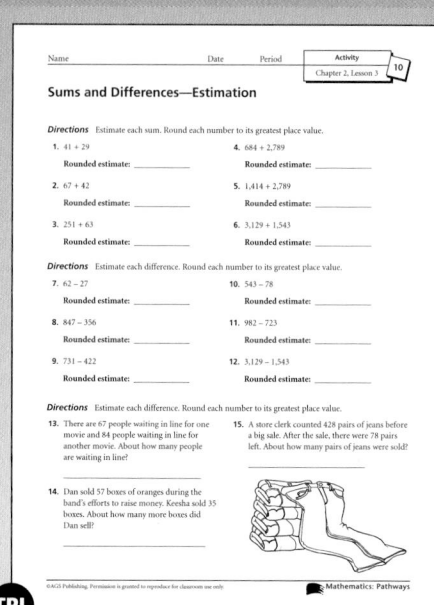

©AGS Publishing. Permission is granted to reproduce for classroom use only. ▲ Mathematics: Pathways

Activity 10

Exercise A Estimate each sum.

1. 643 + 821   1,400

2. 3,916 + 542   4,500

3. 21,647 + 912 + 385   21,300

4. 40,429 + 6,950 + 532   47,500

5. 105,990 + 67,192 + 8,915 + 78   179,080

Exercise B Estimate each difference.

6. 875 − 397   500

7. 1,980 − 529   1,500

8. 18,401 − 8,640   11,000

9. 101,600 − 36,970   60,000

10. 214,401 − 67,801   130,000

Exercise C Estimate. Then find the exact answer.

11. 100; 101

12. 1,400; 1,468

13. 1,500; 1,468

14. 40; 38

15. 1,400; 1,408

16. 400; 389

17. 13,000; 13,294

18. 150,000; 152,393

19. 30,000; 29,853

20. 70,000; 70,665

11. 28 + 73

12. 643 + 825

13. 912 + 556

14. 85 − 47

15. 864 + 544

16. 753 − 364

17. 10,642 + 2,652

18. 63,467 + 88,926

19. 95,110 − 65,257

20. 100,354 − 29,689

You could estimate the number of apples in each box.

LEARNING STYLES

LEP/ESL

Give students practice in identifying place values. Create a grid on posterboard, identifying the ones, tens, hundreds, thousands, and ten-thousands places with column headings. Give students numerals on sticky notes that fit in the grid squares. Have each student create a number that you dictate, for example, "a 9 in the ones place, a 2 in the tens place, a 4 in the hundreds, a 6 in the thousands, a 7 in the ten thousands." After the student has placed the numbers, he or she reads the number aloud—76,429.

LEARNING STYLES

Auditory/Verbal

Provide students with addition and subtraction problems. Have them estimate the sum or difference orally, including an explanation of the rounding process they use. Then ask them to calculate the exact answers and comment on their accuracy. Ask, "When is estimation helpful? When would it be a poor method?" *(when you need only a "ballpark" answer; when you must be precise)*

KNOWING YOUR STUDENTS

With all of the distractions that seek to capture an adolescent student's attention, the ability to estimate can be a great time saver and a good way for students to gain some control over their day. Students can use the ability to estimate to quickly decide whether there is time for a phone call before their next class, for example, or whether they have enough money to go to a movie tonight without having to put pencil to paper or pull out a calculator. Most students will have been introduced to estimates in earlier grades, but they may still need help in knowing when to use estimation and why. Help students generalize what they know by providing them with concrete situations to help them judge whether an estimate is reasonable. Students need to learn when to use a higher estimate, when a ballpark figure is enough, and so on.

LEARNING STYLES

Interpersonal/ Group Learning

Have small groups of students study creatively the vocabulary words from Lessons 1, 2, and 3. Ask them to make posters, create characters, invent songs, or write skits that illustrate what each term is or does. For example, "Abby Addend" could always be trying to join the group. "Iggy Inverse" could always say the opposite of what others say.

Lesson at a Glance

Chapter 2 Lesson 4

Overview This lesson explains multiplication as repeated addition and introduces algebraic multiplication.

Objectives

- To multiply whole numbers
- To identify the symbols that indicate multiplication
- To multiply whole numbers times algebraic expressions

Student Pages 30–31

Teacher's Resource Library **TRL**

Workbook Activity 10

Activity 11

Alternative Activity 11

....

Mathematics Vocabulary

factor
product

....

1 Warm-Up Activity

Ask students to imagine that they are buying a CD and write down the amount it costs. Tell them that they must pay a sales tax of 5 cents for every dollar. Have them determine the total they must pay and explain how they calculated it. Discuss which is easier: adding 5 cents for each dollar or multiplying 5 times the number of dollars.

2 Teaching the Lesson

Review the process of renaming places in multiplication. As you work through Example 3 on page 30, ask students to explain the meaning of the 3 and the 1 above the 5. (*The 3 represents the 3 tens of 4 times 8; the 1 represents the 1 ten of 3 times 4.*)

Lesson 4 — Multiplying Whole Numbers

Factor
The numbers in a multiplication statement

Product
The result of multiplication

Remember that multiplication gives the same result as repeated addition. The numbers you multiply are the **factors**, and the answer is the **product**.

$$\begin{array}{r} 4 \\ 4 \\ + 4 \\ \hline \end{array} \quad 4 \text{ three times}$$

$$4 \times 3 = 12$$
factors — product

Different symbols are used to indicate multiplication.
× means "multiply," so $6 \times 2 = 12$.
• means "multiply," so $6 \cdot 2 = 12$.
Parentheses can mean "multiply," so $6(2) = 12$.

EXAMPLE 1 $42 \times 7 = \blacksquare$

$$\begin{array}{r} 42 \\ \times\ 7 \\ \hline 14 \\ +\ 280 \\ \hline 294 \end{array}$$

14 Multiply the ones, 2×7.
+ 280 Multiply the tens, 40×7.
294 Add.

In algebra, you multiply numbers with letters, such as $3x$ times 3. You multiply in the same way as in arithmetic.

EXAMPLE 2 $3x \cdot 3$

$$\begin{array}{r} 3x \\ \times\ 3 \\ \hline 9x \end{array}$$

or

$3x \cdot 3$
$x + x + x$
$x + x + x$
$x + x + x$
$9x$

$3x$ three times

When the product of the ones is greater than 9, you must rename the tens and ones.

EXAMPLE 3 $54 \times 38 = \blacksquare$

Step 1	Step 2	Step 3
3	1	
54	54	54
× 38	× 38	× 38
432	432	432
	1,620	+ 1,620
		2,052
Multiply the ones.	Multiply the tens.	Add.

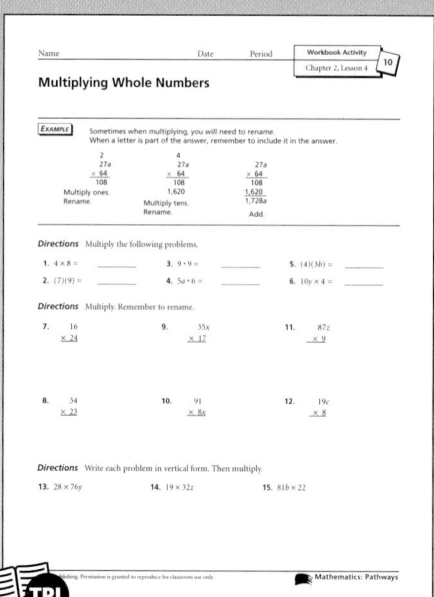

Workbook Activity 10

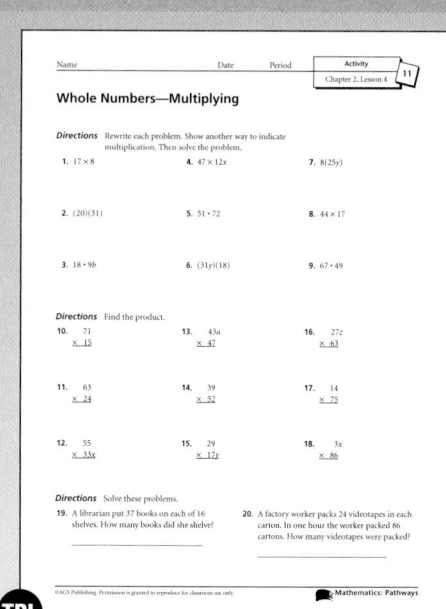

Activity 11

You multiply the same way in algebra, but you also must include the letter as part of the answer.

EXAMPLE 4 $21a • 22 = $ ◼

Step 1	Step 2	Step 3
21a	21a	21a
× 22	× 22	× 22
42a	42a	42a
	420	+ 420
Write the letter and multiply the ones.	Multiply the tens.	462a
		Add.

Exercise A Multiply the following problems.

1. 4		**5.** 8		**9.** 96	**13.** 5		**17.** 9a		
× 6		× 4		× 63	× 9		× 6		
24		32		6,048	45		54a		

2. 24	**6.** 85	**10.** 64	**14.** 86	**18.** 73
× 4	× 34	× 64	× 6	× 8x
96	2,890	4,096	516	584x

3. 54	**7.** 93	**11.** 7	**15.** 88	**19.** 64
× 46	× 87	× 8	× 41	× 9x
2,484	8,091	56	3,608	576x

4. 65	**8.** 56	**12.** 74	**16.** 37	**20.** 24a
× 45	× 7	× 82	× 84	× 78
2,925	392	6,068	3,108	1,872a

Exercise B Rewrite these problems in vertical form. Then multiply.

21. 237 × 456   **22.** 971 × 365   **23.** 147 × 447
108,072   354,415   65,709

PROBLEM SOLVING

Exercise C Solve each problem.

24. A complex has 4 office buildings. Each building has 26 offices. How many offices are there in the complex? 104 offices

25. Jessica bought 3 reams of paper. Each ream has 500 sheets of paper. How many sheets of paper did Jessica buy? 1,500 sheets

Whole Numbers and Algebra   Chapter 2   31

GROUP PROBLEM SOLVING

Organize students into groups of four. Each group is to manage a concert tour for a rock group. Group members must decide:

• What price(s) to charge for tickets

• How many tickets are available per stadium

• How much money will be made in each of three cities if all stadium seats are sold

Have each group share its work with the other groups.

COMMON ERROR

While reviewing the symbols that indicate multiplication, point out to students that the use of *x* in algebra is usually reserved for unknowns. Therefore, they should avoid using it as a multiplication symbol in problems involving algebraic expressions.

3 **Reinforce and Extend**

LEARNING STYLES

Logical/Mathematical
Help students understand the connection between multiplication and adding by moving their finger along a number line.

3(4)

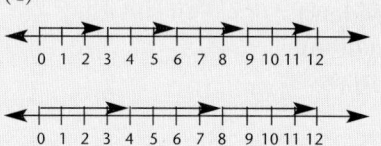

Move the finger to the right three spaces four different times or four spaces three different times.

MENTAL MATH

A quick review of the multiplication tables will help prepare students to calculate the problems in the exercises and allow them to focus on renaming and alignment. Make flash cards, and have students work in pairs to develop speed in naming products through 12 times 12. Students may also use the Multiplication Table on page 500 in their textbooks.

Lesson at a Glance

Chapter 2 Lesson 5

Overview This lesson presents the process of dividing whole numbers and algebraic expressions.

Objectives

- To explain the steps in division
- To identify the numbers in a division problem and their proper placement

Student Pages 32–33

Teacher's Resource Library TRL

Workbook Activities 11–12

Activity 12

Alternative Activity 12

Mathematics Vocabulary

divisor
dividend
quotient
remainder

---

1 Warm-Up Activity

Ask students to imagine that they are chefs for a hotel restaurant. Food service delivers 13 dozen (156) eggs. About 50 people usually order an omelet for breakfast. Ask, "How many eggs can you put in each omelet?" *(about 3)* Encourage students to explain how they estimated the answer. Have the class read the lesson to compare their methods with that in the text.

2 Teaching the Lesson

To ensure that vocabulary is not a stumbling block, give students time to work with the lesson terms. Draw a large division symbol on the board.

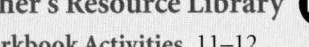

As you point to the left, inside, and top of the symbol, have students name the division-problem component that belongs there. *(divisor, dividend, quotient)* Then give problems orally ("6 divided into 36; 100 divided by 4"), and have students write the division problems and name the numbers.

Divisor
The number that is used to divide

Dividend
The number that is divided

Quotient
The result of division

Remainder
Amount left over when dividing

Division is the arithmetic operation of finding how many times a number, the **divisor,** goes into another number, the **dividend.** To check the answer to a division problem, multiply the **quotient,** or answer, by the divisor.

Division is the same in algebra as in arithmetic.

EXAMPLE 1 $42 \div 7 = \blacksquare$

$$\text{Divisor} \rightarrow 7\overline{)42} \begin{array}{l} \leftarrow \text{Quotient} \\ \leftarrow \text{Dividend} \end{array}$$

$$\begin{array}{r} \text{Check.} \quad 6 \quad \leftarrow \text{Quotient} \\ \underline{\times\ 7} \quad \leftarrow \text{Divisor} \\ 42 \quad \leftarrow \text{Dividend} \end{array}$$

EXAMPLE 2 $8a \div 2 = \blacksquare$

$$\underbrace{a + a + a + a}_{4a} | \underbrace{a + a + a + a}_{4a}$$

$$8a \div 2 = 4a \quad \text{Check.} \quad \begin{array}{r} 4a \\ \underline{\times\ 2} \\ 8a \end{array}$$

or $8a \div 2 = \blacksquare$
$(8 \div 2)a = \frac{8}{2}a = 4a$

When dividing, place the numbers correctly in each step. A **remainder** is always written as part of the quotient.

EXAMPLE 3 $144 \div 6 = \blacksquare$

$$\begin{array}{r} 24 \\ 6\overline{)144} \\ \underline{-\ 12} \\ 24 \\ \underline{-\ 24} \\ 0 \end{array}$$

6 goes into 14 two times. Multiply 6 by 2.
Subtract 12 from 14. Bring down the 4.
6 goes into 24 four times. Multiply 6 by 4.
Subtract 24 from 24. The remainder is 0.

Check. $24 \times 6 = 144$

EXAMPLE 4 $300 \div 8 = \blacksquare$

$$\begin{array}{r} 37\ \text{r4} \\ 8\overline{)300} \\ \underline{-\ 24} \\ 60 \\ \underline{-\ 56} \\ 4 \end{array}$$

8 does not go into 3.
8 goes into 30 three times. Multiply 8 by 3.
Subtract 24 from 30. Bring down the 0.
8 goes into 60 seven times. Multiply 8 by 7.
Subtract 56 from 60. Write the remainder 4 as part of the quotient.

Check. $(37 \times 8) + 4 = 296 + 4 = 300$

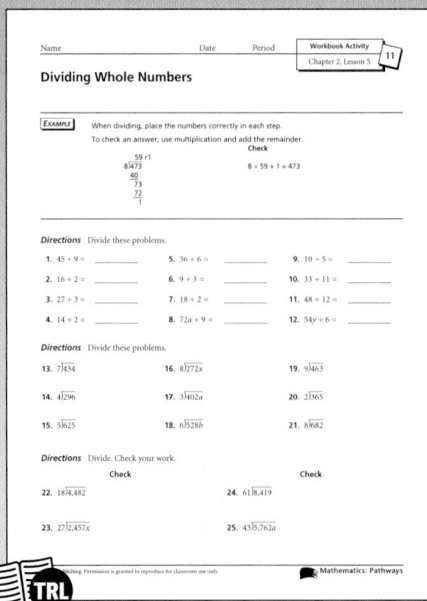

Workbook Activity 11

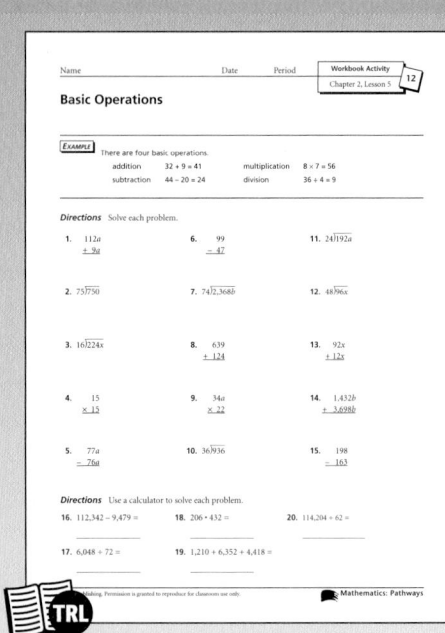

Workbook Activity 12

Try This

Identify the inverse, or opposite, operation of division. Provide examples that illustrate the inverse relationship.

Multiplication.
Sample example:
24 ÷ 6 = 4,
4 • 6 = 24

Exercise A Divide these problems.

1. 5)45   9
2. 8)96   12
3. 3)27   9
4. 5)120   24
5. 9)72   8
6. 6)378   63
7. 6)48c   8c
8. 4)116b   29b
9. 8)64a   8a
10. 9)621x   69x

Exercise B Divide. Check your work.

11. 5)412   82 r2
12. 9)566   62 r8
13. 2)347   173 r1
14. 8)659   82 r3
15. 8)489   61 r1
16. 6)623   103 r5
17. 6)827   137 r5
18. 5)403   80 r3

Exercise C Divide. Be sure to show your work.

19. 4,650 ÷ 8   581 r2
20. 27,542 ÷ 9   3,060 r2
21. 61,923 ÷ 64   967 r35
22. 42,450 ÷ 89   476 r86

PROBLEM SOLVING

Exercise D Solve each problem.

23. A restaurant orders 320 packages of crackers in cartons. If 20 packages are in each carton, how many cartons of crackers does the restaurant receive? 16 cartons

24. A local movie critic sees 3 movies every week that she works. If she has seen 141 movies this year, how many weeks has she worked this year? 47 weeks

25. The new hotel purchased uniforms for its 420 employees. Each employee needs 2 uniforms. The uniforms are packaged 6 to a carton. How many cartons were shipped to the hotel?
140 cartons

Math in Your Life

Say What?
Mathematics is very precise. Each number represents a specific quantity. Each operation defines a special function with a specific result. For example, when you divide any number or shape in half, you end up with two identical and equal parts. So, the next time you hear someone say, "I want the *bigger* half," you will know that mathematically speaking a bigger *half* is not possible.

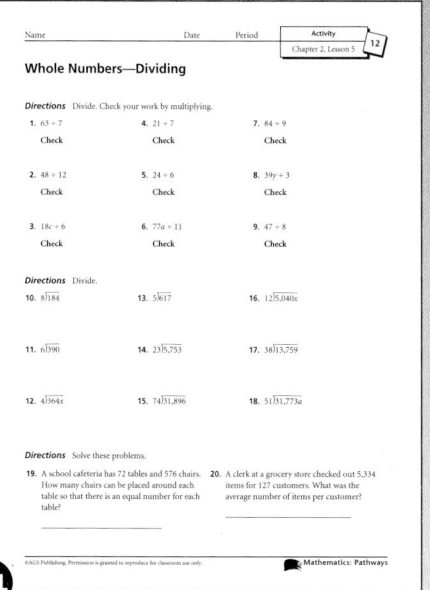

Activity 12

Try This

Assess students' understanding of division by asking them to explain why multiplication may be used to check division calculations. (*Division and multiplication are inverse, or opposite, processes.*) Have students pick other "families" of numbers (5, 12, 60; 9, 11, 99; 15, 6, 90) and use them to show inverse processes.

LEARNING STYLES

Auditory/Verbal
Have students take turns solving the problems in Exercise A on the board. Have them explain what they are doing as they complete each step.

CAREER CONNECTION

Invite a restaurant manager or chef to speak to the class and demonstrate math skills he or she uses frequently. Have students write questions beforehand that they wish to ask the speaker about his or her career. Make sure that students question in particular how the speaker uses multiplication and division; for example, to determine quantities to order and to use in recipes for various numbers of customers.

MODELING

Display three ranges of numbers (0–100, 101–500, 501–1,000). Explain that these ranges represent quotients. Provide each student in one group with a two- to five-digit dividend and one of the three ranges. Provide a second group of students with one- to two-digit divisors. Direct students with dividends to find a peer whose divisor results in a quotient that falls in the required range.

Example:
> Dividend = 7,230
> Range = **101–500**

The student must find a peer with a number between 15 and 71 (7,230 / 15 = **482**, 7,230 / 71 = **101.8**).

Students may use calculators if necessary to check answers or to solve problems involving remainders. After completing an equation successfully, students may use different numbers or switch roles. Ranges may be modified to meet students' needs.

Lesson at a Glance

Chapter 2 Lesson 6

Overview This lesson explains how to estimate the product or quotient of two numbers.

Objectives

- To estimate the product of two numbers
- To estimate the quotient of two compatible numbers
- To round dividends and divisors to create compatible numbers

Student Pages 34–35

Teacher's Resource Library TRL

Workbook Activity 13

Activity 13

Alternative Activity 13

Mathematics Vocabulary

compatible numbers

------

1 Warm-Up Activity

Find out the exact population of your school and the amount spent per pupil per year by the school district. Write this information on the board, explain it, and ask students to express *about* how much the school district spends on their school in a year. (For example, 624 students at $4,197 per pupil might generate answers of $2,400,000 to $2,500,000.) Have students explain how they estimated. Read the lesson to learn how to extend their skills of estimation to the operations of multiplication and division.

2 Teaching the Lesson

When dealing with large divisors and dividends, help students focus on the portions of the two numbers that can be isolated and converted to a division fact.

$$32\overline{)739} \quad \text{3 and 6} \qquad 30\overline{)600}^{20}$$

$$37\overline{)8,489} \quad \text{40 and 80} \qquad 40\overline{)8,000}^{200}$$

Point out to students that finding compatible numbers simplifies estimating quotients but may generate

------

Compatible numbers
Two numbers that form a basic division fact

Remember, when rounding to the greatest place value, round up if the numeral next to the greatest place value is 5 or more. Round down if the numeral is less than 5.

You can use estimation to check whether a product or quotient makes sense.

EXAMPLE 1 $54 \times 62 = $

Round each factor to its greatest place value.

$54 \rightarrow 50$
$62 \rightarrow 60$

Multiply the rounded factors.

$50 \times 60 = 3,000$

An estimate of the product 54×62 is 3,000.

Two numbers that form a basic division fact are **compatible numbers.** Compatible numbers can be used to estimate quotients.

EXAMPLE 2 $1,515 \div 42 = n$

The numbers 15 and 4 are not compatible.

$1,515 \div 42$

Write compatible numbers for the dividend and divisor.

$1,515 \div 42$
$\downarrow \qquad \downarrow$
$1,600 \div 40 \qquad 16 \div 4$ is a basic fact.

Divide.

$1,600 \div 40 = 40$

An estimate of the quotient $1,515 \div 42$ is 40.

Workbook Activity 13

Name _____ Date _____ Period _____

Workbook Activity 13
Chapter 2, Lesson 6

Estimating Products and Quotients

EXAMPLE To estimate a product, round to the greatest place value. Round up if 5 or more. Round down if less than 5.

$23 \times 67 =$
estimate $20 \times 70 = 1,400$

To estimate a quotient, use two numbers that form a basic division fact.

$1,721 \div 61 =$
$17 \div 6$ is not a basic fact.
$18 \div 6$ is a basic fact.
estimate $1,800 \div 60 = 300$

Directions Round. Estimate. Then find the exact product.

Problem	Rounded	Estimate	Exact Product
1. 63×24			
2. 85×36			
3. 17×42			
4. 44×75			
5. 59×14			
6. 32×55			
7. 73×64			
8. 27×83			

Directions Round. Estimate. Then find the exact quotient.

Problem	Rounded	Estimate	Exact Quotient
9. $534 \div 6$			
10. $736 \div 8$			
11. $1,380 \div 23$			
12. $2,862 \div 54$			
13. $6,290 \div 74$			
14. $4,758 \div 78$			
15. $11,613 \div 49$			

TRL

Workbook Activity 13

Activity 13

Name _____ Date _____ Period _____

Activity 13
Chapter 2, Lesson 6

Products and Quotients—Estimating

Directions Round each set of numerals.

1. 42×81 _____
2. 37×63 _____
3. 88×51 _____
4. 128×17 _____
5. $3,261 \times 243$ _____
6. $23,615 \times 5,260$ _____

Directions Write the compatible numbers for the dividend and divisor.

7. $115 \div 5$ _____
8. $273 \div 43$ _____
9. $792 \div 36$ _____
10. $3,328 \div 64$ _____
11. $2,784 \div 79$ _____
12. $19,698 \div 76$ _____

Directions Estimate each product or quotient.

13. 64×8 _____
14. 19×54 _____
15. 27×17 _____
16. 39×86 _____
17. 44×37 _____
18. $138 \div 6$ _____
19. $476 \div 54$ _____
20. $1,702 \div 74$ _____
21. $9,027 \div 59$ _____
22. $12,285 \div 35$ _____

Directions Estimate each answer. Then find the exact answer.

23. There are 36 pickles in each jar of a certain brand. How many pickles are in 368 jars?

Estimate: _____

Exact: _____

24. In each birdhouse kit there are 6 pieces of wood. How many kits can be made from 234 pieces of wood?

Estimate: _____

Exact: _____

25. For a class fund-raising project, 386 muffins were sold at 55¢ each. How much money was raised?

Estimate: _____

Exact: _____

TRL

Activity 13

EXAMPLE 3 4,639 ÷ 89 = ■

Write the compatible numbers.

4,639 ÷ 89
↓ ↓
4,500 ÷ 90

Divide.

4,500 ÷ 90 = 50

An estimate of the quotient 4,639 ÷ 89 is 50.

Exercise A Estimate each product.

1. 92 × 64   5,400
2. 65 × 95   7,000
3. 72 × 46   3,500
4. 476 × 39   20,000

5. 872 × 404   360,000
6. 76 × 88   7,200
7. 28 × 32   900
8. 234 × 61   12,000

9. 1,654 × 24   40,000
10. 5,176 × 486   2,500,000

Exercise B Estimate each quotient.

11. 375 ÷ 6   60
12. 826 ÷ 9   90
13. 2,386 ÷ 24   100
14. 19,995 ÷ 54   400

15. 16,115 ÷ 41   400
16. 712 ÷ 8   90
17. 335 ÷ 4   80
18. 6,428 ÷ 33   200

19. 65,454 ÷ 63   1,000
20. 41,118 ÷ 38   1,000

Exercise C Estimate. Then find the exact answer. You may use a calculator.

21. 3,412 × 653   2,100,000; 2,228,036
22. 62,338 ÷ 31   2,000; 2,010 r28 or 2,010.9
23. 41,392 ÷ 13   4,000; 3,184
24. 986 × 744   700,000; 733,584
25. 9,800 ÷ 46   200; 213 r2 or 213.04

 Try This

Write 10 division problems, some with compatible numbers and some with numbers that are not compatible. Read each problem to a partner and challenge him or her to identify whether the numbers in the problem are compatible.

Answers will vary.

---

rougher estimates. For example, rounding 1,515 to the closest hundred would give 1,500, not 1,600, but the divisor 4 is compatible with the larger number. The exact quotient of the original problem is 36.07; the estimated quotient using a dividend of 1,500 is 37.5, closer than the 40 estimated using 1,600.

Explain that students can use their calculators to check their estimates. However, remainders in division will appear as decimals.

Try This
You may make this activity a game by having students write their division problems on 3 × 5 cards, collecting them, and presenting them one at a time to teams. Each team member takes a turn, answering yes for compatible numbers and no for incompatible ones. The team with the most correct responses wins.

3 Reinforce and Extend

LEARNING STYLES

 **Visual/Spatial**
Students who have difficulty establishing appropriate boundaries for compatible numbers within dividends and divisors may be helped by using colors to isolate the relevant portions of numbers in examples written on the board:

94 **53,499**   10 **50**   100)50,000 (with 500 above)

LEARNING STYLES

 **LEP/ESL**
Have students who have difficulty understanding compatible numbers review basic division facts. Make a set of 3 × 5 cards with compatible numbers on one side and the quotient they produce on the other. Pair students, and have them take turns quizzing each other until they know these division facts.

Chapter 2 Lesson 7

Overview This lesson introduces open statements including algebraic terms and differentiates true, false, and open statements.

Objectives

- To identify true, false, and open statements
- To recognize the meaning and operations involved in terms with unknowns

Student Pages 36–37

Teacher's Resource Library **TRL**

Workbook Activity 14

Activity 14

Alternative Activity 14

Mathematics Vocabulary

open statement
terms
expression

---

1 ⚡ Warm-Up Activity

Present students with a series of statements to classify as true or false:

Multiplication and division are inverse operations. *(true)*

$3 + 4 = 4 + 3$ *(true)*

25 is a product. *(can't tell)*

$7 \times 4 = 14 + 10$ *(false)*

Ask, "Why can you classify the first, second, and fourth statements as true or false?" *(They are facts and provable or disprovable.)* "Why is the third statement neither true nor false?" *(You don't have enough information to tell.)*

2 ⚡ Teaching the Lesson

Provide students with extra practice in "reading" algebraic terms. Write expressions like the following on the board. Ask volunteers to circle each term and use words to describe its meaning.

$25n - 12n$
[(twenty-five times some number) minus (twelve times that same number)]

Open statement
A sentence that is neither true nor false

Terms
Parts of an expression separated by operation signs such as +, −, •, ×, or ÷

Expression
A mathematical statement that usually includes numbers, variables, and symbols

These exercises show the four basic operations.

$15 + 6 = \blacksquare$
$15 - 8 = \blacksquare$
$4 \times 5 = \blacksquare$
$15 \div 3 = \blacksquare$

If you perform each operation correctly, the statements are *true*. If you make a mistake, the statements are *false*.

EXAMPLE 1

True Statements	False Statements
$15 + 6 = 21$	$15 + 6 = 23$
$15 - 8 = 7$	$15 - 8 = 9$
$4 \times 5 = 20$	$4 \times 5 = 25$
$15 \div 3 = 5$	$15 \div 3 = 8$

4n means 4 times n. In algebra, the multiplication sign can be confused with the letter x. This is how you show multiplication in algebra: 4n or 4 • n or 4(n).

In algebra, statements include letters as well as numbers. Letters are used as placeholders for numbers. Suppose n is a placeholder for an unknown number.

- $15 + n$ means 15 plus *some number.*
- $15 - n$ means 15 minus *some number.*
- $4n$ means 4 times *some number.*
- $15 \div n$ means 15 divided by *some number.*

The statement $4n = 20$ is neither true nor false. It is an **open statement.**

EXAMPLE 2 Open Statements

$15 + n = 21$
$15 - n = 7$
$4n = 20$
$15 \div n = 5$

In these examples, 15 and n are called **terms.** Terms are the parts of an **expression** separated by an operation sign.

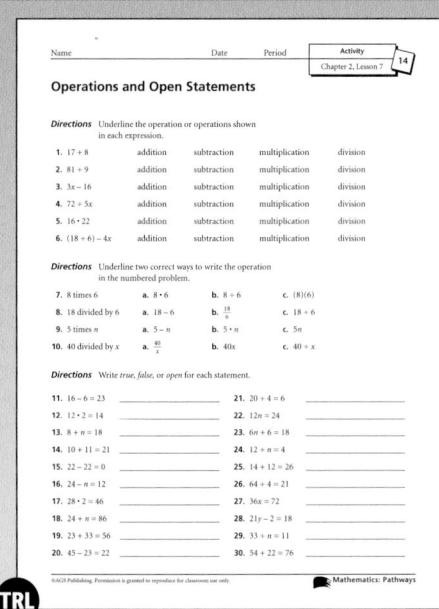

Exercise A Write *true* or *false* for each statement.

1. $5 + 4 = 9$ true   **6.** $16 + 6 = 22$ true

2. $12 - 8 = 3$ false   **7.** $35 - 11 = 14$ false

3. $6 \times 9 = 54$ true   **8.** $8 \times 8 = 56$ false

4. $81 \div 9 = 9$ true   **9.** $21 \div 7 = 3$ true

5. $5 \times 5 = 30$ false   **10.** $14 - 4 = 9$ false

Exercise B Tell whether each statement is *true, false,* or *open.*

11. $7 + 5 = 12$ true   **16.** $14 + n = 32$ open

12. $5n = 45$ open   **17.** $15 \div n = 5$ open

13. $17 - n = 10$ open   **18.** $10n = 100$ open

14. $36 \div 12 = 2$ false   **19.** $31 - 18 = 13$ true

15. $15 + 14 = 30$ false   **20.** $15 + 8 = 22$ false

Exercise C Use words to write the meaning of each of the following.

21. $34 \div n$ Thirty-four divided by some number

22. $14n$ Fourteen times some number

23. $16 - n$ Sixteen minus some number

24. $24 + n$ Twenty-four plus some number

25. $n \div 8$ Some number divided by eight

Estimation Activity

Estimate: A gallon of gasoline costs $\$1.49\frac{9}{10}$. How many gallons can you buy for $10?

Solution: Round price to $1.50

Think: $1.50 for 1 gal
        $3.00 for 2 gal   } add: $9.00 for 6 gallons
        $6.00 for 4 gal

You get a little more than 6 gallons for $10.

     $10 \div 1.50 = 6.67$ gallons or $6\frac{2}{3}$ gallons

Whole Numbers and Algebra Chapter 2 **37**

$36a \div 9$

[(thirty-six times some number) divided by 9]

$(12 \div 2a)a$

[(twelve divided by 2 times some number) multiplied by that same number]

3   Reinforce and Extend

MENTAL MATH

You may wish to have students complete Exercise A orally. For additional practice, read additional statements, such as those below, and have students classify them orally.

$2 \div 2 = 1$	*(true)*
$30 \times 5 = 145$	*(false)*
$20 + 30 = 50$	*(true)*
$800 - 200 = 500$	*(false)*
$25 \div 6 = 5$	*(false)*
$4 \times 80 = 320$	*(true)*
$16 + 4 = 30$	*(false)*
$16 - 4 = 12$	*(true)*

LEARNING STYLES

Interpersonal/ Group Learning

After students complete the exercises for Lesson 7, have them work in small groups to write ten new true statements, false statements, and open statements. Members of the group can check one another's statements and write each on a 3 × 5 card. Ask them to shuffle their 30 cards and exchange them with another group. Then groups can sort the statements into true, false, and open piles. Have students correct false statements and change open statements into true statements, writing the information on the backs of the cards.

Whole Numbers and Algebra **37**

Lesson at a Glance

Chapter 2 Lesson 8

Overview This lesson differentiates algebraic and numerical expressions.

Objectives

- To identify and name variables
- To identify operations in algebraic expressions
- To classify expressions as algebraic or numerical

Student Pages 38–39

Teacher's Resource Library

Workbook Activity 15

Activity 15

Alternative Activity 15

Mathematics Vocabulary

variable
algebraic expression
numerical expression

---

1 Warm-Up Activity

On the board, write two formulas that students are likely to know or can easily understand, such as:

$$A = l \cdot w$$

$$P = 2(l + w)$$

Ask students to explain what the letters represent. Then give numbers for two unknown quantities in each equation, and have students explain what has changed. (*Only one unknown quantity remains—the one still represented by a letter.*) Explain that algebra presents mathematical expressions that include both numbers and letters (unknowns). Have students read the lesson to learn how to "read" these expressions.

2 Teaching the Lesson

Draw on vocabulary from the preceding lessons to relate numerical and algebraic expressions to the four operations. Write expressions on the board. Ask students to

- identify them as numerical or algebraic.

Lesson 8 Using Letters to Represent Numbers

Variable
A letter that represents an unknown number

Algebraic expression
A mathematical statement that includes at least one operation and variable

Numerical expression
A mathematical sentence that uses operations and numbers

Recall that a letter can be used as a placeholder for a number. This letter is known as a **variable**.

An expression with at least one variable and one operation is called an **algebraic expression**.

An expression that includes only numbers is called a **numerical expression**.

EXAMPLE 1

Numerical Expressions	Algebraic Expressions
$6 + 5$	$6 + n$
$16 - 3$	$n - 3$
14×5	$14 \times a$
$24 \div 4$	$y \div 4$

When describing an expression, you decide whether it is a numerical or algebraic expression. You identify the operations and name any variable.

Remember that any letter can be used as the variable in an algebraic expression.

EXAMPLE 2 Classify the expression, name the operation(s), and identify any variables.

$4n + 5$

The expression $4n + 5$ is an algebraic expression.

There are two operations in the expression— multiplication and addition.

There is one variable—the letter n.

Square: $3x + 3x + 3x + 3x$, or $4(3x)$

Rectangle: $(m + 6) + (m + 4) + (m + 6) + (m + 4)$, or $2(m + 6) + 2(4 + m)$

Equilateral triangle: $(2 + g) + (2 + g) + (2 + g)$, or $3(2 + g)$

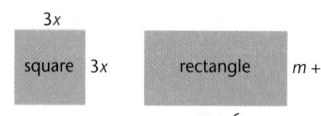

Build a Model

Use construction paper to cut out the three shapes below. Then write an expression to find the distance around each shape.

square $3x$

rectangle $m + 4$ / $m + 6$

equilateral triangle $2 + g$

38 Chapter 2 Whole Numbers and Algebra

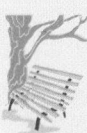
Exercise A Name the variable in each expression.

1. $18 + x$ x
2. $2n$ n
3. $6a + 15$ a
4. $15 - y$ y
5. $36 \div t$ t
6. $5 + b$ b
7. $40h$ h
8. $k - 11$ k
9. $n \div 16$ n
10. $2d + 3$ d

Exercise B Identify the operation(s) in each expression.

11. $n + 10$ addition
12. $4n - 3$ multiplication, subtraction
13. $x \div 7$ division
14. $7n$ multiplication
15. $6x + 14$ multiplication, addition
16. $8m \div 2$ multiplication, division
17. $2y + 5$ multiplication, addition
18. $6y - 3$ multiplication, subtraction
19. $d - 10$ subtraction
20. $5n$ multiplication

Exercise C Classify each expression as numeric or algebraic, name the operation(s), and identify any variables.

21. $15 + 22$
22. $14 - 8$
23. $y \div 10$
24. $11 - x$
25. $2y + 5$
26. $14 \cdot 12$
27. $3m + 6$
28. $18 + 4$
29. $25n$
30. $12 \div 6$

21. numerical, addition
22. numerical, subtraction
23. algebraic, division, y
24. algebraic, subtraction, x
25. algebraic, multiplication, addition, y
26. numerical, multiplication
27. algebraic, multiplication, addition, m
28. numerical, addition
29. algebraic, multiplication, n
30. numerical, division

- identify the operation involved.
- name the parts of the expression.

(For example, $16 \div a$ is an algebraic expression using division; 16 is the dividend, and a is the divisor.) For further practice, draw a rectangle on the board, and introduce area and perimeter problems, providing only two numbers. For example, $P = 50$, $l = 15$. Have students create equations and explain which contain numerical expressions and which contain algebraic expressions. For example, $50 = 2(15 + w)$ contains an algebraic expression, but $P = 2(15 + 10)$ contains a numerical expression.

3 Reinforce and Extend

LEARNING STYLES

Body/Kinesthetic

Give each student two 4×6 cards, one with an operation sign and the other with a number on one side and an algebraic variable, such as a, n, or c, on the other side. Randomly call groups of three to the front of the class, and have the class instruct the three to form an algebraic or numerical expression by holding up cards. Classmates can then read the expressions using words. For example, $n + 10$ is an algebraic expression meaning "Add 10 to some number n."

IN THE COMMUNITY

Ask students to gather information about a business or another school in the area: dimensions of the building, number of parking spaces and rows in the parking lot, number of employees and administrators, and so on. Have students write a paragraph explaining the information they gathered. Then ask them to exchange papers and use the information they receive to create a numerical expression and an algebraic expression and explain their meaning. (For example, if there are 66 parking spaces and 6 rows in the school parking lot, $66 \div 6$ would tell how many spaces are in one row. If there are 66 people in one business office and 58 are employees, then $58 + n = 66$, where n is the number of administrators.)

Chapter 2 Lesson 9

Overview This lesson explains how to evaluate algebraic expressions.

Objective

■ To write and evaluate (or find the numerical value) of algebraic expressions

Student Pages 40–41

Teacher's Resource Library   **TRL**

Workbook Activity 16

Activity 16

Alternative Activity 16

Mathematics Vocabulary

substitute
evaluate

1 Warm-Up Activity

Ask a volunteer to write an algebraic expression on the board. Ask the class to interpret it in words. Have a second volunteer add an equal sign and a number value to create an equation. Ask, "What has to be done to solve this equation?" *(Find the exact value of the unknown that makes it a true expression.)* Explain that in algebra, the job is usually to replace unknowns (letters) with numbers. In this lesson, students will learn to evaluate whether a statement is true or false when they replace variables with numbers.

2 Teaching the Lesson

To provide extra practice, have students evaluate problems in Exercise B with other values for each unknown.

11. $m = 51$ *(66)*; $m = 11$ *(26)*

12. $n = 50$ *(33)*; $n = 25$ *(8)*

13. $n = 12$ *(48)*; $n = 16$ *(64)*

14. $n = 5$ *(20)*; $n = 10$ *(10)*

15. $m = 7$ *(21)*; $m = 5$ *(17)*

16. $m = 3$ *(4)*; $m = 5$ *(12)*

17. $y = 5$ *(1)*; $y = 2$ *(10)*

18. $n = 30$ *(12)*; $n = 26$ *(16)*

19. $n = 48$ *(4)*; $n = 144$ *(12)*

20. $m = 3$ *(14)*; $m = 10$ *(35)*

Lesson 9 Replacing Variables

Substitute
To put a number in place of a variable

Evaluate
To find the numerical value of an algebraic expression

Recall that statements such as $4n = 20$ are open statements. An open statement becomes a true or false statement when you **substitute** a number for the variable. When you substitute a number for the variable, follow these steps to **evaluate** the expression.

Step 1 First, substitute a number.

Step 2 Perform the operations from left to right.

EXAMPLE 1 Evaluate $8 + m$ when $m = 3$.

Step 1 Substitute the number for the variable.

$8 + 3$

Step 2 Perform the operation.

$8 + 3 = 11$

The statement $8 + 3 = 11$ is a true statement.

EXAMPLE 2 Is $4n = 12$ a true or false statement when $n = 1, 2,$ or 3?

When $n = 1$,
$4n = 12 \rightarrow 4 \cdot 1 = 4$, or $4 = 12 \rightarrow$ false statement

When $n = 2$,
$4n = 12 \rightarrow 4 \cdot 2 = 8$, or $8 = 12 \rightarrow$ false statement

When $n = 3$,
$4n = 12 \rightarrow 4 \cdot 3 = 12$, or $12 = 12 \rightarrow$ true statement

Exercise A Write an algebraic expression.

1. add 5 to some number $n + 5$
2. some number times 3 $3n$
3. 15 divided by some number $15 \div n$
4. some number minus 8 $n - 8$
5. 2 times some number plus 5 $2n + 5$
6. subtract 46 from some number $n - 46$
7. 10 minus some number $10 - n$
8. some number plus 16 $n + 16$
9. some number divided by 9 $n \div 9$
10. 23 times some number $23n$

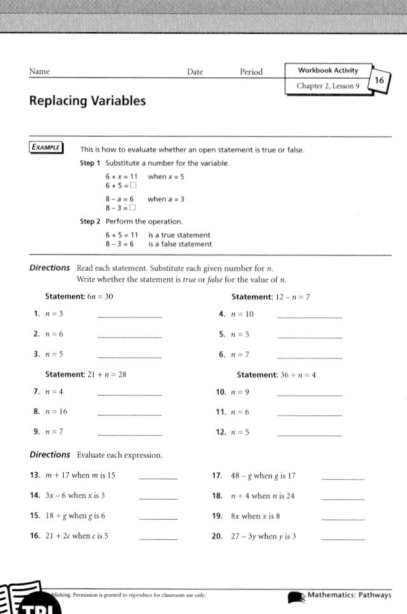

Workbook Activity 16

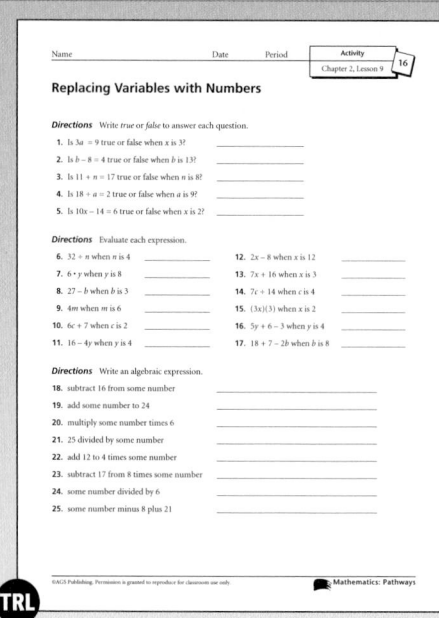

Activity 16

Exercise B Evaluate each expression.

11. $m + 15$ when $m = 14$ 29
16. $4m - 8$ when $m = 2$ 0

12. $n - 17$ when $n = 30$ 13
17. $16 - 3y$ when $y = 3$ 7

13. $4n$ when $n = 21$ 84
18. $42 - n$ when $n = 27$ 15

14. $100 \div n$ when $n = 20$ 5
19. $n \div 12$ when $n = 60$ 5

15. $2m + 7$ when $m = 3$ 13
20. $5 + 3m$ when $m = 8$ 29

Exercise C Write *true* or *false*.

Is $5 + n = 12$ a true or false statement when

21. $n = 3$?   false
22. $n = 5$?   false
23. $n = 7$?   true

Calculator Practice

You can use the calculator to help you evaluate algebraic expressions easily.

EXAMPLE 3 $49 \div x = 7$ when $x = 7$.

Press 49 ÷ 7 =. The display reads 7.

The statement $49 \div x = 7$ when $x = 7$ is true.

EXAMPLE 4 $8x = 56$ when $x = 6$.

Press 8 × 6 =. The display reads 48.

The statement $8x = 56$ when $x = 6$ is false.

Exercise D Use your calculator to evaluate each expression. Then identify the expression as *true* or *false*.

24. $35 \div x = 5$ when $x = 7$.   true
28. $49 \div x = 8$ when $x = 9$.   false

25. $182 + x = 186$ when $x = 3$.   false
29. $x + 22 = 30$ when $x = 7$.   false

26. $184 - x = 134$ when $x = 50$.   true
30. $22x = 132$ when $x = 6$.   true

27. $25 \div x = 5$ when $x = 5$.   true

MANIPULATIVES

 Replacing Variables

Materials: Pattern Blocks, Cuisenaire Rods

Group Practice: Build models of various algebraic expressions (excluding division), using shapes to represent variables and rods to model constants. For example, model $4n + 3$ with 4 triangles and a 3-rod. Write operation signs as needed. Evaluate an expression by replacing each variable with a rod of the indicated value. Combine rods to find sums. To find differences, place one rod model on top of the other, and find the value of the uncovered part of the rod. To multiply, place the rods perpendicular to each other to form a rectangle, and multiply the dimensions of the rectangle to find the product. Write the symbolic equivalent for each step.

Student Practice: Have students build models and draw sketches for Exercise A, problems 1–2, 4–8. For Exercise B, problems 11–13, 15–18, have students evaluate each expression, drawing sketches of each model.

3 **Reinforce and Extend**

AT HOME

 Have students create algebraic expressions to represent situations at home or in other classes. They must also write an explanation of what the numbers and the letters represent. Here are some starter suggestions:

- Earnings and allowance saved over a month's time, when the total deposited in the account is known

- Points received in a subject this grading period (Hint: Break into points received so far and possible points remaining or into categories such as homework, tests, and extra credit.)

CALCULATOR

 Some students may enjoy the challenge of actually solving algebraic equations with their calculators. Present equations such as the following, and discuss what operation is required to find the values of a and b.

$$15 + a = 75$$

$$5 \cdot b = 30$$

(Students should see that the inverse process needs to be performed.)

- Press 75 − 15 =.

  The display reads 60.

  The statement $15 + 60 = 75$ is true.

- Press 30 ÷ 5 =.

  The display reads 6.

  The statement $5 \cdot 6 = 30$ is true.

Chapter 2 Application

Overview This lesson provides an application of using patterns.

Objective

- To identify a pattern and complete and extend a number sequence

Student Page 42

Teacher's Resource Library

Application Activity 2

Everyday Math 2

1 Warm-Up Activity

Call out students' names according to a pattern, and encourage students to identify the pattern. Patterns may be based on gender, height, hair color, syllables in the name, and so on.

2 Teaching the Lesson

Explain to students that patterns follow a rule. This explains how it is possible to predict what numbers will appear later in a pattern.

COMMON ERROR

Students may predict a number in the pattern by going through the numbers one by one. Encourage them to create an algebraic expression to find the number more easily.

MENTAL MATH

Students may be able to mentally predict numbers in a sequence. Encourage mental estimates if students are also checking their answers.

Application

Using Patterns After you identify the pattern in a series of numbers, you will be able to find any number in that sequence.

EXAMPLE 1 Name the next number in the sequence.

1, 4, 9, 16, 25, . . .

Step 1 Look at the sequence. Notice that each number is a square number, the product of two identical numbers. For example:

$1 \times 1 = 1 \quad 2 \times 2 = 4 \quad 3 \times 3 = 9 \quad 4 \times 4 = 16 \quad 5 \times 5 = 25,$ and so on.

Step 2 The next number in this sequence would be $6 \times 6 = 36$, and the next number after that would be $7 \times 7 = 49$.

The sequence would be 1, 4, 9, 16, 25, 36, 49, . . .

EXAMPLE 2 Name the twentieth number in the sequence.

6, 7, 8, 9, 10, 11, . . .

Step 1 Make a table.

Order of Number	1st	2nd	3rd	4th	5th	6th
	6	7	8	9	10	11

Step 2 Look at the Order of Number and the numbers. Notice that each number is 5 more than the order number.

Step 3 Let x represent the order number. Then the algebraic expression for this sequence is $x + 5$.

If $x = 20$, then $x + 5 = 20 + 5 = 25$.

So, the twentieth number in this sequence is 25.

Exercise Solve each problem.

1. Name the twentieth number in the sequence: 400

   1, 4, 9, 16, 25, . . .

2. Name the 250th number in the sequence: 255

   6, 7, 8, 9, 10, 11, . . .

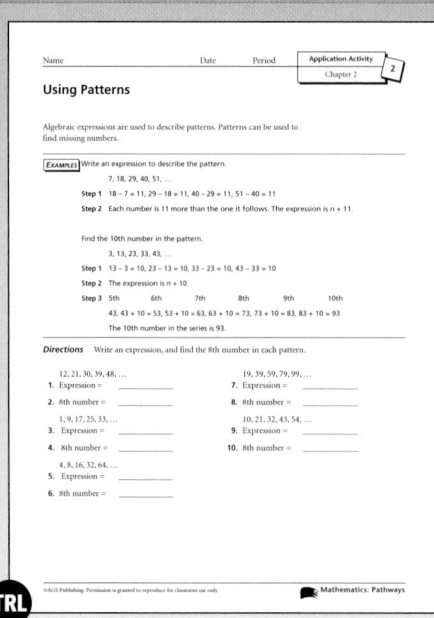

Application Activity 2

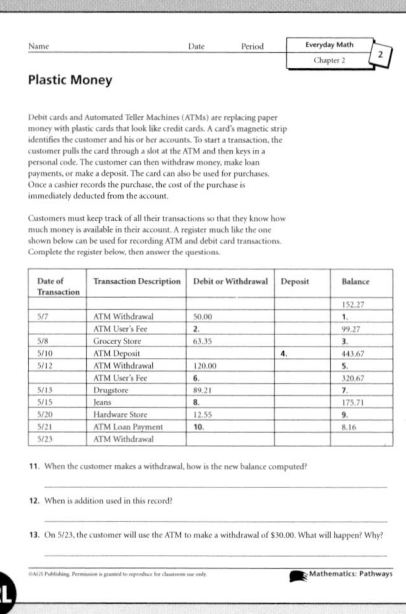

Everyday Math 2

Chapter 2 REVIEW

Write the letter of the correct answer.

1. Find the sum of 9,273 + 291 C
- **A** 9,464
- **B** 8,982
- **C** 9,564
- **D** 12,183

2. Find the difference of 111 − 99 D
- **A** 11
- **B** 22
- **C** 200
- **D** 12

3. Find the product of 42 × 53 A
- **A** 2,226
- **B** 2,136
- **C** 95
- **D** 126

4. Find the quotient of 23,670 ÷ 31 C
- **A** 789
- **B** 763
- **C** 763 r17
- **D** 673 r11

5. Evaluate the expression $n + 7$ when $n = 8$ C
- **A** 16
- **B** 1
- **C** 15
- **D** 14

6. Evaluate the expression $60 ÷ y$ when $y = 5$ B
- **A** 300
- **B** 12
- **C** 15
- **D** 65

CAREER CONNECTION

Biologists and naturalists use patterns to identify how a species multiplies in the wild. Invite students to research population trends in nature and look for patterns. How could this affect the job of a naturalist?

Cell division in the human body also follows a pattern. Contact a biology teacher or resource book for more information. How do biologists use their knowledge of this type of pattern?

CALCULATOR

Have students explore how to use calculators to extend patterns. Ask them to find a method and share it with the class. Ask students whether they can find one method that works for all patterns.

Challenge students to explain whether a calculator can *identify* a pattern and then extend it. Students should justify their answers with examples from their explorations.

Chapter 2 Review

Each set of problems in the Chapter Review includes an example and solution to illustrate the concept. Use the given examples for reteaching the materials in Chapter 2. For additional practice, refer to the Supplementary Problems for Chapter 2 (pages 434–435).

Chapter 2 Mastery Test

The Teacher's Resource Library includes parallel forms of the Chapter 2 Mastery Test. The difficulty level of the two forms is equivalent. You may wish to use one form as a pretest and the other form as a posttest.

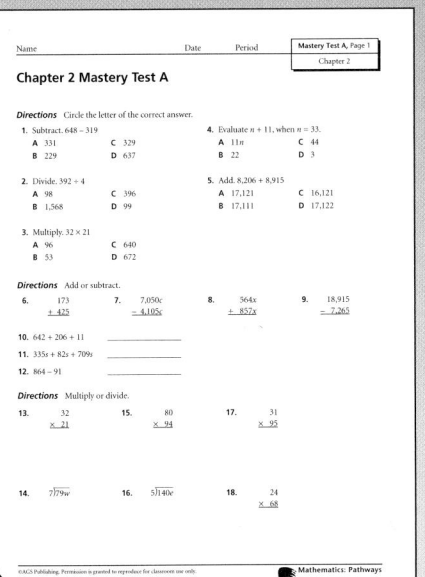

Chapter 2 Mastery Test A

Alternative Assessment items correlate with student Goals for Learning at the beginning of this chapter.

■ To review addition and subtraction using whole numbers

Have students work in teams to add and subtract several problems. Make a contest of solving the problems. Allow a few minutes for strategizing before the team begins working the problems. Discuss the strategies the winning team used to complete the most problems correctly.

■ To learn to estimate sums and differences

Have students make a list of strategies that they use for estimating sums and differences. After individual students have compiled their lists, have the entire class share their strategies. List them on the board or on a poster, and display the list in a prominent place in the classroom so that students have the option to practice and learn one another's strategies.

■ To review multiplication and division using whole numbers

Have students work in pairs. Using manipulatives such as toothpicks, have students demonstrate simple multiplication and division problems. The products, divisors, and dividends of the problems should not be greater than 100. One partner should write a problem, and the other partner should demonstrate how the problem could be solved with the toothpicks.

■ To learn to estimate products and quotients

Have students work in groups of three or four to discuss and list strategies they can use for estimating products and quotients. Remind groups to determine which of the same strategies work for estimating products and quotients as well as estimating sums and differences. Have the groups share their strategies with the whole class. Create a list of class strategies, and display it in a prominent place so that students can practice and learn one anothers' strategies. *(Strategies will vary but should include finding compatible numbers.)*

Chapter 2 REVIEW - continued

Find each sum.

Example: 2,158 + 1,682

Solution:
$$\begin{array}{r} 2,158 \\ +\ 1,682 \\ \hline 3,840 \end{array}$$

7. 37,104   **7.** 32,105 + 4,999   **9.** 295 + 638   933

8. 112,110   **8.** 105,213 + 6,897   **10.** 12,683 + 75,922   88,605

Find each difference.

Example: 3,422 − 2,193

Solution:
$$\begin{array}{r} 3,422 \\ -\ 2,193 \\ \hline 1,229 \end{array}$$

11. 38,788   **11.** 42,647 − 3,859   **13.** 131,050 − 29,682   101,368

12. 1,701   **12.** 2,218 − 517   **14.** 486,982 − 321,518   165,464

Find each product.

Example: 28 × 16

Solution:
$$\begin{array}{r} 28 \\ \times\ 16 \\ \hline 168 \\ +\ 280 \\ \hline 448 \end{array}$$

15. 363 × 249   90,387   **17.** 16 × 8   128

16. 42 × 39   1,638   **18.** 760 × 5   3,800

Find each quotient. Remember to write any remainder as part of the quotient.

Example: 434 ÷ 7

Solution:
$$\begin{array}{r} 62 \\ 7\overline{)434} \\ -\ 42 \\ \hline 14 \\ -\ 14 \\ \hline 0 \end{array}$$

19. 1,438 ÷ 42   34 r10   **21.** 158 ÷ 30   5 r8

20. 625 ÷ 25   25   **22.** 9,696 ÷ 8   1,212

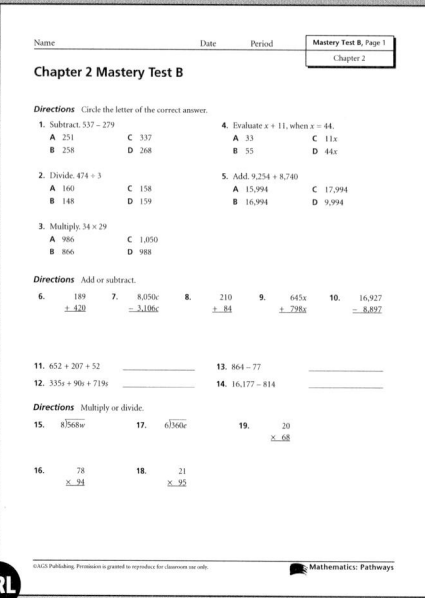

Chapter 2 Mastery Test B

Name _____ Date _____ Period _____ | Mastery Test B, Page 1 / Chapter 2

Chapter 2 Mastery Test B

Directions Circle the letter of the correct answer.

1. Subtract. 537 − 279
   A 251   C 337
   B 258   D 268

2. Divide. 474 ÷ 3
   A 160   C 158
   B 148   D 159

3. Multiply. 34 × 29
   A 986   C 1,050
   B 866   D 988

4. Evaluate x + 11, when x = 44.
   A 33   C 11x
   B 55   D 44x

5. Add. 9,254 + 8,740
   A 15,994   C 17,994
   B 16,994   D 9,994

Directions Add or subtract.

6. 189 + 420
7. 8,050c − 3,106c
8. 210 + 84
9. 645x + 798x
10. 16,927 − 8,897

11. 652 + 207 + 52 _____
12. 335z + 90z + 719z _____
13. 864 − 77 _____
14. 16,177 − 814 _____

Directions Multiply or divide.

15. 8)568w
17. 6)360r
19. 20 × 68

16. 78 × 94
18. 21 × 95

©AGS Publishing. Permission is granted to reproduce for classroom use only.   Mathematics: Pathways

---

Name _____ Date _____ Period _____ | Mastery Test B, Page 2 / Chapter 2

Chapter 2 Mastery Test B, continued

Directions Estimate each product by rounding to the greatest place value.

20. 94 × 21 _____
21. 407 × 192 _____

Directions Use compatible numbers to estimate each quotient.

22. 642f ÷ 6 _____
24. 499 ÷ 5 _____
23. 3,517 ÷ 9 _____

Directions Write an algebraic expression.

25. twenty subtracted from some number _____
26. eight more than six times some number _____

Directions Evaluate.

27. 5m when m = 140 _____
28. 2,000 + b when b = 10 _____

Directions Solve.

29. In 2 weeks, an employee worked 80 hours of regular time and 15 hours of overtime. How many hours total did the employee work during that period?

30. A machine that is programmed to print 8,500 pages breaks after printing only 2,176 pages. How many pages still need to be printed?

©AGS Publishing. Permission is granted to reproduce for classroom use only.   Mathematics: Pathways

Estimate each answer.

Example: 1,921 − 473   Solution: 2,000
                                      − 500
                                    1,500

23. 120,000   **23.** $65,402 + 54,410$ **25.** $103,412 − 49,205$ 50,000

24. 270,000   **24.** 321×856 **26.** $33,464 \div 74$ 500

Tell whether each statement is true, false, or open.

Example: 6 + 7 = 12   Solution: 6 + 7 = 13, so 6 + 7 = 12 is false.

27. open   **27.** $15 − n = 8$ **29.** $14 + 6 = 21$ false

28. true   **28.** $7 \times 4 = 28$ **30.** $30 \div 5 = n$ open

31. algebraic, multiplication, addition, m

32. numerical, multiplication, addition

33. algebraic, division, g

Classify each expression, name the operation(s), and identify any variables.

Example: 4 − x   Solution: algebraic expression, subtraction, x

31. $2m + 9$ **34.** $15 − x$
                                       algebraic, subtraction, x

32. $5 \times 6 + 3$ **35.** $3x$
                                       algebraic, multiplication, x

33. $g \div 58$ **36.** $918 + 413$
                                       numerical, addition

Write true or false.

Example: 21 ÷ n = 7 when n = 3.   Solution: $3\overline{)21}^{\,7}$ True

37. $5y = 80$ when $y = 14$.   false

38. $q \div 16 = 8$ when $q = 128$.   true

39. $14 + n = 22$ when $n = 8$.   true

40. $19 − n = 14$ when $n = 4$.   false

Test-Taking Tip

Remember an expression can have numbers, operations, and variables, but it does not have an equal sign.

■ **To recognize true, false, and open statements**

Have individual students write two open, two false, and two true statements. Then separate students into pairs, and have them solve their partners' questions. Students should explain why the statements are true, false, or open. (*Answers will vary. Check students' work for accuracy.*)

■ **To recognize algebraic and numerical expressions**

Arrange students into two teams—one algebraic expression team and one numerical expression team. Have each team line up near the board, and when you say go, have the first person go to the board and write an expression for his or her team (algebraic or numeric, depending on the team). Ask that each student not use the same numbers and/or operators as the student immediately preceding him or her.

■ **To evaluate algebraic expressions**

Have students use manipulatives such as paper clips to evaluate simple algebraic expressions. Have students do problems, such as $6 + r$ when r is 9, $17 − q$ when q is 14, $2 + 3x$ when x is 4, and so on. (*Check students' work for accuracy.*)

Chapter

Planning Guide

Decimals

Lesson		Student Pages	Vocabulary	Practice Exercises	Problem Solving	Try This	Solutions Key
1	Place Value and Decimals	48–49	✔	✔		49	✔
2	Comparing and Rounding Decimals	50–51		✔		51	✔
3	Adding and Subtracting Decimals	52–53	✔	✔	53		✔
4	Multiplying Decimals by Powers of 10	54–55		✔			✔
5	Multiplying Decimals	56–57	✔	✔	57		✔
6	Dividing Decimals by Powers of 10	58–59		✔			✔
7	Dividing Decimals	60–61		✔	61		✔
8	Decimals and Fractions	62–63	✔	✔	63		✔
9	Repeating Decimals	64–65	✔	✔		65	✔
10	Renaming Percents to Decimals	66–67	✔	✔	67		✔
11	Evaluating Expressions with Decimals	68–69		✔			✔
Application	Converting a Measurement	70		✔			✔

Chapter Activities

Teacher's Resource Library
Estimation Exercise 3: Estimating with Decimals
Application Activity 3: Converting a Measurement
Everyday Math 3: Metric Measures
Community Connection 3: The Better Buy

Teacher's Edition
Chapter 3 Project

Assessment Options

Student Text
Chapter 3 Review

Teacher's Resource Library
Chapter 3 Mastery Tests A and B

Teacher's Edition
Chapter 3 Alternative Assessments

	Student Text Features						Teaching Strategies									Learning Styles						Teacher's Resource Library			
Estimation Activity	Math in Your Life	Technology Connection	Writing About Mathematics	Build a Model	Calculator Practice	Online Connection	Common Error	Applications Home, Career, Community	Mental Math	Manipulatives	Calculator	Group Problem Solving	Modeling	Knowing Your Students	Auditory/Verbal	Visual/Spatial	Logical/Mathematical	Body/Kinesthetic	Interpersonal/Group Learning	LEP/ESL	Activities	Alternate Activities	Workbook Activities	Self-Study Guide
															49	49					17	17	17	✔
					51			51		51		51		51							18	18	18	✔
					53						53	53						53			19	19	19	✔
		55	55						55											55	20	20	20	✔
					57						57	57									21	21	21	✔
	59						59	59								59					22	22	22	✔
					61	61					61	61									23	23	23–24	✔
							63											63			24	24	25	✔
65							65				65								65		25	25	26	✔
								67				67	67								26	26	27	✔
								69							69				69		27	27	28	✔
							70					71				71								✔

Software Options

Skill Track Software

Use the Skill Track Software for *Mathematics: Pathways* for additional reinforcement of this chapter. The software provides multiple-choice assessment items for students to access by computer.

Solutions Key

Use the Solutions Key with this chapter to help students who may need additional assistance. The Solutions Key CD provides solutions for every exercise in the student edition.

Other Resources

Alternative Activities

The Teacher's Resource Library (TRL) contains a set of worksheets written at a second-grade reading level called Alternative Activities. They cover the same content as the regular Activities.

Manipulatives

See the Manipulative activities in this chapter for hands-on modeling of the content.
Base Ten Blocks

Chapter at a Glance

Chapter 3: Decimals
pages 46–73

Lessons

Skill Track for Mathematics: Pathways

Teacher's Resource Library TRL

- Workbook Activities 17–28
- Activities 17–27
- Alternative Activities 17–27
- Application Activity 3
- Estimation Exercise 3
- Everyday Math 3
- Community Connection 3
- Chapter 3 Self-Study Guide
- Chapter 3 Mastery Tests A and B (Answer Keys for the Teacher's Resource Library begin on page 528 of this Teacher's Edition.)

Name Date Period — Estimation Exercise, Chapter 3 — 3

Estimating with Decimals

You can use rounding to estimate the sums and differences in problems with decimals. Line up the decimal points as always, then round to the nearest tenth.

EXAMPLE Estimate 5.2 + 0.8 + 6.07

Step 1 Round to the nearest tenth.

5.2 + 0.8 + 6.1

Step 2 Rewrite the problem vertically, line up the decimal points, and add.

$$\begin{array}{r} 5.2 \\ 0.8 \\ +\underline{6.1} \\ 12.1 \end{array}$$

The estimated sum is 12.1, which is close to the actual sum of 12.07.

There are many ways to round decimals and estimate. You can round to the nearest tenth, the nearest hundredth, the nearest thousandth, or the nearest whole number. The estimated sum or difference can be very close or not very close to the actual sum or difference. It depends on the numbers you are working with and how you round them.

Directions Estimate the sum of each problem by rounding to the nearest tenth.

1. 5.44 + 10.9 + 3.07 ______
2. 31.2 + 10.09 ______
3. 16.08 + 0.72 + 4 ______
4. 7.008 + 3.081 + .05 ______
5. 23.5 + 5 + 87.03 ______

Directions Estimate the sum of each problem by rounding to the nearest whole number.

6. 3.62 + 9.5 + 0.006 ______
7. 0.63 + 0.063 + 0.0063 ______
8. 10.5 + 4.09 + 3.49 ______
9. 64.6 + 0.9345 + 1.2 ______
10. 13.895 + 22.567 + 18.0995 ______

 Mathematics: Pathways

TRL

Estimation Exercise 3

Name Date Period — Community Connection, Chapter 3 — 3

The Better Buy

When you shop for groceries, you often try to get the best buy. You want the most cereal, juice, or milk for the least amount of money. For example, an 8-ounce box of cereal may be marked \$1.39 while a 20-ounce box of the same cereal may be marked \$3.29. To find which box of cereal represents the better buy, you need to find the unit price, or cost for 1 ounce of each.

\$1.39 ÷ 8 = \$0.17 The unit price is 17¢ for one ounce.
\$3.29 ÷ 20 = \$0.16 The unit price is 16¢ for one ounce.

If the cereals are the same brand, 20 ounces of cereal at \$3.29 is a better buy than 8 ounces of cereal at \$1.39.

Go to a supermarket or grocery store to collect data to complete the chart. Choose two sizes of the same item. For example, you might choose a quart carton and a half-gallon jug of Brand X orange juice for item 1. Then answer the questions that follow.

Item	Brand	Size	Unit Price
1.			
2.			
3.			
4.			
5.			
6.			
7.			
8.			

9. How often was the larger size the better buy? ______
   How often was the smaller size the better buy? ______
10. Were there any items marked "sale" that were not the better buy?
    ______

 Mathematics: Pathways

TRL

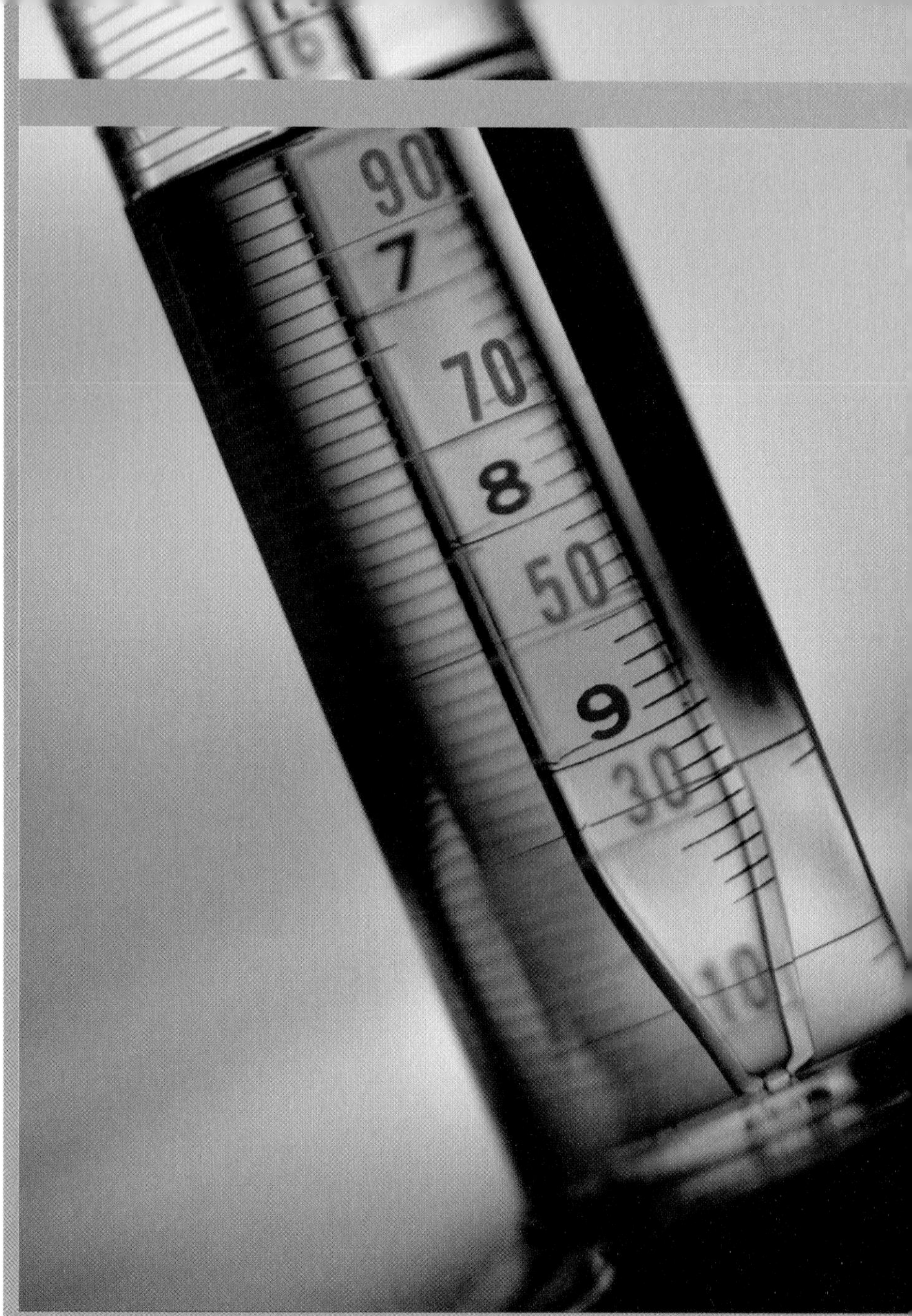

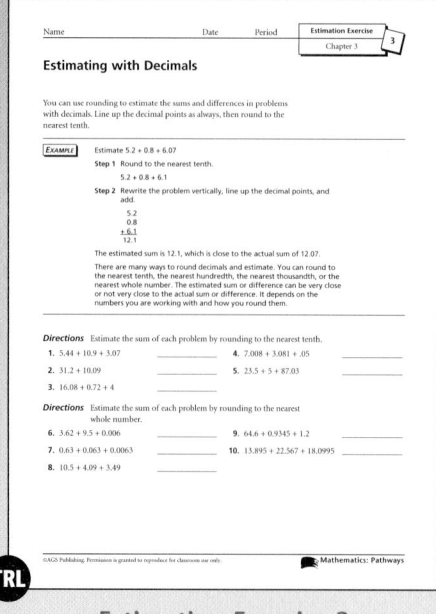

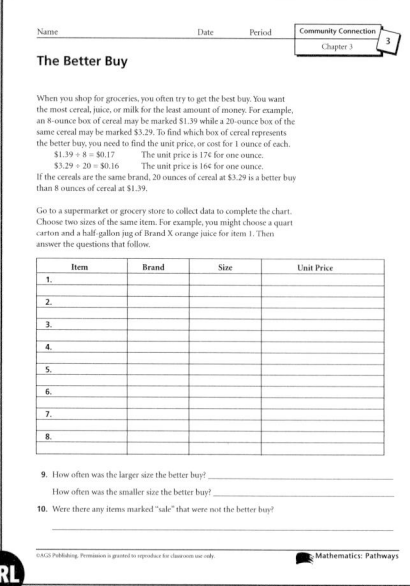

Community Connection 3

Chapter

3 Decimals

The next time you are in the science lab, take a look at the scales, weights, and beakers—like the beaker in the picture. You will notice that many, if not all, are marked in metric measures. In the photograph, the scale of measure runs up the side of the beaker. That makes it easy for the scientist or student to pour in just the right amount.

In the early 1600s, the decimal system became a popular way to sort and count things. In Europe, mathematicians such as John Napier started to use the decimal system to represent numbers greater than 0 and less than 1. The decimal point separated the whole number from its fractional part.

Today, the decimal system is used in metric measurements, money, calculators, tools, and many other areas.

In Chapter 3, you will perform basic operations with decimals.

Goals for Learning

◆ To identify the place value of digits
◆ To compare and round decimals
◆ To add and subtract decimals
◆ To multiply and divide decimals
◆ To change decimals to fractions and fractions to decimals
◆ To use a bar to identify a repeating decimal
◆ To rename percents as decimals
◆ To evaluate algebraic expressions with decimals

47

Introducing the Chapter

Tell students that although every chapter in this book will use numbers, the two previous chapters used only *whole* numbers. Write a mixed decimal on the board, and have students compare and contrast it with a whole number. Identify the decimal point and the digit to the right of the decimal point. Ask students to brainstorm common uses of *decimals*.

CHAPTER PROJECT

 Have students select a science subject that interests them or one of those listed below and do research to gather facts and statistics about the subject.

- Space travel
- The stock market
- Microscopic organisms

As they complete each lesson, ask students to apply the skills they learn to their science reports.

TEACHER'S RESOURCE

The AGS Publishing Teaching Strategies in Math Transparencies may be used with this chapter. They add an interactive dimension to expand and enhance the program content.

CAREER INTEREST INVENTORY

The AGS Publishing Harrington-O'Shea Career Decision-Making System-Revised (CDM) may be used with this chapter. Students can use the CDM to explore their interests and identify careers. The CDM defines career areas that are indicated by students' responses on the inventory.

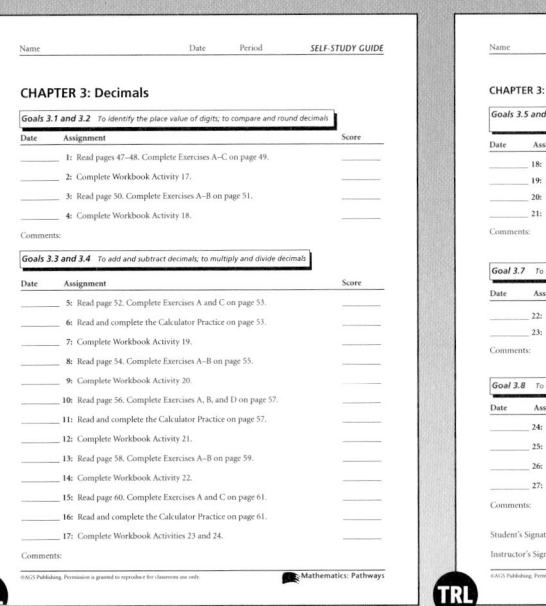

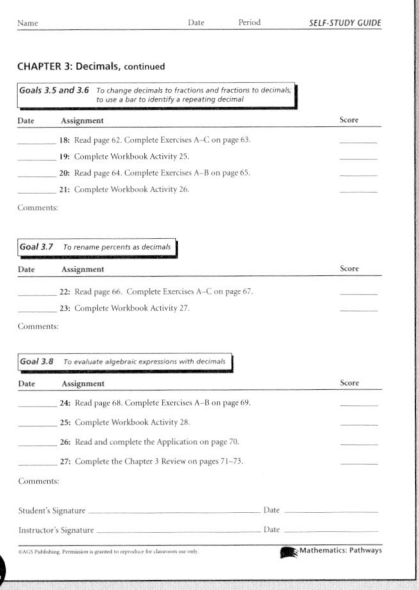

Chapter 3 Self-Study Guide

Decimals **47**

Lesson at a Glance

Chapter 3 Lesson 1

Overview This lesson demonstrates the place values of numbers with decimals.

Objectives

- To identify tenths, hundredths, thousandths, ten-thousandths, and millionths places
- To name the values of various decimal places

Student Pages 48–49

Teacher's Resource Library

Workbook Activity 17

Activity 17

Alternative Activity 17

....

Mathematics Vocabulary

decimal
decimal point

....

1 Warm-Up Activity

Produce on the board or an overhead a labeled grid showing place values for whole numbers.

ten-thousands	thousands	hundreds	tens	ones	•
					•

Have volunteers enter whole numbers into the chart and read them aloud. Have students explain what happens as you move from left to right on the place value chart. (*Number values are smaller by 10 with each step.*) Then ask, "How could you express numbers that are between whole numbers?" (*Add a decimal point and columns or places to the right of the ones column.*) Revise the chart as shown:

ten-thousands	thousands	hundreds	tens	ones	•	tenths	hundredths	thousandths	ten-thousandths
					•				

Decimal
A number that has a decimal point in it

Decimal point
A period that separates digits representing numbers that are one or more from digits representing numbers that are less than one

You use **decimals** every day when you handle money. In money, the digits to the left of the decimal point represent dollars, or numbers greater than or equal to 1. The digits to the right of the **decimal point** represent cents, or parts of a dollar.

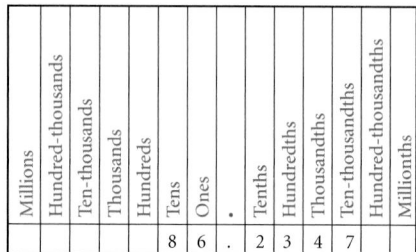

$2.35

- dollars
- values greater than or equal to 1

- cents
- values that are part of a whole

The chart of place values shows the value of each digit based on its position in a numeral.

Places to the right of the decimal point end in *th* to indicate that they are part of a whole. For example, 0.2 is read "two tenths," 0.03 is read "three hundredths," and 0.004 is read "four thousandths."

Millions	Hundred-thousands	Ten-thousands	Thousands	Hundreds	Tens	Ones	•	Tenths	Hundredths	Thousandths	Ten-thousandths	Hundred-thousandths	Millionths
					8	6	•	2	3	4	7		

EXAMPLE 1 Write the place of the underlined digit in 86.23<u>4</u>7.

The digit 4 is three places to the right of the decimal point.

The digit 4 is in the thousandths place, so its value is 4 × 0.001, or 0.004.

EXAMPLE 2 What is the value of the digit 2 in the numeral <u>2</u>,345.167?

The digit 2 is in the thousands place, so its value is 2 × 1,000, or 2,000.

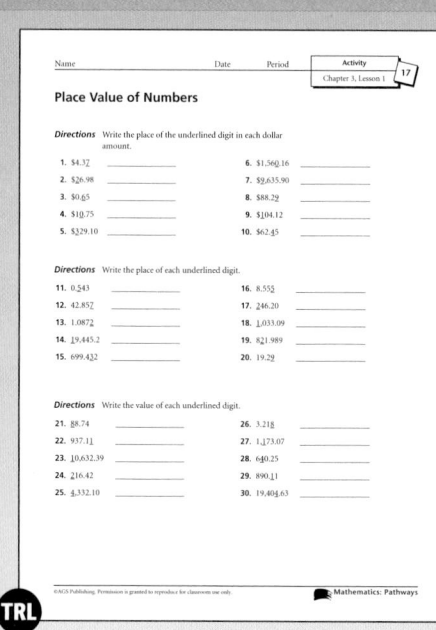

Name _____ Date _____ Period _____ **Workbook Activity** 17

Chapter 3, Lesson 1

Place Value and Decimals

EXAMPLE 165.8742   The digit 1 is in the hundreds place.
The digit 6 is in the tens place.
The digit 5 is in the ones place.
The digit 8 is in the tenths place.
The digit 7 is in the hundredths place.
The digit 4 is in the thousandths place.
The digit 2 is in the ten-thousandths place.
The value of the digit 6 is 60. The value of the digit 7 is 0.07.
0.7 = seven tenths   0.42 = forty-two hundredths

Directions Write each number in words.

1. 0.3 _____
2. 0.81 _____
3. 0.12 _____
4. 0.077 _____
5. 0.325 _____

Directions Write the number expressed by each phrase.

6. forty-two one-hundredths
7. seven tenths
8. two one-hundredths
9. thirty-three one-thousandths
10. twenty-five one-hundredths

Workbook Activity 17

Name _____ Date _____ Period _____ **Activity** 17

Chapter 3, Lesson 1

Place Value of Numbers

Directions Write the place of the underlined digit in each dollar amount.

1. $4.3<u>7</u>
2. $26.9<u>8</u>
3. $0.<u>6</u>5
4. $<u>1</u>0.75
5. $3<u>2</u>9.10
6. $1,5<u>6</u>0.16
7. $<u>9</u>,635.90
8. $88.<u>2</u>9
9. $<u>1</u>04.12
10. $62.4<u>5</u>

Directions Write the place of each underlined digit.

11. 0.<u>5</u>43
12. 42.8<u>5</u>7
13. 1.08<u>7</u>2
14. <u>1</u>9,445.2
15. 699.4<u>3</u>2
16. 8.5<u>5</u>5
17. <u>2</u>46.20
18. <u>1</u>,033.09
19. 8<u>2</u>1.989
20. 19.<u>2</u>9

Directions Write the value of each underlined digit.

21. <u>8</u>8.74
22. 937.1<u>1</u>
23. 1<u>0</u>,632.39
24. 2<u>1</u>6.42
25. <u>4</u>,332.10
26. 3.21<u>8</u>
27. 1,<u>1</u>73.07
28. 6<u>4</u>0.25
29. 890.1<u>1</u>
30. 19,40<u>4</u>.63

Activity 17

Exercise A Write the place of each underlined digit.

1. tenths
2. ones
3. thousandths
4. ten-thousandths
5. hundreds
6. hundredths
7. tens
8. thousands
9. ones

1. 164.1<u>3</u>　　**4.** 0.432<u>6</u>　　**7.** <u>6</u>4.021

2. 2<u>4</u>.267　　**5.** <u>7</u>65.92　　**8.** <u>1</u>,234.567

3. 624.55<u>5</u>　　**6.** 6,423.9<u>2</u>5　　**9.** 4<u>0</u>.12

Exercise B Write the value of each underlined digit.

10. 786.<u>3</u>4　0.3　　**15.** 84<u>2</u>.167　2　　**20.** 95.7<u>7</u>28　0.07

11. 2.635<u>9</u>　0.0009　**16.** 0.6<u>5</u>78　0.05　**21.** 0.64<u>7</u>　0.007

12. <u>4</u>81.73　400　　**17.** <u>1</u>,482　1,000　**22.** <u>9</u>7.84　90

13. <u>8</u>7.665　80　　**18.** 8.<u>2</u>9　0.2　　**23.** 3.2679<u>8</u>　0.0009

14. 6.795<u>6</u>　0.0006　**19.** <u>3</u>,675.8　3,000　**24.** 346.88<u>7</u>　0.007

Exercise C Write the value of the last digit in each numeral.

25. 42.361　0.001　　**28.** 0.5　0.5

26. 0.25　0.05　　**29.** 365.066　0.006

27. 98.5623　0.0003　　**30.** 5.00004　0.00004

> When reading a number with a decimal out loud, say "and" or "point" for the decimal point. So 40.12 would be read "forty and twelve hundredths" or "forty point one two."

Try This

Write instructions for placing a digit in a specific place; for example, place 3 in the tenths place. Ask a partner to follow your instructions. Check his or her answer.

Answers will vary.

Have students speculate about the place value of each column to the right of the decimal.

2 Teaching the Lesson

Make sure that students understand the significance of the decimal place. Ask them to complete the following statements:

- Any digit to the left of the decimal place represents a number that is _____. *(greater than or equal to 1)*

- Any digit to the right of the decimal place represents a number that is _____. *(less than 1)*

- The farther right you go from the decimal, the (larger, smaller) the value of the number. *(smaller)*

Try This

To extend the activity, have partners write a series of instructions until all place values from hundreds to hundredths are filled. Then have all students compare numbers and place them in order from least to greatest.

3 Reinforce and Extend

LEARNING STYLES

Visual/Spatial
Students can create a bulletin board display that will help them visualize the "weight" of each decimal place compared with 1. Have students make 3 squares of equal size. One square represents the whole number 1. Students can use ruler and pencil to divide one square into tenths, another into hundredths, and so on. Direct students to color in one unit of each square and create bold, clear labels for each: *one tenth, one hundredth,* and so on.

LEARNING STYLES

Auditory/Verbal
To help students learn decimal notation, provide practice in identifying and reading decimal numbers aloud. Make sure that students pronounce the words clearly; *tenths* and *tens, hundredths* and *hundreds* sound similar.

0.5　*(five tenths)*

0.33　*(thirty-three hundredths)*

0.185　*(one hundred eighty-five thousandths)*

2,999.99　*(two thousand, nine hundred ninety-nine and ninety-nine hundredths)*

Ask students to explain in their own words how these pairs are related.

tens and tenths

hundreds and hundredths

Chapter 3 Lesson 2

Overview This lesson explains methods for comparing decimals with unlike numbers of places and for rounding decimals.

Objectives

■ To identify one decimal as greater than or less than another

■ To round decimals to the nearest tenth, hundredth, and thousandth

Student Pages 50–51

Teacher's Resource Library

Workbook Activity 18

Activity 18

Alternative Activity 18

1 ⋮ Warm-Up Activity

Ask students which number is larger: 0.2 or 0.22. Have them explain why they think as they do. *(0.2, or two-tenths, is the same as twenty hundredths, which is less than twenty-two hundredths.)* Have them use graph paper to create grid squares and verify their guesses.

Then add the number 0.3, and have students identify which is closer to 0.22. *(0.2)* Explain that working with decimals is far easier if students know how to compare and approximate their values.

2 ⋮ Teaching the Lesson

Students will be unable to round decimals without a firm grasp of decimal place values. Display a large chart, like the one on page 48, illustrating place values.

Provide additional practice in comparing decimals by having students compare and order their answers in Exercise B.

Lesson 2   Comparing and Rounding Decimals

Remember, you can use signs to show how one number is related to another. For example, = means equals; < means less than; > means greater than; ≤ means less than or equal to; ≥ means greater than or equal to.

One of the reasons it's easy to compare $2.45 and $2.50 is because both decimals have the same number of places to the right of the decimal point.

EXAMPLE 1 Compare 14.256 and 14.26.

First, add one zero to 14.26 so that each decimal has the same number of places to the right of the decimal point.

14.256   14.260   (add one zero)

Next, compare the decimals.

14.256 *is less than* 14.260 because 256 *is less than* 260.

14.256 < 14.260

EXAMPLE 2 Compare 0.0576 and 0.05.

Add two zeros to 0.05.

0.0576   0.0500   (add two zeros)

Compare the two decimals.

0.0576 *is greater than* 0.0500 because 576 *is greater than* 500.

0.0576 > 0.0500

Sometimes, when working with decimals, you may need to round.

EXAMPLE 3 Round 13.036 to the nearest hundredth.

Step 1   Find the place to be rounded.

13.036   The place to be rounded is the hundredths place.

Step 2   Find the digit to the right of the place you are rounding to.

13.036   If the digit is 5 or greater, add 1 to the digit in the place you are rounding to. If the digit is less than 5, do not change the digit in the place you are rounding to.

Step 3   13.04   Since 6 is greater than 5, add 1 to the digit in the hundredths place. Drop the digits to the right of the place you are rounding to.

So, 13.036 rounded to the nearest hundredth is 13.04.

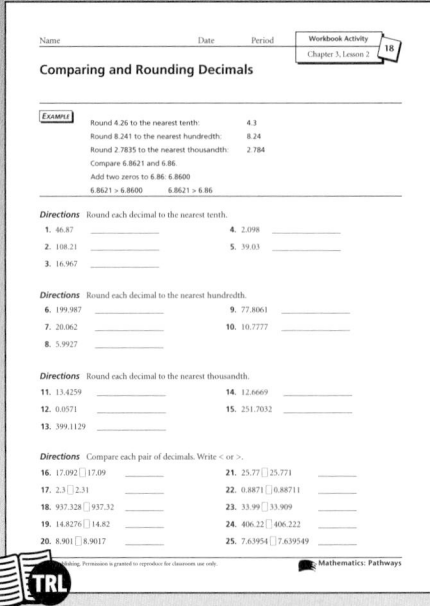

Workbook Activity 18

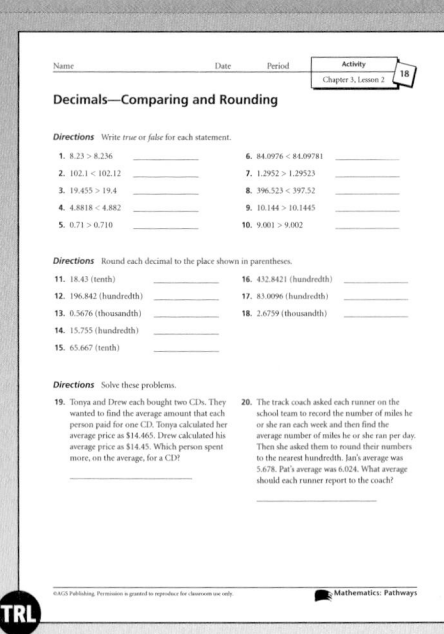

Activity 18

Try This

Find numerals with decimal points in a newspaper or magazine. Cut the numbers out. In a group, round the numerals you found to the digit left of the last digit.

Answers will vary.

Exercise A Compare each pair of decimals. Write < or >.

1. 5.403 ▪ 5.03	>	**6.** 7.0 ▪ 0.77	>
2. 8.43 ▪ 8.340	>	**7.** 403.079 ▪ 403.07	>
3. 91.8 ▪ 91.8135	<	**8.** 0.653924 ▪ 0.65394	<
4. 2.2210 ▪ 2.223	<	**9.** 30.19 ▪ 300.19	<
5. 2.04 ▪ 2.044	<	**10.** 634.5 ▪ 634.203	>

Exercise B 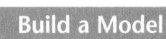 Make a chart. Then round these decimals to the nearest tenth, hundredth, and thousandth.

	Tenth	Hundredth	Thousandth
11. 2.6345	2.6	2.63	2.635
12. 1.8092	1.8	1.81	1.809
13. 0.9024	0.9	0.90	0.902
14. 37.2099	37.2	37.21	37.210
15. 6.4625	6.5	6.46	6.463
16. 0.6502	0.7	0.65	0.650
17. 2.7995	2.8	2.80	2.800
18. 88.0092	88.0	88.01	88.009
19. 14.0365	14.0	14.04	14.037
20. 53.4798	53.5	53.48	53.480

Students should draw number lines with the following points labeled in this order:

A 4.0, 4.2, 4.7, 4.9, 5.1

B 17.0, 17.6, 18.0, 18.2, 18.5

C 32.8, 32.9, 33.1, 33.4, 33.9

Build a Model

On a sheet of graph paper, draw three number lines like the one below. Be sure to insert 20 equally spaced marks.

◄─┼─►

On a separate sheet of paper, list each set of numbers from least to greatest. Then, graph each set of numbers on a number line.

A 4.7, 4.0, 4.2, 4.9, 5.1
B 18.2, 17.6, 18.5, 17.0, 18.0
C 33.4, 32.8, 32.9, 33.9, 33.1

Try This

Have students select five of the numbers they have gathered and rounded and

- write them in word form.

- order them from smallest to largest.

3 Reinforce and Extend

GROUP PROBLEM SOLVING

Have students work in groups of three to research how batting averages are computed and if and when they are rounded. If possible, allow students to work with actual game data to compute averages. Finally, have the groups write a summary report about what they learned.

AT HOME

Have students select two small objects at home to measure using a centimeter ruler. (Remind students that each centimeter is divided into ten millimeters on their rulers.) They are to record an estimate of the object's size in centimeters; the object's exact measurement in millimeters; and the object's measurement rounded to the nearest centimeter.

KNOWING YOUR STUDENTS

While in elementary school, students lived and worked in a concrete world. As they now transition from childhood to adolescence, their abstract abilities will begin to mature. But in secondary school, most students will still benefit from using manipulatives to help visualize abstract concepts. For example, the concept of tenths and hundredths can be difficult for students to visualize. Allow students to use manipulatives such as strips of paper divided into equal parts, multicolored connecting cubes, or graph paper when comparing decimals. Using manipulatives such as these, students will be able to more easily compare each digit's place value.

MANIPULATIVES

M **Comparing Decimals**

Materials: Base Ten Blocks

Group Practice: Write any two decimals from 0.1 to 0.99999. Organize students into two groups and assign one number to each group. Each student will choose a place value and model the digit in that place with Base Ten Blocks. For example, if the numbers were *eight thousand, four hundred twelve ten-thousandths* and *eight hundred forty-one thousandths,* the two students (one from each group) responsible for the tenths place would display eight cubes. Two students would then show four cubes for the hundredths place and the next two students would show one for the thousandths place. Only one group would produce Base Ten Blocks for the ten-thousandths place. Therefore, students should identify the number *eight thousand, four hundred twelve ten-thousandths* as the greater number. If both numbers have an equal amount of digits, students should identify the larger digit to find the greater number. Encourage students to choose a different place value for the next round.

Student Practice: For individual practice, students should receive or choose pairs of numbers and again model digits' place values with Base Ten Blocks.

Lesson at a Glance

Chapter 3 Lesson 3

Overview This lesson explains how to add and subtract decimals.

Objectives
- To add and subtract decimals
- To find the perimeter of a triangle

Student Pages 52–53

Teacher's Resource Library **TRL**

Workbook Activity 19

Activity 19

Alternative Activity 19

Mathematics Vocabulary

perimeter
formula

---

1 Warm-Up Activity

Dictate amounts of money for students to add: $25, $15.73, $5.49. Observe as they write the addition problem, and have them comment about how they line up the figures when some amounts contain decimals and others do not. Ask them to read the lesson to compare their strategy with that of the book.

2 Teaching the Lesson

Make sure that students understand that subtracting to the right of the decimal uses the same process of renaming or "borrowing" as they use in whole number subtraction. Ask, "How many hundredths are in a tenth?" *(10)* "How many thousandths are in a hundredth?" *(10)*

Lesson 3 — Adding and Subtracting Decimals

Adding and subtracting decimals is like adding and subtracting money or whole numbers. To add or subtract decimals, line up the decimal points. Then add or subtract each place value.

Perimeter
The distance around the outside of a shape

Formula
A combination of symbols used to state a rule

EXAMPLE 1 Find the **perimeter** of the triangle at the right.

14.25 cm
6.5 cm
9.755 cm

To find the perimeter of a triangle, you can use the **formula** $P = a + b + c$, where a, b, and c are the lengths of the sides of the triangle and P is the perimeter.

First, substitute the lengths of the sides into the formula.
$$P = 6.5 \text{ cm} + 9.755 \text{ cm} + 14.25 \text{ cm}$$

Next, line up the decimal points.

```
   6.5
   9.755
+ 14.25
```
. Bring down the decimal point.

Then add.

```
   6.5
   9.755
+ 14.25
  30.505
```

EXAMPLE 2 Suppose you pay $13.99 for a CD (including sales tax). You give the clerk $20. How much change do you receive?

First, include zeros to help you subtract.
$20 = $20.00

Next, line up the decimal points.

```
  $20.00
 − 13.99
```
. Bring down the decimal point.

Then subtract.

```
  $20.00
 − 13.99
  $ 6.01
```

You receive $6.01 in change.

52 *Chapter 3 Decimals*

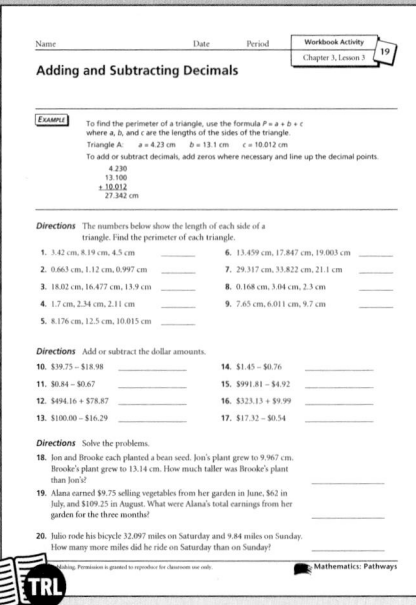

Workbook Activity 19

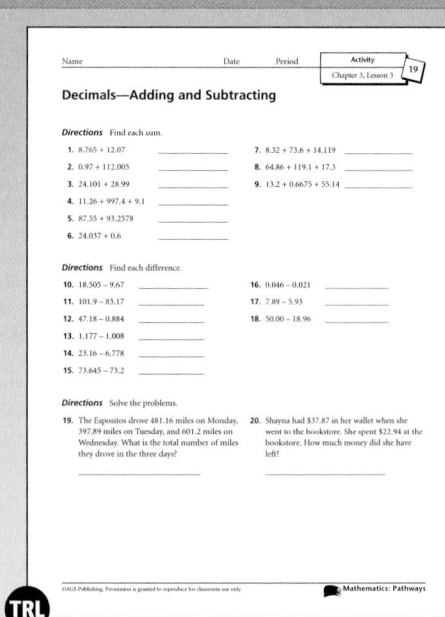

Activity 19

Exercise A Add or subtract.

1. $3.2 + 0.91 + 6$
   10.11
2. $4.3 + 0.455 + 0.6$
   5.355
3. $4.13 - 2.6$
   1.53
4. $0.34 - 0.023$
   0.317

5. $32.1 - 0.8$
   31.3
6. $0.9 - 0.099$
   0.801
7. $23.5 + 5 + 96.9$
   125.4
8. $9.5 + 3.52 + 0.004$
   13.024

9. $16 + 0.72 + 3.2 + 3$
   22.92
10. $1 - 0.674$
    0.326
11. $38.5 - 21.392$
    17.108
12. $74.4 + 0.3904 + 5.04$
    79.8304

 **Calculator Practice**   You can use a calculator to add or subtract decimals.

EXAMPLE 3 $34.543 - 28.698 = \blacksquare$

Press $34 \cdot 543 - 28 \cdot 698 =$.

The display reads 5.845.

Exercise B Use a calculator to find each sum or difference.

13. $1.5 + 0.21 + 0.35 + 0.611$ 2.671
14. $9 + 2.1 + 0.62 + 0.1711$ 11.8911
15. $6 - 0.04321$ 5.95679
16. $246.62 - 18.7346$ 227.8854
17. $891.289 + 42.6758$ 933.9648

18. $0.9325 - 0.7439$ 0.1886
19. $\$50 - \$32.46$ \$17.54
20. $\$5.62 + \$10.30 + \$6.40 + \$0.32$ \$22.64
21. $\$0.34 + \$2.50 + \$13.18 + \$113.54$ \$129.56

 **PROBLEM SOLVING**

Exercise C Solve these problems.

22. Troy jogs 5 miles on Monday, 6.05 miles on Tuesday, and 8.7 miles on Wednesday. How many total miles does Troy jog in the 3 days?
    19.75 miles

23. Amar's school supplies cost \$15.95 with tax. If he gives the clerk \$20, how much change does he receive? \$4.05

24. Anna has a pet-sitting service. She earns \$8.50 for walking a dog, \$6.50 for sitting a cat, and \$12.75 for overnight care. How much does she earn for walking one dog, sitting for one cat, and taking care of a bird for a night? \$27.75

25. Station A charges \$1.312 for a gallon of gasoline. Station B charges \$1.295. How much more does Station A charge per gallon of gasoline?
    \$0.017 or about \$0.02 more

LEARNING STYLES

Body/Kinesthetic
To model subtraction of decimals, have students create grids using graph paper, color in the number of squares indicated by the first decimal, and then cross out the number of colored squares indicated by the second number. For example,

$0.39 - 0.14$

CALCULATOR

   As a challenge, have students work in pairs to first add and subtract selected problems in Exercise B without a calculator and then use their calculators to check their answers.

GROUP PROBLEM SOLVING

   Have students work in groups of four to research the currency of another country (the Mexican peso, the Swedish krona, the Japanese yen). Suggest that they find the most recent dollar value for the currency by checking an online source or using a newspaper exchange rate. Record values on the board as each group reports on its currency. Then have the groups select other currencies and use them with their information to create addition and subtraction problems.

Lesson at a Glance

Chapter 3 Lesson 4

Overview This lesson presents a method for multiplying decimals by powers of 10.

Objectives

- To identify the product of a given power of 10
- To multiply decimal numbers by powers of 10

Student Pages 54–55

Teacher's Resource Library 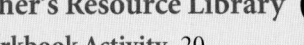 **TRL**

Workbook Activity 20

Activity 20

Alternative Activity 20

---

1 Warm-Up Activity

Write on the board 2^2, 3^2, and 4^2, and ask students to explain the meaning of the superscript 2 and what operation is to be performed in each instance. *(The number is to be squared, or multiplied by itself.)* Introduce the definition for powers of 10, and have students read to find out what the superscript beside each 10 is telling them to do.

2 Teaching the Lesson

To assess students' understanding, give practice in reversing the process. Inform the class that astronomers who deal with very large numbers generally express them in powers of 10 so that they are not so unwieldy. Have students change the following numbers into decimals with powers of 10:

250,000,000 (2.5×10^8)

8,975,421,000 (8.975421×10^9)

13,400,000,000 (1.34×10^{10})

Review the meanings of *true, false,* and *open statements* before students complete Exercise B.

There are an infinite number of powers of 10.

$$10^1 = 10$$
$$10^2 = 10 \times 10 = 100$$
$$10^3 = 10 \times 10 \times 10 = 1,000$$
$$10^4 = 10 \times 10 \times 10 \times 10 = 10,000$$
$$10^5 = 10 \times 10 \times 10 \times 10 \times 10 = 100,000$$
$$10^6 = 10 \times 10 \times 10 \times 10 \times 10 \times 10 = 1,000,000$$
$$\vdots$$
$$10^n = \underbrace{10 \times 10 \times 10 \ldots 10}_{n \text{ times}}$$

The power of a number, or the number of times it should be multiplied by itself, is shown by a small number written on the upper right side. This number is called an exponent. For example, in 10^2, the raised 2 indicates that 10 should be multiplied by itself 2 times. 2 is the exponent.
$10 \times 10 = 100.$

The small number next to the 10s above are called *exponents.* An exponent tells the number of times another number is a factor.

To multiply any number by a power of 10, count the number of zeros in the power of 10 and move the decimal point that many places to the right. If the number does not have a decimal point, add one after the last digit. Then move it to the right to multiply by a power of 10.

EXAMPLE 1 4.34×100

In 100, there are 2 zeros. Move the decimal point 2 places to the right.

$4 . 3 4 \rightarrow 4 . 3 \underset{\smile}{4} \rightarrow 4 3 4$

So, $4.34 \times 100 = 434.$

645×10^3

$645 \times 10^3 = 645 \times 1,000$

Add a decimal point. In 1,000, there are 3 zeros. Move the decimal point 3 places to the right. You need to add zeros.

$6 4 5 . \rightarrow 6 4 5 0 0 0 \rightarrow 6 4 5 , 0 0 0$

So, $645 \times 10^3 = 645,000.$

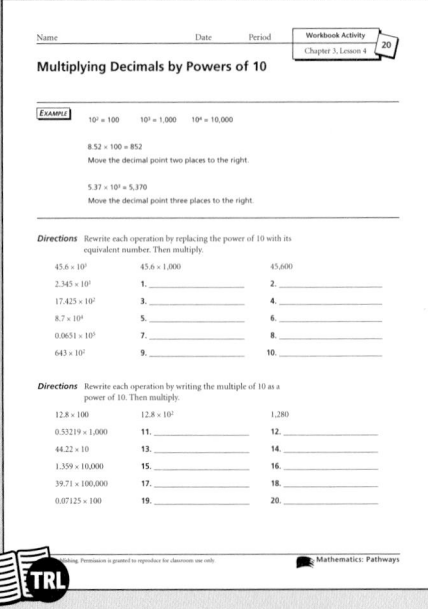

Workbook Activity 20

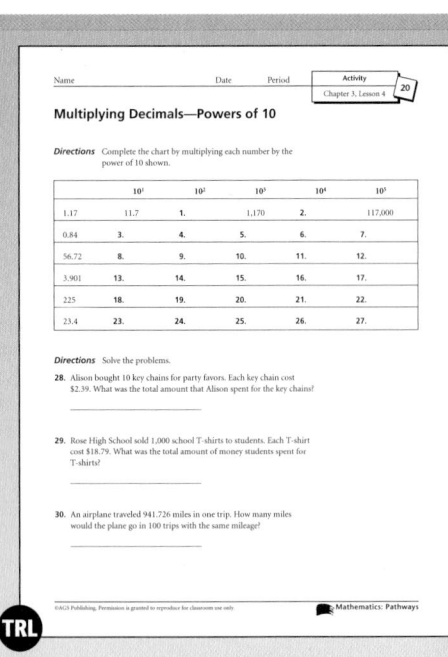

Activity 20

Exercise A Multiply.

1. 2.36×10^2 236
2. 0.05×10 0.5
3. 2.7×10^3 2,700
4. 5.36×100 536
5. $1.441 \times 1,000$ 1,441
6. 0.00276×100 0.276
7. 7.710×10^5 771,000
8. $18.8 \times 10,000$ 188,000
9. 7.3×10^4 73,000
10. $5.02 \times 100,000$ 502,000
11. 8.4104×10^1 84.104
12. $0.0565 \times 1,000$ 56.5
13. $0.769 \times 10,000$ 7,690
14. 2.2×10^6 2,200,000
15. 4.044×10^3 4,044
16. $0.25 \times 100,000$ 25,000
17. $1.0112 \times 1,000,000$ 1,011,200
18. $0.0063 \times 10,000$ 63
19. 8.907×10^2 890.7
20. $162.5 \times 1,000$ 162,500

Exercise B Write *true*, *false*, or *open* for each statement.

21. $3.3 \times 10^1 = 33$ true
22. $35.04 \times 1,000 = 3,504$ false
23. $0.204 \times 100 = 2.04$ false
24. $8.9 \times n = 89$ open
25. $60.4 \times 100 = n$ open
26. $2.87 \times 10^2 = 287$ true
27. $0.64 \times 10 = 6.4$ true
28. $0.94 \times 1,000 = 94$ false
29. $n \times 10^3 = 5,140$ open
30. $1.15 \times 100 = 1,150$ false

Technology Connection

Microscopes Multiply Size

An electron microscope lets you look at things that are very small. Suppose an object measures 0.05 inches long. That's too small for your eye to see it clearly. But an electron microscope will multiply the size by as much as 10^5. How big does the object appear now? At this size, you can see even the smallest details easily. Even at 10^1, you can see some of the details. How big does an object that is 0.005 inches long appear at 10^3?

LEARNING STYLES

LEP/ESL

Students who have difficulty translating the exponential notation directly into a product can make a table like this:

Power of 10	10^1	10^2	10^3
Multiply	10	10×10	$10 \times 10 \times 10$
Product	10	100	1,000
# of zeros	1	2	3

MENTAL MATH

Discuss the relationship between the power of 10 and the number of zeros it adds. (Where *n* is the power, add *n* zeros.) Familiarity in handling exponential notation is useful in both math and science. Give students powers of 10 orally, and have them give the problem and product orally. For example,

Ten to the fourth power
(*Ten times itself four times gives ten thousand.*)

Ten to the sixth power
(*Ten times itself six times gives one million.*)

Lesson at a Glance

Chapter 3 Lesson 5

Overview This lesson uses the formula for the circumference of a circle to illustrate multiplication of decimals.

Objectives

- To introduce the formula for the circumference of a circle
- To calculate the product when one or both factors are decimals

Student Pages 56–57

Teacher's Resource Library **TRL**

Workbook Activity 21

Activity 21

Alternative Activity 21

Mathematics Vocabulary

circumference
pi
diameter

---

1 Warm-Up Activity

Ask, "What do addition and multiplication have in common?" *(Multiplying is adding again and again.)* Write on the board:

$$25 \times 4 = 25 + 25 + 25 + 25$$

Then ask students how the solution would be different if one number were a decimal:

$$25.4 \times 4 = 25 + 25 + 25 + 25 + ?$$

(Students should see that 0.4 must be added four times as well.) Then have students read the lesson to learn to multiply decimals.

2 Teaching the Lesson

Make sure that students understand that pi is a constant (the ratio of the circumference of a circle to its diameter is the same for any circle) and that 3.14 is rounded from 3.14159265....

Provide extra practice in using the formula and in multiplying decimals by having students measure the diameter of circles found in the classroom and calculate their circumferences.

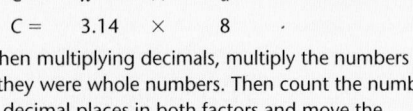

Circumference
Distance around a circle
Pi (π)
Ratio of the circumference of a circle to its diameter
Diameter
Distance across a circle through the center

Circumference is the distance around a circle. The formula for finding the circumference of a circle is $C = \pi d$, where

C = circumference
π = **pi**   π is about 3.14
d = **diameter**

EXAMPLE 1 Find the circumference of a circle with a diameter of 8 inches.

Substitute the numbers into the formula. Let π be equal to 3.14. Then multiply.

$$C = \quad \pi \quad \times \quad d$$
$$C = \quad 3.14 \quad \times \quad 8$$

When multiplying decimals, multiply the numbers as if they were whole numbers. Then count the number of decimal places in both factors and move the decimal point that many places in the product.

```
   3.14   two decimal places
×     8   zero decimal places
 25.12   two decimal places
```

The circumference is 25.12 inches.

EXAMPLE 2 Find the circumference of a circle with a diameter of 3.5 centimeters.

$$C = \quad \pi \quad \times \quad d$$
$$C = \quad 3.14 \quad \times \quad 3.5$$

```
    3.14   two decimal places
×   3.5   one decimal place
   1570
+  942
 10.990   three decimal places
```

The circumference is 10.99 cm.

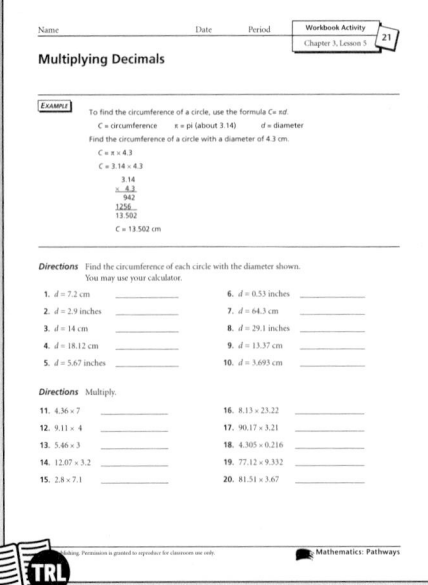

Workbook Activity 21

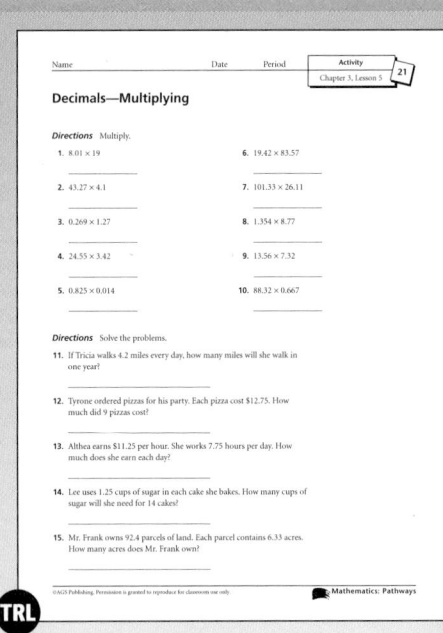

Activity 21

Exercise A Multiply.

1. 2.36
× 9
21.24

3. 7.82
× 5
39.1

5. 2.9
× 7.1
20.59

7. 8.31
× 0.8
6.648

9. 3.18
× 0.09
0.2862

11. 23.14
× 3.7
85.618

2. 4.5
× 7
31.5

4. 3.2
× 6.4
20.48

6. 4.7
× 2.6
12.22

8. 2.65
× 2.4
6.36

10. 0.26
× 0.8
0.208

12. 3.14
× 3.14
9.8596

Exercise B Find the circumference of each circle. Use 3.14 for π.

13. Diameter = 10 inches   31.4 in.

14. Diameter = 15 inches   47.1 in.

15. Diameter = 50 inches   157 in.

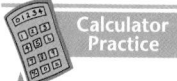
Calculator Practice   A calculator can be used to multiply decimals.

EXAMPLE 3 4.321 × 63.7 = ■
Press 4 · 321 × 63 · 7 = .
The display reads 275.2477.

Exercise C Use a calculator to find each product.

16. 3.2 × 6.4 × 0.018
0.36864

17. 0.423 × 7.6 × 0.05
0.16074

18. 6.19 × 0.53 × 23
75.4561

19. 8.9 × 0.33 × 5.2
15.2724

20. 65.9 × 0.08 × 0.004
0.021088

21. 0.03 × 0.04 × 0.05
0.00006

PROBLEM SOLVING

Exercise D Solve these problems.

22. Brian works 35.5 hours a week. If he earns $15.75 an hour, how much does Brian make in a week? Round your answer to the nearest cent. $559.13

23. At the supermarket, bananas cost $0.59 per pound. How much do 3.5 pounds of bananas cost? Round your answer to the nearest cent. $2.07

24. Venus buys 13 CDs at $18.99 each. How much does she spend on CDs? $246.87

25. Vang drives for 3.5 hours at an average speed of 45.5 miles per hour. How far does he drive? 159.25 miles

Decimals Chapter 3 **57**

3 Reinforce and Extend

CALCULATOR

Have students measure the circumference and diameter of a circle. Write the circumference formula on the board. Ask students to decide how they can find pi. *(Divide diameter into circumference.)* Have them do this using their calculators and report the result. (Note: Answers should have more places than the 3.14 approximation in the text.)

GROUP PROBLEM SOLVING

Organize the class into groups of three, and give each group a square grid with a 100 squares. Give each group a problem with two factors less than one, such as the following:

0.5 × 0.2
0.3 × 0.6
0.7 × 0.4
0.4 × 0.3

Ask the groups to decide how they might color in squares to model the solution to this problem. (Hint: Color in the squares representing the first number vertically in one color; color those representing the second number horizontally in another color. The portion where the colored squares overlap shows the product of the numbers.) Ask students to complete this statement: "When you multiply two numbers less than 1, the product is _____." *(smaller than either factor)*

Lesson at a Glance

Chapter 3 Lesson 6

Overview This lesson explains how to divide a decimal by a power of 10.

Objective

■ To divide decimals by powers of 10 by moving the decimal left

Student Pages 58–59

Teacher's Resource Library

Workbook Activity 22

Activity 22

Alternative Activity 22

1 ⟩ Warm-Up Activity

Review exponential forms for powers of 10. Have students explain in their own words how to multiply numbers by powers of 10. *(Move the decimal to the right one place for each power of 10.)* Ask, "How are multiplication and division related?" *(They are opposite or inverse processes.)* "How do you think you divide a number by a power of 10?" *(Move the decimal to the left.)* Have students read the lesson to see whether they are correct.

2 ⟩ Teaching the Lesson

Assess students' understanding of division by powers of 10. Have them solve problems in Exercise A dividing by three different powers of 10:

$$6.6 \div 10 = 0.66$$

$$6.6 \div 10^2 = 0.066$$

$$6.6 \div 10^3 = 0.0066$$

Ask students to explain why the quotient value becomes smaller as the power of 10 grows larger. *(The quantity is being divided into ten times more equal pieces with each additional power of 10.)*

Recall that when you multiply a decimal by a power of 10, you move the decimal point to the right. When dividing by a power of 10, move the decimal point to the left.

EXAMPLE 1 $35 \div 10 = $ ■

In 10, there is one zero. To divide by 10, move the decimal point one place to the left.

$3\,5\,. \quad \to \quad 3\,.\,5 \quad \to \quad 3.5$

So, $35 \div 10 = 3.5$.

EXAMPLE 2 $20.4 \div 1{,}000 = $ ■

In 1,000, there are three zeros. To divide by 1,000, move the decimal point three places to the left. You may need to insert zeros.

$2\,0\,.\,4 \quad \to \quad .\,0\,2\,0\,4 \quad \to \quad 0.0204$

So, $20.4 \div 1{,}000 = 0.0204$.

EXAMPLE 3 $9.4 \div 10^2 = $ ■

$9.4 \div 10^2 = 9.4 \div 100$

In 100, there are two zeros. To divide by 100, move the decimal point two places to the left.

$9\,.\,4 \quad \to \quad .\,0\,9\,4 \quad \to \quad 0.094$

So, $9.4 \div 10^2 = 0.094$.

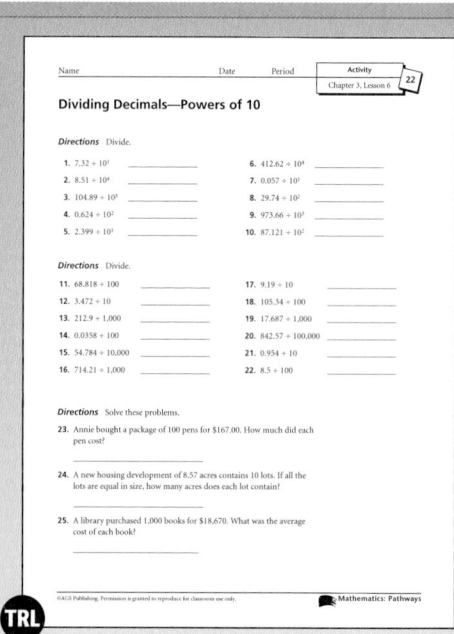

Workbook Activity 22   Activity 22

Exercise A Divide.

1. $6.6 \div 10$ *0.66*
2. $0.08 \div 100$ *0.0008*
3. $93 \div 1{,}000$ *0.093*
4. $47.6 \div 10^1$ *4.76*
5. $2.03 \div 100$ *0.0203*
6. $4.8 \div 1{,}000$ *0.0048*
7. $11.5 \div 1{,}000$ *0.0115*
8. $0.45 \div 10$ *0.045*
9. $24.4 \div 10^2$ *0.244*
10. $0.004 \div 100$ *0.00004*

11. $243.2 \div 1{,}000$ *0.2432*
12. $0.56 \div 1{,}000$ *0.00056*
13. $73.6 \div 10^2$ *0.736*
14. $125.3 \div 10{,}000$ *0.01253*
15. $0.0005 \div 1{,}000$ *0.0000005*
16. $48.84 \div 10^3$ *0.04884*
17. $0.03 \div 10{,}000$ *0.000003*
18. $123.4 \div 100{,}000$ *0.001234*
19. $300.05 \div 10^1$ *30.005*
20. $324 \div 10^4$ *0.0324*

Exercise B Write *true*, *false*, or *open* for each statement.

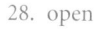

21. true
22. false
23. true
24. open
25. true
26. open
27. false
28. open
29. true
30. true

21. $6.5 \div 10 = 0.65$
22. $55.1 \div 10{,}000 = 0.0551$
23. $0.007 \div 100 = 0.00007$
24. $75.4 \div n = 0.0754$
25. $3.91 \div 10^2 = 0.0391$

26. $3.63 \div 10^1 = n$
27. $9.94 \div 1{,}000 = 0.0994$
28. $n \div 10^3 = 0.001$
29. $35.6 \div 100 = 0.356$
30. $135.79 \div 1{,}000 = 0.13579$

Math in Your Life

All Shook Up

In 1989, a major earthquake centered in southern California became the wake-up call for many residents in the Los Angeles area. To measure the strength of earthquakes, scientists depend on the Richter Scale, which uses decimals. A quake of 1.5 is recorded, but not felt. A quake of 6.1 can tumble buildings. Any quake above 7.9 will cause major destruction in crowded city settings.

3 **Reinforce and Extend**

Lesson at a Glance

Chapter 3 Lesson 7

Overview This lesson demonstrates division of a decimal by a whole number.

Objectives
- To divide decimals
- To transform decimal divisors into whole numbers before dividing

Student Pages 60–61

Teacher's Resource Library TRL

Workbook Activities 23–24

Activity 23

Alternative Activity 23

1 Warm-Up Activity

Give students three bags of drinking straws, 20 per bag, and a fourth bag with 10 straws. Ask, "How many bags of straws do you have?" *(3.5)* Have students reason how they would share the straws equally among 7 people. Create the 7 piles of straws; there will be 10 in each. Ask, "What part of a bag does each person get?" *(0.5 or half)* Have students read the lesson to see how to represent this division problem mathematically.

2 Teaching the Lesson

Assess students' understanding by having them explain to a partner what additional steps are required when both the divisor and dividend in a problem are decimals. *(Move decimal in divisor to make a whole number; move decimal in dividend same number of spaces.)*

Placement of the decimal is crucial in dividing decimals. Complete several problems on the board or overhead, using a contrasting color to highlight decimals and to trace decimal movements in the divisor and dividend. Have students highlight the decimal and its movement path on their exercise papers.

Lesson 7 — Dividing Decimals

When dividing with decimals, the divisor must be a whole number.

> Remember, the divisor is the number by which you divide, the dividend is the number that you divide, and the quotient is the result of the division.

EXAMPLE 1 Ricky earns $16.50 in 3 hours. How much does he earn in 1 hour?

Write the division.

$$3\overline{)\$16.50}$$

Since the divisor is a whole number, write a decimal point in the quotient.

$$3\overline{)\$16.50}^{\,.}$$

Divide.

$$\begin{array}{r} \$5.50 \\ 3\overline{)\$16.50} \\ -\,15 \\ \hline 15 \\ -\,15 \\ \hline 00 \end{array}$$

Ricky earns $5.50 in 1 hour.

Sometimes you must make the divisor a whole number before you divide.

EXAMPLE 2 $0.5\overline{)1.86}$

Move the decimal point in the divisor and in the dividend one place to the right.

$$0.5\overline{)1.86} \quad \text{}$$

Place a decimal point in the quotient.

$$5\overline{)18.6}^{\,.}$$

Divide.

$$\begin{array}{r} 3.72 \\ 5\overline{)18.6} \\ -\,15 \\ \hline 3\,6 \\ -\,3\,5 \\ \hline 10 \\ -\,10 \\ \hline 0 \end{array}$$

So, $1.86 \div 0.5 = 3.72$

Name _____ Date _____ Period _____ **Workbook Activity 23**
Chapter 3, Lesson 7

Dividing Decimals

EXAMPLE
$$\begin{array}{r} 3.68 \\ 5\overline{)18.40} \\ -15 \\ \hline 34 \\ -30 \\ \hline 40 \\ -40 \\ \hline 0 \end{array} \qquad \begin{array}{r} 6.5 \\ 1.5\overline{)9.75} \\ -90 \\ \hline 75 \\ -75 \\ \hline 0 \end{array}$$

Directions Divide.

1. $18.76 \div 4$ _____
2. $78.84 \div 8$ _____
3. $48.96 \div 3$ _____
4. $18.84 \div 12$ _____
5. $28.71 \div 9$ _____

6. $59.90 \div 5$ _____
7. $121.28 \div 32$ _____
8. $223.14 \div 6$ _____
9. $154.62 \div 9$ _____
10. $119.32 \div 4$ _____

Directions Divide. Round your answer to the nearest hundredth. You may use your calculator.

11. $58.86 \div 0.6$ _____
12. $4.851 \div 0.3$ _____
13. $137.28 \div 5.2$ _____
14. $35.87 \div 1.74$ _____
15. $155.52 \div 8.1$ _____

16. $728.52 \div 1.2$ _____
17. $34.84 \div 0.04$ _____
18. $0.8665 \div 0.05$ _____
19. $75.12 \div 0.823$ _____
20. $385.14 \div 2.1$ _____

Mathematics: Pathways

Workbook Activity 23

Name _____ Date _____ Period _____ **Workbook Activity 24**
Chapter 3, Lesson 7

Using Decimals

1. Luis brought 12 pounds of aluminum cans to the recycling center. He received $3.36. How much does the recycling center pay for each pound of aluminum? _____

2. The average temperature in Key West, Florida, is 77.7°F. The average temperature in International Falls, Minnesota, is 36.4°F. On average, how much warmer is it in Key West than in International Falls? _____

3. A small swimming pool holds 5,263 gallons of water. A bathtub holds 55.4 gallons of water. How many times would you have to fill the bathtub to use the amount of water it takes to fill the pool? _____

4. Sam earned $5.75 for mowing the lawn, $14.50 for delivering newspapers, and $12.00 for washing windows last week. How much did he earn? _____

5. The George Washington Bridge is 1,066.8 m long. The Golden Gate Bridge is 213.4 m longer than the George Washington Bridge. How long is the Golden Gate Bridge? _____

6. Gina rode 496.24 miles on a bicycle trip. The trip took 9 days. What was the average number of miles Gina rode each day? Round your answer to the nearest tenth. _____

7. A recipe for fruit salad calls for 1.5 pounds of apples, 2 pounds of oranges, and 1.25 pounds of grapes. At the market, apples cost $0.69 per pound, oranges cost $0.79 per pound, and grapes cost $0.86 per pound. How much will it cost to make the fruit salad? _____

8. Jim's grandparents sent him $35.00 for his birthday. He bought a CD for $12.99 and put $15.00 in his savings account. How much did Jim have left? _____

9. Kay purchased 16 tomato plants for $0.48 each. How much did she spend? _____

10. A camper hiked 41.7 kilometers on the first day, 21.2 kilometers on the second day, and 37.4 kilometers on the third day. How many more kilometers did the camper hike on the first two days than on the third day? _____

Mathematics: Pathways

Workbook Activity 24

Exercise A Divide. Round your answer to the nearest hundredth.

1. $5.21 \div 4$ 1.30
2. $142.51 \div 53$ 2.69
3. $8.65 \div 0.6$ 14.42
4. $1.7571 \div 0.21$ 8.37
5. $0.2360 \div 0.05$ 4.72
6. $2 \div 0.83$ 2.41
7. $221 \div 0.14$ 1,578.57
8. $0.285 \div 0.012$ 23.75
9. $9.63 \div 0.036$ 267.50
10. $512.68 \div 0.009$ 56,964.44

 **Calculator Practice**   You can use a calculator to divide decimals.

EXAMPLE 3 $0.55543 \div 0.67 = \blacksquare$
Press $\boxed{\cdot}$ 55543 $\boxed{\div}$ $\boxed{\cdot}$ 67 $\boxed{=}$.
The display reads *0.829*.

Exercise B Use a calculator to find each quotient. Round your answer to the nearest thousandth.

11. $16.5 \div 27.58$ 0.598
12. $207.7 \div 538.92$ 0.385
13. $609 \div 4,710.5$ 0.129
14. $58.493 \div 237.6$ 0.246
15. $2 \div 4.5 \div 0.198$ 2.245
16. $8.6 \div 77.1 \div 41.9$ 0.003

PROBLEM SOLVING

Exercise C Solve these problems.

17. Carlos buys 8 pounds of dog food for $8.45. What is the price per pound? Round your answer to the nearest cent. $1.06

18. Carrie drives 262.85 miles in 4.5 hours. What is her average speed in miles per hour? Round your answer to the nearest hundredth.
58.41 miles per hour

19. Vernon earns $558.25 a week. If he works 38.5 hours each week, how much does Vernon earn an hour? $14.50

20. Megan spent $54.18 on food for her dinner party. If she is having five friends over for dinner, what is the average amount of money she spent for food per person? (Hint: Include Megan.) $9.03

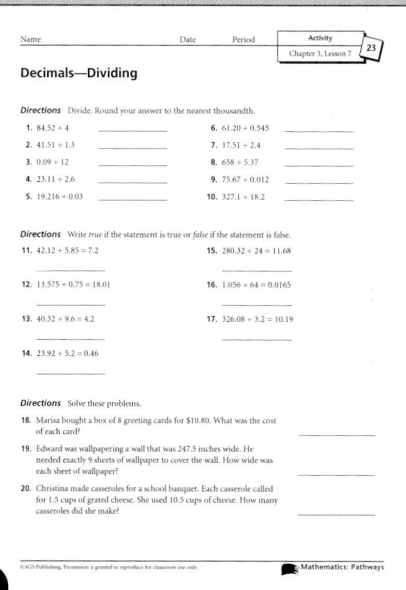

CALCULATOR

After students calculate the quotient with their calculators, have them check their answers by multiplying the quotient times the divisor.

Enter the quotient, and press $\boxed{\times}$.

Enter the divisor, and press $\boxed{=}$.

If the product does not agree exactly with the dividend in the original problem, discuss the result of having rounded answers to the nearest thousandth.

GROUP PROBLEM SOLVING

Have students bring in empty food cartons and labels from cans that show values in decimals. Organize students into groups of three or four; give each group a carton or label. The group's tasks are to

- write the decimal values and label them clearly.

- write three word problems requiring division of a decimal by a whole number and by a decimal.

Have the groups exchange and solve the problems and then retrieve their original papers. Discuss whether the solutions turned out as they expected.

ONLINE CONNECTION

For a birds-eye view of the Portland, Oregon, transit system, have students visit www.trimet.org/fares/index.htm. They can practice using decimals to figure out how much they can save by buying books of 10 tickets over 10 single tickets. As a bonus, have students figure out how many trips they would have to take in order to save money on a monthly pass.

Lesson at a Glance

Chapter 3 Lesson 8

Overview This lesson presents the steps for changing a decimal to a fraction and a fraction to a decimal.

Objectives
- To convert decimals to fractions
- To convert fractions to decimals
- To simplify fractions and create equivalent fractions

Student Pages 62–63

Teacher's Resource Library

Workbook Activity 25

Activity 24

Alternative Activity 24

Mathematics Vocabulary

fraction
denominator
numerator
simplify
equivalent fraction

1 Warm-Up Activity

Write the fraction $\frac{1}{4}$ and the decimal 0.25 on the board. Have students identify each quantity and list things they share in common. *(They have the same value, they are both less than 1, they are different ways of writing the same amount.)* Explain that decimals and fractions are different ways of describing numbers between whole numbers and that it is useful to know how to convert one form to the other.

2 Teaching the Lesson

Review the vocabulary terms by having students identify denominators and numerators in several example fractions and identify equivalent fractions, given trios such as $\frac{1}{2}, \frac{5}{10}, \frac{50}{100}$. Use money to help model examples. Display three quarters, and have students explain why $0.75 is $\frac{3}{4}$ of a dollar.

Lesson 8 Decimals and Fractions

Fraction
Part of a whole number such as $\frac{1}{2}$

Denominator
The number below the fraction bar

Numerator
The number above the fraction bar

Simplify
State as a fraction whose only common factor of the numerator and denominator is 1

Equivalent fraction
A fraction that has the same value as another fraction

To change a decimal to a **fraction,** follow these steps.

Step 1 Find the place of the last digit. The place value for this digit becomes the **denominator.**

Step 2 Use the numeral in the decimal for the **numerator.**

Step 3 **Simplify** the fraction.

EXAMPLE 1 Write 0.75 as a fraction.

Step 1 Find the place value of the last digit.

5 is in the hundredths place

The denominator of the fraction is 100.

Step 2 Use the numeral in the decimal for the numerator.

$0.75 \rightarrow \frac{75}{100}$

Step 3 Simplify the fraction.

$\frac{75}{100} = \frac{75 \div 25}{100 \div 25} = \frac{3}{4}$

Sometimes you may need to change a fraction to a decimal.

EXAMPLE 2 Write $\frac{17}{100}$ as a decimal.

When the denominator is a power of 10, identify the place value of the denominator.

$\frac{17}{100}$ Place value is hundredths.

Write the decimal using the numeral in the numerator.

$\frac{17}{100} = 0.17$

EXAMPLE 3 Write $\frac{8}{25}$ as a decimal.

Since the denominator is not a power of 10, write an **equivalent fraction** whose denominator is a power of 10.

$\frac{8}{25} = \frac{8 \times 4}{25 \times 4} = \frac{32}{100}$

Write the decimal for $\frac{32}{100}$.   0.32

$\frac{8}{25} = 0.32$

Workbook Activity 25

Name _____ Date _____ Period _____ Workbook Activity 25 / Chapter 3, Lesson 8

Decimals and Fractions

EXAMPLE Write 0.25 as a fraction. 5 is in the hundredths place. The denominator is 100.

$\frac{25}{100} = \frac{1}{4}$

Write $\frac{29}{100}$ as a decimal.   0.29

Write $\frac{30}{50}$ as a decimal. $\frac{30}{50} = \frac{30 \times 2}{50 \times 2} = \frac{60}{100}$ $\frac{60}{100} = 0.60$

Directions Write the denominator that would be used to change each decimal to a fraction.

1. 0.7 _____
2. 0.21 _____
3. 0.03 _____
4. 0.1 _____
5. 0.119 _____

Directions Write each decimal as a fraction. Simplify.

6. 0.34 _____
7. 0.24 _____
8. 0.45 _____
9. 0.010 _____
10. 0.2 _____
11. 0.13 _____
12. 3.08 _____
13. 0.006 _____
14. 0.36 _____
15. 7.8 _____

Directions Write each fraction as a decimal.

16. $\frac{8}{25}$ _____
17. $\frac{3}{4}$ _____
18. $1\frac{1}{50}$ _____
19. $\frac{29}{40}$ _____
20. $\frac{11}{20}$ _____
21. $3\frac{18}{25}$ _____
22. $\frac{5}{8}$ _____
23. $7\frac{1}{5}$ _____
24. $\frac{91}{100}$ _____
25. $\frac{19}{25}$ _____

_____ Publishing. Permission is granted to reproduce for classroom use only. Mathematics: Pathways

---

Activity 24

Name _____ Date _____ Period _____ Activity 24 / Chapter 3, Lesson 8

Fractions and Decimals

Directions Write each decimal as a fraction. Simplify.

1. 0.018 _____
2. 2.96 _____
3. 0.36 _____
4. 1.255 _____
5. 0.344 _____
6. 9.21 _____

Directions Write each fraction as a decimal.

7. $\frac{11}{100}$ _____
8. $\frac{15}{20}$ _____
9. $2\frac{4}{25}$ _____
10. $\frac{39}{50}$ _____
11. $\frac{185}{200}$ _____
12. $\frac{32}{250}$ _____

Directions Write *true* if the statement is true or *false* if it is false.

13. $\frac{33}{100} = 0.33$ _____
14. $\frac{7}{8} = 0.88$ _____
15. $3\frac{4}{5} = 3.8$ _____
16. $0.62 = \frac{1}{5}$ _____
17. $2.32 = 2\frac{8}{25}$ _____
18. $1.09 = 1\frac{9}{100}$ _____
19. $0.84 = \frac{21}{25}$ _____
20. $\frac{7}{11} = 0.79$ _____
21. $0.18 = \frac{7}{25}$ _____
22. $\frac{22}{25} = 0.88$ _____

Directions Solve these problems.

23. The Randall farm has 22.82 acres. The Schneider farm has $22\frac{7}{8}$ acres. Which farm is larger? _____

24. Gina pays $18.75 per hour for piano lessons. In March she took $7\frac{1}{2}$ hours of lessons. How much did she pay for piano lessons in March? _____

25. Jackie bought $16\frac{1}{2}$ yards of ribbon. She paid $74.52. What was cost of the ribbon per yard? _____

©AGS Publishing. Permission is granted to reproduce for classroom use only. Mathematics: Pathways

Exercise A Write each decimal as a fraction. Simplify your answer.

1. 0.28 $\frac{7}{25}$

2. 0.05 $\frac{1}{20}$

3. 0.54 $\frac{27}{50}$

4. 0.60 $\frac{3}{5}$

5. 0.004 $\frac{1}{250}$

6. 8.4 $8\frac{2}{5}$

7. 0.29 $\frac{29}{100}$

8. 0.625 $\frac{5}{8}$

9. 0.0075 $\frac{3}{400}$

10. 0.875 $\frac{7}{8}$

11. 5.05 $5\frac{1}{20}$

12. 0.202 $\frac{101}{500}$

13. 0.0011 $\frac{11}{10,000}$

14. 2.5 $2\frac{1}{2}$

15. 0.045 $\frac{9}{200}$

16. 0.0032 $\frac{2}{625}$

Exercise B Write each fraction as a decimal.

17. $\frac{3}{10}$ 0.3

18. $\frac{23}{100}$ 0.23

19. $\frac{250}{1,000}$ 0.25

20. $\frac{4}{5}$ 0.8

21. $\frac{15}{25}$ 0.6

22. $2\frac{3}{5}$ 2.6

23. $\frac{62}{500}$ 0.124

24. $\frac{11}{20}$ 0.55

25. $\frac{12}{40}$ 0.3

26. $\frac{175}{10,000}$ 0.0175

27. $6\frac{1}{2}$ 6.5

28. $\frac{124}{250}$ 0.496

29. $\frac{63}{125}$ 0.504

30. $\frac{21}{200}$ 0.105

31. $\frac{9}{16}$ 0.5625

32. $\frac{15}{80}$ 0.1875

PROBLEM SOLVING

Exercise C Solve these problems.

33. Elena bought $3\frac{1}{2}$ yards of fabric for $32.75. What was the cost of the fabric per yard to the nearest cent?
$9.36 per yard

34. Julia has a length of string that measures $15\frac{3}{4}$ feet. If she cuts a piece 6.5 feet long, how much of the string will she have left?
9.25 feet of string

35. Alex earns $15 an hour for writing insurance reports. If he works for $5\frac{2}{5}$ hours, how much will Alex earn?
$81

Make sure that students understand that any fraction must be expressed as a power of 10 before it can be converted to a decimal. This process is the inverse of simplifying.

3 Reinforce and Extend

LEARNING STYLES

Logical/Mathematical
Have students create a table showing decimal equivalents for one of the following fraction families:

$\frac{1}{5}, \frac{2}{5}, \frac{3}{5}, \frac{4}{5}, \frac{5}{5}$

$\frac{1}{6}, \frac{2}{6}, \frac{3}{6}, \frac{4}{6}, \frac{5}{6}, \frac{6}{6}$

$\frac{1}{7}, \frac{2}{7}, \frac{3}{7}, \frac{4}{7}, \frac{5}{7}, \frac{6}{7}, \frac{7}{7}$

$\frac{1}{8}, \frac{2}{8}, \frac{3}{8}, \frac{4}{8}, \frac{5}{8}, \frac{6}{8}, \frac{7}{8}, \frac{8}{8}$

Students should round decimals to the nearest hundredth. As they complete their tables, instruct them to look for patterns. Post each table in logical order (fifths, then sixths, and so on), and have students study the tables to look for other patterns.

IN THE COMMUNITY

Have students locate information about state parks with hiking trails and note whether the lengths of the trails are expressed in kilometers or miles, using decimals or fractions. Instruct students to convert trail lengths (from fractions to decimals, or vice versa) and make trail signposts listing distances in both forms.

Lesson at a Glance

Chapter 3 Lesson 9

Overview This lesson defines repeating decimals and explains how to express them.

Objectives

- To convert fractions into repeating decimals
- To convert degrees Celsius to degrees Fahrenheit and vice versa

Student Pages 64–65

Teacher's Resource Library (TRL)

Workbook Activity 26

Activity 25

Alternative Activity 25

....

Mathematics Vocabulary

repeating decimal

....

1 Warm-Up Activity

Read a postcard from Africa to the class: "Today we drove across the savannah and saw lions, giraffes, zebras, and elephants. At noon we rested in the shade, for it was burning hot, 32 degrees!" Have students explain how this can be true and tell what they know about the Celsius and Fahrenheit systems of temperature measurement. Have them read the lesson to find out how to convert temperatures from one scale to the other.

2 Teaching the Lesson

Make sure that students understand that the C in this formula stands for degrees Celsius, not circumference, as it did in Lesson 5.

Review the procedure for multiplying a fraction by a whole number:

$$\frac{5}{9}(3) = \frac{5}{9}\left(\frac{3}{1}\right) = \frac{15}{9} = 1\frac{6}{9} \text{ or } 1\frac{2}{3}$$

As students compute the repeating decimal equivalents to fractions, have them circle or highlight the portions of the division problem that repeat (aside from the quotient pattern). *(Students should realize that the subtractions from the point at which the decimal repeats will also repeat.)*

64 *Chapter 3*

Repeating decimal

A decimal in which one or more digits repeat

The formula for changing degrees Fahrenheit to degrees Celsius is

$$C = \frac{5}{9}(F - 32),$$

where F is degrees Fahrenheit and C is degrees Celsius.

EXAMPLE 1 If it is 35°F outside, what is the Celsius temperature?

First, substitute 35° Fahrenheit into the formula.

$$C = \frac{5}{9}(F - 32)$$
$$C = \frac{5}{9}(35 - 32)$$

Then simplify.

$$C = \frac{5}{9}(3)$$
$$C = \frac{15}{9}$$

Temperature is usually given as a decimal, not as a fraction. So change $\frac{15}{9}$ to a decimal.

```
      1.666
  9 ) 15.0
     - 9
       6 0
     - 5 4
         60
       - 54
```

In the quotient, the digit 6 repeats. The quotient is a **repeating decimal.**

To write a repeating decimal, place a bar over the repeating digit(s).

$$1.666 = 1.\overline{6}$$

If you are asked to write $1.\overline{6}$°C as a whole number, round $1.\overline{6}$°C to 2°C.

Exercise A Write each fraction as a repeating decimal.

1. $\frac{1}{3}$ $0.\overline{3}$ **4.** $\frac{1}{9}$ $0.\overline{1}$ **7.** $\frac{9}{11}$ $0.\overline{81}$

2. $\frac{1}{11}$ $0.\overline{09}$ **5.** $\frac{2}{3}$ $0.\overline{6}$ **8.** $\frac{4}{9}$ $0.\overline{4}$

3. $\frac{5}{6}$ $0.8\overline{3}$ **6.** $\frac{4}{11}$ $0.\overline{36}$ **9.** $\frac{8}{9}$ $0.\overline{8}$

Exercise B Use the formula $C = \frac{5}{9}(F - 32)$ to find the Celsius temperature for each Fahrenheit temperature. Round your answer to the nearest whole degree.

10. F = 62° 17°C **16.** F = 55° 13°C

11. F = 54° 12°C **17.** F = 39° 4°C

12. F = 73° 23°C **18.** F = 102° 39°C

13. F = 88° 31°C **19.** F = 78° 26°C

14. F = 49° 9°C **20.** F = 115° 46°C

15. F = 95° 35°C

Estimation Activity

Estimate: Compare these fractions. Which statement is true?

$\frac{3}{5} < \frac{3}{4}$
$\frac{3}{5} = \frac{3}{4}$
$\frac{3}{5} > \frac{3}{4}$

Solution:
Draw a scale from 0 to 1.

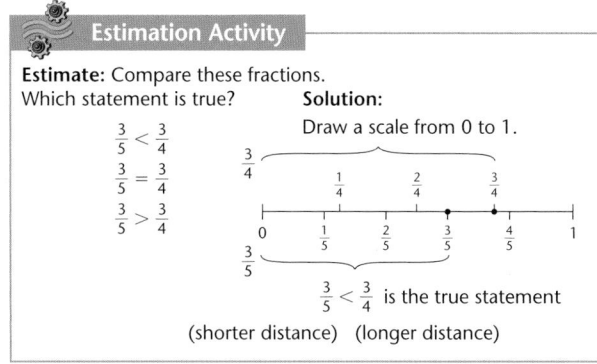

$\frac{3}{5} < \frac{3}{4}$ is the true statement
(shorter distance) (longer distance)

Try This

The formula for changing degrees Celsius to degrees Fahrenheit is $F = \frac{9}{5}(C) + 32$. Change 25° Celsius to degrees Fahrenheit.

77°F

Try This

Write both formulas (C to F and F to C) on the board, and have students compare them and point out how they are related. Draw arrows connecting inversely related portions of the formulas.

COMMON ERROR

Make sure that students realize that the bar denoting a repeating decimal goes only over the portion of the decimal that repeats. It does not necessarily involve the entire decimal.

3 Reinforce and Extend

CALCULATOR

Students can use their calculators to convert fractions to repeating decimals. Have them note how their calculator shows this value. For example, to convert $\frac{2}{3}$ to a decimal:

Enter $2 \div 3 =$.

Is the answer displayed as 0.66666666 or 0.6666667? The first expression simply truncates, or cuts off, the repeating decimal after the eighth place; the second rounds the value.

LEARNING STYLES

Interpersonal/ Group Learning

Have students work in pairs to calculate the answers to the problems in Exercise B. After papers have been collected, dictate answers from the papers to the class, and have pairs check the accuracy of answers by using the formula

$$F = \frac{9}{5}(C) + 32$$

to convert degrees Celsius back to degrees Fahrenheit.

Lesson at a Glance

Chapter 3 Lesson 10

Overview This lesson introduces the formula for simple interest and explains how to change percentages to decimals in order to calculate interest.

Objectives

- To convert percents to decimals
- To calculate simple interest

Student Pages 66–67

Teacher's Resource Library **TRL**

Workbook Activity 27

Activity 26

Alternative Activity 26

Mathematics Vocabulary

interest
percent

---

1 Warm-Up Activity

Display a passbook savings statement form. (If possible, create a transparency of one.) Enter hypothetical deposits and earnings on the form. Point out to students the interest earnings on the account. Ask them to define interest in their own words, and discuss different rates of interest commonly paid on different types of savings and investments. Encourage speculation about how bankers compute interest on your account. Write $5\frac{1}{2}\%$ on the board, and ask students to suggest ways they would calculate the interest they would earn at this rate.

2 Teaching the Lesson

Make sure that students realize that simple interest is calculated annually, not monthly. Ask them to determine the percent of interest effectively paid on a 6% rate if the money remains for the following lengths of time:

6 months	*(3%)*
2 months	*(1%)*
8 months	*(4%)*
9 months	*(4.5%)*

Interest
The amount of money paid or received for the use of money

Percent
Part per one hundred; hundredth

When you deposit money in a bank, your money earns **interest.** Interest is stated in **percents,** or parts per hundred. The formula for simple interest is one way to determine the amount of money you will earn.

The simple interest formula is $I = p \times r \times t$ or $I = prt$ where I is the interest in dollars, p is the principal in dollars, r is the rate in percent, and t is the time in years.

EXAMPLE 1 Suppose you deposit $500 into an account that earns 6% for 1 year. How much interest will you be paid?

First, you need to change 6% to a decimal. $6\% = \frac{6}{100}$. Write 6% as 0.06.

$$6\% \rightarrow 0.06$$

Next, substitute the values into the formula and solve.

$p = \$500$	$I = prt$
$r = 6\% = 0.06$	$= (500)(0.06)(1)$
$t = 1$ year	$I = 30$

The interest you will be paid is $30.

Sometimes the amount of time is not a whole number of years.

EXAMPLE 2 Sara borrows $1,000 at a rate of $9\frac{1}{2}\%$ for 6 months. How much interest will she pay?

First, write $9\frac{1}{2}\%$ as a decimal. To change the percent to a decimal, move the decimal point two places to the left.

$$9\frac{1}{2}\% \rightarrow 9.5\% \rightarrow 09.5 \rightarrow 0.095$$

Because 6 months represents $\frac{1}{2}$ of a year, and $\frac{1}{2} = 0.5$, use 0.5 for t.

$p = \$1,000$	$I = prt$
$r = 9\frac{1}{2}\% = 0.095$	$= (1,000)(0.095)(0.5)$
$t = 6$ months or 0.5 year	$I = \$47.50$

The interest Sara will pay is $47.50.

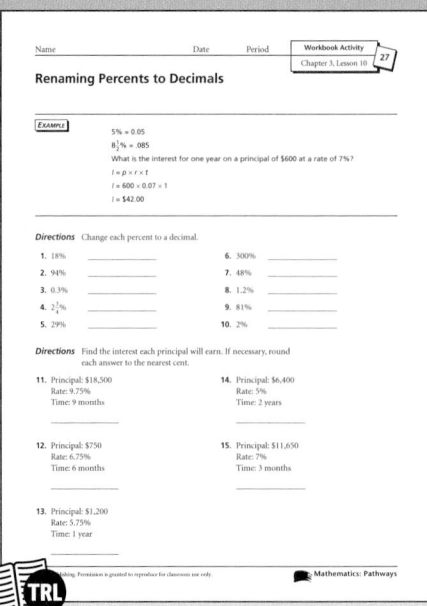

Workbook Activity 27

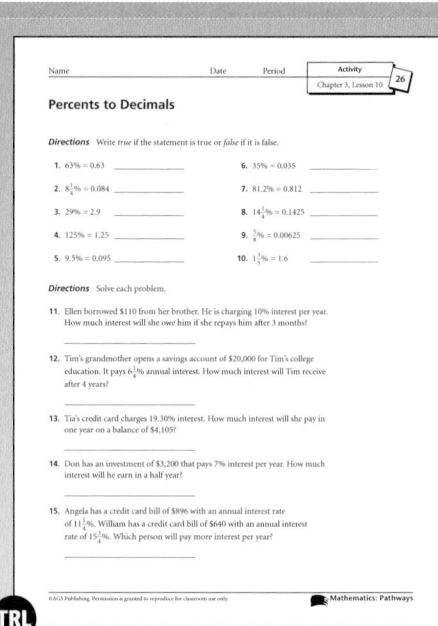

Activity 26

1. 5% 0.05   **3.** $4\frac{1}{2}$% 0.045 **5.** 0.6% 0.006 **7.** 0.8% 0.008

2. 32% 0.32   **4.** 150% 1.5   **6.** $\frac{7}{8}$% 0.00875 **8.** $\frac{1}{2}$% 0.005

Exercise B Find the interest each principal will earn. If
necessary, round your answer to the nearest cent.

9. Principal: $3,000   **11.** Principal: $5,000
   Rate: 5.5% per year   Rate: 11.5% per year
   Time: 1 year $165   Time: 6 months $287.50

10. Principal: $8,000
   Rate: 8% per year
   Time: 3 months $160

PROBLEM SOLVING

Exercise C Solve each problem.

12. Gail opens a savings account with a
deposit of $2,000 at 5.5% annual
interest. How much interest will she
receive after 2 years? $220

13. Suppose you lend a relative $800 for
1 year. You loan the money at a rate
of 4.75%. How much will your
relative pay you in interest at the end
of 1 year? $38

14. Chen wants to know which would
earn more interest: $10,000 earning
$6\frac{3}{4}$% for a year or $100,000 earning
$3\frac{1}{2}$% for a year. Tell him which
deposit would earn more interest.

$100,000 at $3\frac{1}{2}$%

15. Credit cards usually have high
interest rates. Cathy has a credit
card bill of $1,350. The annual
interest rate is 16.25%. How much
interest would she pay at the end
of 1 month? (Hint: one month is $\frac{1}{12}$
of a year.) $219.38 per year
                     $18.28 per month

Decimals   Chapter 3   **67**

MODELING

Ask students to write a
decimal to the tenths or
hundredths place on a
sheet of paper. Instruct
each student to pass his or her paper
to a partner. Students should rename
their partners' decimals as percents and
form a line in the classroom. The line
should display the percents in order
from least to greatest.

To modify the activity, direct half of
the class to write a decimal that will
produce the largest percent (up to
100%). The other half should write a
decimal that will produce the smallest
percent (down to 0%). Students in
each group will read their decimals and
have their peers rename the decimals as
percents. Students will identify the
largest and smallest percents.

Provide extra practice in changing
percents to decimals, including
fractional percents.

  2.3%   *(0.023)*

  $7\frac{1}{4}$%   *(0.0725)*

  20%   *(0.2)*

  $87\frac{1}{3}$%   *(0.8733)*

 3 **Reinforce and Extend**

GROUP PROBLEM SOLVING

Bring several credit card
advertisements to class.
Organize students into
groups of four or five, and
have each group study the contract
terms of one credit card to determine

- the promotional interest rate
  charged.

- how long the lower rate stays
  in effect.

- the regular interest rate that will
  be charged at the end of the
  promotional period.

Ask the groups to calculate the interest
they would pay in a year on a $1,500
charge card debt at the lower rate and
then at the higher rate.

CAREER CONNECTION

Have interested students
investigate trends in
banking, including average
interest paid over the past
ten years, expected changes in the
future, and advice to young wage
earners about managing money and
using credit cards wisely. Suggest that
students write at least five questions to
which they would like to find the
answers before they begin their
research. Encourage them to share
their findings with their classmates.

Lesson at a Glance

Chapter 3 Lesson 11

Overview This lesson shows how to evaluate algebraic expressions including decimals by substituting a number for the variable.

Objectives

- To substitute numbers for variables in expressions and perform the indicated arithmetic operation
- To evaluate whether the resulting statement is true or false

Student Pages 68–69

Teacher's Resource Library

Workbook Activity 28

Activity 27

Alternative Activity 27

---

1 ⎰ Warm-Up Activity

Ask students to explain how they evaluate something. *(judge its worth, find out its value)* Remind them that in mathematics *evaluate* has a different meaning: to find the numerical value of an expression. Ask, "When you have an unknown in an expression, how can you evaluate it?" *(Substitute different values into the expression, then perform the operations.)*

2 ⎰ Teaching the Lesson

Have students write out the complete problem for each problem in the exercises. Suggest that they stack the problems vertically for ease in working with decimals.

NOT $4(3.479) + 7.26$

BUT
$$\begin{array}{cc} 3.479 & 13.916 \\ \underline{\times\quad 4} & \underline{+\ 7.260} \end{array}$$

You may wish to give students more practice in estimation by having them round decimals in Exercise A and write an estimated answer for each problem before calculating answers. If possible, have students check their answers using calculators.

Point out that problem 9 in Exercise A produces a repeating decimal.

When you evaluate expressions, you substitute a number for the variable and then perform arithmetic operations from left to right.

> Remember, different symbols are used in mathematics to indicate multiplication.
> $\times$ means multiply, so $6 \times 2 = 12$.
> • means multiply, so $6 • 2 = 12$.
> Parentheses can mean multiply, so $6(2) = 12$.

EXAMPLE 1 Evaluate $8.25 + m$ when $m = 6.008$.

In the expression, substitute 6.008 for m.

$8.25 + 6.008$

Perform the arithmetic operation.

$8.25 + 6.008 = 14.258$

EXAMPLE 2 Evaluate $1.3m + 2.5n$ when $m = 6$ and $n = 3.14$.

In the expression, substitute 6 for m and 3.14 for n.

$1.3(6) + 2.5(3.14)$

Multiply. Then add.

$7.8 + 7.85 = 15.65$

When you evaluate an open statement, you determine whether the number that is substituted for the variable makes the statement true or false.

EXAMPLE 3 Is $4.5n = 13.5$ a true or false statement when $n = 1$, 2, or 3?

When $n = 1$, $4.5n = 13.5 \rightarrow 4.5 \times 1 = 4.5$, or
$4.5 = 13.5 \rightarrow$ false statement

When $n = 2$, $4.5n = 13.5 \rightarrow 4.5 \times 2 = 9.0$, or
$9.0 = 13.5 \rightarrow$ false statement

When $n = 3$, $4.5n = 13.5 \rightarrow 4.5 \times 3 = 13.5$, or
$13.5 = 13.5 \rightarrow$ true statement

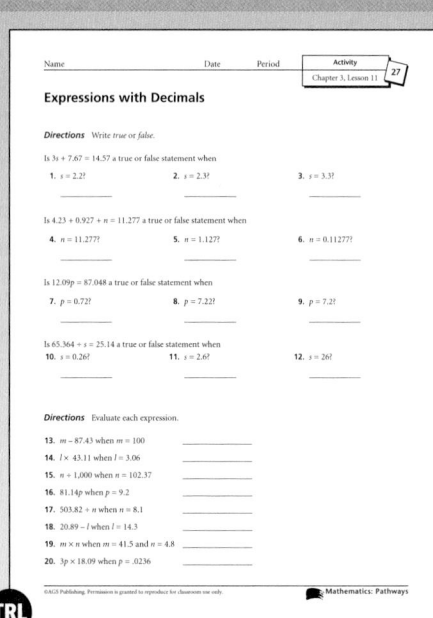

Workbook Activity 28   **Activity 27**

Exercise A Evaluate each expression.

1. $m + 2.07$ when $m = 3.085$ 5.155

2. $n - 6.257$ when $n = 20$ 13.743

3. $3.14d$ when $d = 2.6$ 8.164

4. $n \div 100$ when $n = 0.572$ 0.00572

5. $4m + 7.26$ when $m = 3.479$ 21.176

6. $2l + 2w$ when $l = 10.75$ and $w = 5.5$ 32.50

7. $l \times w$ when $l = 16.29$ and $w = 3.4$ 55.386

8. $16 - n$ when $n = 0.0825$ 15.9175

9. $n \div 1.23$ when $n = 6.42$ 5.21951

10. $2.4a + 2.67b$ when $a = 6.8$ and $b = 0.02$ 16.3734

Exercise B Write true or false.

Is $4s = 18$ a true or false statement when

11. $s = 3.5$?   false   **12.** $s = 4.5$?   true   **13.** $s = 5.5$?   false

Is $\$1,200 \times n \times 3 = \$216$ a true or false statement when

14. $n = 4\%$?   false   **15.** $n = 5\%$?   false   **16.** $n = 6\%$?   true

Is $8.5n = 8.585$ a true or false statement when

17. $n = 1.01$?   true   **18.** $n = 1.1$?   false   **19.** $n = 1.001$? false

20. $n = 1.0085$? false

Lesson at a Glance

Chapter 3 Application

Overview This lesson provides an application of converting between measurement systems.

Objective

- To find equivalent metric and linear measurements

Student Page 70

Teacher's Resource Library

Application Activity 3

Everyday Math 3

---

1 ⟩ Warm-Up Activity

Give students options involving mixed measurements, and have them vote for their choices. For example, students may be asked to choose between a piece of pizza three inches long or a piece 200 centimeters long. After students have voted, identify the smaller and larger item in each option.

2 ⟩ Teaching the Lesson

As students are doing conversions, ask them the difference in size between each unit of measure. Encourage students to remember these differences because they have practical applications for activities such as cooking or reading a map.

It is important that measurements be exact. Therefore, the name of the correct unit must accompany the number when writing the answer.

COMMON ERROR

Remind students of the process of multiplying with decimals. The decimal point must be in the correct position to ensure accurate conversions.

Application

Converting a Measurement Sometimes you may need to change measures from one measurement system to another. For example, while visiting a foreign country, you might see metric measures. How do you change the metric measurements?

> **EXAMPLE 1** 1 kilometer is equal to about 0.6 miles. About how far away in miles is a distance of 7 kilometers?
>
> **Step 1** Use the decimal to convert the measurement.
>
> **Step 2** Multiply: $7 \times 0.6 = 4.2$
>
> 7 kilometers = 4.2 miles

> **EXAMPLE 2** 1 square foot is equal to about 0.09 square meters. About how big is an area of 150 square feet when measured in square meters?
>
> **Step 1** Use the decimal to convert the measurement.
>
> **Step 2** Multiply: $150 \times 0.09 = 13.5$
>
> 150 square feet = 13.5 square meters

Exercise

1. One gallon is equal to about 3.8 liters. About how many liters are in 22 gallons? 83.6 liters

2. One inch is equal to about 2.5 centimeters. About how many centimeters are in a standard 12-inch ruler? 30 centimeters

3. One foot is equal to about 0.3 meters.

   A The length of a long-course pool is 164 feet. About how many meters long is this pool? 49.2 meters

   B The length of a short-course pool is 82 feet. About how many meters long is this pool? 24.6 meters

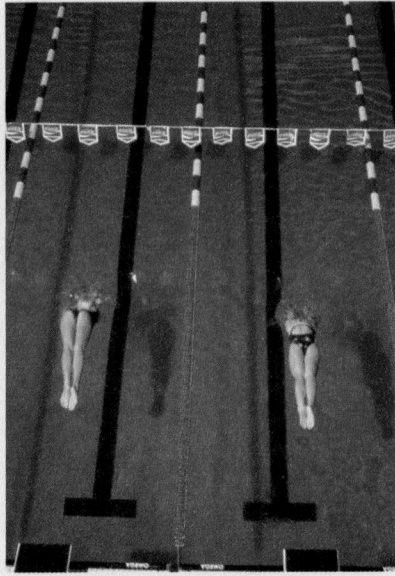

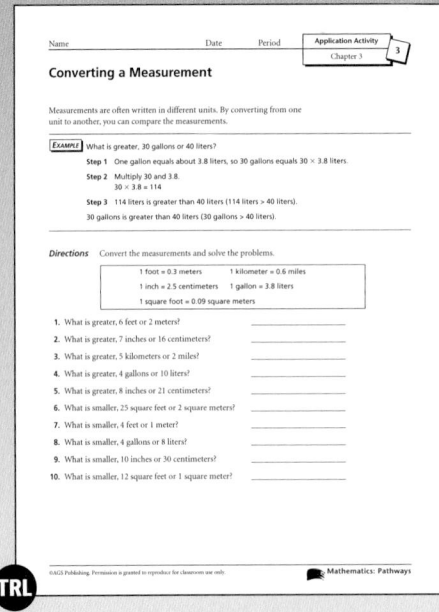

Application Activity 3

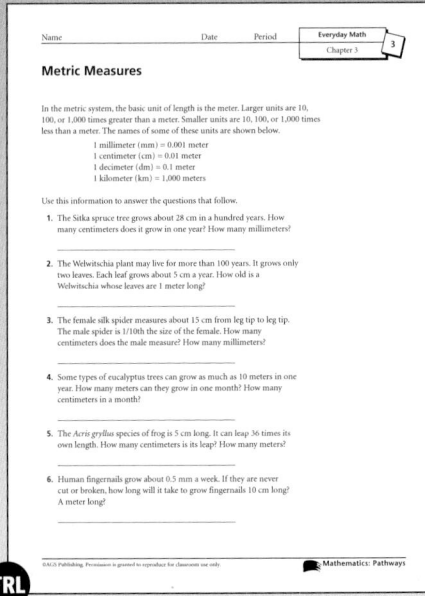

Everyday Math 3

Chapter 3 R E V I E W

Write the letter of the correct answer.

1. Add 22.56 + 0.385. B
  A 23.0   **C** 22.175
  B 22.945   **D** 22.96

2. Subtract 3.658 − 2.31. C
  A 3.427   **C** 1.348
  B 5.968   **D** 1.34

3. Multiply 4.1804 × 100. A
  A 418.04   **C** 4180.4
  B 41.804   **D** 0.041804

4. Multiply $9.20 × 40.5. D
  A $3726   **C** $3.726
  B $37.26   **D** $372.60

5. Divide 62.85 ÷ 10^2. Round the answer to the nearest thousandth. B
  A 6.285   **C** 62.900
  B 0.629   **D** 0.063

6. Write the fraction $\frac{19}{100}$ as a decimal. A
  A 0.19   **C** 19
  B 1.9   **D** 0.02

7. Evaluate the expression $2l + 2w$ when $l = 6.3$ and $w = 5.75$. D
  A 17.8   **C** 12.05
  B 18.35   **D** 24.1

GROUP PROBLEM SOLVING

Have groups of students use a map to plan a trip. They must travel a required distance, and all data must be written in miles and kilometers. Data may also be written in inches and centimeters, according to the distance traveled on one page of the map.

LEARNING STYLES

Visual/Spatial
Provide concrete examples of units of measure. A gallon jug, liter container, tape measure, and ruler will help students comprehend different measurements. Allow students to transfer a liquid between the containers or to measure something in the classroom in different units.

Chapter 3 Review

Each set of problems in the Chapter Review includes an example and solution to illustrate the concept. Use the given examples for reteaching the materials in Chapter 3. For additional practice, refer to the Supplementary Problems for Chapter 3 (pages 436–437).

Chapter 3 Mastery Test

The Teacher's Resource Library includes parallel forms of the Chapter 3 Mastery Test. The difficulty level of the two forms is equivalent. You may wish to use one form as a pretest and the other form as a posttest.

Name _____ Date _____ Period _____ | Mastery Test A, Page 1
                                              | Chapter 3

Chapter 3 Mastery Test A

Directions Circle the letter of the correct answer.

1. Round the decimal to the hundredths place.   4. Divide. 0.135 ÷ 0.45
   5.217   A 0.3   C 0.03
   A 5.22   C 5.2   B 3   D 0.003
   B 100   D 5.0
                                                  5. Evaluate the expression z + 4, when z = 1.28.
2. Subtract. 21 − 6.75   A 0.32   C 0.34
   A 26.75   C 14.25   B 5.12   D 3.2
   B 15.75   D 16.25

3. Multiply. 0.0045 × 100
   A 0.045   C 4.500
   B 0.45   D 0.000045

Directions Write the place *and* the value of each underlined digit.

6. 21.6   8. 0.03941

7. 1.525

Directions Compare each pair of decimals. Write > or <.

9. 17.7 ☐ 16.3   11. 20.4 ☐ 2.04

10. 0.5457 ☐ 0.5754   12. 911.6 ☐ 911.61

Directions Round each decimal to the place shown.

13. 19.34 (tenth)   14. 0.0865 (thousandth)

Directions Add or subtract.

15. 29.03 + 6.7   18. 12.6 − 8.17

16. 85.41 − 17.06   19. 116.5 + 0.033 + 10

17. 0.16 + 0.4 + 0.903

Name _____ Date _____ Period _____ | Mastery Test A, Page 2
                                              | Chapter 3

Chapter 3 Mastery Test A, continued

Directions Multiply.

20. 3.7 × 10^4 23. 0.05 × 0.6

21. 11.7 × 1.3   24. 12 × 70.1

22. 6.14 × 3

Directions Divide.

25. 0.02 ÷ 100   27. 24.1 ÷ 10^2

26. 4.6 ÷ 0.23   28. 40 ÷ 0.8

Directions Write each decimal as a fraction in simplest form.

29. 0.35   30. 0.004

Directions Write each fraction as a terminating or repeating decimal.

31. $\frac{5}{25}$ 33. $\frac{7}{11}$

32. $\frac{41}{500}$

Directions Rename each percent as a decimal.

34. 15%   35. 6%

Directions Evaluate.

36. a + 1.09 when a = 2.6   38. 6a + 0.5b when a = 1.3 and b =16

37. 19.61 − w when w = 10.3   39. n ÷ 2.55 when n = 3.57

Directions Solve.

40. One centimeter is equal to 0.3937 inches. Determine the height in feet and inches of a person who is 183 centimeters tall.

Chapter 3 Mastery Test A

Alternative Assessment items correlate with student Goals for Learning at the beginning of this chapter.

■ To identify the place value of digits
Have at least 10 students line up across the front of the room. Designate one student as the decimal point. Then have a student to the right or left of the designated decimal point step forward and ask seated students to identify which place value that student represents. Repeat several times.

■ To compare and round decimals
Have students explain in words and/or use graph paper (or some other grid device) to explain which is smaller and why: 0.003 or 0.03; 0.1 or 0.01; 0.01 or 0.002; 0.6 or 0.77. *(0.003 < 0.03 because thousandths are smaller than hundredths, and so on)*

■ To add and subtract decimals
Have students create two word problems that involve adding and subtracting decimals. Encourage them to think of problems using decimals other than money—batting averages, for example. Students can trade questions with a partner and solve the problems.

■ To multiply and divide decimals
Have students do the following activity. Each student stands for a place value to the right of a decimal point. Write a multiplication problem with decimals in both multiplier and multiplicand on the board. Have a number of students stand up to represent the place values to the right of the multiplicand. Then have an additional group of students stand up to represent the place values to the right of the multiplier. Ask seated students to guess how many decimal places the product will need. Solve the problem on the board. After several repetitions, ask students to give a rule for multiplying decimal numbers. *(The product will always have a number of places equal to the sum of the places to the right of the multiplier and multiplicand.)*

Then, write several division problems with decimals in the divisor on the board. Have students mark where the decimal point must move in both the divisor and the dividend before the problem can be solved.

Chapter 3   R E V I E W - continued

Identify place or value.

Example: the place of 6 in 5.062   Solution: 6 is in the hundredths place.

8. the value of 3 in the decimal 324.15   300

9. the place of 5 in the decimal 26.9875   ten-thousandths

10. the value of 2 in 1,204.5   200

11. the place of 8 in 75.832   tenths

Add or subtract.

Example: $1.23 - 0.45$ Solution: $\begin{array}{r} 1.23 \\ -\ 0.45 \\ \hline 0.78 \end{array}$

12. $0.963 + 1.58$ 2.543   **14.** $\$60 - \$24.63$ $35.37

13. $3 - 0.746$ 2.254   **15.** $5.9 + 5.32 + 0.496$ 11.716

Multiply. Round to the nearest thousandth when necessary.

Example: 2.48×3.1 Solution: $\begin{array}{r} 2.48 \\ \times\ 3.1 \\ \hline 248 \\ +\ 7440 \\ \hline 7.688 \end{array}$

16. 0.568×23.3 13.234   **18.** 32.41×7.3 236.593

17. 6.872×9.18 63.085   **19.** 8.72×10^3 8,720

Divide. If necessary, round your answer to the nearest thousandth.

Example: $2.829 \div 1.23$ Solution: $\begin{array}{r} 2.3 \\ 1.23\overline{)2.829} \\ -\ 2\ 46 \\ \hline 369 \\ -\ 369 \\ \hline 0 \end{array}$

20. $8.4 \div 1,000$ 0.008   **22.** $72.85 \div 5.3$ 13.745

21. $68.5 \div 0.6$ 114.167   **23.** $63.7 \div 10^2$ 0.637

Chapter 3 Mastery Test B

Directions Circle the letter of the correct answer.

1. Round the decimal to the hundredths place.
7.867
A 7.86   C 7.9
B 8.0   D 7.87

2. Subtract. 31 − 7.68
A 23.32   C 23.42
B 24.32   D 24.42

3. Multiply. 0.0076 × 1,000
A 76,000   C 0.00000076
B 0.076   D 7.6

4. Divide. 0.684 ÷ 0.75
A 0.0912   C 0.912
B 9.12   D 0.00912

5. Evaluate the expression b ÷ 3, when b = 1.14.
A 0.38   C 0.038
B 3.8   D 0.4

Directions Write the place *and* the value of each underlined digit.

6. 2.1_2_5

7. 22._3_

Directions Compare each pair of decimals. Write > or <.

9. 18.8 ☐ 19.3

10. 0.7375 ☐ 0.7573

8. 21._9_1

11. 40.1 ☐ 4.01

12. 711.71 ☐ 711.7

Directions Round each decimal to the place shown.

13. 17.24 (tenth)

14. 0.0775 (thousandth)

Directions Add or subtract.

15. 22.04 + 7.6

16. 95.41 − 27.05

17. 0.17 + 0.3 + 0.705

18. 13.6 − 7.18

19. 118.9 + 0.066 + 9

■Mathematics: Pathways

Chapter 3 Mastery Test B, continued

Directions Multiply.

20. 3.8 × 10⁶ _____

21. 11.6 × 1.4 _____

22. 7.32 × 5 _____

23. 0.07 × 0.2 _____

24. 11 × 70.3 _____

Directions Divide.

25. 0.04 ÷ 10 _____

26. 5.7 ÷ 0.24 _____

27. 24.2 ÷ 10² _____

28. 60 ÷ 0.5 _____

Directions Write each decimal as a fraction in simplest form.

29. 0.45 _____

30. 0.005 _____

Directions Write each fraction as a terminating or repeating decimal.

31. $\frac{4}{36}$ _____

32. $\frac{47}{500}$ _____

33. $\frac{5}{20}$ _____

Directions Rename each percent as a decimal.

34. 25% _____

35. 9% _____

Directions Evaluate.

36. a + 2.09 when a = 3.7 _____

37. 19.61 − w when w = 13.7 _____

38. 7a + 0.5b when a = 3.1 and b = 17 _____

39. n + 2.975 when n = 3.57 _____

Directions Solve.

40. One centimeter is equal to 0.3937 inches. Determine the height in feet and inches of a person who is 192 centimeters tall. _____

■Mathematics: Pathways

Chapter 3 Mastery Test B

Write each decimal as a fraction. Simplify your answer.

Example: 0.50   Solution: $0.50 = \frac{50}{100} = \frac{1}{2}$

24. 0.625 $\frac{5}{8}$

26. 0.045 $\frac{9}{200}$

25. 0.250 $\frac{1}{4}$

27. 0.875 $\frac{7}{8}$

Write each fraction as a decimal. Round to the nearest hundredth if necessary.

Example: $\frac{1}{4}$ Solution: $\frac{1}{4} \times \frac{25}{25} = \frac{25}{100} = 0.25$

28. $\frac{2}{7}$ 0.29

30. $\frac{5}{9}$ 0.56

29. $\frac{7}{8}$ 0.88

Find the interest earned.

Example: What is the interest earned on $500 at 8% for 1 year?

Solution: I (interest) $= p$ (principal) r (rate) t (time) $\$500 \times .08(1) = \$40$

31. What is the interest earned on $24,000 at $8\frac{1}{2}$% for 2 years?
$4,080

32. What is the interest earned on $1,500 at 5.2% for 3 years?
$234

Evaluate each expression. Round to the nearest hundredth if necessary.

Example: $y + 18$ when $y = 2.1$ Solution: 2.1
                                               + 18.0
                                                20.1

33. $x - 6.25$ when $x = 11.99$ 5.74

34. $6.3a - 5.2b$ when $a = 2.3$ and $b = 2$ 4.09

35. $n \div 4.5$ when $n = 125.25$ 27.83

 Test-Taking Tip

Use an estimate to check your answers, especially when working with decimals. Use the whole number part of the decimal to estimate, and then compare your answer. Are they close?

■ **To change decimals to fractions and fractions to decimals**

Have students use a calculator to change all the fractional parts of 9 and 11 ($\frac{1}{9}$ through $\frac{8}{9}$ and $\frac{1}{11}$ through $\frac{10}{11}$) to decimals. Then have them determine the patterns in the decimals and define a relationship between the numbers 9 and 11. ($\frac{1}{9}$ = *repeating decimal 0.11;* $\frac{1}{11}$ = *repeating decimal 0.09;* $\frac{2}{9}$ = *repeating decimal 0.22;* $\frac{2}{11}$ = *repeating decimal 0.18, and so on*)

■ **To use a bar to identify a repeating decimal**

Have students explain two advantages of using a bar to identify a repeating decimal. (*Answers will vary; a repeating decimal goes on to infinity, and the bar provides a good device for showing that concept.*)

■ **To rename percents as decimals**

Have students use simple manipulatives such as paper clips to show the relationship between percents and their decimal equivalents. Students should work with 100 paper clips and demonstrate the relationship between a percent of the total number of paper clips and the percentage that represents.

■ **To evaluate algebraic expressions with decimals**

Have students take five to six decimal problems and substitute a variable such as x or n for one of the numbers. Then have them solve the problems by substituting at least two different numbers for each variable. The numbers they substitute should be decimal numbers.

Chapter 4

Planning Guide

Number Theory

Lesson	Student Text Lesson: Student Pages	Vocabulary	Practice Exercises	Problem Solving	Try This	Solutions Key
1 Divisibility Rules	76–79	✔	✔	79		✔
2 Prime and Composite Numbers	80–81	✔	✔	81	80	✔
3 Greatest Common Divisor	82–83	✔	✔		83	✔
4 Factoring	84–87	✔	✔	87		✔
5 Least Common Multiple	88–91	✔	✔	91		✔
6 Scientific Notation	92–93	✔	✔		93	✔
Application Finding Perfect Numbers	94		✔			✔

Chapter Activities

Teacher's Resource Library

Estimation Exercise 4: Estimating Quotients

Application Activity 4: Finding Perfect Numbers

Everyday Math 4: Light Goes the Distance

Community Connection 4: Sports Figures

Teacher's Edition

Chapter 4 Project

Assessment Options

Student Text

Chapter 4 Review

Teacher's Resource Library

Chapter 4 Mastery Tests A and B

Teacher's Edition

Chapter 4 Alternative Assessments

Student Text Features						Teaching Strategies									Learning Styles						Teacher's Resource Library			
Estimation Activity	Math in Your Life	Technology Connection	Writing About Mathematics	Build a Model	Calculator Practice	Online Connection	Common Error	Applications Home, Career, Community	Mental Math	Manipulatives	Calculator	Group Problem Solving	Modeling	Knowing Your Students	Auditory/Verbal	Visual/Spatial	Logical/Mathematical	Body/Kinesthetic	Interpersonal/Group Learning	LEP/ESL	Activities	Alternate Activities	Workbook Activities	Self-Study Guide
77			79								78	79		77	77	77	78				28	28	29	✔
			81					81		81		81								81	29	29	30	✔
							83			83								83			30	30	31	✔
		85					85			85		87			86				86	86	31	31	32	✔
	90		89		90	91		90	90	89	90	91									32	32	33	✔
			93	93			93						93							93	33	33	34	✔
							94		95					95										✔

Software Options

Skill Track Software

Use the Skill Track Software for *Mathematics: Pathways* for additional reinforcement of this chapter. The software provides multiple-choice assessment items for students to access by computer.

Solutions Key

Use the Solutions Key with this chapter to help students who may need additional assistance. The Solutions Key CD provides solutions for every exercise in the student edition.

Other Resources

Alternative Activities

The Teacher's Resource Library (TRL) contains a set of worksheets written at a second-grade reading level called Alternative Activities. They cover the same content as the regular Activities.

Manipulatives

See the Manipulative activities in this chapter for hands-on modeling of the content. The following TRL pages can also be used:

Manipulatives Master 1 (Factor Frame)
Cuisenaire Rods; Algebra Tiles

74B

Chapter at a Glance

Chapter 4: Number Theory
pages 74–97

Skill Track for Mathematics: Pathways

Teacher's Resource Library TRL

- Workbook Activities 29–34
- Activities 28–33
- Alternative Activities 28–33
- Application Activity 4
- Estimation Exercise 4
- Everyday Math 4
- Community Connection 4
- Chapter 4 Self-Study Guide
- Chapter 4 Mastery Tests A and B

(Answer Keys for the Teacher's Resource Library begin on page 528 of this Teacher's Edition.)

Career Interest Inventory

The AGS Publishing Harrington-O'Shea Career Decision-Making System-Revised (CDM) may be used with this chapter. Students can use the CDM to explore their interests and identify careers. The CDM defines career areas that are indicated by students' responses on the inventory.

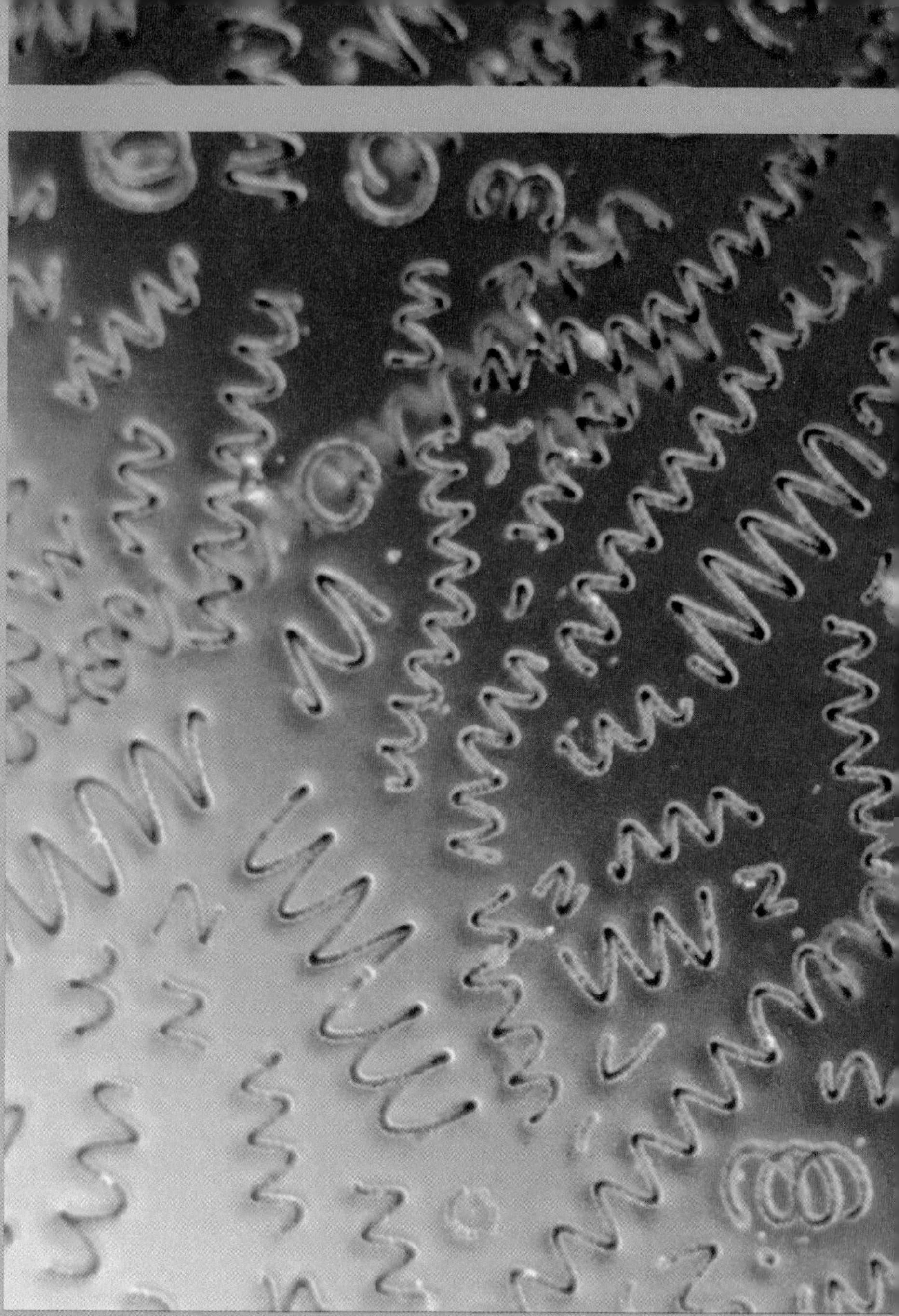

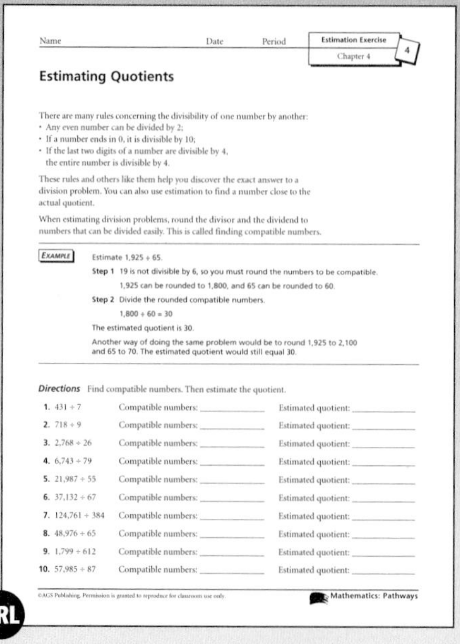

Name Date Period | Estimation Exercise | Chapter 4 | 4

Estimating Quotients

There are many rules concerning the divisibility of one number by another:
- Any even number can be divided by 2;
- If a number ends in 0, it is divisible by 10;
- If the last two digits of a number are divisible by 4, the entire number is divisible by 4.

These rules and others like them help you discover the exact answer to a division problem. You can also use estimation to find a number close to the actual quotient.

When estimating division problems, round the divisor and the dividend to numbers that can be divided easily. This is called finding compatible numbers.

EXAMPLE Estimate 1,925 ÷ 65.

Step 1 19 is not divisible by 6, so you must round the numbers to be compatible. 1,925 can be rounded to 1,800, and 65 can be rounded to 60.

Step 2 Divide the rounded compatible numbers.
1,800 ÷ 60 = 30

The estimated quotient is 30.

Another way of doing the same problem would be to round 1,925 to 2,100 and 65 to 70. The estimated quotient would still equal 30.

Directions Find compatible numbers. Then estimate the quotient.

1. 431 ÷ 7 Compatible numbers: ____________ Estimated quotient: ____________
2. 718 ÷ 9 Compatible numbers: ____________ Estimated quotient: ____________
3. 2,768 ÷ 26 Compatible numbers: ____________ Estimated quotient: ____________
4. 6,743 ÷ 79 Compatible numbers: ____________ Estimated quotient: ____________
5. 21,987 ÷ 55 Compatible numbers: ____________ Estimated quotient: ____________
6. 37,132 ÷ 67 Compatible numbers: ____________ Estimated quotient: ____________
7. 124,761 ÷ 384 Compatible numbers: ____________ Estimated quotient: ____________
8. 48,976 ÷ 65 Compatible numbers: ____________ Estimated quotient: ____________
9. 1,799 ÷ 612 Compatible numbers: ____________ Estimated quotient: ____________
10. 57,985 ÷ 87 Compatible numbers: ____________ Estimated quotient: ____________

 Mathematics: Pathways

TRL

Estimation Exercise 4

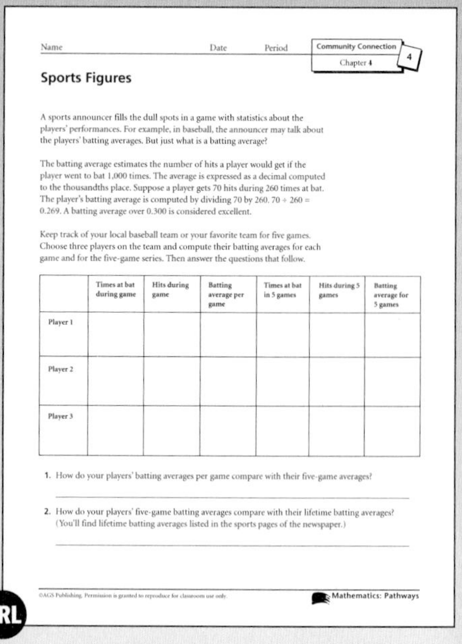

Name Date Period | Community Connection | Chapter 4 | 4

Sports Figures

A sports announcer fills the dull spots in a game with statistics about the players' performances. For example, in baseball, the announcer may talk about the players' batting averages. But just what is a batting average?

The batting average estimates the number of hits a player would get if the player went to bat 1,000 times. The average is expressed as a decimal computed to the thousandths place. Suppose a player gets 70 hits during 260 times at bat. The player's batting average is computed by dividing 70 by 260. 70 ÷ 260 = 0.269. A batting average over 0.300 is considered excellent.

Keep track of your local baseball team or your favorite team for five games. Choose three players on the team and compute their batting averages for each game and for the five-game series. Then answer the questions that follow.

	Times at bat during game	Hits during game	Batting average per game	Times at bat in 5 games	Hits during 5 games	Batting average for 5 games
Player 1						
Player 2						
Player 3						

1. How do your players' batting averages per game compare with their five-game averages?

   ____
2. How do your players' five-game batting averages compare with their lifetime batting averages? (You'll find lifetime batting averages listed in the sports pages of the newspaper.)

   ____

 Mathematics: Pathways

TRL

Community Connection 4

4 Number Theory

Many amazing and beautiful images are found in enlarged photographs. Bacteria like this *Anabaena Spiroides* are not visible to our naked eye. However, once magnified, even the smallest details of the twisting spirals are clear. Hundreds of thousands of these little bacteria can exist on a teaspoon.

However, very large or very small numbers are not easy to work with. Keeping track of all the zeros can be hard to do. Mistakes can happen when place value is confused. Scientific notation is sometimes a better way to express these numbers. In scientific notation, 0.00000001 is written $1.0 \cdot 10^{-8}$.

In Chapter 4, you will identify and use properties of numbers.

Goals for Learning

◆ To identify divisible numbers
◆ To tell prime numbers from composite numbers
◆ To find the greatest common divisor
◆ To use the distributive property to multiply or factor expressions
◆ To find the least common multiple
◆ To use scientific notation for large and small numbers

75

Introducing the Chapter

Bacteria reveal their unique characteristics when examined closely. Explain to students that although bacteria are microorganisms, different bacteria can be identified by their distinctive properties. Inform students that numbers can also be identified by certain properties. These properties, expressed as *number theories,* make all operations consistent. The numbers do not change, but different number theories give different numerical solutions.

CHAPTER PROJECT

Suggest that students work in groups of four to create their own number theory booklet. Have them choose one of the following topics or a topic of their own.

- *Divide and Conquer,* a story of the medieval intrigue between the Primes and the Composites in which each group plots to gain the kingdom of whole numbers.

- *Prime Puzzles,* a collection of puzzles focusing on prime numbers. Examples:

43	61	7
1	37	73
67	13	31

ppp × *pp* = *ppppp*, where each *p* stands for a prime number (775 × 33 = 25,575)

- *Note This!,* an almanac of the very small and the very large described in scientific notation. Entries might include the distance from Earth to Jupiter and the size of a helium atom.

Students should work together to decide what information to include in the booklet. Each team can assign tasks to individual students such as researcher, artist/illustrator, writer, and producer.

TEACHER'S RESOURCE

The AGS Publishing Teaching Strategies in Math Transparencies may be used with this chapter. They add an interactive dimension to expand and enhance the program content.

Name _____ Date _____ Period _____ *SELF-STUDY GUIDE*

CHAPTER 4: Number Theory

Goal 4.1 *To identify divisible numbers*

Date	Assignment	Score
	1: Read pages 75–79. Complete Exercises A–C on page 79.	
	2: Complete Workbook Activity 29.	

Comments:

Goal 4.2 *To tell prime numbers from composite numbers*

Date	Assignment	Score
	3: Read pages 80–81. Complete Exercises A–C on page 81.	
	4: Complete Workbook Activity 30.	

Comments:

Goal 4.3 *To find the greatest common divisor*

Date	Assignment	Score
	5: Red pages 82–83. Complete Exercise A on page 83.	
	6: Complete Workbook Activity 31.	

Comments:

Goal 4.4 *To use the distributive property to multiply or factor expressions*

Date	Assignment	Score
	7: Read pages 84–86. Complete Exercises A–D on pages 86–87.	
	8: Complete Workbook Activity 32.	

Comments:

©AGS Publishing. Permission is granted to reproduce for classroom use only. ■Mathematics: Pathways

---

Name _____ Date _____ Period _____ *SELF-STUDY GUIDE*

CHAPTER 4: Number Theory, continued

Goal 4.5 *To find the least common multiple*

Date	Assignment	Score
	9: Read pages 88–89. Complete Exercises A and C on pages 90–91.	
	10: Read and complete the Calculator Practice on page 90.	
	11: Complete Workbook Activity 33.	

Comments:

Goal 4.6 *To use scientific notation for large and small numbers*

Date	Assignment	Score
	12: Read page 92. Complete Exercises A–C on page 93.	
	13: Complete Workbook Activity 34.	
	14: Read and complete the Application on page 94.	
	15: Complete the Chapter 4 Review on pages 95–97.	

Comments:

Student's Signature _____ Date _____
Instructor's Signature _____ Date _____

©AGS Publishing. Permission is granted to reproduce for classroom use only. ■Mathematics: Pathways

TRL

Chapter 4 Self-Study Guide

Lesson at a Glance

Chapter 4 Lesson 1

Overview This lesson defines divisibility and presents rules for divisibility by the numbers 2 through 6 and 8 through 10.

Objective

■ To determine the divisibility of a number from rules

Student Pages 76–79

Teacher's Resource Library (TRL)

Workbook Activity 29

Activity 28

Alternative Activity 28

Mathematics Vocabulary

divisible

---

1 Warm-Up Activity

Review with students the multiplication and division facts for 2 through 10. Then write a division problem on the board, and ask students to identify the divisor, dividend, and remainder, if any.

2 Teaching the Lesson

Point out to students that they can use remainders as an indicator of divisibility. Help them formulate their own statements relating division, remainders, and divisibility. (*Example: If division results in a remainder of 1 or greater, the numbers are not divisible.*)

Encourage students to confirm the example divisibility tests. Have volunteers complete the long division of 4,320 on the board for each of the example divisors.

Choose another large number, such as 51,840, to use as an example. Have volunteers test its divisibility by 2, 3, 4, 5, 6, 8, 9, and 10. Record the results. (*51,840 is divisible by all the listed whole numbers.*)

Divisible

Able to be divided by a whole number with no remainder

Divisibility is a useful property of whole numbers. For example, 4 divides 8, and 5 divides 25. The symbol | is used to represent the word *divides*.

EXAMPLE 1 Which of these statements are true? Which are false?

2|16   9|19   7|40   3|21

2|16 is true because 2 • 8 = 16.

9|19 is false because 9 • NO WHOLE NUMBER = 19.

7|40 is false because 7 • NO WHOLE NUMBER = 40.

3|21 is true because 3 • 7 = 21.

Divisibility Rule

In general, a whole number *a* divides a whole number *b* if and only if there is a whole number *n* so that *a* • *n* = *b*.

a|*b* if and only if there is a whole number *n* so that *a* • *n* = *b*.

Another way to think about divisibility is to think about remainders. If a division produces a remainder other than zero, then the numbers are not divisible.

EXAMPLE 2 Which of these statements are true? Which are false?

5|32   8|8   4|36   2|9

5|32 is false because 32 ÷ 5 = 6 r2.

8|8 is true because 8 ÷ 8 = 1 r0.

4|36 is true because 36 ÷ 4 = 9 r0.

2|9 is false because 9 ÷ 2 = 4 r1.

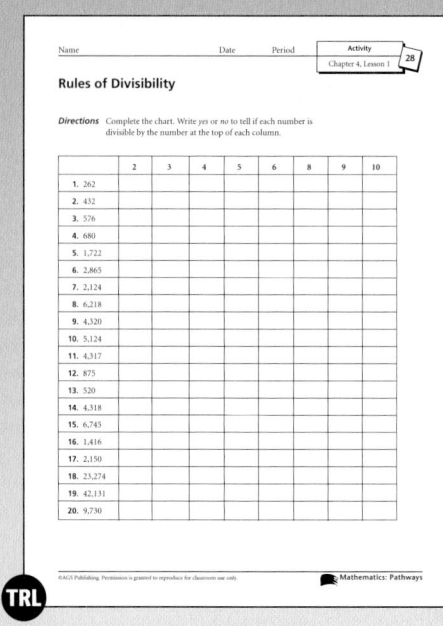

Workbook Activity 29

Name _____ Date _____ Period _____   Workbook Activity 29 · Chapter 4, Lesson 1

Divisibility Rules

EXAMPLE A number that can be divided by a whole number with no remainder is said to be divisible. The symbol | means divides.
2|10 is a true statement because 10 is divisible by 2 and there is no remainder.
10 ÷ 2 = 5 (no remainder)
2|17 is a false statement because 17 is not divisible by 2 without leaving a remainder.
17 ÷ 2 = 8 r1

Directions Write *true* if the statement is true and *false* if the statement is false. Write a division equation to prove your answer.

1. 5|15
2. 4|36
3. 6|39
4. 8|40
5. 9|82
6. 6|46
7. 3|90
8. 5|85
9. 4|128
10. 8|374
11. 2|577
12. 4|634
13. 9|567
14. 7|473
15. 8|688

Activity 28

Name _____ Date _____ Period _____   Activity · Chapter 4, Lesson 1

Rules of Divisibility

Directions Complete the chart. Write *yes* or *no* to tell if each number is divisible by the number at the top of each column.

	2	3	4	5	6	8	9	10
1. 262								
2. 432								
3. 576								
4. 680								
5. 1,722								
6. 2,865								
7. 2,124								
8. 6,218								
9. 4,320								
10. 5,124								
11. 4,317								
12. 875								
13. 520								
14. 4,318								
15. 6,745								
16. 1,416								
17. 2,150								
18. 23,274								
19. 42,131								
20. 9,730								

To test larger numbers for divisibility, use these rules:

Rule—Divisibility by 2

A number is divisible by 2 if its last digit is 0, 2, 4, 6, or 8.

EXAMPLE 3 Is 4,320 divisible by 2?

4,320 is divisible by 2 because its last digit is 0.

Rule—Divisibility by 3

A number is divisible by 3 if the sum of its digits is divisible by 3.

EXAMPLE 4 Is 4,320 divisible by 3?

4,320 is divisible by 3 because the sum of its digits $(4 + 3 + 2 + 0 = 9)$ is divisible by 3. $(9 \div 3 = 3)$

Rule—Divisibility by 4

A number is divisible by 4 if the number represented by its last two digits is divisible by 4.

EXAMPLE 5 Is 4,320 divisible by 4?

4,320 is divisible by 4 because the number represented by its last two digits (20) is divisible by 4. $(20 \div 4 = 5)$

Estimation Activity

Estimate: Find the value of n to the nearest whole number when $3n = 17.8$

Solution: 3 times what whole number = 17 or 18.

Answer: 5 is too small, $3 \cdot 5 = 15$
6 is good, $3 \cdot 6 = 18$
7 is too large, $3 \cdot 7 = 21$
The best estimate is 6.

Determine whether students understand the rules of divisibility by asking questions such as the following. Have students explain their reasoning.

- A number is divisible by 9. What other number(s) also divide the number? *(3)*

- A number is divisible by 8. What other number(s) also divide the number? *(2, 4)*

- A number is divisible by 4. What other number(s) also divide the number? *(2)*

 Reinforce and Extend

LEARNING STYLES

 Visual/Spatial

Invite small groups of students to develop a comic book series titled *Division Rules!* Encourage students to create characters whose actions reveal the rules for divisibility. Display the completed comic books around the classroom. Ask students to vote on the most imaginative comic book as well as the most informative one.

LEARNING STYLES

 Auditory/Verbal

Have students work in pairs to develop number riddles modeled on the following: "I'm thinking of a number. The sum of its digits is divisible by 9. What other whole number(s) are divisors of the number?" *(3)* Pairs should share and solve other pairs' riddles, explaining how they found the answer.

KNOWING YOUR STUDENTS

 Adolescent students frequently question their academic abilities as they strive to learn in a new setting. Teachers, peers, and even the school building may all be different. It is important to provide every student with the necessary tools to achieve. Give students multiple tools by introducing them to different factoring methods. You can display a factor tree, model writing the factors horizontally, or have multiplication charts available. Encourage cooperative learning, as each student's ability using the basic operations may be different from that of his or her classmates. This teaching style also promotes peer interaction. As partners in the academic and social transition, parents should be kept informed of student progress and asked to support learning at home.

Rule—Divisibility by 5

A number is divisible by 5 if its last digit is 0 or 5.

EXAMPLE 6 Is 4,320 divisible by 5?

4,320 is divisible by 5 because its last digit is 0.

Rule—Divisibility by 6

A number is divisible by 6 if it is divisible by 2 and by 3.

EXAMPLE 7 Is 4,320 divisible by 6?

4,320 is divisible by 6 because it is divisible by 2 and by 3.

Rule—Divisibility by 8

A number is divisible by 8 if the number represented by its last three digits is divisible by 8.

EXAMPLE 8 Is 4,320 divisible by 8?

4,320 is divisible by 8 because the number represented by its last three digits (320) is divisible by 8. (320 ÷ 8 = 40)

Rule—Divisibility by 9

A number is divisible by 9 if the sum of its digits is divisible by 9.

EXAMPLE 9 Is 4,320 divisible by 9?

4,320 is divisible by 9 because the sum of its digits (4 + 3 + 2 + 0 = 9) is divisible by 9. (9 ÷ 9 = 1)

> **Rule—Divisibility by 10**
> A number is divisible by 10 if its last digit is 0.

EXAMPLE 10   Is 4,320 divisible by 10?

4,320 is divisible by 10 because its last digit is 0.

Writing About Mathematics

There is no rule given for divisibility by 7. Describe some numbers you know are divisible by 7.

Exercise A Evaluate each statement. Write *true* or *false*.

1. 2|12	true	**7.** 6|742	false
2. 5|48	false	**8.** 8|400	true
3. 9|81	true	**9.** 5|850	true
4. 3|154	false	**10.** 3|907	false
5. 10|375	false	**11.** 4|1,116	true
6. 4|228	true	**12.** 9|2,649	false

Exercise B Is each number divisible by 2? by 3? by 4? by 5? by 6? by 8? by 9? by 10?

13. 90   2, 3, 5, 6, 9, 10   **16.** 51,840   2, 3, 4, 5, 6, 8, 9, 10

14. 812   2, 4   **17.** 248,121   3, 9

15. 5,760   2, 3, 4, 5, 6, 8, 9, 10   **18.** 1,036,800   2, 3, 4, 5, 6, 8, 9, 10

PROBLEM SOLVING

Exercise C Answer each question.

19. Write a whole number greater than ten million that is divisible by 2, 3, 4, 5, 6, 8, 9, and 10.

Answers will vary. Sample answer: 12,000,960

20. If you know that 2,388 is divisible by 6, what other numbers do you know also divide 2,388? Why?

2 and 3 because the rule for divisibility by 6 is the number must be divisible by both 2 and 3

GROUP PROBLEM SOLVING

Have students work in groups of four to develop a divisibility game board as a project. Indicate that the board must have at least 5 squares with numbers that are divisible by 2, 3, 4, 5, 6, 8, 9, and 10. (One of the squares can be labeled 4,320.) Students must find four other numbers to use in the game. Have them present their solution as a "How To" segment for a television show called *Games Are Us*. Encourage groups to assign the tasks needed in producing the show, such as graphic artist, designer, director, and announcer, to their members.

Lesson at a Glance

Chapter 4 Lesson 2

Overview This lesson introduces composite and prime numbers.

Objective

■ To distinguish prime and composite numbers

Student Pages 80–81

Teacher's Resource Library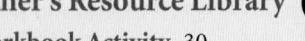

Workbook Activity 30

Activity 29

Alternative Activity 29

Mathematics Vocabulary

prime number
composite number

1 Warm-Up Activity

Demonstrate prime numbers using a 1–12 multiplication table. Point out that some numbers, such as 3, 7, and 11, appear only in the 1 × column or the 1 × row. These numbers do not appear in the body of the multiplication table. In contrast, point out that some numbers, such as 12 and 24, can be found in several cells of the table.

2 Teaching the Lesson

Use a 1–50 table of numbers on the overhead projector. Work with students to find the prime numbers greater than 0 and less than 50. Have volunteers execute each of the steps shown in the example.

Try This

Point out that the number students are seeking must have each of the given numbers as a factor.

Lesson 2 Prime and Composite Numbers

Prime number
A whole number greater than one that has only 1 and itself as factors

Composite number
A whole number that is not a prime number

Some whole numbers have only two factors. For example, $5 = 1 \cdot 5, 7 = 1 \cdot 7, 13 = 1 \cdot 13$. Any whole number greater than one that has only 1 and itself as factors is called a **prime number.**

EXAMPLE 1 Is 29 a prime number?

Since $1 \cdot 29 = 29$, and there are no other ways to make a product of 29 using two whole numbers as factors, 29 is a prime number.

A whole number may have factors other than 1 and itself. For example, 12 has 6 different factors—1, 2, 3, 4, 6, and 12. Any whole number that has factors other than 1 and itself is called a **composite number.** A composite number cannot be prime.

EXAMPLE 2 Is 14 a composite number?

Since $2 \cdot 7 = 14$, 14 is a composite number.

Eratosthenes (ehr uh TAHS thuh neez) was a Greek mathematician who lived more than 2,000 years ago. He developed an organized way to find prime numbers. This organized way is known as the Sieve of Eratosthenes. (A *sieve* is something that is used to separate one thing from another.)

Try This

The numbers 2, 3, and 5 represent the prime factors of a person's age. How old is that person?

30 years old, or any multiple of 30 years

EXAMPLE 3 Find all of the prime numbers greater than 0 and less than 50.

Step 1 Create a table of positive numbers from 1 to 50.

Step 2 Cross out 1; 1 is not a prime number.

Step 3 Circle 2; 2 is a prime number. Then cross out every multiple of 2 because every multiple of 2 is a composite number.

Step 4 Circle 3; 3 is a prime number. Then cross out every multiple of 3.

Step 5 Circle 5. Then cross out every multiple of 5.

Step 6 Circle 7. Then cross out every multiple of 7.

80 *Chapter 4 Number Theory*

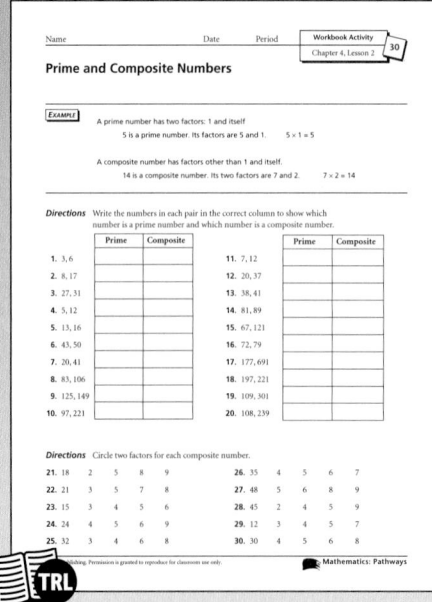

Workbook Activity 30

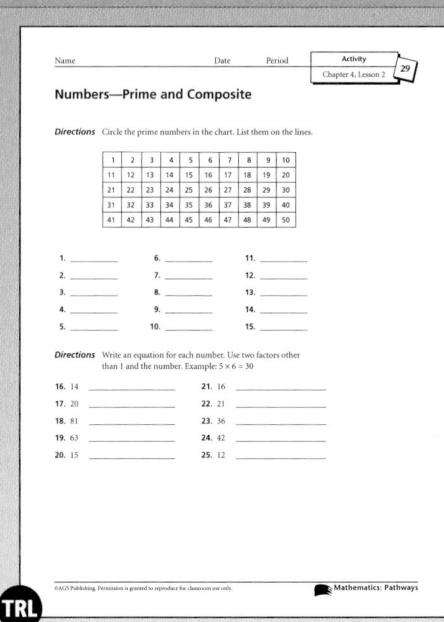

Activity 29

In Lesson 1, you learned how to test a number for divisibility by 2, 3, 4, 5, 6, 8, 9, and 10. You can use these tests to help you decide whether a number is prime or composite.

EXAMPLE 3 *(continued)*

Step 7 Circle the remaining numbers.
The circled numbers —2, 3, 5, 7, 11, 13, 17, 19, 23, 29, 31, 37, 41, 43, 47—are the prime numbers that are greater than 0 and less than 50.

~~1~~	(2)	(3)	~~4~~	(5)	~~6~~	(7)	~~8~~	~~9~~	~~10~~
(11)	~~12~~	(13)	~~14~~	~~15~~	~~16~~	(17)	~~18~~	(19)	~~20~~
~~21~~	~~22~~	(23)	~~24~~	~~25~~	~~26~~	~~27~~	~~28~~	(29)	~~30~~
(31)	~~32~~	~~33~~	~~34~~	~~35~~	~~36~~	(37)	~~38~~	~~39~~	~~40~~
(41)	~~42~~	(43)	~~44~~	~~45~~	~~46~~	(47)	~~48~~	~~49~~	~~50~~

Writing About Mathematics

Read about the Greek mathematician Eratosthenes and write about his contributions to mathematics.

Exercise A

1. On grid paper, copy the example table of numbers from 1 to 50 and extend it to 100. Use the Sieve of Eratosthenes method to find all of the prime numbers from 1 to 100.
numbers circled above plus 53, 59, 61, 67, 71, 73, 79, 83, 89, 97

Exercise B Decide whether each number is prime or composite.

2. 108 composite
3. 109 prime
4. 119 composite
5. 121 composite
6. 137 prime
7. 142 composite
8. 149 prime
9. 177 composite
10. 221 composite
11. 239 prime
12. 691 prime

PROBLEM SOLVING

Exercise C Answer each question.

13. The numbers 2 and 3 are consecutive and prime. Is there another pair of numbers between 1 and 100 that are consecutive and prime? Tell why or why not.
No. See Teacher's Edition page.

14. Prime numbers like 5 and 7, 11 and 13, and 17 and 19 are called *twin primes* because they differ by 2. List all twin primes between 1 and 100. Use your table from Exercise A.
See Teacher's Edition page.

15. Find a number that is greater than 150 and has exactly 3 different factors.
Answers will vary.

MANIPULATIVES

Prime and Composite Numbers

Materials: Cuisenaire Rods

Group Practice: Build models of smaller prime and composite numbers using cubes (1-rods). Arrange each model to form a rectangle. For example, to model 12, arrange the cubes in a 3×4 rectangle and then a 1×12 rectangle. Discuss how the dimensions of the rectangle are factors of the number. Explain that if a number is prime, only one rectangle ($1 \times n$) can be formed. With larger numbers, use the longer rods to build the rectangles.

Student Practice: Have students build models and draw sketches of the numbers from 20 to 30 to determine whether each number is prime or composite. Then have students use this method to complete Exercise A.

3 Reinforce and Extend

GROUP PROBLEM SOLVING

Pose the following problem to small groups of students to discuss.

Jamaal looked at the intervals between prime numbers from 1 to 100. Then he made the following observations.

- For primes 1 to 50, most of the consecutive primes differ by 2.
- For primes from 50 to 100, most consecutive primes differ by 6.

Jamaal predicted that the interval between consecutive prime numbers increases as the numbers increase.

Have the groups determine whether Jamaal's prediction is correct. *(Jamaal is correct.)*

LEARNING STYLES

LEP/ESL

Have students work in pairs. Have one partner explain in his or her own words what composite numbers are. Have the other student explain in his or her own words what prime numbers are.

AT HOME

Ask students to list the ages of the people, both children and adults, who live in their home. Have them determine which ages are prime numbers and explain how they determined this fact.

Answers to Problems 13–14

13. No; for two numbers greater than 3 to be consecutive, one number must be an even number, and every even number is a composite number because it is a multiple of 2.

14. 3 and 5, 5 and 7, 11 and 13, 17 and 19, 29 and 31, 41 and 43, 59 and 61, 71 and 73

Lesson at a Glance

Chapter 4 Lesson 3

Overview This lesson demonstrates how to find the greatest common divisor of two or more numbers.

Objective
- To determine the greatest common divisor of a given number

Student Pages 82–83

Teacher's Resource Library

Workbook Activity 31

Activity 30

Alternative Activity 30

Mathematics Vocabulary

simplest form
greatest common divisor (GCD)
common factor
greatest common factor (GCF)

1 Warm-Up Activity

Write several equivalent fractions on the board, such as $\frac{1}{2}$, $\frac{2}{4}$, $\frac{6}{12}$, $\frac{25}{50}$, and $\frac{360}{720}$. Ask students to discuss what these fractions have in common and which of the fractions is in simplest form. (*They are all equivalent; $\frac{1}{2}$ is in simplest form.*) Write important points or terms from students' discussion on the board for reference.

2 Teaching the Lesson

Using the overhead projector, work through the first example with students. Point out that the first step is to list all the factors of each number. Have a volunteer work through the second example at the overhead projector.

Simplest form
A fraction in which the only common factor of the numerator and denominator is 1

Greatest common divisor (GCD)
The largest factor that two or more numbers or terms have in common

Common factor
A number that will divide each of two or more numbers with no remainder

A factor of a number is also a divisor of the number. You can use either word.

To write a fraction in **simplest form,** divide the numerator and denominator of the fraction by the **greatest common divisor** of the numerator and denominator. The greatest common divisor (GCD) of two or more numbers is the largest **common factor** of two or more numbers.

EXAMPLE 1 Express $\frac{20}{48}$ in simplest form.

$$\frac{20 \div 4}{48 \div 4} = \frac{5}{12}$$

In this example, the greatest common divisor of 20 and 48 is 4.

Step 1 To find a greatest common divisor, first list all of the factors of each number.

20: 1 2 4 5 10 20
48: 1 2 3 4 6 8 12 16 24 48

Step 2 Then circle the factors that are common to, or shared by, each number.

20: ① ② ④ 5 10 20
48: ① ② 3 ④ 6 8 12 16 24 48

Step 3 Choose the greatest common divisor or factor.
The greatest common divisor of 20 and 48 is 4 and can be written GCD (20, 48) = 4.

You can also find the greatest common divisor of algebraic terms.

EXAMPLE 2 Find GCD ($6x$, 21).

Step 1 List all of the factors of each term.
$6x$: 1 2 3 6 x
21: 1 3 7 21

Step 2 Circle the factors that are common to, or shared by, each term.
$6x$: ① 2 ③ 6 x
21: ① ③ 7 21

Step 3 Choose the greatest common divisor:
GCD ($6x$, 21) = 3.

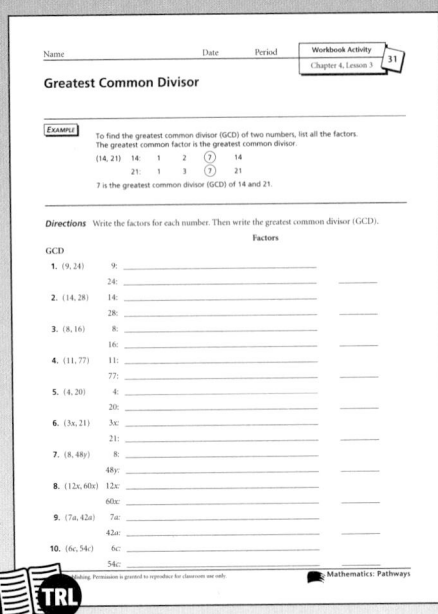

Workbook Activity 31

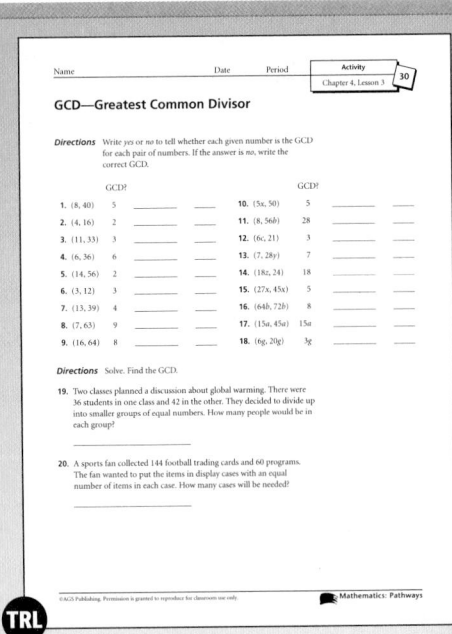

Activity 30

EXAMPLE 3 Find GCD (5a, 17a).

Step 1 List all of the factors of each term.

5a: 1 5 a

17a: 1 17 a

Step 2 Circle the factors that are common to, or shared by, each number.

5a: ① 5 ⓐ

17a: ① 17 ⓐ

Step 3 Choose the greatest common divisor:

GCD (5a, 17a) = a.

The greatest common divisor, or GCD, is sometimes called the **greatest common factor,** or GCF.

Exercise A Find the greatest common divisor.

1. (10, 50)   10

2. (16, 30)   2

3. (9, 24)   3

4. (72, 18)   18

5. (12, 32)   4

6. (54, 1)   1

7. (4x, 8)   4

8. (7, 28c)   7

9. (6a, 12)   6

10. (45r, 15)   15

11. (14, 6e)   2

12. (36, 42q)   6

13. (49y, 21)   7

14. (3b, 9b)   3b

15. (20h, 5h)   5h

16. (18m, 24m)   6m

17. (45d, 27d)   9d

18. (84n, 54n)   6n

19. (26v, 65v)   13v

20. (56p, 72p)   8p

Try This

Find two whole numbers in a newspaper or a magazine. Find their greatest common divisor.

Answers will vary.

Try This

Remind students who find large numbers that they can apply the divisibility rules to determine factors.

COMMON ERROR

In their enthusiasm or haste, students often stop listing all factors as soon as they discover a common factor between two numbers. Failing to list all the factors increases the possibility that students will not find the *greatest* common factor. Encourage them to always list all factors of each number before identifying any common factors.

MANIPULATIVES

 Greatest Common Divisor

Materials: Cuisenaire Rods

Group Practice: Review the connection between the dimensions of a rectangle and the factors of a number. To find common factors of two numbers, build rectangular models of both numbers. Find GCD (20, 48). Use the 5- or 10-rods to model 20. Then try to build 48 with these rods. Because 5 and 10 are not factors of 48, a rectangle cannot be made. Use 4-rods to build both rectangles, showing that 4 is a dimension, or factor, of both 20 and 48.

Student Practice: Have students use the rods for Exercise A, problems 1–13, drawing sketches of rectangles to support their answers.

 Reinforce and Extend

LEARNING STYLES

Body/Kinesthetic

Suggest that pairs of students construct arrays representing the factors of each pair of numbers in Exercise A, problems 1–6. Each partner chooses one of the numbers in the problem. For their chosen number, students use counters to make arrays that represent the factors for that number. Students should use the arrays to list the factors of the chosen number. For example, a student choosing 10 might construct a 1 × 10 array and a 2 × 5 array and conclude that the factors of 10 are 1, 2, 5, and 10. After students have exhausted array possibilities, they can compare factors and identify the greatest common factor.

Lesson at a Glance

Chapter 4 Lesson 4

Overview This lesson shows the usefulness of the distributive property when multiplying or factoring expressions.

Objectives

- To use the distributive property when multiplying expressions
- To use the distributive property when factoring expressions

Student Pages 84–87

Teacher's Resource Library

Workbook Activity 32

Activity 31

Alternative Activity 31

....

Mathematics Vocabulary

distributive property

....

 **Warm-Up Activity**

Draw the following sign on the board:

```
Apples 10¢ each
Oranges 10¢ each
```

Ask, "How much would you pay for 3 apples? For 4 oranges? For 3 apples + 4 oranges?" Tell students that this lesson will show them how to use the distributive property to find the answers.

2 Teaching the Lesson

Begin the lesson by reminding students that multiplication is the same as repeated addition. Then refer to the first example, $2(3 + 5)$, and indicate that the problem is asking for $(3 + 5) + (3 + 5)$. Have a volunteer work through the two additional multiplication examples on the board or overhead projector.

As you introduce factoring using the distributive property, you may wish to have a volunteer list all the factors of $4x$ and 6: $1x \cdot 4$, $2x \cdot 2$, $4x \cdot 1$, $1 \cdot 6$, and $2 \cdot 3$. From these factors students can determine the factors common to both $4x$ and 6.

Distributive property
Numbers within parentheses that can be multiplied by the same factor

The **distributive property** can be used to multiply or to factor expressions. When you *multiply* using the distributive property, the product will have no parentheses.

EXAMPLE 1 $2(3 + 5)$

$2(3 + 5)$ means $(3 + 5) + (3 + 5) = 8 + 8 = 16$. You can use the distributive property as a shortcut to get the same answer.

Apply the distributive property. $2(3 + 5)$

$(2 \cdot 3) + (2 \cdot 5)$
$\quad\quad 6 \quad + \quad 10$
$\quad\quad\quad\quad 16$

EXAMPLE 2 $3(r + 4)$

$3(r + 4)$ means $(r + 4) + (r + 4) + (r + 4) = (r + r + r) + (4 + 4 + 4) = 3r + 12$

Apply the distributive property. $3(r + 4)$

$(3 \cdot r) + (3 \cdot 4)$
$\quad 3r \quad + \quad 12$

EXAMPLE 3 $2(a + 6b + 1)$

$2(a + 6b + 1)$ means $(a + 6b + 1) + (a + 6b + 1) = (a + a) + (6b + 6b) + (1 + 1) = 2a + 12b + 2$

Apply the distributive property. $2(a + 6b + 1)$

$(2 \cdot a) + (2 \cdot 6b) + (2 \cdot 1)$
$\quad 2a \quad + \quad 12b \quad + \quad 2$

The distributive property is also useful whenever you factor expressions. To factor an expression, first find the greatest common divisor. Then use the distributive property to place parentheses between the factors.

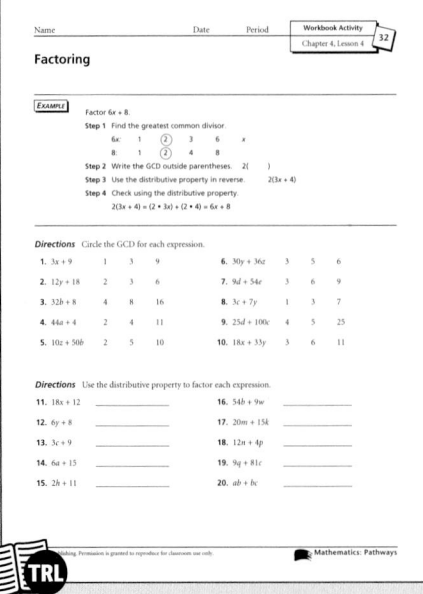

Workbook Activity 32

Activity 31

EXAMPLE 4 Factor $4x + 6$.

Step 1 First find the greatest common divisor, or GCD, of each term.

$4x$: ①②④ x
6: ①②③⑥

The GCD of $4x$ and 6 is 2.

Step 2 Write the GCD outside parentheses.

$2(\quad)$

Step 3 To complete the factoring, use the distributive property in reverse.

$2(2x + 3)$

Step 4 Check your work using the distributive property.

$2(2x + 3) = (2 \bullet 2x) + (2 \bullet 3) = 4x + 6$

EXAMPLE 5 Factor $3x + 3y$.

Step 1 First find the GCD of each term.

$3x$: ①③ x
$3y$: ①③ y

The GCD of $3x$ and $3y$ is 3.

Step 2 Write the GCD outside parentheses.

$3(\quad)$

Step 3 To complete the factoring, use the distributive property in reverse.

$3(x + y)$

Step 4 Check your work using the distributive property.

$3(x + y) = (3 \bullet x) + (3 \bullet y) = 3x + 3y$

Technology Connection

Spell Check This!

A spell-check program on a computer works something like factoring. Suppose you've written the word "algebra." First, it factors out all the words that have the same number of letters as *algebra*. Then it works through the alphabet. It looks at all words that begin with *a*. Then it looks at all words that begin with the letters *al*, and so on, until it has made sure that the word "algebra" that you wrote matches the word *algebra* in the computer's dictionary.

COMMON ERROR

Students sometimes fail to multiply each term in the parentheses by the multiplier. Instead of $2(3 + 5)$, students may compute $2(3) + 5$. Stress the importance of multiplying each term within the parentheses by the multiplier outside the parentheses.

MANIPULATIVES

 Factoring

Materials: Algebra Tiles, two copies of Manipulatives Master 1 (Factor Frame) for each student

Group Practice: Identify the Algebra Tiles for students (see pages T8–T9). Model the expression $4x + 6$. Place each term on the inside of a Factor Frame. Arrange the pieces in each frame to form rectangles that have a common dimension (2). The largest common dimension represents the GCD and is written outside the parentheses: $2(\quad)$. The remaining dimensions, or factors, are written inside the parentheses: $2(2x + 3)$. To check, multiply the pieces that represent the terms inside the parentheses by the GCD, and compare this model with the original expression.

Student Practice: Have students use the Algebra Tiles to check their answers for Exercise A, problems 3–4, 6. Have them draw sketches and write the symbolic equivalent for each model. Use the Algebra Tiles to solve Exercise B, problems 11–12, 16 and Exercise C, problems 17–20.

LEARNING STYLES

Auditory/Verbal

Invite students to work in pairs. Each partner can demonstrate and explain the steps he or she used to find the products in Exercise A. Partners can exchange roles after completing each problem.

LEARNING STYLES

LEP/ESL

Ask pairs of students to explain to one another the steps to use to find the greatest common factor for the problems in Exercise B.

LEARNING STYLES

**Interpersonal/
Group Learning**

Have groups of five students work progressively to factor the expressions in Exercise B. One student writes one of the expressions on a sheet of paper. The second student lists the factors and passes the sheet to the third student who identifies the GCD. The fourth student writes the GCD outside the parentheses, and the fifth student completes the factoring. Groups should rotate roles with each expression so that all members have a chance to perform each step in the process.

EXAMPLE 6 Factor $ab + ac$.

Step 1 First find the GCD of each term.

ab: (a) b

ac: (a) c

The GCD of ab and ac is a.

Step 2 Write the GCD outside parentheses.

$a(\ \ )$

Step 3 To complete the factoring, use the distributive property in reverse.

$a(b + c)$

Step 4 Check your work using the distributive property.

$a(b + c) = (a \cdot b) + (a \cdot c) = ab + ac$

Some expressions cannot be factored.

EXAMPLE 7 Factor $4x + 7y$.

First find the GCD of each term.

$4x$: (1) 4 x

$7y$: (1) 7 y

The GCD of $4x$ and $7y$ is 1. When the GCD of any group of numbers or terms is 1, the expression cannot be factored.

> The greatest common divisor, or GCD, is sometimes called the greatest common factor, or GCF. A factor is also a divisor.

Whenever you factor an expression, you are rewriting the expression as the product of two or more factors.

Exercise A Use the distributive property to multiply each expression.

6. $9q + 99$	**1.** $3(2 + 6)$ 24	**6.** $9(q + 11)$
7. $4n + 12p + 8$	**2.** $15(3 + 4)$ 105	**7.** $4(n + 3p + 2)$
8. $48k + 8h + 80$	**3.** $2(a + 5)$ $2a + 10$	**8.** $8(6k + h + 10)$
9. $2v + 26 + 4x$	**4.** $7(8 + w)$ $56 + 7w$	**9.** $2(v + 13 + 2x)$
10. $225 + 25b +$ $125d$	**5.** $20(m + 1)$ $20m + 20$	**10.** $25(9 + b + 5d)$

86 *Chapter 4 Number Theory*

Exercise B Find the GCD of each term.

11. $2x + 10$ 2   **13.** $4m + 4n$ 4   **15.** $3z + 8y$ 1

12. $28 + 7p$ 7   **14.** $15c + 5d$ 5   **16.** $6x + 8$ 2

Exercise C Use the distributive property to factor each expression.

17. $2d + 9$ $2d + 9$ **22.** $13g + 39h$ $13(g + 3h)$

18. $10s + 20$ $10(s + 2)$ **23.** $23b + 4n$ $23b + 4n$

19. $9j + 3$ $3(3j + 1)$ **24.** $6h + 27f$ $3(2h + 9f)$

20. $12t + 18$ $6(2t + 3)$ **25.** $22x + 2y$ $2(11x + y)$

21. $15w + 6y$ $3(5w + 2y)$ **26.** $bc + cd$ $c(b + d)$

PROBLEM SOLVING

Exercise D Use the distributive property to solve each problem.

27. Jarrod has 6 CDs and his sister Nadine has 5. If they both double the number of CDs they have, how many do they have altogether?   22 CDs

28. Carmen has written 3 letters to each of 2 people this month. Last month she wrote 3 letters to each of 4 people. How many letters has she written in the past 2 months?   18 letters

29. Megan earns $18 baby-sitting on Friday night and $24 baby-sitting on Saturday night. The amount she earns in an hour is the GCD of $18 and $24. Find the GCD and factor the expression to show the number of hours she baby-sits each night. $6(3 + 4)$

30. Justin collects sports cards. He has 9 times 25 baseball cards and 9 times 14 basketball cards. How many sports cards does he have?   351 cards

 Suggest that students plan a used-book sale to raise $1,000 for the school library. Every paperback sells for 10¢; every hardcover book sells for 50¢. Have students use the distributive property to complete the following chart showing how many of each kind of book they would need to sell to make $1,000. (Answers are shown in parentheses.)

Paperback	Hardcover
10,000	*(none)*
7,500	*(500)*
(5,000)	1,000
2,500	*(1,500)*
(none)	2,000

Lesson at a Glance

Chapter 4 Lesson 5

Overview This lesson introduces the least common multiple (LCM).

Objectives

- To determine the least common multiple of a pair of numbers
- To use prime factorization as a method of finding the least common multiple

Student Pages 88–91

Teacher's Resource Library **TRL**

Workbook Activity 33

Activity 32

Alternative Activity 32

Mathematics Vocabulary

least common multiple (LCM)
prime factorization

---

1 Warm-Up Activity

Review with students the multiples of several numbers including 2, 3, 6, 7, 8, and 9.

2 Teaching the Lesson

Point out to students that the fractions in the first example are in their simplest forms. However, in order to add the fractions, the denominators must be the same. One way to ensure that the denominators will be the same is to use the least common multiple of the denominators.

Work through the example with students. After finding the LCM in step 3, point out that students now know that to add $\frac{1}{3}$ and $\frac{3}{5}$, each of the denominators must be 15. That is, they will need to multiply the denominator of $\frac{1}{3}$ by 5 (to get 15) and the denominator of $\frac{3}{5}$ by 3 (to get 15). Remind students that whenever they multiply the denominator of a fraction by a number, they must multiply the numerator by the same number in order to keep the value of the fraction the same. Help students recognize that this means they will need to multiply $\frac{1}{3}$ by $\frac{5}{5}$ and $\frac{3}{5}$ by $\frac{3}{3}$. Then work through step 4 with students.

Least common multiple (LCM)
The smallest number divisible by all numbers in a group

Prime factorization
An expression showing a composite number as a product of its prime factors

The **least common multiple**, or LCM, is useful in working with fractions. The least common multiple is the smallest number that is a common multiple of two or more numbers. You find a LCM whenever you add or subtract fractions with unlike denominators.

EXAMPLE 1 Find $\frac{1}{3} + \frac{3}{5}$.

Step 1 Find the LCM of the denominators by first writing several multiples (M) of each denominator.

$M_3 = \{3, 6, 9, 12, 15, 18, 21, 24, 27, 30, 33, ...\}$
$M_5 = \{5, 10, 15, 20, 25, 30, 35, ...\}$

Step 2 Determine common multiples.

$M_3 = \{3, 6, 9, 12, ⑮, 18, 21, 24, 27, ㉚, 33, ...\}$
$M_5 = \{5, 10, ⑮, 20, 25, ㉚, 35, ...\}$

Step 3 Choose the least (smallest) common multiple.

LCM (3, 5) = 15

Step 4 Write equivalent fractions using 15 as the denominator. Then add.

$$\frac{1}{3} + \frac{3}{5} =$$
$$\frac{1}{3} \cdot \frac{5}{5} + \frac{3}{5} \cdot \frac{3}{3} =$$
$$\frac{5}{15} + \frac{9}{15} =$$
$$\frac{14}{15}$$

In this example, the method of writing multiples of a number works well if the numbers are small. If, however, the numbers are large, this method will take too much time. To find the LCM of greater numbers, use **prime factorization.**

Workbook Activity 33

Name _____ Date _____ Period _____ Workbook Activity **33**
Chapter 4, Lesson 5

Least Common Multiple

EXAMPLE Find the least common multiple (LCM) of 48 and 63.

Step 1 Write the prime factorization of each number.

$2 \cdot 2 \cdot 2 \cdot 2 \cdot 3$ or $2^4 \cdot 3$ (prime factorization)

$3 \cdot 3 \cdot 7$ or $3^2 \cdot 7$ (prime factorization)

Step 2 Identify the greatest power of each prime factor.
The greatest power of the prime factor 2 is 2^4.
The greatest power of the prime factor 3 is 3^2.
The greatest power of the prime factor 7 is 7.

Step 3 Find the product.
$2^4 \cdot 3^2 \cdot 7 = 16 \cdot 9 \cdot 7 = 1,008$
The LCM of 48 and 63 is 1,008.

Directions Complete each factor tree.

1. 72

2. 27

Directions Write the prime factorization for each factor tree above.

3. _____ 4. _____

Directions Find each least common multiple (LCM).

5. LCM (4, 12) _____
6. LCM (5, 18) _____
7. LCM (30, 60) _____
8. LCM (16, 35) _____
9. LCM (10, 28) _____
10. LCM (21, 24) _____

...hing. Permission is granted to reproduce for classroom use only. **Mathematics: Pathways**

TRL

Workbook Activity 33

Activity 32

Name _____ Date _____ Period _____ Activity **32**
Chapter 4, Lesson 5

LCM—Least Common Multiple

Directions Find the value of each expression.

1. $3^2 \cdot 2^3$ _____
2. $4^3 \cdot 4^2$ _____
3. $5^2 \cdot 2^3$ _____
4. $10 \cdot 5^3$ _____
5. $6^2 \cdot 4^2$ _____
6. $8^2 \cdot 5$ _____
7. $7^3 \cdot 2$ _____
8. $8^2 \cdot 4 \cdot 2^2$ _____
9. $3^3 \cdot 2^3 \cdot 5$ _____
10. $9 \cdot 4^2 \cdot 6^2$ _____

Directions Find each LCM.

11. (17, 34) _____
12. (3, 63) _____
13. (8, 57) _____
14. (5, 81) _____
15. (14, 38) _____
16. (6, 19) _____
17. (4, 9, 18) _____
18. (16, 21, 32) _____

Directions Solve these problems.

19. A bread-truck driver makes 24 stops a month at a grocery store. A produce driver makes 15 stops at the grocery store. If the two drivers meet today, how many stops will it be before they meet again?

_____

20. A frozen-pizza inspector in a factory checks every twelfth pizza for weight and every fifteenth pizza for proper sealing of the package. What number pizza each day will be the first the inspector will check for both?

_____

©*ACB Publishing. Permission is granted to reproduce for classroom use only.* **Mathematics: Pathways**

TRL

Activity 32

EXAMPLE 2 Find LCM (54, 120).

Step 1 Write the prime factorization of each number.

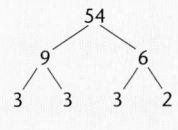 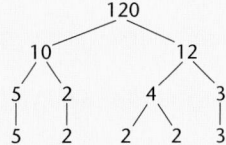

$2 \cdot 3 \cdot 3 \cdot 3$ or $2 \cdot 3^3$ $2 \cdot 2 \cdot 2 \cdot 3 \cdot 5$ or $2^3 \cdot 3 \cdot 5$

Step 2 Identify the greatest power of each prime factor.

The greatest power of the prime factor 2 is 2^3.

The greatest power of the prime factor 3 is 3^3.

The greatest power of the prime factor 5 is 5.

Step 3 Find the product of the greatest power of each prime factor.

$2^3 \cdot 3^3 \cdot 5 = 8 \cdot 27 \cdot 5 = 1{,}080$

LCM (54, 120) = 1,080

Find the LCM of three numbers the same way you find the LCM of two numbers.

EXAMPLE 3 Find LCM (18, 55, 125).

Step 1 Write the prime factorization of each number.

$18 = 2 \cdot 3^2$

$55 = 5 \cdot 11$

$125 = 5^3$

Step 2 Identify the greatest power of each prime factor.

The greatest power of the prime factor 2 is 2.

The greatest power of the prime factor 3 is 3^2.

The greatest power of the prime factor 5 is 5^3.

The greatest power of the prime factor 11 is 11.

Step 3 Find the product of the greatest power of each prime factor.

$2 \cdot 3^2 \cdot 5^3 \cdot 11 = 2 \cdot 9 \cdot 125 \cdot 11 = 24{,}750$

LCM (18, 55, 125) = 24,750

> **Writing About Mathematics**
>
> Is the least common multiple of two different positive numbers always greater than the greatest common divisor of those numbers? Do some examples. Explain.

Number Theory   *Chapter 4*   **89**

Before discussing the prime factorization method to find the LCM, students may need a quick review of primes and powers. Remind them that they know that $10 \cdot 10$ is 10^2 and $10 \cdot 10 \cdot 10$ is 10^3. Point out to students that they can use this knowledge to read the shorthand for raising any number to a power.

Write the following information on the board or overhead projector: $2 \cdot 2 = (2^2)$, $2 \cdot 2 \cdot 2 = (2^3)$, $3 \cdot 3 = (3^2)$, and $3 \cdot 3 \cdot 3 = (3^3)$. Then have a volunteer write the equivalent of $5 \cdot 5 \cdot 5$ (5^3) and $2 \cdot 2 \cdot 2 \cdot 2$ (2^4). When students have grasped this shorthand, point out that prime factorization requires that all the factors of a number be written in the form of prime numbers. Then work through the LCM examples with students.

MANIPULATIVES

M | **Least Common Multiples**

Materials: Cuisenaire Rods, Manipulatives Master 1 (Factor Frame)

Group Practice: Review prime numbers and factoring (Lessons 2 and 3), as necessary. Identify rods that represent prime numbers. Use Example 2, LCM (54, 120). Model 54 with a 6×9 rectangle on the Factor Frame. Place 6- and 9-rods on the left and top of the frame. Because 6 and 9 are not prime numbers, remove the 6×9 rectangle, and repeat the factoring for 6 and 9. When only prime number rods are left, factoring is complete. Repeat for the prime factors of 120. Stack same-value rods to model powers of factors, and write their symbolic equivalents. The greatest power of each prime factor is the highest stack of each. These models represent the factors of the LCM.

Student Practice: Have students use the rods for Exercise A, problems 1–11.

3 Reinforce and Extend

CALCULATOR

Suggest that students use a calculator to find the value of each expression.

$2^5 \cdot 3^5$ *(7,776)*

$2^2 \cdot 3^2 \cdot 5^2 \cdot 7^2$ *(44,100)*

$5^2 \cdot 7^2 \cdot 11^2$ *(148,225)*

MENTAL MATH

Ask students to identify the prime factorization of the following numbers:

12   $(2^2 \cdot 3)$ 24 $(2^3 \cdot 3)$

15   $(3 \cdot 5)$ 36 $(2^2 \cdot 3^2)$

18   $(2 \cdot 3^2)$ 48 $(2^4 \cdot 3)$

CAREER CONNECTION

Identify students who are knowledgeable about models or carpentry, and invite them to speak to the class about how they use mathematics when assembling or building things. Encourage the speakers to stress any computations they might do involving fractions. Encourage the students in the audience to ask questions not only about the role of mathematics but also the nature and appeal of the work.

Exercise A Find each LCM.

1. LCM (8, 12)   24   **7.** LCM (72, 32)   288

2. LCM (10, 18)   90   **8.** LCM (21, 25)   525

3. LCM (13, 3)   39   **9.** LCM (64, 42)   1,344

4. LCM (15, 25)   75   **10.** LCM (5, 14, 18)   630

5. LCM (16, 22)   176   **11.** LCM (45, 30, 9)   90

6. LCM (48, 54)   432   **12.** LCM (100, 144, 250) 18,000

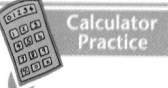 **Calculator Practice**   You can use a calculator to check the prime factorization of any number.

EXAMPLE 4   Suppose you determine that the prime factorization of 48 is $2^4 \cdot 3$.

To check with a calculator, use the $\boxed{y^x}$ or $\boxed{x^y}$ key on your calculator.

Press 2 $\boxed{y^x}$ 4 $\boxed{\times}$ 3 $\boxed{=}$.

The calculator display reads *48*.

Exercise B Use a calculator and find the value of each expression.

13. 5 $\boxed{y^x}$ 3 $\boxed{\times}$ 2 $\boxed{=}$ 250

14. 7 $\boxed{y^x}$ 2 $\boxed{\times}$ 2 $\boxed{y^x}$ 3 $\boxed{=}$ 392

15. $3^3 \cdot 2^2$ 108

16. $11^3 \cdot 5 \cdot 3^2$ 59,895

17. $7^2 \cdot 13 \cdot 19^2$ 229,957

 Math in Your Life

10-Day Week

Did you know that in 1795, the French government actually adopted a 10-day week? Along with it came 10-hour days and 100-minute hours. Then, ten years later, this movement was abandoned. Think about how your life would change on a 10-day week with 10-hour days and 100-minute hours.

90   *Chapter 4*   *Number Theory*

90   *Chapter 4*

Exercise C Solve these problems.

18. Kayla and Tia work at the same business. Kayla has every sixth and seventh day off. Tia has every fourth and fifth day off. If both Kayla and Tia are off work today, what is the minimum number of days until both will be off again on the same day?

19. Marcus and Dan decide to ride their bicycles around a circular track. At the start/finish line, both riders begin riding at the same time. If Marcus completes a lap every 42 seconds, and Dan completes a lap every 48 seconds, in how many minutes will Marcus and Dan cross the start/finish line at the same time?

20. Tiffany earns 8¢ for every newspaper she delivers. Last week she used all of the money she saved from delivering newspapers to give a gift of $10.00 to each of her 2 brothers and 2 sisters. What is the least number of newspapers Tiffany could have delivered to give the gifts?

18. One day; if today represents Kayla's sixth day off and today represents Tia's fourth day off, both Kayla and Tia will be off again tomorrow

19. 5.6 min or 5 min 36 sec

20. 500 newspapers

Lesson at a Glance

Chapter 4 Lesson 6

Overview This lesson shows how to write very large and very small numbers using scientific notation.

Objectives

- To write large and small numbers in scientific notation
- To write the decimal equivalents of numbers in scientific notation

Student Pages 92–93

Teacher's Resource Library (TRL)

Workbook Activity 34

Activity 33

Alternative Activity 33

....

Mathematics Vocabulary

scientific notation

....

1 Warm-Up Activity

Write the following pairs of numbers on the board:

4.6   40.2

460,000,000   4,020,000,000

Ask students which two numbers seem easier to add, subtract, or multiply. Point out that this lesson will show students how to write very large and very small numbers so that they are easier to work with.

2 Teaching the Lesson

Remind students that they can factor large numbers. For example, they can write 2,300 as the product of 230×10, 23×100, or $2.3 \times 1,000$. Also, remind students that they can write 1,000 as 10^3.

Work through the examples with students, pointing out that in scientific notation there is always one digit in the ones place. All other digits are to the right of the decimal point.

Exponents are covered in greater detail in Chapter 9.

Lesson 6   Scientific Notation

Scientific notation
A number written as the product of a number between 1 and 10 and a power of 10   *Any number in scientific notation =* $(1 \leq x < 10)(10^n)$

Recall that you learned about the powers of 10 in Chapter 3. 10^1 equals 10. 10^2 equals 100. 10^3 equals 1,000   and so on.

Did you know that Earth has a weight of about 6.6×10^{21} tons? The number 6.6×10^{21} is written in **scientific notation.** Scientific notation is a way of writing very large numbers.

$$6.6 \times 10^{21} \quad \text{exponent}$$

a number from 1 to 10   power of 10

EXAMPLE 1 Write 43,000,000 in scientific notation.

There is a decimal point at the end of every whole number. The decimal point is usually not written. Move the decimal point so that 43,000,000 becomes a number between 1 and 10.

43,000,000.   →   4.3

Count the number of place values the decimal point was moved.

43,000,000

The decimal point was moved seven places to the left. Seven places to the left means 10^7.

In scientific notation, 43,000,000 becomes 4.3×10^7.

EXAMPLE 2 Write 234,000,000,000 in scientific notation.

Move the decimal point eleven places to the left.

234,000,000,000   →   2.34

In scientific notation, 234,000,000,000 becomes 2.34×10^{11}.

You can also write decimals in scientific notation.

EXAMPLE 3 Write 0.643 in scientific notation.

Move the decimal point so that 0.643 becomes a number between 1 and 10.

0.643   →   6.43

The decimal point was moved one place to the right. When you move the decimal point to the right, the exponent is negative. One place to the right means 10^{-1}.

In scientific notation, 0.643 becomes 6.43×10^{-1}.

Workbook Activity 34

Name _____ Date _____ Period _____ | Workbook Activity 34 / Chapter 4, Lesson 6

Scientific Notation

EXAMPLE   To write large numbers using scientific notation, move the decimal to make a number between 1 and 10.
 Count the number of places the decimal was moved.
 65,000,000 = 6.5 × 10⁷
 7 654 321 (number of places from the decimal point = 7)
 0.658 = 6.58 × 10⁻¹ (number of places from the decimal point = 1)
 If the decimal is moved to the left, the exponent is positive. (10¹)
 If the decimal is moved to the right, the exponent is negative. (10⁻¹)

Directions To write the number in scientific notation: Write how many places each decimal must be moved. Write *left* or *right* to tell in which direction to move the decimal point.

	Number	Places Moved	Direction	Scientific Notation
1.	325,000			
2.	27,800			
3.	105,000,000			
4.	0.653			
5.	0.0325			
6.	0.0000817			
7.	681,000,000,000			
8.	0.000000783			
9.	0.00001818			
10.	86,000,000,000			

Directions Write the number that each example of scientific notation stands for.

11. 6.2×10^2 _____   14. 7.15×10^{-1} _____

12. 8.7×10^4 _____   15. 3.84×10^{-2} _____

13. 3.87×10^6 _____

AGS Publishing. Permission is granted to reproduce for classroom use only.   Mathematics: Pathways

---

Activity 33

Name _____ Date _____ Period _____ | Activity 33 / Chapter 4, Lesson 6

Using Scientific Notation

Directions Write *true* or *false* for each statement. If the statement is false, write the correct expression in scientific notation.

1. $3.5 \times 10^3 = 3,500$ _____
2. $7.3 \times 10^{-2} = 0.073$ _____
3. $8.3 \times 10^5 = 83,000$ _____
4. $6.5 \times 10^3 = 0.00065$ _____
5. $7.8 \times 10^{-4} = 0.0078$ _____
6. $7.68 \times 10^5 = 768,000$ _____
7. $6.72 \times 10^6 = 6,720,000$ _____
8. $5.6 \times 10^{-3} = 0.00056$ _____
9. $9.37 \times 10^{-2} = 0.0937$ _____
10. $4.37 \times 10^7 = 437,000,000$ _____

Directions Write these numbers in scientific notation.

11. 24,000 _____   15. 0.000438 _____
12. 606,000,000 _____   16. 84,000,000,000 _____
13. 0.00347 _____   17. 0.0000947 _____
14. 517,000,000,000 _____   18. 0.000000346 _____

Directions Solve. Write each answer using scientific notation.

19. One city has a population of about 2,840,000 people. Another city has about 3,120,000 people. About how many people live in both cities?

20. The width of one fiber is 0.1016 cm and the width of another fiber is 0.1024 cm. What is the average width of the fibers?

AGS Publishing. Permission is granted to reproduce for classroom use only.   Mathematics: Pathways

Exercise A Write each number in scientific notation.

1. 62,000
  6.2×10^4

2. 524,000
  5.24×10^5

3. 306,000,000
  3.06×10^8

4. 32,000,000
  3.2×10^7

5. 12,000
  1.2×10^4

6. 312,000
  3.12×10^5

7. 6,221,000
  6.221×10^6

8. 800,000,000
  8.0×10^8

9. 33,400
  3.34×10^4

10. 51,000,000,000
  5.1×10^{10}

11. 119,400,000,000
  1.194×10^{11}

12. 445,000,000,000,000
  4.45×10^{14}

Exercise B Write each decimal in scientific notation.

13. 0.005
  5.0×10^{-3}

14. 0.03
  3.0×10^{-2}

15. 0.4402
  4.402×10^{-1}

16. 0.00002089
  2.089×10^{-5}

17. 0.000666
  6.66×10^{-4}

18. 0.00000506
  5.06×10^{-6}

19. 0.0000000004
  4.0×10^{-10}

20. 0.000000000062
  6.2×10^{-11}

Exercise C Write *true* or *false* for each statement.

21. $2.4 \times 10^4 = 24,000$ true

22. $8.416 \times 10^3 = 84,160$ false

23. $7.83 \times 10^5 = 78,300$ false

24. $4.75 \times 10^{-3} = 0.0475$ false

25. $9.3 \times 10^{-1} = 0.93$ true

Build a Model

Scientific notation is used to write the masses in kilograms of the planets in our solar system.

Copy the name and mass of each planet on 9 separate index cards. Then, arrange the cards so that the masses of the planets are ordered from least to greatest.

Mercury	3.30×10^{23}	Saturn	5.69×10^{26}
Venus	4.87×10^{24}	Uranus	8.69×10^{25}
Earth	5.98×10^{24}	Neptune	1.02×10^{26}
Mars	6.42×10^{23}	Pluto	1.32×10^{22}
Jupiter	1.90×10^{27}		

HINT: To order the masses, first look at the powers of 10.

3 **Reinforce and Extend**

IN THE COMMUNITY

Ask students to find out one of the following facts:

- the weight of garbage collected in their community in a day, week, month, or year

- the dollar amount of the yearly school budget

- the volume of water used by their community in an hour, day, or week

Have students write these numbers in both decimal form and scientific notation.

MODELING

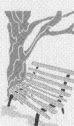

Ask students to divide a sheet of paper into ten even sections. Then provide students with appropriate hands-on materials. Write a number in scientific notation, and ask students to write the digits and display the zeros represented by the exponent. For example, if students receive the number 7.7×10^7, they should write the number 7 in the first two places on the paper and place one item in each of the next six places. Students should count the items and write the number 77,000,000. Alternatively, you can model the number for the students and ask them to write it in scientific notation. Either activity can be done as a class, in groups, or with partners.

LEARNING STYLES

LEP/ESL

Have pairs of students design a storyboard or comic strip that shows, frame by frame, how to write a large number in scientific notation. Suggest that partners choose one of the numbers from Exercise A to illustrate.

Lesson at a Glance

Chapter 4 Application

Overview This lesson provides an application of perfect numbers.

Objectives

- To use an algebraic expression to find perfect numbers
- To identify the factors of a whole number

Student Page 94

Teacher's Resource Library

Application Activity 4

Everyday Math 4

---

1 Warm-Up Activity

Allow students to find the factors of their ages. Each student should share his or her factors with a peer of the same age (to check work) and a peer of a different age (to identify the factors of a different whole number).

2 Teaching the Lesson

Encourage students to share their factoring methods. Some students may use a multiplication chart, and others might make a factor tree. Explain that different methods can be effective.

Explain the order of operations. If this is not followed, students' responses may be incorrect even if the calculations are done correctly.

Have students continue their practice with exponents by changing each variable to a negative and solving the expressions.

COMMON ERROR

Students may forget to include 1 and the number as factors.

Application

Finding Perfect Numbers A perfect number is a whole number that is equal to the sum of its factors, including 1 but *not* the number itself.

EXAMPLE 1 Is 6 a perfect number?

Step 1 Find the factors for 6: 1, 2, 3, 6

Step 2 Is the sum of the factors, *not* including 6, equal to 6?

$$1 + 2 + 3 = 6$$

Yes, 6 is a perfect number.

EXAMPLE 2 Is 8 a perfect number?

Step 1 Find the factors for 8: 1, 2, 4, 8

Step 2 Is the sum of the factors, *not* including 8, equal to 8?

$$1 + 2 + 4 = 7 \quad 7 \neq 8$$

No, 8 is not a perfect number.

Exercise Is the number a perfect number? Write *yes* or *no*. Show your work.

1. 9
2. 4
3. 28
4. 10
5. 25
6. 496 (HINT: You might wish to use a calculator to find the factors of 496.)

94   *Chapter 4   Number Theory*

---

1. Sum of factors: $1 + 3 = 4 \neq 9$
   No, 9 is not a perfect nu[mber]

2. Sum of factors: $1 + 2 = 3 \neq 4$
   No, 4 is not a perfect nu[mber]

3. Sum of factors:
   $1 + 2 + 4 + 7 + 14 = 2[8]$
   Yes, 28 is a perfect numb[er]

4. Sum of factors:
   $1 + 2 + 5 = 8, 8 \neq 10$
   No, 10 is not a perfect n[umber]

5. Sum of factors: $1 + 5 = 6 \neq 25$
   No, 25 is not a perfect n[umber]

6. Sum of factors:
   $1 + 2 + 4 + 8 + 16 + 3[1 +]$
   $62 + 124 + 248 = 496$
   Yes, 496 is a perfect num[ber]

Name _____ Date _____ Period _____ **Application Activity** 4 Chapter 4

Finding Perfect Numbers

EXAMPLE Factor 32 to see if it is a perfect number.

Step 1 List the factors.
1, 2, 4, 8, 16

Step 2 Add the factors.
$1 + 2 + 4 + 8 + 16 = 31$

Step 3 $31 \neq 32$, so 32 is not a perfect number.

Directions Factor the number. Tell whether it is a perfect number. Use a calculator if necessary.

8,128

1. $2 \times$ _____ = 8,128
2. $4 \times$ _____ = 8,128
3. $8 \times$ _____ = 8,128
4. $16 \times$ _____ = 8,128
5. $32 \times$ _____ = 8,128
6. $64 \times$ _____ = 8,128
7. List the factors of 8,128 in order, including 1, from least to greatest. _____
8. Add all the factors of 8,128 (except the number itself). _____
   Explain why 8,128 is or is not a perfect number.

Directions Find the pattern.

9. The first five factors of 8,128, not including 1, are: 2, 4, 8, 16, 32, 64. What is the pattern?

10. The next five factors of 8,128 are: 127, 254, 508, 1,016, 2,032, 4,064. What is the pattern?

©AGS Publishing. Permission is granted to reproduce for classroom use only.   Mathematics: Pathways

  Application Activity 4

Name _____ Date _____ Period _____ **Everyday Math** 4 Chapter 4

Light Goes the Distance

Light travels at a speed of approximately 186,000 miles per second.

The table below gives the length of time it takes light from the sun to reach each of the planets. Use the speed of light and the information in the table to find the distance from the sun to each planet. Then answer the questions below the table. You may use a calculator. Express your answer in scientific notation.

Planet	Time it takes light from sun to reach planet	Distance from sun to planet in miles
Mercury	3.2 minutes	1.
Venus	6.1 minutes	2.
Earth	8.3 minutes	3.
Mars	12.7 minutes	4.
Jupiter	43.2 minutes	5.
Saturn	79.3 minutes	6.
Uranus	2.7 hours	7.
Neptune	4.2 hours	8.
Pluto	5.5 hours	9.

10. What is the distance between Earth and Mars?

11. How long does it take light to travel from Earth to Neptune?

12. A deep space probe has just passed Saturn. How many miles does it need to travel to reach Uranus?

©AGS Publishing. Permission is granted to reproduce for classroom use only.   Mathematics: Pathways

  Everyday Math 4

Chapter 4 REVIEW

Write the letter of the correct answer.

1. Find the greatest common divisor of 15 and 28. C
- **A** 5
- **B** 3
- **C** 1
- **D** 7

2. Find the greatest common divisor of 9 and 27c. D
- **A** c
- **B** 3
- **C** 3c
- **D** 9

3. Find the GCD of $12z + 32y$. A
- **A** 4
- **B** 4zy
- **C** 6zy
- **D** 8

4. Factor $5s + 15$. B
- **A** $3(s + 5)$
- **B** $5(s + 3)$
- **C** $s(1 + 3)$
- **D** $s(5 + 15)$

5. Factor $19b + 7n$. A
- **A** $19b + 7n$
- **B** $7(3b + n)$
- **C** $4(5b + 2n)$
- **D** $bn(19 + 7)$

6. Find the LCM of 24 and 36. B
- **A** 60
- **B** 72
- **C** 36
- **D** 3

7. Find the LCM of 8 and 16. D
- **A** 32
- **B** 24
- **C** 2
- **D** 16

MENTAL MATH

Ask students to do a portion of the factoring mentally. Remind students of the inverse relationship between multiplication and division and to use either or both when finding factors.

MODELING

Students can demonstrate factoring by using small objects to represent the multiplication problems present in the process. Encourage students to check one another's work, and invite each student to share his or her representations with you.

Chapter 4 Review

Each set of problems in the Chapter Review includes an example and solution to illustrate the concept. Use the given examples for reteaching the materials in Chapter 4. For additional practice, refer to the Supplementary Problems for Chapter 4 (pages 438–439).

Chapter 4 Mastery Test

The Teacher's Resource Library includes parallel forms of the Chapter 4 Mastery Test. The difficulty level of the two forms is equivalent. You may wish to use one form as a pretest and the other form as a posttest.

Name _____ Date _____ Period _____

Mastery Test A, Page 1
Chapter 4

Chapter 4 Mastery Test A

Directions Circle the letter of the correct answer.

1. What is the greatest common divisor of 12 and 20?
   - A 3
   - B 12
   - C 5
   - D 4

2. Factor $2x + 6y$.
   - A $2(x + 3y)$
   - B $2 + 6(x + y)$
   - C $2x(3y)$
   - D $6(2x + y)$

3. Simplify $7(m + 4n)$.
   - A $7m + 4n$
   - B $(7m + 4)n$
   - C $7(m + 28n)$
   - D $7m + 28n$

4. Find the least common multiple of (18, 54).
   - A 972
   - B 54
   - C 18
   - D 1

5. Find the least common multiple of the numbers (5, 7, 35).
   - A 7
   - B 1,225
   - C 70
   - D 35

Directions Evaluate each statement. Write *true* or *false*.

6. 2|18 _____
7. 9|90 _____
8. 10|475 _____
9. 6|105 _____
10. 4|218 _____
11. 3|4,002 _____
12. 5|45 _____
13. 3|31 _____
14. 8|328 _____
15. 2|127 _____
16. 10|1,200 _____

Directions Tell whether each number is *prime* or *composite*.

17. 47 _____
18. 117 _____
19. 87 _____

Directions Find the greatest common divisor.

20. 24w; 18w _____
21. 4x + 12 _____
22. 9g + 17h _____
23. 3a, 15a _____
24. 13, 7 _____
25. 9 + 30y _____
26. 10p + 50q _____

©AGS Publishing. Permission is granted to reproduce for classroom use only.

Mathematics: Pathways

Name _____ Date _____ Period _____

Mastery Test A, Page 2
Chapter 4

Chapter 4 Mastery Test A, *continued*

Directions Factor or simplify each expression.

27. $12(d + r)$ _____
28. $15p + 40q$ _____
29. $24g + 8h$ _____
30. $ab + bc$ _____

Directions Find the least common multiple of the numbers.

31. (10, 16) _____
32. (2, 12, 30) _____
33. (8, 9) _____
34. (20, 45) _____

Directions Write each whole number in scientific notation.

35. 5,400 _____
36. 208,000 _____
37. 31,000,000,000 _____

Directions Write each decimal number in scientific notation.

38. 0.007 _____
39. 0.0000081 _____

Directions Solve.

40. Jan and Tyrell are running laps for exercise on a circular track. Tyrell takes 3 minutes (or 180 seconds) to complete a lap around the track. Jan takes $2\frac{1}{2}$ minutes (or 150 seconds). If they are both together now at the start/finish line, how long will it be until they are together again at the start/finish line?

©AGS Publishing. Permission is granted to reproduce for classroom use only.

Mathematics: Pathways

Chapter 4 Mastery Test A

ALTERNATIVE ASSESSMENT

Alternative Assessment items correlate with student Goals for Learning at the beginning of this chapter.

■ **To identify divisible numbers**
Have students use calculators to determine numbers other than those provided in Lesson 1 that are divisible by 2, 3, 5, 6, 8, 9, and 10. Have them discuss how they found these numbers.

■ **To tell prime numbers from composite numbers**
Have students use calculators to determine larger primes by adding consecutive prime numbers. (*Possible answers: 2 + 3 = 5, 23 + 29 + 31 + 41 + 43 + 47 = 214. Have students note that not all consecutive primes added together result in another prime number.*)

■ **To find the greatest common divisor**
Have students find the greatest common divisors of several pairs of objects in their classroom. For example, 24 desks and 6 computer stations would have a greatest common divisor of 6.

■ **To use the distributive property to multiply or factor expressions**
Have students write two algebraic expressions that can be multiplied and two expressions that can be factored. Have students exchange their work with a partner and solve the expression using the distributive property to multiply or factor the expressions.

■ **To find the least common multiple**
Have students find the least common multiple for the following fractions. Then have them find the sum.

$\frac{1}{9} + \frac{1}{3} =$

$\frac{1}{21} + \frac{3}{7} =$

$\frac{1}{4} + \frac{1}{9} =$

$\frac{3}{8} + \frac{2}{7} =$

$\left(\frac{4}{9}, \frac{10}{21}, \frac{13}{36}, \frac{37}{56}\right)$

Evaluate each statement. Write true or false.

Example: 5|15   Solution: 5 • 3 = 15   True

8. 3|19   false   **10.** 7|91   true

9. 4|40   true   **11.** 2|103   false

Is each number divisible by 2? by 3? by 4? by 5? by 6? by 8? by 9? by 10?

Example: 20   Solution: 20 is divisible by 2, 4, 5, and 10.

12. 52   2, 4   **14.** 1,080   2, 3, 4, 5, 6, 8, 9, 10

13. 624   2, 3, 4, 6, 8   **15.** 90,200   2, 4, 5, 8, 10

Decide whether each number is prime or composite.

Example: 123   Solution: 123 is composite because it is divisible by 3 and 41 as well as itself and 1.

16. 113   prime   **18.** 135   composite

17. 124   composite   **19.** 147   composite

Use the distributive property to find the product of each expression.

Example: 2(14 + 3)   Solution: 2 • 14 + 2 • 3 = 28 + 6 = 34

20. 6(3 + 1)   24   **22.** 18(3 + 2h)   54 + 36h

21. 2(12 + 5)   34   **23.** 3(b + 10 + 5x)   3b + 30 + 15x

Find the GCD of each term.

Example: 6b + 8ab   Solution: 6b: ① ② 3 6 ⓑ
8ab: ① ② 4 a ⓑ   GCD = 2b

24. 4d + 12   4   **26.** 9c + 3b   3

25. 14 + 7p   7   **27.** 3g + 11p   1

Name ___ Date ___ Period ___   Mastery Test B, Page 1
Chapter 4

Chapter 4 Mastery Test B

Directions Circle the letter of the correct answer.

1. What is the greatest common divisor of 14 and 21?
   A 2   C 14
   B 7   D 21

2. Factor. 5y + 35x
   A 5(y + 7x)   C y(5 + 7x)
   B (5y + 35)x   D 5(y + x)7

3. Simplify. 5(a + 8b)
   A 5a + 13b   C 5a + 40b
   B (5a + 8)b   D 13a + 40b

4. Find the least common multiple of (22, 33).
   A 11   C 33
   B 55   D 66

5. Find the least common multiple of (8, 16, 64).
   A 8,192   C 128
   B 64   D 96

Directions Evaluate each statement. Write *true* or *false*.

6. 2|20 ___   10. 9|96 ___   14. 8|320 ___

7. 10|495 ___   11. 5|214 ___   15. 2|134 ___

8. 7|70 ___   12. 7|36 ___   16. 7|47 ___

9. 7|49 ___   13. 4|16 ___

Directions Tell whether each number is *prime* or *composite*.

17. 93 ___   19. 7 ___

18. 121 ___

Directions Find the greatest common divisor.

20. 21w, 18w ___   23. 6a, 24a ___   26. 25p + 50q ___

21. 6x + 12 ___   24. 21, 14 ___

22. 9g + 18h ___   25. 7 + 30y ___

Name ___ Date ___ Period ___   Mastery Test B, Page 2
Chapter 4

Chapter 4 Mastery Test B, continued

Directions Factor or simplify each expression.

27. 14(d + e) ___   29. 28q + 7h ___

28. 35p + 70q ___   30. cb + ca ___

Directions Find the least common multiple of the numbers.

31. (10, 14) ___   33. (7, 9) ___

32. (2, 15, 45) ___   34. (20, 35) ___

Directions Write each whole number in scientific notation.

35. 6,400 ___   37. 33,000,000,000 ___

36. 308,000 ___

Directions Write each decimal number in scientific notation.

38. 0.006 ___   39. 0.0000072 ___

Directions Solve.

40. Jan and Tyrell are running laps for exercise on a circular track. Tyrell takes 5 minutes (or 300 seconds) to complete a lap around the track. Jan takes $2\frac{1}{2}$ minutes (or 150 seconds). If they are both together now at the start/finish line, how long will it be until they are together again at the start/finish line?

___

TRL   TRL

Chapter 4 Mastery Test B

Factor.

Example: $9b + 6$ Solution: 9b: ① ③ 9 b
6: ① 2 ③ 6   GCD = 3
$3(3b + 2)$

28. $2x + 8$ $2(x + 4)$ **31.** $18w + 6k$ $6(3w + k)$

29. $8j + 4$ $4(2j + 1)$ **32.** $12g + 36t$ $12(g + 3t)$

30. $10t + 32$ $2(5t + 16)$ **33.** $9f + 24m$ $3(3f + 8m)$

Find each LCM.

Example: (12, 24) Solution: 12: 12 ㉔ 36 ㊸ 60 ㉒
24: ㉔ ㊸ ㉒   LCM (12, 24) = 24

34. LCM (14, 35)   70   **36.** LCM (7, 29)   203

35. LCM (15, 40)   120   **37.** LCM (12, 50)   300

Use a calculator and find the value of each expression.

Example: $3^3 \cdot 5^3$ Solution: 3 $\boxed{y^x}$ 3 $\boxed{\times}$ 5 $\boxed{y^x}$ 3 $\boxed{=}$ 3,375

38. $5 \cdot 7^2$ 245   **40.** $7 \cdot 17 \cdot 19^3$ 816,221

39. $2^6 \cdot 3^3$ 1,728   **41.** $2^3 \cdot 3^3 \cdot 4^3$ 13,824

Write in scientific notation.

Example: 18,000 Solution: 1.8×10^4

42. 26,160,000 2.616×10^7 **44.** 0.0002402 2.402×10^{-4}

43. 8,900,000,000 8.9×10^9 **45.** 0.0428 4.28×10^{-2}

Test-Taking Tip

Don't confuse *factor* with *multiple*. Remember that multiples can go on infinitely, while there is an exact set of numbers for factors.

Number Theory   **97**

Planning Guide

Rational Numbers and Fractions

Lesson		Student Pages	Vocabulary	Practice Exercises	Problem Solving	Try This	Solutions Key
				Student Text Lesson			
1	Proper Fractions	100–101	✔	✔	101		✔
2	Improper Fractions and Mixed Numbers	102–105	✔	✔	105		✔
3	Equivalent Fractions	106–109	✔	✔		109	✔
4	Simplest Form	110–111		✔	111		✔
5	Comparing and Ordering Fractions	112–115		✔	115	115	✔
6	Fractions—Like Denominators	116–119		✔			✔
7	Fractions—Unlike Denominators	120–123		✔			✔
8	Subtracting Fractions with Regrouping	124–125		✔	125		✔
9	Multiplying Fractions and Mixed Numbers	126–127		✔			✔
10	Dividing Fractions and Mixed Numbers	128–131	✔	✔	131	131	✔
Application	Moving with the Beat	132		✔			✔

Chapter Activities

Teacher's Resource Library
Estimation Exercise 5: Estimating Using
  Mixed Numbers
Application Activity 5: Moving with
  the Beat
Everyday Math 5: Survey Says
Community Connection 5: A Fractional
  Market

Teacher's Edition
Chapter 5 Project

Assessment Options

Student Text
Chapter 5 Review

Teacher's Resource Library
Chapter 5 Mastery Tests A and B

Teacher's Edition
Chapter 5 Alternative Assessments

Estimation Activity	Math in Your Life	Technology Connection	Writing About Mathematics	Build a Model	Calculator Practice	Online Connection	Common Error	Applications Home, Career, Community	Mental Math	Manipulatives	Calculator	Group Problem Solving	Modeling	Knowing Your Students	Auditory/Verbal	Visual/Spatial	Logical/Mathematical	Body/Kinesthetic	Interpersonal/Group Learning	LEP/ESL	Activities	Alternate Activities	Workbook Activities	Self-Study Guide
										101		101							101		34	34	35	✔
		105								103		105			104	104					35	35	36	✔
					109		107				109							107	108		36	36	37	✔
							110	111		111		111									37	37	38	✔
							112			113		115				113				114	38	38	39	✔
117	119		119				117		119	117									118	118	39	39	40	✔
		123					121	123		121					122				122		40	40	41	✔
										125	125					125				125	41	41	42	✔
			127			127				127	127								127		42	42	43	✔
			130	130		130	130					131			129						43	43	44–45	✔
							132						133	133						132				✔

Software Options

Skill Track Software

Use the Skill Track Software for *Mathematics: Pathways* for additional reinforcement of this chapter. The software provides multiple-choice assessment items for students to access by computer.

Solutions Key

Use the Solutions Key with this chapter to help students who may need additional assistance. The Solutions Key CD provides solutions for every exercise in the student edition.

Other Resources

Alternative Activities

The Teacher's Resource Library (TRL) contains a set of worksheets written at a second-grade reading level called Alternative Activities. They cover the same content as the regular Activities.

Manipulatives

See the Manipulative activities in this chapter for hands-on modeling of the content. The following TRL pages can also be used:

Manipulatives Master 1 (Factor Frame)
Manipulatives Master 2 (Blank Number Lines)
Cuisenaire Rods

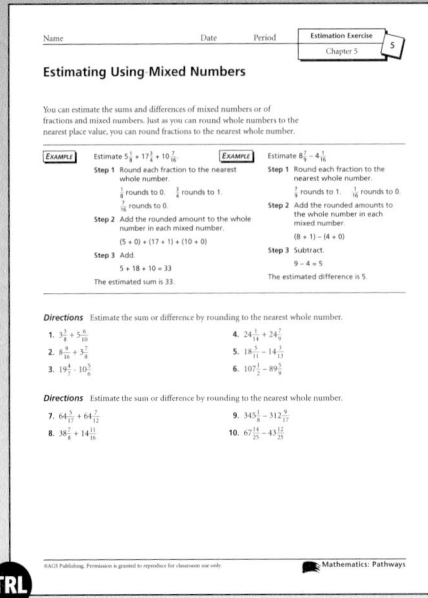

Estimation Exercise 5

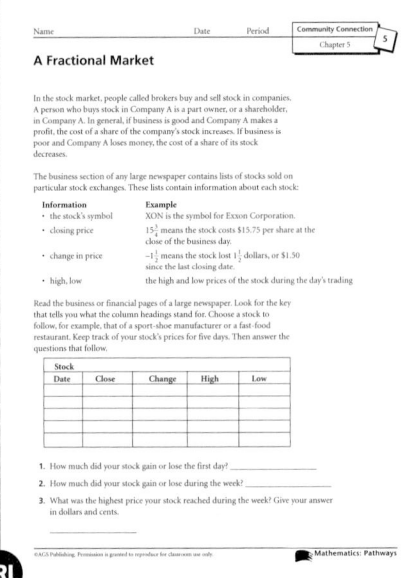

Community Connection 5

5 Rational Numbers and Fractions

Does the picture of the pizza look so good that you feel like saying, "I'll take two slices, please!" How many times have you said that in the past at your favorite pizza place? Did you know that you were "speaking" fraction?

Fractions are numbers that stand for part of a whole or part of a set. These numbers are used to specify the portions of ingredients in a recipe (half a cup, three quarters of a teaspoon). They are used for timing of events (quarter of an hour, half a day) and shopping discounts (half off regular price). Fractions, used as ratios, compare quantities with the same units. As a rate, they compare quantities with different units. Fractions can represent numbers smaller than 1, such as $\frac{1}{3}$, or greater than 1 such as $\frac{7}{5}$ or $1\frac{2}{5}$.

In Chapter 5, you will identify and use fractions and mixed numbers.

Goals for Learning

◆ To identify proper and improper fractions and mixed numbers

◆ To write equivalent fractions

◆ To express fractions in simplest form

◆ To compare and order fractions

◆ To add and subtract fractions and mixed numbers with like or unlike denominators

◆ To multiply and divide fractions and mixed numbers

99

Introducing the Chapter

Review the purpose of decimals, and encourage students to compare decimals and *fractions.* Model a fraction, and discuss the numerator and the denominator (both *rational numbers*). Review the text accompanying the Chapter Opener. Ask students to identify the fraction two slices represent of the whole pizza and the numerator and denominator of the fraction. Tell students that this chapter will allow them to use different types of fractions in different operations.

CHAPTER PROJECT

Suggest that small groups of students complete a project on fractions. Have the groups choose one of the following topics or a topic of their own.

• *Survey* Students survey their school's population about likes and dislikes. They prepare a television news brief, including narrative and pie graphs, to present their results.

• *Web Site* Students prepare a draft of AllAboutFractions.edu, a Web site that includes information about proper and improper fractions, equivalent fractions, and arithmetic operations involving fractions.

TEACHER'S RESOURCE

The AGS Publishing Teaching Strategies in Math Transparencies may be used with this chapter. They add an interactive dimension to expand and enhance the program content.

CAREER INTEREST INVENTORY

The AGS Publishing Harrington-O'Shea Career Decision-Making System-Revised (CDM) may be used with this chapter. Students can use the CDM to explore their interests and identify careers. The CDM defines career areas that are indicated by students' responses on the inventory.

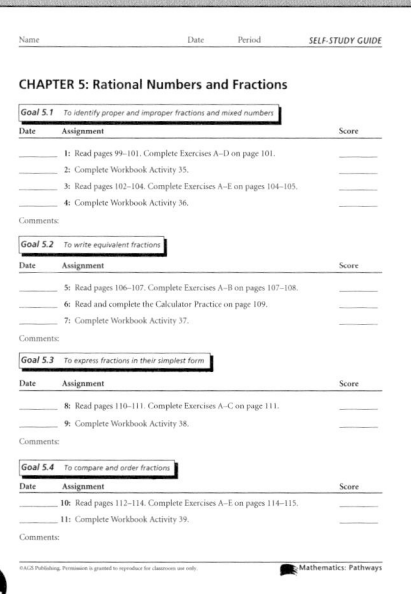

Chapter 5 Self-Study Guide

Chapter 5 Lesson 1

Overview This lesson introduces fractions in which the numerator is less than the denominator.

Objectives
- To identify proper fractions
- To illustrate proper fractions

Student Pages 100–101

Teacher's Resource Library **TRL**

Workbook Activity 35

Activity 34

Alternative Activity 34

Mathematics Vocabulary

proper fraction

---

1 Warm-Up Activity

Engage students in a discussion about eating a piece of a pie or cake. Ask them to list ways they can describe what part of the pie was eaten and what part of the pie remains. Record their suggestions on the board. Reinforce responses suggesting fractions.

2 Teaching the Lesson

Help students recognize that there are two steps in naming or identifying a fraction. Draw a circle divided in fourths on the overhead projector or on the board. Indicate that students must first determine the number of equal-sized parts in the whole. Stress that the number of parts in the whole is always the denominator of the fraction. Then shade three parts of the circle. Tell students that the number of shaded parts is the numerator of a fraction. Have a volunteer write a sentence that uses a fraction to describe the shaded parts of the circle. *(Three-fourths of the circle is shaded.)* Have another volunteer describe the unshaded parts of the circle. *(One-fourth of the circle is not shaded.)* Point out that the two fractions describe different parts of the circle, yet each has a denominator of 4—the number of parts in the whole.

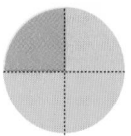

Proper fraction

A fraction in which the numerator is less than the denominator

Remember that the numerator of a fraction is the number above the fraction bar, and the denominator is the number below the fraction bar.

Fractions can be used to represent part of a whole or part of a set.

In this whole circle, three of four equal parts are yellow. The fraction $\frac{3}{4}$ can be used to describe the number of parts that are yellow.

$\dfrac{3 \leftarrow \text{number of yellow parts}}{4 \leftarrow \text{total number of parts}}$

In this set of shapes, two out of five shapes are squares. The fraction $\frac{2}{5}$ can be used to describe the part of the set that is made up of squares.

$\dfrac{2 \leftarrow \text{number of squares in set}}{5 \leftarrow \text{total number of shapes in set}}$

In any fraction, the number above the fraction bar is the numerator of the fraction. The number below the fraction bar is the denominator of the fraction.

$\dfrac{3}{4} \begin{array}{l} \leftarrow\text{numerator} \\ \leftarrow\text{denominator} \end{array}$ $\dfrac{2}{5} \begin{array}{l} \leftarrow\text{numerator} \\ \leftarrow\text{denominator} \end{array}$

The fraction $\frac{3}{4}$ is read "three-fourths," and the fraction $\frac{2}{5}$ is read "two-fifths."

A fraction of the form $\frac{a}{b}$ where $0 \leq a < b$ is a **proper fraction.** In other words, a proper fraction is a fraction in which the numerator is less than the denominator.

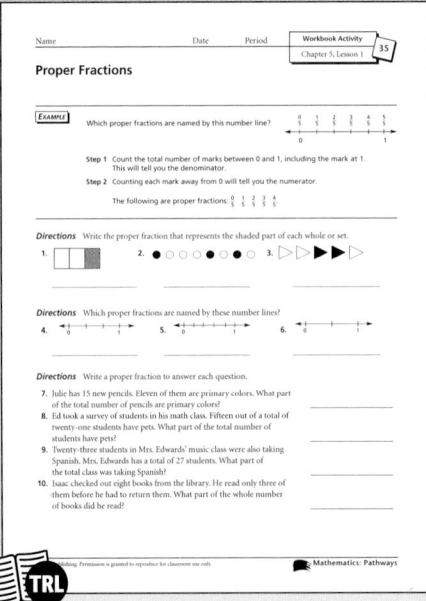

Workbook Activity 35

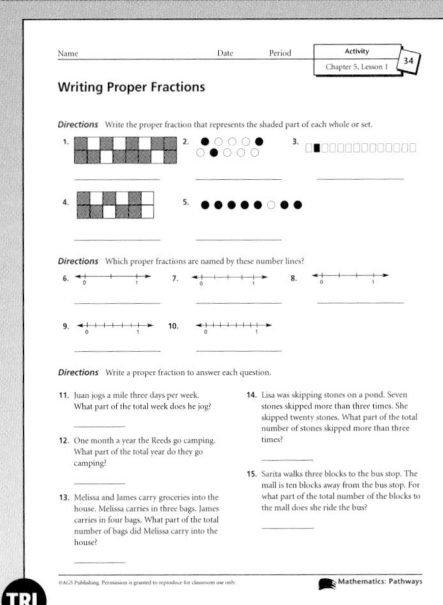

Activity 34

EXAMPLE 1 Which proper fractions are named by this number line?

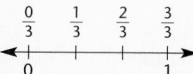

$$\frac{0}{3} \quad \frac{1}{3} \quad \frac{2}{3} \quad \frac{3}{3}$$

Step 1 Recall that in any proper fraction, the numerator is less than the denominator.

Step 2 Choose the fractions in which the numerator is less than the denominator. The proper fractions $\frac{0}{3} \quad \frac{1}{3} \quad \frac{2}{3}$ are named by the number line.

Exercise A Write the proper fraction that represents the shaded part of each whole or set.

1. 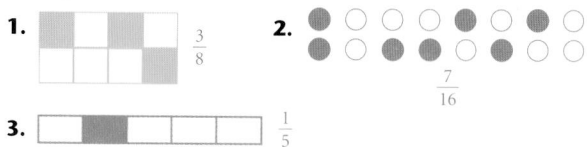 $\frac{3}{8}$

2. $\frac{7}{16}$

3. 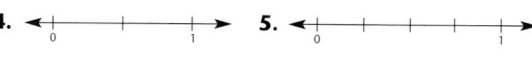 $\frac{1}{5}$

Exercise B Which proper fractions are named by these number lines?

4.   **5.**

Exercise C

6. Write five different proper fractions that have a denominator of 8.

7. Draw a picture or diagram in which $\frac{7}{10}$ of a set is shaded.

8. Draw a picture or diagram in which $\frac{3}{4}$ of a whole is *not* shaded.

4. $\frac{0}{2}, \frac{1}{2}$

5. $\frac{0}{4}, \frac{1}{4}, \frac{2}{4}, \frac{3}{4}$

6. Sample answer: $\frac{2}{8}, \frac{3}{8}, \frac{4}{8}, \frac{5}{8}, \frac{6}{8}$

7. $\frac{7}{10}$ of a set should be shaded

8. $\frac{3}{4}$ of a whole should not be shaded

PROBLEM SOLVING

Exercise D Solve each problem.

9. Jamal lives 6 blocks from school. He has walked 5 blocks. What part of the total distance has he walked?
$\frac{5}{6}$ of the total distance

10. Cathy wants to read all 20 of her favorite author's books. So far she has read 13 of them. What part of the total number has she read?
$\frac{13}{20}$ of the books

 Proper Fractions

Materials: Cuisenaire Rods, Manipulatives Master 2 (Blank Number Lines)

Group Practice: Label a number line so that each unit represents $\frac{1}{4}$ and four units represent a whole. Model $\frac{3}{4}$ by placing a 3-rod on the number line. Write the symbolic equivalent of the model, and discuss the numerator and denominator. Model several other fractions with various denominators, labeling a new number line as necessary.

Student Practice: Have students label one number line so that each unit represents $\frac{1}{2}$, another $\frac{1}{3}$, and so on. Then have students sketch models of fractions (by shading the number line) and write the symbolic equivalent of each sketch.

3 **Reinforce and Extend**

LEARNING STYLES

 **LEP/ESL**
Have pairs of students prepare a denominator dictionary. Suggest that they record the singular and plural words used to describe fractions with denominators of 2, 3, 4, 5, 8, 10, 12, and 16.

GROUP PROBLEM SOLVING

 Suggest that students work in small groups to develop five fractions describing the students at their school. Prime their responses by asking questions such as these: What fraction of the students are girls? wear glasses? have long hair? own pets? and so on. Have students illustrate their categories. Display students' work, and have the class vote on the most inventive, unusual, and useful descriptions.

Chapter 5 Lesson 2

Overview This lesson introduces fractions in which the numerator is greater than the denominator as well as mixed numbers.

Objectives

- To distinguish proper and improper fractions
- To write improper fractions as mixed numbers
- To convert mixed numbers to improper fractions

Student Pages 102–105

Teacher's Resource Library

Workbook Activity 36

Activity 35

Alternative Activity 35

....

Mathematics Vocabulary

improper fraction
mixed number
rational number

....

1 Warm-Up Activity

Write a series of proper fractions on the board. Ask a volunteer to rewrite the fractions so that the numerator becomes the denominator. Have students discuss whether the newly formed number is a proper fraction or even a fraction at all. Encourage all responses.

2 Teaching the Lesson

Stress to students that mixed numbers, as well as improper and proper fractions, are all rational numbers because they can be written in the form $\frac{a}{b}$, where $b \neq 0$.

Draw two circles on the board or overhead projector. Divide each circle in fourths. Stress that the number of parts in the whole is always the denominator of the fraction. Ask a volunteer to name the denominator of a fraction describing these circles. Then shade one entire circle and one part of the second circle. Point out that the number of shaded parts is the numerator of a fraction. Have a volunteer write a sentence that uses

---

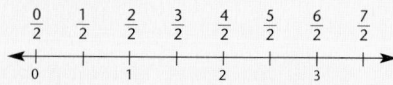

Lesson 2 Improper Fractions and Mixed Numbers

Improper fraction
A fraction in which the numerator is greater than or equal to the denominator

Mixed number
A whole number and a proper fraction

Rational number
Any number that can be represented by $\frac{a}{b}$ where a and b are integers and $b \neq 0$

A fraction of the form $\frac{a}{b}$ where $0 < b \leq a$ is an **improper fraction**. In other words, an improper fraction is a fraction in which the numerator is greater than or equal to the denominator.

EXAMPLE 1 What improper fractions are named by this number line?

$$\frac{0}{2} \quad \frac{1}{2} \quad \frac{2}{2} \quad \frac{3}{2} \quad \frac{4}{2} \quad \frac{5}{2} \quad \frac{6}{2} \quad \frac{7}{2}$$

Step 1 Recall that in any improper fraction, the numerator is greater than or equal to the denominator.

Step 2 Choose the fractions in which the numerator is greater than or equal to the denominator.

The improper fractions
$$\frac{2}{2} \quad \frac{3}{2} \quad \frac{4}{2} \quad \frac{5}{2} \quad \frac{6}{2} \quad \frac{7}{2}$$
are named by the number line.

Improper fractions, and proper fractions that you studied earlier, are examples of **rational numbers.** A rational number is any number that can be represented by $\frac{a}{b}$ where a and b are integers and $b \neq 0$.

The following are examples of rational numbers.
$$\frac{0}{4} \quad \frac{5}{6} \quad \frac{14}{14} \quad \frac{32}{20} \quad \frac{-5}{10} \quad \frac{10}{-11} \quad -\frac{1}{2}$$

Mixed numbers are also examples of rational numbers. A mixed number is the sum of a whole number and a proper fraction. Mixed numbers belong to the set of rational numbers because mixed numbers can be expressed as improper fractions.

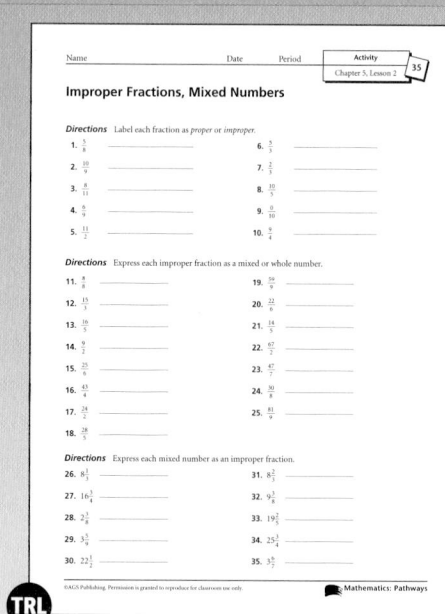

Workbook Activity 36   **Activity 35**

EXAMPLE 2 Express $\frac{11}{2}$ as a mixed number.

Step 1 In any fraction, the fraction bar (or line segment) that separates the numerator from the denominator means "divide." To express an improper fraction as a mixed number, divide the numerator by the denominator.

Step 2 Divide.

$$\frac{11}{2} = 11 \div 2 = 2\overline{\smash{\big)}11} \atop {\underline{-10} \atop 1}$$

Step 3 List the remainder as a fraction of the divisor 2.

$$\frac{11}{2} = 11 \div 2 = 2\overline{\smash{\big)}11} = 5\frac{1}{2} \atop {\underline{-10} \atop 1}$$

Sometimes when you change an improper fraction to a mixed number, the remainder will be zero. When this happens, the answer is a whole number.

EXAMPLE 3 Express $\frac{45}{5}$ as a mixed number.

Step 1 To express an improper fraction as a mixed number, divide the numerator by the denominator.

Step 2 Divide.

$$\frac{45}{5} = 45 \div 5 = 5\overline{\smash{\big)}45} \atop {\underline{-45} \atop 0}$$

Step 3 Since the remainder is zero, the answer is a whole number.

$$\frac{45}{5} = 45 \div 5 = 5\overline{\smash{\big)}45} = 9 \atop {\underline{-45} \atop 0}$$

a fraction to describe the shaded parts of the circles. (*Five-fourths of the circles are shaded.*)

Help students understand that even though improper fractions have numerators greater than the denominators, the following statements are still true: The denominator tells the number of equal parts in (one) whole, and the numerator tells the number of shaded parts.

MANIPULATIVES

 Improper Fractions and Mixed Numbers

Materials: Cuisenaire Rods, Manipulatives Master 2 (Blank Number Lines)

Group Practice: Begin with Example 2 to express $\frac{11}{2}$ as a mixed number. Label a line in $\frac{1}{2}$ units with improper fractions through $\frac{12}{2}$. Explain that the expression $\frac{11}{2}$ means eleven $\frac{1}{2}$ units and that on this number line, a cube (1-rod) represents a $\frac{1}{2}$ unit and a 2-rod represents a whole unit. Place 11 cubes on the number line, and write the symbolic equivalent. Next, place a 2-rod over each pair of cubes. Explain that two $\frac{1}{2}$ units are the same as one whole unit. Write the symbolic equivalent of this mixed number model. Repeat with additional examples.

To reverse the process, use Example 4 to express $13\frac{1}{2}$ as an improper fraction. Label a number line in $\frac{1}{2}$ units. Place 13 2-rods and one cube on the number line. Place two cubes over each 2-rod, and count the cubes to find the improper fraction. Write the symbolic equivalent for each step, reminding students that the values of the rods change according to how the number line is labeled.

Student Practice: Have students use the rods for Exercise C, problems 11–20; Exercise D, problems 21–27; and Exercise E, problems 31–35.

It is also possible to express a mixed number as an improper fraction.

EXAMPLE 4 Express $13\frac{1}{2}$ as an improper fraction.

Step 1 To express a mixed number as an improper fraction, multiply the whole number by the denominator of the fraction.

$$13\frac{1}{2} \quad 13 \cdot 2 = 26$$

Step 2 Add the numerator to the product you found in Step 1.

$$26 + 1 = 27$$

Step 3 Write the sum from Step 2 as the numerator of an improper fraction. Write the denominator of the mixed number as the denominator of your improper fraction.

$$13\frac{1}{2} = \frac{27}{2}$$

Exercise A Use the number line below for problems 1 and 2.

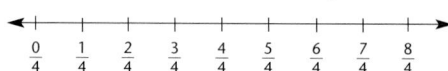

1. $\frac{4}{4}, \frac{5}{4}, \frac{6}{4}, \frac{7}{4}, \frac{8}{4}$ **1.** Name the improper fractions shown by the number line.

2. $\frac{0}{4}, \frac{1}{4}, \frac{2}{4}, \frac{3}{4}, \frac{4}{4}, \frac{5}{4},$ **2.** Name the rational numbers shown by the number line.
$\frac{6}{4}, \frac{7}{4}, \frac{8}{4}$

Exercise B Label each fraction *proper* or *improper*.

3. $\frac{3}{8}$ proper   **7.** $\frac{13}{16}$ proper

4. $\frac{4}{1}$ improper   **8.** $\frac{0}{3}$ proper

5. $\frac{5}{12}$ proper   **9.** $\frac{23}{6}$ improper

6. $\frac{38}{32}$ improper   **10.** $\frac{7}{10}$ proper

Writing About Mathematics

Can the sum of a proper fraction and an improper fraction ever be exactly 1? Explain.

Exercise C Express each improper fraction as a mixed or whole number.

11. $\frac{2}{2}$ 1

12. $\frac{15}{2}$ $7\frac{1}{2}$

13. $\frac{11}{4}$ $2\frac{3}{4}$

14. $\frac{14}{9}$ $1\frac{5}{9}$

15. $\frac{29}{10}$ $2\frac{9}{10}$

16. $\frac{8}{3}$ $2\frac{2}{3}$

17. $\frac{19}{12}$ $1\frac{7}{12}$

18. $\frac{24}{5}$ $4\frac{4}{5}$

19. $\frac{31}{8}$ $3\frac{7}{8}$

20. $\frac{19}{6}$ $3\frac{1}{6}$

Exercise D Express each mixed number as an improper fraction.

21. $4\frac{1}{3}$ $\frac{13}{3}$

22. $7\frac{1}{4}$ $\frac{29}{4}$

23. $12\frac{1}{2}$ $\frac{25}{2}$

24. $2\frac{5}{6}$ $\frac{17}{6}$

25. $9\frac{3}{8}$ $\frac{75}{8}$

26. $15\frac{7}{10}$ $\frac{157}{10}$

27. $8\frac{5}{16}$ $\frac{133}{16}$

28. $20\frac{4}{5}$ $\frac{104}{5}$

29. $100\frac{1}{20}$ $\frac{2,001}{20}$

30. $2\frac{4}{9}$ $\frac{22}{9}$

PROBLEM SOLVING

Exercise E Solve each problem. Give each answer as a whole or mixed number.

31. Eric has 31 golf balls that he bought in sets of 9. How many sets of golf balls does Eric still have? $3\frac{4}{9}$ or 3 complete sets

32. Maria has 15 sets of earrings. Each set has 2 earrings. How many earrings does she have? 30 earrings

33. Lali is adding 29 photographs to her photo album. How many sheets of the album will she use if each sheet holds 6 photographs? $4\frac{5}{6}$ or 5 sheets

34. Leroy is making word cards for Spanish class. He needs 35 cards. If he cuts 8 cards from each sheet of paper, how many sheets will he use? $4\frac{3}{8}$ or 5 sheets

35. Anton pours 17 ounces of juice into 3 glasses. If he pours the same amount of juice into each glass, how many ounces of juice will be in each glass? $5\frac{2}{3}$ ounces

GROUP PROBLEM SOLVING

Pose the following problems for small groups of students to solve:

Chopin School is so over-crowded that the school board is planning to use portable classrooms until the new wing is built. Each portable classroom has facilities for 20 students. How many portable classrooms will the school need to make room for 235 students? How many portable classrooms will the school board need to buy?

$(11\frac{15}{20}; 12)$

The portable classrooms are assembled in clusters of four. How many clusters will Chopin School have?

$(\frac{12}{4}$ or 3$)$

Have students investigate overcrowding at their own or a nearby school. Suggest that they find out whether any classes are held in rooms that were not originally designed for classroom use. Then have them determine how many students might use a portable classroom. Finally, have them compute how many portable classrooms the school might use.

Lesson at a Glance

Chapter 5 Lesson 3

Overview This lesson presents equivalent fractions.

Objectives
- To identify equivalent fractions
- To write equivalent fractions

Student Pages 106–109

Teacher's Resource Library **TRL**

Workbook Activity 37

Activity 36

Alternative Activity 36

Mathematics Vocabulary

Fundamental Law of Fractions

---

1 Warm-Up Activity

Draw three circles on the board or overhead projector. Divide one into halves, one into fourths, and one into eighths. Shade one-half of each circle. Ask students to describe each of the shaded areas. Prompt with questions such as these: How many parts of the whole are shaded? How do the shaded parts compare with one another? Lead students to the generalization that $\frac{1}{2}$, $\frac{2}{4}$, and $\frac{4}{8}$ can all represent the same amount of a whole.

2 Teaching the Lesson

Point out to students that one way to find an equivalent fraction is to multiply by 1 written in fraction form. Ask several volunteers to come to the board and complete the following number sentence with a fraction:

$$1 = \frac{\blacksquare}{\blacksquare}$$

Pose the following problem: Suppose that each student in the class supplies a different fraction. Will all the forms of 1 have been shown? Ask students to explain why. (*No; there is an infinite number of numbers that can be used.*)

Fundamental Law of Fractions

The value of a fraction does not change if its numerator and its denominator are multiplied by the same number

Study these figures.

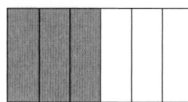 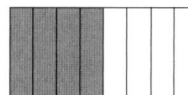

In the figure at the left, three of six congruent parts (or $\frac{3}{6}$) of the figure are shaded. In the figure at the right, four of eight congruent parts (or $\frac{4}{8}$) of the figure are shaded. Although the fractions $\frac{3}{6}$ and $\frac{4}{8}$ do not look alike, both fractions represent the same rational number. Fractions that name the same rational number are equivalent fractions.

For any rational number, there are an infinite number of equivalent fractions. You can create equivalent fractions by applying the **Fundamental Law of Fractions.**

Remember that an equivalent fraction is a fraction that has the same value as another fraction.

> **Fundamental Law of Fractions**
>
> For any rational number $\frac{a}{b}$ and any whole number $c \neq 0$,
>
> $$\frac{a}{b} = \frac{ac}{bc}.$$
>
> This is true because $\frac{c}{c} = 1$, which is the same as multiplying by 1.

The Fundamental Law of Fractions states that the value of a fraction does not change if its numerator and its denominator are multiplied by the same number.

EXAMPLE 1 Write an equivalent fraction for $\frac{2}{3}$.

Apply the Fundamental Law of Fractions—choose a number, then multiply the numerator and the denominator of $\frac{2}{3}$ by that number.

$$\frac{2}{3} \cdot \frac{5}{5} = \frac{10}{15}$$

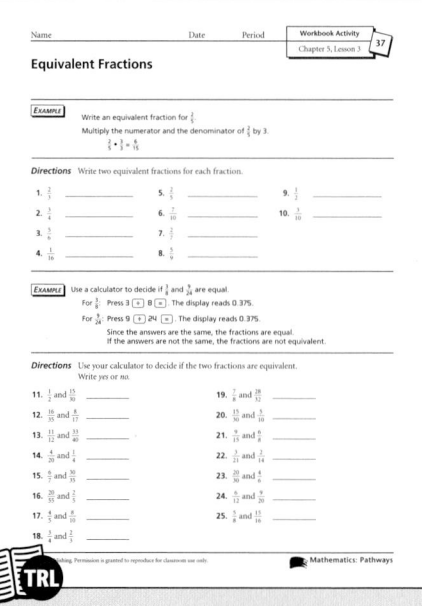

Workbook Activity 37

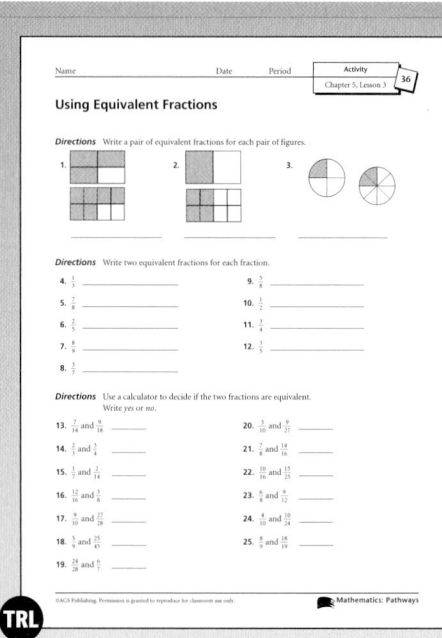

Activity 36

The fractions $\frac{2}{3}$ and $\frac{10}{15}$ are equivalent fractions. In this example, the numerator and denominator were multiplied by 5. You could have chosen a different number.

EXAMPLE 2 Write an equivalent fraction for $\frac{2}{3}$.

Multiply the numerator and the denominator of $\frac{2}{3}$ by 4.

$$\frac{2}{3} \cdot \frac{4}{4} = \frac{8}{12}$$

The following fractions are equivalent fractions.

$$\frac{2}{3} \quad \frac{10}{15} \quad \frac{8}{12}$$

Whenever you must write equivalent fractions, choose any number you want to multiply by. Just remember to multiply the numerator and the denominator by the number you chose.

Exercise A Write two equivalent fractions for each fraction.

1. $\frac{1}{3}$ $\frac{2}{6}$ and $\frac{3}{9}$ 6. $\frac{5}{16}$ $\frac{10}{32}$ and $\frac{15}{48}$

2. $\frac{5}{6}$ $\frac{10}{12}$ and $\frac{15}{18}$ 7. $\frac{3}{8}$ $\frac{6}{16}$ and $\frac{9}{24}$

3. $\frac{7}{8}$ $\frac{14}{16}$ and $\frac{21}{24}$ 8. $\frac{1}{6}$ $\frac{2}{12}$ and $\frac{3}{18}$

4. $\frac{2}{5}$ $\frac{4}{10}$ and $\frac{6}{15}$ 9. $\frac{9}{10}$ $\frac{18}{20}$ and $\frac{27}{30}$

5. $\frac{3}{10}$ $\frac{6}{20}$ and $\frac{9}{30}$ 10. $\frac{11}{16}$ $\frac{22}{32}$ and $\frac{33}{48}$

Sample answers shown for 1–10.

3 **Reinforce and Extend**

Exercise B Write two equivalent fractions for each pair of figures.

11.

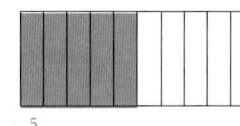

$\frac{1}{2}$ and $\frac{5}{10}$

12.

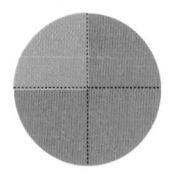 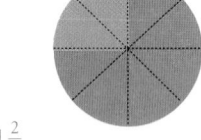

$\frac{1}{4}$ and $\frac{2}{8}$

13.

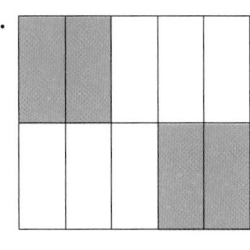 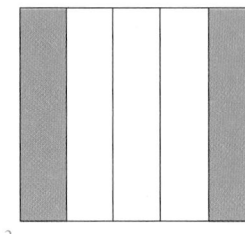

$\frac{4}{10}$ and $\frac{2}{5}$

14.

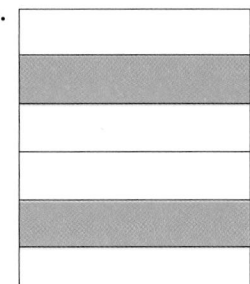 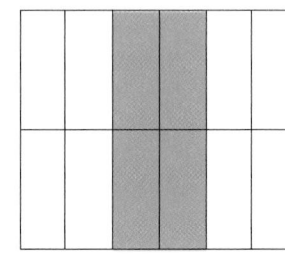

$\frac{2}{6}$ and $\frac{4}{12}$

108 Chapter 5   *Rational Numbers and Fractions*

 **Calculator Practice**

You can use a calculator to check if two or more fractions are equivalent fractions.

EXAMPLE 3 Are $\frac{3}{4}$ and $\frac{6}{8}$ equivalent fractions?

Since a fraction bar (the line segment that separates the numerator from the denominator) in any fraction means "divide," use a calculator to divide each fraction.

$\frac{3}{4}$ Press *3* ÷ *4* =. The display reads *0.75*.

$\frac{6}{8}$ Press *6* ÷ *8* =. The display reads *0.75*.

Since the fractions name the same decimal value, the fractions are equivalent.

Exercise C Use a calculator to decide if each pair of fractions are equivalent. Write *yes* or *no*.

15. $\frac{1}{5}$ $\frac{10}{50}$ yes

16. $\frac{4}{20}$ $\frac{1}{4}$ no

17. $\frac{7}{9}$ $\frac{2}{3}$ no

18. $\frac{1}{6}$ $\frac{8}{48}$ yes

19. $\frac{7}{19}$ $\frac{14}{39}$ no

20. $\frac{4}{7}$ $\frac{20}{35}$ yes

 Try This

Write 3 fractions on a sheet of paper. Exchange papers with a partner. Write 5 equivalent fractions for each fraction your partner wrote.

Answers will vary.

Try This

Encourage students to check their answers by drawing a picture to represent each of the equivalent fractions.

CALCULATOR

 Some calculators have a $\boxed{1/x}$ key. Students can use this key to find the value of all fractions with a given denominator. For example, to find the value of $\frac{3}{16}$:

Press *16*.

Press $\boxed{1/x}$.

The display reads *0.0625*.

Press $\boxed{\times}$ *3* $\boxed{=}$.

The display reads *0.1875*.

Encourage students to use this method to decide whether the fractions in the following pairs are equivalent.

$\frac{3}{64}$ $\frac{6}{128}$ *(yes)*

$\frac{5}{8}$ $\frac{42}{64}$ *(no)*

$\frac{12}{36}$ $\frac{2}{6}$ *(yes)*

$\frac{14}{16}$ $\frac{42}{48}$ *(yes)*

$\frac{6}{40}$ $\frac{3}{20}$ *(yes)*

Lesson at a Glance

Chapter 5 Lesson 4

Overview This lesson discusses how to present fractions in their simplest forms (lowest terms).

Objective

■ To express fractions in their simplest forms

Student Pages 110–111

Teacher's Resource Library TRL

Workbook Activity 38

Activity 37

Alternative Activity 37

1 Warm-Up Activity

Discuss with students the many ways in which they can write the rational number 1. Point out that by convention we write it in the simplest possible form. Ask students to conjecture why this is so. Help them generalize their ideas to other fractions, leading to the understanding that, by convention, we express all fractions in their lowest terms.

2 Teaching the Lesson

Students may benefit from writing out the complete factorizations of 9 and 21.

9: $1 \times 9, 3 \times 3, 9 \times 1$ gives factors of 1, 3, and 9.

21: $1 \times 21, 3 \times 7, 7 \times 3, 21 \times 1$ gives factors of 1, 3, 7, and 21.

COMMON ERROR

Students who are eager to complete problems may stop listing factors as soon as they discover a common factor. Stress to students that it is best to write out all the factors because they are looking for the *greatest* common factor.

Recall that the greatest common divisor (GCD) of two or more numbers is the greatest factor the numbers have in common.

EXAMPLE 1 Find GCD (9, 21).

Step 1 List all of the factors of each number.

9:     1   3   9

21:    1   3   7   21

Step 2 Circle the factors that are common, or shared by, each number.

9:     ①   ③   9

21:    ①   ③   7   21

Step 3 Choose the greatest common divisor.

GCD (9, 21) = 3.

The GCD is used to express a fraction in simplest form. A fraction is said to be in simplest form when the greatest common divisor of its numerator and denominator is 1.

> Expressing a fraction in simplest form means the same as reducing the fraction to lowest terms.

EXAMPLE 2 Express $\frac{9}{21}$ in simplest form.

Step 1 Find the GCD of the numerator and the denominator. (Look again at the previous example.)

GCD (9, 21) = 3.

Step 2 Divide the numerator and denominator of $\frac{9}{21}$ by 3, the GCD.

$$\frac{9 \div 3}{21 \div 3} = \frac{3}{7}$$

The fraction $\frac{3}{7}$ is in simplest form because the GCD of its numerator and denominator is 1.

---

110 *Chapter 5 Rational Numbers and Fractions*

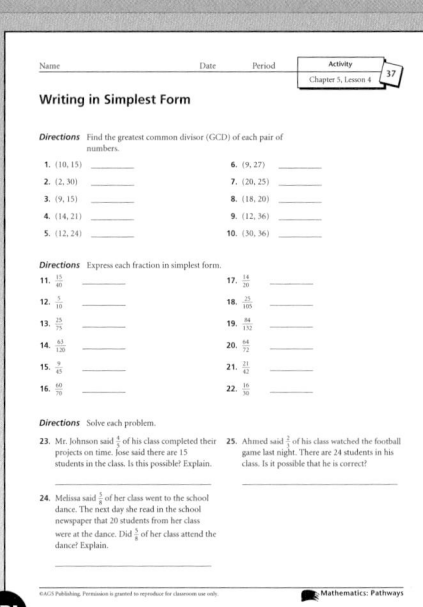

EXAMPLE 3 Express $\frac{15}{60}$ in simplest form.

Step 1 Find the GCD of 15 and 60. GCD (15, 60) = 15.

Step 2 Divide the numerator and denominator of $\frac{15}{60}$ by 15, the GCD.

$$\frac{15 \div 15}{60 \div 15} = \frac{1}{4}$$

Exercise A Find the greatest common divisor (GCD) of each pair of numbers.

1. (8, 16)   8
2. (10, 35)   5
3. (12, 18)   6
4. (8, 20)   4
5. (16, 42)   2
6. (6, 27)   3

Exercise B Express each fraction in simplest form.

7. $\frac{10}{16}$ $\frac{5}{8}$
8. $\frac{4}{8}$ $\frac{1}{2}$
9. $\frac{5}{15}$ $\frac{1}{3}$
10. $\frac{4}{6}$ $\frac{2}{3}$
11. $\frac{9}{15}$ $\frac{3}{5}$
12. $\frac{12}{40}$ $\frac{3}{10}$

13. $\frac{15}{18}$ $\frac{5}{6}$
14. $\frac{7}{42}$ $\frac{1}{6}$
15. $\frac{28}{35}$ $\frac{4}{5}$
16. $\frac{30}{80}$ $\frac{3}{8}$
17. $\frac{55}{60}$ $\frac{11}{12}$
18. $\frac{42}{60}$ $\frac{7}{10}$

19. $\frac{56}{64}$ $\frac{7}{8}$
20. $\frac{78}{96}$ $\frac{13}{16}$
21. $\frac{60}{144}$ $\frac{5}{12}$
22. $\frac{72}{108}$ $\frac{2}{3}$

PROBLEM SOLVING

Exercise C Answer each question. In a mathematics class, $\frac{5}{8}$ of the students are female. In another mathematics class, $\frac{3}{8}$ of the students are male.

23. Is it possible for both classes to have the same numbers of female and male students? Explain.

24. Is it possible for both classes to have different numbers of female and male students? Explain.

23. Yes, if there are the same number of students in each class.

25. How many students are in each class? Tell how you know.

24. Yes, if the number of students in each class is different.

25. The enrollment in each class is 8, or a multiple of 8, because the fractions are in eighths.

GROUP PROBLEM SOLVING

Ask students to imagine that they are in charge of ordering school uniforms for grades 6, 7, 8, and 9. The manufacturer wants to know what fraction of all the uniforms will be girls' uniforms and what fraction will be boys' uniforms. Have students work in pairs to compose a letter that gives the manufacturer the necessary information. The letter should also include how many girls' and boys' uniforms are needed for each grade.

MANIPULATIVES

M Simplest Form

Materials: Cuisenaire Rods, two copies of Manipulatives Master 1 (Factor Frame) for each student

Group Practice: Use the first example to find GCD (9, 21). Build rectangles of areas 9 and 21 inside the Factor Frames. Place rods representing the factors of each rectangle in the left and top portions of the frame. The GCD will be the rod common to both rectangles. The remaining rods represent the *simplest form* of the numerator and denominator after being divided by the GCD. Explain that to find the *greatest* common divisor, the rectangles must use the largest dimension common to both rectangles.

Student Practice: Have students use the rods for problems 1–6 in Exercise A and problems 7–15 in Exercise B.

3 Reinforce and Extend

IN THE COMMUNITY

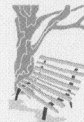

Have students collect newspaper and magazine articles and advertisements that contain fractions. Suggest that they look for stock quotes, automobile financing, bank interest rates, and so on. Have students create a bulletin board showing the variety of fractions they found. Ask them to circle any fractions not in lowest terms and rewrite these in lowest terms. Have them draw boxes around any mixed numbers and rewrite these as improper fractions. Finally, have them write one equivalent fraction for every fraction in lowest terms they find.

Chapter 5 Lesson 5

Overview This lesson shows how to use a number line to compare fractions.

Objectives

- To compare fractions
- To order fractions from least to greatest

Student Pages 112–115

Teacher's Resource Library TRL

Workbook Activity 39

Activity 38

Alternative Activity 38

1 Warm-Up Activity

Ask students which they would rather have: $\frac{5}{8}$ of a dollar or $\frac{9}{16}$ of a dollar. Encourage them to explain their choices. Reward answers that indicate that students are comparing fractions with similar denominators.

2 Teaching the Lesson

Duplicate the first example on an overhead projector. Point out that using the number line to show that $\frac{5}{4} > \frac{3}{4}$ is similar using the number line to show that $5 > 3$. Lead students to a generalization of how they can use the numerators of fractions to compare fractions with like denominators.

COMMON ERROR

As students try to write each fraction with the LCM as the denominator, they may multiply only the numerator or the denominator of the fraction. Stress that as they find equivalent fractions, they should write out the multiplication, writing 1 as a fraction (for example, $\frac{5}{8} \cdot \frac{5}{5} = \frac{25}{40}$) to help them remember that they must multiply both the numerator and denominator.

A number line can be used to compare fractions. To compare fractions means to decide which fraction is greater or smaller.

EXAMPLE 1 Which is greater, $\frac{3}{4}$ or $\frac{5}{4}$?

Step 1 The number line below is divided into fourths. Find each fraction on the number line.

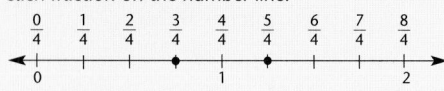

Step 2 On the line, the fraction farther to the right is the greater fraction.

$\frac{5}{4}$ is greater than $\frac{3}{4}$ or $\frac{5}{4} > \frac{3}{4}$

Number lines can also be used to compare fractions with different, or unlike, denominators.

EXAMPLE 2 Which is smaller, $\frac{2}{3}$ or $\frac{2}{5}$?

Step 1 One number line below is divided into thirds. The other is divided into fifths. Find each fraction.

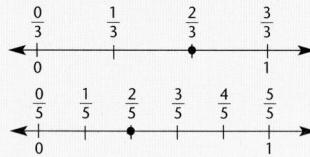

Step 2 The fraction farther to the left is the smaller fraction.

$\frac{2}{5}$ is less than $\frac{2}{3}$ or $\frac{2}{5} < \frac{2}{3}$

112 Chapter 5 *Rational Numbers and Fractions*

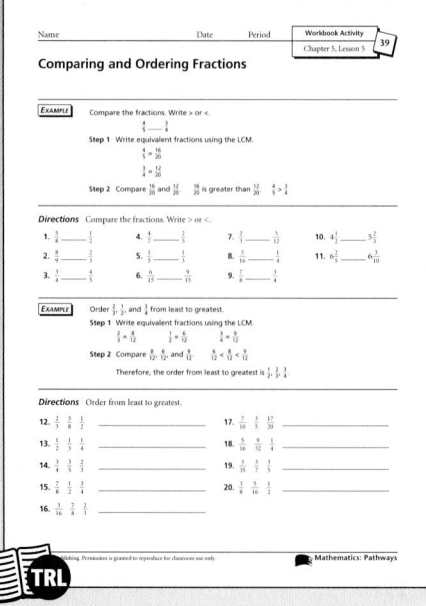

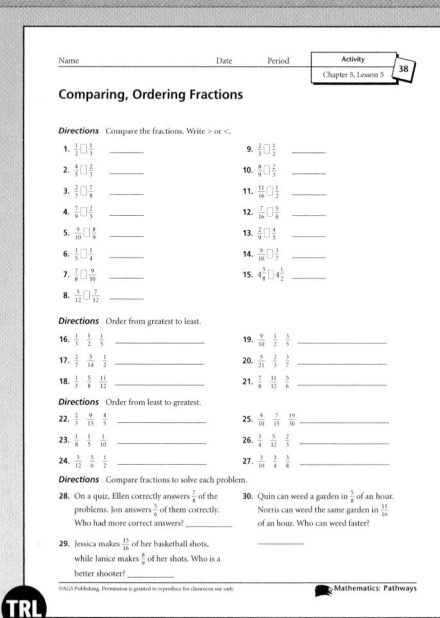

Using a number line to compare fractions is not always practical, especially when the denominators of the fractions to be compared are unlike.

EXAMPLE 3 Suppose that $\frac{5}{8}$ of the students in a mathematics class earned a perfect score on the first quiz of the year. On the second quiz of the year, $\frac{3}{5}$ of the students earned a perfect score. On which quiz did a greater number of students earn a perfect score? Compare $\frac{5}{8}$ and $\frac{3}{5}$ to find the greater fraction.

Step 1 Find the least common multiple (LCM) of the denominators of the fractions.

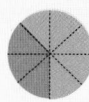

$$8 \rightarrow \quad 8 \quad 16 \quad 24 \quad 32 \quad \textcircled{40} \quad 48 \quad 56 \quad 64 \quad 72$$
$$5 \rightarrow \quad 5 \quad 10 \quad 15 \quad 20 \quad 25 \quad 30 \quad 35 \quad \textcircled{40} \quad 45$$

The LCM of 8 and 5 is 40.

Step 2 Write equivalent fractions for $\frac{5}{8}$ and $\frac{3}{5}$ using the LCM (40) as the denominator.

$$\frac{5}{8} \cdot \frac{5}{5} = \frac{25}{40} \qquad \frac{3}{5} \cdot \frac{8}{8} = \frac{24}{40}$$

Step 3 Compare $\frac{25}{40}$ and $\frac{24}{40}$. $\quad \frac{25}{40} > \frac{24}{40}$ and $\frac{5}{8} > \frac{3}{5}$

A greater number of students earned a perfect score on the first quiz.

It is also possible to compare improper fractions and mixed numbers.

EXAMPLE 4 Compare $2\frac{1}{5}$ and $\frac{9}{4}$. Which is smaller?

Step 1 Change $2\frac{1}{5}$ to an improper fraction. $\qquad 2\frac{1}{5} = \frac{11}{5}$

Step 2 Find the LCM of the denominators of the fractions $\frac{11}{5}$ and $\frac{9}{4}$.

$$5 \rightarrow \quad 5 \quad 10 \quad 15 \quad \textcircled{20} \quad 25 \quad 30 \quad 35$$
$$4 \rightarrow \quad 4 \quad 8 \quad 12 \quad 16 \quad \textcircled{20} \quad 24 \quad 28$$

Step 3 Write equivalent fractions for $\frac{11}{5}$ and $\frac{9}{4}$ using the LCM (20) as the denominator.

$$\frac{11}{5} \cdot \frac{4}{4} = \frac{44}{20} \qquad \frac{9}{4} \cdot \frac{5}{5} = \frac{45}{20}$$

Step 4 Compare $\frac{44}{20}$ and $\frac{45}{20}$. $\quad \frac{44}{20}$ is less than $\frac{45}{20}$ and $2\frac{1}{5} < \frac{9}{4}$.

The value of a fraction does not change if its numerator and its denominator are multiplied by the same number.

Comparing fractions is the first step in ordering two or more fractions or mixed numbers.

EXAMPLE 5 Order the following from least to greatest.

$$1\frac{2}{3} \qquad \frac{3}{4} \qquad 1\frac{1}{2}$$

Step 1 Change $1\frac{2}{3}$ and $1\frac{1}{2}$ to improper fractions.

$$1\frac{2}{3} = \frac{5}{3}$$
$$1\frac{1}{2} = \frac{3}{2}$$

Step 2 Find the LCM of the denominators of these fractions.

$$\frac{5}{3} \qquad \frac{3}{4} \qquad \frac{3}{2}$$

$$3 \rightarrow \quad 3 \quad 6 \quad 9 \quad ⑫ \quad 15 \quad 18 \quad 21$$
$$4 \rightarrow \quad 4 \quad 8 \quad ⑫ \quad 16 \quad 20 \quad 24 \quad 28$$
$$2 \rightarrow \quad 2 \quad 4 \quad 6 \quad 8 \quad 10 \quad ⑫ \quad 14$$

Step 3 Write equivalent fractions for the following using the LCM (12) as the denominator. $\frac{5}{3} \quad \frac{3}{4} \quad \frac{3}{2}$

$$\frac{5}{3} \bullet \frac{4}{4} = \frac{20}{12}$$
$$\frac{3}{4} \bullet \frac{3}{3} = \frac{9}{12}$$
$$\frac{3}{2} \bullet \frac{6}{6} = \frac{18}{12}$$

Step 4 Compare these fractions. $\frac{20}{12} \quad \frac{9}{12} \quad \frac{18}{12}$

$\frac{9}{12}$ is less than $\frac{18}{12}$ and $\frac{18}{12}$ is less than $\frac{20}{12}$.

The order from least to greatest is $\frac{3}{4} \quad 1\frac{1}{2} \quad 1\frac{2}{3}$.

Exercise A Use the number lines below for problems 1–2.

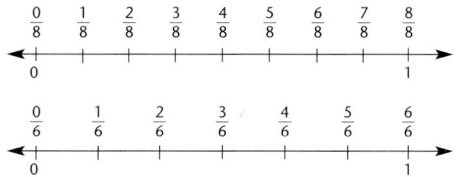

1. Which is greater, $\frac{3}{8}$ or $\frac{1}{6}$? $\quad \frac{3}{8}$

2. Which is smaller, $\frac{5}{6}$ or $\frac{5}{8}$? $\quad \frac{5}{8}$

Exercise B Compare the fractions. Write $>$ or $<$.

3. $\frac{4}{5} \blacksquare \frac{3}{5}$ $>$

4. $\frac{3}{10} \blacksquare \frac{7}{10}$ $<$

5. $\frac{1}{2} \blacksquare \frac{1}{3}$ $>$

6. $\frac{5}{8} \blacksquare \frac{1}{2}$ $>$

7. $\frac{3}{10} \blacksquare \frac{2}{5}$ $<$

8. $\frac{2}{3} \blacksquare \frac{7}{12}$ $>$

9. $\frac{11}{16} \blacksquare \frac{5}{8}$ $>$

10. $\frac{3}{5} \blacksquare \frac{3}{4}$ $<$

11. $\frac{4}{7} \blacksquare \frac{9}{14}$ $<$

12. $\frac{1}{6} \blacksquare \frac{2}{9}$ $<$

13. $1\frac{1}{3} \blacksquare 1\frac{4}{15}$ $>$

14. $4\frac{11}{12} \blacksquare 4\frac{4}{5}$ $>$

Exercise C Order from greatest to least.

15. $\frac{1}{2}$ $\frac{2}{3}$ $\frac{3}{4}$ $\frac{3}{4}$ $\frac{2}{3}$ $\frac{1}{2}$

16. $\frac{1}{4}$ $\frac{1}{3}$ $\frac{1}{5}$ $\frac{1}{3}$ $\frac{1}{4}$ $\frac{1}{5}$

17. $\frac{11}{12}$ $\frac{5}{6}$ $\frac{7}{8}$ $\frac{11}{12}$ $\frac{7}{8}$ $\frac{5}{6}$

18. $\frac{3}{10}$ $\frac{2}{5}$ $\frac{1}{3}$ $\frac{2}{5}$ $\frac{1}{3}$ $\frac{3}{10}$

Exercise D Order from least to greatest.

19. $\frac{3}{4}$ $\frac{5}{8}$ $\frac{1}{2}$ $\frac{1}{2}$ $\frac{5}{8}$ $\frac{3}{4}$

20. $\frac{2}{5}$ $\frac{1}{3}$ $\frac{7}{15}$ $\frac{1}{3}$ $\frac{2}{5}$ $\frac{7}{15}$

21. $\frac{4}{7}$ $\frac{9}{14}$ $\frac{1}{2}$ $\frac{1}{2}$ $\frac{4}{7}$ $\frac{9}{14}$

22. $\frac{7}{12}$ $\frac{2}{3}$ $\frac{5}{8}$ $\frac{7}{12}$ $\frac{5}{8}$ $\frac{2}{3}$

 **PROBLEM SOLVING**

Exercise E Compare fractions to solve each problem.

23. On a test, Gina got $\frac{5}{6}$ of the answers correct, and Terrence got $\frac{7}{8}$ of the answers correct. Who had more correct answers? Terrence

24. Jacob can mow $\frac{4}{5}$ of Mr. Albert's lawn in an hour. Lin can mow $\frac{7}{9}$ of the same lawn in an hour. Who mows more of the lawn in an hour? Jacob

25. James lives $\frac{7}{10}$ of a mile from school, and Matt lives $\frac{13}{18}$ of a mile from school. Who lives closer to school?

James

Try This

Students should recognize that they can find the decimal equivalent of each fraction and then order the decimals.

GROUP PROBLEM SOLVING

 Suggest that small groups of students develop a series of equal-length number lines that can be used to compare fractions with different denominators. Ask the groups to describe fractions with denominators of 2, 4, 5, 8, and 10 as well as three additional denominators of students' choosing. Encourage students to present their work as a draft of an Internet Web page on fractions. Students may assign tasks to group members such as researcher, graphic artist, writer, and link coordinator.

Lesson at a Glance

Chapter 5 Lesson 6

Overview This lesson introduces addition and subtraction of fractions with like denominators.

Objective

■ To add and subtract fractions and mixed numbers with like denominators

Student Pages 116–119

Teacher's Resource Library TRL

Workbook Activity 40

Activity 39

Alternative Activity 39

1 Warm-Up Activity

Pose this situation to students: "Jacob has $\frac{1}{2}$ of a cherry pie, and his twin sister Jean has $\frac{1}{2}$ of a cherry pie. Together, how much pie do they have?" *(one whole pie)* Ask students to explain how they found their answer.

2 Teaching the Lesson

Draw a rectangle on the board or overhead projector. Divide the rectangle into 5 parts. Have a volunteer use the rectangle to demonstrate the first example, $\frac{2}{5} + \frac{1}{5} = \frac{3}{5}$.

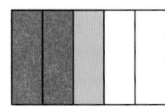

To stress the need for simplest form, use two rectangles, each divided into 8 equal parts, and have a volunteer demonstrate the example $\frac{3}{8} + \frac{7}{8} = 1\frac{1}{4}$.

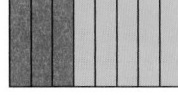 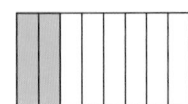

Some of the work you will perform in algebra involves computations. Some of these computations include adding fractions with like denominators. You perform computations in algebra in the same way you do in arithmetic.

EXAMPLE 1 Add $\frac{2}{5} + \frac{1}{5}$.

Step 1 Add the numerators of the fractions.

$$\frac{2}{5} + \frac{1}{5} = \frac{2+1}{5} = \frac{3}{5}$$

Step 2 Write the denominator of the fractions.

$$\frac{2}{5} + \frac{1}{5} = \frac{3}{5}$$

EXAMPLE 2 Add $\frac{2x}{5} + \frac{1x}{5}$.

Step 1 Add the numerators of the fractions.

$$\frac{2x}{5} + \frac{1x}{5} = \frac{2x+1x}{5} = \frac{3x}{5}$$

Step 2 Write the denominator of the fractions.

$$\frac{2x}{5} + \frac{1x}{5} = \frac{3x}{5}$$

You can also add fractions that have like variables as denominators.

EXAMPLE 3 Add $\frac{b}{x} + \frac{c}{x}$.   Add $\frac{2}{y} + \frac{d}{y}$.

Step 1 Add the numerators of the fractions.

$$\frac{b}{x} + \frac{c}{x} = \frac{b+c}{}$$ $$\frac{2}{y} + \frac{d}{y} = \frac{2+d}{}$$

Step 2 Write the denominator of the fractions.

$$\frac{b}{x} + \frac{c}{x} = \frac{b+c}{x}$$ $$\frac{2}{y} + \frac{d}{y} = \frac{2+d}{y}$$

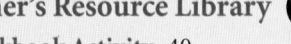

Workbook Activity 40   **Activity 39**

Some of the computations you will perform in algebra include subtracting fractions with like denominators.

EXAMPLE 4 Subtract $\frac{2}{3} - \frac{1}{3}$.   Subtract $\frac{2x}{3} - \frac{x}{3}$.

Step 1 Subtract the numerators of the fractions.

$$\frac{2}{3} - \frac{1}{3} = \frac{2-1}{3} = 1 \qquad \frac{2x}{3} - \frac{1x}{3} = \frac{2x-1x}{3} = \frac{1x}{3} = \frac{x}{3}$$

Step 2 Write the denominator of the fractions.

$$\frac{2}{3} - \frac{1}{3} = \frac{1}{3} \qquad \frac{2x}{3} - \frac{x}{3} = \frac{x}{3}$$

Whenever you add or subtract fractions, write your answer in simplest form.

EXAMPLE 5 Add $\frac{3}{8} + \frac{7}{8}$.   Add $\frac{3x}{8} + \frac{7x}{8}$.

Step 1 Add the fractions.

$$\frac{3}{8} + \frac{7}{8} = \frac{3+7}{8} = \frac{10}{8} \qquad \frac{3x}{8} + \frac{7x}{8} = \frac{3x+7x}{8} = \frac{10x}{8}$$

Step 2 Simplify.

$$\frac{10}{8} = 8\overline{)10} = 1\frac{2}{8} = 1\frac{1}{4} \qquad \frac{10x}{8} = 8\overline{)10x} = 1\frac{2}{8}x = 1\frac{1}{4}x$$

You can also subtract fractions with like variables as denominators.

EXAMPLE 6 Subtract $\frac{b}{x} - \frac{c}{x}$.   Subtract $\frac{d}{y} - \frac{3}{y}$.

Step 1 Subtract the numerators of the fractions.

$$\frac{b}{x} - \frac{c}{x} = \frac{b-c}{x} \qquad \frac{d}{y} - \frac{3}{y} = \frac{d-3}{y}$$

Step 2 Write the denominator of the fractions.

$$\frac{b}{x} - \frac{c}{x} = \frac{b-c}{x} \qquad \frac{d}{y} - \frac{3}{y} = \frac{d-3}{y}$$

Estimation Activity

Estimate: $9\frac{1}{5} - 1\frac{3}{5}$

Solution: Round to the nearest whole number.

$9\frac{1}{5}$ to 9

$1\frac{3}{5}$ to 2

Subtract whole numbers: $9 - 2 = 7$

COMMON ERROR

When adding or subtracting fractions, most students will recognize that the denominator stays the same. However, if the fractions have variables as denominators, students may become confused and add denominators as well as numerators. Help them avoid this error by encouraging them to remember that the variables stand for numbers. For instance, in $\frac{1}{x}$, if $x = 2$, the denominator of the sum or difference would be 2.

MANIPULATIVES

  Fractions with Like Denominators

Materials: Cuisenaire Rods, Manipulatives Master 2 (Blank Number Lines)

Group Practice: Label a number line in $\frac{1}{3}$ units. Place two cubes on the line for $\frac{2}{3}$. Remove one cube to model the example $\frac{2}{3} - \frac{1}{3} = \frac{1}{3}$. For the next example, label a number line in $\frac{1}{8}$ units. Model $\frac{3}{8} + \frac{7}{8} = \frac{10}{8}$ by adding seven cubes to three. Then place an 8-rod (whole unit) over the ten cubes to show that $\frac{8}{8}$ equals one whole unit. Write the symbolic equivalents of the improper fraction and the mixed number. Model Example 7 on page 118 using the same process.

Student Practice: Have students use the rods for Exercise A, problems 1–6, and Exercise C, problems 16–21.

Some of the computations you will perform in algebra will
also include adding and subtracting mixed numbers
with like denominators.

EXAMPLE 7 Find $(2\frac{1}{10} + 5\frac{7}{10}) - 3\frac{3}{10}$. Find $(2\frac{1}{10}x + 5\frac{7}{10}x) - 3\frac{3}{10}x$.

Step 1 Perform the computation inside ( ) first.

$(2\frac{1}{10} + 5\frac{7}{10}) - 3\frac{3}{10}$ $\qquad$ $(2\frac{1}{10}x + 5\frac{7}{10}x) - 3\frac{3}{10}x$
$\downarrow$ $\qquad$ $\downarrow$
$7\frac{8}{10}$ $\qquad$ $7\frac{8}{10}x$

Step 2 Perform the remaining computation.

$(2\frac{1}{10} + 5\frac{7}{10}) - 3\frac{3}{10}$ $\qquad$ $(2\frac{1}{10}x + 5\frac{7}{10}x) - 3\frac{3}{10}x$
$\downarrow \qquad \downarrow$ $\qquad$ $\downarrow \qquad \downarrow$
$7\frac{8}{10} \qquad - 3\frac{3}{10}$ $\qquad$ $7\frac{8}{10}x \qquad - 3\frac{3}{10}x$
$\downarrow$ $\qquad$ $\downarrow$
$4\frac{5}{10}$ $\qquad$ $4\frac{5}{10}x$

Step 3 Simplify if possible.

$4\frac{5}{10} = 4\frac{1}{2}$ $\qquad$ $4\frac{5}{10}x = 4\frac{1}{2}x$

Exercise A Add or subtract. Write your answer in simplest form.

1. $\frac{3}{4} - \frac{1}{4}$ $\qquad \frac{1}{2}$ $\qquad\qquad$ **5.** $10\frac{7}{12} - 4\frac{5}{12}$ $\qquad 6\frac{1}{6}$

2. $\frac{2}{3} + \frac{2}{3}$ $\qquad 1\frac{1}{3}$ $\qquad\qquad$ **6.** $5\frac{9}{10} - 3\frac{3}{10}$ $\qquad 2\frac{3}{5}$

3. $\frac{4}{5} - \frac{2}{5}$ $\qquad \frac{2}{5}$ $\qquad\qquad$ **7.** $6\frac{7}{12} + 9\frac{11}{12}$ $\qquad 16\frac{1}{2}$

4. $2\frac{13}{16} + 1\frac{11}{16}$ $\qquad 4\frac{1}{2}$

Writing About Mathematics

Explain how to subtract $7\frac{3}{4}$ from $15\frac{1}{4}$.

Exercise B Add or subtract. Write your answer in simplest form.

8. $\frac{7x}{8} - \frac{x}{8}$ $\frac{3x}{4}$ **12.** $\frac{2x}{6} - \frac{x}{6}$ $\frac{x}{6}$

9. $\frac{5x}{6} - \frac{x}{6}$ $\frac{2x}{3}$ **13.** $\frac{y}{x} - \frac{3}{x}$ $\frac{y-3}{x}$

10. $\frac{5}{x} + \frac{3}{x}$ $\frac{8}{x}$ **14.** $\frac{5}{6} + \frac{x}{6}$ $\frac{5+x}{6}$

11. $\frac{x}{y} - \frac{1}{y}$ $\frac{x-1}{y}$ **15.** $\frac{3x}{5} + \frac{2x}{5}$ $\frac{5x}{5} = x$

Exercise C Perform each computation inside the ( ) first. Write your answer in lowest terms.

16. $(\frac{4}{5} - \frac{1}{5}) + \frac{2}{5}$ 1 **21.** $\frac{1}{12} + (\frac{11}{12} - \frac{5}{12})$ $\frac{7}{12}$

17. $\frac{2}{3} + (\frac{2}{3} - \frac{1}{3})$ 1 **22.** $(\frac{13}{16} - \frac{7}{16}) + \frac{9}{16}$ $\frac{15}{16}$

18. $\frac{3}{4} - (\frac{1}{4} + \frac{1}{4})$ $\frac{1}{4}$ **23.** $(\frac{x}{8} + \frac{7x}{8}) - \frac{5x}{8}$ $\frac{3x}{8}$

19. $(\frac{5}{6} - \frac{1}{6}) + \frac{5}{6}$ $1\frac{1}{2}$ **24.** $\frac{2x}{5} + (\frac{3x}{5} - \frac{3x}{5})$ $\frac{2x}{5}$

20. $(\frac{5}{8} - \frac{3}{8}) + \frac{7}{8}$ $1\frac{1}{8}$ **25.** $\frac{3x}{10} + (\frac{9x}{10} - \frac{7x}{10})$ $\frac{x}{2}$

 Math in Your Life

Discounts

End-of-Season sales often declare: $\frac{1}{3}$ *Off All Prices Marked.* It helps to be able to do a quick calculation mentally. To figure out the price of an item marked down by one-third, you divide by 3, and then double the quotient. This quickly gives you the discounted price. Try it:

$36 ÷ 3 = $12 → $12 × 2 = $24
$150 ÷ 3 = $50 → $50 × 2 = $100

MENTAL MATH

 Ask students to solve each of the following problems without using pencil and paper. Remind them that their answers should be in lowest terms.

$\frac{1}{10} + \frac{1}{10}$ $(\frac{1}{5})$

$\frac{x}{10} + \frac{x}{10}$ $(\frac{x}{5})$

$\frac{2}{10} + \frac{3}{10}$ $(\frac{1}{2})$

$\frac{2x}{10} + \frac{3x}{10}$ $(\frac{x}{2})$

$\frac{7}{10} + \frac{3}{10}$ (1)

$\frac{7x}{10} + \frac{3x}{10}$ (x)

$\frac{1}{4} + \frac{3}{4}$ (1)

$\frac{1}{5x} + \frac{3}{5x}$ $(\frac{4}{5x})$

$\frac{1}{3} + 1\frac{2}{3}$ (2)

Lesson at a Glance

Chapter 5 Lesson 7

Overview This lesson introduces addition and subtraction of fractions with unlike denominators.

Objective

- To add and subtract fractions and mixed numbers with unlike denominators

Student Pages 120–123

Teacher's Resource Library

Workbook Activity 41

Activity 40

Alternative Activity 40

1 Warm-Up Activity

Remind students of their work with LCMs from Lesson 5. Ask volunteers to supply the LCMs for the following groups of numbers:

2, 3	*(6)*	3, 4	*(12)*
2, 4, 8	*(8)*	6, 4	*(12)*
8, 3	*(24)*	6, 5	*(30)*

2 Teaching the Lesson

Use the example $\frac{5x}{8} - \frac{x}{3}$ in a demonstration on the overhead projector. Ask a volunteer to explain why, in the second step, $\frac{5}{8}$ is multiplied by $\frac{3}{3}$ and $\frac{1}{3}$ is multiplied by $\frac{8}{8}$. Make sure that students understand that the goal is to have the least common multiple, 24, as the denominator for both fractions. If necessary, present the example with unlike denominators $\frac{3}{k} - \frac{2}{m}$ in a demonstration. First, ask students to identify the LCM for the two fractions. *(km)* Then ask students what they can do to the fraction $\frac{3}{k}$ to make the denominator km. *(Multiply by $\frac{m}{m}$.)* Have students explain why this multiplication does not change the value of the fraction. *(It is multiplication by 1.)* Then present steps 1, 2, and 3 of the example.

Sometimes your work in algebra will include subtracting fractions with unlike denominators.

EXAMPLE 1 Subtract $\frac{5}{8} - \frac{1}{3}$. Subtract $\frac{5x}{8} - \frac{x}{3}$.

Step 1 Find the LCM of the denominators.

LCM (8, 3) = 24 LCM (8, 3) = 24

Step 2 Write an equivalent fraction for each fraction using the LCM (24) as the denominator.

$\frac{5}{8} \cdot \frac{3}{3} = \frac{15}{24}$ $\frac{5x}{8} \cdot \frac{3}{3} = \frac{15x}{24}$

$\frac{1}{3} \cdot \frac{8}{8} = \frac{8}{24}$ $\frac{x}{3} \cdot \frac{8}{8} = \frac{8x}{24}$

Step 3 Subtract.

$\frac{15}{24} - \frac{8}{24} = \frac{15-8}{24} = \frac{7}{24}$ $\frac{15x}{24} - \frac{8x}{24} = \frac{15x-8x}{24} = \frac{7x}{24}$

In the examples, it is not necessary to simplify because $\frac{7}{24}$ and $\frac{7x}{24}$ are in simplest form.

You can also subtract fractions that have unlike variables as denominators.

EXAMPLE 2 Subtract $\frac{3}{k} - \frac{2}{m}$.

Step 1 Find equivalent fractions by multiplying each fraction's numerator and denominator by the other fraction's denominator.

$\frac{3}{k}$ $\frac{3}{k} \cdot \frac{m}{m} = \frac{3m}{km}$

$\frac{2}{m}$ $\frac{2}{m} \cdot \frac{k}{k} = \frac{2k}{km}$

Step 2 Write the equivalent fractions into the equation.

$\frac{3}{k} - \frac{2}{m}$ $\frac{3m}{km} - \frac{2k}{km}$

Step 3 Subtract.

$\frac{3m}{km} - \frac{2k}{km} = \frac{3m-2k}{km}$

120 Chapter 5 Rational Numbers and Fractions

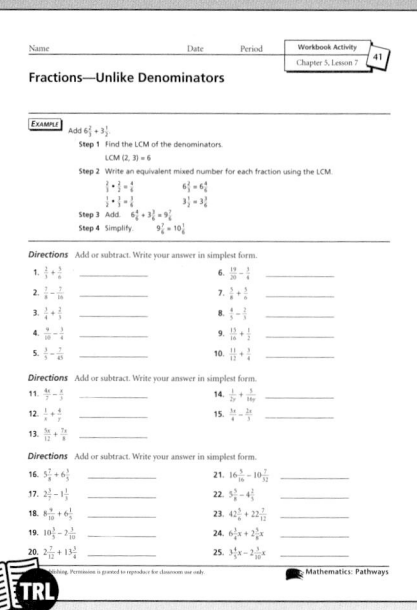

Workbook Activity 41

Activity 40

Sometimes your work in algebra will include adding fractions with unlike denominators.

EXAMPLE 3 Add $\frac{3}{4} + \frac{2}{3}$. Add $\frac{3x}{4} + \frac{2x}{3}$.

Step 1 Find the LCM of the denominators.

LCM (4, 3) = 12 LCM (4, 3) = 12

Step 2 Write an equivalent fraction for each fraction using the LCM (12) as the denominator.

$\frac{3}{4} \cdot \frac{3}{3} = \frac{9}{12}$ $\frac{3x}{4} \cdot \frac{3}{3} = \frac{9x}{12}$

$\frac{2}{3} \cdot \frac{4}{4} = \frac{8}{12}$ $\frac{2x}{3} \cdot \frac{4}{4} = \frac{8x}{12}$

Step 3 Add.

$\frac{9}{12} + \frac{8}{12} = \frac{9+8}{12} = \frac{17}{12}$ $\frac{9x}{12} + \frac{8x}{12} = \frac{9x+8x}{12} = \frac{17x}{12}$

Step 4 Simplify.

$\frac{17}{12} = 1\frac{5}{12}$ $\frac{17x}{12} = \frac{17}{12}x = 1\frac{5}{12}x$

You can also add fractions that have unlike variables as denominators.

EXAMPLE 4 Add $\frac{5}{x} + \frac{2}{y}$.

Step 1 Find equivalent fractions by multiplying each fraction's numerator and denominator by the other fraction's denominator.

$\frac{5}{x}$ $\frac{5}{x} \cdot \frac{y}{y} = \frac{5y}{xy}$

$\frac{2}{y}$ $\frac{2}{y} \cdot \frac{x}{x} = \frac{2x}{xy}$

Step 2 Write the equivalent fractions into the equation.

$\frac{5}{x} + \frac{2}{y}$ $\frac{5y}{xy} + \frac{2x}{xy}$

Step 3 Add.

$\frac{5y}{xy} + \frac{2x}{xy} = \frac{5y+2x}{xy}$

COMMON ERROR

Some students may have difficulty finding equivalent fractions for fractions with variables as the denominator. They may correctly identify the LCM but fail to multiply both numerator and denominator by the appropriate factor. Stress to students that when they multiply by one in any form, they must multiply both the numerator and denominator of the fraction.

MANIPULATIVES

 Fractions with Unlike Denominators

Materials: Cuisenaire Rods, Manipulatives Master 2 (Blank Number Lines)

Group Practice: Review LCM and common denominators from Lesson 5. Using the example $\frac{5}{8} - \frac{1}{3}$, model Steps 1–2 with the rods. For Step 3, label a number line in $\frac{1}{24}$ units, and then place $\frac{15}{24}$ on the number line. Subtract eight cubes to find the difference. Write the symbolic equivalent for each step. Repeat to model Example 3 on page 121.

Student Practice: Have students use the rods to model problems 1–6 in Exercise A and problem 16 in Exercise C.

3 Reinforce and Extend

Your work in algebra will also include computing with
mixed numbers.

EXAMPLE 5 Add $6\frac{4}{5} + 1\frac{7}{10}$. Add $6\frac{4}{5}x + 1\frac{7}{10}x$.

Step 1 Find the LCM of the denominators.

LCM (5, 10) = 10   LCM (5, 10) = 10

Step 2 Write an equivalent mixed number for each fraction
using the LCM (10) as the denominator.

$\frac{4}{5} \cdot \frac{2}{2} = \frac{8}{10}$ $\frac{4}{5}x \cdot \frac{2}{2} = \frac{8}{10}x$

$6\frac{4}{5} = 6\frac{8}{10}$ $6\frac{4}{5}x = 6\frac{8}{10}x$

Step 3 Add.

$6\frac{8}{10} + 1\frac{7}{10} = 7\frac{15}{10}$ $6\frac{8}{10}x + 1\frac{7}{10}x = 7\frac{15}{10}x$

Step 4 Simplify.

$7\frac{15}{10} = 8\frac{1}{2}$ $7\frac{15}{10}x = 8\frac{1}{2}x$

Exercise A Add or subtract. Write your answer in simplest form.

1. $\frac{1}{3} + \frac{3}{4}$ $1\frac{1}{12}$ 6. $\frac{3}{4} - \frac{2}{3}$ $\frac{1}{12}$

2. $\frac{7}{8} - \frac{2}{3}$ $\frac{5}{24}$ 7. $\frac{3}{16} + \frac{4}{5}$ $\frac{79}{80}$

3. $\frac{1}{4} + \frac{2}{5}$ $\frac{13}{20}$ 8. $\frac{3}{5} - \frac{1}{8}$ $\frac{19}{40}$

4. $\frac{5}{8} - \frac{1}{4}$ $\frac{3}{8}$ 9. $\frac{4}{9} + \frac{4}{7}$ $1\frac{1}{63}$

5. $\frac{3}{10} - \frac{1}{6}$ $\frac{2}{15}$ 10. $\frac{7}{12} + \frac{13}{16}$ $1\frac{19}{48}$

Exercise B Add or subtract. Write your answer in simplest form.

11. $\frac{5}{6}x - \frac{1}{2}x \qquad \frac{1}{3}x$

12. $\frac{1}{x} + \frac{5}{y} \qquad \frac{y + 5x}{xy}$

13. $\frac{7x}{12} + \frac{3x}{8} \qquad \frac{23x}{24}$

14. $\frac{3}{x} - \frac{1}{y} \qquad \frac{3y - x}{xy}$

15. $\frac{9x}{10} - \frac{7x}{8} \qquad \frac{x}{40}$

Exercise C Add or subtract. Write your answer in simplest form.

16. $2\frac{3}{4} - 1\frac{1}{2} \qquad 1\frac{1}{4}$

17. $7\frac{7}{8} + 3\frac{1}{4} \qquad 11\frac{1}{8}$

18. $8\frac{9}{10} + 6\frac{2}{5} \qquad 15\frac{3}{10}$

19. $9\frac{4}{5} - 8\frac{1}{8} \qquad 1\frac{27}{40}$

20. $1\frac{5}{12} + 12\frac{3}{4} \qquad 14\frac{1}{6}$

21. $34\frac{3}{8} - 11\frac{1}{12} \qquad 23\frac{7}{24}$

22. $15\frac{15}{16} - 5\frac{1}{3} \qquad 10\frac{29}{48}$

23. $27\frac{5}{12} + 19\frac{3}{10} \qquad 46\frac{43}{60}$

24. $5\frac{1}{4}x + 4\frac{2}{3}x \qquad 9\frac{11}{12}x$

25. $7\frac{9}{16}x - 2\frac{1}{5}x \qquad 5\frac{29}{80}x$

Technology Connection

Changing Crude Oil into Fractions

You may have seen a movie or TV show where oil rushes out of the ground. How does that thick, black liquid change into the thin, golden liquid we pump into our cars' gasoline tanks? A process called *fractional distillation* separates crude oil into different products. The crude oil is heated up. At different temperatures, the vapor is collected and cooled down so that it becomes a liquid again. The liquid is then refined into gasoline, kerosene, or diesel fuel.

CAREER CONNECTION

Ask groups of four students to investigate a career as a water-quality technician or water-treatment engineer. Have the groups find out what skills, education, and training are needed for each career. Also, suggest that they find out about future employment opportunities in these areas. Invite each group to present its findings in a brochure titled *Your Future in Water Quality.* Students can assign roles to members of the group—the researcher who finds out about the career, the writer who composes text for the brochure, the designer who designs and illustrates the brochure, and the producer who coordinates the efforts of team members.

Chapter 5 Lesson 8

Overview This lesson explains how to subtract fractions using regrouping or borrowing.

Objective

■ To subtract fractions using regrouping as a technique

Student Pages 124–125

Teacher's Resource Library TRL

Workbook Activity 42

Activity 41

Alternative Activity 41

1 Warm-Up Activity

Write the following subtraction problems on the board:

$$\begin{array}{cccc} 23 & 34 & 56 & 81 \\ -19 & -28 & -48 & -72 \end{array}$$

Ask students how they are able to subtract 9 ones from 3 ones, 8 ones from 4 ones, and so on. Lead students in a discussion about regrouping in subtraction of whole numbers.

2 Teaching the Lesson

Using the first example as a guide, point out to students that any mixed number can be written as a mixed number with an improper fraction. Draw students' attention to the renaming of $9\frac{1}{5}$: $9\frac{1}{5}$ equals $8 + 1 + \frac{1}{5}$ equals $8 + \frac{5}{5} + \frac{1}{5}$ equals $8 + \frac{6}{5}$ equals $8\frac{6}{5}$. Point out the similarity of this process to the process of borrowing or renaming used when subtracting whole numbers.

Sometimes it is necessary to rename before you can subtract. Renaming is sometimes called *regrouping* or *borrowing*.

EXAMPLE 1 Subtract $9\frac{1}{5} - 1\frac{3}{5}$.

Step 1 Since you cannot subtract $\frac{3}{5}$ from $\frac{1}{5}$, you must rename.

$$9\frac{1}{5} = 8\frac{6}{5}$$ Think: $9\frac{1}{5} = 9 + \frac{1}{5} = \boxed{8} + \boxed{1} + \boxed{\frac{1}{5}}$

$$\boxed{8} + \boxed{\frac{5}{5}} + \boxed{\frac{1}{5}} = 8\frac{6}{5}$$

Step 2 Subtract.

$$\begin{array}{r} 8\frac{6}{5} \\ - 1\frac{3}{5} \\ \hline 7\frac{3}{5} \end{array}$$

In this example, the whole number 1 was renamed as $\frac{5}{5}$. There are an infinite number of ways to rename the whole number 1. These are some of the ways.

$$\frac{2}{2} \quad \frac{3}{3} \quad \frac{4}{4} \quad \frac{6}{6} \quad \frac{8}{8} \quad \frac{10}{10}$$

When subtracting fractions with unlike denominators, you must write equivalent fractions using the LCM before you perform any other operations.

EXAMPLE 2 Subtract $4\frac{2}{5} - 2\frac{7}{12}$.

Step 1 Find the LCM of the denominators.

LCM (5, 12) = 60

Step 2 Write equivalent mixed numbers for $\frac{2}{5}$ and $\frac{7}{12}$ using the LCM (60) as the denominator.

$$\frac{2}{5} \cdot \frac{12}{12} = \frac{24}{60}$$

$$\frac{7}{12} \cdot \frac{5}{5} = \frac{35}{60}$$

Workbook Activity 42

Activity 41

EXAMPLE 2 (continued)

Step 3 Since you cannot subtract $\frac{35}{60}$ from $\frac{24}{60}$, you must rename.

$4\frac{24}{60} = 3\frac{84}{60}$ Think: $4\frac{24}{60} = 4 + \frac{24}{60} = \boxed{3} + \boxed{1} + \boxed{\frac{24}{60}}$
$-\ 2\frac{35}{60}$

$ = \boxed{3} + \boxed{\frac{60}{60}} + \boxed{\frac{24}{60}} = 3\frac{84}{60}$

Step 4 Subtract. $3\frac{84}{60}$
$\ -\ 2\frac{35}{60}$
$\overline{\ \ 1\frac{49}{60}}$

Always check to make sure your answer is in simplest form.

Exercise A Subtract. Write your answer in simplest form.

1. $3\frac{1}{4} - 1\frac{3}{4}$ $1\frac{1}{2}$

2. $7\frac{2}{5} - 4\frac{4}{5}$ $2\frac{3}{5}$

3. $8\frac{3}{10} - 2\frac{7}{10}$ $5\frac{3}{5}$

4. $11\frac{1}{8} - 10\frac{5}{8}$ $\frac{1}{2}$

5. $6\frac{1}{3} - 3\frac{2}{3}$ $2\frac{2}{3}$

6. $5\frac{1}{6} - 2\frac{5}{6}$ $2\frac{1}{3}$

7. $9\frac{7}{12} - 8\frac{11}{12}$ $\frac{2}{3}$

8. $17\frac{1}{10} - 14\frac{1}{2}$ $2\frac{3}{5}$

9. $18\frac{3}{8} - 4\frac{7}{16}$ $13\frac{15}{16}$

10. $9\frac{1}{4} - 6\frac{1}{3}$ $2\frac{11}{12}$

11. $10\frac{5}{8} - 1\frac{1}{5}$ $9\frac{17}{40}$

12. $21\frac{3}{4} - 17\frac{5}{6}$ $3\frac{11}{12}$

13. $8\frac{3}{10} - 7\frac{1}{3}$ $\frac{29}{30}$

14. $19\frac{9}{16} - 12\frac{2}{5}$ $7\frac{13}{80}$

15. $31\frac{5}{12} - 9\frac{5}{7}$ $21\frac{59}{84}$

PROBLEM SOLVING

Exercise B Add or subtract.

16. Yesterday Lin worked $3\frac{3}{4}$ hours. She has worked $5\frac{1}{2}$ hours today. How many hours has she worked altogether? $9\frac{1}{4}$ hours

17. Justin weighs $188\frac{3}{16}$ pounds. He wants to lose $9\frac{7}{8}$ pounds. How much will he weigh if he loses the weight? $178\frac{5}{16}$ pounds

18. Tisha studies $3\frac{1}{2}$ hours after school. If she has studied for $2\frac{5}{8}$ hours, how much longer will she study? $\frac{7}{8}$ hour

19. Rafael lives $18\frac{3}{4}$ miles from the amusement park. His friend lives $53\frac{2}{3}$ miles from the park. How much closer to the park does Rafael live? $34\frac{11}{12}$ miles

20. For a project, Tracy needs $5\frac{1}{2}$ yards of blue yarn, $8\frac{3}{4}$ yards of yellow yarn, and $2\frac{1}{3}$ yards of green yarn. How many yards of yarn does she need altogether? $16\frac{7}{12}$ yards

---

MANIPULATIVES

 Subtracting Fractions with Regrouping

Materials: Cuisenaire Rods, Manipulatives Master 2 (Blank Number Lines)

Group Practice: Label a number line in $\frac{1}{5}$ units. Model the first example, $9\frac{1}{5} - 1\frac{3}{5}$. Place $9\frac{1}{5}$ on the number line. (The whole unit is the 5-rod.) To rename $9\frac{1}{5}$, remove the last 5-rod and replace it with five cubes. Write the symbolic equivalent for regrouping. Remove three cubes and one 5-rod. Realign the remaining rods to find the difference. Repeat with a second example, $3\frac{1}{3} - 2\frac{3}{4}$, labeling a number line in $\frac{1}{12}$ units.

Student Practice: Use the rods with Exercise A, problems 1–2, 5–6, 10 and Exercise B, problems 16, 18.

 Reinforce and Extend

GROUP PROBLEM SOLVING

 Present the following problem for small groups of students to solve:

Brooks School is collecting handmade toys for children in the local hospital. Students need $\frac{1}{2}$ yard of felt to make faces on 12 sock puppets. They also need $\frac{1}{3}$ yard of felt and $3\frac{3}{4}$ yards of fleece to make 12 tiny beanbag animals. Ask the groups to determine how many yards of felt and fleece are needed to complete the project.

Invite students to plan a craft project of their own. Have them create designs and draw up a materials list showing how much material is needed to complete the project.

LEARNING STYLES

 LEP/ESL

Ask students to tell which of the following steps or operations they used to solve problem 8 in Exercise A. Have them number the steps in the correct order.

(5) Find the GCF to put fractions in simplest form.

(2) Multiply numerators and denominators by 1 to get common denominators.

(3) Regroup.

(1) Find the LCM.

(4) Subtract.

LEARNING STYLES

Visual/Spatial

Have students fashion fraction strips and model the subtraction, including the regrouping, of problems 1 and 2 in Exercise A.

Chapter 5 Lesson 9

Overview This lesson shows students how to multiply fractions and mixed numbers.

Objective

■ To multiply fractions and mixed numbers

Student Pages 126–127

Teacher's Resource Library **TRL**

Workbook Activity 43

Activity 42

Alternative Activity 42

1 Warm-Up Activity

Have half of the class stand up and count off by twos. Then have all the students who said "two" sit down. Ask the class to describe the fraction of students who are still standing. ($\frac{1}{4}$) Point out that $\frac{1}{4} = \frac{1}{2}$ of $\frac{1}{2}$, or $\frac{1}{2} \times \frac{1}{2}$.

2 Teaching the Lesson

Some students may have difficulty grasping that the product of a fraction and a number is smaller than the original number. Help them grasp this concept by discussing what happens when both multipliers are greater than one. (*The product is greater than either number.*) Then have students discuss what happens when one of the multipliers is 1. (*The product is equal to the second number.*) Ask students to generalize about what happens if one of the multipliers is less than 1. (*The product is less than the second multiplier.*)

Lesson 9 — Multiplying Fractions and Mixed Numbers

Sometimes you must multiply fractions. To multiply two or more fractions, multiply the numerators and multiply the denominators. Then simplify your answer if possible.

EXAMPLE 1 Multiply $\frac{5}{6} \cdot \frac{2}{3}$. Multiply $\frac{5x}{6y} \cdot \frac{2}{3}$.

Step 1 Multiply the numerators.

$$\frac{5}{6} \cdot \frac{2}{3} = \frac{5 \cdot 2}{} = \frac{10}{}$$

$$\frac{5x}{6y} \cdot \frac{2}{3} = \frac{5x \cdot 2}{} = \frac{10x}{}$$

Step 2 Multiply the denominators.

$$\frac{5}{6} \cdot \frac{2}{3} = \frac{10}{6 \cdot 3} = \frac{10}{18}$$

$$\frac{5x}{6y} \cdot \frac{2}{3} = \frac{10x}{6y \cdot 3} = \frac{10x}{18y}$$

Step 3 If possible, simplify by dividing the numerator and denominator by the GCD.

$$\frac{10}{18} \div \frac{2}{2} = \frac{5}{9}$$

$$\frac{10x}{18y} \div \frac{2}{2} = \frac{5x}{9y}$$

Multiplication sometimes includes a mixed number.

EXAMPLE 2 Multiply $1\frac{3}{4} \cdot \frac{3}{8}$. Multiply $1\frac{3}{4}x \cdot \frac{3}{8}$.

Step 1 Change the mixed number to an improper fraction.

$$1\frac{3}{4} = \frac{7}{4}$$

$$1\frac{3}{4}x = \frac{7}{4}x$$

Step 2 Multiply the numerators.

$$\frac{7}{4} \cdot \frac{3}{8} = \frac{7 \cdot 3}{} = \frac{21}{}$$

$$\frac{7}{4}x \cdot \frac{3}{8} = \frac{7 \cdot 3}{}x = \frac{21}{}x$$

Step 3 Multiply the denominators.

$$\frac{7}{4} \cdot \frac{3}{8} = \frac{21}{32}$$

$$\frac{7}{4}x \cdot \frac{3}{8} = \frac{21}{32}x$$

The fractions cannot be simplified.

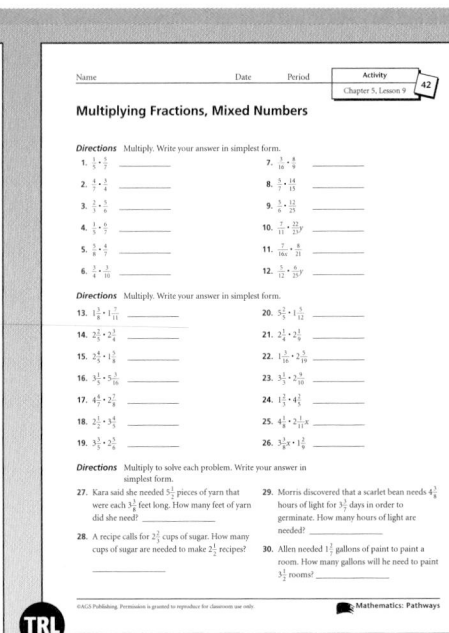

Workbook Activity 43   **Activity 42**

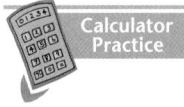
Exercise A Multiply. Write your answer in simplest form.

1. $\frac{1}{4} \cdot \frac{1}{3}$ $\frac{1}{12}$ **5.** $\frac{5}{6} \cdot \frac{1}{8}$ $\frac{5}{48}$ **9.** $\frac{5}{8y} \cdot \frac{1}{10}$ $\frac{1}{16y}$

2. $\frac{2}{5} \cdot \frac{1}{8}$ $\frac{1}{20}$ **6.** $\frac{3}{5} \cdot \frac{3}{10}$ $\frac{9}{50}$ **10.** $\frac{5}{7}x \cdot \frac{1}{20}y$ $\frac{1}{28}xy$

3. $\frac{2}{3} \cdot \frac{1}{5}$ $\frac{2}{15}$ **7.** $\frac{1}{12} \cdot \frac{3}{16}$ $\frac{1}{64}$

4. $\frac{3}{8} \cdot \frac{4}{5}$ $\frac{3}{10}$ **8.** $\frac{1}{6} \cdot \frac{3}{4}x$ $\frac{1}{8}x$

Exercise B Multiply. Write your answer in simplest form.

11. $1\frac{1}{2} \cdot 1\frac{1}{2}$ $2\frac{1}{4}$ **15.** $5\frac{2}{3} \cdot 1\frac{1}{3}$ $7\frac{5}{9}$ **19.** $1\frac{1}{2}x \cdot 2\frac{1}{4}$ $3\frac{3}{8}x$

12. $2\frac{1}{4} \cdot 2\frac{1}{4}$ $5\frac{1}{16}$ **16.** $3\frac{3}{4} \cdot 4\frac{1}{2}$ $16\frac{7}{8}$ **20.** $2\frac{3}{8}y \cdot 1\frac{1}{4}$ $2\frac{31}{32}y$

13. $3\frac{1}{3} \cdot 1\frac{1}{6}$ $3\frac{8}{9}$ **17.** $1\frac{3}{10} \cdot 1\frac{2}{5}$ $1\frac{41}{50}$

14. $2\frac{2}{5} \cdot 3\frac{1}{5}$ $7\frac{17}{25}$ **18.** $2\frac{5}{8} \cdot 2\frac{1}{16}$ $5\frac{53}{128}$

Calculator Practice

Suppose you use pencil and paper to determine that $\frac{1}{2} \cdot \frac{2}{5} = \frac{1}{5}$. To check your answer using a calculator, follow these steps.

EXAMPLE 3 Find the decimal equivalent for your answer.

Press $1 \div 5 =$. The calculator display reads 0.2.

Perform the computation using a calculator.

Press $1 \div 2 \times 2 \div 5 =$. The calculator display reads 0.2.

Compare your first answer to your second answer. If the answers are different, use pencil and paper to perform the computation again.

Exercise C Use a calculator to perform these computations. If the answer is correct, write *correct*. If the answer is not correct, write *not correct*.

21. $\frac{1}{4} \cdot \frac{7}{8} = 0.583$ not correct   **24.** $\frac{7}{16} \cdot \frac{3}{16} = 0.1346$ not correct

22. $\frac{4}{5} \cdot \frac{1}{2} = 0.4$ correct   **25.** $\frac{9}{17} \cdot \frac{2}{5} = 0.2117647$ correct

23. $\frac{3}{8} \cdot \frac{1}{6} = 0.0625$ correct

Lesson at a Glance

Chapter 5 Lesson 10

Overview This lesson teaches students how to divide fractions and mixed numbers.

Objectives

- To divide fractions and mixed numbers
- To identify and use reciprocals of numbers for division with fractions

Student Pages 128–131

Teacher's Resource Library **TRL**

Workbook Activity 44–45

Activity 43

Alternative Activity 43

Mathematics Vocabulary

reciprocal

---

1 Warm-Up Activity

Use a rectangular cake to model the following situation: There is one-half of a birthday cake left from yesterday's party. Four students share the remaining cake equally. How much of the cake did each get? $\left(\frac{1}{8}\right)$

---

2 Teaching the Lesson

Use the first two examples in demonstrations on the overhead projector or board. Encourage volunteers to explain each of the steps in division by fractions.

Suggest that students adopt a formal process for dividing with fractions. Point out that they might perform each operation in the same relative order for all division problems. Remind them that the last step is to check to see that the answer is in simplest form.

Reciprocal

The reciprocal of any non-zero number x is $\frac{1}{x}$, sometimes called the multiplicative inverse of that number

Computations sometimes involve dividing fractions or mixed numbers. Whenever you are asked to divide fractions or mixed numbers, use a **reciprocal.** The reciprocal of any non-zero number x is $\frac{1}{x}$.

EXAMPLE 1 What is the reciprocal of $\frac{1}{2}$?

The reciprocal of $\frac{1}{2}$ is $\frac{2}{1}$.

What is the reciprocal of $\frac{y}{3}$?

The reciprocal of $\frac{y}{3}$ is $\frac{3}{y}$.

You can also write the reciprocal of a mixed number.

EXAMPLE 2 What is the reciprocal of $2\frac{3}{4}$ and of $2\frac{3}{4}x$?

Step 1 Express the mixed number as an improper fraction.

$$2\frac{3}{4} = \frac{11}{4} \qquad\qquad 2\frac{3}{4}x = \frac{11}{4}x = \frac{11x}{4}$$

Step 2 Write the reciprocal of the improper fraction.

The reciprocal of $\frac{11}{4}$ is $\frac{4}{11}$.

The reciprocal of $\frac{11x}{4}$ is $\frac{4}{11x}$.

The product of any number (x) and its reciprocal $\left(\frac{1}{x}\right)$ is 1.

EXAMPLE 3 5 and $\frac{1}{5}$ are reciprocals. $\qquad$ $5x$ and $\frac{1}{5x}$ are reciprocals.

$$5 \cdot \frac{1}{5} = \frac{5}{1} \cdot \frac{1}{5} = \frac{5}{5} = 1 \qquad 5x \cdot \frac{1}{5x} = \frac{5x}{1} \cdot \frac{1}{5x} = \frac{5x}{5x} = 1$$

Workbook Activity 44

Workbook Activity 45

The reciprocal of a number is sometimes called the *multiplicative inverse* of that number. Use the reciprocal or multiplicative inverse to divide fractions or mixed numbers.

> When simplifying fractions, the value of a fraction is not changed if both the numerator and denominator are divided by the same number.

EXAMPLE 4 Divide $\frac{3}{4} \div \frac{3}{8}$. Divide $\frac{3}{4} \div \frac{3}{8x}$.

Step 1 Find the reciprocal of the divisor.

The reciprocal of $\frac{3}{8}$ is $\frac{8}{3}$. The reciprocal of $\frac{3}{8x}$ is $\frac{8x}{3}$.

Step 2 Multiply the dividend by the reciprocal of the divisor.

$$\frac{3}{4} \div \frac{3}{8} = \frac{3}{4} \bullet \frac{8}{3} = \frac{24}{12} \qquad \frac{3}{4} \div \frac{3}{8x} = \frac{3}{4} \bullet \frac{8x}{3} = \frac{24x}{12}$$

Step 3 If possible, simplify.

$$\frac{24}{12} = 2 \qquad \frac{24x}{12} = 2x$$

Rule

To divide two fractions, multiply by the reciprocal of the second fraction, which is the divisor.

$$\frac{a}{b} \div \frac{c}{d} = \frac{a}{b} \bullet \frac{d}{c}$$

Also use a reciprocal whenever you divide one or more mixed numbers.

EXAMPLE 5 Divide $1\frac{1}{2} \div 2\frac{3}{8}$. Divide $1\frac{1}{2}y \div 2\frac{3}{8}$.

Step 1 Express each mixed number as an improper fraction.

$$1\frac{1}{2} = \frac{3}{2} \qquad 1\frac{1}{2}y = \frac{3}{2}y$$

$$2\frac{3}{8} = \frac{19}{8} \qquad 2\frac{3}{8} = \frac{19}{8}$$

Step 2 Multiply the dividend by the reciprocal of the divisor.

$$1\frac{1}{2} \div 2\frac{3}{8} \qquad 1\frac{1}{2}y \div 2\frac{3}{8}$$
$$\downarrow \qquad \downarrow \qquad\qquad \downarrow \qquad \downarrow$$
$$\frac{3}{2} \div \frac{19}{8} = \frac{3}{2} \bullet \frac{8}{19} = \frac{24}{38} \qquad \frac{3}{2}y \div \frac{19}{8} = \frac{3}{2}y \bullet \frac{8}{19} = \frac{24}{38}y$$

Step 3 If possible, simplify.

$$\frac{24}{38} = \frac{12}{19} \qquad \frac{24}{38}y = \frac{12}{19}y$$

LEARNING STYLES

Auditory/Verbal

Help students practice naming reciprocals. Present a fraction or mixed number on a card, or write it on the board. Ask students to name its reciprocal as quickly as possible. Sample fractions and mixed numbers include:

$\frac{1}{2}$	(2)	$\frac{3}{5}$	$\left(\frac{5}{3}\right)$
$1\frac{1}{2}$	$\left(\frac{2}{3}\right)$	$3\frac{3}{5}$	$\left(\frac{5}{18}\right)$
$\frac{7}{8}$	$\left(\frac{8}{7}\right)$	$\frac{8}{9}$	$\left(\frac{9}{8}\right)$
$5\frac{7}{8}$	$\left(\frac{8}{47}\right)$	$3\frac{8}{9}$	$\left(\frac{9}{35}\right)$

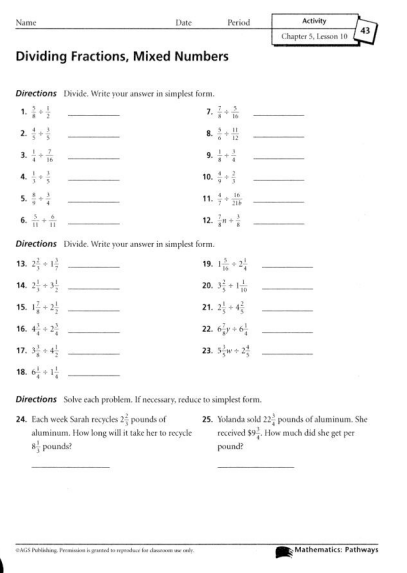

RL

Activity 43

Writing About Mathematics

Write one or more sentences to answer this question. How can you check your work when finding the reciprocal of a number or fraction?

Exercise A Divide. Write your answer in simplest form.

1. $\frac{3}{4} \div \frac{5}{8}$ $1\frac{1}{5}$

2. $\frac{7}{10} \div \frac{3}{4}$ $\frac{14}{15}$

3. $\frac{1}{4} \div \frac{2}{3}$ $\frac{3}{8}$

4. $\frac{5}{16} \div \frac{5}{8}$ $\frac{1}{2}$

5. $\frac{1}{2} \div \frac{3}{10}$ $1\frac{2}{3}$

6. $\frac{7}{8}b \div \frac{1}{3}$ $2\frac{5}{8}b$

7. $\frac{1}{3} \div \frac{1}{2m}$ $\frac{2m}{3}$

8. $\frac{11}{12} \div \frac{3x}{4}$ $\frac{11}{9x}$

Exercise B Divide. Write your answer in simplest form.

9. $2\frac{1}{2} \div 1\frac{1}{5}$ $2\frac{1}{12}$

10. $3\frac{3}{4} \div 1\frac{1}{4}$ 3

11. $1\frac{1}{3} \div 4\frac{1}{6}$ $\frac{8}{25}$

12. $2\frac{7}{8} \div 5\frac{1}{2}$ $\frac{23}{44}$

13. $1\frac{1}{2} \div 1\frac{3}{4}$ $\frac{6}{7}$

14. $4\frac{2}{3} \div 2\frac{1}{10}$ $2\frac{2}{9}$

15. $2\frac{1}{4}h \div 1\frac{5}{8}$ $1\frac{5}{13}h$

16. $2\frac{5}{12} \div 6\frac{2}{3}y$ $\frac{29}{80y}$

17. $3\frac{3}{8}k \div 5\frac{1}{4}$ $\frac{9}{14}k$

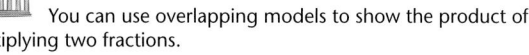

Build a Model

You can use overlapping models to show the product of multiplying two fractions.

Draw 2 identical squares on tracing paper, and cut them out. Divide square A into 3 equal columns. Color one of the columns. Divide square B into 6 equal rows. Color 5 of the rows.

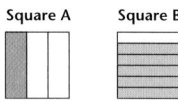

Square A   Square B

Next, overlap the 2 squares. You will see a total of 18 units. The overlapping area, which includes 5 units out of 18, is equal to the product of $\frac{1}{3} \times \frac{5}{6}$.

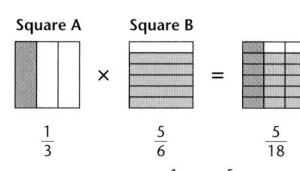

Square A   Square B

$\frac{1}{3}$ $\frac{5}{6}$ $\frac{5}{18}$

Make models for $\frac{1}{6}$, $\frac{1}{2}$, and $\frac{4}{5}$. Use these and the $\frac{1}{3}$ and $\frac{5}{6}$ models. Overlap them to show the products of:

$\frac{1}{3} \cdot \frac{1}{6}$ $\frac{1}{2} \cdot \frac{4}{5}$ $\frac{1}{4} \cdot \frac{4}{5}$

$\frac{1}{3} \times \frac{1}{6} = \frac{1}{18}$

$\frac{1}{2} \times \frac{4}{5} = \frac{4}{10}$

$\frac{1}{4} \times \frac{4}{5} = \frac{4}{20}$

Exercise C Solve each problem.

18. A tennis court is 36 feet wide. The half-court playing width for singles is $13\frac{1}{2}$ feet. What part of the full width does each half-court take up?

$\frac{3}{8}$ of the court

19. Shanelle has a bolt of material that is $17\frac{1}{2}$ feet long. She cuts the material into pieces $\frac{2}{5}$ foot long. How many $\frac{2}{5}$-foot long pieces does she have?

$43\frac{3}{4}$ pieces

20. The national park has $19\frac{1}{3}$ miles of road. If Claire skates the entire length of the road in $3\frac{3}{4}$ hours, how many miles per hour does she skate?

$5\frac{7}{45}$ mph

 Try This

Find the quotient $\frac{1}{2} \div \frac{2}{3} \div \frac{3}{4} \div \frac{4}{5}$.

Hint: Do the operations from left to right in the order they appear.

$1\frac{1}{4}$

Try This

When reciprocals are employed, the problem becomes $[(\frac{1}{2} \cdot \frac{3}{2}) \cdot \frac{4}{3}] \cdot \frac{5}{4}$. Students can confirm their answers with a calculator.

GROUP PROBLEM SOLVING

 Suggest that small groups of students investigate the possibility of placing a traffic circle at a busy intersection near the school. Have them report on what fraction of the school's traffic passes through the intersection and what fraction of the total traffic is caused by the school. They should also find out what fraction of the homes and businesses within one block of the intersection would favor a traffic circle. Have them contact the local Department of Transportation or the mayor's office to find out what requirements must be met to implement a traffic circle.

Chapter 5 Application

Overview This lesson provides an application of breaking a whole number into parts.

Objectives

- To find whole-number equivalency using fractions
- To find whole-number equivalency using the basic operations

Student Page 132

Teacher's Resource Library **TRL**

Application Activity 5

Everyday Math 5

1 Warm-Up Activity

Play or sing a song for the class. Choose two measures, and ask students to identify the number of beats per measure. Have students choose or create a rhythm and sing or clap measures with different numbers of beats.

2 Teaching the Lesson

Remind students to check the picture of the musical notes so that they identify them properly in the problems. Ask students to think about songs they know and the number of possible note combinations. Have students rewrite all answers as fractions. Students can then write equations for adding the fractions to equal the whole.

MENTAL MATH

 Students can count by $\frac{1}{2}$, $\frac{1}{4}$, or $\frac{1}{8}$ as they complete the problems. If music is playing, have students identify the beats per measure by converting the numbers to fractions and using mental addition.

LEARNING STYLES

 **LEP/ESL**
Students should count aloud and become familiar with numbers in fraction form. Allow students to share musical genres from different cultures.

Moving with the Beat In music, rhythm is set by the beat of each note. How long you play a note is determined by the type of note it is. There are 6 common types of notes:

If you have 4 beats for any set of notes, then a whole note gets 4 beats, a half note gets 2 beats, a quarter note gets 1, and so on.

EXAMPLE 1 The total number of beats is 4. How many beats will each note get?

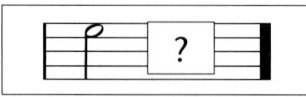

EXAMPLE 2 The total number of beats is 4. What is the beat of the missing note?

The beat of the missing note is a half note (2 beats).

Exercise

1. The total number of beats is 4. How many beats will the whole note get?

   4 beats

2. The total number of beats is 4. How many beats will the quarter note get?

   1 beat

3. The total number of beats is 4. How many beats will the eighth note get?

   $\frac{1}{2}$ beat

4. The total number of beats is 4. One note is missing. Which is it? half note
   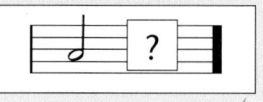

5. The total number of beats is 4. One note is missing. Which is it? quarter note
   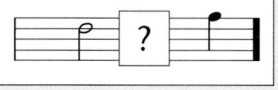

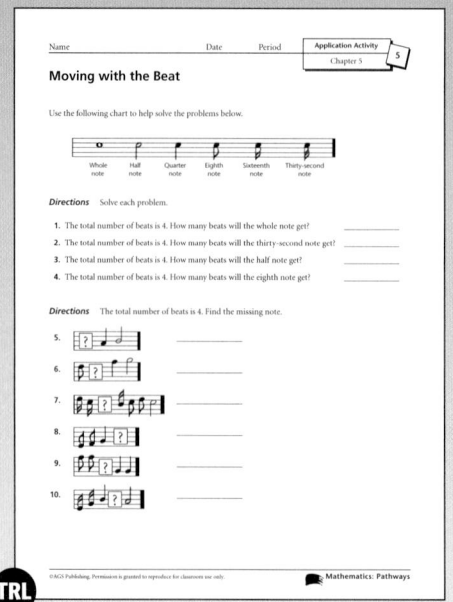

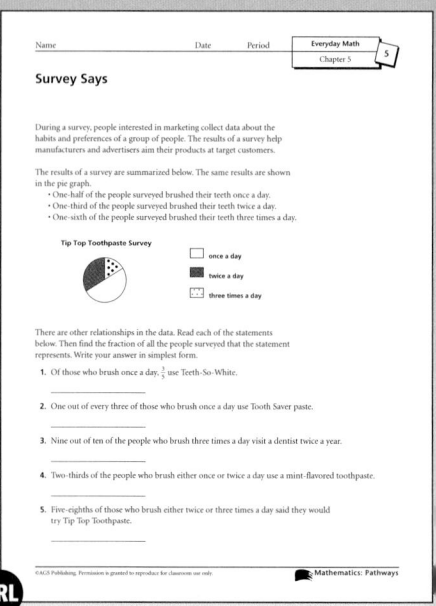

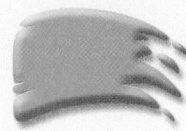

Chapter 5 REVIEW

Write the letter of the correct answer.

1. How would $1\frac{2}{3}$ be expressed as an improper fraction? B

   A $\frac{3}{3}$ C $\frac{7}{3}$

   B $\frac{5}{3}$ D $\frac{3}{5}$

2. How would $\frac{15}{2}$ be expressed as a mixed number? A

   A $7\frac{1}{2}$ C $8\frac{1}{2}$

   B $2\frac{1}{7}$ D $6\frac{1}{2}$

Add, subtract, multiply, or divide.

3. $2\frac{1}{5} \cdot 2\frac{1}{5} =$ C

   A $1\frac{1}{5}$ B $4\frac{2}{5}$ C $4\frac{21}{25}$ D 1

4. $\frac{5}{8} - \frac{3}{8} =$ A

   A $\frac{1}{4}$ B $\frac{2}{0}$ C $\frac{25}{64}$ D $\frac{8}{8}$

5. $\frac{1}{3} \div \frac{2}{3} =$ C

   A $\frac{3}{2}$ B 1 C $\frac{1}{2}$ D $\frac{1}{6}$

6. $1\frac{1}{2} \cdot 4\frac{1}{2} =$ B

   A 6 B $6\frac{3}{4}$ C $5\frac{3}{4}$ D $5\frac{1}{2}$

7. $\frac{1}{2}x + \frac{1}{4}x =$ D

   A $\frac{2}{8}x$ B $\frac{1}{6}x$ C $\frac{1}{8}x$ D $\frac{3}{4}x$

Rational Numbers and Fractions   **133**

---

3 Reinforce and Extend

MODELING

Using prerecorded music or musical instruments, invite students to familiarize themselves with different musical genres. Help students identify different styles of music by different beats per measure.

KNOWING YOUR STUDENTS

The importance of popular music to most secondary school students should not be underestimated. Relating math activities to music is a good way to capture students' attention. Students may extend the lesson and improve abstract thinking skills by using "if-then" steps to evaluate beats per measure. Provide music, and ask students to form a hypothesis about the number of beats per measure within a song and across a genre. *If* a song begins with four beats per measure, *then* will this number remain consistent throughout the song? *If* a song from a genre has six beats per measure, *then* is this number the same for songs across the genre?

Chapter 5 Review

Each set of problems in the Chapter Review includes an example and solution to illustrate the concept. Use the given examples for reteaching the materials in Chapter 5. For additional practice, refer to the Supplementary Problems for Chapter 5 (pages 440–441).

Chapter 5 Mastery Test

The Teacher's Resource Library includes parallel forms of the Chapter 5 Mastery Test. The difficulty level of the two forms is equivalent. You may wish to use one form as a pretest and the other form as a posttest.

Chapter 5 Mastery Test A

Alternative Assessment items correlate with student Goals for Learning at the beginning of this chapter.

■ **To identify proper and improper fractions and mixed numbers**
Have students describe and give examples of a proper fraction, an improper fraction, and a mixed number.

■ **To write equivalent fractions**
Have students create a series of six equivalent fractions with increasingly greater numerators and denominators. Examples of fractions you may use include the following:

$$\frac{1}{4} \quad \frac{1}{2} \quad \frac{2}{3} \quad \frac{3}{5}$$

■ **To express fractions in simplest form**
Have students come up with three questions or problems to pose to a partner (or the class) that involve fractions. Encourage them to think of things most students in the class are involved in. For example, "What fraction of our class is wearing sneakers or running shoes today?" or "What fraction of our school day is spent changing classes?"

■ **To compare and order fractions**
Direct students to choose five random numbers from 1 to 15 and write them in order from greatest to least on a sheet of paper. Then have them choose five random numbers from 16 to 30 and write them from least to greatest below the numbers they just wrote. Tell students to draw a fraction bar between the two numbers. Have students order the fractions they've created from least to greatest (or greatest to least). Remind students to check their work by finding the LCD of all the fractions and comparing them mathematically.

Express each improper fraction as a mixed number and express each mixed number as an improper fraction.

Example: $\frac{11}{6}$ and $3\frac{1}{8}$ Solution: $\frac{11}{6} = 1\frac{5}{6}$ and $3\frac{1}{8} = \frac{3 \cdot 8 + 1}{8} = \frac{25}{8}$

$$6\overline{)11}$$
$$\underline{-6}$$
$$5$$

8. $\frac{5}{4}$ $1\frac{1}{4}$

9. $\frac{10}{3}$ $3\frac{1}{3}$

10. $4\frac{5}{6}$ $\frac{29}{6}$

11. $2\frac{2}{5}$ $\frac{12}{5}$

12. $\frac{24}{7}$ $3\frac{3}{7}$

13. $3\frac{1}{3}$ $\frac{10}{3}$

Write two equivalent fractions for each fraction.

Example: $\frac{5}{8}$ Solution: $\frac{5}{8} \cdot \frac{2}{2} = \frac{10}{16}$ $\frac{5}{8} \cdot \frac{3}{3} = \frac{15}{24}$

14. $\frac{2}{3}$ $\frac{4}{6}$ and $\frac{6}{9}$

15. $\frac{1}{4}$ $\frac{2}{8}$ and $\frac{3}{12}$

16. $\frac{3}{5}$ $\frac{6}{10}$ and $\frac{9}{15}$

17. $\frac{7}{10}$ $\frac{14}{20}$ and $\frac{21}{30}$

18. $\frac{1}{16}$ $\frac{2}{32}$ and $\frac{3}{48}$

19. $\frac{5}{12}$ $\frac{10}{24}$ and $\frac{15}{36}$

Sample answers shown for problems 14–19.

Express each fraction in simplest form.

Example: $\frac{10}{16}$ Solution: GCD(10, 16) = 2 $\frac{10}{16} \div \frac{2}{2} = \frac{5}{8}$

20. $\frac{6}{8}$ $\frac{3}{4}$

21. $\frac{4}{6}$ $\frac{2}{3}$

22. $\frac{8}{10}$ $\frac{4}{5}$

23. $\frac{2}{8}$ $\frac{1}{4}$

24. $\frac{3}{15}$ $\frac{1}{5}$

25. $\frac{14}{30}$ $\frac{7}{15}$

Chapter 5 Mastery Test B

Order from least to greatest.

Example: $\frac{1}{2}$ $\frac{2}{5}$ $\frac{3}{4}$ Solution: $\frac{1}{2} = \frac{10}{20}$ $\frac{2}{5} = \frac{8}{20}$ $\frac{3}{4} = \frac{15}{20}$

$\frac{8}{20} < \frac{10}{20} < \frac{15}{20}$ so $\frac{2}{5}$ $\frac{1}{2}$ $\frac{3}{4}$

26. $\frac{1}{5}$ $\frac{1}{3}$ $\frac{4}{15}$ $\frac{1}{5}$ $\frac{4}{15}$ $\frac{1}{3}$ **28.** $\frac{7}{10}$ $\frac{3}{5}$ $\frac{1}{2}$ $\frac{1}{2}$ $\frac{3}{5}$ $\frac{7}{10}$

27. $\frac{11}{12}$ $\frac{5}{6}$ $\frac{2}{3}$ $\frac{2}{3}$ $\frac{5}{6}$ $\frac{11}{12}$ **29.** $\frac{5}{8}$ $\frac{13}{24}$ $\frac{9}{16}$ $\frac{13}{24}$ $\frac{9}{16}$ $\frac{5}{8}$

Add, subtract, multiply, or divide. Simplify your answer if possible.

Example: Add $\frac{1}{3} + \frac{1}{12}$.   Solution: $\frac{1}{3} + \frac{1}{12} = \frac{4}{12} + \frac{1}{12} = \frac{5}{12}$

30. $\frac{2}{5} + \frac{1}{5}$ $\frac{3}{5}$ **38.** $2\frac{5}{8} - 1\frac{1}{6}$ $1\frac{11}{24}$

31. $\frac{3}{4} \cdot \frac{3}{4}$ $\frac{9}{16}$ **39.** $5\frac{1}{8} - 2\frac{7}{12}$ $2\frac{13}{24}$

32. $\frac{3}{16} + \frac{7}{8}$ $1\frac{1}{16}$ **40.** $8\frac{1}{3} \div 4\frac{1}{6}$ 2

33. $\frac{4}{5} \div \frac{9}{10}$ $\frac{8}{9}$ **41.** $3\frac{1}{2} \cdot 1\frac{11}{16}$ $5\frac{29}{32}$

34. $3\frac{1}{8} - 1\frac{3}{4}$ $1\frac{3}{8}$ **42.** $4\frac{1}{4} \div 2\frac{1}{8}$ 2

35. $6\frac{5}{12} + 10\frac{2}{3}$ $17\frac{1}{12}$ **43.** $6\frac{2}{3}h + 6\frac{3}{4}h$ $13\frac{5}{12}h$

36. $1\frac{1}{6} \div 3\frac{1}{2}$ $\frac{1}{3}$ **44.** $2\frac{1}{6}y \cdot 3\frac{2}{5}$ $7\frac{11}{30}y$

37. $5\frac{3}{8} + 8\frac{1}{3}$ $13\frac{17}{24}$ **45.** $\frac{5a}{6} - \frac{2a}{3}$ $\frac{a}{6}$

 Test-Taking Tip

When taking a test, it helps to know the different ways to name the same thing. For example, the *smallest common denominator* is also known as the *least common denominator*, or LCD. Sometimes, *common denominator* is used instead of *like denominator*.

■ **To add and subtract fractions and mixed numbers with like or unlike denominators**

Have students write one fraction and one mixed number on separate slips of scrap paper and label one slip *a* and the other *b*. Put the papers in two containers (one for *a* slips and one for *b* slips). Have students draw one slip from each container. Direct students to find the sum of the two slips (*a* and *b*). Next, have students subtract and find the difference between the mixed number and the fraction.

■ **To multiply and divide fractions and mixed numbers**

Have students take a survey of friends and/or relatives to record statistics such as height, weight, foot size, age, and so on. Then have them formulate word problems requiring multiplication and division of fractions to express one person's statistics with respect to others surveyed. For example, I am $\frac{7}{8}$ as tall as Dad, who is $\frac{6}{5}$ as tall as Danielle. Danielle is 5 feet 2 inches tall. How tall am I? Have students trade problems and solve them.

6

Planning Guide

Basic Operations and Rational Expressions

Lesson	Student Pages	Vocabulary	Practice Exercises	Problem Solving	Try This	Solutions Key
1 The Order of Operations	138–141	✔	✔		141	✔
2 Evaluating Algebraic Expressions	142–145	✔	✔	145		✔
3 Equations—Solution by Substitution	146–147	✔	✔			✔
4 Solving Addition Equations	148–149		✔			✔
5 Solving Subtraction Equations	150–151		✔	151	151	✔
6 Complex Fractions	152–155	✔	✔			✔
7 Simplifying by Addition	156–157	✔	✔			✔
8 Simplifying by Subtraction	158–159		✔	159		✔
9 Multiplying Rational Expressions	160–161		✔	161		✔
Application Converting Measurements	162		✔			✔

Student Text Lesson

Chapter Activities

Teacher's Resource Library
Estimation Exercise 6: Estimating
   Solutions for Equations
Application Activity 6: Converting
   Measurements
Everyday Math 6: Order, Order
Community Connection 6: Voter
   Registration

Teacher's Edition
Chapter 6 Project

Assessment Options

Student Text
Chapter 6 Review

Teacher's Resource Library
Chapter 6 Mastery Tests A and B

Teacher's Edition
Chapter 6 Alternative Assessments

Estimation Activity	Math in Your Life	Technology Connection	Writing About Mathematics	Build a Model	Calculator Practice	Online Connection	Common Error	Applications Home, Career, Community	Mental Math	Manipulatives	Calculator	Group Problem Solving	Modeling	Knowing Your Students	Auditory/Verbal	Visual/Spatial	Logical/Mathematical	Body/Kinesthetic	Interpersonal/Group Learning	LEP/ESL	Activities	Alternate Activities	Workbook Activities	Self-Study Guide
141			141		140	139	140				141		141			140				139	44	44	46	✔
							143		144			145			144		143				45	45	47	✔
		147						147												147	46	46	48	✔
	149						149		149										149		47	47	49	✔
								151	151			151									48	48	50	✔
		154			155		153	154			155							153			49	49	51	✔
		157	157												157	157					50	50	52	✔
							159					159									51	51	53	✔
									161										161		52	52	54	✔
							162						163	163										✔

Software Options

Skill Track Software

Use the Skill Track Software for *Mathematics: Pathways* for additional reinforcement of this chapter. The software provides multiple-choice assessment items for students to access by computer.

Solutions Key

Use the Solutions Key with this chapter to help students who may need additional assistance. The Solutions Key CD provides solutions for every exercise in the student edition.

Other Resources

Alternative Activities

The Teacher's Resource Library (TRL) contains a set of worksheets written at a second-grade reading level called Alternative Activities. They cover the same content as the regular Activities.

Manipulatives

See the Manipulative activities in this chapter for hands-on modeling of the content. The following TRL pages can also be used:

Manipulatives Master 3 (Sentence Mat)
Algebra Tiles

Skill Track for Mathematics: Pathways

Teacher's Resource Library **TRL**

Workbook Activities 46–54

Activities 44–52

Alternative Activities 44–52

Application Activity 6

Estimation Exercise 6

Everyday Math 6

Community Connection 6

Chapter 6 Self-Study Guide

Chapter 6 Mastery Tests A and B
(Answer Keys for the Teacher's Resource Library begin on page 528 of this Teacher's Edition.)

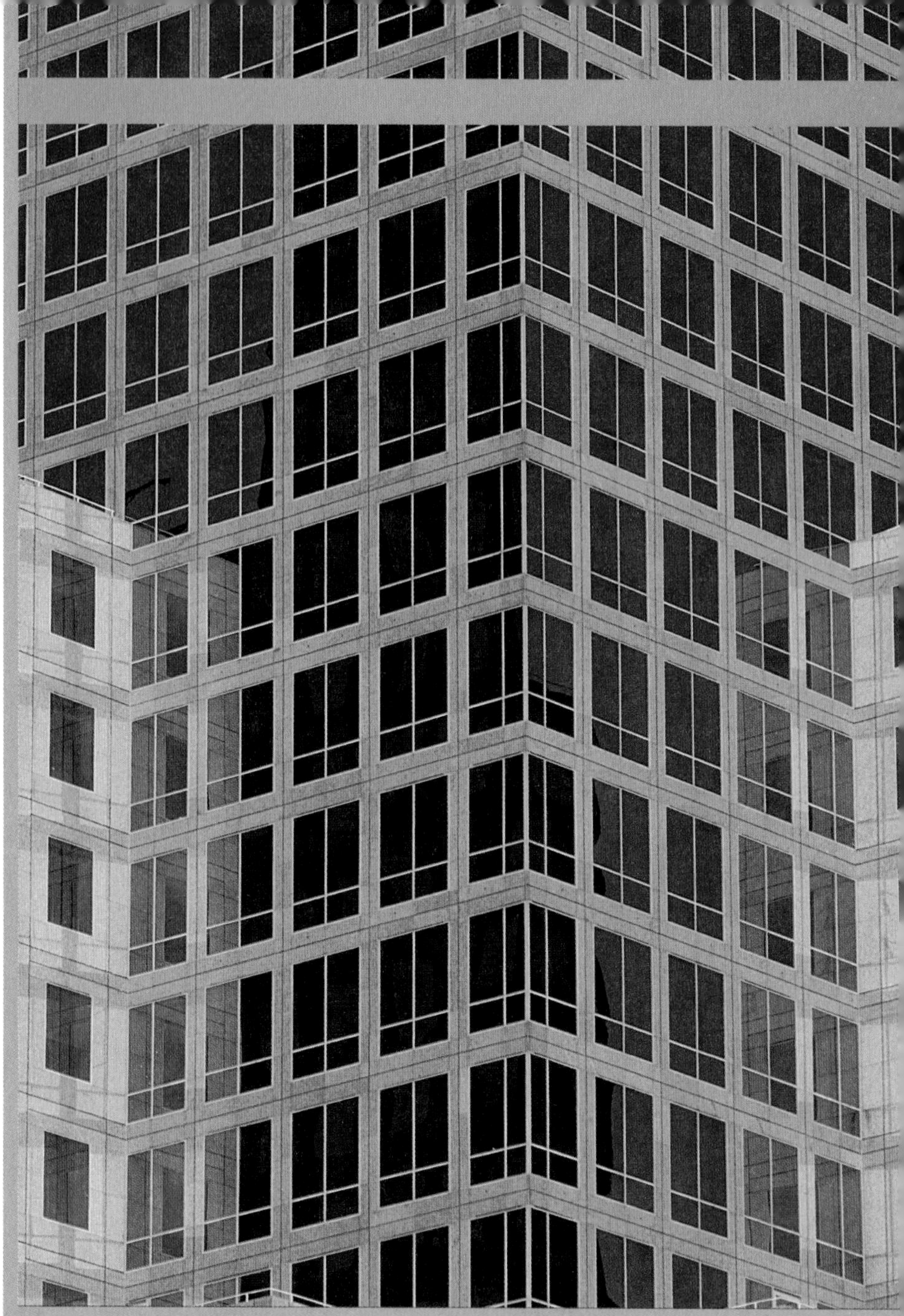

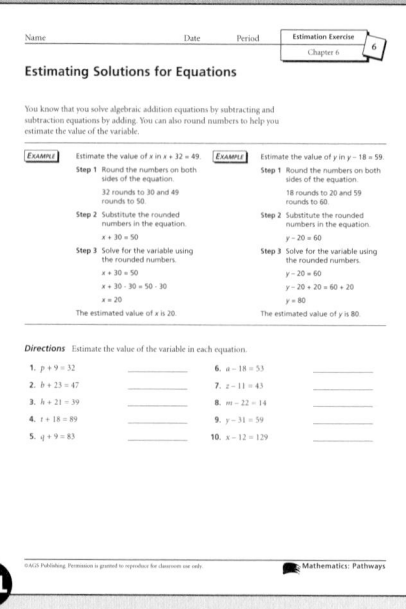

Estimation Exercise 6

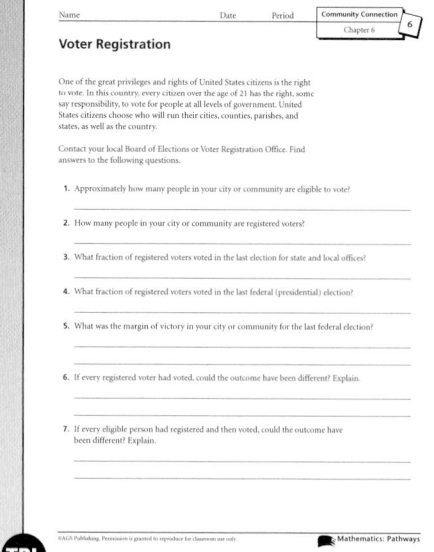

Community Connection 6

6 Basic Operations and Rational Expressions

Many cities are known for the buildings that define their skylines. Some structures are so unique that just seeing their images lets you name the location. For example, when you see the Statue of Liberty, can you instantly name New York City? What about the Arch in St. Louis? Or the Golden Gate Bridge in San Francisco?

Architects and engineers use algebraic equations when designing buildings. They use them to design skyscrapers, bridges, and single family homes. They use algebraic equations to calculate the amount of concrete needed. Engineers use algebra to determine the stress levels of the steel beams. They need to calculate the amount of weight the building materials can handle.

In Chapter 6, you will use basic operations to solve problems with rational numbers.

Goals for Learning

◆ To use the order of operations to solve problems correctly

◆ To evaluate algebraic expressions

◆ To solve algebraic equations through substitution

◆ To solve equations by adding and subtracting

◆ To simplify complex fractions

◆ To add and subtract to simplify rational expressions

◆ To multiply rational expressions

137

Introducing the Chapter

Remind students of the variables used in Chapter 2. Add that this chapter will allow students to continue using the *basic operations* to solve algebraic *expressions*. In addition, this chapter introduces algebraic equations. Point out that many workers, such as builders, retailers, architects, and scientists, use algebra skills to complete tasks.

CHAPTER PROJECT

Have students research the population of your town or city, county, and state, finding the following:

• current population

• population 20 years ago

Also ask that they determine the K–12 student population for these geopolitical areas. Then have small groups of students manipulate the data to find out the following facts:

• How have city, county, and state populations grown or declined?

• What fraction of your total city, county, and state population is enrolled in K–12?

As they progress through the chapter, students will learn the procedures they need to make these calculations.

TEACHER'S RESOURCE

The AGS Publishing Teaching Strategies in Math Transparencies may be used with this chapter. They add an interactive dimension to expand and enhance the program content.

CAREER INTEREST INVENTORY

The AGS Publishing Harrington-O'Shea Career Decision-Making System-Revised (CDM) may be used with this chapter. Students can use the CDM to explore their interests and identify careers. The CDM defines career areas that are indicated by students' responses on the inventory.

Name _____ Date _____ Period _____ *SELF-STUDY GUIDE*

CHAPTER 6: Basic Operations and Rational Expressions

| Goal 6.1 | To use the order of operations to solve problems correctly |

Date	Assignment	Score
	1: Read pages 137–139. Complete Exercise A on page 140.	
	2: Read and complete the Calculator Practice on pages 140–141.	
	3: Complete Workbook Activity 46.	

Comments:

| Goal 6.2 | To evaluate algebraic expressions |

Date	Assignment	Score
	4: Read pages 142–144. Complete Exercises A–C on page 145.	
	5: Complete Workbook Activity 47.	

Comments:

| Goal 6.3 | To solve algebraic equations through substitution |

Date	Assignment	Score
	6: Read page 146. Complete Exercises A–B on page 147.	
	7: Complete Workbook Activity 48.	

Comments:

| Goal 6.4 | To solve equations by adding and subtracting |

Date	Assignment	Score
	8: Read pages 148–149. Complete Exercises A–B on page 149.	
	9: Complete Workbook Activity 49.	
	10: Read page 150. Complete Exercises A–B on page 151.	
	11: Complete Workbook Activity 50.	

Comments:

Name _____ Date _____ Period _____ *SELF-STUDY GUIDE*

CHAPTER 6: Basic Operations and Rational Expressions, continued

| Goal 6.5 | To simplify complex fractions |

Date	Assignment	Score
	12: Read pages 152–154. Complete Exercise A on page 154.	
	13: Read and complete the Calculator Practice on page 155.	
	14: Complete Workbook Activity 51.	

Comments:

| Goal 6.6 | To add and subtract to simplify rational expressions |

Date	Assignment	Score
	15: Read page 156. Complete Exercises A–B on page 157.	
	16: Complete Workbook Activity 52.	
	17: Read page 158. Complete Exercises A–C on page 159.	
	18: Complete Workbook Activity 53.	

Comments:

| Goal 6.7 | To multiply rational expressions |

Date	Assignment	Score
	19: Read page 160. Complete Exercises A–B on page 161.	
	20: Complete Workbook Activity 54.	
	21: Read and complete the Application on page 162.	
	22: Complete the Chapter 6 Review on pages 163–165.	

Comments:

Student's Signature _____ Date _____

Instructor's Signature _____ Date _____

(TRL)

Chapter 6 Self-Study Guide

Basic Operations and Rational Expressions **137**

Lesson at a Glance

Chapter 6 Lesson 1

Overview This lesson specifies the order in which basic operations in a number sentence must be performed.

Objectives

- To comprehend the sequence in which addition, subtraction, multiplication, and division must be performed in an expression
- To simplify expressions using the order of operations

Student Pages 138–141

Teacher's Resource Library

Workbook Activity 46

Activity 44

Alternative Activity 44

Mathematics Vocabulary

order of operations

1 Warm-Up Activity

Ask students to think of a task they perform that requires a number of steps, such as mowing the grass or making a favorite recipe. Have them list the steps in the order in which they are performed. What would happen if the steps were mixed up? Explain to students that in mathematics, operations must be completed in a certain order, and have them read page 138 to find out what that order is.

2 Teaching the Lesson

Students must master and remember the order of operations to solve equations accurately. A mnemonic device can help them remember the proper order of operations:

Please	(*p*arentheses)
Excuse	(*e*xponent)
My **D**ear	(*m*ultiply, *d*ivide)
Aunt **S**usan	(*a*dd, *s*ubtract)

Order of operations

Rules that describe the order that addition, subtraction, multiplication, and division must be performed

Examples of operations include addition, subtraction, multiplication, and division. Number sentences and expressions often contain more than one operation.

When expressions and number sentences contain two or more operations, the order in which you perform those operations is very important.

EXAMPLE 1 Find $2 + 8 \div 2$.

By looking at the problem, you may think you could do the problem in two ways—add then divide, or divide then add. But there is only one correct solution. According to the rules for the **order of operations,** you must divide first.

Step 1 Divide first. $2 + 8 \div 2$
↓
4

Step 2 Then add. $2 + 4$
↓
6

The solution $2 + 8 \div 2 = 6$ is correct. Whenever a number sentence or expression contains more than one operation, the operations must be performed in a specific order.

Order of Operations

1. If grouping symbols such as parentheses are used, perform the operations inside the grouping symbols first.
2. Evaluate powers.
3. Multiply and divide in order from left to right.
4. Add and subtract in order from left to right.

These rules are known as the order of operations. Follow the order of operations whenever an expression or number sentence contains two or more operations.

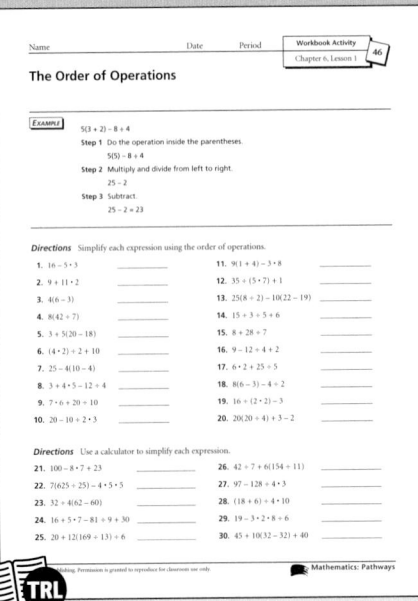

Workbook Activity 46

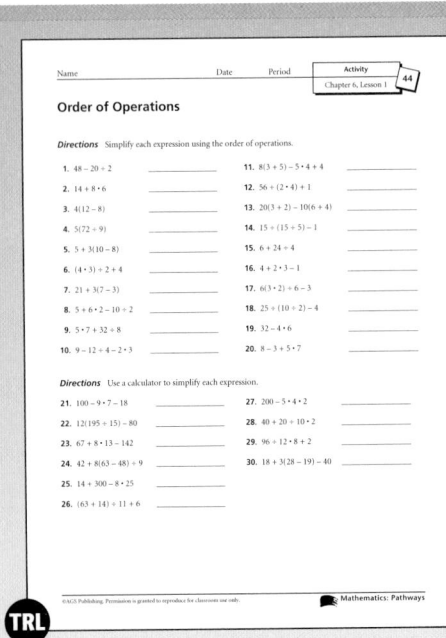

Activity 44

Expressions and number sentences sometimes contain three or more operations.

EXAMPLE 2 4 ÷ 2 + 16 • 2

Step 1 Since the number sentence does not contain grouping symbols, multiply and divide in order from left to right.

$$4 ÷ 2 + 16 • 2$$
$$\downarrow \qquad \downarrow$$
$$2 \ + \ 32$$

Step 2 Add and subtract in order from left to right.

$$4 ÷ 2 + 16 • 2$$
$$\downarrow \qquad \downarrow$$
$$2 \ + \ 32$$
$$\downarrow$$
$$34$$

EXAMPLE 3 2(7 − 4) − 9 ÷ 3

Follow the order of operations.

2(7 − 4) − 9 ÷ 3   Perform the operations inside
$\downarrow$ the grouping symbols.

2(3)   − 9 ÷ 3   Multiply and divide from left
$\downarrow$ $\downarrow$ to right.

6   −   3   Add and subtract from left
$\downarrow$ to right.
3

Check students' understanding of the order of operations by posing questions such as the following:

- Which is greater: $3 + 4^2$ or $(3 + 4)^2$? *[$(3 + 4)^2$ is 49; $3 + 4^2$ is 19]*

- Which answer is correct for the expression $25 + 3 • (10 − 4)$—43 or 51? *(43)*

- What value do you get from the first operation performed in $8 − 5 + 20 ÷ 5$? *(4)*

3 Reinforce and Extend

COMMON ERROR

Because English is read from left to right, most students will have a natural tendency to compute operations from left to right. Until they have adequate practice in using the four steps, students need to refer frequently to the order of operations chart on page 138 to avoid errors.

Students who come from cultures in which the written material is read from right to left may need extra reminders to perform each step in left-to-right order.

LEARNING STYLES

Visual/Spatial

To provide stronger visual cues to the order of operations, have students copy problems from Exercise A on the board, underline each step, and number it, as the following example shows:

$$\overset{1}{10\underline{(2+8)}} + 3 \cdot 2$$

$$\overset{2}{10\underline{(10)}} + 3 \cdot 2$$

$$100 + \overset{3}{\underline{3 \cdot 2}}$$

$$\overset{4}{\underline{100 + 6}}$$

$$106$$

Exercise A Simplify each expression by applying the rules for the order of operations.

1. $24 - 8 \div 4$	22	**9.** $3 \cdot 5 + 10 \div 5$	17
2. $11 + 9 \cdot 3$	38	**10.** $8 - 4 \div 2 - 2 \cdot 1$	4
3. $3(6 - 2)$	12	**11.** $10(2 + 8) + 3 \cdot 2$	106
4. $9(12 \div 3)$	36	**12.** $28 \div (4 \cdot 7) - 0$	1
5. $1 + 17(7 - 5)$	35	**13.** $20(2 + 6) - 10(32 \div 4)$	80
6. $(6 \cdot 6) \div 12 + 6$	9	**14.** $(10 \div 2) \div 5 + 1$	2
7. $11 + 4(5 - 1)$	27	**15.** $7 + 12 \div 3$	11
8. $2 + 4 \cdot 6 - 8 \div 4$	24		

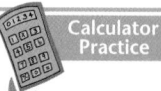

Calculator Practice

You can use a scientific calculator to find the solution to a numerical expression. Input the expression exactly as it appears. Include the $\times$ to multiply the amount within the parentheses.

EXAMPLE 4 $(15 \div 4 - 1) + 4(3 - 2)$

Press $(\ |5\ \div\ 4\ -\ |\ )\ +\ 4\ \times$

$(\ 3\ -\ 2\ )\ =$.

The display reads 6.75.

If you have a standard calculator, it may not follow the order of operations. Before relying on the calculator, work one problem with paper and pencil to verify the answer on your calculator. Follow these steps and the order of operations to work the problem with a standard calculator.

EXAMPLE 5 $(15 \div 4 - 1) + 4(3 - 2)$

Press $15\ \div\ 4\ =\ -\ |\ =$.

The display reads 2.75.

Press $\boxed{M+}$.

Press $3\ -\ 2\ =\ \times\ 4\ =$.

Press $\boxed{M+}$.

The display reads 4.

Press $\boxed{MRC}$.

The display reads 6.75.

Exercise B Use a scientific calculator to simplify each expression. Input each expression exactly as it appears.

16. $10 - 2 \cdot 4 + 1$ 3

17. $5(4 - \frac{1}{5})$ 19

18. $16 \div 4(3 - 1)$ 8

19. $5 + 2(12 - 4) + 20 \div 4$ 26

20. $2 + 3 \cdot 4 - 6 \div 2 + 9 - 18 \div 3$ 14

Estimation Activity

Estimate: A bag of dry dog food weighs $8\frac{1}{2}$ pounds. If a dog eats $\frac{1}{2}$ pound each day, how many days will a bag last?

Solution: $2(\frac{1}{2}$ lb$) = 1$ lb lasts 2 days

            8 lb lasts 16 days

            $8\frac{1}{2}$ lb lasts 17 days

Try This

Write a numerical expression that contains $+$, $-$, $\bullet$, and $\div$. Simplify the expression incorrectly. Then show the expression and its incorrect solution to a classmate and challenge him or her to find the error that you made.

Answers will vary. Sample answer:
$2 + 3(4) = 20$. Error: First multiply and then add.
$2 + 3(4) = 14$.

Try This

Before students can learn to simplify expressions, they will first need to fully understand the correct order of operations. Go over each of the lesson exercises in class to make sure that students have accurately completed them. Use the problems below and similar problems to help students who need extra practice develop this skill.

$15 + 24 \div 2 \cdot 4$ *(63)*

$5 \cdot 3^2 - (9 + 8)$ *(28)*

$(50 \cdot 2) + (12 - 7)^2 \div 5$ *(105)*

$7(5) - 60 \div 4$ *(20)*

CALCULATOR

Have pairs of students work with two different calculators—one scientific and one standard—to input the following expressions:

$3 + 4 \cdot 6$

$42 \div 7 + 3$

$(5 \cdot 2) \div 2 + 8$

Have partners make a chart noting differences in the values they get from each calculator. Then have them use pencil and paper to simplify each expression and determine which calculator uses the order of operations. Finally, pairs can read manual instructions and recalculate to find the correct answer with the standard calculator.

MODELING

Provide students with a number sentence and a solution. Ask students to brainstorm, individually or in groups, to identify the method used to obtain the solution. Groups may use counters, number lines, or other materials. Allow groups to share strategies. Discuss the order of operations with students.

Place students in groups, and give each group a number sentence. Ask each student in the group to choose one operation and calculate the section of the number sentence that uses that operation. Students must follow the order of operations. For example, if the problem is $4 - 3 + 6^2$, one student will calculate with the exponent (first), one will do the subtraction (second), and one will do the addition (third). Encourage groups to repeat these steps as their equations and solutions are shared. Direct students to use concrete materials to model their process.

Lesson at a Glance

Chapter 6 Lesson 2

Overview This lesson explains how to evaluate expressions by substituting values and using the order of operations.

Objectives

- To substitute given values for variables in algebraic expressions
- To follow the order of operations to simplify expressions

Student Pages 142–145

Teacher's Resource Library **TRL**

Workbook Activity 47

Activity 45

Alternative Activity 45

Mathematics Vocabulary

constant

---

1 Warm-Up Activity

Have students discuss jobs they do and how they figure the amount of money they will earn in a given week. Does this amount vary? What causes it to vary? Create a chart like the following on the board:

Hrs. Worked	$ Earned
1	$5.15
2	$10.30
3	$15.45
4	$20.60

Have students decide what variable, or number, is multiplied by the number of hours to determine earnings. ($5.15)

2 Teaching the Lesson

Point out to students that x is not used to specify multiplication in algebraic expressions because it is frequently used as a variable. Parentheses, a dot, or simply placement is used to indicate this operation.

Constant

A number in an expression that does not change such as 2, −6, and $\frac{1}{3}$ in an expression such as $2x - 6y + \frac{1}{3}z$

Enclosing a number in parentheses does not change its value. For example, $2 = (2)$ and $3 \cdot 5 = (3) \cdot (5)$.

Recall that an algebraic expression is made up of one or more variables and usually includes one or more **constants** and one or more operations.

It is possible to evaluate an expression. To evaluate means to substitute given values for the variable(s), then simplify by following the order of operations.

EXAMPLE 1 Evaluate $3x + 5$ when $x = 1, 2,$ and 3.

Step 1 For each variable x in the expression, substitute a given number. Write the number inside parentheses.

Step 2 Simplify the expression by following the order of operations.

$$3x + 5 \text{ when } x = 1.$$
$$\downarrow$$
$$3(1) + 5$$
$$\downarrow \quad \text{Multiply.}$$
$$3 + 5$$
$$\downarrow \quad \text{Add.}$$
$$8$$

$$3x + 5 \text{ when } x = 2.$$
$$\downarrow$$
$$3(2) + 5$$
$$\downarrow \quad \text{Multiply.}$$
$$6 + 5$$
$$\downarrow \quad \text{Add.}$$
$$11$$

$$3x + 5 \text{ when } x = 3.$$
$$\downarrow$$
$$3(3) + 5$$
$$\downarrow \quad \text{Multiply.}$$
$$9 + 5$$
$$\downarrow \quad \text{Add.}$$
$$14$$

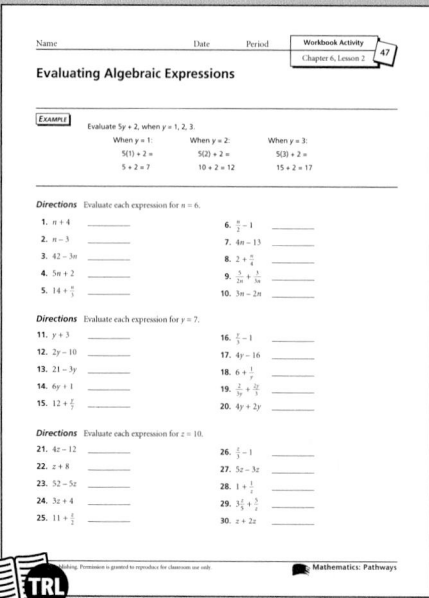

Workbook Activity 47

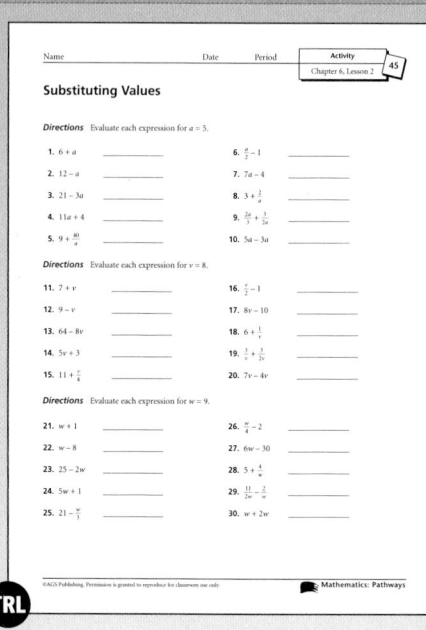

Activity 45

EXAMPLE 2 Evaluate $\frac{3}{x} + x$ when $x = 1$, 2, and 3.

Step 1 For each variable x in the expression, substitute a given number.

Step 2 Simplify the expression by following the order of operations.

$$\frac{3}{x} + x \text{ when } x = 1.$$
$$\downarrow$$
$$\frac{3}{1} + 1$$
$$\downarrow \quad \text{Divide.}$$
$$3 + 1$$
$$\quad \downarrow \quad \text{Add.}$$
$$4$$

$$\frac{3}{x} + x \text{ when } x = 2.$$
$$\downarrow$$
$$\frac{3}{2} + 2$$
$$\downarrow \quad \text{Divide.}$$
$$1\frac{1}{2} + 2$$
$$\quad \downarrow \quad \text{Add.}$$
$$3\frac{1}{2}$$

$$\frac{3}{x} + x \text{ when } x = 3.$$
$$\downarrow$$
$$\frac{3}{3} + 3$$
$$\downarrow \quad \text{Divide.}$$
$$1 + 3$$
$$\quad \downarrow \quad \text{Add.}$$
$$4$$

COMMON ERROR

When students substitute a value for the variable in expressions that lack a multiplication sign, such as $5n$, they may forget to multiply. For example, where $n = 12$, $5n$ might simply become 512. Remind students that placing the two values side by side with no space between them means that they must be multiplied, just as if an $\times$ or a $\cdot$ or ( ) were used.

 Reinforce and Extend

LEARNING STYLES

Body/Kinesthetic
Have students work with paper cups and small identical objects such as paper clips to model algebraic expressions for different values. For example, for $3x + 5$, provide three paper cups, and explain that x will equal 3. Place three paper clips in each cup and 5 in a separate pile. Have students count clips and evaluate the expression for $x = 3$. *(14)* Then have a volunteer model the expression when $x = 4$. *(17)*

Auditory/Verbal

Increase students' understanding of what each numerical expression means by calling out expressions and having students write them in numerical form. For example,

"15 more than *n*" *(n + 15)*

"6 less than *a*" *(a − 6)*

"the product of 24 and *k*" *(24k)*

"*x* to the fourth power divided by 5" *(x⁴ ÷ 5)*

Repeat the process, using phrases from word problems for practice in recognizing the needed operation.

"how many more this week than last week?" *(subtraction)*

"all together" *(addition)*

"three times farther" *(multiplication)*

"shared equally" *(division)*

MENTAL MATH

Review the order of operations by first asking a volunteer to list the steps, explaining any mnemonic device used. Then call out simple expressions such as the following, and have students use mental math to name the first operation to be performed:

$12 + 3 \cdot 2$	*(3 • 2)*
$5 \cdot 2 \div 3$	*(5 • 2)*
$(6 - 3)^2$	*(6 − 3)*
$27 + 14 \cdot 4 \div 10$	*(14 • 4)*
$20 \cdot (8 - 5)$	*(8 − 5)*

EXAMPLE 3 Evaluate $4 - \frac{2}{y}$ when $y = 1$, 2, and 3.

Step 1 For each variable y in the expression, substitute a given number.

Step 2 Simplify the expression by following the order of operations.

$$4 - \frac{2}{y} \text{ when } y = 1.$$
$$\downarrow$$
$$4 - \frac{2}{1}$$
$$\downarrow \text{ Divide.}$$
$$4 - 2$$
$$\downarrow \quad \text{Subtract.}$$
$$2$$

$$4 - \frac{2}{y} \text{ when } y = 2.$$
$$\downarrow$$
$$4 - \frac{2}{2}$$
$$\downarrow \text{ Divide.}$$
$$4 - 1$$
$$\downarrow \quad \text{Subtract.}$$
$$3$$

$$4 - \frac{2}{y} \text{ when } y = 3.$$
$$\downarrow$$
$$4 - \frac{2}{3}$$
$$\downarrow \text{ Divide.}$$
$$4 - \frac{2}{3}$$
$$\downarrow \quad \text{Subtract.}$$
$$3\frac{1}{3}$$

Exercise A Evaluate each expression.

1. $a - \frac{2}{3}$ when $a = 9$ $8\frac{1}{3}$

2. $a + \frac{3}{4}$ when $a = 13$ $13\frac{3}{4}$

3. $3a - 1$ when $a = 5$ 14

4. $15 - 7a$ when $a = 2$ 1

5. $\frac{a}{2} - 4$ when $a = 10$ 1

6. $17 + \frac{a}{2}$ when $a = 5$ $19\frac{1}{2}$

7. $8 + 9a$ when $a = 3$ 35

8. $2a + \frac{1}{a}$ when $a = 4$ $8\frac{1}{4}$

9. $\frac{a}{4} + \frac{a}{4}$ when $a = 3$ $1\frac{1}{2}$

10. $30a - 32 \div 2a$ when $a = 4$ 56

Exercise B Evaluate each expression for $x = 12$.

11. $x + 2(x)$ 36

12. $\frac{x}{6} + 3 - \frac{1}{2}$ $4\frac{1}{2}$

13. $18(\frac{9}{x}) \div x$ $1\frac{1}{8}$

14. $3(x - 2)$ 30

15. $\frac{1}{x} + (\frac{10}{5} - \frac{1}{2})$ $1\frac{7}{12}$

16. $4x - (15 \div 3)$ 43

17. $38 \div 19 \cdot x$ 24

PROBLEM SOLVING

Exercise C Write and solve an equation.

18. Kareem is one year younger than his sister. The sum of their ages is 29. How old is Kareem? How old is his sister? (Hint: Let x = Kareem's age and $x + 1$ = his sister's age.)
Kareem is 14; his sister is 15.

19. Sherry is two years younger than Sara. The sum of their ages is 46. How old is Sherry? How old is Sara? (Hint: Let x = Sherry's age and $x + 2$ = Sara's age.)
Sherry is 22; Sara is 24.

20. The Shore Building is two feet taller than the Everly Building. The sum of their heights is 1,424 feet. How tall is each building? (Hint: Let x = the Everly Building and $x + 2$ = the Shore Building.)
The Everly Building is 711 feet tall; the Shore Building is 713 feet tall.

GROUP PROBLEM SOLVING

Provide groups of four students with the same set of expressions.

$$60 \div 5 = 12$$
$$16 + 21 = 37$$
$$25 \cdot 4 = 100$$
$$100 - x = 89$$

For each expression, have them write a word problem that has this solution. Students should not use the words *add, subtract, multiply,* or *divide* in their problems. (Hint: First translate each expression into a phrase, and then think of a situation that fits.) When groups are finished, have them compare and discuss the problems they wrote for each expression.

Lesson at a Glance

Chapter 6 Lesson 3

Overview This lesson demonstrates solving equations by substituting numbers for the variable.

Objectives

- To comprehend when a solution, or root of an equation, has been found
- To solve equations by substitution

Student Pages 146–147

Teacher's Resource Library

Workbook Activity 48

Activity 46

Alternative Activity 46

Mathematics Vocabulary

equation
root of the equation

---

1 Warm-Up Activity

Display a jar of pennies, and ask students how they would determine how many dollars it represents. Encourage them to write this as an algebraic expression on the board. ($\frac{p}{100}$ where p = *number of pennies*) Ask, "Why is p called a variable?" (*It can vary.*) Discuss ways to find out how many dollars' worth of pennies are in the jar. Explain that students will now learn to find values such as p in equations by substituting.

2 Teaching the Lesson

Label the jar of pennies with a dollar total (say, $3.49). Have students write an equation based on this information ($\frac{p}{100}$ = 3.49) and explain what each number and symbol represents. Create a table for ease in substituting values for p:

No. of pennies	No. of $
100	$1
150	$1.50
	$2
	$2.50
	$3
	$3.50

One way to solve an **equation** is to substitute numbers for the variable. You continue substituting other numbers until you have an equation with sides equal to one another.

Equation

A mathematical sentence stating that two quantities are equal and written as two expressions separated by an equal sign

Root of the equation

The number substituted for a variable that makes the equation a true statement

EXAMPLE 1 Evaluate $3x + 2 = 14$. Substitute 0 for the variable.

Step 1 Write the equation.

$$3x + 2 = 14$$

Step 2 Choose a number to substitute for the variable.

$$3(0) + 2 = 14$$

Step 3 Solve the one side of the equation to see if it matches the other side.

$$0 + 2 = 14$$

$$2 = 14 \quad \text{False. So } x \text{ is not 0.}$$

Continue substituting other numbers until you have an equation with both sides equal to one another.

Evaluate $3x + 2 = 14$ when $x = 1$.

$$3x + 2 = 14$$
$$3(1) + 2 = 14$$
$$3 + 2 = 14$$
$$5 = 14 \quad \text{False}$$

Evaluate $3x + 2 = 14$ when $x = 2$.

$$3x + 2 = 14$$
$$3(2) + 2 = 14$$
$$6 + 2 = 14$$
$$8 = 14 \quad \text{False}$$

Evaluate $3x + 2 = 14$ when $x = 3$.

$$3x + 2 = 14$$
$$3(3) + 2 = 14$$
$$9 + 2 = 14$$
$$11 = 14 \quad \text{False}$$

Evaluate $3x + 2 = 14$ when $x = 4$.

$$3x + 2 = 14$$
$$3(4) + 2 = 14$$
$$12 + 2 = 14$$
$$14 = 14 \quad \text{True}$$

When $x = 4$, $3x + 2 = 14$ is true. Therefore, $x = 4$ is called a solution, or **root of the equation** $3x + 2 = 14$.

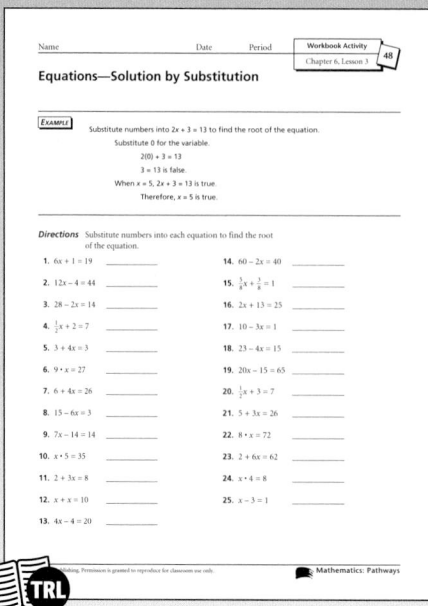

Exercise A Tell whether each equation is true or false when the given number is substituted for x.

1. $4x - 3 = 13$ when $x = 2$ false

2. $35 - 2x = 15$ when $x = 10$ true

3. $\frac{3}{4}x = 36$ when $x = 48$ true

4. $2x + 14 = 26$ when $x = 5$ false

5. $12 - 3x = 9$ when $x = 4$ false

Exercise B Substitute numbers into each equation to find the root of the equation.

6. $17 - 3x = 11$ 2

7. $22x + 5 = 93$ 4

8. $\frac{1}{2}x + 15 = 20$ 10

9. $7 + 14x = 7$ 0

10. $6 \cdot x = 12$ 2

11. $7 + 4x = 11$ 1

12. $4x - 10 = 26$ 9

13. $x \cdot 4 = 12$ 3

14. $3 + 6x = 21$ 3

15. $x + x = 14$ 7

Answers may vary. Remove one [x] for every row of [1][1][1] .

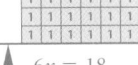
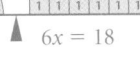
$6x = 18$

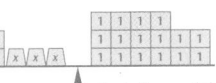
$2 + 3x = 16$

$\frac{1}{3}x = 6$

Build a Model

The balance scale below represents the equation $3x = 9$. Explain what would you do to isolate x and still keep the two sides balanced.

On separate sheets of paper, draw models like the one above to show each of the equations below:

$6x = 18$
$2 + 3x = 16$
$\frac{1}{3}x = 6$

Have students complete the table and use a caret to insert the exact number of pennies at the appropriate place in the table. Explain that this is the root, or solution, of the equation.

3 Reinforce and Extend

CAREER CONNECTION

Ask a small group of students to research the way in which a travel agent works with clients to arrange travel and lodging within a budget. Have students prepare questions in advance.

- What information do you get from the client before making plans?

- How many options do you usually give?

- On what math operations do you rely?

- Do you substitute different values for transportation and lodging costs?

- Do quality lodging and transportation costs vary greatly?

Have students report on several possible cost distributions for a trip in which they have specified the place they want to go, how long they will stay, and how much they can spend.

LEARNING STYLES

LEP/ESL

Suggest that students who are having difficulty with Exercise B construct tables to keep track of substituted values and note how close each is to the solution. Model such a table for problem 8:

$\frac{1}{2}x + 15 = 20$

If x is	Then $\frac{1}{2}x + 15$ is
1	$\frac{1}{2} + 15 = 15\frac{1}{2}$ (too low)
2	$1 + 15 = 16$ (too low; try higher value)
8	$4 + 15 = 19$ (low but close)
10	$5 + 15 = 20$ (correct value)

The table organizes information so that students can quickly compare results, avoid using the same value twice, and keep track of whether a substitution is too low or too high. It also helps students avoid extra steps by showing when substitutions are way off or close to the correct solution.

Lesson at a Glance

Chapter 6 Lesson 4

Overview This lesson presents a method for solving addition equations by using subtraction.

Objectives

- To isolate variables by applying inverse operations to both sides of an equation
- To solve addition equations, reduce answers to lowest form, and check by adding

Student Pages 148–149

Teacher's Resource Library **TRL**

Workbook Activity 49

Activity 47

Alternative Activity 47

1 Warm-Up Activity

Use a balance scale to model an equation. Place various weights on each side until the scale is balanced. Give students the mass of each item except one, and ask them to experiment to discover the mass of the unknown. Have them explain how they kept the scale balanced and why this must be done. (*Remove the same mass from each side; if the scale does not balance, then the masses on each side are not equal.*)

2 Teaching the Lesson

Remind students that the object of this method is to get the variable alone on one side of the equation. To help students remember that they must apply the subtraction operation to both sides of the equation, show examples using a balance scale form.

$$x + 4 = 18$$

$$x + 4 - 4 = 18$$

In Lesson 3, you solved equations by substituting numbers for the variable. You can also solve equations by using mathematics operations. In this lesson, you will solve addition problems by using subtraction.

EXAMPLE 1 Solve $x + 1 = 3$ for x.

Step 1 Subtract 1 from each side of the equation.

$$x + 1 = 3$$
$$x + 1 - 1 = 3 - 1$$

Step 2 Perform the operation.

$$x + 1 - 1 = 3 - 1$$
$$x = 2$$

Step 3 Check by substituting your answer into the equation.

$$x + 1 = 3$$
$$2 + 1 = 3 \quad \text{True}$$

> Whenever you apply an inverse operation to solve an equation, always remember to apply that operation to both sides of the equation.

In this example, you subtracted from each side of the equation so that the variable x would be by itself on one side of the equation. This is called isolating the variable. To isolate a variable, you perform an *inverse operation*. Subtraction is the inverse operation of addition.

EXAMPLE 2 Solve $x + \frac{1}{4} = \frac{3}{4}$ for x.

Step 1 Isolate the variable x by subtracting $\frac{1}{4}$ from each side of the equation.

$$x + \frac{1}{4} = \frac{3}{4}$$
$$x + \frac{1}{4} - \frac{1}{4} = \frac{3}{4} - \frac{1}{4}$$

Step 2 Perform each operation.

$$x + \frac{1}{4} - \frac{1}{4} = \frac{3}{4} - \frac{1}{4}$$
$$x = \frac{2}{4}$$

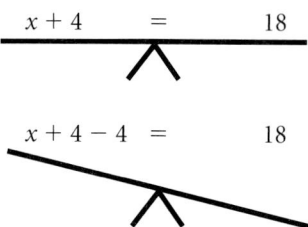

Workbook Activity 49

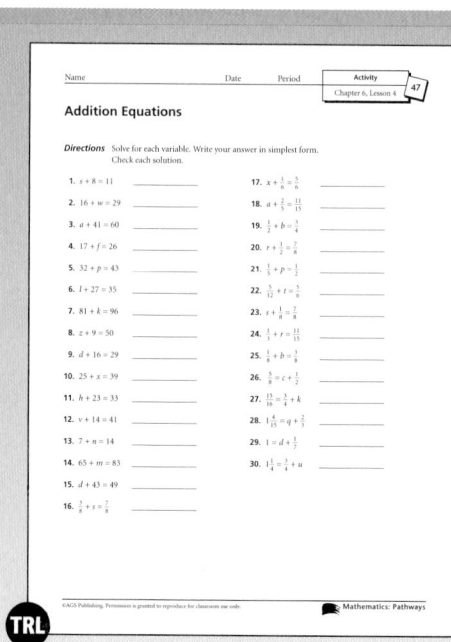

Activity 47

EXAMPLE 2 (continued)

Step 3 Simplify.
$$x = \frac{2}{4} \div \frac{2}{2} = \frac{1}{2}$$

Step 4 Check by substituting your answer (before it was simplified) into the original equation.
$$x + \frac{1}{4} = \frac{3}{4}$$
$$\frac{2}{4} + \frac{1}{4} = \frac{3}{4}$$
$$\frac{3}{4} = \frac{3}{4} \quad \text{True}$$

Exercise A Write what you would subtract to isolate the variable in each expression.

1. $x + \frac{2}{3}$ $\quad \frac{2}{3}$ **3.** $y + 4$ $\quad 4$

2. $x + \frac{9}{10}$ $\quad \frac{9}{10}$ **4.** $y + 12$ $\quad 12$

Exercise B Solve for each variable. Write your answer in simplest form. Check each solution.

5. $a + 3 = 17$ $\quad 14$ **11.** $\frac{5}{12} + k = \frac{11}{12}$ $\quad \frac{1}{2}$

6. $h + 15 = 38$ $\quad 23$ **12.** $1\frac{3}{5} = w + \frac{2}{5}$ $\quad 1\frac{1}{5}$

7. $32 + q = 49$ $\quad 17$ **13.** $\frac{3}{8} = d + \frac{1}{8}$ $\quad \frac{1}{4}$

8. $s + 18 = 25$ $\quad 7$ **14.** $\frac{9}{16} = x + \frac{7}{16}$ $\quad \frac{1}{8}$

9. $x + \frac{1}{5} = \frac{3}{5}$ $\quad \frac{2}{5}$ **15.** $\frac{3}{4} = \frac{3}{8} + m$ $\quad \frac{3}{8}$

10. $\frac{1}{6} + y = \frac{5}{6}$ $\quad \frac{2}{3}$

 Math in Your Life

Go Figure!
An average family of two adults and two children uses almost 250 gallons of water on a daily basis. For example, a typical shower uses up to 4 gallons of water per minute. Economists and conservationists rely on complex algebraic equations to calculate consumer needs and society's ability to meet the demands.

---

3 Reinforce and Extend

LEARNING STYLES

 Interpersonal/ Group Learning

Have students work in groups of three or four to write a paragraph explaining why and how subtraction can be used to solve addition equations. They should select two equations from Exercise B and use them as examples.

In their paragraphs, groups should include

- the terms *inverse operation* and *variable*.

- illustrations using a balance scale comparison.

- the reason for subtracting an equal amount from each side.

$$\frac{x + 4 - 4 \;=\; 18 - 4}{}$$

Review equivalent fractions and simplest forms of fractions before students complete Exercise B.

MANIPULATIVES

M **Solving Addition Expressions**

Materials: Algebra Tiles, Manipulatives Master 3 (Sentence Mat)

Group Practice: Review the Algebra Tiles with students (see pages T8–T9). Fill in an equal sign in the empty box between the two sides of the balance on the Sentence Mat. Model the first example, $x + 1 = 3$. Add -1 to each side of the equation, and discuss the Zero Rule (see pages T8–T9). Simplify by removing pairs of inverses. The variable piece is isolated on the left, and the root of the equation (2) is on the right. To check, rebuild the original equation, replacing the unknown piece with its known value. To model fractions in the next example, let each unit represent $\frac{1}{4}$, and build the equation using 3 unit pieces to represent $\frac{3}{4}$.

Student Practice: Have students use the Algebra Tiles for Exercise B, problems 5, 8–11, 13–14.

COMMON ERROR

 Make sure that students do not try to solve by adding the number on the right side of the equation that they subtracted on the left. You may wish to require students to use a different color to write the $-$ sign and number subtracted on each side.

$$n + 7 = 24$$
$$n + 7 - 7 = 24 - 7$$
$$n = 17$$

Chapter 6 Lesson 5

Overview This lesson applies inverse operations to solving subtraction equations.

Objectives

■ To add a quantity to both sides of a subtraction equation to isolate the variable

■ To solve addition and subtraction problems using subtraction and addition

Student Pages 150–151

Teacher's Resource Library

Workbook Activity 50

Activity 48

Alternative Activity 48

1 Warm-Up Activity

Write the following on the board:

$50 + d = 72$

Have students direct you in the steps to solving the equation, or isolating the unknown. *(Subtract 50 from each side.)* Then write on the board

$w - 40 = 27$

and have students suggest a similar method for solving this equation. *(Add 40 to each side.)* Have a student describe the relationship of addition and subtraction. *(They are inverse, or opposite, operations.)*

2 Teaching the Lesson

Review addition and simplification of fractions. Ask students to explain why unsimplified fractions are used in checking the solution. *(Only fractions with like denominators can be added and subtracted accurately.)*

As in the preceding lesson, use the balance scale symbol to model imbalance when the same operation is not done to both sides of the equation.

Try This

Students may find it easier to solve the equations mentally if the reader says "what number" in place of "x." Thus $x - 5 = 14$ becomes "What number minus 5 equals 14?"

Lesson 5 **Solving Subtraction Equations**

In Lesson 4, you solved addition equations by using the mathematics operation of subtraction. In this lesson, you will solve subtraction problems by using addition.

Remember to apply the operation to both sides of the equation whenever you use the inverse operation of addition or subtraction to solve an equation.

EXAMPLE 1 Solve $x - \frac{1}{4} = \frac{3}{4}$ for x.

Step 1 Isolate the variable x by adding $\frac{1}{4}$ to each side of the equation.

$$x - \frac{1}{4} = \frac{3}{4}$$
$$x - \frac{1}{4} + \frac{1}{4} = \frac{3}{4} + \frac{1}{4}$$

Step 2 Perform each operation.

$$x - \frac{1}{4} + \frac{1}{4} = \frac{3}{4} + \frac{1}{4}$$
$$x = \frac{4}{4}$$

Step 3 Simplify.

$$x = \frac{4}{4} = 1$$

Step 4 Check by substituting your answer (before it was simplified) into the original equation.

$$x - \frac{1}{4} = \frac{3}{4}$$
$$\frac{4}{4} - \frac{1}{4} = \frac{3}{4}$$
$$\frac{3}{4} = \frac{3}{4} \quad \text{True}$$

In this example, you added to each side of the equation so that the variable x would be by itself on one side of the equation. To isolate the variable, you used addition as the inverse operation of subtraction.

Workbook Activity 50

Activity 48

Exercise A Solve for each variable. Write your answer in simplest form. Check each solution.

1. $x - 14 = 22$ 36

2. $c - 6 = 36$ 42

3. $p - 52 = 13$ 65

4. $c - \frac{3}{8} = \frac{1}{8}$ $\frac{1}{2}$

5. $h - \frac{5}{10} = \frac{3}{10}$ $\frac{4}{5}$

6. $n - \frac{2}{3} = \frac{1}{3}$ 1

7. $1 = q - \frac{1}{4}$ $1\frac{1}{4}$

8. $\frac{3}{8} = d - \frac{1}{8}$ $\frac{1}{2}$

PROBLEM SOLVING

Exercise B Use addition and subtraction to solve these problems.

9. Mars is about 48 million miles farther away from the Sun than the Earth. Earth is about 93 million miles from the Sun. How far is Mars from the Sun?
(Hint: $x - 48 = 93$ million miles)
141 million miles

10. Mercury is about 57 million miles closer to the Sun than the Earth. How far is Mercury from the Sun?
(Hint: $x + 57 = 93$ million miles)
36 million miles

Basic Operations and Rational Expressions   Chapter 6   **151**

MANIPULATIVES

M Solving Subtraction Equations

Materials: Algebra Tiles, Manipulatives Master 3 (Sentence Mat)

Group Practice: Model the equation $x - 4 = 3$. Isolate the variable by adding 4 to both sides of the equation. Use the Zero Rule, and simplify. Check by rebuilding the original equation, replacing the unknown piece with its known value. To model $x - \frac{1}{4} = \frac{3}{4}$ in the example, let each unit represent $\frac{1}{4}$, reviewing that $\frac{4}{4}$ is a whole, or 1. Repeat with several more equations that students generate.

Student Practice: Have students use the Algebra Tiles for Exercise A, problems 1, 4–8.

 3 **Reinforce and Extend**

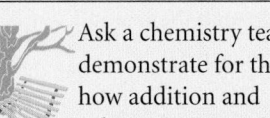

IN THE COMMUNITY

Ask a chemistry teacher to demonstrate for the class how addition and subtraction equations are used to show chemical reactions and calculate results. (If the teacher is unable to visit the class, arrange to videotape the demonstration.) Prepare students by discussing several common atoms (for example, hydrogen and oxygen), molecules (H_2O for water and NaCl for sodium chloride, or table salt), and elements as well as the symbols used to represent these elements (H for hydrogen, O for oxygen, and so on).

GROUP PROBLEM SOLVING

Display an illustration of the planets in our solar system, complete with interplanetary distances, sizes of planets, number of moons, time required for one rotation, and so on. Organize the class in groups of four or five, and have each group use the solar system statistics to create five interplanetary riddles requiring the use of addition and subtraction, such as the following:

"I am from a planet that is 48 million miles farther from the Sun than Earth. What planet is my home?"

Have each group present its riddles to the class for solution.

Lesson at a Glance

Chapter 6 Lesson 6

Overview This lesson defines complex fractions and presents a method for dividing complex fractions.

Objective

- To simplify complex fractions by multiplying the dividend by the reciprocal of the divisor

Student Pages 152–155

Teacher's Resource Library (TRL)

Workbook Activity 51

Activity 49

Alternative Activity 49

Mathematics Vocabulary

complex fraction

---

1 ⟩ Warm-Up Activity

Write several fractions on the board, and ask students to read them aloud.

$\frac{1}{2}$ *(one-half)*

$\frac{3}{4}$ *(three-fourths)*

$\frac{2}{3}$ *(two-thirds)*

Ask, "What operation does the fraction bar direct you to do?" *(divide)* Have students read the expressions to reflect this operation.

$\frac{1}{2}$ *(one divided by two)*

$\frac{3}{4}$ *(three divided by four)*

$\frac{2}{3}$ *(two divided by three)*

Have students read Lesson 6 to discover how this operation can be carried out if the numerator and the denominator are both fractions.

2 ⟩ Teaching the Lesson

Review the concept of *reciprocal* until you are confident that students understand that the reciprocal of any fraction reverses the fraction's numbers. This means that

$$\frac{a}{b} \cdot \frac{b}{a} = \frac{ab}{ab} = 1$$

Lesson 6 Complex Fractions

Complex fraction

A fraction in which the numerator, the denominator, or both the numerator and the denominator are fractions

Recall that to divide two fractions, you multiply the dividend by the reciprocal of the divisor.

$$\frac{2}{3} \div \frac{7}{8} = \frac{2}{3} \cdot \frac{8}{7} = \frac{16}{21}$$

This idea—to multiply the dividend by the reciprocal of the divisor—can also be used to simplify **complex fractions**. A complex fraction is a fraction in which the numerator, the denominator, or both the numerator and the denominator are fractions.

The following fractions are examples of complex fractions.

$$\frac{2}{\frac{1}{3}} \qquad \frac{\frac{4}{5}}{8} \qquad \frac{\frac{3}{4}}{\frac{1}{2}}$$

Recall that the fraction bar separating the numerator from the denominator means "divide."

The complex fraction $\dfrac{2}{\frac{1}{3}}$ means "two divided by one-third."

The complex fraction $\dfrac{\frac{4}{5}}{8}$ means "four-fifths divided by eight."

The complex fraction $\dfrac{\frac{3}{4}}{\frac{1}{2}}$ means "three-fourths divided by one-half."

Look again at the example $\frac{2}{3} \div \frac{7}{8}$. It shows division of two fractions, written horizontally.

The complex fraction $\dfrac{\frac{2}{3}}{\frac{7}{8}}$ shows division of the same two fractions, written vertically.

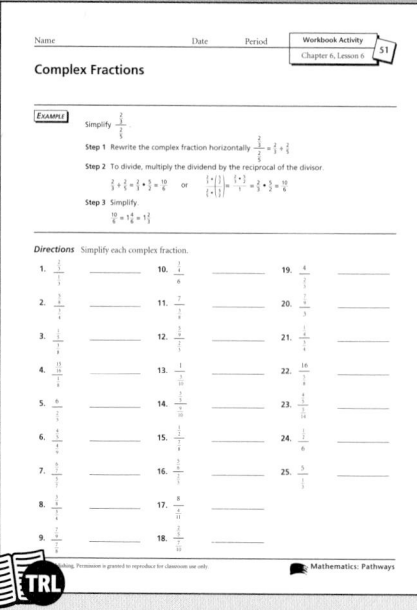

Workbook Activity 51

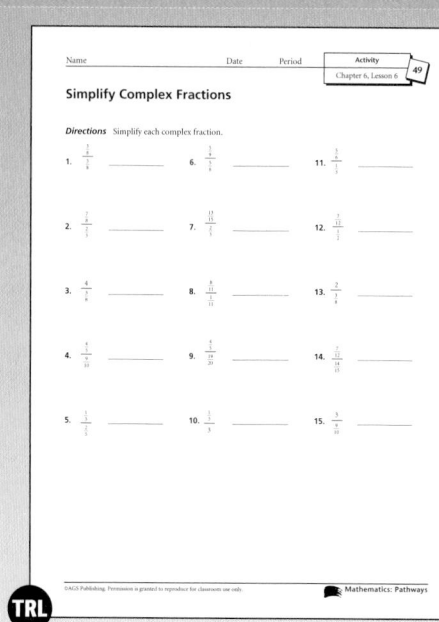

Activity 49

Expressions involving complex fractions can be simplified.

EXAMPLE 1 Simplify $\dfrac{\frac{1}{2}}{\frac{3}{4}}$.

Step 1 Rewrite the complex fraction horizontally.

$$\frac{\frac{1}{2}}{\frac{3}{4}} = \frac{1}{2} \div \frac{3}{4} \qquad \textbf{Think: } \frac{\frac{1}{2}}{\frac{3}{4}} \text{ means "one-half divided by three-fourths."}$$

Step 2 To divide two fractions, multiply the dividend by the reciprocal of the divisor.

$$\frac{1}{2} \div \frac{3}{4} = \frac{1}{2} \bullet \frac{4}{3} = \frac{4}{6}$$

Step 3 Simplify.

$$\frac{4}{6} = \frac{2}{3}$$

The numerator of a complex fraction is sometimes a whole number.

EXAMPLE 2 Simplify $\dfrac{2}{\frac{1}{3}}$.

Step 1 Rewrite the complex fraction horizontally.

$$\frac{2}{\frac{1}{3}} = 2 \div \frac{1}{3} \qquad \textbf{Think: } \frac{2}{\frac{1}{3}} \text{ means "two divided by one-third."}$$

Step 2 Write 2 as an improper fraction, then multiply the dividend by the reciprocal of the divisor.

$$2 \div \frac{1}{3} = \frac{2}{1} \div \frac{1}{3} = \frac{2}{1} \bullet \frac{3}{1} = \frac{6}{1}$$

Step 3 Simplify.

$$\frac{6}{1} = 6$$

This table may prove helpful:

Number	Reciprocal	No. × Reciprocal
1	$\frac{1}{1}$	1
$\frac{1}{2}$	$\frac{2}{1}$	1
$\frac{1}{3}$	$\frac{3}{1}$	1
$\frac{2}{5}$	$\frac{5}{2}$	1
$\frac{15}{6}$	$\frac{6}{15}$	1

COMMON ERROR

Make sure that students remember to reverse the divisor (that is, form the reciprocal) before multiplying. Have them write out each problem in three steps, as in the text examples, to avoid this error.

3 Reinforce and Extend

LEARNING STYLES

Body/Kinesthetic
Have students cut paper strips and fold the strips to divide them into fractions. They can then color in the fractions represented by problems such as the following:

$$\frac{2}{3} \div \frac{1}{6}$$

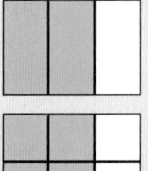

The number of segments that fit under the first fraction gives the whole number that solves the equation. (In this case, 4 because 4 of the one-sixth portions fit below $\frac{2}{3}$.)

AT HOME

Ask students to choose an object or area and measure its length and width two ways.

- Make up a unit of measurement that can be reliably used, such as foot length or the width of a textbook. Use the unit to measure the chosen object or area. Record the measurements.

- Next, measure the area using standard measurement (metric or customary). Record these measurements also.

Have students use their knowledge of complex fractions to discover how many of their original units it takes to make one unit of the standard form used.

The denominator of a complex fraction is sometimes a whole number.

EXAMPLE 3 Simplify $\dfrac{\frac{4}{5}}{8}$.

Step 1 Rewrite the complex fraction horizontally.

$$\frac{\frac{4}{5}}{8} = \frac{4}{5} \div 8 \qquad \textbf{Think: } \frac{\frac{4}{5}}{8} \text{ means "four-fifths divided by eight."}$$

Step 2 Write 8 as an improper fraction, then multiply the dividend by the reciprocal of the divisor.

$$\frac{4}{5} \div 8 = \frac{4}{5} \div \frac{8}{1} = \frac{4}{5} \cdot \frac{1}{8} = \frac{4}{40}$$

Step 3 Simplify.

$$\frac{4}{40} = \frac{1}{10}$$

Exercise A Simplify each complex fraction.

Writing About Mathematics

Write a brief description of how you might use a calculator to check a complex fraction that includes mixed numbers.

1. $\dfrac{\frac{1}{2}}{\frac{2}{3}}$ $\frac{3}{4}$ 7. $\dfrac{5}{\frac{1}{2}}$ 10   13. $\dfrac{12}{\frac{5}{12}}$ $28\frac{4}{5}$

2. $\dfrac{\frac{1}{5}}{\frac{3}{4}}$ $\frac{4}{15}$ 8. $\dfrac{\frac{7}{12}}{3}$ $\frac{7}{36}$ 14. $\dfrac{9}{\frac{1}{3}}$ 27

3. $\dfrac{3}{\frac{1}{3}}$ 9   9. $\dfrac{\frac{5}{6}}{\frac{1}{5}}$ $4\frac{1}{6}$ 15. $\dfrac{\frac{7}{8}}{16}$ $\frac{7}{128}$

4. $\dfrac{\frac{4}{5}}{4}$ $\frac{1}{5}$ 10. $\dfrac{8}{\frac{2}{3}}$ 12   16. $\dfrac{\frac{3}{4}}{\frac{7}{12}}$ $1\frac{2}{7}$

5. $\dfrac{\frac{5}{8}}{\frac{1}{6}}$ $3\frac{3}{4}$ 11. $\dfrac{\frac{1}{8}}{\frac{3}{16}}$ $\frac{2}{3}$ 17. $\dfrac{20}{\frac{7}{10}}$ $28\frac{4}{7}$

6. $\dfrac{\frac{1}{16}}{2}$ $\frac{1}{32}$ 12. $\dfrac{\frac{4}{5}}{10}$ $\frac{2}{25}$ 18. $\dfrac{15}{\frac{3}{5}}$ 25

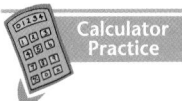

Calculator Practice

Suppose you use pencil and paper to determine that $\dfrac{\frac{1}{2}}{\frac{5}{8}} = \dfrac{4}{5}$.

To check your answer using a calculator, follow these steps.

EXAMPLE 4 **Step 1** Find the decimal equivalent for your answer.

Press $4 \div 5 =$.

The display reads 0.8.

Step 2 Use the calculator to find the decimal equivalent of $\dfrac{\frac{1}{2}}{\frac{5}{8}}$.

Press $(1 \div 2) \div (5 \div 8) =$.

The display reads 0.8.

If the decimal answer you found in Step 1 does not match the decimal answer you found in Step 2, use pencil and paper to simplify the fraction again.

If you have a calculator with a fraction key $a^{b/c}$, follow these steps:

Press $1 \; a^{b/c} \; 2 \div 5 \; a^{b/c} \; 8 =$.

The display will read $\dfrac{4}{5}$.

Exercise B Use a calculator to perform these computations. If the answer is correct, write *correct*. If the answer is not correct, write *not correct*.

19. $\dfrac{1}{4} \div \dfrac{1}{8} = 0.002$
  not correct

20. $\dfrac{3}{10} \div \dfrac{1}{5} = 0.15$
  not correct

21. $\dfrac{1}{8} \div \dfrac{4}{5} = 0.15625$
  correct

22. $\dfrac{1}{4} \div \dfrac{1}{16} = 2$
  not correct

23. $\dfrac{2}{5} \div \dfrac{4}{5} = 0.05$
  not correct

24. $\dfrac{5}{12} \div \dfrac{1}{3} = 1.25$
  correct

25. $\dfrac{3}{4} \div \dfrac{1}{4} = 0.3$
  not correct

CALCULATOR

Work with students to help them discover whether their calculators have a fraction key. If so, they should find out the following:

- What order of operations does the calculator use?

- Must each fraction be placed inside ( )?

- Does the calculator give answers as percents, fractions, or both?

Lesson at a Glance

Chapter 6 Lesson 7

Overview This lesson presents a method of adding rational expressions using the least common multiple of the denominators.

Objectives

- To simplify rational expressions
- To convert fractions to equivalent fractions with like denominators

Student Pages 156–157

Teacher's Resource Library (TRL)

Workbook Activity 52

Activity 50

Alternative Activity 50

Mathematics Vocabulary

rational expression

---

1 Warm-Up Activity

Write a number of fractions in large size with magic marker on 4 × 6 cards. Have students group the fractions according to common denominators. Draw models of two simple fractions with like denominators (for example, $\frac{1}{5}, \frac{3}{5}$). Manipulate the model pieces by adding and subtracting.

Encourage students to suggest ways they might convert fractions with unlike denominators so that the fractions have the same denominator.

2 Teaching the Lesson

Model addition of fractions with like denominators to show why denominators are not added. (*The denominator represents the number of parts into which we agree to divide a whole; it does not double when two fractions are added.*)

Make sure that students understand *terms, least common denominator,* and *simplify.* Work with additional examples, and have students use this vocabulary as they explain the steps in adding.

Lesson 7   Simplifying by Addition

Rational expression
An algebraic expression that can be written like a fraction

Rational expressions often contain operation signs such as $+, -, \bullet,$ or $\div$. The parts of an expression that are separated by operation signs are known as the terms of the expression.

$$\frac{1}{2}x + \frac{1}{4}x \qquad 10 + \frac{7}{8}c - d$$
$$\uparrow \quad \uparrow \qquad \uparrow \quad \uparrow \quad \uparrow$$
terms terms

You can simplify some rational expressions by collecting like terms and adding them. Like terms have the same variable.

EXAMPLE 1 Simplify $\frac{a}{2} + \frac{a}{2}$. Simplify $\frac{2x}{3} + \frac{x}{3}$.

Step 1 Add the fractions.
$$\frac{a}{2} + \frac{a}{2} = \frac{2a}{2} \qquad \frac{2x}{3} + \frac{x}{3} = \frac{3x}{3}$$

Step 2 If possible, simplify your answer.
$$\frac{2a}{2} = a \qquad \frac{3x}{3} = x$$

Before you can add rational expressions with unlike denominators, you must convert the fractions to equivalent fractions with like denominators.

> Remember when you add or subtract a fraction with the same denominator, you add or subtract the numerator only. You do not add or subtract the denominator.

EXAMPLE 2 Simplify $\frac{a}{2} + \frac{a}{3}$.

Step 1 Find the least common multiple of the denominators.
$$LCM = 6$$

Step 2 Multiply both the numerators and denominators by numbers to make the denominator of both fractions alike.
$$\frac{a \bullet 3}{2 \bullet 3} + \frac{a \bullet 2}{3 \bullet 2} = \frac{3a}{6} + \frac{2a}{6}$$

Step 3 Add the equivalent fractions.
$$\frac{3a}{6} + \frac{2a}{6} = \frac{5a}{6}$$

Step 4 If possible, simplify your answer.
$$\frac{5a}{6} \text{ is in simplest form.}$$

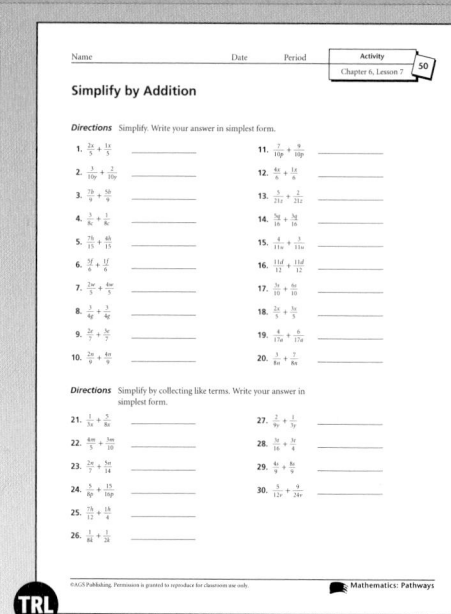

Workbook Activity 52

Activity 50

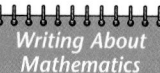
Exercise A Simplify. Write your answer in simplest form.

1. $\frac{1}{8a} + \frac{5}{8a}$ $\frac{3}{4a}$

2. $\frac{2x}{4} + \frac{x}{4}$ $\frac{3x}{4}$

3. $\frac{2}{5c} + \frac{4}{5c}$ $\frac{6}{5c}$

4. $\frac{4}{6m} + \frac{1}{6m}$ $\frac{5}{6m}$

5. $\frac{3y}{8} + \frac{7y}{8}$ $\frac{5y}{4}$ or $1\frac{1}{4}y$

6. $\frac{4x}{7} + \frac{6x}{7}$ $\frac{10x}{7}$ or $1\frac{3}{7}x$

7. $\frac{6}{9t} + \frac{1}{9t}$ $\frac{7}{9t}$

8. $\frac{14x}{17} + \frac{3x}{17}$ x

9. $\frac{1}{8b} + \frac{3}{8b}$ $\frac{1}{2b}$

10. $\frac{7g}{10} + \frac{5g}{10}$ $\frac{6g}{5}$ or $1\frac{1}{5}g$

Exercise B Simplify by collecting like terms. Write your answer in simplest form.

11. $\frac{7}{10n} + \frac{5}{10n}$ $\frac{6}{5n}$

12. $\frac{1}{4r} + \frac{9}{16r}$ $\frac{13}{16r}$

13. $\frac{11d}{12} + \frac{d}{3}$ $\frac{5d}{4}$ or $1\frac{1}{4}d$

14. $\frac{3z}{5} + \frac{z}{6}$ $\frac{23z}{30}$

15. $\frac{2}{3b} + \frac{3}{4b}$ $\frac{17}{12b}$

Technology Connection

Technology Simplifies Your Life

Imagine writing a term paper on a typewriter instead of a computer. Every time you wanted to rewrite a sentence or delete a paragraph, you'd have to start over. Word processing has simplified that problem.

Imagine hauling your water from a well in a bucket instead of turning on a faucet. Whenever you washed clothes or did the dishes, you'd have to refill the bucket. Modern plumbing technology has simplified your life.

Technology has simplified almost every area of our lives.

$\frac{4}{12} + \frac{2}{12}$ (*Add like terms.*)

$\frac{6 + 2}{12}$ (*Have common denominator.*)

$\frac{6}{12} = \frac{1}{2}$ (*Simplify by reducing to lowest terms.*)

$\frac{1}{5} + \frac{3}{10}$ (*Make terms like.*)

$\frac{2}{10} + \frac{3}{10}$ (*Add like terms.*)

$\frac{2 + 3}{10}$ (*Have common denominator.*)

$\frac{5}{10} = \frac{1}{2}$ (*Simplify by reducing to lowest terms.*)

Explain simplest terms for problems 5, 6, 10, 11, 13, and 15. For example, for problem 5, $\frac{10y}{8}$ simplifies to $\frac{5y}{4}$ or $1\frac{1}{4}y$.

3 Reinforce and Extend

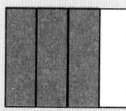 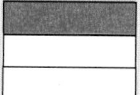
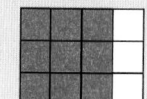 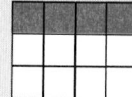

Chapter 6 Lesson 8

Overview This lesson demonstrates a method for making fractions equivalent and subtracting them.

Objectives

- To simplify fractions with like denominators by subtraction
- To convert fractions with unlike denominators to equivalent fractions

Student Pages 158–159

Teacher's Resource Library

Workbook Activity 53

Activity 51

Alternative Activity 51

1 Warm-Up Activity

Make a pie shape divided into six equal wedges with one wedge removed, and ask students to identify what part has been eaten and what part remains. ($\frac{1}{6}$; $\frac{5}{6}$) Ask students to write an equation on the board to show this problem. ($\frac{6}{6} - \frac{1}{6} = \frac{5}{6}$) Have students remove other wedges and revise the equation appropriately. Then refer to the $\frac{5}{6}$ model and ask, "What part remains if someone eats $\frac{1}{4}$ of the pie?" ($\frac{7}{12}$) Have students read the lesson to learn how to change unlike fractions to like fractions.

2 Teaching the Lesson

This lesson can be taught at the same time as Lesson 7 because its conversions are identical to those for addition of terms with fractions.

Remind students that $\frac{x}{4}$ is the same as $\frac{1x}{4}$.

Some students may have difficulty following the conversion to lowest common denominator. The following alternative explanation may prove helpful:

1. Find the LCD by listing multiples of each denominator until a common number is found. For example, $\frac{1}{4} - \frac{1}{5}$

   Multiples of 4: 4, 8, 12, 16, <u>20</u>

   Multiples of 5: 5, 10, 15, <u>20</u>

You can simplify some rational expressions by collecting like terms and subtracting them.

EXAMPLE 1 Simplify $\frac{5y}{4} - \frac{2y}{4}$.

Step 1 Subtract the fractions.

$$\frac{5y}{4} - \frac{2y}{4} = \frac{3y}{4}$$

Step 2 If possible, simplify your answer.

$\frac{3y}{4}$ is in simplest form.

Before you can subtract rational expressions with unlike denominators, you must convert the fractions to equivalent fractions with like denominators.

EXAMPLE 2 Simplify $\frac{a}{2} - \frac{a}{3}$.

Step 1 Find the least common multiple of the denominators.

LCM = 6

Step 2 Multiply both the numerators and denominators by numbers to make the denominator of both fractions alike.

$$\frac{a \cdot 3}{2 \cdot 3} - \frac{a \cdot 2}{3 \cdot 2} = \frac{3a}{6} - \frac{2a}{6}$$

Step 3 Subtract the equivalent fractions.

$$\frac{3a}{6} - \frac{2a}{6} = \frac{1a}{6} = \frac{a}{6}$$

Step 4 If possible, simplify your answer.

$\frac{a}{6}$ is in simplest form.

Name _____ Date _____ Period _____

Simplifying by Subtraction

EXAMPLE Simplify $\frac{7}{10} - \frac{2}{5}$

Step 1 Find the LCM of the denominators.   LCM = 10

Step 2 Write equivalent fractions. $\frac{7}{10} - \frac{2}{5} = \frac{7}{10} - \frac{4}{10}$

Step 3 Subtract the equivalent fractions. $\frac{7}{10} - \frac{4}{10} = \frac{3}{10}$

Step 4 Simplify if possible. $\frac{3}{10}$ is in simplest form.

Directions Simplify. Write your answer in simplest form.

Directions Simplify by collecting like terms. Write your answer in simplest form.

Directions Solve these problems.

18. Ed spends $\frac{3}{5}$ of his study time on history. How much of his study time does he have left!

19. Juan has $\frac{7}{8}$ yards of string. He used $\frac{1}{4}$ yards of string. How much does he have left?

20. Jenny's survey showed that $\frac{11}{20}$ of her class picked blue as their favorite color. What part of her class picked a different color?

Name _____ Date _____ Period _____

Simplify by Subtraction

Directions Simplify. Write your answer in simplest form.

Directions Simplify by collecting like terms. Write your answer in simplest form.

Directions Solve these problems.

23. Sue walked $\frac{7}{10}$ of the way to the park. What fraction of her walk to the park remains?

24. Ali's stock gained $\frac{1}{4}$ dollar today. The price is now $\frac{9}{16}$ of a dollar. How much was the price yesterday?

25. Charlotte used $\frac{2}{3}$ yards of twine. She started with $\frac{7}{8}$ yards of twine. How much does she have left?

Exercise A Simplify. Write your answer in simplest form.

1. $\frac{5}{8a} - \frac{1}{8a}$ $\quad \frac{1}{2a}$

2. $\frac{3x}{4} - \frac{x}{4}$ $\quad \frac{x}{2}$

3. $\frac{4}{5c} - \frac{2}{5c}$ $\quad \frac{2}{5c}$

4. $\frac{5}{6m} - \frac{1}{6m}$ $\quad \frac{2}{3m}$

5. $\frac{7y}{8} - \frac{3y}{8}$ $\quad \frac{y}{2}$

6. $\frac{6x}{7} - \frac{4x}{7}$ $\quad \frac{2x}{7}$

7. $\frac{6}{9t} - \frac{1}{9t}$ $\quad \frac{5}{9t}$

8. $\frac{14x}{17} - \frac{3x}{17}$ $\quad \frac{11x}{17}$

9. $\frac{3}{8b} - \frac{1}{8b}$ $\quad \frac{1}{4b}$

10. $\frac{7g}{10} - \frac{5g}{10}$ $\quad \frac{g}{5}$

Exercise B Simplify by collecting like terms. Write your answer in simplest form.

11. $\frac{7}{10n} - \frac{1}{2n}$ $\quad \frac{1}{5n}$

12. $\frac{9r}{16} - \frac{r}{4}$ $\quad \frac{5r}{16}$

13. $\frac{11}{12d} - \frac{1}{3d}$ $\quad \frac{7}{12d}$

14. $\frac{3x}{5} - \frac{x}{6}$ $\quad \frac{13x}{30}$

15. $\frac{2}{3b} - \frac{1}{4b}$ $\quad \frac{5}{12b}$

16. $\frac{7}{8y} - \frac{5}{16y}$ $\quad \frac{9}{16y}$

17. $\frac{8q}{9} - \frac{q}{6}$ $\quad \frac{13q}{18}$

 **PROBLEM SOLVING**

Exercise C Solve these problems.

18. Henry has $\frac{1}{2}$ dollar and Kari had $\frac{1}{4}$ dollar. How much more money does Henry have? $\frac{1}{4}$ dollar more

19. Ron spends $\frac{1}{3}$ of his allowance on pet supplies. How much of his allowance does he have left? $\frac{2}{3}$ left

20. Ling has $\frac{2}{3}$ yards of material. She uses $\frac{1}{4}$ of the material. How much material does she have left? $\frac{1}{2}$ yards

2. Multiply each numerator and denominator by the numbers that create the same denominator for both fractions. For example,

$$\frac{1}{4} \cdot \frac{5}{5} = \frac{5}{20}$$
$$\frac{1}{5} \cdot \frac{4}{4} = \frac{4}{20}$$

3. Subtract.
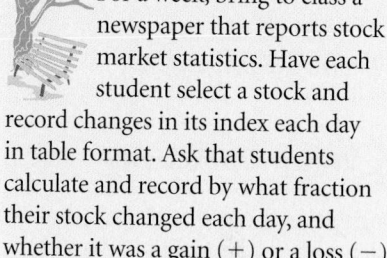
$$\frac{5}{20} - \frac{4}{20} = \frac{1}{20}$$

3 **Reinforce and Extend**

IN THE COMMUNITY

For a week, bring to class a newspaper that reports stock market statistics. Have each student select a stock and record changes in its index each day in table format. Ask that students calculate and record by what fraction their stock changed each day, and whether it was a gain ($+$) or a loss ($-$). Finally, have them list the following:

- their stock's greatest gain
- their stock's greatest loss
- their stock's net gain or loss for the week

Basic Operations and Rational Expressions Chapter 6 **159**

GROUP PROBLEM SOLVING

 Publish results of students' stock analyses in the preceding activity (or compile a set of data showing fractional gains and losses for various stocks). Part of the resulting table might look like this:

Stock	Mon.	Tues.	Wed.
A	$+\frac{5}{8}$	$-\frac{1}{8}$	$+\frac{1}{16}$
B	$-\frac{1}{4}$	$+\frac{7}{8}$	$+\frac{2}{8}$

Organize students in groups of four. Each group is to select and use portions of the stock data to create two addition and two subtraction word problems. Have groups exchange problems and choose one problem to solve, then exchange again and solve another, and so on until all problems have been solved. Return papers to the original group to be checked. Problems solved incorrectly can be corrected and modeled on the board.

Chapter 6 Lesson 9

Overview This lesson explains how to multiply fractions in rational expressions.

Objective

- To multiply fractions by multiplying numerators and denominators

Student Pages 160–161

Teacher's Resource Library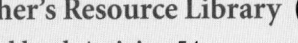

Workbook Activity 54

Activity 52

Alternative Activity 52

1 Warm-Up Activity

Bring to class a cardboard egg carton. Ask students how they might purchase six eggs. Tear the carton in half, and ask students to name the fraction they have purchased. ($\frac{1}{2}$) Then have students decide on the number of these eggs they will use to make a cake and express this number as a fraction of the half dozen. *(for example, $\frac{3}{6}$, or $\frac{1}{2}$)* Have the class think about how they would calculate the part of the original carton that they used. *($\frac{1}{2}$ of 12 = 6 and $\frac{1}{2}$ of 6 = 3; $\frac{3}{12} = \frac{1}{4}$)* Explain that this lesson will show how to multiply fractions—a task they have just done.

2 Teaching the Lesson

Provide a grid model of $\frac{3}{5} \cdot \frac{2}{3}$ to help students visualize the product of two fractions. Shade the areas using different colors so that the overlapping green portion is clearly a combination of the blue and yellow grid sections:

$$\frac{3}{5} \cdot \frac{2}{3} \qquad\qquad \frac{6}{15}$$

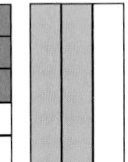
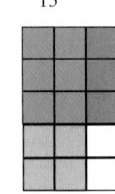

Lesson 9 Multiplying Rational Expressions

Just as you can add and subtract the terms of a rational expression, you can multiply the terms of rational expressions.

When you multiply fractions, you multiply the numerators and the denominators.

> Recall that to divide a fraction, you multiply the dividend by the reciprocal of the divisor.
> $$\frac{a}{b} \div \frac{c}{d} = \frac{a}{b} \cdot \frac{d}{c}$$

EXAMPLE 1 Multiply $\frac{3}{5} \cdot \frac{2}{3}$.

Step 1 Multiply the numerators and the denominators.
$$\frac{3}{5} \cdot \frac{2}{3} = \frac{3 \cdot 2}{5 \cdot 3} = \frac{6}{15}$$

Step 2 If possible, simplify the fraction.
$$\frac{6}{15} = \frac{2}{5}$$

Step 3 Check by dividing your answer by one of the terms to find the other term.
$$\frac{2}{5} \div \frac{2}{3} = \frac{2}{5} \cdot \frac{3}{2} = \frac{2 \cdot 3}{5 \cdot 2} = \frac{6}{10} = \frac{3}{5}$$

$\frac{3}{5}$ is the other term in your rational expression, so $\frac{3}{5} \cdot \frac{2}{3} = \frac{2}{5}$ is true.

EXAMPLE 2 Multiply $\frac{3}{5} \cdot \frac{2a}{3}$.

Step 1 Multiply the numerators and the denominators.
$$\frac{3}{5} \cdot \frac{2a}{3} = \frac{3 \cdot 2a}{5 \cdot 3} = \frac{6a}{15}$$

Step 2 If possible, simplify the fraction.
$$\frac{6a}{15} = \frac{2a}{5}$$

Step 3 Check by dividing your answer by one of the terms to find the other term.
$$\frac{2a}{5} \div \frac{2a}{3} = \frac{2a}{5} \cdot \frac{3}{2a} = \frac{2a \cdot 3}{5 \cdot 2a} = \frac{3}{5}$$

$\frac{3}{5}$ is the other term in your rational expression, so $\frac{3}{5} \cdot \frac{2a}{3} = \frac{2a}{5}$ is true.

Workbook Activity 54

Activity 52

Exercise A Multiply. Write your answer in simplest form.

1. $\frac{1}{4} \cdot \frac{2}{3}$ $\frac{1}{6}$
2. $\frac{5}{6} \cdot \frac{1}{8}$ $\frac{5}{48}$
3. $\frac{3}{10} \cdot \frac{9}{11}$ $\frac{27}{110}$
4. $\frac{2}{5} \cdot \frac{2}{7}$ $\frac{4}{35}$
5. $\frac{4}{15} \cdot \frac{4}{9}$ $\frac{16}{135}$
6. $\frac{1}{12} \cdot \frac{3}{8}$ $\frac{1}{32}$
7. $\frac{4}{15} \cdot \frac{2}{9}$ $\frac{8}{135}$
8. $\frac{3}{5} \cdot \frac{9}{13}$ $\frac{27}{65}$

9. $\frac{8}{9a} \cdot \frac{4}{7}$ $\frac{32}{63a}$
10. $\frac{3}{13} \cdot \frac{7b}{9}$ $\frac{7b}{39}$
11. $\frac{2}{3x} \cdot \frac{5x}{8}$ $\frac{5}{12}$
12. $\frac{12}{17h} \cdot \frac{2}{5}$ $\frac{24}{85h}$
13. $\frac{7}{9y} \cdot \frac{6}{7}$ $\frac{2}{3y}$
14. $\frac{4}{11s} \cdot \frac{11s}{12}$ $\frac{1}{3}$
15. $\frac{15}{16} \cdot \frac{5p}{7}$ $\frac{75p}{112}$

PROBLEM SOLVING

Exercise B Solve each problem. Write your answer in simplest form.

16. Libby is $\frac{3}{5}$ Rachel's age. Rachel is 35 years old. How old is Libby? (Hint: Remember to make the whole number a fraction by placing it over 1 before multiplying.)

    21 years old

17. $\frac{2}{3}$ of the cereal that was in a box is left. After Tyrone pours $\frac{1}{3}$ of the remaining cereal out of the box, how much will be left in the box?

    $\frac{4}{9}$ of the cereal

18. Stacy drove $\frac{1}{4}$ of the way to Atlanta in one day. The next day she drove $\frac{3}{5}$ of the remaining distance. How much farther does she have to drive?

    $\frac{3}{10}$ of the distance

19. Justin has $\frac{5}{8}$ of a casserole left over. If he eats $\frac{1}{4}$ of that, how much of the casserole is left?

    $\frac{15}{32}$ of the casserole

20. The Statue of Liberty is about $\frac{15}{28}$ the height of the Washington Monument. The Washington Monument is almost 560 feet tall. How tall is the Statue of Liberty?

    300 feet

LEARNING STYLES

Logical/Mathematical
Have students determine which sale gives the better price for a coat costing $100.

Sale of the Century:
Last month we slashed $\frac{1}{4}$ of the price off every coat in our stock. This month we are marking another $\frac{1}{4}$ off that sale price. You can't beat this deal!

Crazy Super Sale:
You can't beat our quality coats, and now you can't beat the price. All coats are reduced to half cost. That's right. Pay only $\frac{1}{2}$ the original retail price!

Have students explain their choice and show calculations to prove which sale coat costs less. *[The Crazy Super Sale coat will cost $50 ($\frac{1}{2} \cdot \frac{100}{1}$), but the Sale of the Century coat will cost $56.25. (It is discounted $43.75 because $\frac{1}{4} + \frac{3}{4} \cdot \frac{1}{4} = \frac{7}{16}$; $\frac{7}{16} \cdot \frac{100}{1} = $43.75.)]*

3   Reinforce and Extend

MENTAL MATH

Demonstrate this way of simplifying larger fractions to make multiplying easier:

$$20\ \overset{1}{\cancel{\frac{4}{100}}} \cdot \frac{\overset{1}{\cancel{8}}}{6}$$

$$5\ \overset{1}{\cancel{\frac{4}{20}}} \cdot \frac{1}{6} = \frac{1}{5} \cdot \frac{1}{6}$$

$$\frac{1}{30}$$

Use the greatest common factor to divide numerators and denominators.

Point out that either numerator may be divided into either denominator. Write the following examples on the board, and have students use mental math to simplify the fractions, using this method before finding a product using paper and pencil.

$$\frac{2}{5} \cdot \frac{10}{12}$$

$$\overset{1}{\cancel{\Big(\frac{2}{5}}} \cdot \overset{2}{\underset{6}{\cancel{\frac{10}{12}}}} = \frac{2}{6} = \frac{1}{3}\Big)$$

$$\frac{1}{4} \cdot \frac{8}{10}$$

$$\overset{}{\cancel{\Big(\frac{1}{4}}} \cdot \underset{1}{\overset{2}{\cancel{\frac{8}{10}}}} = \frac{2}{10} = \frac{1}{5}\Big)$$

$$\frac{6}{7} \cdot \frac{21}{22}$$

$$\overset{3}{\underset{1}{\cancel{\Big(\frac{6}{7}}}} \cdot \underset{11}{\overset{3}{\cancel{\frac{21}{22}}}} = \frac{9}{11}\Big)$$

Lesson at a Glance

Chapter 6 Application

Overview This lesson provides an application of converting linear measurements.

Objective
- To identify equivalent measurements

Student Page 162

Teacher's Resource Library

Application Activity 6

Everyday Math 6

1 Warm-Up Activity

Provide each student with a ruler. Ask that he or she measure something in the classroom. All measurements should be in inches. Have students identify the objects as "less than one ruler," "equal to one ruler," or "greater than one ruler." Students should identify the length of a ruler as one foot. The measured objects can then be described as "less than one foot," "equal to one foot," or "more than one foot."

2 Teaching the Lesson

It may be necessary to provide a list of the linear measurement units organized from least to greatest. Students can use this list to check the reasonableness of their answers. It is important that measurements be exact. Therefore, the name of the correct unit must accompany the number when writing the answer.

Allow students to make predictions as the problems are introduced. Invite students to share predictions with their peers. Students should compare actual answers with predictions as problems are completed.

COMMON ERROR

 Remind students that when a whole number is written as a fraction, the 1 is on the bottom. If the whole number is put below the 1, the answer will be incorrect.

Converting Measurements Sometimes when working with measurements, you need to convert a larger measurement into a smaller one, or the other way around. You can use simple equations to help you calculate the conversions.

EXAMPLE 1 Convert 18 ounces into pounds.

$$1 \text{ ounce} = \frac{1}{16} \text{ pound}$$

Step 1 Set up the conversion. $\frac{1}{16} \cdot 18$

Step 2 Multiply to find the number of pounds. $\frac{1}{16} \cdot \frac{18}{1} = \frac{1 \cdot 18}{16 \cdot 1} = \frac{18}{16}$

Step 3 Simplify the fraction. $\frac{18}{16} = 1\frac{2}{16} = 1\frac{1}{8}$

$$18 \text{ ounces} = 1\frac{1}{8} \text{ pounds}$$

Exercise Solve the problems.

1. The hallway rug measures 84 inches long. How many feet is this?

   12 inches = 1 foot   7 feet

2. Nature Valley Farm is located on 50 acres. How many square feet is the farm?   2,178,000 square feet

   1 acre = 43,560 square feet

3. The cross-country course measures 5 kilometers from beginning to end. How many meters is this?   5,000 meters

   1 kilometer = 1,000 meters

4. Ana's recipe calls for 3 quarts of broth. She has a $\frac{1}{2}$-gallon can. Is this enough? Explain your answer.

   1 quart = $\frac{1}{4}$ gallon

   No; Ana needs more broth.
   3 quarts is equal to $\frac{3}{4}$ gallon.

Application Activity 6

Everyday Math 6

Chapter 6 R E V I E W

Write the letter of the correct answer.
Simplify each expression by following the order of operations.

1. $2(7 - 3) - 12 \div 6$ B

  A $\frac{1}{6}$ **C** 3

  B 6   **D** 10

2. $10(15 \div 5)$ A

  A 30   **C** 3

  B 6   **D** 10

3. $18 \div 6 + 3(7 - 2)$ D

  A 40   **C** 7

  B 11   **D** 18

Evaluate each expression for $m = 5$.

4. $m - 4$ B

  A 9   **C** 0

  B 1   **D** 20

5. $3m + 1$ D

  A 14   **C** 9

  B 20   **D** 16

6. $2 + \frac{1}{m}$ D

  A $\frac{1}{7}$ **C** $\frac{1}{10}$

  B $1\frac{4}{5}$ **D** $2\frac{1}{5}$

7. $5m + 2m$ C

  A 7   **C** 35

  B 25   **D** 250

GROUP PROBLEM SOLVING

Provide students with a measurement challenge that relates to the classroom or school building. Encourage students to use the appropriate tools to find measurements. All answers should be recorded and converted to at least one different unit.

KNOWING YOUR STUDENTS

Teenage students are very visual. They typically enjoy television as well as video games, magazines, and other visual stimulation. Also, because most adolescents are still developing their abstract thinking skills, concrete models or diagrams of different-sized objects may be helpful. Students can use visual representations as resources during the lesson. Gradually remove items as students are able to describe differences in units of measurement.

Chapter 6 Review

Each set of problems in the Chapter Review includes an example and solution to illustrate the concept. Use the given examples for reteaching the materials in Chapter 6. For additional practice, refer to the Supplementary Problems for Chapter 6 (pages 442–443).

Chapter 6 Mastery Test

The Teacher's Resource Library includes parallel forms of the Chapter 6 Mastery Test. The difficulty level of the two forms is equivalent. You may wish to use one form as a pretest and the other form as a posttest.

Chapter 6 Mastery Test A

Chapter 6 Mastery Test A

Name _____ Date _____ Period _____ Mastery Test A, Page 1 — Chapter 6

Directions Circle the letter of the correct answer.

1. Simplify $2 + 9(8 - 1)$ using the order of operations.
  A 77   C 87
  B 65   D 68

2. Evaluate $10 - 3n$ when $n = 3$.
  A 1   C 19
  B 21   D −21

3. What is the sum of $\frac{2x}{5} + \frac{x}{5}$ in simplest form?
  A $\frac{2x}{5}$ C $\frac{3x}{5}$
  B $\frac{3x}{5}$ D x

4. Find the product. $\frac{7}{11} \cdot \frac{4y}{5}$
  A $\frac{28y}{55}$ C $\frac{11}{16}$
  B $\frac{11y}{55}$ D $\frac{28y}{55y}$

5. Evaluate $\frac{12}{n} + \frac{n}{4}$ when $n = 2$. Give the answer in simplest form.
  A $12\frac{2}{4}$ C $\frac{14}{n}$
  B $6\frac{1}{2}$ D $2\frac{1}{2}$

Directions Simplify each expression using the order of operations.

6. $32 - 16 \div 4$ _____
7. $5 + 3(4)$ _____
8. $(27 - 9) + 3$ _____
9. $6(8 - 7) + 4 \cdot 1$ _____

Directions Evaluate each expression for $n = 3$.

10. $n + 1$ _____
11. $n - 2$ _____
12. $7n - 11$ _____
13. $18 + \frac{n}{3}$ _____

Directions Tell whether each equation is *true* or *false* when the given number is substituted for x.

14. $10x + 5 = 25$ when $x = 2$ _____
15. $15 - 3x = 14$ when $x = 1$ _____
16. $5x = 3\frac{3}{4}$ when $x = \frac{3}{4}$ _____
17. $7x = 8\frac{1}{2}$ when $x = 1\frac{1}{4}$ _____
18. $10 + 12x = 56$ when $x = 4$ _____

Directions Solve for x. Write your answer in simplest form.

19. $x + 11 = 23$ _____
20. $44 - x = 29$ _____
21. $x + 5 = 6\frac{1}{2}$ _____
22. $39 - x = 5$ _____
23. $\frac{7}{5} = \frac{3}{5} + x$ _____
24. $125 = 53 + x$ _____

©AGS Publishing. Permission is granted to reproduce for classroom use only. ▲ Mathematics: Pathways

---

Name _____ Date _____ Period _____ Mastery Test A, Page 2 — Chapter 6

Chapter 6 Mastery Test A, continued

Directions Simplify each complex fraction.

25. $\frac{\frac{1}{2}}{\frac{1}{4}}$ _____
26. $\frac{\frac{2}{3}}{\frac{1}{3}}$ _____
27. $\frac{\frac{1}{5}}{10}$ _____
28. $\frac{\frac{3}{16}}{\frac{3}{8}}$ _____
29. $\frac{\frac{2}{3}}{12}$ _____
30. $\frac{\frac{5}{8}}{\frac{5}{2}}$ _____

Directions Find each sum or difference. Write your answer in simplest form.

31. $\frac{7}{6n} - \frac{1}{6n}$ _____
32. $\frac{11b}{5} - \frac{2b}{5}$ _____
33. $\frac{1}{6m} + \frac{3}{4m}$ _____
34. $\frac{4}{3r} - \frac{7}{20y}$ _____

Directions Find each product. Write your answer in simplest form.

35. $\frac{2}{5} \cdot \frac{1}{2}$ _____
36. $\frac{3}{4} \cdot \frac{1}{4}$ _____
37. $\frac{1}{6a} \cdot \frac{2}{3}$ _____
38. $\frac{8y}{10} \cdot \frac{1}{2r}$ _____
39. $\frac{11}{16p} \cdot \frac{8p}{11}$ _____

Directions Solve.

40. On their first day of vacation, the DiCosolas drove $\frac{2}{3}$ of the distance to their destination. On the second day, they drove $\frac{1}{4}$ of the remaining distance. What fraction of the total distance do they still have to drive?

©AGS Publishing. Permission is granted to reproduce for classroom use only. ▲ Mathematics: Pathways

---

Chapter 6 Mastery Test A

ALTERNATIVE ASSESSMENT

Alternative Assessment items correlate with student Goals for Learning at the beginning of this chapter.

■ **To use the order of operations to solve problems correctly**

Have students create a unique way (such as rhyme or illustration) of remembering the correct order of operations. You can use the mnemonic device **P**lease **E**xcuse **M**y **D**ear **A**unt **S**usan as an example, where **P** = parentheses, **E** = exponent, **M** = multiply, **D** = divide, **A** = add, and **S** = subtract.

■ **To evaluate algebraic expressions**

Have students work in pairs and use manipulatives such as toothpicks or paper clips to visually evaluate algebraic expressions you have written on the board, such as $x + 5$, $2x + 1$, $3x - 5$, and $27x$. Have students use manipulatives to evaluate the expressions for given values of x.

■ **To solve algebraic equations through substitution**

Have students work in groups of three or four, and give each student two half-sheets of paper with a different equation written at the top of each paper. Then instruct students to draw a table, substitute a number for x, and solve to see whether the equation is true. If it is true, that student keeps the sheet. If it is false, have him or her pass it to the person on the left and go on to the next equation. A student gets to try each problem only once before passing it on. If no student in the group solves the equation in the first round, keep the sheet going until the problem is solved. The students with the most sheets at the end are the "winners."

■ **To solve equations by adding and subtracting**

Have students each write one addition equation and one subtraction equation. Then have students work in pairs. Partners should exchange equations and then take turns explaining the appropriate method for solving the equation.

Tell whether each equation is true or false when the given number is substituted for x.

Example: $2x - 3 = 13$ when $x = 8$ Solution: $2x - 3 = 13$
$$2(8) - 3 = 13$$
$$16 - 3 = 13 \quad \text{True}$$

8. true   **8.** $4(9) - x = 27$ when $x = 9$ **12.** $22 + 3x = 34$ when $x = 4$

9. false   **9.** $3(x) + x = 18$ when $x = 6$ **13.** $6x \cdot 4 = 48$ when $x = 2$

10. true   **10.** $x + 31 = 38$ when $x = 7$ **14.** $7 + 8x = 54$ when $x = 6$

11. true   **11.** $29 - 5x = 4$ when $x = 5$ **15.** $2x \div 3 = 9$ when $x = 8$

12. true

13. true

14. false

15. false

Solve for x. Write your answer in simplest form.

Example: $3 + x = 25$ Solution: $3 + x = 25$
$$3 + x - 3 = 25 - 3$$
$$x = 22$$

16. $x + 13 = 17$ 4   **20.** $2\frac{5}{8} - x = \frac{1}{8}$ $2\frac{1}{2}$

17. $25 - x = 19$ 6   **21.** $\frac{2}{3}x - \frac{1}{3} = 3\frac{2}{3}$ 6

18. $\frac{3}{4}x + \frac{3}{4} = 6\frac{3}{4}$ 8   **22.** $\frac{3}{4} + \frac{1}{4}x = 3\frac{3}{4}$ 12

19. $\frac{1}{9} + 4x = 44\frac{1}{9}$ 11

Simplify each complex fraction.

Example: Simplify $\dfrac{\frac{1}{2}}{\frac{2}{3}}$ Solution: $\dfrac{\frac{1}{2}}{\frac{2}{3}} = \frac{1}{2} \div \frac{2}{3} = \frac{1}{2} \cdot \frac{3}{2} = \frac{3}{4}$

23. $\dfrac{\frac{1}{3}}{\frac{1}{2}}$ $\frac{2}{3}$ **26.** $\dfrac{\frac{5}{6}}{3}$ $\frac{5}{18}$ **29.** $\dfrac{\frac{8}{5}}{\frac{5}{8}}$ $12\frac{4}{5}$

24. $\dfrac{\frac{3}{4}}{\frac{3}{5}}$ $1\frac{1}{4}$ **27.** $\dfrac{\frac{1}{8}}{\frac{1}{16}}$ 2   **30.** $\dfrac{\frac{11}{12}}{6}$ $\frac{11}{72}$

25. $\dfrac{\frac{2}{1}}{4}$ 8   **28.** $\dfrac{\frac{2}{3}}{9}$ $\frac{2}{27}$

Chapter 6 Mastery Test B

Simplify. Write your answer in simplest form.

Example: Simplify $\frac{5}{12a} + \frac{19}{12a}$ Solution: $\frac{5}{12a} + \frac{19}{12a} = \frac{24}{12a} = \frac{2}{a}$

31. $\frac{1}{8c} + \frac{3}{8c}$ $\frac{1}{2c}$ **35.** $\frac{5}{6z} - \frac{1}{5z}$ $\frac{19}{30z}$

32. $\frac{11}{12m} - \frac{1}{2m}$ $\frac{5}{12m}$ **36.** $\frac{3}{16h} + \frac{7}{16h} + \frac{5}{16h}$ $\frac{15}{16h}$

33. $\frac{9}{16r} + \frac{3}{4r}$ $\frac{21}{16r}$ **37.** $\frac{11}{12w} - \frac{1}{12w} + \frac{7}{12w}$ $\frac{17}{12w}$

34. $\frac{7}{8b} - \frac{2}{3b}$ $\frac{5}{24b}$ **38.** $\frac{2}{3z} - \frac{1}{6z} + \frac{3}{4z}$ $\frac{5}{4z}$

Multiply. Write your answer in simplest form.

Example: $\frac{3r}{5} \cdot \frac{3}{4}$ Solution: $\frac{3r}{5} \cdot \frac{3}{4} = \frac{3r \cdot 3}{5 \cdot 4} = \frac{9r}{20}$

39. $\frac{4}{9x} \cdot \frac{1}{4}$ $\frac{1}{9x}$ **43.** $\frac{4}{9} \cdot \frac{7p}{10}$ $\frac{14p}{45}$

40. $\frac{3q}{16} \cdot \frac{3}{10}$ $\frac{9q}{160}$ **44.** $\frac{3}{5y} \cdot \frac{2}{15}$ $\frac{2}{25y}$

41. $\frac{9}{11w} \cdot \frac{1}{8}$ $\frac{9}{88w}$ **45.** $\frac{2}{3a} \cdot \frac{5}{12}$ $\frac{5}{18a}$

42. $\frac{14}{19h} \cdot \frac{5}{6}$ $\frac{35}{57h}$

Test-Taking Tip

When solving an equation, always start each step on a new line. Check to be sure that you have the equal sign lined up under one another.

Basic Operations and Rational Expressions   Chapter 6   **165**

ALTERNATIVE ASSESSMENT, CONTINUED

■ **To simplify complex fractions**
Have students explain the relationship between simplifying a complex fraction and dividing a number or fraction by a fraction.

■ **To add and subtract to simplify rational expressions**
Organize the class in four teams. Divide the board into four or more sections. Team members should take turns using addition and subtraction to simplify rational expressions written on the board. Have each team work a problem step by step.

■ **To multiply rational expressions**
Have students bring in a favorite recipe that serves several people. Have students figure out the amounts of ingredients for one person and for 100 people. For example, tell students that if the recipe makes enough for five people, they would multiply the amounts by $\frac{1}{5}$ to find the ingredients for one person. For 100 people, they would multiply all amounts by 20.

Planning Guide

Ratios, Proportions, and Percents

Lesson		Student Pages	Vocabulary	Practice Exercises	Problem Solving	Try This	Solutions Key
1	Ratios	168–169	✔	✔	169		✔
2	Proportions	170–171	✔	✔			✔
3	Ratios and Proportions	172–173	✔	✔	173		✔
4	Proportional Relationships	174–175		✔	175		✔
5	Solving Distance, Rate, and Time Problems	176–177		✔	177		✔
6	Percents and Fractions	178–181		✔		181	✔
7	Percents and Decimals	182–185		✔	185		✔
8	Finding the Percent of a Number	186–187		✔			✔
9	Finding the Percent	188–189		✔			✔
10	Percent of Increase and Decrease	190–191		✔	191		✔
11	Formulas and Percents	192–193	✔	✔		193	✔
12	Scale Drawings and Models	194–197	✔	✔	197		✔
Application	Rates of Change	198		✔			✔

Chapter Activities

Teacher's Resource Library
Estimation Exercise 7: Estimating the Percent of a Number
Application Activity 7: Rates of Change
Everyday Math 7: Mapping Distances
Community Connection 7: A Home Loan

Teacher's Edition
Chapter 7 Project

Assessment Options

Student Text
Chapter 7 Review

Teacher's Resource Library
Chapter 7 Mastery Tests A and B
Chapters 1–7 Midterm Mastery Test

Teacher's Edition
Chapter 7 Alternative Assessments

Estimation Activity	Math in Your Life	Technology Connection	Writing About Mathematics	Build a Model	Calculator Practice	Online Connection	Common Error	Applications Home, Career, Community	Mental Math	Manipulatives	Calculator	Group Problem Solving	Modeling	Knowing Your Students	Auditory/Verbal	Visual/Spatial	Logical/Mathematical	Body/Kinesthetic	Interpersonal/Group Learning	LEP/ESL	Activities	Alternate Activities	Workbook Activities	Self-Study Guide
							169								169	169					53	53	55	✔
		171							171							171				171	54	54	56	✔
								173		173		173									55	55	57	✔
								175				175		175							56	56	58	✔
						177		177				176						177			57	57	59	✔
		181	180				179	180				181						180			58	58	60	✔
	183		184				183	185	185	184		185				185					59	59	61–62	✔
187							187		187										187		60	60	63	✔
						189			189		189	189									61	61	64	✔
					191			191				191									62	62	65	✔
						193		193				193							193		63	63	66	✔
							194	195, 196	196		197		195			197					64	64	67	✔
												199												✔

Software Options

Skill Track Software

Use the Skill Track Software for *Mathematics: Pathways* for additional reinforcement of this chapter. The software provides multiple-choice assessment items for students to access by computer.

Solutions Key

Use the Solutions Key with this chapter to help students who may need additional assistance. The Solutions Key CD provides solutions for every exercise in the student edition.

Other Resources

Alternative Activities

The Teacher's Resource Library (TRL) contains a set of worksheets written at a second-grade reading level called Alternative Activities. They cover the same content as the regular Activities.

Manipulatives

See the Manipulative activities in this chapter for hands-on modeling of the content. The following TRL pages can also be used:

Manipulatives Master 4 (100-Square Grid)
Cuisenaire Rods

Chapter at a Glance

Chapter 7: Ratios, Proportions, and Percents
pages 166–201

Lessons

Skill Track for Mathematics: Pathways

Teacher's Resource Library TRL

(Answer Keys for the Teacher's Resource Library begin on page 528 of this Teacher's Edition.)

Name Date Period | Estimation Exercise 7 | Chapter 7

Estimating the Percent of a Number

There are many times when you have to work out percents in your head. For example, you might want to figure out how much sales tax you are going to pay on a purchase or how much to leave for a tip in a restaurant.

EXAMPLE Estimate 13% of $23.00.

Step 1 Move the decimal point one place to the left and drop the final zero. That will give you 10% of the number.

10% of $23.00 = $2.30.

Step 2 Mentally divide the result by 2. (Half of 10% is 5%.) Then add the two amounts together to get 15% of the number.

$2.30 ÷ 2 = $1.15 $1.15 + $2.30 = $3.45

Step 3 You know that 13% is between 10% and 15%, so 13% of $23.00 is between $2.30 and $3.45.

13% of $23.00 is about $3.00.

You can use a similar method for higher percentages as well. There are other ways to estimate percents of a number. To find 50% of a number you divide the number by 2. To find 25% of a number you divide the number by 4. You can then estimate a percentage between the two numbers.

Directions Estimate the amount of each percentage.

1. 11% of $34.00 ______
2. 14% of 43 ______
3. 18% of 322 ______
4. 72% of 364 ______
5. 39% of 4,600 ______
6. 23% of 128 ______
7. 12% of $56.79 ______
8. 45% of 2,386 ______
9. Justin's family was on vacation and took a taxi from the airport to their hotel. The fare for the ride was $26.85. Justin's father tipped the cab driver 12%. About how much did the ride cost altogether? ______
10. Paula and her three friends were at a restaurant. The total bill came to $43.89. They decided to tip their server 14%, so each person put $1.00 on the table. Did they leave enough? Explain. ______

 Mathematics: Pathways

TRL

Estimation Exercise 7

Name Date Period | Community Connection 7 | Chapter 7

A Home Loan

When you take out a mortgage, you are borrowing money from a lender. The mortgage is a legal document that entitles the lender to your home if you do not repay the money you borrowed.

There are several costs associated with a mortgage. The cost of greatest concern is the *interest*. Newspapers regularly publish the average mortgage rates for the region. A specific lender may have a rate that matches the rate in the newspaper or may have a slightly higher or lower rate.

Visit a local lender and make inquiries about mortgage rates and costs. Then answer these questions.

1. What is the current mortgage rate for a 15-year fixed mortgage? 30-year fixed mortgage?
2. What type of mortgage currently has the best interest rate?
3. What percent of a home's price does the lender expect as a down payment on the home?
4. How much is the application fee? What other costs are associated with the mortgage?

Suppose you want a $50,000 mortgage for 30 years.

5. What would your monthly payment be? ______
6. During the first year of the mortgage, how much of that payment would be interest? ______ How much would go toward the principal? ______
7. How much will you have paid for the $50,000 mortgage after 15 years? ______ after 30 years? ______

 Mathematics: Pathways

TRL

Community Connection 7

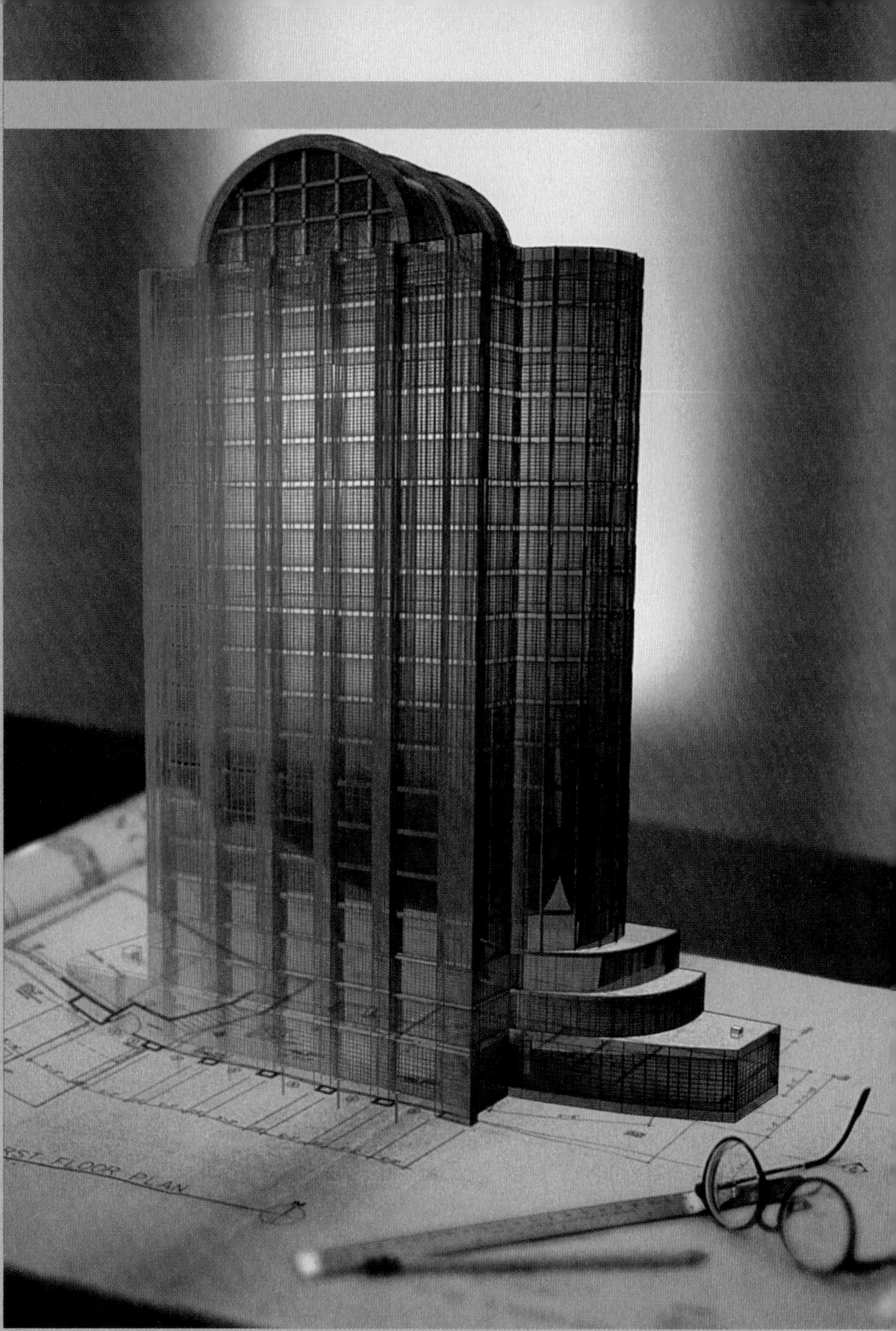

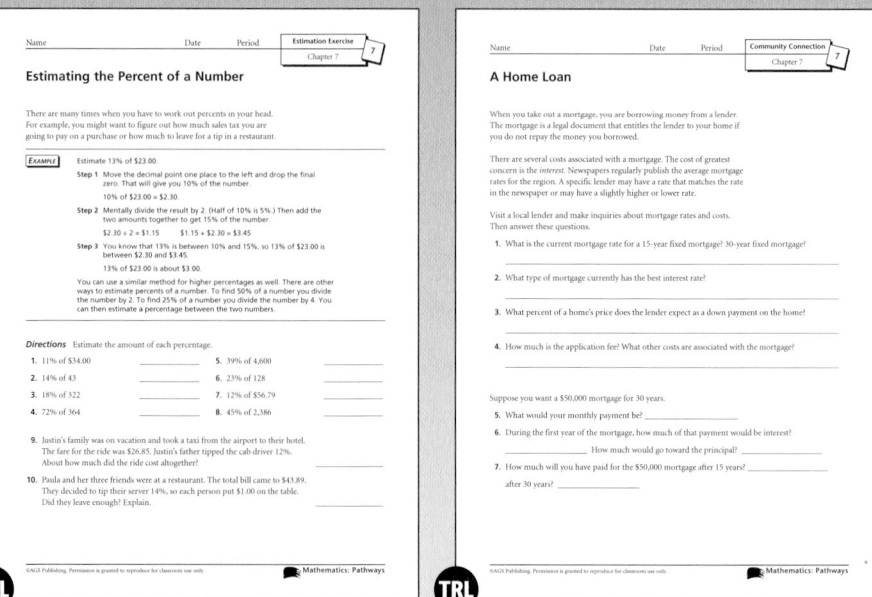

7 Ratios, Proportions, and Percents

In Jonathan Swift's novel *Gulliver's Travels*, Gulliver finds himself in a world called Lilliput that looks exactly like his homeland, but where everything is reduced in size. The details are the same, but everything is much, much smaller. The model in the picture is a smaller version of the real building it represents. Notice the size of the model compared to the glasses and pencil on the desk.

Ratios, proportions, and percents are tools we use to compare quantities. Ratios and proportions show the relative size or scale of similar things. For example, the model is a tiny copy of the actual building. Each feature in the model corresponds in size and location to the feature on the real building.

In Chapter 7, you will work with ratios, proportions, and percents.

Goals for Learning

- ◆ To express ratios in different forms
- ◆ To solve problems using proportions
- ◆ To use proportions to find length, weight, capacity, and volume
- ◆ To solve distance and rate problems
- ◆ To change fractions and decimals to percents
- ◆ To solve problems using percents
- ◆ To read and draw scale drawings

167

Introducing the Chapter

Use the information in the chapter opener to help students understand that they are likely to encounter ratios, proportions, and percents often in their personal lives and in their careers. You might choose to ask students to name different nonclassroom situations in which they have already encountered ratios, proportions, and/or percents.

CHAPTER PROJECT

Remind students that the use of percents is pervasive in society. As they complete their work in the chapter, ask students to periodically identify and list various situations in which percents occur. They will encounter these situations as they complete various lessons in the chapter. Each time students add situations to their lists, provide them with an opportunity to use the situations as discussion springboards and talk about other situations in life that are likely to involve percents. These situations can then be added to the lists. Upon completion of their work in the chapter, invite students to review their lists and form an opinion about the importance of being familiar with percents.

TEACHER'S RESOURCE

The AGS Publishing Teaching Strategies in Math Transparencies may be used with this chapter. They add an interactive dimension to expand and enhance the program content.

CAREER INTEREST INVENTORY

The AGS Publishing Harrington-O'Shea Career Decision-Making System-Revised (CDM) may be used with this chapter. Students can use the CDM to explore their interests and identify careers. The CDM defines career areas that are indicated by students' responses on the inventory.

Name _____ Date _____ Period _____ *SELF-STUDY GUIDE*

CHAPTER 7: Ratios, Proportions, and Percents

Goals 7.1 and 7.2 To express ratios in different forms; to solve problems using proportions

Date	Assignment	Score
_____	1: Read pages 167–169. Complete Exercises A–C on page 169.	_____
_____	2: Complete Workbook Activity 55.	_____
_____	3: Read pages 170–171. Complete Exercises A–B on page 171.	_____
_____	4: Complete Workbook Activity 56.	_____
_____	5: Read pages 172–173. Complete Exercise A on page 173.	_____
_____	6: Complete Workbook Activity 57.	_____

Comments:

Goals 7.3 and 7.4 To use proportions to find length, weight, capacity, and volume; to solve distance and rate problems

Date	Assignment	Score
_____	7: Read pages 174–175. Complete Exercise A on page 175.	_____
_____	8: Complete Workbook Activity 58.	_____
_____	9: Read pages 176–177. Complete Exercise A on page 177.	_____
_____	10: Complete Workbook Activity 59.	_____

Comments:

Goal 7.5 To change fractions and decimals to percents

Date	Assignment	Score
_____	11: Read pages 178–179. Complete Exercises A–C on pages 180–181.	_____
_____	12: Complete Workbook Activity 60.	_____
_____	13: Read pages 182–183. Complete Exercises A–D on pages 184–185.	_____
_____	14: Complete Workbook Activities 61 and 62.	_____

Comments:

©AGS Publishing. Permission is granted to reproduce for classroom use only. ▸ Mathematics: Pathways

---

Name _____ Date _____ Period _____ *SELF-STUDY GUIDE*

CHAPTER 7: Ratios, Proportions, and Percents, continued

Goal 7.6 To solve problems using percents

Date	Assignment	Score
_____	15: Read pages 186–187. Complete Exercise A on page 187.	_____
_____	16: Complete Workbook Activity 63.	_____
_____	17: Read pages 188–189. Complete Exercise A on page 189.	_____
_____	18: Read and complete the Calculator Practice on page 189.	_____
_____	19: Complete Workbook Activity 64.	_____
_____	20: Read pages 190–191. Complete Exercises A–B on page 191.	_____
_____	21: Complete Workbook Activity 65.	_____
_____	22: Read pages 192–193. Complete the Calculator Practice on page 193.	_____
_____	23: Complete Workbook Activity 66.	_____

Comments:

Goal 7.7 To read and draw scale drawings

Date	Assignment	Score
_____	24: Read pages 194–195. Complete Exercises A–C on pages 196–197.	_____
_____	25: Complete Workbook Activity 67.	_____
_____	26: Read and complete the Application on page 198.	_____
_____	27: Complete the Chapter 7 Review on pages 199–201.	_____

Comments:

Student's Signature _____ Date _____

Instructor's Signature _____ Date _____

©AGS Publishing. Permission is granted to reproduce for classroom use only. ▸ Mathematics: Pathways

---

TRL

Chapter 7 Self-Study Guide

Lesson at a Glance

Chapter 7 Lesson 1

Overview This lesson introduces ratios.

Objective

- To express ratios in simplest form

Student Pages 168–169

Teacher's Resource Library **TRL**

Workbook Activity 55

Activity 53

Alternative Activity 53

....

Mathematics Vocabulary

ratio

....

1 Warm-Up Activity

Invite students to name as many different modes of transportation as they can. These modes may include flying in a commercial aircraft, walking, traveling in an automobile, and sailing. After each mode of transportation is identified, ask students to estimate the speed at which that mode typically occurs. The average adult, for example, walks at a speed of about 4 miles per hour. Then point out that each speed mentioned is an example of a rate or a ratio. In this case, the rate or ratio describes the relationship between distance and time.

2 Teaching the Lesson

Students are likely to be familiar with fractions that include $\frac{1}{2}$, $\frac{3}{4}$, $\frac{5}{8}$, and $\frac{9}{16}$ because the denominators of the fractions are increments into which the customary unit of measure *inch* is divided. Choose a fraction such as $\frac{1}{2}$, write it on the board, and ask students to describe, with respect to an inch, the relationship between the numerator and the denominator of the fraction. *[The denominator represents the number of equal parts into which the whole (inch) is divided. The numerator represents the quantity of those equal parts that has been selected.]* Then have students compare their answers with the definition of a ratio given on page 168 and identify the similarities that are shared by each definition.

Lesson 1   Ratios

Ratio
A comparison of two like quantities using a fraction

Recall that examples of fractions include proper fractions such as $\frac{3}{4}$ and improper fractions such as $\frac{5}{2}$. Proper and improper fractions are examples of **ratios**. A ratio is a comparison of two quantities using a fraction.

EXAMPLE 1 In a class of 15 students, 7 students are female and 8 students are male. The following ratios can be written to describe that class.

$\frac{7}{8}$ The ratio of female students to male students

$\frac{8}{7}$ The ratio of male students to female students

$\frac{7}{15}$ The ratio of female students to the total number of students

$\frac{8}{15}$ The ratio of male students to the total number of students

$\frac{15}{7}$ The ratio of the total number of students to the number of female students

$\frac{15}{8}$ The ratio of the total number of students to the number of male students

The word *to* and the symbol : can also be used to express a ratio.

To find the simplest form of a fraction, find the GCD of the numerator and denominator, then divide both the numerator and denominator by the GCD.

EXAMPLE 2 In a collection of 32 books, 13 books are fiction and 19 books are nonfiction. Write the ratio of nonfiction books to the total number of books three different ways.

1. Write the ratio as a fraction $\frac{19}{32}$

2. Write the ratio using the word *to*   19 to 32

3. Write the ratio using the symbol :   19:32

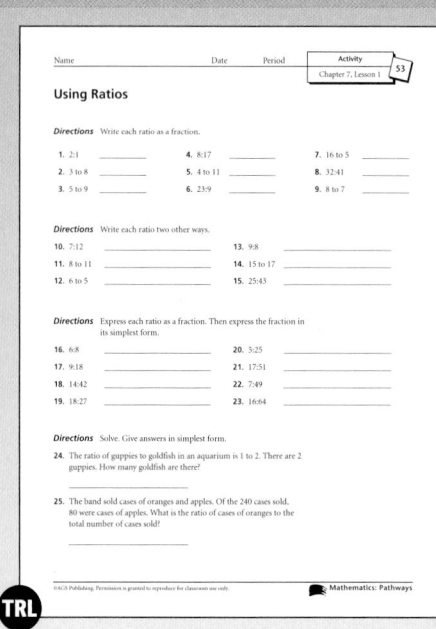

Workbook Activity 55

Name _____ Date _____ Period _____ **Workbook Activity** 55
Chapter 7, Lesson 1

Ratios

EXAMPLE A ratio is a comparison of two quantities using fractions.
Here are some ways to write a ratio: $\frac{3}{8}$ 3 to 8   3:8
Express a ratio in simplest form.
$\frac{18}{24} = \frac{18 \div 2}{24 \div 2} = \frac{9}{12}$ 5 to 12   or   5:12

Directions Complete the chart to show how to write each ratio two other ways.

1. $\frac{9}{11}$		
2.	4 to 11	
3.		5:17
4.	16 to 9	
5. $\frac{12}{7}$		
6.		21:14
7. $\frac{13}{11}$		
8.	27 to 41	
9.		37:19
10.	53 to 61	

Directions Write *OK* if each ratio is a fraction expressed in its simplest form. If the fraction is not expressed in its simplest form, write the simplest form.

11. $\frac{3}{15}$ _____
12. $\frac{4}{5}$ _____
13. $\frac{9}{6}$ _____
14. $\frac{9}{4}$ _____
15. $\frac{12}{7}$ _____
16. $\frac{14}{56}$ _____
17. $\frac{5}{9}$ _____
18. $\frac{9}{24}$ _____
19. $\frac{9}{6}$ _____
20. $\frac{32}{12}$ _____

Mathematics: Pathways

Activity 53

Name _____ Date _____ Period _____ **Activity** 53
Chapter 7, Lesson 1

Using Ratios

Directions Write each ratio as a fraction.

1. 2:1 _____
2. 3 to 8 _____
3. 5 to 9 _____
4. 8:17 _____
5. 4 to 11 _____
6. 23:9 _____
7. 16 to 5 _____
8. 32:41 _____
9. 8 to 7 _____

Directions Write each ratio two other ways.

10. 7:12 _____
11. 8 to 17 _____
12. 6 to 5 _____
13. 9:8 _____
14. 15 to 17 _____
15. 25:43 _____

Directions Express each ratio as a fraction. Then express the fraction in its simplest form.

16. 6:8 _____
17. 9:18 _____
18. 14:42 _____
19. 18:27 _____
20. 5:25 _____
21. 17:51 _____
22. 7:49 _____
23. 16:64 _____

Directions Solve. Give answers in simplest form.

24. The ratio of guppies to goldfish in an aquarium is 1 to 2. There are 2 guppies. How many goldfish are there?

25. The band sold cases of oranges and apples. Of the 240 cases sold, 80 were cases of apples. What is the ratio of cases of oranges to the total number of cases sold?

Mathematics: Pathways

EXAMPLE 3 Express the ratios 10:2 and 24 to 16 in simplest form.

Write each ratio as a fraction. Use division to find the simplest form of each fraction. Then rewrite each fraction.

$$10:2 = \frac{10}{2} = \frac{10 \div 2}{2 \div 2} = \frac{5}{1} = 5:1 \qquad 24 \text{ to } 16 = \frac{24}{16} = \frac{24 \div 8}{16 \div 8} = \frac{3}{2} = 3 \text{ to } 2$$

Exercise A Express each ratio two different ways.

1. 4 to 3 $\frac{4}{3}$; 4:3

3. $\frac{7}{2}$ 7 to 2; 7:2

5. $\frac{5}{11}$ 5 to 11; 5:11

2. 1:8 $\frac{1}{8}$; 1 to 8

4. 100:9 $\frac{100}{9}$; 100 to 9

6. 29 to 41 $\frac{29}{41}$; 29:41

Exercise B Express each ratio as a fraction in simplest form.

7. 9:18 $\frac{1}{2}$

9. $\frac{34}{4}$ $\frac{17}{2}$

11. 64:18 $\frac{32}{9}$

13. 7 to 42 $\frac{1}{6}$

8. 26 to 13 $\frac{2}{1}$

10. 10 to 42 $\frac{5}{21}$

12. $\frac{6}{16}$ $\frac{3}{8}$

14. 17:24 $\frac{17}{24}$

PROBLEM SOLVING

Exercise C Solve these problems. Give the answers in simplest form.

15. In a class of 14 students, 6 students are male. What is the ratio of female students to the total number of students in the class? $\frac{4}{7}$

16. Of the 120 compact discs in a music collection, 45 compact discs contain jazz music. What is the ratio of non-jazz compact discs to the total number of compact discs in the collection? $\frac{5}{8}$

17. The ratio of girls to boys in a family is 1:2. If there are two girls in the family, how many boys are in the family? 4 boys

18. If the ratio of males to females in each of two different mathematics classes is 5 to 4, is the ratio of males to females still 5 to 4 if the classes were considered as one large class instead of two smaller classes? Yes

19. In a coin collection, the ratio of coins minted before 1940 to those minted in 1940 or after is 3 to 1. Is there an odd or even number of coins in the collection? Explain.

20. Suppose one person describes the number of sunny days to cloudy days in June as 18 to 12, and another person describes the number of sunny days to cloudy days in June as 3 to 2. Can each person be describing the same month in the same year? Explain.

19. Even, because there are 3 + 1 coins, or some multiple of 4 coins, in the collection.

20. Yes; In simplest form, the ratio 18 to 12 is 3 to 2.

Ratios, Proportions, and Percents Chapter 7 **169**

Lesson at a Glance

Chapter 7 Lesson 2

Overview This lesson introduces proportions.

Objective

- To solve for the unknown in a proportion

Student Pages 170–171

Teacher's Resource Library **TRL**

Workbook Activity 56

Activity 54

Alternative Activity 54

....

Mathematics Vocabulary

proportion
cross product

....

1 Warm-Up Activity

Invite students who have experience preparing food from a recipe to explain how different amounts of a recipe are determined. For example, if a recipe serves 6 persons, how does one alter the recipe to serve 9 people, 12 people, or 3 people? Summarize the discussion by pointing out that each time a recipe is increased or decreased with respect to the number of its servings, *proportional* amounts of ingredients are used.

2 Teaching the Lesson

You might choose to share the following background material with students. A proportion is a statement of the form $\frac{a}{b} = \frac{c}{d}$ in which a, b, c, and d are *terms* of the proportion. In the proportion $\frac{a}{b} = \frac{c}{d}$, b and c represent the *means* of the proportion, and a and d represent the *extremes* of the proportion. In a true proportion, the product of the extremes is equal to the product of the means: $a \cdot d = b \cdot c$.

As students solve for the variable in Examples 2 and 3, remind them that the equation that results from setting cross products equal to each other is solved by performing an opposite operation. In these cases of cross products set equal to each other, the value of the variable is

170 *Chapter 7*

Lesson 2 Proportions

Proportion
An equation made up of two equal ratios

Cross product
The result of multiplying the denominator of one fraction with the numerator of another

For any ratio, you can write an infinite number of equivalent ratios. The following are examples of equivalent ratios for $\frac{1}{2}$.

$$\frac{2}{4} \quad \frac{3}{6} \quad \frac{4}{8} \quad \frac{5}{10} \quad \text{and so on}$$

Any ratio (such as $\frac{1}{2}$) and an equivalent ratio (such as $\frac{2}{4}$) can be combined to form a **proportion**. A proportion is a statement of the form $\frac{a}{b} = \frac{c}{d}$. Examples of proportions include

$$\frac{1}{2} = \frac{2}{4} \qquad \frac{5}{7} = \frac{15}{21} \qquad \frac{6}{10} = \frac{24}{40}$$

In any true proportion written in the form $\frac{a}{b} = \frac{c}{d}$, a, b, c, and d are terms of the proportion, and $ad = bc$.

EXAMPLE 1 Is $\frac{3}{4} = \frac{6}{8}$ a true proportion?

Decide if $ad = bc$.

$$\frac{a}{b} = \frac{c}{d} \quad \rightarrow \quad a \bullet d = b \bullet c$$
$$\downarrow \qquad \qquad \downarrow \quad \downarrow \quad \downarrow \quad \downarrow$$
$$\frac{3}{4} = \frac{6}{8} \quad \rightarrow \quad 3 \bullet 8 \ \blacksquare \ 4 \bullet 6$$
$$24 = 24$$

Because $ad = bc$, $\frac{3}{4} = \frac{6}{8}$ is a true proportion.

The terms ad and bc are sometimes called the **cross products** of a proportion. You can use cross products to find the missing value in a proportion.

EXAMPLE 2 Solve $\frac{24}{15} = \frac{8}{n}$ for n.

Step 1 Set the cross products of the proportion equal to each other.
$$(24)(n) = (15)(8)$$

Step 2 Multiply.
$$24n = 120$$

Step 3 Divide each side of the equation by 24.
$$\frac{24n}{24} = \frac{120}{24}$$

Step 4 Simplify.
$$n = 5$$

170 *Chapter 7 Ratios, Proportions, and Percents*

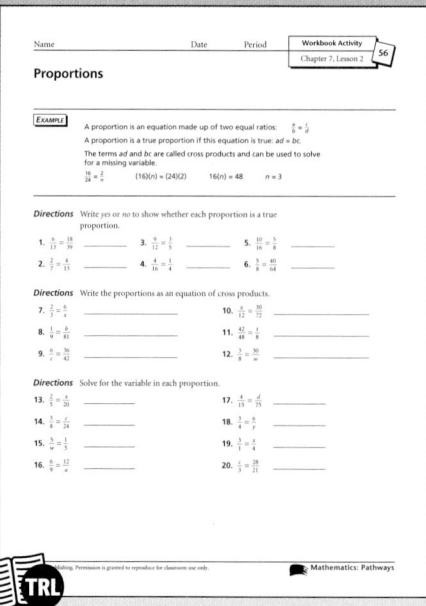

Workbook Activity 56

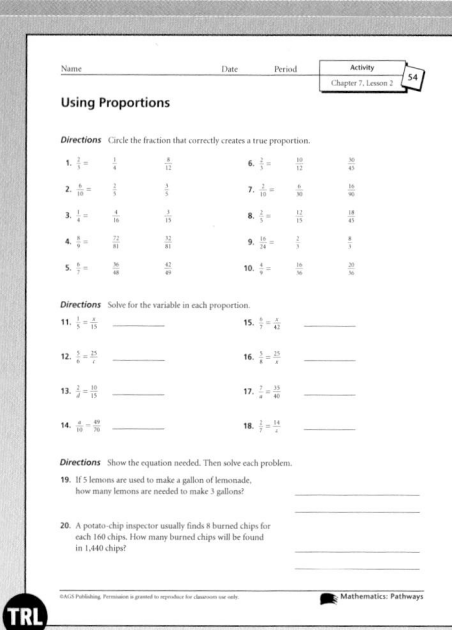

Activity 54

The variable can appear anywhere in a proportion.

EXAMPLE 3 Solve $\frac{2}{x} = \frac{6}{30}$ for x.

Step 1 Set the cross products of the proportion equal to each other.
$$(2)(30) = (x)(6)$$

Step 2 Multiply.
$$60 = 6x$$

Step 3 Divide each side of the equation by 6.
$$\frac{60}{6} = \frac{6x}{6}$$

Step 4 Simplify.
$$x = 10$$

Each time you solve for the variable in a proportion, check your work by finding the cross products of the proportion. If the cross products are equal to each other, your answer is correct.

Exercise A Is each proportion a true proportion? Write *yes* or *no*.

1. $\frac{3}{10} = \frac{10}{30}$ No   **3.** $\frac{1}{4} = \frac{6}{27}$ No   **5.** $\frac{4}{5} = \frac{16}{20}$ Yes

2. $\frac{16}{24} = \frac{2}{3}$ Yes   **4.** $\frac{9}{12} = \frac{12}{15}$ No   **6.** $\frac{10}{28} = \frac{2}{7}$ No

Exercise B Solve for the variable in each proportion.

7. $\frac{2}{n} = \frac{8}{12}$ 3   **10.** $\frac{m}{10} = \frac{2}{5}$ 4   **13.** $\frac{g}{16} = \frac{3}{4}$ 12

8. $\frac{3}{7} = \frac{c}{28}$ 12   **11.** $\frac{8}{56} = \frac{1}{b}$ 7   **14.** $\frac{1}{7} = \frac{9}{r}$ 63

9. $\frac{4}{h} = \frac{1}{4}$ 16   **12.** $\frac{3}{d} = \frac{18}{24}$ 4   **15.** $\frac{5}{h} = \frac{25}{30}$ 6

Technology Connection

Making Microchips Takes a Toll

Microchips are small, but they require a huge amount of fossil fuels to make. Compare making one chip to making one car. A single microchip takes about 3.5 pounds of fossil fuel. Making a car requires more than 3,300 pounds of fossil fuel. If you look at the ratio of fossil fuel to weight, the ratio to make a car is about 2 to 1. For a microchip, it is about 630 to 1. Proportionally, it takes a lot more energy to make a microchip.

determined by division, the opposite operation of multiplication.

 3 **Reinforce and Extend**

LEARNING STYLES

Visual/Spatial

Invite students to observe all of the students presently in their classroom and use a ratio to compare the number of males in the classroom with the number of females. Then ask students to determine the number of males and the number of females they would expect to find in the classroom if the number of students was

- halved.
- doubled.
- tripled.

LEARNING STYLES

LEP/ESL

Ask students to name and write on the board native language words or phrases that mean the same as, or nearly the same as, the terms *ratio* and *proportion*. Invite them also to describe one or more aspects of their native culture using a ratio.

MENTAL MATH

 Have students mentally compute and compare the cross products of these proportions and then decide whether the proportion is a true proportion.

$\frac{1}{2} = \frac{5}{10}$ *(yes)*

$\frac{1}{3} = \frac{9}{6}$ *(no)*

$\frac{1}{4} = \frac{5}{20}$ *(yes)*

$\frac{3}{10} = \frac{1}{5}$ *(no)*

$\frac{2}{24} = \frac{1}{8}$ *(no)*

$\frac{3}{18} = \frac{1}{6}$ *(yes)*

Chapter 7 Lesson 3

Overview This lesson introduces proportions that are used to solve for an unknown.

Objective

- To solve for an unknown using a proportion

Student Pages 172–173

Teacher's Resource Library (TRL)

Workbook Activity 57

Activity 55

Alternative Activity 55

Mathematics Vocabulary

equivalent

---

1 Warm-Up Activity

Invite students to consider the following scenario and mentally compute its solution.

Suppose that an adult is walking at an average speed of 4 miles per hour. At that speed, what distance would the adult be expected to walk in 1 hour *(4 miles)*, 2 hours *(8 miles)*, or $\frac{1}{2}$ hour *(2 miles)*?

Invite volunteers to use the board to model how each answer was obtained. Then point out how the models shown on the board are, to varying degrees, proportions.

2 Teaching the Lesson

After discussing the lesson development and the two examples on page 172, help students identify general strategies that can be used to understand and solve word problems, such as those they must solve on page 173. Invite students to use the board and list problem-solving strategies they find to be effective. Then as students solve the word problems on page 173, encourage them to refer to the hints and strategies shown on the board as often as necessary.

Equivalent
The same in value

A proportion is made up of two equal ratios. In some problems, one ratio and part of an **equivalent** ratio are given. One way to solve these problems is to make a table.

EXAMPLE 1 The ratio of computers to students in a classroom is 1 to 3. If there are 15 students in the class, how many computers are in the classroom?

Step 1 Make a table that displays the data in the problem. In the table, write the proportion that is given.

Number of computers	1	
Number of students	3	

Step 2 Complete the table using the remaining data in the problem.

Number of computers	1	n
Number of students	3	15

Step 3 Solve the proportion shown in the table.

$$\frac{1}{3} = \frac{n}{15}$$

$(1)(15) = (3)(n)$ Set the cross products equal to each other.

$15 = 3n$ Divide each side of the equation by 3.

$5 = n$

There are 5 computers in the classroom.

You can also solve proportion problems by just writing and solving a proportion.

EXAMPLE 2 In one hour, a bicyclist pedaled 16 miles. At that rate, how far can the bicyclist pedal in 4 hours?

Step 1 Write a proportion.

$$\frac{1 \text{ hour}}{16 \text{ miles}} = \frac{4 \text{ hours}}{x \text{ miles}}$$

Step 2 Set the cross products equal to each other.

$(1)(x) = (16)(4)$

$1x = 64$

$x = 64$

The bicyclist can pedal 64 miles in 4 hours.

Name _____ Date _____ Period _____ **Workbook Activity**

Chapter 7, Lesson 3 57

Ratios and Proportions

EXAMPLE A table can be helpful in solving proportion problems.

A record store sold 1 tape for every 5 CDs. If 60 CDs were sold, how many tapes were sold?

Number of Tapes	1	x
Number of CDs	5	60

Write an equation and solve it.

$\frac{1}{5} = \frac{x}{60}$ $(1)(60) = (5)(x)$ $60 = 5x$ $x = 12$

Directions Fill in each chart. Solve the problem.

1. Three cans of peas cost $1.80. How much do 9 cans cost?

Number of Cans		
Cost		

2. A soccer player averaged 1 goal for every 18 tries. If the player made 6 goals, how many tries were made?

Goals		
Tries		

3. A bag of pecans has 2 broken pecans for each 84 nuts. How many broken pecans were found in a sack of 504 nuts?

Number of Broken Pecans		
Total Nuts		

4. In a class, two out of every nine students were left-handed. How many left-handers would be found in a group of 63 students?

Left-handers		
Total Students		

5. If 20 pounds of bird seed cost $4.40, how much would 3 pounds cost?

Number of Pounds		
Cost		

TRL ...shing, Permission is granted to reproduce for classroom use only.   Mathematics: Pathways

Workbook Activity 57

Name _____ Date _____ Period _____ **Activity**

Chapter 7, Lesson 3 55

Ratios, Proportions

Directions Solve each proportion problem.

1. To announce a school's fun fair, the fair committee makes posters. Three sheets of poster board cost $1.50. How much will 27 sheets cost?

2. One can of orange juice concentrate makes 2 gallons of juice. How many cans of concentrate are needed to make 140 gallons of juice?

3. On the ring toss game, players score two ringers for every 18 tries. How many ringers are scored in 360 tries?

4. It takes 64 feet of crepe paper streamers to decorate 8 feet of booths. How many feet of streamers will be needed to decorate 246 feet of booths?

5. When the fair opens, 8 people enter the grounds every two minutes. How many people enter in an hour?

6. In a box of 144 plastic toy prizes, 2 are broken. How many broken toys will be found among 864 toys?

7. In a crowd of 177 children, 2 out of every 3 children are girls. How many girls are in the crowd?

8. For every 30¢ entrance fee, 40¢ is profit. How much money has to be taken in to earn $200?

9. Ice costs $163.50 for 150 pounds. How much does 100 pounds of ice cost?

10. For every 8 hot dogs sold, 3 are ordered with mustard. How many hot dogs with mustard are ordered if 272 hot dogs are sold?

TRL   ©AGS Publishing. Permission is granted to reproduce for classroom use only.   Mathematics: Pathways

Activity 55

Each time you solve a proportion, remember to check your work by making sure the cross products in your completed proportion are equal to each other.

PROBLEM SOLVING

Exercise A Solve each problem.

1. A baseball player averages 1 hit in every 3 at bats. If the player bats 480 times during a season, how many hits can the player be expected to get? 160 hits

2. On a basketball team, the ratio of players less than 6 feet tall to players 6 feet or taller is 2 to 5. If 10 players on the team are 6 feet or taller, how many players are less than 6 feet tall? 4 players

3. Last year during league bowling, Jeremy averaged 1 strike for every 5 frames he bowled. If he bowled 84 strikes last season, how many frames did he bowl? 420 frames

4. In a 72-hole golf tournament, Pat scored under par every 2 out of 9 holes. For the tournament, how many times did Pat score under par? 16 times

5. In a gymnastics meet, a gymnast earned a perfect score of 10 from 1 out of every 4 judges. If there were 8 judges altogether at the meet, how many perfect scores did the gymnast earn? 2 perfect scores

8. More than 9 minutes. $\frac{50 \text{ m}}{34 \text{ sec}} = \frac{800 \text{ m}}{n \text{ sec}}$. 544 seconds, or 9 minutes 4 seconds to complete the race.

9. 105 children

6. In a track-and-field meet, a runner ran the first 200 meters of an 800-meter race in 24 seconds. If the runner runs the remainder of the race at that speed, how many minutes and seconds will it take the runner to complete the race? 1 min 36 sec

7. On a football team, 7 out of every 9 players weigh 190 pounds or more. If 42 players weigh more than 190 pounds, how many players are on the team? 54 players

8. At a swim meet, a swimmer completes the first 50 meters of the 800-meter freestyle race in 34 seconds. If the swimmer does not swim faster or slower for the remainder of the race, will the swimmer complete the race in more than or less than 9 minutes? Explain.

9. Twelve hundred fans are attending a tennis match. If the ratio of adult fans to children is 73 to 7, how many children are attending the match?

10. The ratio of goals scored by a soccer team to the goals scored by opponents is 3:2. If 55 goals were scored altogether last season by the team and its opponents, how many goals were scored by the opponents? 22 goals

Ratios, Proportions, and Percents Chapter 7 **173**

MANIPULATIVES

M Ratios and Proportions

Materials: Cuisenaire Rods

Group Practice: Introduce Example 1 on page 172. Place a 3-rod under a cube (1-rod) to model the ratio 1:3. Place five 3-rods (15) across from the model of 3. Have students tell how many times 3 is multiplied to make 15. (5) Multiply the cube 5 times to maintain the ratio, and find the missing term in the proportion. Write the symbolic equivalent of the ratio. Repeat for the next example and other problems generated by students.

Student Practice: Have students use the rods to check their answers for Exercise A, problems 2, 4–5, and 7.

3 Reinforce and Extend

AT HOME

Invite volunteers to bring a recipe from home that includes the number of servings. Ask students to exchange recipes and use proportions to determine how much of each ingredient would be required to double the recipe, halve the recipe, and so on.

GROUP PROBLEM SOLVING

Have students work in small groups to consider the following problem:

Measure the length of your shoe and your height. Create a ratio from the data you collect. The numerator of your ratio should be the length of your shoe to the nearest inch. The denominator should be your height to the nearest inch. Compare your ratio with the ratios of your group members and with the ratios of the rest of your classmates. Using all the data, can you create one ratio that can be used to predict the height of a person if the shoe length of that person is known?

Lesson at a Glance

Chapter 7 Lesson 4

Overview This lesson introduces the use of proportions to find measures of length, weight, capacity, and volume.

Objective

■ To solve word problems using proportions

Student Pages 174–175

Teacher's Resource Library **TRL**

Workbook Activity 58

Activity 56

Alternative Activity 56

1 Warm-Up Activity

Begin by showing the class two different-sized containers. These containers should look relatively the same but should differ in that one is a larger version of the other. Have the class guess how much bigger the one container is than the other. Ask students how many times bigger the container is (ex. 2:1, 4:1). Pass the containers around the room, and let students examine them. Tell students that they can take measurements if they like. After guesses have been made, tell students the correct answer. Have the students who guessed the right answer state their methods.

Explain the word *proportion* and how it relates to the two objects. Tell students that if the larger container is three times the size of the smaller container, they can use the length of one side of one container to find the length of the corresponding side of the other container. Relate this to the weight, capacity, and volume of each container.

2 Teaching the Lesson

Use Example 1 in the lesson to show the class how to set up the proportion/ratio problem. Begin by reading the entire problem aloud. Ask the class what the unknown in this problem is, or what they are trying to find. Tell the class that the unknown variable can be called *x* until it is found. Ask the class whether any proportions/ratios can be set up to help

---

You can use proportions to solve many problems involving length, weight, capacity, and volume. Here are some examples:

> Capacity is the amount that a container can hold and volume is the number of cubic units in a figure.

EXAMPLE 1 The tank of a walk-behind lawn mower has a capacity of 2 liters, and the tank of a riding mower can hold 10 times as much. Set up a proportion and solve it.

Step 1: Set up a proportion.

$$\frac{\text{capacity of small tank}}{\text{capacity of large tank}} = \frac{1}{10}$$

Step 2: Let x = capacity of large tank.

$$\frac{2\text{ L}}{x} = \frac{1}{10} \qquad x = (10)(2\text{ L})$$
$$x = 20\text{ L}$$

The capacity of the large tank is 20 liters.

EXAMPLE 2 Double the height of a triangle, but keep the base the same. How does the area of the larger triangle compare with the area of the smaller?

Step 1: Set up a proportion: $A = \frac{1}{2}(\text{base})(\text{height}) = \frac{1}{2}bh$

Let h = height of smaller triangle; then $2h$ = height of larger triangle.

Step 2: $\dfrac{\text{area of smaller }\Delta}{\text{area of larger }\Delta} = \dfrac{\frac{1}{2}bh}{\frac{1}{2}b(2h)}$

Because $\dfrac{\frac{1}{2}}{\frac{1}{2}} = 1$, $\dfrac{\text{area of smaller }\Delta}{\text{area of larger }\Delta} = \dfrac{bh}{2bh} = \dfrac{1}{2}$

Therefore, the area of the larger triangle is double the area of the smaller triangle.

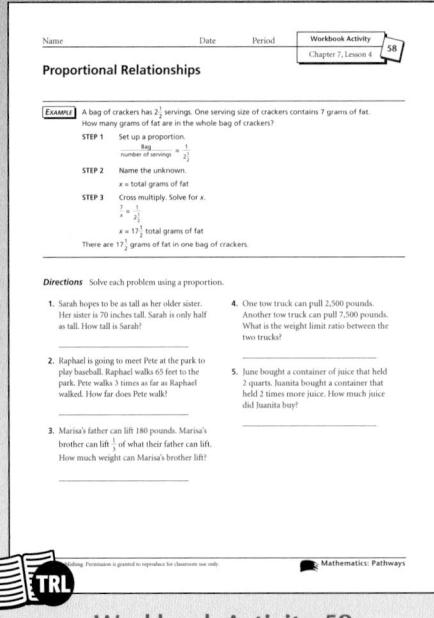

Workbook Activity 58

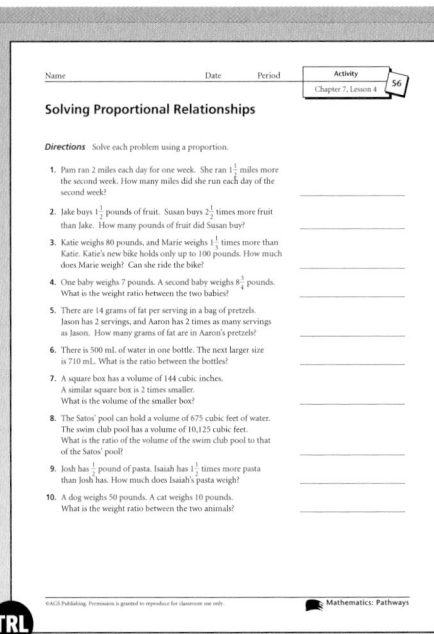

Activity 56

EXAMPLE 3 The weight limit on two types of trucks is in the ratio of 1:5. If the larger truck can carry 12 tons, what is the weight limit of the smaller?

Step 1: Set up a proportion.

Let x = weight limit of smaller truck.

Step 2: $\dfrac{\text{smaller truck}}{\text{larger truck}} = \dfrac{1}{5}$ $\qquad \dfrac{x}{12 \text{ tons}} = \dfrac{1}{5}$ $\qquad 5x = 12 \text{ tons}$

$x = \dfrac{12}{5}$ tons or $2\frac{2}{5}$ tons

So the smaller truck can carry up to $2\frac{2}{5}$ tons.

EXAMPLE 4 The volume of a cube = length • width • height, or side^3.
The side of a cube is 3 meters. If you double the side, by what factor is the volume increased?

Step 1: Set up a proportion to compare volumes.
Double 3m = 6m.

Step 2: $\dfrac{\text{volume of smaller cube}}{\text{volume of larger cube}} = \dfrac{(3m)^3}{(6m)^3} = \dfrac{27m^3}{216m^3}$

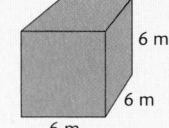

So the volume of the smaller cube is to the larger cube as 27 is to 216. The volume of the smaller cube is increased by a factor of 8:

$\dfrac{27}{216} = \dfrac{1}{8}$ $\qquad$ or $\qquad$ $\dfrac{216}{27} = 8$

PROBLEM SOLVING

Exercise A Set up a proportion, and then solve the problem.

1. The capacity of two tanks is in the ratio of 1:15. If the larger tank contains 75 liters, how many liters does the smaller tank hold?
   5 liters

2. If the height of a triangle is increased from 12 cm to 60 cm while the base remains the same, what is the ratio of the larger area to the smaller?
   The ratio is 5:1.

3. If you triple the edge of a cube from 2 m to 6 m, by what factor do you increase the volume of the smaller cube to obtain the larger?
   A factor of 27

4. Daphne drives 10 miles to the library. When Earl goes to the library, he drives 3 times as many miles as Daphne. How far does Earl drive?
   30 miles

5. A box of newspapers weighs 15 pounds. A box of magazines weighs 60 pounds. What is the weight ratio between the box of newspapers and the box of magazines? 1:4

Ratios, Proportions, and Percents Chapter 7 **175**

solve for x. Set up the proportion so that one side equals the other, and cross multiply to find x.

As students solve for x, remind them that they followed a process to get to this point. The process is to understand what they are solving for, set up a proportion, and then solve for x.

COMMON ERROR

A proportion/ratio can be set up two different ways. If the problem is "x is 3 times more than y," students could write this problem two ways. The correct way to read the ratio is 3:1 ($x{:}y$) or $\frac{3}{1}$ $(\frac{x}{y})$. However, the ratio could also be written 1:3 ($y{:}x$) or $\frac{1}{3}$ $(\frac{y}{x})$. It is important to stress to students that either way is correct, but they need to stick with one order throughout the problem. If mistakes occur, then the problem cannot be solved correctly.

3 ⌇ Reinforce and Extend

GROUP PROBLEM SOLVING

Pair students, and ask the pairs to solve problem 1 in class. Allow 5 to 10 minutes before asking for their answers and how they approached the problem. If students did not get the correct answer, ask them how they approached the problem. In a positive manner, describe what the students did incorrectly.

KNOWING YOUR STUDENTS

In the secondary school years, students are keen on avoiding social embarrassment and are determined to look good in the eyes of their peers. For this reason, they want to appear to be keeping up with the rest of the class. Moreover, students may get frustrated if they are not grasping the material as fast as other students are. Although their problem-solving strategies may be equal, some students may benefit by having more examples shown to them and working with other students on in-class projects.

Lesson at a Glance

Chapter 7 Lesson 5

Overview This lesson introduces formulas for distance, rate, and time.

Objective
- To apply formulas to determine distance, rate, or time

Student Pages 176–177

Teacher's Resource Library **TRL**

   Workbook Activity 59

   Activity 57

   Alternative Activity 57

---

1   Warm-Up Activity

Have students name various modes of transportation (walking, driving, flying, and so on), name the city or community in which they live, and name another city in their state. For each mode of transportation, ask students to estimate the time it would take to travel from one city to the other.

2   Teaching the Lesson

Write the formulas $d = rt$, $r = \frac{d}{t}$, and $t = \frac{d}{r}$ on the board. Point out that multiplication is used to solve for d and division is used to solve for r or t.

3   Reinforce and Extend

GROUP PROBLEM SOLVING

 Suggest that students work in small groups. Ask each group member to estimate how long it takes to travel to school in the morning and the distance that is traveled to get to school. Ask the group to then work cooperatively and determine the average speed in miles per hour for each student's morning commute.

Lesson 5   Solving Distance, Rate, and Time Problems

The total distance traveled is equal to the average rate of speed multiplied by the total time.

Formulas for Distance, Rate, and Time	
Total distance = Average rate of speed • Total time	$d = rt$
Average rate of speed = $\frac{\text{total distance}}{\text{total time}}$	$r = \frac{d}{t}$
Total time = $\frac{\text{total distance}}{\text{average rate of speed}}$	$t = \frac{d}{r}$

Average rate of speed can be expressed as miles per (one) hour or kilometers per (one) hour.

EXAMPLE 1 Suppose you drive for $3\frac{1}{2}$ hours at 50 miles per hour (mph). How many miles have you driven?

50 mph means 50 miles in one hour.

50 miles	50 miles	50 miles	25 miles	= 175 miles
1 hour	2 hours	3 hours	$3\frac{1}{2}$ hours	

This diagram shows that you drove 50 miles in 1 hour, 100 miles in 2 hours, 150 miles in 3 hours, and 175 miles in $3\frac{1}{2}$ hours.

Or, you can use the formula $d = rt$ to find out how many miles, or the distance, you drove.

$d = rt$

$d = (50)(3\frac{1}{2}) = 175$ miles

EXAMPLE 2 Suppose you travel 378 miles in 7 hours.

What is your average rate of speed?
(Hint: How many miles did you travel in one hour?)

1 hour	2 hours	3 hours	4 hours	5 hours	6 hours	7 hours	378 miles

Divide the total number of miles driven (378 miles) by the number of hours (7 hours) to find average speed.

$\frac{378}{7} = 54$ miles per (one) hour.

The formula $r = \frac{d}{t}$ uses the same steps to find average rate of speed.

$r = \frac{d}{t}$ $r = \frac{378}{7} = 54$ miles per hour

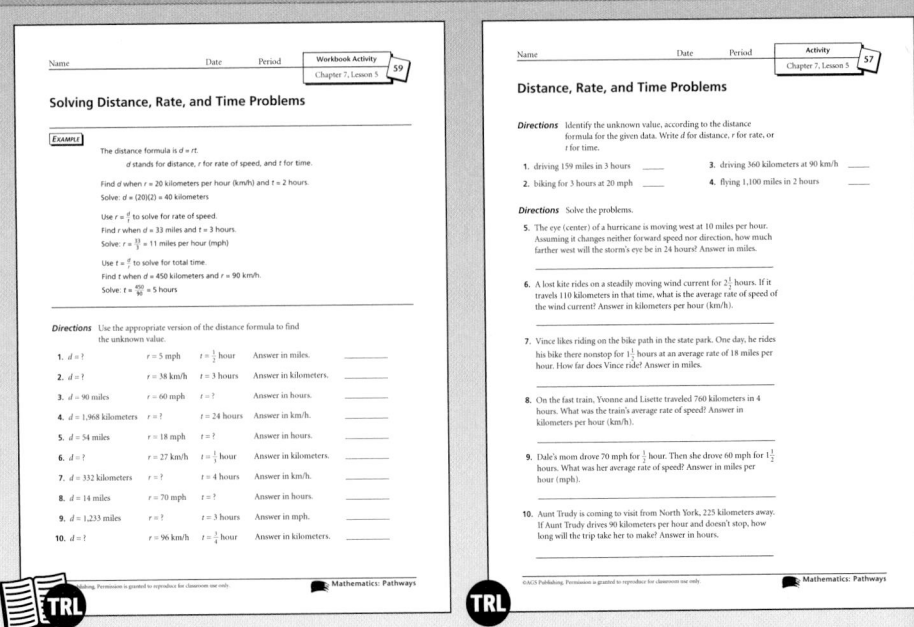

Workbook Activity 59   **Activity 57**

EXAMPLE 3 Suppose you drive 80 kilometers per hour for $1\frac{1}{2}$ hours and 90 kilometers per hour for $\frac{1}{2}$ hour. What is your average rate of speed?

80 km/h means 80 kilometers in one hour, or 120 kilometers in $1\frac{1}{2}$ hours.

90 km/h means 90 kilometers in one hour, or 45 kilometers in $\frac{1}{2}$ hour.

$\quad$ 120 kilometers in $1\frac{1}{2}$ hours
$\underline{+\ \ 45}$ kilometers in $\frac{1}{2}$ hour
$\quad$ 165 kilometers in 2 hours, or $165 \div 2 = 82.5$ kilometers in 1 hour

Use the formula Average rate $= \frac{\text{Total distance}}{\text{Total time}}$ and solve for r.

$$r = \frac{d}{t} = \frac{(80)(1\frac{1}{2})\ +\ 90(\frac{1}{2})}{1\frac{1}{2}\ +\ \frac{1}{2}}$$

$$= \frac{120 + 45}{2} \quad = \frac{165}{2} \quad = 82.5 \text{ km/h}$$

PROBLEM SOLVING

Exercise A Solve each problem.

1. Fernando drives 165 miles at a constant speed of 55 miles per hour. How many hours does he drive? 3 hours

2. Maria and Julia live 690 miles apart. They decide to meet. Maria drives toward Julia at 60 miles per hour and Julia drives toward Maria at 55 miles per hour. How long will it take for them to meet? 6 hours

3. Jessica rides her bicycle for $2\frac{3}{4}$ hours at an average rate of speed of $14\frac{1}{2}$ kilometers per hour. How many kilometers does she ride? $39\frac{7}{8}$ km

4. On Saturday, Erica and Bianca travel 324 kilometers. They reach their destination in 4 hours. What is their average speed? 81 km per hour

5. Jake and Lisa walk at a rate of 9 kilometers per hour for $1\frac{1}{4}$ hours and 6 kilometers per hour for 15 minutes. What is their average speed? $8\frac{1}{2}$ km per hour

Lesson at a Glance

Chapter 7 Lesson 6

Overview This lesson introduces percents.

Objective

- To explore the relationship shared by fractions and percents

Student Pages 178–181

Teacher's Resource Library

Workbook Activity 60

Activity 58

Alternative Activity 58

1 Warm-Up Activity

Ask the class to suppose that a student received a quiz score of 90%. Ask volunteers to describe what the expression 90% means. *(Sample answer: 90% refers to the rate at which questions on the quiz were answered correctly.)* Help students understand that a quiz score of 90% does not refer directly to the number of questions on the quiz; a score of 90% can be earned on quizzes containing various numbers of questions. Point out instead that 90% is a *ratio* of questions answered correctly to questions asked.

2 Teaching the Lesson

As students read the introductory paragraphs on page 178, help them understand that a percent is a reference to a whole. When working with percents, the whole is 100. If the percent includes a grid, the length of the grid is 10 unit squares, and the width of the grid is also 10 unit squares. To determine the area of the entire percent grid, use the formula that determines the area of a square: $A = s^2$ where $s = 10$.

As students work through Example 1 on page 178, have them note that they are finding a ratio by pointing out the word *ratio* in the first sentence of the example. Help them recall that a ratio is a comparison of two quantities using a fraction. In this example, the numerator of the ratio is the number of shaded unit squares *(29)*, and the denominator of the ratio is the number of unit squares in the whole *(100)*.

178 *Chapter 7*

Lesson 6 **Percents and Fractions**

A great deal of data is given as percents. For example, a weather forecaster might say that the chance of rain is 40%, and the state might charge a sales tax of 7%.

The word *percent* comes from the Latin phrase *per centum*, which means "per hundred." In general, a percent is the numerator of a fraction whose denominator is 100.

> Remember, percent means part per one hundred.

A hundreds grid is a grid that measures 10 units by 10 units and contains 100 unit squares.

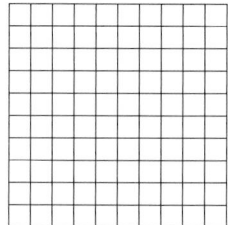

A hundreds grid can be used to show percents.

EXAMPLE 1 What is the ratio of the number of shaded squares to the total number of squares in this figure?

Step 1 Determine the number of shaded squares.
The figure contains 29 shaded squares.

Step 2 Determine the total number of squares.
The figure contains 100 squares altogether.

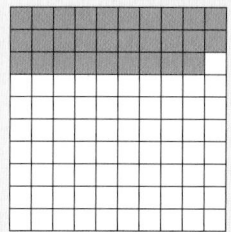

Step 3 Write the ratio. The ratio of the number of shaded squares to the total number of squares in the figure is 29 to 100.

178 *Chapter 7 Ratios, Proportions, and Percents*

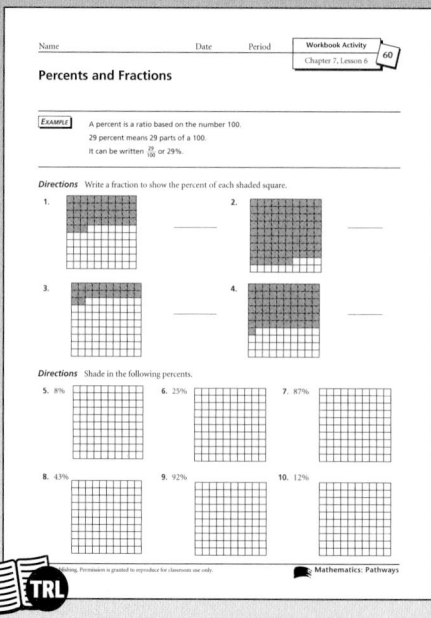

Workbook Activity 60

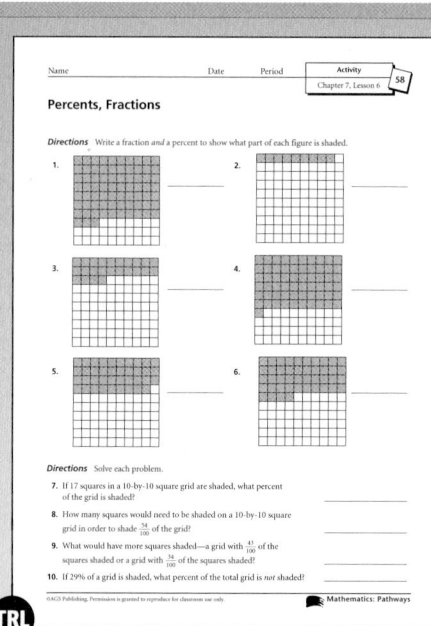

Activity 58

Recall that any ratio written in the form a to b can also be written in the form $\frac{a}{b}$.

EXAMPLE 2 What fraction of this figure is shaded?

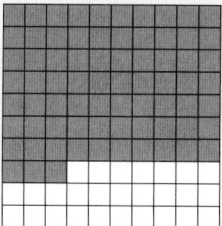

Step 1 Determine the number of shaded squares. The figure contains 73 shaded squares.

Step 2 Determine the total number of squares. The figure contains 100 squares altogether.

Step 3 Write the fraction: $\frac{73}{100}$ of the figure is shaded.

To write a fraction whose denominator is 100 as a percent, write the numerator and use the % symbol.

EXAMPLE 3 What percent of this figure is shaded?

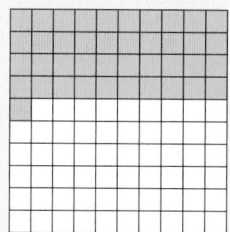

Since 41 out of 100 or $\frac{41}{100}$ of the figure is shaded, 41% of the figure is shaded.

After students complete Example 2 on page 179, ask them to write, as a percent, the fraction of the whole that is shaded. *(73%)*

After students complete Example 3 on page 179, ask them to find the percent of the figure that is *not* shaded. *(59%)* Then invite volunteers to tell how the quantities 41% and 59% are related to the whole. *[The sum of the percent of the figure that is shaded (41%) and the percent of the figure that is not shaded (59%) is 100%; 100% represents the whole in any percent problem.]*

Ask students to pause for a moment after they complete problem 1 on page 180. Use the pause to explain that their answer for problem 1 can be checked using subtraction. Point out that the correct answer is $\frac{53}{100}$. To check the answer, subtract $\frac{53}{100}$ (the shaded region) from $\frac{100}{100}$ (the whole). $\frac{100}{100} - \frac{53}{100} = \frac{47}{100}$; there should be 47 unshaded squares in the region.

COMMON ERROR

Remind students that the denominator of a fraction must be 100 if the numerator of the fraction is used to represent a percent.

AT HOME

Each state of the United States has a Web site dedicated to disseminating information about that state. Invite students with home access to the World Wide Web to visit the Web site for their state and search it to find interesting data in the form of ratios, proportions, fractions, or percents. Invite volunteers to share their findings with their classmates.

State Web sites can be found at www.state.xx.us where xx represents the state abbreviation. For example, to visit the state of Texas Web site, go to www.state.tx.us.

LEARNING STYLES

Body/Kinesthetic

Invite students to cut a 10 by 10 grid from a piece of graph paper and then fold the grid in half. Ask, "The size of the grid has been reduced by what percent?" *(50%)* Have students fold the grid in half again. Ask, "The size of the 50% grid has been reduced by what amount?" *(50%)* "The grid is now what percent of the original grid?" *(25%)*

Exercise A Write a fraction to describe the percent of each figure that is shaded.

1.
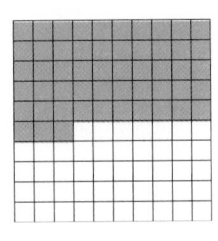
$\frac{53}{100}$

2.
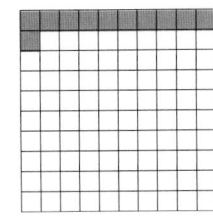
$\frac{11}{100}$

3.
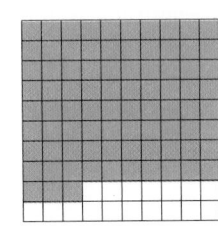
$\frac{83}{100}$

Build a Model

Make a golden section spiral. On a sheet of graph paper, start with one square. Add squares until you have 7 in all, like the diagram. Color the squares. Then use your compass to draw a quarter-circle in each square. Connect the quarter-circles from square to square until you have the spiral as shown.

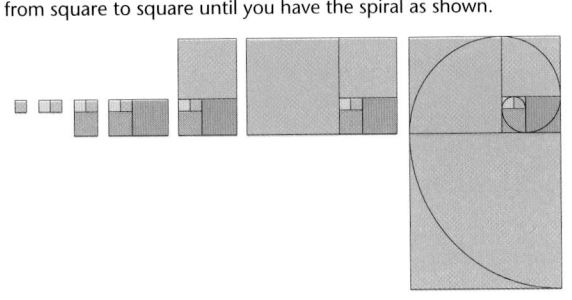

Exercise B What percent of each figure is shaded?

4.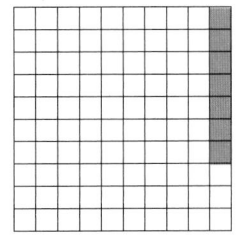

7%

5.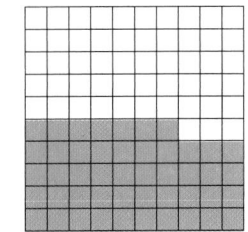

47%

6.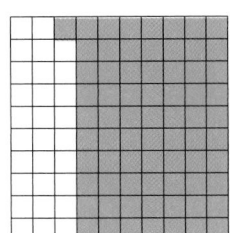

71%

7.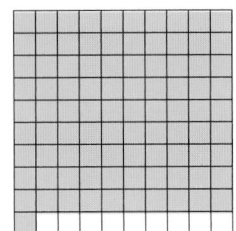

91%

Exercise C Write each fraction as a percent.

8. $\frac{22}{100}$ 22%

9. $\frac{95}{100}$ 95%

10. $\frac{40}{100}$ 40%

11. $\frac{53}{100}$ 53%

12. $\frac{82}{100}$ 82%

13. $\frac{33}{100}$ 33%

14. $\frac{67}{100}$ 67%

15. $\frac{9}{100}$ 9%

Try This

In a figure measuring 100 by 100 units, 4,000 units are shaded. In simplest form, what fraction of the figure is shaded? What fraction of the figure is not shaded? What is the sum of the shaded and not shaded regions?

$\frac{4,000}{10,000} = \frac{4}{10} = \frac{2}{5}$ is shaded $\frac{6,000}{10,000} = \frac{3}{5}$ is not shaded

$\frac{2}{5} + \frac{3}{5} = 1$

Try This

Explain that any fraction used to represent the shaded region of a grid measuring 100 by 100 units must have a denominator of 100 • 100 or 10,000.

GROUP PROBLEM SOLVING

 Ask students to work in groups of three to discuss and solve the following problem:

Suppose that 100 identical wooden cubes are glued together to form a 10 by 10 square. You may use a Base 10 Flat manipulative to visualize this concept. After the glue dries, the square is picked up, and each face of the square is painted red. After the paint dries, the square is broken apart into 100 identical cubes.

What percent of the cubes have six faces painted? *(0%)*

What percent of the cubes have five faces painted? *(0%)*

What percent of the cubes have four faces painted? *(4%)*

What percent of the cubes have three faces painted? *(32%)*

What percent of the cubes have two faces painted? *(64%)*

What percent of the cubes have one face painted? *(0%)*

Invite groups to share any sketches or drawings that were used to help solve the problem.

Lesson at a Glance

Chapter 7 Lesson 7

Overview This lesson introduces percents and decimals.

Objective

■ To explore the relationship shared by percents and decimals

Student Pages 182–185

Teacher's Resource Library

    Workbook Activities 61–62

    Activity 59

    Alternative Activity 59

---

1 Warm-Up Activity

Invite students to consider and solve the following problem.

Suppose that one bowl of a breakfast cereal contained 0.25% of the minimum daily requirement of a vitamin. How many bowls of that cereal would you need to eat to get 100% of the minimum daily requirement of that vitamin? *(400 bowls)*

2 Teaching the Lesson

As students explore the examples shown on page 182, they are likely to find the "shortcut" shown in Example 2 an attractive way to change a decimal to a percent. Although it is an attractive and efficient way to change a decimal to a percent, make sure that students understand *why* the "shortcut" works. Emphasize that each time a decimal is changed to a percent, the decimal must be multiplied by 100. It is the configuration of our base 10 number system that enables students to simply move the decimal point two places to the right and create the same result as they would get by taking the time to multiply by 100.

After completing Example 3 on page 183, point out that it is also possible to encounter a percent that is greater than or equal to 100 and that it is possible to write such percents as decimals. Write the following percents on the board, and ask volunteers to change each percent to a decimal by moving the decimal point in each percent two places to the left.

Recall that percent is the numerator of a fraction whose denominator is 100. You can express any decimal as a percent by first writing the decimal as a fraction that has a denominator of 100.

EXAMPLE 1 Express 0.5 as a percent.

  Step 1 Write the decimal as a fraction that has 100 as its denominator.

$$0.5 = \frac{0.5}{1} \cdot \frac{100}{100} = \frac{(0.5)(100)}{1 \cdot 100}$$

  Step 2 Multiply.

$$\frac{0.5 \cdot 100}{100} = \frac{50}{100}$$

  Step 3 Write the fraction as a percent.

$$\frac{50}{100} = 50\%$$

    The decimal 0.5 is equivalent to 50%.

You can use a shortcut to change the decimal to a percent.

EXAMPLE 2 Write 0.12 as a percent.

  Step 1 Move the decimal two places to the right. This is the same as multiplying by 100.

$$0.12 \cdot 100 = 0.12 \quad \rightarrow \quad 12$$

  Step 2 Write the decimal as a percent by adding the percent symbol.

$$0.12 = 12\%$$

Multiplying by 100 and then adding the percent symbol is the same as multiplying by $\frac{100}{100}$.

Workbook Activity 61

Name   Date   Period   **Workbook Activity**
Chapter 7, Lesson 7   61

Percents and Decimals

EXAMPLE
Change a decimal to a percent.   0.35 to 35%   0.07 to 7%
Change a percent to a decimal.   46% to $\frac{46}{100}$ to 0.46
Change a fraction to a percent. $\frac{46}{100}$ to 46%
Change a fraction with a denominator that is not 100.
$\frac{3}{4}$ to 3 ÷ 4 to 0.75 to 75%

Directions Complete the chart by filling in the missing numbers.

	Decimal	Percent	Fraction
1.		63%	
2.			$\frac{2}{5}$
3.	0.10		
4.		25%	
5.			$\frac{51}{100}$
6.	0.41		
7.		55%	
8.	0.67		
9.			$\frac{9}{25}$
10.			$\frac{17}{20}$
11.	0.50		
12.		93%	
13.			$\frac{21}{50}$
14.			$\frac{7}{20}$
15.		88%	

Mathematics: Pathways

Workbook Activity 62

Name   Date   Period   **Workbook Activity**
Chapter 7, Lesson 7   62

More Percents and Decimals

Directions Change each fraction to a percent.

1. $\frac{1}{10}$ _____   6. $\frac{3}{5}$ _____
2. $\frac{4}{5}$ _____   7. $\frac{1}{4}$ _____
3. $\frac{1}{2}$ _____   8. $\frac{12}{25}$ _____
4. $\frac{7}{8}$ _____   9. _____
5. $\frac{1}{5}$ _____   10. $\frac{7}{10}$ _____

Directions Change each percent above to a decimal.

11. _____   16. _____
12. _____   17. _____
13. _____   18. _____
14. _____   19. _____
15. _____   20. _____

Directions Read each problem and write a percent *and* a decimal for the fraction used in the problem. Then solve the problem.

21. One-third of a school's students went to the football game. There are 270 students in the school. Then solve the problem.

22. Two-fifths of a school's 640 students eat a school lunch each day. How many students eat school lunches each day?

23. Of the 200 trees in the park by the lake. How many trees are by the lake?

24. Three-tenths of the birds in the zoo live in the rainforest. The zoo has 470 birds. How many of the zoo's birds live in the rainforest?

25. Nine hundred people visit the elephants every day. That is three-fourths of the visitors to the zoo. How many people visit the zoo each day?

Mathematics: Pathways

To express a percent as a decimal, write the percent as a fraction with a denominator of 100. Then write it as a decimal.

EXAMPLE 3 Write 46% as a decimal.

Step 1 Write the percent as a fraction. Since percent means "per one hundred," write $46\% = \frac{46}{100}$.

$$46\% = \frac{46}{100}$$

Step 2 Write the fraction as a decimal.

$$\frac{46}{100} = 0.46$$

Recall that to express a fraction whose denominator is 100 as a percent, you write the numerator of the fraction and use the % symbol. To express a fraction whose denominator is not 100 as a percent, first express the fraction as a decimal. Then express the decimal as a percent.

> Remember, moving the decimal point two places to the right is the same as multiplying by 100. Adding the percent symbol is the same as dividing by 100.

EXAMPLE 4 Express $\frac{3}{8}$ as a percent.

Step 1 First change the fraction to a decimal. Remember, a fraction bar means "divide."

$$\frac{3}{8} = 3 \div 8 = 0.375$$

Step 2 Write the decimal as a percent by moving the decimal point two places to the right. Then add the percent symbol.

$$0.375 = 37.5\%$$

Math in Your Life

Tip on Tips

Here is a quick way to calculate a 15% tip on any bill. Suppose that the total of your bill comes to $28.35. To work with an easier number, round up to $30. Think: 10% of $30 is $3. Add to it half of $3, or $1.50. So, the tip equals $4.50, which is about 15%.

100%	*(1.00 or 1)*
150%	*(1.50 or 1.5)*
225%	*(2.25)*
375%	*(3.75)*

Explain that using a grid to represent a percent can never result in a percent greater than 100 or a decimal greater than 1 because the maximum area in any grid that can be shaded is 100 of 100 squares or 100%.

After completing Example 4 on page 183, point out that the answer shown in Step 1—0.375—is a terminating decimal. Explain that although some decimals are terminating, others are not. Write the fraction $\frac{1}{3}$ on the board, and invite students to share ideas about how the fraction can be expressed as a decimal.

COMMON ERROR

Remind students that each time they express a percent as a decimal by moving the decimal point, they should not forget to erase the percent symbol or not show the percent symbol if the percent is rewritten as a decimal.

Name _____ Date _____ Period _____ | **Activity** Chapter 7, Lesson 7 | **59**

Percents, Decimals

Directions Draw a line to match each fraction with its equivalent percent.

1. $\frac{1}{2}$ 40%   6. $\frac{1}{5}$ 75%

2. $\frac{1}{4}$ 50%   7. $\frac{3}{8}$ 55%

3. $\frac{5}{8}$ 87.5%   8. $\frac{7}{4}$ 70%

4. $\frac{2}{8}$ 25%   9. $\frac{11}{20}$ 20%

5. $\frac{29}{50}$ 58%   10. $\frac{7}{10}$ 37.5%

Directions Express each decimal as a percent.

11. 0.46 _____   15. 0.17 _____

12. 0.91 _____   16. 0.05 _____

13. 0.83 _____   17. 0.357 _____

14. 0.03 _____   18. 0.413 _____

Directions Solve these problems.

19. A politician's approval rating increased by $\frac{2}{5}$. By what percent did the politician's rating increase?

20. Energy use in a home decreased by $\frac{1}{4}$. By what percent did energy use in the home decrease?

©AGS Publishing. Permission is granted to reproduce for classroom use only.   ■ Mathematics: Pathways

Activity 59

MANIPULATIVES

 Percents and Decimals

Materials: Cuisenaire Rods, Manipulatives Master 4 (100-Square Grid)

Group Practice: The 100-Square Grid represents one whole, and each square is $\frac{1}{100}$ of the whole. Explain to students that the cube (1-rod) represents 1 out of 100. Similarly, the 10-rod represents 10 out of 100. Write the fraction, decimal, and percent symbolic equivalents.

To express a decimal as a percent, model 0.5 by placing five 10-rods on the 100-Square Grid. Write the fraction and percent symbolic equivalents. Repeat for 0.12 using a 10-rod and two cubes. To write a percent as a decimal, place the appropriate number of 10-rods and cubes on the grid to represent the percent. Write the fraction and decimal symbolic equivalents. Use $\frac{1}{5}$, $\frac{3}{10}$, and $\frac{3}{20}$ to practice changing fractions to percents. For example, change $\frac{1}{5}$ to a percent by placing a cube on one of every five squares until each group of five squares on the grid has one cube. Group the cubes to model $\frac{20}{100}$, and discuss the decimal and percent symbolic equivalents.

Student Practice: Use the rods and grid for all problems in Exercises A, B, and C (except problems 12 and 16), and for problems 29–30, 32–33 in Exercise D.

Writing About Mathematics

Suppose you double in weight between your ninth and fifteenth birthdays. Express the change in percent. Do you need to know the actual weight? Why or why not?

Exercise A Express each decimal as a percent.

1. 0.75	75%		**6.** 0.24	24%
2. 0.80	80%		**7.** 0.88	88%
3. 0.18	18%		**8.** 0.04	4%
4. 0.42	42%		**9.** 0.1	10%
5. 0.78	78%			

Exercise B Express each fraction as a percent.

10. $\frac{1}{2}$	50%		**15.** $\frac{7}{10}$	70%
11. $\frac{1}{4}$	25%		**16.** $\frac{15}{16}$	93.75%
12. $\frac{7}{8}$	87.5%		**17.** $\frac{19}{25}$	76%
13. $\frac{2}{5}$	40%		**18.** $\frac{64}{100}$	64%
14. $\frac{3}{4}$	75%			

Exercise C Express each percent as a decimal.

19. 11%	0.11		**24.** 27%	0.27
20. 46%	0.46		**25.** 5%	0.05
21. 68%	0.68		**26.** 91%	0.91
22. 3%	0.03		**27.** 83%	0.83
23. 17%	0.17			

Exercise D Solve these problems.

28. Can a percent ever be greater than 100? Explain. Yes, if something increases.

29. Jessica purchased $2,000 worth of stocks. The stocks value increased by $\frac{1}{5}$ each month. What is the percent of increase per month? 20%

30. At the beginning of a day, a floppy computer disk contains 840 kilobytes of data. By the end of the day, the disk contains 630 kilobytes of data. The disk is $\frac{3}{4}$ full. What percent of the disk is full of data? 75%

31. Between 9 A.M. and 11 A.M., a cafe expects to serve 40 meals. The number of meals served increases 3 and a half times between 11 A.M. and 1 P.M. What percent does the number increase? 350%

32. Alex is scheduled to work 37.5 hours each week. Last week he was only able to work 33.75 hours. He worked 10% less. Write a fraction to show the decrease in number of hours. $\frac{1}{10}$

33. Two hundred people attended the first performance of a school play. The second performance was attended by 220 people. The attendance increased by $\frac{1}{10}$. What is the percent of increase? 10%

34. When asked to describe the soccer team's winning rate, Jan said 60%, Allison said 0.6, and Jesse said $\frac{3}{5}$. Is it possible that each person is describing the same winning rate? Tell why or why not.

35. Suppose Marc is receiving an allowance increase. If he could choose the amount of the increase, should he choose an increase of $\frac{1}{5}$ or an increase of 15%? Why?

34. Yes; 60%, 0.6, and $\frac{3}{5}$ are equivalent.

35. Sample answer: Marc should choose an increase of $\frac{1}{5}$ because $\frac{1}{5} = 0.2 = 20\%$.

Ratios, Proportions, and Percents Chapter 7 **185**

3 **Reinforce and Extend**

IN THE COMMUNITY

Reference books such as *The World Almanac and Book of Facts* or *Information Please Almanac* contain a wealth of data related to percents. Have students use reference materials such as these to discover interesting percent-related data about their community or their state. Then invite volunteers to share their findings with their classmates.

LEARNING STYLES

Visual/Spatial

Ask each student to outline a 10 by 10 grid on graph paper and shade a portion of the grid. Collect and display the grids, and invite students to work in small groups to develop an estimate (in the form of a percent) of the shaded area of each grid. After the estimates have been made, the exact number of shaded unit squares in each grid can be counted and compared with the estimates.

MENTAL MATH

Invite volunteers to name "common" fractions such as $\frac{1}{2}$ and $\frac{3}{4}$ and identify the decimal and percent equivalents of each fraction.

GROUP PROBLEM SOLVING

Have students work in groups of three to consider the following problem:

The numerators and denominators of fractions are usually whole numbers. But they can also be decimal numbers and/or percents. Find the whole number or decimal equivalent of each of these fractions.

$\frac{0.4}{2}$	(0.2)
$\frac{8}{0.1}$	(80)
$\frac{20\%}{5}$	(0.04)
$\frac{10}{50\%}$	(20)
$\frac{0.25}{200\%}$	(0.125)

Invite the groups to compare answers and share their problem-solving approaches with one another.

Lesson at a Glance

Chapter 7 Lesson 8

Overview This lesson introduces the use of proportions and equations to find the percent of a number.

Objective

■ To find a percent of a number

Student Pages 186–187

Teacher's Resource Library **TRL**

  Workbook Activity 63

  Activity 60

  Alternative Activity 60

---

1 ⟩ Warm-Up Activity

Write the following equations on the board, and invite volunteers to identify the solution to each equation without using pencil and paper.

$2x = 8$	$(x = 4)$
$7x = 21$	$(x = 3)$
$3x = 3$	$(x = 1)$
$5x = 45$	$(x = 9)$
$9x = 63$	$(x = 7)$
$4x = 20$	$(x = 5)$
$6x = 12$	$(x = 2)$
$8x = 48$	$(x = 6)$

Remind students that an opposite operation is used to find the value of a variable in an equation. In these equations, division is used to find the value of each variable.

2 ⟩ Teaching the Lesson

After students explore Example 1 on page 186, explain that each fraction of the proportion represents a ratio of a part to the whole. In the case of the first fraction of the proportion, the numerator (40) represents the percent of the whole that is being considered, and the denominator (100) represents the whole. (Have students recall that with respect to percents, the whole is always given to be 100.) In the case of the second fraction of the proportion, the numerator (x) represents the part of the whole that is being sought, and the denominator (72) represents the whole.

186   *Chapter 7*

As you work with percents, you sometimes will be asked to find the percent of a number. To find a percent of a number, you can use a proportion.

EXAMPLE 1   40% of 72 is what number?

  Step 1   Use a proportion. Express the percent as a ratio.

$$40\% = \frac{40}{100}$$

  Step 2   Let x represent the part of 72 you are trying to find.

$$\frac{40}{100} = \frac{x}{72}$$

  Step 3   Solve the proportion by setting the cross products equal to each other. Then solve for x.

$$\frac{40}{100} = \frac{x}{72} \quad \rightarrow \quad (40)(72) = (100)(x)$$
$$2,880 = 100x$$

  Divide both sides by 100. $28.80 = x$

  40% of 72 is 28.8.

Another way to find a portion of a number is using the 1% solution method.

EXAMPLE 2   25% of 200 is what number?

  Step 1   Write an equation for 100%.

$$100\% = 200$$

  Step 2   Divide both sides of the equation by 100 to find 1% of the number.

$$\frac{100\%}{100} = \frac{200}{100}$$
$$1\% = 2$$

  Step 3   Multiply both sides by 25 to find the number.

$$1\% \bullet 25 = 2 \bullet 25$$
$$25\% = 50$$

  25% of 200 is 50.

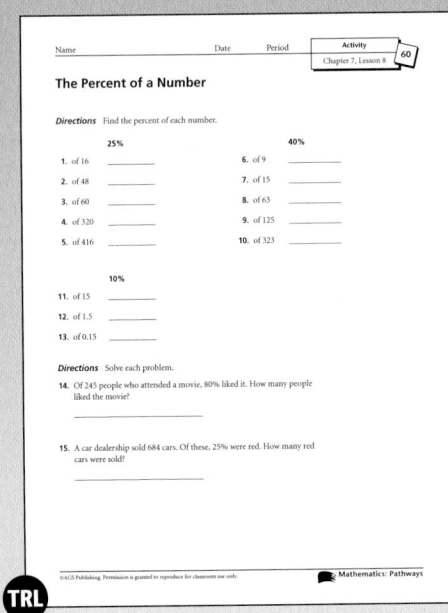

You can also write and solve an equation to find what number is a percent of another number.

EXAMPLE 3 80% of 48 is what number?

Step 1 Write an equation.

80% of 48 is what number?
↓ ↓ ↓ ↓
$(80\%)(48) = n$

Step 2 Change the percent to a decimal, then solve for n.

$(80\%)(48) = n$
↓
$(0.80)(48) = n$
$38.4 = n$

80% of 48 is 38.4.

Exercise A Solve to answer each question.

1. 12% of 12 is what number?   1.44
2. 30% of 18 is what number?   5.4
3. 150% of 320 is what number?   480
4. 60% of 125 is what number?   75
5. 39% of 2,400 is what number?   936

6. 125% of 10 is what number?   12.5
7. 67% of 200 is what number?   134
8. 42% of 442 is what number?   185.64
9. 75% of 874 is what number?   655.5
10. 200% of 0.5 is what number?   1

Estimation Activity

Estimate: A gas station owner earns 2% of the price for each gallon of gas sold. If the price of gasoline is $1.63 per gallon, how much does he make on a 10 gallon sale?

Solution: Find the approximate value of 1%, double, multiply by ten.

100% = $1.63
1% = $0.0163   is about 1.6 cents
2% = 3.2 cents is about 3 cents
(10)(3¢) = 30 cents

He earns a little more than 30 cents for 10 gallons.

Write the following proportion on the board to remind students of the need for consistency when a proportion is used to find a percent of a number.

$$\frac{\text{part}}{\text{whole}} = \frac{\text{part}}{\text{whole}}$$

Encourage students to remember the part/whole relationship of the ratios (fractions) in a proportion.

3 Reinforce and Extend

LEARNING STYLES

Interpersonal/ Group Learning

Suggest that students work in groups of three and use an equation *and* a proportion to solve the following problem:

What is the cost of a sweater if the price of the sweater is $36.00 and the sales tax added to the price of the sweater is 6%? *($38.16)*

Ask students to compare the answer that was generated using a proportion to the answer that was generated using an equation and explain any discrepancies that might be found.

MENTAL MATH

Invite students to mentally compute 50% of the following numbers:

100	50	8
600	80	2
300	30	6
420	94	5
710	58	3

Lesson at a Glance

Chapter 7 Lesson 9

Overview This lesson introduces the use of proportions and equations to find what percent one number is of another.

Objective

■ To find what percent one number is of another

Student Pages 188–189

Teacher's Resource Library

Workbook Activity 64

Activity 61

Alternative Activity 61

1 Warm-Up Activity

Using graph paper, invite students to work in small groups and perform these steps:

- Draw a rectangle that measures 2 unit squares by 4 unit squares.

- The 2 by 4 rectangle you drew represents 50% of a larger rectangle. Draw the larger rectangle.

- The larger rectangle you drew represents 50% of an even larger rectangle. Draw the even larger rectangle.

- How is the final rectangle you drew related to the 2 by 4 rectangle you began with? *(Sample answer: The area of the final rectangle is 4 times larger than the area of the 2 by 4 rectangle.)*

2 Teaching the Lesson

After discussing Step 1 of Example 1 on page 188, point out that although the fraction $\frac{35}{10}$ is an improper fraction, it is written in the form $\frac{\text{part}}{\text{whole}}$ because 10 represents the whole in the problem and 35 represents the part (in this case, a large part) of the whole that is being sought. Help students develop a sense that when the part being sought is greater than the whole, the percent will be greater than 100%. After discussing Step 2 of the example, point out that the fractions $\frac{35}{10}$ and $\frac{x}{100}$ are both written in the form $\frac{\text{part}}{\text{whole}}$.

Sometimes you will be asked to find what percent one number is of another. To find what percent one number is of another, you can use a proportion.

EXAMPLE 1 What percent of 10 is 35?

Step 1 Express the ratio of part to whole as a fraction.

$$\frac{\text{part}}{\text{whole}} = \frac{35}{10}$$

Step 2 Write the unknown percent as a ratio.

$$\frac{35}{10} = \frac{x}{100}$$

Step 3 Solve the proportion by setting the cross products equal to each other. Then solve for x.

$$\frac{35}{10} = \frac{x}{100} \quad \rightarrow \quad (35)(100) = (10)(x)$$
$$3,500 = 10x$$
$$350 = x$$

350% of 10 is 35.

You can use the 1% solution method to find what percent one number is of the total.

EXAMPLE 2 What percent of 300 is 36?

Step 1 Write an equation to show the amount that is equal to 100%.

100% = 300

Step 2 Divide both sides by 100.

$$\frac{100\%}{100} = \frac{300}{100}$$
$$1\% = 3$$

Step 3 Divide 36 by the 1% amount to find the percent.

$$\frac{36}{3} = 12\%$$

12% of 300 is 36.

You can also write and solve an equation to find what percent one number is of another.

Name _____ Date _____ Period _____ | **Workbook Activity**
Chapter 7, Lesson 9 | 64

Finding the Percent

EXAMPLE What percent of 800 is 200?
Here are some ways to find out.

Use a ratio. $\frac{200}{800} = \frac{x}{100}$ to $(200)(100) = (800)(x)$ to $20,000 = 800x$ to $x = 25\%$

Use the 1% solution. $100\% = 800$ to $\frac{100\%}{100} = \frac{800}{100}$

$1\% = 8$ $\frac{200}{8} = 25\%$

Use an equation. $(x)(800) = 200$ to $800x = 200$ to $x = \frac{2}{8} = \frac{1}{4} = 25\%$

Directions Find the missing percent.

1. 15 is _____% of 20.   4. 300 is _____% of 120.
2. 64 is _____% of 320.   5. 44 is _____% of 11.
3. 48 is _____% of 96.   6. 900 is _____% of 45.

Directions Find the given percentage of each number.

	18% of	26% of	73% of
21	**7.** _____	**8.** _____	**9.** _____
73	**10.** _____	**11.** _____	**12.** _____
65	**13.** _____	**14.** _____	**15.** _____
56	**16.** _____	**17.** _____	**18.** _____
82	**19.** _____	**20.** _____	**21.** _____
37	**22.** _____	**23.** _____	**24.** _____
28	**25.** _____	**26.** _____	**27.** _____
45	**28.** _____	**29.** _____	**30.** _____

Workbook Activity 64

Name _____ Date _____ Period _____ | **Activity**
Chapter 7, Lesson 9 | 61

What Percent?

Directions Find the percent of each number.

1. What percent of 120 is 45? _____
2. What percent of 64 is 16? _____
3. What percent of 82 is 26? _____
4. What percent of 150 is 45? _____
5. What percent of 40 is 8? _____
6. What percent of 62 is 122? _____
7. What percent of 42 is 324? _____
8. What percent of 320 is 444? _____
9. What percent of 62 is 18? _____
10. What percent of 54 is 24? _____

Directions Solve each problem.

11. A school with 512 students had an average weekly attendance of 478 students. What percent of the total student population was this? _____

12. At an egg hatchery, 962 out of 1,000 eggs hatched into baby chicks. What percent of the eggs hatched? _____

13. In an opinion survey of 250 people, 78 people favored a new landfill. What percent of the people surveyed favored the landfill? _____

14. A monthly weather chart showed that out of 31 days, 21 were sunny. What percent of the days during the month were *not* sunny? _____

15. In a clothing store, out of 215 suits that were sold, 183 were navy blue. What percent of the suits sold were some other color? _____

Activity 61

EXAMPLE 3 What percent of 20 is 8?

Step 1 Write an equation.

What percent of 20 is 8?

$\downarrow$ $\downarrow$ $\downarrow$

(n) $(20) = 8$

Step 2 Solve for n.

$(n)(20) = 8$

$20n = 8$

$n = \frac{8}{20}$

Step 3 Rewrite the fraction as a decimal, then as a percent.

$n = \frac{8}{20} = 0.4 = 40\%$

40% of 20 is 8.

These examples help show that you can solve percent problems in different ways.

Exercise A Solve to answer each question.

1. What percent of 4 is 10?
2. What percent of 72 is 18?
3. What percent of 40 is 15?
4. What percent of 65 is 195?
5. What percent of 900 is 45?

Calculator Practice

Some calculators have a percent key. You can use these calculators to solve percent problems.

EXAMPLE 4 Use a calculator to find 15% of 60.

To find a percent of a number, multiply.

Press 60 $\times$ 15 $\%$ $=$.

The display reads 9.

Exercise B Find the given percent of the given number.

6. Find 18% of 75.   13.5
7. Find 6% of 2.5.   0.15
8. Find 300% of 800.   2,400
9. Find 28% of 1,400.   392
10. Find 95% of 9.   8.55

Answers (left margin):
1. 250%
2. 25%
3. 37.5%, $37\frac{1}{2}\%$
4. 300%
5. 5%

Remind students that ratios in the form of fractions that are used in a proportion must always be written and used in the form $\frac{part}{whole}$.

3   Reinforce and Extend

MENTAL MATH

Invite students to mentally compute the answer to each question.

What percent of 2 is 4?	*(200%)*
What percent of 5 is 10?	*(200%)*
What percent of 1 is 6?	*(600%)*
What percent of 3 is 9?	*(300%)*
What percent of 4 is 16?	*(400%)*
What percent of 10 is 50?	*(500%)*
What percent of 8 is 8?	*(100%)*

CALCULATOR

Although many calculators have a $\%$ key, some do not. Remind students that percent computations can be performed using a calculator that does not have a percent key by dividing the percent by 100. For example, to find 15% of 60,

Press 60 $\times$ 15 $\div$ 100 $=$.

The display shows 9.

15% of 60 = 9

GROUP PROBLEM SOLVING

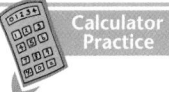
Ask students to work in groups of four to discuss and solve the following problem:

At a company, Employee X earns $20,000 per year, and Employee Y earns $30,000 per year. The company is considering giving a 6% "across-the-board" raise to all employees. You are Employee X. Tell why Employee Y gets a larger raise than you do.

(Before the raise is given, the difference between Employee Y's income and my income is $10,000. If the raise is given, the difference between our incomes becomes $10,600. The raise Employee Y receives is $600 more than the raise I receive.)

Lesson at a Glance

Chapter 7 Lesson 10

Overview This lesson introduces percent of increase and decrease.

Objective

■ To use a proportion to determine the percent of increase or decrease

Student Pages 190–191

Teacher's Resource Library

Workbook Activity 65

Activity 62

Alternative Activity 62

1 ⟋ Warm-Up Activity

Invite students to react to the following hypothetical conversation:

Mark: I heard that you moved.

Tanya: Yes, we moved to a bigger house. We had lived in our old house for quite a few years, and we made a nice profit on its sale because we received 150% more than we paid for it.

Mark: That's impossible! 100% is all there is of something—there can never be more than 100% of *anything.*

Is Mark correct? Explain. *(Mark is not correct; explanations may vary.)*

2 ⟋ Teaching the Lesson

After students discuss the examples on pages 190 and 191, ask them to look again at Step 1 of each example. Point out that in any situation that involves an increase or a decrease, the first step that must be performed is the identification of the exact amount of increase or decrease. Also point out that when the exact amount of increase or decrease is substituted into a proportion or equation to find the related percent, the increase or decrease always represents part of the whole.

Help students develop a sense of the magnitude of an increase or decrease by explaining that percents such as 10% and 20% reflect a relatively small part of the whole. As a result, a 10% or 20% increase or decrease will only be a small part of the whole. The opposite is also true—an

---

Percent problems sometimes ask you to find the percent of increase or decrease. To find the percent of increase or decrease, first find the amount of increase or decrease. Then write and solve a proportion, the 1% solution, or an equation.

EXAMPLE 1 On his fourth birthday, Lon was 40 inches tall. On his fifth birthday, he was 43 inches tall. By what percent did his height increase between his fourth and fifth birthdays?

Step 1 Find the amount of increase.

43 inches − 40 inches = 3 inches

Step 2 Write an equation.

3 inches is what percent of 40 inches?
$$\downarrow \qquad \downarrow \quad \downarrow \qquad \downarrow$$
$$(3) \qquad = \quad (x) \qquad 40$$

Step 3 Solve the equation for x.

$$3 = (x)(40)$$
$$\frac{3}{40} = x$$

Step 4 Change the fraction to a decimal, then to a percent.

$$\frac{3}{40} = 3 \div 40 = 0.075 = 7.5\%$$

Lon's height increased by 7.5%.

Some percent problems ask you to find the percent of decrease.

EXAMPLE 2 The price of a pair of shoes has been reduced from $60 to $48. By what percent has the price been reduced?

Step 1 Find the amount of decrease.

$60 − $48 = $12

Step 2 Write a proportion.

$$\frac{\text{amount of decrease}}{\text{original price}} = \frac{x}{100} \rightarrow \frac{12}{60} = \frac{x}{100}$$

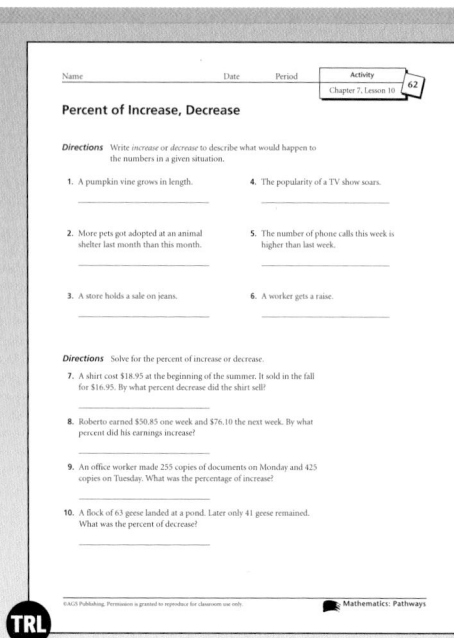

Workbook Activity 65   **Activity 62**

EXAMPLE 2 (continued)

Step 3 Set the cross products of the proportion equal to each other, then solve for x.

$$\frac{12}{60} = \frac{x}{100}$$

$$(12)(100) = (60)(x)$$

$$1,200 = 60x$$

$$20 = x$$

The percent of decrease was 20%.

A proportion, the 1% solution, or an equation can be used to solve a percent problem.

If a percent problem asks you to solve for the percent of increase or decrease, remember to first find the amount of the increase or decrease.

Exercise A What is the amount of increase or decrease in each situation?

1. Each Wednesday, the cost of museum admission for senior citizens is $4.00. On days other than Wednesday, the cost for senior citizens is $7.50. $3.50

2. In 1996, the amount of precipitation during the month of June totaled 4.2 inches. In 1997, the amount of precipitation during the month of June totaled 5.1 inches. 0.9 in.

PROBLEM SOLVING

Exercise B Solve each problem.

3. Suppose an investment in the stock market cost $1,600 to purchase and was worth $1,850 one year later. Did the value of the investment increase or decrease during that year? By what percent? Increase; 15.625%

4. On the first quiz of the year, Roberto answered 6 of 10 questions correctly. On the second quiz, he answered 8 of 10 questions correctly. By what percent did the number of questions he answered correctly increase? 20%

5. Leslie's old car had an average fuel economy of 30 miles per gallon of gasoline. Her new car has an average fuel economy of 27.6 miles per gallon of gasoline. By what percent did the fuel economy decrease? 8%

Ratios, Proportions, and Percents Chapter 7 **191**

---

increase or decrease of 80% or 90% will represent a large part of the whole. This sense of magnitude can be used to check the reasonableness of answers.

3 Reinforce and Extend

AT HOME

Ask students to find out the cost of the previous two months' electric or other utility bills and then determine the percent of increase or decrease from one month's bill to the next. Students may need the help of a family member with this activity.

GROUP PROBLEM SOLVING

Encourage students to work in groups of four or five to discuss the following question and debate its answer:

Can a percent of decrease ever be greater than 100%? Explain.

(Answers and explanations will vary. Sample answer and explanation: No; for example, if a shopper begins shopping with $50 and spends all of it, the percent of decrease of the shopper's money is 100%.)

Invite groups to exchange opinions about the solution.

ONLINE CONNECTION

Have students go to www.newsengin.com/ neFreeTools.nsf. Click on All items, and choose an area of the United States. Students can use the currency converter to calculate the percent change of $100 within 3 different time periods. Then, using an average percent, have students create tables on paper to approximate how much $100 will be worth in 10, 30, and 50 years. Have students use the tables they've created to calculate how much groceries, CDs, shoes, and so on will cost in 10, 30, and 50 years.

Chapter 7 Lesson 11

Overview This lesson introduces formulas that include percents.

Objective

■ To apply the compound interest formula

Student Pages 192–193

Teacher's Resource Library **TRL**

　Workbook Activity 66

　Activity 63

　Alternative Activity 63

....

Mathematics Vocabulary

compound interest
compounding period

....

1 　Warm-Up Activity

Students may be interested to learn about the Rule of 72. Explain that the Rule of 72 is an algorithm that can be used to quickly estimate the length of time it will take an investment to double in value if the percent of interest the investment earns is known. To estimate how long it would take an investment earning 9% interest per year to double in value, divide 72 by 9; it will take an investment earning 9% interest per year about 8 years to double in value. To estimate how long it would take an investment earning 12% interest per year to double in value, divide 72 by 12; it would take an investment earning 12% interest per year about 6 years to double.

2 　Teaching the Lesson

In Step 2 of Example 1 on page 192, have students note that the compound interest formula always includes a set of parentheses. Remind students of the order of operations and the importance of performing the computation inside the parentheses *before* the value of the parentheses is raised to a power.

After discussing Example 2 on page 193, invite one or more volunteers to demonstrate how to solve the problem using a calculator that does not have a parentheses key or function.

Compound interest

Interest paid on both the original amount of money plus any interest added to date; compound interest is usually computed on deposits placed into savings accounts

Compounding period

The amount of time that the interest rate is calculated

The **compound interest** formula is an example of a formula that includes a percent. The compound interest formula is used to find the amount of money earned after a given number of **compounding periods**.

> **The Compound Interest Formula**
>
> $A = P(1 + i)^n$ where A = the amount of money in the account, P = the principal or original deposit, i = the interest rate per period expressed as a decimal, and n = the number of compounding periods.

To use the formula, substitute values for P, i, and n.

EXAMPLE 1 $2,000 is deposited in a savings account that pays 6% interest compounded annually. Find the amount of money in the account after 2 years.

Step 1 Determine the values that represent P, i, and n. In this example:

P is $2,000, the amount of the deposit.

i is 0.06, the interest rate per period (6%) expressed as a decimal.

n is 2, the number of compounding periods. (In this example, compounding occurs annually. Annually means once at the end of each year. The number of compounding periods in this example is 2—once at the end of each year for two years.)

Step 2 Substitute P, i, and n into the compound interest formula. Then solve for A.

$A = P(1 + i)^n$

$A = 2,000(1 + 0.06)^2$

$A = 2,000(1.06)^2$

$A = 2,000(1.1236)$

$A = 2,247.20$

After two years, the value of the account will be $2,247.20.

Name _____ Date _____ Period _____ | **Workbook Activity** 66 | Chapter 7, Lesson 11

Formulas and Percents

EXAMPLE The formula for compound interest involves percents.

$A = P(1 + i)^n$
A = amount of money
P = principal or original deposit
i = interest rate per period (shown as a decimal)
n = number of compounding periods

$A = $200(1 + 0.04)^2$
$A = $200(1.04)^2$
$A = $200(1.0816)$
$A = 216.32

Directions Write each percentage rate as a decimal.

1. $3\frac{3}{4}$ _____
2. $4\frac{1}{4}$ _____
3. $2\frac{1}{2}$ _____
4. $1\frac{1}{4}$ _____
5. $3\frac{1}{2}$ _____
6. $2\frac{1}{4}$ _____
7. $5\frac{1}{2}$ _____
8. $4\frac{1}{4}$ _____
9. $8\frac{3}{4}$ _____

Directions Solve each problem. Round to the fourth digit.

10. $(1.04)^3$ _____
11. $(1.04)^2$ _____
12. $(1.0425)^2$ _____
13. $(1.0375)^2$ _____
14. $(1.0875)^3$ _____
15. $(1.025)^2$ _____

Directions Solve each problem.

A bank advertised an interest rate on a savings account of $3\frac{1}{2}$% annually. How much did each person have at the end of two years?

Original Deposit　　**Amount After Two Years**

16. $250 _____
17. $1,800 _____
18. $735 _____
19. $2,145 _____
20. $8,620 _____

Workbook Activity 66

Name _____ Date _____ Period _____ | **Activity** 63 | Chapter 7, Lesson 11

Percents and Formulas

Directions Use a calculator to find out how much more a saver would earn by depositing money in Bank A rather than in Bank B after two years. Use the compound interest formula $A = P(1 + i)^n$.

	Bank A $2\frac{3}{4}$% interest per year	Bank B $2\frac{1}{4}$% interest per year	Difference
1. $120			
2. $950			
3. $635			
4. $2,675			
5. $5,210			
6. $10,265			

Directions Solve each problem.

7. How much money will you earn in interest in three years if you deposit $600 at 4% annually?

8. Two years ago Allen deposited $50 in a savings account earning $2\frac{1}{4}$% interest. Two years ago Sara deposited $50 at $2\frac{1}{2}$%. Who has a bigger balance? How much bigger?

9. How much interest will you pay after two years if you borrow $150 at 5%?

10. A car dealer offers a three-year loan of $12,000 at 5% per year. How much will a buyer pay for the car and the loan?

Activity 63

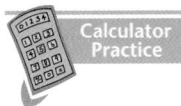

Calculator Practice

A calculator is a very helpful tool to use whenever you need to find compound interest.

EXAMPLE 2 $5,000 is deposited in a savings account that pays $4\frac{1}{2}\%$ interest compounded annually. Find the amount of money in the account after 5 years.

Step 1   Determine the values that represent P, i, and n.

P is $5,000, the amount of the deposit.

i is 0.045, the interest rate per period ($4\frac{1}{2}\%$) expressed as a decimal.

n is 5, the number of compounding periods. (You need to find the amount of money in the account after 5 years. The number of compounding periods is 5—once at the end of each year for five years.)

Step 2   Substitute P, i, and n into the compound interest formula. Then use a calculator to solve for A.

$$A = P(1 + i)^n$$
$$A = 5,000(1 + 0.045)^5$$
$$A = 5000 \; \boxed{\times} \; \boxed{(} \; \boxed{1} \; \boxed{+} \; \boxed{0.045} \; \boxed{)} \; \boxed{y^x} \; \boxed{5} \; \boxed{=}$$
$$A = 6230.90968827$$

After five years, the value of the account will be $6,230.91.

Try This

How many years will it take an account to double in value at 10% interest compounded annually? Round your answer to the nearest whole number of years.

7 years

Exercise A In problems 1–4, the interest is compounded annually. Find the value of each account at the end of each period of time.

1. $P = \$500$; $i = 5\%$; $t = 2$ years $551.25
2. $P = \$10,000$; $i = 8\%$; $t = 4$ years $13,604.89
3. $P = \$2,500$; $i = 7.5\%$; $t = 5$ years $3,589.07
4. $P = \$1,000$; $i = 5\%$; $t = 3$ years $1,157.63
5. Suppose that on your tenth birthday, you deposit $108 into an account that pays an average of 12% interest compounded annually. If you do not make additional deposits to that account and you do not withdraw money from that account, what will be the value of the account on your fiftieth birthday? $10,049.50

Ratios, Proportions, and Percents   Chapter 7   **193**

LEARNING STYLES

Interpersonal/ Group Learning

Ask small groups of students to solve the following problem:

Find the value of an account after two years, given $P = \$100$ and $i = 10\%$ compounded every 6 months. Round your answer to the nearest penny. *($121.55)*

Then have the groups write and solve several similar compound interest problems.

GROUP PROBLEM SOLVING

Encourage students to work in groups of three to discuss and solve the following problem:

On the day of a baby's birth, suppose that $1.00 is invested in the stock market in an account for that baby. Also suppose that over time, the investment will earn an average interest rate of 10% compounded annually.

- Estimate the value of the baby's account on his or her sixty-fifth birthday. Round your answer to the nearest penny. *($490.37)*

- Determine the number of times the original investment of $1.00 will double in 65 years. *(between 8 and 9 times)*

Invite groups to share their problem-solving approach and their answers with one another.

CAREER CONNECTION

Realtors, bankers, and stockbrokers, as well as employees of many other professions, need to be proficient with percents. If possible, obtain a calculator that financial professionals use (examples of such calculators include business or statistical calculators), and invite students to explore how computations using such calculators are performed.

Lesson at a Glance

Chapter 7 Lesson 12

Overview This lesson explains how to use ratios to understand and construct scale drawings.

Objective

- To solve word problems using scale drawings

Student Pages 194–197

Teacher's Resource Library TRL

Workbook Activity 67

Activity 64

Alternative Activity 64

....

Mathematics Vocabulary

scale drawing
dimension

....

1 Warm-Up Activity

Use a map of the United States to show that even though a ruler is used to measure distance between two cities, the actual driving distance is much greater. Stress to students that the map is drawn to a certain scale so that we can read it. Define the word *scale* for students.

2 Teaching the Lesson

Show pictures of animals to students, and ask them which pictures show an animal to scale and which do not. Review the meaning of the words *to scale* and how they are used when describing an object.

Ask students what they know about scale drawings. Ask students why scale drawings are important and when they would need to use a scale drawing.

COMMON ERROR

 Make sure that students understand that most of the problems they are solving have two different units of measure (for example, 4 ft = 120 mi). Errors can occur when setting up the problem. Be sure to show an example problem to make students aware of the different measurements.

Scale drawing
A picture in which the relative sizes have been kept

Dimension
The measure, such as length, width, or height, of the size of an object

Scale drawings are drawings of real-life objects that are usually much smaller than their true **dimensions.** The scale, or ratio, is expressed in whole numbers such as 1:2 or 1:3 (1 to 2 or 1 to 3). The 1 represents the dimension in the scale drawing, and the real-life dimensions are double for 1:2 and triple for 1:3.

EXAMPLE 1 How long is the bird in real life? The scale is 1:2, and the length of the drawing is $2\frac{5}{8}$ inches between the arrows.

Let n = real dimension.

Scale: 1:2 means $\frac{\text{Drawing}}{\text{Real}} = \frac{1}{2} = \frac{2\frac{5}{8} \text{ inches}}{n}$

Cross multiply $(2)(2\frac{5}{8}) = n$

$5\frac{1}{4} = n$

The bird is $5\frac{1}{4}$ inches long.

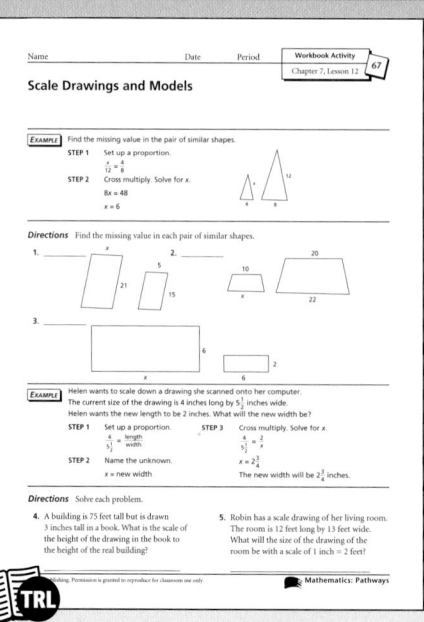

Workbook Activity 67

Activity 64

Maps are scale drawings of the location of roads and cities. The scale is usually printed at the bottom of the map.

EXAMPLE 2   In the sample scale at the right, $1\frac{1}{4}$ inches represents 2 miles in real life.
1 centimeter represents 1 kilometer.

Scale in Miles

Scale in Kilometers

How many miles apart are the two cities if the distance on the map is $3\frac{3}{4}$ inches?

Step 1   Given $1\frac{1}{4}$ inches = 2 miles

$2\frac{1}{2}$ inches = 4 miles

3 and $\frac{3}{4}$ inches = 6 miles

How many miles apart are the two cities if the distance on the map is $5\frac{1}{2}$ centimeters?

Step 2   Given 1 centimeter (cm) = 1 kilometer (km)

$5\frac{1}{2}$ cm = $5\frac{1}{2}$ km

EXAMPLE 3   Floor plans for houses and apartments are drawn to scale. Plans for houses drawn by architects are called blueprints. Use a ruler and the given scale to determine the actual dimensions of the room.

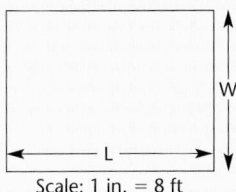

Scale: 1 in. = 8 ft

Length of drawing = $1\frac{1}{2}''$ Width of drawing = $1\frac{1}{8}''$

$\frac{\text{Drawing}}{\text{Real}} \quad \frac{1}{8} = \frac{1\frac{1}{2}}{n}$ $\frac{\text{Drawing}}{\text{Real}} \quad \frac{1}{8} = \frac{1\frac{1}{8}}{n}$

$8 \times 1\frac{1}{2} = 1 \times n$ $8 \times 1\frac{1}{8} = 1 \times n$

$8 \times \frac{3}{2} = n$ $8 \times \frac{9}{8} = n$

$12 = n$ $9 = n$

The living room is 12 feet long.   The living room is 9 feet wide.

MODELING

Have students work in small groups. Ask them to use an inch ruler to measure the length and width of a desk. Give each group one sheet of $8\frac{1}{2} \times 11$ paper. Have students make a scale drawing of the desk from their measurements.

AT HOME

Ask students to think about how far away they live from school. Have students note all the turns they make on the way home and the length of the streets. If students had to make a map of their trip, what scale would they have to use to fit it on an $8\frac{1}{2} \times 11$ sheet of paper?

Invite students to mentally compute the answer to each of the following questions. Remind students to cross-multiply and then divide to solve for x. Ask a volunteer to take the class through the steps that he or she followed to solve the first problem. Go through the first three problems in this manner until the class feels comfortable with the process.

1. $\frac{x}{2} = \frac{10}{4}$ $(x = 5)$

2. $\frac{3}{x} = \frac{6}{8}$ $(x = 4)$

3. $\frac{11}{x} = \frac{2}{4}$ $(x = 22)$

4. $\frac{8}{10} = \frac{x}{5}$ $(x = 4)$

5. $\frac{6}{4} = \frac{x}{6}$ $(x = 9)$

6. $\frac{2}{x} = \frac{6}{9}$ $(x = 3)$

7. $\frac{14}{4} = \frac{x}{2}$ $(x = 7)$

8. $\frac{12}{x} = \frac{6}{5}$ $(x = 10)$

CAREER CONNECTION

Invite an architect to talk to students about the importance of scale drawings in his or her job. Ask the architect to bring in blueprints, drawings, or models for the class to look at. Tell students to be prepared with questions to ask the architect.

Exercise A Measure the distance between the points of the arrows to the nearest $\frac{1}{8}$ inch. Use the scale to write a proportion. Solve the proportions to find the length of the real-life object in inches.

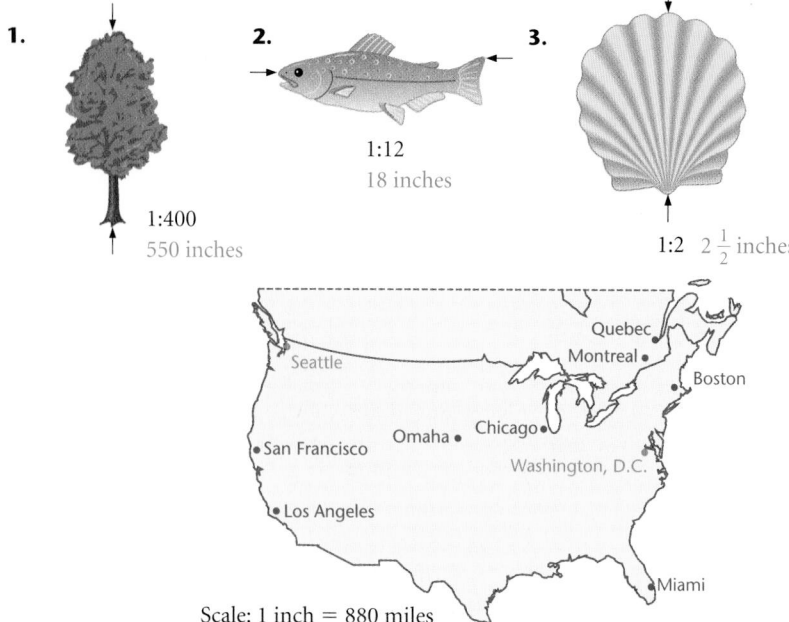

1.

2. 1:12
18 inches

3.

1:400
550 inches

1:2 $2\frac{1}{2}$ inches

Scale: 1 inch = 880 miles

Exercise B Measure to the nearest eighth of an inch. Use a ruler. Copy and complete this chart. You may use a calculator.

	Trip	Map Distance (inches)	Real Distance (miles)
4.	Los Angeles to Miami	$2\frac{3}{4}$	2,420
5.	Seattle to Chicago	$1\frac{7}{8}$	1,650
6.	Boston to Omaha	$1\frac{5}{8}$	1,430
7.	Montreal to Washington, D.C.	$\frac{5}{8}$	550
8.	Quebec to San Francisco	3	2,640

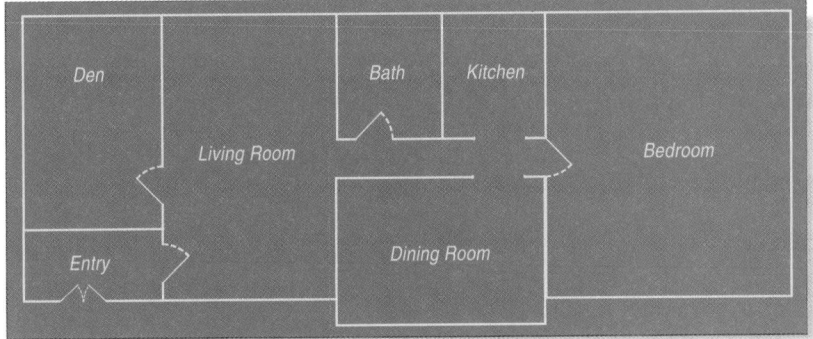

Scale: 1 inch = 8 feet
length ←→ width ↕

PROBLEM SOLVING

Exercise C Use the scale to convert your answer to feet.

9. What is the length and the width of the kitchen? 6 feet by 7 feet

10. If the length and the width of the kitchen was 2 times larger than the original, what would be the new length and width? 12 feet by 14 feet

11. What is the length and the width of the bedroom? 14 feet by 16 feet

12. Would the larger size of the kitchen be larger than the bedroom? No

13. What is the ratio between the width of the bedroom and the width of the dining room? 2:1

14. What is the length and the width of the den? 8 feet by 12 feet

15. What is the length and the width of the entry? 8 feet by 4 feet

CALCULATOR

In this lesson, students have been using scales or ratios to solve word problems. An example of a scale or ratio students are now familiar with is inches-to-feet. Have students use their calculators to convert feet to inches. Remind students that 1 foot = 12 inches.

1. 2 feet   *(24 inches)*

2. 10 feet   *(120 inches)*

3. 5 feet   *(60 inches)*

4. 250 feet   *(3,000 inches)*

5. 431 feet   *(5,172 inches)*

LEARNING STYLES

Visual/Spatial

Gather pictures or illustrations of animals from books or magazines. Ask the class whether each picture is to scale. Some pictures should be obvious, and some should challenge students. If pictures are difficult to locate, have students create a scaled-down or full-size sketch of an animal. Write the names of animals on separate sheets of paper. After each animal's name, write the words "scaled" or "full size." (Examples: crocodile (scaled), rabbit (full size), bee (full size), ant (full size), bear (scaled), and so on) Have students select the name of an animal from a hat or bag. Hold completed sketches up, and have the class guess whether they are scaled drawings or full-size sketches.

Lesson at a Glance

Chapter 7 Application

Overview This lesson presents an application of rates of change to solve word problems.

Objective

- To solve word problems using rates of change

Student Page 198

Teacher's Resource Library

Application Activity 7

Everyday Math 7

---

1 Warm-Up Activity

Begin by explaining the difference between a ratio and a rate. Using the example in the lesson, ask students what two rates they are comparing. If the students are unsure of the answer, it might help to give an example. Example: We go to a grocery store and want to buy some bananas. The sign says that bananas are $0.49 per pound. Cents or dollars per pound are examples of rates that we will encounter in everyday life. Explain to students that when a rate is written, the word *per* is included. *Per* means "for each." Therefore, the example could also read "The sign says that bananas are $0.49 for each pound." Ask students to identify any other rates that use the word *per*. Students can be asked to think of riding in a car or bus (miles per hour) or earning money (dollars per hour).

2 Teaching the Lesson

Explain that finding a rate uses subtraction and division. In the example, students must subtract the temperatures and find the difference in time. After those values have been determined, they can divide to find the rate of change. Be sure to tell students to read the problem carefully so that when they calculate the rate of change, the correct numbers are in the numerator and denominator.

Rates of Change Ratios compare the relationship between two quantities. A rate compares two quantities with different units of measure.

EXAMPLE 1 At 9 A.M. the outside temperature was 80° Fahrenheit. By 3 P.M., it had reached 92° Fahrenheit. What was the rate of change in temperature per hour?

Step 1 Find the difference in temperature.

$92 - 80 = 12$

Step 2 Find the elapsed time.

9 A.M. to 3 P.M. is 6 hours

Step 3 Divide to find the rate per hour.

$$\frac{\text{temperature}}{\text{time}} = \frac{12}{6} = \frac{2}{1}$$

The temperature increased at a rate of 2° Fahrenheit per hour.

Exercise Solve each problem.

1. In 1995 the number of cellular phones sold was about 36,000,000. By 1998 the number reached over 60,000,000. What was the rate of change in sales per year? 8,000,000 cellular phones per year

2. Emily baby-sits the Goodall children from 5:30 P.M. until 10:30 P.M. She is paid $37.50. What is Emily's rate per hour? $7.50 per hour

3. The 540-mile drive from home to Chicago takes Arlo 9 hours. At what speed is he driving? 60 miles per hour

4. The bank teller can process about 4 customers in 12 minutes. At this rate, how many customers can be served in one hour? about 20 customers

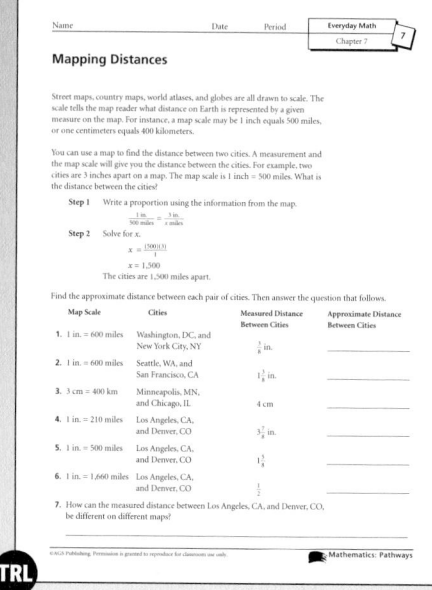

Application Activity 7

Everyday Math 7

Chapter 7 REVIEW

Write the letter of the correct answer.

1. Express the ratio 3:15 as a fraction in simplest form. D

   A $\frac{3}{15}$ **C** $\frac{15}{3}$

   B 5   **D** $\frac{1}{5}$

2. Choose the true proportion to $\frac{3}{8}$. B

   A $\frac{9}{28}$ **C** $\frac{8}{3}$

   B $\frac{9}{24}$ **D** $\frac{6}{24}$

3. Solve for d. $\frac{6}{d} = \frac{18}{39}$ A

   A $d = 13$ **C** $d = 3$

   B $d = 236$ **D** $d = 24$

4. Solve for v. $\frac{5}{6} = \frac{v}{12}$ B

   A $v = 30$ **C** $v = 5$

   B $v = 10$ **D** $v = 11$

5. Express 0.94 as a percent. C

   A 9.4%   **C** 94%

   B 0.94%   **D** 940%

Solve each problem.

6. Ryan is 30″ tall. His brother is $2\frac{1}{3}$ times taller than Ryan. How tall is Ryan's brother? 70″ tall

7. The weight of a small bag of potatoes is 8 pounds. The ratio between a small bag and a large bag is 1:3. What is the weight of the larger bag? 24 pounds

8. One container can hold a volume of 36 mL³ of milk. Another container can hold 12 mL³. What is the ratio between the two containers? 3:1

CALCULATOR

 Invite students to use their calculators to complete the following chart. You may draw this on the board and ask students to fill in the blanks.

Start time	End time	Hourly pay	Total pay
9 A.M.	3 P.M.		$60.00
7:30 A.M.	4:30 P.M.		$80.19
6:30 A.M.	3:00 P.M.		$215.22
8 A.M.	12 P.M.		$22.60
12 P.M.	12 A.M.		$145.44

($10.00, $8.91, $25.32, $5.65, $12.12)

Chapter 7 Review

Each set of problems in the Chapter Review includes an example and solution to illustrate the concept. Use the given examples for reteaching the materials in Chapter 7. For additional practice, refer to the Supplementary Problems for Chapter 7 (pages 444–445).

Chapter 7 Mastery Test

The Teacher's Resource Library includes parallel forms of the Chapter 7 Mastery Test. The difficulty level of the two forms is equivalent. You may wish to use one form as a pretest and the other form as a posttest.

Chapters 1–7 Midterm Mastery Test TRL

The Teacher's Resource Library includes the Midterm Mastery Test. This test is pictured on page 525 of the Teacher's Edition. The Midterm Mastery Test assesses the major learning objectives for Chapters 1–7.

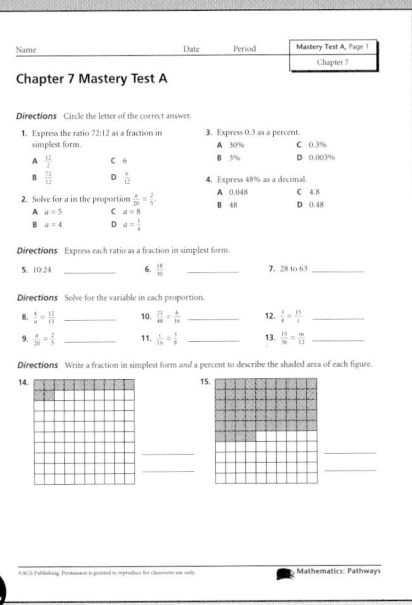

Chapter 7 Mastery Test A

ALTERNATIVE ASSESSMENT

Alternative Assessment items correlate with student Goals for Learning at the beginning of this chapter.

■ **To express ratios in different forms**

List several ratios and several numbers that are not ratios on the board. Have students identify whether each is a ratio. If it is a ratio, students should express the ratio in two other ways. If the numbers given are not ratios, have students explain why. If the ratios are not in simplest form, have students simplify them.

■ **To solve problems using proportions**

Have students bring in the nutrition fact panel from a box of their favorite cereal or other packaged food product. Have them calculate the calories, fat, carbohydrates, and other nutrients they consume if they double, triple, or quadruple the recommended serving size. Then have them calculate what nutrients they consume if they eat half or one-third of the recommended serving size.

■ **To use proportions to find length, weight, capacity, and volume**

Pair students, and instruct them to write a word problem that contains a proportion. Assign each pair a unit of measure [length (ft), weight (lb), capacity (mL), volume (in.³)] and a topic. Some topic examples you might use could include the height of a building or the length of a race; lifting weights at a gym or carrying books for weight; a glass of milk or a container of water for capacity; or a kitchen sink or a fish bowl for volume. Tell the class that they can use their books for help. Make sure that the students provide an answer to the problem on a separate sheet of paper. Have pairs trade problems with other pairs. Check for correct answers.

■ **To solve distance and rate problems**

Conduct an experiment using toy cars. Use five cars (or any objects that can slide across the floor) in a variety of sizes, weights, and materials. Organize students into groups of three to record the time on paper, use a stopwatch

Solve each problem. Distance = (rate)(time).

9. Jenny ran the 9-mile race in $1\frac{1}{2}$ hours. What was her constant speed? 6 miles per hour

10. An airplane has a constant speed of 512 mph. The total time of the trip is $3\frac{1}{4}$ hours. How many miles did the airplane travel? 1,664 miles

11. Sheila, 0.26 hours; Tonya, 0.21 hours. Tonya will arrive there first.

11. Sheila and Tonya are going to meet for lunch. Sheila drives at a constant speed of 38 miles per hour for a distance of 10 miles. Tonya drives at a constant speed of 35 miles per hour for a distance of $7\frac{1}{2}$ miles. How long does it take for each girl to get to the restaurant? Who will arrive first if both girls leave at the same time?

Express each decimal as a percent.

Example: 0.60   Solution: 0.60 = 60%

12. 0.40   40%   **15.** 0.03   3%

13. 0.12   12%   **16.** 0.5   50%

14. 0.09   9%   **17.** 0.81   81%

Express each fraction as a percent.

Example: $\frac{3}{4}$ Solution: $\frac{3}{4} = 3 \div 4 = 0.75 = 75\%$

18. $\frac{1}{10}$ 10%   **21.** $\frac{4}{25}$ 16%

19. $\frac{5}{16}$ 31.25%   **22.** $\frac{11}{25}$ 44%

20. $\frac{1}{4}$ 25%   **23.** $\frac{29}{50}$ 58%

Express each percent as a decimal.

Example: 12%   Solution: 12% = 0.12

24. 54%   0.54   **27.** 95%   0.95

25. 19%   0.19   **28.** 79%   0.79

26. 6%   0.06   **29.** 61%   0.61

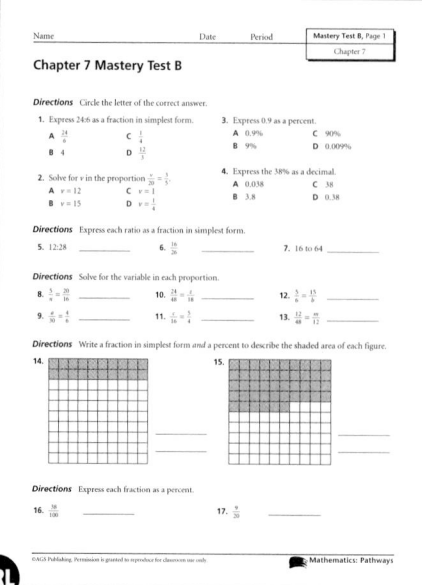

Chapter 7 Mastery Test B

Solve each problem.

Example: The tax in Lake County is 7%. How much tax will you pay if you buy a T-shirt for $14.00?   Solution: 7% = 0.07

$$0.07 \cdot \$14 = \$0.98 \qquad 7\% \text{ of } \$14 \text{ is } \$0.98.$$

30. Kara is buying a used car for $2,580. The tax on the car is 11%. How much is the total cost of the car with tax? $2,863.80

31. Mike deposits $1,500 in a savings account that pays 7% interest compounded annually. How much money will he have in the account after 3 years? Remember, the compound interest formula is $A = P(1 + i)^n$. $1,837.56

32. Rosa works in the local library. On Wednesday she checked out 50 books. On Thursday she checked out 65 books. What was the percent of increase in the number of books she checked out? 30%

33. The distance from Shelley's house to her aunt's house measures $5\frac{1}{4}$ inches on a map. The scale of the map is $1'' = 4$ miles. How far is it to Shelley's aunt's house? 21 miles

34. Jamal is assembling a bookcase. Looking at the directions, he finds that the next piece he needs measures $4''$ long on the drawing. The scale of the drawing is $1'' = 6''$. What is the actual length of the piece Jamal needs? 24″ long

35. Find the missing value in the pairs of shapes. The ratio is 3:1.

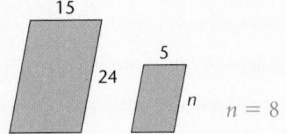

$n = 8$

Test-Taking Tip

Remember that the word *of* means *times,* so you can rewrite 12% of 40 as 0.12 × 40.

MANIPULATIVES

 Review

Materials: Cuisenaire Rods, Manipulatives Master 4 (100-Square Grid)

Group Practice: Review the procedures for modeling fractions, decimals, and percents and writing equivalent values.

Student Practice: Have students use the rods and grid to solve Chapter Review problems 8–14 and 17–30.

(time in seconds), and push the cars. Define a start and finish line on the floor for the cars, and have students measure this distance (no longer than 4 feet). After all the groups have completed the experiment, ask the students to solve for speed. Compare answers. *(Answers for each car should be similar between the groups because of the different sizes, weights, and materials.)*

■ **To change fractions and decimals to percents**
Have students work in groups to design a matching game. Have them create a variety of fractions and decimals and convert them to percentages. Have each group write its fractions and decimals and the corresponding percents on separate sheets of paper, mix them up, and hand them to a different group to match the percent with the correct fraction or decimal.

■ **To solve problems using percents**
Have students work in pairs to solve the following problem. Then discuss it as a class. Family A paid $4,000 in federal income taxes last year, which was 12% of its adjusted gross income. Family B paid $5,000, which is 12% of its adjusted gross income. Have students figure out the adjusted gross annual incomes for both families. *(Adjusted gross annual income for Family A is about $33,333 and for Family B is about $41,666.)*

■ **To read and draw scale drawings**
Using a map of the United States that shows only capital cities and which uses a scale equating inches with another measurement, ask students to use the scale to find the distance between cities such as Sacramento, California, to Austin, Texas, or Boston, Massachusetts, to Lansing, Michigan. Ask questions to help students find the city. (For example, what city is 1,000 miles directly west of Columbus, Ohio?) Students will have to convert the measurement back to inches and use their rulers to find the city.

Planning Guide

Integers

Lesson		Student Pages	Vocabulary	Practice Exercises	Problem Solving	Try This	Solutions Key
1	The Real Number Line and Integers	204–207	✔	✔	207		✔
2	Comparing Integers	208–209	✔	✔	209		✔
3	Even and Odd Integers	210–211		✔		211	✔
4	Adding Positive Integers	212–213		✔			✔
5	Adding Negative Integers	214–215		✔	215		✔
6	Subtracting Positive and Negative Integers	216–219		✔	219		✔
7	Multiplying by Positive Integers	220–221		✔			✔
8	Multiplying by Negative Integers	222–223		✔	223		✔
9	Dividing Positive and Negative Integers	224–225		✔	225	225	✔
Application	Ice Cold	226		✔			✔

Chapter Activities

Teacher's Resource Library
Estimation Exercise 8: Estimating
   Products and Quotients
Application Activity 8: Ice Cold
Everyday Math 8: Up and Away
Community Connection 8: Utility Bills

Teacher's Edition
Chapter 8 Project

Assessment Options

Student Text
Chapter 8 Review

Teacher's Resource Library
Chapter 8 Mastery Tests A and B

Teacher's Edition
Chapter 8 Alternative Assessments

Estimation Activity	Math in Your Life	Technology Connection	Writing About Mathematics	Build a Model	Calculator Practice	Online Connection	Common Error	Applications Home, Career, Community	Mental Math	Manipulatives	Calculator	Group Problem Solving	Modeling	Knowing Your Students	Auditory/Verbal	Visual/Spatial	Logical/Mathematical	Body/Kinesthetic	Interpersonal/Group Learning	LEP/ESL	Activities	Alternate Activities	Workbook Activities	Self-Study Guide
	206											207	207		205	206				206	65	65	68	✔
							209					209						209	209		66	66	69	✔
									211											211	67	67	70	✔
			213	213						213	213							213			68	68	71	✔
		214		215						215	215	215									69	69	72	✔
	218					217			218	217		219		219	218					219	70	70	73–74	✔
221									221							221					71	71	75	✔
		223						223									223				72	72	76	✔
									225			225							225		73	73	77	✔
								226																✔

Chapter 8: Integers

pages 202–229

Lessons

**Skill Track for
  Mathematics: Pathways**

Teacher's Resource Library (TRL)

(Answer Keys for the Teacher's Resource Library begin on page 528 of this Teacher's Edition.)

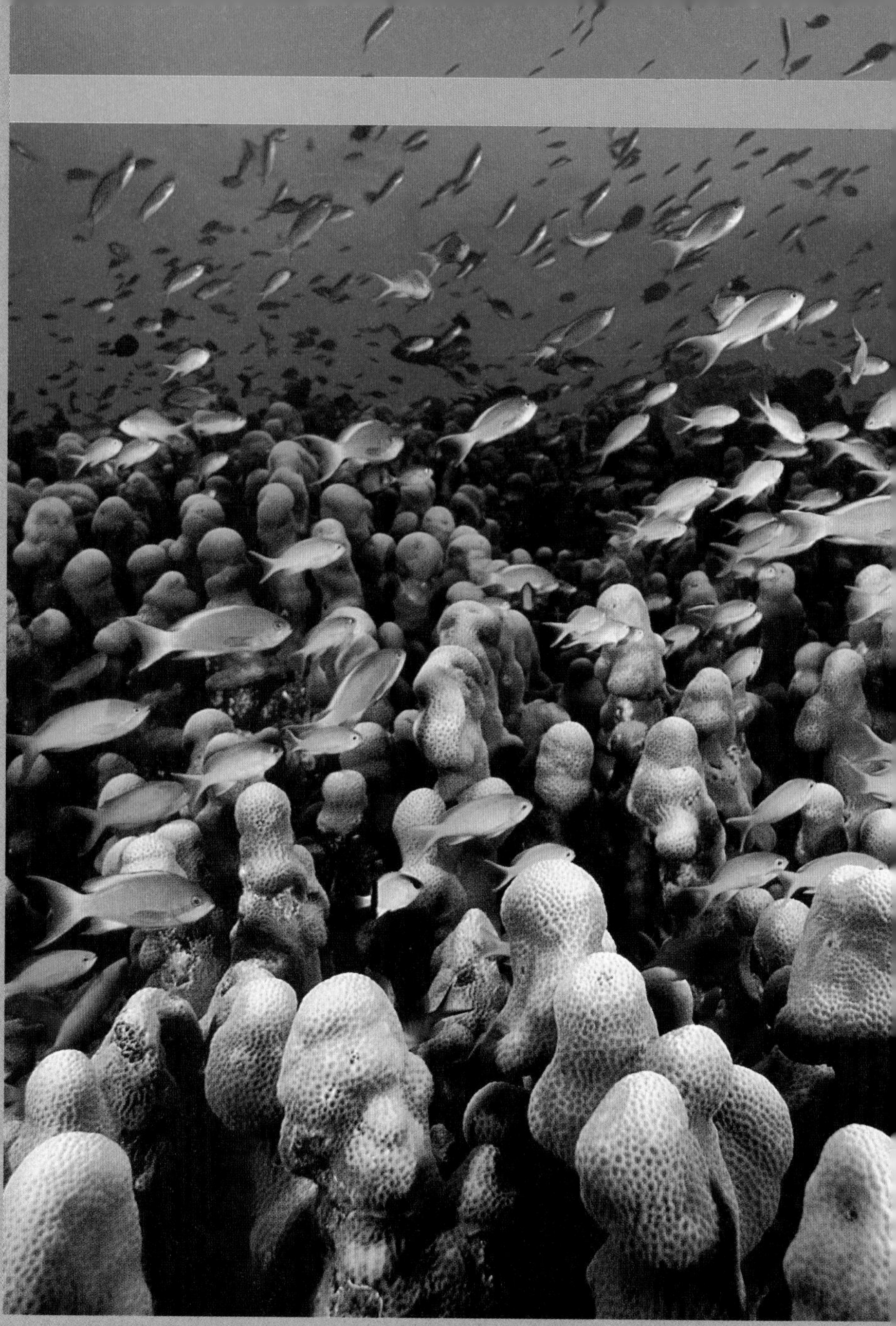

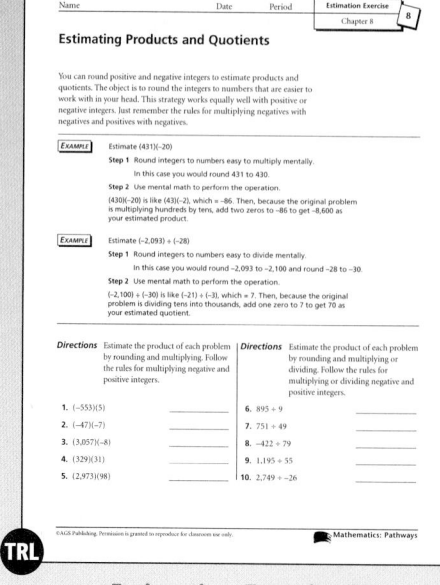

Estimation Exercise 8

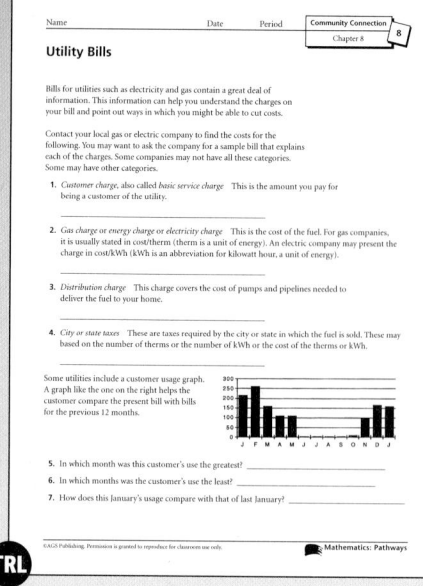

Community Connection 8

8 Integers

The fish in the photograph swim in the warm tropical waters of a coral reef. In geography any depth below sea level has *negative* altitude. A mountain towering into the sky has *positive* altitude. When you put money in your bank account, it is recorded as a positive amount. But when you take money out of your account, it is recorded as a negative amount.

The Chinese were the first to work with positive and negative numbers a long time ago. They used two sets of counting rods, one color for positive and a second one for negative. It wasn't until the 1500s that mathematicians in Europe started to work with negative numbers. Today, positive and negative numbers are used widely. In many fields, positive and negative numbers mark values above or below a starting point.

In Chapter 8, you will work with positive and negative integers.

Goals for Learning

◆ To identify the absolute value of integers
◆ To compare the values of negative and positive whole numbers
◆ To add and subtract integers
◆ To multiply and divide integers

203

Introducing the Chapter

After students read the chapter opener, brainstorm a list of objects that can be found both above and below sea level. *(an iceberg, a boat, rocks, and so on)* Challenge students to describe ways we use positive and negative numbers today. *(rising and falling temperatures, money withdrawn from a bank account, a financial loss in the stock market, and so on)*

CHAPTER PROJECT

 Students will select three corporations currently in the news and create a chart for each company listing its name, its product or service, and the price per share of its stock. Students will "own" 100 shares of each company's stock and provide updates each week on news that affects the stock, such as announcements of new products or reductions in workforce. Students should consult the *Wall Street Journal*, the *New York Times*, and national or local news programs. Help students keep tables, charts, or graphs showing changes in revenue, employees, stock value, and so on.

TEACHER'S RESOURCE

The AGS Publishing Teaching Strategies in Math Transparencies may be used with this chapter. They add an interactive dimension to expand and enhance the program content.

CAREER INTEREST INVENTORY

The AGS Publishing Harrington-O'Shea Career Decision-Making System-Revised (CDM) may be used with this chapter. Students can use the CDM to explore their interests and identify careers. The CDM defines career areas that are indicated by students' responses on the inventory.

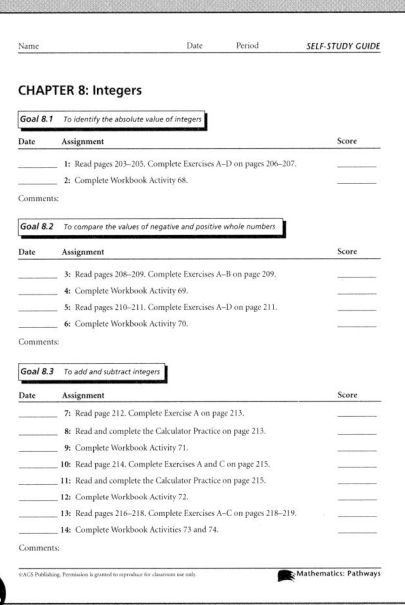

Chapter 8 Self-Study Guide

Lesson at a Glance

Chapter 8 Lesson 1

Overview This lesson uses the number line to introduce absolute value, negative integers, and positive integers.

Objectives

- To comprehend the opposite nature of positive and negative integers
- To read a number line to determine absolute value of real numbers

Student Pages 204–207

Teacher's Resource Library **TRL**

Workbook Activity 68

Activity 65

Alternative Activity 65

Mathematics Vocabulary

integer
real number
negative integer
positive integer
absolute value
opposites

1 Warm-Up Activity

Ask students whether they can think of a situation in which 5 is less than 1. Draw a portion of a thermometer on the board, and have students model when this is true:

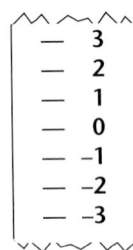

```
— 3
— 2
— 1
— 0
— −1
— −2
— −3
```

(At 5 degrees below zero, the temperature is less than at 1 degree above zero.) Ask students to list other times when we use negative numbers to show value. *(market losses, wind chill, annual reports, graph of the coordinate plane, and so on)* Have students read the lesson to learn the mathematical framework for dealing with positive and negative numbers.

Integer
Any positive or negative whole number including zero

Real number
Any number on the number line

Negative integer
A whole number less than zero

Positive integer
A whole number greater than zero

In arithmetic, you learned to add, subtract, multiply, and divide whole numbers greater than zero. In algebra, you also use whole numbers less than zero.

You can use a number line to show the relation between positive and negative whole numbers, also called **integers.**

Every point on the number line corresponds to a specific **real number.** A real number can be used to describe one and only one point on the number line. The arrows at the ends of the number line show that the line continues.

Numbers to the left of zero are **negative integers.** They are read as "negative 1, negative 2," and so on.

Whole numbers are the counting numbers 1, 2, 3, 4, . . . and zero.

Numbers to the right of zero are **positive integers.** They are read as "positive 1, positive 2," and so on.

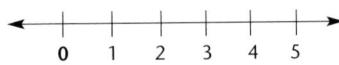

Zero is neither positive nor negative.

A negative integer is always indicated by the use of a minus ($-$) sign. A positive integer may be indicated by a plus ($+$) sign or no sign at all.

Name _____ Date _____ Period _____ | **Workbook Activity** **68** Chapter 8, Lesson 1

The Real Number Line and Integers

EXAMPLE |−3| = 3   −3 is 3 units from 0.
The absolute value of |−3| is 3.

Directions Find the absolute value.

1. |−6| _____
2. |4| _____
3. |−8| _____
4. |0| _____
5. |11| _____
6. |−72| _____
7. |−31| _____
8. |25| _____
9. |−92| _____
10. |16| _____

Directions Name the opposite of each integer.

11. −6 _____
12. −9 _____
13. 15 _____
14. −24 _____
15. 11 _____
16. −52 _____
17. 84 _____
18. −5 _____
19. −42 _____
20. 38 _____

Directions Write an integer that describes each situation.

21. The Chicago Bulls make a three-point shot in basketball. _____
22. The Green Bay Packers lose ten yards in a football game. _____
23. The stock of Company XYZ falls eight dollars in value. _____
24. School Inc., gains five dollars on the stock market. _____
25. Eighty dollars is taken out of a paycheck for taxes. _____
26. Pay fifty-five dollars for electric. _____
27. Win three hundred dollars in a raffle. _____
28. The temperature falls to twenty degrees below zero. _____
29. In five minutes, the test begins. _____
30. The test began four minutes ago. _____

AGS Publishing. Permission is granted to reproduce for classroom use only. ■ *Mathematics: Pathways*

TRL **Workbook Activity 68**

Name _____ Date _____ Period _____ | **Activity** **65** Chapter 8, Lesson 1

Real Number Line and Integers

Directions Find each absolute value.

1. |−8| _____
2. |−14| _____
3. |15| _____
4. |−23| _____
5. |−99| _____
6. |87| _____
7. |−7| _____
8. |29| _____
9. |−43| _____
10. |12| _____

Directions Name the opposite of each integer.

11. −17 _____
12. 50 _____
13. −62 _____
14. −9 _____
15. 13 _____
16. −51 _____
17. 38 _____
18. 25 _____
19. −47 _____
20. 4 _____

Directions Write an integer that describes each situation.

21. A hockey player is sent to the time-out box for five minutes. _____
22. Mike can jump three inches higher than the average jumper. _____
23. Susie can run the 100-m dash 4 seconds faster than Nancy. _____
24. Lisa deposited $75 into her checking account. _____
25. Jerry wrote a check for $85. _____
26. Albert can dive 200 feet below sea level. _____
27. Beth went sky-diving. The plane was 2,000 feet above the ground. _____
28. The temperature dropped fifteen degrees. _____
29. The temperature rose ten degrees. _____
30. Carla missed three problems on the quiz. _____

AGS Publishing. Permission is granted to reproduce for classroom use only. ■ *Mathematics: Pathways*

TRL **Activity 65**

Absolute value

The distance from zero of a number on a number line

Opposites

Numbers the same distance from zero but on different sides of zero on the number line

The **absolute value** of an integer is the distance between the integer and zero on the number line. The integer can be either to the left or to the right of zero. The symbol for absolute value is | |.

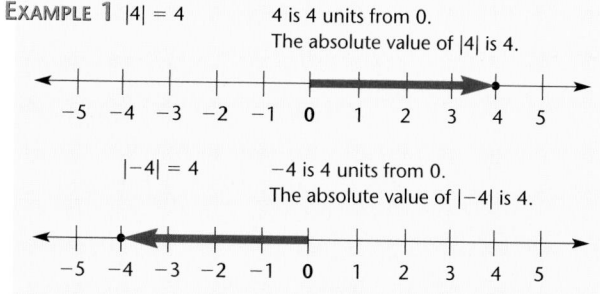

EXAMPLE 1 |4| = 4   4 is 4 units from 0.
The absolute value of |4| is 4.

|−4| = 4   −4 is 4 units from 0.
The absolute value of |−4| is 4.

Every number other than 0 has an **opposite** number. Opposites are the same distance from zero.

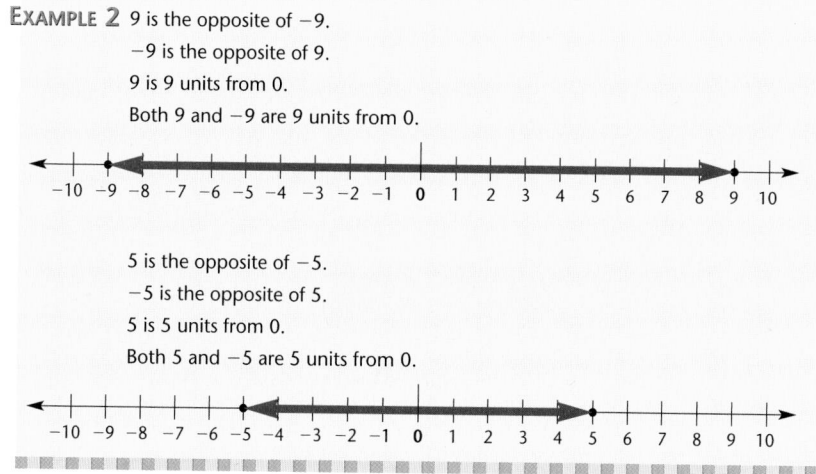

EXAMPLE 2 9 is the opposite of −9.
−9 is the opposite of 9.
9 is 9 units from 0.
Both 9 and −9 are 9 units from 0.

5 is the opposite of −5.
−5 is the opposite of 5.
5 is 5 units from 0.
Both 5 and −5 are 5 units from 0.

2 Teaching the Lesson

To dramatize the concept of absolute value, tape a number line measured in one-foot units on the floor, and have students walk in both directions away from zero. Ask each student to describe how far he or she walked. Distance is a positive number no matter which direction. Explain that, because absolute value measures *only* distance (number of units) from zero on the number line, it cannot be negative. Have students use string to measure the distance to zero for opposite pairs of numbers on your number line to confirm that opposites are equal distances from zero.

3 Reinforce and Extend

LEARNING STYLES

Auditory/Verbal

To help the class learn the lesson vocabulary, print the terms clearly on the board. Then read aloud examples such as the following. Have students name the concept(s) represented.

5 and −5 (*opposites, real numbers, integers*)

10,000 (*positive integer, real number*)

−10 (*negative integer, real number*)

a number inside || marks (*absolute value*)

what 12 is to −12 (*either absolute value or opposite*)

Learning Styles

Visual/Spatial

Draw a number line on the board that extends to +15 and −15. Call on students to name the values for the following sentences, and place the values on the number line:

You earn $6 baby-sitting. *(+6)*

The wind chill is 12 below zero. *(−12)*

The Lions took a ten-yard loss on the play. *(−10)*

We realized a net profit of $15 on the bake sale. *(+15)*

A mailbox post rises 4 feet above the ground; it is set 2 feet into the ground. *(+4; −2)*

Learning Styles

LEP/ESL

Some students may need help differentiating the right-left orientation of the number line. Post a laminated number line (labeled with *Right* and *Left*) on a bulletin board. As students complete Exercise A, have them use water-based markers to place absolute values on the line. Ask them to state what this display shows. *(All absolute values are positive numbers, to the right of zero.)* Clean the line, and have students add pairs of opposites from Exercise B, explaining how they are alike and different. *(They are the same number of units from zero; negatives are to the left of zero, and positives are to the right of zero.)*

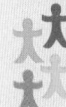

Exercise A Find each absolute value.

1. |3| 3

2. |−3| 3

3. |10| 10

4. |−6| 6

5. |−12| 12

6. |24| 24

7. |−73| 73

8. |−4| 4

Exercise B Name the opposite of each integer.

9. 4 −4

10. −7 7

11. −73 73

12. 73 −73

13. 8 −8

14. −12 12

15. 1 −1

16. −9 9

Exercise C Solve these problems using the number line.

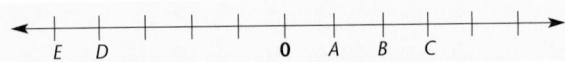

17. Which letters represent positive real numbers? *A, B, C*

18. Which letters represent negative real numbers? *D, E*

19. Which letter is the greatest distance from zero? *E*

20. Which letter represents the greatest absolute value? *E*

Math in Your Life

In the Red

Positive and negative numbers play an important role in finance and accounting. The bank transfer of money is noted as positive or negative when money is moved from one account to another. In accounting, negative sums are often written inside brackets in red. For example, ($250) means a debt of $250.

PROBLEM SOLVING

Exercise D Give an integer that describes each situation.

21. A gain of 3 yards in a football game
+3

22. A loss of 15 yards in a football game
−15

23. A withdrawal of $40 from a bank account
−40

24. A deposit of $100 in a bank account
+100

25. A temperature of 13°F below zero
−13

26. A temperature of 32°F above zero
+32

27. Ten seconds before space shuttle launch time
−10

28. Thirty seconds after launch time
+30

29. An altitude of 2,500 feet above sea level
+2,500

30. An ocean depth of 900 feet below sea level
−900

Have small groups of students search reference books, online encyclopedias, or the Internet (check under GIS Maps in search engine) to find the heights of several landmarks and the depths of several undersea features. Ask students to make a number line on which they can show these features and decide which numbers will be positive and which negative. Suggest that they first decide what unit to use (one unit such as an inch might need to stand for 1,000 feet, for example). Then have groups use rulers and pencils to construct their number lines.

MODELING

Have students make a human number line. Ask for three volunteers; these students will work in shifts to put the other students on the number line. Have the number line face the three students. Write a variety of integers on separate sheets of paper, and randomly hand them out to members of the number line. The three students will observe the order and put each student into line according to the number he or she holds (from left to right). They can only exchange the numbers (for example, if −2 is before −10, then the student will tell −2 to switch places with −10); they cannot move and squeeze students into place. Each of the three students moving the numbers will take a turn controlling the number line.

Lesson at a Glance

Chapter 8 Lesson 2

Overview This lesson introduces the concepts of consecutive order among integers and "greater than" and "less than" in comparing integers.

Objectives

- To compare two numbers and determine which is greater
- To compare two numbers and determine which is smaller
- To compare integers using the < and > symbols

Student Pages 208–209

Teacher's Resource Library

Workbook Activity 69

Activity 66

Alternative Activity 66

Mathematics Vocabulary

consecutive

---

1 Warm-Up Activity

Read a list of basketball game final scores (some with winning score first, some not), and have students write the scores as you read them. Ask students to describe how they wrote the scores down. (Most will pair scores in the order they were given.) Discuss reasons why it might be useful to list the winning score first. Putting sets of numbers in order is a common task. Have students read to learn about ordering and comparing numbers.

2 Teaching the Lesson

Assess students' understanding of number order and consecutive order by giving them sets of numbers to place in number line order. After students write the numbers in order on the board, have them star sets that are consecutive.

6, 2, 51, −20, −3, 12
(−20, −3, 2, 6, 12, 51)

4, −2, 0, 1, −1, 2, 3
(−2, −1, 0, 1, 2, 3, 4; ★)

Lesson 2 Comparing Integers

Consecutive
Following one after the other in order

Integers can be arranged in an increasing or decreasing order. **Consecutive** integers are integers arranged from least to greatest or greatest to least without any missing integers. The integers on a number line are consecutive integers.

You can use a number line to compare two integers. On a number line, the greater of two numbers is the number farthest to the right.

EXAMPLE 1 Compare 2 and −3.

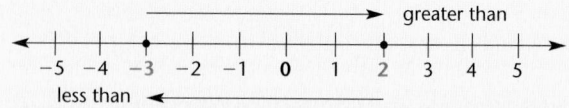

2 is to the *right* of −3 on the number line.
2 is *greater* than −3.
In symbols: 2 > −3   > means "is greater than"

−3 is to the *left* of 2 on the number line.
−3 is *less* than 2.
In symbols: −3 < 2   < means "is less than"

EXAMPLE 2 Compare −1 and −5.

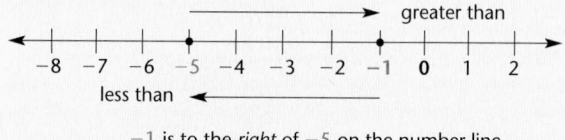

−1 is to the *right* of −5 on the number line.
−1 is *greater* than −5.
In symbols: −1 > −5

−5 is to the *left* of −1 on the number line.
−5 is *less* than −1.
In symbols: −5 < −1

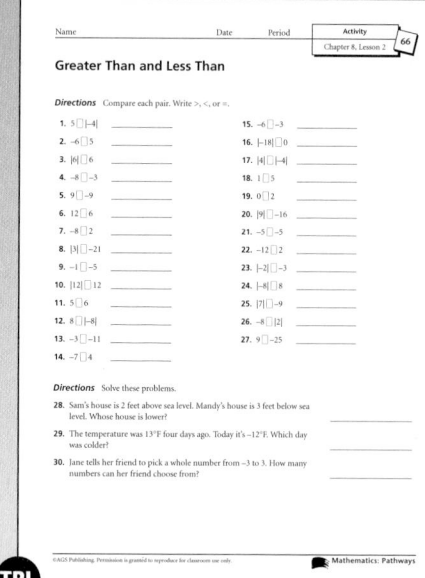

Workbook Activity 69   **Activity 66**

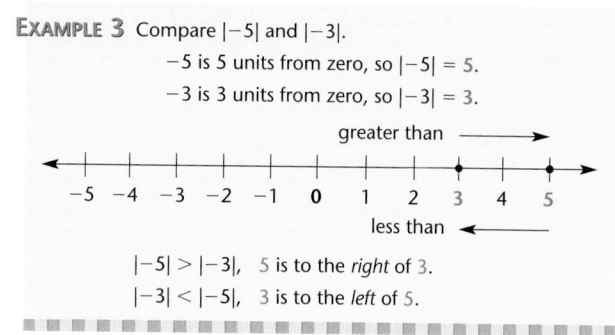

EXAMPLE 3 Compare $|-5|$ and $|-3|$.

-5 is 5 units from zero, so $|-5| = 5$.

-3 is 3 units from zero, so $|-3| = 3$.

greater than →

$$-5 \quad -4 \quad -3 \quad -2 \quad -1 \quad 0 \quad 1 \quad 2 \quad 3 \quad 4 \quad 5$$

← less than

$|-5| > |-3|$, 5 is to the *right* of 3.

$|-3| < |-5|$, 3 is to the *left* of 5.

Exercise A Compare each pair. Use $>$, $<$, or $=$.

1. $5 \blacksquare 2$ $>$
2. $11 \blacksquare -10$ $>$
3. $12 \blacksquare 11$ $>$
4. $8 \blacksquare 3$ $>$
5. $-4 \blacksquare 0$ $<$
6. $2 \blacksquare -2$ $>$
7. $|-5| \blacksquare 1$ $>$

8. $|-3| \blacksquare |-2|$ $>$
9. $8 \blacksquare -8$ $>$
10. $|1| \blacksquare |-2|$ $<$
11. $|13| \blacksquare |-7|$ $>$
12. $-11 \blacksquare -4$ $<$
13. $6 \blacksquare -2$ $>$
14. $5 \blacksquare |-5|$ $=$

15. $|-6| \blacksquare -6$ $>$
16. $-7 \blacksquare -6$ $<$
17. $15 \blacksquare 11$ $>$
18. $-4 \blacksquare -2$ $<$
19. $|-7| \blacksquare -2$ $>$
20. $-5 \blacksquare -7$ $>$

PROBLEM SOLVING

Exercise B Solve these problems.

21. Marlene lists these five numbers and says that they are consecutive integers: $-2, -1, 0, 1, 2, 3$. Is she right? Tell why or why not.

22. Kito is drawing and labeling a number line. Where would she place -9 in relation to $+3$? Why?

23. Aaron wants to know which is less, -3 or -5. Draw a number line to show him which number is less.

24. The temperature was 0°F on Saturday and -11°F today. Which temperature is higher? Explain.

25. Cory says that he is thinking of an integer that is 8 units from 0. Can you be sure that the integer he is thinking of is greater than 0? Explain.

See Teacher's Edition for answers.

Integers Chapter 8 **209**

Lesson at a Glance

Chapter 8 Lesson 3

Overview This lesson presents patterns for adding and subtracting odd and even integers.

Objectives

■ To identify integers as odd or even

■ To add, subtract, and multiply integers

■ To note the pattern of answers obtained by operations on odd and even numbers

Student Pages 210–211

Teacher's Resource Library **TRL**

Workbook Activity 70

Activity 67

Alternative Activity 67

1 Warm-Up Activity

Count by twos to 20, and ask students to describe this set of numbers. (*Answers may include even numbers and numbers divisible by 2.*) Write the words *even* and *odd* on the board, and ask students what they mean in math. (*divisible by 2; not divisible by 2*) Have students read the lesson to find out whether an odd number can ever be even and vice versa.

2 Teaching the Lesson

Discuss why zero is considered an even integer. (*It is consecutive with −1 and +1 on the number line; even numbers alternate with odd numbers. Moreover, any number ending with 0 is a multiple of 2.*)

Use the marginal note to review the concept of place. Students who are skeptical about relying only on the ones digit can use a calculator to check various large numbers by dividing them by 2.

Have students create additional examples to test the patterns for adding, subtracting, and multiplying even and odd integers.

Lesson 3 Even and Odd Integers

Integers that have a factor of 2 without leaving a remainder are even integers. $-6, -4, -2, 0, +2, +4,$ and $+6$ are examples of even integers.

Integers that do not have a factor of 2 are odd integers. $-5, -3, -1, +1, +3,$ and $+5$ are examples of odd integers.

Zero is an even integer.

You can tell whether a number is even or odd by checking the digit in the ones position. If the digit in the ones position is odd, the number is odd; if the digit in the ones position is even, the number is even.

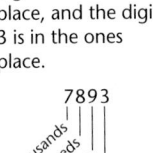

In 7,893, the digit 7 is in the thousands place, the digit 8 is in the hundreds place, the digit 9 is in the tens place, and the digit 3 is in the ones place.

EXAMPLE 1 2,987,654,321 is an odd integer because 1 is odd.
12,345,678 is an even integer because 8 is even.

Consecutive even integers are even integers arranged in order without any missing even integers. For example, $-10, -8, -6, -4, -2, 0, +2, +4, +6, +8, +10$ are consecutive even integers. Consecutive odd integers are odd integers arranged in order without any missing integers. For example, $-9, -7, -5, -3, -1, +1, +3, +5, +7, +9$ are consecutive odd integers. In both of these examples, the integers are ordered from least to greatest.

When you add or subtract integers, you can predict whether the sum or difference will be odd or even.

Adding Integers	Subtracting Integers
even + even = even	even − even = even
even + odd = odd	even − odd = odd
odd + odd = even	odd − odd = even

EXAMPLE 2

4 + 6 = 10	6 − 4 = 2
4 + 5 = 9	6 − 1 = 5
5 + 3 = 8	5 − 3 = 2

210 *Chapter 8 Integers*

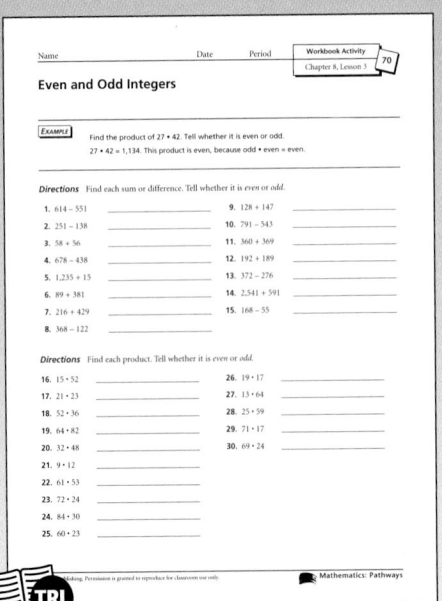

Workbook Activity 70

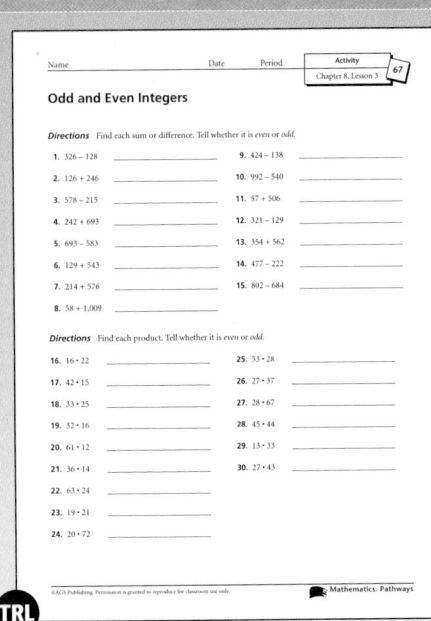

Activity 67

You can also predict whether or not a product will be even.

Multiplying Integers

even • even = even

even • odd = even

odd • odd = odd

EXAMPLE 3   4 • 6 = 24   4 • 5 = 20   3 • 5 = 15

Try This

Make a table showing the result of dividing even by even, even by odd, and odd by odd numbers.

Try This

even ÷ even = even or odd;
64 ÷ 8 = 8,
44 ÷ 4 = 11

even ÷ odd = even;
24 ÷ 3 = 8

odd ÷ odd = odd;
35 ÷ 5 = 7

Exercise A Tell whether the following numbers are odd or even.

1. 24,004   even

2. 35,793   odd

3. 15,378   even

4. 210,244,663   odd

5. 13,459,235,743,221   odd

Exercise B Find each sum or difference. Tell whether it is even or odd.

6. 432 + 444   876, even

7. 523 − 352   171, odd

8. 134 + 235   369, odd

9. 793 + 583   1,376, even

10. 669 − 571   98, even

11. 1,224 + 3,468   4,692, even

12. 554 + 33   587, odd

13. 221 − 123   98, even

14. 334 − 55   279, odd

15. 664 − 334   330, even

Exercise C Find each product. Tell whether it is even or odd.

16. 24 • 36   864, even

17. 39 • 36   1,404, even

18. 27 • 23   621, odd

19. 22 • 43   946, even

20. 59 • 73   4,307, odd

Exercise D Tell which operation will give the desired even or odd integer. Then solve each problem. There may be more than one correct answer.

21. 4 ☐ 5 = ■ (even)   •, 20

22. 6 ☐ 3 = ■ (even)   •, 18

23. 6 ☐ 3 = ■ (odd)   +, 9 or −, 3

24. 9 ☐ 3 = ■ (even)   +, 12 or −, 6

25. 9 ☐ 3 = ■ (odd)   •, 27

Try This

Students will avoid the frustration of working with remainders (or decimals) if they construct their tables using familiar fact families:

2, 3, 6	2, 2, 4	3, 5, 15
6, 7, 42	4, 5, 20	8, 9, 72

3 **Reinforce and Extend**

MENTAL MATH

Before students compute answers for Exercises B and C, have them predict even or odd answers by referring to the tables in the lesson. Ask students to put this paper aside; compute the sums, differences, and products; and see whether their predictions (and the tables) are correct.

LEARNING STYLES

LEP/ESL

Give students hands-on experience of the meanings of *even* and *odd*. Create bulletin-board "banks" (boxes, envelopes, or lists) of even and odd numbers. As each number is presented, have students divide it by 2 on the board. If there is a remainder, the number cannot be divided into two even pieces without parts left over, and it is deposited in the Odd Bank. If there is no remainder, the number can be divided into two even pieces and can be added to the Even Bank.

Lesson at a Glance

Chapter 8 Lesson 4

Overview This lesson establishes rules for adding two positive integers and a positive and a negative integer.

Objectives

■ To visualize sums of integers on the number line

■ To add positive integers to positive or negative integers

Student Pages 212–213

Teacher's Resource Library

Workbook Activity 71

Activity 68

Alternative Activity 68

1 ⚡ Warm-Up Activity

On the board, draw a simple glass beaker filled with fluid. Label the fluid *−4 degrees*. Have students place the temperature of the fluid on a number line. Ask, "If you add heat to the fluid and raise the temperature 3 degrees, what is the new temperature?" *(−1 degree)* Have students explain how they found the answer, demonstrating on the number line.

2 ⚡ Teaching the Lesson

Students may wonder why Example 2 is not expressed as $5 − 3 = 2$. Remind them that this is an addition problem, and $−3$ is simply one of the addends. In fact, the problem could be written $5 + (−3) = 2$. However, it is easier to visualize the operation on the number line if you begin with the negative, left of zero. Work several problems in Exercise A together, using a number line on the board to demonstrate, before assigning the remainder of the exercise for independent work.

You can use the number line to help you find and understand how to add positive integers to other positive or negative integers.

EXAMPLE 1 Find the sum of $3 + 5$.

Begin at 3.
Then move to the right 5 units.
$3 + 5 = 8$

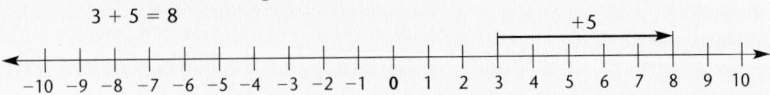

> **Rule**
> Adding a positive to a positive gives a result farther to the right on the number line.

EXAMPLE 2 Find the sum of $−3 + 5$.

Begin at $−3$.
Then move to the right 5 units.
$−3 + 5 = 2$

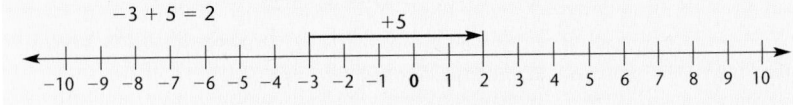

> **Rule**
> Adding a positive to a negative gives a result farther to the right on the number line.

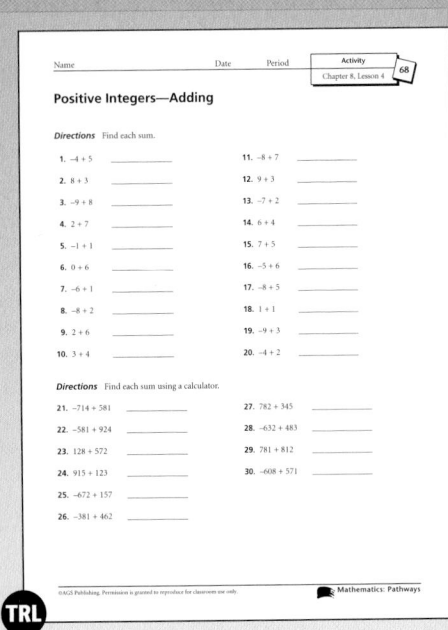

Workbook Activity 71

Activity 68

Exercise A Find each sum.

1.	3 + 8	11		
2.	4 + 6	10		
3.	−2 + 7	5		
4.	−6 + 4	−2		
5.	−6 + 6	0		
6.	−2 + 9	7		
7.	−4 + 7	3		
8.	−7 + 3	−4		

9.	−7 + 2	−5		
10.	6 + 9	15		
11.	−12 + 4	−8		
12.	10 + 9	19		
13.	0 + 5	5		
14.	−7 + 7	0		
15.	−6 + 8	2		
16.	−8 + 2	−6		

 **Calculator Practice**

You can use the [+/−] key on a calculator to add positive and negative integers.

EXAMPLE 3 Find the sum −3 + 5.

Press *3* [+/−] [+] *5* [=].

The display reads *2*.

Exercise B Find each sum using a calculator.

17. −441 + 239   −202   **19.** −57 + 784   727

18. 485 + 332   817   **20.** 888 + 424   1,312

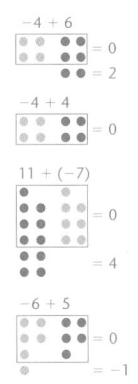

Build a Model

Use any 2-color manipulatives to represent positive and negative numbers. For example, you may use red and blue tiles, black and white counters, or red and white beans.

−7   4   −7 + 4   −7 + 4

Use one color to show −7.   Use the second color to show 4.   Pair off the two colors. Remove the pairs.   The remaining color is the answer, or −3.

Use the 2-color manipulatives to show:

−4 + 6   −4 + 4   11 + (−7)   −6 + 5

Integers   *Chapter 8*   **213**

Lesson at a Glance

Chapter 8 Lesson 5

Overview This lesson uses the number line to demonstrate adding negative integers.

Objectives

- To move left along the number line to represent the sum of a positive or negative integer and a negative integer
- To add negative integers to positive or negative integers

Student Pages 214–215

Teacher's Resource Library

Workbook Activity 72

Activity 69

Alternative Activity 69

1 Warm-Up Activity

Encourage students to discuss this question: "When could you add two numbers and get a sum with a value smaller than either addend?" *(when you add two negative numbers)* Have the class read the lesson to learn how to model the addition of negative integers.

2 Teaching the Lesson

Some students may try to locate both addends on the number line, confusing the issue. Explain that the vital part of this procedure is a movement.

First, place a finger on the first addend.

Next, slide the finger left the number of units in the second addend.

Your new location is the sum.

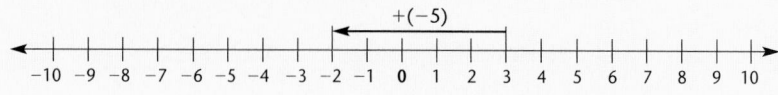

You can use the number line to help you find and understand how to add negative integers to other positive or negative integers.

EXAMPLE 1 Find the sum of $3 + (-5)$.

Begin at 3.
Then move to the left 5 units.
$3 + (-5) = -2$

Rule
Adding a negative to a positive gives a result farther to the left on the number line.

EXAMPLE 2 Find the sum of $-3 + (-5)$.

Begin at -3.
Then move to the left 5 units.
$-3 + (-5) = -8$

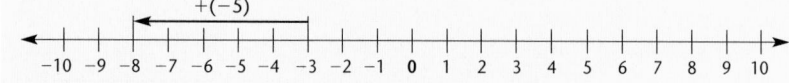

Writing About Mathematics

Will you always get a negative number if you add a negative number to another number? Explain.

Rule
Adding a negative to a negative gives a result farther to the left on the number line.

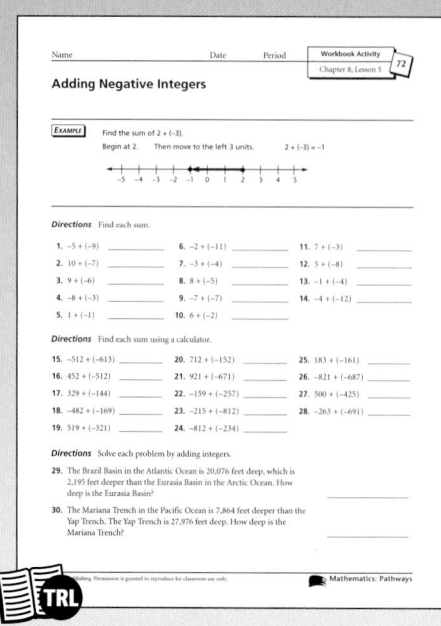

Workbook Activity 72

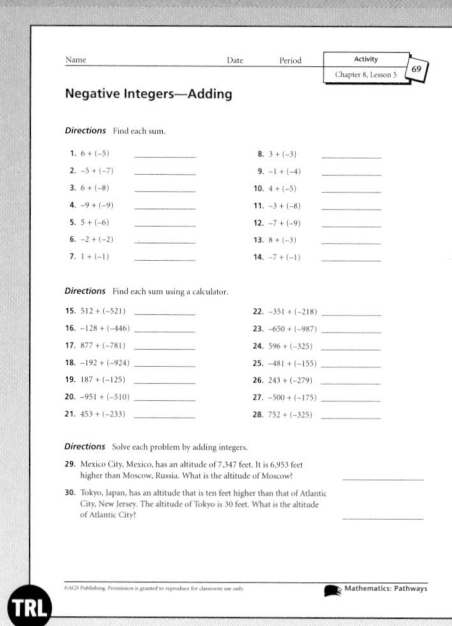

Activity 69

Exercise A Find each sum.

1. $-2 + (-7)$ -9 **4.** $4 + (-8)$ -4

2. $-6 + (-6)$ -12 **5.** $12 + (-4)$ 8

3. $-2 + (-9)$ -11 **6.** $28 + (-32)$ -4

 **Calculator Practice** You can use the +/− key on a calculator to add positive and negative integers.

EXAMPLE 3   Find the sum of $5 + (-7)$.
Press 5 + 7 +/− =.
The display reads -2.

Exercise B Find each sum using a calculator.

7. $-359 + (-243)$ -602 **10.** $233 + (-873)$ -640

8. $112 + (-444)$ -332 **11.** $975 + (-105)$ 870

9. $-576 + (-495)$ $-1,071$ **12.** $-649 + (-573)$ $-1,222$

 **PROBLEM SOLVING**

Exercise C Solve each problem by adding integers.

13. An airplane flying at 25,000 feet climbs an additional 2,000 feet. What is the final altitude of the airplane?   27,000 ft

14. At midnight the temperature was 29°C. During the day the temperature fell 4 degrees. What was the temperature at the end of the day?   25°C

15. A sky diver 2,351 feet above a cornfield suddenly drops 1,334 feet. How far above the cornfield is the sky diver?   1,017 ft

GROUP PROBLEM SOLVING

 Organize the class into groups of six. Each group forms a club. Give each club a treasury balance and a list showing money spent and earned by the club. The group's task is to determine the current balance, using a chart to show how the balance changes after each expense or deposit. Have students show their operations on another sheet of paper.

MANIPULATIVES

 Adding Negative Integers

Materials: Cuisenaire Rods, Manipulatives Master 5 (Number Line)

Group Practice: Follow the procedures for adding positive integers in Lesson 4. Build models of the addends on page 214. Find the sum of two negative integers by placing rods end to end below the Number Line. For sums of opposite sign integers, place the negative model below the Number Line and the positive model directly above the negative model. Find the sum. Repeat with several more problems generated by students.

Student Practice: Use the rods and Number Line for Exercise A, problems 1–5.

3 Reinforce and Extend

CALCULATOR

 Have students use a calculator to compute answers to the problems in Exercise B. To enter factors with different signs (as in problem 8):

Press 112 + 444 +/− =.

The display shows -332.

Have students note where their calculator places the minus sign. (It may follow the number instead of preceding it.)

Lesson at a Glance

Chapter 8 Lesson 6

Overview This lesson explains subtraction as adding a number's opposite and models subtraction on the number line.

Objectives

- To model subtraction of positive and negative integers on the number line
- To convert subtraction expressions to addition expressions
- To subtract positive and negative integers from positive and negative integers

Student Pages 216–219

Teacher's Resource Library TRL

Workbook Activities 73–74

Activity 70

Alternative Activity 70

1 Warm-Up Activity

Remind students that subtraction means "taking away." On the board, use + and − tiles to model the expression 3 − 5 (read aloud as "three take away five"):

Add three − tiles; these cancel, or take away, the + tiles.

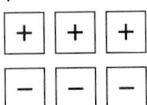

Then ask students how they could take away two more. (*Possible answer: Add two +/− pairs—each equal to zero— then remove the two + tiles. Two − tiles remain.*) Tell students that they will now explore ways of showing subtraction problems with answers less than zero.

2 Teaching the Lesson

Use + and − tiles as an alternative to the number line to show subtraction. The second example [−3 − (−5)] appears as:

216 *Chapter 8*

A number line can be used to show that subtracting a number gives the same result as adding the opposite of the number.

EXAMPLE 1 Find the difference of 3 − (+5).

Begin at 3.
Then move to the left 5 units.
3 − (+5) = −2

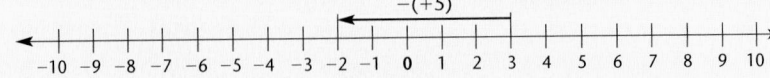

Note that 3 − (+5) = −2 and 3 + (−5) = −2 because subtracting 5 is the same as adding −5.

> **Rule**
> Subtracting a positive from a positive gives a result farther to the left on the number line.

EXAMPLE 2 Find the difference of −3 − (−5).

Begin at −3.
Then move to the right 5 units.
−3 − (−5) = 2

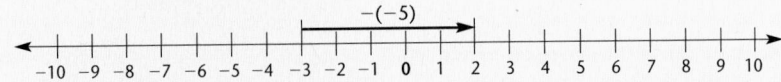

Note that −3 − (−5) = 2 and −3 + 5 = 2 because 5 and −5 are opposites. Subtracting is the same as adding the opposite.

> **Rule**
> Subtracting a negative from a negative gives a result farther to the right on the number line.

216 *Chapter 8 Integers*

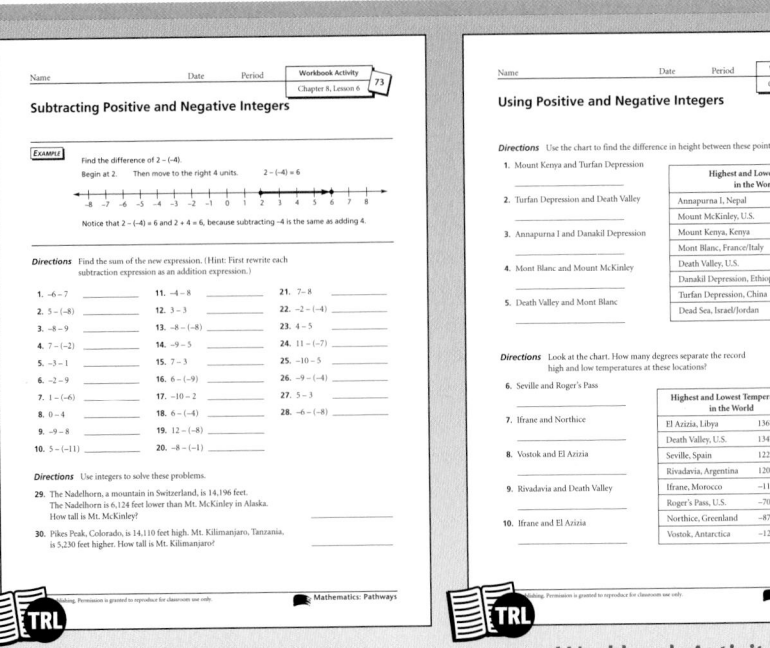

Workbook Activity 73   **Workbook Activity 74**

EXAMPLE 3 Find the difference of $3 - (-5)$.

Begin at 3.
Then move to the right 5 units.
$3 - (-5) = 8$
This is the same as $3 + 5 = 8$.

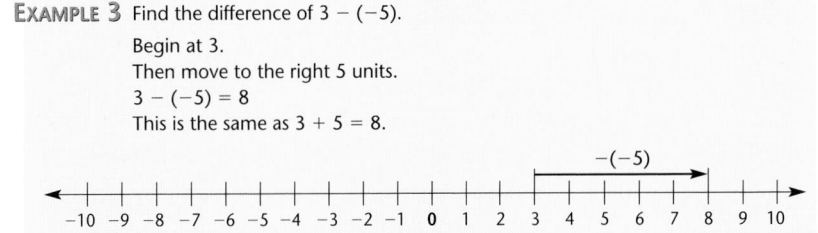

Rule

Subtracting a negative from a positive gives a result farther to the right on the number line.

EXAMPLE 4 Find the difference of $-3 - (+5)$.

Begin at -3.
Then move to the left 5 units.
$-3 - (+5) = -8$

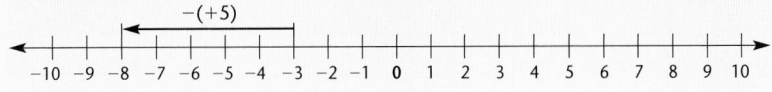

Rule

Subtracting a positive from a negative gives a result farther to the left on the number line.

Look again at addition of positive and negative integers. Compare the results with subtraction of integers.

Subtraction		Addition
$3 - (+5) = -2$	is the same as	$3 + (-5) = -2$
$-3 - (-5) = 2$	is the same as	$-3 + 5 = 2$
$3 - (-5) = 8$	is the same as	$3 + 5 = 8$
$-3 - (+5) = -8$	is the same as	$-3 + (-5) = -8$
Subtraction	is the same as	adding the opposite.

Assess students' understanding of subtraction of negative integers by asking them to explain how subtracting a negative integer is like addition. (*To subtract a negative integer, you change its sign to make it opposite, and add.*)

As students explain their answers to Exercise C, they can write each problem on the board and refer to a number line to indicate "direction moved." (*Large numbers preclude the actual use of a number line to solve the problems.*)

MANIPULATIVES

Subtracting Integers

Materials: Cuisenaire Rods, Manipulatives Master 5 (Number Line)

Group Practice: Review how to change subtraction to addition of the opposite, using the examples on pages 216–217. Follow the procedures introduced in Lessons 4 and 5 to find sums using the Cuisenaire Rods and the Number Line.

Student Practice: Use the rods and Number Line for problems 1–10 in Exercise A and problems 11–20 in Exercise B.

ONLINE CONNECTION

Have students visit www.airproducts.com/ productstewardship. Click on *Fast Facts* and then *Properties* to learn about atmospheric gases and to practice subtracting negative integers. Have them write down the boiling points of six gases and then order the boiling points from highest to lowest. Direct students to find the differences in the boiling points of several pairs of gases—hydrogen and carbon dioxide, for example.

Name _____ Date _____ Period _____

Activity — Chapter 8, Lesson 6 — 70

Subtracting Positive, Negative Integers

Directions Rewrite each subtraction expression as an addition expression. Find the sum of the new expression.

1. $4 - (-8)$ _____
2. $-6 - 7$ _____
3. $8 - 6$ _____
4. $-2 - (-5)$ _____
5. $7 - 3$ _____
6. $-8 - (-1)$ _____
7. $0 - 1$ _____
8. $-2 - 7$ _____
9. $-6 - (-5)$ _____
10. $8 - 5$ _____
11. $4 - (-8)$ _____
12. $-5 - 0$ _____
13. $1 - (-6)$ _____
14. $-3 - (-5)$ _____
15. $5 - (-4)$ _____

16. $-3 - 3$ _____
17. $9 - (-8)$ _____
18. $-2 - 6$ _____
19. $-8 - 4$ _____
20. $7 - (-9)$ _____
21. $9 - 5$ _____
22. $-5 - (-6)$ _____
23. $1 - 7$ _____
24. $-3 - 4$ _____
25. $-5 - 2$ _____
26. $7 - (-8)$ _____
27. $-9 - (-5)$ _____
28. $0 - (-3)$ _____

Directions Use integers to solve these problems.

29. Black Mountain, Kentucky, is 3,820 feet lower than Mt. Olympus, Washington. Mt. Olympus is 7,965 feet high. How tall is Black Mountain?

30. The tallest peak of the Kirkpatrick mountains in Antarctica is 2,855 feet taller than the highest peak of the Coman mountains in Antarctica. The highest peak of the Coman is 12,000 feet. How tall is the tallest peak of the Kirkpatrick mountains?

©AGS Publishing. Permission is granted to reproduce for classroom use only.   Mathematics: Pathways

RL

Activity 70

LEARNING STYLES

Auditory/Verbal

To give students extra practice in subtracting integers, provide them with problems such as the following:

7 − 6	*(1)*
6 − 7	*(−1)*
−7 − 6	*(−13)*
7 − (−6)	*(13)*

Explaining each step as students model the subtractions on a number line will help them remember the rules for subtracting integers with different signs.

MENTAL MATH

Duplicate the following table on the board, and have students solve the subtraction problems mentally. As they provide answers, add them to the table. Suggest that students watch carefully for patterns.

10 − 1 = *(9)*	10 − (−1) = *(11)*
10 − 2 = *(8)*	10 − (−2) = *(12)*
10 − 3 = *(7)*	10 − (−3) = *(13)*
10 − 4 = *(6)*	10 − (−4) = *(14)*

Create a second table, making all the 10s negative, and repeat the process. Have the class answer true or false to each statement, referring to the table for confirmation:

Subtracting a positive number takes away, or decreases, value. *(true)*

Subtracting a negative number takes away, or decreases, value. *(false)*

A minus next to a negative is the same as a positive. *(true)*

> **Rule**
>
> To subtract a positive or negative integer, add the opposite of the integer.

Exercise A Rewrite each subtraction expression as an addition expression. Find the sum of the new expression.

1. $4 - (+5)$
   $4 + (-5) = -1$

2. $8 - 4$
   $8 + (-4) = 4$

3. $-6 - (-5)$
   $-6 + 5 = -1$

4. $-9 - (-11)$
   $-9 + 11 = 2$

5. $7 - (+5)$
   $7 + (-5) = 2$

6. $-6 - 4$
   $-6 + (-4) = -10$

7. $-2 - (+4)$
   $-2 + (-4) = -6$

8. $10 - (+7)$
   $10 + (-7) = 3$

9. $7 - (-4)$
   $7 + 4 = 11$

10. $5 - 4$
   $5 + (-4) = 1$

Exercise B Find each difference.

11. $3 - (+7)$ $\quad -4$

12. $6 - 2$ $\quad 4$

13. $-7 - (-7)$ $\quad 0$

14. $-8 - (-13)$ $\quad 5$

15. $9 - (+2)$ $\quad 7$

16. $-5 - 2$ $\quad -7$

17. $-3 - (+5)$ $\quad -8$

18. $12 - (+5)$ $\quad 7$

19. $9 - (-3)$ $\quad 12$

20. $6 - 3$ $\quad 3$

Technology Connection

Bookkeeper—A Job Title of the Past?
Bookkeepers keep track of business expenses and income. Bookkeepers used to write down the business expenses and income in big books called ledgers. Back then, the name of the job fit the work. Today, most bookkeepers no longer "keep books." They use computer software programs instead. These programs are designed specially to do the bookkeeping. They can automatically and quickly calculate expenses and income that in the past had to be done by hand. Perhaps now bookkeepers need a new name.

Exercise C Solve these problems.

21. The highest point on Earth is Mount Everest, 29,028 feet above sea level. The shore of the Dead Sea, at 1,312 feet below sea level, is the lowest place on Earth's surface. What is the vertical distance from the shore of the Dead Sea to the top of Mount Everest? 30,340 ft

22. The average depth of the Arctic Ocean is 3,950 feet below sea level. The average depth of the Pacific Ocean is 12,900 feet below sea level. How much deeper is the Pacific Ocean? 8,950 ft

23. The highest recorded temperature in North America was 134°F, recorded at Death Valley, California. The lowest recorded temperature was −87°F, recorded at Northice, Greenland. How many degrees separate the two temperatures? 221°F

24. What is the difference between Alaska's record low temperature of −80°F and Utah's record low temperature of −69°F? 11°F

25. Astronauts board a space shuttle at T−90 minutes. Actual news coverage begins at T−15 minutes. How long are the astronauts on board before the news coverage begins?

75 minutes

KNOWING YOUR STUDENTS

Adolescents typically have active social lives and may be involved in drama, music, sports, and socializing. Because of this, you may find that homework (and even classroom work) does not get the attention it deserves. Students may be in a hurry to complete an assignment and might make common mistakes, such as misreading a sentence or skipping a word. If they read too quickly, they may miss critical information. Watch students as they subtract negative integers. Although a parenthesis may be used between the two negative signs, the student might omit the parenthesis and see only one negative. This would cause the student to subtract the two numbers instead of adding them.

LEARNING STYLES

LEP/ESL

Have students create a number line from +6 to −6. Use two paper number cubes (or dice) of different colors, and designate one color a + and the other color a −. Have students do the following:

- Pick one cube, toss it, and place it at the appropriate point on the number line.

- Toss the second cube. Move the first cube the number of units shown on the second cube. To subtract, move in the opposite direction that the cube's sign (color) indicates. Move left to subtract positive numbers; right to subtract negative numbers.

- Write out the subtraction problem in standard form on paper.

GROUP PROBLEM SOLVING

Ask the class to use history books or encyclopedias to find and list 12 dates (both B.C. and A.D.) when important events in history occurred. Make a large time line on the board to incorporate all these dates. Discuss the similarity between this line and a number line. (B.C. dates are left of 0 and, like subtracted negative numbers, must be added to get the total number of years since their occurrence.) Organize the class into groups of four, and assign each group three sets of dates:

- one A.D. and one B.C.

- two A.D.

- two B.C.

Students are to find how much time elapsed between the two events in each pair. They should write out each addition or subtraction problem and be prepared to model the solution using the time line.

Lesson at a Glance

Chapter 8 Lesson 7

Overview This lesson models the multiplication of integers on the number line.

Objectives

- To count multiples on the number line to model the product of a positive times a positive or negative integer
- To identify the sign of a product as positive or negative
- To multiply positive and negative integers

Student Pages 220–221

Teacher's Resource Library **TRL**

Workbook Activity 75

Activity 71

Alternative Activity 71

1 Warm-Up Activity

Review multiplication; remind students that it is the same as repeated addition. Ask, "If you walk up 5 flights of stairs, and each flight of stairs is 20 feet tall, how many feet have you gone up?" *(5 • 20 = 20 + 20 + 20 + 20 + 20 = 100)* Discuss how the equation would differ if you walked down those stairs. *[5 • (−20) = −20 + (−20), etc. = −100]* Tell students that they will now learn how to multiply positive and negative integers.

2 Teaching the Lesson

After reviewing the examples, have students use a number line on the board to model multiplication of several problems in Exercise A. Make sure that they understand that the numerical portion of the products in this lesson and the next are identical to those for whole numbers. The only new step here is calculating the *sign* of the product. As students complete problems in Exercise A, have them refer to the rules on page 220 to check the accuracy of the signs they have used.

Your study of arithmetic showed you that multiplication is the same as repeated addition. For example, 4 • 3 is the same as 3 + 3 + 3 + 3 = 12. You can use the idea of repeated addition and the number line to learn about multiplying two positive integers and multiplying a negative and a positive integer.

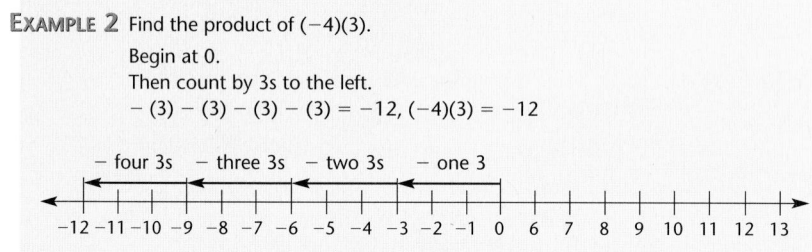

EXAMPLE 1 Find the product of (+4)(+3).

Begin at 0.
Then count by 3s to the right.
You will reach 12.
(+4)(+3) = 12

Rule

(Positive) • (Positive) = (Positive)

EXAMPLE 2 Find the product of (−4)(3).

Begin at 0.
Then count by 3s to the left.
− (3) − (3) − (3) − (3) = −12, (−4)(3) = −12

Rule

(Negative) • (Positive) = (Negative)

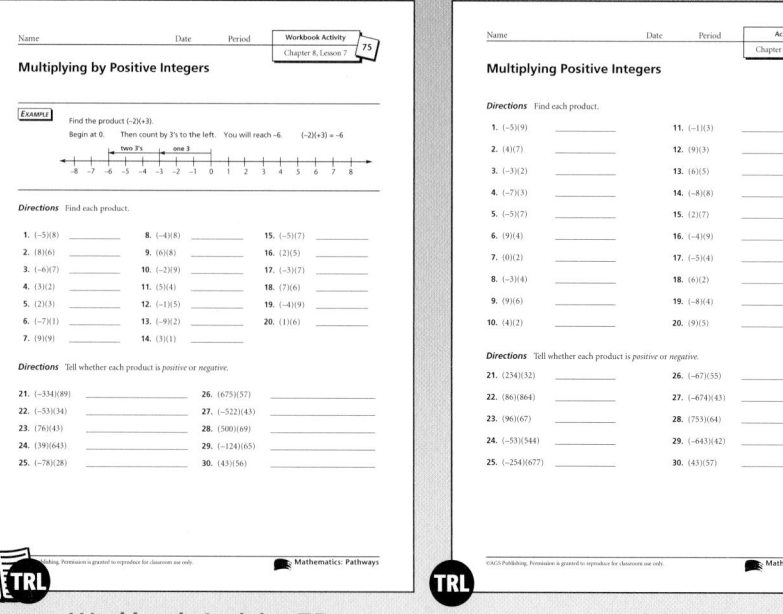

Workbook Activity 75   **Activity 71**

Exercise A Find each product.

1. (4)(5)	20	**11.** (−7)(3)	−21
2. (−4)(8)	−32	**12.** (2)(6)	12
3. (−6)(4)	−24	**13.** (7)(7)	49
4. (−6)(5)	−30	**14.** (5)(2)	10
5. (9)(11)	99	**15.** (−3)(5)	−15
6. (7)(5)	35	**16.** (−5)(12)	−60
7. (−4)(5)	−20	**17.** (−8)(13)	−104
8. (−4)(2)	−8	**18.** (−2)(9)	−18
9. (−7)(10)	−70	**19.** (−3)(9)	−27
10. (−4)(7)	−28	**20.** (−3)(6)	−18

Exercise B Tell whether each product is positive or negative.

21. (167)(192)	positive	**26.** (−64)(20)	negative
22. (−19)(421)	negative	**27.** (−15)(45)	negative
23. (−8)(58)	negative	**28.** (102)(10)	positive
24. (67)(76)	positive	**29.** (914)(4)	positive
25. (9)(74)	positive	**30.** (−72)(3)	negative

Estimation Activity

Estimate: Suppose you owe your friend $12.75. You help your friend with his paper route and get $3.00 deducted per week. How many weeks must you work to pay back your friend?

Solution: −$3.00 per week
$$4(−3) = −12$$

You must work a little longer than 4 weeks.

Integers   **221**

MANIPULATIVES

M Multiplying by Positive Integers

Materials: Cuisenaire Rods, Manipulatives Master 1 (Factor Frame)

Group Practice: To illustrate a product as the area of a rectangle, with factors as the dimensions of the rectangle, place the rod value of each factor on the left and top portions of the Factor Frame. Fill in the frame with rods, building a rectangle with the dimensions of the factors on the outside of the frame. Discuss the symbolic equivalent of the model in the frame. Apply rules for multiplying integers with same and different signs.

Student Practice: Use the rods and Factor Frame for Exercise A, problems 1–4, 6–8, 10–15, 18–20.

3 Reinforce and Extend

LEARNING STYLES

Visual/Spatial

Use a chart like the following to help students perceive patterns in multiplication of integers:

−25	−20	−15	−10	−5	5	5	10	15	20	25
−20	−16	−12	−8	−4	4	4	8	12	16	20
−15	−12	−9	−6	−3	3	3	6	9	12	15
−10	−8	−6	−4	−2	2	2	4	6	8	10
−5	−4	−3	−2	−1	1	1	2	3	4	5
−5	−4	−3	−2	−1	0	1	2	3	4	5

Ask volunteers to explain the pattern of the chart in their own words, using examples. You might also have students check their answers to Exercise A against the chart.

1 Warm-Up Activity

Write -20 on the board, and ask students to list all pairs of factors that can produce this product. *(20, -1; -20, 1; 2, -10; -2, 10; 4, -5; -4, 5)* Then ask, "What factors can produce the product $+20$?" *(Students will likely mention only the positive integer pairs 1, 20; 2, 10; and 4, 5.)* Explain that they will now read about positive products that result from negative factors.

2 Teaching the Lesson

A review of the commutative property will help students see that multiplying a positive by a negative integer gives the same result as multiplying a negative by a positive integer (modeled in Lesson 7). That is,

$$(4)(-3) = (-3)(4) = -12$$

and because the product of two numbers with opposite signs is negative, then

$$(-4)(3) = -12$$

as well.

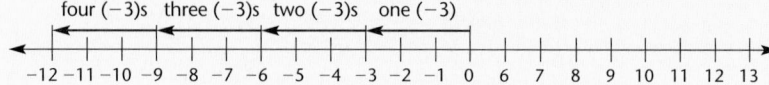
Remember that multiplication is the same as repeated addition. You can use the idea of repeated addition and the number line to learn about multiplying a negative and a positive integer and multiplying two negative integers.

EXAMPLE 1 Find the product of $(4)(-3)$.

Begin at 0.

Then count by -3s to the left.

$(-3) + (-3) + (-3) + (-3) = -12$, $(4)(-3) = -12$

four (-3)s   three (-3)s   two (-3)s   one (-3)

$-12\ -11\ -10\ -9\ -8\ -7\ -6\ -5\ -4\ -3\ -2\ -1\ 0\ \ 6\ 7\ 8\ 9\ 10\ 11\ 12\ 13$

Rule

(Positive) • (Negative) = (Negative)

EXAMPLE 2 Find the product of $(-4)(-3)$.

This case, $(-4)(-3)$ or a negative times a negative, cannot be shown on a number line. The product of $(-4)(-3)$ is $+12$. When you multiply a negative times a negative, use the following rule.

Rule

(Negative) • (Negative) = (Positive)

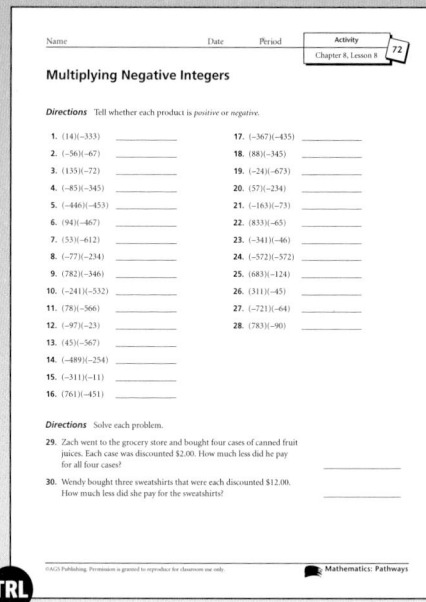

Workbook Activity 76   **Activity 72**

Exercise A Tell whether each product is positive, negative, or zero.

1. $(-322)(-457)$ positive
2. $(745)(-63)$ negative
3. $(433)(-221)$ negative
4. $(21)(-989)$ negative
5. $(-100)(-13)$ positive
6. $(923)(0)$ zero
7. $(444)(-333)$ negative
8. $(-197)(-842)$ positive
9. $(-2,093)(-22)$ positive
10. $(12)(-294)$ negative

PROBLEM SOLVING

Exercise B Solve each problem.

11. In each game of a three-game golf tournament, Nathaniel scored 5 under par. How many points under par did he score in the tournament?

12. During one winter day, the temperature fell 4 degrees each hour for 6 hours. How great was the total temperature drop?

13. The price of a stock fell $4 each day for 9 days. What was the total change in price?

14. Every year for the past five years, the forest preserve has lost 16 trees to disease or weather. How many trees have been lost in the past 5 years?

15. At a local movie theater, senior citizens receive a $2.00 discount. How much less will a senior pay to attend 15 movies in a year?

5 points under par

$-24°$

$-$36

-80 trees; 80 trees have been lost

$-$30.00

3   Reinforce and Extend

LEARNING STYLES

Logical/Mathematical

What happens when more than two negative integers are multiplied? Remind students that they know that a negative and a positive give a negative, and a negative and a negative give a positive. Have students experiment with powers of 10 to discover a pattern in numbers of negative factors compared with negative products. Students should complete a table similar to the one shown below. Have them use their tables and multiplication problems to explain the pattern they discover.

Power	Factors	Product
$(-10)^1$	$-10 \cdot 1$	-10
$(-10)^2$	$-10 \cdot (-10)$	100
$(-10)^3$	$-10 \cdot (-10) \cdot (-10)$	$-1,000$
$(-10)^4$		
$(-10)^5$		

(Students should conclude that odd numbers of negative factors produce negative products. To show the multiplications, students should pair up negative 10s. Every pair of -10s will result in a positive product that, when multiplied times any "leftover" or odd negative factor, will give a negative product.)

AT HOME

Have students research the costs of going to a movie theater in your community, including regular admission, youth admission, and any discount for early showings. Have them organize the information in table format and calculate the cost for a family of four to go to a movie in the following situations:

- at 7:15 P.M. if one person is a youth
- at 3:30 P.M. if two are youths
- at 9:30 P.M. if three are youths

Ask students to show their calculations.

Lesson at a Glance

Chapter 8 Lesson 9

Overview This lesson models the division of positive and negative integers and develops rules for identification of quotient and product signs.

Objectives

■ To model division of negative and positive integers on the number line

■ To divide negative and positive integers and identify the sign of a quotient

Student Pages 224–225

Teacher's Resource Library TRL

Workbook Activity 77

Activity 73

Alternative Activity 73

1 Warm-Up Activity

Remind students that, like addition and subtraction, multiplication and division are opposite operations. Write the following on the board:

3 • 6 = 18

Add groups of 3 six times.

18 ÷ 3 = 6

Subtract groups of 3 six times.

18 ÷ 6 = 3

Subtract groups of 6 three times.

Ask volunteers to explain how each division problem is related to the multiplication problem. Add a negative sign to a factor and discuss how the product changes. Have students read page 224 to learn how a negative dividend or divisor affects the sign of the quotient.

2 Teaching the Lesson

Point out to students that Example 1 could also show the 12 units divided into 3 equal segments of 4 units.

If students have trouble perceiving the relationship between multiplication and division, ask them to work a division

---

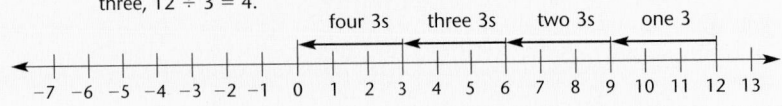

Recall that multiplication is the same as repeated addition. Division is the opposite of multiplication—repeated subtraction.

EXAMPLE 1 Find the quotient of 12 ÷ 3.

Begin at 12.
Then count by 3s to the left until you reach zero. You will have four groups of three, 12 ÷ 3 = 4.

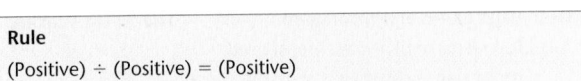

four 3s   three 3s   two 3s   one 3

−7 −6 −5 −4 −3 −2 −1 0 1 2 3 4 5 6 7 8 9 10 11 12 13

Rule

(Positive) ÷ (Positive) = (Positive)

Because multiplication and division are opposite operations, the rules for multiplying positive and negative integers are similar to the rules for dividing positive and negative integers.

Multiplication		Division
(3)(4) = 12 Rule (+)(+) = (+)	and	12 ÷ 4 = 3 Rule (+) ÷ (+) = (+)
(3)(−4) = −12 Rule (+)(−) = (−)	and	12 ÷ (−4) = −3 Rule (+) ÷ (−) = (−)
(−3)(4) = −12 Rule (−)(+) = (−)	and	(−12) ÷ (4) = −3 Rule (−) ÷ (+) = (−)
(−3)(−4) = 12 Rule (−)(−) = (+)	and	(−12) ÷ (−4) = 3 Rule (−) ÷ (−) = (+)

A general statement can be made that covers all the multiplication and division rules.

Rules

Like signs give positive products and quotients.

Unlike signs give negative products and quotients.

---

224 *Chapter 8 Integers*

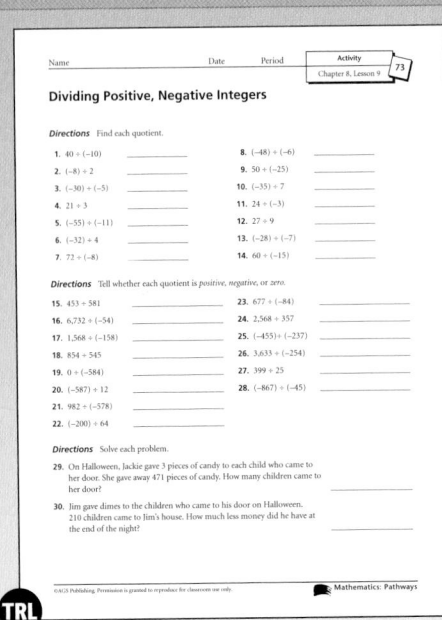

Workbook Activity 77   **Activity 73**

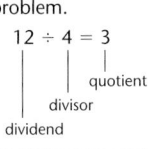

A quotient is the answer to a division problem.

$$12 \div 4 = 3$$

- quotient
- divisor
- dividend

Exercise A Find each quotient.

1. $4 \div 2$	2	**11.** $(-21) \div (-7)$	3
2. $32 \div (-4)$	-8	**12.** $(-12) \div (-6)$	2
3. $(-24) \div (4)$	-6	**13.** $(-7) \div (7)$	-1
4. $(30) \div (-5)$	-6	**14.** $(-50) \div (2)$	-25
5. $(-9) \div (-3)$	3	**15.** $(-15) \div (5)$	-3
6. $(45) \div (5)$	9	**16.** $(-60) \div (-5)$	12
7. $(20) \div (-4)$	-5	**17.** $(-88) \div (11)$	-8
8. $(-20) \div (-4)$	5	**18.** $(-18) \div (-2)$	9
9. $(10) \div (-5)$	-2	**19.** $(9) \div (-3)$	-3
10. $(-28) \div (-4)$	7	**20.** $(6) \div (-3)$	-2

Exercise B Tell whether each quotient is positive, negative, or zero.

21. $3{,}956 \div 43$	positive	**25.** $100 \div 20$	positive
22. $-6{,}324 \div 17$	negative	**26.** $-976 \div -331$	positive
23. $-221 \div -11$	positive	**27.** $671 \div -13$	negative
24. $-989 \div 21$	negative	**28.** $-1{,}970 \div 3$	negative

PROBLEM SOLVING

Exercise C Solve each problem.

29. The theater complex has 1,440 seats in six theaters. All theaters have the same number of seats. How many seats does each have? 240 seats

30. A submarine is moving underwater at -390 meters. It dives to that level in 13 minutes. How many meters does it dive per minute?
30 meters per minute

Try This

The sum of two integers is -25. The quotient of the integers is 4. What are the integers?

$-20, -5$

problem and check the answer. Ask, "What do you do to check your division?" *(multiply)* Students can then easily see the relationship and formulate many division problems from fact groups.

Try This

Help students begin the process of deduction by thinking about how much they know about the integers.

- Are the integers positive, negative, or both? *(Their sum is negative, so at least one is negative. The quotient is positive, and like signs give positive quotients, so both must be negative.)*

- What pairs of negative numbers add up to -25? *($-1, -24; -2, -23; -3, -22; -4, -21; -5, -20;$ and so on)*

3 Reinforce and Extend

LEARNING STYLES

Interpersonal/ Group Learning

Make 3×5 cards with positive and negative integers—one each for each integer from -20 to $+20$ except 0. Shuffle the cards, and have students play a division game. All players draw cards and place them face up on the table at the same time. The first player to correctly name the sign of the quotient of these two numbers wins a point. He or she also has the first chance to give the quotient of the two numbers for another point.

GROUP PROBLEM SOLVING

Review averaging (finding the mean by adding a set of numbers and then dividing by the number of items in the set). Have groups of five or six students record how many minutes it takes each member to get to school and find the average time for the group. As time allows, students can repeat this process for an expense that everyone in the group incurs, such as weekly lunches or snacks.

MANIPULATIVES

 Dividing Integers

Materials: Cuisenaire Rods, Manipulatives Master 1 (Factor Frame)

Group Practice: Review rules for multiplying and dividing same and opposite sign integers. Establish the connection between factors and products and between dividends, divisors, and quotients. Using Example 1 on page 224, build a rectangle of area 12 inside the Factor Frame using 3-rods (because 3 is the divisor and, therefore, one of the factors, or dimensions, of the rectangle). Place a 3-rod on the left side of the frame to represent the divisor. The rectangle represents the dividend. To find the quotient, place the rod that represents the missing dimension, or factor, on the top portion of the frame. Discuss the symbolic equivalent of the division model on the frame.

Student Practice: Use the rods and Factor Frame for Exercise A, problems 1–13, 15, 18–20.

Lesson at a Glance

Chapter 8 Application

Overview This lesson requires students to solve word problems relating to the height and depth of icebergs and to add, subtract, and divide integers.

Objectives

- To relate elevations involving sea level to positive and negative integers
- To solve word problems using positive and negative integers

Student Page 226

Teacher's Resource Library

Application Activity 8

Everyday Math 8

---

1 Warm-Up Activity

Explain that sea level is given an altitude of 0 feet. Have students suggest how integers would be assigned to elevations above and below sea level. (*Negative integers express elevations below sea level; positive, above.*)

2 Teaching the Lesson

Solve Exercise 1 as a class, following the steps used in the example in the lesson. On the board, create a vertical number line using multiples of 1,000 for students to use as a visual reference. Use the number line to show how far above and below sea level the iceberg floats.

3 Reinforce and Extend

CAREER CONNECTION

Have students search an online encyclopedia to learn about civil engineering. What skills and training are needed to design, create, repair, or replace roads, bridges, railroad lines, airports, harbors, tunnels, and other large structures built by civil engineers? Encourage students to learn about and name the accomplishments of a specific civil engineer.

Application

Ice Cold An iceberg is a floating mass of freshwater ice that has broken from a glacier or a polar ice sheet.

Usually a newly formed iceberg is lighter than a older iceberg, so about $\frac{1}{8}$ of it rises above the waterline. An older iceberg that has tumbled over several times becomes more compact and much heavier. As a result only $\frac{1}{10}$ of it rises above the surface.

> **EXAMPLE 1** Scientists estimate that the new iceberg measures about 5,600 feet in total height. Use positive and negative signs to write the height of the iceberg above and below the waterline.
>
> **Step 1** Multiply by $\frac{1}{8}$ to find the height above the waterline.
>
> $5,600 \times \frac{1}{8} = \frac{5,600}{8} = 700$
>
> **Step 2** Subtract to find the depth below the waterline.
>
> $5,600 - 700 = 4,900$
>
> **Step 3** Use positive and negative signs to indicate the height above and below the waterline.
>
> above waterline: $+700$ feet
> below waterline: $-4,900$ feet

Exercise Solve each problem.

1. Many of the older icebergs in the Arctic measure about 1,350 feet in total height. Use positive and negative signs to write the height above and below the waterline. $+135$ feet, $-1,215$ feet
2. In 1985 the wreck of the *Titanic* was found 12,612 feet below the surface on the ocean floor. Write this number as an integer. $-12,612$ feet
3. While in a kayak in Alaska you see the top of an iceberg. It rises about 300 feet above the waterline. What is the possible depth of this iceberg?
   $-2,700$ feet, total height 3,000 feet
   $-2,100$ feet, total height 2,400 feet

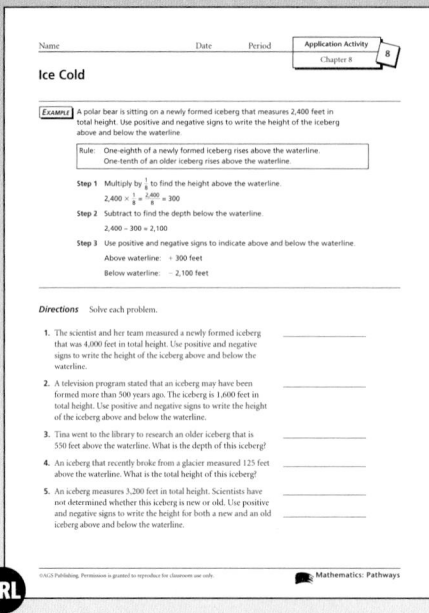

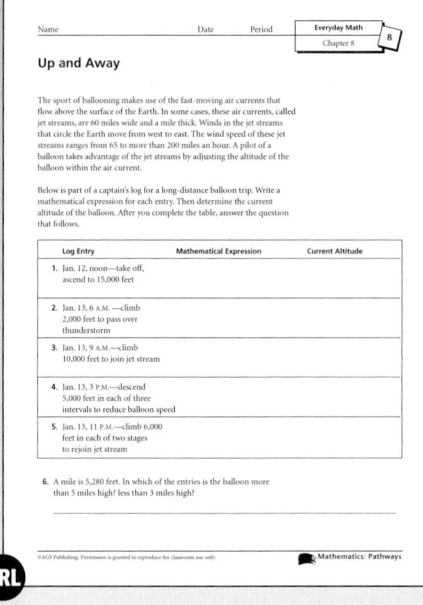

Application Activity 8

Everyday Math 8

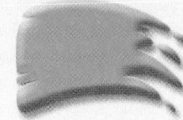

Chapter 8 R E V I E W

Write the letter of the correct answer.

1. What is the absolute value of $|-5|$? B

   A -5 **C** $-2\frac{1}{2}$

   B 5 **D** -10

2. Name the opposite of the integer -23. D

   A -23 **C** -11.5

   B -46 **D** 23

3. Find the sum. $9 + (-2) =$ D

   A 11 **C** -11

   B -7 **D** 7

4. Find the sum. $-7 + (-3) =$ B

   A 4 **C** -4

   B -10 **D** 10

5. Find the difference. $7 - (+5) =$ A

   A 2 **C** -2

   B 12 **D** -12

6. Find the product. $(8)(-3) =$ B

   A 24 **C** 5

   B -24 **D** 11

7. Find the quotient. $-60 \div 12 =$ C

   A -72 **C** -5

   B 5 **D** 48

Find each absolute value or distance from zero.

Example: $|-4|$ Solution: $|-4| = 4$

8. $|-9|$ 9   **10.** $|-5|$ 5

9. $|14|$ 14   **11.** $|-71|$ 71

Chapter 8 Review

Each set of problems in the Chapter Review includes an example and solution to illustrate the concept. Use the given examples for reteaching the materials in Chapter 8. For additional practice, refer to the Supplementary Problems for Chapter 8 (pages 446–447).

Chapter 8 Mastery Test

The Teacher's Resource Library includes parallel forms of the Chapter 8 Mastery Test. The difficulty level of the two forms is equivalent. You may wish to use one form as a pretest and the other form as a posttest.

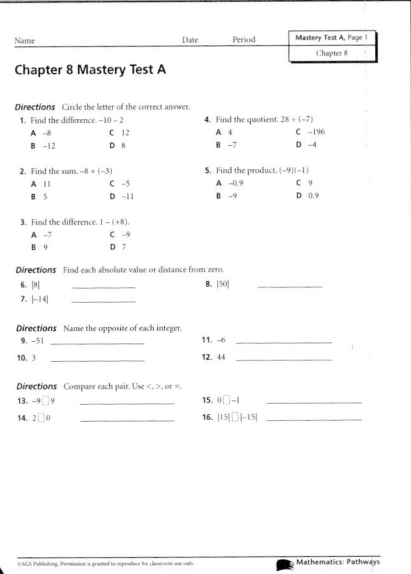

Chapter 8 Mastery Test A

ALTERNATIVE ASSESSMENT

Alternative Assessment items correlate with student Goals for Learning at the beginning of this chapter.

■ **To identify the absolute value of integers**

Have students use maps to determine opposite distances from a central point. For example, if the central point is Chicago, label that 0, and then find points 3 inches east and 3 inches west. Find several central points, distances, and directions. Label each central point 0. Have students explain the importance of absolute value to determining distances.

■ **To compare the values of negative and positive whole numbers**

Have students draw three number lines and then plot two numbers on their lines to show how "farther right is always greater." Have them write the inequality below their number lines; for example, $-2 > -5$. Make sure that students include examples of negative number pairs such as -5 and -2. Create a poster, and glue all the students' number lines on the poster. Title the poster "Farther Right Is Always Greater."

■ **To add and subtract integers**

Have students create a large table illustrating the textbook rules for adding and subtracting positive and negative integers to hang in the classroom. Have each group of students create a line of the table for one of the eight rules. Have the groups then illustrate a different part of the table with an example number line and two points. Below the table, have a designated class artist illustrate the last rule: Subtraction is the same as adding the opposite. Have another person include an example to illustrate the rule.

■ **To multiply and divide integers**

Have groups of students each create a line of another table. This table should illustrate the rules for multiplying and dividing integers. Have different groups provide examples of each rule. Let the groups decide whether their examples will be shown on number lines or as equations.

Name the opposite of each integer.

Example: -5 Solution: 5 is the opposite of -5

12. 8 -8

13. -4 4

14. 7 -7

15. 43 -43

Compare each pair. Use $<$, $>$, or $=$.

Example: 9 ■ -2 Solution: $9 > -2$

16. 7 ■ -7 $7 > -7$

17. 4 ■ 0 $4 > 0$

18. -4 ■ 0 $-4 < 0$

19. -2 ■ $|-5|$ $-2 < |-5|$

Find each sum.

Example: $-8 + 3$ Solution: $-8 + 3 = -5$

20. $8 + 3$ 11

21. $6 + 4$ 10

22. $-6 + (-6)$ -12

23. $6 + (-6)$ 0

24. $-9 + (-2)$ -11

25. $-7 + 4$ -3

26. $8 + (-3)$ 5

27. $-9 + (-9)$ -18

Find each difference.

Example: $-8 - (-5)$ Solution: $-8 - (-5) = -3$

28. $-9 - (-11)$ 2

29. $-6 - (-4)$ -2

30. $10 - (-7)$ 17

31. $-7 - (-4)$ -3

32. $5 - (-4)$ 9

33. $-9 - (-2)$ -7

Find each product.

Example: $(4)(-7)$ Solution: $(4)(-7) = -28$

34. $(3)(5)$ 15

35. $(-6)(7)$ -42

36. $(-6)(-6)$ 36

37. $(-8)(-12)$ 96

38. $(9)(5)$ 45

39. $(5)(-8)$ -40

---

228   Chapter 8   Integers

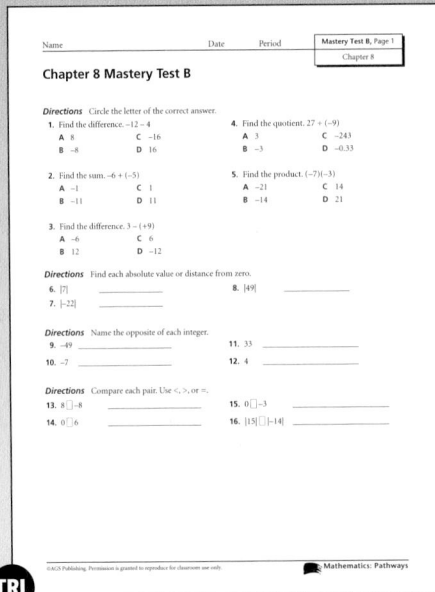

Chapter 8 Mastery Test B

Find each quotient.

Example: 28 ÷ (−7)   Solution: 28 ÷ (−7) = −4

40. 30 ÷ 5   6   **43.** −120 ÷ (−30)   4

41. 8 ÷ (−2)   −4   **44.** 45 ÷ 5   9

42. −6 ÷ (−6)   1   **45.** 56 ÷ (−8)   −7

Solve each problem.

Example: The team loses by 84 points in a total of 12 games. They lose by the same number of points in each game. By how many points did they lose per game?

Solution: 84 ÷ 12 = 7 points

46. A submarine dives 96 feet in a minute. At what depth will the submarine be in 15 minutes? −1,440 feet

47. What is the difference in elevation of a mountain 22,834 feet tall and an ocean basin floor at −16,896 feet? 39,730 feet

48. The temperature was −9°C yesterday and 3°C today. How much did the temperature increase? 12°C

49. A pro golf player has these scores for the three games of a tournament: −3, −6, and +2. Find out his score for the tournament by adding the three scores together. −7

50. Karen walked down 7 flights of stairs. If each flight has 12 steps, how many steps did she walk down? 84 steps

Test-Taking Tip

To help you work through computation quicker and more accurately, review your multiplication tables before a test.

MANIPULATIVES

 **Review**

Materials: Cuisenaire Rods, Manipulatives Master 1 (Factor Frame), Manipulatives Master 5 (Number Line)

Group Practice: Review the procedures for adding, subtracting, multiplying, and dividing integers in Lessons 4–7 and 9.

Student Practice: Have students use the rods, Factor Frame, and Number Line to help with problems 20–27, 34–36, 40–42, and 44–45.

Planning Guide

Exponents, Radicals, and the Pythagorean Theorem

Lesson		Student Pages	Vocabulary	Practice Exercises	Problem Solving	Try This	Solutions Key
1	Exponents	232–233	✔	✔			✔
2	Multiplying with Exponents	234–235		✔		235	✔
3	Dividing with Exponents	236–237		✔		237	✔
4	Squares	238–239	✔	✔	239		✔
5	Cubes	240–241	✔	✔	241		✔
6	Square Roots	242–245	✔	✔			✔
7	Irrational Numbers and Square Roots	246–247	✔	✔		247	✔
8	Irrational Numbers as Decimals	248–249	✔	✔	249		✔
9	Radicals in Equations	250–253		✔	252–253		✔
10	The Pythagorean Theorem	254–257	✔	✔		257	✔
11	More About Triangles	258–259	✔	✔			✔
Application	Applying the Pythagorean Theorem	260		✔			✔

Chapter Activities

Teacher's Resource Library
Estimation Exercise 9: Estimating Square
  Roots
Application Activity 9: Applying the
  Pythagorean Theorem
Everyday Math 9: Triangle Two-Step
Community Connection 9: Triangle Tally

Teacher's Edition
Chapter 9 Project

Assessment Options

Student Text
Chapter 9 Review

Teacher's Resource Library
Chapter 9 Mastery Tests A and B

Teacher's Edition
Chapter 9 Alternative Assessments

Estimation Activity	Math in Your Life	Technology Connection	Writing About Mathematics	Build a Model	Calculator Practice	Online Connection	Common Error	Applications Home, Career, Community	Mental Math	Manipulatives	Calculator	Group Problem Solving	Modeling	Knowing Your Students	Auditory/Verbal	Visual/Spatial	Logical/Mathematical	Body/Kinesthetic	Interpersonal/Group Learning	LEP/ESL	Activities	Alternate Activities	Workbook Activities	Self-Study Guide
			233		233	233	233			233						233					74	74	78	✔
	235									235									235	235	75	75	79	✔
							237			237					237						76	76	80	✔
								239		239		239	239								77	77	81	✔
					241					241	241	241									78	78	82	✔
245					244			245	244	243	244			245		243					79	79	83	✔
												247					247				80	80	84	✔
									249												81	81	85	✔
		253						252, 253				251							251		82	82	86	✔
				257	257	256	256	257			255	255			255				256	257	83	83	87	✔
																		259		259	84	84	88	✔
								261	261															✔

Software Options

Skill Track Software

Use the Skill Track Software for *Mathematics: Pathways* for additional reinforcement of this chapter. The software provides multiple-choice assessment items for students to access by computer.

Solutions Key

Use the Solutions Key with this chapter to help students who may need additional assistance. The Solutions Key CD provides solutions for every exercise in the student edition.

Other Resources

Alternative Activities

The Teacher's Resource Library (TRL) contains a set of worksheets written at a second-grade reading level called Alternative Activities. They cover the same content as the regular Activities.

Manipulatives

See the Manipulative activities in this chapter for hands-on modeling of the content.

Cuisenaire Rods
Pattern Blocks

Chapter 9: Exponents, Radicals, and the Pythagorean Theorem
pages 230–263

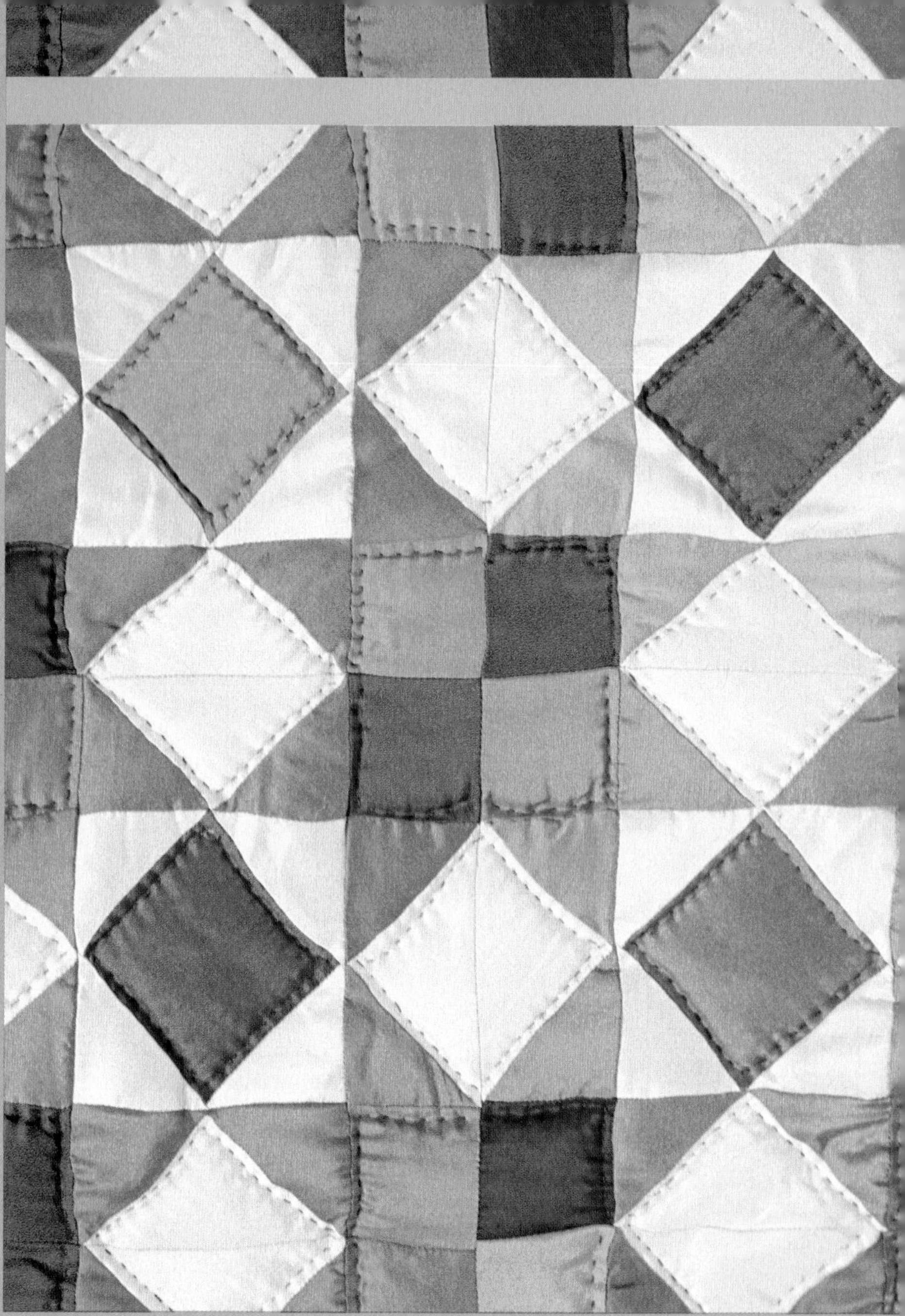

**Skill Track for
  Mathematics: Pathways**

Teacher's Resource Library **TRL**

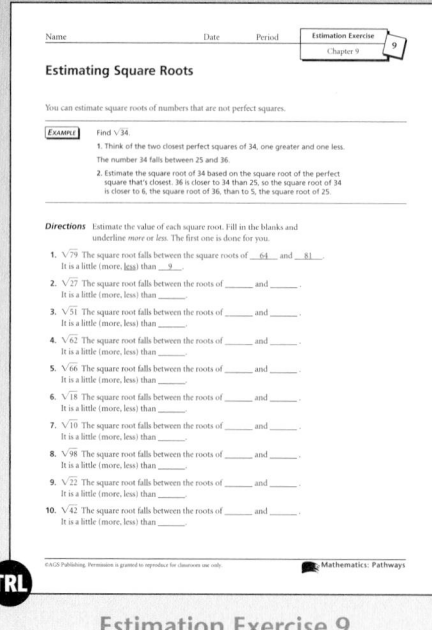

Estimation Exercise 9

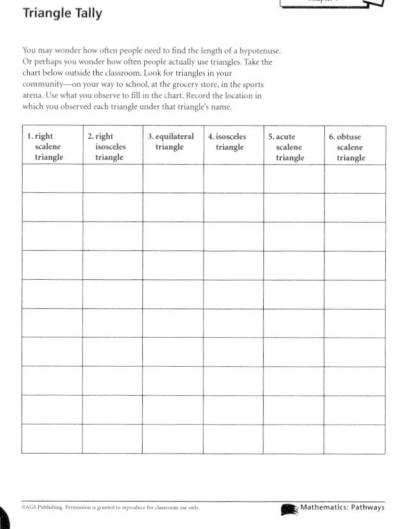

Community Connection 9

9 Exponents, Radicals, and the Pythagorean Theorem

The colorful quilt is warm and comforting, but did you know that it is also mathematical? You may notice the rectangles and triangles in the pattern of the quilt. The ancient Greeks developed the study of right-angled triangles and the Pythagorean theorem. The Pythagorean theorem can be used to find the distance between two points, the height of a building, or even the length of fabric needed for a quilt block.

The Greek mathematician Pythagoras found a way to calculate the lengths of sides of right-angled triangles. If you know the length of two sides, you can use the Pythagorean theorem to figure out the length of the third.

In Chapter 9, you will find the powers and roots of numbers and learn how to use the Pythagorean theorem.

Goals for Learning

◆ To find the value of numbers raised to a certain power

◆ To multiply and divide terms with exponents

◆ To find area and volume by using numbers with exponents

◆ To find the square roots of numbers

◆ To understand and operate with irrational numbers

◆ To solve equations with radicals

◆ To use the Pythagorean theorem to solve problems

231

Introducing the Chapter

In this chapter, students will combine concepts in algebra and geometry to learn the practical skills involved in calculating area and volume. They will also learn about square roots and how to apply them to the Pythagorean theorem to find the side lengths of a right triangle. Mention to students that without the use of algebra and geometry, civilizations (such as those of the ancient Greeks and Romans) could not have designed and built cities, bridges, or roads.

CHAPTER PROJECT

As a class project, create a plan for a town using squares and right triangles. After a grid for the overall street layout has been mapped on posterboard, assign small groups or pairs of students their own area to plan in more detail. As they progress through the chapter, students will use what they learn to measure the area taken up by parks, businesses, and residences. They will plan streets, sidewalks, and buildings. They will decide the length, width, and height of buildings, build them from heavy weight paper, and measure their volumes.

TEACHER'S RESOURCE

The AGS Publishing Teaching Strategies in Math Transparencies may be used with this chapter. They add an interactive dimension to expand and enhance the program content.

CAREER INTEREST INVENTORY

The AGS Publishing Harrington-O'Shea Career Decision-Making System-Revised (CDM) may be used with this chapter. Students can use the CDM to explore their interests and identify careers. The CDM defines career areas that are indicated by students' responses on the inventory.

Name _____ Date _____ Period _____ SELF-STUDY GUIDE

CHAPTER 9: Exponents, Radicals, and the Pythagorean Theorem

Goals 9.1 and 9.2 *To find the value of numbers raised to a certain power; to multiply and divide terms with exponents*

Date	Assignment	Score
_____	1: Read pages 231–232. Complete Exercises A–B on page 233.	_____
_____	2: Read and complete the Calculator Practice on page 233, and Workbook Activity 78.	_____
_____	3: Read page 234. Complete Exercises A–B on page 235.	_____
_____	4: Complete Workbook Activity 79.	_____
_____	5: Read page 236. Complete Exercises A–B on page 237.	_____
_____	6: Complete Workbook Activity 80.	_____

Comments:

Goal 9.3 *To find area and volume by using numbers with exponents*

Date	Assignment	Score
_____	7: Read page 238. Complete Exercises A–C on page 239.	_____
_____	8: Complete Workbook Activity 81.	_____
_____	9: Complete Exercises A, B, and D on pages 240–241.	_____
_____	10: Read and complete the Calculator Practice on page 241, and Workbook Activity 82.	_____

Comments:

Goal 9.4 *To find the square roots of numbers*

Date	Assignment	Score
_____	11: Read pages 242–243. Complete Exercise B on page 245.	_____
_____	12: Read and complete the Calculator Practice on page 244, and Workbook Activity 83.	_____
_____	13: Read pages 246–247. Complete Exercise A on page 247.	_____
_____	14: Complete Workbook Activity 84.	_____

Comments:

RL ©AGS Publishing. Permission is granted to reproduce for classroom use only. ▲ Mathematics: Pathways

Name _____ Date _____ Period _____ SELF-STUDY GUIDE

CHAPTER 9: Exponents, Radicals, and the Pythagorean Theorem, continued

Goals 9.5 and 9.6 *To understand and operate with irrational numbers; to solve equations with radicals*

Date	Assignment	Score
_____	15: Read pages 248–249. Complete Exercises A–B on page 249.	_____
_____	16: Complete Workbook Activity 85.	_____
_____	17: Read pages 250–251. Complete Exercises A–C on pages 252-253.	_____
_____	18: Complete Workbook Activity 86.	_____

Comments:

Goal 9.7 *To use the Pythagorean theorem to solve problems*

Date	Assignment	Score
_____	19: Read pages 254–255. Complete Exercise A on page 256.	_____
_____	20: Read and complete the Calculator Practice on pages 256–257.	_____
_____	21: Complete Workbook Activity 87.	_____
_____	22: Read pages 258–259. Complete Exercise A on page 259.	_____
_____	23: Complete Workbook Activity 88.	_____
_____	24: Read and complete the Application on page 260.	_____
_____	25: Complete the Chapter 9 Review on pages 261-263.	_____

Comments:

Student's Signature _____ Date _____

Instructor's Signature _____ Date _____

TRL ©AGS Publishing. Permission is granted to reproduce for classroom use only. ▲ Mathematics: Pathways

Lesson at a Glance

Chapter 9 Lesson 1

Overview This lesson explains exponential notation.

Objectives

- To define and identify *exponent* and *base*
- To express factors in exponential form
- To find the values of powers of numbers

Student Pages 232–233

Teacher's Resource Library **TRL**

Workbook Activity 78

Activity 74

Alternative Activity 74

....

Mathematics Vocabulary

power
exponent
base

....

1 Warm-Up Activity

Have students compare what happens to a number

- when it is added to itself again and again
- when it is multiplied by itself again and again

and describe the difference. Students should note that the numbers grow much more rapidly with multiplication. Explain that such products are called powers of a number. Assign the lesson, asking students to read to learn or review the method for representing powers in math.

2 Teaching the Lesson

Have students create definitions in their own words for *base*, *exponent*, and *power*. *(For example, the base is the number that is to be multiplied by itself a certain number of times; the exponent is the number of times the base is multiplied; the power is the result.)*

Have students suggest reasons why a negative base number is placed in ( ). *(so that the negative will not be mistaken for a subtraction sign)*

Power

The product of multiplying any number by itself once or many times

Exponent

Number that tells how many times another number is a factor

Base

The number being multiplied; a factor

You can use the symbols $3 \cdot 3$ to show 3 multiplied by itself. You can also use the symbol 3^2 (read "3 to the second **power**") to show $3 \cdot 3$.

$$3^2$$

2 is the **exponent**.

3 is the **base**.

EXAMPLE 1 $2 \cdot 2 \cdot 2 = 2^3$

2^3 is read "2 to the third power."

2 is the base.   3 is the exponent.

To write a negative number with an exponent, first place the negative number in parentheses and then write the exponent. For example, the second power of -2 is written $(-2)^2$.

EXAMPLE 2 $(-4)(-4) = (-4)^2$

$(-4)^2$ is read "negative four to the second power."

(-4) is the base.   2 is the exponent.

You can use the same symbols in algebra.

EXAMPLE 3 $a \cdot a \cdot a$ is a to the third power or a^3.

a is the base.   3 is the exponent.

$z \cdot z \cdot z \cdot z \cdot z$ is z to the fifth power or z^5.

z is the base.   5 is the exponent.

Terms such as x^2 or x^3 do not have a numerical value until you substitute numbers for x.

EXAMPLE 4 If $x = 3$, $x^2 = 3 \cdot 3 = 9$ and $x^3 = 3 \cdot 3 \cdot 3 = 27$.

3 to the second power is 9.

3 to the third power is 27.

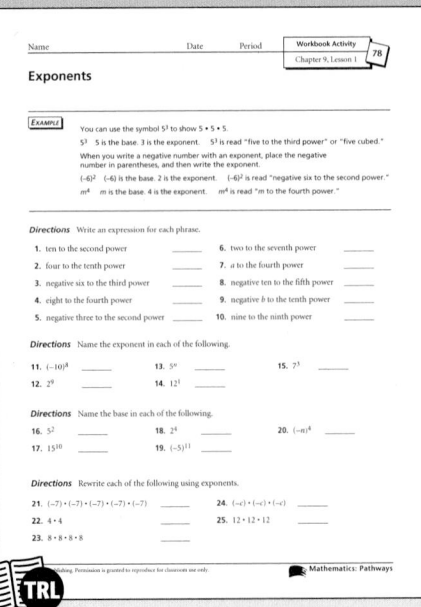

Workbook Activity 78   **Activity 74**

Writing About Mathematics

Can a negative number to the power of 2 be negative? Explain.

Any number to the first power is the number itself.

$$2^1 = 2 \qquad x^1 = x$$

Any number to the zero power is 1.

$$2^0 = 1 \qquad y^0 = 1$$

Exercise A Name the exponent in each of the following items.

1. 4^2 2
5. 4^3 3
9. x^1 1

2. $(-5)^3$ 3
6. x^3 3
10. x^n n

3. 2^3 3
7. a^5 5

4. 10^2 2
8. $(-y)^{10}$ 10

Exercise B Rewrite each of the following using exponents.

11. $2 \cdot 2 \cdot 2$ 2^3
16. $(-a)$ $(-a)^1$ or $-a$

12. $3 \cdot 3$ 3^2
17. $x \cdot x \cdot x \cdot x$ x^4

13. $4 \cdot 4 \cdot 4$ 4^3
18. $(-y) \cdot (-y) \cdot (-y)$ $(-y)^3$

14. $(-5) \cdot (-5)$ $(-5)^2$
19. $m \cdot m \cdot m \cdot m \cdot m \cdot m$ m^6

15. $5 \cdot 5 \cdot 5 \cdot 5$ 5^4
20. $p \cdot p \cdot p$ p^3

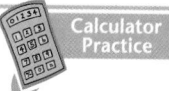
Calculator Practice

Use the $\boxed{y^x}$ or $\boxed{x^y}$ key on your calculator to find the value of expressions with exponents.

EXAMPLE 5 Find 4^5.

Press 4 $\boxed{y^x}$ 5 $\boxed{=}$.

The display reads *1024*.

Exercise C Use a calculator to find the value of each expression.

21. 2^{10} 1,024
24. $(0.02)^3$ 0.000008

22. $(-5)^3$ -125
25. $(-0.5)^2$ 0.25

23. 16^3 4,096

ONLINE CONNECTION

Students can read about exponential growth at www.science.org.au/nova/020/020box03.htm. After they read this article, have students do an exponential experiment. Ask them to figure out how they would make more money: having a steady salary of $1,000 per day for a month or starting with a salary of two dollars the first day and squaring each day's salary for a week.

COMMON ERROR

Failure to place the negative sign within parentheses when finding a power of a negative integer may cause errors. Remind students that a negative times a negative gives a positive. Illustrate for students the difference in products:

$$(-4)^2 = (-4) \cdot (-4) = 16$$
$$-(4^2) = -(4 \cdot 4) = -16$$

3 Reinforce and Extend

LEARNING STYLES

Visual/Spatial

Extend Exercise A by having students write out the factors representing each power. As a student writes the problem on the board, he or she should explain the relationship between the exponential notation and the multiplication expression. Reverse the sign of each base in the exercise, and repeat so that students explore what happens to negative bases raised to a power. *(Raised to an odd power such as 1 or 3, they result in a negative product; raised to an even power such as 2 or 4, they become positive products.)*

CALCULATOR

The symbol used to enter expressions with exponents varies with different calculators. For example, on the scientific calculator TI-83, the key for the power of a number has the symbol ^. To find 4^5,

Press 4 $\boxed{\wedge}$ 5 (not $\boxed{=}$).

Have students determine whether their calculators have a key for exponential notation. Compare differences. Discuss how problems in Exercise C could be solved using a calculator with no exponent key.

Lesson at a Glance

Chapter 9 Lesson 2

Overview This lesson illustrates multiplication of exponential numbers with the same base.

Objectives

- To multiply numbers with the same base by adding exponents
- To identify the accuracy of such multiplications

Student Pages 234–235

Teacher's Resource Library TRL

Workbook Activity 79

Activity 75

Alternative Activity 75

1 Warm-Up Activity

Write the following on the board:

$7 \cdot 7 \cdot 7 \cdot 7 \cdot 7$

Have students describe the expression and tell how they would simplify it. Next, write 7^2, and ask students to explain its meaning. (*7 squared or multiplied by itself*) Discuss ways to give the first expression in this kind of shorthand. (*one possibility: $7^2 \cdot 7^2 \cdot 7$*) Have the class read the lesson to find how exponents can be multiplied in a shorthand way.

2 Teaching the Lesson

Have students verify the accuracy of the rule for multiplying with exponents. Write out the factors in each part of the expressions in Exercise A, repeating these questions for each problem:

$(4 \cdot 4) \cdot (4 \cdot 4)$

How many times is 4 used as a factor? (*4*) What is the exponent? (*4*) What is the sum of the original exponents? (*2 + 2 = 4*)

If two terms with exponents have the same base, you can multiply the terms by adding exponents.

EXAMPLE 1

$$2^2 \cdot 2^3 = (2 \cdot 2) \cdot (2 \cdot 2 \cdot 2)$$
$$= 2 \cdot 2 \cdot 2 \cdot 2 \cdot 2$$
$$= 2^5$$
$$\text{or } 2^2 \cdot 2^3 = 2^{2+3} = 2^5$$

$$-5 \cdot (-5)^2 = (-5) \cdot (-5) \cdot (-5)$$
$$= (-5) \cdot (-5) \cdot (-5)$$
$$= (-5)^3$$
$$\text{or } -5 \cdot (-5)^2 = (-5)^{1+2} = (-5)^3$$

$$y^3 \cdot y^3 = (y \cdot y \cdot y) \cdot (y \cdot y \cdot y)$$
$$= y \cdot y \cdot y \cdot y \cdot y \cdot y$$
$$= y^6$$
$$\text{or } y^3 \cdot y^3 = y^{3+3} = y^6$$

$$5^n \cdot 5^n = 5^{n+n}$$
$$= 5^{2n}$$

Rule

To multiply numbers with the same base, add their exponents.

Workbook Activity 79

Name _____ Date _____ Period _____ **Workbook Activity** 79
Chapter 9, Lesson 2

Multiplying with Exponents

EXAMPLE If two terms with exponents have the same base, you can multiply the terms by adding exponents.

$4^2 \cdot 4^1$	$b^2 \cdot b^2$	$3^n \cdot 3^n$
The base of both terms is 4.	The base of both terms is b.	The base of both terms is 3.
$4^2 \cdot 4^1 = (4 \cdot 4) \cdot (4 \cdot 4 \cdot 4)$	$b^2 \cdot b^2 = (b \cdot b) \cdot (b \cdot b)$	$3^n \cdot 3^n = 3^{n+n}$
$= 4 \cdot 4 \cdot 4 \cdot 4$	$b^2 \cdot b^2 = b^4$	$3^n \cdot 3^n = 3^{2n}$
$4^2 \cdot 4^1 = 4^5$		

Directions Simplify each expression.

1. $7^4 \cdot 7^2$ _____
2. $6^2 \cdot 6$ _____
3. $(-m)^2 \cdot (-m)^8$ _____
4. $2^4 \cdot 2^3$ _____
5. $n^3 \cdot n$ _____
6. $14^3 \cdot 14^7$ _____
7. $a^3 \cdot a^2$ _____
8. $(-10)^2 \cdot (-10)^3$ _____

9. $3^{2r} \cdot 3^r$ _____
10. $6^5 \cdot 6^5$ _____
11. $2^{3y} \cdot 2^{3y}$ _____
12. $15^3 \cdot 15^6$ _____
13. $3^3 \cdot 3^4$ _____
14. $b^3 \cdot b^3$ _____
15. $(-n)^2 \cdot (-n)^2$ _____

Directions Tell whether each statement is *true or false*. If a statement is false, tell why.

16. $(-8)^8 \cdot (-8)^8 = (-8)^{16}$ _____
17. $5^5 \cdot 5^4 = 5^{12}$ _____
18. $6^{4n} \cdot 6^{3n} = 6^{7n}$ _____
19. $b^2 \cdot b^2 = b^5$ _____
20. $25^3 \cdot 25 = 25^5$ _____

21. $3^4 \cdot 3^2 = 3^8$ _____
22. $2^6 \cdot 2^6 = 2^{12}$ _____
23. $2^n \cdot 2^{3n} = 2^{4n}$ _____
24. $7^7 \cdot 7^4 = 7^{11}$ _____
25. $b^2 \cdot b^{10} = b^{12}$ _____

©AGS Publishing. Permission is granted to reproduce for classroom use only. *Mathematics: Pathways*

Activity 75

Name _____ Date _____ Period _____ **Activity** 75
Chapter 9, Lesson 2

Exponents—Multiplying

Directions Simplify each expression.

1. $m^4 \cdot m^2$ _____
2. $10^2 \cdot 10^5$ _____
3. $r^2 \cdot r^2$ _____
4. $12^4 \cdot 12^5$ _____
5. $n^3 \cdot n^5$ _____

6. $6^4 \cdot 6^{10}$ _____
7. $q^6 \cdot q^9$ _____
8. $18^2 \cdot 18^7$ _____
9. $2^{5r} \cdot 2^r$ _____
10. $100^3 \cdot 100^5$ _____

Directions Tell whether each statement is *true or false*. If a statement is false, give the correct answer.

11. $4^{3n} \cdot 4^{3n} = 4^{9n}$ _____
12. $10^5 \cdot 10^6 = 10^{11}$ _____
13. $14^3 \cdot 14^5 = 14^8$ _____
14. $b^2 \cdot b^2 = b^4$ _____
15. $10^{2x} \cdot 10^x = 10^{3x}$ _____
16. $a^8 \cdot a^{10} = a^{80}$ _____
17. $2^3 \cdot 2^4 = 2^7$ _____
18. $9^{4n} \cdot 9^{4n} = 9^{8n}$ _____
19. $p^2 \cdot p^2 = p^5$ _____
20. $5^3 \cdot 5 = 5^5$ _____
21. $20^4 \cdot 20^2 = 20^6$ _____

22. $6^6 \cdot 6^6 = 6^{12}$ _____
23. $3^y \cdot 3^y = 3^y$ _____
24. $a^7 \cdot a^4 = a^{11}$ _____
25. $15^2 \cdot 15^2 = 15^4$ _____
26. $8^{10} \cdot 8^{10} = 8^{10}$ _____
27. $4^5 \cdot 4^{5b} = 4^{6b}$ _____
28. $m^1 \cdot m^1 = m^2$ _____
29. $11^5 \cdot 11^6 = 11^{11}$ _____
30. $x^8 \cdot x^8 = x^{16}$ _____

©AGS Publishing. Permission is granted to reproduce for classroom use only. *Mathematics: Pathways*

Workbook Activity 79   **Activity 75**

Exercise A Simplify each expression.

1. $4^2 \cdot 4^2$ 4^4
2. $5^3 \cdot 5^2$ 5^5
3. $2^4 \cdot 2^3$ 2^7
4. $10^3 \cdot 10^2$ 10^5
5. $4^5 \cdot 4^3$ 4^8
6. $x^7 \cdot x^3$ x^{10}
7. $a^5 \cdot a^3$ a^8
8. $y^{10} \cdot y^7$ y^{17}
9. $x^4 \cdot x^3$ x^7
10. $p^4 \cdot p^2$ p^6
11. $2^n \cdot 2^n$ 2^{2n}
12. $3^{4x} \cdot 3^x$ 3^{5x}

Try This

Multiply.
$x^n \cdot x^m$
$a^x \cdot a^y$

x^{n+m}, a^{x+y}

Exercise B Tell whether each statement is *true* or *false*. If a statement is false, tell why.

13. $2^3 \cdot 2^5 = 2^8$
True
14. $3 \cdot 3^2 = 3^3$
True
15. $4^3 \cdot 5^3 = 9^3$
False, bases not same
16. $5^3 \cdot 5^2 = 5^6$
False, $5^{3+2} = 5^5$
17. $3^3 \cdot 3 = 3^3$
False, $3^{3+1} = 3^4$
18. $a^3 \cdot a^5 = a^8$
True
19. $y^5 \cdot y^3 = y^8$
True
20. $a^5 \cdot a^5 = a^{25}$
False, $a^{5+5} = a^{10}$
21. $n^6 \cdot n^2 = n^{12}$
False, $n^{6+2} = n^8$
22. $p^1 \cdot p^1 = p^1$
False, $p^{1+1} = p^2$
23. $2^y \cdot 2^y = 2^{2y}$
True
24. $3^{2n} \cdot 3^{4n} = 3^{8n}$
False, $3^{2n+4n} = 3^{6n}$
25. $7^{3x} \cdot 7^x = 7^{4x}$
True

Math in Your Life

The word *exponential* is used to describe something that increases very quickly. For example, it can be used to describe a sudden rise in population. When bacteria reproduce, their numbers increase very fast. This is called exponential growth. Numbers experience this type of increase when they have exponents.

Try This

Use this exercise to assess students' understanding of the rule for multiplying with exponents. If students multiply factors instead of adding them (x^{nm}, a^{xy}), assign numerical values for each letter, and have them carry out the operation to see why it is wrong.

MANIPULATIVES

 Multiplying with Exponents

Materials: Cuisenaire Rods, Pattern Blocks

Group Practice: Model numbers with exponents by stacking one rod for each factor. Use shapes to model variables with exponents, stacking one shape for each factor. For example, $y^3 = y \cdot y \cdot y =$ stack of three shapes. Stack the models of each term, and add rods or shapes to find the product. Write the symbolic equivalent for each model. Emphasize that different shapes or rods, like different variables or numbers, cannot be combined or simplified.

Student Practice: Have students use the rods and shapes for problems 1–7, 9–10 in Exercise A and problems 13–19, 21–22 in Exercise B.

 3 Reinforce and Extend

LEARNING STYLES

Interpersonal/ Group Learning

Organize the class into groups of four, and assign each group a false statement from Exercise B. Their task is to write a paragraph explaining what the original solver did wrong and demonstrating the correct answer. Then have the groups write and solve three expressions involving multiplying exponents. They should make one or more solutions false and exchange problems with another group to find and correct the false statements.

LEARNING STYLES

LEP/ESL

Some students will consistently multiply exponents instead of adding them. Have them make a poster illustrating the rule, with color coding to clearly separate the bases from the exponents. The words *same base* and the algebraic bases might be blue, and the words *add . . . exponents* and the algebraic exponents might be red:

$$a^x \cdot a^y = a^{x+y}$$

Have students refer to the poster as they solve problems, first underlining bases in blue and exponents in red. Ask, "Are the blue bases the same?" Only if they are the same can the red exponents be added.

Chapter 9 Lesson 3

Overview This lesson shows how to divide exponential terms by subtracting.

Objectives

- To divide numbers with the same base by subtracting exponents
- To identify the accuracy of such division

Student Pages 236–237

Teacher's Resource Library (TRL)

Workbook Activity 80

Activity 76

Alternative Activity 76

---

1 ⬤ Warm-Up Activity

You may wish to teach this lesson concurrently with Lesson 2. Remind students that multiplication and division are opposite operations, just as addition and subtraction are. Ask, "How do you multiply with exponents? *(Add them.)* "How do you think you would divide with exponents?" *(Subtract them.)* Have students study the examples on page 236 to see how this is done.

2 ⬤ Teaching the Lesson

Make sure that students follow each step of the process in the examples.

a) Express the division problem in fractional form.

b) Write out the factors of the numerator and denominator.

c) Cross out element pairs that equal 1 (and therefore do not change value).

d) Express the remaining numerator elements in base and exponent form.

If two terms with exponents have the same base, you can divide the terms by subtracting exponents.

Recall that any number to the 0 power is 1, and any number to the first power is the number itself.

EXAMPLE 1

$$35 \div 33 = \frac{3^5}{3^3}$$

$$= \frac{3 \cdot 3 \cdot 3 \cdot 3 \cdot 3}{3 \cdot 3 \cdot 3}$$

$$= 3^2$$

or $3^5 \div 3^3 = 3^{5-3} = 3^2$

$$5^4 \div 5^3 = \frac{5^4}{5^3}$$

$$= \frac{5 \cdot 5 \cdot 5 \cdot 5}{5 \cdot 5 \cdot 5}$$

$$= 5$$

or $5^4 \div 5^3 = 5^{4-3} = 5$

$$x^4 \div x^3 = \frac{x^4}{x^3}$$

$$= \frac{x \cdot x \cdot x \cdot x}{x \cdot x \cdot x}$$

$$= x^1 = x$$

or $x^4 \div x^3 = x^{4-3} = x^1 = x$

$$5^{2x} \div 5^x = \frac{5^{2x}}{5^x}$$

$$= \frac{5^x \cdot 5^x}{5^x}$$

$$= 5^x$$

or $5^{2x} \div 5^x = 5^{2x-x} = 5^x$

Rule

To divide numbers with the same base, subtract their exponents.

Dividing with Exponents

EXAMPLE If two terms with exponents have the same base, you can divide the terms by subtracting exponents.

$8^6 \div 8^3 = \frac{8^6}{8^3}$ $a^4 \div a^2 = \frac{a^4}{a^2}$ $6^{2n} \div 6^n = \frac{6^{2n}}{6^n}$

The base of both terms is 8. $= \frac{(a \cdot a \cdot a \cdot a)}{(a \cdot a)}$ $= \frac{(6^n \cdot 6^n)}{(6^n)}$

$= \frac{(8 \cdot 8 \cdot 8 \cdot 8 \cdot 8 \cdot 8)}{(8 \cdot 8 \cdot 8)}$ $a^4 \div a^2 = a^{4-2} = a^2$ $6^{2n} \div 6^n = 6^{2n-n} = 6^n$

$= (8 \cdot 8 \cdot 8)$

$8^6 \div 8^3 = 8^{6-3} = 8^3$

Directions Simplify each expression.

1. $7^{6n} \div 7^{5n}$ _____
2. $8^6 \div 8^2$ _____
3. $m^4 \div m^4$ _____
4. $22^8 \div 22^4$ _____
5. $k^2 \div k$ _____
6. $10^9 \div 10^7$ _____
7. $(-y)^6 \div (-y)^3$ _____
8. $11^{10} \div 11^{10}$ _____

9. $7^{14} \div 7^7$ _____
10. $10^5 \div 10$ _____
11. $(-6)^{6n} \div (-6)^{2n}$ _____
12. $2^5 \div 2^5$ _____
13. $30^4 \div 30^3$ _____
14. $d^3 \div d^2$ _____
15. $17^8 \div 17^2$ _____

Directions Tell whether each statement is *true or false*. If a statement is false, tell why.

16. $4^4 \div 4^4 = 4$ _____
17. $12^3 \div 12 = 12^2$ _____
18. $3^{6n} \div 3^{2n} = 3^{2n}$ _____
19. $9^7 \div 9^2 = 9^5$ _____
20. $1^5 \div 1^2 = 1^3$ _____

21. $16^8 \div 16^2 = 16^6$ _____
22. $4^6 \div 4^4 = 4^2$ _____
23. $10^{10} \div 10^3 = 10^7$ _____
24. $(-j)^{17} \div (-j)^2 = (-j)^9$ _____
25. $5^{12} \div 5^2 = 5^{10}$ _____

Exponents—Dividing

Directions Simplify each expression.

1. $a^4 \div a^2$ _____
2. $3^{12} \div 3^5$ _____
3. $r^2 \div r^2$ _____
4. $12^6 \div 12^4$ _____
5. $t^3 \div t$ _____

6. $9^9 \div 9^5$ _____
7. $q^6 \div q^1$ _____
8. $8^6 \div 8$ _____
9. $4^{26} \div 4^2$ _____
10. $100^5 \div 100^5$ _____

Directions Tell whether each statement is *true or false*. If a statement is false, give the correct answer.

11. $9^{6n} \div 9^{3n} = 9^{6n}$ _____
12. $11^3 \div 11^3 = 1$ _____
13. $24^4 \div 24^2 = 24^2$ _____
14. $m^2 \div m^2 = 1$ _____
15. $7^8 \div 7 = 7^7$ _____
16. $a^{12} \div a^6 = a^2$ _____
17. $2^5 \div 2 = 2^4$ _____
18. $9^{6n} \div 9^{4n} = 9^{2n}$ _____
19. $4^7 \div 4^2 = 4^5$ _____
20. $10^5 \div 10 = 10^4$ _____
21. $6^4 \div 6^1 = 6^3$ _____

22. $6^8 \div 6^8 = 6$ _____
23. $9^{10} \div 9^2 = 9^7$ _____
24. $a^7 \div a^4 = a^{11}$ _____
25. $15^2 \div 15^2 = 15^4$ _____
26. $5^{10} \div 5^5 = 5^5$ _____
27. $(-m)^7 \div (-m)^3 = (-m)^4$ _____
28. $n^{10} \div n^1 = n^9$ _____
29. $3^5 \div 3^3 = 3^2$ _____
30. $x^2 \div x^1 = x^1$ _____

Exercise A Simplify each expression.

1. $7^3 \div 7^2$ 7
2. $6^7 \div 6^3$ 6^4
3. $2^4 \div 2^3$ 2
4. $10^{18} \div 10^2$ 10^{16}
5. $9^4 \div 9^2$ 9^2
6. $x^8 \div x^4$ x^4

7. $h^7 \div h^4$ h^3
8. $w^{14} \div w^7$ w^7
9. $k^5 \div k^2$ k^3
10. $s^4 \div s$ s^3
11. $y^2 \div y^1$ y
12. $8^n \div 8^n$ 1

Try This

Divide.
$19^x \div 19^w$
$m^y \div m^y$

19^{x-w}, 1

Exercise B Tell whether each statement is *true* or *false*. If a statement is false, tell why.

13. $2^8 \div 2^2 = 2^4$
    False, $2^{8-2} = 2^6$
14. $6^6 \div 6^2 = 6^4$
    True
15. $9^3 \div 9^1 = 9^3$
    False, $9^{3-1} = 9^2$
16. $(-3)^6 \div (-3)^2 = (-3)^4$
    True
17. $3^3 \div 3 = 3^3$
    False, $3^{3-1} = 3^2$
18. $a^{10} \div a^5 = a^5$
    True
19. $x^{12} \div x^3 = x^4$
    False, $x^{12-3} = x^9$

20. $r^5 \div r^5 = 1$
    True, $r^{5-5} = r^0 = 1$
21. $(-s)^6 \div (-s)^2 = (-s)^3$
    False, $(-s)^{6-2} = (-s)^4$
22. $b^2 \div b^1 = b$
    True
23. $x^{15} \div x^3 = x^5$
    False, $x^{15-3} = x^{12}$
24. $k^{10} \div k^2 = k^8$
    True
25. $7^{3n} \div 7^{2n} = 7^n$
    True

Try This

Remind students that any number to the zero power is 1. Then ask them to prove that $m^y \div m^y = 1$ by

- using the rule.

- substituting numbers for letters and using mathematical operations.

($y - y = 0$, and $m^0 = 1$; $3^2 \div 3^2 = \frac{3 \cdot 3}{3 \cdot 3} = \frac{1}{1} = 1$)

COMMON ERROR

In this lesson and the last, because the operation called for is multiplication or division, the natural inclination is for students to multiply exponents instead of adding them or to divide exponents instead of subtracting them. Those who make such errors should rework problems, expressing the exponential forms as factors. Explain that these numbers are actually what is being divided; exponents are just a command, telling how many times the base is a factor.

MANIPULATIVES

Dividing with Exponents

Materials: Cuisenaire Rods, Pattern Blocks

Group Practice: Review Lesson 2, representing numbers and variables with exponents using rods and shapes. Use the rods and shapes to model the terms in the examples. To divide, place the model of the divisor (denominator) directly below the model of the dividend (numerator). Pair shapes or rods from the numerator and denominator, and remove them, explaining that each pair represents 1. The quotient is represented by the remaining rods or shapes.

Student Practice: Have students use the rods and shapes for Exercise A, problems 1–3, 5–7, 9–11 and Exercise B, problems 13–22.

3 Reinforce and Extend

LEARNING STYLES

Auditory/Verbal

When students understand the rule, give them practice in the subtraction operation. For each expression, have students identify each element (base, exponent, division sign) and give oral instructions about how to carry out the subtraction:

$7^9 \div 7^5$

$5^6 \div 5^2$

$20^7 \div 20^6$

(Example: 7 is the base; 9 and 5 are exponents. To divide 7 to the ninth power by 7 to the fifth power, subtract 5 from 9. The answer is 7 to the fourth power.)

For each false statement in Exercise B, have students explain to each other what error has been made and how to correct it.

Lesson at a Glance

Chapter 9 Lesson 4

Overview This lesson relates the area of a square to its exponential expression (s^2).

Objectives

- To recognize the relationship of the length and width of a square with the factors of s^2
- To find the area of a square, given the length of a side

Student Pages 238–239

Teacher's Resource Library TRL

　Workbook Activity 81

　Activity 77

　Alternative Activity 77

....

Mathematics Vocabulary

area

square

....

1 Warm-Up Activity

Review the formula for finding the area of a quadrilateral: $A = lw$. Draw a square on the board, and ask students to describe its sides. *(They are all the same length.)* Have the class formulate a rule for finding the area of a square. *(Possible statement: To find the area of a square, multiply the length of one side by itself.)* Ask, "How is this rule related to exponents?" *(A number times itself is raised to the second power; it has the exponent 2.)*

2 Teaching the Lesson

For visual reinforcement, represent the area of a square as a grid of units. This models the multiplication of one side by another, illustrating how it "covers" the whole area:

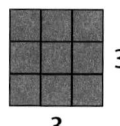

3

3

Students can then add the unit squares to confirm that it takes 9 to cover the area of the square.

If students have difficulty with the multiplication of 800^2 in problem 15,

---

You can use exponents to describe the **area** of a **square**.

> **Area**
> *The number of square units inside a closed region*
>
> **Square**
> *A four-sided shape with sides of equal length and four right angles*

EXAMPLE 1 Write an expression for the area of the square.

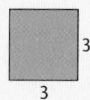

3

3

Area of a square = length • width = $3 • 3 = 3^2$

You can read 3^2 as "three squared."

The formula for the area of a square can also be written s^2 because the sides of a square are the same length.

You can read s^2 as "side squared."

Area = $s^2 = 5 • 5 = 5^2$

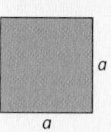

5

5

Area = $s^2 = a • a = a^2$

a

a

You can find the area of a square in square units by multiplying.

EXAMPLE 2 Find the area of a square with sides of six inches.

$s^2 = 6^2$

$= 6 • 6 = 36$ square inches

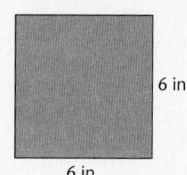

6 in.

6 in.

Name _____ Date _____ Period _____ **Workbook Activity**
Chapter 9, Lesson 4 **81**

Squares

EXAMPLE Write an expression for the area of a square.
Area of a square = length • width = $4 • 4 = 4^2$
or　Area of a square = side squared, or $s^2 = 4 • 4 = 4^2$
That is why 4^2 can be read as "4 squared."

4

4

Find the area of a square in square units by multiplying.
Area of a square = $s^2 = 5^2$
　　　　　　　　= $5^2 = 5 • 5 = 25$ sq cm

5 cm

5 cm

Directions Write an expression for the area of each square.

3
3
1. _____

x
x
2. _____

y
y
3. _____

Directions Multiply to find the area of each square. Use the formula Area = s^2.

4. Square with sides 7 centimeters long _____

5. Square with sides 2 centimeters long _____

6. Square with sides 6 centimeters long _____

Directions Write an expression to describe the problem. Then solve the problem.

7. Alicia has a board game that is 18 inches wide and 18 inches long. What is the area of the board game?

8. Harris is cultivating a garden that is 20 feet long and 20 feet wide. What is the area of his garden?

9. The floor plan for the game room in the new recreation center is 40 feet by 40 feet. What is the floor area in the game room?

10. Iris bought a new square tablecloth for the kitchen table. The cloth is 5 feet by 5 feet. What is its area?

TRL ○Publishing. Permission is granted to reproduce for classroom use only.　Mathematics: Pathways

Workbook Activity 81

Name _____ Date _____ Period _____ **Activity**
Chapter 9, Lesson 4 **77**

Area of Squares

Directions Write an expression for the area of each square.

2
2
1.

5
5
2.

1
1
3.

p
p
4.

d
d
5.

h
h
6.

Directions Multiply to find the area of each square. Use the formula Area = s^2.

7. Square with sides 4 centimeters long _____

8. Square with sides 9 centimeters long _____

9. Square with sides 7 centimeters long _____

10. Square with sides 11 centimeters long _____

11. Square with sides 14 centimeters long _____

12. Square with sides 22 centimeters long _____

Directions Solve each problem.

13. How many square yards of carpeting will Ms. Sereto need to buy for a room that is 15 feet long by 15 feet wide?

14. Bailey is painting one wall of his bedroom. The wall is 10 feet high and 10 feet long. What is the area of the wall Bailey is painting?

15. Enrico has drawn a picture on a square piece of paper that has an area of 169 sq in. Will the paper fit on a square scrapbook page that has sides 16 inches long?

TRL ○Publishing. Permission is granted to reproduce for classroom use only.　Mathematics: Pathways

Activity 77

Exercise A Write an expression for the area of each of these squares.

1. 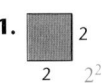 2
2 2^2

2.  4
4 4^2

3. 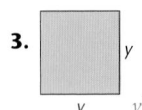 y
y y^2

4. 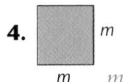 m
m m^2

5. p
p p^2

Exercise B Multiply to find the area of each square. Use the formula area = s^2.

6. Square with sides 7 centimeters long   49 sq cm

7. Square with sides 9 centimeters long   81 sq cm

8. Square with sides 2 centimeters long   4 sq cm

9. Square with sides 4 centimeters long   16 sq cm

10. Square with sides 3 centimeters long   9 sq cm

 **PROBLEM SOLVING**

Exercise C Solve each problem.

11. A room is 12 feet wide and 12 feet long. What is the area of a rug that covers the floor? 144 sq ft

12. The new classroom measures 35 feet on each side. How many square feet of tile cover the entire floor? 1,225 sq ft

13. Anika buys a fleece blanket that is seven feet long and seven feet wide. What is the area of the blanket? 49 sq ft

14. A can of paint covers 100 square feet. Dwayne wants to paint a wall that is 8 feet high and 8 feet long. Will one can of paint be enough for one coat? two coats? Explain. Yes, $8^2 = 64, 64 < 100$; No, $64 + 64 = 128, 128 > 100$

15. The farmer is harvesting a field that is 800 meters long and 800 meters wide. How many square meters is the field? 640,000 sq m

remind them that they need only know 8 • 8. They then add to the product one zero for each zero in the factors. Because there are 4 zeros, the answer is 640,000 sq m.

MANIPULATIVES

 Squares

Materials: Cuisenaire Rods

Group Practice: Use 3-rods to build a 3×3 square, as in the example. Write the symbolic equivalent for the model. Show students how to add the values of the rods to find the area of the square. Then use multiplication to find the area. Repeat using squares of other dimensions.

Student Practice: Have students use the rods for Exercise B, problems 6–10 and Exercise C, problems 13–14.

3 **Reinforce and Extend**

AT HOME

 Have students inventory and list items at home that are square. They must measure each to make sure that all the sides are the same length. Have students find the area of each square and add side length and area to the items on their lists. Ask them to select one item and devise a way to "prove" its area by covering it with paper units. (Hint: Students may choose to divide a square of paper into a grid.)

MODELING

 Have students use their rulers to find the area of a square object either on or in their desks. Have them measure one side of the object and then solve for the area. For a group project, have students work in pairs or teams to measure one side of the classroom. Then, ask students to use this measurement to find the area of the classroom. For the purposes of this project, assume that the room is a perfect square.

GROUP PROBLEM SOLVING

 Have students work in groups of three, using a T square and straightedge to draw squares of different sizes on butcher paper or cardboard. Ask students to record the length of a side in inches, feet, centimeters, or meters on the back of each square. Assign each group another group's square. The groups are to measure the lengths of the sides, divide each side into equal units of measure, and then find the area of the square, first by multiplication and second by drawing straight lines to form a grid of squares and counting these units. Finally, students should turn the squares over and see whether the unit of measure they used agrees with the original group's measurements.

Chapter 9 Lesson 5

Overview This lesson relates the volume of a cube to exponential notation.

Objectives

- To comprehend volume as area times height, or the number of units that completely fill a solid
- To recognize that the volume of a cube is equal to the length of its side to the third power
- To find the volume of a cube, given the length of a side

Student Pages 240–241

Teacher's Resource Library

Workbook Activity 82

Activity 78

Alternative Activity 78

Mathematics Vocabulary

volume

cube

1 Warm-Up Activity

Use a die or a box as a model cube. Have students name the shape of each face (*a square*) and count the number of squares (*6*). Ask, "How is the cube different from a square?" (*It has a third dimension—height.*) Encourage students to suggest ways in which they might measure the amount it would take to fill the cube. Have them read page 240 to test their ideas.

2 Teaching the Lesson

Keep on hand a model of a cube for reference. Write 2^3 on the board, and ask students how they might read the expression. (*two to the third power, two times itself three times, two cubed*) Explain that a number used as a factor three times is said to be *cubed* because the length, width, and height of a cube are the same value. Whereas s^2 calculates the area covered by a square, s^3 calculates the capacity of all of the interior of a cube, which is "built" from six squares.

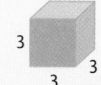

Lesson 5 Cubes

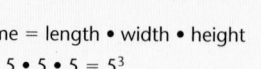

Volume

The number of cubic units that fill the interior of a solid

Cube

A solid with six square faces

You can also use exponents to describe the **volume** of a **cube**. The volume of the cube is given in cubic units.

EXAMPLE 1 Write an expression for the volume of the cube.

Volume = length • width • height

$= 3 \cdot 3 \cdot 3 = 3^3$

You can read 3^3 as "three cubed."

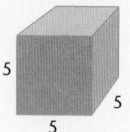

Volume = length • width • height

$= 5 \cdot 5 \cdot 5 = 5^3$

Volume = length • width • height

$= a \cdot a \cdot a = a^3$

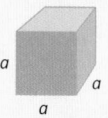

The formula for the volume of a cube can also be written s^3 because the sides of the cube are the same length.

You can read s^3 as "side cubed."

Volume $= s^3 = 5 \cdot 5 \cdot 5 = 5^3$

Volume $= s^3 = a \cdot a \cdot a = a^3$

You can find the volume of a cube in cubic units by multiplying.

EXAMPLE 2 Find the volume of a cube with sides of six inches.

$s^3 = 6^3 = 6 \cdot 6 \cdot 6 = 216$ cubic inches

Exercise A Multiply to find the volume of each cube. Use the formula volume $= s^3$.

1. Cube with sides 3 inches long   27 cu in.

2. Cube with sides 7 inches long   343 cu in.

3. Cube with sides 5 inches long   125 cu in.

240   *Chapter 9 Exponents, Radicals, and the Pythagorean Theorem*

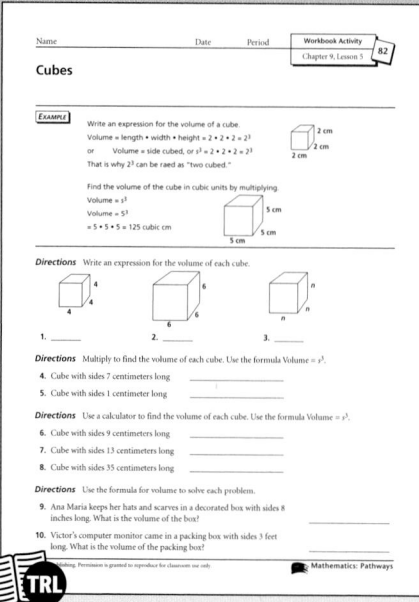

Workbook Activity 82

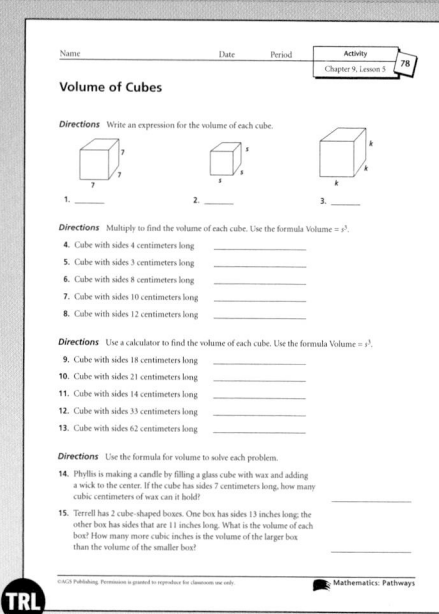

Activity 78

Exercise B Write an expression for the volume of each of these cubes.

4. 4^3

5. 2^3

6. 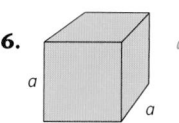 a^3

7. 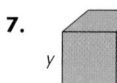 y^3

8. 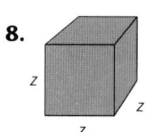 z^3

Calculator Practice

You can use a scientific calculator to find the volume of a cube. You will use the y^x or x^y key.

EXAMPLE 3 Find the volume of a cube with sides of 4 centimeters. Volume = s^3 = 4^3

Press 4 y^x 3 =.

The display reads 64.

The volume of the cube is 64 cubic centimeters.

Exercise C Use the calculator to find the volume of each cube.

9. Cube with sides of 8 centimeters   512 cu cm

10. Cube with sides of 15 centimeters   3,375 cu cm

11. Cube with sides of 2 centimeters   8 cu cm

12. Cube with sides of 12 centimeters   1,728 cu cm

13. Cube with sides of 18 centimeters   5,832 cu cm

PROBLEM SOLVING

Exercise D Use the formula for volume to solve each problem.

14. Marlene is filling an aquarium that is 1 foot high, 1 foot long, and 1 foot deep. What is the volume of water in cubic feet that will fit in the tank?
1 cu ft

15. A television is shipped in a packing box that is a cube. One side is 3 feet long. What is the volume of the packing box? 27 cu ft

Exponents, Radicals, and the Pythagorean Theorem   Chapter 9   **241**

MANIPULATIVES

 Cubes

Materials: Cuisenaire Rods

Group Practice: Use 3-rods to build a cube with sides of 3 units, as in the example. Write the symbolic equivalent for the model. Unstack the rods, and arrange them to form a rectangle. Use multiplication to calculate the volume of the cube. Repeat for the next example.

Student Practice: Have students use the rods for Exercise A, problems 1–3 and Exercise D, problems 14–15.

3   Reinforce and Extend

CALCULATOR

 Students who use arithmetic calculators should have no trouble calculating the volume of a cube, which uses the length of a side as a factor three times. For a cube with sides 9 inches long,

Enter 9 × 9 × 9 =.

The display reads 729.

The volume of the cube is 729 cubic inches.

GROUP PROBLEM SOLVING

Explore the relationship between the length of a cube's side and its volume. Have students work in groups of four or five to

- calculate the volumes of cubes with sides whose lengths are 1, 2, 3, 4, 5, 6, 7, 8, 9, and 10 inches.

- make a table comparing these measurements.

(Possible table format shown)

Cube	Factors	Volume	Increase
1^3	1 • 1 • 1	1 cu. in.	0 units
2^3	2 • 2 • 2	8 cu. in.	7 units

- construct cubes with sides of 2, 6, and 10 inches for comparison.

- write a paragraph summarizing their findings. (Have students think in terms of the difference an inch would make if they were allowed to fill their cubes with gold.)

Lesson at a Glance

Chapter 9 Lesson 6

Overview This lesson explains how to take the square root of a number.

Objectives

- To perceive finding the root as the opposite of finding the area of a square—that is, discovering the "length of a side"
- To identify a as the square root of a^2
- To estimate and calculate square roots of whole numbers

Student Pages 242–245

Teacher's Resource Library

Workbook Activity 83

Activity 79

Alternative Activity 79

Mathematics Vocabulary

root
square root

1 Warm-Up Activity

Write on the board

$$a^2 = b$$

and have students describe each unknown. (*a is a number squared, or multiplied by itself; b is the product of that operation.*) Assign *b* a value (say, 36) and ask students how they would find the value of *a*. (*They might evaluate what number times itself gives 36.*) Inform students that this factor *a* is called the square root of *b*. This lesson shows how to find it.

2 Teaching the Lesson

Representing numbers as an area of a square helps students visualize finding the square root (or length of a side). Tell students that the text examples represent perfect squares (the square root is a whole number). However, substituting areas such as 8, 10, and 12 should demonstrate quickly that most integers do not have whole number square roots. It should also prepare students for the logic of estimating square roots using

---

Root
An equal factor of a number

Square root
A factor of a power of two

The opposite of raising a number to a power is called taking the **root** of a number. The symbol $\sqrt{}$ is used to indicate taking a **square root**.

EXAMPLE 1

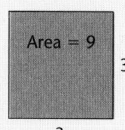

Area = 9

Area = 3^2
Area = (3)(3) = 9 square units
3 squared equals 9.

$\sqrt{9} = 3$
The square root of 9 equals 3.
Side of square = $\sqrt{9} = 3$

EXAMPLE 2

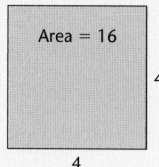

Area = 16

Area = 4^2
Area = (4)(4) = 16 square units
4 squared equals 16.

$\sqrt{16} = 4$
The square root of 16 equals 4.
Side of square = $\sqrt{16} = 4$

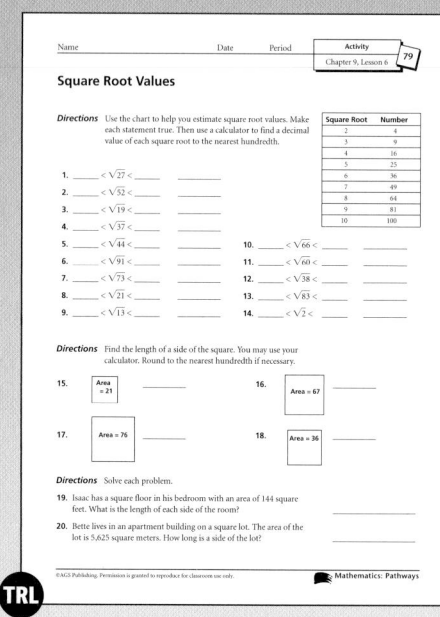

Workbook Activity 83   **Activity 79**

EXAMPLE 3

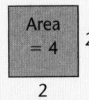

Area = 2^2

Area = $(2)(2)$ = 4 square units

2 squared equals 4.

$\sqrt{4} = 2$

The square root of 4 equals 2.

Side of square = $\sqrt{4} = 2$

EXAMPLE 4

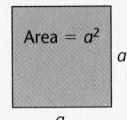

Area = a^2

Area = $(a)(a)$

$\sqrt{a^2} = a$

The square root of a^2 equals a.

Side of square = $\sqrt{a^2} = a$

You can use a number line like the one below to help you estimate the square roots of numbers that are not perfect squares.

1	2	3	4

$1 < \ 2 < \ 3 < \ 4 < \ 5 < \ 6 < \ 7 < \ 8 < \ 9 < \ 10 < \ 11 < \ 12 < \ 13 < \ 14 < \ 15 < \ 16$

$\sqrt{1} < \sqrt{2} < \sqrt{3} < \sqrt{4} < \sqrt{5} < \sqrt{6} < \sqrt{7} < \sqrt{8} < \sqrt{9} < \sqrt{10} < \sqrt{11} < \sqrt{12} < \sqrt{13} < \sqrt{14} < \sqrt{15} < \sqrt{16}$

$\sqrt{2}$ is between 1 and 2.

$\sqrt{7}$ is between 2 and 3.

$\sqrt{13}$ is between 3 and 4.

---

the number line chart on page 243. As students estimate a square root, ask them to plug it into a square model and see whether the square root squared gives the original number.

MANIPULATIVES

 Square Roots

Materials: Cuisenaire Rods

Group Practice: To find the square root of a number, try to build a square using the same number of cubes as the number inside the radical. If a square can be built, the number is a perfect square, and the length of one side represents the square root.

If a square cannot be made with the cubes, make the largest square possible, noting how many cubes are left over. Then add more cubes to build the next largest square, noting how many more cubes are needed. Use the two squares to estimate the square root of the original number. For example, to estimate $\sqrt{8}$, the largest square with eight cubes has area 4, sides of $\sqrt{4}$, with four cubes left over. By adding one cube to the eight, you can make a square with sides $\sqrt{9}$. Therefore, $\sqrt{8}$ is between $\sqrt{4}$ and $\sqrt{9}$, but closer to $\sqrt{9}$. Repeat for $\sqrt{5}, \sqrt{13}$, and $\sqrt{17}$.

Student Practice: Have students use the rods for problems 1–8 in Exercise A.

 3 Reinforce and Extend

LEARNING STYLES

Visual/Spatial

Provide models of squares whose areas are 16, 20, and 25 square inches, respectively, without providing the lengths of their sides. Ask students to determine the length of each side without using a ruler. Then have them use a ruler to check their answers. *(Sides are 4, 4.472, and 5.)*

Have students memorize these simple square roots so that they are able to estimate irrational square roots more quickly.

$$\sqrt{1} = 1 \qquad \sqrt{49} = 7$$
$$\sqrt{4} = 2 \qquad \sqrt{64} = 8$$
$$\sqrt{9} = 3 \qquad \sqrt{81} = 9$$
$$\sqrt{16} = 4 \qquad \sqrt{100} = 10$$
$$\sqrt{25} = 5 \qquad \sqrt{121} = 11$$
$$\sqrt{36} = 6 \qquad \sqrt{144} = 12$$

Then give students numbers that fall between these squares, and have them use mental math to place the numbers on a number line and estimate their roots in this way.

30: "30 is between the perfect squares 25 and 36. The square root of 25 is 5, and the square root of 36 is 6. Therefore, the square root of 30 is between 5 and 6."

CALCULATOR

Calculators vary in their handling of square root calculations. For example, to find the square root of 7, the TI-83 scientific calculator requires that you enter the square root symbol (which first requires pressing the A-lock key to access the symbol) before entering the number 7. Press ENTER to display the root—2.645751311. Have students note the number of places their calculator shows, and review rounding of decimals to the nearest hundredth and thousandth.

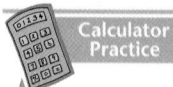

Calculator Practice You can use a calculator to find a more accurate decimal value of a square root. You will need a calculator with a $\sqrt{}$ key.

EXAMPLE 5 Use a calculator to find the value of $\sqrt{2}$.

First, estimate the value of $\sqrt{2}$: $1 < \sqrt{2} < 2$. You know the value of $\sqrt{2}$ will be between the whole numbers 1 and 2.

Next, use a calculator to find a decimal approximation of $\sqrt{2}$.

Press *2* $\sqrt{}$.

The display reads *1.414213562*.

Exercise A Find the positive whole numbers that make each statement true. Then use a calculator to find a decimal value of each square root. Round to the nearest hundredth.

1. $\blacksquare < \sqrt{3} < \blacksquare$
   1, 2; 1.73
2. $\blacksquare < \sqrt{5} < \blacksquare$
   2, 3; 2.24
3. $\blacksquare < \sqrt{6} < \blacksquare$
   2, 3; 2.45
4. $\blacksquare < \sqrt{7} < \blacksquare$
   2, 3; 2.65
5. $\blacksquare < \sqrt{8} < \blacksquare$
   2, 3; 2.83
6. $\blacksquare < \sqrt{11} < \blacksquare$
   3, 4; 3.32
7. $\blacksquare < \sqrt{13} < \blacksquare$
   3, 4; 3.61
8. $\blacksquare < \sqrt{23} < \blacksquare$
   4, 5; 4.80

9. $\blacksquare < \sqrt{99} < \blacksquare$
   9, 10; 9.95
10. $\blacksquare < \sqrt{101} < \blacksquare$
    10, 11; 10.05
11. $\blacksquare < \sqrt{105} < \blacksquare$
    10, 11; 10.25
12. $\blacksquare < \sqrt{122} < \blacksquare$
    11, 12; 11.05
13. $\blacksquare < \sqrt{216} < \blacksquare$
    14, 15; 14.70
14. $\blacksquare < \sqrt{331} < \blacksquare$
    18, 19; 18.19
15. $\blacksquare < \sqrt{427} < \blacksquare$
    20, 21; 20.66

Exercise B Find the length of a side of each square. You may use your calculator. Round to the nearest tenth.

16.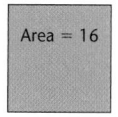
Area = 16

4

17.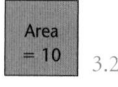
Area = 10

3.2

18.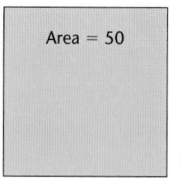
Area = 50

7.1

19.
Area = 8

2.8

20.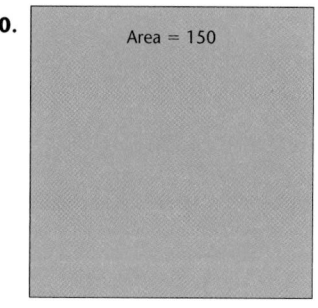
Area = 150

12.2

Estimation Activity

Estimate: "Square Roots" to the nearest whole number.

Solution: Try to "squeeze" $\sqrt{16}$, $\sqrt{23}$, $\sqrt{25}$ between perfect square 4, $\sqrt{23}$, 5

But $\sqrt{23}$ is closer to $\sqrt{25}$ than to $\sqrt{16}$, so 5 is the best estimate.

Chapter 9 Lesson 7

Overview This lesson explains irrational roots and models a way to approximate their values on a graph.

Objectives

- To differentiate numbers whose roots are irrational from those whose roots are rational
- To use a graph to estimate square roots involving decimals

Student Pages 246–247

Teacher's Resource Library

Workbook Activity 84

Activity 80

Alternative Activity 80

Mathematics Vocabulary

irrational number

graph

---

1 Warm-Up Activity

Write on the board

1 2 3 4 5 6 7 8 9

and ask students to circle the numbers with whole number roots. (*1, 4, and 9*) Remind students that these numbers are called perfect squares, and tell them that the whole number roots of these numbers are called rational numbers. Ask, "What do the square roots of the other numbers have in common?" (*They are not whole numbers.*) Have the class read the lesson to learn about irrational numbers and a new way to estimate irrational square roots.

2 Teaching the Lesson

Make a large copy of the graph on page 247 on the overhead or the board. Explain that the *x*-axis represents square roots and the *y*-axis represents squares. The point on the grid where lines from the two numbers meet forms the curving line, or graph. The dots on the line mark the points at which perfect squares and their rational square roots come together. The larger-size graph will make it easier for

---

Irrational number

A real number such as $\sqrt{2}$ that cannot be written in the form $\frac{a}{b}$ in which a and b are whole numbers and $b \neq 0$

Graph

A diagram showing how one quantity depends on another

The square roots of some numbers are whole numbers. Often, however, the square root of a number is not a whole number.

Roots of numbers that equal a whole number are called rational numbers. Roots of numbers that do not equal whole numbers are called **irrational numbers.**

EXAMPLE 1 $\sqrt{9}$ is a rational number (3).

$\sqrt{16}$ is a rational number (4).

$\sqrt{3}$ is an irrational number.

$\sqrt{7}$ is an irrational number.

It is important to note that not all roots are irrational. For instance, $\sqrt{4} = 2$, and $\sqrt{25} = 5$. In these cases, the root is equal to a rational number, so these roots are *not* irrational.

You can use a **graph** to find the approximate value of an irrational number.

When you draw the line from 45 to the graph, think "45 is closer to 49 than 36." You will graph your point so that it is closer to the point where 49 crosses 7 than the point where 6 crosses 36.

EXAMPLE 2 Find the value of $\sqrt{45}$.

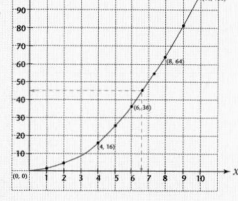

Step 1 Estimate the value of $\sqrt{45}$. 45 is between 36 and 49, so $\sqrt{45}$ is between 6 and 7. $\sqrt{45}$ is an irrational number.

Step 2 Find 45 on the left-hand scale. Draw a straight line from 45 to the graph.

Step 3 Draw a straight line from that point of the graph to the bottom axis. That line will cross the bottom axis at the value $\sqrt{45}$. In this case, the value is approximately 6.7, so $\sqrt{45} \approx 6.7$.

Step 4 Compare this value to the calculator value. Press 45 √ .

The display reads 6.7082039.

So 6.7 from the graph agrees with the calculator value of 6.7082039 rounded to nearest tenth.

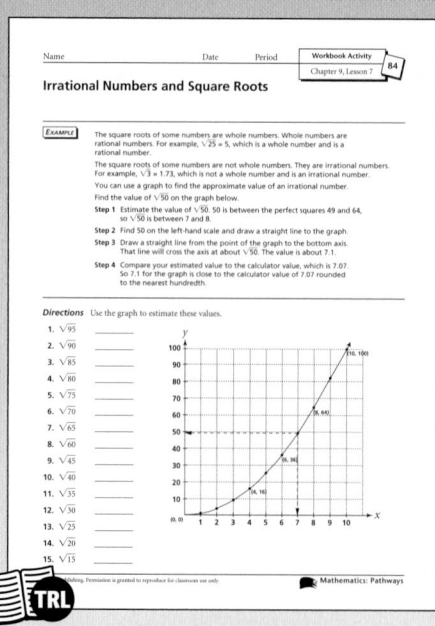

Workbook Activity 84

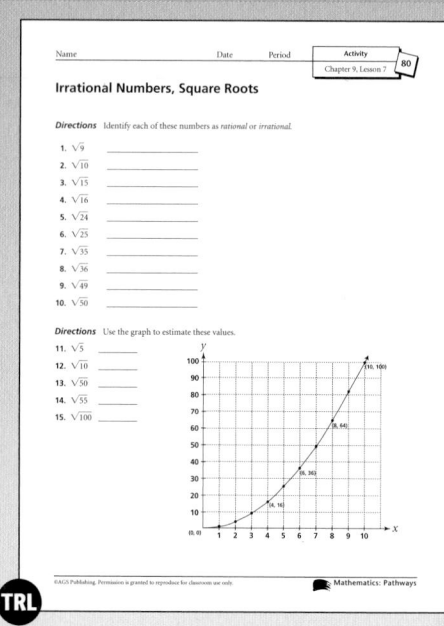

Activity 80

EXAMPLE 3 Find the value of $\sqrt{55}$.

Step 1 Estimate the value of $\sqrt{55}$. 55 is between 49 and 64, so $\sqrt{55}$ is between 7 and 8 and is an irrational number.

Step 2 Find 55 on the left-hand scale. Draw a straight line from 55 to the graph.

Step 3 Draw a straight line from the point of the graph to the bottom axis. The line will cross the bottom axis at the value $\sqrt{55}$. In this case, the value is approximately 7.5, so $\sqrt{55} \approx 7.5$.

Step 4 Compare this value to the calculator value. Press 55 $\sqrt{}$.

The display reads 7.4161984.

So 7.5 from the graph roughly agrees with the calculator value of 7.4161984.

The symbol $\approx$ means "is approximately equal to"

Exercise A Use the graph to estimate these values.

Estimates are shown.

1. $\sqrt{10}$	3.2	**6.** $\sqrt{60}$	7.7
2. $\sqrt{20}$	4.5	**7.** $\sqrt{65}$	8.1
3. $\sqrt{30}$	5.5	**8.** $\sqrt{75}$	8.7
4. $\sqrt{40}$	6.3	**9.** $\sqrt{85}$	9.2
5. $\sqrt{50}$	7.1	**10.** $\sqrt{95}$	9.7

 Try This

Use a calculator to find the square roots of these numbers: 81, 91, 111, 121. Tell whether each square root is a rational or an irrational number. If irrational, round to the nearest tenth.

$\sqrt{81} = 9$, rational

$\sqrt{91} \approx 9.5$, irrational

$\sqrt{111} \approx 10.5$, irrational

$\sqrt{121} = 11$, rational

Exponents, Radicals, and the Pythagorean Theorem Chapter 9 **247**

---

students to follow the path straight out to the curve and straight down to locate irrational square roots.

Try This

If a calculator is not available, students can determine rational squares by remembering multiplication facts: $9 \cdot 9 = 81$ and $11 \cdot 11 = 121$, so 81 and 121 have rational square roots. $10 \cdot 10 = 100$, so the square root of 111 must be a decimal between 10 and 11, and that of 91 must be between 9 and 10; the square roots of 91 and 111 are irrational.

3 Reinforce and Extend

GROUP PROBLEM SOLVING

 How many numbers between 1 and 200 are perfect squares? How many have irrational square roots? Have students work in groups of three to answer these questions. You may wish to suggest that they make a table or that they review what they already know from multiplication tables. (Hint: The square roots of perfect squares between 1 and 196 are integers from 1 to 14.) *(14 numbers between 1 and 200 are perfect squares; 186 have irrational square roots.)*

LEARNING STYLES

 **Logical/Mathematical**

Display a table of perfect squares less than 100 and their square roots.

Perfect Square	Square Root
1	1
4	2
9	3
. . . *and so on.*	

Have students find the square roots of the following numbers by the guess-and-check method, referring to the chart for a beginning guess and refining the factors with each multiplication. Students should show all calculations and check their answers using a calculator.

12	*(3.464)*
24	*(4.899)*
42	*(6.481)*

Exponents, Radicals, and the Pythagorean Theorem **247**

Chapter 9 Lesson 8

Overview This lesson introduces rational and irrational roots of integers.

Objective

- To use a calculator to find the roots of radicals and identify the roots as rational or irrational

Student Pages 248–249

Teacher's Resource Library TRL

Workbook Activity 85

Activity 81

Alternative Activity 81

Mathematics Vocabulary

radical
radical sign

---

1 Warm-Up Activity

Remind students that the integer 5, when multiplied by itself, creates a product of 25. Working in groups of four, challenge students to use a calculator and find a decimal value in tenths that, when multiplied by itself, as closely approximates 12 as possible without being greater than 12. Repeat the activity several times, using other whole numbers. Each time, challenge each group to find the number, with a goal of using fewer guesses or trials than the other groups in the classroom use.

2 Teaching the Lesson

Not all calculators require a user to perform the same steps when finding the root of a number. For example, to find the root of 36, some calculators will require the user to input 36 and then press the radical key. Other calculators will require a user to first press the radical key, then enter 36, and then press the equals key. Prior to assigning homework exercises, make sure that each student understands the sequence that is required by his or her calculator for generating roots.

Radical

A number that is written with the radical sign

Radical sign

The mathematical symbol (√) placed before a number or algebraic expression to indicate that the root should be found

Recall that the set of real numbers can be grouped into two groups—rational numbers and irrational numbers.

Irrational numbers include the square root, cube root, and *n*th root of many numbers. $\sqrt[3]{\ }$ is a cube root, and $\sqrt[n]{\ }$ is an *n*th root. These numbers are sometimes called roots, or **radicals**, because they are written with the **radical sign** (√). These are examples: $\sqrt{2}$, $\sqrt{3}$, $\sqrt[3]{2}$, and so on. It is important to note that not all radicals or roots are irrational. For instance, $\sqrt{4} = 2$, because $2 \cdot 2 = 4$; $\sqrt[3]{-8} = -2$, because $(-2)(-2)(-2) = -8$; $\sqrt[5]{32} = 2$, because $2 \cdot 2 \cdot 2 \cdot 2 \cdot 2 = 32$. In each case, the root is an integer. You know that integers are also rational numbers, so these roots are *not* irrational.

Use your calculator to find the decimal expansion of irrational numbers.

Remember, a root is an equal factor of a number or expression. Roots, or radicals, that cannot be written in the form $\frac{a}{b}$ in which *a* and *b* are whole numbers and $b \neq 0$ are called irrational numbers.

EXAMPLE 1 Write the decimal expansion for $\sqrt{2}$.

Use a calculator to find the decimal expansion of $\sqrt{2}$.

Press 2 $\boxed{\sqrt{\ }}$. On many calculators, the answer will be displayed after the $\boxed{\sqrt{\ }}$ is pressed. On some calculators, you will have to press $\boxed{=}$ for the answer to be displayed.

The display reads *1.4142136*.

This expansion does *not* end in zeroes and it does *not* have a repeating pattern. Therefore, $\sqrt{2}$ is *not* a rational number. Because the display of some calculators is limited to 8 digits, $\sqrt{2} = 1.4142136 \ldots$ is an approximation of the complete decimal expansion. This is often written using " ≈," a symbol standing for *approximately equal*.

So $\sqrt{2} \approx 1.4142136$, which is an irrational number. The decimal expansion of an irrational number does not end, and does not repeat. In other words, an irrational number is nonterminating and nonrepeating.

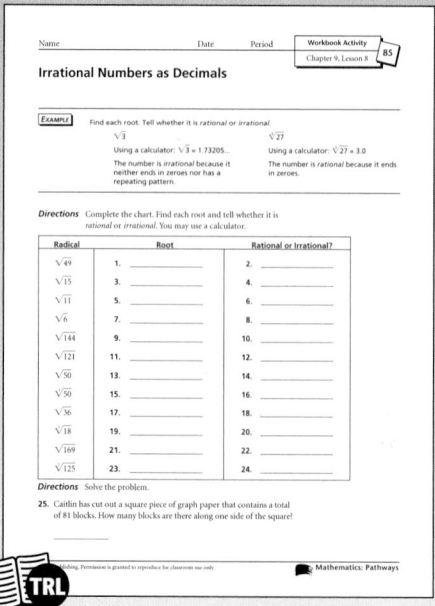

Workbook Activity 85

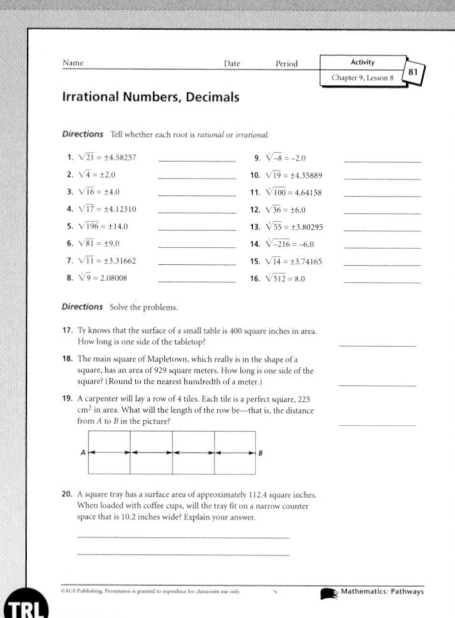

Activity 81

EXAMPLE 2 Write a decimal expansion for $\sqrt[3]{2}$. Tell whether it is rational or irrational.

Use a calculator to find the cube root. Note that the cube root key may look like $\sqrt[3]{x}$, $\sqrt[3]{\ }$, or $\sqrt[3]{y}$ depending on the calculator.

Press 2 $\sqrt[3]{x}$. The display shows 1.259921.

The decimal is not terminating and not repeating, so $\sqrt[3]{2}$ is irrational.

EXAMPLE 3 The area of a square is 30 cm². What is the length of one side (s) of the square?

Area $= s^2$, so $\sqrt{\text{area}} = s$

You can estimate the length of one side by comparing the area to known squares:

$\sqrt{25} < \sqrt{30} < \sqrt{36}$ so $5 < s < 6$

Use a calculator to make a closer approximation.

Press 30 $\sqrt{\ }$. The display shows 5.477225.

s | 30 cm²

s

Exercise A Use your calculator to find the roots for these radicals. Tell whether they are rational or irrational.

1. $\sqrt[3]{400}$
7.368, irrational

3. $\sqrt[5]{400}$
3.314, irrational

5. $\sqrt[3]{45}$
3.557, irrational

7. $\sqrt[10]{1,024}$
2, rational

9. $\sqrt[8]{256}$
2, rational

2. $\sqrt[4]{400}$
4.472, irrational

4. $\sqrt[3]{512}$
8, rational

6. $\sqrt[9]{512}$
2, rational

8. $\sqrt[2]{30}$
5.477, irrational

10. $\sqrt{55}$
7.416, irrational

PROBLEM SOLVING

Exercise B Answer the following questions. You may use a calculator.

11. Hisako is building a square birdhouse with a 36 in.² floor. How long will each side of the birdhouse floor be? 6 in.

12. Sharon wants to make a square poster with an area of about 500 cm². What will be the length of each side of the square, rounded to the nearest hundredth? 22.36 cm

13. Jesse's room has an area of 160 ft². What is the length of one side of the square room? Round to the nearest hundredth. 12.65 ft

14. A store has a square floor space with an area of 1,600 ft². Can you find the exact length of a side of this square? Explain.

15. A building is divided into four square offices with each having 49 square units. What is the area of the building (larger square)? What is the length of a side of the larger square?

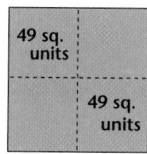

49 sq. units

49 sq. units

MENTAL MATH

Invite volunteers to name the following roots:

$\sqrt{100}$	(10)
$\sqrt[3]{8}$	(2)
$\sqrt{64}$	(8)
$\sqrt[3]{64}$	(4)
$\sqrt[3]{27}$	(9)
$\sqrt{144}$	(12)
$\sqrt{400}$	(20)
$\sqrt[4]{16}$	(2)
$\sqrt{900}$	(30)
$\sqrt[3]{8,000}$	(20)

$= 40^2$.
se
00 is
nal
er, it

units;

Lesson at a Glance

Chapter 9 Lesson 9

Overview This lesson introduces equations that contain a radical and a variable or an unknown.

Objective

- To determine the value of a variable in an equation that contains a radical

Student Pages 250–253

Teacher's Resource Library (TRL)

Workbook Activities 86

Activity 82

Alternative Activity 82

1 Warm-Up Activity

Invite students to consider and solve the following riddles:

"I am thinking of a fraction. When you subtract $\frac{3}{4}$ and add $\frac{1}{2}$ to the fraction, the result is $\frac{1}{4}$. What is the fraction?" $\left(\frac{1}{2}\right)$

"I am thinking of a positive integer. When you subtract -3 and add -7 to the number, the result is 6. What is the integer?" *(10)*

"I am thinking of a negative integer. When you add 11 to the integer and then find the square root of the sum, the result is 3. What is the integer?" *(-2)*

"I am thinking of a positive whole number. When you cube the number and then take its square root, the result is 8. What is the number?" *(4)*

"I am thinking of a fraction. When you square the fraction and then take its fourth root, the answer is $\frac{1}{3}$. What is the fraction?" $\left(\frac{1}{9}\right)$

2 Teaching the Lesson

Prior to discussing the examples beginning on page 250, write the equation $x + 2 = 9$ on the board, and remind students that the answer, $x = 7$, is found by subtracting 2 from both sides of the equation. Explain that adding, subtracting, multiplying, or dividing both sides of an equation by the same number helps *isolate* the variable. When an

Suppose you were asked to solve this puzzle: "The square root of a number is 10. What is the number?" You could solve the puzzle by letting n equal the number and writing the puzzle in terms of an equation:

$$\sqrt{n} = 10$$

If the sides of two squares are equal, then the squares are equal. If $\square a = \square b$, then $a^2 = b^2$. Therefore, you can "square" both sides of the equation: $(\sqrt{n})^2 = (10)^2$

And then solve for n: $n = 100$

EXAMPLE 1 Find x when $\sqrt{3x} = 4$.

First, square both sides of the equation.

$(\sqrt{3x})^2 = 4^2$ Then solve for x.

$3x = 16$

$x = \frac{16}{3}$

Check: $\sqrt{3\left(\frac{16}{3}\right)} = 4$ $\sqrt{16} = 4$ True

EXAMPLE 2 Find x when $\sqrt{x - 1} = 5$.

Square both sides of the equation, then solve for x.

$[\sqrt{(x - 1)}]^2 = 5^2$

$x - 1 = 25$

$x = 26$

Check: $\sqrt{(26 - 1)} = 5$ $\sqrt{25} = 5$ True

EXAMPLE 3 Find x when $12 - \sqrt{3x} = 4$.

Step 1 In this case, you must first isolate the variable. Place the term with the variable on one side of the equation and place all other terms on the opposite side of the equation.

$12 - \sqrt{3x} = 4$ is the same as $-\sqrt{3x} = -8$.

Workbook Activity 86

Activity 82

EXAMPLE 3 *(continued)*

Step 2 Square both sides of the equation and solve for x.

$$-\sqrt{3x} = -8$$
$$(-\sqrt{3x})^2 = (-8)^2$$
$$3x = 64$$
$$x = \frac{64}{3}$$

Check: $12 - \sqrt{3x} = 4$

$$12 - \sqrt{3\left(\frac{64}{3}\right)} = 4$$
$$12 - \sqrt{64} = 4$$
$$12 - 8 = 4 \quad \text{True}$$

You may also need to use radicals when presented with some formulas.

EXAMPLE 4 What is the length of the side of a square whose area is A?

Write the question in equation form: $A = s^2$. Then solve for s.
Your answer is in simplified radical form.

$$A = s^2, \sqrt{A} = s \text{ or } s = \sqrt{A}$$

What is the length of the side of a square whose area is 25 cm²?

$$s = \sqrt{A}$$
$$s = \sqrt{25} \text{ or } 5 \text{ cm}$$

EXAMPLE 5 What is the radius of a circle whose area is A?

Write the question in equation form: $A = \pi r^2$.

Isolate r^2 on one side of the equation.

$$A = \pi r^2 \text{ is the same as } \frac{A}{\pi} = r^2.$$

Solve for r.

$$\sqrt{\left(\frac{A}{\pi}\right)} = r \text{ or } r = \sqrt{\left(\frac{A}{\pi}\right)}$$

What is the radius of a circle whose area is 12 cm²? Let $\pi \approx 3$.

$$r = \sqrt{\left(\frac{A}{\pi}\right)}$$
$$r = \sqrt{\frac{12}{3}}$$
$$r = \sqrt{4} \text{ or } 2 \text{ cm}$$

Diameter (d) is the distance across a circle through its center. Radius (r) is one half the diameter, the distance from the center of a circle to the edge of the circle.

unknown in the form of a variable is isolated in any equation, the value of the variable becomes known.

After discussing Example 5 at the bottom of page 251, explain that the formula $\frac{A}{\pi} = r^2$ is derived from the formula $A = \pi r^2$ by isolating r^2. This isolation is accomplished by dividing both sides of the equation by π:

$$A = \pi r^2$$
$$\frac{A}{\pi} = \frac{\pi r^2}{\pi}$$
$$\frac{A}{\pi} = r^2$$

3 **Reinforce and Extend**

LEARNING STYLES

Body/Kinesthetic
Invite students to use graph paper or other classroom materials to model problems 14–20 on pages 252 and 253.

GROUP PROBLEM SOLVING

Encourage students to work in groups of three to discuss and solve the following problem:

Does $\sqrt{x} - \sqrt{y} = \sqrt{(x - y)}$? Explain.

(The statement is true if $y = 0$ or if $x = 0$ and $y = 0$. The statement is false for all other values of x and y.)

Exercise A Solve each equation for the variable.

1. $\sqrt{n} = 7$ $n = 49$
2. $\sqrt{x} = 4$ $x = 16$
3. $\sqrt{2y} = 6$ $y = 18$
4. $\sqrt{4m} = 8$ $m = 16$
5. $\sqrt{5y} = 35$ $y = 245$
6. $\sqrt{z} = \frac{3}{2}$ $z = \frac{9}{4}$
7. $\sqrt{3x} = 7$ $x = 16\frac{1}{3}$
8. $\sqrt{4x} = 6$ $x = 9$

Exercise B Solve each equation for x. Check your answers.

9. $13 - \sqrt{x} = 5$ $x = 64$
10. $29 - \sqrt{x} = 13$ $x = 256$
11. $43 - \sqrt{x} = 18$ $x = 625$
12. $\sqrt{x} - 9 = 16$ $x = 625$
13. $\sqrt{(2x - 1)} = 16$ $x = 128\frac{1}{2}$

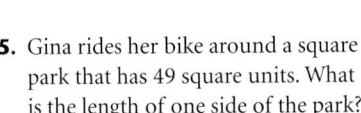

PROBLEM SOLVING

Exercise C Solve each problem.

14. In the new mall, each store has a square floor space of 36 square units. What is the length of one side of the store?   6 units

$A = 36$ sq. units s

s

15. Gina rides her bike around a square park that has 49 square units. What is the length of one side of the park?   7 units

16. Carrie has drawn a right triangle. She asks you to determine the lengths of the sides of the triangle by using the formula $a^2 + b^2 = c^2$. Solve for a, b, and c.

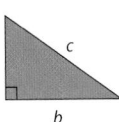

a c

b

$a^2 + b^2 = c^2$

$a = \sqrt{c^2 - b^2}$
$b = \sqrt{c^2 - a^2}$
$c = \sqrt{a^2 + b^2}$

The formula for the area of a circle with radius r is $A = \pi r^2$. Use this formula for Problems 17 and 18.

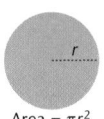

Area = πr^2

17. The small, circular area rug in Jackson's room has an area of 1,200 square inches. What is the length of the rug's radius? (Use $\pi \approx 3$.) You may use radicals in your answer. 20 in.

18. Juanita draws a chalk circle on the sidewalk after tying the chalk to a length of string and taping the string to the ground. The length of the string is equal to the radius of the circle. How long is her string if the circle has an area of 81 square units? (Use $\pi \approx 3$.) $\sqrt{27}$ units or 5.196 units

The formula for the volume of a cylinder with radius r is $V = \pi r^2 h$. Use this formula for Problems 19 and 20.

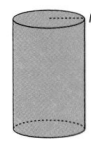

$V = \pi r^2 h$

19. Cal is making a lid for a can shaped like a cylinder. What is the radius of the circle Cal must make for the lid? The volume (V) of the cylinder is 600 cubic units and its height is 200 units. What is its radius? (Use $\pi \approx 3$.) 1 unit

20. An auto mechanic pours used oil into a cylindrical drum. What is the radius of the lid of the drum if the drum's volume is 1,200 cubic units and its height is 16 units? (Use $\pi \approx 3$.) 5 units

Technology Connection

Designing Buildings on a Computer
Most architects use computer-aided design (CAD) software programs to design buildings. Many of these CAD programs contain basic designs that an architect can change to suit his or her needs. CAD programs can be great time-savers, because the architect doesn't have to start over each time. The program can show a 3-D picture of the building from all sides. This is a great aid to their clients. Some people have a hard time imagining what a building will look like from paper drawings.

AT HOME

Have students note the scenario presented in problem 17 on page 253, and invite them to name other home-improvement formulas that are sometimes used by homeowners.

[Sample answers: Use A = lw (where l = the measure of the length and w = the measure of the width) to find the area of a rectangular floor to carpet or to find the area of a rectangular wall or other rectangular surface to paint; use n = $\frac{A}{9}$ (where A = area of a surface in square feet) to find the number of square yards in a given number of square feet; use x = 144y, where y = a measure in square feet, to find the number of square inches in a given number of square feet.]

Lesson at a Glance

Chapter 9 Lesson 10

Overview This lesson models the proof of the Pythagorean theorem and shows how to calculate the length of a side of a right triangle, given the other two side lengths.

Objectives

- To visualize why the hypotenuse of a right triangle squared equals the sum of the other two sides squared
- To use the Pythagorean theorem to find the length of an unknown side of a right triangle

Student Pages 254–257

Teacher's Resource Library **TRL**

Workbook Activity 87

Activity 83

Alternative Activity 83

....

Mathematics Vocabulary

triangle
right triangle
angle
right angle
hypotenuse
Pythagorean theorem

....

1 Warm-Up Activity

Construct several right triangles of different shapes on the board. Ask students to observe and list traits that all the figures share. *(three sides, three points, three angles, one angle of 90 degrees, and so on)* Explain that each triangle has one right angle and that right triangles have special characteristics. In this lesson, students will learn a formula that applies only to right triangles.

2 Teaching the Lesson

Use the right triangles on the board to review the vocabulary until students can identify their angles, right angle, and hypotenuse easily. Make sure that students follow the logic leading from $c^2 = a^2 + b^2$ to $c = \sqrt{a^2 + b^2}$. (This is so because c is the square root of c^2.)

Triangle
A closed figure with three sides

Right triangle
A three-sided figure, or triangle, with one right, or 90°, angle

Angle
A figure made up of two sides or rays with a common endpoint

Right angle
A 90° angle

Hypotenuse
The longest side in a right triangle

Pythagorean theorem
A formula that states that in a right triangle, the length of the hypotenuse c squared is equal to the length of side a squared plus the length of side b squared

You know that $9 + 16 = 25$.

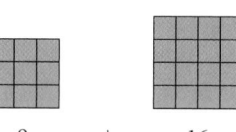 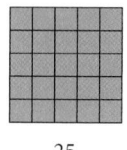

$$9 \quad + \quad 16 \quad = \quad 25$$

You can rearrange the squares to form a **right triangle.** The two legs of the triangle, a and b, form a **right angle.** The side opposite the right angle, c, is called the **hypotenuse.**

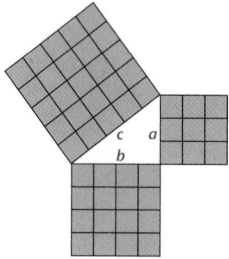

We can let $a^2 = 9$, $b^2 = 16$, and $c^2 = 25$. Since $9 + 16 = 25$, we can say $a^2 + b^2 = c^2$. This is true for any right triangle.

This formula is called the **Pythagorean theorem.**

In a right triangle, the square of the hypotenuse is equal to the sum of the squares of the other two sides.

$$c^2 = a^2 + b^2$$

You can use this formula to find the length of any side of a right triangle.

To find the length of the hypotenuse, take the square root of each side of the equation.

$$c = \sqrt{a^2 + b^2}$$

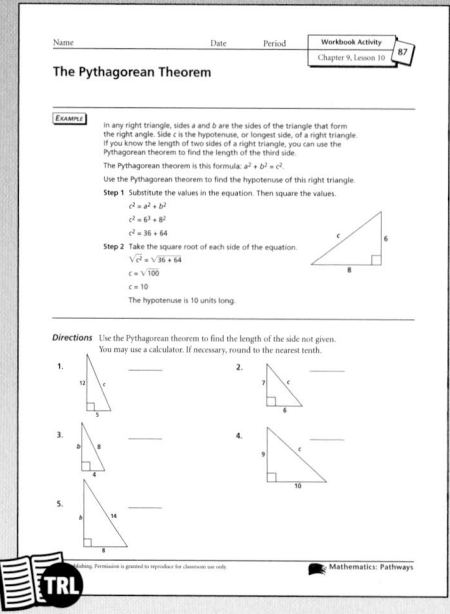

Workbook Activity 87

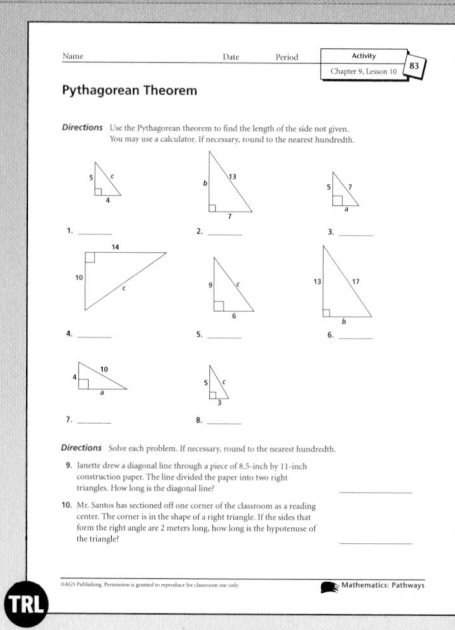

Activity 83

To find the length of side a, use this formula.

$$a^2 = c^2 - b^2$$

Take the square root of each side of the equation.

$$a = \sqrt{c^2 - b^2}$$

To find the length of side b, use this formula.

$$b^2 = c^2 - a^2$$

Take the square root of each side of the equation.

$$b = \sqrt{c^2 - a^2}$$

EXAMPLE 1 Find the length of the hypotenuse of this right triangle.

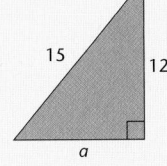

Step 1 Substitute the values in the equation $a^2 + b^2 = c^2$ and square the numbers.

$$c^2 = 5^2 + 12^2$$
$$c^2 = 25 + 144$$

Step 2 Take the square root of each side of the equation.

$$c = \sqrt{25 + 144}$$
$$c = \sqrt{169}$$
$$c = 13$$

EXAMPLE 2 Find the length of side a of this right triangle.

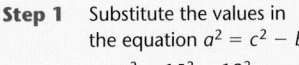

Step 1 Substitute the values in the equation $a^2 = c^2 - b^2$.

$$a^2 = 15^2 - 12^2$$
$$a^2 = 225 - 144$$

Step 2 Take the square root of each side of the equation.

$$a = \sqrt{225 - 144}$$
$$a = \sqrt{81}$$
$$a = 9$$

LEARNING STYLES

Auditory/Verbal
Have students make illustrations modeling each vocabulary term for the lesson and use the illustrations to explain the terms' meanings in their own words.

CALCULATOR

Students must use a calculator with a square root function key to complete Exercise B as directed. Lacking this, they may use a standard calculator to find squares and add or subtract them. For $8^2 + 6^2 = x$,

Press 8 $\times$ 8 $=$.

The display reads 64.

Press $+$, then 6 $\times$ 6 $=$.

The display reads 36.

Press $+$ once more.

The display reads 100.

To find the square root of 100, students can use the calculator to multiply reasonable factors and check the product.

GROUP PROBLEM SOLVING

Have students recall that the Pythagorean theorem ($a^2 + b^2 = c^2$ where c represents the hypotenuse, or longest side of a right triangle, and a and b represent the legs opposite the hypotenuse) can be used to determine the measure of one side of a right triangle if the measures of the other two sides are known. Encourage students to work in pairs and use a calculator to find the diagonal measure of each square described in problems 11–15 on page 249. Ask students to round their answers to the nearest tenth. *[11) 8.5 in. 12) 31.6 cm 13) 17.9 ft 14) 56.6 ft 15) 9.9 units and/or 19.8 units]*

Exercise A Use the Pythagorean theorem to find x.

1.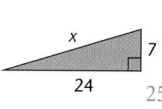
25

2.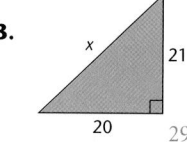

3.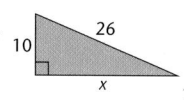
29

4.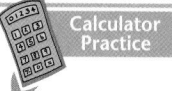
9

5.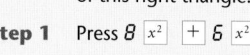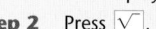
24

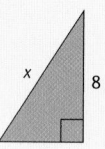

Calculator Practice

You can use a calculator and the Pythagorean theorem to find the length of a side of a right triangle.

EXAMPLE 3 Find the length of the hypotenuse of this right triangle.

Step 1 Press 8 $\boxed{x^2}$ $\boxed{+}$ 6 $\boxed{x^2}$ $\boxed{=}$.
The display reads *100*.

Step 2 Press $\boxed{\sqrt{}}$.
The display reads *10*.
The hypotenuse is 10 units long.

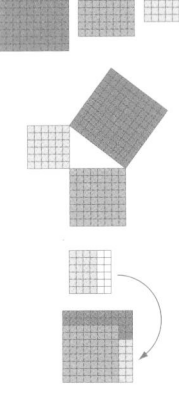
Exercise B Use the Pythagorean theorem and a calculator to find *x*. Round your answer to the nearest tenth.

6.
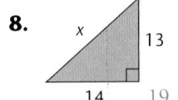
10
x
9
4.4

7.
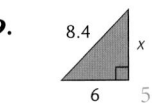
x
29
28
40.3

8.
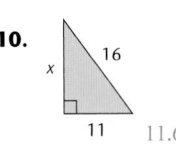
x
13
14
19.1

9.
8.4
x
6
5.9

10.
16
x
11
11.6

Build a Model

Here is how you can make a model that shows that the Pythagorean theorem really does work.

On graph paper, draw the three squares as shown. Cut out each of the squares, and place them on your desk.

3 × 3   4 × 4   5 × 5

Fit the squares together to make a right triangle as shown.

Next, lay the middle square on top of the large square. Notice that a row of squares is left uncovered on the large square. Cover those remaining squares by cutting the small square into rows and placing the rows on top.

So, $a^2 + b^2$ does equal c^2.

Try the same steps for these three squares: a 6 × 6 square, a 8 × 8 square, and a 10 × 10 square.

Exponents, Radicals, and the Pythagorean Theorem Chapter 9   **257**

Overview This lesson defines scalene, isosceles, and equilateral triangles and shows which may also be right triangles.

Objectives

- To identify triangles according to the relative lengths of their sides
- To identify triangles as right triangles, given only the lengths of their sides

Student Pages 258–259

Teacher's Resource Library

Workbook Activity 88

Activity 84

Alternative Activity 84

Mathematics Vocabulary

scalene triangle
isosceles triangle
equilateral triangle

1 Warm-Up Activity

Display three triangles that are very different in shape and size. As students analyze them, ask, "What makes all triangles similar?" (*All have three sides and three angles.*) "What are some ways triangles may differ?" (*They may have sides and angles of different sizes.*) Have the class read page 258 to learn to classify triangles by the lengths of their sides.

2 Teaching the Lesson

Students must first learn to differentiate the three types of triangles and then test which of the types can be a right triangle. Refer students to Exercise B of Lesson 10, in which it is immediately clear that right triangles generally are scalene triangles. You may also wish to use logic to help students perceive that an equilateral triangle cannot be a right triangle:

- In a right triangle, the hypotenuse *c* is the longest side. The legs *a* and *b* are shorter than the hypotenuse. Therefore, $c > a$ and $c > b$.

Scalene triangle
A triangle with no equal sides
Isosceles triangle
A triangle with two sides of equal length
Equilateral triangle
A triangle with three equal sides

You know that some triangles, called right triangles, have one angle of 90°. However, there are other ways to identify triangles. One way to name and identify triangles uses the lengths of the sides of the triangle.

If no two sides of a triangle are of equal length, the triangle is a **scalene triangle.**

Scalene

If two sides of a triangle are of equal length, the triangle is an **isosceles triangle.**

Isosceles

If three sides of a triangle are of equal length, the triangle is an **equilateral triangle.**

Equilateral

Can a scalene triangle also be a right triangle? You can use the Pythagorean formula to find out.

EXAMPLE 1 The sides of this scalene triangle measure 3, 4, and 5 units.

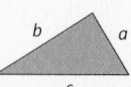

Step 1 Let $a = 3$, $b = 4$, and $c = 5$.

Step 2 In a right triangle, $a^2 + b^2 = c^2$. Substitute values for *a*, *b*, and *c*.

$$3^2 + 4^2 = 5^2$$

$$9 + 16 = 25 \quad \text{True, so the triangle is a right triangle.}$$

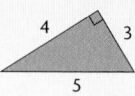

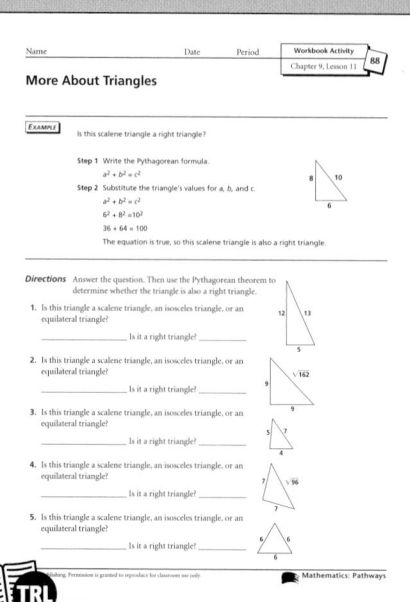

Workbook Activity 88

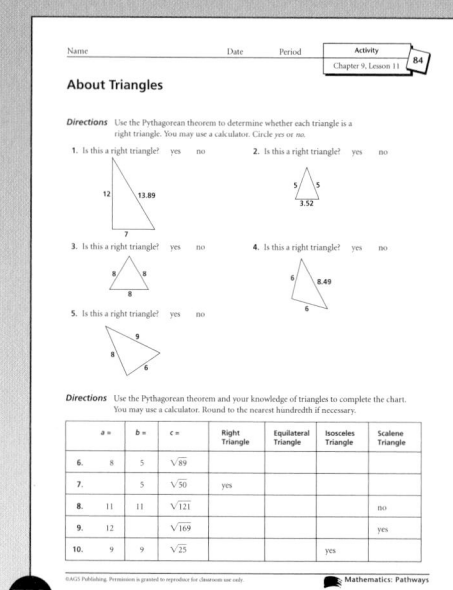

Activity 84

Use the Pythagorean formula to find out if these triangles are right triangles.

EXAMPLE 2 Two sides of this triangle are $\sqrt{2}$ units long. The third side is 2 units long.

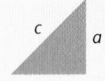

Step 1 Let $a = \sqrt{2}$, $b = \sqrt{2}$, and $c = 2$.

Step 2 In a right triangle, $a^2 + b^2 = c^2$. Substitute values for a, b, and c.

$$\sqrt{2}^2 + \sqrt{2}^2 = 2^2$$

$2 + 2 = 4$ True, so the triangle is a right triangle.

EXAMPLE 3 Each side of this triangle is 4 units long. Is this a right triangle?

Step 1 Let $a = 4$, $b = 4$, and $c = 4$.

Step 2 In a right triangle, $a^2 + b^2 = c^2$. Substitute values for a, b, and c.

$$4^2 + 4^2 = 4^2$$

$16 + 16 = 16$ False, so the triangle is not a right triangle.

Exercise A Use the Pythagorean theorem and your knowledge of triangles to complete the following table.

$a =$	$b =$	$c =$	Right Triangle	Equilateral Triangle	Isosceles Triangle	Scalene Triangle
1.	3 in.	4 in.	5	yes	no	no	yes
2.	18	24	30	yes	no	no	yes
3.	4 ft	4 ft	4 ft	no	yes	no	no
4.	6 m	6 m	$\sqrt{72}$	yes	no	yes	no
5.	6	8	10	yes	no	no	yes

- In an equilateral triangle, all three sides are equal length: $a = b = c$. Therefore, a right triangle cannot be an equilateral triangle. If $a = b$, then a cannot be greater than b.

3 Reinforce and Extend

LEARNING STYLES

LEP/ESL

As students work with labeled models of each kind of triangle, they may benefit from learning about the history of the terms.

- *Scalene* is from the Greek *skalenos*, meaning "uneven" or "odd." Scalene triangles are uneven because their sides are different lengths.

- *Equilateral* is compounded from Latin *aequalis* ("equal, even") and *latus* ("side"). All sides of an equilateral triangle are equal.

- *Isosceles* comes from two Greek words: *isos* ("equal") and *skelos* ("leg"). Two adjacent sides of a triangle are its legs; these are equal in an isosceles triangle.

LEARNING STYLES

Body/Kinesthetic

Provide students with a drawing of a polygon that has been divided into triangular "puzzle" pieces. Ask them to cut out the triangles and sort them according to type: scalene, equilateral, isosceles. When in doubt, students should measure before classifying.

Lesson at a Glance

Chapter 9 Application

Overview This lesson provides an application in which students draw diagrams representing real-life problems and use the Pythagorean theorem to find solutions.

Objectives

- To map distances and diagram heights in geographic and architectural contexts
- To compute unknown measures of distance using the Pythagorean theorem

Student Page 260

Teacher's Resource Library

Application Activity 9

Everyday Math 9

1 Warm-Up Activity

Use two books placed on a tabletop to create a ramp. Have students identify the right triangle created by this structure and show that the diagonal part is its hypotenuse. Point out that right triangles exist all around us. Tell students that in this application they will have a chance to use what they know about right triangles to solve everyday problems.

2 Teaching the Lesson

Review the parts of the right triangle represented by *a*, *b*, and *c* in the Pythagorean theorem and the steps in finding a square root. Before assigning the problems, give students practice in interpreting word problems that require the drawing of a diagram.

A rectangular park has a sidewalk around its perimeter. The park is 300 feet by 150 feet. If you contract to build a sidewalk running diagonally across the park, how long will the sidewalk be?

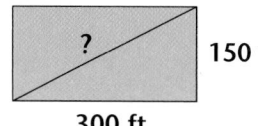

(The diagonal line is approximately 334 ft.)

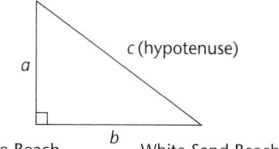

Applying the Pythagorean Theorem The Greek mathematician Pythagoras (c. 582–500 B.C.) is best remembered for his study of shapes and angles. The theorem stating the relationship for the three sides of a right triangle is named for him.

EXAMPLE 1 White Sand Beach is 8 miles due east of Pebble Beach. Blue Water Cove is 6 miles due north of Pebble Beach. What is the direct distance from White Sand Beach to Blue Water Cove?

Step 1 Use the Pythagorean theorem.

$$c^2 = a^2 + b^2$$

Step 2 Substitute the values. Let $a = 6$ and $b = 8$.

$$c^2 = a^2 + b^2 = 6^2 + 8^2 = 36 + 64 = 100$$
$$c = \sqrt{100} = \sqrt{10 \times 10} = 10$$

The direct distance from White Sand Beach to Blue Water Cove is 10 miles.

Exercise Use the Pythagorean theorem to solve each problem.

1. The sail measures 18 yards wide by 24 yards tall. What is the length of the diagonal edge? 30 yards

2. The picket fence is 4 feet tall. It casts a shadow that measures 3 feet long. What is the distance from the top of the fence to the end of the shadow? 5 feet

3. Steve's vegetable garden measures 12 feet long by 16 feet wide. He builds in a path from one corner of the plot to the other. How long is the path? 20 feet

4. A transmitter tower is 60 meters tall. It is anchored with 3 sets of wire braces. The anchors are 80 meters from the base of the tower. Is 100 meters of wiring enough to do the job? Explain your answer. No; you will need at least 300 meters for all 3 sets.

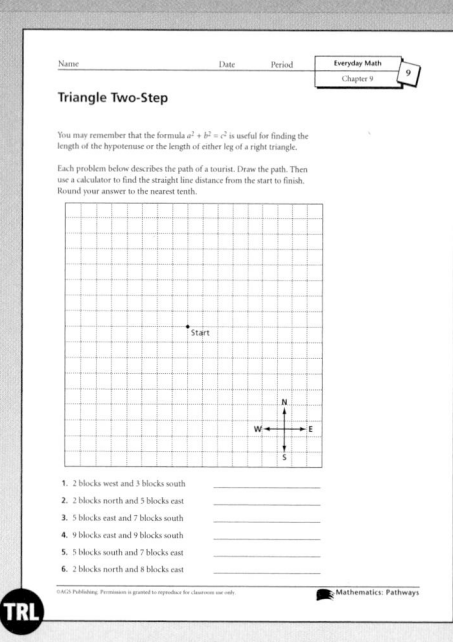

Application Activity 9   **Everyday Math 9**

Chapter 9 REVIEW

Write the letter of the correct answer.

1. Rewrite $4 \cdot 4 \cdot 4$ using exponents. B
  A 64   C 12
  B 4^3 D 3^4

2. Rewrite $(-a) \cdot (-a) \cdot (-a)$ using exponents. D
  A a^3 C $3(-a)$
  B a^2 D $(-a)^3$

3. Find the value of 16^2. B
  A 32   C 8
  B 256   D 18

4. Find the value of $(-5)^3$. A
  A -125 C -25
  B -15 D 125

5. Simplify the expression $5^2 \cdot 5^2$. D
  A 25^4 C 125
  B $2(5^2)$ D 5^4

6. Simplify the expression $3^5 \div 3^4$. C
  A 1^9 C 3
  B 3^9 D 9^3

Write an expression for the area of each square. Then find the area.

Example: 2   Solution: $2 \cdot 2 = 2^2 = 4$

7.
4
$4^2, 16$

8.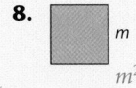
m
m^2

9. 1
$1^2, 1$

10. between 1 and 2

11. between 8 and 9

12. between 6 and 7

Estimate the square root of each number.

Example: $\sqrt{12}$ Solution: 3 squared is 9 and 4 squared is 16, so $\sqrt{12}$ is between 3 and 4.

10. $\sqrt{3}$ **11.** $\sqrt{69}$ **12.** $\sqrt{43}$

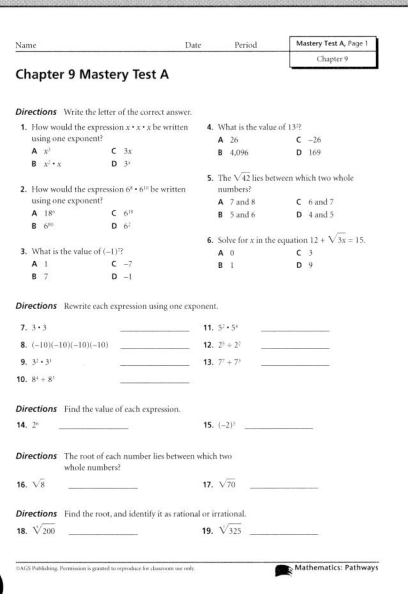

Chapter 9 Mastery Test A   *Exponents, Radicals, and the Pythagorean Theorem*   **261**

 **3** **Reinforce and Extend**

AT HOME

Have students measure the length and width of two rectangular objects (such as windows or cupboard doors). Ask them to suppose that they want to create an X-shaped lattice decoration for the front of each rectangle. Have them calculate how long each piece of wood or plastic in the X must be. Then have them measure the diagonal to check their calculations.

Chapter 9 Review

Each set of problems in the Chapter Review includes an example and solution to illustrate the concept. Use the given examples for reteaching the materials in Chapter 9. For additional practice, refer to the Supplementary Problems for Chapter 9 (pages 448–449).

Chapter 9 Mastery Test

The Teacher's Resource Library includes parallel forms of the Chapter 9 Mastery Test. The difficulty level of the two forms is equivalent. You may wish to use one form as a pretest and the other form as a posttest.

MANIPULATIVES

 Review

Materials: Cuisenaire Rods

Group Practice: Review how to model and simplify numbers and variables with exponents and how to build squares and cubes to calculate area and volume.

Student Practice: Have students use the rods to help solve or check their work in problems 7, and 13–14.

ALTERNATIVE ASSESSMENT

Alternative Assessment items correlate with student Goals for Learning at the beginning of this chapter.

■ To find the value of numbers raised to a certain power

Have students determine whether the following statements are true or false. Note: For some of the calculations, students may use a calculator.

$3^4 = 3 \cdot 3 \cdot 3 \cdot 3$ *(true)*

$5^8 = 5 \cdot 5 \cdot 5 \cdot 5 \cdot 5 \cdot 5 \cdot 5 \cdot 5$ *(true)*

$-(14)^2 = -14 \cdot -14$ *(false)*

$10^3 = 30$ *(false)*

$4^4 = 256$ *(true)*

$7^2 = 14$ *(false)*

■ To multiply and divide terms with exponents

Have students work in small groups to write a jingle, a rap, or another memory device that will help them remember to add exponents when multiplying terms with the same base and to subtract exponents when dividing terms with the same base.

■ To find area and volume by using numbers with exponents

Have students determine which formula to use—area or volume— and solve the following problems. Tell them to be sure to include the appropriate unit labels.

A square 4 inches on each side *(area = s^2, A = 4 in. • 4 in. = 16 in.²)*

A cube 3 cm on each side *(volume = s^3, V = 3 cm • 3 cm • 3 cm = 27 cm³)*

A square 7 mm on each side *(area = s^2, A = 7 mm • 7 mm = 49 mm²)*

■ To find the square roots of numbers

Have students draw a number line from 1 to 144, similar to the one shown on page 243 in the textbook for estimating square roots. Have pairs of students draw different portions of the number line, using different colors for numbers that are perfect squares— 1, 4, 9, 16, 25, 36, 49, 64, 81, 100, 121, and 144. Have each pair include an example of an irrational root between each of the square roots. Have students use their calculators to find the approximate decimal equivalent.

Write an expression for the volume of each cube. Then find the volume.

Example: 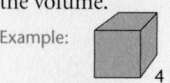 Solution: $4 \cdot 4 \cdot 4 = 4^3 = 64$

13. $6^3, 216$ **14.** $2^3, 8$

Find the approximate length of a side of each square.

Example: Area = 4   Solution: $A = s^2 = 4$ $s = 2$

15. Area = 250   15.8   **17.** Area = 28   5.3

16. Area = 75   8.7   **18.** Area = 1,000   31.6

Tell whether the radicals are rational or irrational.

Example: $\sqrt[4]{69}$ Solution: $\sqrt[4]{69} = 2.88$, the number is irrational

19. rational (7)

20. irrational (4.86)

21. irrational (6.93)

19. $\sqrt[2]{49}$ **20.** $\sqrt[4]{560}$ **21.** $\sqrt[3]{333}$

Find the roots for these radicals. Round to the nearest hundredth.

Example: $\sqrt[2]{86}$ Solution: $\sqrt[2]{86} = 9.27$

22. $\sqrt[2]{126}$ 11.22   **23.** $\sqrt[3]{9}$ 2.08

Solve the problem.

Example: A square has an area of 225 square inches. What is the length of one side of the square?

Solution: $x^2 = 225$, $x = \sqrt{225}$, $x = 15$ inches. The length of a side of the square is 15 inches.

24. A square living room has an area of 121 square feet. A couch is 10 feet long. What is the length of a side of the living room? Will the couch fit in the room?   11 feet; yes

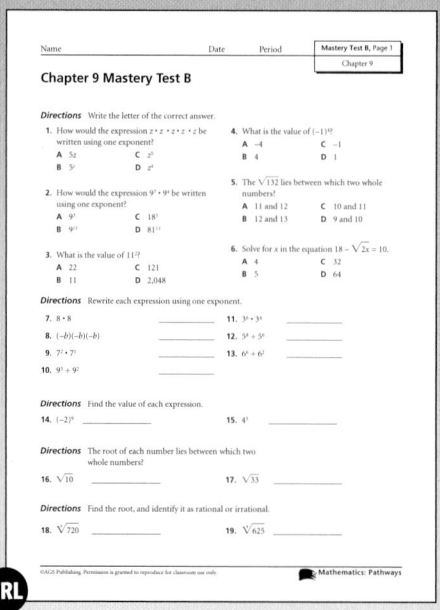

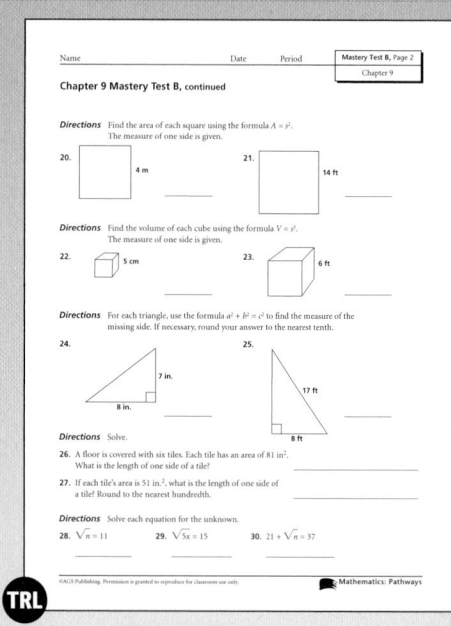

Chapter 9 Mastery Test B

Solve equations for each unknown. Check your answers.

Example: $\sqrt{28 - 4x} = 8$ Solution: $(\sqrt{28 - 4x})^2 = (8)^2$, $28 - 4x = 64$, $-4x = 36$, $x = -9$

25. $p = 32$

26. $x = 81$

27. $x = 6$

25. $\sqrt{2p} = 8$ **26.** $\sqrt{x} - 4 = 5$ **27.** $\sqrt{3x - 2} = 4$

Solve each problem. Use the formula for an area of a circle ($A = \pi r^2$) or the volume of a cylinder ($V = \pi r^2 h$) for the following problems. r = radius, h = height, $\pi = 3$

Example: A circular mirror has an area of 93 square inches. What is the radius of the mirror?

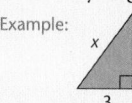

Solution: $\pi r^2 = 93$; $r = \dfrac{\sqrt{93}}{3} = \sqrt{31}$; $r = 5.57$ inches.

The radius of the mirror is 5.57 inches.

28. A disk has an area of 250 square inches. What is the radius of the disk? 9.13 in.

29. Wilma is using a cylindrical coffee can for a project. The can has a volume of 150 cubic inches and a height of 8 inches. What is the radius of the can? 2.5 in.

Use the Pythagorean theorem to find x.

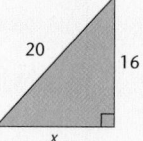

Example: Solution: $a^2 + b^2 = c^2$ $4^2 + 3^2 = x^2$
$16 + 9 = x^2$
$\sqrt{25} = x$ $5 = x$

30.

Test-Taking Tip

Before taking a test, find out what tools, such as a calculator, you need to bring with you.

Exponents, Radicals, and the Pythagorean Theorem   *Chapter 9*   **263**

Chapter

10

Planning Guide

Equations from Geometry

Lesson		Student Pages	Vocabulary	Practice Exercises	Problem Solving	Try This	Solutions Key
1	Perimeters of Polygons	266–269	✔	✔	269	269	✔
2	Perimeters of Regular Polygons	270–273	✔	✔	273	273	✔
3	Perimeters of Irregular Polygons	274–277	✔	✔			✔
4	Areas of Rectangles and Squares	278–281		✔	281		✔
5	Areas of Triangles	282–283	✔	✔	283		✔
6	Areas of Trapezoids and Parallelograms	284–285	✔	✔			✔
7	Areas of Irregular Polygons	286–287		✔			✔
8	Circumferences and Areas of Circles	288–291	✔	✔			✔
9	Solid Figures	292–293	✔	✔			✔
10	Surface Areas of Prisms and Cylinders	294–297		✔	297		✔
11	Surface Areas of Pyramids and Cones	298–301		✔	301		✔
12	Volumes of Cubes, Prisms, and Pyramids	302–305		✔	305		✔
13	Volumes of Cylinders, Cones, and Spheres	306–307	✔				✔
Application	Dilation	308	✔				✔

Chapter Activities

Teacher's Resource Library
Estimation Exercise 10: Estimating the Perimeters of Polygons
Application Activity 10: Dilation
Everyday Math 10: Packaging a Volume
Community Connection 10: School Measures Up

Teacher's Edition
Chapter 10 Project

Assessment Options

Student Text
Chapter 10 Review

Teacher's Resource Library
Chapter 10 Mastery Tests A and B

Teacher's Edition
Chapter 10 Alternative Assessments

Student Text Features						Teaching Strategies									Learning Styles						Teacher's Resource Library			
Estimation Activity	Math in Your Life	Technology Connection	Writing About Mathematics	Build a Model	Calculator Practice	Online Connection	Common Error	Applications Home, Career, Community	Mental Math	Manipulatives	Calculator	Group Problem Solving	Modeling	Knowing Your Students	Auditory/Verbal	Visual/Spatial	Logical/Mathematical	Body/Kinesthetic	Interpersonal/Group Learning	LEP/ESL	Activities	Alternate Activities	Workbook Activities	Self-Study Guide
												269				268				267	85	85	89	✔
							271	272				273									86	86	90	✔
		276				275									275			276	277		87	87	91	✔
				281	280	279					280	281						280		279	88	88	92	✔
												283								283	89	89	93	✔
			285																285	285	90	90	94	✔
	287					287	287									287					91	91	95–96	✔
291					291		289				291				289				289	290	92	92	97	✔
							293						293	293							93	93	98	✔
						295	296									295				297	94	94	99	✔
					301						301	300								299	95	95	100	✔
					305		303				305	305							304	304	96	96	101	✔
																307	307				97	97	102	✔
																				309				✔

Software Options

Skill Track Software

Use the Skill Track Software for *Mathematics: Pathways* for additional reinforcement of this chapter. The software provides multiple-choice assessment items for students to access by computer.

Solutions Key

Use the Solutions Key with this chapter to help students who may need additional assistance. The Solutions Key CD provides solutions for every exercise in the student edition.

Other Resources

Alternative Activities

The Teacher's Resource Library (TRL) contains a set of worksheets written at a second-grade reading level called Alternative Activities. They cover the same content as the regular Activities.

Manipulatives

See the Manipulative activities in this chapter for hands-on modeling of the content.

Craft sticks or straws

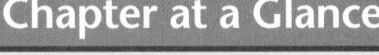
Chapter 10: Equations from Geometry
pages 264–311

**Skill Track for
   Mathematics: Pathways**

Teacher's Resource Library

Workbook Activities 89–102

Activities 85–97

Alternative Activities 85–97

Application Activity 10

Estimation Exercise 10

Everyday Math 10

Community Connection 10

Chapter 10 Self-Study Guide

Chapter 10 Mastery Tests A and B
(Answer Keys for the Teacher's
Resource Library begin on page 528
of this Teacher's Edition.)

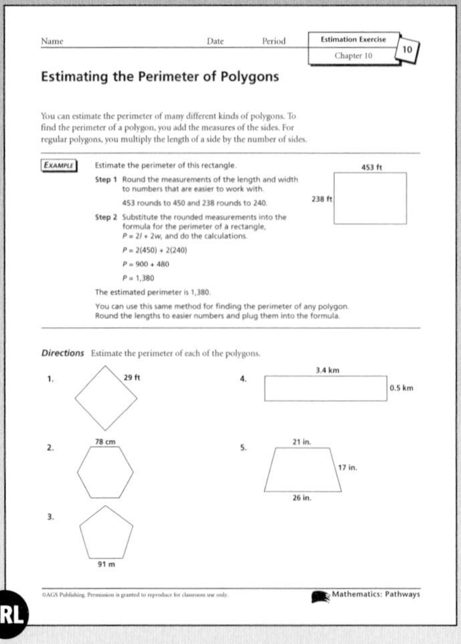

Name _____ Date _____ Period _____ | Estimation Exercise 10 | Chapter 10

Estimating the Perimeter of Polygons

You can estimate the perimeter of many different kinds of polygons. To find the perimeter of a polygon, you add the measures of the sides. For regular polygons, you multiply the length of a side by the number of sides.

EXAMPLE Estimate the perimeter of this rectangle.

Step 1 Round the measurements of the length and width to numbers that are easier to work with.
453 rounds to 450 and 238 rounds to 240.

Step 2 Substitute the rounded measurements into the formula for the perimeter of a rectangle, $P = 2l + 2w$, and do the calculations.
$P = 2(450) + 2(240)$
$P = 900 + 480$
$P = 1,380$

The estimated perimeter is 1,380.
You can use this same method for finding the perimeter of any polygon. Round the lengths to easier numbers and plug them into the formula.

Directions Estimate the perimeter of each of the polygons.

1. 29 ft
2. 78 cm
3. 91 m
4. 3.4 km 0.5 km
5. 21 in. 17 in. 26 in.

Estimation Exercise 10

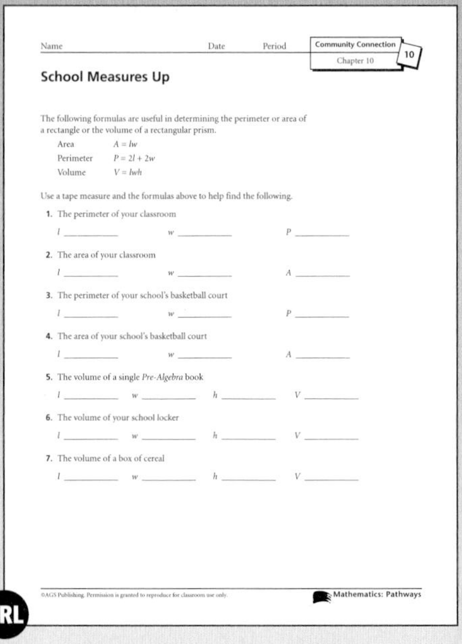

Name _____ Date _____ Period _____ | Community Connection 10 | Chapter 10

School Measures Up

The following formulas are useful in determining the perimeter or area of a rectangle or the volume of a rectangular prism.

Area $A = lw$
Perimeter $P = 2l + 2w$
Volume $V = lwh$

Use a tape measure and the formulas above to help find the following.

1. The perimeter of your classroom
   l _____ w _____ P _____
2. The area of your classroom
   l _____ w _____ A _____
3. The perimeter of your school's basketball court
   l _____ w _____ P _____
4. The area of your school's basketball court
   l _____ w _____ A _____
5. The volume of a single *Pre-Algebra* book
   l _____ w _____ h _____ V _____
6. The volume of your school locker
   l _____ w _____ h _____ V _____
7. The volume of a box of cereal
   l _____ w _____ h _____ V _____

Community Connection 10

10 Equations from Geometry

When it's time to paint a room, apply your math knowledge to figure out how much paint you will need for the job. Start by measuring the height and width of each of the walls to find the total surface area. Then, buy the right amount of paint to cover that much area. The coverage is listed on the label of the can of paint.

In the mid-1600s, mathematicians first used algebraic equations to define geometric structures. By setting up these principles, they created methods that we still use today. The formula for figuring out the area of a figure is the same as it was when René Descartes (re-nay day-kart) first applied algebra to geometry in 1637.

In Chapter 10, you will use equations to solve geometry problems.

Goals for Learning

◆ To find the perimeter of regular and irregular polygons
◆ To calculate the area of regular and irregular polygons
◆ To determine the circumference and area of circles
◆ To use formulas to find the surface area of cubes, prisms, cylinders, pyramids, and cones
◆ To use formulas to find the volume of cubes, prisms, pyramids, cylinders, cones, and spheres

265

Introducing the Chapter

Use the chapter opener as a discussion starter for geometry and its equations. Encourage students to think about instances when designers need to use equations from geometry, such as calculating surface area for creating wall coverings or painting walls. Suggest to students that the formulas associated with area and volume are among the most used formulas in everyday life.

CHAPTER PROJECT

Suggest that students work in small groups to complete a project suggested below. Have groups choose one of the following topics or a topic of their own.

• *Recycled Volume* Students can investigate their school's recycling program and determine the volume of recyclable materials collected in a day, a week, and a month. Students present their results in a television news brief, including narrative and visuals.

• *Web Site* Students prepare a draft of a Web site which includes information about the oldest estimates of pi and some of the more novel equations used to describe pi.

Each group can assign tasks to its members such as researcher, artist, writer, and producer.

TEACHER'S RESOURCE

The AGS Publishing Teaching Strategies in Math Transparencies may be used with this chapter. They add an interactive dimension to expand and enhance the program content.

CAREER INTEREST INVENTORY

The AGS Publishing Harrington-O'Shea Career Decision-Making System-Revised (CDM) may be used with this chapter. Students can use the CDM to explore their interests and identify careers. The CDM defines career areas that are indicated by students' responses on the inventory.

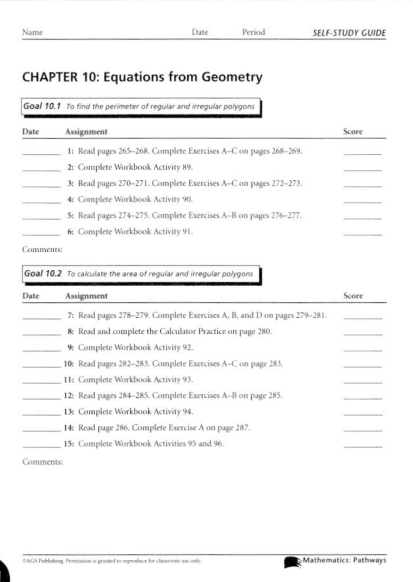

Chapter 10 Self-Study Guide

Chapter 10 Lesson 1

Overview This lesson introduces polygons, the names of selected polygons, and how to find the perimeters of polygons.

Objectives

- To identify selected regular polygons
- To find the perimeter of a regular polygon

Student Pages 266–269

Teacher's Resource Library (TRL)

Workbook Activity 89

Activity 85

Alternative Activity 85

....

Mathematics Vocabulary

geometry
polygon
parallel
quadrilateral
rectangle
rhombus

....

1 ⬛ Warm-Up Activity

Draw the following figures on the board.

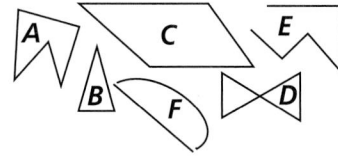

Use the figures in conjunction with the following descriptions, asking students which of the figures match each of the descriptions.

- formed by line segments *(ABCDE)*
- each line segment is a side of the figure *(ABCE)*
- figure is closed *(ABCD)*

2 ⬛ Teaching the Lesson

Draw a scalene, an isosceles, and an equilateral triangle on the board. Point out that for any triangle, the perimeter (*P*) is the sum of the lengths of the sides.

Geometry	**Geometry** is the branch of mathematics that studies points, lines, angles, surfaces, and solids. In geometry, you compare and measure figures, including **polygons.**
The study of points, lines, angles, surfaces, and solids	
Polygon	A polygon is a closed, many-sided figure that is made up of line segments. Each line segment of a polygon is a side of the polygon. Line segments can be **parallel** to one another.
A closed, many-sided figure that is made up of line segments	
Parallel	Polygons are named by the number of sides they have. Polygons with three sides are triangles.
Lines that are always the same distance apart; parallel lines never meet	

scalene triangle

isosceles triangle

equilateral triangle

Perimeter is a measure of the distance around a figure or shape. The letter *P* is used to indicate perimeter.

scalene triangle

$$P = a + b + c$$

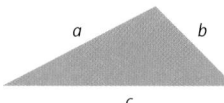

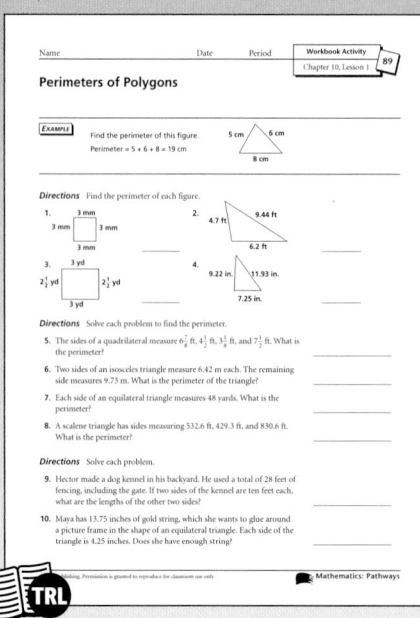

Workbook Activity 89

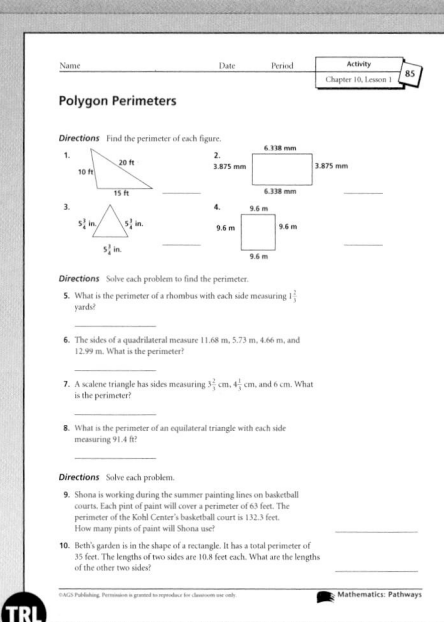

Activity 85

isosceles triangle

$P = a + a + b$
 or
$P = 2a + b$

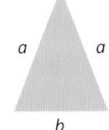

equilateral triangle

$P = s + s + s$
 or
$P = 3s$

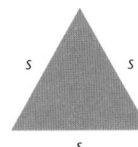

Polygons with four sides are **quadrilaterals.** Examples of quadrilaterals include a **rectangle** and a **rhombus.**

quadrilateral

$P = a + b + c + d$

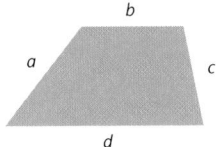

rectangle

$P = l + l + w + w$
 or
$P = 2l + 2w$

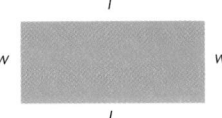

rhombus

$P = s + s + s + s$
 or
$P = 4s$

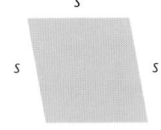

Help students use that information as well as the drawings to identify the primary characteristic of each triangle. *(scalene: no sides of equal length; isosceles: two sides of equal length; equilateral: three sides of equal length)*

Have students identify the same patterns in the formulas for perimeters of quadrilaterals. Help them use the drawings and the perimeter formulas to identify a primary characteristic of a quadrilateral *(no sides the same length)*, a rectangle *(two pairs of equal-length sides)*, and a square *(four sides of equal length)*.

3 Reinforce and Extend

LEARNING STYLES

LEP/ESL

Suggest that students create their own picture dictionary. Have them work in pairs to create pictures of the polygons introduced in the lesson. Next to each polygon have them write its name. Encourage students to add other words to their picture dictionary. For example, they can create a drawing to show distance around and use it as the illustration for *perimeter*.

Use a formula to find the perimeter of a polygon.

EXAMPLE 1   Two sides of an isosceles triangle measure 4.5 inches. The remaining side measures 7.5 inches. Find the perimeter of the triangle.

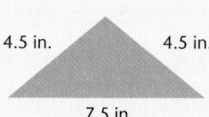

Step 1   Choose a formula. Since the triangle is isosceles, choose $P = a + a + b$ or $P = 2a + b$. If used correctly, either formula will give the correct answer.

$$P = a + a + b \qquad P = 2a + b$$

Step 2   Substitute the given measures into the formula.

$$P = a + a + b \qquad P = 2a + b$$
$$P = 4.5 + 4.5 + 7.5 \qquad P = 2(4.5) + 7.5$$
$$P = 16.5 \qquad P = 9.0 + 7.5$$
$$P = 16.5$$

Step 3   Check to make sure your answer is written in simplest form. Then label your answer. In this example, the unit of measure is inches.
$$P = 16.5 \text{ inches}$$

Exercise A   Find the perimeter of each figure.

1.

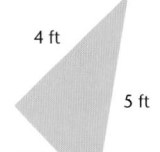

4 ft
5 ft
3 ft
12 ft

2.

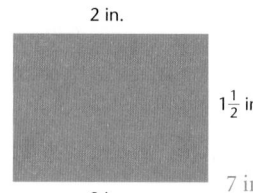

2 in.
$1\frac{1}{2}$ in.
$1\frac{1}{2}$ in.
2 in.
7 in.

3.

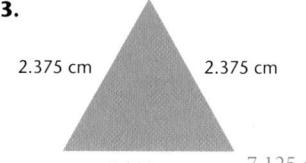

2.375 cm   2.375 cm
2.375 cm   7.125 cm

Exercise B Solve each problem to find the perimeter.

4. Two sides of an isosceles triangle measure $5\frac{1}{8}$ inches. The remaining side of the triangle measures $8\frac{1}{2}$ inches. Find the perimeter of the triangle. $18\frac{3}{4}$ in.

5. The sides of a quadrilateral are 1.15 m, 1.06 m, 1.2 m, and 1.25 m. What is the perimeter of the quadrilateral? 4.66 m

6. Two sides of a rectangle measure 18 cm each and each of the other sides measures 9 cm. Find the perimeter of the rectangle. 54 cm

7. A scalene triangle has sides measuring 203.25 feet, 197.5 feet, and 211 feet. What is the perimeter of the triangle? 611.75 ft

PROBLEM SOLVING

Exercise C Solve each problem.

8. Bell Park is a playground shaped like a rectangle. Two sides of the park are each 42.5 meters long. What is the measure of each of the other 2 sides of the park if the park's perimeter is 257.4 meters? 86.2 m

9. Delaney is designing a pin for the Shelby Company in the shape of the company's logo. The logo is an equilateral triangle. Delaney has designed the pin with a 95-millimeter perimeter. How long is each side of the pin? 31.67 mm or $31\frac{2}{3}$ mm

10. Jackson is framing a picture of swans he took today. It is a rectangle that measures 70 centimeters long and 40 centimeters wide. Will he be able to put the picture in a rectangular frame that is 45 centimeters wide and has a perimeter of 200 centimeters? Why or why not? No, because the perimeter of the picture is 220 cm whereas the perimeter of the frame is only 200 cm. The length of the frame is too short.

Try This

Write two formulas that can be used to find the perimeter of a square.

$P = s + s + s + s$,
$P = 4s$

Try This
Remind students they can write the formulas as either a repeated addition expression or a multiplication expression.

GROUP PROBLEM SOLVING

Have small groups of students make suggestions for improvements to the school's grounds. Encourage them to consider flower borders or fences around parking lots, edging along building walls, and so on. Ask students to include any appropriate measurements of perimeters in their plans. They should use the measurements to estimate the costs of materials needed to implement their suggestions. Students can present their plans to classmates, and the class can vote on the best plan. Students might assign tasks to group members—surveyor (measures each border), analyst (finds the perimeter), researcher (finds the costs of materials), and report writer (prepares the information for presentation).

Lesson at a Glance

Chapter 10 Lesson 2

Overview This lesson presents how to find the perimeters of regular polygons.

Objective

■ To find the perimeters of selected regular polygons

Student Pages 270–273

Teacher's Resource Library TRL

Workbook Activity 90

Activity 86

Alternative Activity 86

....

Mathematics Vocabulary

regular polygon

....

1 Warm-Up Activity

Open the lesson with the following teaser: "I'm thinking of a polygon. Its perimeter is 4*s*. What kind of polygon is it?" *(square)* Be sure to ask students to explain their response.

2 Teaching the Lesson

Discuss the characteristics of each regular polygon shown in the text. Then use the example on page 271 to demonstrate that the addition and multiplication formulas produce the same result.

Regular polygon
A polygon in which each side and each angle has the same measure

Each side and each angle of a **regular polygon** has the same measure.

equilateral triangle

$$P = s + s + s$$
or
$$P = 3s$$

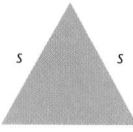

square

$$P = s + s + s + s$$
or
$$P = 4s$$

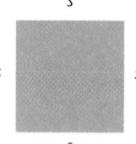

regular pentagon

$$P = s + s + s + s + s$$
or
$$P = 5s$$

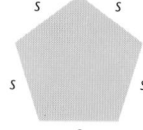

regular hexagon

$$P = s + s + s + s + s + s$$
or
$$P = 6s$$

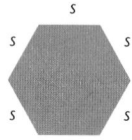

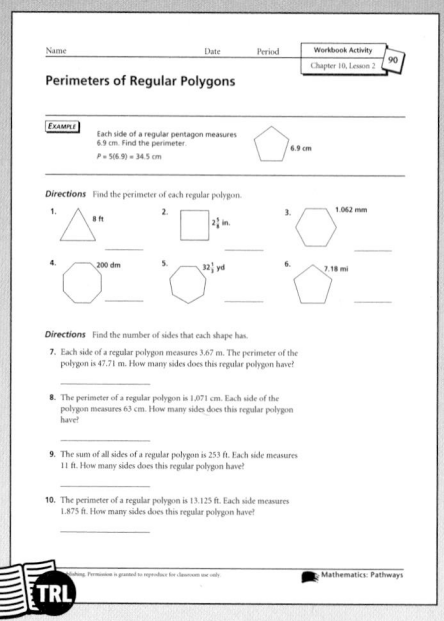

Workbook Activity 90

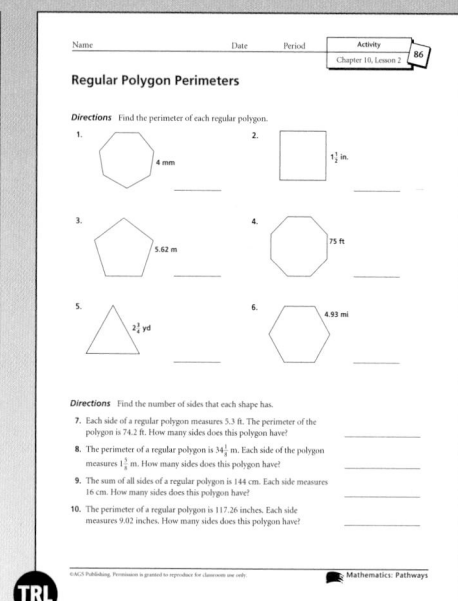

Activity 86

regular heptagon

$$P = s + s + s + s + s + s + s$$
or
$$P = 7s$$

regular octagon

$$P = s + s + s + s + s + s + s + s$$
or
$$P = 8s$$

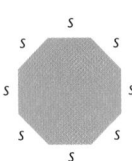

Use a formula to find the perimeter of a regular polygon.

EXAMPLE 1   Each side of a square measures 2.5 feet. Find the perimeter of the square.

 2.5 ft

Step 1   Choose a formula. To find the perimeter of a square, use $P = s + s + s + s$ or $P = 4s$. If used correctly, either formula will give the correct answer.

$P = s + s + s + s$ $P = 4s$

Step 2   Substitute the given measures into the formula.

$P = s + s + s + s$	$P = 4s$
$P = 2.5 + 2.5 + 2.5 + 2.5$	$P = 4(2.5)$
$P = 10.0$	$P = 10.0$

Step 3   Check to make sure your answer is written in simplest form. Then label your answer. In this example, the answer can be simplified and the unit of measure is feet.

$P = 10$ feet

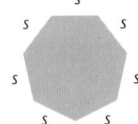

IN THE COMMUNITY

Enlist students in a regular polygon hunt. Suggest that they find examples of regular polygons in their community. Have them keep a list of the polygons they see, where they see them, and what function they serve. You may start students by indicating that some traffic signs are squares, and others are octagons. Point out that many corporations have logos that are regular polygons. If possible, have students take instant photos of their finds. Students can use their observations to create a class list. Vote on the most unusual use of a regular polygon.

Exercise A Find the perimeter of each regular polygon.

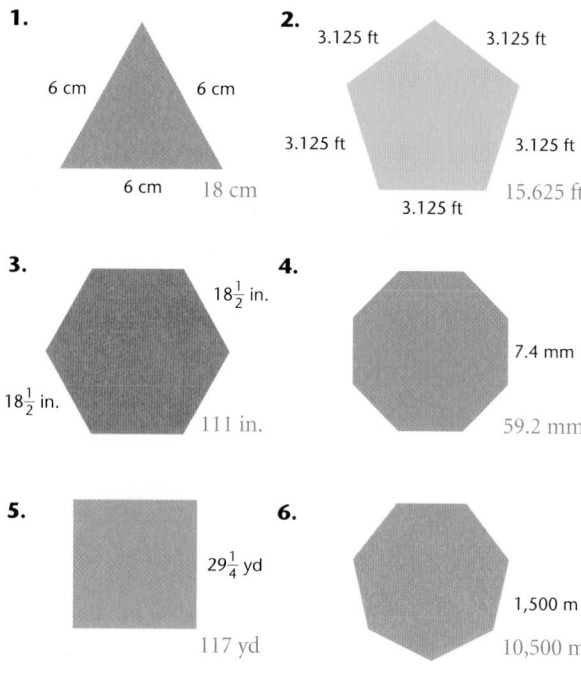

1.

6 cm   6 cm

6 cm   18 cm

2.

3.125 ft   3.125 ft

3.125 ft   3.125 ft

3.125 ft   15.625 ft

3.

$18\frac{1}{2}$ in.

$18\frac{1}{2}$ in.   111 in.

4.

7.4 mm

59.2 mm

5.

$29\frac{1}{4}$ yd

117 yd

6.

1,500 m

10,500 m

Exercise B Find the number of sides that each shape has.

7. Each side of a regular decagon measures 8.25 inches. The perimeter of the decagon is 82.5 inches. How many sides does a decagon have? 10 sides

8. The perimeter of a regular dodecagon is 52 centimeters. Each side of the dodecagon measures $4\frac{1}{3}$ centimeters. How many sides does a dodecagon have? 12 sides

PROBLEM SOLVING

Exercise C Solve each problem.

9. Titus is making two drawings of volcanoes. One drawing is on a sheet of square-shaped paper. The other is on a rectangular-shaped paper. The square paper has a side length of 15 inches. The rectangular paper is 20 inches long and 10 inches wide. Titus is decorating the perimeters of his drawings with colored tape. Is it possible that he will use the same amount of tape on both drawings? Explain.

Try This

Write a general formula that can be used to find the perimeter of any regular polygon.

Sample answer:
$P = nm$ where
n = the number of sides of a regular polygon and
m = the measure of one side.

10. The stop sign that a crossing guard uses is an octagon with a perimeter of 64 inches. The handle of the sign is 12 inches long. How much shorter or longer is the handle than each side of the octagon? the handle is 4 in. longer

9. Yes. Sample explanation: Find the perimeters of the square and rectangle. A 20 by 10 rectangle has the same perimeter (60 in.) as a 15 by 15 square.

Try This

Suggest that students look for the pattern in the perimeters of polygons with 3, 4, 5, 6, 7, and 8 sides.

GROUP PROBLEM SOLVING

Invite your class to frame a class photograph. Students can use a group photo or make a class photo by grouping together photos of individual students. Ask groups of four students to suggest ways in which to arrange the individual photos in a single frame. Students should find the perimeter of the arrangement. They can then compute the costs of several framing alternatives, for example, shrink wrap, tension or spring frames, and traditional metal or wood framing. Have the groups present their proposals to the class and allow the class to choose their favorite.

Lesson at a Glance

Chapter 10 Lesson 3

Overview This lesson demonstrates how to compute the perimeters of irregular polygons.

Objective

- To find the perimeters of irregular polygons

Student Pages 274–277

Teacher's Resource Library

Workbook Activity 91

Activity 87

Alternative Activity 87

....

Mathematics Vocabulary

irregular polygon

....

1 Warm-Up Activity

Draw a series of darts and kites on the board or overhead projector.

Ask students to describe how they would find the perimeter of each of the figures. Encourage all responses, and reward responses that suggest adding the lengths of all the sides or line segments.

2 Teaching the Lesson

Point out to students the conventions associated with naming and writing line segments. Ask students to read the following symbols: $\overline{AB}$, $\overline{CD}$, $\overline{BD}$, and $\overline{CA}$. Then ask students if there is any difference between $\overline{AB}$ and $\overline{BA}$. Ask them to explain their reasoning. (*No; each symbol indicates a line segment and its endpoints. It makes no difference whether the notation goes from right to left or left to right.*)

Use the first example as a demonstration on the board or overhead projector. Help students understand that the distance around the polygon is the sum of the measures of all the sides.

Irregular polygon
A polygon that is not uniform in shape or size

Recall that a polygon is a closed, many-sided figure that is made up of line segments. In the previous two lessons, you explored how to find the perimeters of ordinary and regular polygons. There are also **irregular polygons.**

You can find the perimeter of an irregular polygon by adding the lengths of all its line segments together.

Note that a line segment is identified by its endpoints with a line drawn over the letters, such as $\overline{AB}$. This line symbol means "line segment," so $\overline{AB}$ is read "line segment AB."

EXAMPLE 1 Find the perimeter of polygon *ABDC.*

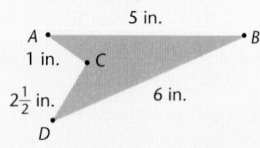

To find the perimeter of an irregular polygon, find the sum of the measures of the sides of the polygon.

$$P = \overline{AB} + \overline{BD} + \overline{DC} + \overline{CA}$$
$$\downarrow \qquad \downarrow \qquad \downarrow \qquad \downarrow$$
$$P = 5 + 6 + 2\tfrac{1}{2} + 1$$
$$P = 14\tfrac{1}{2} \text{ in.}$$

Irregular polygons can be many different shapes and sizes.

EXAMPLE 2 Find the perimeter of polygon *UVWXYZ.*

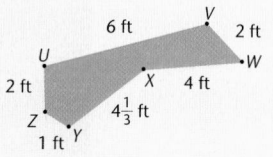

To find the perimeter of an irregular polygon, find the sum of the measures of the sides of the polygon.

$$P = \overline{UV} + \overline{VW} + \overline{WX} + \overline{XY} + \overline{YZ} + \overline{ZU}$$
$$\downarrow \qquad \downarrow \qquad \downarrow \qquad \downarrow \qquad \downarrow \qquad \downarrow$$
$$P = 6 + 2 + 4 + 4\tfrac{1}{3} + 1 + 2$$
$$P = 19\tfrac{1}{3} \text{ ft}$$

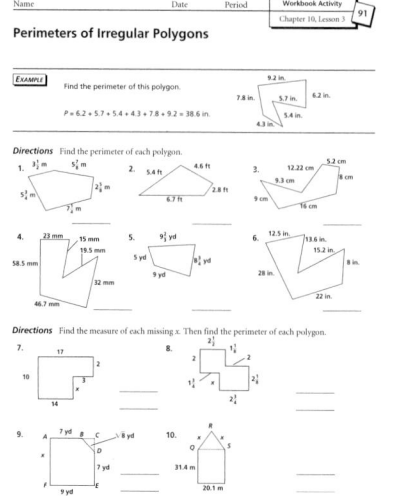

Workbook Activity 91

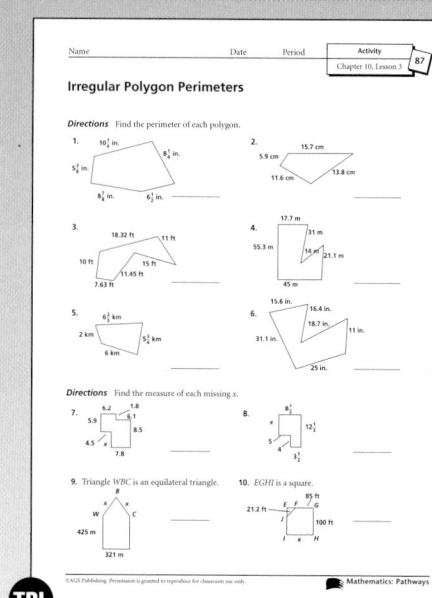

Activity 87

You can also find the perimeters of some irregular polygons that have a missing measure.

EXAMPLE 3 Find the perimeter of this polygon.

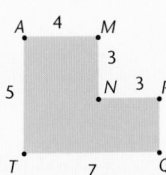

Step 1 Determine the measure of $\overline{PQ}$. Since the measure of $\overline{AT}$ is 5, the measure of $\overline{MN} + \overline{PQ} = 5$. The measure of $\overline{PQ} = 5 - 3$ or 2.

Step 2 Determine the perimeter by finding the sum of the measures of the sides. Begin at a point such as A and move around the figure.

$$P = 4 + 3 + 3 + 2 + 7 + 5$$
$$P = 24 \text{ units}$$

Polygons may sometimes have more than one missing measure.

EXAMPLE 4 Find the perimeter of this polygon.

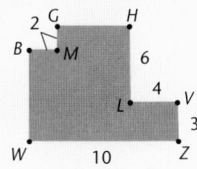

Step 1 Determine the measure of $\overline{GH}$. Since the measure of $\overline{WZ}$ is 10, the measure of $\overline{BM} + \overline{GH} + \overline{LV} = 10$. The measure of $\overline{GH} = 10 - 2 - 4$ or 4.

Step 2 Determine the measure of $\overline{WB}$. Since the measure of $\overline{ZV} + \overline{LH}$ is 3 + 6 or 9, the measure of $\overline{WB} = 9 - 2$ or 7.

Step 3 Determine the perimeter by finding the sum of the measures of the sides. Begin at a point such as G and move around the figure.

$$P = 4 + 6 + 4 + 3 + 10 + 7 + 2 + 2 = 38$$
$$P = 38 \text{ units}$$

Direct students' attention to polygon *AMNPQT*. Point out that before they can find the perimeter of the entire polygon, students will need to find the measure of $\overline{PQ}$. Ask a volunteer to explain why $\overline{PQ} = 2$. ($\overline{AT} = 5$, $\overline{MN} + \overline{PQ} = \overline{AT}$, $\overline{MN} = 3$, $\overline{PQ} = 5 - 3$ or 2)

Point out to students that the perimeter of polygon *MNPQTA* is the same as the perimeter of polygon *AMNPQT* or the perimeter of *TQPNMA*. Ask students how they could show that these perimeters are equal. (*The lengths of the sides can be added in any order and the sum would be the same.*)

3 Reinforce and Extend

LEARNING STYLES

Auditory/Verbal

Have pairs of students explain to one another the steps they used to find the perimeters of the polygons in Exercise A.

MANIPULATIVES

M **Irregular Polygons**

Materials: Craft sticks or straws

Review the definition of perimeter. Provide each student with craft sticks or straws. Explain that they are to use the straws to create an irregular polygon. Students should use letters to name polygons. Ask each student to draw his or her polygon on a sheet of paper. Students should then label each line segment with letters and record the perimeter by counting the number of straws or sticks used in its construction. Have students use the same number of straws to create a different irregular polygon. This should also be drawn, labeled, and measured, and all information should be recorded. Students will then repeat the process a third time. Encourage students to share their irregular polygons on the overhead. Each time a new polygon is formed, choose a student to identify its perimeter. Students should recognize that the perimeter remains the same for each student's three irregular polygons.

Exercise A Find the perimeters.

1.

2   $2\frac{1}{3}$

3   $1\frac{1}{2}$

$8\frac{5}{6}$

2.

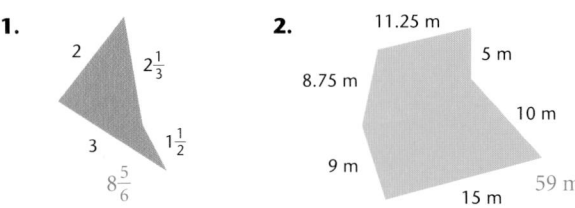

11.25 m
5 m
8.75 m
10 m
9 m
15 m   59 m

3.

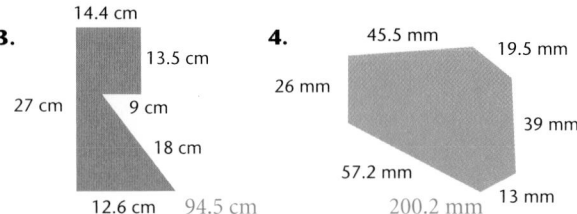

14.4 cm
13.5 cm
27 cm
9 cm
18 cm
12.6 cm   94.5 cm

4.

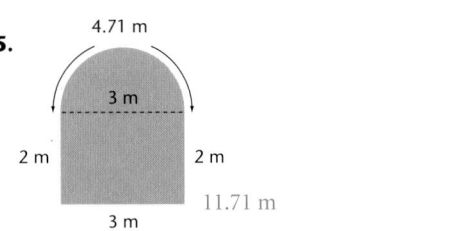

45.5 mm   19.5 mm
26 mm
39 mm
57.2 mm
13 mm
200.2 mm

5.

4.71 m
3 m
2 m   2 m
3 m
11.71 m

Technology Connection

Fencing in Fido

Invisible fencing is a high-tech way to keep a dog in its own yard. The "fence" is a cable, buried around the perimeter of the yard. The dog wears a special collar that picks up radio waves transmitted through the cable. When the dog gets too close to the cable, it hears a beep. If it doesn't move away, the collar gives the dog a mild electric shock. The owner can train the dog to move away as soon as it hears the beep.

Exercise B Find each missing measure *x*. Then find the perimeter of each colored polygon.

6.

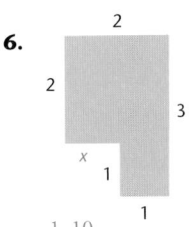

1, 10

7.

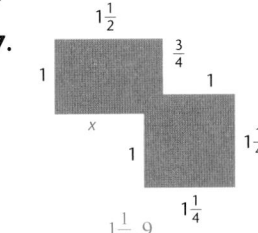

$1\frac{1}{4}$, 9

8.

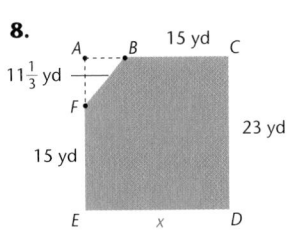

ACDE is a square.

23 yd, $87\frac{1}{3}$ yd

9.

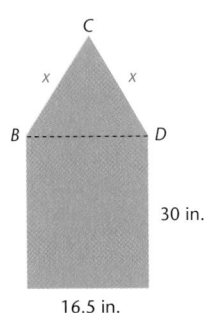

Triangle *BCD* is an equilateral triangle.

16.5 in., 109.5 in.

10.

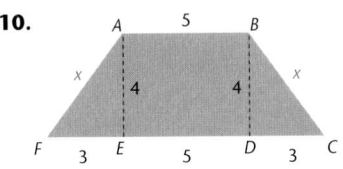

ABDE is a rectangle.

5, 26

Lesson at a Glance

Chapter 10 Lesson 4

Overview This lesson presents the formulas used to find the areas of rectangles and squares.

Objective

■ To find the area of a rectangle or square given the length of the side(s)

Student Pages 278–281

Teacher's Resource Library 🆃🆁🅻

Workbook Activity 92

Activity 88

Alternative Activity 88

1 Warm-Up Activity

Draw an array of squares on the board or overhead projector as shown below. Tell students that each of the small squares is 1 unit wide and 1 unit long. Ask them to describe two ways in which to find the area of the large rectangle. *(Count squares; multiply 3 by 7.)*

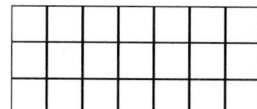

2 Teaching the Lesson

Ask a volunteer to explain Example 1. Suggest that he or she draws the rectangle on the board or overhead projector. Make certain that students understand how the answer was simplified and why the answer is given in cm².

The area of a figure is a measure of the number of square units in that figure. Each of the smaller squares in the rectangle below measures 1 unit by 1 unit. Altogether, there are 15 unit squares in the rectangle. The rectangle has an area of 15 units² or 15 square units.

> Recall that area is given in square units, such as square feet. You can use ft² for square feet.

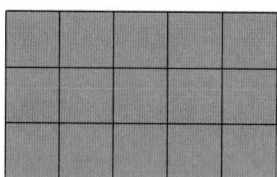

The formula $A = lw$ is used to determine the area of a rectangle. In the formula, l represents the measure of the length of the rectangle and w represents the measure of the width.

> For finding the area of a rectangle, the formula $A = bh$ is sometimes used instead of $A = lw$. In the formula $A = bh$, b stands for "base" and h stands for "height." Either formula is correct.

EXAMPLE 1 Find the area of rectangle *ABCD*.

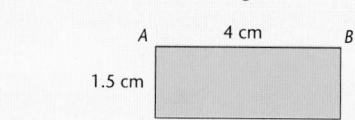

Step 1 Substitute the measures of the length and width of the rectangle into the formula $A = lw$.

$A = lw$

$A = (4)(1.5)$

Step 2 Simplify and label your answer.

$A = (4)(1.5)$

$A = 6.0$

$A = 6 \text{ cm}^2$

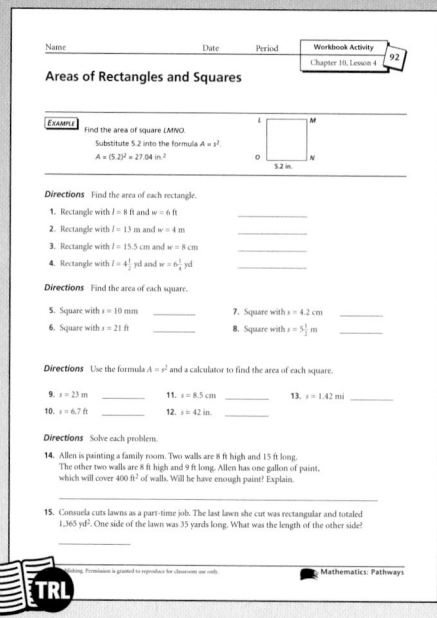

Workbook Activity 92

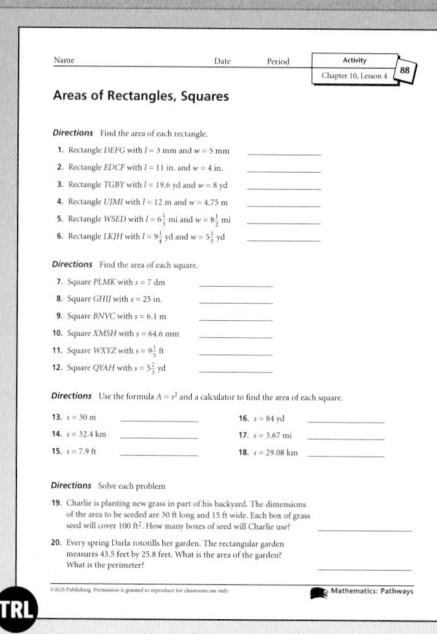

Activity 88

Recall that the formula $A = s^2$ is used to determine the area of a square. In the formula, s represents the measure of any side of the square.

EXAMPLE 2 Find the area of square *JKLM*.

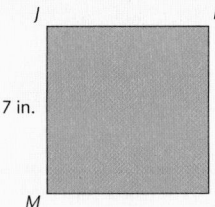

Step 1 Substitute the measure of one side of the square into the formula $A = s^2$.

$A = s^2$

$A = (7)^2$

Step 2 Simplify. Label your answer.

$A = 7^2$

$A = (7)(7)$

$A = 49 \text{ in.}^2$

Exercise A Find the area of each rectangle.

1. Rectangle *ABCD* with $l = 12$ cm and $w = 7$ cm
   84 cm^2

2. Rectangle *KLMN* with $l = 10$ in. and $w = 6$ in.
   60 in.^2

3. Rectangle *WXYZ* with $l = 20.4$ mm and $w = 5$ mm
   102 mm^2

4. Rectangle *GHPQ* with $l = 8$ ft and $w = 1.25$ ft
   10 ft^2

5. Rectangle *ABCD* with $l = 2\frac{1}{2}$ yd and $w = 1\frac{1}{2}$ yd
   $3\frac{3}{4} \text{ yd}^2$

6. Rectangle *JKRS* with $l = 3\frac{1}{4}$ mi and $w = 2\frac{1}{3}$ mi
   $7\frac{7}{12} \text{ mi}^2$

Students often complete the multiplication correctly but fail to completely or correctly label their answer. Stress to students that they must develop consistent habits when determining areas. After they multiply, they should always check their work, making sure that they have correctly labeled the answer with the appropriate square units. Review with students the meanings of the following notations: ft^2, m^2, yd^2, $in.^2$, and cm^2.

3 **Reinforce and Extend**

LEARNING STYLES

LEP/ESL

Provide graph paper and rulers to pairs of students. Ask them to make and label full-size drawings from problems 1–3 in Exercise A. Circulate, helping students recognize that they should label the vertices of the rectangles in order. Then have the student pairs make and label scale drawings from problems 4–6.

Exercise B Find the area of each square.

7. Square *RSTU* with $s = 9$ mm $\qquad$ 81 mm^2

8. Square *DCBA* with $s = 15$ in. $\qquad$ 225 in.^{2}

9. Square *QRMS* with $s = 4.4$ m $\qquad$ 19.36 m^2

10. Square *MLKJ* with $s = 12.5$ cm $\qquad$ 156.25 cm^2

11. Square *HSYB* with $s = 2\frac{1}{2}$ ft $\qquad$ $6\frac{1}{4}$ ft^2

12. Square *CQDX* with $s = 5\frac{1}{3}$ yd $\qquad$ $28\frac{4}{9}$ yd^2

 **Calculator Practice** A calculator can be used to find the areas of geometric figures.

EXAMPLE 3 Find the area of this square.

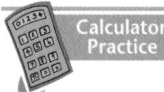

1.04 m

The formula for the area of a square is $A = s^2$.

Press 1 $\cdot$ 04 x^2.

The display reads 1.0816. Round to the nearest tenth.

$A = 1.1$ m^2

Exercise C Use the formula $A = s^2$, a calculator, and the x^2 key of the calculator to find the area of each square.

13. $s = 20$ m $\qquad$ 400 m^2

14. $s = 14.3$ cm $\qquad$ 204.49 cm^2

15. $s = 7.5$ ft $\qquad$ 56.25 ft^2

16. $s = 36$ in. $\qquad$ 1,296 in.^{2}

17. $s = 1.12$ mi $\qquad$ 1.2544 mi^2

18. $s = 11.06$ mi $\qquad$ 122.3236 mi^2

Exercise D Solve each problem.

19. Ivan is a gymnast whose best events are the floor exercise and the pommel horse. For the floor exercise, he must stay within the perimeter of the mat, which is a square with sides 12 meters long. What is the area in which Ivan performs his floor exercise? 144 m²

20. The Shipleys' living room is a rectangle 14 feet wide with an area of 224 ft². They are installing floorboards around the perimeter of the room. What is the length of the room? What is its perimeter?
16 ft, 60 ft

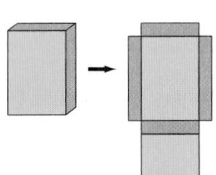

Build a Model

What does your cereal box look like in two dimensions? Follow the steps below to create a net for your box. A *net* is an unfolded three-dimensional figure.

On a large sheet of paper, trace the net of your box. Use the tracing to find
• the perimeter of your cereal box.
• the surface area of your cereal box.

Answers will vary depending on the size of students' boxes. Help students recognize that the perimeter is the distance around the outermost sides of the net. To find the surface area, help students identify duplicate shapes in their nets. Students can then find the area of one shape and multiply by 2 to find the area for both shapes. From this activity, students should see that surface area is the sum of all the surfaces in a 3-dimensional shape.

GROUP PROBLEM SOLVING

Have pairs of students find the best price for carpeting their classroom. Encourage the partners to bring in newspaper ads and take notes from television ads about carpet prices. Make sure that students define the area they want carpeted (the entire room or a portion of it), compute the area to be carpeted, and find the cost of carpeting that area. Remind students to pay close attention to the units they use and the units they find in the advertisements. Have them post their findings and then have the class determine which represents the best purchase price and the best value.

Build a Model

Mention to students that a *net* is a 2-dimensional drawing of a 3-dimensional object. The drawing is cut, folded, and sometimes taped or glued to recreate a version of the original object. Students may be familiar with books that have nets that, once assembled, recreate well-known objects such as the Space Shuttle, the Washington Monument, or the Empire State Building. All of the objects start out as flat pages and use various shapes and polyhedra to assemble into 3-dimensional paper "sculptures." The Build a Model for this chapter has students work with the net for a simple yet very familiar polyhedron (rectangular prism): a cereal box.

Lesson at a Glance

Chapter 10 Lesson 5

Overview This lesson discusses how to find the areas of triangles.

Objective

■ To find the area of a triangle using $A = \frac{1}{2}bh$

Student Pages 282–283

Teacher's Resource Library

  Workbook Activity 93

  Activity 89

  Alternative Activity 89

....

Mathematics Vocabulary

perpendicular

....

1 ⫶ Warm-Up Activity

Draw rectangle *ABCD* on the board or overhead projector. Draw a diagonal to form triangle *DCB*. Ask, "If the area of *ABCD* is y^2, what is the area of *DCB*?" Encourage students to offer opinions. Pursue responses of "$\frac{1}{2}y^2$," asking students to explain their reasoning.

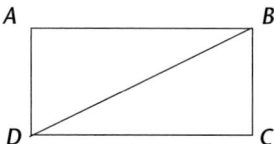

2 ⫶ Teaching the Lesson

As you discuss Example 1, make certain that students understand that the height of the triangle could also be a line from *B* perpendicular to the base of the triangle, $\overline{AC}$. In this instance, the height was drawn outside the triangle to make it easy to see.

As you discuss Example 2, tell the students they are solving by substitution.

Lesson 5   **Areas of Triangles**

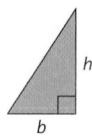

Perpendicular

Two intersecting lines forming right angles

The height of a triangle is measured by a line **perpendicular** to the base of the triangle. Sometimes the line is real and a part of the triangle. Other times it is imaginary and shown as a broken line. But the height of a triangle is never a slant measure.

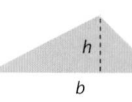

The height of a right triangle is perpendicular to the base. Therefore, the height line is real and part of the triangle.

The height of a scalene triangle is an imaginary line that is perpendicular to the base. It is represented by a broken line.

When you know the measures of a triangle's height and base, you can find its area.

$$A = \frac{1}{2}bh \text{ or } A = \frac{bh}{2}$$

In the formula, *A* equals area, *b* equals base, and *h* equals height.

Remember that dividing is the same as multiplying by the inverse of a number.

EXAMPLE 1 Find the area of triangle *ABC*.

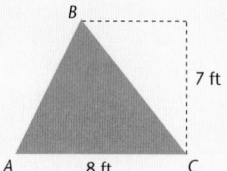

Use the formula $A = \frac{1}{2}bh$ or $A = \frac{bh}{2}$. Substitute the values of *b* and *h* into the formula, then simplify. Label your answer with the unit of measurement.

$A = \frac{1}{2}bh$

$A = \frac{1}{2}(8)(7)$

$A = \frac{1}{2}(56)$

$A = 28 \text{ ft}^2$

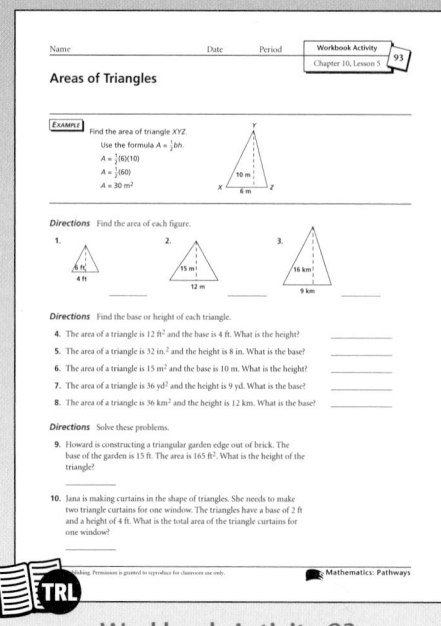

Workbook Activity 93

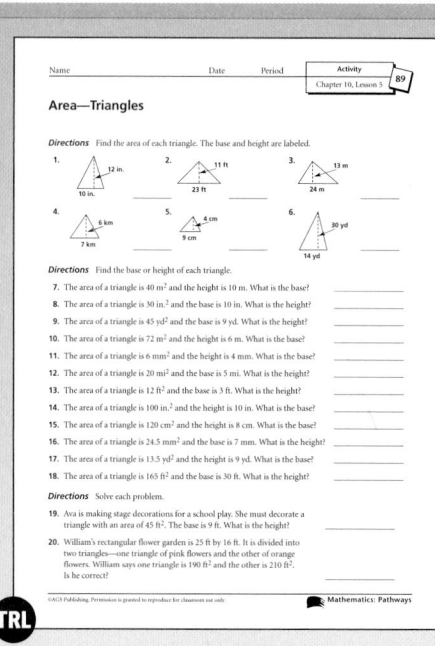

Activity 89

You can use the formula to find the base or height when you know the area and the height or base of a triangle.

EXAMPLE 2   Find the base of a triangle with a height of 6 inches and an area of 12 square inches.

$$A = \frac{1}{2}bh$$

$$12 = \frac{1}{2}b(6)$$

$$12 = \frac{1}{2}(6)b$$

$$12 = 3b$$

$$4 = b \quad \text{The base is 4 inches.}$$

Exercise A Find the area of each figure.

1. 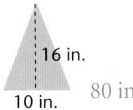 80 in.²

2. 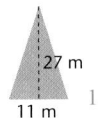 148.5 m²

3. 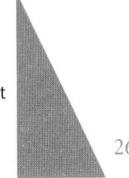 261 ft²

4. 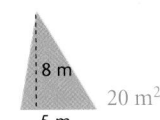 20 m²

5. 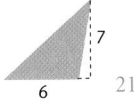 21

Exercise B Find the base or height of each triangle.

6. The area of a triangle is 36 in.² and the base is 18 in. What is its height? 4 in.

7. The area of a triangle is 2 ft² and the height is 1 ft. What is its base? 4 ft

8. The area of a triangle is 42 in.² and its base is 12 in. What is its height? 7 in.

 **PROBLEM SOLVING**

Exercise C Solve each problem.

9. The landscapers are planting flowers in a garden area shaped like a triangle. The base of the triangle is 12 feet and the area is 60 square feet. What is the height of the triangle? 10 ft

10. Sara is lining the bottom of a triangular box with paper. The base of the triangle is 15 inches and the height is 30 inches. What is the area of the bottom of the box? 225 in.²

Equations from Geometry   Chapter 10   **283**

LEARNING STYLES

LEP/ESL
Suggest that students add terms such as *perpendicular, height of a triangle,* and *base of a triangle* to any picture dictionary they may have started.

GROUP PROBLEM SOLVING

Suggest that groups of four students design pennants for their school's pep squad. The groups should decide the most appropriate size for the triangle-shaped pennants and compute the perimeter and area for a range of sizes. The groups can investigate the costs associated with making several dozen of the pennants. They can then determine what selling price would cover expenses and offer a modest profit. Have the groups present their plans and findings as a small business plan.

Lesson at a Glance

Chapter 10 Lesson 6

Overview This lesson presents the formulas needed to find the areas of trapezoids and parallelograms.

Objectives

- To find the area of a parallelogram using the formula $A = bh$
- To find the area of a trapezoid using the formula $A = \dfrac{b_1 + b_2}{2}h$

Student Pages 284–285

Teacher's Resource Library **TRL**

Workbook Activity 94

Activity 90

Alternative Activity 90

Mathematics Vocabulary

parallelogram
trapezoid

---

1 Warm-Up Activity

Place the following two drawings on the board or overhead projector without comment.

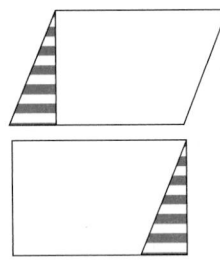

Ask students to describe any relationships they see between the two figures. Accept all responses. Reward responses identifying the second figure as a rectangle made from the parts of the first figure. Encourage responses indicating that the areas of the two figures are probably the same.

Parallelogram
A four-sided polygon with two pairs of equal and parallel sides

Trapezoid
A four-sided polygon with one pair of parallel sides and one pair of sides that are not parallel

You have found the areas of rectangles, squares, and triangles. Now you will find the areas of quadrilaterals such as **parallelograms** and **trapezoids.**

The height of a parallelogram or a trapezoid is measured by a line perpendicular to its base. Just as with some triangles, the line is imaginary and shown as a broken line. The height of a parallelogram or a trapezoid is never a slant measure.

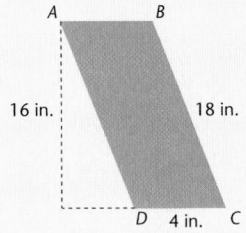

parallelogram   trapezoid

$$A = bh \qquad\qquad A = \frac{b_1 + b_2}{2}h$$

Use $A = bh$ to find the area of a parallelogram.

EXAMPLE 1 Find the area of parallelogram *ABCD*.

16 in.   18 in.

D   4 in.   C

Use the formula $A = bh$. Substitute the values of b and h into the formula, then simplify.

$A = bh$

$A = (4)(16)$

$A = 64$ in.^{2}

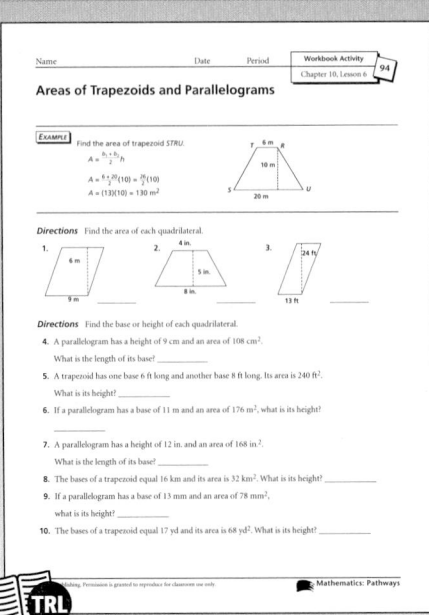

Workbook Activity 94

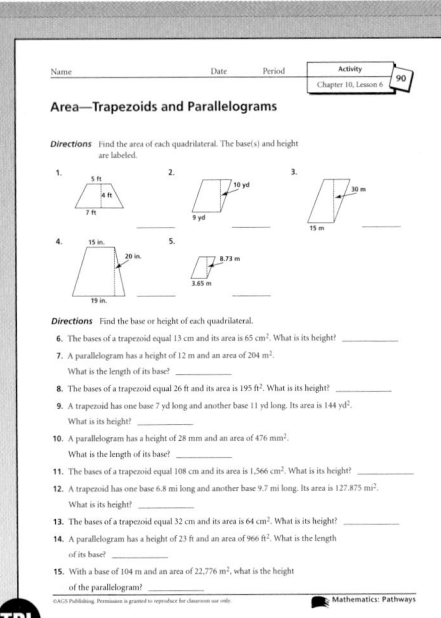

Activity 90

Use $A = \frac{b_1 + b_2}{2}h$ to find the area of a trapezoid.

EXAMPLE 2 Find the area of trapezoid *WXYZ*.

Use the formula $A = \frac{b_1 + b_2}{2}h$. Substitute the values of b_1, b_2, and h into the formula, then simplify. Label your answer.

$A = \frac{b_1 + b_2}{2}h$

$A = \frac{24 + 8}{2}(14)$

$A = \frac{32}{2}(14)$

$A = (16)(14)$

$A = 224 \text{ cm}^2$

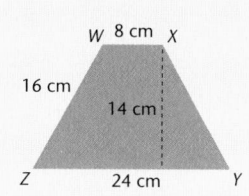

Exercise A Find the area of each quadrilateral.

1.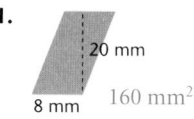
20 mm
8 mm
160 mm²

2.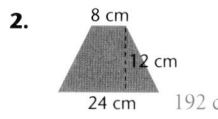
8 cm
12 cm
24 cm
192 cm²

3.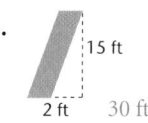
15 ft
2 ft
30 ft²

4.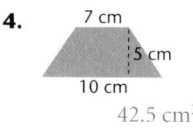
7 cm
5 cm
10 cm
42.5 cm²

5.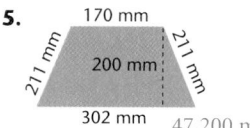
170 mm
211 mm
200 mm
211 mm
302 mm
47,200 mm²

6.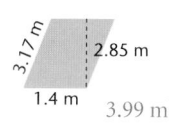
3.17 m
2.85 m
1.4 m
3.99 m²

Exercise B Find the base or height of each quadrilateral.

7. A parallelogram has a height of 2 feet and an area of 7 square feet. What is the length of its base? 3.5 ft

8. A trapezoid has one base 2 inches long and another base 4 inches long. Its area is 21 square inches. What is its height? 7 in.

9. With a base of 14 inches and an area of 28 square inches, what is the height of a parallelogram? 2 in.

10. The bases of a trapezoid equal 10 inches and its area is 35 square inches. What is its height? 7 in.

2 Teaching the Lesson

Have a volunteer work through Example 1 on page 284, showing how to use the formula $A = bh$ to find the area of a parallelogram. Point out that in the example, the height could have been drawn inside the parallelogram—from B perpendicular to $\overline{DC}$. The height was drawn outside the figure to make it easier to see.

3 Reinforce and Extend

LEARNING STYLES

Body/Kinesthetic

Students can trace the parallelogram on page 284. Have them mark the height with a dotted line. Ask them to cut out their tracing along the outside lines. Then have them cut along the dotted line that indicates the height. Prompt students to use the two polygons to form a rectangle. Ask them to describe the area of the rectangle. Note that students can do a similar activity with the trapezoid on page 284.

LEARNING STYLES

Interpersonal/ Group Learning

Have pairs of students describe why the area of a rectangle, $A = lw$, is a special case of the area of a parallelogram, $A = bh$. Have them present their description in a four-frame comic strip.

Chapter 10 Lesson 7

Overview This lesson explores ways in which to find the areas of irregular polygons.

Objective

■ To find areas of irregular polygons

Student Pages 286–287

Teacher's Resource Library **TRL**

Workbook Activity 95–96

Activity 91

Alternative Activity 91

1 Warm-Up Activity

Ask students to describe the grounds of their school. Prompt them with questions such as the following: "Are all the green or planted areas regular polygons?" "Is the parking lot a regular polygon?" "What parts of the school grounds can be described as irregular polygons?"

2 Teaching the Lesson

Use the example on page 286 as a demonstration on how to find areas of irregular polygons. Make sure that students understand the steps involved in finding the areas of the smaller regions as well as the addition needed to find the area of the entire region.

Formulas that are used to find the areas of figures such as triangles and rectangles can also be used to find the areas of irregular polygons.

EXAMPLE 1 Find the area of this polygon.

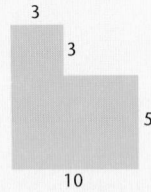

Step 1 Since there is no formula that can be used to determine the area of the entire polygon, plan to divide the polygon into smaller regions.

Step 2 Divide the polygon into smaller regions. Note the shape of each region, then use a formula to find the area of that region.

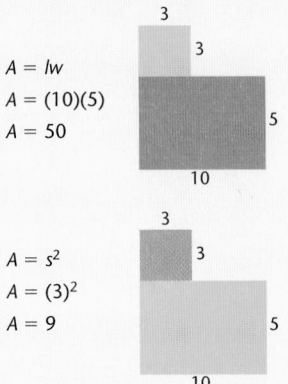

$A = lw$
$A = (10)(5)$
$A = 50$

$A = s^2$
$A = (3)^2$
$A = 9$

Step 3 To find the area of the entire figure, find the sum of the areas of the smaller regions.

$A = ■ + ■$
$A = 50 + 9 = 59$ square units

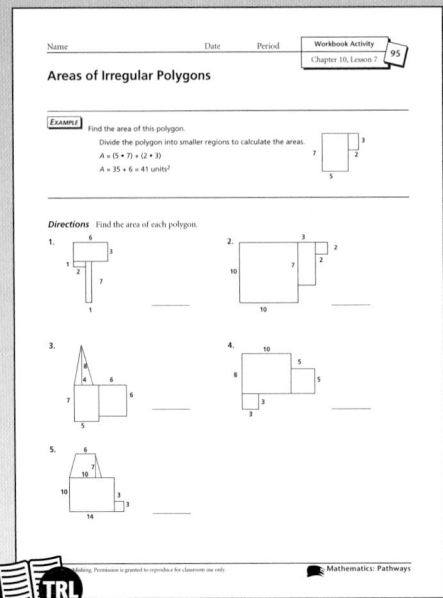

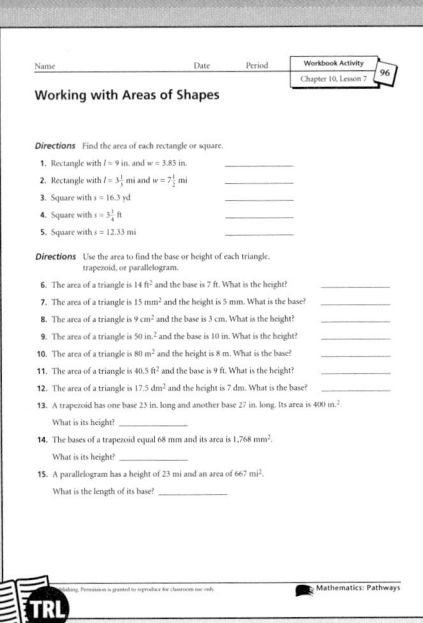

Exercise A Find the area of each polygon.

1.

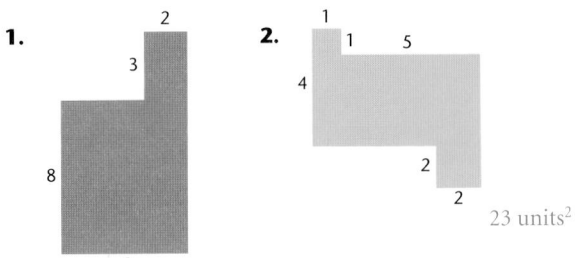

8

70 units²

2.

23 units²

3.

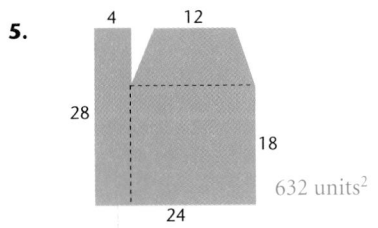

15

11

11

15

442.5 units²

4.

7

10

12

3

18

6

289 units²

5.

4   12

28

18

632 units²

24

Math in Your Life

Going Around in Circles

A circle is considered by mathematicians to be the perfect shape. Look around you, and you'll notice circles occur everywhere. In fact, the organ you use to see, the human eye, is in the shape of a circle. The ripples caused by a stone skipping over water are circles spreading outward from the point of contact. A rainbow is also a collection of circles, each one a different color.

LEARNING STYLES

Visual/Spatial

Have students work in groups of four to design cookie cutters in different kinds of shapes. Each cutter should have a different perimeter. However, all cutters should have approximately the same area so that they produce cookies of a similar size. Ask students to display their designs on a class bulletin board.

CAREER CONNECTION

Point out that landscape designers and architects must take irregular polygons into account as they work on a location. Suggest that students find out about the skills and qualifications needed to be a landscape designer or architect in your state. Encourage them to find out if your state offers a licensing program in landscape design.

ONLINE CONNECTION

Students can learn about calculating field sizes at www.leaprealtors.com/ acreage_calc.htm. Provide students with paper copies of the shapes at the site. Have students calculate the acres of these fields. For the last field, provide measurements for the given polygons and have students find the total area. Then have them divide the polygon in their own shapes. Ask them to recalculate the area and why the areas are equal. Have them explain why 43,560 is used in the given formulas.

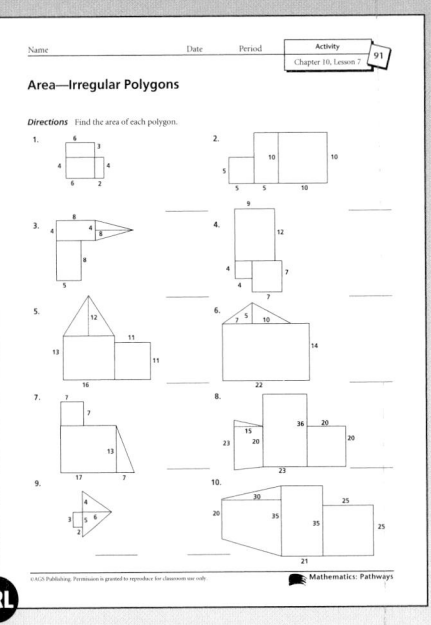

Activity 91

Lesson at a Glance

Chapter 10 Lesson 8

Overview This lesson discusses the circumferences and areas of circles.

Objectives

- To use the formula $C = \pi d$ to find the circumference of a circle
- To use $A = \pi r^2$ to find the area of a circle

Student Pages 288–291

Teacher's Resource Library

Workbook Activity 97

Activity 92

Alternative Activity 92

Mathematics Vocabulary

radius

----

1 Warm-Up Activity

Spread butcher paper or other large paper on the classroom floor. Use a 5-foot length of string and a marker to draw a circle on the paper. Ask one volunteer to walk, heel to toe, along the radius of the circle. Then ask the volunteer to walk, heel to toe, along a diameter of the circle. Record the number of footsteps taken in each instance. Finally, have the same volunteer walk, heel to toe, around the circumference of the circle. Record the number of footsteps taken. Ask the class to describe the ratio of the radius to the diameter and the ratio of the diameter to the circumference.

2 Teaching the Lesson

Use the examples on page 289 to demonstrate how to use the formula for circumference of a circle.

Radius

Distance from the center of a circle to the edge of the circle

Recall that circumference is the distance around a circle, diameter is the distance across a circle through the center, and pi (π) is the ratio of the circumference of a circle to the diameter.

Your study of circles will include the terms *radius,* *diameter,* and *circumference*. The length of a diameter is twice the length of a radius.

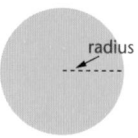 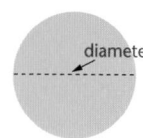 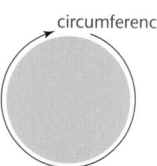

If you would take the time to draw a variety of circles and measure both the diameter and the circumference of each circle, you would find that the circumference of any circle is about three times the length of its diameter.

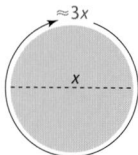

A measure used to describe this relationship is pi—the ratio of the circumference of any circle to the length of its diameter. Because pi is an irrational number, you will use an approximation for it. Three common approximations for pi are 3, 3.14, and $\frac{22}{7}$. The symbol for pi is π. Pi is used in formulas to find the circumference and area of a circle.

To find the circumference of a circle, use the formula $C = \pi d$ where C is circumference and d is diameter.

To find the area of a circle, use the formula $A = \pi r^2$ where A is area and r is radius.

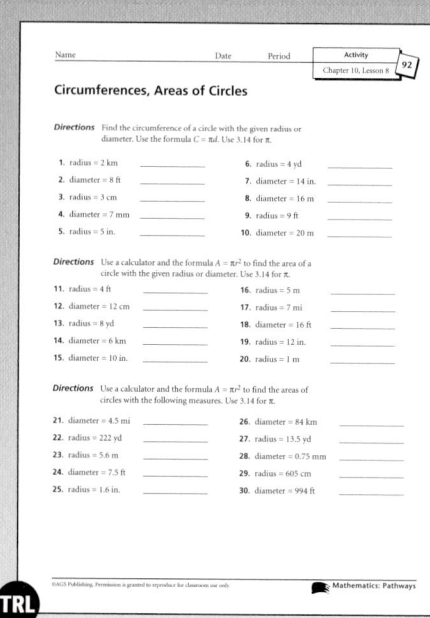

Workbook Activity 97   Activity 92

EXAMPLE 1 Find the circumference of this circle.

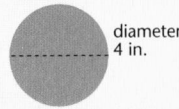

diameter
4 in.

To find the circumference of a circle, use the formula
$C = \pi d$. Substitute 3.14 for π and 4 for d. Then
simplify and label your answer.

$C = \pi d$

$C = (3.14)(4)$

$C = 12.56$ inches

When asked to find the circumference of a circle, you will
sometimes be given the radius of the circle, instead of the
diameter.

EXAMPLE 2 Find the circumference of this circle.

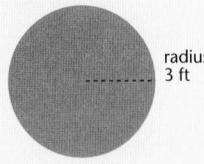

radius
3 ft

Step 1 To find the circumference of a circle, use the formula
$C = \pi d$. In this circle, the diameter is not given.

Since the radius of any circle is one-half the length of
the diameter, multiply the radius by 2 to find the
diameter.

3 ft • 2 = 6 ft; the diameter is 6 feet.

Step 2 In the formula $C = \pi d$, substitute 3.14 for π and 6 for d.
Then simplify and label your answer.

$C = \pi d$

$C = (3.14)(6)$

$C = 18.84$ feet

COMMON ERROR

When working with circles,
students may be prone to
not observing whether the
given measurement is a
radius or a diameter. Remind them
that these characteristics of a circle
are related but are not equivalent.
Encourage them to develop the habit
of checking to make sure they have
properly identified a measurement
as the radius or diameter of a circle
before using formulas.

3 Reinforce and Extend

LEARNING STYLES

**Interpersonal/
Group Learning**

Have students work in pairs
to show that $C = \pi d$ and
$C = 2\pi r$ are equivalent formulas for
finding the circumference of a circle.
They might present their explanations
as an advertisement for the formulas.

LEARNING STYLES

Auditory/Verbal

Ask student pairs to explain,
in detailed steps, how they
solved problems 1–4 in
Exercise A. As one student explains,
the second student can execute the
steps as described. Students should
change roles after each explanation.

When asked to find the area of a circle, you will sometimes be given the diameter of the circle, instead of the radius.

EXAMPLE 3 Find the area of this circle.

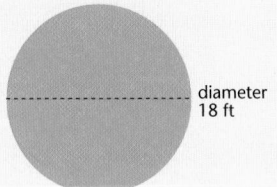

diameter
18 ft

Step 1 To find the area of a circle, use the formula $A = \pi r^2$. In this circle, the radius is not given.

Since the diameter of any circle is twice the length of the radius, divide the diameter by 2 to find the radius.

18 feet ÷ 2 = 9 feet; the radius is 9 feet.

Step 2 In the formula $A = \pi r^2$, substitute 3.14 for π and 9 for r. Then simplify and label your answer.

$$A = \pi r^2$$
$$A = (3.14)(9)^2$$
$$A = (3.14)(9)(9)$$
$$A = 254.34 \text{ ft}^2$$

Exercise A Find the circumference of a circle with the given radius or diameter. Use 3.14 for π.

1. radius = 3 in.   18.84 in.

2. diameter = 3 ft   9.42 ft

3. radius = 6 m   37.68 m

4. diameter = 5 cm   15.7 cm

5. radius = 10 yd   62.8 yd

Exercise B Find the area of a circle with the given radius or diameter. Use 3.14 for π.

6. radius = 4 m   50.24 m²

9. radius = 7 cm   153.86 cm²

7. diameter = 8 in.   50.24 in.²

10. diameter = 12 m   113.04 m²

8. diameter = 2 yd   3.14 yd²

Calculator Practice   Many calculators have a $\boxed{\pi}$ key. When a formula includes π, use the $\boxed{\pi}$ key.

> **EXAMPLE 4** The radius of a circle is 15 mm. Find the area of the circle.
>
> To find the area of a circle, use the formula $A = \pi r^2$.
>
> On the calculator, press $\boxed{\pi}$ $\boxed{\times}$ 15 $\boxed{x^2}$ $\boxed{=}$.
>
> The display may read 706.8583471, depending on how many decimal places the calculator uses for its approximation of π.

Exercise C Use a calculator and the formula $A = \pi r^2$ to find the areas of circles with the following measures.

11. radius = 6.5 in.   132.7322896 in.²

14. radius = 67 mm   14,102.60942 mm²

12. radius = 150 ft   70,685.83471 ft²

15. diameter = 1.15 mi   1.038689071 mi²

13. diameter = 2.4 m   4.523893421 m²

Estimation Activity

Estimate: Using π = 3, estimate the area of a circle with a diameter of 4 feet.

Solution: Use the formula for finding the area of a circle $A = \pi r^2$ where r = radius and 3 is used for π.

diameter = 4 feet → radius = 2 feet

Approximate area of circle = $(3)(2\ \text{ft})^2 = 12\ \text{ft}^2$

Chapter 10 Lesson 9

Overview This lesson introduces solid figures and the names of selected solid figures.

Objective

■ To identify selected solid figures

Student Pages 292–293

Teacher's Resource Library

Workbook Activity 98

Activity 93

Alternative Activity 93

Mathematics Vocabulary

prism
right prism
pyramid
vertex
cylinder
cone
sphere

---

1 Warm-Up Activity

Start by drawing two shapes on the board. One should be a plane figure and the other a three-dimensional version of the same plane figure. Ask students to identify the differences and similarities between the two shapes. Then point out that one figure is called a *plane* figure and one is called a *solid* or *three-dimensional* figure. Explain that a plane figure has length and width, and a solid figure has length, width, and height.

2 Teaching the Lesson

You will be discussing shapes in this lesson, so before class, gather several appropriate objects of varying shapes. During the lesson, hold up the objects one at a time and ask students to identify the shape. Ask students to find the faces, edges, and vertices of each object. Define each as students locate it (or as you show students where it is). Define terms such as *prism, cube, base,* and *pyramid* while showing objects with the corresponding shapes.

Lesson 9 Solid Figures

Prism	

A solid figure with two parallel bases that are polygons of the same shape and size

Right prism

Prism in which the base and the sides are at right angles

Pyramid

A solid figure with a base that is a polygon and triangular sides

Vertex

A common point opposite the base of a pyramid or cone

Solid geometric figures are three-dimensional. They have length, width, and height. The most common forms are shaped like boxes. In geometry they are called **prisms**. A prism is a solid that has two parallel bases that are the same size and shape and whose faces or sides are parallelograms.

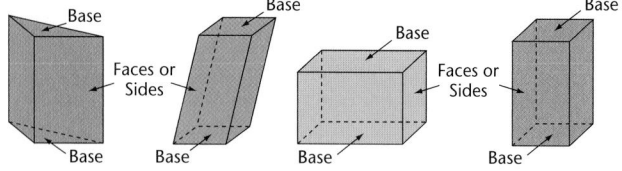

Right prisms are prisms with sides that are rectangles. Prisms are named by the shape of their equal bases.

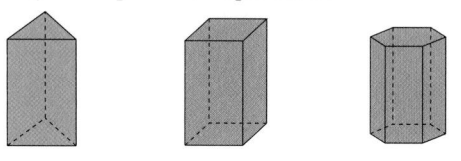

Triangular prism Square prism Hexagonal prism

A **pyramid** has a polygon as a base and triangles as faces or sides with a common **vertex**. The sides of a pyramid meet at a vertex opposite the base. Pyramids are also named by the shape of their bases.

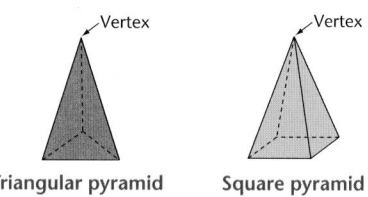

Triangular pyramid Square pyramid

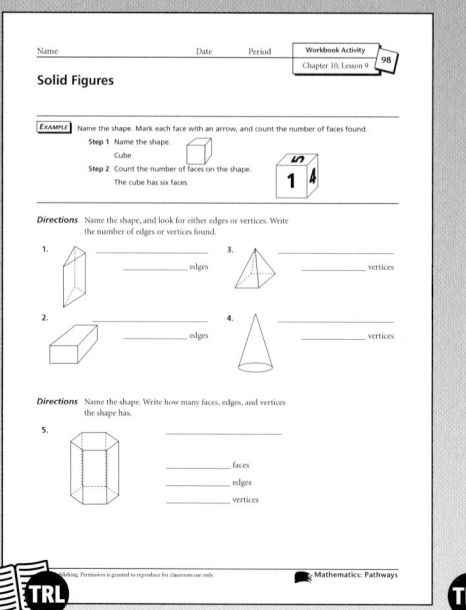

Workbook Activity 98

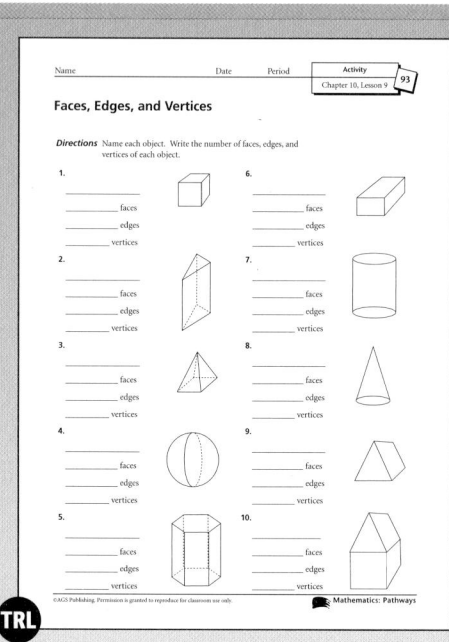

Activity 93

Some solid figures have curved surfaces. A **cylinder** has two equal circular bases that are parallel. A soup can looks like a cylinder. A **cone** has a circular base connected to a vertex. Some ice cream cones look like cones. A **sphere** is a round solid figure with all points on the surface an equal distance from the center. A basketball is a sphere.

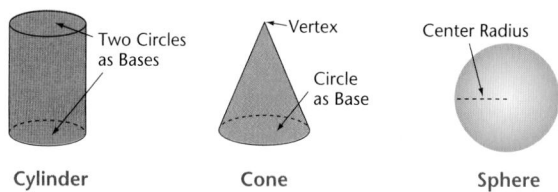

Cylinder   Cone   Sphere

Exercise A Write the name of each solid figure.

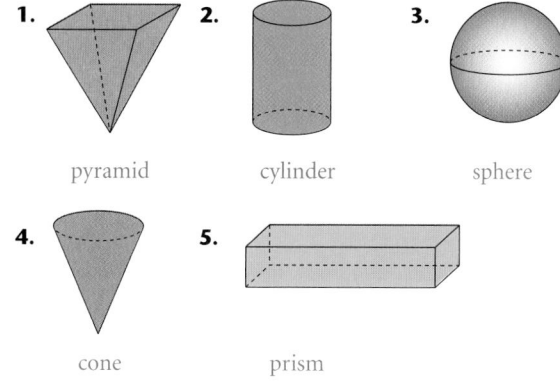

1. pyramid
2. cylinder
3. sphere
4. cone
5. prism

AT HOME

Ask students to look around their homes and find common objects with the shapes discussed in today's lesson. Ask students to list or sketch these objects for discussion tomorrow. They may bring smaller objects to show and discuss.

MODELING

Have students work in pairs. Give each pair several craft sticks and have them make shapes they learned about in the lesson. After students have completed the assignment, select several shapes, and ask the class to identify them.

KNOWING YOUR STUDENTS

Adolescents are under new pressures, both at home and at school. These new pressures can have an effect on their ability to remember even the simplest things. For example, you might expect that students would know the basic shapes by the time they get to the upper grades; however, some students may have difficulty remembering the names of these figures. It may be beneficial to review the names of basic shapes and figures before introducing more complex solid figures. In addition, when students are later asked to identify complex figures, encourage them to refer to their math books for examples and other useful information. You may need to review the simple shapes and figures more than once.

Lesson at a Glance

Chapter 10 Lesson 10

Overview This lesson introduces computations needed to find the surface areas of prisms and cylinders.

Objectives

- To recognize that the surface area of a prism or cylinder is the sum of the surface areas of the faces plus the surface area of the base
- To compute the surface area of selected prisms and cylinders

Student Pages 294–297

Teacher's Resource Library

Workbook Activity 99

Activity 94

Alternative Activity 94

1 Warm-Up Activity

Display a variety of similar-sized prisms and cylinders. Ask students how they could determine how much paint—or paper—they would need to cover each. Point out that in this lesson they will use their intuition to determine formulas for finding the surface areas of some solids.

2 Teaching the Lesson

Use models of each of the solids mentioned in the examples. With a marker, number or *X* each side as you include it in the total surface area. After completing each example, allow students to inspect the model. Make sure that they understand that each side was included once in the computation of the surface area.

Three-dimensional figures have a measurable characteristic—surface area. The surface areas of three-dimensional geometric figures can be computed by adding the areas of the sides, the base, and the top.

Cube

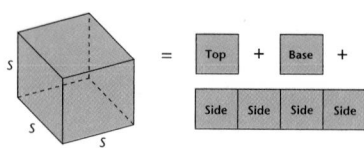

Total surface area of cube = area of 6 squares

Formula

Surface area of cube = $6s^2$

Rectangular Prism

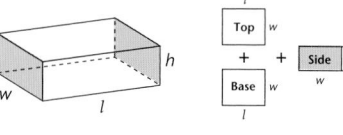

$$= 2(lw) \quad + \quad h(l + w + l + w)$$
$$= 2(lw) \quad + \quad h(2l + 2w)$$
$$= 2lw \quad + \quad 2hl \quad + \quad 2hw$$

Area = base and top + two larger sides + two smaller sides

Formula

Surface area of rectangular prism = $2(lw + hl + hw)$

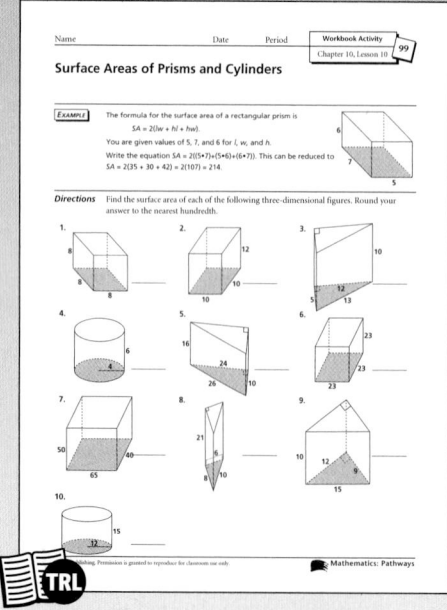

Workbook Activity 99

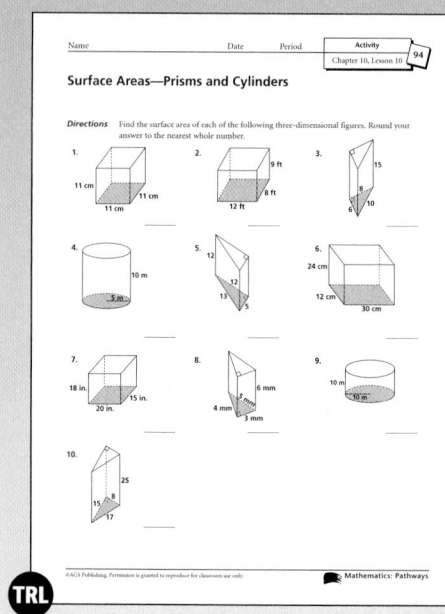

Activity 94

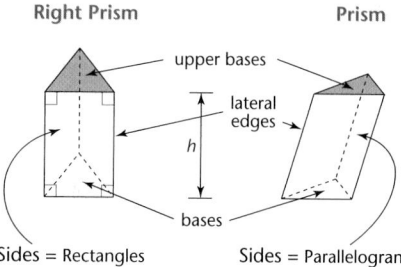

Right Prism　　　　　　**Prism**

upper bases

lateral edges

h

bases

Sides = Rectangles　　Sides = Parallelograms

Cubes and rectangular prisms can be grouped as right prisms. In a right prism, the side surfaces are perpendicular to the base and the upper surface. The total surface area is the sum of the areas of the base, upper base (top), and the sides. The side surfaces are rectangles. In prisms that are not right prisms, the sides are parallelograms.

Right Prism　　　　**Surfaces are two triangles and three rectangles**

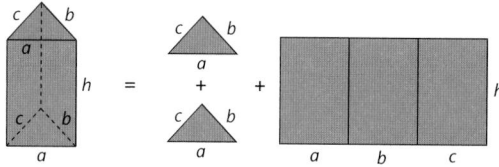

Formula

Surface area of right prism =
2(area of triangle) + $h(a + b + c)$

If the side surfaces of a prism are not perpendicular to the base and top, the sides are parallelograms.

Triangular Prism　　　　**Surfaces are two triangles and three parallelograms**

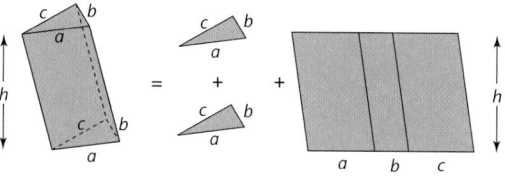

LEARNING STYLES

Visual/Spatial

Invite teams of students to use poster board or construction paper to duplicate each of the solids described in the lesson. Suggest that they also make a model for a cylinder. Have students follow the diagrams to construct each of the solids. Then have them draw, on separate sheets of paper, each of the surfaces used to make up the solid. Encourage them to produce diagrams similar to those shown in the text.

Ask students to label their solids to match those in the text. Challenge them to use their solids to derive the formulas for finding surface area.

COMMON ERROR

When working with prisms, students often forget to include the base as part of the total surface area.

AT HOME

Encourage students to collect several empty boxes, such as cereal or shoe boxes, from home. Encourage them to carefully slit the edges of the box, unfolding it so that it matches the rectangular—or square—diagrams shown in the text. Indicate that a test of such a diagram is that it can be folded again so that it encloses the original space. Mention to students that they may need to make more than one attempt to know which edges to slit. Invite students to share their successful attempts with the class. Have the class compute the surface area of each diagram presented by students.

A cylinder whose parallel bases are circles requires a special formula.

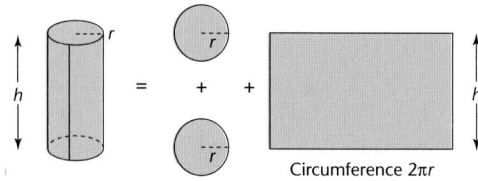

Cylinder   **Surfaces are two circles and one rectangle**

Circumference $2\pi r$

Formula

Surface area of cylinder $= 2\pi r^2 + (2\pi r)h$

You can use these formulas to calculate the surface areas of some of the most common three-dimensional objects.

EXAMPLE 1 What is the total surface area of a cube whose side is 5 units long?

Sketch all the surfaces of the cube.

Surface area of cube $= 6s^2$

$\qquad = 6(5^2) = 6(25)$

$\qquad = 150$ sq units

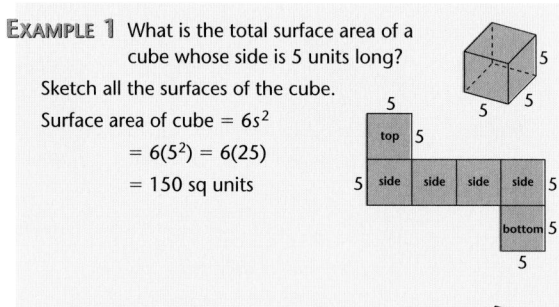

EXAMPLE 2 What is the total surface area of a box that is 10 inches on a side and has no lid?

Sketch all the surfaces of the box.

Surface area of cube $= 5s^2$

$\qquad = 5(10^2) = 5(100)$

$\qquad = 500$ sq in.

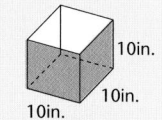

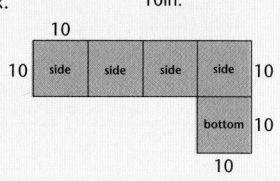

EXAMPLE 3 Calculate the total surface area of a rectangular box whose dimensions are 10 • 8 • 5.

Sketch all the surfaces of the box.

Surface area of rectangular prism = 2(*lw* + *hl* + *hw*)

let *l* = 10, *w* = 5, *h* = 8

Surface area = 2[(10 • 5) + (8 • 10) + (8 • 5)]

= 100 + 160 + 80

= 340 sq units

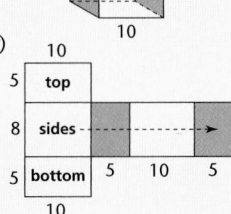

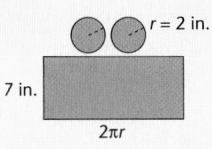

EXAMPLE 4 What size label is needed to cover the sides of a can whose radius is 2 inches and whose height is 7 inches?

Sketch each surface of the cylinder.

surface area = *l* • *w*

w = 7

l = circumference = 2π*r*

= 2π2 = 4π

surface area = 7(4π)

= 28π sq in.

Exercise A Find the surface area of each of the following three-dimensional figures. Some answers may include radicals or π.

1.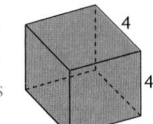

96 sq units

2.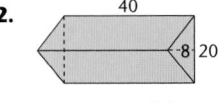

960 + 160 √41 sq units

3.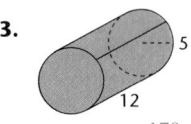

170π sq units

 PROBLEM SOLVING

Exercise B Find the surface area of each of the following three-dimensional figures. Some answers may include radicals or π.

4. What is the surface area of a 12-inch-tall cylindrical vase whose radius is 4 inches?

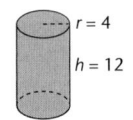

112π sq in.

5. Juanita plans to paint the walls and ceiling of a room bright green. The room is 10 feet wide and 12 feet long. The ceilings are 9 feet above the floor. She has one can of paint that covers 500 sq ft. Will it be enough? Why?

No, she's planning to paint 516 sq ft.

Chapter 10 Lesson 11

Overview This lesson describes methods for finding the surface area of pyramids and cones.

Objectives

- To recognize that the surface area of pyramids and cones is the sum of the surface areas of the sides plus the surface area of the base
- To compute the surface area of selected pyramids and cones

Student Pages 298–301

Teacher's Resource Library

Workbook Activity 100

Activity 95

Alternative Activity 95

1 Warm-Up Activity

Display a variety of poster board or cardboard pyramids and cones. Make certain that the insides of each solid are a color different from the outside. Take each pyramid and cone apart for students. Ask students to speculate on how they might use the parts of the solids to determine their surface areas.

2 Teaching the Lesson

Demonstrate how to find the surface area of a pyramid. Following the example, take apart a paper pyramid and complete the diagram for the solid. Do the same for the cone example at the bottom of the page. Allow a volunteer to reassemble the two-part model, closing the cut with tape.

Help students recognize that finding the surface area of a pyramid or cone is the same as finding the surface area of a prism or cylinder—one must find the surface area of each part or component.

Lesson 11 Surface Areas of Pyramids and Cones

In the previous lesson, you found the area of each side of a three-dimensional figure and then added the areas. You can use the same method to find the surface areas of pyramids and cones. First, separate the base of the pyramid (a polygon) from its sides (triangles). Here is an example using a square pyramid.

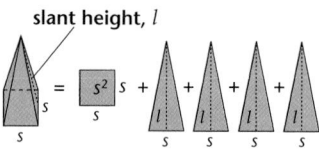

The area of each of the four side triangles is found using the base of the triangle and a measurement called the *slant height* of the pyramid. Think of the slant height as the straight-line distance you would have to climb from the midpoint of a base to the top of the pyramid. The symbol for slant height is *l*. So, the area of a pyramid is:

$$= s \cdot s \quad + \tfrac{1}{2}sl + \tfrac{1}{2}sl + \tfrac{1}{2}sl + \tfrac{1}{2}sl$$
$$= s^2 \quad + \quad 2sl$$

> **Formula**
> Surface area of pyramid =
> (area of base) + areas of four triangles = $s^2 + 2sl$

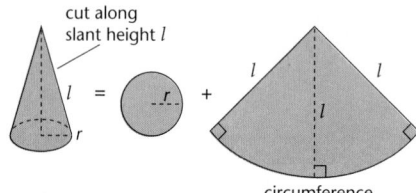

The surface area of a cone is found in much the same way. Think of the surface of the cone cut from the base to the vertex. Then flatten the surface. You will see that the surface of the cone is made up of the surfaces of two areas. One is a circle with radius *r*. The other is like a triangle with a base that is the circumference of the circle and a height that is the slant height of the cone.

> **Formula**
> Surface area of cone =
> (area of circular base) + area of triangle = $\pi r^2 + \tfrac{1}{2}bl$

---

298 *Chapter 10 Equations from Geometry*

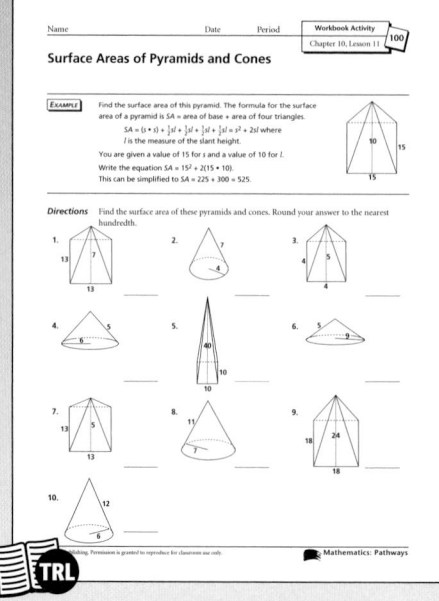

Workbook Activity 100

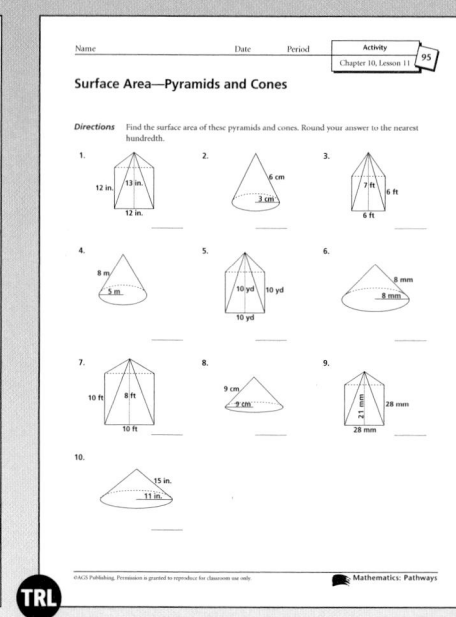

Activity 95

In this case, the base of the triangle, *b*, equals the circumference of the circle. The height of the triangle is the slant height, *l*, of the side's edge.

$$= \pi r^2 + \frac{1}{2}(2\pi r \cdot l)$$
$$= \pi r^2 + \pi r l$$
$$= \pi r (r + l)$$

Each of these formulas can be used to find the total surface areas of pyramids and cones.

EXAMPLE 1 Find the areas of the sides and then the total surface area of the square pyramid with the given dimensions.

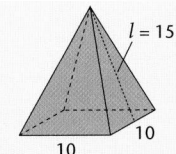

Sketch all the surfaces of the pyramid.
Surface area of pyramid = (area of base) + areas of four triangles
Surface area of pyramid sides = areas of four triangles

$$= 4(\tfrac{1}{2})(bl) \qquad b = 10, l = 15$$

$$= 4(\tfrac{1}{2})(10)(15) = 2(150)$$

$$= 300 \text{ sq units}$$

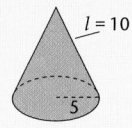

Surface area of base = 10 • 10 = 100 sq units
Surface area of pyramid = 100 sq units + 300 sq units
$$= 400 \text{ sq units}$$

EXAMPLE 2 What is the surface area of a cone whose radius is 5 and whose slant height is 10?

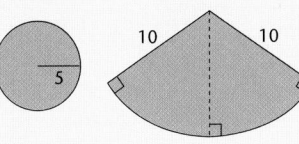

Sketch the surface.

Surface area of cone = (area of circular base) + area of triangle

$$= \pi r^2 + \tfrac{1}{2}bl$$

b = the circumference of the circle = $2\pi r = 2\pi 5$, *l* = 10

$$= \pi 5^2 + \tfrac{1}{2}(2\pi 5)(10)$$

$$= \pi 25 + \pi 50$$

$$= 75\pi$$

As with cylinders, you can substitute 3, 3.1, 3.14, or any other approximation for π.

GROUP PROBLEM SOLVING

Engage students in a discussion of soft-drink sizes available at fast-food restaurants. Have students work in groups of four. If feasible, encourage students to bring in a selection of paper cups used for soft drinks, noting the price, without tax, for each size. Challenge students to determine how to find the volume of the cups (most are frustums of cones). Groups should investigate how many cubic centimeters of liquid each cup holds, what is the price per cubic centimeter of a soft drink, and how much paper is needed to make the cup. Students can present their findings as a Consumer Corner segment of the evening news.

EXAMPLE 3 Find the total surface area of the triangular pyramid whose base measures 10 units on a side and whose slant height is 25 units.

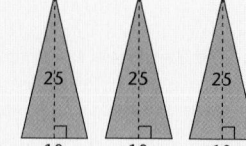

Sketch all the surfaces of the pyramid.

Surface area of pyramid = (area of base) + areas of three triangles

Surface area of pyramid sides = areas of three triangles

$$= 3(\tfrac{1}{2})(bl) \qquad b = 10, l = 25$$

$$= 3(\tfrac{1}{2})(10)(25) = 3(5 \cdot 25)$$

$$= 375 \text{ sq units}$$

Surface area of base $= \tfrac{1}{2}(bh)$

$b = 10$ but you must find the value of h:

Using the Pythagorean theorem:

$$10^2 = 5^2 + h^2$$

$$100 = 25 + h^2$$

$$75 = h^2$$

$$\sqrt{3 \cdot 25} = h$$

$$5\sqrt{3} = h$$

Surface area of base $= \tfrac{1}{2}(bh) = \tfrac{1}{2}(10)(5\sqrt{3})$

$$= 25\sqrt{3}$$

Surface area of pyramid = (area of base) + areas of three triangles

$$= 25\sqrt{3} + 375 \text{ sq units}$$

Exercise A Find the surface areas of these pyramids and cones.

1.

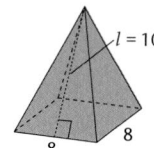

224 sq units

2.

75p sq units

3.

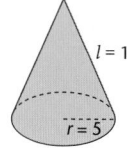

$120 + 16\sqrt{3}$ sq units

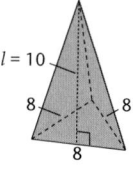

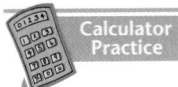

Calculator Practice: When calculating the area of the base of a cone, you may find it helpful to use the key x^2 on your calculator.

EXAMPLE 4 Find the value of 17^2.
Press 17 x^2.
The display reads 289.

Exercise B Find the squares of the following numbers.

4. 16   256   **6.** 24   576   **8.** 19   361

5. 18   324   **7.** 23   529

PROBLEM SOLVING

Exercise C Solve the following problems.

9. Roger has to make a model tepee for social studies class. He has a triangle with the dimensions shown. Can he make a tepee whose base radius is 8 feet? Explain.

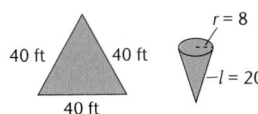

40 ft   40 ft $r = 8$
40 ft $l = 20$

No, he needs a triangle whose base > 50 ft, the circumference of the base.

10. The largest of the Egyptian pyramids, built for Pharaoh Khufu, is a square pyramid with the dimensions shown. What is the surface area of the sides of Khufu's pyramid?
86,394 m²

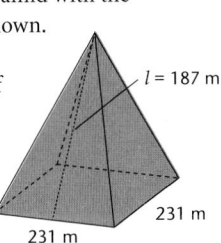

$l = 187$ m
231 m
231 m

CALCULATOR

Point out that another useful key is the $\sqrt{}$ key which takes the square root of a number. Have students use their calculators to find the following square roots.

$\sqrt{625}$ (25)

$\sqrt{169}$ (13)

$\sqrt{225}$ (15)

$\sqrt{100}$ (10)

Lesson at a Glance

Chapter 10 Lesson 12

Overview This lesson addresses finding the volumes of cubes, rectangular prisms, and square pyramids.

Objectives

- To use the formula $V = e^3$ to find the volume of a cube
- To use the formula $V = lwh$ to find the volume of a rectangular prism
- To use $V = \frac{s^2 h}{3}$ to find the volume of a square pyramid

Student Pages 302–305

Teacher's Resource Library

Workbook Activity 101

Activity 96

Alternative Activity 96

1 Warm-Up Activity

If feasible, present three-dimensional models of a cube, a rectangular prism, and a square pyramid to students. If models are not available, collect and display photos of the solids. Help students become aware of the different shapes of solid objects.

2 Teaching the Lesson

Use unit cubes, such as sugar cubes, to build a $2 \times 2 \times 2$ unit cube. Have a volunteer count the number of cubes in the unit cube and compare it to the volume found by using the formula $V = e^3$.

If necessary, repeat the demonstration with a $4 \times 4 \times 4$ cube and a $10 \times 2 \times 3$ rectangular prism.

Ask a volunteer to explain why $V = e^3$ is a special case of $V = lwh$. ($l = e$, $w = e$, and $h = e$)

 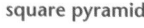
Three-dimensional figures such as cubes, rectangular prisms, and square pyramids have volume.

cube   rectangular prism   square pyramid

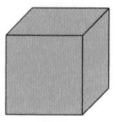 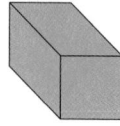 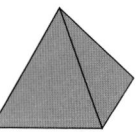

Recall that a cube is a solid with six square faces. You can also define a cube as a prism with six square faces.

Volume is a measure of the number of cubic units contained in a three-dimensional figure. The unit of measure for volume must be a shape that will fill all of the space inside a figure.

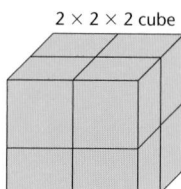

$2 \times 2 \times 2$ cube

The volume of this cube, for example, can be measured in unit cubes. The cube is made up of 8 unit cubes. A 2 by 2 by 2 cube has a volume of 8 cubic units or 8 units^3.

302 Chapter 10 Equations from Geometry

Workbook Activity 101

Activity 96

The formula $V = e^3$, where V is the volume and e is the measure of any edge of the cube, can be used to find the volume of a cube.

EXAMPLE 1 Find the volume of this cube.

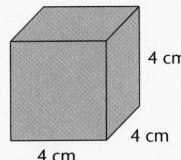

4 cm
4 cm
4 cm

Determine the measure of one edge of the cube. Then use the formula $V = e^3$.

$V = e^3$

$V = (4)^3$

$V = (4)(4)(4)$

$V = 64 \text{ cm}^3$

The formula $V = lwh$, where l is length, w is width, and h is height, can be used to find the volume of a rectangular prism.

EXAMPLE 2 Find the volume of this rectangular prism.

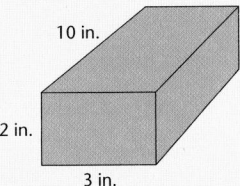

10 in.

2 in.

3 in.

Determine the length, the width, and the height of the prism. Then use the formula $V = lwh$.

$V = lwh$

$V = (10)(3)(2)$

$V = 60$

$V = 60 \text{ in.}^3$

AT HOME

Ask students to collect measurements and find the volumes of several common household solids. Encourage them by pointing out that shoe boxes, bar soap, and books can all be described as rectangular prisms.

The formula $V = \frac{Bh}{3}$ can also be used to find the volume of a square pyramid. In the formula, B represents the area of the base of the pyramid.

The formula $V = \frac{s^2h}{3}$ (where s is the measure of one side of the square base and h is the height as measured by a line perpendicular to the base) can be used to find the volume of a square pyramid.

EXAMPLE 3 Find the volume of this square pyramid.

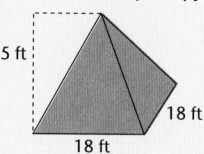

Determine the measure of one side of the square base and the height of the pyramid. Then use the formula $V = \frac{s^2h}{3}$.

$$V = \frac{s^2h}{3}$$
$$V = \frac{(18)^2(25)}{3}$$
$$V = \frac{18 \cdot 18 \cdot 25}{3}$$
$$V = \frac{8,100}{3}$$
$$V = 2,700 \text{ ft}^3$$

Whenever you find volume, remember to label your answer in cubic units.

Exercise A Find the volume of each three-dimensional figure.

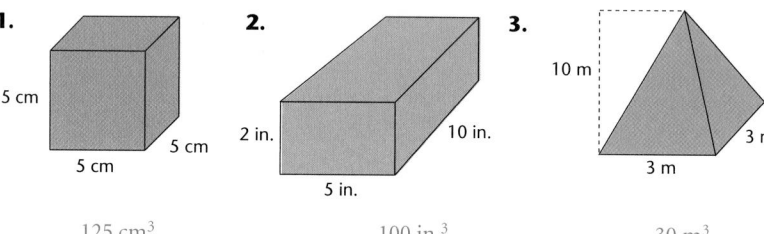

1. 125 cm³
2. 100 in.³
3. 30 m³

 **Calculator Practice**

A calculator can be used to help find the volume of three-dimensional figures.

EXAMPLE 4 Each edge of a cube measures 12.5 mm. Find the volume of the cube.

Press 12 $\cdot$ 5 y^x 3 $=$.

The display reads *1953.125*.

4. 27,000 mm³

5. 262.144 in.³

6. 1,225.043 cm³

7. 1,906,624 in.³

8. 1.157625 m³

Exercise B Use the formula $V = e^3$ and a calculator to find the volume of each cube.

4. $e = 30$ mm   **7.** $e = 124$ in.

5. $e = 6.4$ in.   **8.** $e = 1.050$ m

6. $e = 10.7$ cm

 **PROBLEM SOLVING**

Exercise C Solve each problem.

9. A cube measuring 4 inches by 4 inches by 4 inches has a square hole cut in it. If the hole measures 1 inch by 1 inch and goes all the way through the cube, what is the volume of the cube? 60 in.³

10. The basket of Rosa's shopping cart is a rectangular prism 18 inches wide, 30 inches long, and 15 inches high. What is the cart's volume? 8,100 in.³

 **CALCULATOR**

Ask students to use their calculators to find the volumes of cubes with the following edge lengths.

3.4 in.   *(39.304 in.³)*

4.5 m   *(91.125 m³)*

4.01 ft   *(64.481201 ft³)*

5.04 cm   *(128.024064 cm³)*

2.05 m   *(8.615125 m³)*

7.3 mm   *(389.017 mm³)*

0.08 in.   *(0.000512 in.³)*

0.02 mm   *(0.000008 mm³)*

 **GROUP PROBLEM SOLVING**

Have pairs of students estimate the amount of air inside their school. The partners should present their answers in either cubic feet or cubic yards of air. They can use their estimates as part of a museum exhibit that includes a life-size model of a cubic yard.

Lesson at a Glance

Chapter 10 Lesson 13

Overview This lesson presents the formulas for finding the volume of a cylinder, sphere, or cone.

Objective

■ To use the appropriate formula to compute the volume of a cylinder, sphere, or cone

Student Pages 306–307

Teacher's Resource Library **TRL**

Workbook Activity 102

Activity 97

Alternative Activity 97

---

1 Warm-Up Activity

Ask students to provide examples of cylinders, spheres, or cones from their daily lives. Responses may include the balls used in their favorite sport, such as volleyballs or baseballs; different containers such as soup or juice cans; or shapes found in the cafeteria, such as ice cream cones. Discuss why they might need to know the volume of a cylinder or cone. *(to know how much the container can hold)*

2 Teaching the Lesson

Use the examples on page 306 and 307 to show how to use the formulas for the volume of a cylinder, sphere, or cone. Be sure to point out to students that each of the formulas uses *r*, or *radius*. Remind them that cylinders and spheres can be described using their diameters. Encourage students to always check their work to ensure that they have properly identified a measurement as either the radius or diameter, and remind them that their answers must be in "units cubed."

Volumes of cylinders and cones are related in a very special way.

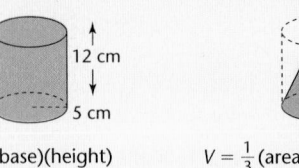

EXAMPLE 1 Find the volume of the cylinder and cone. Use 3.14 for π.

12 cm / 5 cm

$V = $ (area of base)(height)
$V = (\pi r^2)(h)$
$V = (3.14)(5)^2(12)$
$V = (3.14)(25)(12)$
$V = 942$ cm^3

$V = \frac{1}{3}$ (area of base)(height)
$V = \frac{1}{3}(\pi r^2)(h)$
$V = \frac{1}{3}(3.14)(5)^2(12)$
$V = \frac{1}{3}(942)$
$V = 314$ cm^3

Volume of cone $= \frac{1}{3}$ volume of cylinder with equal base and height.

Volumes of square prisms and square pyramids are related in a similar way.

The formula $\frac{4\pi r^3}{3}$ can also be used to find the volume of a sphere.

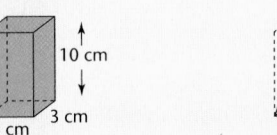

EXAMPLE 2 Find the volume of this square prism and square pyramid.

10 cm / 3 cm

$V = $ (area of base)(height)
$V = 90$ cm^3

$V = \frac{1}{3}$ (area of base)(height)
$V = 30$ cm^3

Volume of pyramid $= \frac{1}{3}$ volume of prism with equal base and height.

---

306 Chapter 10 *Equations from Geometry*

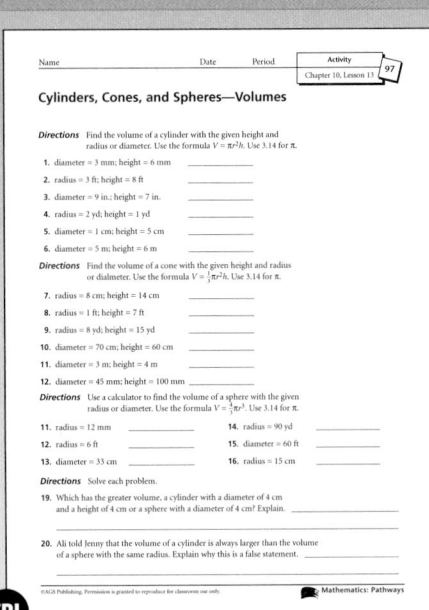

Workbook Activity 102

Activity 97

To find the volume of a sphere, use the formula $V = \frac{4}{3}\pi r^3$.

EXAMPLE 3 Calculate the volume of a sphere with
$r = 2$ m. Use 3.14 for π.

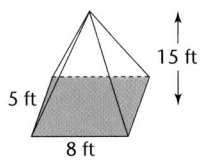

2 m

$V = \frac{4}{3}\pi(2)^3$

$V = \frac{4}{3}(3.14)(2)(2)(2)$

$V = \frac{4}{3}(25.12)$

$V = \frac{4}{3} \cdot \frac{25.12}{1} = \frac{100.48}{3} = 33.49\overline{3}$ m^3

Exercise A Find the volume of a cylinder with the given height
and radius or diameter. Use 3.14 for π.

1. diameter = 4 in.; height = 10 in.   125.6 in.^{3}

2. radius = 20 cm; height = 50 cm   62,800 cm^3

3. diameter = 16 mm; height = 10 mm   2,009.6 mm^3

Exercise B Find the volume of a sphere with the given radius
or diameter. Use 3.14 for π. You may use a calculator.

4. radius = 5 cm   523.$\overline{3}$ cm^3

5. diameter = 24 in.   7,234.56 in.^{3}

Exercise C Find the volume of each pyramid. Be sure to make
and label a sketch for each.

6. $s = 10$ in.,
$h = 10$ in.

$333\frac{1}{3}$ in^3

10 in.

10 in.

10 in.

7. $l = 8$ ft,
$w = 5$ ft,
$h = 15$ ft

200 ft^3

15 ft

5 ft

8 ft

Exercise D Use a calculator to find the volume of each cone. Use 3.14 for π.

8.
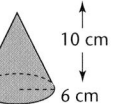
10 cm

6 cm

376.8 cm^3

9. $r = 7$ cm, $h = 10$ cm   512.8$\overline{6}$ cm^3

10. $r = 14$ cm, $h = 20$ cm   4,102.9$\overline{3}$ cm^3

*Equations from Geometry   Chapter 10   **307***

LEARNING STYLES

Visual/Spatial

To help students visualize
the volumes of different
cylinders, suggest that the
class make a collection of common
cylinders such as soup, tuna fish, and
potato chip cans as well as oatmeal
and cornmeal boxes. Have students
compute the volume of each. They
can then label each container with
its volume and put the containers
in a display.

LEARNING STYLES

Logical/Mathematical

Have students investigate
the sizes of cylinders used
to package common foods.
Have them use their investigation
to show that taller cans do not
necessarily have a greater volume
than shorter cans. In addition, ask
them to find two common food
containers of different heights or
shapes that have the same volume.

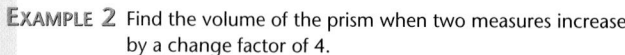

Lesson at a Glance

Chapter 10 Application

Overview This application uses the formula for finding the volume of a rectangular prism and demonstrates how the volume changes when its dimensions are scaled.

Objective

- To use the formula for the volume of a rectangular prism to solve scale problems

Student Page 308

Teacher's Resource Library **TRL**

Application Activity 10

Everyday Math 10

1 Warm-Up Activity

Define the term *dilation* for students as "an enlargement." Ask students to identify something that might be enlarged, such as a photograph. Ask the students why someone would want to enlarge a photograph. The term dilation can now be applied to other objects, such as the solid objects that will be explored in this lesson.

2 Teaching the Lesson

Remind students how to find the volume of a rectangular prism by completing some examples from the lesson on the board. To make sure that students understand the word *dilation*, ask them the following questions:

- What would happen to an object if you dilated it by a scale factor less than 1?
- Greater than 1?
- Equal to 1?

Be sure to make students aware that when the problem involves an *increase*, the scale factor is a number *larger* than one and when the problem indicates a *decrease*, the scale factor is *less* than one.

Dilation means to increase in size. The volume of a rectangular prism changes when its measures change. If one measure of the prism is dilated by a change factor of 4, that means the measure of one side is multiplied by 4. To find the volume of a prism when it changes by:

- *one* dimension: Multiply the original volume by the scale factor.
- *two* dimensions: Multiply the original volume by the *square* of the scale factor.
- *three* dimensions: Multiply the original volume by the *cube* of the scale factor.

EXAMPLE 1 A rectangular prism measures 10 cm by 4 cm by 6 cm. Find its volume when one measure increases by a change factor of 4.

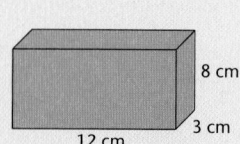

Step 1 Find the original volume.
$V = lwh = 10$ cm $\times 4$ cm $\times 6$ cm $= 240$ cm^3

Step 2 Multiply the original volume by 4.
240 cm$^3 \times 4 = 960$ cm^3

Step 3 Check your answer. If the side that was 10 cm dilated by a change factor of 4, it would become 40 cm.
$V = 40 \times 4 \times 6 = 960$ cm^3

EXAMPLE 2 Find the volume of the prism when two measures increase by a change factor of 4.

Step 1 Multiply the original volume by $(4)^2$.
240 cm$^3 \times (4)^2 = 240$ cm$^3 \times 16 = 3,840$ cm^3

Step 2 Check your answer.
$V = 10 \times 4(4) \times 6(4) = 3,840$ cm^3

Exercise Solve each problem. Use your calculator.

1. A rectangular prism measures 12 cm by 3 cm by 8 cm. The change factor is 2. Find the new volume when:

A one dimension increases 576 cm^3

B two dimensions increase 1,152 cm^3

C three dimensions increase 2,304 cm^3

2. How does the volume of a rectangular prism change when the change factor is greater than 1? Less than 1?
Volume gets bigger; Volume gets smaller

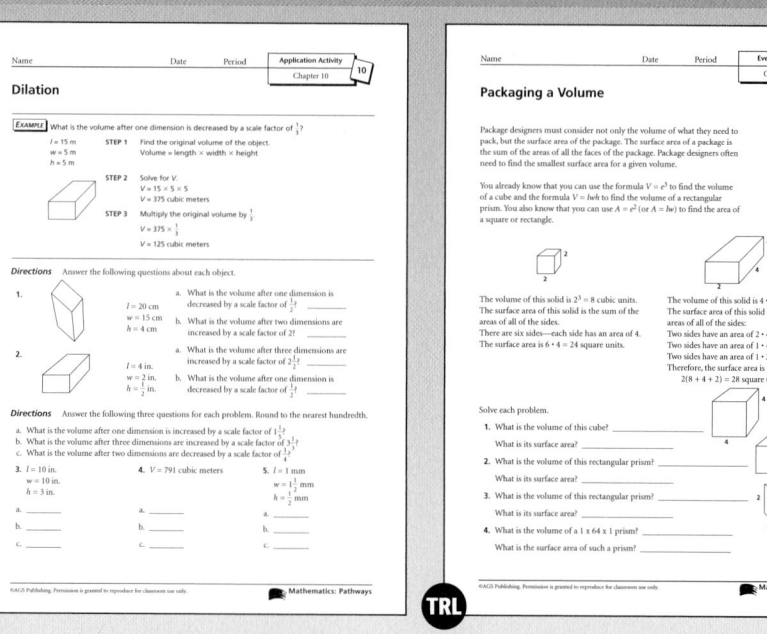

TRL **Application Activity 10**

Everyday Math 10

Chapter 10 REVIEW

Write the letter of the correct answer.

1. Find the area of square *PQRS* with *s* = 1.5 m. B

   A   2 m²   **C**   2.5 m²

   B   2.25 m²   **D**   2.50 m²

2. Find the area of rectangle *ABCD* with *l* = 6 cm, *w* = 2 cm. C

   A   8 cm²   **C**   12 cm²

   B   6 cm²   **D**   24 cm²

3. Find the area of triangle *EFG* with *b* = 2 in. and *h* = 3 in. C

   A   6 in.²   **C**   3 in.²

   B   7 in.²   **D**   4 in.²

Find the perimeter of each polygon.

4. **A**   15 m   **C**   6 m

     B   9 m   **D**   12 m

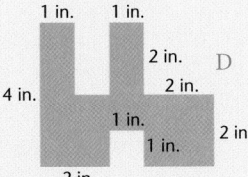

5. **A**   12 cm   **C**   13 cm

     B   9 cm   **D**   8 cm

6. **A**   17 in.   **C**   26 in.

     B   32 in.   **D**   24 in.

Choose the correct name for each shape.

7. 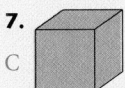 **8.** 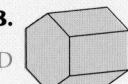 **9.** 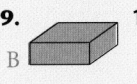 **10.**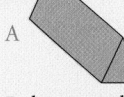

C   D   B   A

  A triangular **B** rectangular **C** square **D** hexagonal
     prism   prism   prism   prism

LEARNING STYLES

LEP/ESL

Encourage pairs of students to draw and label an illustration for each of the problems in the Application Exercise. They can then use the illustrations to find solutions to the problems.

Chapter 10 Review

Each set of problems in the Chapter Review includes an example and solution to illustrate the concept. Use the given examples for reteaching the materials in Chapter 10. For additional practice, refer to the Supplementary Problems for Chapter 10 (pages 450–451).

Chapter 10 Mastery Test

The Teacher's Resource Library includes parallel forms of the Chapter 10 Mastery Test. The difficulty level of the two forms is equivalent. You may wish to use one form as a pretest and the other form as a posttest.

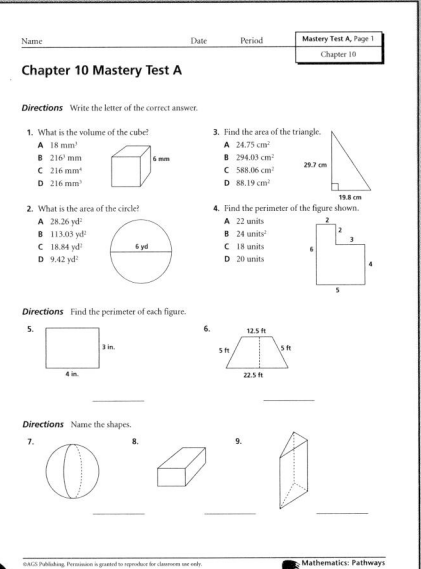

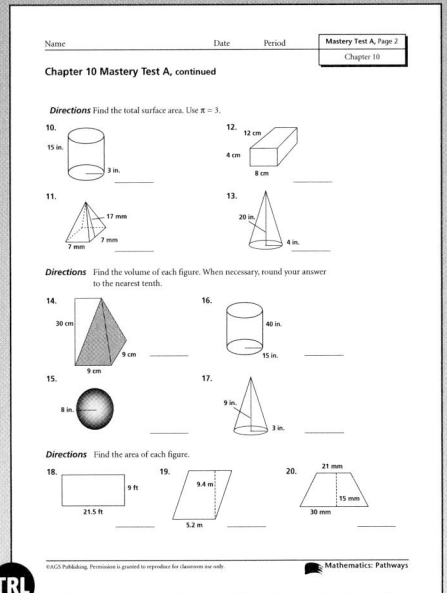

Chapter 10 Mastery Test A

Alternative Assessment

Alternative Assessment items correlate with student Goals for Learning at the beginning of this chapter.

- **To find the perimeter of regular and irregular polygons**
Have students use metric rulers to draw four regular and four irregular polygons. The sides of the polygons should be in even numbers of centimeters. Students should label the length of each side. Encourage students to draw irregular polygons with a "reasonable" number of sides. Have students trade their drawings with a partner. Students should then find the perimeter of each of their partner's polygons. After they are finished, partners can check each other's work.

- **To calculate the area of regular and irregular polygons**
Have students use metric rulers to draw four regular and two irregular polygons. The sides of the polygons should be in even numbers of centimeters. Students should label the length of each side. Students may use some of the same polygons they drew for the previous assessment about finding the perimeters. Have students trade their drawings with a partner. Students should then find the area of each of their partner's polygons. After they are finished, partners can check each other's work.

- **To determine the circumference and area of circles**
Have students identify a number of circles or circular items in their classroom, for example a wastepaper basket or a clock. You could also ask students to bring different items from home. Have students work in groups of three or four to calculate the circumferences and areas of at least four different items. They will have to measure the diameter of the different circles, or they can stretch a string around the object, measure the string, and calculate the diameter using $C = \pi d$.

Find the area of each shape.

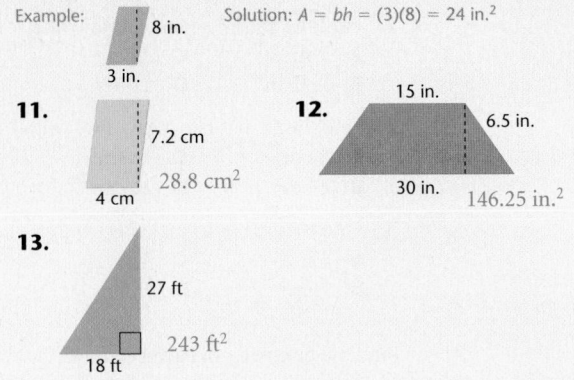

Example:

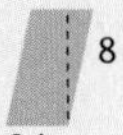
8 in.
3 in.

Solution: $A = bh = (3)(8) = 24$ in.^{2}

11.

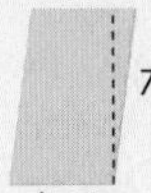
7.2 cm
4 cm

28.8 cm^2

12.

15 in.
6.5 in.
30 in.

146.25 in.^{2}

13.

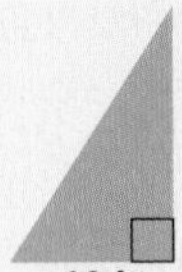
27 ft
18 ft

243 ft^2

Find the surface area. Use $\pi = 3.14$.

Example: Find the surface area of a cylinder with a radius of 2 inches and a height of 10 inches. Formula is $A = (2\pi r^2) + (2\pi rh)$.

Solution: $(2\pi r^2) + (2\pi rh) = (2 \times 3.14 \times 2^2) + (2 \times 3.14 \times 2 \times 10)$
$= 25.12 + 125.6$
$= 150.72$ square inches

14. What is the surface area of the cube? $A = 294$ sq units

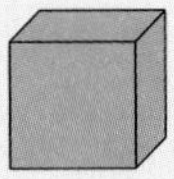
7

15. A cylindrical container has a radius of 5 and a height of 20. What is the total surface area of the container? 785 sq units

16. What is the surface area of the pyramid? $A = 1{,}095$ sq units

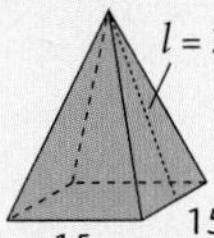
l = 29
15
15

17. If a cone has a length of 6 inches and a radius of 1 inch, what is the surface area of the cone? $A = 21.98$ in.^{2}

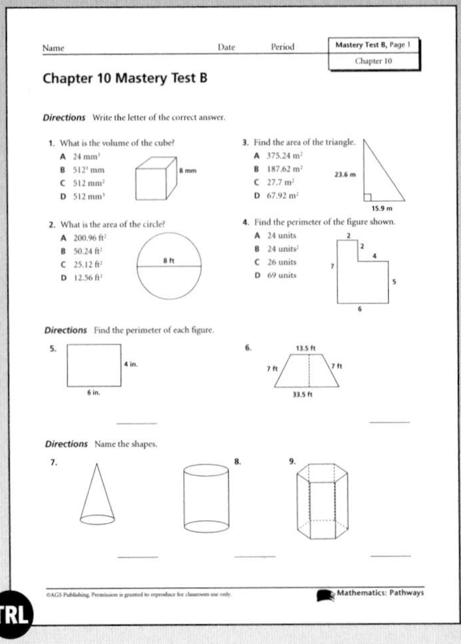

Name Date Period | Mastery Test B, Page 1 | Chapter 10

Chapter 10 Mastery Test B

Directions Write the letter of the correct answer.

1. What is the volume of the cube? (8 mm)
   A 24 mm^3
   B 512^3 mm
   C 512 mm^2
   D 512 mm^3

2. What is the area of the circle? (8 ft)
   A 200.96 ft^2
   B 50.24 ft^2
   C 25.12 ft^2
   D 12.56 ft^2

3. Find the area of the triangle. (23.6 m, 15.9 m)
   A 375.24 m^2
   B 187.62 m^2
   C 27.7 m^2
   D 67.92 m^2

4. Find the perimeter of the figure shown. (2, 2, 4, 7, 5, 6)
   A 24 units
   B 24 units^2
   C 26 units
   D 69 units

Directions Find the perimeter of each figure.

5. (4 in., 6 in.) ______
6. (13.5 ft, 7 ft, 7 ft, 33.5 ft) ______

Directions Name the shapes.

7. ______ 8. ______ 9. ______

©AGS Publishing. Permission is granted to reproduce for classroom use only. Mathematics: Pathways

TRL

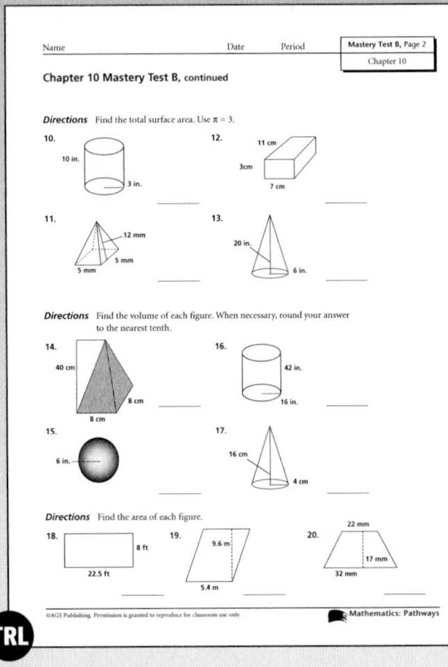

Name Date Period | Mastery Test B, Page 2 | Chapter 10

Chapter 10 Mastery Test B, continued

Directions Find the total surface area. Use $\pi = 3$.

10. (10 in., 3 in.) ______
11. (12 mm, 5 mm, 5 mm) ______
12. (11 cm, 3cm, 7 cm) ______
13. (20 in., 6 in.) ______

Directions Find the volume of each figure. When necessary, round your answer to the nearest tenth.

14. (40 cm, 8 cm, 8 cm) ______
15. (6 in.) ______
16. (42 in., 16 in.) ______
17. (16 cm, 4 cm) ______

Directions Find the area of each figure.

18. (8 ft, 22.5 ft) ______
19. (9.6 m, 5.4 m) ______
20. (22 mm, 17 mm, 32 mm) ______

©AGS Publishing. Permission is granted to reproduce for classroom use only. Mathematics: Pathways

TRL

Chapter 10 Mastery Test B

Find the volume of each shape.

Example: 13 cm   Solution: $V = e^3$ $V = (13)^3 =$
(13)(13)(13) = 2,197 cm³

18. 20 cm
8,000 cm³

19. 0.5 m 3 m 1 m
1.5 m³

Use 3.14 for π to find area and circumference.

Example: Christina is tracing and coloring a circle with a radius of 10 cm on a poster she is making. What is the circle's circumference? What is its area?

Solution: $C = \pi d = (3.14)(20) = 62.8$ cm
$A = \pi r^2 = (3.14)(10)^2 = (3.14)(10)(10) = 314$ cm²

20. The clock in the train station has a clock face with a 9-inch radius. What are the circumference and area of the clock face? $C = 56.52$ in. $A = 254.34$ in.²

21. The company's logo is drawn inside a circle with a diameter of 12.2 cm. What are the circumference and area of the circle? $C = 38.308$ cm $A = 116.8394$ cm²

Use 3.14 for π to find the volume of each figure.

Example: 16 in. 4 in.   Solution: $V = \pi r^2 h = (3.14)(4)^2(16) =$
(3.14)(4)(4)(16) = 803.84 in.³

22. 16 cm 3 cm
452.16 cm³

23. 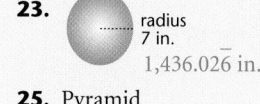 radius 7 in.
1,436.026 in.³

24. Cone
Diameter = 20 cm
Height = 43 cm
$V = 4,500.67$ cm³

25. Pyramid
Side = 2 inches
Height = 10 inches
$V = 13.33$ in.³

Test-Taking Tip

Remember that _circumference_ refers to the distance around a _circle_. The formula to use is $2\pi r$.

Chapter

Planning Guide

Graphing

Lesson	Student Pages	Vocabulary	Practice Exercises	Problem Solving	Try This	Solutions Key
1 Graphing Equalities	314–315	✔	✔			✔
2 Graphing Inequalities	316–319	✔	✔			✔
3 Graphing Solutions of Equalities	320–321	✔	✔	321		✔
4 Graphing Solutions of Inequalities	322–323		✔	323		✔
5 The Coordinate System—Locating Points	324–327	✔	✔	327		✔
6 The Coordinate System—Plotting Points	328–329		✔			✔
7 Determining the Points of a Line	330–333	✔	✔			✔
8 Lines as Functions	334–335	✔	✔			✔
9 Domain and Range of a Function	336–339	✔	✔			✔
10 Graphing Lines	340–341		✔		341	✔
11 The Slope of a Line	342–343	✔	✔			✔
12 Formula for the Slope of a Line	344–347		✔	347	347	✔
13 The Slope-Intercept Form of a Line	348–351	✔	✔			✔
Application The Story Line	352		✔			✔

Chapter Activities

Teacher's Resource Library
Estimation Exercise 11: Estimating Slope
Application Activity 11: The Story Line
Everyday Math 11: Talk Isn't Cheap
Community Connection 11: Line Graphs

Teacher's Edition
Chapter 11 Project

Assessment Options

Student Text
Chapter 11 Review

Teacher's Resource Library
Chapter 11 Mastery Tests A and B

Teacher's Edition
Chapter 11 Alternative Assessments

Estimation Activity	Math in Your Life	Technology Connection	Writing About Mathematics	Build a Model	Calculator Practice	Online Connection	Common Error	Applications Home, Career, Community	Mental Math	Manipulatives	Calculator	Group Problem Solving	Modeling	Knowing Your Students	Auditory/Verbal	Visual/Spatial	Logical/Mathematical	Body/Kinesthetic	Interpersonal/Group Learning	LEP/ESL	Activities	Alternate Activities	Workbook Activities	Self-Study Guide
								315											315		98	98	103	✔
	319						316								317				318	318	99	99	104	✔
							320		321			321							321		100	100	105	✔
							322		323			323								323	101	101	106	✔
		325					325	326										327		325	102	102	107	✔
							329												329		103	103	108	✔
			332		333				333	331	332								331		104	104	109–110	✔
			335									335			335	335					105	105	111	✔
		339					338										339			337	106	106	112	✔
341									341							341					107	107	113	✔
					343			343				343	342								108	108	114	✔
					346	346	345					346	347		345						109	109	115	✔
		351	351				350												350		110	110	116	✔
							352	353																✔

Software Options

Skill Track Software

Use the Skill Track Software for *Mathematics: Pathways* for additional reinforcement of this chapter. The software provides multiple-choice assessment items for students to access by computer.

Solutions Key

Use the Solutions Key with this chapter to help students who may need additional assistance. The Solutions Key CD provides solutions for every exercise in the student edition.

Other Resources

Alternative Activities

The Teacher's Resource Library (TRL) contains a set of worksheets written at a second-grade reading level called Alternative Activities. They cover the same content as the regular Activities.

Manipulatives

See the Manipulative activities in this chapter for hands-on modeling of the content. The following TRL pages can also be used:
Manipulatives Master 3 (Sentence Mat)
Algebra Tiles
Pattern Blocks

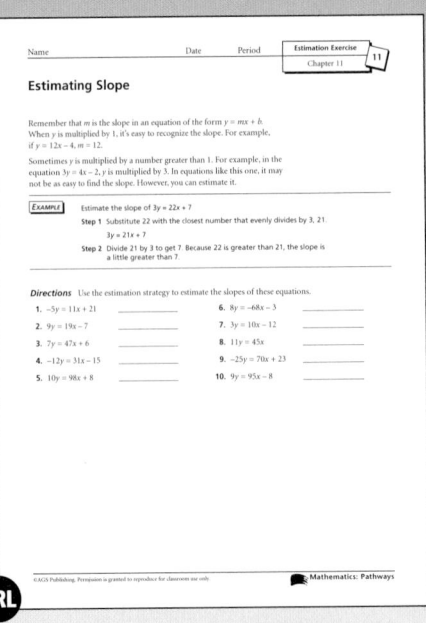

Estimation Exercise 11

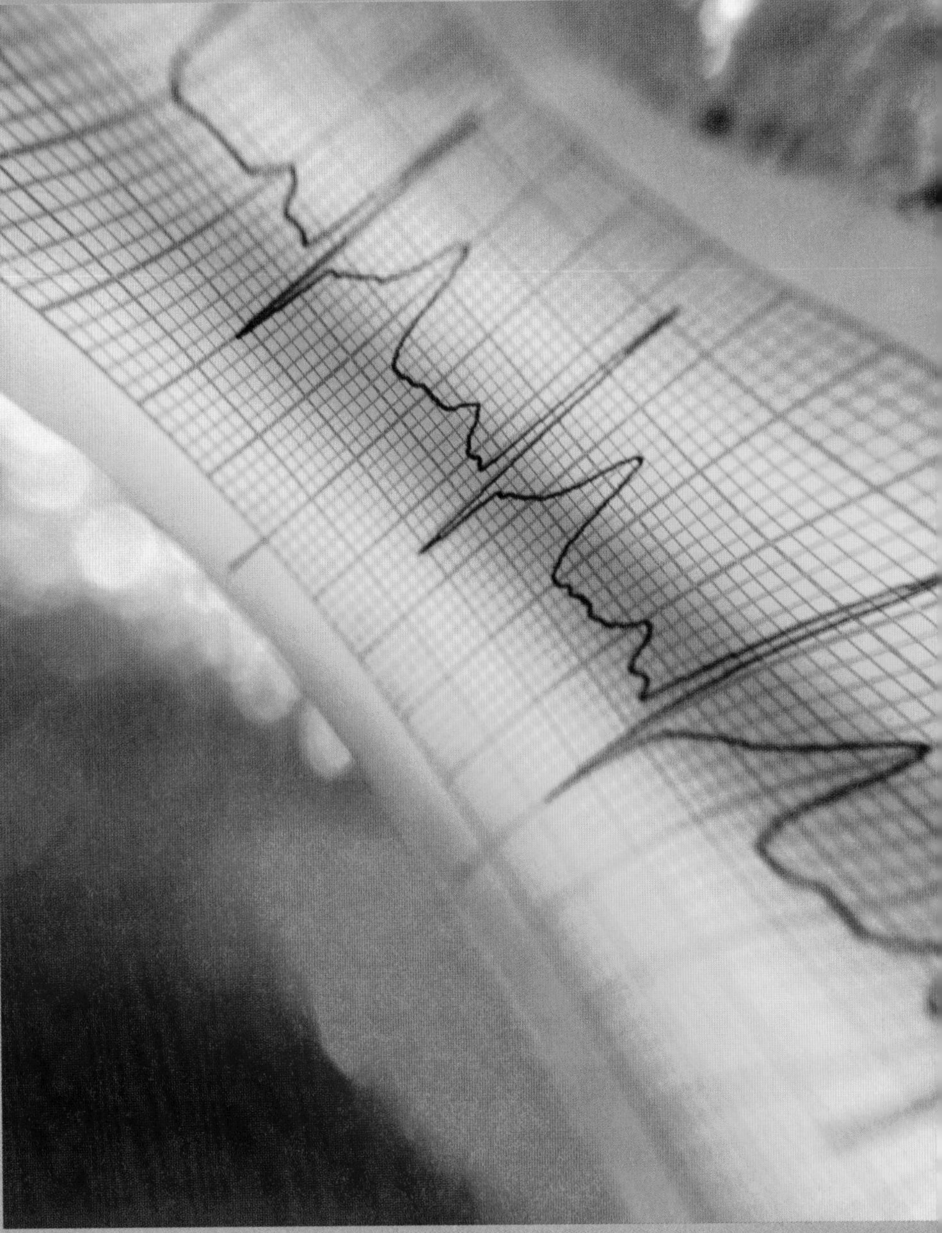

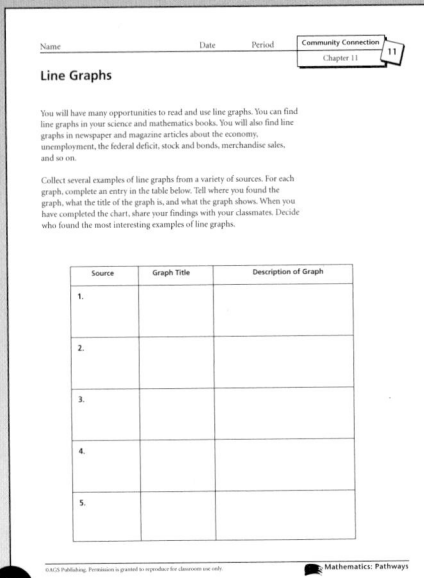

Community Connection 11

Chapter

11 Graphing

In medicine, doctors can use electrocardiograms (EKGs) to see whether a patient's heart is healthy. The EKG is an electrical recording of a heart's condition. *Cardio* simply means *heart*. When you run or do other exercises that work your heart, you are doing *cardio* work. The data collected by the EKG let doctors see heart activity over time. A line graph is used to show the information recorded.

Line graphs are diagrams that show the relationships between pairs of numbers. Points plotted on a graph reflect changes along the horizontal *x*-axis and the vertical *y*-axis. Trends, patterns, and important changes are easy to spot on line graphs.

In Chapter 11, you will use the coordinate system to graph linear equations.

Goals for Learning

◆ To graph solutions to equalities and inequalities on number lines

◆ To identify and graph ordered pairs of values

◆ To write equations for straight lines as functions

◆ To identify the domain and range of functions

◆ To determine and graph points of a linear equation

◆ To identify the slope of a line

◆ To determine the values of slope, the *y*-intercept, and the *x*-intercept

313

Introducing the Chapter

Ask students where line graphs are used today. (*Answers may include hospitals, government, scientific experiments, and marketing companies.*) Point out that there is a variety of applications for line graphs and that understanding graphs is an important skill in the study of mathematics.

CHAPTER PROJECT

Have students work in groups of four to produce a five-minute documentary. Each documentary should tell what coordinate grids are, tell how they are useful, and focus on a specific grid use. Allow students to choose one of the following uses or to choose their own use.

- *Wide, Wide World of Grids*, a documentary in which students indicate how grids are essential to worldwide coordinate systems because they are used to locate specific places on Earth. The documentary should include a description of latitude/longitude.

- *View from Beyond*, an introduction to weather satellites and how coordinate systems are used to relay and analyze data from these satellites. The documentary may explore how some automobiles use a global positioning system to keep drivers from getting lost.

TEACHER'S RESOURCE

The AGS Publishing Teaching Strategies in Math Transparencies may be used with this chapter. They add an interactive dimension to expand and enhance the program content.

CAREER INTEREST INVENTORY

The AGS Publishing Harrington-O'Shea Career Decision-Making System-Revised (CDM) may be used with this chapter. Students can use the CDM to explore their interests and identify careers. The CDM defines career areas that are indicated by students' responses on the inventory.

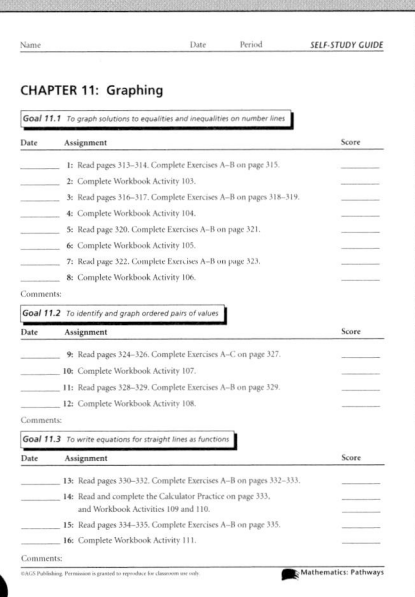

Chapter 11 Self-Study Guide

Lesson at a Glance

Chapter 11 Lesson 1

Overview This lesson teaches how to graph equalities on a number line.

Objective

■ To graph equalities and solutions to equalities on a number line

Student Pages 314–315

Teacher's Resource Library

Workbook Activity 103

Activity 98

Alternative Activity 98

Mathematics Vocabulary

equality
graphing
solution

---

1 Warm-Up Activity

Begin by asking students to describe their idea of what a graph is and what uses it might have. Invite volunteers to draw their ideas of a graph on the board or overhead projector. Continue by asking the same questions about a number line. Guide students to the conclusion that a number line can be used as a type of graph.

2 Teaching the Lesson

Use the examples as demonstrations on the overhead projector. Offer students an opportunity to graph several other solutions, such as $x = 9$, $y = -1$, $b = 3$, $r = -2$.

Point out to students that intervals on the number lines in the examples are marked by consecutive integers. Tell them that number line intervals can be marked in a variety of ways, such as by even numbers or multiples of five. Mention that number line intervals can also be marked in fractions such as $\frac{1}{2}$, $\frac{1}{4}$, or $\frac{1}{3}$.

Equality
The state of being equal; shown by the equal sign
Graphing
Showing on a number line the relationship of a set of numbers
Solution
The value of a variable that makes an open statement true

Recall that an equation is a mathematical sentence with an equal sign. Equations such as $4 + 5 = 9$ and $w = 12$ are examples of **equalities.** **Graphing** is a way to show the **solution** on a number line.

EXAMPLE 1 Suppose that $x = 3$ is the solution of an equality. Graph the solution on a number line.

Step 1 Draw a number line.

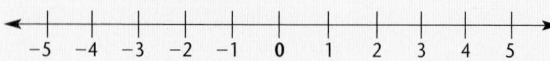

Step 2 A shaded circle is used to indicate an integer solution. Since the solution is $x = 3$, make a shaded circle on the number line at 3.

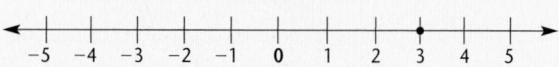

The solution to an equality will sometimes be a negative integer.

EXAMPLE 2 Suppose that $q = -4$ is the solution of an equality. Graph the solution on a number line.

Step 1 Draw a number line.

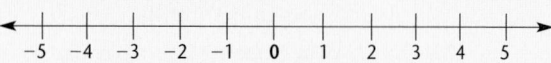

Step 2 A shaded circle is used to indicate an integer solution. Since the solution is $q = -4$, make a shaded circle on the number line at -4.

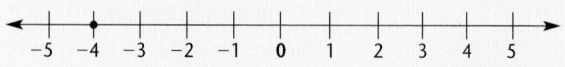

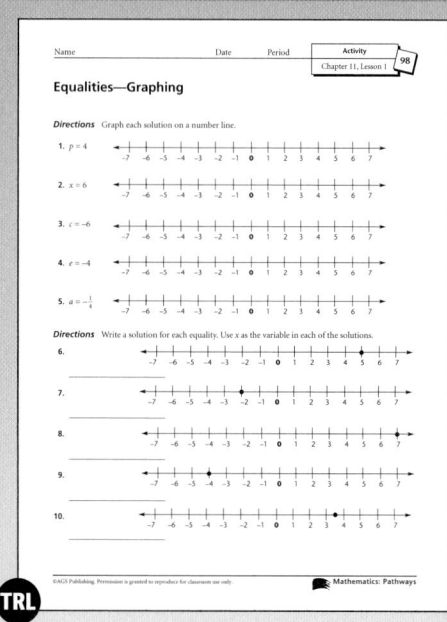

Workbook Activity 103   **Activity 98**

Exercise A Graph each solution on a number line.

1. $x = 8$

2. $r = -2$

3. $s = -6$

4. $p = 6$

5. $n = -\frac{1}{2}$

Exercise B Write a solution for each equality. Use x as the variable in each of the solutions.

6. $x = 5$

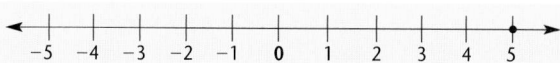

7. $x = 0$

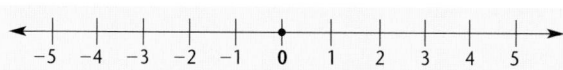

8. $x = -2$

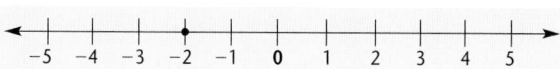

9. $x = 1\frac{1}{2}$

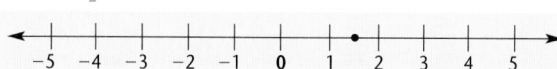

10. $x = -3\frac{1}{2}$

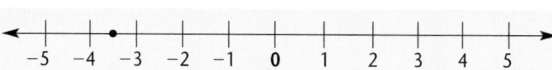

3 Reinforce and Extend

LEARNING STYLES

Body/Kinesthetic

Students can play a number line version of Simon Says. Put butcher paper on the classroom floor. Have students draw a number line on the paper and mark the number line with consecutive integers from −20 to +20. Then have them prepare 41 number cards, corresponding to the numbers shown on the number line. One student, acting as moderator, draws a number and tells another student to stand at that number's position on the number line, but the second student does so only if the moderator prefaces the direction with "Simon says."

AT HOME

Encourage students to begin and maintain a list of number lines they encounter outside school. Help them recognize everyday number lines such as temperature scales.

Lesson at a Glance

Chapter 11 Lesson 2

Overview This lesson teaches how to graph inequalities on a number line.

Objective

■ To graph inequalities and solutions to inequalities on a number line

Student Pages 316–319

Teacher's Resource Library TRL

Workbook Activity 104

Activity 99

Alternative Activity 99

Mathematics Vocabulary

inequality

1️⃣ Warm-Up Activity

Ask students who are five feet, five inches tall to stand. Then ask students who are more than five feet, five inches tall to stand. Ask the class to describe the heights of the students who are standing. *(five feet, five inches and taller)*

2️⃣ Teaching the Lesson

Review with students the meanings of the symbols $<$, $\leq$, $>$, $\geq$, and $\neq$. Ask them to offer any mnemonics they use to remember the meanings of the symbols.

Demonstrate each of the examples on the overhead projector. Stress to students the difference in meaning between open circles and completely shaded circles.

COMMON ERROR

Students sometimes overlook the distinction between $<$ and $\leq$ and between $>$ and $\geq$. Encourage them to develop the habit of double-checking their work to make sure that they have correctly interpreted the symbols.

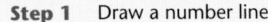

Inequality
Two quantities that are not the same; shown by the less than, greater than, and unequal to signs

Recall that a shaded circle is used to show the solution to an equality. It can also be used to show an integer that is a solution to an inequality. An open circle is used to show an integer that is not a solution to an inequality.

An **inequality** is a mathematical sentence that contains a symbol such as $>$ (greater than), $<$ (less than), $\geq$ (greater than or equal to), $\leq$ (less than or equal to), and $\neq$ (unequal to). A number line can be used to graph the solution of an inequality.

EXAMPLE 1 Suppose that $n > 16$ is the solution of an inequality. Graph the solution on a number line.

Step 1 Draw a number line.

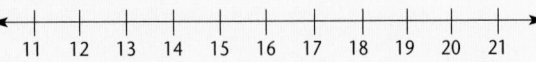

Step 2 Note that the inequality $n > 16$ means "n is greater than 16." The integer 16 is not a solution of the inequality.

Step 3 Graph the solution. To show all numbers greater than 16, but not including 16, make an open circle at 16. Draw a line extending to the right and place an arrow at the end of the line.

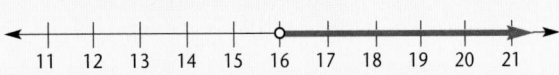

EXAMPLE 2 Suppose that $c < -5$ is the solution of an inequality. Graph the solution on a number line.

Step 1 Draw a number line.

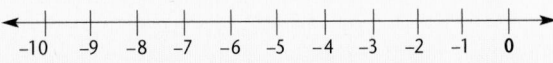

Step 2 Note that the inequality $c < -5$ means "c is less than -5." The integer -5 is not a solution of the inequality.

Step 3 Graph the solution. To show all numbers less than -5, but not including -5, make an open circle at -5. Draw a line extending to the left and place an arrow at the end of the line.

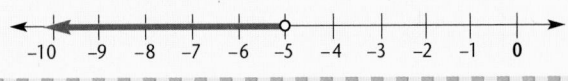

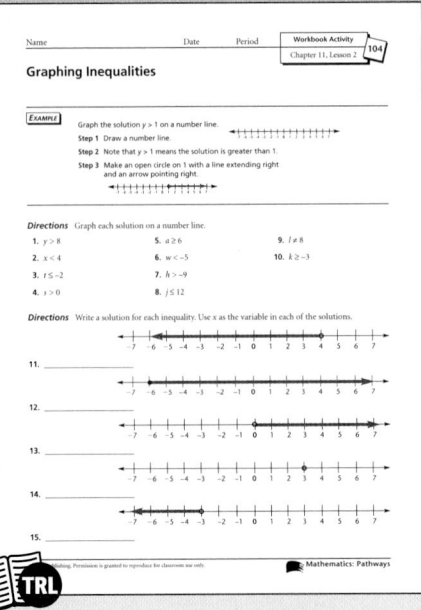

Workbook Activity 104

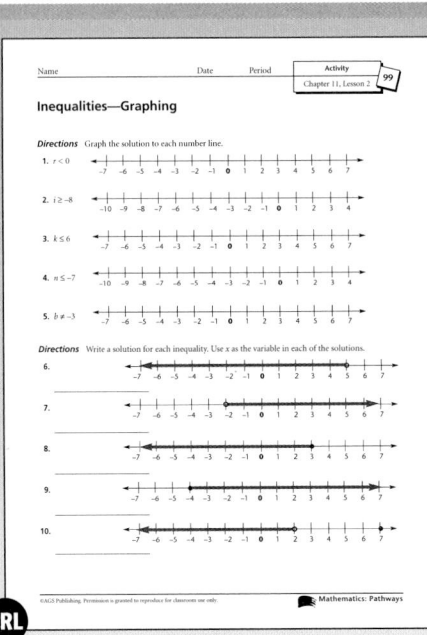

Activity 99

EXAMPLE 3 Suppose that $h \le 10$ is the solution of an inequality. Graph the solution on a number line.

Step 1 Draw a number line.

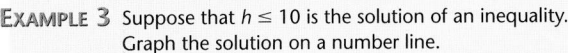

Step 2 Note that the inequality $h \le 10$ means "h is less than or equal to 10." The integer 10 and all numbers less than 10 are solutions of the inequality.

Step 3 Graph the solution. To show all numbers that are less than or equal to 10, make a shaded circle at 10. Draw a line extending to the left and place an arrow at the end of the line.

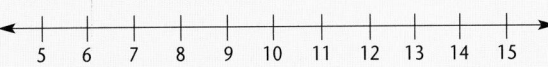

EXAMPLE 4 Suppose that $a \ge -2$ is the solution of an inequality. Graph the solution on a number line.

Step 1 Draw a number line.

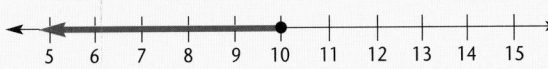

Step 2 Note that the inequality $a \ge -2$ means "a is greater than or equal to -2." The integer -2 and all numbers greater than -2 are solutions of the inequality.

Step 3 Graph the solution. To show all numbers that are greater than or equal to -2, make a shaded circle at -2. Draw a line extending to the right and place an arrow at the end of the line.

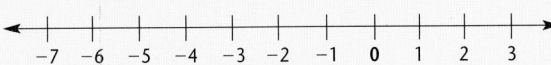

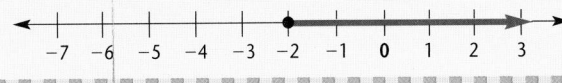

1. Number line shows an open circle at 8 with an arrow extending to the left.

2. Number line shows an open circle at −1 with an arrow extending to the left.

3. Number line shows an open circle at 12 with an arrow extending to the right.

4. Number line shows an open circle at −4 with an arrow extending to the right.

5. Number line shows a shaded circle at −1 with an arrow extending to the right.

6. Number line shows a shaded circle at 11 with an arrow extending to the left.

Exercise A Graph each solution on a number line.

1. $x < 8$

2. $b < -1$

3. $v > 12$

4. $r > -4$

5. $m \geq -1$

6. $d \leq 11$

Exercise B Write a solution for each inequality. Use *x* as the variable in each of the solutions.

7. $x < -7$

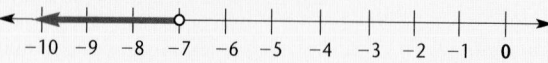

8. $x > 3$

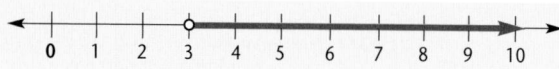

9. $x \leq 1$

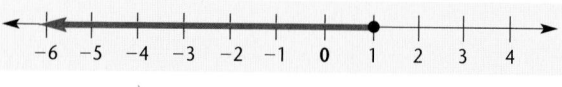

10. $x \geq -2$

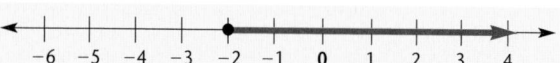

11. $x \geq 5$

12. $x < -3$

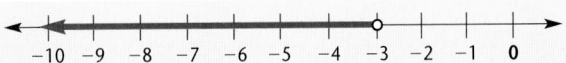

13. $x \leq 0$

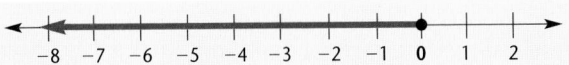

14. $x > 2$

15. $x \leq -4$

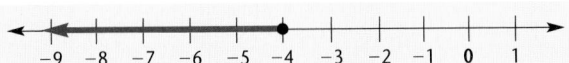

Math in Your Life

Ups or Downs

As a student, one of the most important things about school is your grades. In high school, what grades your teachers give you will determine what you will do after high school. So, to keep track of your work, you can use a graph to plot your grades. At a glance, you can tell the direction you are headed. With that information and your need to succeed, the possibilities are endless.

Chapter 11 Lesson 3

Overview This lesson introduces graphing solutions of equalities.

Objective

■ To graph the solution to an equality on a number line

Student Pages 320–321

Teacher's Resource Library TRL

Workbook Activity 105

Activity 100

Alternative Activity 100

....

Mathematics Vocabulary

relationship
function

....

1 Warm-Up Activity

Introduce the lesson with the following teaser: "I'm thinking of a number. Twelve more than this number is 20. What is the number?" *(12 + x = 20, x = 8)*

2 Teaching the Lesson

Use each of the examples as a demonstration of graphing a solution. Invite volunteers to explain each step.

COMMON ERROR

Students may forget to perform an operation on each side of the equation. Encourage them to carefully write out each step of the solution. This practice will allow students to review their work, checking to see that they performed an operation on each side of the equation.

Relationship
A set of grouped pairs

Function
A rule that associates every x-value with one and only one y-value

Number **relationships** are shown in the expressions in Lessons 1 and 2. Every problem has a *number* and a *variable*. The sign between them shows the relationship. Lessons 3 and 4 will show how algebraic expressions represent **functions**. Functions are rules used to determine a solution (or *output*) based on the numbers and variables in the equation (the *input*).

EXAMPLE 1 Solve $x - 3 = 6$ for x. Then graph the solution.

Step 1 Solve for x by adding 3 to each side of the equality.
$$x - 3 = 6$$
$$x - 3 + 3 = 6 + 3$$
$$x = 6 + 3$$
$$x = 9$$

Step 2 Graph the solution on a number line.

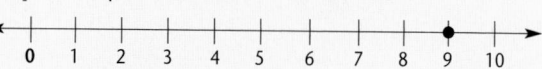

$$\begin{array}{ccccccccccc} 0 & 1 & 2 & 3 & 4 & 5 & 6 & 7 & 8 & 9 & 10 \end{array}$$

Step 3 To check your work, substitute 9 for x in the given equality.
$$x - 3 = 6$$
$$9 - 3 = 6$$
$$6 = 6 \quad \text{True}$$

EXAMPLE 2 Solve $x + 2 = -5$ for x. Then graph the solution.

Step 1 Solve for x by adding -2 to each side of the equality.
$$x + 2 = -5$$
$$x + 2 + (-2) = -5 + (-2)$$
$$x = -5 + (-2)$$
$$x = -7$$

Step 2 Graph the solution on a number line.

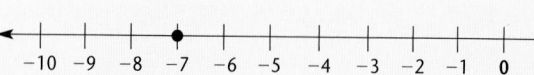

$$\begin{array}{ccccccccccc} -10 & -9 & -8 & -7 & -6 & -5 & -4 & -3 & -2 & -1 & 0 \end{array}$$

Step 3 To check your work, substitute -7 for x in the given equality.
$$x + 2 = -5$$
$$(-7) + 2 = -5$$
$$-5 = -5 \quad \text{True}$$

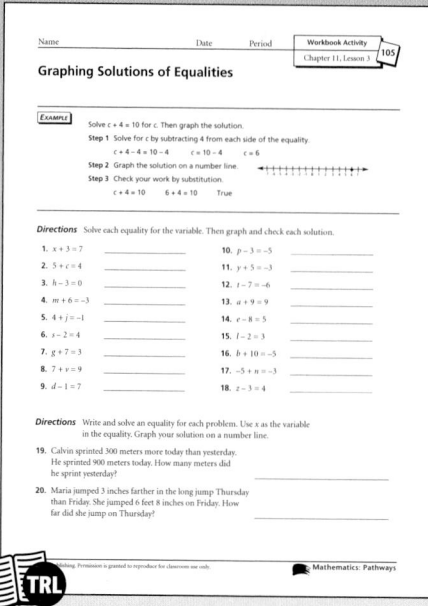

Workbook Activity 105

Activity 100

Exercise A Find the output of each function by solving for the variable. Then graph and check each solution.

1. $d + 4 = 7$ $d = 3$ **4.** $t - 4 = -2$ $t = 2$

2. $x + 1 = 10$ $x = 9$ **5.** $n - 6 = 0$ $n = 6$

3. $g + 12 = 7$ $g = -5$ **6.** $-3 + w = -6$ $w = -3$

PROBLEM SOLVING

Exercise B Write and solve an equality for each problem. Use x as the variable in the relationship. Graph your solution on a number line.

7. Luis has competed in 17 hurdle races this year. He has lost 8 of the races. How many has he won?

8. Kito has seen 13 movies he liked and 9 he disliked this year. How many movies has he seen this year?

9. Yesterday, the high temperature was 45°F. Today's high temperature is 15°F lower. What is today's high temperature?

10. The stock market was up 29 points today. If it gains 5 points tomorrow, how many points will it have gained in the two days?

7. $x + 8 = 17$ or $17 - x = 8$; $x = 9$

8. $x - 13 = 9$ or $x - 9 = 13$; $x = 22$

9. $45 - x = 15$ or $15 + x = 45$; $x = 30$

10. $x - 29 = 5$ or $x - 5 = 29$; $x = 34$

Students should graph their solutions on a number line.

MANIPULATIVES

 Solving Equations

Materials: Algebra Tiles, Manipulatives Master 3 (Sentence Mat)

Group Practice: Review the Algebra Tiles with students (see pages T8–T9). Model the first example equation, $x - 3 = 6$ on the Sentence Mat. Add $+3$ to each side of the equation. Simplify the model by applying the Zero Rule (see pages T8–T9), removing pairs of inverses. The variable is isolated on the left, and the root of the equation (9) is modeled on the right. Write the symbolic equivalent, and graph the solution. To check, replace the variable with its known value in the original equation. Repeat with the next example.

Student Practice: Have students use the Algebra Tiles for Exercise A, problems 1–6.

3 Reinforce and Extend

LEARNING STYLES

 Interpersonal/ Group Learning

Have groups of four students discuss the problems in Exercise A. Ask the groups to describe a way in which they could use the number line itself to find the solution to the equality. *(Count on or back to find the solution to addition or subtraction problems.)*

GROUP PROBLEM SOLVING

 Invite students to make graphs of the wins of local sports teams. They should determine how many games the teams have played, how many games they have lost, and how many they have won. Students can then write an equality for each team's wins. Finally, students can graph the solution to the equality on a number line.

Chapter 11 Lesson 4

Overview This lesson introduces graphing solutions of inequalities.

Objective

■ To graph the solution to an inequality on a number line

Student Pages 322–323

Teacher's Resource Library

Workbook Activity 106

Activity 101

Alternative Activity 101

1 Warm-Up Activity

Introduce the lesson with the following teaser. "I'm thinking of a range of numbers. If I add 6 to any of these numbers, the sum is greater than 15. What are the numbers?" ($6 + x > 15, x > 9$)

2 Teaching the Lesson

Demonstrate the first example on the overhead projector. Ask a volunteer to explain why 3 is added to each side of the inequality. Have another volunteer explain step 3 to show how to check the work.

COMMON ERROR

Even students who consistently perform operations on each side of an equality may not grasp the importance of doing the same for an inequality. Emphasize that an inequality, like an equality, must be preserved to find the correct solution by performing operations on each side. Encourage students to carefully write out each step of the solution, checking to see that they performed an operation on each side of the equation.

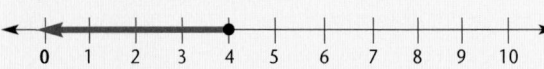
Lesson 4 Graphing Solutions of Inequalities

To graph an inequality on a number line, use the same steps as you did for graphing an equality—first solve for the variable.

EXAMPLE 1 Solve $n - 3 \leq 1$ for n. Then graph the solution.

Step 1 Solve for n by adding 3 to each side of the inequality.

$$n - 3 \leq 1$$
$$n - 3 + 3 \leq 1 + 3$$
$$n \leq 1 + 3$$
$$n \leq 4$$

Step 2 Graph the solution on a number line.

Step 3 To check your work, substitute 4 for n in the given inequality.

$$n - 3 \leq 1$$
$$4 - 3 \leq 1$$
$$1 \leq 1 \quad \text{True}$$

Substituting the value of the variable into the given equality or inequality is one way to check your work. Another way is to choose several points from the graph and substitute those points into the given equality or inequality.

To solve $k + 5 > 8$ for k, subtract 5 from each side of the inequality.
$$k + 5 - 5 > 8 - 5$$
$$k > 3$$

EXAMPLE 2 Suppose this number line is a graph of the solution $k + 5 > 8$. Check the solution.

Substitute the points 2, 3, and 4 into the given inequality. Since the graph shows that 4 is a part of the solution, 4 is the only point that should make the given equation true.

$k + 5 > 8$	$k + 5 > 8$	$k + 5 > 8$
$(2) + 5 > 8$	$(3) + 5 > 8$	$(4) + 5 > 8$
$7 > 8$ False	$8 > 8$ False	$9 > 8$ True

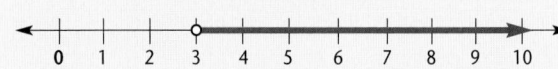

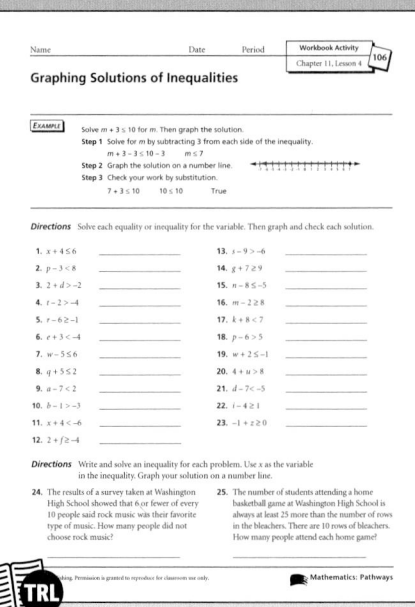

Workbook Activity 106

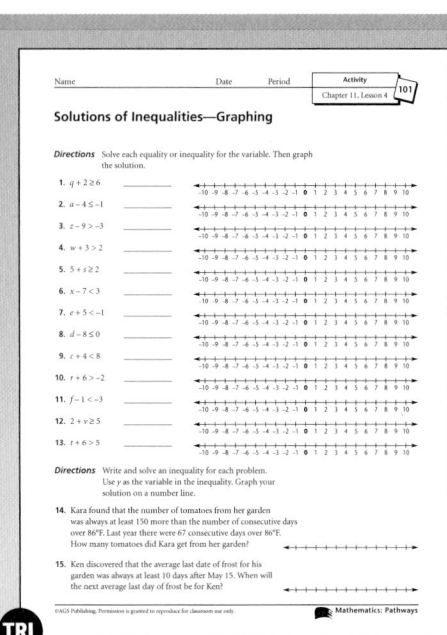

Activity 101

Exercise A Find the output of each function by solving for the variable. Then graph and check each solution.

1. $d + 4 < 7$ $d < 3$
2. $h - 7 > 0$ $h > 7$
3. $1 + c < 4$ $c < 3$
4. $s - 1 \geq -5$ $s \geq -4$
5. $-9 + w \leq -7$ $w \leq 2$
6. $p + 4 > 10$ $p > 6$
7. $6 + r \leq -4$ $r \leq -10$
8. $-1 + m < -1$ $m < 0$
9. $z - 2 > -3$ $z > -1$
10. $-5 + f \geq 5$ $f \geq 10$
11. $-2 + v < -9$ $v < -7$
12. $a + 11 < 6$ $a < -5$

PROBLEM SOLVING

Exercise B Write and solve an inequality for each problem. Use x as the variable in the relationship. Graph your solution on a number line.

13. This month Bette used her cellular phone for 52 or more minutes. If she has to pay for any time over 35 minutes, how many minutes does she have to pay for?

14. One basketball player scores more than 18 points. The other players score 45 points together. How many points were scored in all?

15. For every ten people polled, three or fewer said they bought new cars this year. For every ten people, how many didn't buy new cars?

13. $x + 35 \geq 52$;
$x \geq 17$

14. $x - 45 > 18$; $x > 63$

15. $10 - x \leq 3$; $7 \leq x$

Lesson at a Glance

Chapter 11 Lesson 5

Overview This lesson introduces the coordinate grid system.

Objectives

- To locate points corresponding to ordered pairs of numbers in a coordinate system
- To identify points in a coordinate grid using ordered pairs

Student Pages 324–327

Teacher's Resource Library **TRL**

Workbook Activity 107

Activity 102

Alternative Activity 102

Mathematics Vocabulary

vertical
horizontal
coordinate system
x-axis
y-axis
quadrant
origin
ordered pair

---

1 Warm-Up Activity

Ask students about the kinds of directions that might be given in a treasure hunt, for example, 4 paces east, 9 paces north to the tree, 3 paces west, and so on. Draw an unnumbered grid on the board with a starting point and the cardinal directions. Ask a volunteer to draw a line that follows the directions to the treasure. Encourage students to keep these kinds of directions in mind as they begin their study of coordinate systems.

2 Teaching the Lesson

Help students recognize the differences in the ordered pairs that are located in different quadrants. Encourage them to make generalizations such as "Each of the numbers in the ordered pairs in Quadrant I has a positive sign" and "Each of the numbers in the ordered pairs in Quadrant III has a negative sign."

Lesson **5** **The Coordinate System—Locating Points**

Vertical

Straight up and down

Horizontal

Left to right or parallel to the horizon

Coordinate system

A way of using number lines to locate points on a plane or in space

x-axis

The horizontal, or left-to-right, axis in a coordinate system

y-axis

The vertical, or up-and-down, axis in a coordinate system

Quadrant

One of four regions of a coordinate system bounded by the x-axis and y-axis

Origin

The point at which the x-axis and y-axis intersect in the coordinate system

Ordered pair

A set of two real numbers that locate a point in a plane

Have you ever used a mercury or alcohol thermometer to see the temperature? A mercury thermometer is an example of a **vertical** number line. A vertical number line and a **horizontal** number line can be combined to form a **coordinate system**. A coordinate system is a way of using numbers to locate points on a plane or in space.

A coordinate system is shown here.

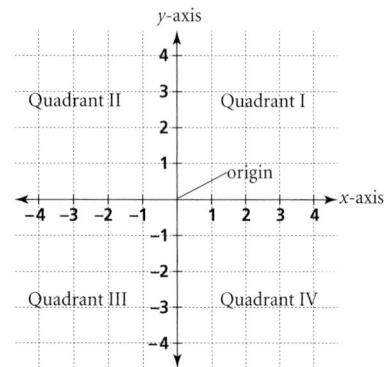

In a coordinate system, the **x-axis** and **y-axis** separate the system into four regions called **quadrants.** The intersection of the x-axis and y-axis is known as the **origin.**

Points in a coordinate system are given as **ordered pairs** of the form (x, y). All ordered pairs show number relationships. To locate points in a coordinate system, write an ordered pair of the form (x, y) for each point.

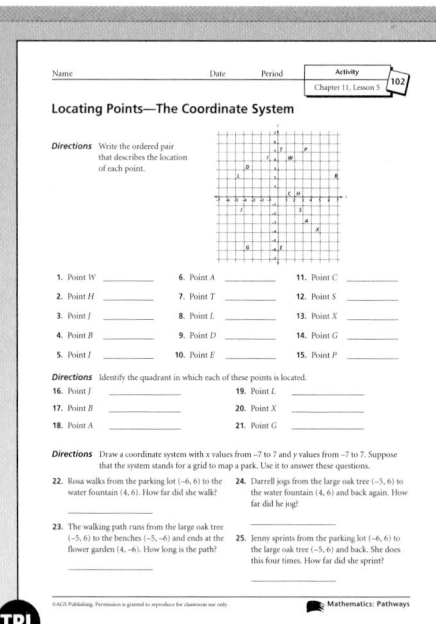

EXAMPLE 1 Locate Point *A*.

Step 1 Determine the *x*-value of the ordered pair of the form (*x, y*) that will be used to describe the location of Point *A*. Begin at the origin and count the number of units the point is to the right or to the left of the *y*-axis. Since Point *A* is located 3 units to the right of the *y*-axis, the *x*-value is +3.

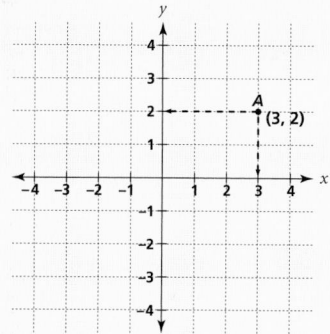

Step 2 Count the number of units the point is above or below the *x*-axis. Since Point *A* is located 2 units above the *x*-axis, the *y*-value is +2.

Step 3 Write the ordered pair (3, 2) to describe the location of Point *A*.

The ordered pair (3, 2) describes the location of Point *A* with respect to the *x*- and *y*-axes.

> In a coordinate system, ordered pairs are listed so that the *x*-value is always given first and the *y*-value second.

In the coordinate system, the location of a point may sometimes be on an axis.

> Whenever a point lies exactly on one axis, one value of the ordered pair describing the location of that point will be zero.

Technology Connection

Graphing Calculators

People used to have to draw their own graphs. Now calculators can draw graphs for you. Some graphing calculators have libraries of equations so that you just choose the one you need and presto— the calculator graphs the equation for you. Some calculators graph in three dimensions. You can plug some graphing calculators into a computer. Then you can see your graphs on a large monitor, print them out, and even share them over the Internet.

Graphing *Chapter 11* **325**

Play a game with students in which you offer an ordered pair, and they tell which is the *x*-coordinate, which is the *y*-coordinate, and in which quadrant the point is located.

(3, 2)	(*I*)
(3, −2)	(*IV*)
(−2, 3)	(*II*)
(−3, −2)	(*III*)
(9, 7)	(*I*)
(−9, 7)	(*II*)
(−7, −9)	(*III*)
(9, −7)	(*IV*)

COMMON ERROR

Some students are apt to confuse the order of the numbers in an ordered pair. Point out that when they recite the alphabet, they reach *x* before *y*. The same is true in ordered pairs: *x* is before *y*.

3 **Reinforce and Extend**

LEARNING STYLES

LEP/ESL

Have pairs of students describe the locations of the points in Exercise A. A typical description would be "Point *K* is one unit to the right of the *y*-axis and six units above the *x*-axis." Ask students to take turns giving their descriptions. Circulate to ensure that they always give the location of the *x*-coordinate first and the location of the *y*-coordinate second.

Emphasize to students that there are times when it is important that a description of a point applies to only one location. For example, the legal description of a parcel of land must describe only one land parcel. Encourage students to determine the legal description of the land occupied by their school. The information is kept by the county and is usually accessible through the county clerk's office. (The description may include terms such as *meridians*, *ranges*, *townships*, *sections*, and *subdivisions*.) Students might investigate how this older version of land description can be converted to a geographic coordinate system.

EXAMPLE 2 Locate each point.

Step 1 Locate Point M. The ordered pair (0, 3) describes the location of Point M.

Step 2 Locate Point N. The ordered pair (4, −1) describes the location of Point N.

Step 3 Locate Point B. The ordered pair (−4, 0) describes the location of Point B.

Step 4 Locate Point T. The ordered pair (−2, −3) describes the location of Point T.

Step 5 Locate Point W. The ordered pair (0, −4) describes the location of Point W.

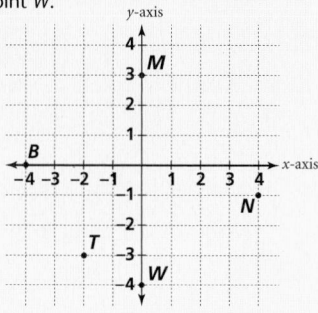

A point can be located in a specific quadrant by its x- and y-values. The values represent the ordered pair, which defines the number relationship.

In the coordinate system, Quadrant I is the upper-right quarter of the system, Quadrant II is the upper-left quarter of the system, Quadrant III is the lower-left quarter, and Quadrant IV is the lower-right quarter of the system.

EXAMPLE 3 Identify the quadrants in which Point G, Point C, Point R, and Point P are located.

Point G is located in Quadrant I.

Point C is located in Quadrant II.

Point R is located in Quadrant III.

Point P is located in Quadrant IV.

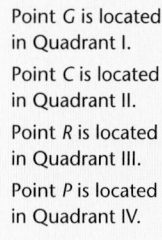
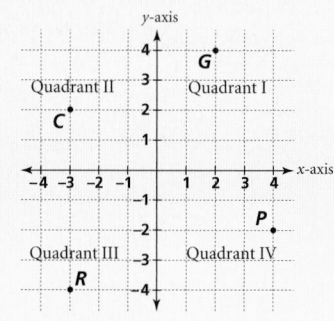

Exercise A Write an ordered pair to describe the location of each point.

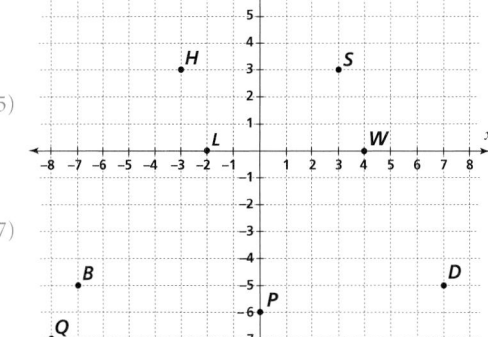

1. Point K $(1, 6)$
2. Point H $(-3, 3)$
3. Point M $(0, 7)$
4. Point W $(4, 0)$
5. Point B $(-7, -5)$
6. Point S $(3, 3)$
7. Point P $(0, -6)$
8. Point Q $(-8, -7)$
9. Point D $(7, -5)$
10. Point L $(-2, 0)$

Exercise B Identify the quadrant in which each of these points is located.

11. Point K Quadrant I
12. Point H Quadrant II
13. Point B Quadrant III

14. Point S Quadrant I
15. Point Q Quadrant III
16. Point D Quadrant IV

PROBLEM SOLVING

Exercise C Draw a coordinate system with x-values from -10 to 10 and y-values from -10 to 10. Suppose that the system stands for a grid of city blocks. Use it to answer the questions.

17. Kafi walks from $(0, 0)$ to $(2, 0)$. How many units does he walk?   2 units

18. Every morning, Mark jogs from $(0, 0)$ to $(0, -4)$ and back again. How many units does he jog?
8 units

19. Wendy left her home at $(3, 4)$, picked up Jessie at $(3, 5)$, and went to the library at $(5, 5)$. How far did Wendy go?   3 units

20. Part of the mail carrier's route takes her from $(-2, 6)$ to $(-2, -4)$ to $(6, -4)$ to $(6, 8)$. How many units is this part of her route?   30 units

Lesson at a Glance

Chapter 11 Lesson 6

Overview This lesson presents how to plot points on a coordinate grid.

Objective

- To plot a point, an ordered pair of numbers, on a coordinate grid

Student Pages 328–329

Teacher's Resource Library **TRL**

  Workbook Activity 108

  Activity 103

  Alternative Activity 103

1 Warm-Up Activity

Discuss with students the instructions needed to get to a specific location. Conclude that the instructions generally include two components: an indication of direction (for example, north, south, left, or right) and an indication of distance (such as 4 blocks or 30 miles).

2 Teaching the Lesson

Demonstrate Example 1, Point *J* located at (−4, 4), at the board or on an overhead projector. Indicate to students that the *x*-value of *J* is 4 units to the left of the origin and the *y*-value of *J* is 4 units up from the *x*-axis.

Ask a volunteer to describe how to plot Point *D*, (2, −1), from Example 2. Encourage the volunteer to describe how many units he or she needs to count as well as in which direction to count to plot point *D*.

You may want to ask volunteers to locate Points *Q* (−2, 1), *R* (1, −2), and *S* (−1, −2) on the same coordinate system.

In the coordinate system, the *x*-value of an ordered pair (x, y) is a description of the horizontal distance a point is to the left or to the right of the *y*-axis, and the *y*-value of an ordered pair is a description of the vertical distance a point is above or below the *x*-axis. The values together represent a number relationship. This concept of horizontal and vertical distance is used when plotting points in the coordinate system.

EXAMPLE 1 Plot a point at (−4, 4). Label the point Point *J*.

  Step 1 Construct a coordinate system. Since the greatest value of the ordered pair (−4, 4) is 4, show at least four units on each axis. Label the *x*- and *y*-axes.

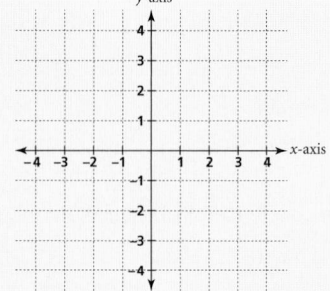

  Step 2 To plot a point at (−4, 4), begin at the origin. Move 4 units to the left.

  Step 3 Then move 4 units up.

  Step 4 Make a shaded circle at (−4, 4).

  Step 5 Label the point *J*.

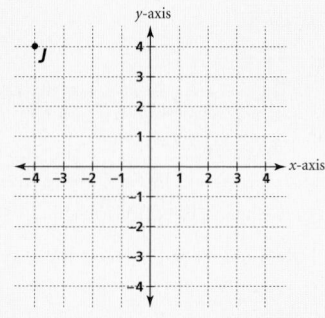

Each time you plot a point in the coordinate system, remember that the *x*-value of the ordered pair describes the horizontal distance a point is to the left or to the right of the *y*-axis, and the *y*-value of the ordered pair describes the vertical distance a point is above or below the *x*-axis.

328   Chapter 11   Graphing

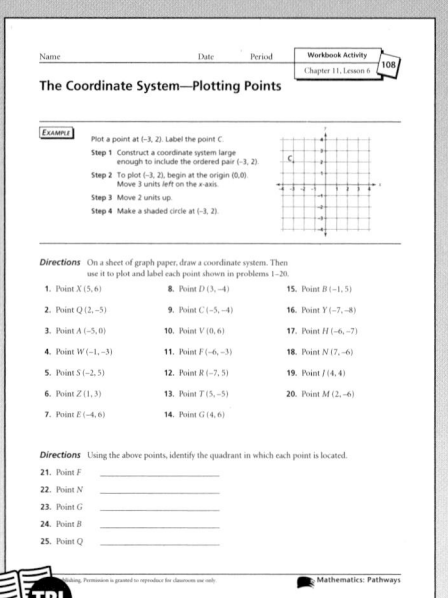

Workbook Activity 108

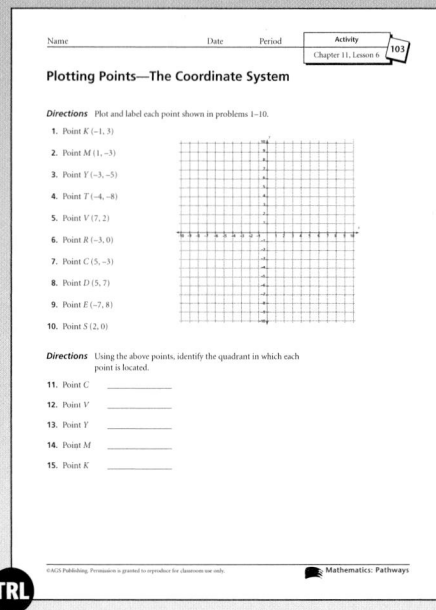

Activity 103

EXAMPLE 2 Plot a point at $(2, -1)$. Label the point Point D.

Step 1 To plot a point at $(2, -1)$, begin at the origin. Move 2 units to the right.

Step 2 Then move 1 unit down.

Step 3 Make a shaded circle at $(2, -1)$.

Step 4 Label the point D.

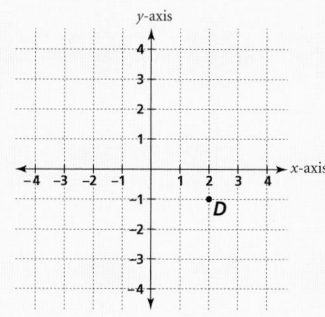

Exercise A On a sheet of graph paper, draw a coordinate system. Then use it to plot and label each point shown in problems 1–11.

1. Point $Z \, (-4, -2)$

2. Point $C \, (2, 3)$

3. Point $R \, (-5, 0)$

4. Point $N \, (6, 4)$

5. Point $Q \, (-3, 5)$

6. Point $B \, (-1, -6)$

7. Point $M \, (0, -1)$

8. Point $P \, (3, 0)$

9. Point $W \, (4, 1)$

10. Point $S \, (-2, 4)$

11. Point $V \, (0, 3)$

Exercise B The sign of each coordinate of an ordered pair is shown. In which quadrant is each point found?

12. $(+, +)$ Quadrant I

13. $(-, -)$ Quadrant III

14. $(+, -)$ Quadrant IV

15. $(-, +)$ Quadrant II

As they gain familiarity with coordinate systems, students may again lose track of the order in ordered pairs. Help them establish consistent graphing skills by always plotting the *x*-value of an ordered pair first.

3 **Reinforce and Extend**

LEARNING STYLES

Body/Kinesthetic

Mark a coordinate grid on the classroom floor. If the floor is covered in square tiles, use the corners of the tiles as grid intersections. Have students choose which point from Exercise A they wish to represent and then write that point and its coordinates on a sheet of paper. Ask each student to move to the location on the coordinate grid that matches the ordered pair that he or she chose. Have students hold up their papers to indicate their location.

Answers to Problems 1–11

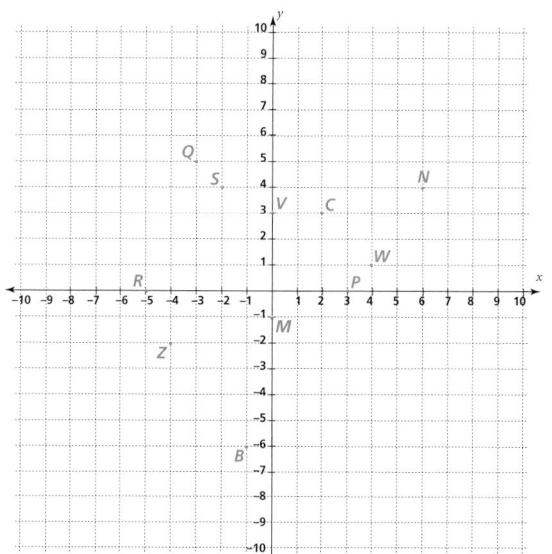

Chapter 11 Lesson 7

Overview This lesson demonstrates how to produce an ordered pair solution to an equation and use the ordered pair to graph the line of the equation.

Objectives

- To produce ordered pairs that represent solutions to equations
- To graph the line of an equation using ordered pairs

Student Pages 330–333

Teacher's Resource Library (TRL)

Workbook Activities 109–110

Activity 104

Alternative Activity 104

....

Mathematics Vocabulary

linear equation
pattern

....

 Warm-Up Activity

Remind students that in equations involving x and y, they can choose a value of x, substitute it in the equation, and find the value for y for which the equation is true.

2 **Teaching the Lesson**

Use the example $y = x + 2$ to demonstrate for students how to choose a value for x and then solve for the appropriate value of y. Then, using a coordinate system on the board or overhead projector, work with students to plot points to determine the graph of the equation $y = x + 2$.

Invite a volunteer to work through the steps of Example 1, $y = x - 1$.

Help students grasp that this process of choosing a value for x and then solving for y is designed to produce ordered pairs that represent points along the line of the equation.

Linear equation
An equation whose graph is a straight line

Pattern
A list of numbers, shapes, colors, and so on that repeats in such a way that the next item can be guessed

The equation $y = x + 2$ is an example of a **linear equation** because its graph is a straight line. The graph of any linear equation will intersect an infinite number of points in the coordinate system.

For example, the graph of the line $y = x + 2$ intersects $(-4, -2), (-2, 0),$ $(1, 3)$, and many other points.

This table of values shows several points that are intersected by the line $y = x + 2$.

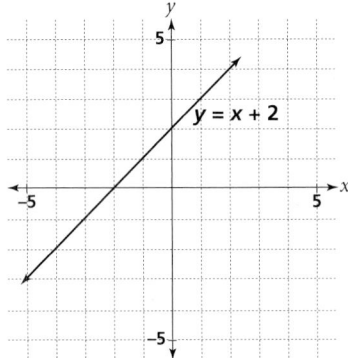

In order to graph an equation of a line in the coordinate system, you must first find two or more points that the graph will intersect. To find two or more points, make a table of values. The table shows the function as "add two." Because the function in the table remains the same, a **pattern** develops between the x- and y- values.

$y = x + 2$	
x	**y**
-4	-2
-2	0
1	3
2	4

EXAMPLE 1 Make a table of values for the line $y = x - 1$.

Step 1 Create a table that displays the equation of the line and space for at least three x and y values.

$y = x - 1$	
x	**y**

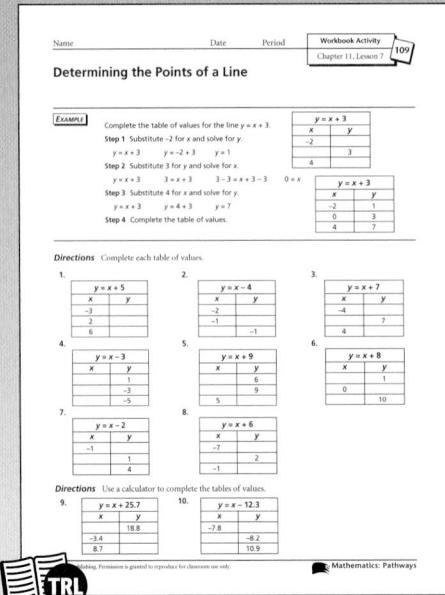

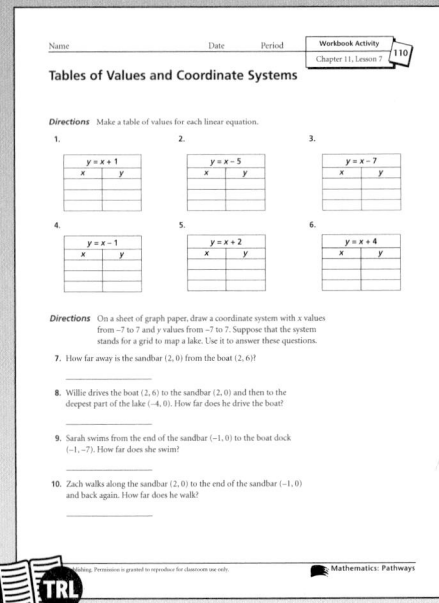

EXAMPLE 1 (continued)

Step 2 Choose a value for x. For example, choose $x = -3$.
Write -3 in the table for x, then substitute $x = -3$
into the equation of the line $y = x - 1$ and solve for y.

$y = x - 1$	
x	y
-3	

$y = x - 1$
$y = (-3) - 1$
$y = -4$

$y = x - 1$	
x	y
-3	-4

The line passes through $(-3, -4)$.

Step 3 Repeat Step 2. Choose a different value for x.
For example, choose $x = 0$.

$y = x - 1$	
x	y
-3	
0	

$y = x - 1$
$y = 0 - 1$
$y = -1$

$y = x - 1$	
x	y
-3	-4
0	-1

The line passes through $(0, -1)$.

Step 4 Repeat Step 2. Choose a different value for x.
For example, choose $x = 2$.

$y = x - 1$	
x	y
-3	
0	
2	

$y = x - 1$
$y = 2 - 1$
$y = 1$

$y = x - 1$	
x	y
-3	-4
0	-1
2	1

The line passes through $(2, 1)$.

A completed table of values shows that
the graph of the line $y = x - 1$ passes
through $(-3, -4)$, $(0, -1)$, and $(2, 1)$.
As long as you substitute a value for
either x or y, you can solve for the
other variable and find the pattern.

$y = x - 1$	
x	y
-3	-4
0	-1
2	1

Determining Points on a Line

Materials: Algebra Tiles, Pattern
Blocks, Manipulatives Master 3
(Sentence Mat)

Group Practice: Use Algebra Tiles unit
squares for numbers, and choose
Pattern Block shapes to represent
variables x and y. On the Sentence
Mat, model the equation in the
example, $y = x + 2$. To find ordered
pairs, substitute values (unit squares)
for x and y and make a table of values.
To solve for y, choose a value for x and
replace the variable with unit squares.
Apply the Zero Rule, and simplify. To
solve for x, remove the constant (2)
from the right by adding -2 to both
sides and simplify. Choose a value for
y, and simplify. The value of x is on the
left side of the equation.

Student Practice: Have students use
the unit squares and shapes for
problems 1–3 in Exercise A and
problems 5–6 in Exercise B.

 3 **Reinforce and Extend**

LEARNING STYLES

Interpersonal/ Group Learning

Have small groups of
students write the inverses of
the equations in problems 1–4 in
Exercise A. For example, $y = x + 1$
becomes $x = y + 1$; $y = x - 2$
becomes $x = y - 2$. Have students
create and complete a table of values
for each of the new equations.

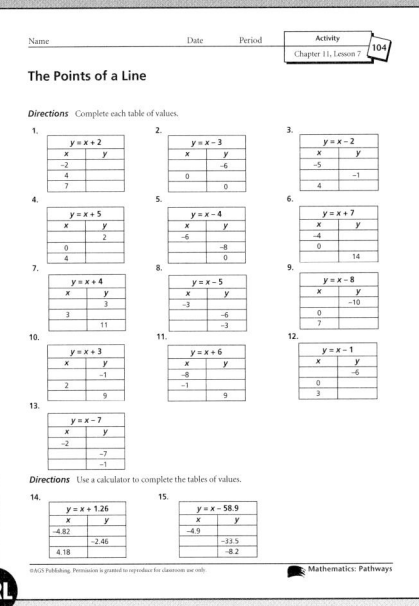

Activity 104

TRL

CALCULATOR

Encourage students to use the $+/-$ key on a calculator to complete these tables of values.

$y = x - 14$	
x	y
1	(-13)
0	(-14)
14	(0)

$y = x + 9$	
x	y
(-2)	7
(-3)	6
(0)	9

$y = x - 8$	
x	y
0	(-8)
(-4)	-12
-8	(-16)

Writing About Mathematics

In several short sentences, explain why you can substitute a value for y or x in a linear equation and still graph the same line.

EXAMPLE 2 Complete the table of values for the line $y = x + 4$.

$y = x + 4$	
x	y
-5	
	3
6	

Step 1 Substitute -5 for x and solve for y.

$$y = x + 4$$
$$y = (-5) + 4$$
$$y = -1$$

Step 2 Substitute 3 for y and solve for x.

$$y = x + 4$$
$$3 = x + 4$$
$$3 + (-4) = x + 4 + (-4)$$
$$-1 = x$$

Step 3 Substitute 6 for x and solve for y.

$$y = x + 4$$
$$y = 6 + 4$$
$$y = 10$$

Step 4 Complete the table of values.

$y = x + 4$	
x	y
-5	-1
-1	3
6	10

Exercise A Complete each table of values.

1.

$y = x + 1$	
x	y
-1	0
0	1
1	2

2.

$y = x - 2$	
x	y
-3	-5
2	0
3	1

3.

$y = x + 3$	
x	y
-7	-4
-1	2
-4	-1

4.

$y = 2x$	
x	y
-2	-4
0	0
1	2

Answers will vary.
Sample answers
shown for 5–6.

Exercise B Create a table of values for each equation of a line.

5.

y = x + 6	
x	y
−1	5
0	6
1	7

6.

y = x − 5	
x	y
−2	−7
0	−5
2	−3

Calculator
Practice

Use the [+/−] key on a calculator to help complete a table of values.

EXAMPLE 3 Complete the table of values for the line $y = x − 3$.

y = x − 3	
x	y
2	−1
0	−3
−2	

In the equation $y = x − 3$, substitute $(−2)$ for x and use a calculator to find y.

$y = (−2) − 3$

Press 2 [+/−] [−] 3 [=].

The display reads −5.
Complete the table.

y = x − 3	
x	y
2	−1
0	−3
−2	−5

Exercise C Use a calculator to complete this table of values.

y = x − 12	
x	y
−53.2	**7.**
8.	−25
−89.9	**9.**
10.	−52.7

7. −65.2
8. −13
9. −101.9
10. −40.7

Lesson at a Glance

Chapter 11 Lesson 8

Overview This lesson introduces students to functions.

Objectives

- To identify graphs that represent functions
- To evaluate functions

Student Pages 334–335

Teacher's Resource Library **TRL**

Workbook Activity 111

Activity 105

Alternative Activity 105

Mathematics Vocabulary

dependent variable
independent variable
vertical line test

1 ⚡ Warm-Up Activity

Help students relate the term *function* to their everyday lives. Pose situations in which one event is a function of another: whether a car moves is a function of (depends on) how much gas is in the tank; whether a team wins is a function of (depends on) how well the team plays, and so on. Indicate to students that in mathematical circles, functions have specific characteristics.

2 ⚡ Teaching the Lesson

Indicate to students that $y = mx + b$ and $f(x) = mx + b$ are two ways of stating the same information. Point out that the significant characteristic of a function is that for every value of x, there is only one related value of y.

| **Dependent variable** |
| The value of the y variable that depends on the value of x |
| **Independent variable** |
| The value of x that determines the value of y |
| **Vertical line test** |
| A way of determining whether a graph is a function; if a vertical line intersects a graph at more than 1 point, the graph is not a function |

If you make a table of values for the equation $y = \frac{3}{2}x + 7$, you will find that for each value you choose for x, the value of y changes. Because the value of y depends on the value you choose for x, y is known as the **dependent variable** and x is known as the **independent variable**. Another way to describe the same idea is to say that y is a function of x.

To use the language of functions, use the symbol $f(x)$ in place of y.

$$y = mx + b \text{ is the same as } f(x) = mx + b.$$

The symbol $f(x)$ is read "the function of x."

Rewrite $y = \frac{3}{2}x + 7$ as $f(x) = \frac{3}{2}x + 7$.

> **Rule** A function is a rule that associates every *x*-value with one and only one *y*-value.

All equations of the form $f(x) = mx + b$ are functions. To decide whether the graph of an equation is a function, perform a **vertical line test**—if a vertical line crosses the graph more than once, the graph is not a function because the x-value of the vertical line is associated with more than one y-value.

EXAMPLE 1 Is the graph at the right a function?

Solution No; a vertical line crosses the graph more than once—for every x-value, there is more than one y-value.

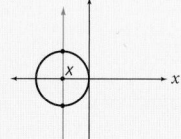

EXAMPLE 2 Is the graph at the right a function?

Solution Yes; a vertical line crosses the graph only once—for every x-value, there is one and only one y-value.

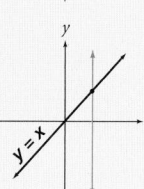

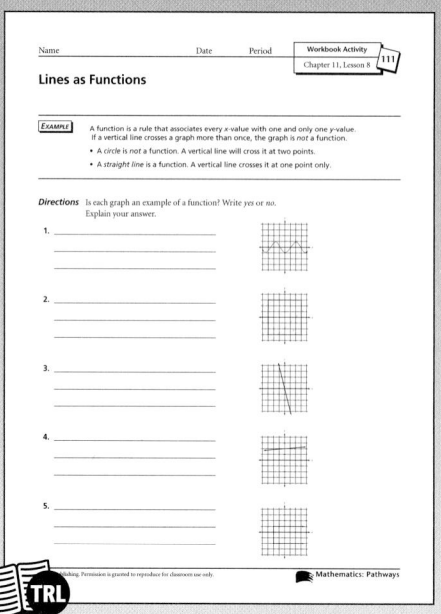

Workbook Activity 111

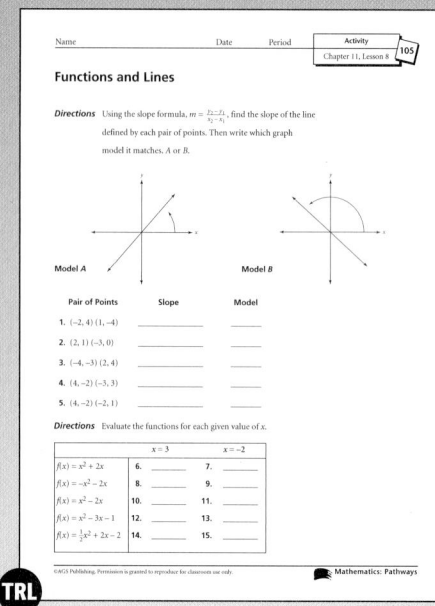

Activity 105

To evaluate a function means to substitute a value for x and solve for $f(x)$.

EXAMPLE 3 Evaluate $f(x) = x^2 + x - 1$ given $x = 3$.

Solution $f(x) = x^2 + x - 1$

$f(3) = 3^2 + 3 - 1$

$f(3) = 11$

Exercise A Is each graph an example of a function? Write yes or no.

1. yes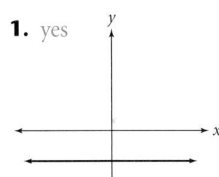

2. no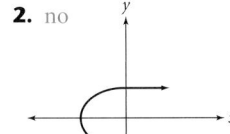

3. yes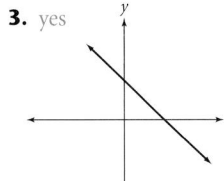

4. yes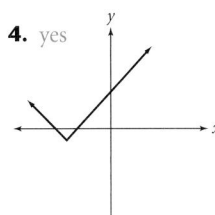

5. yes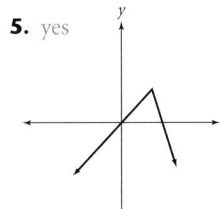

6. no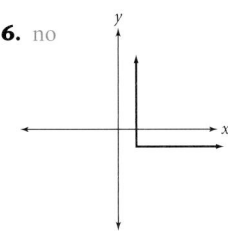

Exercise B Evaluate each function two times. Use $x = 2$ and $x = -4$.

7. $f(x) = x^2 + x$
$f(2) = 6; f(-4) = 12$

8. $f(x) = x^2 - x$
$f(2) = 2; f(-4) = 20$

9. $f(x) = 4x^2 - x$
$f(2) = 14; f(-4) = 68$

10. $f(x) = -2x^2 + x$
$f(2) = -6; f(-4) = -36$

11. $f(x) = -x^2 + 3x$
$f(2) = 2; f(-4) = -28$

12. $f(x) = x^2 - 6x$
$f(2) = -8; f(-4) = 40$

13. $f(x) = -3x^2 + x - 1$
$f(2) = -11; f(-4) = -53$

14. $f(x) = 4x^2 - x - 4$
$f(2) = 10; f(-4) = 64$

15. $f(x) = 1.5x^2 + 3x$
$f(2) = 12; f(-4) = 12$

Graphing   Chapter 11   **335**

Lesson at a Glance

Chapter 11 Lesson 9

Overview This lesson demonstrates several different ways to determine the domain and range of a graphed function.

Objectives

- To find the domain and range using two sets of ordered pairs on a line
- To calculate the range of a function given the domain
- To determine the domain and range of a function using a graph

Student Pages 336–339

Teacher's Resource Library TRL

  Workbook Activity 112

  Activity 106

  Alternative Activity 106

....

Mathematics Vocabulary

domain

range

....

1 Warm-Up Activity

Reinforce the concept of an algebraic function by asking students whether they have auto-dial or a speed dial feature on their telephones or cell phones. Explain that programming a speed dial is similar to an algebraic function—a single key or "function" button is programmed to produce a series of numbers (a phone number). For a phone, $f(x)$ is a phone number. On the keypad of the phone, $f(1)$ might be the fire department phone number, $f(3)$ might be a parent's telephone number at work, $f(5)$ might be a friend's phone number in another state, and so on. Remind students that in algebra, a function is a rule that sets up a relationship between an x-value and a y-value.

Lesson	9	Domain and Range of a Function

Domain

The independent variables, or set of x-values, of a function

Range

The dependent variables, or set of y-values, of a function

The set of x-values, the independent variables that are used in a function, is called the **domain** of the function. The corresponding set of y-values, the dependent variables, is called the **range** of the function.

EXAMPLE 1 $y = f(x) = 2x - 1$

Let the domain be $-1, 0, 2, 5$.

Determine the range.

Substitute the domain values in $f(x)$ to determine the range.

$x = -1$ $y = f(-1) = 2(-1) - 1 = -3$ so $y = -3$

$x = 0$ $y = f(0) = 2(0) - 1 = -1$ so $y = -1$

$x = 2$ $y = f(2) = 2(2) - 1 = 3$ so $y = 3$

$x = 5$ $y = f(5) = 2(5) - 1 = 9$ so $y = 9$

The range is $-3, -1, 3, 9$.

EXAMPLE 2 Look at the graph for
$f(x) = x - 1$ for $1 \le x \le 4$

What is the range?

Find the endpoints of the range by evaluating $f(1)$ and $f(4)$.

$f(1) = 1 - 1 = 0$

$f(4) = 4 - 1 = 3$

So the range is $0 \le y \le 3$.

Note: domain: $1 \le x \le 4$

      range: $f(1) \le y \le f(4)$

The range of the dependent variable depends on the domain.

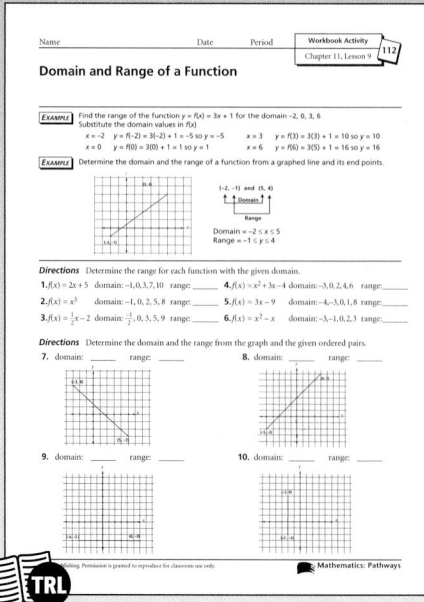

Workbook Activity 112

Activity 106

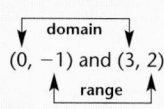

EXAMPLE 3 Use the graph at the right to determine the domain and range of the graphed function.

The ordered pairs $(0, -1)$ and $(3, 2)$ give the endpoints of the intervals of domain and range.

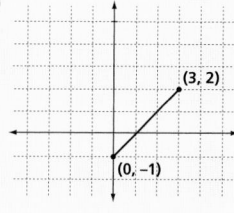

domain
$(0, -1)$ and $(3, 2)$
range

domain: $0 \leq x \leq 3$
range: $-1 \leq y \leq 2$

Remember:

1. The domain includes all the x-values needed to define the function. The domain is found on the x-axis. You can choose the domain. It is independent.

2. The range includes all the y-values, which depend directly on the domain-values substituted in the function. The range is found on the y-axis. It is dependent on the domain.

Exercise A Determine the range for each function with the given domain.

1. $f(x) = 2x - 5$ domain: $-1, 0, 3, 7, 10$

2. $f(x) = -x^2$ domain: $-1, 0, 5, 9, 100$

3. $f(x) = \frac{1}{2}x + 2$ domain: $-\frac{1}{2}, 0, 2, 3, 4$

4. $f(x) = x^2 + 2x + 3$ domain: $-2, 0, 1, 2, 3$

5. $f(x) = 2x + 6$ domain: $-4, -3, -\frac{1}{2}, 1, 8$

1. Range: $-7, -5, 1, 9, 15$

2. Range: $-1, 0, -25, -81, -10{,}000$

3. Range: $\frac{7}{4}, 2, 3, \frac{7}{2}, 4$

4. Range: $3, 3, 6, 11, 18$

5. Range: $-2, 0, 5, 8, 22$

2 Teaching the Lesson

Begin by drawing a coordinate plane on the board and drawing a line between the points $(-3, -3)$ and $(4, 4)$. Using the diagram in the example box as a guide, discuss the meanings of range and domain using the plane you drew. Explain that the domain is $-3, -1, 2, 4$. Because $y = f(x) = x$, the range is the same as the domain in this example. It is important that students understand that the domain contains x-values and that the range contains y-values. Discuss the examples shown in the lesson, emphasizing that there are different ways of determining the domain and range: you can calculate range by using the function and a given domain; you can find the range and domain by using the ordered pairs of the two end points of a graphed line; and you can determine the range and domain from a line on a coordinate plane.

3 Reinforce and Extend

LEARNING STYLES

LEP/ESL

The words *range* and *domain* both have several meanings, which might be confusing to some students. For example, *range* can mean the distance a vehicle can travel on a full tank of fuel, a cooking stove, a prairie (as in "Home on the Range"), or a series of things in a row (the algebraic meaning). *Domain* can mean an area of land owned by someone, a country or territory that is controlled by a government, the sphere of knowledge that someone has, or a set of numbers or variables in a function. Reinforce the definitions that are used in this lesson.

Exercise B Determine the range for each function, given the domain and the graph.

6. $f(x) = -x + 2$ for $-2 \leq x \leq 4$
Range: $-2 \leq y \leq 4$

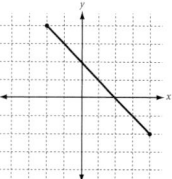

7. $f(x) = 3$ for $-3 \leq x \leq 4$
Range: $y = 3$

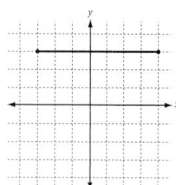

8. $f(x) = \frac{1}{3}x + 2$ for $-7 \leq x \leq 10$
Range: $-\frac{1}{3} \leq y \leq 5\frac{1}{3}$

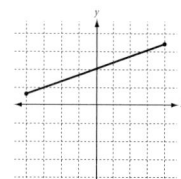

9. $f(x) = x^2$ for $-2 \leq x \leq 2$
Range: $0 \leq y \leq 4$

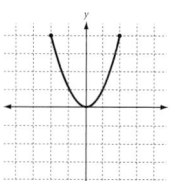

10. $f(x) = |x|$ for $-5 \leq x \leq 5$
Range: $0 \leq y \leq 5$

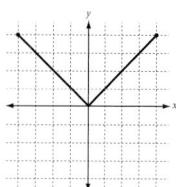

Exercise C Determine the domain and the range from the graph and the given ordered pairs.

11. Domain: $-4 \le x \le 6$
    Range: $-2 \le y \le 5$

12. Domain: $-5 \le x \le 3$
    Range: $-\frac{1}{2} \le y \le 2$

13. Domain: $-4 \le x \le 5$
    Range: $y = 2$

14. Domain: $-2 \le x \le 3$
    Range: $-2 \le y \le 3$

15. Domain: $-2 \le x \le 2$
    Range: $0 \le y \le 4$

11.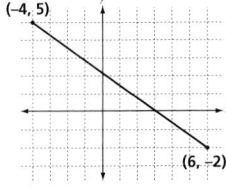
(-4, 5) (6, -2)

14.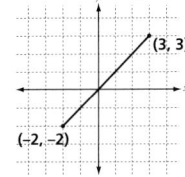
(3, 3) (-2, -2)

12.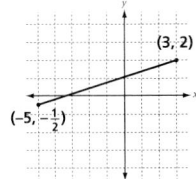
(3, 2) (-5, -$\frac{1}{2}$)

15.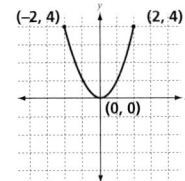
(-2, 4) (2, 4) (0, 0)

13.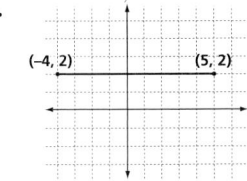
(-4, 2) (5, 2)

Technology Connection

Graphing Tools

If you have access to the Internet, there are lots of graphing tools available. Go to a search engine, type in the words "online graphing tools," and you'll find several you can download for free. (There are many you can buy, as well.) Computer spreadsheet and even word-processing programs are capable of making graphs, too. All these graphing tools function the same way. You plug in a formula or data, and the tool will display the resulting graph.

LEARNING STYLES

Logical/Mathematical

Have students explain how the range of a function depends on the value of x. (The range of a function contains y-values based on a function. The function might be $y = 3x - 7$ or $y = x + 29$. The value of x determines the value of y. y is a dependent variable, so the range is dependent.)

Lesson at a Glance

Chapter 11 Lesson 10

Overview This lesson demonstrates how to use a table of values to graph a linear equation.

Objective

■ To graph a linear equation using a table of values to produce three points on the line

Student Pages 340–341

Teacher's Resource Library **TRL**

Workbook Activity 113

Activity 107

Alternative Activity 107

---

1 Warm-Up Activity

Remind students that in equations involving x and y, they can choose a value of x, substitute it in the equation, and find the value for y for which the equation is true. Point out that, as an alternative, they can choose a value of y, substitute it in the equation, and find the value for x for which the equation is true.

2 Teaching the Lesson

Use the example $y = 3x - 1$ to demonstrate how to choose a value for x and then solve for the appropriate value of y. Then, using a coordinate system on the board or overhead projector, help students plot points to determine the graph of the equation $y = 3x - 1$.

Ask a series of volunteers to describe the steps that can be used to graph the linear equation in Example 2, $y = -x + 1$.

Discuss with students how to proceed if they find that the three points are not on the same line. Have them describe what they would do to check their work.

The graph of a straight line can be drawn using only two points. However, if you use only two points, you may find it difficult to tell whether an error has been made in graphing. For this reason, use three points whenever you graph linear equations.

EXAMPLE 1 Graph the linear equation $y = 3x - 1$.

Step 1 Create a table of values.

$y = 3x - 1$	
x	y

Step 2 Choose three different values for x.

$y = 3x - 1$	
x	y
-2	
0	
2	

Step 3 Solve for y.

$y = 3x - 1$	
x	y
-2	-7
0	-1
2	5

Step 4 Draw a coordinate system. Plot the points shown in the table of values. Draw a line to connect the points, make an arrow at each end of the line, and label the line $y = 3x - 1$.

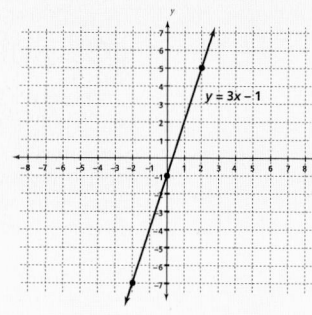

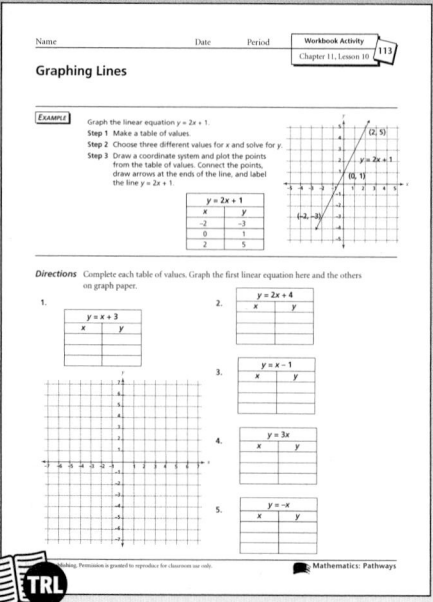

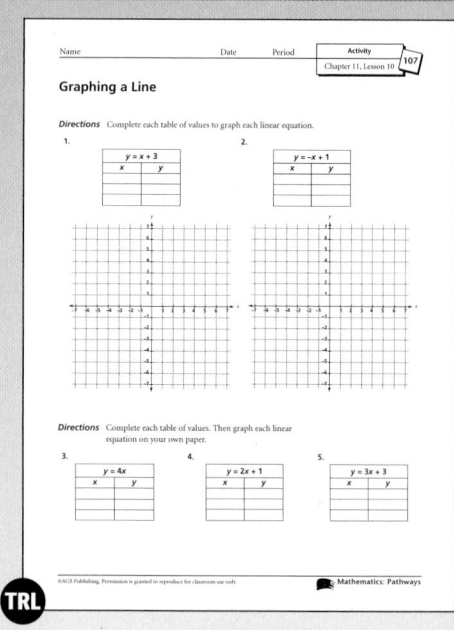

Workbook Activity 113

Activity 107

EXAMPLE 2 Graph the linear equation $y = -x + 1$.

Create and complete a table of values and then plot the points shown in the table and graph the line.

$y = -x + 1$	
x	y
-3	4
0	1
3	-2

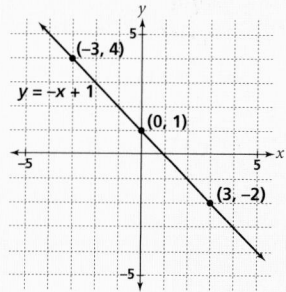

Exercise A Graph each linear equation.

See Teacher's Edition page for answers to problems 1–10.

1. $y = x + 5$

2. $y = x - 4$

3. $y = x$

4. $y = 2x + 2$

5. $y = -2x$

6. $y = -x + 2$

7. $y = 3x + 1$

8. $y = 2x - 3$

9. $y = -x - 1$

10. $y = 3x - 3$

 Try This

On a grid, draw a straight line. Choose three points on the line. Give the ordered pairs for the points to a partner. Ask your partner to write a linear equation based on the ordered pairs given. For example, if your ordered pairs are (0, 2), (2, 4), and (3, 5), the equation would be $y = x + 2$.

Answers will vary.

 Estimation Activity

Estimate: Estimate the population in 2010 based on the given graph.

Solution: The straight line increases by 10,000 every ten years. So in 2010 the population would be about 40,000.

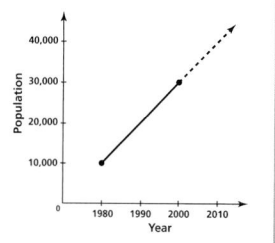

Answers to Problems 1–10

1 and 2.

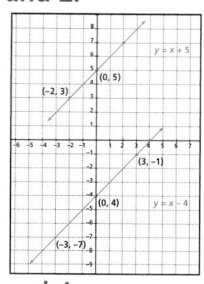

5 and 6.

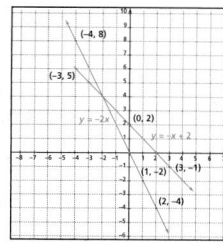

9 and 10.

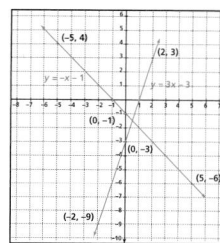

3 and 4.

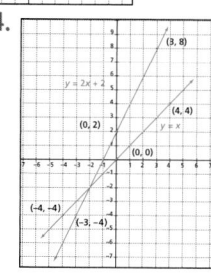

7 and 8.

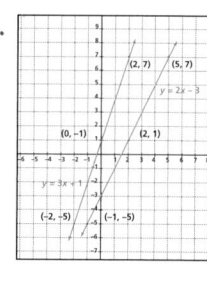

MANIPULATIVES

M Graphing Lines

Materials: Algebra Tiles, Pattern Blocks, Manipulatives Master 3 (Sentence Mat)

Group Practice: Review Lesson 7 to complete the table of values for Example 1 on page 340. For equations where the x-coefficient is not 1, show that *each* x-variable shape is replaced with the indicated number of unit squares. For example, if $x = -2$, then $3x$ (three x-shapes) is replaced with six negative unit squares, two for each x. Simplify and solve for y as in the previous lesson, choosing three different values for x. Plot the three points on the coordinate system, and graph the line.

Student Practice: Have students use the unit squares and shapes to complete a table of values for problems 1–10 in Exercise A.

Try This

Remind students that each of the ordered pairs represents values for which the equation is true. Students might find it helpful to place the values in a table like those they have used to find ordered pairs.

3 **Reinforce and Extend**

LEARNING STYLES

Visual/Spatial

Have students work in groups of four to analyze the graphs of the equations in Exercise A. Suggest that they compare the following groups of graphs.

$y = x + 5$, $y = x - 4$, and $y = x$

$y = 2x + 2$ and $y = 2x - 3$

$y = -x + 2$ and $y = -x - 1$

$y = 3x + 1$ and $y = 3x - 3$

Ask the groups to describe the similarities and differences between the graphs in each group.

Chapter 11 Lesson 11

Overview This lesson introduces the concept of the slope of a line.

Objective

- To determine the slope of a line $\frac{rise}{run}$.

Student Pages 342–343

Teacher's Resource Library (TRL)

Workbook Activity 114

Activity 108

Alternative Activity 108

Mathematics Vocabulary

slope

---

1 Warm-Up Activity

Engage students in a discussion about slope. Ask them to give examples such as hills, ski slopes, and toboggan slides. Have them identify characteristics of slope such as length, height, steepness, shallowness, and so on.

2 Teaching the Lesson

Work with students to develop an intuitive notion of slope. Point out that slope is a measure of how steeply a line rises or falls. Slope tells how many units a line goes up or down (rise) for every unit the line goes to the left or right (run).

MODELING

Organize the class in four or five groups. Invite students to the board to create their own coordinate axes. Ask them to choose two random points. Make sure that students pick points that will make an angled line when connected. Have groups connect their two points. Ask groups to find the slope of the line. Go over each of the group's problems in class.

Lesson 11 The Slope of a Line

Slope
The measure of the steepness of a line
$$slope = \frac{rise}{run}$$

If you've ever pedaled a bicycle up a hill and coasted down the other side, you know that pedaling a bicycle up a hill requires a great deal more energy than coasting a bicycle down a hill. This happens because the slope of the hill in one direction is different from the slope of the hill in the other direction.

The **slope** of a line is the ratio of the vertical rise to the horizontal run and is written in the form $slope = \frac{rise}{run}$.

Recall that the fraction bar means *divide*. You can use the division symbol on the calculator to divide the rise by the run.

EXAMPLE 1 What is the slope of a street that is 800 feet long and rises 10 feet in that distance?

Step 1 Express the slope as the fraction $\frac{rise}{run}$.

Step 2 $\frac{rise}{run} = \frac{+10}{+800}$

Step 3 Simplify if possible. $\frac{+10}{+800} = \frac{1}{80}$

A slope of $\frac{1}{80}$ means for every 80 feet of horizontal distance, the street rises 1 foot.

The slope of a line may sometimes be a negative number.

EXAMPLE 2 What is the slope of a driveway that is 60 feet long and falls 2 feet in that distance?

Step 1 Express the slope as the fraction $\frac{rise}{run}$.

Step 2 $\frac{rise}{run} = \frac{-2}{+60}$

Step 3 Simplify if possible. $\frac{-2}{+60} = \frac{-1}{30}$

A slope of $\frac{-1}{30}$ means for every 30 feet of horizontal distance, the driveway falls 1 foot.

The slope of the line depends on the numerical relationship between the rise and the run. It is possible to decide whether the slope of a line is positive or negative simply by looking at the line.

A line has a *positive slope* if it moves upward when viewed from left to right.

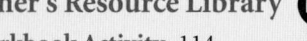

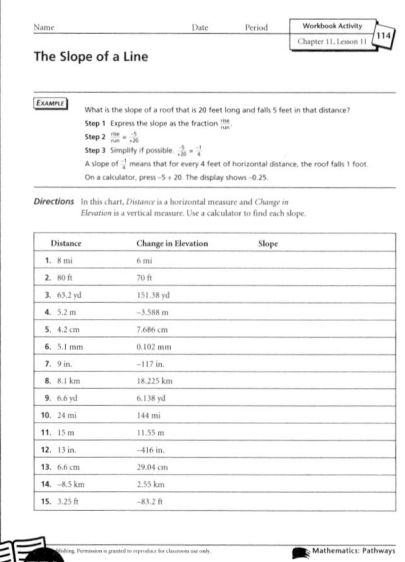

Workbook Activity 114

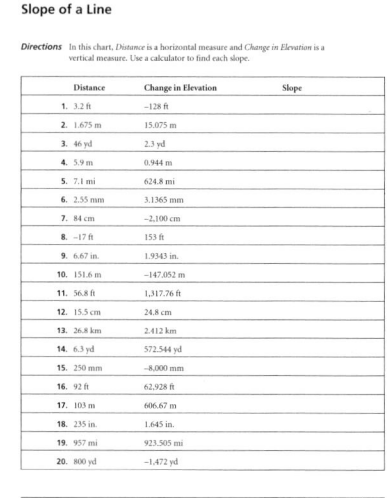

Activity 108

A line has a *negative slope* if it moves downward when viewed from left to right.

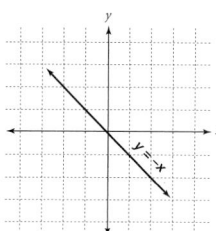

A line has *zero slope* if it is parallel to the *x*-axis.

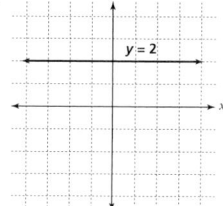

 You can use a calculator and the formula slope = $\frac{rise}{run}$ to determine slope of lines. Your answer will be given in decimal points.

EXAMPLE 3 Find the slope of a line that is 14.7 miles long and has a −9 mile change in elevation.
Press 9 [+/−] [÷] 14 [.] 7 [=].
The display reads *−0.612244898*.

Exercise A In this chart, *Distance* is a horizontal measure and *Change in Elevation* is a vertical measure. Use a calculator to find slope.

	Distance	Change in Elevation		Distance	Change in Elevation
1.	16 in.	0.2 in.	**5.**	100 m	200 m
2.	1,200 mi	5 mi	**6.**	2.4 mm	−0.6 mm
3.	180 cm	−12 cm	**7.**	0.5 in.	6 in.
4.	10 yd	−50 yd			

1. 0.0125
2. 0.004166667
3. −0.066666667
4. −5
5. 2
6. −0.25
7. 12

Exercise B Describe the slope of each line. Write *positive slope*, *negative slope*, or *zero slope*.

8.
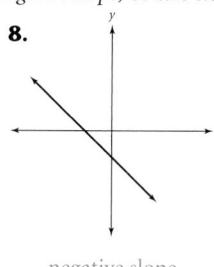
negative slope

9.
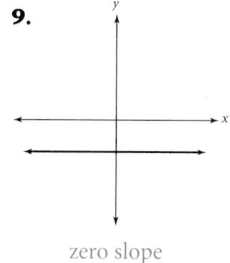
zero slope

10.
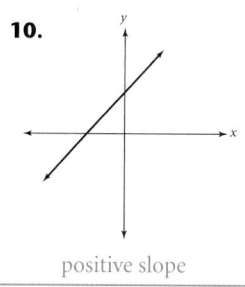
positive slope

AT HOME

 Have students find the slope $\frac{rise}{run}$ of any stairs they might have at home. Suggest that they draw a picture of the stairs, showing the rise (height) and the run (width) of each stair. They can find the slope of one stair, or, by counting the number of stairs and multiplying, they can find the slope of an entire staircase. Post students' findings as part of a class bulletin board.

CALCULATOR

 Provide these additional opportunities for students to find slope using the formula $\frac{rise}{run}$. After students determine the slope, have them describe the general direction of the slope, that is, upward from left to right (positive slope) or downward from left to right (negative slope). Remind students to watch for consistent units.

Distance	Change in Elevation	Slope
4 mi	$\frac{1}{4}$ mi	(0.0625)
1 m	10 cm	(0.1)
150 yd	−1 yd	(−0.00667)
15 yd	6 in.	(0.011)

Chapter 11 Lesson 12

Overview This lesson offers a more refined method for finding the slope of a line.

Objective

■ To determine the slope of a line using the formula $m = \frac{y_2 - y_1}{x_2 - x_1}$

Student Pages 344–347

Teacher's Resource Library **TRL**

Workbook Activity 115

Activity 109

Alternative Activity 109

---

1 ⚡ Warm-Up Activity

Ask students to describe ways in which they can find the distance between two points on the *x*-axis. (*Subtract one x-coordinate from the other.*) Then have them describe how they can find the horizontal distance between any two points on the coordinate plane. (*Subtract one x-coordinate from the other.*)

2 ⚡ Teaching the Lesson

Work through the example with students. Make sure that they understand that making (0, 0) correspond to (x_1, y_1) is an arbitrary choice. Help students substitute values in the formula as shown in step 2. Finally, have them confirm that the slope is $\frac{1}{2}$ by asking them to compare the vertical rise (1) to the horizontal run (2) of the line.

To persuade students who may not believe that they can assign either ordered pair the value (x_1, y_1), work through the second example. Make sure that students realize that in the first instance, (x_1, y_1) is assigned to (−2, 3), and in the second instance, the same ordered pair is assigned (x_2, y_2). Have students explain in their own words why the slope of the line is the same no matter which ordered pair is chosen as (x_1, y_1).

The ratio $\frac{\text{rise}}{\text{run}}$ is one way to determine the slope of a line. Another way is to use the formula $m = \frac{y_2 - y_1}{x_2 - x_1}$ where (x_1, y_1) and (x_2, y_2) are any two points on the line. In the formula, *m* represents slope. Use the formula whenever you are given two points through which a line passes.

EXAMPLE 1 A line passes through the points (0, 0) and (4, 2). Find the slope of the line.

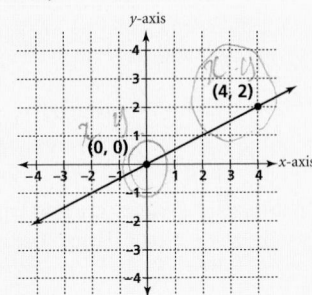

Step 1 Recall that points such as (0, 0) and (4, 2) are written in the form (*x*, *y*). Designate one of the points (x_1, y_1) and designate the other point (x_2, y_2).

$$(0, 0) \qquad (4, 2)$$
$$\downarrow \downarrow \qquad \downarrow \downarrow$$
$$(x_1, y_1) \qquad (x_2, y_2)$$

Step 2 Substitute the values for x_1, y_1, x_2, and y_2 into the formula.

$$m = \frac{y_2 - y_1}{x_2 - x_1} = \frac{2 - 0}{4 - 0}$$

Step 3 Simplify.

$$\frac{2 - 0}{4 - 0} = \frac{2}{4} = \frac{1}{2}$$

The slope of a line passing through the points (0, 0) and (4, 2) is $\frac{1}{2}$.

When you use two points and the formula $m = \frac{y_2 - y_1}{x_2 - x_1}$ to find the slope of a line, it does not matter which point you designate (x_1, y_1) and which point you designate (x_2, y_2).

---

344 *Chapter 11 Graphing*

EXAMPLE 2 Find the slope of a line that passes through the points $(-2, 3)$ and $(1, 0)$.

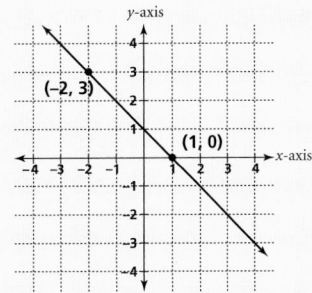

Step 1 Designate the point $(-2, 3)$ as (x_1, y_1) and designate the point $(1, 0)$ as (x_2, y_2).

$$(-2, 3) \qquad (1, 0)$$
$$\downarrow \downarrow \qquad\quad \downarrow \downarrow$$
$$(x_1, y_1) \qquad (x_2, y_2)$$

Step 2 Substitute the values for x_1, y_1, x_2, and y_2 into the formula.

$$m = \frac{y_2 - y_1}{x_2 - x_1} = \frac{0 - 3}{1 - (-2)}$$

Step 3 Simplify.

$$\frac{0 - 3}{1 - (-2)} = \frac{-3}{3} = -1$$

Step 1 Designate the point $(1, 0)$ as (x_1, y_1) and designate the point $(-2, 3)$ as (x_2, y_2).

$$(1, 0) \qquad (-2, 3)$$
$$\downarrow \downarrow \qquad\quad \downarrow \downarrow$$
$$(x_1, y_1) \qquad (x_2, y_2)$$

Step 2 Substitute the values for x_1, y_1, x_2, and y_2 into the formula.

$$m = \frac{y_2 - y_1}{x_2 - x_1} = \frac{3 - 0}{-2 (-1)}$$

Step 3 Simplify.

$$\frac{3 - 0}{-2 - 1} = \frac{3}{-3} = -1$$

The slope of a line passing through the points $(-2, 3)$ and $(1, 0)$ is -1.

Exercise A Find the slope of a line that passes through the given points.

1. $(5, 1)$ and $(0, 0)$ $\frac{1}{5}$

2. $(4, 4)$ and $(8, 8)$ 1

3. $(-2, 10)$ and $(6, 1)$ $\frac{-9}{8}$

4. $(1, -5)$ and $(2, -10)$ -5

5. $(-8, 3)$ and $(3, 8)$ $\frac{5}{11}$

6. $(7, 5)$ and $(3, 15)$ $\frac{-5}{2}$

7. $(-4, -6)$ and $(4, -6)$ 0

8. $\frac{3}{10}$

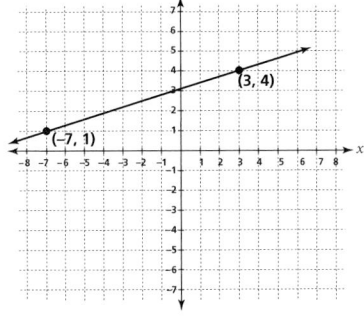

COMMON ERROR

Make sure that students understand that to find the slope of a line, they need to subtract one x-coordinate from the other x-coordinate and one y-coordinate from the other y-coordinate. Some students may incorrectly try to determine slope by subtracting the x- and y-coordinates of one point and dividing that by the difference between the x- and y-coordinates of the second point, essentially computing $(x_1 - y_1) \div (x_2 - y_2)$.

3 **Reinforce and Extend**

LEARNING STYLES

Auditory/Verbal

Suggest that students work in pairs. Each student should take a turn explaining slope in his or her own words. Students can use the problems in Exercise B and make statements such as "The slope of the line is two-elevenths. This means that the line moves two units upward for every eleven units it moves to the right."

 A calculator can be used to help find the slope of a line that passes through two points. Use the [+/-] key to calculate negative integers.

EXAMPLE 3 Find the slope of a line that passes through the points $(-4, 6)$ and $(8, -1)$.

Step 1 Designate one of the points (x_1, y_1) and designate the other point (x_2, y_2).

$$\begin{array}{cc} (-4, 6) & (8, -1) \\ \downarrow \ \downarrow & \downarrow \ \downarrow \\ (x_1, y_1) & (x_2, y_2) \end{array}$$

Step 2 Substitute the values for x_1, y_1, x_2, and y_2 into the formula.

$$m = \frac{y_2 - y_1}{x_2 - x_1} = \frac{-1 - 6}{8 - (-4)}$$

Step 3 Use a calculator to compute the numerator. Press 1 [+/-] [−] 6 [=].
The display reads -7.

Step 4 Use a calculator to compute the denominator. Press 8 [−] 4 [+/-] [=].
The display reads 12.

Step 5 Write the numerator over the denominator. Simplify if possible. The slope of a line passing through the points $(-4, 6)$ and $(8, -1)$ is $\frac{-7}{12}$.

Exercise B Find the slope of a line that passes through the given points. You may use a calculator.

9. $(-7, 3)$ and $(4, 5)$ $\quad \frac{2}{11}$

10. $(2, -9)$ and $(1, -10)$ $\quad 1$

11. $(8, -1)$ and $(4, 8)$ $\quad \frac{-9}{4}$

12. $(2, 2)$ and $(-1, 1)$ $\quad \frac{1}{3}$

13. $(-10, -5)$ and $(8, -7)$ $\quad \frac{-1}{9}$

Exercise C Answer each question.

14. Suppose the first half of a hiking trail has a slope of $\frac{-2}{25}$ and the last half of the trail has a slope of $\frac{1}{25}$. Which part of the trail is more difficult to hike? Explain. Last half; positive slope, so it's uphill

15. Suppose the first half of a bicycle trail has a slope of $\frac{3}{20}$ and the last half of the trail has a slope of $\frac{5}{40}$. Which part of the trail is more difficult to bicycle? Explain.

First half; greater slope

 Try This

Look at these shapes. Tell whether each line has a negative slope, a positive slope, or zero slope.

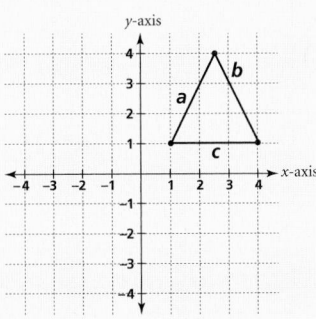

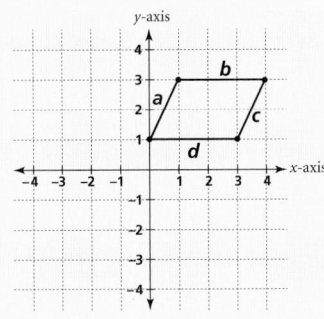

Triangle: *a* has a positive slope, *b* has a negative slope, and *c* has zero slope.

Parallelogram: *a* and *c* have positive slopes and *b* and *d* have zero slopes.

GROUP PROBLEM SOLVING

Suggest that small groups of students work together to find the slope of the auditorium seating in their school or of their school's main staircase. Indicate that the groups will have to present their methods including an explanation of how they measured, estimated, or computed the *y* and *x* values they used. Invite students to present their findings as a Math World break for a local TV program.

Chapter 11 Lesson 13

Overview This lesson introduces students to the slope-intercept form for all linear equations: $y = mx + b$.

Objectives

- To recognize $y = mx + b$ as the slope-intercept form for a linear equation
- To write an equation that describes a line with a given slope and passing through given points

Student Pages 348–351

Teacher's Resource Library **TRL**

Workbook Activity 116

Activity 110

Alternative Activity 110

....

Mathematics Vocabulary

x-intercept
y-intercept
slope-intercept form

---

1 Warm-Up Activity

Point out to students that most of the lines they have graphed have crossed the x-axis at some point. The lines have also crossed the y-axis at some point. Invite students to confirm this by looking back at the graphs of the examples in Lessons 7–12.

2 Teaching the Lesson

Use the graph of $y = 2x + 4$ to introduce students to the terms x-*intercept* and y-*intercept*. Make sure that they understand that the equation $y = 2x + 4$ is in the form $y = mx + b$, where m is the slope of the line and b is the y-intercept, the point at which $x = 0$.

Use Example 1 as a demonstration vehicle. In step 2, ask students to offer a proof that 4 is the y-intercept. (*The y-intercept is the point at which $x = 0$. Substitute $x = 0$ in equation. $y = 0 + 4$*)

---

x-intercept
The point at which a line crosses or intersects the x-axis

y-intercept
The point at which a line crosses or intersects the y-axis

Slope-intercept form
The slope-intercept form of a line in which
$m = slope$ and
$b = y$-intercept is
$y = mx + b$

The graph of $y = 2x + 4$ is shown in this coordinate system.

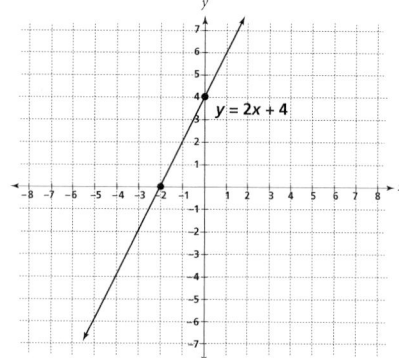

The line has three characteristics: it has slope, a point at which it crosses the x-axis, and a point at which it crosses the y-axis. The point at which a line crosses the x-axis is the **x-intercept** of the line. The point at which a line crosses the y-axis is the **y-intercept** of the line.

The graph of $y = 2x + 4$ can be used to determine that the x-intercept of the line is -2, the y-intercept is 4, and the slope is 2 (the line moves $+2$ units vertically for every $+1$ unit horizontally).

When a graph of a line is not given, it is still possible to determine the slope, x-intercept, and y-intercept of the line if the equation of the line is written in **slope-intercept form.** The slope-intercept form of a line is $y = mx + b$, where $m =$ slope and $b = y$-intercept.

Workbook Activity 116

Activity 110

EXAMPLE 1 Suppose the graph was not given and instead only the equation $y = 2x + 4$ was given. Find the slope, x-intercept, and y-intercept of the line $y = 2x + 4$.

Step 1 Determine the slope. Since $y = 2x + 4$ is written in slope-intercept form, the corresponding value for m is the slope of the line.

$$y = mx + b$$
$$\downarrow \qquad \text{The slope of the line is 2.}$$
$$y = 2x + 4$$

Step 2 Determine the y-intercept. Since $y = 2x + 4$ is written in slope-intercept form, the corresponding value for b is the y-intercept of the line.

$$y = mx + b$$
$$\downarrow \qquad \text{The y-intercept of the line is 4.}$$
$$y = 2x + 4$$

Step 3 To determine the x-intercept of a line written in slope-intercept form, substitute 0 for y in the equation of the line and solve for x.

$$y = 2x + 4$$
$$0 = 2x + 4$$
$$-4 = 2x$$
$$-2 = x \qquad \text{The x-intercept of the line is } -2.$$

To write the equation of a line in slope-intercept form, solve the equation for y.

EXAMPLE 2 Write the equation of the line $3y = 3x - 12$ in slope-intercept form.

Solve the equation for y.
$$3y = 3x - 12$$
$$\frac{3}{3}y = \frac{3}{3}x - \frac{12}{3}$$
$$y = x - 4$$

The slope-intercept form of $3y = 3x - 12$ is $y = x - 4$.

For reinforcement, list or read the following equations for students. Ask them to identify the slope of each as well as the y-intercept.

$$y = x + 2$$
$$(m = 1, \text{y-}intercept = 2)$$

$$y = x + 1$$
$$(m = 1, \text{y-}intercept = 1)$$

$$y = 2x$$
$$(m = 2, \text{y-}intercept = 0)$$

$$y = 2x + 2$$
$$(m = 2, \text{y-}intercept = 2)$$

$$y = -2x + 2$$
$$(m = -2, \text{y-}intercept = 2)$$

$$y = 3x - 3$$
$$(m = 3, \text{y-}intercept = -3)$$

COMMON ERROR

Some students may incorrectly identify an equation such as $3y = 6x + 1$ as an equation of the form $y = mx + b$. Help them avoid this error by stressing that in the general equation, the coefficient of y must equal 1.

Point out to students that they can use their knowledge of algebra to rewrite equations so that they are in the form $y = mx + b$. Tell students that this is the case with Example 3 on page 350. The first step in finding the slope and the y-intercept is to rewrite the equation in the general form.

 3 Reinforce and Extend

LEARNING STYLES

 Interpersonal/Group Learning

Have small groups of students develop a five-question True-or-False quiz. Questions should focus on the relationships between slope, the y-intercepts, and the general equation $y = mx + b$. Students might prepare questions such as "In $y = mx + b$, b gives the value of y when $x = 0$." *(true)* Have the groups answer one another's quiz questions. Students might vote on the best questions and post them for use as study aids.

To find the slope, x-intercept, and y-intercept of a line, first write the equation of the line in slope-intercept form.

EXAMPLE 3 Find the slope, x-intercept, and y-intercept of the line $2y = -4x + 1$.

Step 1 Write the equation of the line in slope-intercept form by solving the equation for y.

$$2y = -4x + 1$$
$$\frac{2}{2}y = \frac{-4}{2}x + \frac{1}{2}$$
$$y = -2x + \frac{1}{2} \quad \text{slope-intercept form}$$

Step 2 Determine the slope. Since $y = -2x + \frac{1}{2}$ is written in slope-intercept form, the corresponding value for m is the slope of the line.

$$\begin{array}{c} y = \quad mx + b \\ \quad\quad \downarrow \\ y = -2x + \frac{1}{2} \end{array} \quad \text{The slope of the line is } -2.$$

Step 3 Determine the y-intercept. Since $y = -2x + \frac{1}{2}$ is written in slope-intercept form, the corresponding value for b is the y-intercept of the line.

$$\begin{array}{c} y = \quad mx + b \\ \quad\quad\quad\quad \downarrow \\ y = -2x + \frac{1}{2} \end{array} \quad \text{The } y\text{-intercept of the line is } \frac{1}{2}.$$

Step 4 Determine the x-intercept. Substitute 0 for y in the equation of the line and solve for x.

$$y = -2x + \frac{1}{2}$$
$$0 = -2x + \frac{1}{2}$$
$$2x = \frac{1}{2}$$
$$x = \frac{1}{4} \quad \text{The } x\text{-intercept of the line is } \frac{1}{4}.$$

Exercise A Identify the slope, x-intercept, and y-intercept of each line.

1.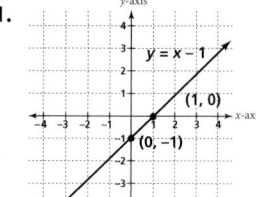

1. slope $= m = 1$
   x-intercept $= 1$
   y-intercept $= -1$

2.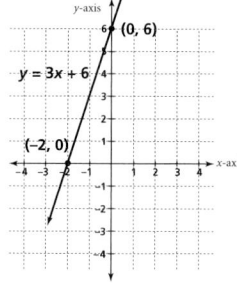

2. slope $= m = 3$
   x-intercept $= -2$
   y-intercept $= 6$

Writing About Mathematics

Describe a line that does not have an x-intercept. Describe a line that does not have a y-intercept.

3. $y = x + 5$
4. $y = x - 2$
5. $y = 2x - 1$
6. $y = 3x + 1$
7. $y = -x - 1$
8. $y = -2x - 2$
9. m 1; x 3; y -3
10. m 2; x -5; y 10
11. m -2; x -2; y -4
12. m -1; x 1; y 1
13. m 1; x -1; y 1
14. m 3; x 2; y -6
15. m 1; x 5; y -5
16. m -3; x 1; y 3
17. m -1; x -1; y -1
18. m 2; x $\frac{1}{4}$; y $\frac{-1}{2}$
19. m $\frac{1}{2}$; x -2; y 1
20. m $\frac{-1}{2}$; x 3; y $1\frac{1}{2}$

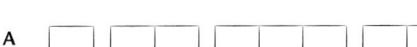

Exercise B Write each of these equations of a line in slope-intercept form.

3. $2y = 2x + 10$

4. $3y = 3x - 6$

5. $-4y = -8x + 4$

6. $-5y = -15x - 5$

7. $-2y = 2x + 2$

8. $-y = 2x + 2$

Exercise C Determine the slope, x-intercept, and y-intercept of each line.

9. $y = x - 3$

10. $y = 2x + 10$

11. $y = -2x - 4$

12. $y = -x + 1$

13. $-3y = -3x - 3$

14. $5y = 15x - 30$

15. $7y = 7x - 35$

16. $-6y = 18x - 18$

17. $-2y = 2x + 2$

18. $2y = 4x - 1$

19. $4y = 2x + 4$

20. $2y = -x + 3$

Build a Model

Use art sticks or toothpicks to make the figures shown. Make the fifth figure for each pattern.

A

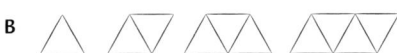

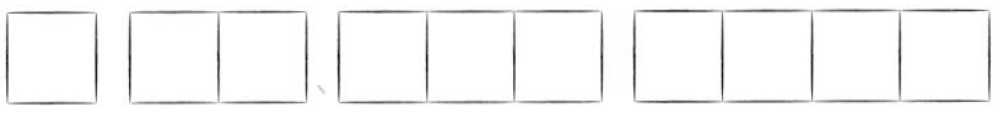

B

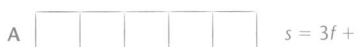

Write an algebraic equation to represent the patterns.

Let f = figure number
s = number of sticks

A $s = 3f + 1$

B $s = 2f + 1$

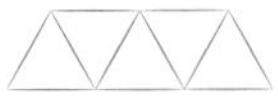

Chapter 11 Application

Overview This lesson provides an application of using graphs to visualize data.

Objective

■ To interpret data on a graph

Student Page 352

Teacher's Resource Library **TRL**

Application Activity 11

Everyday Math 11

1 ⬤ Warm-Up Activity

Explain to students that some patients in hospitals are connected to heart monitors. A heart monitor is a machine that allows doctors and nurses to observe a patient's heartbeat. Each time the heart beats, an electric pulse appears on the monitor. Draw a model of the pulses on a heart monitor, identify the peaks and valleys, and encourage students to interpret the diagram.

2 ⬤ Teaching the Lesson

Review how all graphs have lines (line graphs have a series of points connected as a line, and bar graphs have lines connected to one another to create bars). Review the fact that every time the data change, the line or lines on a graph change direction.

COMMON ERROR

Students attempting to model an object at a complete stop may not bring the line all the way down to the *x*-axis.

COMMON ERROR

The direction of the line on the graph is not dependent on the object's direction (as long as the object is moving forward). A line traveling up from the *x*-axis represents all acceleration.

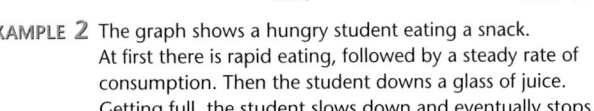

Application

The Story Line Graphs help us visualize data. Behind every graph lies a story. The examples below show two interpretations of the speed/time graph.

EXAMPLE 1 The graph records the workout pace of a jogger. The line first shows the jogger warming up, increasing speed over time. Then the jogger maintains a steady pace for a bit. There is a sprint that is reflected in the sharp incline. After that, the jogger cools down as the speed steadily drops.

EXAMPLE 2 The graph shows a hungry student eating a snack. At first there is rapid eating, followed by a steady rate of consumption. Then the student downs a glass of juice. Getting full, the student slows down and eventually stops.

1. Answers will vary. Possible answer: trai

2. Answers will vary. Possible answer: the temperature warms gradually, and then starts to cool off.

3. Answers will vary.

Exercise Interpret each graph.

1. What type of transportation do you think Graph A represents? Is it more likely to be the ups and downs of an airplane or the stop and go of a train? Explain your thinking.

2. Tell a story about the change/time Graph B. What do you think it represents?

3. Draw a graph of your own. Give it to several classmates to interpret. Keep a list of how many different readings you get.

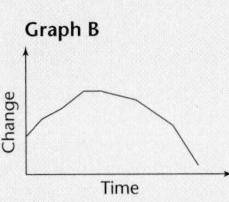

Graph A

Graph B

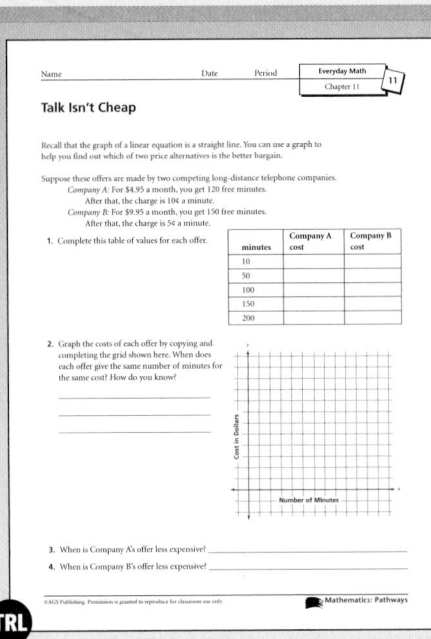

Application Activity 11

Everyday Math 11

Chapter 11 REVIEW

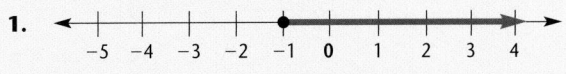

Write the letter of the correct answer.
Identify the solution shown by the number line.

1.

 *(number line from −5 to 4 with a shaded dot at −1 and an arrow to the right)*

A $x \geq -1$ C $x \geq 1$ A

B $x < 1$ D $x = -1$

2. Find the slope of a line that passes through points $(3, -6)$ and $(6, 12)$. D

A 3   C 2

B −6   D 6

3. How would the equation of the line $3y = 3x + 3$ be written in slope-intercept form? B

A $y = 3x$ C $y = x + 3$

B $y = x + 1$ D $y = x - 1$

Number lines to show—

4. a shaded circle at 9

5. an open circle at −4, arrow right

6. a shaded circle at 5, arrow right

Graph each solution on a number line.

Example: Graph the solution $x < -16$ on a number line.
Solution:

(number line from −19 to −11 with an open circle at −16 and an arrow to the left)

4. $n = 9$ **5.** $m > -4$ **6.** $p \geq 5$

7.

$y = x + 1$	
x	y
−2	−1
−1	0
3	4

8.

$y = x - 2$	
x	y
−2	−4
−1	−3
5	3

Graph the equation of each line.

Example: $y = x - 3$

Solution: Complete a table of values and graph the points shown in the completed table.

$y = x - 3$	
x	y
−2	−5
0	−3
2	−1

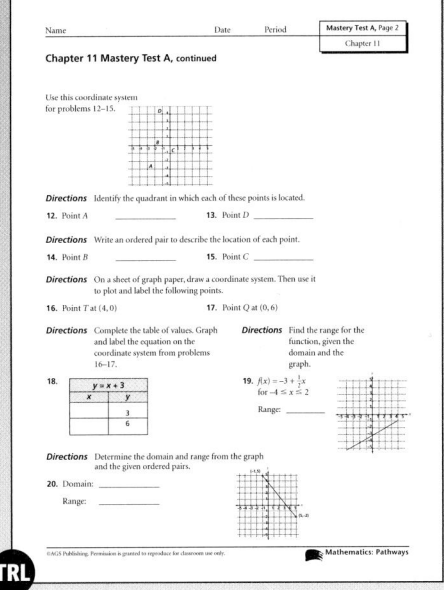

7. $y = x + 1$

8. $y = x - 2$

Lines on student's graphs should match tables of values.

CAREER CONNECTION

Invite students to research occupations that use graphs to visualize data. Encourage students to use the Internet to learn about professionals in these fields.

Chapter 11 Review

Each set of problems in the Chapter Review includes an example and solution to illustrate the concept. Use the given examples for reteaching the materials in Chapter 11. For additional practice, refer to the Supplementary Problems for Chapter 11 (pages 452–453).

Chapter 11 Mastery Test TRL

The Teacher's Resource Library includes parallel forms of the Chapter 11 Mastery Test. The difficulty level of the two forms is equivalent. You may wish to use one form as a pretest and the other form as a posttest.

Chapter 11 Mastery Test A

ALTERNATIVE ASSESSMENT

Alternative Assessment items correlate with student Goals for Learning at the beginning of this chapter.

■ To graph solutions to equalities and inequalities on number lines

Have groups of students create large number lines. They may draw the lines on the floor in chalk or use a large sheet of paper taped to the floor. One group should give an equality or inequality to another group and ask that group to graph it on the number line. Students may display the data by standing in the correct spots on the number line, using manipulatives, and so on. Groups will then change roles. Each group should graph both an equality and an inequality.

■ To identify and graph ordered pairs of values

Direct each student to draw a picture on a coordinate plane. Then have students trade their drawings with partners and identify the coordinates used on their partners' drawings. Students may also trade coordinates and then draw the pictures.

■ To write equations for straight lines as functions

In a bag on your desk, place a set of large cards showing different vertical line graphs. Next, divide the board into two sections. Label the left section, "Function" and the right section, "Not a Function." Choose students to come up one by one and select a card. After examining the graph, the student should place the card under the correct heading and explain why the graph is or is not a function. The rest of the class can participate by explaining why the graph was categorized correctly or, if they disagree, by explaining why they think the graph should be placed in the other category.

■ To identify the domain and range of functions

Ask each student to write the steps used to determine the domain and range of functions, given the graph and ordered pairs. Students should

Solve each inequality for the variable. Then graph and check each solution.

Example: $h - 1 > 0$ for h Solution: $h - 1 > 0 = h > 1$

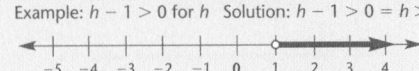

9. $b - 2 \geq -3$ $b \geq -1$

10. $5 + m < 6$ $m < 1$

Number lines to s

9. a shaded cir
   -1, arrow ri

10. a open circle
    arrow left

Is the graph an example of a function?

Example:

Solution: It is not a function because more than one y-value exists for each x-value.

11.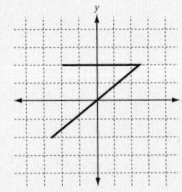

No

Evaluate each function two times.   Use $x = -3$ and 2.

Example: Use $x = -2$ and 1 for $f(x) = 2x + 1$

Solution: $f(-2) = 2(-2) + 1 = -4 + 1 = -3$
$f(1) = 2(1) + 1 = 2 + 1 = 3$

12. $f(x) = 3x - 1.5$

13. $f(x) = -x^2 + x + 9$

12. $f(-3) = -10.5$
    $f(2) = 4.5$

13. $f(-3) = -3$
    $f(2) = 7$

Determine the range for each function with the given domain.

Example: $f(x) = x + x^2$
domain: $-3, -2, 1, 4, 7$

Solution: $f(-3) = -3 + -3^2 = 6$
$f(-2) = -2 + -2^2 = 2$
$f(1) = 1 + 1^2 = 2$
$f(4) = 4 + 4^2 = 20$
$f(7) + 7 + 7^2 = 56$
Range: 2, 2, 6, 20, 56

14. $f(x) = -3x^2 - 3$
domain: $-6, -2, 3, 5, 100$

Range: $-111, -15,$
$-30, -78,$
$-30,003$

Determine the range for the function, given the domain and the graph.

Example: $f(x) = x + 3$ for $-2 \leq x \leq 3$
Solution: $f(-2) = -2 + 3 = 1$
$f(3) = 3 + 3 = 6$
Range: $1 \leq y \leq 6$

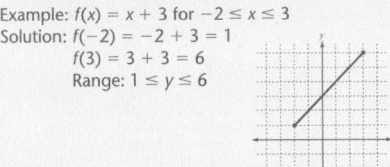

15. $f(x) = x - 2$ for $-1 \leq x \leq 5$

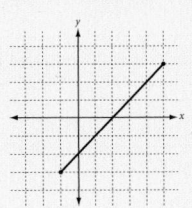

Range: $-3 \leq y \leq 3$

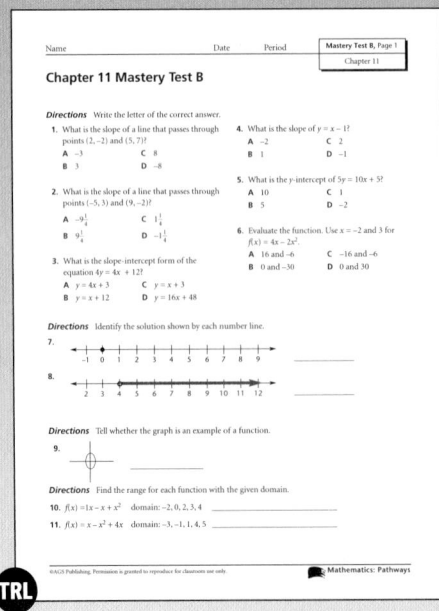

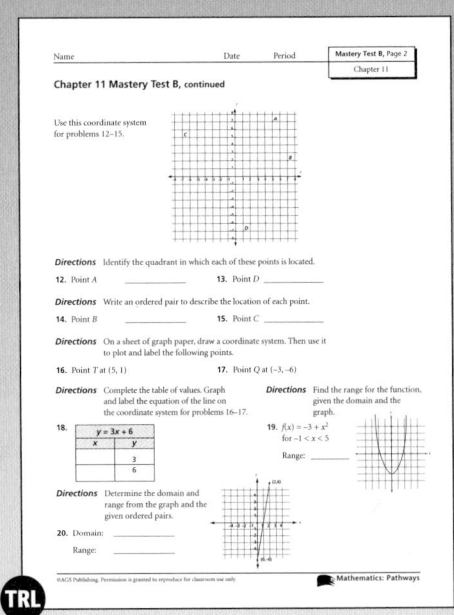

Chapter 11 Mastery Test B

Determine the domain and the range from the graph and the given ordered pairs.

Example: 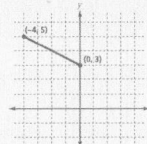   Solution: Domain: $-4 \le x \le 0$ **16.**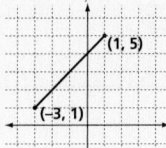
Range: $3 \le y \le 5$

Domain: $-3 \le x \le 1$
Range: $1 \le y \le 5$

Use this coordinate system for problems 17–22.

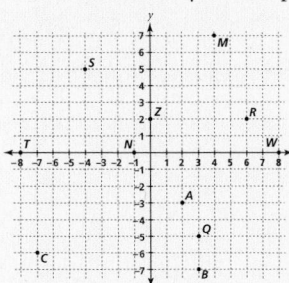

Identify the quadrant in which each of these points is located.

Example: Point M
Solution: Since Point M is located 4 units to the right of the y-axis and 7 units above the x-axis, the point is located in Quadrant I.

17. Point B   **18.** Point C   **19.** Point R

Quadrant IV   Quadrant III   Quadrant I

Write an ordered pair to describe the location of each point.

Example: Point A Solution: (2, −3)

20. Point B $(3, -7)$ **21.** Point S $(-4, 5)$ **22.** Point C $(-7, -6)$

On a sheet of graph paper, draw a coordinate system like the one above. Then use it to plot and label the following points.

Example: Point Q (3, −5)   Solution: The graph of Point Q above.

23. Point D $(-1, -2)$ **24.** Point Y $(0, 5)$ **25.** Point V $(-7, 7)$

See Teacher's Edition page for answers to problems 23–25.

Test-Taking Tip

To keep the inequality symbols ($<$ and $>$) straight, remember that the larger number is always at the open end. Use a simple expression as a reminder: $5 < 7$.

**Answers to Problems 23–25
in the Chapter Review**

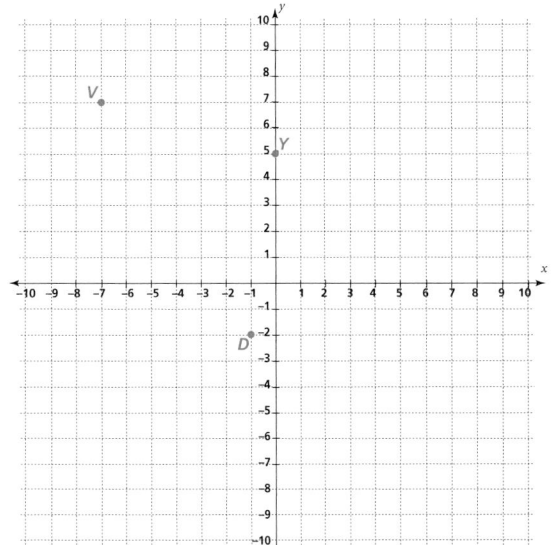

share their steps with partners and modify as needed. Each pair should share with one other pair and create one list. All of the students should work together to combine each group's list into one document, which will be posted in the classroom for future reference.

■ **To determine and graph points of a linear equation**
Organize the class in two groups. On the board or overhead, draw two coordinate planes and two tables of value. Put an X on each plane, and enter a linear equation and the first x- and y-values into each table of values. Have groups take turns choosing x- and y-values for their tables and using the linear equation to plot the points on their coordinate planes. Continue until one group can draw a straight line from the first ordered pair to the X.

■ **To identify the slope of a line**
Organize students in groups of four, and give each student a paper containing a coordinate plane. One student from each group will choose the height and length of an incline. The second student will determine the slope, the third student will check the answer, and the fourth student will draw a line representing a positive, negative, or zero slope on the plane. Calculators may be used if necessary. Students will then change roles and continue.

■ **To determine the values of slope, the y-intercept, and the x-intercept**
Organize the class in two groups. On the board or overhead, draw two coordinate planes. Depending on the ability of students, the equation may be written in slope-intercept form. One student from each group will then draw a line on the group's coordinate plane that displays the correct slope, x-intercept, and y-intercept.

Chapter 12

Planning Guide

Geometry

Lesson		Student Pages	Vocabulary	Practice Exercises	Problem Solving	Try This	Solutions Key
		Student Text Lesson					
1	Angles and Angle Measures	358–359	✔	✔			✔
2	Identifying and Classifying Angles	360–361	✔	✔			✔
3	Complementary and Supplementary Angles	362–365	✔	✔		365	✔
4	Angle Measure in a Triangle	366–369	✔	✔	369		✔
5	Naming Triangles	370–371	✔	✔			✔
6	Congruent Triangles	372–373	✔	✔			✔
7	Similar Triangles	374–375	✔	✔			✔
8	Parallelograms	376–377		✔	377		✔
9	Quadrilaterals and Diagonals	378–379	✔	✔			✔
10	Polygons and Diagonals	380–381		✔			✔
11	Reflections in the Coordinate Plane	382–385	✔	✔			✔
12	Special Reflections: Symmetries	386–387	✔	✔		387	✔
13	Slides and Translations	388–389	✔	✔			✔
14	Rotations	390–393	✔	✔			✔
Application	Plane Cover-Up	394		✔			✔

Chapter Activities

Teacher's Resource Library

Estimation Exercise 12: Estimating the Measure of Acute Angles

Application Activity 12: Plane Cover-Up

Everyday Math 12: Tangram Teasers

Community Connection 12: Similar or Congruent

Teacher's Edition

Chapter 12 Project

Assessment Options

Student Text

Chapter 12 Review

Teacher's Resource Library

Chapter 12 Mastery Tests A and B

Teacher's Edition

Chapter 12 Alternative Assessments

Student Text Features						Teaching Strategies									Learning Styles						Teacher's Resource Library			
Estimation Activity	Math in Your Life	Technology Connection	Writing About Mathematics	Build a Model	Calculator Practice	Online Connection	Common Error	Applications Home, Career, Community	Mental Math	Manipulatives	Calculator	Group Problem Solving	Modeling	Knowing Your Students	Auditory/Verbal	Visual/Spatial	Logical/Mathematical	Body/Kinesthetic	Interpersonal/Group Learning	LEP/ESL	Activities	Alternate Activities	Workbook Activities	Self-Study Guide
			359															359	359		111	111	117	✔
							361									361					112	112	118	✔
365			364				364								365			363		363	113	113	119	✔
		367						368	368							367	369				114	114	120	✔
	371		371						371									371		371	115	115	121	✔
						373	373												373		116	116	122	✔
							375									375					117	117	123	✔
												377	377		377						118	118	124	✔
				379							379				379						119	119	125	✔
		381				381		381												381	120	120	126	✔
								384						385			383				121	121	127–128	✔
								387		387						387					122	122	129	✔
			389																	389	123	123	130	✔
			393	393			391	393	392						391						124	124	131	✔
							395																	✔

Software Options

Skill Track Software

Use the Skill Track Software for *Mathematics: Pathways* for additional reinforcement of this chapter. The software provides multiple-choice assessment items for students to access by computer.

Solutions Key

Use the Solutions Key with this chapter to help students who may need additional assistance. The Solutions Key CD provides solutions for every exercise in the student edition.

Other Resources

Alternative Activities

The Teacher's Resource Library (TRL) contains a set of worksheets written at a second-grade reading level called Alternative Activities. They cover the same content as the regular Activities.

Manipulatives

See the Manipulative activities in this chapter for hands-on modeling of the content.

Yardstick, rulers

Chapter at a Glance

Chapter 12: Geometry
pages 356–397

Lessons

Skill Track for Mathematics: Pathways

Teacher's Resource Library TRL

(Answer Keys for the Teacher's Resource Library begin on page 528 of this Teacher's Edition.)

Name Date Period | Estimation Exercise Chapter 12 | 12

Estimating the Measure of Acute Angles

EXAMPLE You know that an acute angle is an angle with a measure greater than 0° and less than 90°.

You recognize a 90° angle. It is also called a right angle.

You can learn to estimate acute angles.

A 45° angle is an acute angle. It is half of a right angle.

If you divide both of those 45° in half, you'll get four equal angles with measures of $22\frac{1}{2}$°.

You can use those four angles to estimate the measure of all acute angles.

Here are some questions you can ask to help you estimate the measure of an acute angle:

Is the angle smaller than half of 90°?
If YES, the angle will measure less than 45°.
If NO, the angle will measure more than 45°.

Is the angle closer to 90° than it is to 45°?
If YES, the angle will be more than $67\frac{1}{2}$°.
If NO, it will be less than $67\frac{1}{2}$°.

Is the angle closer to 0° than it is to 45°?
If YES, the angle will be less than $22\frac{1}{2}$°.
If NO, it will be more than $22\frac{1}{2}$°.

Directions Estimate the measurements of the following angles.

1. Estimate: ______
2. Estimate: ______
3. Estimate: ______
4. Estimate: ______
5. Estimate: ______

 Mathematics: Pathways

TRL

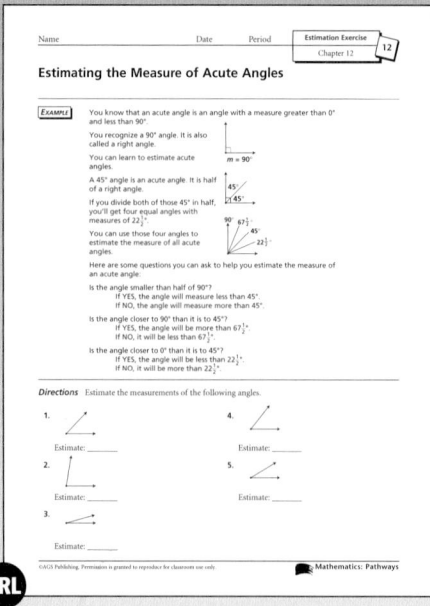

Estimation Exercise 12

Name Date Period | Community Connection Chapter 12 | 12

Similar or Congruent

The properties of similar and congruent are not confined to triangles and polygons in textbooks. There are everyday instances in which you rely on two objects being similar or congruent. For instance, when you take photographs in for enlargement, you expect the new and old photos to be similar, that is, they will be the same shape, but different sizes. On the other hand, when you use the copy machine, you expect the copy and the original to be congruent, the same size and shape.

Find examples of similar and congruent items in your home or school. Record your observations in this chart. Two entries have been completed for you. After you complete the chart, share your findings with your classmates.

Similar	Congruent
Streets on a street map are similar to actual streets.	Several birdhouses made from kits are congruent, the same size and shape.

 Mathematics: Pathways

TRL

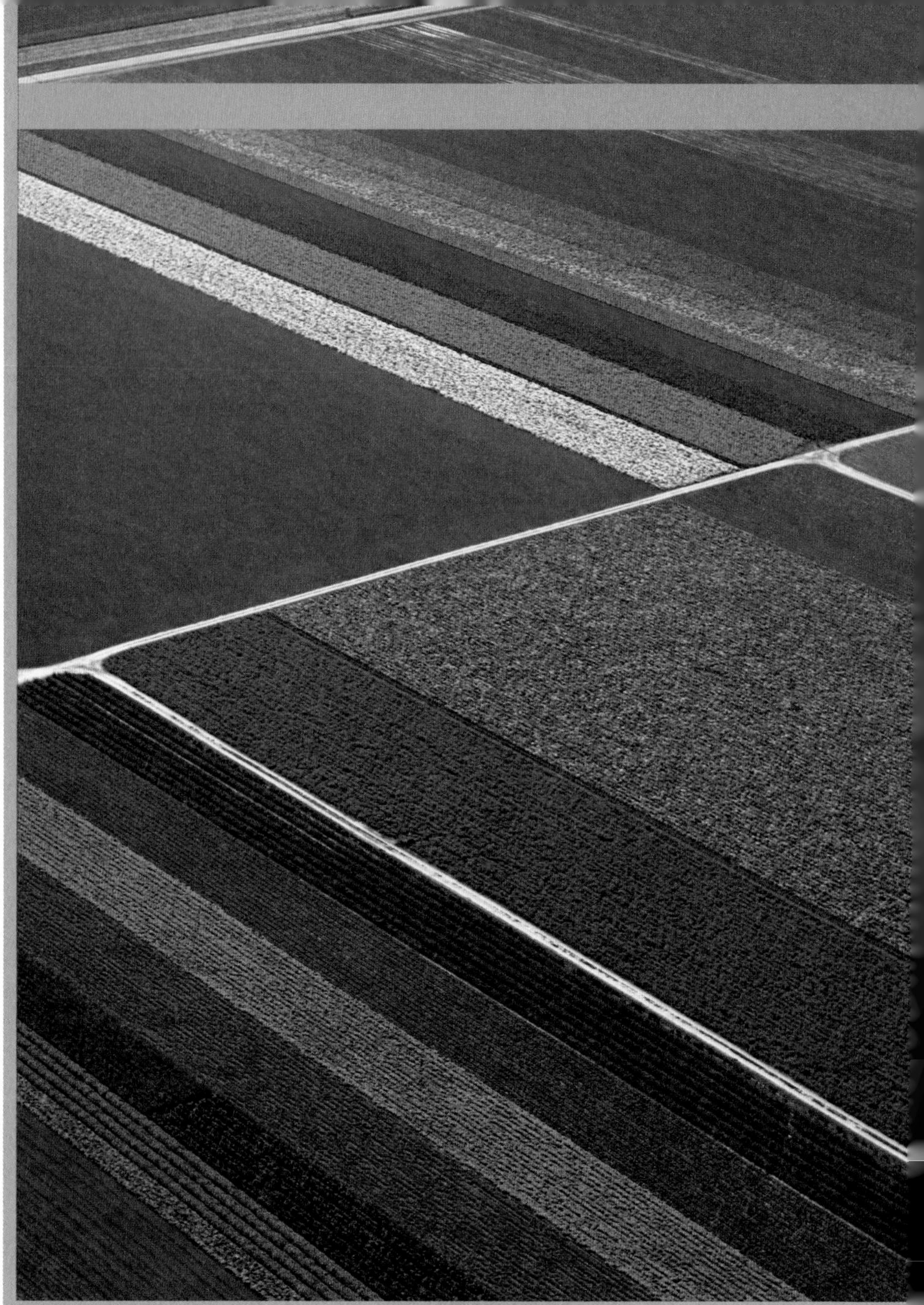

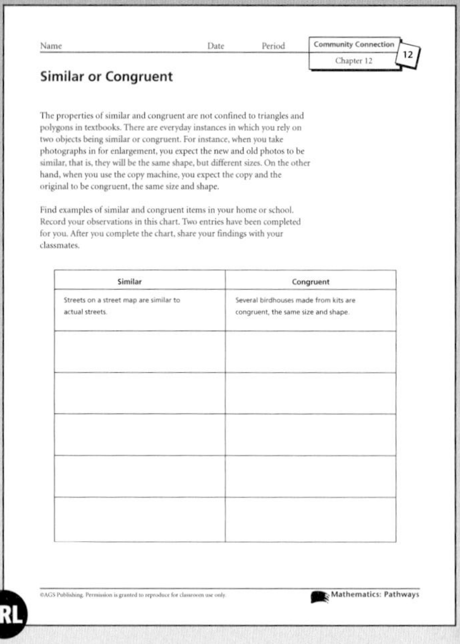

Community Connection 12

12 Geometry

N otice the geometric shapes and angles in this eagle-eye view of flower fields and the roads between them. The different areas are seen as narrow and wide rectangular shapes and lines. Farmers use photos like this to help them manage large pieces of land.

The study of points, lines, angles, surfaces, and solids is the basis of geometry. The understanding of this subject has made it possible for us to build tall buildings. It lets us model the spiral structure of DNA and fly to the Moon and back.

In Chapter 12, you will use geometry to learn about polygons.

Goals for Learning

◆ To measure and classify angles
◆ To name and classify triangles
◆ To find the measures of angles in triangles
◆ To identify quadrilaterals
◆ To determine the number of degrees in polygons
◆ To identify reflections across a line of symmetry
◆ To identify lines of symmetry and symmetric shapes
◆ To carry out slides and translations in the plane
◆ To carry out and identify rotations in the plane

357

Introducing the Chapter

Use the introductory picture to make students aware that geometry is all around them—in the yards in which they play, in the buildings in which they live, in the products they buy, even in the structures created by nature. Have students identify and list geometric shapes and figures they find within their field of vision. In the chapter, they will learn names and ways of measuring these shapes.

CHAPTER PROJECT

Divide the class into teams of "teachers." For each lesson in the chapter, a team is to create visual aids, such as models, charts, posters, or drawings, and write a clear, simple explanation of the main terms and ideas. These materials should be aimed at students at least two years younger. Suggest possible "building" materials for models of angles, triangles, and polygons: toothpicks and small gumdrops, pasta and glue, cardboard and markers, and so on. If possible, arrange for students to teach their lessons to younger students during the chapter study.

TEACHER'S RESOURCE

The AGS Publishing Teaching Strategies in Math Transparencies may be used with this chapter. They add an interactive dimension to expand and enhance the program content.

CAREER INTEREST INVENTORY

The AGS Publishing Harrington-O'Shea Career Decision-Making System-Revised (CDM) may be used with this chapter. Students can use the CDM to explore their interests and identify careers. The CDM defines career areas that are indicated by students' responses on the inventory.

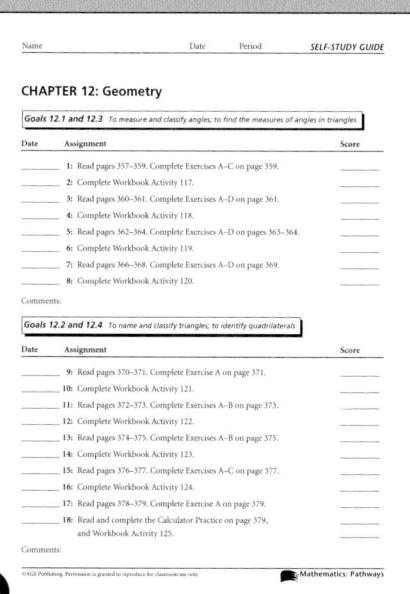

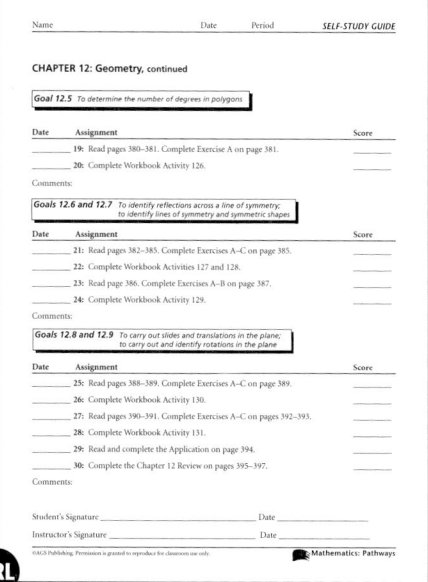

Chapter 12 Self-Study Guide

Lesson at a Glance

Chapter 12 Lesson 1

Overview This lesson defines angles and their parts and explains the use of a protractor to measure angles.

Objectives

- To identify angles by their labeled rays and endpoint
- To use a protractor to measure angles

Student Pages 358–359

Teacher's Resource Library (TRL)

Workbook Activity 117

Activity 111

Alternative Activity 111

....

Mathematics Vocabulary

intersection
ray
vertex
protractor

....

1 Warm-Up Activity

Let students demonstrate what they already know about angles by drawing angles on the board, identifying angles in the classroom, and explaining what makes up an angle. Draw intersecting lines on the board and ask, "What must happen for an angle to form?" (*Lines must intersect.*) Ask students to read to find out the parts of an angle and how to name and measure angles.

2 Teaching the Lesson

Make sure that students understand that the ray indicated by a line with an arrow extends forever in the direction of the arrow. Line segments, which have a definite length, are used to construct geometric shapes.

Describe the organization of a protractor and demonstrate its use. Have students use a straightedge and a pencil to construct an angle and then measure it using a protractor.

Intersection
A point at which two or more lines cross in a figure

Ray
Part of a line—a ray has one endpoint and extends indefinitely in one direction

Vertex
A common point to both sides of an angle

Protractor
A tool used to draw or measure angles

In geometry, you study the size, shape, and position of objects. One way to make that study easier is to concentrate on the outline of a figure, looking closely at the lines, angles, and **intersections** that make up the figure. Two of the most important geometric forms are **rays** and angles. Two rays form an angle, and their shared endpoint is called a **vertex.**

The symbol ∠ is used to show an angle. Any angle can be named in two ways. An angle is sometimes named by one letter or number.

 ∠1 and ∠2   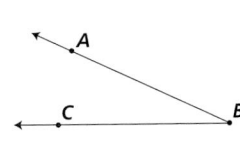 ∠a and∠b

Recall that an angle is a figure made up of two sides, or rays, with a common endpoint.

The angle at the right can be named ∠*ABC* or ∠*CBA*. Each name has the letter *B*, the letter at the vertex, as the middle letter.

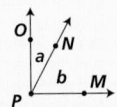

EXAMPLE 1 Name ∠*a* in two other ways.

Point *P* is the vertex of ∠*a*, so *P* must be the middle letter of the angle name. The angle has sides *OP* and *PN*. The angle can be named ∠*OPN* or ∠*NPO*.

A **protractor** is used to measure an angle in degrees. The basic unit of angle measure (m) is the degree (°).

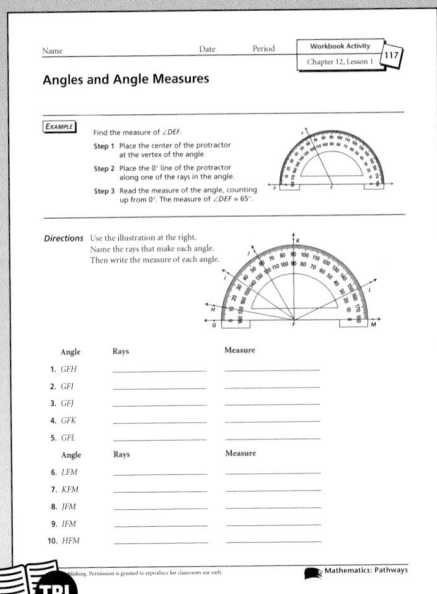

Workbook Activity 117

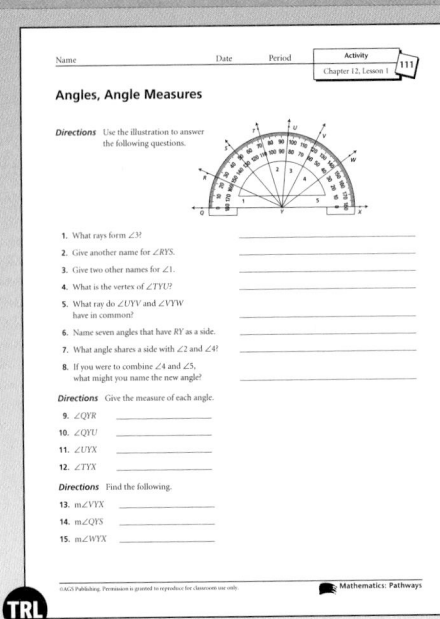

Activity 111

EXAMPLE 2 What is the measure, m, of ∠XRT?

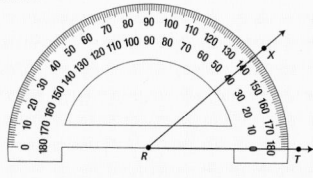

Step 1 Place the center point of the protractor at the vertex of the angle.

Step 2 Place the 0° line of the protractor along one side of the angle.

Step 3 Read the measure of the angle shown by the second side of the angle, m∠XRT = 40°

Exercise A Use the illustration to answer the following questions.

1. ∠XPA, ∠APX

2. P

3. ∠3, ∠GPF

4. ∠EPF

5. $\overrightarrow{PD}$ and $\overrightarrow{PE}$

6. ∠CPB, ∠CPA, ∠CPX, ∠CPD, ∠CPE, ∠CPF, ∠CPG, ∠CPY

1. Give two other names for ∠1.

2. What is the vertex of ∠2?

3. What are two other names for ∠FPG?

4. What angle shares a side with both ∠2 and ∠3?

5. What rays form ∠2?

6. Name eight angles that have CP as a side.

Writing About Mathematics

Write directions telling how to find the measure of ∠2 in the illustration for the Exercises.

Exercise B Give the measure of each angle.

7. ∠DPY   90°   **10.** ∠FPX   140°

8. ∠DPX   90°   **11.** ∠XPA   35°

9. ∠FPY   40°   **12.** ∠APY   145°

Exercise C Find the following.

13. m∠CPY   110°   **14.** m∠CPX   70°   **15.** m∠EPY   60°

Lesson at a Glance

Chapter 12 Lesson 2

Overview This lesson explains the relationships of angles based on their positions and classifies angles according to their measures.

Objectives

- To identify angles formed by intersecting lines as adjacent or vertical
- To classify angles as acute, right, obtuse, or straight

Student Pages 360–361

Teacher's Resource Library

Workbook Activity 118

Activity 112

Alternative Activity 112

Mathematics Vocabulary

adjacent angles
vertical angles
acute
obtuse

---

1 ⚡ Warm-Up Activity

Draw a right angle and a straight angle on the board and have students describe them as angles. Review right angles, if necessary, and relate the straight angle to "two right angles added together." Ask, "How can you use these two angles as a standard to divide any angles into similar groups?" *(Any angle could be greater than, equal to, or less than each standard.)* In the lesson, students will classify angles according to their characteristics.

2 ⚡ Teaching the Lesson

Have students look up *adjacent* in a dictionary. Recognizing that the word means "next to" should help them identify adjacent angles. An alternative explanation of the equality of vertical angles is to have students picture them as mirror images, or exact opposites. To assess students' understanding of vertical and adjacent angles, have them explain what elements are shared by a pair of each type of angle.

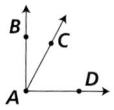

Adjacent angles

Two angles that have the same vertex and one side in common

Vertical angles

Pairs of opposite angles formed by intersecting lines—vertical angles have the same measure

Acute

An angle less than 90 degrees

Obtuse

An angle with a measure between 90 and 180 degrees

The symbol □ is sometimes used to show a right angle.

You can identify some angles by their position relative to other angles. Angles that share a common vertex and a common side are called **adjacent angles.**

∠BAC and ∠DAC are adjacent.

Vertical angles are opposite pairs of angles formed by the intersection of two lines. Vertical angles have the same measure.

∠a and ∠b are vertical angles.

You can classify an angle using its measure.

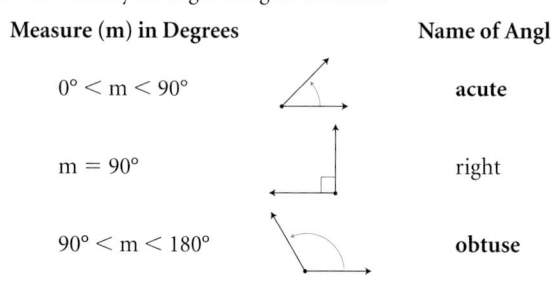

Measure (m) in Degrees		Name of Angle
0° < m < 90°		**acute**
m = 90°		right
90° < m < 180°		**obtuse**
m = 180°		straight

EXAMPLE 1 Name two angles adjacent to ∠APB. Tell what kind of angle each is.

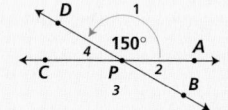

Step 1 To be adjacent, the angle must share the vertex, P. It must also share a common side. ∠APD and ∠BPC are each adjacent to ∠APB.

Step 2 m∠APD is greater than 90° but less than 180°, so m∠APD is an obtuse angle.

Step 3 ∠APD and ∠BPC form a pair of vertical angles, so m∠APD = m∠BPC. Therefore, ∠BPC must also be an obtuse angle.

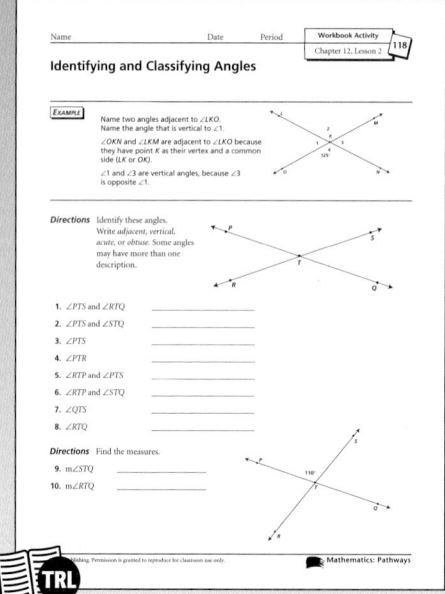

Workbook Activity 118

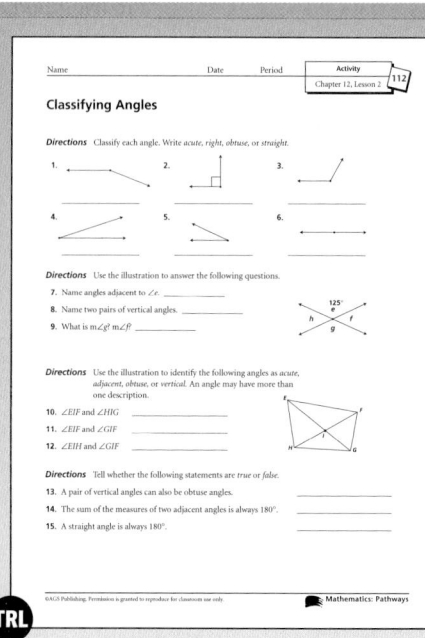

Activity 112

The measure of a straight line is 180°.

EXAMPLE 2 Give two names for the angle vertical to ∠2 in Example 1 on page 360. Tell what kind of angle it is.

Step 1 The angle opposite to ∠2 will be the vertical angle. ∠4 is opposite ∠2, so it is the vertical angle. ∠4 can also be named ∠CPD or ∠DPC.

Step 2 m∠4 is less than 90°, so ∠4 is an acute angle.

Exercise A Classify each angle. Write *acute, right, obtuse,* or *straight.*

1.  right

2. 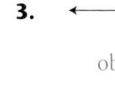 acute

3. obtuse

4. 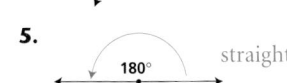 acute 78°

5. 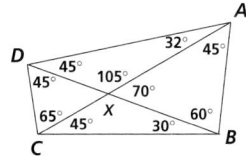 180° straight

Exercise B Use this illustration to answer the following questions.

6. Name any angles adjacent to ∠a.   *d, b*

7. Name any pairs of vertical angles.   *a, c; b, d*

8. What is m∠a? m∠b?   140°, 40°

9. What is m∠c? m∠d? Explain.   140°, 40°; Vertical angles have the same measure, so m∠a = m∠c and m∠b = m∠d.

a, 140°
d
b
c

Exercise C Identify these angles. Write *vertical* or *adjacent, acute, right, obtuse,* or *straight.* An angle may have more than one description.

10. ∠AXB and ∠DXC   vertical, acute

11. ∠DXC and ∠AXD   adjacent, one acute and one obtuse

12. ∠BXC and ∠AXD   vertical, both obtuse

Exercise D Tell whether the following statements are *true* or *false.*

13. A pair of vertical angles can also be acute angles.   true

14. The sum of the measures of two obtuse angles is always greater than 180°.   true

15. The sum of the measures of a right angle and a straight angle is 270°.   true

LEARNING STYLES

Visual/Spatial
Provide magazines and have students locate angles and label them as acute, right, or obtuse. To identify angles, students may check them using the corner of an index card as a right angle. If the angle extends beyond the edge of the card, it is larger than 90 degrees and must be obtuse. If it falls within, it must be acute.

MENTAL MATH

Reproduce the figure from Exercise C on the board or overhead. Use a pointer to trace each angle and have students identify it as acute, right, obtuse, or straight. Continue until students are confident in their ability to categorize angles.

Lesson at a Glance

Chapter 12 Lesson 3

Overview This lesson defines and models pairs of angles that are complementary and supplementary.

Objectives

- To identify complementary and supplementary angles
- To calculate the measure of one complementary angle, given the measure of the other
- To calculate the measure of one supplementary angle, given the measure of the other

Student Pages 362–365

Teacher's Resource Library **TRL**

Workbook Activity 119

Activity 113

Alternative Activity 113

....

Mathematics Vocabulary

complementary angles
supplementary angles

....

1 Warm-Up Activity

Explain that some angles are related to each other by the shape they make when they are joined together. On the overhead, join complementary angles and ask, "What new angle is formed?" *(a right angle)* Model supplementary angles in the same way. *(a straight angle)* Have students turn to page 362 and find out what these special pairs of angles are called and how their relationships can be used to solve problems.

2 Teaching the Lesson

Make sure that students can distinguish between the words *complementary* and *complimentary*. (A complement is an amount needed to complete or perfect.) To help students associate *complementary* with 90-degree pairs and *supplementary* with 180-degree pairs, point out that *c* comes before *s*, and 90 comes before 180. Thus, *complementary* = 90, and *supplementary* = 180.

> **Complementary angles**
> Two angles whose sum of their measures is 90 degrees
>
> **Supplementary angles**
> Two angles whose sum of their measures is 180 degrees

Some pairs of angles are related by their measures. If the sum of the measures of two angles is 90°, the angles are **complementary angles.** Angles do not have to be adjacent to be complementary.

Examples of Complementary Angles

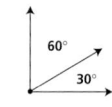 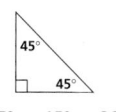 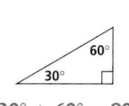

$60° + 30° = 90°$ $45° + 45° = 90°$ $30° + 60° = 90°$

EXAMPLE 1 Angles *a* and *b* are complementary. $m\angle b = 37°$. What is the $m\angle a$?

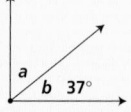

Step 1 The sum of the measures of complementary angles is 90°. Write an equation for the sum of the measures of $\angle a$ and $\angle b$.

$m\angle a + 37° = 90°$

Step 2 Solve the equation for $m\angle a$.

$m\angle a + 37° = 90°$

$m\angle a = 90° - 37°$

$m\angle a = 53°$

Step 3 Check. $53° + 37° = 90°$

If the sum of the measures of two angles is 180°, the angles are **supplementary angles.** Angles do not have to be adjacent to be supplementary.

Examples of Supplementary Angles

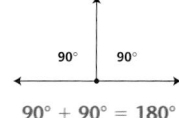 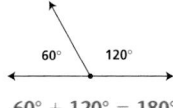 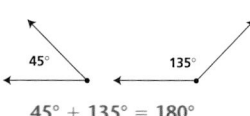

$90° + 90° = 180°$ $60° + 120° = 180°$ $45° + 135° = 180°$

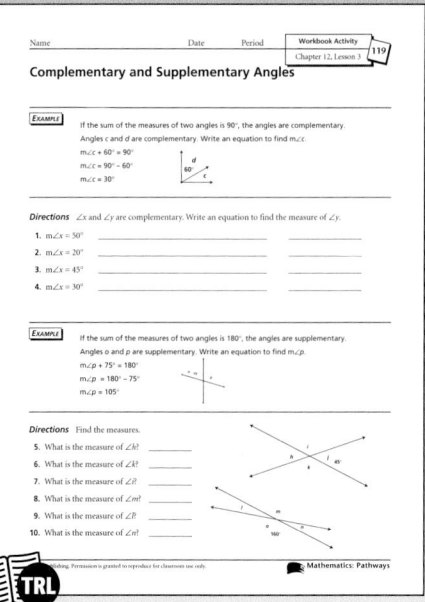

Workbook Activity 119

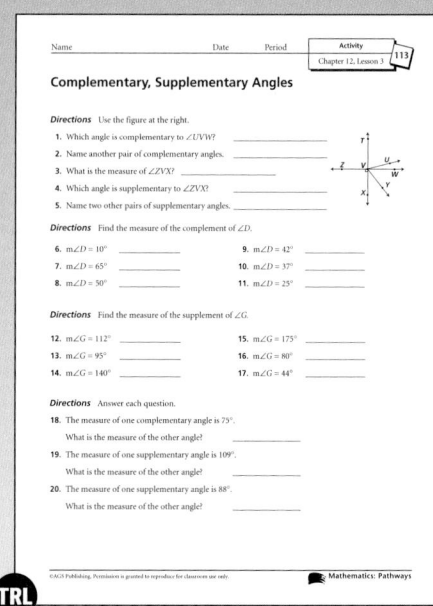

Activity 113

EXAMPLE 2 Angles *a* and *b* are supplementary angles. m∠*b* is two times greater than m∠*a*. What is the measure of each angle?

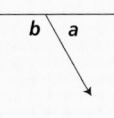

Step 1 The sum of the measures of supplementary angles is 180°. Write an equation for the sum of the measures of ∠*a* and ∠*b*. Let m∠*b* = 2m∠*a*.

m∠*a* + 2m∠*a* = 180°

Step 2 Solve the equation for m∠*a*.

m∠*a* + 2m∠*a* = 180°
3m∠*a* = 180°
m∠*a* = 180° ÷ 3
m∠*a* = 60°

Since m∠*b* = 2m∠*a*, m∠*b* = 2(60°) = 120°.

Step 3 Check. 60° + 120° = 180°

EXAMPLE 3 The measure of ∠*a* = 30°. What is m∠*b*? m∠*c*? m∠*d*?

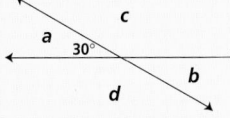

Step 1 Find the measure of ∠*c*. Note that ∠*a* and ∠*c* are adjacent and supplementary angles. The sum of the measures of supplementary angles is 180°.

m∠*a* + m∠*c* = 180°
30° + m∠*c* = 180°
m∠*c* = 180° − 30°
m∠*c* = 150°

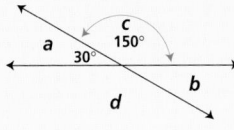

(continued)

To emphasize the fact that complements and supplements do not have to be adjacent, copy the example triangles on page 362 onto notebook paper, cut out their acute points, and line them up to show that they form a right angle.

As the class works through the examples on pages 362–364, point out the algebraic equations that are set up to find the unknown angles' measures.

3 Reinforce and Extend

LEARNING STYLES

LEP/ESL

Students will need to be comfortably familiar with the terms and definitions in Lessons 2 and 3. Make flash cards using index cards. On the front, write the term in bold letters. Above it, draw an example illustration. On the back, provide simple definitions. Have students work in pairs, showing the front of each card to a partner, who explains its meaning using the illustration.

LEARNING STYLES

Body/Kinesthetic

Draw several pairs of supplementary and complementary angles on paper and cut them out. Have students sort through the angles independently, pairing them and checking the total measure of each pair, until all angles have been paired as complements or supplements. Then students can measure each angle using a protractor to confirm their choices.

CALCULATOR

Have students use a calculator to determine the measure of an angle's complement or supplement.

To find the complement of an angle whose measure is 33 degrees,

Press 90 $-$ 33 $=$.

The display reads 57.

To find the supplement of the same angle,

Press 180 $-$ 33 $=$.

The display reads 147.

To check their answers, have students add the angle measures using their calculators.

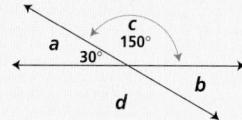

Writing About Mathematics

Tell how you could use the fact that vertical angles are equal to find the measures of the angles in the figure shown in the example to the right.

EXAMPLE 3 *(continued)*

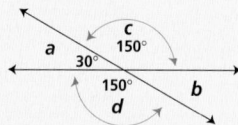

Step 2 Find the measure of ∠d. Note that ∠a and ∠d are adjacent and supplementary angles.

$$m\angle a + m\angle d = 180°$$
$$30° + m\angle d = 180°$$
$$m\angle d = 180° - 30°$$
$$m\angle d = 150°$$

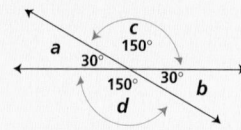

Step 3 Find the measure of ∠b. Note that ∠b and ∠d are adjacent and supplementary angles.

$$m\angle b + m\angle d = 180°$$
$$m\angle b + 150° = 180°$$
$$m\angle b = 180° - 150°$$
$$m\angle b = 30°$$

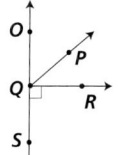

Exercise A Use the figure at the right.

1. ∠OQP and ∠PQR

2. ∠OQR and ∠SQR or ∠OQP and ∠PQS

3. ∠PQR and ∠RQS

1. Which angles are complementary?

2. Which angles are supplementary?

3. Which angles are adjacent but neither complementary nor supplementary?

Exercise B Find the measure of the complement of ∠X.

4. m∠X = 45°	45°	**7.** m∠X = 55°	35°
5. m∠X = 20°	70°	**8.** m∠X = 75°	15°
6. m∠X = 30°	60°	**9.** m∠X = 80°	10°

Exercise C Find the measure of the supplement of ∠Y.

10. m∠Y = 20°	160°	**13.** m∠Y = 150°	30°
11. m∠Y = 105°	75°	**14.** m∠Y = 135°	45°
12. m∠Y = 90°	90°	**15.** m∠Y = 120°	60°

Exercise D Answer each question.

16. The measure of one supplementary angle is 120°. What is the measure of the other angle? 60°

17. The measure of one complementary angle is 22°. What is the measure of the other angle? 68°

18. The measure of one supplementary angle is 100°. What is the measure of the other angle? 80°

19. The measure of one supplementary angle is 3 times greater than the measure of the other angle. What is the measure of each angle? 45°, 135°

20. The measure of one complementary angle is 3 times greater than the measure of the other angle. What is the measure of each angle? 22.5°, 67.5°

Estimation Activity

Estimate: Estimate the measure of the angle at the right.
Solution: Think of a circle and a 90° angle over the given angle. The length of the arc between the sides of the angle is about $\frac{1}{2}$ of the 90° arc. So the angle is about $\frac{1}{2}$ of 90° or about 45°.

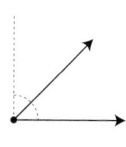

Try This

Remind students that supplements, when joined, form a straight angle. Place a right angle on top of a straight angle for visual clues. Have students complete a written proof as well as diagrams showing the pairing of two right angles.

LEARNING STYLES

Auditory/Verbal

Have students construct the angles for Exercise D on the board. Then have them explain how they found the answers by using their diagrams and equations. Repeat the process for these additional problems:

A pair of supplementary angles is 85 degrees and _____ degrees. *(95)*

A pair of complementary angles is 25 degrees and _____ degrees. *(65)*

Find the measures of the supplementary angles *a* and *3a*.

($a + 3a = 180$; $4a = 180$; $a = \frac{180}{4}$; $a = 45$; $3a = 135$)

Lesson at a Glance

Chapter 12 Lesson 4

Overview This lesson discusses the relationships of the angles within a triangle and among the angles formed by extending the sides at the vertexes.

Objectives

■ To demonstrate that the sum of the measures of the angles in a triangle is 180 degrees

■ To demonstrate that an exterior angle is supplementary to the adjacent interior angle of a triangle

■ To calculate the measures of angles inside and outside a triangle

Student Pages 366–369

Teacher's Resource Library **TRL**

Workbook Activity 120

Activity 114

Alternative Activity 114

....

Mathematics Vocabulary

exterior angle
interior angle

....

1 Warm-Up Activity

Draw a triangle on the board and ask students to identify its angles. Then extend the lines used to form the triangle and have volunteers point out the angles formed outside the triangle. Ask them to identify all vertical angles they see and recall a true statement about vertical angles. *(There are six pairs; they are opposite and equal in measure.)* Then have volunteers point out adjacent angles in the figure and observe something that is true for all of them. *(All pairs of adjacent angles are supplementary.)* As they complete Lesson 4, students will learn about the relationships of all these angles inside and outside a triangle.

2 Teaching the Lesson

To verify that the measures of the angles in any triangle total 180 degrees, have students create two identical triangles on scrap paper.

Buildings, signs, staircases, and kites all depend on one geometric figure, the triangle. A triangle is a closed geometric figure with three sides and three angles. There are many different relationships among the sides and angles of triangles. If you try this experiment with several different triangles, you will find the results will be the same.

The symbol $\triangle$ is used to denote a triangle.

EXAMPLE 1 Discover the relationship among the measures of the three angles of a triangle.

Step 1 Draw a triangle similar to $\triangle ABC$. Be sure to label each angle.

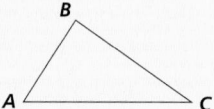

Step 2 Using scissors, cut off each angle of the triangle.

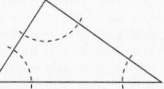

Step 3 Place the angles adjacent to each other along a straight line.

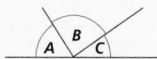

The angles form a straight angle.

$$m\angle A + m\angle B + m\angle C = 180°$$

The sum of the measures of the angles in a triangle is 180°.

You can use this information to find the missing measure of an angle in a triangle.

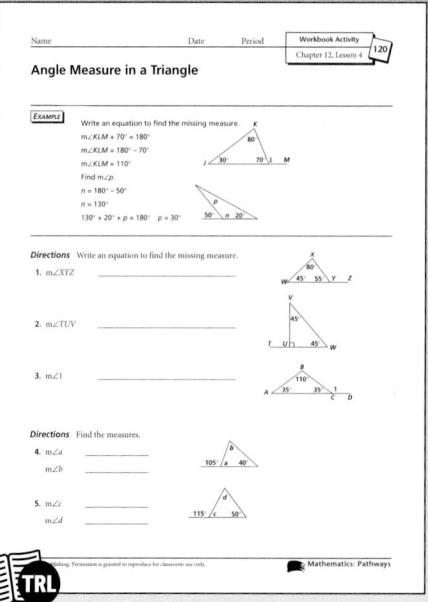

Workbook Activity 120

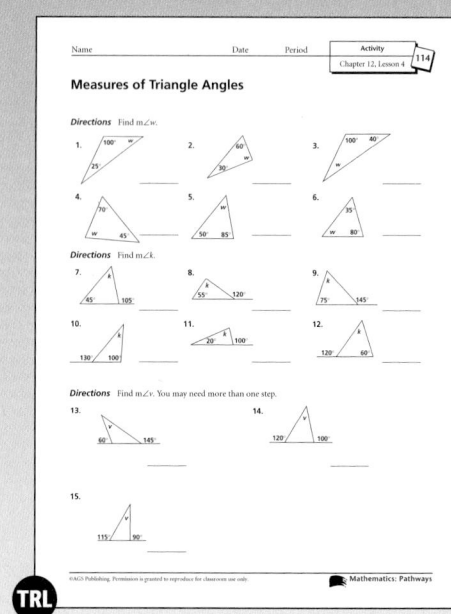

Activity 114

EXAMPLE 2 One angle in a triangle measures 45°. Another angle measures 30°. What is the measure of the third angle?

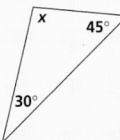

Step 1 Write an equation for the sum of the measures of the angles.

$$x + 45° + 30° = 180°$$

Step 2 Solve the equation for x.

$$x + 45° + 30° = 180°$$
$$x = 180° - (+45°) - (+30°)$$
$$x = 180° - 75°$$
$$x = 105°$$

Step 3 Check. $105° + 45° + 30° = 180°$

There are many other relationships that exist in triangles. In $\triangle ABC$, for example, angles A, B, and C are **interior angles.** Extending one side of the triangle at any vertex forms an **exterior angle.**

In $\triangle ABC$, $\angle DCB$ is an exterior angle.

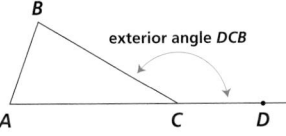

Note that $\angle DCB$ and $\angle ACB$ are supplementary angles.

Any exterior angle of a triangle is supplementary to the adjacent interior angle.

Technology Connection

Making Tracking and Navigation Easy

A global positioning system (GPS) works on a geometric principle called *triangulation*. GPS uses satellites to calculate a location. GPS shows a location by the intersection of distances from the location and three (and sometimes four) satellites. GPS was built by the U.S. government, but now GPS is available to everyone. Many cities use GPS to get their police and ambulances to people who call 911. Some people who fish even use GPS so they can return to their best fishing spots.

Geometry Chapter 12 **367**

Students can tear the angles off of one triangle and place them adjacent on a straight line drawn across the board. Above the "proof," have students tape the second triangle. As students compare the differences among the triangles, they should see that, regardless of shape, the triangles all have angles whose measures total 180 degrees.

Use your diagram of a triangle with exterior angles from the Warm-Up Activity to demonstrate why any given exterior angle is supplementary to the adjacent interior angle. (*They form a straight angle, which equals 180 degrees.*) Help students prove why the measure of the exterior angle must equal the sum of the measures of the other two interior angles:

- The measure of the exterior angle = 180 − the measure of the adjacent interior angle.

- The sum of the measures of all three interior angles = 180 degrees.

- The sum of the measures of the other two interior angles = 180 − the measure of the adjacent interior angle.

3 Reinforce and Extend

LEARNING STYLES

Visual/Spatial

For visual proof that the measures of the nonadjacent interior angles equal the measure of the exterior angle supplementary to the remaining interior angle, have students

- trace triangle *ABC* from Example 3 onto unlined paper.

- cut off angles *A* and *B*. (Trim away the portion of paper outside these vertexes.)

- join angles *A* and *B* and place over angle 1.

The two angles should be identical in measure.

MENTAL MATH

Draw a triangle on the board and give the measures of two of its angles. Have students determine, without using paper and pencil, the measure and type of the remaining angle.

50 degrees, 50 degrees
(80 degrees, acute)

35 degrees, 55 degrees
(90 degrees, right)

60 degrees, 20 degrees
(100 degrees, obtuse)

IN THE COMMUNITY

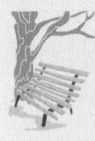

Have students bring in photographs, drawings, or graphic art representations of local buildings, bridges, or street patterns that form triangles. After students highlight the triangles in each illustration, have them measure and add the angles. Post the pictures on a bulletin board. Lead a classroom discussion on the reason why these triangles are useful or pleasing in each construction.

EXAMPLE 3 Find the measure of exterior angle 1.

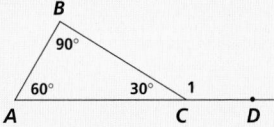

Step 1 Angle 1 and ∠BCA are supplementary. Write an equation using this information.

$$m\angle 1 + 30° = 180°$$

Step 2 Solve the equation for m∠1.

$$m\angle 1 + 30° = 180°$$
$$m\angle 1 = 180° - 30°$$
$$m\angle 1 = 150°$$

Step 3 Check. $150° + 30° = 180°$

Note that $m\angle B + m\angle A = 90° + 60° = 150°$. So for this triangle, the measure of the exterior angle at one vertex is equal to the sum of the measures of the two nonadjacent interior angles. In fact, this is true for any triangle.

> The measure of the exterior angle is equal to the sum of the measures of the two nonadjacent interior angles.

EXAMPLE 4 Given △RST, find m∠x.

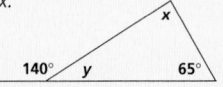

Step 1 The measure of the exterior angle is 140°. Angle x is one of the two nonadjacent angles. The measure of the other nonadjacent angle is 65°. Write an equation using this information.

$$140° = x + 65°$$

Step 2 Solve the equation for x.

$$140° = x + 65°$$
$$140° - 65° = x$$
$$75° = x$$

Step 3 Check. $65° + 75° = 140°$

Exercise A Find m∠*x*.

1.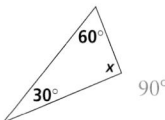
60°
x
30° 90°

2.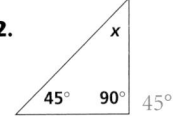
x
45° 90° 45°

3.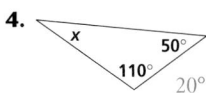
x 40°
30°
110°

4.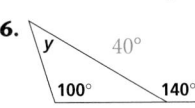
x 50°
110° 20°

5.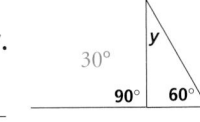
75°
35° *x* 70°

Exercise B Find ∠*y*.

6.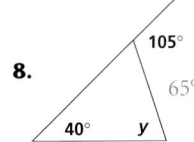
y 40°
100° 140°

7.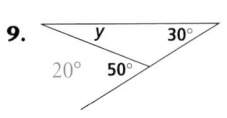
y
30°
90° 60°

8.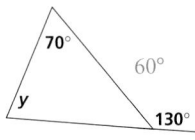
105°
65°
40° *y*

9.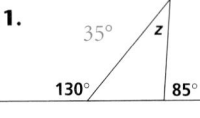
y 30°
20° 50°

10.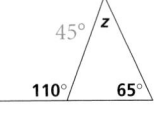
70°
60°
y
130°

Exercise C Find ∠*z*. You may need more than one step.

11.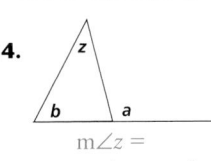
35° *z*
130° 85°

12.
45° *z*
110° 65°

13.
36° *z*
110° 106°

14.
z
b *a*
m∠*z* =
m∠*a* − m∠*b*

PROBLEM SOLVING

Exercise D Solve the problem.

15. The pitch (m∠*ABC*) of the roof is 38°. What is the m∠1, the angle the roof makes with the outside wall of the house? 128°

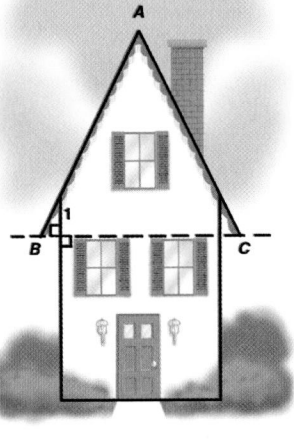

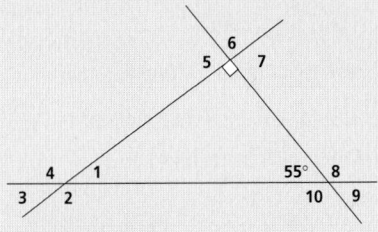

Lesson at a Glance

Chapter 12 Lesson 5

Overview This lesson classifies triangles by the lengths of their sides and the sizes of their angles.

Objective

- To identify and name triangles according to their angle sizes and side lengths

Student Pages 370–371

Teacher's Resource Library

Workbook Activity 121

Activity 115

Alternative Activity 115

Mathematics Vocabulary

tick
acute triangle
obtuse triangle
equiangular triangle

---

1 Warm-Up Activity

Provide students with straight strips of paper, wood, or plastic in sets of various lengths. Have them create triangles with three sides of equal length, with two sides of equal length, and with three sides of differing lengths. Ask, "What happens to the angles within a triangle as you change the lengths of the sides in this way?" *(With three equal sides, the angles are equal. With two equal sides, two angles are equal. With no equal sides, no angles are equal.)* Tell the class that Lesson 5 explains how to name triangles according to their sides and angles.

2 Teaching the Lesson

Check to make sure that students understand the meanings of tick marks and arcs. Draw several triangles on the board and have students direct you to use ticks and arcs to show comparative side lengths and angle sizes.

In Exercise A, students may note that triangle 7 is obtuse (for one angle is clearly greater than 90 degrees) scalene. They may also point out that triangle 9, like 3, is equilateral as well as equiangular.

 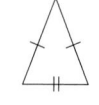

Tick
A short line used to mark the side of a triangle

Acute triangle
A triangle with three acute angles

Obtuse triangle
A triangle with one obtuse angle

Equiangular triangle
A triangle with three equal angles, each measuring 60°

Arcs are used like ticks to show angles. If a triangle has two angles marked with a single arc, those two angles are of equal measure.

You've already learned to name and identify triangles using the lengths of the sides of the triangle. Short lines, called **ticks,** may be used to mark the sides of a triangle or other geometric figure. One tick represents one length, two ticks represent another, and three ticks represent a third length. For example, a triangle that has a single tick marking each side has three sides of equal length.

Scalene Triangle   Isosceles Triangle   Equilateral Triangle

Recall that each side of a scalene triangle is a different length, two sides of an isosceles triangle have the same length, and all sides of an equilateral triangle have the same length.

Triangles can also be classified by their angles. In addition to right triangles, which you've already studied, there are **acute, obtuse,** and **equiangular** triangles.

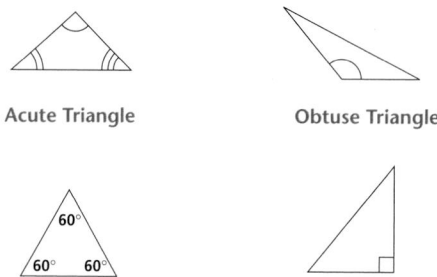

Acute Triangle   Obtuse Triangle

Equiangular Triangle   Right Triangle

Each angle of an acute triangle measures less than 90°.
One angle of an obtuse triangle measures more than 90°.
Each angle of an equiangular triangle measures 60°.
You can use the characteristics of triangles to name or classify triangles.

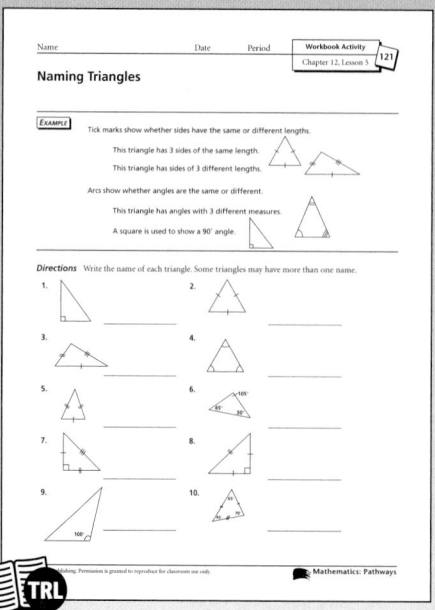

Workbook Activity 121

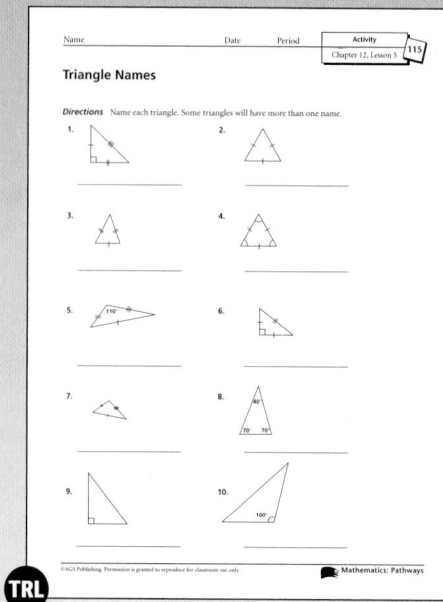

Activity 115

EXAMPLE 1 What name or names best describe this triangle?

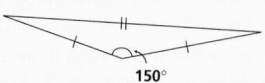

150°

Step 1 Look at the angles of the triangle. Because one angle measures more than 90°, it is an obtuse triangle.

Step 2 Look at the sides of the triangle. Two of the sides are the same length. Therefore, the triangle is an isosceles triangle.

Step 3 Name the triangle. The triangle is an obtuse, isosceles triangle.

Exercise A Name each triangle.

1.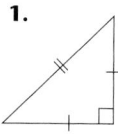
2.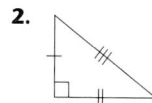
3.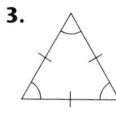
4.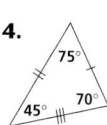

75°
45° 70°

5.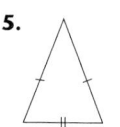
6.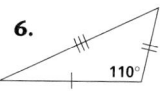
110°
7.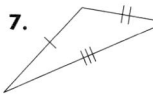
8.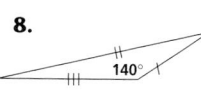
140°

9.
10. 120°

1. right isosceles
2. right scalene
3. equilateral and equiangular
4. acute scalene
5. isosceles
6. obtuse scalene
7. scalene
8. obtuse scalene
9. equiangular
10. obtuse isosceles

Math in Your Life

Honeycombs

The cells in a honeycomb consist of hexagons made of wax. Hexagons fit together compactly. This prevents the comb from falling apart easily. Other shapes, such as squares or triangles, would fit equally as well but hexagons provide the largest storage volume for the amount of wax used to create the comb.

Geometry Chapter 12 **371**

Point out that visual clues are often not clear-cut enough to allow this kind of analysis. To be accurate, students must rely on measurement or mathematical proofs.

3 Reinforce and Extend

Geometry **371**

Lesson at a Glance

Chapter 12 Lesson 6

Overview This lesson introduces congruence and the theorems that prove congruence of triangles.

Objectives

- To identify triangles that are congruent
- To comprehend that triangles are congruent if they have two sides and an included angle that are equal
- To comprehend that triangles are congruent if they have three equal corresponding sides
- To comprehend that triangles are congruent if they have two angles and an included side that are equal

Student Pages 372–373

Teacher's Resource Library **TRL**

Workbook Activity 122

Activity 116

Alternative Activity 116

....

Mathematics Vocabulary

congruent

....

1 Warm-Up Activity

Cut out congruent triangles from heavy paper or cardboard. Have students verify that the triangles are the same size and shape and state why this is so. (*They are the same size and shape because their side lengths and angles are the same.*) Tell students that this lesson will introduce rules that make it easy to determine when two triangles are the same.

2 Teaching the Lesson

The triangles from the Warm-Up Activity may be used to reinforce the concept of congruence. Place them on a tabletop. Slide and rotate the triangles into different positions, with each change asking, "Are the two triangles still the same size and shape?" (*yes*) "What does this show about congruence?" (*Congruent figures remain congruent no matter how they are oriented.*)

372 *Chapter 12*

Geometric figures, such as triangles, that have exactly the same size and shape are **congruent.** The symbol for congruent is ≅. $\triangle ABC \cong \triangle DEF$ is read "triangle *ABC* is congruent to triangle *DEF*."

> **Congruent**
> *Figures that have the same size and shape*

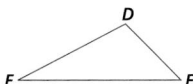

There are three sets of conditions that determine whether two triangles are congruent.

Side-Angle-Side (SAS)
If two sides and the included angle of two triangles are equal, then the triangles are congruent.

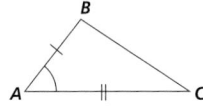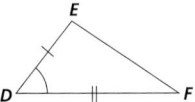

Side-Side-Side (SSS)
If the corresponding sides of two triangles are equal, then the triangles are congruent.

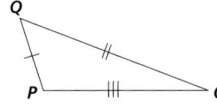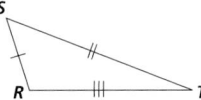

Angle-Side-Angle (ASA)
If two angles and the included side of two triangles are equal, then the triangles are congruent.

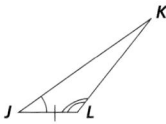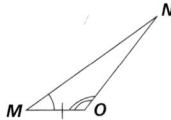

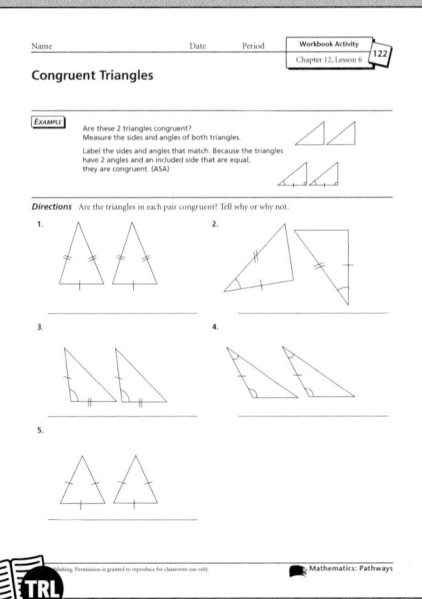

Workbook Activity 122

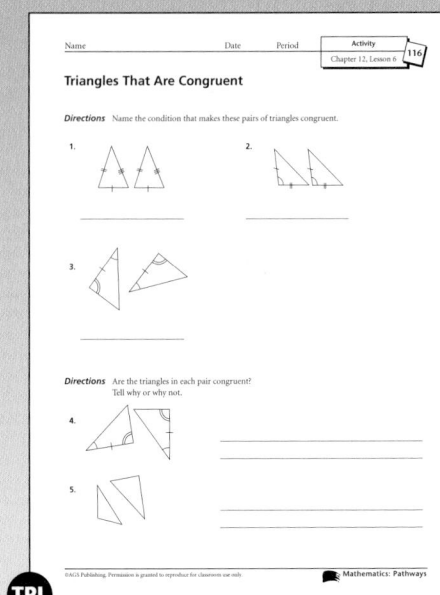

Activity 116

EXAMPLE 1 Determine if △ABC is congruent to △DEF. m∠A = m∠D, side AB = side DE and side AC = side DF. If the triangles are congruent, tell which condition they satisfy.

Step 1 Make a sketch and label the conditions.

Step 2 Note that two sides and the included angles of the triangles are equal.

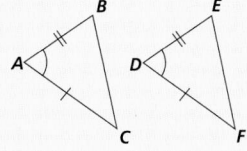

△ABC ≅ △DEF.

They satisfy the SAS condition.

EXAMPLE 2 Determine if triangles HJK and DFG are congruent. m∠H = m∠D, side JK = side FG, and side HJ = side DF. If the triangles are congruent, name the condition they satisfy.

Step 1 Make a sketch and label the conditions.

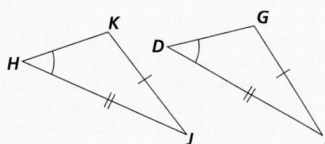

Step 2 The triangles have two sides and an angle that are equal. However, the angle that is equal is not the angle included between the two equal sides. Therefore, the triangles are not congruent.

Exercise A Name the condition that makes these pairs of triangles congruent.

1.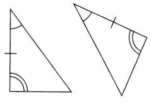

ASA

2.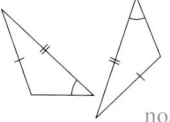

SSS

3.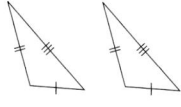

SAS

Exercise B Tell whether each pair of triangles is congruent. Tell why or why not.

4.

yes, ASA

5.

no, angle is not included

Geometry   Chapter 12   **373**

Point out the symbol for congruence and have students note similar math symbols they have seen. Make a comparison chart of the symbols and their meanings to help students differentiate among them:

Symbol	Meaning
≈	approximately equal to
≅	congruent to
∼	similar to

COMMON ERROR

Some students may have difficulty perceiving the congruence of figures that are not positioned the same way. Remind them that they may need to rotate and turn the figures mentally to determine congruence.

3 Reinforce and Extend

LEARNING STYLES

Interpersonal/ Group Learning

Draw pairs of triangles, some congruent and some not. For each pair, provide information about some sides and angles, but do not always give enough information for students to apply the SAS, SSS, or ASA rules. Give small groups of students pairs of the triangles and have them identify the relationship between each pair of triangles or state that not enough information is given. If the triangles are congruent, have students name the rule they used to determine congruence. Groups can exchange triangles until they have analyzed all the pairs.

AT HOME

Provide students with a copy of a tangram. Have them experiment at home, cutting pieces apart, determining which are congruent, and fitting them together in different ways to make new shapes. Once the desired shape is formed, students should trace it and exchange tracings with others to see whether their new puzzles can be solved.

Lesson at a Glance

Chapter 12 Lesson 7

Overview This lesson defines corresponding angles and similar triangles and shows that corresponding sides of similar triangles form equal ratios.

Objectives

- To identify similar triangles
- To comprehend the proportionality of sides of similar triangles
- To reason about the similarity of various classes of triangles

Student Pages 374–375

Teacher's Resource Library **TRL**

Workbook Activity 123

Activity 117

Alternative Activity 117

Mathematics Vocabulary

similar
corresponding angles

1 Warm-Up Activity

Display examples of boxes or forms that nest inside one another. Have students think about and discuss what makes the shapes similar. Ask, "Are these items congruent?" *(No; although they are the same shape, they are not the same size.)* In this lesson, students will learn about the characteristics of similar triangles.

2 Teaching the Lesson

Make sure that students understand that saying $\triangle ABC \sim \triangle DEF$ means that angles A and D, B and E, and C and F are equal in measure.

Before introducing the concept of equal ratios among corresponding sides, review ratios and give examples of ratios in two forms: 3 : 8 and $\frac{3}{8}$.

Have students measure the sides of similar triangles and form ratios to confirm that $\frac{AB}{DE} = \frac{BC}{EF} = \frac{AC}{DF}$.

Lesson 7 Similar Triangles

Similar
Figures that have the same shape but not the same size

Corresponding angles
Interior or exterior angles of figures in the same position as those of figures with the same shape

Sometimes, geometric figures such as triangles can have exactly the same shape but be different sizes. Figures that have the same shape but not the same size are **similar.** The symbol for similar is ~. $\triangle ABC \sim \triangle DEF$ is read "triangle ABC is similar to triangle DEF."

Similar triangles have equal **corresponding angles** but not equal corresponding sides. These triangles are similar because their corresponding angles are equal.

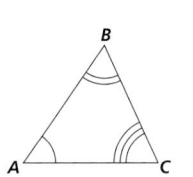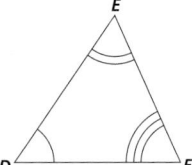

Corresponding angles are marked like this. If the corresponding angles of two triangles are equal, then the triangles are similar.

EXAMPLE 1 $\triangle ABC \sim \triangle DEF$, m$\angle A = 60°$, m$\angle C = 50°$. Find m$\angle E$.

Step 1 Since the triangles are similar, their corresponding angles are equal, and m$\angle E =$ m$\angle B$.

Step 2 Find m$\angle B$.

$$m\angle A + m\angle B + m\angle C = 180°$$
$$60° + m\angle B + 50° = 180°$$
$$m\angle B = 180° - 60° - 50°$$
$$m\angle B = 70°$$
$$m\angle E = 70° \text{ (from Step 1)}$$

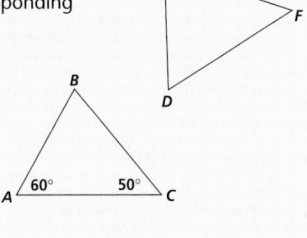

Similar triangles have other characteristics in common. In similar triangles, the lengths of the corresponding sides form equal ratios. You may remember from an earlier chapter that a ratio can be expressed as a fraction. For example,

if $\triangle ABC \sim \triangle DEF$, then $\frac{AB}{DE} = \frac{BC}{EF} = \frac{AC}{DF}$.

374 Chapter 12 Geometry

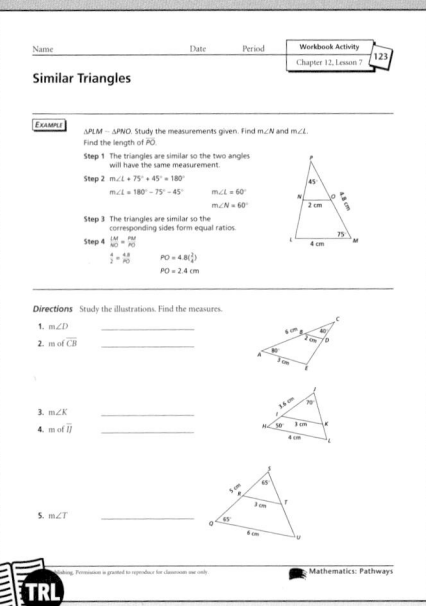

Workbook Activity 123

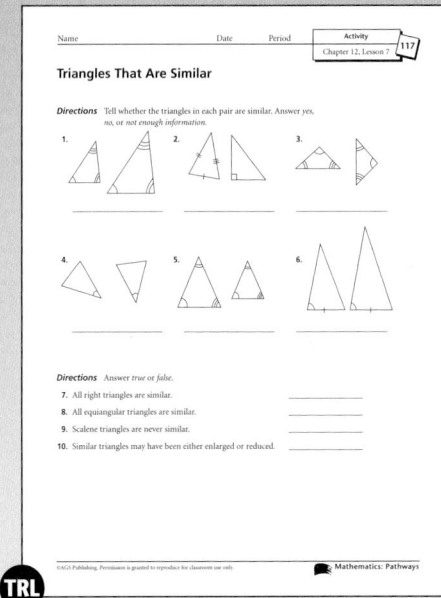

Activity 117

EXAMPLE 2 $\triangle ABC \sim \triangle DEC$, $m\angle B = 100°$, $m\angle C = 30°$, $AB = 8$, $AC = 10$, and $DE = 4$.
Find $m\angle D$ and length DC.

Step 1 The triangles are similar so corresponding angles are equal and $m\angle D = m\angle A$.

Step 2 Find $m\angle A$.

$$m\angle A + m\angle B + m\angle C = 180°$$
$$m\angle A + 100° + 30° = 180°$$
$$m\angle A = 180° - 100° - 30°$$
$$m\angle A = 50°$$
$$m\angle D = 50° \text{ (from Step 1)}$$

Step 3 The triangles are similar so corresponding sides form equal ratios.

$$\frac{AB}{DE} = \frac{AC}{DC}$$
$$\frac{8}{4} = \frac{10}{DC} \text{ ; thus } 2 = \frac{10}{DC}$$
$$2DC = 10$$
$$DC = 5$$

Exercise A Tell whether the triangles in each pair are similar.
Answer *yes*, *no*, or *not enough information*.

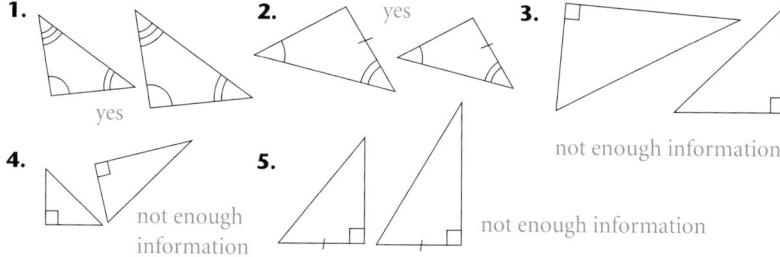

1. yes

2. yes

3. not enough information

4. not enough information

5. not enough information

Exercise B Answer *true* or *false*.

6. All isosceles triangles are similar.
   false

7. All equilateral triangles are similar.
   true

8. All right isosceles triangles are similar.
   true

9. All congruent triangles are similar.
   true

10. All similar triangles are congruent.
    false

LEARNING STYLES

Visual/Spatial

Give students practice in distinguishing congruent and similar triangles and using the symbols for "congruent to" and "similar to." Have each student write the symbols $\cong$ and $\sim$ on separate sheets of paper using black marker so that the symbols are easily visible. On the overhead or board, show pairs of triangles with tick marks, arcs, or side measurements that give adequate clues. Students hold up the appropriate card ($\cong$ or $\sim$) to identify the triangles' relationship.

AT HOME

Geometric patterns that repeat are pleasing and useful in many aspects of our lives. Have students use a computer graphics program or drawing tools to create a design that uses congruent and similar shapes. They can use color coding or another visual means to differentiate the congruent from the similar shapes.

Lesson at a Glance

Chapter 12 Lesson 8

Overview This lesson classifies and names quadrilaterals according to their sides.

Objectives

- To differentiate trapezoids, rhombuses, squares, rectangles, and parallelograms
- To identify quadrilaterals by the length and orientation of their lines

Student Pages 376–377

Teacher's Resource Library

Workbook Activity 124

Activity 118

Alternative Activity 118

1 Warm-Up Activity

List these terms on the board: *quadruplets, quarters, quadrants, quadruple, quartets.* Ask "What do all these words have in common?" *(All have the letters* quadr *or* quar; *all involve the number 4.)* Explain that in this lesson they will analyze figures that have four sides—quadrilaterals. Have students name and draw examples of as many different four-sided figures as they can.

2 Teaching the Lesson

Create a flow chart on the board that shows the relationships among the types of quadrilaterals.

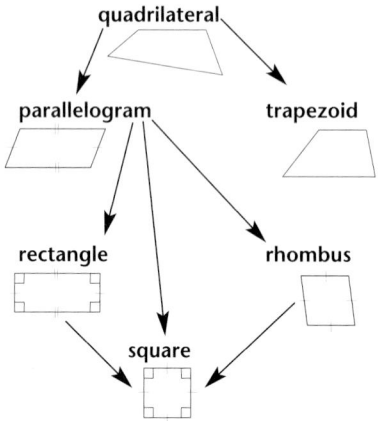

Have students refer to the chart to create true statements such as these:

- A rhombus is a parallelogram with sides of equal length.

You've studied triangles—polygons made up of three intersecting lines. There are other types of polygons, and some of these polygons are made of sets of parallel lines. The symbol for parallel is ||. $m||n$ is read "*m* is parallel to *n*."

m and n are intersecting lines   **m and n are parallel lines**

Polygons with four sides and four angles are called quadrilaterals. Quadrilaterals can be classified by whether or not they are made up of parallel lines.

Quadrilateral
- four sides

Parallelogram
- two pairs of parallel sides
- opposite sides are the same length
- opposite angles are equal

Rectangle
- parallelogram
- all angles 90°

Square
- rectangle
- all sides same length

Rhombus
- parallelogram
- all sides same length

Trapezoid
- quadrilateral
- one pair of parallel sides

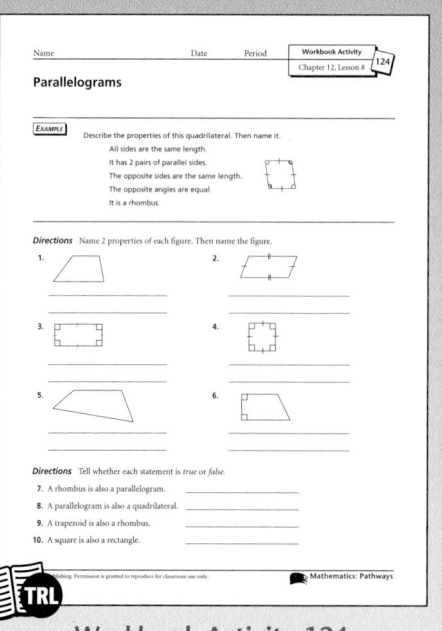

Name _____ Date _____ Period _____ **Workbook Activity 124**
Chapter 12, Lesson 8

Parallelograms

EXAMPLE Describe the properties of this quadrilateral. Then name it.
All sides are the same length.
It has 2 pairs of parallel sides.
The opposite sides are the same length.
The opposite angles are equal.
It is a rhombus.

Directions Name 2 properties of each figure. Then name the figure.

1. _____ 2. _____

3. _____ 4. _____

5. _____ 6. _____

Directions Tell whether each statement is *true* or *false.*

7. A rhombus is also a parallelogram. _____
8. A parallelogram is also a quadrilateral. _____
9. A trapezoid is also a rhombus. _____
10. A square is also a rectangle. _____

Mathematics: Pathways

Workbook Activity 124

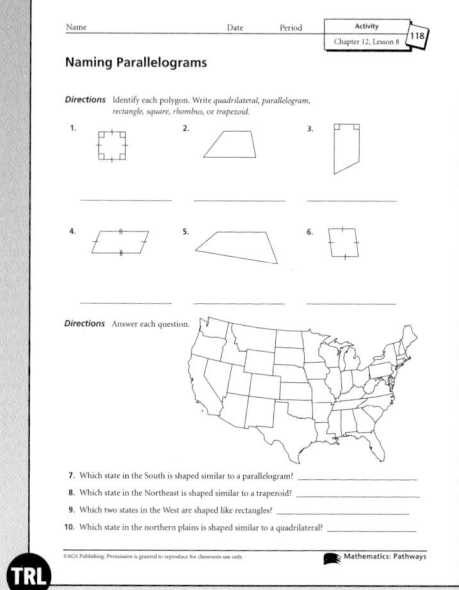

Name _____ Date _____ Period _____ **Activity 118**
Chapter 12, Lesson 8

Naming Parallelograms

Directions Identify each polygon. Write *quadrilateral, parallelogram, rectangle, square, rhombus,* or *trapezoid.*

1. _____ 2. _____ 3. _____

4. _____ 5. _____ 6. _____

Directions Answer each question.

7. Which state in the South is shaped similar to a parallelogram? _____
8. Which state in the Northeast is shaped similar to a trapezoid? _____
9. Which two states in the West are shaped like rectangles? _____
10. Which state in the northern plains is shaped similar to a quadrilateral? _____

Mathematics: Pathways

Activity 118

EXAMPLE 1 Identify this quadrilateral. *AB∥DC*,
∠*A* and ∠*D* are right angles.

Step 1 The figure has only two
right angles so it cannot
be a square or a rectangle.

Step 2 *ABCD* has one set of parallel sides.
Therefore, *ABCD* is a trapezoid.

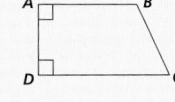

Exercise A Identify each polygon. Write *quadrilateral, parallelogram, rectangle, square, rhombus,* or *trapezoid.*

1.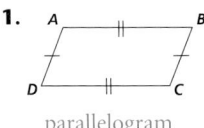
parallelogram

2.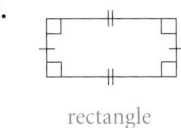
rectangle

3.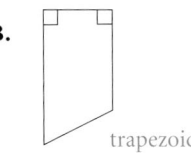
trapezoid

Exercise B Tell whether each statement is *true* or *false.*

4. All squares are rectangles. true

5. A square is a rhombus with right angles. true

6. A rhombus has only two parallel sides, four equal sides,
and equal opposite angles. false

7. A trapezoid is a parallelogram with two pairs of parallel sides. false

8. A rectangle with four equal sides is a square. true

 **PROBLEM SOLVING**

Exercise C Solve each problem.

9. Anna Marie wants to make a
log-cabin quilt. What kinds of
quadrilaterals will she need to use
to duplicate this quilt pattern?

square,
rectangle,
parallelogram

10. Armand plans to make
several birdhouses. He
is using this completed
house as a model. What
kind of quadrilaterals
will he use for the base,
sides, front, back, and
roof of the house?

base, square; sides, trapezoids;
front, back and roof, rectangles

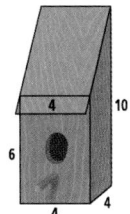

GROUP PROBLEM SOLVING

 Draw the following figures on
the board. Explain that each
figure is classified incorrectly.
Have groups of three students
study each figure, write a paragraph
explaining why the classification is
wrong, and give the correct
classification:

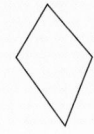

parallelogram

*(Congruent sides must be opposite
and parallel in a parallelogram; this
figure is a quadrilateral.)*

rectangle

*(The figure does not have congruent
opposite sides and has only one pair
of parallel lines; it has no 90-degree
angles; this figure is a trapezoid.)*

- A trapezoid is not a parallelogram
because it has only one pair of
parallel sides.

Explain that a figure should be identified
as specifically as possible. For example,
although a square is a quadrilateral, a
parallelogram, and a rectangle, the
name *square* most precisely explains
its characteristics to a reader or listener.

3 Reinforce and Extend

LEARNING STYLES

 **Auditory/Verbal**

Each answer in Exercise B is
either true or false. Assess
students' understanding of
quadrilaterals by having them explain
why. Add statements such as the
following and continue the process:

Parallelograms must have two sets
of equal angles. *(true)*

A trapezoid is a quadrilateral. *(true)*

All parallelograms are rhombuses.
(false)

A trapezoid must have a right angle.
(false)

MODELING

 Organize students into
groups and tell each group
that they are to create a new
superhero. The superhero
will have a definitive characteristic of
each group's design, such as the ability
to leap over tall polyhedra or to see
through solid geodesic domes. Students
will design a logo for this new
superhero that, similar to Superman's
logo, will be based on a polygonal shape
such as a rhombus, parallelogram,
trapezoid, or square. The logo can
include additional geometric shapes as
well as a letter or other distinguishing
feature. Students will draw and color
the logo and cut it out from stiff paper.
Groups will take turns introducing their
new superhero and explaining why
the logo meets the superhero's
promotional needs.

Lesson at a Glance

Chapter 12 Lesson 9

Overview This lesson addresses the characteristics of diagonals of quadrilaterals, and the triangles they form.

Objectives

■ To demonstrate that every quadrilateral contains angles totaling 360 degrees

■ To use the Pythagorean theorem to find the lengths of quadrilateral sides and diagonals

■ To find squares and square roots using a calculator

Student Pages 378–379

Teacher's Resource Library

Workbook Activity 125

Activity 119

Alternative Activity 119

....

Mathematics Vocabulary

diagonal

....

1 ⁍ Warm-Up Activity

Draw a square on the board and have students list its characteristics. Then draw a diagonal joining opposite corners of the square. Ask, "What has happened to the square?" *(It has been divided into two triangles.)* "What facts do you know about the triangles?" *(They are congruent equilateral right triangles; they have angles 45, 45, and 90 degrees each; the diagonal's length = $\sqrt{2s^2}$, where s is the length of a side.)* Tell students that they will now learn about the triangles that make up quadrilaterals.

2 ⁍ Teaching the Lesson

If students have difficulty understanding why the triangles formed by a diagonal in a rectangle are congruent, have them draw rectangles and diagonals. By cutting the triangles apart and placing one on top of the other, they will have visual proof of congruence.

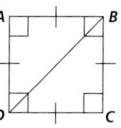

Diagonal

A line segment connecting two vertices that are not next to each other

A line connecting the opposite vertices of a quadrilateral is called a **diagonal.** A diagonal can be used to divide quadrilaterals into two triangles. For example, *BD* is a diagonal of square *ABCD*. If you fold the square along the diagonal, the two triangles would match exactly. That is, $\triangle BAD \cong \triangle DCB$.

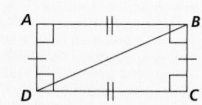

EXAMPLE 1 *ABCD* is a rectangle, with *DB* the diagonal. Determine if $\triangle BAD \cong \triangle DCB$.

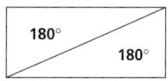

Step 1 Because *ABCD* is a rectangle, $\angle A = \angle C$, $AD = CB$, and $AB = DC$.

Step 2 Because triangles *BAD* and *DCB* meet the Side-Angle-Side condition, $\triangle BAD \cong \triangle DCB$.

There are more relationships you can discover about the diagonals of quadrilaterals. For instance, the sum of the angle measures in any quadrilateral is 360°. You can show this using the diagonal of a quadrilateral. Two triangles make up every quadrilateral, and the sum of the angle measures in each triangle is 180°.

EXAMPLE 2 In trapezoid *ABCD*, m∠A = 90°, m∠B = 50°, ∠A and ∠D are supplementary angles. What is the m∠C? m∠D?

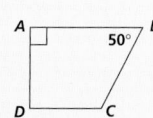

Step 1 ∠A and ∠D are supplementary angles so

m∠A + m∠D = 180°

90° + m∠D = 180°

m∠D = 90°

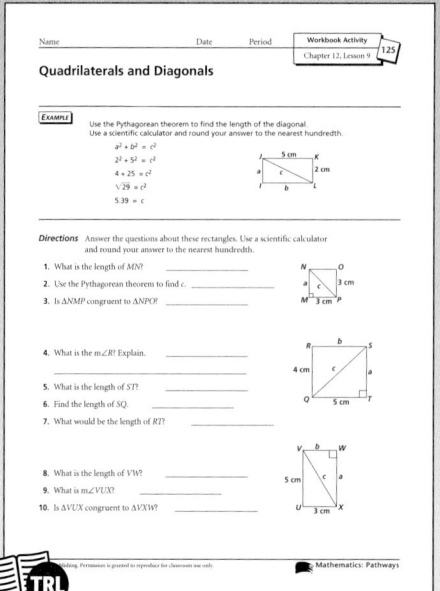

Workbook Activity 125

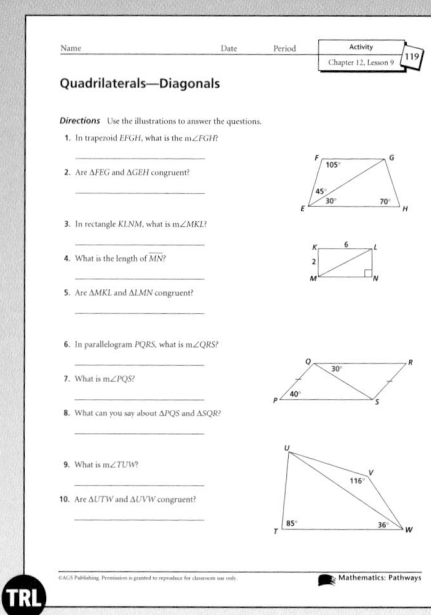

Activity 119

EXAMPLE 2 *(continued)*

Step 2 The sum of the angles in a quadrilateral is 360°.

$$m\angle A + m\angle B + m\angle C + m\angle D = 360°$$
$$90° + 50° + m\angle C + 90° = 360°$$
$$m\angle C = 360° - 90° - 50° - 90°$$
$$m\angle C = 130°$$

EXAMPLE 3 The lengths of the sides of a rectangle are shown in the illustration. What is the length of the diagonal *DB*?

Step 1 Because *ABCD* is a rectangle, $\angle A$ is a right angle and $\triangle DAB$ is a right triangle with legs *AD* and *AB*.

Step 2 From the Pythagorean theorem,

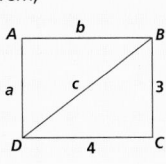

$$a^2 + b^2 = c^2$$
$$3^2 + 4^2 = c^2$$
$$9 + 16 = c^2$$
$$25 = c^2$$
$$\sqrt{25} = \sqrt{c^2}$$
$$5 = c$$

Exercise A Answer the questions about rectangle *ABCD*. Remember, $\triangle ABD$ and $\triangle CDB$ are congruent.

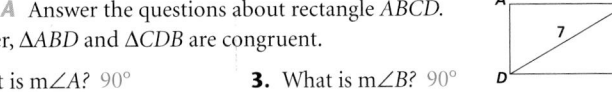

1. What is $m\angle A$? 90°

3. What is $m\angle B$? 90°

2. What is *x*? $\sqrt{33} \approx 5.7$

4. What is the length of *AC*? 7

Calculator Practice   You can use a calculator to find the squares and square roots of numbers.

EXAMPLE 4 Use a calculator to find the value of 17^2.

Press 17 $\boxed{x^2}$.   The displays reads *289*.

Find the value of $\sqrt{63}$.

Press 63 $\boxed{\sqrt{}}$.   The display reads *7.937*.

Exercise B Use a scientific calculator to find these values. Round to the nearest hundredth.

5. 6.9^2 47.61

7. $\sqrt{124}$ 11.14

9. $\sqrt{42}$ 6.48

6. $\sqrt{7.3}$ 2.70

8. 7.4^2 54.76

10. $\sqrt{53}$ 7.28

Have students test the two-triangles-to-a-quadrilateral statement by having them create many different four-sided figures and divide them diagonally. You may wish to review the ASA, SAS, and SSS rules from Lesson 6 and the Pythagorean theorem from Chapter 9 since students must apply them here.

3 **Reinforce and Extend**

LEARNING STYLES

Auditory/Verbal

Have students explain their answers for Exercise A. Reproduce rectangle *ABCD* on the board and have volunteers describe the figure, what they know to be true about it, and how they used one or more of the following to find answers:

- the rules for proving congruence (SSS, SAS, ASA)

- the Pythagorean theorem

- the rule for the sum of angle measures in a triangle

Students should write any calculations on the board as they explain them.

CALCULATOR

Basic math calculators do not have a square or a square root key, but they can be used to find exact squares and approximate square roots. To find 38^2,

Press 38 $\boxed{\times}$ 38 $\boxed{=}$.

The display reads *1444*.

To find $\sqrt{38}$, multiply a number between 6 and 7 (the square roots for perfect squares 36 and 49) times itself.

Press 6.5 $\boxed{\times}$ 6.5 $\boxed{=}$.

The display reads *42.25*. A smaller decimal is needed. Try 6.2.

Press 6.2 $\boxed{\times}$ 6.2 $\boxed{=}$.

The display reads *38.44*.

$\sqrt{38}$ is about 6.2.

Lesson at a Glance

Chapter 12 Lesson 10

Overview This lesson demonstrates that the total number of degrees in a polygon equals the number of triangles formed by drawing diagonals from one vertex times 180 degrees.

Objectives

- To construct all possible diagonals from one vertex of a polygon
- To identify polygons by the number of their sides
- To calculate the number of degrees in a polygon as $(n - 2)180°$, where $n =$ number of sides

Student Pages 380–381

Teacher's Resource Library

Workbook Activity 126

Activity 120

Alternative Activity 120

1 Warm-Up Activity

Draw and label a triangle and a quadrilateral on the board. Ask for a definition of each type of figure. (*a three-sided figure; a four-sided figure*) Have students name and draw as many polygons as they can, noting the number of sides in each. Explain that in Lesson 10, they will learn about a special relationship between the number of sides and the number of degrees in any polygon.

2 Teaching the Lesson

Name each polygon in the table and have students count the number of vertexes. Note that it is the same as the number of sides. Have students draw or trace polygons of five or more sides and construct diagonals. Point out that no diagonals can be drawn to the vertexes next to the vertex from which they start. These form the other two sides of the triangle. Every other vertex can accept a diagonal, forming another triangle. This is why there are $n - 2$ triangles in a polygon of n sides.

You've seen that the sum of the measures of the angles in a triangle is 180°. And you've seen that the sum of the measures of the angles in a quadrilateral is 360°. It is possible to predict the total number of degrees in any polygon. In each of these polygons, all the possible diagonals from one vertex have been drawn.

Polygon	Number of Sides	Number of Triangles	Sum of the Angle Measures
	3	1	180°
	4	2	$2 \cdot 180° = 360°$
	5	3	$3 \cdot 180° = 540°$
	6	4	$4 \cdot 180° = 720°$
	7	5	$5 \cdot 180° = 900°$
	8	6	$6 \cdot 180° = 1,080°$
n-gon	n	$n - 2$	$(n - 2)180°$

EXAMPLE 1 Find the sum of the angle measures of a dodecagon, a polygon with 12 sides.

For a dodecagon, $n = 12$ and $n - 2 = 10$.

$(10)180° = 1,800°$. The sum of the angle measures in a dodecagon is 1,800°.

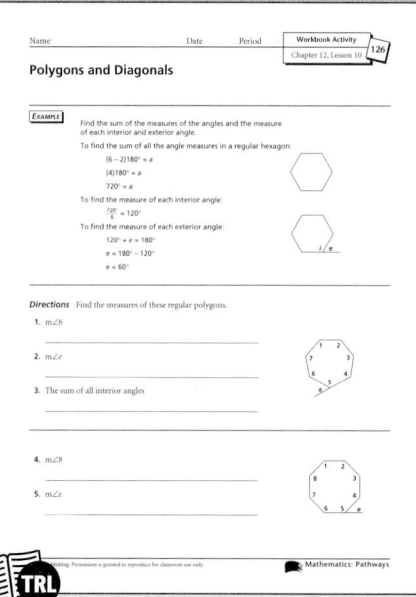

Workbook Activity 126

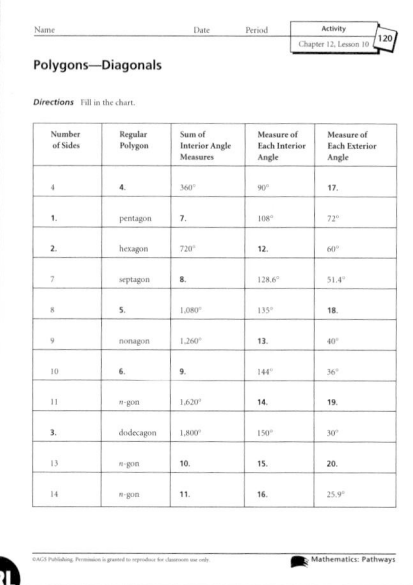

Activity 120

In a regular polygon, all the angles are of equal measure.

EXAMPLE 2 Find the measure of each angle of a regular pentagon, a five-sided polygon.

Step 1 First find the sum of all the angles in a pentagon.

$$(5 − 2)180° = (3)180° = 540°$$

Step 2 The measure of one angle equals the sum of the measures of all angles divided by the number of angles.

$$540° ÷ 5 = 108°$$

EXAMPLE 3 What is the measure of each exterior angle, ∠*e* of a regular pentagon, a five-sided polygon?

The interior and exterior angles are supplementary.

$$m∠i + m∠e = 180°$$
$$108° + m∠e = 180°$$
$$m∠e = 180° − 108°$$
$$m∠e = 72°$$

Exercise A Copy the chart and fill in the missing information. The first two answers are given.

Regular Polygon, Number of Sides	Sum of Interior Angles Measures	Measure of Each Interior Angle	Measure of Each Exterior Angle
3 (triangle)	180°	60°	120°
4 (quadrilateral)	360°	90°	90°
5 (pentagon)	540°	**6.** 108°	**10.** 72°
1. 6 (hexagon)	720°	**7.** 120°	60°
8 (octagon)	**4.** 1,080°	135°	**11.** 45°
2. 10 (decagon)	1,440°	144°	**12.** 36°
12 (dodecagon)	**5.** 1,800°	**8.** 150°	**13.** 30°
20	3,240°	**9.** 162°	**14.** 18°
3. 100	17,640°	176.4°	**15.** 3.6°

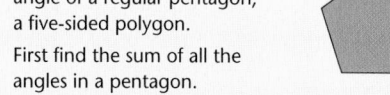

382 *Chapter 12*

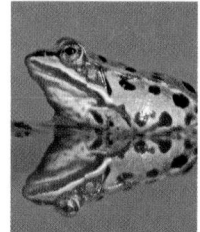

Image
Reflection of an object

You've probably noticed reflections of trees in a pond or lake or even reflections of buildings in puddles of water. In fact, you probably see a reflection of yourself every day when you look in a mirror! As you may already know, the reflection of an object is called its **image.**

In the picture, the object is a frog. The image is the reflection of the frog in the water.

As you work with objects and their reflections, or images, you will also work with the *line of reflection.* The object and its image are at equal distances from the line of reflection.

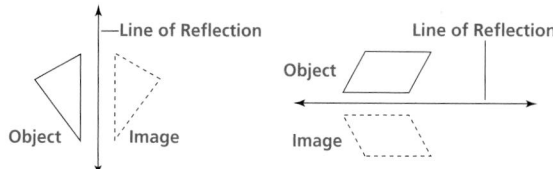

The distance between the object and its image can be shown and calculated if both are placed in a coordinate plane.

The point (3, 2) reflected over the *x*-axis has as its image point (3, −2).

The same point, (3, 2), reflected over the *y*-axis has as its image point (−3, 2).

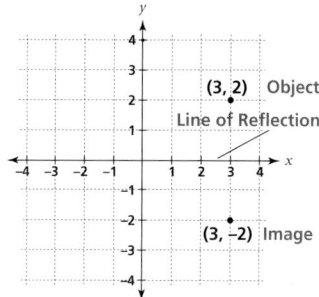
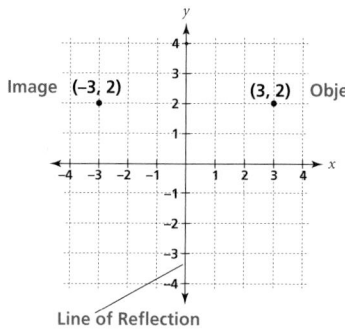

382 *Chapter 12 Geometry*

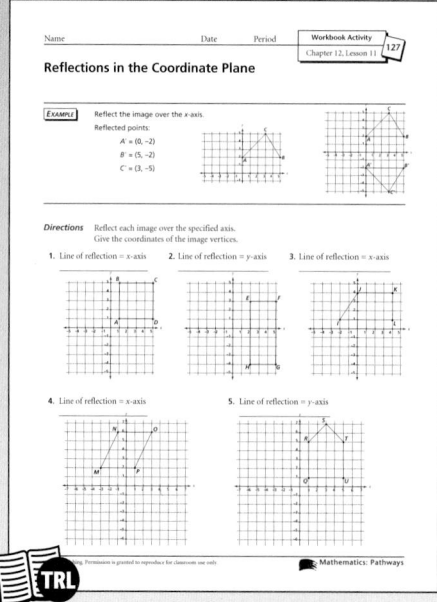

Workbook Activity 127

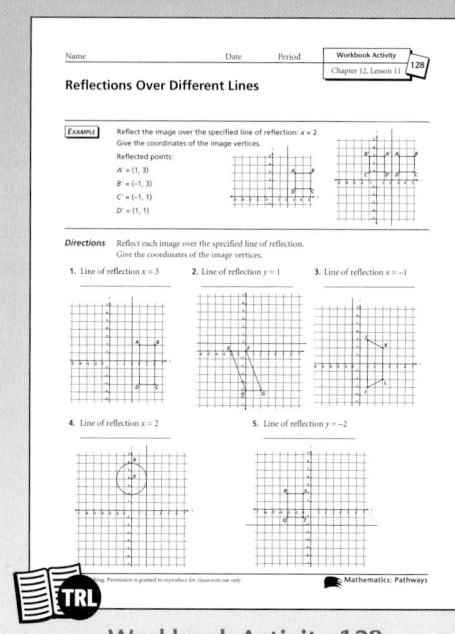

Workbook Activity 128

In fact, you can make the following generalizations or statements.

Reflection over x-axis

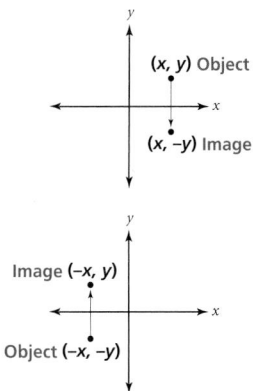

Reflection over y-axis

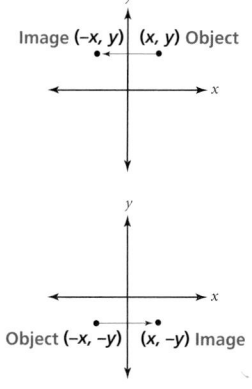

Image: has constant x-value
y-value has opposite sign

Image: has constant y-value
x-value has opposite sign

You can use this information to reflect entire geometric figures over either the x- or y-axis. You need only reflect the vertices of the figures and then draw the line segments. Here are some examples.

EXAMPLE 1 Reflect $\triangle ABC$ over the x-axis.

$A = (2, 5)$, $B = (2, 2)$, $C = (5, 2)$

Object vertices	Image vertices
$A = (2, 5)$	$A' = (2, -5)$
$B = (2, 2)$	$B' = (2, -2)$
$C = (5, 2)$	$C' = (5, -2)$

Notice that the y-values of the image are opposite the y-values of the object.

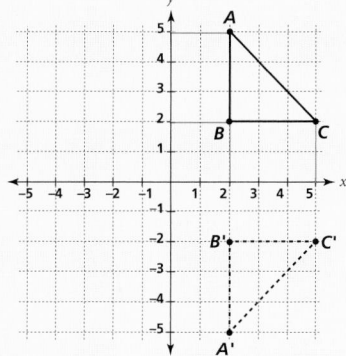

LEARNING STYLES

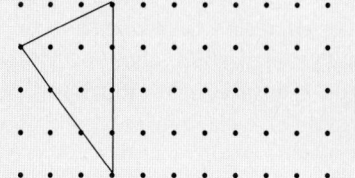

Logical/Mathematical
Have students use dotted grid paper to draw and label a polygon.

Tell students to add the x-axis and the y-axis and write the ordered pairs for the image's vertices. Have them make a horizontal or vertical reflection of their polygon on the grid and name the vertices of the reflection.

EXAMPLE 2 Reflect △*DEF* over the *y*-axis.

$D = (3, 2)$, $E = (5, 2)$, $F = (3, -1)$

Object vertices	Image vertices
$D = (3, 2)$	$D' = (-3, 2)$
$E = (5, 2)$	$E' = (-5, 2)$
$F = (3, -1)$	$F' = (-3, -1)$

Notice that the *x*-values of the image are opposite the *x*-values of the object.

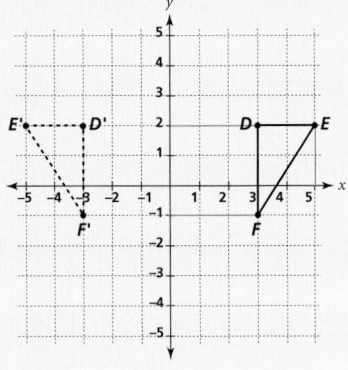

In Examples 1 and 2, you were able to find the coordinates of the image by finding the distance from the object points to the line of reflection and then using that same distance to place the image points.

You may, of course, use a line other than the *x*- or *y*-axis as the line of reflection. The geometry is still the same—the object points and their images are the same distance from the line of reflection.

EXAMPLE 3 Reflect △*LMN* over the line *y* = 2.

$L = (1, 5)$, $M = (5, 5)$, $N = (4, 3)$

To locate the image, you need to find the distance of each object point to the line of reflection, $y = 2$. Then apply this same distance in the opposite direction from $y = 2$.

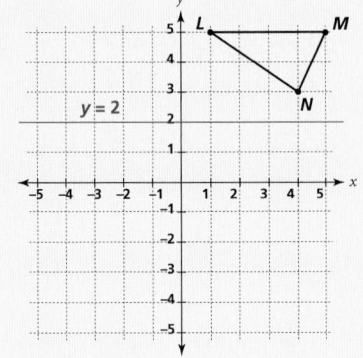

EXAMPLE 3 (continued)

Object Point	Distance to Line of Reflection (y = 2)	Image Point
L = (1, 5)	5 − 2 = 3	L' = (1, 2 − 3) L' = (1, −1)
M = (5, 5)	5 − 2 = 3	M' = (5, 2 − 3) M' = (5, −1)
N = (4, 3)	3 − 2 = 1	N' = (4, 2 − 1) N' = (4, 1)
Vertices for object △LMN (1, 5), (5, 5), (4, 3)		Vertices for image △L'M'N' (1, −1), (5, −1), (4, 1)

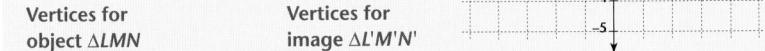

Exercise A Reflect each point over the x-axis. Give the coordinates of the image.

1. A = (3, 5)
A' = (3, −5)

2. C = (−3, 5)
C' = (−3, −5)

3. E = (2, 0)
E' = (2, 0)

Exercise B Reflect each point over the y-axis. Give the coordinates of the image.

4. G = (4, 2)
G' = (−4, 2)

5. I = (−4, 2)
I' = (4, 2)

6. K = (3, 0)
K' = (−3, 0)

7. H = (4, −2)
H' = (−4, −2)

Exercise C Reflect each image over the specified line of reflection. Give the coordinates of the image vertices.

8. x = 2

9. y = −3

10. x = 1

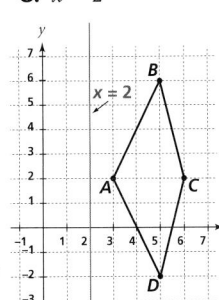 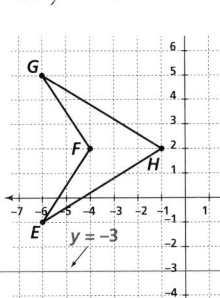 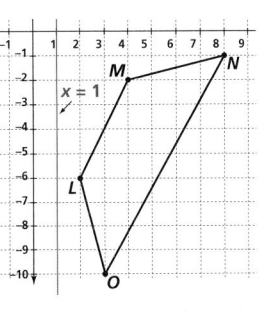

A = (3, 2) B = (5, 6)
C = (6, 2) D = (5, −2)

E = (−6, −1) F = (−4, 2)
G = (−6, 5) H = (−1, 2)

L = (2, −6) M = (4, −2)
N = (8, −1) O = (3, −10)

Geometry Chapter 12 **385**

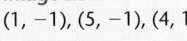

Adolescents are under pressure to succeed academically and socially in ways they may not have been when they were youngsters in elementary school. You can help them make the transition from concrete thinking to abstract thinking by using manipulatives. Give students concrete objects that they can examine, touch, and rotate in their hands as they solve problems.

9.

10.

Answers to Problems 8–10

8.

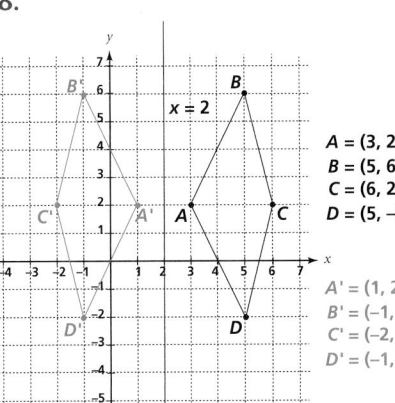

A = (3, 2)
B = (5, 6)
C = (6, 2)
D = (5, −2)

A' = (1, 2)
B' = (−1, 6)
C' = (−2, 2)
D' = (−1, −2)

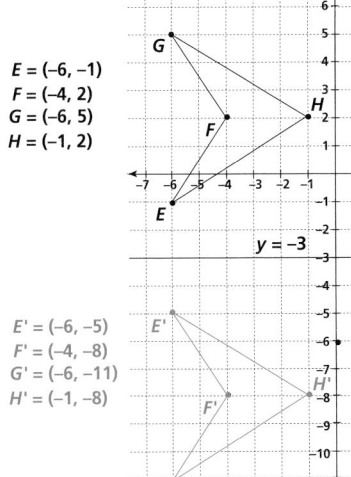

E = (−6, −1)
F = (−4, 2)
G = (−6, 5)
H = (−1, 2)

E' = (−6, −5)
F' = (−4, −8)
G' = (−6, −11)
H' = (−1, −8)

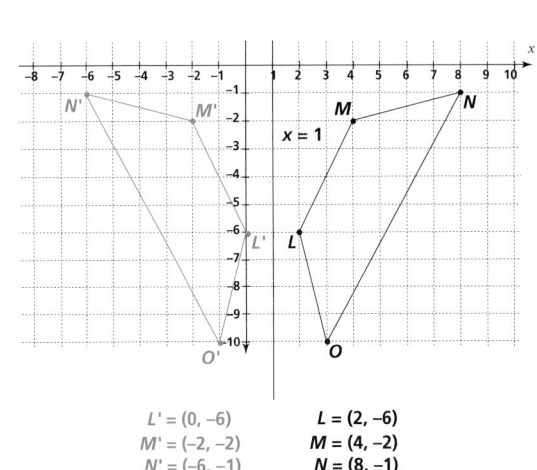

L' = (0, −6)
M' = (−2, −2)
N' = (−6, −1)
O' = (−1, −10)

L = (2, −6)
M = (4, −2)
N = (8, −1)
O = (3, −10)

Geometry **385**

Lesson at a Glance

Chapter 12 Lesson 12

Overview This lesson introduces the concept of symmetry and explains how to determine whether a geometric figure is symmetrical.

Objectives

- To determine if a line of reflection is also a line of symmetry
- To determine the total number of lines of symmetry of a polygon
- To draw conclusions about lines of symmetry in relation to a given symmetrical figure

Student Pages 386–387

Teacher's Resource Library TRL

Workbook Activity 129

Activity 122

Alternative Activity 122

....

Mathematics Vocabulary

line of symmetry

....

1 Warm-Up Activity

Have students draw a figure that contains at least two line segments. Tell them to position a mirror so that the edge lies on the line segment. Ask, "How is the image in the mirror the same as the figure you drew? How is it different?" *(It has the same size and shape. It differs in the direction it faces.)*

2 Teaching the Lesson

Provide students with mirrors and blank sheets of white paper. Draw a square and ask for suggestions for positioning the mirror so that the image matches up with a part of the figure on the other side of the mirror. Each time you find a line of symmetry, draw the line on the figure. Repeat until all four lines of symmetry have been drawn on the square. Repeat this procedure with other polygons, both symmetrical and nonsymmetrical. Be sure to include regular and irregular polygons. Help students draw conclusions about the characteristics of symmetrical and nonsymmetrical figures.

Line of symmetry

Reflection line of an object that leaves the object and the image in the same place

A special class of geometric reflections leaves the object and image in the same location. That is, the object and its image appear as one. If you reflect a square over one of its diagonals, you get a triangle in which the object and image meet. The reflection line is called a **line of symmetry**. A figure with at least one line of symmetry is called *symmetric*.

EXAMPLE 1 A square has four lines of symmetry. Each diagonal is a line of symmetry. Each line connecting the midpoints of opposite sides of the square are also lines of symmetry.

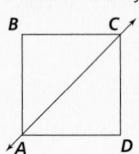 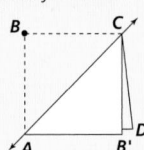 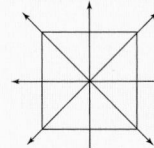

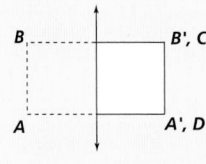 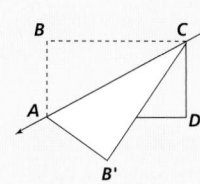

You can see that for rectangles, the lines connecting the midpoints of opposite sides are lines of symmetry.

However, unlike the square, the diagonals of a rectangle are not lines of symmetry.

An isosceles triangle has one line of symmetry. The line of symmetry divides Angle *B* into two equal parts and passes through the midpoint of the base $\overline{AC}$.

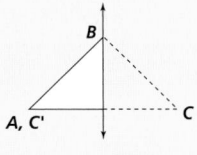

An equilateral triangle has three lines of symmetry. Each line of symmetry passes through the midpoint of a side. It divides the opposite angle into two equal parts.

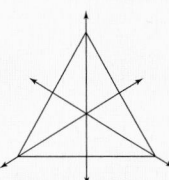

Sometimes you may see the terms *vertical symmetry* or *horizontal symmetry*. The letter A has vertical symmetry. The letter E has horizontal symmetry.

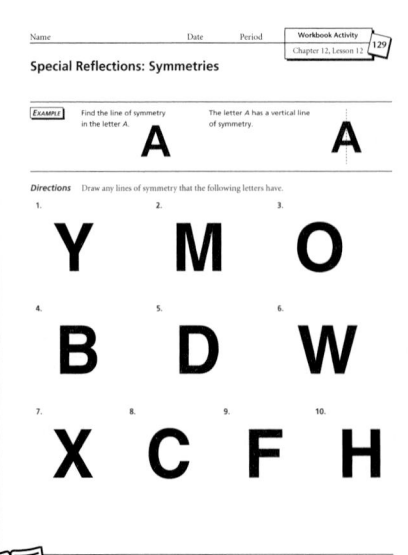

Workbook Activity 129

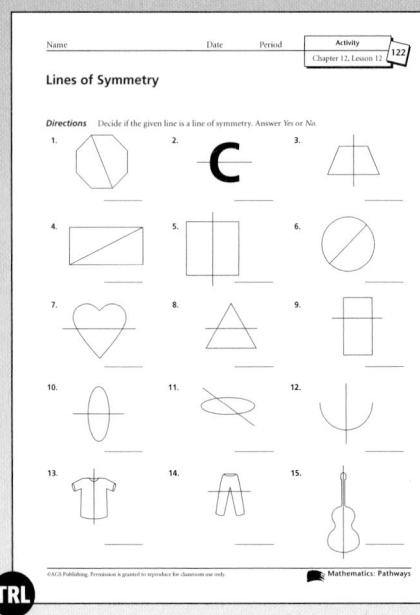

Activity 122

Exercise A Decide if the given line of reflection is also a line of symmetry. Answer *yes* or *no*.

1.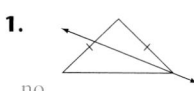

no

2.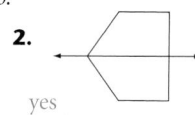

yes

3.

no

4.

yes

5.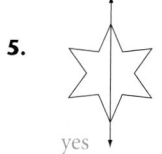

yes

6.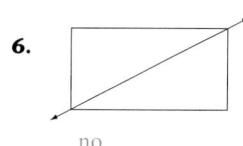

no

Exercise B Complete the following table. Then answer the questions.

	Polygon	Number of Sides	Diagonals Acting as Lines of Symmetry	Total Number of Lines of Symmetry
7. 	equilateral triangle	3	none	3
8.	square	4	2	4
9.	regular pentagon	5	none	5

10. What appears to be necessary for a diagonal to be a line of symmetry?

10. It divides an interior angle into two equal parts.

> **Try This**
>
> What do you think is the relationship between a diameter (distance across a circle through the center) of a circle and a circle's symmetry? How many lines of symmetry do you think a circle has?

Any diameter appears to be a line of symmetry. There are an infinite number of diameters so there must be an infinite number of lines of symmetry.

CAREER CONNECTION

 Many artists have used symmetry in their work. Ask students to choose an artist whose work includes symmetry. Suggest that they research information about the artist and his or her work. Ask them to write a report that discusses the artist's work, specifically identifying three or four pieces that include symmetry. The report should describe each piece and identify its artistic genre. If possible, students should provide sketches or prints of the artwork, highlighting its symmetry. Ask volunteers to share what they discovered about symmetry in the artist's work.

LEARNING STYLES

 Visual/Spatial

Have students draw and cut out large copies of each Exercise B figure. Ask them to verify the lines of symmetry shown in Exercise B by folding their figures so that the sides of the fold match up. They should draw a line on each fold to represent a line of symmetry. They can then use their figures to complete the exercise.

MANIPULATIVES

M **Symmetry**

Materials: Yardstick, rulers

Group Practice: Provide students with rulers and blank sheets of paper and ask that they experiment with you during the following demonstration. Draw a square on the board and have students draw it on their papers. Ask for volunteers to position the yardstick on the board so that the image matches up with a part of the figure on the other side of the yardstick. Each time a line of symmetry is found, have the volunteer draw it on the figure, while students draw it at their desks. Repeat this procedure with other polygons, both symmetrical and nonsymmetrical. Be sure to include regular and irregular polygons, such as a regular pentagon and an irregular pentagon. Help students draw conclusions about the characteristics of symmetrical and nonsymmetrical figures.

Lesson at a Glance

Chapter 12 Lesson 13

Overview This lesson describes what a translation is and explains how to map a given translation on a coordinate plane.

Objectives

- To graph the image of a geometric figure according to a given translation
- To identify an image point when an object point is mapped by a given translation
- To find the image point of any object point under a given translation

Student Pages 388–389

Teacher's Resource Library (TRL)

Workbook Activity 130

Activity 123

Alternative Activity 123

....

Mathematics Vocabulary

transformation
translation

....

 **1 Warm-Up Activity**

Ask students to observe as you slide any object on your desk from one place to another. Encourage students to discuss what they observed. Ask questions, such as "What changed about the object?" (*its position*) "What remained the same?" (*its size, shape, and composition*) Explain that Lesson 13 discusses such movement on a coordinate grid.

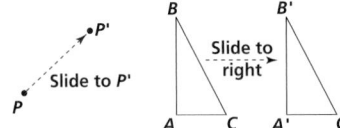

> **Transformation**
> *Movement of a geometric figure from one location to another*
>
> **Translation**
> *Transformation in which a geometric figure slides from one location to another without affecting its size or shape*

A **transformation** is the movement of a figure from one place to another. Reflections are one group of geometric transformations. A *slide,* or **translation,** is another example of a transformation. A slide is a transformation in which you "slide" the figure from one location to another. You do this without changing its size or shape. Sometimes this transformation is called *mapping;* you map point *A* onto point *A'*. A slide, or translation, leaves the object in one location and its image in another.

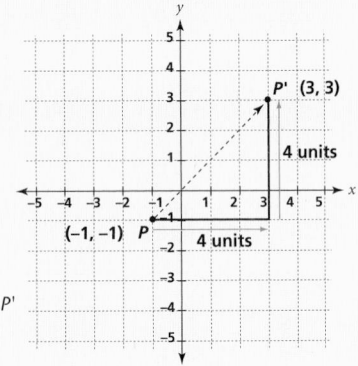

One way to study this kind of transformation is to look at slides or translations that occur in the coordinate plane.

EXAMPLE 1 Slide point *P* (−1, −1) to location *P'*.

Looking at the grid you can see that to reach *P'* you need to move 4 units to the right (*x* + 4) and 4 units up (*y* + 4).

Here is how you can use the coordinates of *P* to find the coordinates of *P'*.

$P = (-1, -1)$

$P' = [(x + 4), (y + 4)]$

$P' = [(-1 + 4), (-1 + 4)] = (3, 3) = P'$

> **Formula**
> To translate or slide point *P a* units horizontally (change in *x*) and *b* units vertically (change in *y*), you must change the *x*- and *y*-values of the coordinates of *P*.
>
> $P = (x, y)$ translates to $P' = (x + a, y + b)$

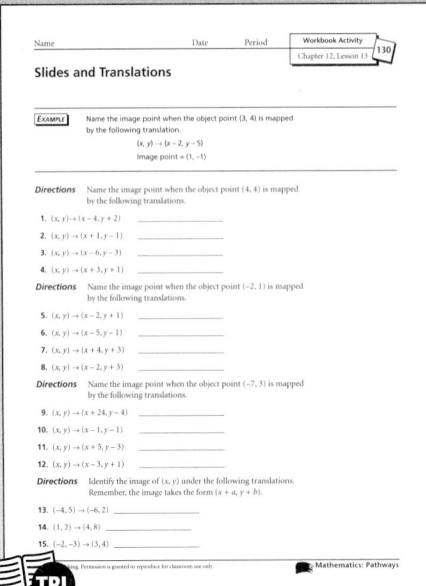

Workbook Activity 130   **Activity 123**

Note that if $a > 0$, the image is to the right, if $a < 0$, the image is to the left; if $b > 0$, the image is above the object, if $b < 0$, the image is below the object.

EXAMPLE 2 Slide $\triangle ABC$ 4 units to the right and 3 units down.

First slide each vertex.
$A = (1, 1)$, $B = (2, 7)$, and $C = (3, 2)$
$a = 4$ (4 units to the right)
$b = -3$ (3 units down)
$P = (x, y)$ translates to $P' = (x + a, y + b)$
$A = (1, 1)$ translates to $A' = (1 + 4, 1 + -3) = (5, -2)$
$B = (2, 7)$ translates to $B' = (2 + 4, 7 + -3) = (6, 4)$
$C = (3, 2)$ translates to $C' = (3 + 4, 2 + -3) = (7, -1)$
Once you have located each image vertex, draw $\triangle A'B'C'$.

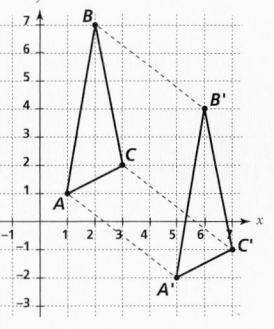

Exercise A Slide each point 3 units to the left and 2 units up. Graph the point and its image, naming the coordinates of the image.

1. $A = (3, 6)$ $A' = (0, 8)$

2. $B = (-3, 6)$ $B' = (-6, 8)$

3. $C = (3, -6)$ $C' = (0, -4)$

4. $D = (-3, -6)$ $D' = (-6, -4)$

5. $E = (0, 5)$ $E' = (-3, 7)$

Exercise B Slide each triangle according to the given translation. Graph the image triangle and name the vertices of the image triangle.

6. $\triangle ABC$: $A = (-7, 3)$, $B = (-2, 1)$, $C = (4, 6)$; slide 4 right, 2 up

7. $\triangle EFG$: $E = (-3, -2)$, $F = (2, 2)$, $G = (2, -3)$; slide 2 left, 3 up

6. $A' = (-3, 5)$
    $B' = (2, 3)$
    $C' = (8, 8)$

7. $E' = (-5, 1)$
    $F' = (0, 5)$
    $G' = (0, 0)$

Writing About Mathematics

Describe how you would slide a circle with a radius of 5 and center at (0, 0) 5 units to the left and 3 units up. What is the center of the image?

Exercise C Name the image point when the object point $(3, -1)$ is mapped by the following translations.

8. $(x, y) \rightarrow (x + 1, y + 5)$ $(4, 4)$

9. $(x, y) \rightarrow (x + 3, y - 2)$ $(6, -3)$

10. $(x, y) \rightarrow (x - 2, y - 4)$ $(1, -5)$

3 Reinforce and Extend

LEARNING STYLES

LEP/ESL

Students may be familiar with the meaning of *translation* as it applies to language but not to geometry. Suggest that students with limited English proficiency work with students with greater proficiency.

Encourage them to find *translation*'s etymology in a dictionary. (trans-, *Latin prefix meaning "across" or "through"* and latus, *Latin verb meaning "carry"*) Help them consider how the meanings of the Latin words relate to the meaning of the term *translation* as it applies to language and geometry.

To provide practice moving, or translating, points on a coordinate grid, tell students to make a coordinate grid on graph paper, marking both axes in one-unit intervals from −5 to 5. Then have students plot the point (−5, −5). As you read the directions below, tell students to follow the directions to move from point to point, plotting each new point as they go. After the last step, ask students where they ended up. *(the origin)* Tell them that what they were doing was making a translation of each point to a different location on the coordinate grid.

Directions to move from point to point Start at (−5, −5).
    1. 3 units right; 2 units up
    2. 4 units right; 1 unit down
    3. 1 unit left; 3 units up
    4. 1 unit right; 2 units up
    5. 2 units left; 1 unit down

After reviewing Example 2 on page 389, refer students to the drawing and ask, "How would the location of the image change if it were mapped four units to the left of the object instead of four units to the right?" *(It would be the same distance away from and below the object, but it would be to the left of the object rather than to the right.)*

Discuss the similarities and differences between reflections and translations. Guide students to realize that they are similar in that each pair of object and image points in a translation is also a reflection (that is, there is a line of reflection for each pair). They are also similar in that both reflected images and translated images are congruent to the original object. They are different because in a translation the image faces the same way as the object, and therefore there is no line of reflection for the image as a whole.

Lesson at a Glance

Chapter 12 Lesson 14

Overview This lesson defines what a rotation is and demonstrates how to transform an object using a rotation.

Objectives

■ To draw an object image using a 90° rotation

■ To draw an object image using a 180° rotation

Student Pages 390–393

Teacher's Resource Library **TRL**

Workbook Activity 131

Activity 124

Alternative Activity 124

Mathematics Vocabulary
rotation

1 Warm-Up Activity

Briefly discuss clockwise and counterclockwise directions of movement. Then have students (in multiples of four) form a circle around one student. The student directly facing the student in the center holds a sign labeled 0°, and the students standing at each 90° position and the 180° position hold signs indicating their positions. The center student tells the circle of students to move either 90° or 180° clockwise or counterclockwise. The circle of students must then move to reflect this rotation and when done, the center student determines if the circle responded correctly to his or her instructions. Repeat the activity several times, allowing students to take turns being in the center.

390 *Chapter 12*

Lesson 14 Rotations

Rotation
Transformation in which a geometric figure turns around a center without affecting its size or shape

Remember, an object that moves clockwise moves in the same direction as the hands on a clock move. An object that moves counterclockwise moves in the direction opposite to the direction the hands on a clock move.

The final group of transformations you will study are called **rotations.** You see and use rotations every day. Wheels on a bus, door knobs, and swivel chairs are examples of objects that turn, or rotate.

Below are diagrams of the rotations of some common geometric figures. Notice that each diagram shows an O, the center of rotation. This is the point that remains in place as the geometric figure turns around it. It is rather like the needle of a drawing compass.

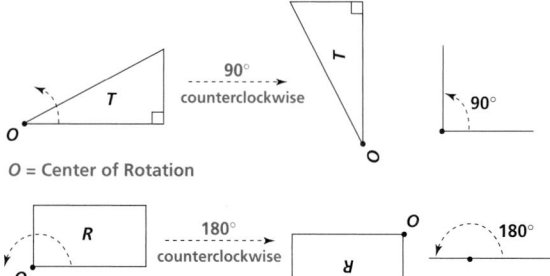

As with other transformations, you can specify a rotation by placing the figure on a coordinate plane.

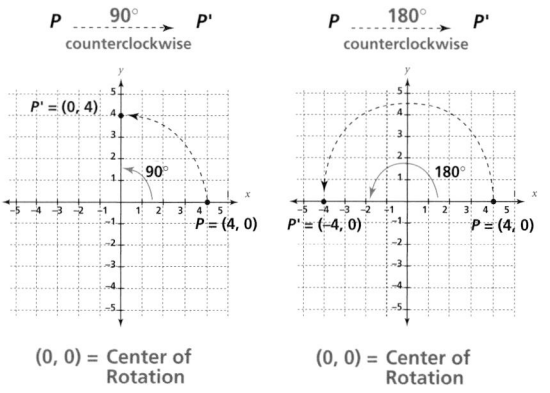

390 *Chapter 12 Geometry*

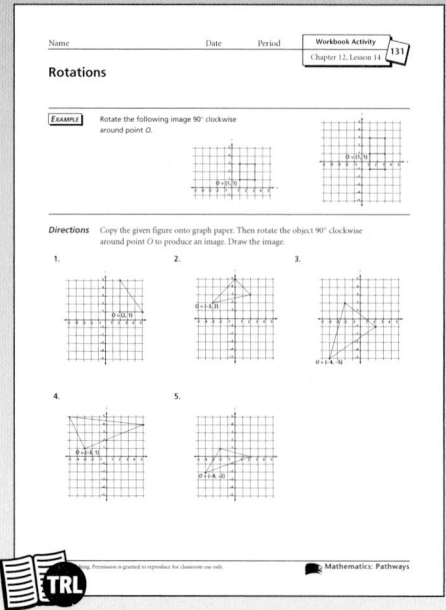

Workbook Activity 131

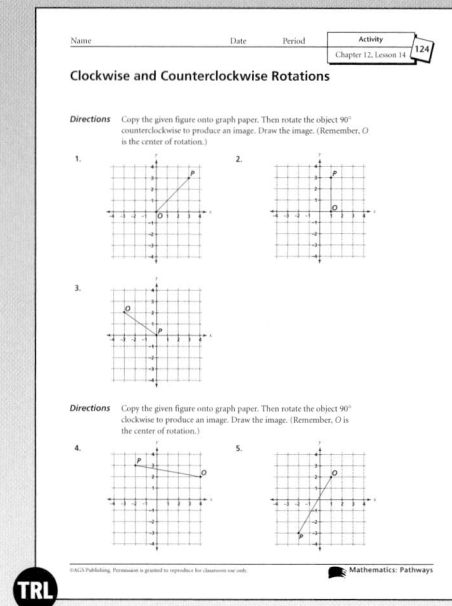

Activity 124

These examples show that knowing the location of the center of rotation, *O*, is key to making the transformation. Without knowing the center of rotation, you have no way of knowing how the object figure is transformed.

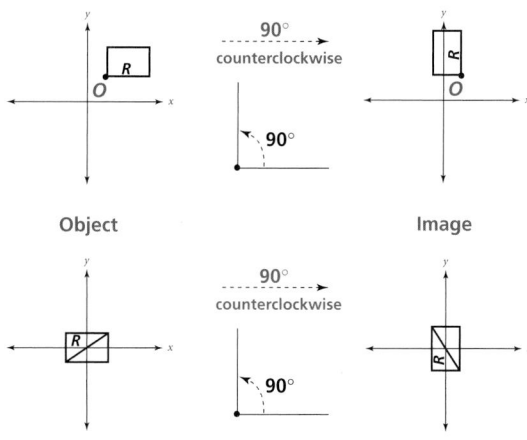

Object   Image

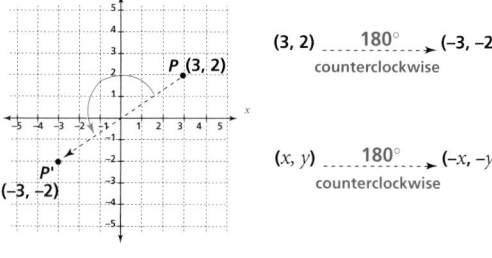

Object   Image

Center of Rotation
(0, 0)

(3, 2) ----180°----> (−3, −2)
        counterclockwise

(*x*, *y*) ----180°----> (−*x*, −*y*)
        counterclockwise

Center of Rotation
(0, 0)

(−3, 2) ----180°----> (3, −2)
        counterclockwise

(−*x*, *y*) ----180°----> (*x*, −*y*)
        counterclockwise

Remember, always check the location of the center of rotation before finding the image of the rotated object.

Remind students that a rotation is a transformation that *rotates* a figure around a given fixed point. This point is called the center of rotation. Rotations can turn in either a clockwise or a counterclockwise direction. How far the object rotates is measured in degrees. On the board, draw the diagram shown below, drawing the 90°/270° and the 0°/180° lines first and labeling them, and the 45°/225° and 135°/315° lines next. Indicate to students that the degrees move in a counterclockwise direction. Suggest to students that they sketch the diagram on scrap paper as a memory aid when solving rotation problems.

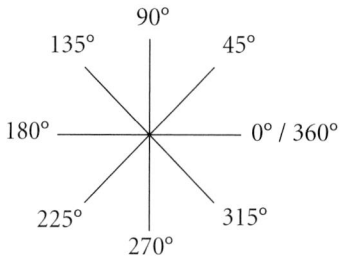

3 **Reinforce and Extend**

LEARNING STYLES

Auditory/Verbal

Have students examine the examples of rotations and read the paragraph at the top of page 391 aloud. Ask them to explain in their own words why it is necessary to know the center of rotation in order to know how an object figure is transformed.

CAREER CONNECTION

Invite a graphic artist to speak to your class about the use of transformations in his or her work. Ask students to prepare questions ahead of time to ask the speaker about his or her work and how he or she uses transformations. Have students write a brief summary of the visitor's presentation.

GROUP PROBLEM SOLVING

Discuss briefly with the class how animated cartoons can be made by translating and rotating the figures in a series of pictures. Then have groups of three or four students make "flip books." They can cut and staple 10 to 15 sheets of grid paper together to form a book and draw a series of pictures that involve gradual and sequential transformations of one or more aspects of the picture. When the book is flipped through quickly, the figures in the picture should appear to be moving. Each group should pick a theme or idea for its flip book. Encourage students to focus on animating one or two simple aspects of a given scene and to make the pictures colorful and clearly drawn. Invite groups to share their flip books with the class.

Exercise A Copy the given figure onto graph paper. Then rotate the object 90° counterclockwise to produce an image. Draw the image. (Remember, *O* is the center of rotation.)

1.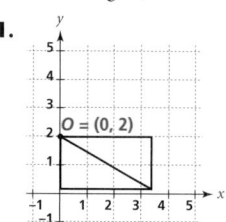

2.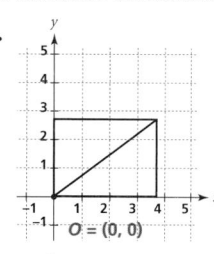

3.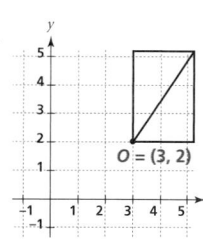

4.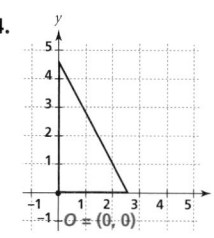

5.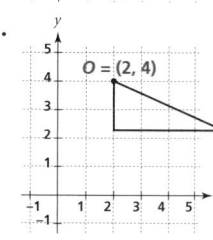

6.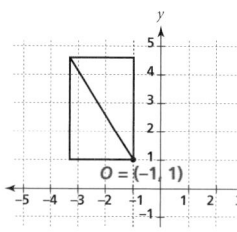

7.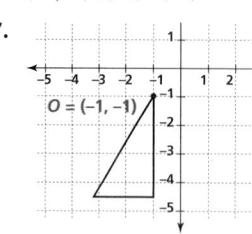

See Teacher's Edition page for answers.

Exercise B Copy the given figure onto graph paper. Then rotate the object 180° counterclockwise to produce an image. Draw the image. (Remember, *O* is the center of rotation.)

See Teacher's Edition page for answers.

8.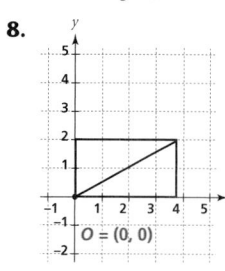

9.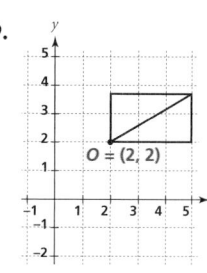

10.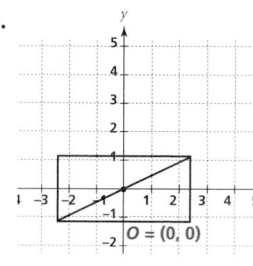

Answers to Exercises A and B

1.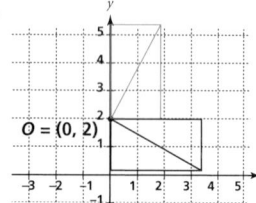

2.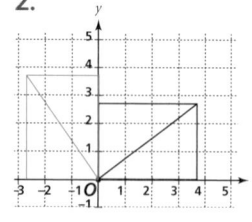

3.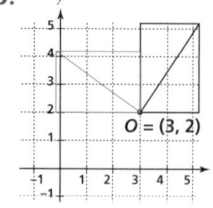

4.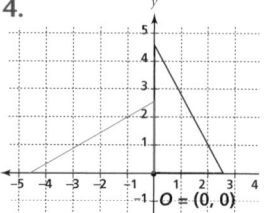

5.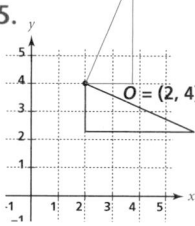

6.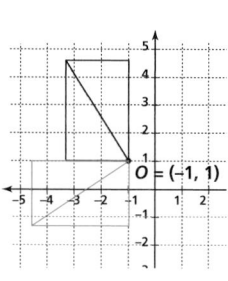

7.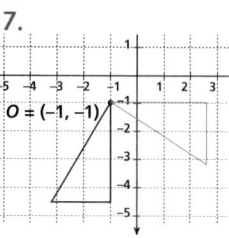

8.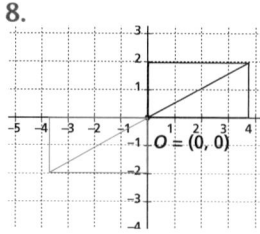

9.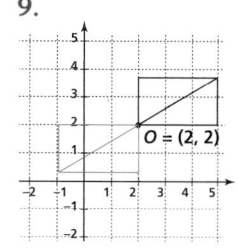

10.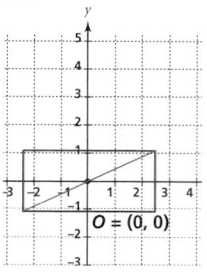

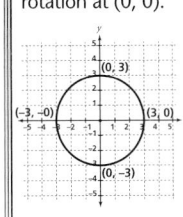
11.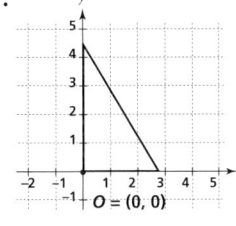

12.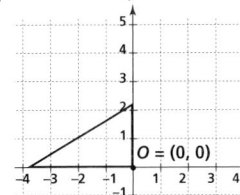

13.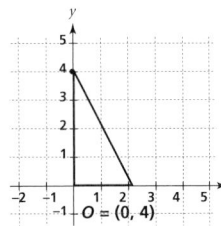

14.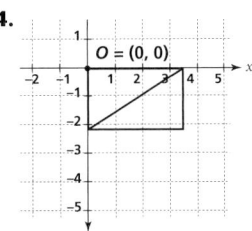

Exercise C Rotate each of the following points 180° counterclockwise around the origin. Give the coordinates of the image point.

15. $(4, -5)$ $(-4, 5)$

18. $(-8, 3)$ $(8, -3)$

16. $(5, 5)$ $(-5, -5)$

19. $(8, -3)$ $(-8, 3)$

17. $(7, 1)$ $(-7, -1)$

20. $(4, -6)$ $(-4, 6)$

Build a Model

You can create a tessellation pattern just by starting with a square. Look at the diagrams below. Follow the steps to create a design of your own.

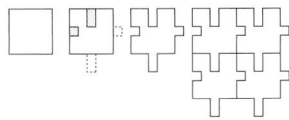

On graph paper, draw a square. → Draw some simple shapes in the square. → Move the shapes to the opposite side as shown. → Repeat the shapes to create a pattern.

MENTAL MATH

Write the following points on the board, and ask students to mentally calculate the image point as indicated, rotated around the origin.

(90° counterclockwise)

$(1, 0)$	*(0, 1)*
$(-3, 0)$	*(0, -3)*
$(0, 1)$	*(-1, 0)*
$(0, -2)$	*(2, 0)*

(180° clockwise)

$(4, -1)$	*(-4, 1)*
$(-5, 3)$	*(5, -3)*
$(-2, -1)$	*(2, 1)*
$(6, 8)$	*(-6, -8)*

11.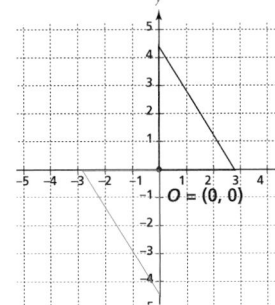

12.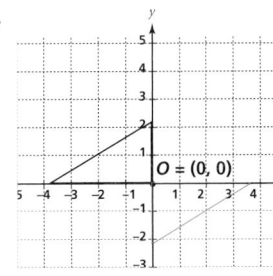

13.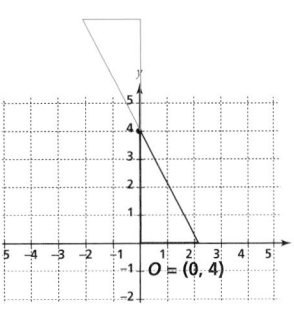

14.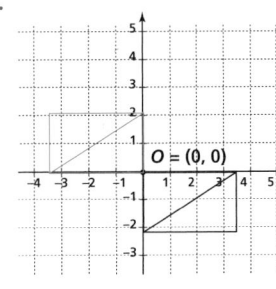

Lesson at a Glance

Chapter 12 Application

Overview This application explains tessellations and challenges students to form tessellations with various polygons.

Objectives

- To identify true tessellations
- To draw tessellations using several different polygons

Student Page 394

Teacher's Resource Library **TRL**

Application Activity 12

Everyday Math 12

1 Warm-Up Activity

If possible, show students copies of artworks by Dutch artist M. C. Escher, who makes extensive use of patterned geometric figures. Encourage students to explore the ways in which the artist has combined shapes for an effect.

2 Teaching the Lesson

The key point in creating tessellations is for students to make sure that the arrangement of regular polygons at every vertex is identical. Students will need to make a template in order to create each tessellation suggested in the lesson. Provide a sample square, rectangle, and equilateral triangle, and have students trace them, copy them onto cardboard, and cut them out.

Sample Answers for Application Problem 3

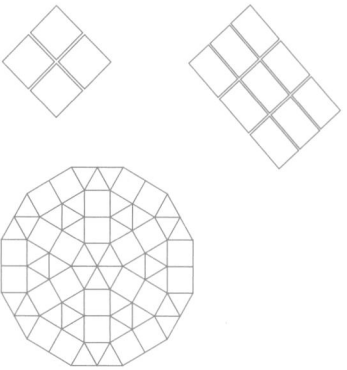

Application

Plane Cover-Up A *tessellation* is a repeating pattern of figures that covers a plane (flat surface) without gaps or overlaps. Using what you learned about reflection (flip), rotation (turn), and translation (slide), you can create beautiful designs.

EXAMPLE 1 Name the transformation in this pattern.

Step 1 Look for recognizable patterns.

Step 2 Name the transformation.

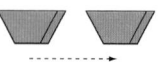 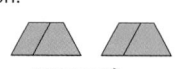

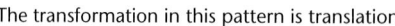

The transformation in this pattern is translation.

EXAMPLE 2 Name all the transformations you see in the pattern.

Step 1 Look for an example of reflection.

Step 2 Look for translation.

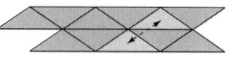

Step 3 Look for rotation.

Exercise Solve each problem.

1. Name the transformations you see in this tessellation. reflection; translation

2. Name the translations you see in this tessellation. reflection; translation

3. Draw 3 polygon tessellations. See Teacher's Edition.

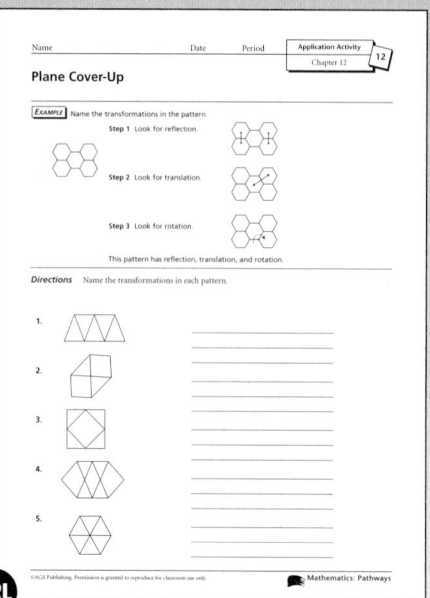

Application Activity 12

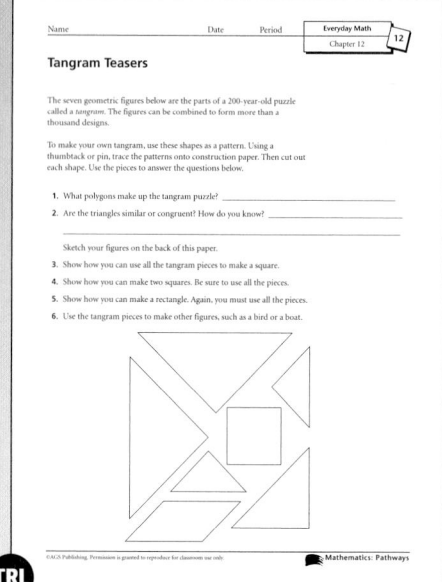

Everyday Math 12

Chapter 12 R E V I E W

Write the letter of the correct answer.

1. Find *x* in the triangle. C
  A 90°   **C** 110°
  B 100°   **D** 290°

2. Is this pair of triangles congruent?
  If yes, why? C
  A yes, SSS   **C** yes, ASA
  B no   **D** yes, SAS

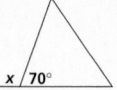

3. Name this polygon. A
  A rhombus   **C** trapezoid
  B pentagon   **D** square

4. *ABCD* is a rectangle. What the value
  of *x* to the tenths place? A
  A 12.2   **C** 14.9
  B 149   **D** 122

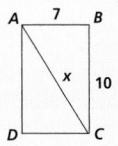

Use this illustration for problems 5 to 12.

Example: m∠*BXC*
Solution: *C* at 90°, *B* at 35°
90° − 35° = 55° = m∠*BXC*

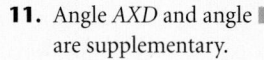

5. 35°
6. 110°
7. 40°
8. 140°
9. AXC and CXF
10. BXF, AXE, AXD, BXE
11. DXF
12. DXF

5. m∠*AXB*

6. m∠*AXD*

7. m∠*FXE*

8. m∠*AXE*

9. Name two right angles.

10. Name three obtuse angles.

11. Angle *AXD* and angle ▇ are supplementary.

12. Angle *CXD* and angle ▇ are complementary.

Chapter 12 Review

Each set of problems in the Chapter Review includes an example and solution to illustrate the concept. Use the given examples for reteaching the materials in Chapter 12. For additional practice, refer to the Supplementary Problems for Chapter 12 (pages 454–455).

Chapter 12 Mastery Test TRL

The Teacher's Resource Library includes parallel forms of the Chapter 12 Mastery Test. The difficulty level of the two forms is equivalent. You may wish to use one form as a pretest and the other form as a posttest.

Chapter 12 Mastery Test A

Alternative Assessment items correlate with student Goals for Learning at the beginning of this chapter.

■ To measure and classify angles

Have students take five angle measurements of the sun at varying times of the day, defining 0 degrees as the eastern horizon and 180 degrees as the western horizon. Use a protractor to measure the degree between level ground and a pole pointed at the direction of the sun, but warn students not to look directly at the sun. (Approximations are acceptable.)

■ To name and classify triangles

Have students bring in examples from magazines or newspapers of several different kinds of triangles. Have them name and classify these triangles and create a poster using these triangles.

■ To find the measures of angles in triangles

Have students measure the angles in their example triangles from the previous assessment. Then have them discuss the relationships of the angles in these triangles. Make sure that they understand the relationship of angles in all kinds of triangles—the angle measurements must always add up to 180 degrees.

■ To identify quadrilaterals

Have students draw a picture of a three-dimensional object such as a table, desk, or book. You could draw a box on the board as an example. When students have finished their drawings, have them identify the number of quadrilaterals that are in their drawing and then name each of them.

■ To determine the number of degrees in polygons

Have students draw a shape such as a star or a pine tree and estimate the total number of the degrees in the structure. Next, have them break the shape into various polygons. Finally, have them figure out the actual number of the degrees in the structure by adding the sums of the degrees in the polygons. Ask students what kinds of polygons they used and how their estimations compared with the actual numbers.

Use the intersecting lines for problems 13 to 17. Write *vertical, adjacent, complementary, equal,* or *supplementary.* More than one name may apply.

Example: ∠2 and ∠3   Solution: adjacent and supplementary

13. adjacent, supplementary
14. vertical and equal
15. adjacent, supplementary
16. 130°
17. 50°
18. 60°
19. 110°
20. 140°

13. ∠1 and ∠2 are ___ angles.

14. ∠1 and ∠3 are ___ angles.

15. ∠1 and ∠4 are ___ angles.

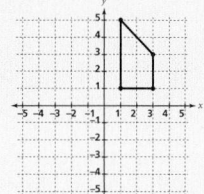

Find the measure of each angle.

Example: m∠4   Solution: 180° − 130° = 50° = m∠4

16. m∠3   **17.** m∠2

Find *x* in the triangles.

Example:

Solution: $180° = 55° + 90° + x$ $180° = 145° + x$ $x = 35°$

18.   **19.**   **20.**

Use graph paper to reflect each point over the specified axis.

Example: (2, 5) *x*-axis = (−2, 5) *y*-axis = (2, −5)

21. *x*-axis
$A = (3, -1)$ $A' = (3, 1)$
$B = (-2, 4)$ $B' = (-2, -4)$
$C = (0, -3)$ $C' = (0, 3)$

22. *y*-axis
$D = (-1, -3)$ $D' = (1, -3)$
$E = (5, 1)$ $E' = (-5, 1)$
$F = (4, -2)$ $F' = (-4, -2)$

Reflect the object shown over the specified line.

23. $A' = (-3, 1)$,
   $B' = (-5, 1)$,
   $C' = (-5, 3)$,
   $D' = (-3, 5)$

23. *x* = −1
$A = (1, 1)$ $C = (3, 3)$
$B = (3, 1)$ $D = (1, 5)$

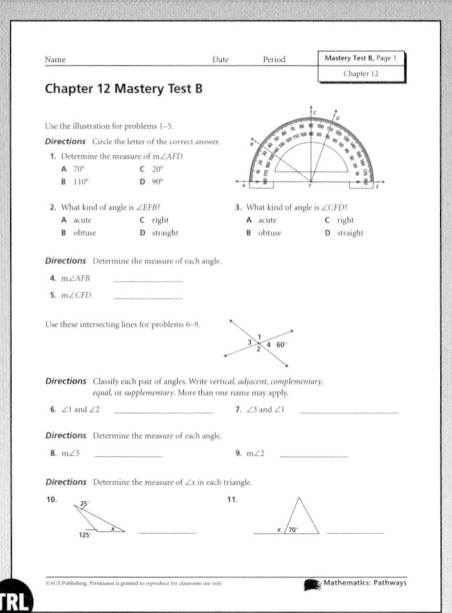

24. **A**

25. none

26. **M**

27. $A' = (-2, -1)$,
$B' = (1, -1)$,
$C' = (-1, 2)$

28. $D' = (0, -2)$,
$E' = (4, -1)$,
$F' = (1, 2)$

Draw one line of reflection for each letter. If none exists, write none.

Example:

24. **A** 25. **Z** 26. **M**

Slide each triangle as directed.
Use your own graph paper.

Example: $\triangle XYZ$ Slide 3 to the left and 2 down.

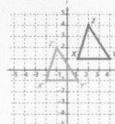

27. $\triangle ABC$
$A = (1, 1)$
$B = (4, 1)$
$C = (2, 4)$
3 to the left
2 down

28. $\triangle DEF$
$D = (-4, -5)$
$E = (0, -4)$
$F = (-3, -1)$
4 to the right
3 up

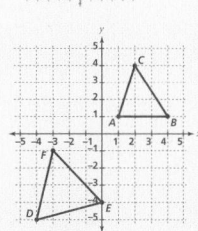

Use your own graph paper to draw object.
Rotate the object around specified point.

Example: Reflect the object shown
90° and 180° about point A.

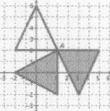

29. Object A
Rotate 90° around point $(-3, -2)$

30. Object B
Rotate 180° around point $(1, -5)$

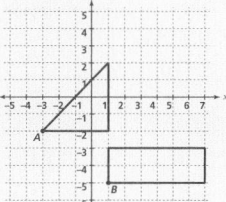

Test-Taking Tip

Avoid confusing the meaning of math symbols by reading them in full. For example, when you see the symbol $\approx$, you should say *is almost equal to.*

■ **To identify reflections across a line of symmetry**

Have students draw an object on the coordinate plane to the left or right of the x-axis. Objects can be a square, rectangle, triangle, or a more difficult shape like a hexagon or star. Have students list the points of their objects on the same sheet of paper. Pair students, and have them exchange papers. Tell them to reflect the object over the x-axis. Remind students that if you reflect an object or a point over the x-axis, the y-coordinate stays the same and if you reflect over the y-axis, the x-coordinate stays the same. *(Answers will vary; check for accuracy of reflection.)*

■ **To identify lines of symmetry and symmetric shapes**

Write the entire alphabet as large as you can on the board. Assign each student a letter, and have each draw all lines of symmetry for his or her letter on the board. If no lines of symmetry exist, students can write "none" under the letter.

■ **To carry out slides and translations in the plane**

Solve problem 1 in Exercise D (Lesson 13) as a class. Tell students that the final form of the answer should be $(x + a, y + b)$ and that they are solving for a and b. Explain that $(4, -1)$ is the start point and $(0, 3)$ is the end point. Ask students the following questions: "How do you get from $(4, -1)$ to $(0, 3)$?" "Starting with the x-coordinates of the ordered pairs, how do you get from 4 to 0?" *(Subtract 4.)* "Looking at the y-coordinates of the ordered pairs, how do you get from -1 to 3?" *(Add 4.)* Replace a and b in the equation above to get $(x - 4, y + 4)$. Have students independently finish the remainder of the problems. Work one of the solutions in class to make sure that students solved the problem correctly.

■ **To carry out and identify rotations in the plane**

Draw four shapes on the board, and rotate them either 90° or 180° clockwise or counterclockwise. Ask students to identify the rotation. Challenge students by rotating an object 45°. Ask whether they can identify the rotation.

Planning Guide

Data, Statistics, and Probability

Lesson		Student Pages	Vocabulary	Practice Exercises	Problem Solving	Try This	Solutions Key
1	Bar Graphs	400–401	✔	✔			✔
2	Frequency Tables	402–403	✔	✔			✔
3	Circle Graphs	404–405	✔	✔			✔
4	Histograms	406–407	✔	✔		407	✔
5	Scatterplots	408–409	✔	✔			✔
6	Mean	410–411	✔	✔	411		✔
7	Median	412–413	✔	✔	413		✔
8	Mode	414–415	✔	✔			✔
9	Range	416–417	✔	✔	417		✔
10	Box-and-Whiskers Plots	418–419	✔	✔			✔
11	The Probability Fraction	420–421	✔	✔		421	✔
12	Dependent and Independent Events	422–425	✔	✔		425	✔
13	The Fundamental Principle of Counting	426–427	✔	✔			✔
Application	Tally Up	428		✔			✔

Student Text Lesson

Chapter Activities

Teacher's Resource Library
Estimation Exercise 13: Estimating the
    Mean
Application Activity 13: Tally Up
Everyday Math 13: Data Check
Community Connection 13: Number
    Please

Teacher's Edition
Chapter 13 Project

Assessment Options

Student Text
Chapter 13 Review

Teacher's Resource Library
Chapter 13 Mastery Tests A and B
Chapters 1–13 Final Mastery Test

Teacher's Edition
Chapter 13 Alternative Assessments

| Student Text Features | | | | | | Teaching Strategies | | | | | | | | | Learning Styles | | | | | | Teacher's Resource Library | | | |
Estimation Activity	Math in Your Life	Technology Connection	Writing About Mathematics	Build a Model	Calculator Practice	Online Connection	Common Error	Applications Home, Career, Community	Mental Math	Manipulatives	Calculator	Group Problem Solving	Modeling	Knowing Your Students	Auditory/Verbal	Visual/Spatial	Logical/Mathematical	Body/Kinesthetic	Interpersonal/Group Learning	LEP/ESL	Activities	Alternate Activities	Workbook Activities	Self-Study Guide
						401	401	401								401					125	125	132	✔
		403					403					403									126	126	133	✔
			405				405		405						405						127	127	134	✔
						407	407						407								128	128	135	✔
								409					409	409							129	129	136	✔
					411						411	411							411		130	130	137	✔
413		412					413					413			413						131	131	138	✔
							415					415							415		132	132	139	✔
									417			417								417	133	133	140–141	✔
							419										419				134	134	142	✔
	420						421			421									421		135	135	143	✔
			424	424			423	424	424			425			425				424		136	136	144	✔
											427							427	427		137	137	145	✔
						429	429																	✔

Software Options

Skill Track Software

Use the Skill Track Software for *Mathematics: Pathways* for additional reinforcement of this chapter. The software provides multiple-choice assessment items for students to access by computer.

Solutions Key

Use the Solutions Key with this chapter to help students who may need additional assistance. The Solutions Key CD provides solutions for every exercise in the student edition.

Other Resources

Alternative Activities

The Teacher's Resource Library (TRL) contains a set of worksheets written at a second-grade reading level called Alternative Activities. They cover the same content as the regular Activities.

Manipulatives

See the Manipulative activities in this chapter for hands-on modeling of the content.

Two-Color Counters (or coins)
1–6 Number Cubes

Chapter 13: Data, Statistics, and Probability

pages 398–431

Lessons

Skill Track for Mathematics: Pathways

Teacher's Resource Library **TRL**

(Answer Keys for the Teacher's Resource Library begin on page 528 of this Teacher's Edition.)

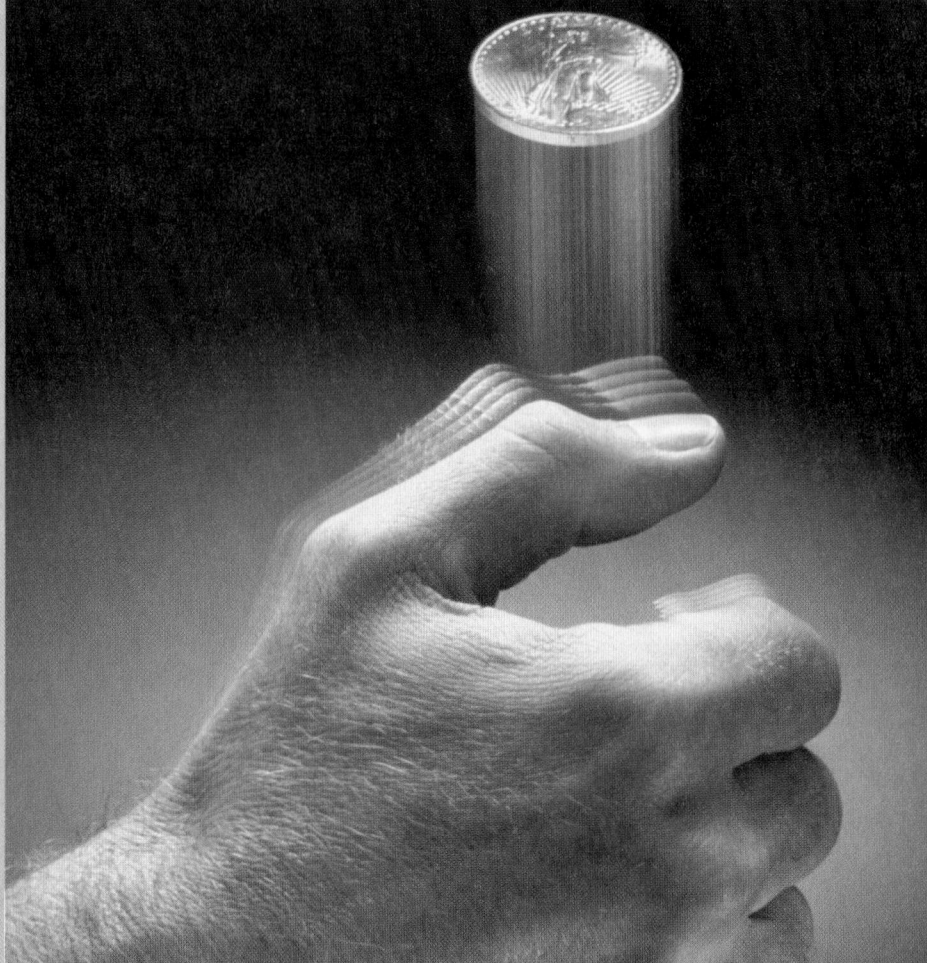

Chapter

13 Data, Statistics, and Probability

H ow many times have you been asked "Heads or tails?" Did you ever make a decision based on the toss of a coin?

You know that each coin toss has two possible results: It will land either head side up or tail side up. The probability of one or the other is said to be 1 in 2, or 50-50.

Data, statistics, and probability are useful in many tasks, from forecasting stock prices and writing insurance policies to predicting coin tosses. Researchers design surveys to collect data. They look at the patterns they find in the data. Then they use mathematics to figure out what the patterns mean. Statistics have been studied since as far back as the time of Columbus.

In Chapter 13, you will solve problems involving data, statistics, and probability.

Goals for Learning

- ◆ To construct bar graphs, frequency tables, circle graphs, histograms, and scatterplots and interpret information illustrated by them
- ◆ To find measures of central tendency and range
- ◆ To construct and understand box-and-whiskers plots
- ◆ To solve problems involving probability and the fundamental principle of counting

399

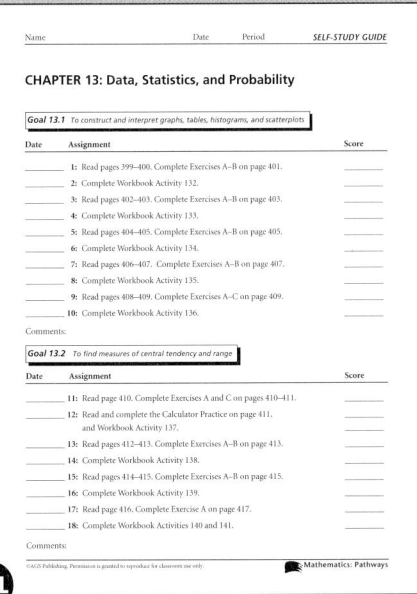

Chapter 13 Self-Study Guide

Introducing the Chapter

Use the information in the chapter opener to help students cultivate an understanding of the importance of statistics. Remind students that a proliferation of statistics exists in our world today. If possible, distribute statistical references such as *The World Almanac and Book of Facts* or *Information Please Almanac* and give students an opportunity to peruse the myriad statistics that are contained in such publications.

CHAPTER PROJECT

Give each student an opportunity to access the World Wide Web and visit the federal government's statistical Web site at www.fedstats.gov. While students are at the Web site, ask them to locate and record a statistic they find interesting. Upon completion of the chapter, schedule time for students to share their statistical findings with each other.

TEACHER'S RESOURCE

The AGS Publishing Teaching Strategies in Math Transparencies may be used with this chapter. They add an interactive dimension to expand and enhance the program content.

CAREER INTEREST INVENTORY

The AGS Publishing Harrington-O'Shea Career Decision-Making System-Revised (CDM) may be used with this chapter. Students can use the CDM to explore their interests and identify careers. The CDM defines career areas that are indicated by students' responses on the inventory.

Chapter 13 Lesson 1

Overview This lesson introduces bar graphs.

Objective
■ To organize and interpret data in a bar graph

Student Pages 400–401

Teacher's Resource Library
Workbook Activity 132
Activity 125
Alternative Activity 125

Mathematics Vocabulary
statistics
data
bar graph
interval

---

1 Warm-Up Activity

Invite volunteers to describe various graphs with which they are familiar. Then ask them to organize themselves in a line from greatest height to least. After the line is formed, point out that each person in line represents a data value, and the height of each person determines the exact value. In much the same way, a bar graph uses various heights of data bars to display exact data values.

2 Teaching the Lesson

As students read the lesson text on page 400, have them note that the vertical axis of the bar graph is broken—it is not continuous. Explain that a requirement of any bar graph is that the axis that displays the data interval (in this case, the vertical axis) must begin at zero and display regular intervals throughout the axis. When the axis begins at zero but does not display *regular* data intervals, the axis must be broken. The function of a broken axis is to indicate that the data interval is not consistent and to help prevent a graph from being misleading to a reader.

Lesson 1 Bar Graphs

Statistics are numerical facts about people or things. Facts, information, and statistics are examples of **data.** Data can be organized and displayed in different ways.

A **bar graph** is a way to organize and display data using rectangular bars. A bar graph has the following parts:

Statistics
Numerical facts about people, places, or things
Data
Information given in numbers
Bar graph
A way of comparing information using rectangular bars
Interval
Set of all numbers between two stated numbers

• a title
• a horizontal axis with labels
• a vertical axis with labels
• data

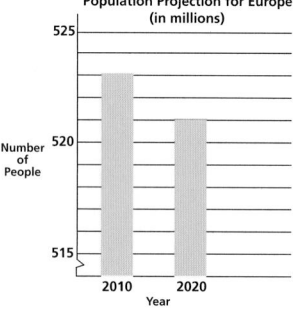

Population Projection for Europe (in millions)

Whenever you see a bar graph with a break in the vertical axis, you know that it does not begin at zero.

In this bar graph, the title tells you that the graph is describing the projected population of Europe, in millions of people. The horizontal axis shows that the graph is describing the years 2010 and 2020. The vertical axis shows the number of people.

The **interval** of this vertical axis is 5 numbers from one labeled number to the next. For example, the interval between 520 and 525 of the vertical axis is 520, 521, 522, 523, and 524. Since the title of the graph tells you the data is stated in millions, the vertical axis represents 516 million, or 516,000,000, people; 517,000,000 people; 518,000,000 people; and so on.

The graph shows that for the year 2010, the projected population of Europe is 523,000,000 people, and for the year 2020, the projected population is 521,000,000 people.

Sometimes an axis of a graph, such as the vertical axis of the graph above, does not begin at zero. Whenever an axis of a graph does not begin at zero, it must be shown as a broken, or jagged, line.

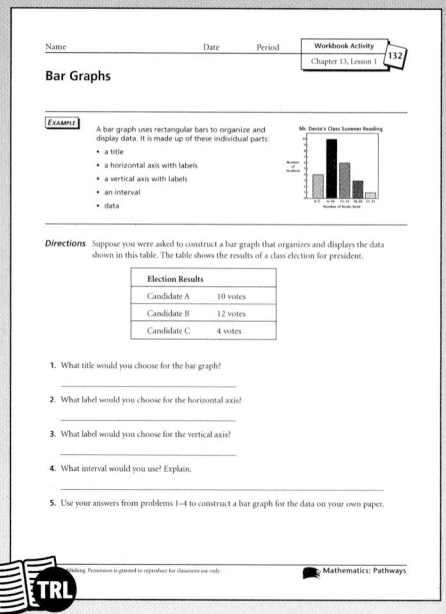

Workbook Activity 132

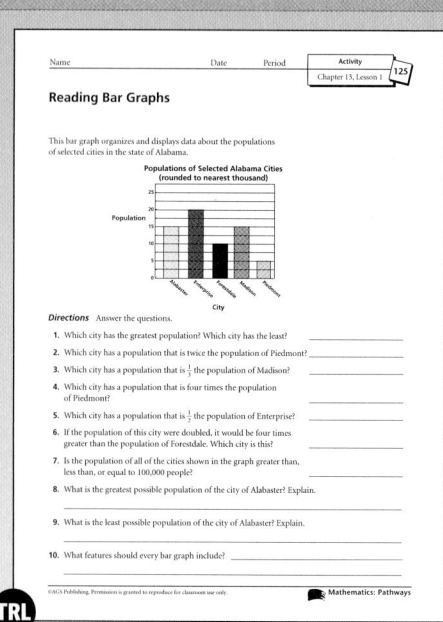

Activity 125

Exercise A Answer the questions about this bar graph.

1. What data is displayed by the graph?
2. What is the interval of the vertical axis?
3. Why is the vertical axis broken and not a straight line?
4. Are all of the counties in the state of Wyoming shown on the graph? Tell how you know.
5. Of the counties shown on the graph, which county covers the greatest number of square miles?
6. Of the counties shown on the graph, which county covers the least number of square miles?
7. Order the counties shown in the graph by area from least to greatest.

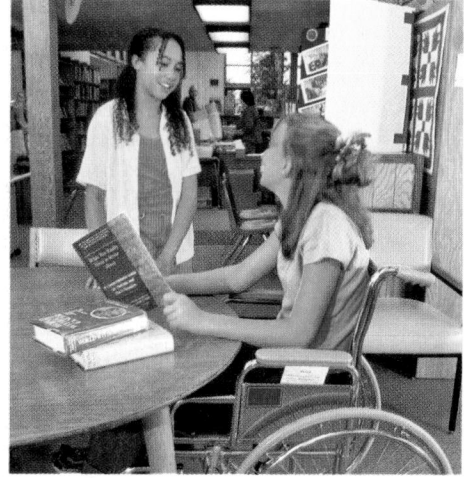

Area of Selected Wyoming Counties
(rounded to nearest hundred square miles)

8. Suppose that two counties were added to the graph and the bar for each county reads 2,500 square miles. Is it likely that both counties have exactly the same area? Explain.
9. Is it possible for the bars of a bar graph to be horizontal instead of vertical? Explain.

Exercise B Draw a bar graph that organizes and displays the data shown in this table.

10.

Number of Minutes of Tutoring This Week	
Monday	35
Tuesday	50
Wednesday	45
Thursday	75

See Teacher's Edition page for answers.

Data, Statistics, and Probability   Chapter 13   **401**

The data interval of a bar graph is the distance between two consecutive tick marks on the data axis. This interval must be regular. In other words, if the interval represented by two consecutive ticks is ten, the intervals between *all* tick marks on the graph must be ten.

COMMON ERROR

Remind students that the interval of the data axis of any bar graph must be consistent, and that the data axis must be shown as broken if the interval is not consistent.

3 **Reinforce and Extend**

LEARNING STYLES

Visual/Spatial

Ask students to use a piece of paper or a finger to cover the vertical axis of the graph on page 400. Then have them order the years shown on the horizontal axis from greatest to least. Repeat the activity using the graph on page 401. This time, however, have students order the counties shown on the horizontal axis from least to greatest.

AT HOME

Many kinds of publications contain bar graphs. Invite students to search in their homes for bar graphs in newspapers, magazines, and other publications. Successful searches can be shared with the class.

ONLINE CONNECTION

Students can learn more about interpreting data in bar graphs at www.census.gov/prod/3/98pubs/cenbr982.pdf. This link will download a pdf file that can be printed. There are two bar graphs. One graph represents changes in the numbers of people who work at home. The other graph compares classes of workers, such as government or self-employed workers, and shows percentages of who works at home or elsewhere. Have students study the graphs and then write short paragraphs about what the graphs tell them.

Answers to Problems 1–10

1. area of selected Wyoming counties 2. five hundred 3. axis does not begin at zero 4. no; selected 5. Crook County 6. Hot Springs County 7. Hot Springs; Platte; Weston; Laramie; Crook 8. no 9. yes 10. sample answer:

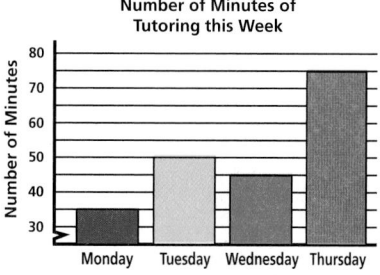

Number of Minutes of Tutoring this Week

Data, Statistics, and Probability   **401**

Lesson at a Glance

Chapter 13 Lesson 2

Overview This lesson introduces frequency tables.

Objective

■ To organize and interpret data in a frequency table

Student Pages 402–403

Teacher's Resource Library **TRL**

Workbook Activity 133

Activity 126

Alternative Activity 126

Mathematics Vocabulary

frequency
frequency table
tally

---

1 Warm-Up Activity

Have students work in groups to estimate the frequency of the following events:

• The number of times a person's eyes blink in one hour

• The number of times a person's heart beats in one year

2 Teaching the Lesson

Explain that the function of a frequency table is the same as the functions of the bar graph and the circle graph studied previously—each represents a way to organize and summarize data. Bar graphs, circle graphs, and frequency tables are visual ways of organizing and summarizing data.

Indicate the frequency table on page 402, and point out that the number of people given in the title (20) must be the same as the sum of the data in the frequency column and must be the same as the number of tallies shown altogether in the tally column. This understanding can be used by students to check the correctness of a frequency table that has been constructed from a set of data. Also have students note that the intervals shown in the first column of the table are regular (just as the intervals shown by the data axis of a bar graph must be regular).

Lesson 2 Frequency Tables

Another way data can be shown is a **frequency table.** A frequency table is a way of **tallying** data in intervals. This frequency table describes the ages of 20 people selected at random.

Frequency

The number of times an event, value, or characteristic occurs

Frequency table

A chart showing the number of times something happened

Tally

A mark of each count

Ages of 20 People Selected at Random

Frequency Table		
Interval	Tally	Frequency
0–9	|||	3
10–19	|	1
20–29	|||	3
30–39	||||	4
40–49		0
50–59	|	1
60–69	||	2
70–79	⊬⊬	5
80–89	|	1
90–99		0
100–109		0

For the tally part of a frequency table, check marks (✓) are sometimes used instead of other kinds of marks.

The column titled *Interval* shows the interval of the frequency table. The interval of this frequency table is ten years: 0–9, 10–19, 20–29, and so on. Other frequency tables may have other intervals—it depends on the table and the data that is described by the table.

The column titled *Tally* contains a tally mark for each time an age in any interval was recorded. Tallies are often arranged in groups of five. Look at the tally marks for the interval 70–79: the fifth tally mark is drawn in a different direction. Grouping tallies in groups of five helps anyone who reads the frequency table interpret the data more quickly.

The column titled *Frequency* shows the exact number of tallies in each interval. In any frequency table, the sum of the numbers in the Frequency column must be the same as the sum of the tallies in the Tally column. Since this frequency table shows the ages of 20 people, the sum of both the Tally column and the Frequency column must be 20.

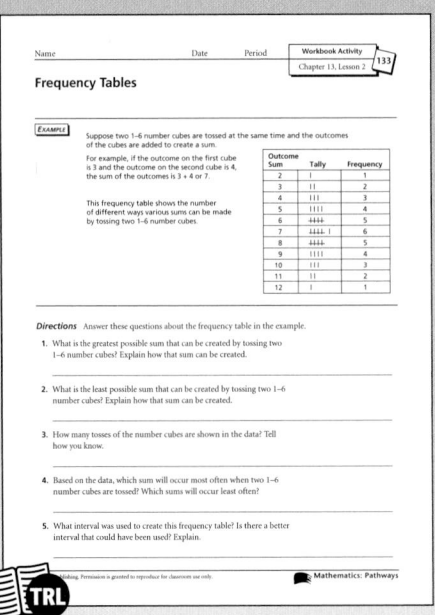

Workbook Activity 133

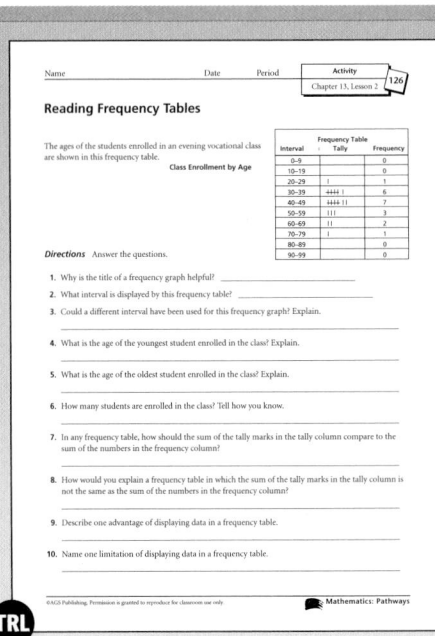

Activity 126

Frequency tables help you interpret data by showing how data is grouped, or clustered. In the frequency table on page 402, the interval 40–49 seems to break the data into halves—about one-half of the data is below the interval and about one-half of the data is above. Also, the interval 70–79 contains the greatest number of tallies, and the intervals 40–49, 90–99, and 100–109 contain the least number of tallies.

Exercise A Use this frequency table for problems 1–4.

Quiz Scores

Frequency Table		
Interval	Tally	Frequency
50–59		0
60–69	||	2
70–79	||||	4
80–89	ⅢⅢ ⅢⅢ ||	12
90–99	ⅢⅢ |	6

1. How many students took the quiz? Tell how you know.

2. What was the highest quiz score? Explain.

3. What was the lowest quiz score? Explain.

4. Suppose that any student who scores 80 or more on the quiz earns an A. How many students earned an A?

Exercise B Take a survey.

5. Survey your classmates and ask each of them to estimate the number of minutes they studied last week. Organize the data you collect and display it in a frequency table.

Technology Connection

Virtual Data Collection and Analysis
Computer software can take the place of paper and pen when it comes to collecting and analyzing data. Some of the professionals who use these "virtual" data collectors are medical researchers, microbiologists, economists, political scientists, and geographers. Look on the Internet, and you can find a dozen products to help these professionals do their work faster and more accurately. Some word processing programs even let you make bar charts and circle graphs.

Data, Statistics, and Probability Chapter 13 **403**

In this frequency table, each interval represents ten possible tallies.

As students read the lesson text at the top of page 403, point out that if the intervals of the frequency table were different (intervals of 20 instead of 10, for example), the clustering of data would be different and the table would generate a slightly different impression than the impression it gives in its present form.

COMMON ERROR

Each time students construct a frequency table, remind them to find the sum of data values in the frequency column and the sum of the tallies in the tally column. Each sum should match the number of data values in the data set used to create the frequency table.

3 **Reinforce and Extend**

GROUP PROBLEM SOLVING

Write the data set shown below on the board. Then have students work in small groups to discuss the data and select the interval that should be used to display the data in a frequency table. Complete the activity by asking groups to share their selections with one another.

2	529
499	487
377	610
512	492
470	989
483	504
558	462
486	541
511	459
524	533

(Intervals will vary.)

Lesson at a Glance

Chapter 13   Lesson 3

Overview This lesson introduces circle graphs.

Objective

- To read and analyze data in a circle graph

Student Pages 404–405

Teacher's Resource Library

  Workbook Activity   134

  Activity   127

  Alternative Activity   127

....

Mathematics Vocabulary

circle graph

....

1   Warm-Up Activity

Display a map of some kind, such as a state or community map. Have students locate north, south, east, and west on the map. Then explain that with respect to compass-oriented directions, north is 0°/360°, east is 90°, south is 180°, and west is 270°. Invite students to describe, using degrees, how to move from one place to another on the map.

2   Teaching the Lesson

After students complete Example 1 on page 404, explain that one way to check an answer derived from a circle graph is to consider the whole of the graph. In this example, the whole is represented by 30 students. Since it was computed that 18 students responded *yes*, the computation can be checked by determining the number of students who responded *no*. If a computation to determine how many students responded *no* generates an answer of 12, the original computation was correct, because 18 + 12 = 30 (the whole).

Before discussing step 4 of Example 2 on page 405, you might choose to review with students the proper procedure for using a protractor to draw angles of various measures.

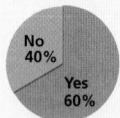

Circle graph

A way to present information using the parts of a circle

A circle graph is also known as a pie chart.

Another way in which data can be shown is a **circle graph.** A circle graph represents data using parts of a circle.

EXAMPLE 1 This circle graph shows how 30 students responded when asked if they listen to music more than two times each week. How many students responded yes? How many students responded no?

To find the number of students who responded yes, find 60% of 30.

60% of 30 = 0.60 • 30 = 18; 18 students responded yes.

To find the number of students who responded no, find 40% of 30.

40% of 30 = 0.40 • 30 = 12; 12 students responded no.

Music Listeners

No 40%

Yes 60%

30 students surveyed

You can use data to make a circle graph.

EXAMPLE 2 Make a circle graph that organizes and displays the data in this table.

Have you ever studied 90 minutes without stopping?	
16 students surveyed	
Yes	12 students
No	4 students

Step 1 Draw a circle.

Step 2 Find the fractional part for the total number of votes for each response.

Yes: $\frac{12}{16}$ votes or $\frac{3}{4}$

No: $\frac{4}{16}$ votes or $\frac{1}{4}$

Step 3 Multiply each fractional part by 360°—the number of degrees in a circle.

$\frac{3}{4} • 360° = 270°$ $\frac{1}{4} • 360° = 90°$

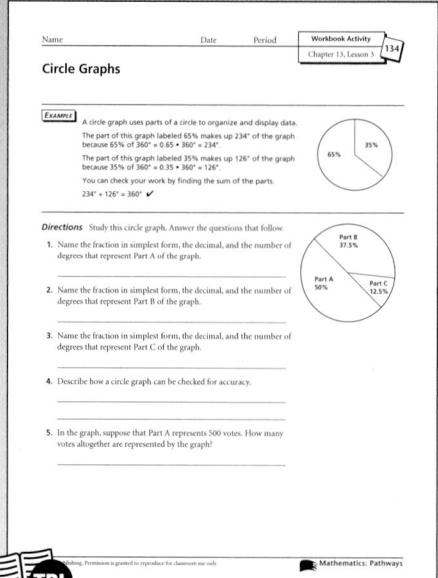

Workbook Activity 134

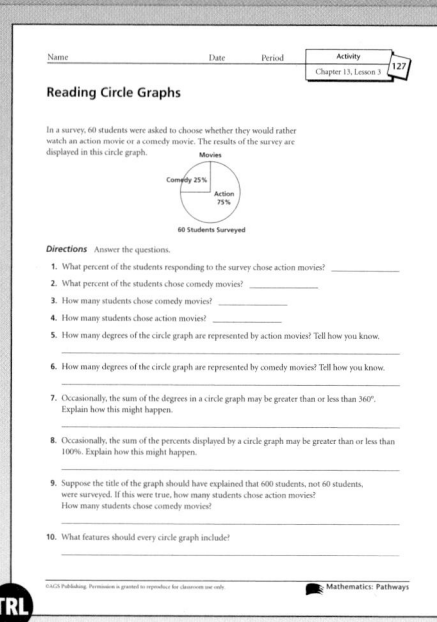

Activity 127

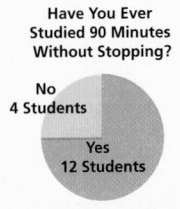
EXAMPLE 2 *(continued)*

Step 4 Use a protractor to divide the circle into two parts. The central angle of one part should measure 270° to represent $\frac{3}{4}$ and the central angle of the other part should measure 90° to represent $\frac{1}{4}$. Label each part and write a title for your graph.

Have You Ever Studied 90 Minutes Without Stopping?

No 4 Students

Yes 12 Students

Exercise A Answer the questions about the circle graph shown.

1. What data does the circle graph organize and display? 40 students' responses

Do You Usually Sleep More Than 8 Hours Each Night?

No 20%

Yes 80%

40 students surveyed

2. What percent of students responded *yes*? 80%

3. What percent of students responded *no*? 20%

4. How many students were surveyed altogether? 40 students

5. How many students responded *yes*? 32 students

6. How many students responded *no*? 8 students

7. How many degrees of the circle are represented by *yes* votes? 288°

8. How many degrees of the circle are represented by *no* votes? 72°

9. Suppose the circle graph represented twice the number of students—80 instead of 40. Would the circle contain twice the number of degrees—720° instead of 360°? Explain. No; A circle cannot measure more than or less than 360°.

Exercise B Draw a circle graph that organizes and displays the data shown in this table.

10.

Class Election	
Candidate A	9 votes
Candidate B	5 votes
Candidate C	10 votes

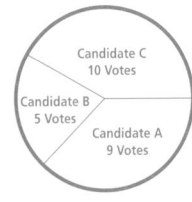

Candidate C 10 Votes

Candidate B 5 Votes

Candidate A 9 Votes

---

3 Reinforce and Extend

Chapter 13 Lesson 4

Overview This lesson introduces histograms.

Objectives

- To read and analyze data from a histogram
- To draw a histogram using data from a frequency table

Student Pages 406–407

Teacher's Resource Library TRL

Workbook Activity 135

Activity 128

Alternative Activity 128

Mathematics Vocabulary

histogram

1 Warm-Up Activity

Have students work in groups to create surveys. Encourage each group to create a question and five responses. Allow students to conduct their surveys with the class and record responses.

2 Teaching the Lesson

Review with students how histograms differ from bar graphs. (*The vertical line between the bars on a histogram has been totally or partially removed. Therefore, the histogram is formed by one continuous line with all the bars touching.*)

Remind students that the skills required to read and analyze graphs and frequency tables can be reviewed in Lessons 1, 2, and 3.

Ask students to check each other's frequency tables from problem 5. The total of the digits in the table should be equal to the number in the problem's directions. (*20*)

Histogram
A bar graph that displays data in equal number groupings with no spaces between the bars

Histograms are like bar graphs in which the bars touch each other. The vertical lines between the bars are erased or dotted so that a continuous area is created. Because histograms are often used to display frequencies, such tables are called frequency histograms.

EXAMPLE 1 Draw a histogram for the number of times heads is obtained when 5 nickels are tossed 20 times.

Frequency Table	
Number of Heads	Frequency
0	1
1	3
2	6
3	5
4	4
5	1
Total	20 tosses

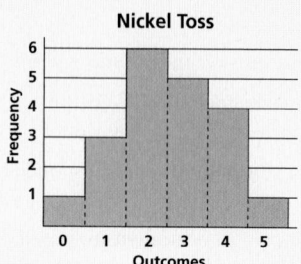

EXAMPLE 2 The given histogram shows the grades received on a test.

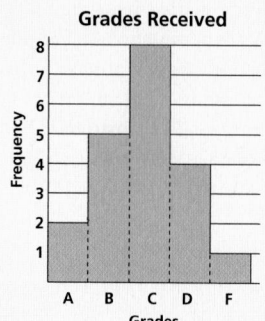

How many students are in the class?

Make a frequency table, and add the frequency for each grade given.

Frequency Table	
Grades	Frequency
A 100–91	2
B 90–81	5
C 80–71	8
D 70–61	4
F 60 and below	1
Total	20 students

A total of 20 students are in the class.

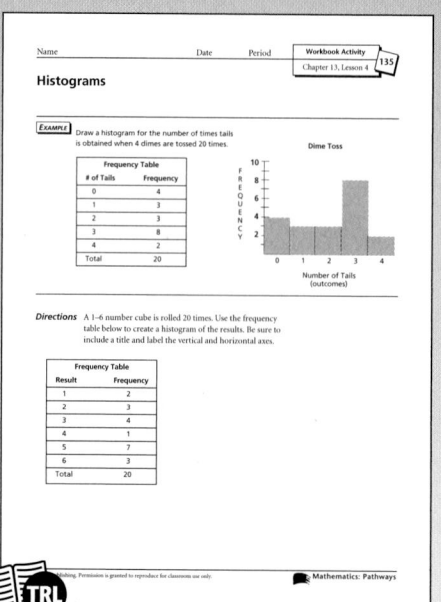

Workbook Activity 135

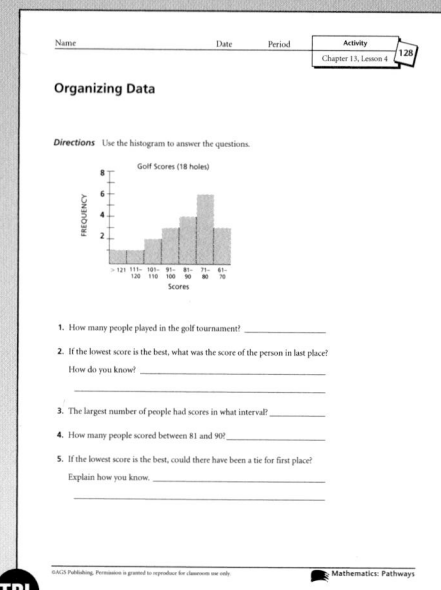

Activity 128

EXAMPLE 2 *(continued)*

What is the most frequently given grade?

Look for the highest point on the histogram. Its height is 8 and corresponds to the grade C.

What is the least frequently given grade?

Look for the lowest point on the histogram. Its height is 1 and corresponds to the grade F.

Exercise A Draw a histogram for the following frequency table.

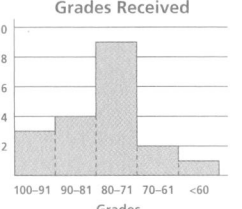

Grades Received

1.

Frequency Table	
Grades	Frequency
A 100–91	3
B 90–81	4
C 80–71	9
D 70–61	2
F 60 and below	1

Exercise B The histogram on the right shows the results of 4 quarters being tossed 20 times. Answer the questions.

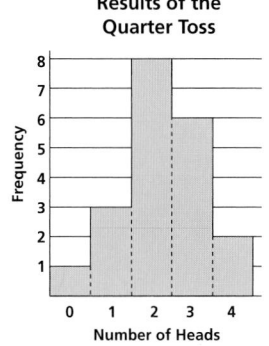

Results of the Quarter Toss

Try This

Find a set of data in a newspaper, in a magazine, in an almanac, or on the Internet. Display the data in a histogram.

Answers will vary.

2. How many times were two heads obtained?   8

3. How many times were no heads obtained?   1

4. How many times were four heads obtained?   2

5. Repeat the experiment above. Toss 4 quarters 20 times. Then make a frequency table for the number of times heads is obtained for each throw. Draw a histogram for the results. Results will vary. Students should make a frequency table and a histogram of their results.

3 **Reinforce and Extend**

MODELING

Have students make life-sized histograms. Provide tape, sidewalk chalk, paper, or other materials, and find a large area indoors or outdoors. Small groups of students should use their data from the Warm-Up Activity to create a histogram.

This activity can be taken further if students are asked to represent specific values (for example, one child equals five students). Students can then model the data by standing in the correct position on the histogram.

Try This

Ask students to check each other's work by exchanging data and graphs.

Lesson at a Glance

Chapter 13 Lesson 5

Overview This lesson introduces scatterplots.

Objective

■ To read and analyze data on a scatterplot

Student Pages 408–409

Teacher's Resource Library

  Workbook Activity 136

  Activity 129

  Alternative Activity 129

....

Mathematics Vocabulary

scatterplot
x-value
y-value

....

1 Warm-Up Activity

Provide a list of five random numbers, and ask each student to choose one. Have each student quickly call out the number as he or she is signaled to do so. Ask students to identify how many times each number was repeated. Explain that the main purpose of a graph or histogram is the same as that for scatterplots: to organize data.

2 Teaching the Lesson

Encourage students to compare and contrast scatterplots and line graphs.

Point out that a scatterplot's appearance allows for easy generalization of the data. This is supported by the examples and by problems 3, and 5.

Have students identify the pattern of the intervals on the *x*- and *y*-axis. Remind students that regular intervals have also appeared on bar graphs, line graphs, and histograms.

Ask for volunteers to identify a situation in which a data model did not have regular intervals. Refer students to Lesson 1 if necessary.

Scatterplot
A graph in which the points plotted show the relationship between two variables

x-value
The value of a given point on a horizontal number line on a coordinate plane; the first number in an ordered pair of coordinates

y-value
The value of a given point on a vertical number line on a coordinate plane; the second number in an ordered pair of coordinates

Scatterplots are graphs of points in the coordinate plane. Each point represents two pieces of data: an **x-value** and a **y-value**.

The word *scatter* means that the points are not on a line. Scientists use scatterplots to analyze pairs of data to discover whether there is any association or relation between the points. In this case, points cluster together around a line or curve.

EXAMPLE 1 Imagine that you are a scientist reviewing the data from 10 sets of twins at age 5. You are viewing the scatterplot of their weights.

Using the scatterplot, can you figure out how many pairs of twins have the same weight?

Look at the line *y* = *x*. There are two points on it, so *two* pairs of twins have the same weight.

Look at the scatterplot again. Is it true that one pair of twins has a weight of 40 pounds each? Yes; the left-most point is 40 pounds on the *x*-axis and 40 pounds on the *y*-axis.

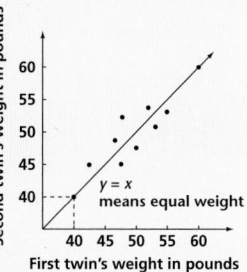

EXAMPLE 2 Look at the scatterplot that shows fathers' heights and their sons' heights when grown. How many sets of fathers and sons have exactly the same height? One set; notice that there is only one point on the *y* = *x* line at 67 inches. That shows that one son has a height of 67 inches (5 feet, 7 inches tall) and his father has that height as well.

Look at the plot again. On the basis of what you see, could you predict the height of the son, knowing the height of the father? Not very well; some points are above and some are below the equal line. Look at the slice between 70 inches and 72 inches (3 points below and 2 points above). This shows that three sons are shorter than their fathers and two sons are taller.

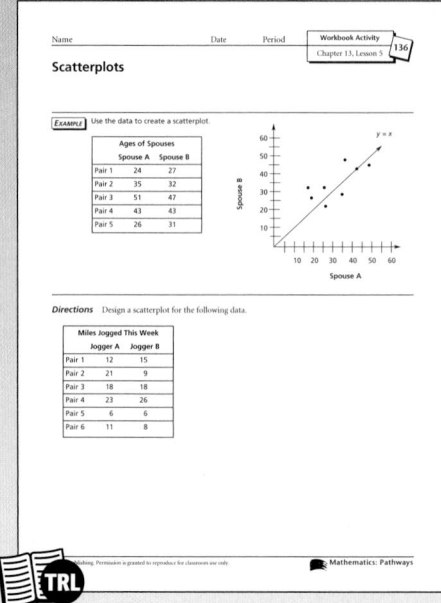

Workbook Activity 136

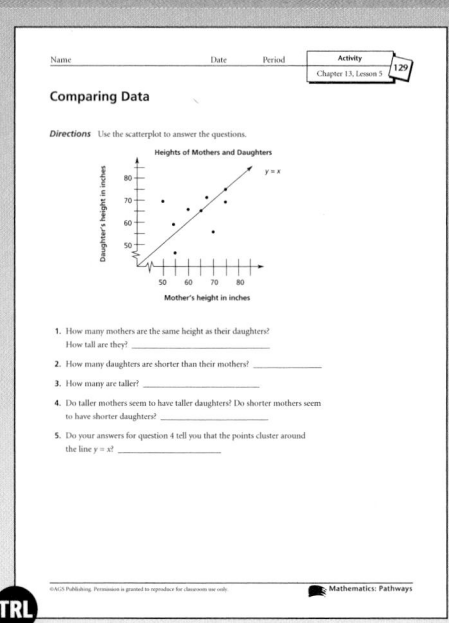

Activity 129

EXAMPLE 3 Which scatterplot shows the points reflecting nearly equal data?
Scatterplot B shows the points reflecting nearly equal data.

Which scatterplot shows the least clustering around the equal line?
Scatterplot A shows the least clustering around the equal line.

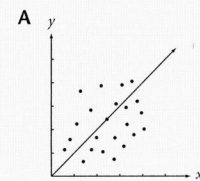 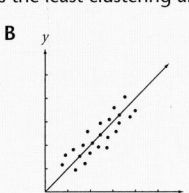 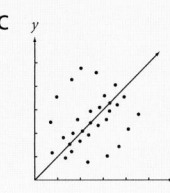

Exercise A Use the scatterplot to answer the questions.

1. How many couples have equal weights? 2

2. What are the weights of the equal points?
150 pounds, 200 pounds

3. Are the points clustered anywhere? no

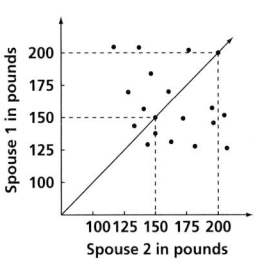

Exercise B Which scatterplot shows the most clustering, A or B?

4.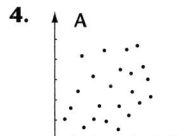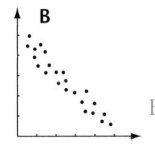

B

Exercise C Use the given scatterplot.

5. Which is the correct description, A or B? B

A As the height increases,
the weight decreases.

B As the height increases,
the weight increases.

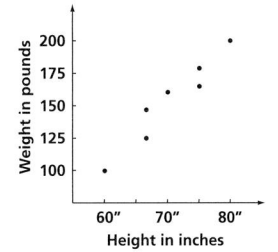

Data, Statistics, and Probability Chapter 13 **409**

3 **Reinforce and Extend**

IN THE COMMUNITY

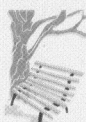 Have each student provide a list of places in the community, such as businesses or parks, where using a scatterplot could be common and helpful.

MODELING

 Ask students to create a large scatterplot on a sheet of paper. Provide students with dice, beans, or other similar objects, and a small cup. Taking turns with a partner, each student should gently roll the items from the cup onto the scatterplot. These objects now represent the data.

Encourage students to keep a tally of the number of times the objects land on the $y = x$ line on each roll. Have each pair compare results with those of the class.

KNOWING YOUR STUDENTS

 In elementary school, most students are good at solving concrete problems. Now that they have arrived at the next academic level, students are being asked to solve more difficult problems that include variables and unknowns. Because of this, solving problems using abstract thinking can be a frustrating new experience for many students. Analyzing data for the purpose of making reasonable predictions or conclusions may take practice. Therefore, pay close attention to students' answers in this lesson. Students may need to do these as a class, in groups, or with a partner. Discussing these problems may help students more fully understand them.

Chapter 13 Lesson 6

Overview This lesson introduces the mean of a set of data.

Objective

- To compute the mean of a set of data

Student Pages 410–411

Teacher's Resource Library

   Workbook Activity 137

   Activity 130

   Alternative Activity 130

Mathematics Vocabulary

mean

---

1 Warm-Up Activity

Point out that some bills received by families on a regular basis (such as monthly utility bills) reflect an average payment instead of an exact payment. Ask a volunteer to describe how such payment plans work. Then provide the class with an opportunity to speculate about or describe potential benefits and/or disadvantages of such payment plans.

2 Teaching the Lesson

The mean described in this lesson is the arithmetic mean. The arithmetic mean is the most commonly used statistical average and is simply referred to as the *mean*. Write the words *mean* and *average* on the board and point out that *mean* and *average* are terms that are used interchangeably. You may introduce the term *measures of central tendency* defined on page 414.

After students read Example 1 on page 410, remind them that a mean is an exact measure. To help reinforce this idea, have students find the mean of the data set {1, 2, 4}. They will discover that if the mean of the data is computed as a decimal, the decimal is repeating. In this case, to describe the mean of the data set as 2.3, 2.33, or 2.333 (and so on) would be incorrect. The mean must be described exactly as $2\frac{1}{3}$ or $2.\overline{3}$.

> **Mean**
>
> *The sum of the values in a set of data divided by the number of pieces of data in the set*

> Another name for *mean* is *average*.

The **mean** of a set of data is the sum of the values in the set divided by the number of data in the set.

EXAMPLE 1 Find the mean of the set of data
{12, 29, 7, 33, 20, 15, 2, 24}.

Step 1 Use addition to find the sum of the values in the set.

$$
\begin{array}{r}
12 \\
29 \\
7 \\
33 \\
20 \\
15 \\
2 \\
+\ 24 \\
\hline
142
\end{array}
$$

Step 2 Count the number of pieces of data.
{12, 29, 7, 33, 20, 15, 2, 24} = 8 pieces of data

Step 3 Divide the sum of the values by the number of pieces of data.
$142 \div 8 = 17.75$
The mean of {12, 29, 7, 33, 20, 15, 2, 24} is 17.75.

Exercise A Find the mean of each set of data.

1. daily newspaper prices each day for a week: $0.35, $0.35, $0.35, $0.35, $0.35, $0.35, $1.75 $0.55

2. minutes of long-distance phone calls on bill: 7, 5, 22, 4, 9, 14, 8, 19, 1, 15   10.4 minutes

3. points scored by high school football team this season: 7, 17, 10, 21, 13, 31, 0, 14   14.125 points

4. height in feet of the 5 tallest buildings in town: 455, 210, 623, 280, 514   416.4 feet

5. height of students in inches: 48, 52, 60, 57, 49, 53, 60, 51, 62, 49   54.1 inches

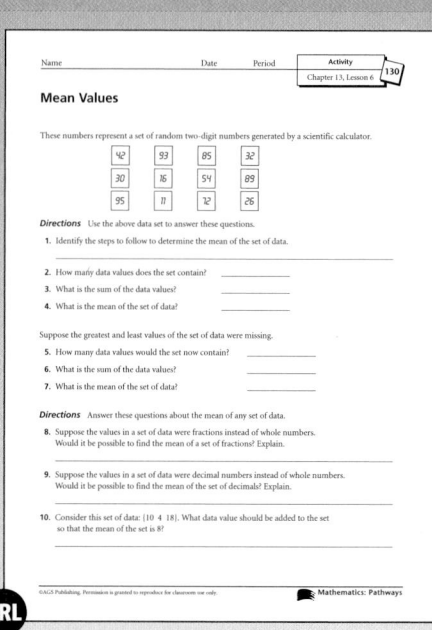

Workbook Activity 137   **Activity 130**

A calculator can be used to find the mean of a set of data.

EXAMPLE 2 Find the mean of this set of data:
{106.25, 181.049, 127.4}

Step 1 Use a calculator to find the sum of the values in the set of data.

Press $106 \cdot 25 + 181 \cdot 049 + 127 \cdot 4 =$.

The display reads *414.699*.

Step 2 Divide the sum by the number of values in the set of data.

Press $\div 3 =$.

The display reads *138.233*.

The mean of {106.25, 181.049, 127.4} is 138.233.

Exercise B Use a calculator to find the mean of each set of data.

6. {18.2, 34, 28.004, 5.080} 21.321

7. {1,099; 1,405; 1,834; 1,970; 1,582} 1,578

8. {13,721; 42,858; 39,121} 31,900

9. {5.075, 3.2, 6.104, 8.4, 6.0605} 5.7679

10. {84, 48, 10, 28, 74, 37, 5, 44, 39, 4} 37.3

11. {14.5, 6.2, 33.1, 25.6, 6} 17.08

12. {121, 218, 483, 912, 219, 555} 418

13. {22, 25, 21, 31, 42, 27, 29, 21} 27.25

PROBLEM SOLVING

Exercise C Find the mean of the set of data in each problem.

14. The ages of five Presidents at their first inauguration were 61, 52, 69, 64, and 46. What is the mean of their ages at the time of inauguration? 58.4 years old

15. The number of times each of the first 16 Presidents vetoed a bill passed by Congress is shown. {2, 0, 0, 7, 1, 0, 12, 1, 0, 10, 3, 0, 0, 9, 7, 7} What is the mean of the number of bills vetoed by the first 16 Presidents? 3.6875 bills

Data, Statistics, and Probability **411**

3 Reinforce and Extend

LEARNING STYLES

Body/Kinesthetic
Write the following data set on the board.

$$\frac{1}{2} \qquad \frac{4}{5} \qquad \frac{3}{10}$$

Invite one or more volunteers to demonstrate on the board how to express the mean of the set as a fraction. $\left(\frac{8}{15}\right)$

CALCULATOR

One way students can use a calculator to check their work is to subtract each data value in the set from the sum of the values that was used to compute the mean. The result of such a series of subtractions should be zero.

GROUP PROBLEM SOLVING

Have groups of three students discuss and solve the following problem.

Suppose Beth must take five mathematics quizzes this month. To date, she has taken three of the five quizzes. Her scores were 82, 78, and 86. What must her average score be on her two remaining quizzes in order to have an average quiz score of 90? *(102)*

Invite the groups to share their problem-solving approaches with one another.

Lesson at a Glance

Chapter 13 Lesson 7

Overview This lesson introduces the median of a set of data.

Objective
- To compute the median of a set of data

Student Pages 412–413

Teacher's Resource Library

Workbook Activity 138

Activity 131

Alternative Activity 131

....

Mathematics Vocabulary
median

....

1 Warm-Up Activity

Invite five volunteers to stand. Ask the remainder of the class to determine which standing student is the "middle" student when the last names of the students are ordered from *A* to *Z*.

2 Teaching the Lesson

After students have worked through the examples on pages 412–413, summarize by pointing out that the median of some data sets will be visible, while the median of other data sets will not. On the board, write the following data sets.

{2, 3, 4}

{1, 8, 10, 25}

Explain that the median in data set {2, 3, 4} is present and visible—it is 3, the middle value. However, the median in data set {1, 8, 10, 25} is not visible. In this set, the median $\frac{8 + 10}{2}$ must be computed.

Median
The middle value in an ordered set of data

Note that one-half of the values of a set of data are above the median and one-half are below the median.

The **median** of a set of data is the middle value when the set is ordered from greatest to least or least to greatest.

EXAMPLE 1 Find the median of this set of data:
{163, 179, 140, 196, 158}

Step 1 Order the values in the set from greatest to least or least to greatest.

140 158 163 179 196

Step 2 Cross off the greatest and least values in the set.

~~140~~ 158 163 179 ~~196~~

Continue crossing off greatest and least pairs until one value remains in the middle of the set.

~~140~~ ~~158~~ 163 ~~179~~ ~~196~~

The median of {163, 179, 140, 196, 158} is 163.

The set of data {163, 179, 140, 196, 158} has an *odd* number of values. Any set of data that has an odd number of values will always have a piece of data as its median. However, a set of data may have an even number of values. To find the median of such a set, arrange the values in order from greatest to least or least to greatest, and cross off greatest and least pairs until two values remain in the middle of the set. The median is the mean, or average, of these two pieces of data.

Writing About Mathematics

Cathryn believes it is possible for a set of data to have the same mean and median. Mario does not believe it is possible. Who is correct? Tell why.

EXAMPLE 2 Find the median of this set of data:
{75, 71, 85, 67, 63, 88}

Step 1 Order the values in the set from greatest to least or least to greatest.

88 85 75 71 67 63

Step 2 Cross off the greatest and least values in the set.

~~88~~ 85 75 71 67 ~~63~~

Continue crossing off greatest and least pairs until two values remain in the middle of the set.

~~88~~ ~~85~~ 75 71 ~~67~~ ~~63~~

412 *Chapter 13 Data, Statistics, and Probability*

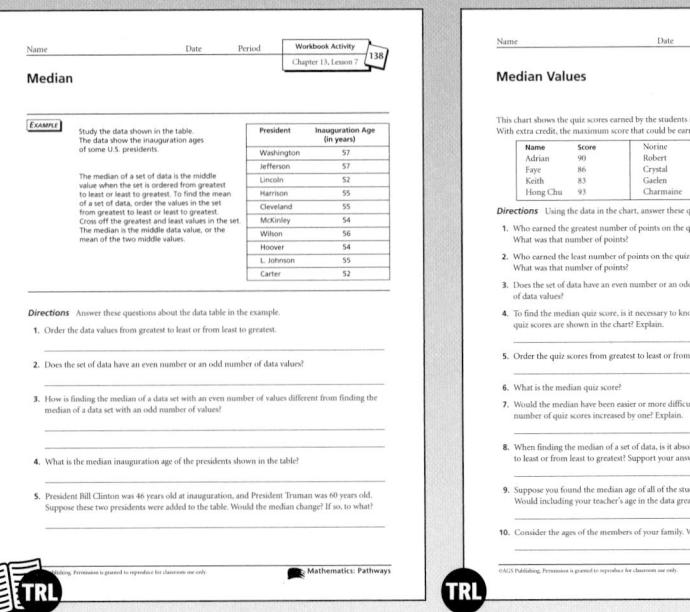

Workbook Activity 138

Activity 131

EXAMPLE 2 *(continued)*

Step 3 Find the mean of the two values in the middle of the set. Add the values, then divide by 2 because there are 2 values in the set.

$$75 + 71 = 146 \qquad 146 \div 2 = 73$$

The median of {75, 71, 85, 67, 63, 88} is 73.

Exercise A Use the data in the following table to answer each question.

Attendance		
	7 P.M.	9:30 P.M.
Movie 1	106	91
Movie 2	85	98
Movie 3	172	180
Movie 4	141	119
Movie 5	52	95

1. Find the median of the data for the movies shown at 7 P.M. 106

2. Find the median of the data for the movies shown at 9:30 P.M. 98

3. Find the median of the data for both times together. 102

PROBLEM SOLVING

Exercise B Find the median for each set of data given.

4. Six cities that have high annual average amounts of snow are Juneau, Alaska, with 101.3 inches; Portland, Maine, with 70.6 inches; Sault Sainte Marie, Ontario, with 115.5 inches; Duluth, Minnesota, with 78.2 inches; Buffalo, New York, with 91.0 inches; and Burlington, Vermont, with 77.5 inches. What is the median amount of annual snowfall? 84.6 in.

5. The heights of several active volcanoes in Africa are 13,354 feet; 1,650 feet; 5,981 feet; 8,000 feet; 3,011 feet; 10,028 feet; 11,400 feet; and 9,469 feet. What is the median height? 8,734.5 ft

Estimation Activity

Estimate: Determine the median from an odd set of ordered data:

30, 9, 7, 39, 4, 31, 21, 18, 9

Solution: Order the values, then strike out the left and right most numbers. Repeat.

4, 7, 9, 9, (18), 21, 30, 31, 39

18 is not an estimate but the actual, correct median. The process, however, is easy and mechanical.

Data, Statistics, and Probability Chapter 13 **413**

3 ⟨ **Reinforce and Extend**

LEARNING STYLES

Auditory/Verbal

Have students work in pairs. Ask one partner to say a simple data set that contains three values, such as {4, 2, 9}. Challenge the other partner to identify the median of the set simply by listening. After partners exchange roles several times, you might choose to challenge them to repeat the activity using data sets that contain five values.

GROUP PROBLEM SOLVING

Have students work in small groups to consider the following problem and debate its solution.

Suppose the annual incomes earned by three people are $20,000, $24,000, and $256,000, respectively. Which best describes the income of the set of those people—the mean or the median? Why?

Invite the groups to share their opinions with one another.

Chapter 13 Lesson 8

Overview This lesson introduces the mode of a set of data.

Objective

■ To compute the mode of a set of data

Student Pages 414–415

Teacher's Resource Library (TRL)

Workbook Activity 139

Activity 132

Alternative Activity 132

Mathematics Vocabulary

mode

measures of central tendency

---

1 Warm-Up Activity

Introduce the idea of frequency and mode by asking the class to decide the following.

- Which student or students in our class smile most often?

- Which student or students in our class are most often diligent about doing homework and trying hard?

- Which student or students in our class most often have something kind to say?

Invite each member of the class to name other polite "most often" characteristics of their classmates.

2 Teaching the Lesson

After students study the information in the examples, point out that in order to identify the mode of a set of data, it is not absolutely necessary to order the data from least to greatest or greatest to least, as is shown in step 1 of each example. To prove this, write the following data set on the board.

{2, 1, 2}

Ask the class to determine the mode of the set, without writing. (2) Explain that the mode could be determined without ordering the data in any way because there were so few data values to consider. However, caution students that when there are many data values in a set to consider, the data must be organized in some way to help ensure that one

---

Mode
The value or values that occur most often in a set of data

Measures of central tendency
The mean, median, and mode of a set of data

The **mode** of a set of data is the value or values that occur most often. The mean, the median, and the mode of a set of data are **measures of central tendency.**

To compute the mode of a set of data, count the number of times each value appears. The value or values that appear most often are the mode.

EXAMPLE 1 Find the mode or modes of the set of data $\{1\frac{1}{2}, 2\frac{1}{8}, 1\frac{1}{4}, 3\frac{3}{4}, 1\frac{1}{2}, 2\frac{5}{8}\}$.

Step 1 Order the data from least to greatest or greatest to least value.

$$1\frac{1}{4} \quad 1\frac{1}{2} \quad 1\frac{1}{2} \quad 2\frac{1}{8} \quad 2\frac{5}{8} \quad 3\frac{3}{4}$$

Step 2 Find the value or values that occur most often.

The value $1\frac{1}{2}$ occurs two times. All other values occur only once. Since $1\frac{1}{2}$ occurs more often than any other value, $1\frac{1}{2}$ is the mode of $\{1\frac{1}{2}, 2\frac{1}{8}, 1\frac{1}{4}, 3\frac{3}{4}, 1\frac{1}{2}, 2\frac{5}{8}\}$.

If two or more values appear the same number of times, the set of data has two or more modes.

EXAMPLE 2 Find the mode or modes of the set of data $\{70, 75, 71, 72, 82, 94, 71, 98, 85, 94\}$.

Step 1 Order the data from least to greatest or greatest to least value.

98 94 94 85 82 75 72 71 71 70

Step 2 Find the value or values that occur most often. The values 94 and 71 occur twice each. All other values occur once. The set of data has two modes: 71 and 94.

If each value in a set of data occurs the same number of times, the set of data has no mode.

EXAMPLE 3 Find the mode of the set of data
{$32.40, $100.00, $67.95, $8.50, $599.99}.

Step 1 Order the data from least to greatest or greatest to least value.

$8.50 $32.40 $67.95 $100.00 $599.99

Step 2 Find the value or values that occur most often. Since each value in the set of data occurs the same number of times (1), the set of data has no mode.

Exercise A Look at each set of data. Identify the number of modes each set has.

1.

Magnitudes of Largest Earthquakes	
Kuril Islands	8.0
Jordan	7.2
Sumatra Island, Indonesia	7.0
Mexico	7.2
Papua New Guinea	7.8
Chile	7.8
Myanmar	7.2
Kermadec Islands, New Zealand	7.1

1 mode

2.

Road Mileage from Chicago	
Atlanta	674 miles
Boston	963 miles
Dallas	917 miles
Denver	996 miles
Detroit	266 miles
Los Angeles	2,054 miles
New York	802 miles
San Francisco	2,142 miles
Washington, DC	671 miles

no modes

3.

Record-High Temperatures in Selected States	
Alaska	100°F
Arizona	128°F
Florida	109°F
Hawaii	100°F
Kansas	121°F
Maryland	109°F
Nevada	125°F
Oregon	119°F

2 modes

Exercise B Determine the mode or modes for each set of data.

4. Number of stories in tallest buildings in Toronto, Ontario:
49, 36, 31, 30, 32, 28, 29, 27, 29, 28.   28, 29

5. Number of stories in tallest buildings in Memphis, Tennessee: 37, 31, 32, 31.   31

6. Number of stories in tallest buildings in Newark, New Jersey:
36, 37, 26, 24, 26, 26, 31, 38.   26

7. Number of stories in tallest buildings in Fort Worth, Texas: 38, 40, 40, 33, 35, 30.   40

8. Number of stories in tallest buildings in Montreal, Quebec: 34, 30, 30, 30.   30

9. Number of stories in tallest buildings in San Diego, California:
34, 34, 39, 30, 41, 23, 27, 27, 27, 24, 25.   27

10. Number of stories in tallest buildings in Phoenix, Arizona:
40, 31, 20, 20, 26, 28, 26.   20, 26

Data, Statistics, and Probability   Chapter 13   **415**

or more data values aren't overlooked. Ordering large sets of data from greatest to least or from least to greatest helps ensure that the correct mode or modes will be identified.

COMMON ERROR

Each time students rewrite a data set from greatest to least or from least to greatest, encourage them to count the number of data values they wrote *before* identifying the mode. If the number of rewritten data values matches the number of data values in the given set, the likelihood of identifying the correct mode or modes is increased.

 3 **Reinforce and Extend**

LEARNING STYLES

Interpersonal/ Group Learning

Suggest that students work in groups of three to discuss the following question.

Is it simple or difficult to determine the mean, median, and mode of data displayed in a frequency table? Why?

(You might choose to have students test their answers by asking them to determine the mean, median, and mode of the data in the frequency table on page 402.)

GROUP PROBLEM SOLVING

Have students work in small groups to consider the following problem and debate its solution.

Suppose that a 70-year-old grandparent is baby-sitting four grandchildren. The ages of the grandchildren are 2, 2, 3, and 4. Which best describes the ages of the grandparent and the grandchildren—the mean, the median, or the mode? Why?

Invite the groups to share their opinions with one another.

Lesson at a Glance

Chapter 13 Lesson 9

Overview This lesson introduces the range of a set of data.

Objective

■ To compute the range of a set of data

Student Pages 416–417

Teacher's Resource Library

Workbook Activities 140–141

Activity 133

Alternative Activity 133

Mathematics Vocabulary

range

1 Warm-Up Activity

Invite students to estimate

- in inches, the difference in height from the tallest member of the class to the shortest.

- in miles, the greatest distance a class member travels to get to class to the least distance a class member travels.

- in hours, the difference between the greatest amount of time a class member has studied to the least amount of time.

2 Teaching the Lesson

After students complete the examples on page 416, remind them that computing a range by subtracting two values can be checked by addition. Ask, "How would you check the answer given in each example?" (*To check the answer 189 in Example 1, add 189 and 181; the sum should be 370.*)

$$
\begin{array}{r}
189 \\
+\ 181 \\
\hline
370\ \checkmark
\end{array}
$$

(*To check the answer 569,329 in Example 2, add 569,329 and 1,045; the sum should be 570,374.*)

$$
\begin{array}{r}
569,329 \\
+\ 1,045 \\
\hline
570,374\ \checkmark
\end{array}
$$

Range
The difference between the greatest and least values in a set of data

The mean, median, and mode of a set of data are measures of central tendency. The **range** of a set of data is the difference between the greatest and least values. To compute the range, subtract the least value from the greatest value.

EXAMPLE 1 Find the range of the set of data {181, 370, 199, 267}.

Step 1 Identify the greatest and least values in the set of data.

$$370 \rightarrow \text{greatest value}$$
$$181 \rightarrow \text{least value}$$

Step 2 Subtract the least value from the greatest value.

$$
\begin{array}{r}
370 \rightarrow \text{greatest value} \\
-\ 181 \rightarrow \text{least value} \\
\hline
189
\end{array}
$$

The range of {181, 370, 199, 267} is 189.

Often, you will be given only the least and greatest values of a set of data. Then you do not have to locate these values in the set. You just subtract the least value from the greatest value to determine the range.

EXAMPLE 2 Find the range of the areas of the 50 states in the United States.

Rhode Island, the smallest state, has an area of 1,045 square miles. Alaska, the largest state, has an area of 570,374 square miles.

$$
\begin{array}{r}
570,374 \rightarrow \text{greatest value} \\
-\ 1,045 \rightarrow \text{least value} \\
\hline
569,329
\end{array}
$$

The range of the areas of the 50 states is 569,329 square miles.

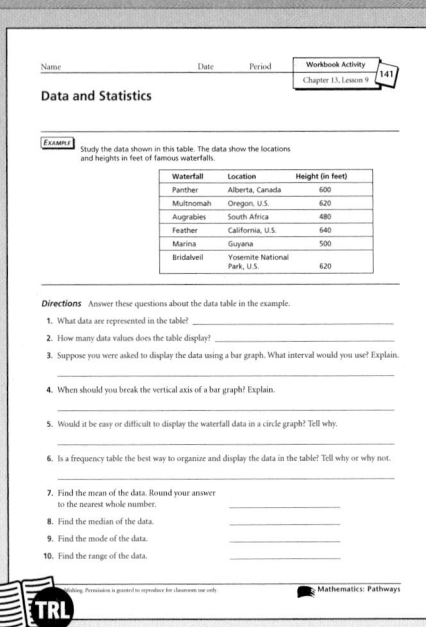

PROBLEM SOLVING

Exercise A Solve each problem.

1. On three math quizzes, Jeremy scored 82, 88, and 99 points. What is the range of his quiz scores? 17 points

2. At 20,320 feet, Mount McKinley is the tallest of the 78 highest mountain peaks in North America. At 14,072 feet, Mount Augusta is the shortest of the 78 peaks. What is the range of the tallest and shortest peaks? 6,248 ft

3. The average daily circulation for specific newspapers follows. Find the range in the papers' circulation. 1,657,516 papers

Austin Tribune	113,031
Long Island Post	684,366
Oakland News	105,624
Orlando Times	1,763,140
Toronto Post	793,660

4. Jenessa bought seven items at the store. Their prices were $3.98, $0.49, $12.99, $6.18, $1.35, $4.32, $0.85. What is the range of the prices? $12.50

5. Lake Ontario, the smallest Great Lake, has an area of 34,850 square miles. Lake Superior, the largest Great Lake, has an area of 81,000 square miles. What is the range of the areas of the Great Lakes? 46,150 sq miles

6. The Olympic gold medal winners in the men's downhill skiing event completed the course in these times: 1 min 45.50 sec, 1 min 45.59 sec, 1 min 59.63 sec, 1 min 50.37 sec, and 1 min 45.75 sec. What is the range of times? 14.13 sec

7. The Olympic gold medal winners in the women's 10-kilometer race had these finishing times: 30 min 31.54 sec, 31 min 44.2 sec, 30 min 08.3 sec, 25 min 53.7 sec, and 27 min 30.1 sec. What is the range of times? 5 min 50.5 sec

8. A general in the military with 26 years of service receives $9,845.40 a month. A general with 2 years of service receives $7,397.10 a month. What is the range of pay? $2,448.30

9. Ten years ago, Americans spent $3,761.2 billion for personal expenses. Five years ago, Americans spent $4,924.9 billion. What is the range in expenses? $1,163.7 billion

10. The more than 600 stone statues on Easter Island have heights from 3.4 meters to 12 meters. What is the range in the statues' heights? 8.6 m

Data, Statistics, and Probability   Chapter 13   417

LEARNING STYLES

LEP/ESL

Invite volunteers to share from their native languages words or phrases that mean the same, or nearly the same, as mean, median, mode, and range.

GROUP PROBLEM SOLVING

Suggest that students work in groups of four or five to design four data sets: one that is best described by the mean, one that is best described by the median, one that is best described by the mode, and one that is best described by the range. Then ask one or more members from each group to describe each set and tell why the given measure of central tendency best describes the set.

MENTAL MATH

Ask volunteers to mentally compute the following ranges.

$\{40, 60\}$	*(20)*
$\{50, 150\}$	*(100)*
$\{10, 7\}$	*(3)*
$\{\frac{4}{5}, \frac{3}{5}\}$	$(\frac{1}{5})$
$\{2.5, 2.2\}$	*(0.3)*
$\{6.1, 6.7\}$	*(0.6)*
$\{10,000, 1,000\}$	*(9,000)*
$\{118, 19\}$	*(99)*

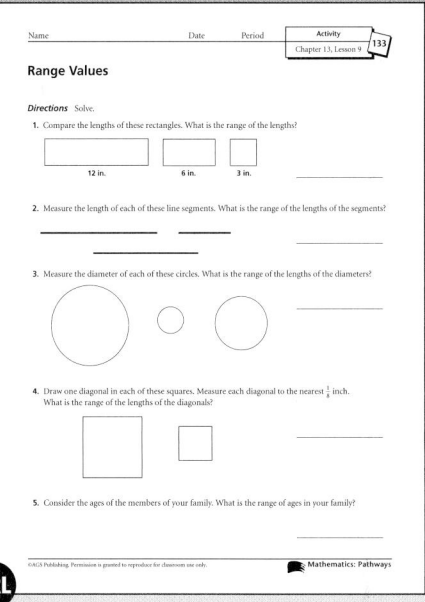

Name   Date   Period   Activity
                                      Chapter 13, Lesson 9   133

Range Values

Directions Solve.

1. Compare the lengths of these rectangles. What is the range of the lengths?

   12 in.   6 in.   3 in.   _____

2. Measure the length of each of these line segments. What is the range of the lengths of the segments?

3. Measure the diameter of each of these circles. What is the range of the lengths of the diameters?

4. Draw one diagonal in each of these squares. Measure each diagonal to the nearest ¼ inch. What is the range of the lengths of the diagonals?

5. Consider the ages of the members of your family. What is the range of ages in your family?

©AGS Publishing. Permission is granted to reproduce for classroom use only.   Mathematics: Pathways

Activity 133

Lesson at a Glance

Chapter 13 Lesson 10

Overview This lesson introduces box-and-whiskers plots.

Objective
- To interpret and construct box-and-whiskers plots

Student Pages 418–419

Teacher's Resource Library (TRL)

Workbook Activity 142

Activity 134

Alternative Activity 134

....

Mathematics Vocabulary

box-and-whiskers plot
lower extreme
upper extreme
lower quartile
upper quartile

....

1 Warm-Up Activity

Have students review how to compute measures of central tendency by asking them to determine the mean, median, mode, and range of the following set of data: {14, 16, 10, 16, 14}. *(mean: 14; median: 14; mode: 14 and 16; range: 6)*

2 Teaching the Lesson

Introduce the lesson by pointing out that some of the skills that are required to construct a box-and-whiskers plot were first encountered when students learned to compute the mean, median, and range of a set of data.

After students have studied the example, help them recall that

- the skill required to complete step 1, step 3, and step 4 of Example 1 can be reviewed in Lessons 7 and 8.

- the skill required to complete step 2 of Example 1 can be reviewed in Lesson 9.

- although the computation of a mean was not required in this example, a mean would have been required had there been an even number of data values in step 3 and step 4. Computing the mean can be reviewed in Lesson 6.

Box-and-whiskers plot
A way to show the spread of data in a set of numbers
Lower extreme
The least value of a set of data
Upper extreme
The greatest value of a set of data
Lower quartile
The median of scores below the median
Upper quartile
The median of scores above the median

A **box-and-whiskers plot** is a visual way to describe the concentration and the spread of data in a set. A box-and-whiskers plot contains a box and two whiskers, and looks like this:

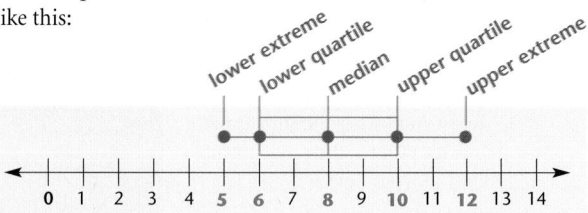

In this example, 5 is the **lower extreme**, 8 is the median, 12 is the **upper extreme**, 6 is the **lower quartile**, and 10 is the **upper quartile.**

EXAMPLE 1 Suppose you were asked to construct a box-and-whiskers plot for the data set below. The data represent the number of years different students have gone to school together.

{12, 5, 8, 16, 15, 9, 19}

Step 1 Arrange the data in order from least to greatest.

5 8 9 12 15 16 19

Step 2 Identify the greatest and least values of the data. These values are called the upper and lower extremes.

5 8 9 12 15 16 19
↑   ↑
lower extreme   upper extreme

Step 3 Find the median of the data.

5 8 9 12 15 16 19
        ↑
      median

Step 4 Find the median of all of the scores below the median. This median is called the lower quartile. Then find the median of all of the scores above the median. This median is called the upper quartile.

5 8 9 12 15 16 19
   ↑   ↑
lower quartile   upper quartile

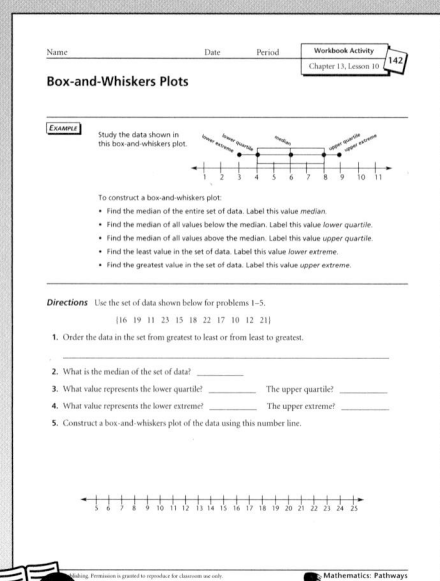

Workbook Activity 142

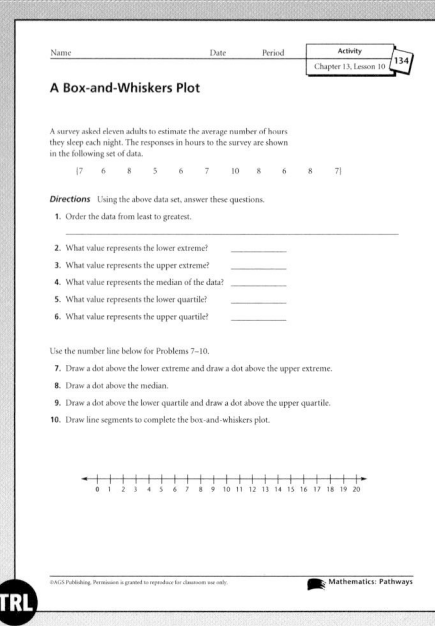

Activity 134

EXAMPLE 1 (continued)

Step 5 Draw a number line that can display all of the data in the set.

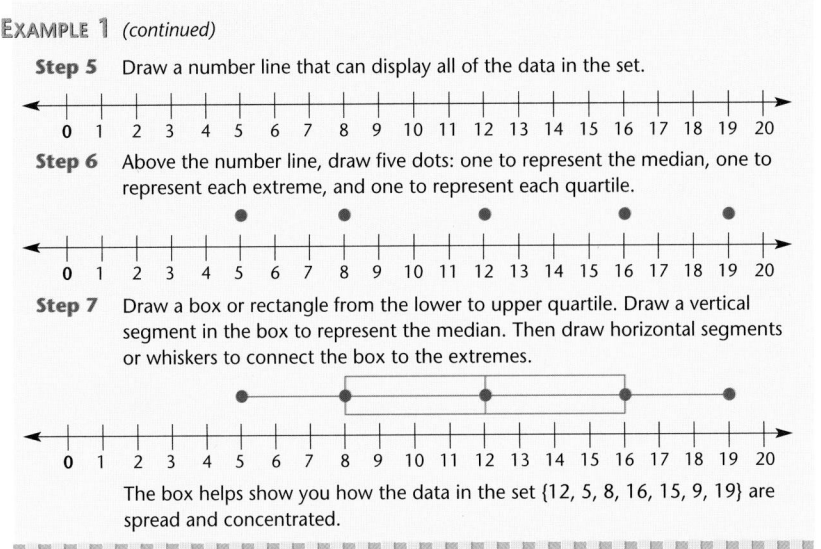

Step 6 Above the number line, draw five dots: one to represent the median, one to represent each extreme, and one to represent each quartile.

Step 7 Draw a box or rectangle from the lower to upper quartile. Draw a vertical segment in the box to represent the median. Then draw horizontal segments or whiskers to connect the box to the extremes.

The box helps show you how the data in the set {12, 5, 8, 16, 15, 9, 19} are spread and concentrated.

Exercise A Use the data set {12, 8, 17, 10, 2, 13, 9, 20, 11, 4, 14}.

2, 4, 8, 9, 10, 11,
2, 13, 14, 17, 20}

20, upper extreme
2, lower extreme
1, median
4, upper quartile
8, lower quartile

Teacher's Edition
ge for 7–9.

1. Arrange the data in order from least to greatest.

2. Identify the greatest value of the data. Label your answer *upper extreme*.

3. Identify the least value of the data. Label your answer *lower extreme*.

4. Find the median of the data. Label your answer *median*.

5. Find the median of all of the scores above the median. Label your answer *upper quartile*.

6. Find the median of all of the scores below the median. Label your answer *lower quartile*.

7. Draw a number line that can display all of the data in the set.

8. Above the number line, draw five dots: one to represent the median, one to represent each extreme, and one to represent each quartile.

9. Draw a box or rectangle from the lower to upper quartile. Draw a vertical segment in the box to represent the median. Then draw horizontal segments or whiskers to connect the box to the extremes.

Sample answer:
Subtract the lower
extreme from the
upper extreme.

Exercise B Answer the question.

10. Suppose a set of data was displayed in a box-and-whiskers plot. How could you use the plot to compute the range of the data?

Data, Statistics, and Probability Chapter 13 **419**

LEARNING STYLES

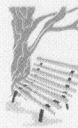

Visual/Spatial
Invite volunteers to draw a variety of number lines on the board and construct a hypothetical box-and-whiskers plot for each number line. Encourage the remainder of the class to observe the various plots and identify the lower extreme, lower quartile, median, upper extreme, and upper quartile of each plot.

IN THE COMMUNITY

This lesson completes the study of graphs and statistical measures. Ask students to generate a list of ten local or state businesses. For each business, have students name a type of graph or statistical measure with which the business must be familiar. Then have them make a list of ten statistical measures or graphs that they themselves will likely need to know how to read and construct in their future lives and careers.

Answers to Problems 7–9

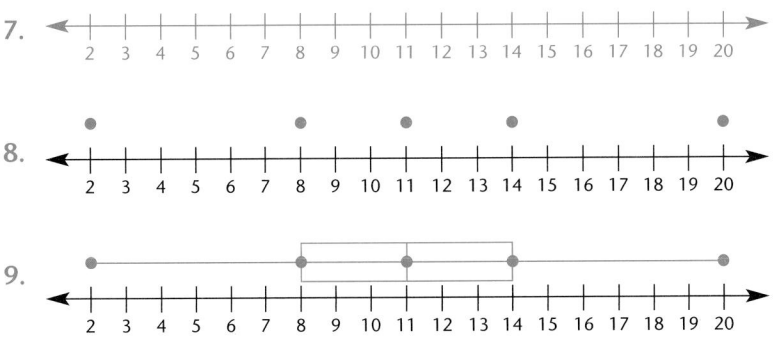

7.

8.

9.

Lesson at a Glance

Chapter 13 Lesson 11

Overview This lesson introduces the probability fraction.

Objective

- To use the probability fraction to determine the probability of an event

Student Pages 420–421

Teacher's Resource Library

  Workbook Activity 143

  Activity 135

  Alternative Activity 135

Mathematics Vocabulary

probability
outcome

1 Warm-Up Activity

A successful backgammon player must have an understanding of probability. If possible, display two 1–6 number cubes and a backgammon game. If a game is not available, ask a volunteer with knowledge of the game to sketch the playing surface on the board and explain how the game is played. Then ask students to discuss and decide which sums are most likely to occur when two 1–6 number cubes are tossed. Invite volunteers to play a game of backgammon and apply their understanding of the likelihood of sums.

2 Teaching the Lesson

Explain that an outcome is often a misunderstood element of probability. To give students a more thorough understanding of what constitutes an outcome, share with them the following scenarios:

- Suppose the letters that form the word *math* are written on four identical slips of paper—one letter per slip—and then placed in a paper bag. If one slip is withdrawn from the bag without looking, how many possible outcomes are in the experiment?

- Now suppose the letter *z* is written on each of four identical slips of paper and the slips are placed in a different

---

Probability
The chance or likelihood of an event occurring

Outcome
A result of a probability experiment

Perhaps you've heard a weather forecaster say something like "Tomorrow there is a 40% chance of rain." A 40% chance of rain is an example of **probability**—the chance or likelihood that something will occur.

Probability experiments always include an event and one or more **outcomes.** A word that means the same as *outcome* is *result*. To find the probability *(P)* that an event in a probability experiment will occur, use the fraction

$$P = \frac{\text{number of favorable outcomes}}{\text{number of possible outcomes}}$$

EXAMPLE 1 Suppose a coin is tossed once. What is the probability that the coin will land with the tails side facing up?

Step 1 Use the probability fraction.

$$P = \frac{\text{number of favorable outcomes}}{\text{number of possible outcomes}}$$

Step 2 Find the denominator. Since there are two possible outcomes when the coin is tossed—the coin will either land heads up or tails up—the denominator is two.

$$P = \frac{\text{number of favorable outcomes}}{2}$$

Step 3 Find the numerator. Since one outcome is favorable—the coin landing tails up—the numerator is one.

$$P = \frac{1}{2}$$

The probability of tossing a coin and having it land tails up is $\frac{1}{2}$.

If you choose to express the probability as a percent, the probability would be 50%, because $\frac{1}{2} = 0.5 = 50\%$.

 Math in Your Life

What's in a Number?
The three most frequently used measures in statistics are the mean, median, and mode. Each one serves a purpose. As a student, these three averages are important. The mean of your test scores could determine your grade in a class. The median of your test scores tells you the halfway point for any set of scores. The mode shows how many students have received the same score.

420 *Chapter 13 Data, Statistics, and Probability*

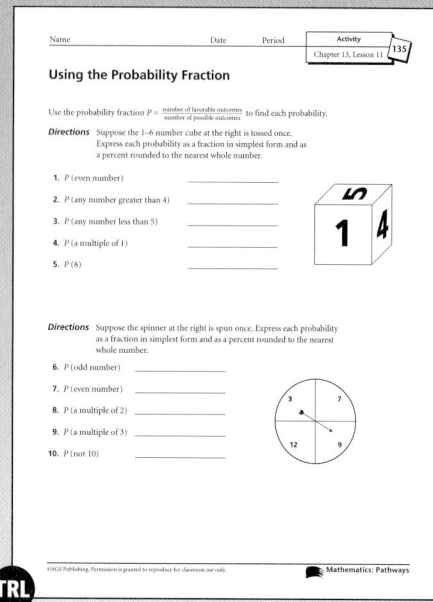

EXAMPLE 2 The faces of the number cube at the right are labeled 1, 2, 3, 4, 5, and 6. Suppose the cube is rolled once. What is the probability of rolling an odd number?

Step 1 Use the probability fraction.

$$P = \frac{\text{number of favorable outcomes}}{\text{number of possible outcomes}}$$

Step 2 Find the denominator. Since there are six possible outcomes when the cube is rolled—1, 2, 3, 4, 5, and 6—the denominator is 6.

$$P = \frac{\text{number of favorable outcomes}}{6}$$

Step 3 Find the numerator. Since three outcomes are favorable—1, 3, and 5—the numerator is 3

$$P = \frac{3}{6}$$

Step 4 Simplify if possible.

$$P = \frac{3}{6} = \frac{1}{2}$$

The probability (P) of rolling a 1–6 number cube and rolling an odd number is $\frac{1}{2}$ or 50%.

Exercise A Answer each question.

1. What is the probability of tossing a coin and getting an outcome of heads? Express your answer as a fraction in simplest form and as a percent. $\frac{1}{2}$; 50%

2. What is the probability of rolling a 1–6 number cube and getting an outcome of an even number? Express your answer as a fraction in simplest form. $\frac{1}{2}$

3. An example of a prime number is the number 3. A prime number has exactly two factors—the number itself and 1. (The factors of 3 are 3 and 1.) What is the probability of tossing a 1–6 number cube and getting an outcome of a prime number? $\frac{3}{6}$ or $\frac{1}{2}$ or 50%

Exercise B In a probability experiment, a painted cube is rolled once. One side of the cube is painted green, two sides are painted blue, and three sides are painted orange. Express the probability of each outcome as a fraction in simplest form.

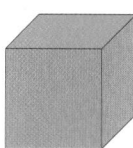

4. P (orange) $\frac{1}{2}$

5. P (blue) $\frac{1}{3}$

 Try This

Integers can be described by the set {..., −3, −2, −1, 0, 1, 2, 3, ...}. The probability of any outcome can never be less than what integer? The probability of any outcome can never be greater than what integer?

0; 1

---

 3 **Reinforce and Extend**

LEARNING STYLES

 **Body/Kinesthetic**

Have students work in small groups. Ask each group member to sketch a circular spinner of his or her own design. Have the groups exchange spinners and then determine the probability of the various outcomes shown on each spinner.

CAREER CONNECTION

Encourage interested students to learn more about how probability is used in meteorology and the science of weather forecasting and to share their findings with their classmates.

---

bag. If one slip is withdrawn from the bag without looking, how many possible outcomes are in the experiment?

Invite students to debate the correct answer to each scenario. If necessary, help them understand that there are four possible outcomes in the first experiment—it is possible to select the letter *m*, the letter *a*, the letter *t*, or the letter *h*. There are also four possible outcomes in the second experiment—it is possible to select the first slip of paper upon which the letter *z* was written, the second slip of paper upon which the letter *z* was written, the third slip of paper upon which the letter *z* was written, or the fourth slip of paper upon which the letter *z* was written.

Try This

If students have difficulty determining the solution, ask them to consider tossing a 1–6 number cube once and determining the probability of the following events.

P (1, 2, 3, 4, 5, or 6)   ($\frac{6}{6}$ or 1)

P (7)   ($\frac{0}{6}$ or 0)

MANIPULATIVES

M The Probability Fraction

Materials: Two-Color Counters (or coins), 1–6 Number Cubes

Group Practice: Use a chip (or coin) to conduct a probability experiment. Toss the chip or coin 10–20 times, having students record the results of each toss. Write the outcome as a fraction in simplest form. Compare the actual outcome to the probability fraction and discuss the results. Repeat the experiment several times. Use a 1–6 Number Cube to perform a similar probability experiment following Example 2 on page 421.

Student Practice: Have students use coins, chips, or cubes to conduct probability experiments for problems 1–3 in Exercise A and then report the actual outcomes as a simplified fraction.

Chapter 13 Lesson 12

Overview This lesson explains how to determine the probability of events that are dependent or independent of one another.

Objectives

- To recognize events in a probability experiment as dependent or independent
- To calculate the probability of successive events that are dependent or independent

Student Pages 422–425

Teacher's Resource Library (TRL)

Workbook Activity 144

Activity 136

Alternative Activity 136

Mathematics Vocabulary

dependent event
independent event

---

1 Warm-Up Activity

Have two students each hold a hand of five different cards including one ace apiece, so that the class can see them, but the students cannot see each other's cards. Ask students to discuss the probability that an ace will be drawn at random. Have each student draw a card from the other. Now ask, "Has the probability of drawing an ace changed? Why?" Explain that some events have an effect on the outcome of other events. In this lesson, students will learn to identify dependent and independent sequences of events and to show how probability is changed when the first event affects the second event.

2 Teaching the Lesson

Assess understanding of the probability calculation in Example 1 by asking students to explain what the multiplicands in the problem $P = \frac{2}{4} \cdot \frac{1}{3}$ each mean. Point out the simplification of $\frac{2}{12}$ to $\frac{1}{6}$ in step 3 of Example 1. Explain that a 2-in-12 chance of occurrence is the same as a 1-in-6 chance.

Probability consists of events, trials, and outcomes. A coin toss, for example, is an event, tossing the coin is a trial, and *heads* and *tails* are the outcomes that could occur. Events in a probability experiment can be dependent or independent.

EXAMPLE 1 Suppose a bag contains 4 marbles, all the same size. Two marbles are red and 2 marbles are yellow. You reach into the bag, choose a marble, record its color, and put the marble in your pocket. Then you take another marble from the bag. What is the probability that you will take out 2 yellow marbles? The experiment contains 2 events. Find the probability of each event.

Step 1 Find the probability of the first event—taking a yellow marble from the bag. Use the probability fraction.

$$P = \frac{\text{number of favorable outcomes}}{\text{number of possible outcomes}}$$

In this event, there are 4 possible outcomes because there are 4 marbles in the bag. The denominator of the fraction is 4. Since choosing either yellow marble that is in the bag is a favorable outcome, the numerator of the fraction is 2. The probability of this event is $\frac{2}{4}$.

Step 2 Find the probability of the second event—taking a yellow marble from the bag. Remember, you put the first marble that was taken from the bag in your pocket.

$$P = \frac{\text{number of favorable outcomes}}{\text{number of possible outcomes}}$$

In this event, there are 3 possible outcomes because there are 3 marbles in the bag. The denominator of the fraction is 3. In the first trial, assume you chose a yellow marble. Since choosing the yellow marble that is still in the bag is a favorable outcome, the numerator of the fraction is 1. The probability of this event is $\frac{1}{3}$.

Step 3 To find the probability of taking out 2 yellow marbles, multiply the probability of the first event by the probability of the second event.

$$P = \frac{2}{4} \cdot \frac{1}{3} = \frac{2}{12} = \frac{1}{6}$$

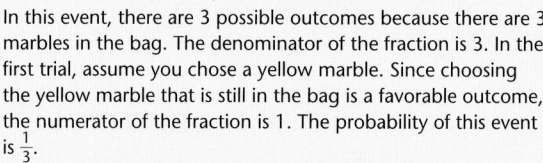

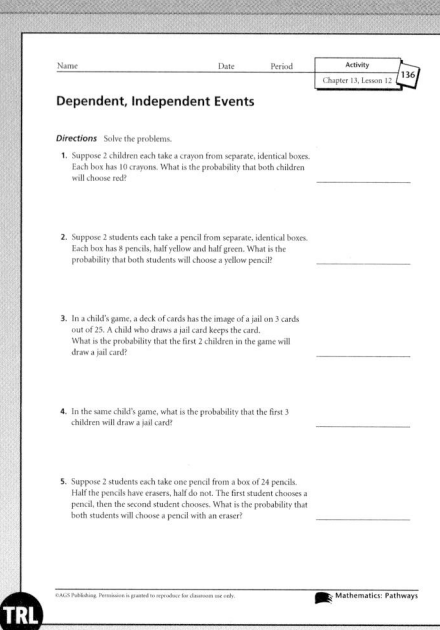

Workbook Activity 144

Activity 136

Dependent event

In a probability experiment, the outcome of one event is affected by the outcome of any other event

The probability of the outcome is $\frac{1}{6}$. The events in this experiment were dependent. In **dependent events,** the outcome of the first event affects the outcome of all other events in the experiment.

EXAMPLE 2 Suppose a bag contains 4 marbles, all the same size. Two marbles are black and 2 marbles are white. You reach into the bag, choose a marble, and record its color. Then you replace the marble in the bag and take out a marble again. What is the probability that you will take out 2 white marbles? The experiment contains 2 events. Find the probability of each event.

Step 1 Find the probability of the first event—taking a white marble from the bag.
Use the probability fraction.

$$P = \frac{\text{number of favorable outcomes}}{\text{number of possible outcomes}}$$

In this event, there are 4 possible outcomes because there are 4 marbles in the bag. The denominator of the fraction is 4. Since choosing either white marble that is in the bag is a favorable outcome, the numerator of the fraction is 2. The probability of this event is $\frac{2}{4}$.

Step 2 Find the probability of the second event—taking a white marble from the bag. Remember, you put the first marble that was taken from the bag back into the bag.

$$P = \frac{\text{number of favorable outcomes}}{\text{number of possible outcomes}}$$

In this event, there again are 4 possible outcomes because there are 4 marbles in the bag. The denominator of the fraction is 4. Since choosing either white marble that is in the bag is a favorable outcome, the numerator of the fraction is 2. The probability of this event is $\frac{2}{4}$.

Step 3 To find the probability of taking out 2 white marbles, multiply the probability of the first event by the probability of the second event.

$$P = \frac{2}{4} \cdot \frac{2}{4} = \frac{4}{16} = \frac{1}{4}$$

COMMON ERROR

Careless thinking may cause some students to forget to adjust the number of possible outcomes when an item is removed. Have them diagram on scratch paper the number of items in the bag before and after each trial.

Independent event

In a probability experiment, the outcome of any event does not affect the outcome of any other event

Writing About Mathematics

You might expect to get 5 heads and 5 tails in 10 coin tosses. Toss a coin 10 times. Tally the results. Compare your results to your prediction.

1. Independent events; any toss does not affect the previous toss or the next toss of the coin.

2. Dependent events; once the consonant is chosen, it cannot be chosen again.

3. These are independent events. The next outcome will be 1, 2, 3, 4, 5, or 6.

The probability of the outcome is $\frac{1}{4}$. The events in this experiment were independent. In **independent events,** the outcome of an event does not affect the outcome of any other event in the experiment.

Exercise A Answer the questions.

1. To find the probability of tossing 5 tails in a row, you toss the same coin 5 times. Are the events in the experiment dependent or independent? Explain.

2. Suppose a consonant of the alphabet is chosen at random and removed. Then a different consonant is chosen. Are the events in the experiment dependent or independent? Explain.

3. Suppose a number cube is rolled and the outcome is 6. The cube is rolled a second time and again the outcome is 6. If the cube is rolled again, what will the outcome be? Explain.

Build a Model

It is snowing outside. Will school be canceled tomorrow? Make the spinners below to find the probability. Use heavyweight paper and a compass. Use a pencil or paper clip for the spinner. Which spinner is most likely to land on yes? Explain.

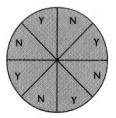 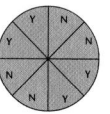 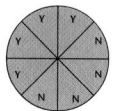

Answers may vary. Students should notice that the probability of each spinner landing on a yes is equal—the probability of each outcome is $\frac{1}{2}$. The placement of the wedges does not affect the outcome.

Exercise B Suppose a bag contains 6 marbles. All the marbles are the same size. One marble is green, 2 marbles are orange, and 3 marbles are purple. A marble will be taken from the bag 2 times. Each time a marble is taken out, it is replaced.

4. Find P (orange and green). $\frac{1}{18}$

5. Find P (green and purple). $\frac{1}{12}$

6. Find P (not purple and not orange). $\frac{1}{3}$

Exercise C Suppose a bag contains 8 marbles. All the marbles are the same size. One marble is red, 2 marbles are white, and 5 marbles are blue. A marble will be taken from the bag 2 times. Each time a marble is taken, it is *not* replaced.

7. Find P (white and red). $\frac{1}{28}$

8. Find P (blue and white). $\frac{5}{28}$

9. Find P (red and not white). $\frac{5}{56}$

10. Find P (blue). $\frac{5}{14}$

 Try This

Look again at Exercise C. Suppose you take out a marble 3 times. What is the probability of (red and white and blue)? Express your answer as a percent rounded to the nearest whole number.

3%

Data, Statistics, and Probability   **425**

Try This

Remind students that the marbles are not replaced in this exercise. Students may wish to simulate the activity and then create other problems for classmates to try.

GROUP PROBLEM SOLVING

 Have students work in small groups to solve the following problem. Eleven teammates want to start in the first game of the season. Set up a drawing that will decide the starting five at random. Decide whether the drawing is independent or dependent. Calculate the probability of being chosen on the first, second, third, fourth, and fifth drawings. Ask groups to write a description of the probability problem and record the steps in their experiment, using the examples in the text as a model. Have groups present their findings and explain their methods to the class.

LEARNING STYLES

 **Auditory/Verbal**

Assess student understanding of independent and dependent events. Number 3 × 5 cards 1 through 10 and place them in a container. Have students explain the probability of drawing an even-numbered card. *(5 in 10, or 1 in 2)* Draw a card at random and record its number before returning it to the container. Ask, "Now what is the probability that the next card drawn will be an even number?" *(the same, 5 in 10, or 1 in 2)* Repeat the process, but do not return the card for the second trial. Have students explain in their own words why the events are *dependent* when the card is not replaced in the container.

Build a Model

Help students recognize that for each of the spinners, the probability of landing on *Yes* or *No* is the same. The probability would change only if, for example, a spinner with 8 wedges had 6 *Yes* wedges and 2 *No* wedges. This would give the spinner a greater probability of landing on *Yes*.

Chapter 13 Lesson 13

Overview This lesson introduces the fundamental principle of counting.

Objective

■ To apply the fundamental principle of counting to determine the total number of arrangements or possibilities

Student Pages 426–427

Teacher's Resource Library **TRL**

Workbook Activity 145

Activity 137

Alternative Activity 137

Mathematics Vocabulary
fundamental principle of counting

---

1 Warm-Up Activity

Share the following scenario with the class.

Every race has an order of finish. For example, if two runners run a race, there can be two orders of finish—either Runner A finishes first and Runner B finishes last, or Runner B finishes first and Runner A finishes last. Now consider a race with 10 runners. True or false: In a race with 10 runners, there are more than *3 million* possible orders of finish.

Encourage class debate. Then tell students that the answer is true.

2 Teaching the Lesson

As well as discussing the example on page 426, you might choose to have three volunteers model the possible arrangements using three desks or chairs at the front of the classroom, and invite the remainder of the class to develop a way to organize and record the various arrangements.

Explain that the fundamental principle of counting is a useful tool because the number of arrangements in some scenarios can often be quite numerous and, as a result, difficult to sketch or record and keep track of in an organized way.

Fundamental principle of counting

A general rule that states if one task can be completed a different ways, and a second task can be completed b different ways, the first task followed by the second task can be completed a • b or ab different ways

There are infinite numbers of arrangements in the world. One example of an arrangement is found in a dictionary. The words in a dictionary are arranged, or ordered, from *A* to *Z*. Another example of an arrangement is found in a library. Books in a library are arranged in a certain order.

Arrangement problems can be solved different ways.

EXAMPLE 1 Suppose a classroom contains 3 desks, all in a row. Three students—Angela, Barry, and Caitlin—enter the classroom. How many different ways can Angela, Barry, and Caitlin sit at the desks?

One way to solve the problem is to draw a diagram.

Step 1 Show all of the possible arrangements with Angela sitting at the first desk.

Angela	Barry	Caitlin
Angela	Caitlin	Barry

Step 2 Show all of the possible arrangements with Barry sitting at the first desk.

Barry	Caitlin	Angela
Barry	Angela	Caitlin

Step 3 Show all of the possible arrangements with Caitlin sitting at the first desk.

Caitlin	Angela	Barry
Caitlin	Barry	Angela

Angela, Barry, and Caitlin can sit at 3 desks 6 different ways. There are 2 ways with Angela first, 2 ways with Barry first, and 2 ways with Caitlin first.

The fundamental principle of counting is also called the *basic counting principle.*

Another way to solve the problem is to use the **fundamental principle of counting.** The fundamental principle of counting is a general rule that states if one task can be completed *a* different ways, and a second task can be completed *b* different ways, the first task followed by the second task can be completed *a • b* or *ab* different ways.

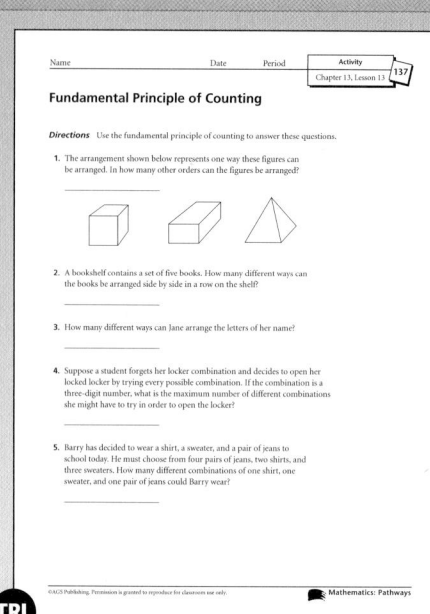

Workbook Activity 145

Activity 137

EXAMPLE 2 Again consider the original problem: suppose a classroom contains 3 desks in a row. Three students—Angela, Barry, and Caitlin—enter the classroom. How many different ways can Angela, Barry, and Caitlin sit at the desks?

Use the fundamental principle of counting.

Any of the 3 students can sit at the first desk.

Once a student is sitting at the first desk, either of the remaining 2 students can sit at the second desk.

Once a student is sitting at the first desk and a student is sitting at the second desk, only 1 student remains, and that student must sit at the last desk.

Three students can arrange themselves 3 • 2 • 1 or 6 different ways.

These examples show you that the problem can be solved by drawing a diagram or by using the fundamental principle of counting. If used correctly, either method will produce the correct answer. However, you may find that as arrangement problems becoming longer, using the fundamental principle of counting requires much less time than drawing a diagram.

Exercise A Use the fundamental principle of counting to answer these questions.

1. Choose any 2 digits. How many different ways can those digits be arranged? 2 ways

2. Choose any 3 letters of the alphabet. How many different ways can those letters be arranged? 6 ways

3. Suppose you had to complete 4 chores, and you could complete the chores in any order. In how many different ways could you complete the chores? 24 ways

Exercise B Use a calculator to find each product.

4. 100 • 99 • 98 970,200

5. 15 • 14 • 13 • 12 • 11 • 10 3,603,600

LEARNING STYLES

Body/Kinesthetic
Encourage students to check their answers to problems 1–3 by substituting people for the items mentioned in each problem and physically modeling each problem by arranging themselves various ways in chairs.

LEARNING STYLES

Logical/Mathematical
Have students discuss and solve the following problem.

How many different phone numbers are possible with an area code of 555 and a prefix of 924? *(10,000)*

CALCULATOR

You might wish to mention that some calculators are programmed to perform the fundamental principle of counting computation. The computation is performed by the factorial or $\boxed{x!}$ key. If possible, display a statistical or scientific calculator that has a factorial key and give students an opportunity to experiment with it. One computation you might have them perform is a proof of the scenario included in the Warm-Up Activity of this lesson. The number of arrangements described in the scenario is true (and greater than 3 million) because 10! = 3,628,800.

Lesson at a Glance

Chapter 13 Application

Overview This lesson presents an application of data collection and analysis.

Objective

■ To test a hypothesis using data and graphs

Student Page 428

Teacher's Resource Library

Application Activity 13

Everyday Math 13

1 Warm-Up Activity

Ask students how they spend time on a computer. Then have students write what they think are the most common reasons their peers use computers. Take a class vote, and ask students to check their predictions by making tally marks after each of the reasons. Remind students that the data they collected can be organized and analyzed with a graph.

2 Teaching the Lesson

Surveys are most effective when the number of people surveyed is large enough to be a reliable resource. Therefore, the issue chosen by each group should be of interest to a large number of students. Help students come up with survey topics such as:

• **After-school sports or clubs:** Which sports are the most popular? Least popular? Which clubs are most popular? Least?

• **After-school jobs:** What percentage of teens work after school? Which group works more hours, boys or girls? What is the most popular occupation?

• **Plans after graduation:** What percentage of the students surveyed plan to go to college? Enter the military? Go to trade school?

Tally Up A survey is a proven way to gather useful information. You review the data you collect to spot trends. For example, are people walking more, driving more, or taking public transportation more often? How good your information is depends on the number of people you survey. This is called the *sample size*.

EXAMPLE 1 The director of your city library has asked you to help her understand who is using the computers at the library and why.

Step 1 Hypothesis (reason for the survey): Computer access provides an important service for the people who live in the city.

Step 2 Decide on the survey questions.

Step 3 Collect data:
• Do a poll for 7 days at the main entrance of the city library.
• Poll during the times the library is busiest.

Step 4 Organize and interpret your data.

How often do you use the computers at the library?	Sometimes 36	Often **52**	Never 12
If you use this service, how important is this to you?	Very important **70**	Somewhat important 21	Not important 9
Do you have access to the Internet anywhere other than at the library?	Yes 21	No **67**	

Step 5 Show your results.

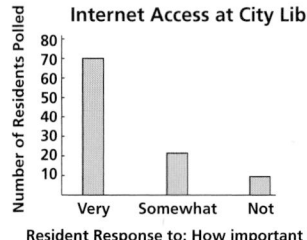

Internet Access at City Library

Exercise Use the steps above to conduct a survey. Work with a small group of friends. Think of an issue important to your group.

428 *Chapter 13 Data, Statistics, and Probability*

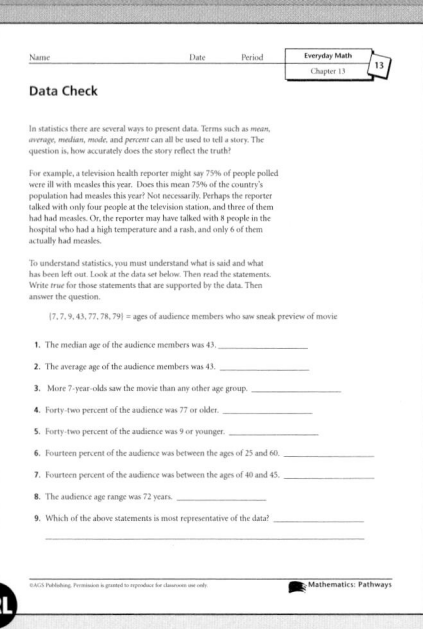

Application Activity 13   Everyday Math 13

Chapter 13 R E V I E W

Write the letter of the correct answer.
Use the table to answer questions 1 through 4.

1. What is the range of the data? B
  A 8   **C** 12
  B 9   **D** 4

7	2	6
4	1	0
5	7	8
3	9	5

2. What is the mean of the data? D
  A 9   **C** 5
  B 7.45   **D** 4.75

3. What is the median of the data? D
  A 7   **C** 4. 75
  B 9   **D** 5

4. What is the mode (or modes) of the data? A
  A 5 and 7   **C** 7 and 2
  B 3   **D** 9

Use the box-and-whiskers plot to answer questions 5 and 6.

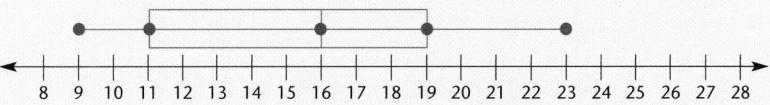

5. Which values represent the extremes? C
  A 11 and 19   **C** 9 and 23
  B 11 and 23   **D** 9 and 11

6. Which values represent the quartiles? B
  A 9 and 23   **C** 16 and 23
  B 11 and 19   **D** 9 and 19

Use the fundamental principle of counting to solve the problem.

Example: How many different ways can three people stand in a straight line?

Solution: Three people can stand in a straight line 3 • 2 • 1 or 6 different ways.

7. Evelyn has a first name, 2 middle names, and a last name. In how many different ways could Evelyn arrange the initials of her name? 24 ways

Data, Statistics, and Probability *Chapter 13* **429**

3 Reinforce and Extend

ONLINE CONNECTION

For data collection and analysis as it relates to the United States census, go to www.census.gov. This site demonstrates practical applications of data collection gathered through surveys and research. The home page offers statistical information divided into six categories. There is a feature titled "Subjects A to Z" that allows students to choose a subject of interest. Click on the For Teachers link under Special Topics for downloadable reference and classroom materials.

Chapter 13 Review

Each set of problems in the Chapter Review includes an example and solution to illustrate the concept. Use the given examples for reteaching the materials in Chapter 13. For additional practice, refer to the Supplementary Problems for Chapter 13 (pages 456–457).

Chapter 13 Mastery Test

The Teacher's Resource Library includes parallel forms of the Chapter 13 Mastery Test. The difficulty level of the two forms is equivalent. You may wish to use one form as a pretest and the other form as a posttest.

Chapters 1–13 Final Mastery Test TRL

The Teacher's Resource Library includes the Final Mastery Test. This test is pictured on pages 526–527 of this Teacher's Edition. The Final Mastery Test assesses the major learning objectives of this text, with emphasis on Chapters 8–13.

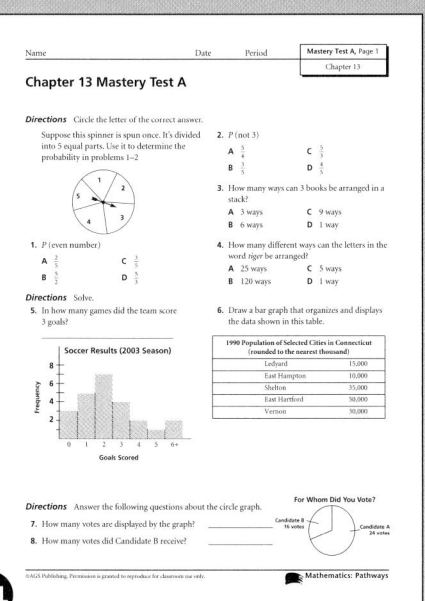

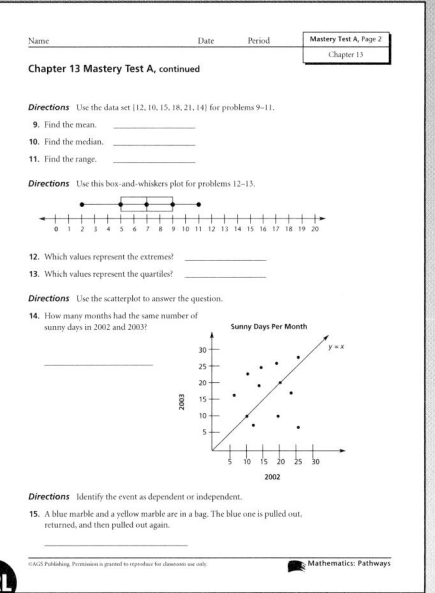

Chapter 13 Mastery Test A

Data, Statistics, and Probability **429**

Alternative Assessment items correlate with student Goals for Learning at the beginning of this chapter.

■ **To construct bar graphs, frequency tables, circle graphs, histograms, and scatterplots and interpret information illustrated by them**
Have students gather data by conducting a survey about something that interests them. (Have students restrict their data to three or four choices such as "Of these four colors, sports, seasons of the year, and so on, which one do you like best?" Otherwise they may have so many responses that constructing a graph will be too difficult.) Using the data they gathered, have students construct a bar graph or circle graph to represent their data. Remind students to label their graphs appropriately so that others will understand them.

• Have students divide into small groups to construct a frequency table from data in a book such as the *World Almanac*. Topics may include a frequency table of the salaries of governors in the 50 states, the 100 most populous cities in the United States, the lengths of the principal world rivers, or tuition costs for your state's colleges and universities. After students have constructed their frequency tables, have them write a brief analysis of three things that the tables show.

• Provide students with a circle or line graph. Ask them to use the data to construct a histogram. Each student should then create up to three questions for another student to answer. Answers should be checked and corrected, if needed, by the students. Questions that involve critical thinking or problem-solving skills may be shared with the class.

Create a bar graph that organizes and displays the data shown in the table below.

Example: Draw a bar graph that organizes and displays the data shown in this table.

Class Attendance Last Week	
Monday	18 students
Tuesday	20 students
Wednesday	19 students
Thursday	15 students
Friday	17 students

Solution:
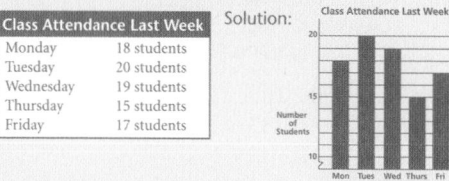

8.
How Do I Spend My Time?	
Sleeping	9 hours
Eating	1 hour
Working/Doing Chores	1 hour
Recreation/Exercise	3 hours
Studying	2 hours
School	8 hours

See Teacher's Edition for answer.

Create a circle graph that organizes and displays the data shown in the table below.

Example: How many degrees of the circle graph are represented by Flavor A?

Solution: 0.70 • 360° = 252°

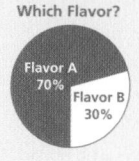

9.
Taste Test— Which Flavors Is Your Favorite?	
Flavor A	12 votes
Flavor B	3 votes
Flavor C	5 votes

See Teacher's Edition for answer.

Use the following frequency table.

Example: How many packages weighing less than 10 pounds were shipped?   Solution: 15

Shipping Weights of Packages		
Weight in Pounds	Tally	Frequency
> 0 but < 10	卌 卌 卌	15
> 10 but < 20	卌 IIII	9
> 20 but < 30	卌 卌 I	11
> 30 but < 40	III	3
> 40 but < 50	I	1

10. How many packages were shipped?

11. What was the weight of the heaviest package? Explain.

10. 39 packages were shipped

11. The heaviest package weighed more pounds but less than 50 pounds. Its weight is not known.

Find the probability. Express your answer as a fraction in simplest form and as a percent rounded to the nearest whole number.

Example: Suppose a coin is tossed once. What is the probability that the coin will land heads up?

Solution: $P = \frac{\text{number of favorable outcomes}}{\text{number of possible outcomes}} = \frac{1}{2} = 0.50 = 50\%$

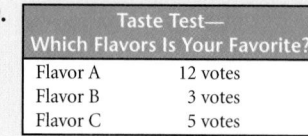

12. Suppose the spinner is spun once. Find the probability of the spinner landing on orange. $\frac{1}{2}$; 50%

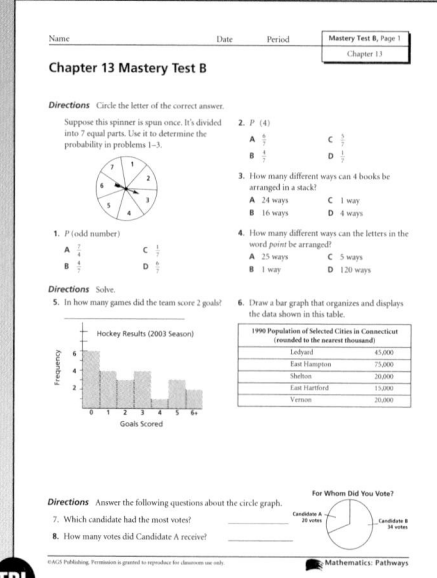

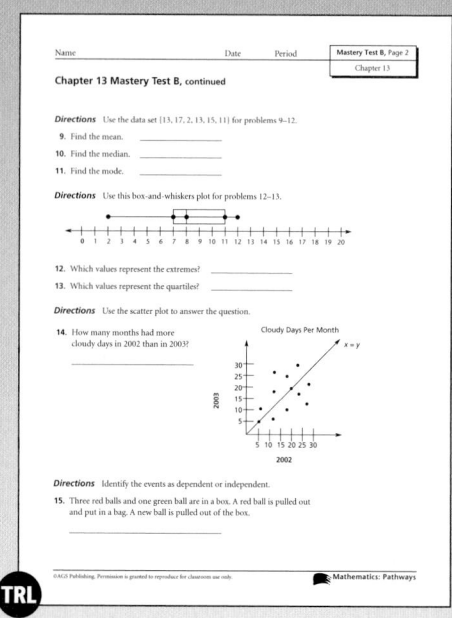

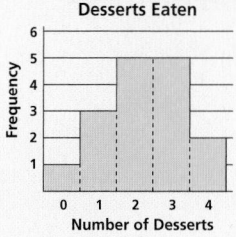

Desserts Eaten

Use the data from the histograms to answer the questions.

Example: Use the histogram. Follow each bar to the top and look at the height. What was the least frequent number of desserts eaten? The top of the shortest bar is above zero, at a height of one. Zero is the least frequent number of desserts eaten.
How many times were four desserts eaten? The height of the bar above four is 2. Four desserts were eaten two times.

13. True or false: every person ate at least one dessert. false

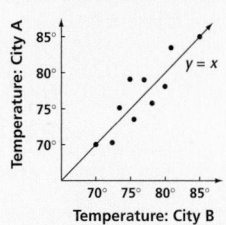

The scatterplot shows temperature readings.

Example: Use the scatterplot for this problem. Look at the points above and below the $y = x$ line.
How many temperatures are on the scatterplot? Count the points on the scatterplot. There are 10 temperatures.
How many times did the cities record different temperatures? Count the number of points that are not on the line. The cities had different temperatures 8 times.

14. Which temperatures were recorded by both cities? 70° and 85°

Read about the dependent experiment, and determine the probability.

Example: Three blocks are put into a box. Two are green and one is white. On the first turn, what is the probability of pulling out a green block?

$$\frac{\text{\# of green blocks}}{\text{total \# of blocks}} = \frac{2}{3} \qquad \text{The probability is } \frac{2}{3}.$$

A green block is pulled and not returned to the box. What is the new probability of pulling a green block?

$$\frac{\text{\# of green blocks}}{\text{total \# of blocks}} = \frac{1}{2} \qquad \text{The probability is } \frac{1}{2}.$$

15.

First draw: $P = \frac{3}{6}$ or $\frac{1}{2}$ (50%)

Second draw: $P = \frac{2}{5}$ (40%)

Third draw: $P = \frac{1}{2}$ (50%)

15. A bag contains 6 blocks. All blocks are the same size. Three blocks are red, 2 are blue, and 1 is yellow. After a block has been removed, it is not used again. A red block is removed, followed by a blue block on the second draw and a red block on the last draw. For each draw, find P for the red blocks.

Test-Taking Tip

To avoid reading the wrong data from a chart, table, or graph, use a straightedge to guide your eye across the information.

■ **To find measures of central tendency and range**
Have students work in pairs or groups of three to write a song, make up a slogan, or create some other memory device to remember the definitions of *mean, median, mode,* and *range.* Ask groups to share their ideas with the class.

■ **To construct and understand box-and-whiskers plots**
Have students each make up a set of data and create a box-and-whiskers plot from the data. Students should exchange their box-and-whiskers plots with a partner. Have partners find and label all the pieces: *lower extreme, lower quartile, median, upper quartile,* and *upper extreme.*

■ **To solve problems involving probability and the fundamental principle of counting**
Have students count the number of pairs of jeans, shirts, and hats they own. Have them assume that they can wear these items of clothing in any combination. Then have them compute the number of different outfits they can make.

Answers to Problems 8 and 9

8.

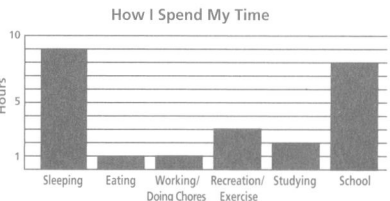

9.

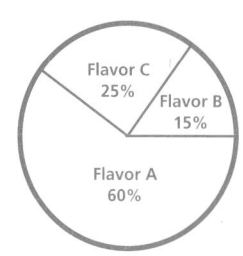

Create a diagram to answer the question.

1. One ten plus 3 = * * * * * * * * * *   * * *

Three tens plus 4 = * * * * * * * * * *   * * * * * * * * * *   * * * * * * * * * *   * * * *

In problems 2 and 3, TT = ten thousands and H = hundreds.
Write the answers using digits.

2. 5TT + 1TT + 3 = ■ 60,003

3. 8TT + 2H = ■ 80,200

Write the number in standard form.

4. $(6 \times 10{,}000) + (7 \times 1{,}000) + (0 \times 100) + (2 \times 10) + (1 \times 1)$ 67,021

Identify the digit in the ten thousands place.

5. 62,091 6

Write the answer using digits.

6. $(1 \times 10^6) + (4 \times 10^5) + (0 \times 10^4) + (1 \times 10^3) + (0 \times 10^2) + (9 \times 10^1) + (5 \times 10^0)$
1,401,095

Write the inverse.

7. 620 + 779 = 1,399   1,399 − 779 = 620

8.
$$\begin{array}{r} 1{,}426 \\ -\ 808 \\ \hline 618 \end{array} \qquad \begin{array}{r} 808 \\ +\ 618 \\ \hline 1{,}426 \end{array}$$

Write the inverse.

9.
$$\begin{array}{r} 411 \\ \times\ 26 \\ \hline 10{,}686 \end{array} \qquad 411\,)\,\overline{10{,}686}\ \ 26$$

10.
$$3\,)\,\overline{411}\ \ 137 \qquad \begin{array}{r} 137 \\ \times\ 3 \\ \hline 411 \end{array}$$

Add the base 2 numbers. Write the answer in base 10.

11. $1\,0\,0\,0_2 + 1\,0\,1\,0_2 = \ 18_{10}$ **12.** $1\,0\,1_2 + 1\,0\,0_2 + 1\,0_2 = \ 11_{10}$

Write the number in base 2.

13. $2^2 + 2^1 \ \ 1\,1\,0_2$ **14.** $2^2 \ \ 1\,0\,0_2$

Provide the next number in the base 5 sequence.

15. $1, 2, 3, 4, ? \ \ 10_5$ **16.** $11, 12, 13, 14, ? \ \ 20_5$

Write the number in base 5.

17. $2(5^0) \ \ 2_5$ **18.** $1(5^1) + 4 \ \ 14_5$

Find the base 10 equivalent.

19. $10100_2 \ \ 20_{10}$

Find the base 5 equivalent.

20. $807_{10} \ \ 11212_5$

Find each sum.

1. 3,289 + 6,573

9,862

2. 324,905 + 8,713

333,618

3. 984 + 321

1,305

4. 5,075 + 837

5,912

5. 64,829 + 92,081

156,910

6. 573 + 43,807

44,380

Find each difference.

7. 12,306 − 8,729

3,577

8. 5,537 − 723

4,814

9. 625 − 98

527

10. 329,610 − 32,106

297,504

11. 485,287 − 251,876

233,411

12. 3,082 − 93

2,989

Find each product.

13. 589 × 251   147,839

14. 41 × 57   2,337

15. 67 × 32   2,144

16. 24 × 9   216

17. 630 × 8   5,040

18. 49 × 34   1,666

Find each quotient. Remember to write any remainder as part of the quotient.

19. 5,544 ÷ 66   84

20. 576 ÷ 24   24

21. 166 ÷ 40   4 r6

22. 23,137 ÷ 32   723 r1

23. 10,908 ÷ 8   1,363 r4

24. 756 ÷ 36   21

Estimate each answer.

25. 82,573 + 15,987   100,000

26. 614 × 321   180,000

27. 5,920 + 5,231   11,000

28. 192,309 − 47,367   150,000

29. 73,582 ÷ 67   1,000

30. 25,308 ÷ 39   750

Tell whether each statement is *true*, *false*, or *open*.

31. $24 - n = 15$ open   **33.** $826n = 24{,}078$ open   **35.** $64 \div 8 = n$ open

32. $11 \times 11 = 111$ false   **34.** $12 + 3 = 36$ false   **36.** $634 \times 7 = 4{,}438$ true

Classify each expression as *numerical* or *algebraic*. Then name the operation(s) and identify any variables.

37. $816 \div 15$ numerical; division   **40.** $w \div 33$ algebraic; division, w

38. $15x$ algebraic; multiplication, x **41.** $4 + 3 \times 9$
                                                      numerical; addition, multiplication
39. $3y - 14$
 algebraic; multiplication, subtraction, y **42.** $5a + 6$
                                                      algebraic; multiplication, addition, a

Evaluate each expression.

43. $16 + n$ when $n = 14$.   30   **45.** $49 - z$ when $z = 13$.   36

44. $125 \div c$ when $c = 5$.   25   **46.** $16 - 3n$ when $n = 3$.   7

Write *true* or *false*.

47. $3m = 42$ when $m = 15$.   false   **49.** $y \div 42 = 6$ when $y = 252$.   true

48. $24 - e = 9$ when $e = 15$.   true   **50.** $31 + n = 49$ when $n = 80$.   false

Identify place or value.

1. the place of 6 in the decimal 135.0861   thousandths place

2. the value of 3 in the decimal 8,346.05 $3 \times 100 = 300$

3. the place of 4 in 267.0914   ten-thousandths place

4. the value of 9 in 89.43 $9 \times 1 = 9$

Add or subtract.

5. $0.978 + 6.84$ 7.818

6. $4.7301 - 2.73$ 2.0001

7. $8 - 0.318$ 7.682

8. $\$80 - \$29.98$ $50.02

9. $35.45 + 1.035$ 36.485

10. $6.4 + 5.31 + 0.675$ 12.385

Multiply. Round to the nearest thousandth when necessary.

11. 200×8.183 1,636.6

12. 0.497×3.25 1.615

13. $\$16.88 \times 3.75$ $63.30

14. 84.51×6.2 523.962

15. 4.135×6.512 26.927

16. 6.57×10^3 6,570

Divide. If necessary, round to the nearest thousandth.

17. $32.6 \div 100$ 0.326

18. $651 \div 9.3$ 70

19. $32.9 \div 0.4$ 82.25

20. $94.58 \div 3.6$ 26.272

21. $57.81 \div 10^2$ 0.578

22. $64.4 \div 10^3$ 0.064

Write each decimal as a fraction. Simplify your answer.

23. 0.750 $\frac{3}{4}$ **25.** 0.375 $\frac{3}{8}$

24. 0.500 $\frac{1}{2}$ **26.** 0.120 $\frac{3}{25}$

Write each fraction as a decimal. Round to the nearest hundredth if necessary.

27. $\frac{3}{11}$ 0.27   **29.** $\frac{27}{100}$ 0.27

28. $\frac{15}{16}$ 0.94   **30.** $\frac{7}{9}$ 0.78

Find the interest earned. Use the formula $I = prt$.

31. What is the interest earned on $32,000 at $6\frac{1}{2}$% for 5 years? $10,400

32. What is the interest earned on $2,500 at 5.3% for 4 years? $530

Evaluate each expression. Round to the nearest hundredth if necessary.

33. $y + 3.14$ when $y = 12.84$ 15.98

34. $2l + 2w$ when $l = 4.6$ and $w = 6.25$ 21.7

35. $4.5c - 6.9b$ when $c = 4.6$ and $b = 2.4$ 4.14

36. $x \div 3.2$ when $x = 45.73$ 14.29

Write *true* or *false*.

37. Is $4.2s = 25.2$ a *true* or *false* statement when $s = 6$?   true

38. Is $403.2 \div s = 4.2$ a *true* or *false* statement when $s = 9.6$?   false

39. Is $21.7 + s = 38.1$ a *true* or *false* statement when $s = 16.4$?   true

40. Is $s + 0.375 = 0.380$ a *true* or *false* statement when $s = 5$?   false

Chapter 4   Supplementary Problems

Evaluate each statement. Write *true* or *false*.

1. $6|32$ false   **4.** $3|265$ false   **7.** $8|448$ true

2. $7|84$ true   **5.** $4|76$ true   **8.** $9|4,509$ true

3. $10|3,560$ true   **6.** $2|843$ false

Is each number divisible by 2? by 3? by 4? by 5? by 6? by 8? by 9? by 10?

9. 84   2, 3, 4, 6   **11.** 3,120   2, 3, 4, 5, 6, 8, 10

10. 430   2, 5, 10   **12.** 32,022   2, 3, 6, 9

Decide whether each number is *prime* or *composite*.

13. 123   composite   **15.** 101   prime

14. 196   composite   **16.** 187   prime

Find the greatest common divisor.

17. $(21, 28)$ 7   **19.** $(3y, 42)$ 3

18. $(6, 16)$ 2   **20.** $(8, 64a)$ 8

Use the distributive property to find the product of each expression.

21. $5(6 + 4)$ 50   **23.** $6(b + 9)$ $6b + 54$ **25.** $4(c + 15 + 5a)$
                                                                         $4c + 60 + 20a$
22. $7(3 + 4)$ 49   **24.** $21(5 + 3x)$ **26.** $17(8 + d + 6p)$
                                                 $105 + 63x$ $136 + 17d + 102p$

Find the greatest common divisor.

27. $12c + 24$ 12   **29.** $9xc + 18x$ $9x$ **31.** $12z + 20h$ 4

28. $15 + 25y$ 5   **30.** $6j + 18k$ 6   **32.** $13y + 21t$ 1

Factor each expression.

33. $3y + 21$ $3(y + 7)$

34. $25x + 35$ $5(5x + 7)$

35. $10c + 5$ $5(2c + 1)$

36. $6u + 4$ $2(3u + 2)$

37. $24s + 28m$ $4(6s + 7m)$

38. $12q + 18n$ $6(2q + 3n)$

39. $7z + 14b$ $7(z + 2b)$

40. $6j + 15k$ $3(2j + 5k)$

Find the LCM.

41. LCM (5, 30)   30

42. LCM (16, 24)   48

43. LCM (9, 30)   90

44. LCM (15, 50)   150

45. LCM (64, 16)   64

46. LCM (12, 20)   60

Use a calculator and find the value of each expression.

47. $6 \cdot 8^3$ 3,072

48. $3^3 \cdot 4^6$ 110,592

49. $8 \cdot 13 \cdot 23^3$ 1,265,368

50. $5^2 \cdot 3^4 \cdot 2^5$ 64,800

Write in scientific notation.

51. 35,210,000,000 $3.521 \cdot 10^{10}$

52. 4,500,000 $4.5 \cdot 10^6$

53. 0.0000375 $3.75 \cdot 10^{-5}$

54. 0.000000089 $8.9 \cdot 10^{-8}$

55. 49.7 $4.97 \cdot 10$

Express each improper fraction as a mixed number and express each mixed number as an improper fraction.

1. $2\frac{2}{3}$ $\frac{8}{3}$

2. $\frac{11}{3}$ $3\frac{2}{3}$

3. $\frac{32}{5}$ $6\frac{2}{5}$

4. $1\frac{7}{8}$ $\frac{15}{8}$

5. $\frac{15}{7}$ $2\frac{1}{7}$

6. $6\frac{5}{9}$ $\frac{59}{9}$

7. $3\frac{3}{4}$ $\frac{15}{4}$

8. $\frac{21}{4}$ $5\frac{1}{4}$

Write two equivalent fractions for each fraction.

9. $\frac{7}{8}$ possible answers: $\frac{14}{16}$ $\frac{21}{24}$

10. $\frac{3}{5}$ possible answers: $\frac{6}{10}$ $\frac{9}{15}$

11. $\frac{1}{8}$ possible answers: $\frac{2}{16}$ $\frac{3}{24}$

12. $\frac{5}{14}$ possible answers: $\frac{10}{28}$ $\frac{15}{42}$

13. $\frac{9}{15}$ possible answers: $\frac{18}{30}$ $\frac{27}{45}$

14. $\frac{11}{12}$ possible answers: $\frac{22}{24}$ $\frac{33}{36}$

15. $\frac{1}{50}$ possible answers: $\frac{2}{100}$ $\frac{3}{150}$

16. $\frac{1}{10}$ possible answers: $\frac{2}{20}$ $\frac{3}{30}$

Express each fraction in simplest form.

17. $\frac{10}{25}$ $\frac{2}{5}$

18. $\frac{4}{30}$ $\frac{2}{15}$

19. $\frac{6}{42}$ $\frac{1}{7}$

20. $\frac{15}{45}$ $\frac{1}{3}$

21. $\frac{3}{27}$ $\frac{1}{9}$

22. $\frac{18}{24}$ $\frac{3}{4}$

23. $\frac{8}{18}$ $\frac{4}{9}$

24. $\frac{21}{30}$ $\frac{7}{10}$

Order from least to greatest.

25. $\dfrac{1}{2}$ $\dfrac{1}{5}$ $\dfrac{3}{10}$ $\dfrac{1}{5}$ $\dfrac{3}{10}$ $\dfrac{1}{2}$

26. $\dfrac{5}{12}$ $\dfrac{2}{3}$ $\dfrac{1}{4}$ $\dfrac{1}{4}$ $\dfrac{5}{12}$ $\dfrac{2}{3}$

27. $\dfrac{2}{9}$ $\dfrac{5}{6}$ $\dfrac{5}{18}$ $\dfrac{2}{9}$ $\dfrac{5}{18}$ $\dfrac{5}{6}$

28. $\dfrac{19}{21}$ $\dfrac{3}{7}$ $\dfrac{2}{3}$ $\dfrac{3}{7}$ $\dfrac{2}{3}$ $\dfrac{19}{21}$

Add, subtract, multiply, or divide. Simplify your answer if possible.

29. $\dfrac{3}{10} + \dfrac{4}{5}$ $1\dfrac{1}{10}$

30. $\dfrac{2}{3} - \dfrac{1}{2}$ $\dfrac{1}{6}$

31. $4\dfrac{1}{2} \cdot 3\dfrac{3}{4}y$ $16\dfrac{7}{8}y$

32. $1\dfrac{3}{24} - \dfrac{11}{12}$ $\dfrac{5}{24}$

33. $\dfrac{5}{6} \div \dfrac{7}{8}$ $\dfrac{20}{21}$

34. $3\dfrac{3}{16} + 5\dfrac{3}{4}$ $8\dfrac{15}{16}$

35. $\dfrac{4}{7} \cdot \dfrac{4}{7}$ $\dfrac{16}{49}$

36. $2\dfrac{5}{8} - 1\dfrac{3}{24}$ $1\dfrac{1}{2}$

37. $9\dfrac{1}{3}g + 6\dfrac{2}{5}g$ $15\dfrac{11}{15}g$

38. $2\dfrac{6}{7} \cdot 2\dfrac{4}{5}$ 8

39. $4\dfrac{7}{8} \div \dfrac{5}{8}$ $7\dfrac{4}{5}$

40. $5\dfrac{1}{2} - 3\dfrac{3}{16}$ $2\dfrac{5}{16}$

41. $\dfrac{4}{7} \div \dfrac{1}{2}$ $1\dfrac{1}{7}$

42. $3\dfrac{1}{8} + 2\dfrac{15}{16}$ $6\dfrac{1}{16}$

43. $3\dfrac{3}{5} \div 2\dfrac{1}{4}$ $1\dfrac{3}{5}$

44. $1\dfrac{7}{12} \div 1\dfrac{1}{3}$ $1\dfrac{3}{16}$

45. $6\dfrac{5}{12}m \cdot 1\dfrac{1}{3}$ $8\dfrac{5}{9}m$

46. $5\dfrac{1}{3}n + 5\dfrac{5}{6}n$ $11\dfrac{1}{6}n$

47. $2\dfrac{1}{4} \cdot 6\dfrac{2}{3}$ 15

48. $3\dfrac{6}{7} \div 4\dfrac{1}{2}$ $\dfrac{6}{7}$

49. $1\dfrac{8}{9} \cdot 3\dfrac{3}{5}$ $6\dfrac{4}{5}$

50. $4\dfrac{1}{4} - 2\dfrac{15}{16}$ $1\dfrac{5}{16}$

Simplify each expression by following the order of operations.

1. $6 + 3 \cdot 8$ 30   **4.** $12(10 - 9) + 3 \cdot 5$ 27   **7.** $11 + 3(10 - 7)$ 20

2. $12 \div 3 \cdot (3 + 4)$ 28   **5.** $6 \cdot 7 \div 3 + 4$ 18   **8.** $5 + 4 - 3 \cdot 6 \div 2$ 0

3. $28 - 20 \div 5$ 24   **6.** $(5 + 7) \div 4 + 3 \cdot 2$ 9

Evaluate each expression from $n = 6$.

9. $n + 6$ 12   **12.** $8n + 5$ 53   **15.** $6n - 30$ 6   **18.** $5n - 3n$ 12

10. $n - 3$ 3   **13.** $\frac{n}{11} + 21$ $21\frac{6}{11}$ **16.** $1 + \frac{1}{n}$ $1\frac{1}{6}$

11. $50 - 3n$ 32   **14.** $\frac{n}{3} - 2$ 0   **17.** $\frac{2n}{3} + \frac{3}{2n}$ $4\frac{1}{4}$

Tell whether each equation is *true* or *false* when the given number is substituted for x.

19. $5(7) - x = 30$ when $x = 5$ true   **23.** $15 + 4x = 23$ when $x = 2$ true

20. $x + 4(x) = 40$ when $x = 10$ false   **24.** $3x \cdot 4 = 16$ when $x = 4$ false

21. $26 + x = 20$ when $x = 6$ false   **25.** $6 + 8x = 62$ when $x = 7$ true

22. $30 - 3x = 9$ when $x = 7$ true

Solve for x. Write your answer in simplest form.

26. $x + 18 = 23$ 5   **30.** $3\frac{3}{4} - x = 2\frac{1}{8}$ $1\frac{5}{8}$

27. $32 - x = 18$ 14   **31.** $\frac{1}{2}x - \frac{1}{2} = 5$ 11

28. $\frac{2}{3}x + \frac{2}{3} = 5\frac{2}{3}$ $7\frac{1}{2}$ **32.** $\frac{7}{8} + \frac{3}{8}x = 6\frac{7}{8}$ 16

29. $\frac{6}{7} + 3x = 12\frac{6}{7}$ 4

Simplify each complex fraction.

33. $\dfrac{\frac{2}{3}}{\frac{1}{3}}$ 2   **35.** $\dfrac{\frac{3}{4}}{2}$ $\dfrac{3}{8}$ **37.** $\dfrac{\frac{1}{4}}{\frac{1}{16}}$ 4   **39.** $\dfrac{10}{\frac{2}{3}}$ 15

34. $\dfrac{\frac{4}{5}}{\frac{4}{7}}$ $1\frac{2}{5}$ **36.** $\dfrac{\frac{6}{7}}{\frac{7}{8}}$ $6\frac{6}{7}$ **38.** $\dfrac{\frac{2}{3}}{6}$ $\dfrac{1}{9}$ **40.** $\dfrac{\frac{15}{16}}{4}$ $\dfrac{15}{64}$

Simplify. Write your answers in simplest form.

41. $\dfrac{2}{7b} + \dfrac{1}{7b}$ $\dfrac{3}{7b}$ **45.** $\dfrac{13}{16a} - \dfrac{1}{2a}$ $\dfrac{5}{16a}$

42. $\dfrac{19}{20x} - \dfrac{1}{4x}$ $\dfrac{7}{10x}$ **46.** $\dfrac{7}{8j} + \dfrac{3}{8j} + \dfrac{5}{8j}$ $\dfrac{15}{8j}$

43. $\dfrac{7}{24g} + \dfrac{3}{8g}$ $\dfrac{2}{3g}$ **47.** $\dfrac{8}{9y} - \dfrac{1}{9y} + \dfrac{2}{9y}$ $\dfrac{1}{y}$

44. $\dfrac{9}{10t} - \dfrac{3}{4t}$ $\dfrac{3}{20t}$ **48.** $\dfrac{3}{4c} - \dfrac{2}{3c} + \dfrac{1}{6c}$ $\dfrac{1}{4c}$

Multiply. Write your answer in simplest form.

49. $\dfrac{3}{5} \cdot \dfrac{5}{6z}$ $\dfrac{1}{2z}$ **53.** $\dfrac{2}{7h} \cdot \dfrac{21}{24}$ $\dfrac{1}{4h}$

50. $\dfrac{3}{8e} \cdot \dfrac{8}{15}$ $\dfrac{1}{5e}$ **54.** $\dfrac{3}{5m} \cdot \dfrac{8}{9}$ $\dfrac{8}{15m}$

51. $\dfrac{24}{25} \cdot \dfrac{5p}{8}$ $\dfrac{3p}{5}$ **55.** $\dfrac{5}{12} \cdot \dfrac{7}{15f}$ $\dfrac{7}{36f}$

52. $\dfrac{15}{16k} \cdot \dfrac{8}{9}$ $\dfrac{5}{6k}$

Chapter 7　Supplementary Problems

Express each ratio as a fraction in simplest form.

1. 50 to 2　$\dfrac{25}{1}$

2. 18:24　$\dfrac{3}{4}$

3. $\dfrac{60}{22}$　$\dfrac{30}{11}$

4. 8 to 64　$\dfrac{1}{8}$

5. $\dfrac{6}{42}$　$\dfrac{1}{7}$

6. 108:9　$\dfrac{12}{1}$

Is each proportion a true proportion? Write *yes* or *no*.

7. $\dfrac{3}{4} = \dfrac{15}{20}$　yes

8. $\dfrac{5}{9} = \dfrac{30}{72}$　no

9. $\dfrac{15}{35} = \dfrac{3}{5}$　no

10. $\dfrac{5}{16} = \dfrac{30}{96}$　yes

Solve for the variable in each proportion.

11. $\dfrac{v}{8} = \dfrac{9}{24}$　3

12. $\dfrac{5}{6} = \dfrac{35}{n}$　42

13. $\dfrac{1}{x} = \dfrac{16}{48}$　3

14. $\dfrac{6}{8} = \dfrac{3}{n}$　4

15. $\dfrac{10}{d} = \dfrac{50}{30}$　6

16. $\dfrac{28}{16} = \dfrac{s}{4}$　7

Express each decimal as a percent.

17. 0.53　53%

18. 0.1　10%

19. 0.91　91%

20. 0.7　70%

Solve each problem.

21. Matthew can lift 70 pounds. Michael can lift $1\frac{1}{4}$ times more weight. How much can Michael lift?　87 lb

22. Jane is on a train that going 70 miles per hour (mph). Her destination is 312 miles away. How long will it take her to get there?　4.46 hours

23. A race car driver finishes a race in 1.3 hours. His constant speed was 180 miles per hour (mph). How many miles did he drive?　234 miles

Express each fraction as a percent.

24. $\frac{3}{10}$ 30%   **26.** $\frac{15}{16}$ 93.75%   **28.** $\frac{6}{25}$ 24%   **30.** $\frac{67}{100}$ 67%

25. $\frac{3}{8}$ 37.5%   **27.** $\frac{3}{4}$ 75%   **29.** $\frac{13}{20}$ 65%   **31.** $\frac{7}{10}$ 70%

Write each percent as a decimal.

32. 25%   0.25   **34.** 8%   0.08   **36.** 16%   0.16   **38.** 79%   0.79

33. 32%   0.32   **35.** 55%   0.55   **37.** 43%   0.43   **39.** 81%   0.81

Solve each problem.

40. Jenny paid $52 for a calculator that originally cost $80. What was her percent of savings on the calculator purchase?   35%

41. Eric is buying two round-trip boat tickets to Alaska for $3,150. The tax on the tickets is 12%. How much is the total cost of the tickets with tax? $3,528

42. Steve works part-time at the local video store. On Thursday, he rented out 200 videos. On Friday, he rented out 354 videos. What was the percent of increase in the number of videos he rented out on Friday?   77%

43. José works as a reporter for a large newspaper. Last year he worked 240 days out of 250 work days. What percent of the year did he work?   96%

Solve each problem.

44. The scale of a building is 1 inch = 41 feet. A picture of the building in a magazine measures 3 inches. How tall is the building in real life?

123 feet tall

45. Find the missing value in the pair of similar shapes. $n = 16$

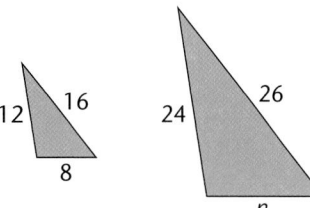

Chapter 8   Supplementary Problems

Find the absolute value or distance from zero.

1. $|6|$ 6   **3.** $|25|$ 25   **5.** $|-93|$ 93

2. $|-40|$ 40   **4.** $|-3|$ 3

Name the opposite of each integer.

6. 15 -15 **8.** -9 9   **10.** -32 32

7. 21 -21 **9.** 5 -5

Compare each pair. Use $<$, $>$, or $=$.

11. $6 \blacksquare -6$ $>$ **13.** $5 \blacksquare -10$ $>$ **15.** $-3 \blacksquare |5|$ $<$

12. $-2 \blacksquare 0$ $<$ **14.** $15 \blacksquare |-15|$ $=$

Find each sum.

16. $8 + 5$ 13   **21.** $-8 + (-6)$ -14

17. $3 + 7$ 10   **22.** $-9 + 5$ -4

18. $7 + (-3)$ 4   **23.** $-3 + (-1)$ -4

19. $-5 + (-4)$ -9 **24.** $2 + (-7)$ -5

20. $-3 + 3$ 0   **25.** $-4 + (-4)$ -8

Find each difference.

26. $-4 - (-10)$ 6 **29.** $15 - (-5)$ 20 **32.** $-5 - (-6)$ 1 **35.** $9 - (+4)$ 5

27. $6 - (+3)$ 3 **30.** $-8 - (-6)$ -2 **33.** $-4 - (-8)$ 4

28. $-7 - (-6)$ -1 **31.** $2 - (-3)$ 5 **34.** $-9 - (-7)$ -2

Find each product or quotient.

36. $(4)(6)$ 24 **41.** $(6)(9)$ 54 **46.** $42 \div 7$ 6 **51.** $72 \div 9$ 8

37. $(6)(-3)$ -18 **42.** $(2)(-12)$ -24 **47.** $10 \div (-5)$ -2 **52.** $64 \div (-8)$ -8

38. $(-5)(4)$ -20 **43.** $(-7)(-5)$ 35 **48.** $-48 \div 12$ -4 **53.** $-24 \div -4$ 6

39. $(-7)(-7)$ 49 **44.** $(-4)(8)$ -32 **49.** $-7 \div -7$ 1 **54.** $50 \div (-5)$ -10

40. $(-12)(-4)$ 48 **45.** $(-5)(9)$ -45 **50.** $-150 \div (-50)$ **55.** $-32 \div (-8)$ 4
  3

Solve each problem.

56. Anita can scuba dive 15 feet in a minute. At what depth will she be in 6 minutes? −90 feet

57. What is the difference between the top of a building, which is 453 feet above ground, and the basement, which is 24 feet below ground? 477 feet

58. The temperature Wednesday was −10°F. Thursday's temperature was 2°F. How much did the temperature increase? 12°F

59. For the first three holes in golf, John scored one point over par $(+1)$, three points under par (-3), and one point under par (-1). What was his score for the first three holes? −3 (three points under par)

60. The top long jump in Phil's gym class was 107 inches. Phil jumped 98 inches. How far was he from the top long jump? 9 inches

Chapter 9   Supplementary Problems

Rewrite each of the following using exponents.

1. $5 \cdot 5 \cdot 5 \cdot 5 \cdot 5$ $\quad\quad 5^5$ $\quad\quad$ **3.** $(-t) \cdot (-t) \cdot (-t) \cdot (-t)$ $\quad (-t)^4$

2. $(-8) \cdot (-8) \cdot (-8)$ $\quad (-8)^3$ $\quad\quad$ **4.** $c \cdot c \cdot c \cdot c$ $\quad\quad\quad\quad c^4$

Find the value of each expression.

5. 2^5 $\quad 32$ $\quad\quad\quad$ **6.** 35^2 $\quad 1{,}225$ $\quad\quad\quad$ **7.** $(-6)^3$ $\quad -216$

Simplify each expression.

8. $6^2 \cdot 6^5$ $\quad 6^7$ $\quad\quad\quad$ **9.** $12^5 \cdot 12^2$ $\quad 12^7$ $\quad\quad\quad$ **10.** $7^4 \div 7^2$ $\quad 7^2$

Write an expression for the area of each square. Then find the area.

11.

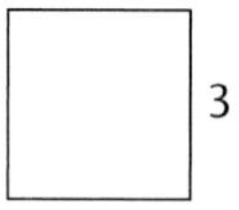

$\square$ $_3$ $\quad\quad 3 \cdot 3 = 3^2 = 9$

12.

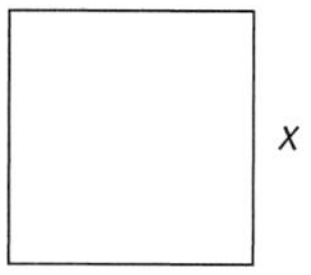

$\square$ $_x$ $\quad\quad x \cdot x = x^2$

Tell whether the radicals are rational or irrational.

13. $\sqrt[5]{243}$ $\quad 3$, rational $\quad\quad$ **14.** $\sqrt[3]{729}$ $\quad 9$, rational $\quad\quad$ **15.** $\sqrt[3]{89}$ $\quad 4.464$, irrational

Write a decimal expansion for each expression. You can use up to three decimal places for your answer.

16. $\sqrt[3]{26}$ $\, 2.96$, irrational $\quad\quad$ **17.** $\sqrt[5]{75}$ $\, 2.371$, irrational $\quad\quad$ **18.** $\sqrt[4]{625}$ $\, 5.000$, rational

Solve each problem.

19. Maria wants to carpet a square room that has an area of 81 square feet. What is the length of one side of the room? 9 feet

20. On a kitchen floor there are 225 square tiles with an area of 0.90 ft² each. What is the area of the entire floor? What is the length of a side of the kitchen? 202.5 ft², 14.23 ft

Write an expression for the volume of each cube. Then find the volume.

21.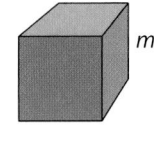

$$m \cdot m \cdot m = m^3$$

22.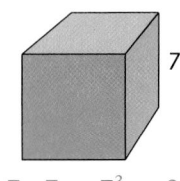

$$7 \cdot 7 \cdot 7 = 7^3 = 343$$

23.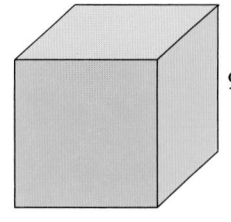

$$9 \cdot 9 \cdot 9 = 9^3 = 729$$

Estimate the square root of each number.

24. $\sqrt{10}$ between 3 and 4   **25.** $\sqrt{37}$ between 6 and 7   **26.** $\sqrt{47}$ between 6 and 7

Find the approximate length of a side of each square. Round to the nearest tenth.

27. Area = 49 $s = 7$ **28.** Area = 67 $s = 8.2$ **29.** Area = 2,000 $s = 44.7$

Solve equations for the unknown.

30. $\sqrt{t} = 6$ $t = 36$ **31.** $\sqrt{4y} = 16$ $y = 64$ **32.** $\sqrt{6x} = 6$ $x = 6$

Solve each equation for x. Check your answers.

33. $\sqrt{x} - 1 = 1$ $x = 4$ **34.** $8 - \sqrt{x} = 4$ $x = 16$ **35.** $27 - \sqrt{x} = 21$ $x = 36$

Solve each problem.

36. Use the formula for the area of a circle for the following problem.
$A = \pi r^2$; r = radius
The circular table in Jackie's kitchen has an area of 800 in.^{2} What is the radius of the table? ($\pi = 3$)
$r = 16.33$ in.

37. Use the formula for the volume of a cylinder for the following problem.
$V = \pi r^2 h$; r = radius, h = height
Patty opens a can of soup. The can has a volume of 75 in.^{3} and a height of 6 in. What is the radius? ($\pi = 3$)
$r = 2.04$ in.

Use the Pythagorean theorem to find x.

38.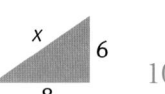

39.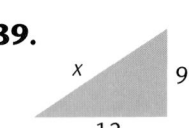

40.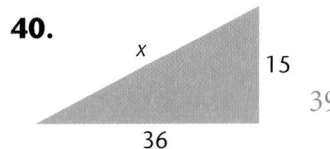

Find each perimeter.

1.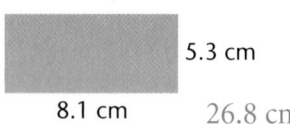

5.3 cm

8.1 cm   26.8 cm

3.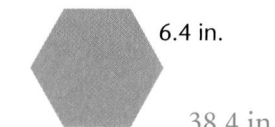

6.4 in.

38.4 in.

2.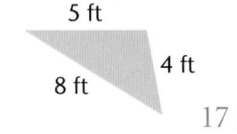

5 ft

4 ft

8 ft

17 ft

4.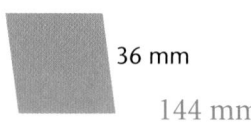

36 mm

144 mm

The measures of various squares and rectangles are given below. Find the area of each.

5. Square *NLIP* with s = 25 mm 625 mm²

6. Rectangle *JHGF* with l = 8.5 in.; w = 3 in. 25.5 in.²

7. Rectangle *CDEF* with l = 9 cm; w = 12 cm 108 cm²

8. Square *ACEG* with s = 7.3 ft 53.29 ft²

Find the area of each shape.

9.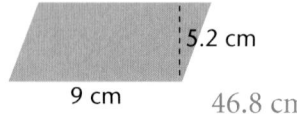

5.2 cm

9 cm   46.8 cm²

11.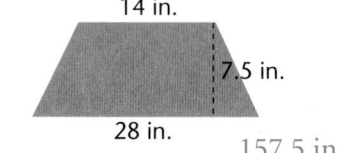

14 in.

7.5 in.

28 in.

157.5 in.²

10.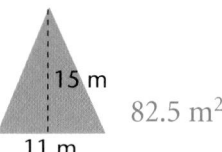

15 m

82.5 m²

11 m

12.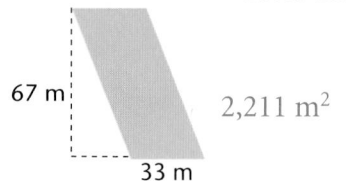

67 m

2,211 m²

33 m

Choose the correct name for each shape.

13. 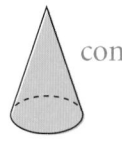 cone

14. 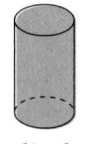 cylinder

15. 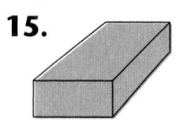 rectangular prism

16. 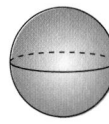 sphere

A sphere

B rectangular prism

C cone

D cylinder

Find the surface area.

17. What is the surface area of the prism?

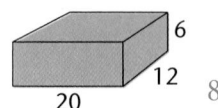

6

12

20

864 units²

18. What is the surface area of a cube with a side length of 12 in.? 864 in.²

Find the volume of each shape.

19.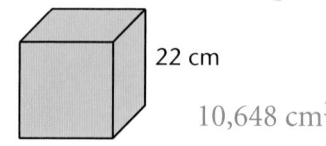

22 cm

10,648 cm³

20.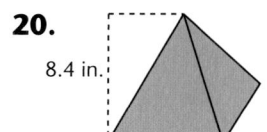

8.4 in.

5 in.

70 in.³

21. Zari mailed a package to her mom that is a cube with sides 23 inches long. What is the volume of the package? 12,167 in.³

22. Melissa is shipping a model boat in a box that is a rectangular prism. Its length is 43 inches, its width is 18 inches, and its height is 15 inches. What is the volume of the box?

11,610 in.³

Find the surface area. Use π = 3.14.

23. What is the surface area of the cone?

$A = 94.2$ units²

$l = 13$

$r = 2$

24. An architect designed a pyramid-shaped building. The building has a length of 200 ft and a base of 40 ft. What is the surface area of the building? $A = 17{,}600$ ft²

Use 3.14 for π to find the area and circumference.

25. On the outside of city hall in Cookport is a clock face with a 24-inch radius. What is the circumference and area of the clock face? 150.72 in.; 1,808.64 in.²

26. A school's logo of a tiger is painted inside a circle on the front door of the building. It has a diameter of 30 cm. What is the circumference and area of the circle? 94.2 cm; 706.5 cm²

Use 3.14 for π to find the volume of each figure. Round to the nearest hundredth.

27.

25 m

14 m

15,386 m³

28.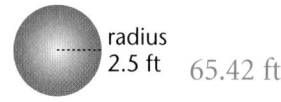

radius
2.5 ft   65.42 ft³

Find the volume for each shape. Use π = 3.14.

29. Cone $V = 41.86$ in.³
Diameter = 4 in.; Height = 10 in.

30. Pyramid $V = 228.67$ mm³
Side = 7 mm; Height = 14 mm

Answers to Problems 1–6

1.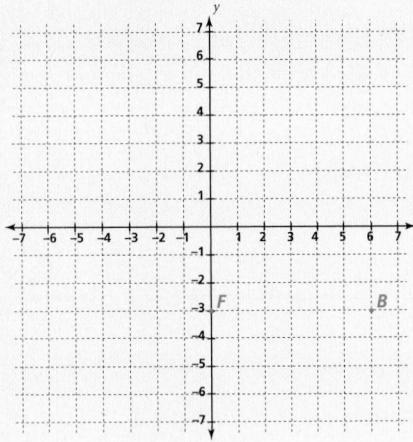

2.

3.

4.

5.

6.

Answers to Problems 8–10

8.

9.

10.

Answers to Problems 16–17

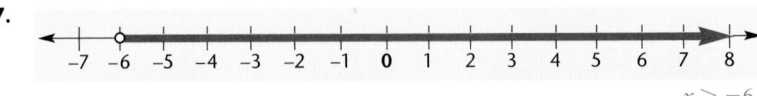

Graph each solution on a number line.

1. $c = 4$
3. $y < -1$
5. $p \le -4$

2. $d > -3$
4. $g \ge 6$
6. $t \ge -5$

See Teacher's Edition page for answers to problems 1–6.

Identify the solution shown by the number line.

7.

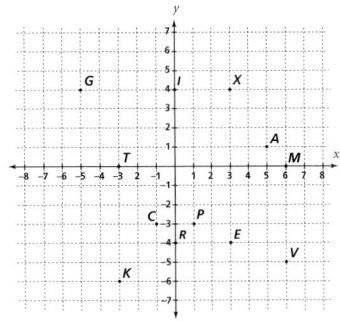

$x > -6$

Solve each equality or inequality for the variable. Then graph and check each solution.

8. $c - 3 \le 5$ $c \le 8$
9. $4 + j > 3$ $j > -1$
10. $t + 16 < 24$ $t < 8$

See Teacher's Edition page for answers to problems 8–10.

Use this coordinate system for problems 11–15.

Identify the quadrant for each point.

11. Point C
    Quadrant III
12. Point A
    Quadrant I
13. Point E
    Quadrant IV

Write an ordered pair to describe the location of each point.

14. Point I $(0, 4)$
15. Point P $(1, -3)$

On a sheet of graph paper, draw a coordinate system as shown above. Then use it to plot and label the following points.

16. Point B $(6, -3)$
17. Point F $(0, -3)$

See Teacher's Edition page for answers to problems 16 and 17.

Is each graph an example of a function?

18. yes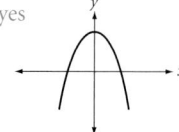

19. no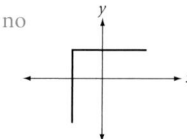

Evaluate each function two times. Use $x = -3$ and $x = 3$.

20. $f(x) = 4x^2 - 2x$
$f(-3) = 42; \ f(3) = 30$

21. $f(x) = -x^2 + x + 5$
$f(-3) = -7; \ f(3) = -1$

Determine the range for each function with the given domain.

22. $f(x) = x + 2x + 4$
domain: $-2, 1, 2, 7, 10$
range: $-2, 7, 10, 25, 34$

23. $f(x) = 4x - x^2 - 1$
domain: $-4, 0, 1, 3, 5$
range: $-33, -1, 2, 2, -6$

Determine the domain and the range from the graph and the given ordered pairs.

24.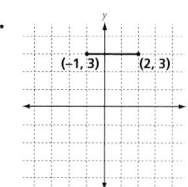

25.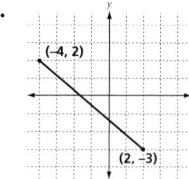

domain: $-1 \le x \le 2$; range: $y = 3$

domain: $-4 \le x \le 2$; range: $-3 \le y \le 2$

Graph the equation of each line.

26. $y = x + 2$ See Teacher's Edition page for answers to problem 26.

Find the slope of a line that passes through the given points.

27. $(6, 13)$ and $(4, 9)$ 2

28. $(-1, -5)$ and $(0, -4)$ 1

Write each of these equations of a line in slope-intercept form.

29. $3y = 6x + 3$ $y = 2x + 1$

30. $-y = -3x - 5$ $y = 3x + 5$

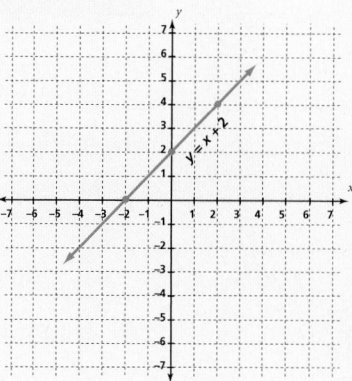

Use a protractor to give the measure of each angle.

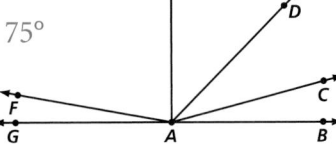

1. angle *BAC*   15°   **3.** angle *CAE*   75°

2. angle *CAD*   30°

Use this illustration to answer the following questions.

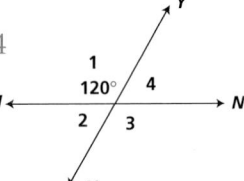

4. Name any angles adjacent to angle 1. angles 2 and 4

5. Name all pairs of vertical angles. angles 1 and 3;
angles 2 and 4

6. What is the measure of angle 3? 120°

Find the measure of the complement and supplement of angle *J*.

7. measure angle *J* = 25°   **8.** measure angle *J* = 75°   **9.** measure angle *J* = 89°
65°; 155°   15°; 105°   1°; 91°

Find the measure of angle *x*.

10.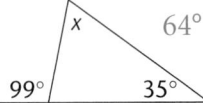

11.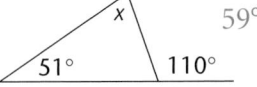

Name each triangle.

12.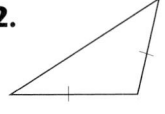

13.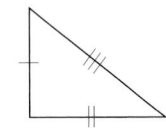

14.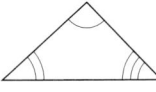

isosceles triangle   scalene triangle   obtuse scalene triangle

Name the condition that makes each pair of triangles congruent.

15. 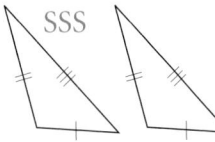 SSS

16. 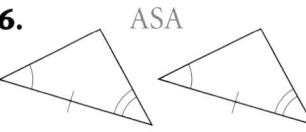 ASA

17.  SAS

Tell whether the triangles in each pair are similar.
Answer *yes*, *no*, or *not enough information*.

18.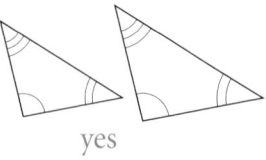

yes

19.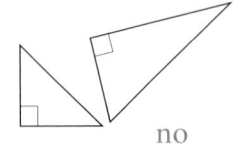

no

20.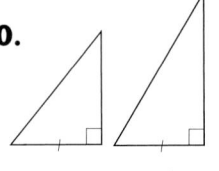

not enough information

Tell whether each statement is *true* or *false*.

21. All polygons with four sides are called quadrilaterals. true

22. All squares have two pairs of parallel sides and are rectangles. true

23. A trapezoid is a parallelogram with one pair of parallel sides. false

24. A rhombus is a square in the shape of a diamond. false

Use graph paper to reflect each point over the specified axis.

x-axis   *y*-axis

25. $A = (1, 1)$ $A' = (1, -1)$ **28.** $D = (2, 3)$ $D' = (-2, 3)$

26. $B = (2, 2)$ $B' = (2, -2)$ **29.** $E = (3, -1)$ $E' = (-3, -1)$

27. $C = (4, 0)$ $C' = (4, 0)$ **30.** $F = (3, 0)$ $F' = (-3, 0)$

Decide whether the given line of reflection is also a line of symmetry.

31. 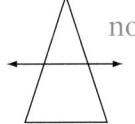 no   **32.** 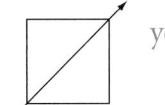 yes   **33.** 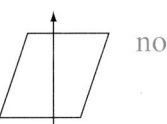 no

Slide the following points 5 units to the left and 4 units up. Graph the points.

34. $A = (0, 0)$ **35.** $B = (-3, -3)$ **36.** $C = (-4, 0)$
$A' = (-5, 4)$ $B' = (-8, 1)$ $C' = (-9, 4)$

Name the image point when the object point is $(-4, 1)$.

37. $(x, y) = (x + 4, y - 2)$ $(0, -1)$

38. $(x, y) = (x - 1, y - 5)$ $(-5, -4)$

Use your own graph paper to rotate the objects
shown in the graph on the right.

39. Object A—Rotate 90° around point $(3, 1)$

40. Object B—Rotate 180° around point $(1, -1)$

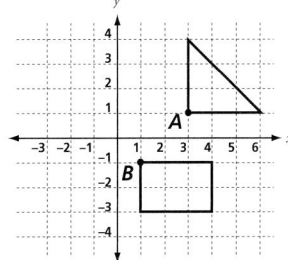

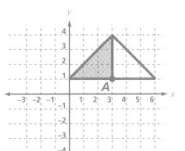 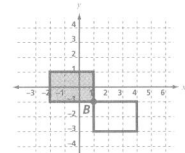

Chapter 13   Supplementary Problems

Create a bar graph that organizes and displays the data shown in the table below.

1.

Type of Music Students Prefer the Most	
Rock	83
Country	25
Heavy Metal	62
Rap	27
Jazz	42
Folk	18
Top 40	73

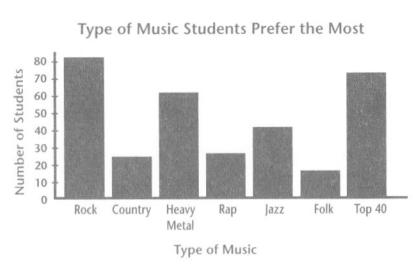

Create a circle graph that organizes and displays the data shown in the table below.

2.

Sales by Student Council	
Tablets	47
T-shirts	16
Notebooks	37

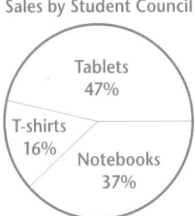

Use the following frequency table.

3. How many items were brought in for the food drive? 36 items

4. How many items were canned? 17 items

Food Drive Results		
Type	Tally	Frequency
Canned Vegetables	⊞ ||||	9
Canned Meats	⊞ |||	8
Boxed Cereal	⊞ ⊞ |||	13
Powdered Milk	||||	4
Boxed Dried Fruit	||	2

Use the table. Find the measures of central tendency and range.

5. Find the range of the data. 8

6. Find the mean of the data. 3.2

7. Find the median of the data. 3

8. Find the mode or modes of the data. 5

Data		
3	0	5
1	0	2
5	5	8

Use the box-and-whiskers plot shown.

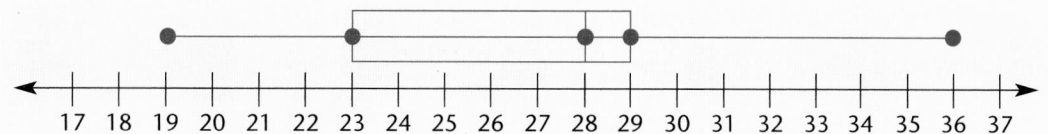

9. Which value represents the quartiles?   23 and 29

Find the probability. Express your answer as a fraction in simplest form and as a percent rounded to the nearest whole number.

10. Suppose that the spinner is spun once. Find the probability of the spinner landing on a prime number. $\frac{1}{2} = 0.50 = 50\%$

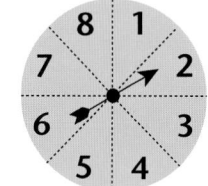

Use the data from the histogram to answer the question.

11. How many times were four activities done? 6

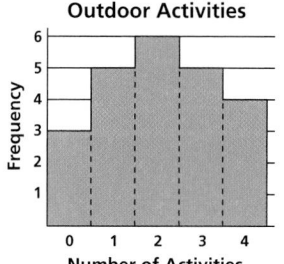

Use the data from the scatterplot to answer the question.

12. Is attendance similar for both rinks? Yes

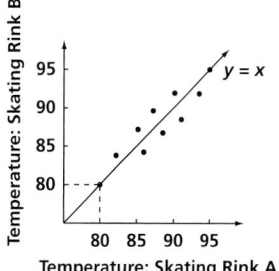

Read about the probability experiment and answer the questions.
A coin is flipped thirty times. After each flip, a new coin is used.

13. Before each flip, what is the probability of getting a head? $\frac{1}{2}$ (50%)

14. Are the events in the experiment dependent or independent?
The events are independent. Even though a new coin is used for each flip, the odds on each flip do not change .

Use the fundamental principle of counting to solve the problem.

15. Eric, Amanda, Alyssa, and Jenny ran in a 100-meter dash. In how many different ways can they place first, second, third, and fourth? 24 ways

CHAPTER 1

Lesson 1, page 3

1. group the stars into 3 sets of 10

☆☆☆☆☆☆☆☆☆☆ ☆☆☆☆☆☆☆☆☆☆ ☆☆☆☆☆☆☆☆☆☆
10   10   10

3. 5; 10; 5H → $\underline{5}$ groups of $\underline{10}$ TENS, or 500, because H equals 100 **5.** 3; 100 **7.** 500; 3,000; 3,500; 5H + 3T = $\underline{500}$ + $\underline{3,000}$ = $\underline{3,500}$, because H equals 100 and T equals 1,000 **9.** 5H; 3,000; 3,500

Lesson 2, page 5

1. hundreds; the digit is 3 places to the left **3.** millions **5.** tens **7.** 4 tens; the digit is 2 places to the left **9.** 9 ones **11.** 1 ten-thousand **13.** (1×100) + $(6 \times 10) + (2 \times 1)$; because 162 = 100 + 60 + 2 **15.** $(4 \times 100,000) + (1 \times 10,000) + (3 \times 1,000) + (0 \times 100) + (7 \times 10) + (8 \times 1)$ **16.** (3×10^3) + $(1 \times 10^2) + (5 \times 10^1) + (8 \times 10^0)$; 3,158 = 3,000 + 100 + 50 + 8 = $(3 \times 1,000) + (1 \times 100) + (5 \times 10) + (8 \times 1)$ **17.** $(7 \times 10^3) + (6 \times 10^2) + (2 \times 10^1) + (3 \times 10^0)$ **19.** $(1 \times 10^4) + (2 \times 10^3) + (5 \times 10^2) + (6 \times 10^1) + (8 \times 10^0)$

Lesson 3, page 7

1. 12; 5 + 7 = 12

5   7
◄─┼─►
0 1 2 3 4 5 6 7 8 9 10 11 12 13 14 15 16 17 18 19 20

3. 15;

11   4
◄─┼─►
0 1 2 3 4 5 6 7 8 9 10 11 12 13 14 15 16 17 18 19 20

4. 23; 17 + 6 = 23; check: 23 − 17 = 6 **5.** 71; 71 − 26 = 45 **7.** 319; 319 − 63 =

256 **8.** Check: 66 + 25 = 91; use the inverse operation to check **9.** 87 − 49 = 38 **11.** 453 + 137 = 590 **13.** 1,693 − 1,009 = 684 **14.** 24 minutes; Alex left home at 11 minutes after 8:00, and she needs to be at school by 35 minutes after 8:00. 35 − 11 = 24 **15.** In 1891

Lesson 4, page 9

1. 35; 5 × 7 = 7 + 7 + 7 + 7 + 7 = 35 **3.** 3 **5.** 63 ÷ 7 = 9 or 63 ÷ 9 = 7; division is the inverse operation of multiplication **7.** 23 × 3 = 69 **9.** 5 feet; Serina's height = 10 × (the length of her hand or 6 inches); height = 10 × 6 inches = 60 inches; 12 inches in 1 foot; 60 inches ÷ 12 (inches per foot) = 5 feet **11.** +; check: 39 $\boxed{+}$ 64 = 103 **13.** − **15.** +

Lesson 5, page 13

1. 1010_2; 10_{10} = 8 + 2; = (1×8) + $(0 \times 4) + (1 \times 2) + (0 \times 1)$ **3.** 11001_2 **5.** 111011_2 **7.** 10_2; $(1 \times 2) + (0 \times 1)$ = 2 + 0 **9.** 7 **11.** 14 **13.** 111_2; 7_{10} = 4 + 2 + 1 = $(1 \times 4) + (1 \times 2) + (1 \times 1)$ = 111_2 **15.** 101000_2 **17.** 4_{10} **19.** 25_{10}

Lesson 6, pages 16–17

1. 130_5; 40_{10} = 25 + 15 = (1×25) + $(3 \times 5) + (0 \times 1) = 130_5$ **3.** 303_5 **5.** 412_5 **7.** 11000_5 **9.** 8_{10}; 13_5 = (1×5) + (3×1) = 5 + 3 = 8_{10} **11.** 31_{10} **13.** 214_{10} **15.** $3,154_{10}$ **17.** 13_{10}; 23_5 = (2×5) + (3×1) = 10 + 3 = 13_{10} **19.** 260_{10}

Try This

10_{10} = 10, 10_2 = 2, 10_5 = 5

Chapter 1 Application, page 18
1. Yes

Chapter 1 Review, pages 19–21
1. B **3.** A **5.** B **7.** B **9.** $(3 \times 10^4) +$ $(0 \times 10^3) + (8 \times 10^2) + (9 \times 10^1) +$ (4×10^0) **11.** $(8 \times 10^6) + (1 \times 10^5) +$ $(7 \times 10^4) + (1 \times 10^3) + (9 \times 10^2) +$ $(8 \times 10^1) + (5 \times 10^0)$ **13.** $54{,}117 +$ $19{,}785 = 73{,}902$ **15.** $850 + 642 = 1{,}492$ **17.** $13 \times 5 = 65$ **19.** $5 \times 25 = 125$ **21.** 15_{10} **23.** 53_{10} **25.** 101100_2 **27.** 1010011_2 **29.** 4121_5 **31.** 100010_5 **33.** 27_{10} **35.** 150_{10}

CHAPTER 2

Lesson 1, page 25
1. 32; To add $23 + 9$, add the ones first; $3 + 9 = 12$. Regroup 12 ones as 1 ten and 2 ones. Write 2 in the ones column. Write 1 in the tens column. Add the tens; $1 + 2 = 3$; $23 + 9 = 32$ **3.** 81 **5.** $12a$ **7.** 574; add the ones, $8 + 4 + 2 = 14$, carry the 1. Add the tens, $5 + 6 + 5 +$ the carried $1 = 17$, carry the one. Add the hundreds $1 + 3 +$ the carried $1 = 5$; 574 **9.** 2,114 **11.** Natawa has $140. Add the ones, $5 + 5 = 10$, carry the 1. Add the tens, $8 + 5 +$ the carried $1 = 14$. $140 **13.** 875 miles **15.** $381

Lesson 2, page 27
1. 6; To subtract $74 - 68$, you cannot subtract 8 from 4. Rename 7 tens 4 ones as 6 tens 14 ones and then subtract; $14 - 8 = 6$; $6 - 6 = 0$ **3.** 49 **5.** 29 **7.** $29a$ **9.** $18x$ **10.** 1,021; To subtract $1{,}400 - 379$ in vertical form, first rename 4 hundreds as 3 hundreds 9 tens and 10 ones. Then subtract the ones; $10 - 9 = 1$. Subtract

the tens; $9 - 7 = 2$. Subtract the hundreds; $3 - 3 = 0$. Subtract the thousands; $1 - 0 = 1$ **11.** 4,252 **13.** $148{,}878y$ **15.** $116{,}189a$ **17.** 162 bushels; To solve, subtract 223 from 385. Subtract the ones first; $5 - 3 = 2$. Then subtract the tens; $8 - 2 = 6$. Subtract the hundreds; $3 - 2 = 1$ **19.** 2,195 books

Try This
Answers will vary. Use subtraction to find the answer. (Price of item) $-$ (Amount on coupon) $=$ Price paid

Lesson 3, page 29
1. 1,400; Round each addend to its greatest place value. Round 643 down to 600. Round 821 down to 800. Add $600 +$ 800. **3.** 21,300 **5.** 179,080 **6.** 500; Round each number to its greatest place value. Round 875 up to 900. Round 397 up to 400. Subtract 400 from 900. **7.** 1,500 **9.** 60,000 **11.** 100; 101; Round 28 up to 30. Round 73 down to 70. Add $30 + 70 =$ 100 for estimated answer; $28 + 73 = 101$ **13.** 1,500; 1,468 **15.** 1,400; 1,408 **17.** 13,000; 13,294 **19.** 30,000; 29,853

Lesson 4, page 31
1. 24; 4 times 6 is the same as $4 + 4 + 4$ $+ 4 + 4 + 4$. **3.** 2,484 **5.** 32 **7.** 8,091 **9.** 6,048 **11.** 56 **13.** 45 **15.** 3,608 **17.** $54a$ **19.** $576x$ **21.** 108,072; To multiply 237 times 456 vertically, multiply the ones first; 237 times $6 = 1{,}422$. Then multiply the tens; 237 times $50 = 11{,}850$. Then multiply the hundreds; 237 times $400 = 94{,}800$. Add the products; $1{,}422 +$ $11{,}850 + 94{,}800$ **23.** 65,709 **24.** 104 offices; Multiply 26 times 4. First multiply

---

the ones; 6 times 4 = 24. Then multiply the tens; 20 times 4 = 80. Add the products; 24 + 80 = 104 **25.** 1,500 sheets

Lesson 5, page 33

1. 9; 45 ÷ 5 = 9. To check, multiply the quotient by the divisor; 9 times 5 = 45 **3.** 9 **5.** 8 **7.** 8*c* **9.** 8*a* **11.** 82 r2; Divide 412 by 5. First see that 5 does not go into 4, but 5 goes into 41 eight times. Multiply 5 by 8. Subtract 40 from 41. Bring down the 2. Next, 5 goes into 12 two times. Multiply 5 by 2. Subtract 10 from 12. The remainder is 2. **13.** 173 r1 **15.** 61 r1 **17.** 137 r5 **19.** 581 r2; Divide 4,650 by 8. First see that 8 does not go into 4, but 8 goes into 46 five times. Multiply 8 by 5. Subtract 40 from 46. Bring down the 5. Next, 8 goes into 65 eight times. Multiply 8 by 8. Subtract 64 from 65. Bring down 0. Eight goes into 10 one time. Multiply 8 by 1. Subtract 8 from 10. The remainder is 2. **21.** 967 r35 **23.** 16 cartons; To find how many cartons, divide 320 (the total number of packages) by 20 (the number of packages in each carton). **25.** 140 cartons

Try This

Multiplication. Sample example:
24 ÷ 6 = 4, 4 · 6 = 24

Lesson 6, page 35

1. 5,400; Round 92 down to 90. Round 64 down to 60. Multiply 90 by 60.
3. 3,500 **5.** 360,000 **7.** 900 **9.** 40,000 **11.** 60; Find compatible numbers for the dividend and divisor. 37 becomes 36, because 36 ÷ 6 is a basic fact. An estimated quotient is 60. **13.** 100 **15.** 400

17. 80 **19.** 1,000 **21.** 2,100,000 and 2,228,036; Round 3,412 down to 3,000 and round 653 up to 700. Multiply 3,000 by 700 for an estimated answer.
23. 4,000 and 3,184 **25.** 200 and 213 r2 or 213.04

Try This

Answers will vary.

Lesson 7, page 37

1. true; To check addition, use subtraction; 9 − 4 = 5 **3.** true **5.** false **7.** false **9.** true **11.** true; To check addition, use subtraction; 12 − 5 = 7. This statement is not open because it does not contain a letter used as a placeholder. **13.** open **15.** false **17.** open **19.** true **21.** Thirty-four divided by some number; The ÷ symbol means division, and *n* is the placeholder for an unknown number. **23.** Sixteen minus some number **25.** Some number divided by eight

Lesson 8, page 39

1. *x*; *x* is the letter used as a placeholder for a number **3.** *a* **5.** *t* **7.** *h* **9.** *n* **11.** addition; The + symbol means addition **13.** division **15.** multiplication, addition **17.** multiplication, addition **19.** subtraction **21.** numerical, addition; This expression does not contain any variables, so it is a numerical expression; the + symbol means addition **23.** algebraic, division, *y* **25.** algebraic, multiplication, addition, *y* **27.** algebraic, multiplication, addition, *m* **29.** algebraic, multiplication, *n*

Lesson 9, pages 40–41

1. $n + 5$; An algebraic expression contains at least one variable and an operation; n is the variable (some number), and the operation is addition $(+)$. **3.** $15 \div n$ **5.** $2n + 5$ **7.** $10 - n$ **9.** $n \div 9$ **11.** 29; Substitute the number 14 for m and then perform the operation (addition); $14 + 15$ **13.** 84 **15.** 13 **17.** 7 **19.** 5 **21.** false; Substitute 3 for n and then perform the operation; $5 + 3$ does not equal 12 **23.** true **24.** true; Substitute 7 for x. Enter 35 and press $\boxed{\div}$. Enter 7 and press $\boxed{=}$. The display reads 5; $35 \div 7 = 5$ **25.** false **27.** true **29.** false

Chapter 2 Application, page 42

1. 400

Chapter 2 Review, pages 43–45

1. C **3.** A **5.** C **7.** 37,104 **9.** 933 **11.** 38,788 **13.** 101,368 **15.** 90,387 **17.** 128 **19.** 34 r10 **21.** 5 r8 **23.** 120,000 **25.** 50,000 **27.** open **29.** false **31.** algebraic, multiplication, addition, m **33.** algebraic, division, g **35.** algebraic, multiplication, x **37.** false **39.** true

CHAPTER 3

Lesson 1, page 49

1. tenths; 1 is in the tenths place **3.** thousandths **5.** hundreds **7.** tens **9.** ones **10.** 0.3; 3 is in the tenths place, so its value is 3 times 0.1 **11.** 0.0009 **13.** 80 **15.** 2 **17.** 1,000 **19.** 3,000 **21.** 0.007 **23.** 0.0009 **25.** 0.001; 1 is in the thousandths place, so its value is 1 times 0.001 **27.** 0.0003 **29.** 0.006

Try This
Answers will vary.

Lesson 2, page 51

1. $5.403 > 5.03$; First add one zero to 5.03 so that each decimal has the same number of places to the right of the decimal point. Next, compare the decimals; 0.403 is greater than 0.030. **3.** $91.8 < 91.8135$ **5.** $2.04 < 2.044$ **7.** $403.079 > 403.07$ **9.** $30.19 < 300.19$ **11.** 2.6; 2.63; 2.635; When rounding 2.6345 to the tenth and hundredth places, there are no changes, since 3 and 4 (digits to the right of the place you are rounding to) are less than 5. When rounding to the thousandth place, one was added to the thousandth place, since 5 was to the right. **13.** 0.9; 0.90; 0.902 **15.** 6.5; 6.46; 6.463 **17.** 2.8; 2.80; 2.800 **19.** 14.0; 14.04; 14.037

Try This
Answers will vary. Sample example: number found 4.179 rounded to 4.18

Lesson 3, page 53

1. 10.11; Include zeros and then line up the decimal points. Add $3.20 + 0.91 + 6.00$. **3.** 1.53 **5.** 31.3 **7.** 125.4 **9.** 22.92 **11.** 17.108 **13.** 2.671; Press 1 $\boxed{\cdot}$ 5 $\boxed{+}$ $\boxed{\cdot}$ 21 $\boxed{+}$ $\boxed{\cdot}$ 35 $\boxed{+}$ $\boxed{\cdot}$ 611 $\boxed{=}$. The display reads 2.671. **15.** 5.95679 **17.** 933.9648 **19.** \$17.54 **21.** \$129.56 **22.** 19.75 miles; Include zeros, line up the decimal points, and then add; $5.00 + 6.05 + 8.70$ **23.** \$4.05 **25.** exactly \$0.017 more or about \$0.02 more

Lesson 4, page 55

1. 236; Since the number of zeros in 10^2 is two, move the decimal point in 2.36 two places to the right. **3.** 2,700 **5.** 1,441 **7.** 771,000 **9.** 73,000 **11.** 84.104 **13.** 7,690 **15.** 4,044 **17.** 1,011,200

19. 890.7 **21.** true; Since the number of zeros in 10^1 is one, the decimal point in 3.3 is moved one place to the right. **23.** false **25.** open **27.** true **29.** open

Lesson 5, page 57

1. 21.24; First multiply the numbers as if they were whole numbers. Then count the number of decimal places in both original factors (two) and move the decimal point that many places in the product. The product 2124 becomes 21.24. **3.** 39.1 **5.** 20.59 **7.** 6.648 **9.** 0.2862 **11.** 85.618 **13.** 31.4 in.; Use the formula $C = \pi d$. Use 3.14 for π. 10 times 3.14 = 31.4. **15.** 157 in. **16.** 0.36864; Press 3 $\boxed{\cdot}$ 2 $\boxed{\times}$ 6 $\boxed{\cdot}$ 4 $\boxed{\times}$ $\boxed{\cdot}$ 018 $\boxed{=}$. The display reads 0.36864. **17.** 0.16074 **19.** 15.2724 **21.** 0.00006 **22.** $559.13; Multiply 355 by 1575. The product is 559125. Since there were three decimal places in the original factors, and you round to the nearest cent, the answer is $559.13. **23.** $2.07 **25.** 159.25 miles

Lesson 6, page 59

1. 0.66; There is one zero in 10. To divide by 10, move the decimal point one place to the left; $6.6 \div 10 = 0.66$ **3.** 0.093 **5.** 0.0203 **7.** 0.0115 **9.** 0.244 **11.** 0.2432 **13.** 0.736 **15.** 0.0000005 **17.** 0.000003 **19.** 30.005 **21.** true; Since there is one zero in 10, to divide 6.5 by 10, move the decimal point one place to the left. This is not an open statement because it does not contain a variable. **23.** true **25.** true **27.** false **29.** true

Lesson 7, page 61

1. 1.30; Since the divisor is a whole number, first write a decimal point in the quotient. Then divide 5.21 by 4. **3.** 14.42 **5.** 4.72 **7.** 1,578.57 **9.** 267.50 **11.** 0.598; Press 16 $\boxed{\cdot}$ 5 $\boxed{\div}$ 27 $\boxed{\cdot}$ 58 $\boxed{=}$. The display reads 0.598. **13.** 0.129 **15.** 2.245 **17.** $1.06; To solve, divide $8.45 by 8. Since the divisor is a whole number, first write a decimal point in the quotient and then divide. **19.** $14.50

Lesson 8, page 63

1. $\frac{7}{25}$; The place value of the last digit in 0.28 is the hundredths place, so the denominator is 100. Use the numeral in the decimal for the numerator; $\frac{28}{100}$. Then simplify the fraction. **3.** $\frac{27}{50}$ **5.** $\frac{1}{250}$ **7.** $\frac{29}{100}$ **9.** $\frac{3}{400}$ **11.** $5\frac{1}{20}$ **13.** $\frac{11}{10,000}$ **15.** $\frac{9}{200}$ **17.** 0.3; Since the denominator of $\frac{3}{10}$ is a power of ten, you can identify the place value as tenths. Write the decimal using the numeral in the numerator; 0.3. **19.** 0.25 **21.** 0.6 **23.** 0.124 **25.** 0.3 **27.** 6.5 **29.** 0.504 **31.** 0.5625 **33.** $9.36 per yard; First change the mixed number $3\frac{1}{2}$ to the decimal 3.5. Then divide $32.75 by 3.5. **35.** $81

Lesson 9, page 65

1. $0.\overline{3}$; 1 divided by 3 is 0.33333 or $0.\overline{3}$. **3.** $0.8\overline{3}$ **5.** $0.\overline{6}$ **7.** $0.\overline{81}$ **9.** $0.\overline{8}$ **10.** 17°C; First, substitute 62° Fahrenheit into the formula; $C = \frac{5}{9}(62 - 32)$. Then simplify; $C = \frac{5}{9}(30)$; $C = \frac{150}{9}$; $C = 16.\overline{6}$. To write $16.\overline{6}$ as a whole number, round up to 17°C. **11.** 12°C **13.** 31°C **15.** 35°C **17.** 4°C **19.** 26°C

Try This

$77°F; F = \frac{9}{5}(25) + 32 = 45 + 32 = 77°F$

Lesson 10, page 67

1. 0.05; Locate the decimal point, move it two places to the left, and drop the % sign. **3.** 0.045 **5.** 0.006 **7.** 0.008 **9.** $165; Before using the formula $I = prt$, change 5.5% to the decimal 0.055; $I = (3,000)(0.055)(1) = \$165$. **11.** $287.50 **12.** $220; Before using the formula $I = prt$, change 5.5% to the decimal 0.055; $I = (2,000)(0.055)(2) = \$220$. **13.** $38 **15.** $219.38 per year; $18.28 per month

Lesson 11, page 69

1. 5.155; Substitute 3.085 for m. Perform the arithmetic operation; $3.085 + 2.07 = 5.155$ **3.** 8.164 **5.** 21.176 **7.** 55.386 **9.** 5.2195121 **11.** false; Substitute 3.5 for s. Perform the arithmetic operation; 4 times 3.5 does not equal 18. **13.** false **15.** false **17.** true **19.** false

Chapter 3 Application, page 70

1. 83.6 liters **3. A** 49.2 meters; **B** 24.6 meters

Chapter 3 Review, pages 71–73

1. B **3.** A **5.** B **7.** D **9.** ten-thousandths **11.** tenths **13.** 2.254 **15.** 11.716 **17.** 63.085 **19.** 8,720 **21.** 114.167 **23.** 0.637 **25.** $\frac{1}{4}$ **27.** $\frac{7}{8}$ **29.** 0.88 **31.** $4,080 **33.** 5.74 **35.** 27.83

CHAPTER 4

Lesson 1, page 79

1. true; 12 is divisible by 2 because its last digit is 2. **3.** true **5.** false **7.** false **9.** true **11.** true **13.** 90 is divisible by 2, 3, 5, 6, 9, and 10; 90 is divisible by 2, 5, and 10

because its last digit is 0; it is divisible by 3 and 9 because the sum of its digits are divisible by 3 and by 9; it is divisible by 6 because it is divisible by 2 and by 3. **15.** by 2, 3, 4, 5, 6, 8, 9, and 10 **17.** by 3 and 9 **19.** Answers will vary. Sample answer: 12,000,960

Try This, page 80

30 years old, or any multiple of 30 years

Lesson 2, page 81

1. numbers circled in the text, plus 53, 59, 61, 67, 71, 73, 79, 83, 89, 97; These numbers were left on the grid after crossing out multiples of 2, 3, 5, and 7. **2.** composite; 108 has factors other than 1 and 108. **3.** prime **5.** composite **7.** composite **9.** composite **11.** prime **13.** No; for two numbers greater than 3 to be consecutive, one number must be an even number, and every even number is a composite number because it is a multiple of 2. **15.** Answers will vary. Sample answer: The factors of 169 are 1, 13, and 169

Lesson 3, page 83

1. 10; List all the factors of each term; 10: 1, 2, 5, 10; 50: 1, 2, 5, 10, 25, 50. They share 1, 2, 5, and 10 as factors. 10 is the greatest common factor. **3.** 3 **5.** 4 **7.** 4 **9.** 6 **11.** 2 **13.** 7 **15.** $5h$ **17.** $9d$ **19.** $13v$

Try This

Answers will vary.

Lesson 4, pages 86–87

1. 24; $3(2 + 6) = (3 \cdot 2) + (3 \cdot 6) = 6 + 18 = 24$ **3.** $2a + 10$ **5.** $20m + 20$ **7.** $4n + 12p + 8$ **9.** $2v + 26 + 4x$ **11.** 2; List all the factors of each term; $2x$:

1, 2, x; 10: 1, 2, 5, 10. The GCD is 2. **13.** 4
15. 1 **17.** 2d + 9; List all the factors of
each term; 2d: 1, 2, d; 9: 1, 3, 9. The GCD
is 1. When the GCD of any group of
numbers or terms is 1, the expression
cannot be factored. **19.** 3(3j + 1)
21. 3(5w + 2y) **23.** 23b + 4n
25. 2(11x + y) **27.** 22 CDs; Jarrod and
Nadine have 6 + 5 CDs. Double that
number is 2(6 + 5); (2 • 6) + (2 • 5) =
12 + 10 = 22 **29.** 6(3 + 4)

Lesson 5, pages 90–91

1. 24; First write the prime factorization
of 8 and 12. Identify the greatest power of
each prime factor. The greatest power of
the prime factor 2 is 2^3. The greatest
power of the prime factor 3 is 3. Find the
product of the greatest power of each
prime factor; $2^3 • 3 = 24$; LCM = 24.
3. 39 **5.** 176 **7.** 288 **9.** 1,344 **11.** 90
13. 250; multiply 5 • 5 • 5 • 2 **15.** 108
17. 229,957 **18.** One day; if today
represents Kayla's sixth day off and today
represents Tia's fourth day off, both Kayla
and Tia will be off again tomorrow
19. 5.6 min or 5 min 36 sec

Lesson 6, page 93

1. 6.2×10^4; Make 62,000 a number
between 1 and 10 by moving the decimal
point to the left; 6.2. The decimal point
was moved four places to the left or 10^4.
The scientific notation is 6.2×10^4.
3. 3.06×10^8 **5.** 1.2×10^4 **7.** 6.221×10^6
9. 3.34×10^4 **11.** 1.194×10^{11}
13. 5.0×10^{-3}; Make 0.005 a number
between 1 and 10 by moving the decimal
point to the right; 5. The decimal point
was moved three places to the right.

Moving the decimal point to the right
makes the exponent negative; 10^{-3}.
The scientific notation is 5.0×10^{-3}.
15. 4.402×10^{-1} **17.** 6.66×10^{-4}
19. 4.0×10^{-10} **21.** true; To check if
$2.4 \times 10^4 = 24,000$, move the decimal
point four places (10^4) to the right; 2.4
becomes 24,000. **23.** false **25.** true

Try This
3.688×10^8

Chapter 4 Application, page 94
1. Sum of factors: $1 + 3 = 4, 4 \neq 9$ *No*, 9
is not a perfect number. **3.** Sum of
factors: $1 + 2 + 4 + 7 + 14 = 28$ *Yes*, 28
is a perfect number. **5.** Sum of factors:
$1 + 5 = 6, 6 \neq 25$ *No*, 25 is not a perfect
number.

Chapter 4 Review, pages 95–97
1. C **3.** A **5.** A **7.** D **9.** true **11.** false
13. 624 is divisible by 2, 3, 4, 6, 8
15. 90,200 is divisible by 2, 4, 5, 8, 10
17. composite **19.** composite **21.** 34
23. 3b + 30 + 15x **25.** 7 **27.** 1
29. 4(2j + 1) **31.** 6(3w + k)
33. 3(3f + 8m) **35.** 120 **37.** 300
39. 1,728 **41.** 13,824 **43.** 8.9×10^9
45. 4.28×10^{-2}

CHAPTER 5

Lesson 1, page 101
1. $\frac{3}{8}$; Three out of eight shapes are
shaded. **3.** $\frac{1}{5}$ **4.** $\frac{0}{2}, \frac{1}{2}$; The number line is
divided into two parts between 0 and 1.
In a proper fraction, the numerator is
less than the denominator; $\frac{2}{2}$ is not a
proper fraction. **5.** $\frac{0}{4}, \frac{1}{4}, \frac{2}{4}, \frac{3}{4}$

6. Sample answer: $\frac{2}{8}, \frac{3}{8}, \frac{4}{8}, \frac{5}{8}, \frac{6}{8}$ **7.** $\frac{7}{10}$ of your set should be shaded.

●●●●●●●○○○

9. $\frac{5}{6}$ of the total distance; Jamal walked 5 of the 6 blocks, or $\frac{5}{6}$ of the total distance.

Lesson 2, pages 104–105

1. $\frac{4}{4}, \frac{5}{4}, \frac{6}{4}, \frac{7}{4}, \frac{8}{4}$; In any improper fraction, the numerator is greater than or equal to the denominator. **3.** proper; The numerator (3) is smaller than the denominator (8). **5.** proper **7.** proper **9.** improper **11.** 1; Divide the numerator by the denominator; $2 \div 2 = 1$. **13.** $2\frac{3}{4}$ **15.** $2\frac{9}{10}$ **17.** $1\frac{7}{12}$ **19.** $3\frac{7}{8}$ **21.** $\frac{13}{3}$; First multiply the whole number by the denominator of the fraction; $4 \cdot 3 = 12$. Add the numerator to this number; $1 + 12 = 13$. Write this sum as the numerator in the improper fraction, and write the denominator of the mixed fraction as the denominator of the improper fraction; $\frac{13}{3}$. **23.** $\frac{25}{2}$ **25.** $\frac{75}{8}$ **27.** $\frac{133}{16}$ **29.** $\frac{2,001}{20}$ **31.** $3\frac{4}{9}$; Begin with the improper fraction $\frac{31}{9}$. Divide the numerator by the denominator and list the remainder as a fraction of the divisor; $31 \div 9 = 3$ r4; $3\frac{4}{9}$; Eric has only 3 complete sets. **33.** $4\frac{5}{6}$, or 5 sheets **35.** $5\frac{2}{3}$ ounces

Lesson 3, pages 107–109

Sample answers shown for **1–13.**

1. $\frac{2}{6}$ and $\frac{3}{9}$ **3.** $\frac{14}{16}$ and $\frac{21}{24}$ **5.** $\frac{6}{20}$ and $\frac{9}{30}$ **7.** $\frac{6}{16}$ and $\frac{9}{24}$ **9.** $\frac{18}{20}$ and $\frac{27}{30}$ **11.** $\frac{1}{2}$ and $\frac{5}{10}$ **13.** $\frac{4}{10}$ and $\frac{2}{5}$ **15.** yes; Press 1 ÷ 5 = .

The display reads 0.2. Press 10 ÷ 50 = . The display reads 0.2. **17.** no **19.** no

Try This
Answers will vary.

Lesson 4, page 111

1. 8; The factors of 8 are 1, 2, 4, 8. The factors of 16 are 1, 2, 4, 8, 16. Shared factors are 1, 2, 4, 8. The greatest common factor is the GCD; 8. **3.** 6 **5.** 2 **7.** $\frac{5}{8}$; GCD (10, 16) = 2. Divide the numerator and denominator of $\frac{10}{16}$ by 2; $\frac{10 \div 2}{16 \div 2} = \frac{5}{8}$. **9.** $\frac{1}{3}$ **11.** $\frac{3}{5}$ **13.** $\frac{5}{6}$ **15.** $\frac{4}{5}$ **17.** $\frac{11}{12}$ **19.** $\frac{7}{8}$ **21.** $\frac{5}{12}$ **23.** Yes. Sample explanation: In each class, $\frac{3}{8}$ of the students are male. If the same number of students are enrolled in each class, each class will have the same number of males $(\frac{3}{8})$ and females $(\frac{5}{8})$. **25.** The enrollment in each class is 8, or a multiple of 8, because the fractions are in eighths.

Lesson 5, pages 114–115

1. $\frac{3}{8}$; On the number line, the fraction farther to the right is greater. **3.** >; When comparing fractions with like denominators, the fraction with the greater numerator is the greater in value. **5.** > **7.** < **9.** > **11.** < **13.** > **15.** $\frac{3}{4}, \frac{2}{3}, \frac{1}{2}$; Write equivalent fractions using the LCM of the denominators (12) as the denominator. $\frac{1}{2} = \frac{6}{12}, \frac{2}{3} = \frac{8}{12}, \frac{3}{4} = \frac{9}{12}$. Then compare the fractions with like denominators. **17.** $\frac{11}{12}, \frac{7}{8}, \frac{5}{6}$ **19.** $\frac{1}{2}, \frac{5}{8}, \frac{3}{4}$; Write equivalent fractions

using the LCM of the denominators (8) as the denominator and then compare the fractions with like denominators.
21. $\frac{1}{2}, \frac{4}{7}, \frac{9}{14}$ **23.** Terrence; Write equivalent fractions for $\frac{5}{6}$ and $\frac{7}{8}$ using the LCM (24) as the denominator and then compare the fractions with like denominators. **25.** James

Try This
Answers will vary. Sample: Change each fraction to a decimal by dividing the numerator of each fraction by its denominator. Align the decimal points, then compare and order the decimals.

Lesson 6, pages 118–119
1. $\frac{1}{2}$; Subtract the numerators of the fractions; $\frac{3-1}{\cdots} = \frac{2}{\cdots}$. Keep the same denominator; $\frac{2}{4}$. Simplify; $\frac{2}{4} = \frac{1}{2}$. **3.** $\frac{2}{5}$
5. $6\frac{1}{6}$ **7.** $16\frac{1}{2}$ **8.** $\frac{3x}{4}$; Subtract the numerators of the fractions; $\frac{7x-x}{\cdots} = \frac{6x}{\cdots}$. Keep the same denominator; $\frac{6x}{8}$. Simplify; $\frac{6x}{8} = \frac{3x}{4}$. **9.** $\frac{2x}{3}$ **11.** $\frac{x-1}{y}$ **13.** $\frac{y-3}{x}$ **15.** x
16. 1; Subtract the numerators of the fractions first; $\frac{4-1}{\cdots} = \frac{3}{\cdots}$. Keep the same denominator; $\frac{3}{5}$. Add $\frac{3}{5} + \frac{2}{5} = \frac{5}{5} = 1$.
17. 1 **19.** $1\frac{1}{2}$ **21.** $\frac{7}{12}$ **23.** $\frac{3x}{8}$ **25.** $\frac{x}{2}$

Lesson 7, pages 122–123
1. $1\frac{1}{12}$; Write equivalent fractions using the LCM of the denominators (12) as the denominator. Add; $\frac{4}{12} + \frac{9}{12} = \frac{13}{12}$. Simplify; $\frac{13}{12} = 1\frac{1}{12}$. **3.** $\frac{13}{20}$ **5.** $\frac{2}{15}$ **7.** $\frac{79}{80}$

9. $1\frac{1}{63}$ **11.** $\frac{1}{3}x$; Write equivalent fractions. Subtract; $\frac{5}{6}x - \frac{3}{6}x = \frac{2}{6}x = \frac{1}{3}x$. **13.** $\frac{23x}{24}$
15. $\frac{x}{40}$ **16.** $1\frac{1}{4}$; Write equivalent fractions. Subtract the numerators of the fractions; subtract the whole numbers; $2\frac{3}{4} - 1\frac{2}{4} = 1\frac{1}{4}$. **17.** $11\frac{1}{8}$ **19.** $1\frac{27}{40}$ **21.** $23\frac{7}{24}$ **23.** $46\frac{43}{60}$
25. $5\frac{29}{80}x$

Lesson 8, page 125
1. $1\frac{1}{2}$; You cannot subtract $\frac{3}{4}$ from $\frac{1}{4}$. You must rename before subtracting; $3\frac{1}{4} = 2\frac{5}{4}$. Subtract; $2\frac{5}{4} - 1\frac{3}{4} = 1\frac{2}{4} = 1\frac{1}{2}$. **3.** $5\frac{3}{5}$
5. $2\frac{2}{3}$ **7.** $\frac{2}{3}$ **9.** $13\frac{15}{16}$ **11.** $9\frac{17}{40}$ **13.** $\frac{29}{30}$
15. $21\frac{59}{84}$ **16.** $9\frac{1}{4}$ hours; Rename $5\frac{1}{2}$ to $5\frac{2}{4}$. Add $3\frac{3}{4} + 5\frac{2}{4} = 8\frac{5}{4} = 9\frac{1}{4}$. **17.** $178\frac{5}{16}$ pounds **19.** $34\frac{11}{12}$ miles

Lesson 9, page 127
1. $\frac{1}{12}$; Multiply the numerators; $\frac{1}{4} \cdot \frac{1}{3} = \frac{1 \cdot 1}{\cdots} = \frac{1}{\cdots}$. Multiply the denominators; $\frac{1}{4} \cdot \frac{1}{3} = \frac{1}{4 \cdot 3} = \frac{1}{12}$. **3.** $\frac{2}{15}$ **5.** $\frac{5}{48}$ **7.** $\frac{1}{64}$ **9.** $\frac{1}{16y}$
11. $2\frac{1}{4}$; Change mixed numbers to improper fractions; $1\frac{1}{2} \cdot 1\frac{1}{2} = \frac{3}{2} \cdot \frac{3}{2}$. Multiply the numerators; $\frac{3 \cdot 3}{\cdots} = \frac{9}{\cdots}$. Multiply the denominators; $\frac{9}{2 \cdot 2} = \frac{9}{4} = 2\frac{1}{4}$. **13.** $3\frac{8}{9}$ **15.** $7\frac{5}{9}$ **17.** $1\frac{41}{50}$ **19.** $3\frac{3}{8}x$
21. not correct; Press 1 ÷ 4 × 7 ÷ 8 =. The display reads 0.21875. **23.** correct
25. correct

Lesson 10, pages 130–131

1. $1\frac{1}{5}$; Find the reciprocal of the divisor (the second fraction). The reciprocal of $\frac{5}{8}$ $\to \frac{8}{5}$. Multiply the dividend by this reciprocal; $\frac{3}{4} \cdot \frac{8}{5} = \frac{24}{20} = 1\frac{1}{5}$. **3.** $\frac{3}{8}$ **5.** $1\frac{2}{3}$ **7.** $\frac{2m}{3}$ **9.** $2\frac{1}{12}$; Express each mixed number as an improper fraction; $2\frac{1}{2} \div 1\frac{1}{5}$ $= \frac{5}{2} \div \frac{6}{5}$. Find the reciprocal of the divisor; $\frac{6}{5} \to \frac{5}{6}$. Multiply the dividend by this reciprocal; $\frac{5}{2} \cdot \frac{5}{6} = \frac{25}{12} = 2\frac{1}{12}$. **11.** $\frac{8}{25}$ **13.** $\frac{6}{7}$ **15.** $1\frac{5}{13}h$ **17.** $\frac{9}{14}k$ **18.** $\frac{3}{8}$ of the court; To solve, divide $13\frac{1}{2}$ by $\frac{36}{1}$. Express the mixed number as an improper fraction; $13\frac{1}{2} = \frac{27}{2}$. Multiply the dividend by the reciprocal of the divisor; $\frac{27}{2} \cdot \frac{1}{36} = \frac{27}{72} = \frac{3}{8}$. **19.** $43\frac{3}{4}$ pieces

Try This

$1\frac{1}{4}$

Chapter 5 Application, page 132

1. 4 beats **3.** $\frac{1}{2}$ beat **5.** quarter note

Chapter 5 Review, pages 133–135

1. B **3.** C **5.** C **7.** D **9.** $3\frac{1}{3}$ **11.** $\frac{12}{5}$ **13.** $\frac{10}{3}$ Sample answers shown for **15–19**. **15.** $\frac{2}{8}$ and $\frac{3}{12}$ **17.** $\frac{14}{20}$ and $\frac{21}{30}$ **19.** $\frac{10}{24}$ and $\frac{15}{36}$ **21.** $\frac{2}{3}$ **23.** $\frac{1}{4}$ **25.** $\frac{7}{15}$ **27.** $\frac{2}{3}, \frac{5}{6}, \frac{11}{12}$ **29.** $\frac{13}{24}, \frac{9}{16}, \frac{5}{8}$ **31.** $\frac{9}{16}$ **33.** $\frac{8}{9}$ **35.** $17\frac{1}{12}$ **37.** $13\frac{17}{24}$ **39.** $2\frac{13}{24}$ **41.** $5\frac{29}{32}$ **43.** $13\frac{5}{12}h$ **45.** $\frac{a}{6}$

Lesson 1, pages 140–141

1. 22; Follow the order of operations and divide first; $8 \div 4 = 2$. Then subtract; $24 - 2 = 22$. **3.** 12 **5.** 35 **7.** 27 **9.** 17 **11.** 106 **13.** 80 **15.** 11 **16.** 3; Press 10 $\boxed{-}$ 2 $\boxed{\times}$ 4 $\boxed{+}$ 1 $\boxed{=}$. The display reads 3. **17.** 19 **19.** 26

Try This

Answers will vary. Sample answer: $2 + 3(4) = 20$. Error: First multiply and then add. $2 + 3(4) = 14$.

Lesson 2, page 145

1. $8\frac{1}{3}$; Substitute 9 for a in the expression. $9 - \frac{2}{3} = \frac{9}{1} - \frac{2}{3} = \frac{27}{3} - \frac{2}{3} = \frac{25}{3} = 8\frac{1}{3}$ **3.** 14 **5.** 1 **7.** 35 **9.** $1\frac{1}{2}$ **11.** 36; Substitute 12 for x in the expression. $12 + 2(12) = 12 + 24 = 36$. **13.** $1\frac{1}{8}$ **15.** $1\frac{7}{12}$ **17.** 24 **18.** Kareem is 14; his sister is 15; $x + (x + 1) = 2x + 1 = 29$; $2x = 28$; $x = 14$; $x + 1 = 15$. **19.** Sherry is 22; Sara is 24

Lesson 3, page 147

1. false; Substitute 2 for x in the equation $4x - 3 = 13$; $4(2) - 3 = 8 - 3 = 5$, not 13. **3.** true **5.** false **6.** 2; Substitute numbers for x in the equation until the sides are equal to each other; $17 - 3(2) = 17 - 6 = 11$ **7.** 4 **9.** 0 **11.** 1 **13.** 3 **15.** 7

Lesson 4, page 149

1. $\frac{2}{3}$; Subtracting $\frac{2}{3}$ from the expression would isolate x. **3.** 4 **5.** 14; Isolate the variable by subtracting 3 from each side of the equation; $a + 3 - 3 = 17 - 3$. Perform each operation; $a = 14$. **7.** 17 **9.** $\frac{2}{5}$ **11.** $\frac{1}{2}$ **13.** $\frac{1}{4}$ **15.** $\frac{3}{8}$

Lesson 5, page 151

1. 36; Isolate the variable by adding 14 to each side of the equation; $x - 14 + 14 = 22 + 14$. Perform each operation; $x = 36$. **3.** 65 **5.** $\frac{4}{5}$ **7.** $1\frac{1}{4}$ **9.** 141 million miles; Isolate the variable by adding 48 to each side of the equation; $x - 48 + 48 = 93 + 48$. Perform each operation; $x = 141$.

Try This

19, 3, 14, 20

Lesson 6, pages 154–155

1. $\frac{3}{4}$; Rewrite the complex fraction horizontally; $\frac{1}{2} \div \frac{2}{3}$. Multiply the dividend by the reciprocal of the divisor; $\frac{1}{2} \cdot \frac{3}{2} = \frac{3}{4}$. **3.** 9 **5.** $3\frac{3}{4}$ **7.** 10 **9.** $4\frac{1}{6}$ **11.** $\frac{2}{3}$ **13.** $28\frac{4}{5}$ **15.** $\frac{7}{128}$ **17.** $28\frac{4}{7}$ **19.** not correct; Press 1 $\boxed{a^{b/c}}$ 4 $\boxed{\div}$ 1 $\boxed{a^{b/c}}$ 8 $\boxed{=}$. The display reads 2. **21.** correct **23.** not correct **25.** not correct

Lesson 7, page 157

1. $\frac{3}{4a}$; To simplify $\frac{1}{8a} + \frac{5}{8a}$ only add the numerators; $\frac{1}{8a} + \frac{5}{8a} = \frac{6}{8a} = \frac{3}{4a}$. **3.** $\frac{6}{5c}$ **5.** $\frac{5y}{4}$ or $1\frac{1}{4}y$ **7.** $\frac{7}{9t}$ **9.** $\frac{1}{2b}$ **11.** $\frac{6}{5n}$; Add the numerators; $\frac{7}{10n} + \frac{5}{10n} = \frac{12}{10n} = \frac{6}{5n}$. **13.** $\frac{5d}{4}$ or $1\frac{1}{4}d$ **15.** $\frac{17}{12b}$

Lesson 8, page 159

1. $\frac{1}{2a}$; To simplify $\frac{5}{8a} - \frac{1}{8a}$ only subtract the numerators; $\frac{5}{8a} - \frac{1}{8a} = \frac{4}{8a} = \frac{1}{2a}$. **3.** $\frac{2}{5c}$ **5.** $\frac{y}{2}$ **7.** $\frac{5}{9t}$ **9.** $\frac{1}{4b}$ **11.** $\frac{1}{5n}$; To simplify $\frac{7}{10n} - \frac{1}{2n}$ convert the fractions to equivalent fractions with like denominators; $\frac{7}{10n} - \frac{5}{10n} = \frac{2}{10n} = \frac{1}{5n}$.

13. $\frac{7}{12d}$ **15.** $\frac{5}{12b}$ **17.** $\frac{13q}{18}$ **18.** $\frac{1}{4}$ dollar more; To solve $\frac{1}{2} - \frac{1}{4}$ convert the fractions to equivalent fractions with like denominators; $\frac{2}{4} - \frac{1}{4} = \frac{1}{4}$. **19.** $\frac{2}{3}$ left

Lesson 9, page 161

1. $\frac{1}{6}$; Multiply the numerators and the denominators; $\frac{1}{4} \cdot \frac{2}{3} = \frac{2}{12} = \frac{1}{6}$. **3.** $\frac{27}{110}$ **5.** $\frac{16}{135}$ **7.** $\frac{8}{135}$ **9.** $\frac{32}{63a}$ **11.** $\frac{5}{12}$ **13.** $\frac{2}{3y}$ **15.** $\frac{75p}{112}$ **16.** 21 years old; $\frac{3}{5} \cdot \frac{35}{1} = \frac{105}{5} = 21$. **17.** $\frac{4}{9}$ of the cereal **19.** $\frac{15}{32}$ of the casserole

Chapter 6 Application, page 162

1. 7 feet **3.** 5,000 meters

Chapter 6 Review, pages 163–165

1. B **3.** D **5.** D **7.** C **9.** false **11.** true **13.** true **15.** false **17.** 6 **19.** 11 **21.** 6 **23.** $\frac{2}{3}$ **25.** 8 **27.** 2 **29.** $12\frac{4}{5}$ **31.** $\frac{1}{2c}$ **33.** $\frac{21}{16r}$ **35.** $\frac{19}{30z}$ **37.** $\frac{17}{12w}$ **39.** $\frac{1}{9x}$ **41.** $\frac{9}{88w}$ **43.** $\frac{14p}{45}$ **45.** $\frac{5}{18a}$

CHAPTER 7

Lesson 1, page 169

1. $\frac{4}{3}$; 4:3 **3.** 7 to 2; 7:2 **5.** 5 to 11; 5:11 **7.** $\frac{1}{2}$; Divide 9 and 18 by 9, the GCD. **9.** $\frac{17}{2}$ **11.** $\frac{32}{9}$ **13.** $\frac{1}{6}$ **15.** $\frac{4}{7}$; There are 14 students and 6 are boys, so $14 - 6$, or 8, are girls. In simplest form, $\frac{8}{14} = \frac{4}{7}$. **17.** 4 boys **19.** Even, because there are $3 + 1$ coins, or some multiple of 4 coins, in the collection.

Lesson 2, page 171

1. no; The cross products are 90 and 100. In a true proportion, the cross products are equal. **3.** No **5.** Yes **7.** 3; Multiply the cross products, $(2)(12) = (n)(8)$, and divide each side of the equation by 8. **9.** 16 **11.** 7 **13.** 12 **15.** 6

Lesson 3, page 173

1. 160 hits; Write and solve the proportion $\frac{1 \text{ hit}}{3 \text{ at bats}} = \frac{n \text{ hits}}{480 \text{ at bats}}$. **3.** 420 frames **5.** 2 perfect scores **7.** 54 players **9.** 105 children

Lesson 4, page 175

1. 5 liters; Set up a proportion; $\frac{1}{15} = \frac{x}{75}$. Cross-multiply and solve for x; $15 \times x = 1 \times 75$; $x = 5$. **3.** A factor of 27 **5.** 1:4

Lesson 5, page 177

1. 3 hours; Time $= \frac{\text{distance}}{\text{rate}}$; Distance $= 165$ miles, rate $= 55$ miles per hour (mph); substitute and solve for time. $\frac{165 \text{ miles}}{55 \text{ mph}} = 3$ hours. **3.** $39\frac{7}{8}$ km **5.** $8\frac{1}{2}$ km per hour

Lesson 6, pages 180–181

1. $\frac{53}{100}$; The grid contains 100 squares; of those squares, 53 are shaded. **3.** $\frac{83}{100}$ **4.** 7%; Seven out of 100 squares are shaded. The ratio 7:100 can be written as the fraction $\frac{7}{100}$. A percent is the numerator of a fraction whose denominator is 100. **5.** 47% **7.** 91% **8.** 22%; Denominator is 100, write numerator with %. **9.** 95% **11.** 53% **13.** 33% **15.** 9%

Try This

$\frac{4,000}{10,000} = \frac{4}{10} = \frac{2}{5}$ is shaded; $\frac{6,000}{10,000} = \frac{3}{5}$ is not shaded; $\frac{2}{5} + \frac{3}{5} = 1$

Lesson 7, pages 184–185

1. 75%; To express a decimal as a percent, move the decimal point two places to the right, and add a percent symbol. **3.** 18% **5.** 78% **7.** 88% **9.** 10% **10.** 50%; To express a fraction as a percent, first use division to change the fraction to a decimal. Then move the decimal point two places to the right and add a percent symbol. **11.** 25% **13.** 40% **15.** 70% **17.** 76% **19.** 0.11; To express a percent as a decimal, move the decimal point two places to the left and leave off the percent symbol. **21.** 0.68 **23.** 0.17 **25.** 0.05 **27.** 0.83 **28.** Yes. Possible answer: For example, a test score can increase by more than 100% when compared to a previous test score. **29.** 20% **31.** 350% **33.** 10% **35.** Sample answer: Marc should choose an increase of $\frac{1}{5}$ because $\frac{1}{5} = 0.2 = 20\%$.

Lesson 8, page 187

1. 1.44; Change the percent to a decimal, then multiply 0.12 by 12. **3.** 480 **5.** 936 **7.** 134 **9.** 655.5

Lesson 9, page 189

1. 250%; $(n)(4) = 10$; $4n = 10$; $n = \frac{10}{4} = 2.5 = 250\%$ **3.** 37.5% or $37\frac{1}{2}\%$ **5.** 5% **6.** 13.5; Press 75 $\boxed{\times}$ 18 $\boxed{\%}$. The display reads 13.5. **7.** 0.15 **9.** 392

Lesson 10, page 191

1. $3.50; Subtract $4.00 from $7.50 **3.** Increase; 15.625%; Find the amount of increase ($1,850 − $1,600 = $250) and

then solve the equation $250 = (x)($1,600)$. **5.** 8%

Lesson 11, page 193

1. $551.25; $A = P(1 + i)^n$;
$A = 500(1 + .05)^2$; $A = 551.25$
3. $3,589.07 **5.** $10,049.50

Try This

7 years

Lesson 12, pages 196–197

1. 550 inches; Measured distance = $1\frac{3}{8}$ in.;

Set up a proportion and solve: $\dfrac{1\frac{3}{8}\text{ in.}}{x} =$
$\dfrac{1}{400}$; $x = 550$ in. **3.** $2\frac{1}{2}$ inches
4. $2\frac{3}{4}$, 2,420; Map distance = measured

distance = $2\frac{3}{4}$ in. To find the real

distance, set up a proportion and solve:
$\dfrac{2\frac{3}{4}}{x} = \dfrac{1}{880}$; $x = 2,420$ miles. **5.** $1\frac{7}{8}$, 1,650
7. $\frac{5}{8}$, 550 **9.** 6 feet by 7 feet; Measured

length = $\frac{3}{4}$ in., measured width = $\frac{7}{8}$ in.

Set up proportions and solve: $\dfrac{\frac{3}{4}\text{ in.}}{x} = \dfrac{1}{8}$,

$\dfrac{\frac{7}{8}}{y} = \dfrac{1}{8}$; $x =$ length = 6 feet, $y =$ width
= 7 feet **11.** 14 feet by 16 feet **13.** 2:1
15. 8 feet by 4 feet

Chapter 7 Application, page 198

1. 8,000,000 cellular phones per year
3. 60 miles per hour

Chapter 7 Review, pages 199–201

1. D **3.** A **5.** C **7.** 24 pounds **9.** 6 miles
per hour **11.** Sheila, 0.26 hours; Tonya,
0.21 hours; Tonya will arrive there first
13. 12% **15.** 3% **17.** 81% **19.** 31.25%
21. 16% **23.** 58% **25.** 0.19 **27.** 0.95

29. 0.61 **31.** $1,837.56 **33.** 21 miles
35. $n = 8$

Lesson 1, pages 206–207

1. 3; 3 is 3 units from zero. **3.** 10 **5.** 12
7. 73 **9.** -4; The opposite of a positive
integer is a negative integer. **11.** 73 **13.** -8
15. -1 **17.** A, B, C; These letters represent
real numbers to the right of zero. **19.** E
21. $+3$; The team moves forward 3 yards.
23. -40 **25.** -13 **27.** -10 **29.** $+2,500$

Lesson 2, page 209

1. $>$; On the number line, 5 is farther to
the right than 2. **3.** $>$ **5.** $<$ **7.** $>$ **9.** $>$
11. $>$ **13.** $>$ **15.** $>$ **17.** $>$ **19.** $>$
21. Yes, the integers follow one another
in order and none are missing. **23.** -5 is
farther left, so $-5 < -3$

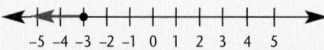

25. No, you need to know whether the
integer is 8 units to the left or to the right
of zero.

Lesson 3, page 211

1. even; Digit in the ones place is even.
3. even **5.** odd **6.** 876, even; Digit in the
ones place is even. **7.** 171, odd **9.** 1,376,
even **11.** 4,692, even **13.** 98, even
15. 330, even **16.** 864, even; Digit in the
ones place is even. **17.** 1,404, even
19. 946, even **21.** ·, 20; even · odd = even
23. +, 9 or $-$, 3 **25.** ·, 27

Try This

even ÷ even = even or odd (64 ÷ 8 = 8,
44 ÷ 4 = 11)
even ÷ odd = even (24 ÷ 3 = 8)
odd ÷ odd = odd (35 ÷ 5 = 7)

Lesson 4, page 213

1. 11; Adding a positive to a positive gives a result farther to the right on a number line. **3.** 5 **5.** 0 **7.** 3 **9.** -5 **11.** -8 **13.** 5 **15.** 2 **17.** -202; 441 $\boxed{+/-}$ $\boxed{+}$ 239 $\boxed{=}$. The display reads -202 **19.** 727

Lesson 5, page 215

1. -9; Adding a negative to a negative gives a result farther to the left on a number line. **3.** -11 **5.** 8 **7.** -602; 359 $\boxed{+/-}$ $\boxed{+}$ 243 $\boxed{+/-}$ $\boxed{=}$. The display reads -602 **9.** $-1,071$ **11.** 870 **13.** 27,000 ft; 25,000 ft + 2,000 ft **15.** 1,017 ft

Lesson 6, pages 218–219

1. $4 + (-5) = -1$; Adding a negative to a positive gives a result farther to the left on the number line. **3.** $-6 + 5 = -1$ **5.** $7 + (-5) = 2$ **7.** $-2 + (-4) = -6$ **9.** $7 + 4 = 11$ **11.** -4; Subtracting 7 is the same as adding -7. **13.** 0 **15.** 7 **17.** -8 **19.** 12 **21.** 30,340 feet; 29,028 ft + 1,312 ft **23.** 221°F **25.** 75 minutes

Lesson 7, page 221

1. 20; $(+5) \cdot (+4) = (+20)$ **3.** -24 **5.** 99 **7.** -20 **9.** -70 **11.** -21 **13.** 49 **15.** -15 **17.** -104 **19.** -27 **21.** positive; (Positive) $\cdot$ (Positive) = (Positive) **23.** negative **25.** positive **27.** negative **29.** positive

Lesson 8, page 223

1. positive; (Negative) $\cdot$ (Negative) = (Positive) **3.** negative **5.** positive **7.** negative **9.** positive **11.** 15 points under par; $-5 \cdot 3 = -15$ **13.** $-\$36$ **15.** $-\$30.00$

Lesson 9, page 225

1. 2; Like signs give positive quotients. **3.** -6 **5.** 3 **7.** -5 **9.** -2 **11.** 3 **13.** -1 **15.** -3 **17.** -8 **19.** -3 **21.** positive; Like signs give positive quotients. **23.** positive **25.** positive **27.** negative **29.** 240 seats; $1,440 \div 6 = 240$

Try This

$-20, -5$

Chapter 8 Application, page 226

1. $+135$ feet, $-1,215$ feet **3.** $-2,700$ feet, total height 3,000 feet; $-2,100$ feet, total height 2,400 feet

Chapter 8 Review, pages 227–229

1. B **3.** D **5.** A **7.** C **9.** 14 **11.** 71 **13.** 4 **15.** -43 **17.** $4 > 0$ **19.** $-2 < |-5|$ **21.** 10 **23.** 0 **25.** -3 **27.** -18 **29.** -2 **31.** -3 **33.** -7 **35.** -42 **37.** 96 **39.** -40 **41.** -4 **43.** 4 **45.** -7 **47.** 39,730 feet **49.** -7

CHAPTER 9

Lesson 1, page 233

1. 2; In 4^2; 4 is the base, 2 is the exponent. **3.** 3 **5.** 3 **7.** 5 **9.** 1 **11.** 2^3; 2 to the third power. **13.** 4^3 **15.** 5^4 **17.** x^4 **19.** m^6 **21.** 1,024; Press 2 $\boxed{y^x}$ 10 $\boxed{=}$. The display reads 1024. **23.** 4,096 **25.** 0.25

Lesson 2, page 235

1. 4^4; To multiply numbers with the same base, add their exponents. **3.** 2^7 **5.** 4^8 **7.** a^8 **9.** x^7 **11.** 2^{2n} **13.** true; $2^3 \cdot 2^5 = 2^{3+5} = 2^8$ **15.** false, the two terms in this expression do not have the same base. **17.** false, $3^{3+1} = 3^4$ **19.** true **21.** false, $n^{6+2} = n^8$ **23.** true **25.** true

Try This

x^{n+m}, a^{x+y}

Lesson 3, page 237

1. 7; To divide numbers with the same base, subtract their exponents. Any number to the first power is the number itself. **3.** 2 **5.** 9^2 **7.** h^3 **9.** k^3 **11.** y
13. false, $2^{8-2} = 2^6$ **15.** false, $9^{3-1} = 9^2$
17. false, $3^{3-1} = 3^2$ **19.** false, $x^{12-3} = x^9$
21. false, $(-s)^{6-2} = (-s)^4$ **23.** false, $x^{15-3} = x^{12}$ **25.** true

Try This

19^{x-w}, 1

Lesson 4, page 239

1. 2^2; Area $= s^2 = 2 \cdot 2 = 2^2$ **3.** y^2 **5.** p^2
6. 49 sq cm; Area $= s^2 = 7 \cdot 7 = 49$
7. 81 sq cm **9.** 16 sq cm **11.** 144 sq ft;
$s^2 = 12^2 = 144$ **13.** 49 sq ft
15. 640,000 sq m

Lesson 5, pages 240–241

1. 27 cu in.; $3 \cdot 3 \cdot 3 = 27$ **3.** 125 cu in.
4. 4^3; Volume $= s^3 = 4 \cdot 4 \cdot 4 = 4^3$ **5.** 2^3
7. y^3 **9.** 512 cu cm; Press 8 $\boxed{y^x}$ 3 $\boxed{=}$. The display reads 512. **11.** 8 cu cm
13. 5,832 cu cm **14.** 1 cu ft; Volume $= s^3 = 1 \cdot 1 \cdot 1 = 1$ **15.** 27 cu ft

Lesson 6, pages 244–245

1. 1, 2; 1.73; Press 3 $\boxed{\sqrt{}}$. The display reads 1.732050808; Round to the nearest hundredth. **3.** 2, 3; 2.45 **5.** 2, 3; 2.83
7. 3, 4; 3.61 **9.** 9, 10; 9.95 **11.** 10, 11; 10.25 **13.** 14, 15; 14.70 **15.** 20, 21; 20.66
16. 4; Side of square $= \sqrt{16}$ **17.** 3.2
19. 2.8

Lesson 7, page 247

Answers will vary. **1.** 3.2; 10 is between 9 and 16, so the $\sqrt{10}$ is between 3 and 4.
3. 5.5 **5.** 7.1 **7.** 8.1 **9.** 9.2

Try This

$\sqrt{81} = 9$, rational
$\sqrt{91} \approx 9.5$, irrational
$\sqrt{111} \approx 10.5$, irrational
$\sqrt{121} = 11$, rational

Lesson 8, page 249

1. 7.368, irrational; Press 400 $\boxed{\sqrt[3]{}}$; The display reads 7.368062997. This is not an integer, so the cube root is irrational. Round to the nearest thousand. **3.** 3.314, irrational **5.** 3.557, irrational **7.** 2, rational **9.** 2, rational **11.** 6 in.; If the area of the floor of a square birdhouse is 36 in.^{2}, one side is $\sqrt{36 \text{ in.}^2} = 6$ in.
13. 12.65 ft **15.** 196 square units, 14 units

Lesson 9, pages 252–253

1. $n = 49$; $\sqrt{n} = 7$, square both sides; $n = 7^2 = 49$ **3.** $y = 18$ **5.** $y = 245$
7. $x = 16\frac{1}{3}$ **9.** $x = 64$; $13 - \sqrt{x} = 5$; $13 - 5 = 8 = \sqrt{x}$. Square both sides: $64 = x$. **11.** $x = 625$ **13.** $x = 128\frac{1}{2}$
14. 6 units; $A = 36$ square units; side $= \sqrt{A} = \sqrt{36 \text{ square units}} = 6$ units
15. 7 units **17.** 20 in. **19.** 1 unit

Lesson 10, pages 256–257

1. 25; $x = \sqrt{7^2 + 24^2}$; $x = \sqrt{625}$; $x = 25$
3. 29 **5.** 24 **6.** 4.4; $x^2 = 10^2 - 9^2$; $x = \sqrt{100 - 81}$; $x = \sqrt{19}$; $x = 4.4$ **7.** 40.3
9. 5.9

Try This

Be sure to draw a triangle with a 90° angle. Check your classmate's calculations.

Lesson 11, page 259

1. 5, no, no, yes; $c = \sqrt{3^2 + 4^2}$; $c = \sqrt{25}$; $c = 5$; This triangle does not have three or two sides of equal length. It is scalene because it has no equal sides. 3. no, yes, no 5. 6, yes, no, yes

Chapter 9 Application, page 260

1. 30 yards 3. 20 feet

Chapter 9 Review, pages 261–263

1. B 3. B 5. D 7. 4^2, 16 9. 1^2, 1 11. between 8 and 9 13. 6^3, 216 15. 15.8 17. 5.3 19. rational (7) 21. irrational (6.93) 23. 2.08 25. $p = 32$ 27. $x = 6$ 29. 2.5 in.

CHAPTER 10

Lesson 1, pages 268–269

1. 12 ft; $P = 3$ ft $+ 4$ ft $+ 5$ ft 3. 7.125 cm 4. $18\frac{3}{4}$ in.; $P = 5\frac{1}{8}$ in. $+ 5\frac{1}{8}$ in. $+ 8\frac{1}{2}$ in. 5. 4.66 m 7. 611.75 ft 8. 86.2 m; Subtract the two given sides (each 42.5 m) from the perimeter. Divide the difference (172.4) by 2. 9. 31.67 mm or $31\frac{2}{3}$ mm

Try This

$P = s + s + s + s$, $P = 4s$

Lesson 2, pages 272–273

1. 18 cm; $P = 6$ cm $+ 6$ cm $+ 6$ cm 3. 111 in. 5. 117 yd 7. 10 sides; Divide 82.5 by 8.25 to find the number of sides. 9. Yes. Sample explanation: Find the perimeters of the square and rectangle. A 20 by 10 rectangle has the same perimeter (60 in.) as a 15 by 15 square.

Try This

Sample answer: $P = nm$ where $n =$ the number of sides of a regular polygon and $m =$ the measure of one side.

Lesson 3, pages 276–277

1. $8\frac{5}{6}$; $P = 2 + 3 + 1\frac{1}{2} + 2\frac{1}{3}$ 3. 94.5 cm 5. 11.71 m 6. 1, 10; Since the measure of the side opposite the missing side is 2, the measure of the missing side is $2 - 1$ or 1. $P = 2 + 3 + 1 + 1 + 1 + 2 = 10$ 7. $1\frac{1}{4}$, 9 9. 16.5 in., 109.5 in.

Lesson 4, pages 279–281

1. 84 cm^2; Use the formula $A = lw$; $A = 12 \cdot 7$. 3. 102 mm^2 5. $3\frac{3}{4}$ yd^2 7. 81 mm^2; Use the formula $A = s^2$; $A = 9^2$ or $9 \cdot 9$. 9. 19.36 m^2 11. $6\frac{1}{4}$ ft^2 13. 400 m^2; Press 20 $\boxed{x^2}$. The display reads 400. 15. 56.25 ft^2 17. 1.2544 mi^2 19. 144 m^2; Use the formula $A = s^2$; $A = 12^2 = 12 \cdot 12$

Lesson 5, page 283

1. 80 in.^{2}; Use the formula $A = \frac{1}{2}bh = \frac{1}{2}(10)(16)$ 3. 261 ft^2 5. 21 6. 4 in.; Use the formula $A = \frac{1}{2}bh$; $36 = \frac{1}{2}(18)h$; $\frac{36}{1} \cdot \frac{2}{18} = \frac{h(18)}{2} \cdot \frac{2}{18} = \frac{72}{18} = 4 = h$ 7. 4 ft 9. 10 ft; Use the formula $A = \frac{1}{2}bh$; $60 = \frac{1}{2}(12)h$; $\frac{60}{1} \cdot \frac{2}{12} = \frac{b(12)}{2} \cdot \frac{2}{12} = \frac{120}{12} = 10 = h$

Lesson 6, page 285

1. 160 mm^2; Use the formula $A = bh$; $A = 8 \cdot 20$ 3. 30 ft^2 5. 47,200 mm^2 7. 3.5 ft; Use the formula $A = bh$; $7 = b(2)$; $7 \cdot \frac{1}{2} = b(\frac{2}{1}) \cdot \frac{1}{2}$; $3\frac{1}{2} = b$ 9. 2 in.

Lesson 7, page 287

1. 70 units^2; $(2 \cdot 3) + (8 \cdot 8) = 6 + 64$
3. 442.5 units^2 **5.** 632 units^2

Lesson 8, pages 290–291

1. 18.84 in.; Since radius = 3, then diameter = 6. Now use the formula $C = \pi d$; $C = 3.14 \cdot 6$ **3.** 37.68 m **5.** 62.8 yd
6. 50.24 m^2; Use the formula $A = \pi r^2$; $A = 3.14 \cdot 4^2 = 3.14 \cdot 16$ **7.** 50.24 in.^{2}
9. 153.86 cm^2 **11.** 132.7322896 in.^{2}; Press $\boxed{\pi}$ $\boxed{\times}$ 6.5 $\boxed{x^2}$ $\boxed{=}$. The display reads 132.7322896. **13.** 4.523893421 m^2
15. 1.038689071 mi^2

Lesson 9, page 293

1. pyramid; The figure has a square base and triangles as faces or sides with a common vertex opposite the base.
3. sphere **5.** prism

Lesson 10, page 297

1. 96 square units; Cube surface area = $6s^2 = 6 \times 4^2 = 6 \times 16$ **3.** 170π sq units
4. 112π sq in.; Cylinder surface area, minus open top of vase = $\pi r^2 + 2\pi rh = \pi (4^2 + 2 \times 4 \times 12)$ **5.** No, she's planning to paint 516 sq ft

Lesson 11, pages 300–301

1. 224 sq units; Surface area = $s^2 + 2sl = 8^2 + 2 \times 8 \times 10 = 64 + 160$ **3.** 120 + $16\sqrt{3}$ sq units **4.** 256; Press 16 $\boxed{x^2}$; display reads 256. **5.** 324 **7.** 529 **9.** No, he needs a triangle whose base > 50 ft, the circumference of the base; The tepee with $r = 8$ has a base circumference of $2\pi(8) = 16\pi$, or about 50.24 feet

Lesson 12, pages 304–305

1. 125 cm^3; Use the formula $V = e^3$; $5 \cdot 5 \cdot 5$ **3.** 30 m^3 **4.** 27,000 mm^3; Press 30 $\boxed{y^x}$ 3 $\boxed{=}$ The display reads 27000
5. 262.144 in.^{3} **7.** 1,906,624 in.^{3} **9.** 60 in.^{3}; $(4 \cdot 4 \cdot 4) - (1 \cdot 1 \cdot 4) = 64 - 4 = 60$

Lesson 13, page 307

1. 125.6 in.^{3}; Use the formula $V = \pi r^2 h$; $V = (3.14)(2)^2(10)$; $(3.14)(2)(2)(10)$ **3.** 2,009.6 mm^3 **5.** 523.$\bar{3}$ cm^3; Use the formula $V = \frac{4}{3}\pi r^3$; $V = \frac{4}{3}(3.14)(5)^3$; $\frac{4}{3}(392.5)$; $\frac{4}{3} \cdot \frac{392.5}{1} = \frac{1,570}{3} = 523.\bar{3}$
6. $333\frac{1}{3}$ in.^{3}; $V = \frac{1}{3}$(area of base)(height) $= \frac{1}{3}(10 \text{ in.})^2(10 \text{ in.}) = \frac{1,000 \text{ in.}^3}{3}$ **7.** 200 ft^3
8. 376.8 cm^3; $V = (\pi r^2)(h) = \frac{1}{3}(6 \text{ cm})^2 (10 \text{ cm})\pi = \frac{360\pi \text{ cm}^3}{3}$ **9.** 512.8$\bar{6}$ cm^3

Chapter 10 Application, page 308

1. A one dimension increases 576 cm^3
  B two dimensions increase 1,152 cm^3
  C three dimensions increase 2,304 cm^3

Chapter 10 Review, pages 309–311

1. B **3.** C **5.** A **7.** C **9.** B **11.** 28.8 cm^2
13. 243 ft^2 **15.** 785 sq units **17.** $A = 21.98$ in.^{2} **19.** 1.5 m^3 **21.** $C = 38.308$ cm, $A = 116.8394$ cm^2 **23.** 1,436.02$\bar{6}$ in.^{3}
25. $V = 13.33$ in.^{3}

CHAPTER 11

Lesson 1, page 315

1. Shaded circle indicates the solution.

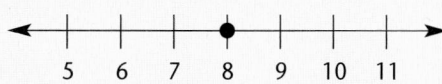

3.

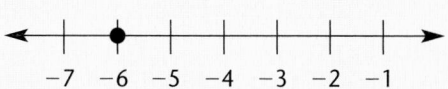

5.

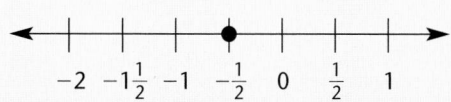

6. $x = 5$; A shaded circle indicates an integer solution. **7.** $x = 0$ **9.** $x = 1\frac{1}{2}$

Lesson 2, pages 318–319

1.

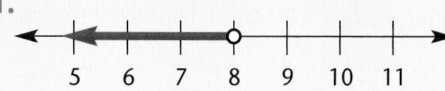

The open circle on 8 and the heavy line to the left show that all numbers less than 8 are solutions to the inequality.

3.

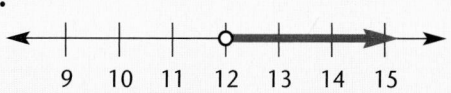

5.

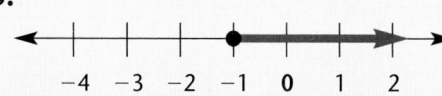

7. $x < -7$; The open circle on -7 and heavy line to the left show that all numbers less than -7 are solutions to the inequality. **9.** $x \leq 1$ **11.** $x \geq 5$ **13.** $x \leq 0$ **15.** $x \leq -4$

Lesson 3, page 321

1. $d = 3$; $3 + 4 = 7$

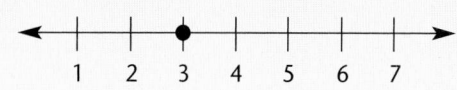

3. $g = -5$

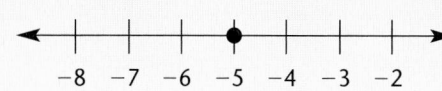

5. $n = 6$

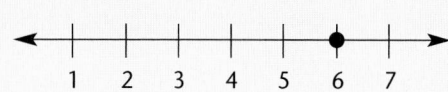

7. $x + 8 = 17$ or $17 - x = 8$; The shaded circle at 9 shows that it is the solution. $9 + 8 = 17$ or $17 - 9 = 8$; $x = 9$

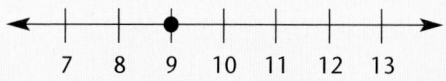

9. $45 - x = 15$ or $15 + x = 45$; $x = 30$

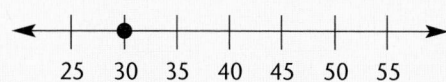

Lesson 4, page 323

1. $d < 3$; All numbers less than 3 solve the inequality.

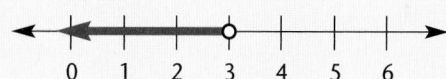

3. $c < 3$

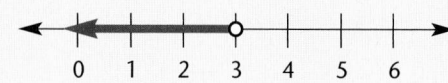

5. $w \leq 2$

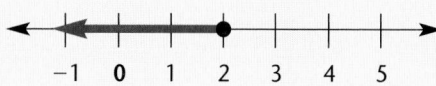

7. $r \leq -10$

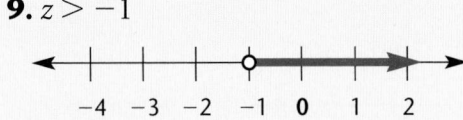

9. $z > -1$

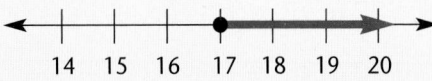

11. $v < -7$

13. $x + 35 \geq 52$; $x \geq 17$; 17 and all numbers greater than 17 solve the inequality.

15. $10 - x \leq 3$; $7 \leq x$

Lesson 5, page 327
1. $(1, 6)$; Point K is 1 unit to the right of the y-axis and 6 units above the x-axis.
3. $(0, 7)$ **5.** $(-7, -5)$ **7.** $(0, -6)$
9. $(7, -5)$ **11.** Quadrant I; Point K is in the upper right quarter of the system.
13. Quadrant III **15.** Quadrant III
17. 2 units; Plot points $(0, 0)$ and $(2, 0)$. The distance between these points is 2 units. **19.** 3 units

Lesson 6, page 329
1, 3, 5, 7, 9, and 11.

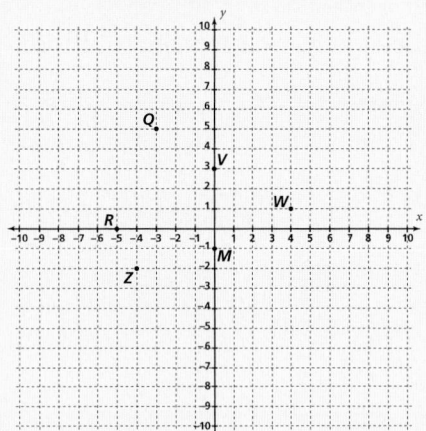

12. Quadrant I; Since the first coordinate of the ordered pair is positive, the point lies to the right of the y-axis, and since the second coordinate of the ordered pair is positive, the point lies above the x-axis.
13. Quadrant III **15.** Quadrant II

Lesson 7, pages 332–333
1. $y = x + 1$; $x = -1, 0, 1$; $y = 0, 1, 2$; Substitute the values for x and y; $0 = -1 + 1$; $1 = 0 + 1$; $2 = 1 + 1$ **3.** $y = x + 3$; $x = -7, -1, -4$; $y = -4, 2, -1$
5. Answers will vary. Sample answer shown. $y = x + 6$; $x = -1, 0, 1$; $y = 5, 6, 7$
7. -65.2; Substitute -53.2 for x in the equation and find y; -53.2 $\boxed{-}$ 12 $\boxed{=}$. The display reads -65.2. **9.** -101.9

Lesson 8, page 335
1. yes; Each x-value has one y-value
3. yes **5.** yes **7.** $f(2) = 6, f(-4) = 12$; $f(2) = 2^2 + 2 = 4 + 2$; $f(-4) = (-4)^2 + (-4) = 16 - 4$ **9.** $f(2) = 14, f(-4) = 68$
11. $f(2) = 2, f(-4) = -28$
13. $f(2) = -11, f(-4) = -53$
15. $f(2) = 12, f(-4) = 12$

Lesson 9, pages 337–339

1. Range $= -7, -5, 1, 9, 15$; $f(-1) =$ $2(-1) - 5 = -2 - 5$; $f(0) = 0 - 5$; $f(3)$ $= 2(3) - 5 = 6 - 5$; $f(7) = 2(7) - 5 =$ $14 - 5$; $f(10) = 2(10) - 5 = 20 - 5$

3. Range: $\frac{7}{4}, 2, 3, \frac{7}{2}, 4$ **5.** Range: $-2, 0, 5,$ $8, 22$ **6.** Range: $-2 \leq y \leq 4$; $f(-2) =$ $-(-2) + 2 = 2 + 2$; $f(4) = -(4) + 2 =$ $-4 + 2$ **7.** Range: $y = 3$ **9.** Range: $0 \leq y$ ≤ 4 **11.** Domain: $-4 \leq x \leq 6$, Range: $-2 \leq y \leq 5$; Endpoints are $(-4, 5)$ and $(6, -2)$, so the x-values range from -4 to 6 and the y-values range from -2 to 5

13. Domain: $-4 \leq x \leq 2$, Range: $y = 2$

15. Domain: $-2 \leq x \leq 2$, Range: $0 \leq y \leq 4$

Lesson 10, page 341

Sample answers shown.

1. $y = x + 5$; $x = -2, 0, 2$; $y = 3, 5, 7$

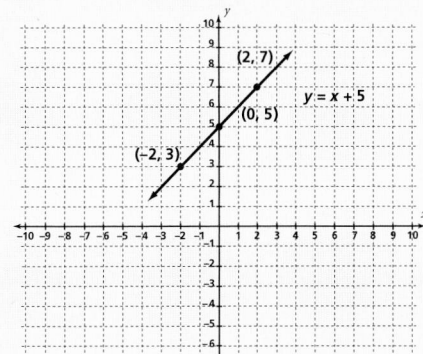

3.

5.

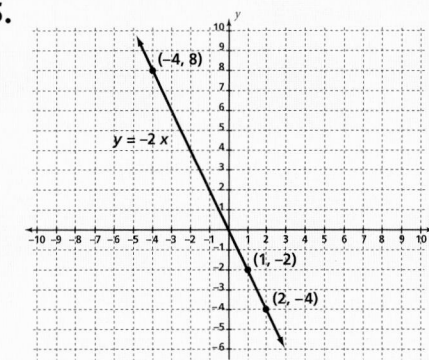

7.

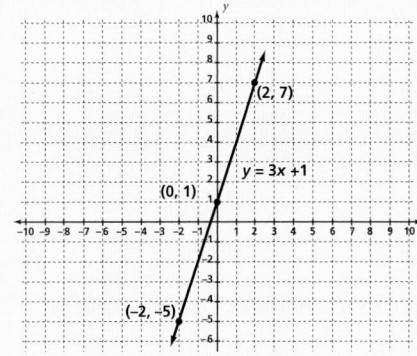

9.

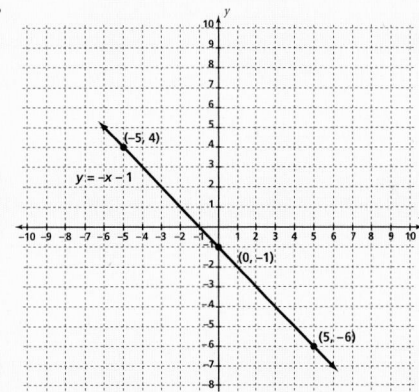

Try This

Check your partner's work to be sure the equation was written correctly.

Lesson 11, page 343

1. 0.0125; Use the formula slope $= \frac{\text{rise}}{\text{run}}$. Press .2 $\boxed{\div}$ 16 $\boxed{=}$. The display reads 0.0125 **3.** -0.066666667 **5.** 2 **7.** 12 **8.** negative slope; The line moves downward when viewed from left to right. **9.** zero slope

Lesson 12, pages 345–347

1. $\frac{1}{5}$; Simplify $\frac{0-1}{0-5} = \frac{-1}{-5} = \frac{1}{5}$. **3.** $\frac{-9}{8}$ **5.** $\frac{5}{11}$ **7.** 0 **9.** $\frac{2}{11}$; $m = \frac{y_2 - y_1}{x_2 - x_1} = \frac{5-3}{4-(-7)}$ $= \frac{2}{11}$ **11.** $\frac{-9}{4}$ **13.** $\frac{-1}{9}$ **14.** Sample answer: The last half of the trail is more difficult because it has a positive, or uphill, slope. The first half of the trail has a negative slope. It is downhill. **15.** Sample answer: The first half of the trail is more difficult. Since an equivalent fraction for $\frac{3}{20}$ is $\frac{6}{40}$, the slope of the first half of the trail $\left(\frac{6}{40}\right)$ is greater than the slope of the second half of the trail $\left(\frac{5}{40}\right)$.

Try This

Triangle: a has a positive slope, b has a negative slope, and c has zero slope. Parallelogram: a and c have positive slopes and b and d have zero slopes.

Lesson 13, pages 350–351

1. slope $= m = 1$; y-intercept $= -1$; x-intercept $= 1$; The slope of the line is 1 because the line moves 1 unit vertically for every 1 unit horizontally. The y-intercept is -1 because the line crosses the y-axis at -1. The x-intercept is 1 because the line crosses the x-axis at $+1$. **3.** $y = x + 5$; Divide each side of the equation by 2. **5.** $y = 2x - 1$ **7.** $y = -x - 1$ **9.** $m = 1$;

y-intercept $= -3$; x-intercept $= 3$; In the equation $y = x - 3$, the slope and y-intercept are the corresponding values for m and b in the equation $y = mx + b$. To find the x-intercept, substitute 0 for y in the equation $y = x - 3$ and solve for x. **11.** $m = -2$; y-intercept $= -4$; x-intercept $= -2$ **13.** $m = 1$; y-intercept $= 1$; x-intercept $= -1$ **15.** $m = 1$; y-intercept $= -5$; x-intercept $= 5$ **17.** $m = -1$; y-intercept $= -1$; x-intercept $= -1$ **19.** $m = \frac{1}{2}$; y-intercept $= 1$; x-intercept $= -2$

Chapter 11 Application, page 352

1. Answers will vary. Possible answer: train. **3.** Answers will vary.

Chapter 11 Review, pages 353–355

1. A **3.** B

5.

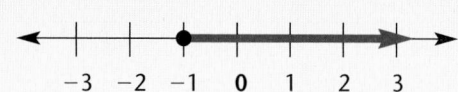

7. Sample answer: $y = x + 1$; $x = -2, 3, -1$; $y = -1, 4, 0$

9. $b \geq -1$

11. No **13.** $f(-3) = -3, f(2) = 7$ **15.** Range: $-3 \leq y \leq 3$ **17.** Quadrant IV **19.** Quadrant I **21.** $(-4, 5)$

23 and 25.

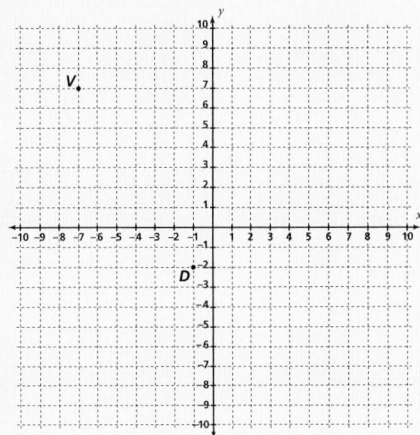

CHAPTER 12

Lesson 1, page 359

1. ∠XPA, ∠APX; Each name has letter P, the vertex, as the middle letter. **3.** ∠3, ∠GPF **5.** $\overrightarrow{PD}$ and $\overrightarrow{PE}$ **7.** 90°; The 0° line of the protractor is on side PY of the angle, and side PD is on 90°. **9.** 40° **11.** 35° **13.** 110°; The 0° line of the protractor is on side PY of the angle, and side PC is on 110°. **15.** 60°

Lesson 2, page 361

1. right; The symbol inside the angle shows a right angle. **3.** obtuse **5.** straight **6.** d, b; These angles share a vertex and a common side with ∠a. **7.** a, c; b, d **9.** 140°, 40°; Vertical angles have the same measure, so m∠a = m∠c and m∠b = m∠d. **10.** vertical, acute; These are opposite pairs of angles formed by the intersection of two lines, and they are less than 90°. **11.** adjacent, one acute and one obtuse **13.** true; Vertical angles are opposite pairs of angles formed by the intersection of two lines. Their angles can be acute or obtuse. **15.** true

Lesson 3, pages 364–365

1. ∠OQP and ∠PQR; The sum of the measures of these angles equals 90°. **3.** ∠PQR and ∠RQS **4.** 45°; The sum of the measures of complementary angles equals 90°; 90° − 45° = 45° **5.** 70° **7.** 35° **9.** 10° **10.** 160°; The sum of the measures of supplementary angles equals 180°; 180° − 20° = 160° **11.** 75° **13.** 30° **15.** 60° **16.** 60°; The sum of the measures of supplementary angles equals 180°; 180° − 120° = 60° **17.** 68° **19.** 45°, 135°

Try This

The sum of the measures of supplementary angles equals 180°; of right angles, 90°. 180° = 90° + x; x = 90°

Lesson 4, page 369

1. 90°; The sum of the measures of the angles in a triangle is 180°; 30° + 60° + x = 180°; x = 90° **3.** 110° **5.** 70° **6.** 40°; The supplement to the exterior angle (140°) is 40°. The sum of the measures of the angles in a triangle is 180°; 100° + 40° + y = 180°; y = 40° **7.** 30° **9.** 20° **11.** 35°; The supplement to the exterior angle (130°) is 50°; the supplement to the other exterior angle (85°) is 95°; 50° + 95° + z = 180°; z = 35° **13.** 36° **15.** 128°; m∠ABC + m(right angle) = m∠1; 38° + 90° = m∠1, m∠1 = 128°

Lesson 5, page 371

1. right isosceles; This triangle has a right angle and two sides of equal length. **3.** equilateral and equiangular **5.** isosceles **7.** scalene **9.** equiangular

Lesson 6, page 373

1. ASA; Two angles and the included side are equal. **3.** SAS **4.** yes, ASA **5.** no, angle is not included angle

Lesson 7, page 375

1. yes; These triangles are the same shape but not the same size. **3.** not enough information **5.** not enough information **6.** false; Isosceles triangles can have many different shapes. For all of them to be similar, they would all need the same shape. **7.** true **9.** true

Lesson 8, page 377

1. parallelogram; This polygon has two pairs of parallel sides, opposite sides of the same length, and opposite angles that are equal. **3.** trapezoid **4.** true; Rectangles are parallelograms with all angles 90°. This also describes squares. **5.** true **7.** false **9.** square, rectangle, parallelogram

Lesson 9, page 379

1. 90°; All angles in a rectangle are right angles. **3.** 90°; All angles in a rectangle are right angles. **5.** 47.61; Press 6.9 $\boxed{x^2}$. The display reads 47.61. **7.** 11.14 **9.** 6.48

Lesson 10, page 381

1. 6; A polygon whose interior angles equal 720° is a hexagon. **3.** 100 **5.** 1,800° **7.** 120° **9.** 162° **11.** 45° **13.** 30° **15.** 3.6°

Lesson 11, page 385

1. $A' = (3, -5)$; Reflected across the x-axis, (x, y) becomes $(x, -y)$, so $(3, -5)$ becomes $(3, 5)$ **3.** $E' = (2, 0)$ **4.** $G' = (-4, 2)$; Reflected across the y-axis, (x, y) becomes $(-x, y)$, so $(4, 2)$ becomes $(-4, 2)$ **5.** $I' = (4, 2)$ **7.** $H' = (-4, -2)$

8.

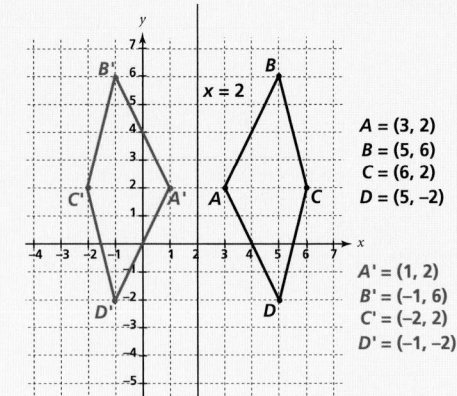

A = (3, 2)
B = (5, 6)
C = (6, 2)
D = (5, –2)

A' = (1, 2)
B' = (–1, 6)
C' = (–2, 2)
D' = (–1, –2)

9. $E' = (-6, -5), F' = (-4, -8),$ $G' = (-6, -11), H' = (-1, -8)$

Lesson 12, page 387

1. no; You cannot reflect the triangle over this diagonal and have the object and the image meet. **3.** No **5.** Yes **7.** 3; A triangle has 3 sides **9.** 5

Try This

Any diameter appears to be a line of symmetry. There are an infinite number of diameters, so there must be an infinite number of lines of symmetry.

Lesson 13, page 389

1. $A' = (0, 8); A = (3, 6), A' = (3 - 3, 6 + 2) = (0, 8)$ **3.** $C' = (0, -4)$ **5.** $E' = (-3, 7)$ **6.** $A' = (-3, 5), B' = (2, 3),$ and $C' = (8, 8); A = (-7, 3), A' = (-7 + 4, 3 + 2) = (-3, 5); B = (-2, 1), B' = (-2 + 4, 1 + 2) = (2, 3); C = (4, 6), C' = (4 + 4, 6 + 2) = (8, 8)$ **7.** $E' = (-5, 1), F' = (0, 5), G' = (0, 0)$ **8.** $(4, 4); (3, -1) \rightarrow (x + 1, y + 5) = (3 + 1, -1 + 5) = (4, 4)$ **9.** $(6, -3)$

1.

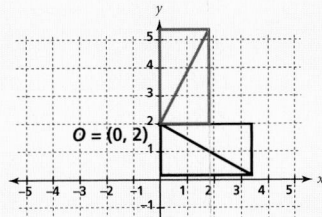

3.

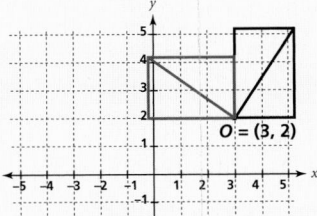

5.

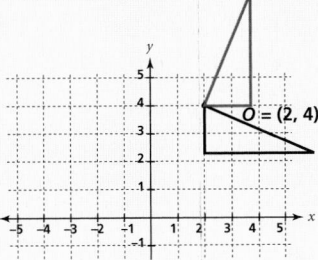

7.

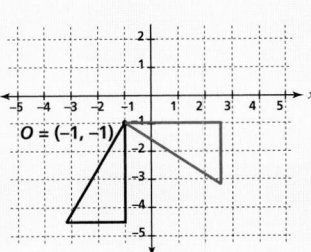

8.

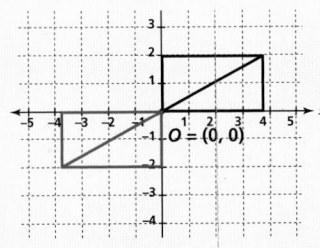

9.

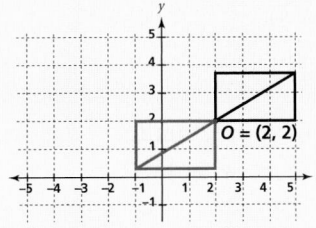

11.

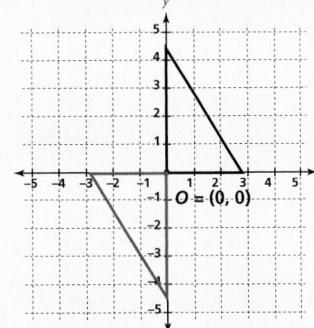

13.

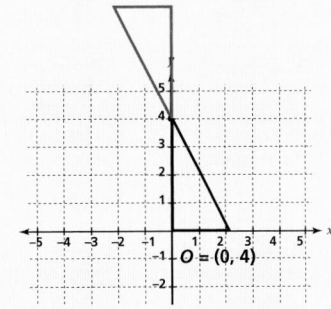

15. $(-4, 5)$; Rotating 180° counterclockwise, $(x, y) \rightarrow (-x, -y)$, so $(4, -5) \rightarrow (-4, -(-5))$, or $(-4, 5)$
17. $(-7, -1)$ **19.** $(-8, 3)$

Chapter 12 Application, page 394
1. reflection; translation
3. Answers will vary.

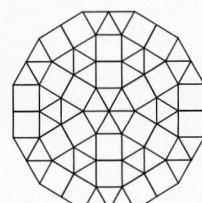

1. C **3.** A **5.** 35° **7.** 40° **9.** *AXC* and *CXF*
11. *DXF* **13.** adjacent, supplementary
15. adjacent, supplementary **17.** 50°
19. 110° **21.** $A' = (3, 1)$, $B' = (-2, -4)$,
$C' = (0, 3)$ **23.** $A' = (-3, 1)$, $B' = (-5, 1)$,
$C' = (-5, 3)$, $D' = (-3, 5)$ **25.** none
27. $A' = (-2, -1)$, $B' = (1, -1)$, $C' =$
$(-1, 2)$ **29.**

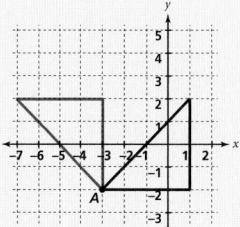

CHAPTER 13

Lesson 1, page 401
1. The graph displays the area, rounded
to the nearest one hundred square miles,
of selected Wyoming counties; the title of
a graph describes the data it displays.
3. The axis does not begin at zero.
5. Crook County **7.** Hot Springs; Platte;
Weston; Laramie; Crook **9.** Yes. Sample
explanation: A horizontal bar graph is a
vertical bar graph rotated 90° clockwise.
10. Sample bar graph:

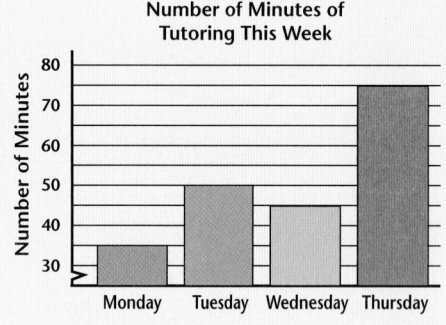

Number of Minutes of Tutoring This Week

Lesson 2, page 403
1. 24 students; there are 24 tallies, and the
sum of the numbers displayed in the
frequency column is 24. **3.** The lowest
quiz score was one number from 60–69.
The interval in which the lowest quiz
scored occurred is 60–69, but the exact
score of the lowest quiz cannot be
determined from the frequency table.
5. Answers will vary. Make a frequency
table with three columns labeled *Interval,
Tally,* and *Frequency.* Determine the
intervals for the minutes studied and list
them. Survey your classmates and make a
tally mark for each interval reported.
Grouping tallies in groups of five will
help anyone reading the frequency table
interpret the data more quickly. Record
the exact number of tallies for each
interval in the *Frequency* column. The
sum of the numbers in the *Frequency*
column must be the same as the sum of
the tallies in the *Tally* column. Write a
title for your frequency table.
Sample frequency table:

Frequency Table		
Interval	Tally	Frequency
0–20	||||	4
21–40	||||	4
41–60	||||	4
61–80	|	1
81–100	|	1

Lesson 3, page 405
1. The graph describes how 40 students
responded when asked if they usually
sleep more than 8 hours each night; the
title of a graph describes the data it
displays. **3.** 20% **5.** 32 students **7.** 288°

9. No; A circle cannot measure more than or less than 360°. **10.** Draw a circle. Find the fractional part for the total number of votes for each candidate. Candidate A: $\frac{9}{24}$ or $\frac{3}{8}$ Candidate B: $\frac{5}{24}$ votes Candidate C: $\frac{10}{24}$ votes or $\frac{5}{12}$ Multiply each fractional part by 360°—the number of degrees in a circle. $\frac{9}{24}$ or $\frac{3}{8} \cdot 360° = 135°$ $\frac{5}{24} \cdot 360° = 75°$ $\frac{10}{24}$ or $\frac{5}{12} \cdot 360° = 150°$ Use a protractor to divide the circle into two parts. Measure and mark a 135° angle; label this part *Candidate A.* Then measure and mark a 75° angle, label this part *Candidate B.* The remaining part of the circle should measure 150°; label it *Candidate C.*
Sample circle graph:

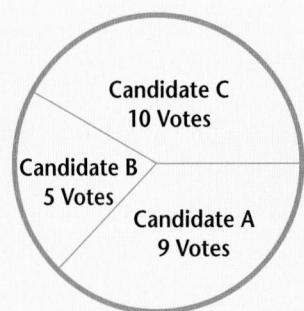

Lesson 4, page 407
1.

Grades Received

2. 8; The height of the histogram at 2 (number of heads) on the horizontal axis is 8 on the vertical axis (frequency), so 2 heads were obtained 8 times **3.** 1
5. Results will vary. Make a frequency table and a histogram of your results.

Try This
Answers will vary. Remember to label the graph.

Lesson 5, page 409
1. 2; Two points fall on the line $y = x$
3. no **4.** B; The points on graph B seem to cluster around a line **5.** B; As the height increases (the graph moves from left to right), the weight increases (the points tend to move upward)

Lesson 6, pages 410–411
1. $0.55; Use addition to find the sum of the values in the set. $0.35 + $0.35 + $0.35 + $0.35 + $0.35 + $0.35 + $1.75 = $3.85 Count the pieces of data in {$0.35, $0.35, $0.35, $0.35, $0.35, $0.35, $1.75} = 7 pieces of data. Divide the sum of the values by the number of pieces of data. $3.85 ÷ 7 = $0.55 **3.** 14.125 points
5. 54.1 inches **6.** 21.321; Press 18.2 [+] [+] 34 [+] 28.004 [+] 5.080 [=]. The display reads 85.284. Divide the sum by the number of values in the set of data. Press [÷] 4 [=]. The display reads 21.321.
7. 1,578 **9.** 5.7679 **11.** 17.08 **13.** 27.25
14. 58.4 years old; Use addition to find the sum of the values in the set. 61 + 52 + 69 + 64 + 46 = 292 Count the pieces of data in {61, 52, 69, 64, 46} = 5 pieces of data. Divide the sum of the values by the number of pieces of data. 292 ÷ 5 = 58.4
15. 3.6875 bills

Lesson 7, page 413

1. 106; Order the values in the set from the greatest to the least or the least to the greatest. 52, 85, 106, 141, 172. Cross off the greatest and least pairs (172, 52; 141, 85) until one value (106) remains in the middle of the set. **3.** 102 **4.** 84.6 in.; Order the values in the set from the greatest to the least or the least to the greatest. 70.6, 77.5, 78.2, 91.0, 101.3, 115.5 Cross off the greatest and least pairs (115.5, 70.6; 101.3, 77.5) until two values (78.2, 91.0) remain in the middle of the set. Add the values, then divide by two because there are two values in the set. 78.2 + 91.0 = 169.2 ÷ 2 = 84.6 **5.** 8,734.5 ft

Lesson 8, page 415

1. 1; Order the data from least to greatest or greatest to least value. 7.0, 7.1, 7.2, 7.2, 7.2, 7.8, 7.8, 8.0. Find the value that occurs most often. 7.2 occurs three times. No other value occurs that often. **3.** 2 modes **4.** 28, 29; Order the data from least to greatest or greatest to least value. 27, 28, 28, 29, 29, 30, 31, 32, 36, 49. Find the values that occur most often. 28 and 29 each occur twice. No other values occur that often. **5.** 31 **7.** 40 **9.** 27

Lesson 9, page 417

1. 17 points; Identify the greatest and least values in the set of data {82, 88, 99}. 99 is the greatest value; 82 is the least value. Subtract the least value from the greatest value. 99 − 82 = 17 **3.** 1,657,516 papers **5.** 46,150 square miles **7.** 5 minutes and 50.5 seconds **9.** $1,163.7 billion

Lesson 10, page 419

1. {2, 4, 8, 9, 10, 11, 12, 13, 14, 17, 20} **3.** 2, lower extreme **5.** 14, upper quartile **7.**

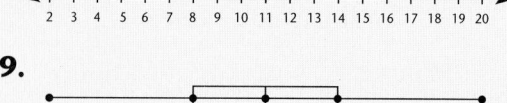

9.

10. Sample answer: Subtract the lower extreme from the upper extreme.

Lesson 11, page 421

1. $\frac{1}{2}$ or 50%; Since there are two possibilities when the coin is tossed—the coin will either land heads up or tails up—the denominator is two. Since one outcome is favorable—the coin landing heads up—the numerator is one. The probability of tossing a coin and having it land heads up is $\frac{1}{2}$ or 50%. **3.** $\frac{3}{6}$ or $\frac{1}{2}$ or 50% **4.** Since there are six possible outcomes when the cube is rolled, the denominator is six. Since there are three orange sides, the numerator is 3. The probability of the cube landing on orange is $\frac{1}{2}$. **5.** $\frac{1}{3}$

Try This

The probability can never be less than 0 and can never be greater than 1.

Lesson 12, pages 424–425

1. Independent events; any toss does not affect the previous toss or the next toss of the coin **3.** These are independent events; the next outcome will be 1, 2, 3, 4, 5, or 6

4. $\frac{1}{18}$; $P(\text{orange and green}) = P(\text{orange}) \times P(\text{green}) = \frac{2}{6} \times \frac{1}{6} = \frac{2}{36} = \frac{1}{18}$

5. $\frac{1}{12}$ **7.** $\frac{1}{28}$; $P(\text{white and red}) = P(\text{white}) \times P(\text{red, one less marble}) = \frac{1}{8} \times \frac{2}{7} = \frac{2}{56} = \frac{1}{28}$ **9.** $\frac{5}{56}$

Try This

$P(\text{red and white and blue}) = P(\text{red}) \times P(\text{white, minus 1 marble}) \times P(\text{blue, minus 2 marbles}) = \frac{1}{8} \times \frac{2}{7} \times \frac{5}{6} = \frac{10}{336}$, which is about 0.03, or 3%

Lesson 13, page 427

1. 2 ways; If, for example, the digits were 5 and 8, the digits could be arranged as 58 or 85. No other arrangements are possible for two digits. **3.** 24 ways **4.** 970,200; Press 100 ×⃞ 99 ×⃞ 98 =⃞ . The display reads 970200. **5.** 3,603,600

Chapter 13 Application, page 428

1. Answers will vary.

Chapter 13 Review, pages 429–431

1. B **3.** D **5.** C **7.** 24 ways

9. Flavor A; $\frac{12}{20} = 60\%$

Flavor B; $\frac{3}{20} = 15\%$

Flavor C; $\frac{5}{20} = 25\%$

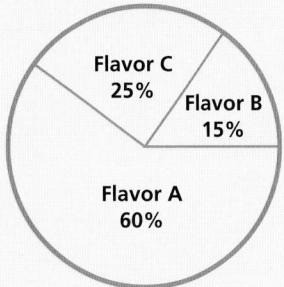

11. The package that weighed the most weighed more than 40 pounds but less than 50 pounds. Its exact weight is not known. **13.** false **15.** First draw: $P = \frac{3}{6}$ or $\frac{1}{2}$ (50%) Second draw: $P = \frac{2}{5}$ (40%) Third draw: $P = \frac{2}{4} = \frac{1}{2}$ (50%)

Supplementary Problems

CHAPTER 1

Chapter 1, pages 432–433

1. ********** ********** ********** ****
2. 60,003 **3.** 80,200 **4.** 67,021 **5.** 6
6. 1,401,095 **7.** 1,399 − 779 = 620

8.
```
   808
 + 618
 1,426
```
9.
```
        26
411 ) 10,686
```
10.
```
   137
 ×   3
   411
```

11. 18_{10} **12.** 11_{10} **13.** 110_2 **14.** 100_2
15. 10_5 **16.** 20_5 **17.** 2_5 **18.** 14_5
19. 20_{10} **20.** 11212_5

CHAPTER 2

Pages 434–435

1. 9,862 **2.** 333,618 **3.** 1,305 **4.** 5,912
5. 156,910 **6.** 44,380 **7.** 3,577 **8.** 4,814
9. 527 **10.** 297,504 **11.** 233,411 **12.** 2,989
13. 147,839 **14.** 2,337 **15.** 2,144 **16.** 216
17. 5,040 **18.** 1,666 **19.** 84 **20.** 24
21. 4 r6 **22.** 723 r1 **23.** 1,363 r4 **24.** 21
25. 100,000 **26.** 180,000 **27.** 11,000
28. 150,000 **29.** 1,000 **30.** 750 **31.** open
32. false **33.** open **34.** false **35.** open
36. true **37.** numerical; division
38. algebraic; multiplication, x
39. algebraic; multiplication, subtraction, y
40. algebraic; division, w
41. numerical; addition, multiplication
42. algebraic; multiplication, addition, a
43. 30 **44.** 25 **45.** 36 **46.** 7 **47.** false
48. true **49.** true **50.** false

CHAPTER 3

Pages 436–437

1. thousandths place **2.** $3 \times 100 = 300$
3. ten-thousandths place **4.** $9 \times 1 = 9$
5. 7.818 **6.** 2.0001 **7.** 7.682 **8.** $50.02
9. 36.485 **10.** 12.385 **11.** 1,636.6
12. 1.615 **13.** $63.30 **14.** 523.962
15. 26.927 **16.** 6,570 **17.** 0.326 **18.** 70
19. 82.25 **20.** 26.272 **21.** 0.578 **22.** 0.064
23. $\frac{3}{4}$ **24.** $\frac{1}{2}$ **25.** $\frac{3}{8}$ **26.** $\frac{3}{25}$ **27.** 0.27
28. 0.94 **29.** 0.27 **30.** 0.78 **31.** $10,400
32. $530 **33.** 15.98 **34.** 21.7 **35.** 4.14
36. 14.29 **37.** true **38.** false **39.** true
40. false

CHAPTER 4

Pages 438–439

1. false **2.** $7 \cdot 12 = 84$ true **3.** $10 \cdot 356 =$
3,560 true **4.** false **5.** $4 \cdot 19 = 76$ true
6. false **7.** $8 \cdot 56 = 448$ true **8.** $9 \cdot 501 =$
4,509 true **9.** 84 is divisible by 2, 3, 4, 6.
10. 430 is divisible by 2, 5, 10. **11.** 3,120
is divisible by 2, 3, 4, 5, 6, 8, 10.
12. 32,022 is divisible by 2, 3, 6, 9.
13. composite **14.** composite **15.** prime
16. prime **17.** 7 **18.** 2 **19.** 3 **20.** 8
21. 50 **22.** 49 **23.** $6b + 54$ **24.** $105 + 63x$
25. $4c + 60 + 20a$ **26.** $136 + 17d + 102p$
27. 12 **28.** 5 **29.** $9x$ **30.** 6 **31.** 4 **32.** 1
33. $3(y + 7)$ **34.** $5(5x + 7)$ **35.** $5(2c + 1)$
36. $2(3u + 2)$ **37.** $4(6s + 7m)$
38. $6(2q + 3n)$ **39.** $7(z + 2b)$
40. $3(2j + 5k)$ **41.** 30 **42.** 48 **43.** 90
44. 150 **45.** 64 **46.** 60 **47.** 3,072

48. 110,592 **49.** 1,265,368 **50.** 64,800
51. $3.521 \cdot 10^{10}$ **52.** $4.5 \cdot 10^{6}$
53. $3.75 \cdot 10^{-5}$ **54.** $8.9 \cdot 10^{-8}$ **55.** $4.97 \cdot 10$

CHAPTER 5

Pages 440–441

1. $\frac{8}{3}$ **2.** $3\frac{2}{3}$ **3.** $6\frac{2}{5}$ **4.** $\frac{15}{8}$ **5.** $2\frac{1}{7}$ **6.** $\frac{59}{9}$
7. $\frac{15}{4}$ **8.** $5\frac{1}{4}$ **9.** possible answers: $\frac{14}{16}$ $\frac{21}{24}$
10. possible answers: $\frac{6}{10}$ $\frac{9}{15}$ **11.** possible
answers: $\frac{2}{16}$ $\frac{3}{24}$ **12.** possible answers: $\frac{10}{28}$
$\frac{15}{42}$ **13.** possible answers: $\frac{18}{30}$ $\frac{27}{45}$
14. possible answers: $\frac{22}{24}$ $\frac{33}{36}$ **15.** possible
answers: $\frac{2}{100}$ $\frac{3}{150}$ **16.** possible answers: $\frac{2}{20}$
$\frac{3}{30}$ **17.** $\frac{2}{5}$ **18.** $\frac{2}{15}$ **19.** $\frac{1}{7}$ **20.** $\frac{1}{3}$ **21.** $\frac{1}{9}$
22. $\frac{3}{4}$ **23.** $\frac{4}{9}$ **24.** $\frac{7}{10}$ **25.** $\frac{1}{5}$ $\frac{3}{10}$ $\frac{1}{2}$
26. $\frac{1}{4}$ $\frac{5}{12}$ $\frac{2}{3}$ **27.** $\frac{2}{9}$ $\frac{5}{18}$ $\frac{5}{6}$ **28.** $\frac{3}{7}$ $\frac{2}{3}$ $\frac{19}{21}$
29. $1\frac{1}{10}$ **30.** $\frac{1}{6}$ **31.** $16\frac{7}{8}y$ **32.** $\frac{5}{24}$ **33.** $\frac{20}{21}$
34. $8\frac{15}{16}$ **35.** $\frac{16}{49}$ **36.** $1\frac{1}{2}$ **37.** $15\frac{11}{15}g$ **38.** 8
39. $7\frac{4}{5}$ **40.** $2\frac{5}{16}$ **41.** $1\frac{1}{7}$ **42.** $6\frac{1}{16}$ **43.** $1\frac{3}{5}$
44. $1\frac{3}{16}$ **45.** $8\frac{5}{9}m$ **46.** $11\frac{1}{6}n$ **47.** 15
48. $\frac{6}{7}$ **49.** $6\frac{4}{5}$ **50.** $1\frac{5}{16}$

CHAPTER 6

Pages 442–443

1. 30 **2.** 28 **3.** 24 **4.** 27 **5.** 18 **6.** 9 **7.** 20
8. 0 **9.** 12 **10.** 3 **11.** 32 **12.** 53 **13.** $21\frac{6}{11}$
14. 0 **15.** 6 **16.** $1\frac{1}{6}$ **17.** $4\frac{1}{4}$ **18.** 12
19. true **20.** false **21.** false **22.** true
23. true **24.** false **25.** true **26.** 5 **27.** 14
28. $7\frac{1}{2}$ **29.** 4 **30.** $1\frac{5}{8}$ **31.** 11 **32.** 16
33. 2 **34.** $1\frac{2}{5}$ **35.** $\frac{3}{8}$ **36.** $6\frac{6}{7}$ **37.** 4 **38.** $\frac{1}{9}$
39. 15 **40.** $\frac{15}{64}$ **41.** $\frac{3}{7b}$ **42.** $\frac{7}{10x}$ **43.** $\frac{2}{3g}$
44. $\frac{3}{20t}$ **45.** $\frac{5}{16a}$ **46.** $1\frac{7}{8j}$ **47.** y **48.** $\frac{1}{4c}$
49. $\frac{1}{2z}$ **50.** $\frac{1}{5e}$ **51.** $\frac{3p}{5}$ **52.** $\frac{5}{6k}$ **53.** $\frac{1}{4h}$
54. $\frac{8}{15m}$ **55.** $\frac{7}{36f}$

CHAPTER 7

Pages 444–445

1. $\frac{25}{1}$ **2.** $\frac{3}{4}$ **3.** $\frac{30}{11}$ **4.** $\frac{1}{8}$ **5.** $\frac{1}{7}$ **6.** $\frac{12}{1}$ **7.** yes
8. no **9.** no **10.** yes **11.** 3 **12.** 42 **13.** 3
14. 4 **15.** 6 **16.** 7 **17.** 53% **18.** 10%
19. 91% **20.** 70% **21.** 87 lb **22.** 4.46
hours **23.** 234 miles **24.** 30% **25.** 37.5%
26. 93.75% **27.** 75% **28.** 24% **29.** 65%
30. 67% **31.** 70% **32.** 0.25 **33.** 0.32
34. 0.08 **35.** 0.55 **36.** 0.16 **37.** 0.43
38. 0.79 **39.** 0.81 **40.** 35% **41.** $3,528
42. 77% **43.** 96% **44.** 123 feet tall
45. $n = 16$

CHAPTER 8

Pages 446–447

1. 6 **2.** 40 **3.** 25 **4.** 3 **5.** 93 **6.** −15
7. −21 **8.** 9 **9.** −5 **10.** 32 **11.** > **12.** <
13. > **14.** = **15.** < **16.** 13 **17.** 10 **18.** 4
19. −9 **20.** 0 **21.** −14 **22.** −4 **23.** −4
24. −5 **25.** −8 **26.** 6 **27.** 3 **28.** −1
29. 20 **30.** −2 **31.** 5 **32.** 1 **33.** 4 **34.** −2
35. 5 **36.** 24 **37.** −18 **38.** −20 **39.** 49
40. 48 **41.** 54 **42.** −24 **43.** 35 **44.** −32
45. −45 **46.** 6 **47.** −2 **48.** −4 **49.** 1
50. 3 **51.** 8 **52.** −8 **53.** 6 **54.** −10 **55.** 4
56. −90 feet **57.** 477 feet **58.** 12°F
59. −3 or three points under par
60. 9 inches

CHAPTER 9

Pages 448–449

1. 5^5 **2.** $(-8)^3$ **3.** $(-t)^4$ **4.** c^4 **5.** 32
6. 1,225 **7.** −216 **8.** 6^7 **9.** 12^7 **10.** 7^2
11. $3 \cdot 3 = 3^2 = 9$ **12.** $x \cdot x = x^2$ **13.** 3,
rational **14.** 9, rational **15.** 4.464,
irrational **16.** 2.96, irrational **17.** 2.371,
irrational **18.** 5, rational **19.** 9 feet
20. 202.5 ft², 14.23 ft **21.** $m \cdot m \cdot m = m^3$
22. $7 \cdot 7 \cdot 7 = 7^3 = 343$ **23.** $9 \cdot 9 \cdot 9 =$
$9^3 = 729$ **24.** $\sqrt{10}$ is between 3 and 4
25. $\sqrt{37}$ is between 6 and 7 **26.** $\sqrt{47}$ is
between 6 and 7 **27.** $s = 7$ **28.** $s = 8.2$
29. $s = 44.7$ **30.** $t = 36$ **31.** $y = 64$
32. $x = 6$ **33.** $x = 4$ **34.** $x = 16$
35. $x = 36$ **36.** $r = 16.33$ in.
37. $r = 2.04$ in. **38.** 10 **39.** 15 **40.** 39

CHAPTER 10

Pages 450–451

1. 26.8 cm **2.** 17 ft **3.** 38.4 in.
4. 144 mm **5.** 625 mm² **6.** 25.5 in.²
7. 108 cm² **8.** 53.29 ft² **9.** 46.8 cm²
10. 82.5 m² **11.** 157.5 in.² **12.** 2,211 m²
13. cone **14.** cylinder **15.** rectangular
prism **16.** sphere **17.** 864 units²
18. 864 in.² **19.** 10,648 cm³ **20.** 70 in.³
21. 12,167 in.³ **22.** 11,610 in.³
23. $A = 94.2$ units² **24.** $A = 17,600$ ft²
25. 150.72 in.; 1,808.64 in.² **26.** 94.2 cm;
706.5 cm² **27.** 15,386 m³ **28.** 65.42 ft³
29. $V = 41.86$ in.³ **30.** $V = 228.67$ mm³

CHAPTER 11

Pages 452–453

1.

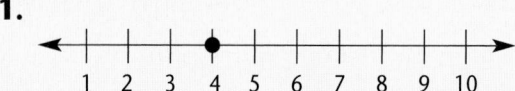

2.

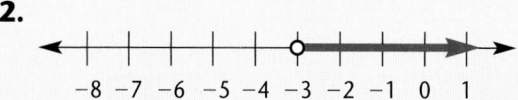

3.

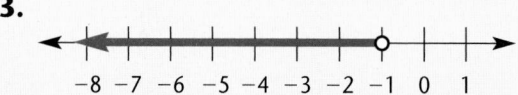

4.

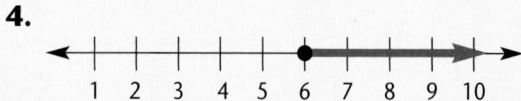

5.

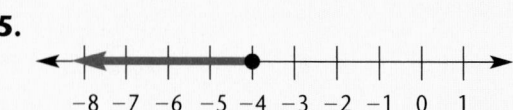

6.

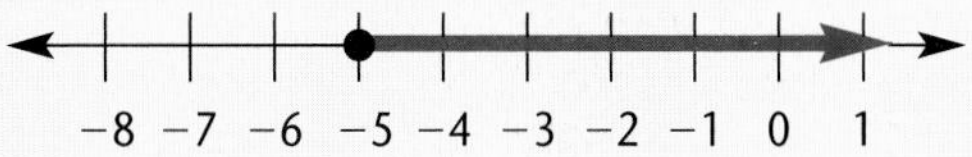

7. $x > -6$

8. $c \leq 8$

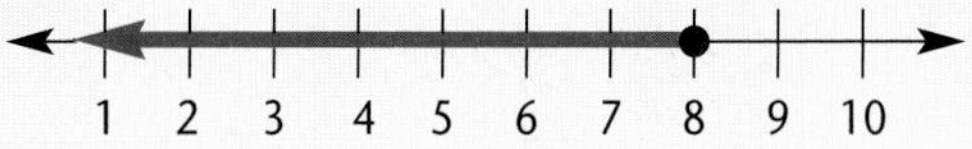

9. $j > -1$

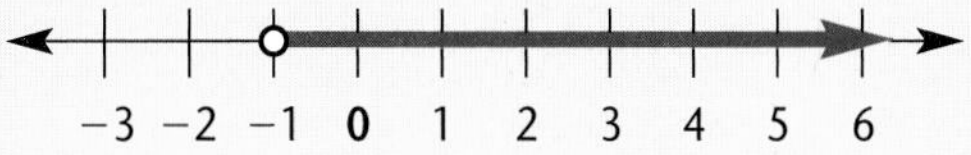

10. $t < 8$

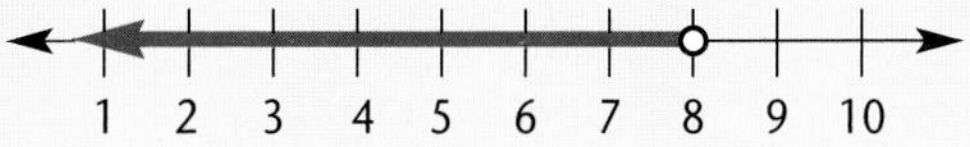

11. Quadrant III **12.** Quadrant I **13.** Quadrant IV **14.** (0, 4) **15.** (1, −3)

16–17.

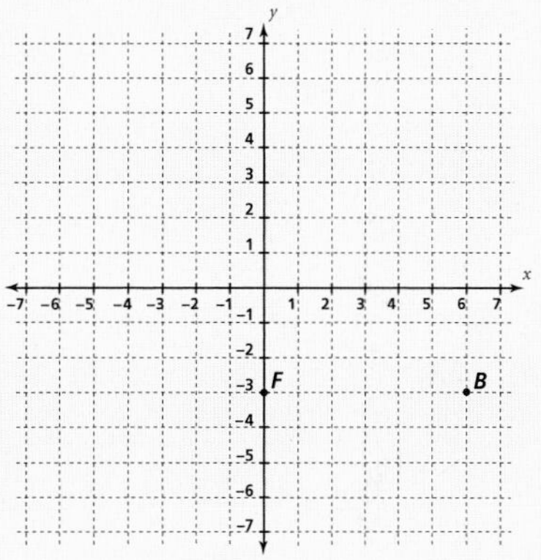

18. yes **19.** no **20.** $f(-3) = 42$; $f(3) = 30$ **21.** $f(-3) = 7$; $f(3) = -1$ **22.** range: −2, 7, 10, 25, 34 **23.** range: −33, −1, 2, 2, −6

24. domain: $-1 \leq x \leq 2$; range = 3

25. domain: $-4 \leq x \leq 2$; range: $-3 \leq y \leq 2$

26. $y = x + 2$

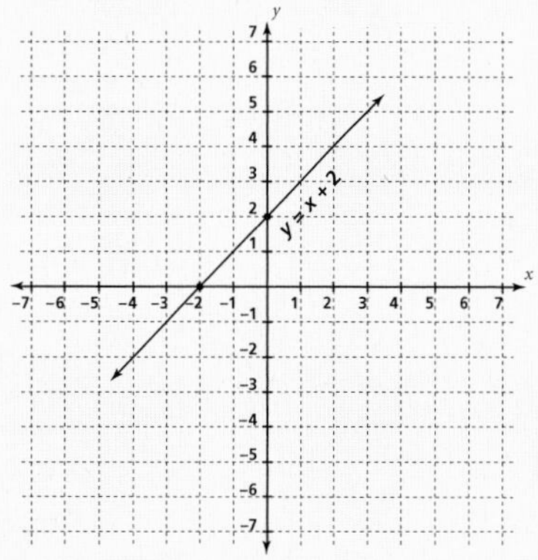

27. 2 **28.** 1 **29.** $y = 2x + 1$ **30.** $y = 3x + 5$

Mathematics: Pathways Selected Answers and Solutions **489**

Pages 454–455

1. 15° **2.** 30° **3.** 75° **4.** angles 2 and 4 **5.** angles 1 and 3; angles 2 and 4 **6.** 120° **7.** 65°; 155° **8.** 15°; 105° **9.** 1°; 91° **10.** 64° **11.** 59° **12.** isosceles triangle **13.** scalene triangle **14.** obtuse scalene triangle **15.** SSS **16.** ASA **17.** SAS **18.** yes **19.** no **20.** not enough information **21.** true **22.** true **23.** false **24.** false **25.** $A' = (1, -1)$ **26.** $B' = (2, -2)$ **27.** $C' = (4, 0)$ **28.** $D' = (-2, 3)$ **29.** $E' = (-3, -1)$ **30.** $F' = (-3, 0)$ **31.** no **32.** yes **33.** no **34.** $A' = (-5, 4)$ **35.** $B' = (-8, 1)$ **36.** $C' = (-9, 4)$ **37.** $(0, -1)$ **38.** $(-5, -4)$

39.

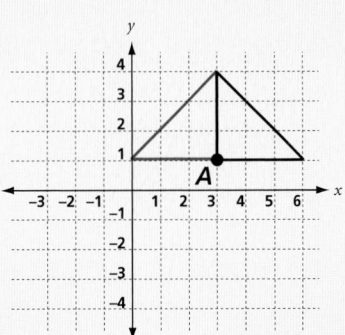

40.

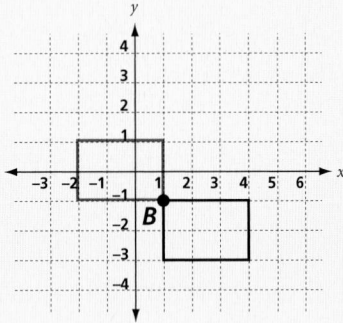

Pages 456–457

1.

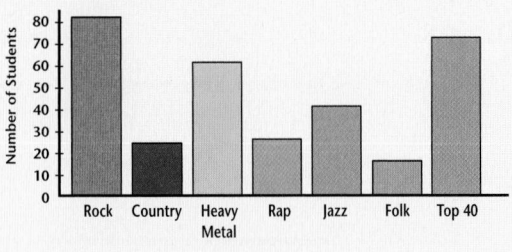

Type of Music Students Prefer the Most

2. Sales by Student Council

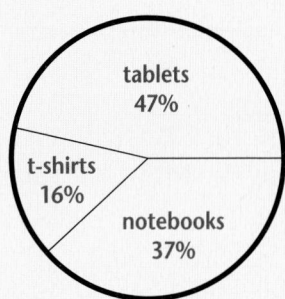

3. 36 items **4.** 17 items **5.** 8 **6.** 3.2 **7.** 3 **8.** 5 **9.** 23 and 29 **10.** $\frac{1}{2} = 0.50 = 50\%$ **11.** 6 **12.** yes **13.** $\frac{1}{2}$ (50%) **14.** The events are independent. Even though a new coin is used for each flip, the odds on each flip do not change. **15.** 24 ways

Calculator Practice

Although the symbols may differ depending on the calculator, most scientific calculators have keys that are useful in algebra. For example,

$\boxed{\sqrt{}}$ or $\boxed{\sqrt{x}}$ for square root; $\boxed{1/x}$ for reciprocals;

$\boxed{y^x}$, $\boxed{x^2}$, or $\boxed{\wedge}$ for powering;

$\boxed{\pi}$ for pi; and $\boxed{x!}$ for factorial;

$\boxed{\pm}$, $\boxed{+/-}$ or $\boxed{-}$ for changing the sign (positive or negative) of a number.

It is easy to use your calculator to help you do arithmetic. Check the display after you key in each number to make sure you have entered the number correctly.

To add:
Press 46 $\boxed{+}$ 31 $\boxed{=}$.
The display will read 77.
$46 + 31 = 77$

To subtract:
Press 84 $\boxed{-}$ 32 $\boxed{=}$.
The display will read 52.
$84 - 32 = 52$

To multiply:
Press 12 $\boxed{\times}$ 6 $\boxed{=}$.
The display will read 72.
$12 \cdot 6 = 72$

To divide:
Press 42 $\boxed{\div}$ 7 $\boxed{=}$.
The display will read 6.
$42 \div 7 = 6$

Use the $\boxed{(}$ and $\boxed{)}$ for expressions to be evaluated separately within another expression. For example, to find $8 \cdot (4 - 2)$, press 8 $\boxed{\times}$ $\boxed{(}$ 4 $\boxed{-}$ 2 $\boxed{)}$ $\boxed{=}$. The display will read 16.
$8 \cdot (4 - 2) = 16$.

Use the $\boxed{\sqrt{}}$ on your calculator to find the square root of a number. For example, to find the square root of 81, press 81 $\boxed{\sqrt{}}$. The display will read 9.

To find the squared value of a number, use $\boxed{x^2}$. For example, to find 12 squared, press 12 $\boxed{x^2}$. The display will read 144.

To raise a number to a specified power, use the $\boxed{y^x}$. For example, to find 5 to the third power, press 5 $\boxed{y^x}$ 3 $\boxed{=}$.
The display will read 125.

To find the decimal value of the reciprocal of the number, use $1/x$. For example, to find the reciprocal of 8, press 8 $1/x$. The display will read 0.125. The decimal for the reciprocal of 8 is 0.125.

To make a calculation including a fraction, use $a^{b/c}$. For example, to find the answer to $3 - \frac{3}{4}$, press 3 $-$ 3 $a^{b/c}$ 4 $=$. The display will read $2\frac{1}{4}$.

$$3 - \frac{3}{4} = 2\frac{1}{4}$$

A scientific calculator contains an exponential shift key EE or EXP. Use this key to enter numbers that are written in scientific notation.

- To multiply $3.64 \cdot 10^6$, press 3.64 EE 6 $=$. The display will read 3640000. The answer is 3,640,000.

- To divide $3.64 \cdot 10^6$ by $1.4 \cdot 10^{-5}$, press 3.64 EE 6 $\div$ 1.4 EE $+/-$ 5 $=$. The display will read $2.6 \; 11$, so the answer is $2.6 \cdot 10^{11}$, or 260,000,000,000.

To find the sine, cosine, or tangent of angles, use SIN, COS, or TAN. For example, to find the cosine of a 30° angle, press 30 COS. The display will read 0.866025404.

Sometimes you want to use the same number, or constant, in a series of calculations. You can store the number in memory. For example, suppose you want to find the answers to 18 • 4, 18 • 12, and 18 • 31.

- Press 18 STO 1. The number 18 is stored in memory 1.

- Press RCL 1 $\times$ 4 $=$. The display will read 72.

- Press RCL 1 $\times$ 12 $=$. The display will read 216.

- Press RCL 1 $\times$ 31 $=$. The display will read 558.

On some calculators, the key used to store a number in memory is $M+$ instead of STO. The key used to display the stored number is MR instead of RCL. On some calculators, you press ON/AC to clear the memory. On other calculators, you must press MC to clear the memory. Read the instructions for your calculator to find out how to store and recall numbers.

Decimal, Percent, and Fraction Conversion

Renaming Decimals as Percents

Example Rename 0.75 as a percent.

Solution 0.75

$0.75 = 75\%$

Step 1 Move the decimal point two places to the right.

Step 2 Then insert a percent symbol.

Example Rename 0.5 as a percent.

Solution $0.5 = .50$

$0.5 = 50\%$

Renaming Percents as Decimals

Example Rename 80% as a decimal.

Solution $80\% = 80.\%$

$80\% = 0.80$

$= 0.8$ ⟵ You can always drop zeros at the end of a decimal.

Step 1 Move the decimal point two places to the left.

Step 2 Then drop the percent symbol.

Renaming Fractions as Decimals

Example Rename $\frac{7}{20}$ as a decimal.

Solution **Method 1**

$$\frac{7}{20} = \frac{7 \times 5}{20 \times 5} = \frac{35}{100}$$

$$= 0.35$$

Choose a multiplier that makes the denominator a power of 10 (10, 100, 1,000, . . .)

Method 2

$$\frac{7}{20} = 20 \overline{)7.00}$$
$$\begin{array}{r} .35 \\ 20\overline{)7.00} \\ -6\,0 \\ \hline 1\,00 \\ -1\,00 \end{array}$$

Divide the numerator by the denominator.

Decimal, Percent, and Fraction Conversion

Renaming Decimals as Fractions

Example Rename 0.025 as a fraction.

Solution First, read the decimal: "25 thousandths."

Then write the fraction and simplify.

$$0.025 = \frac{25}{1,000} = \frac{25 \div 25}{1,000 \div 25} = \frac{1}{40}$$

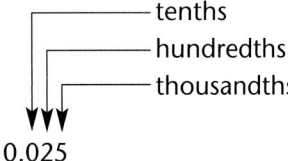

Renaming Fractions as Percents

Example Rename $\frac{9}{25}$ as a percent.

Solution **Method 1**

Write as an equivalent fraction with denominator 100.

$$\frac{9}{25} = \frac{9 \times 4}{25 \times 4} = \frac{36}{100} = 36\%$$

Percent means per 100.
So, 36 hundredths is 36%.

Method 2

$$\frac{9}{25} = 0.36 = 36\%$$

Step 1 Divide the numerator by the denominator.

Step 2 Rewrite the decimal as a percent.

Renaming Percents as Fractions

Example Rename 2% as a fraction.

Solution $2\% = \frac{2}{100}$ ◄── *Percent* means *per 100.*

$\quad\quad\quad = \frac{1}{50}$ ◄── Simplify.

Measurement Conversion Factors

Metric Measures

Length
1,000 meters (m) = 1 kilometer (km)
100 centimeters (cm) = 1 m
10 decimeters (dm) = 1 m
1,000 millimeters (mm) = 1 m
10 cm = 1 decimeter (dm)
10 mm = 1 cm

Area
100 square millimeters (mm^2) = 1 square centimeter (cm^2)
10,000 cm^2 = 1 square meter (m^2)
10,000 m^2 = 1 hectare (ha)

Volume
1,000 cubic meters (m^3) = 1 cubic centimeter (cm^3)
100 cm^3 = 1 cubic decimeter (dm^3)
1,000,000 cm^3 = 1 cubic meter (m^3)

Capacity
1,000 milliliters (mL) = 1 liter (L)
1,000 L = 1 kiloliter (kL)

Mass
1,000 kilograms (kg) = 1 metric ton (t)
1,000 grams (g) = 1 kg
1,000 milligrams (mg) = 1 g

Temperature Degrees Celsius (°C)
0°C = freezing point of water
37°C = normal body temperature
100°C = boiling point of water

Time
60 seconds (sec) = 1 minute (min)
60 min = 1 hour (hr)
24 hr = 1 day

Customary Measures

Length
12 inches (in.) = 1 foot (ft)
3 ft = 1 yard (yd)
36 in. = 1 yd
5,280 ft = 1 mile (mi)
1,760 yd = 1 mi
6,076 feet = 1 nautical mile

Area
144 square inches (sq in.) = 1 square foot (sq ft)
9 sq ft = 1 square yard (sq yd)
43,560 sq ft = 1 acre (A)

Volume
1,728 cubic inches (cu in.) = 1 cubic foot (cu ft)
27 cu ft = 1 cubic yard (cu yard)

Capacity
8 fluid ounces (fl oz) = 1 cup (c)
2 c = 1 pint (pt)
2 pt = 1 quart (qt)
4 qt = 1 gallon (gal)

Weight
16 ounces (oz) = 1 pound (lb)
2,000 lb = 1 ton (T)

Temperature Degrees Fahrenheit (°F)
32°F = freezing point of water
98.6°F = normal body temperature
212°F = boiling point of water

Measurement Conversion Factors

To change	To	Multiply by	To change	To	Multiply by
centimeters	inches	0.3937	meters	feet	3.2808
centimeters	feet	0.03281	meters	miles	0.0006214
cubic feet	cubic meters	0.0283	meters	yards	1.0936
cubic meters	cubic feet	35.3145	metric tons	tons (long)	0.9842
cubic meters	cubic yards	1.3079	metric tons	tons (short)	1.1023
cubic yards	cubic meters	0.7646	miles	kilometers	1.6093
feet	meters	0.3048	miles	feet	5,280
feet	miles (nautical)	0.0001645	miles (statute)	miles (nautical)	0.8684
feet	miles (statute)	0.0001894	miles/hour	feet/minute	88
feet/second	miles/hour	0.6818	millimeters	inches	0.0394
gallons (U.S.)	liters	3.7853	ounces avdp	grams	28.3495
grams	ounces avdp	0.0353	ounces	pounds	0.0625
grams	pounds	0.002205	pecks	liters	8.8096
hours	days	0.04167	pints (dry)	liters	0.5506
inches	millimeters	25.4000	pints (liquid)	liters	0.4732
inches	centimeters	2.5400	pounds avdp	kilograms	0.4536
kilograms	pounds avdp	2.2046	pounds	ounces	16
kilometers	miles	0.6214	quarts (dry)	liters	1.1012
liters	gallons (U.S.)	0.2642	quarts (liquid)	liters	0.9463
liters	pecks	0.1135	square feet	square meters	0.0929
liters	pints (dry)	1.8162	square meters	square feet	10.7639
liters	pints (liquid)	2.1134	square meters	square yards	1.1960
liters	quarts (dry)	0.9081	square yards	square meters	0.8361
liters	quarts (liquid)	1.0567	yards	meters	0.9144

Addition Table

+	0	1	2	3	4	5	6	7	8	9	10
0	0	1	2	3	4	5	6	7	8	9	10
1	1	2	3	4	5	6	7	8	9	10	11
2	2	3	4	5	6	7	8	9	10	11	12
3	3	4	5	6	7	8	9	10	11	12	13
4	4	5	6	7	8	9	10	11	12	13	14
5	5	6	7	8	9	10	11	12	13	14	15
6	6	7	8	9	10	11	12	13	14	15	16
7	7	8	9	10	11	12	13	14	15	16	17
8	8	9	10	11	12	13	14	15	16	17	18
9	9	10	11	12	13	14	15	16	17	18	19
10	10	11	12	13	14	15	16	17	18	19	20

Subtraction Table

−	0	1	2	3	4	5	6	7	8	9	10
0	0	−1	−2	−3	−4	−5	−6	−7	−8	−9	−10
1	1	0	−1	−2	−3	−4	−5	−6	−7	−8	−9
2	2	1	0	−1	−2	−3	−4	−5	−6	−7	−8
3	3	2	1	0	−1	−2	−3	−4	−5	−6	−7
4	4	3	2	1	0	−1	−2	−3	−4	−5	−6
5	5	4	3	2	1	0	−1	−2	−3	−4	−5
6	6	5	4	3	2	1	0	−1	−2	−3	−4
7	7	6	5	4	3	2	1	0	−1	−2	−3
8	8	7	6	5	4	3	2	1	0	−1	−2
9	9	8	7	6	5	4	3	2	1	0	−1
10	10	9	8	7	6	5	4	3	2	1	0

Note: To use this table, look at the numbers in the far left vertical column. Select a number from the vertical column. Then subtract from that number by selecting a number in the top horizontal row. The difference is listed where the column and row meet. For example, subtract 4 in the top horizontal row from 1 in the vertical column. The answer is −3, which is the number located where the column and row meet. You must subtract the numbers in the horizontal row from the numbers in the vertical column for this chart to work.

Multiplication Table

×	2	3	4	5	6	7	8	9	10	11	12
2	4	6	8	10	12	14	16	18	20	22	24
3	6	9	12	15	18	21	24	27	30	33	36
4	8	12	16	20	24	28	32	36	40	44	48
5	10	15	20	25	30	35	40	45	50	55	60
6	12	18	24	30	36	42	48	54	60	66	72
7	14	21	28	35	42	49	56	63	70	77	84
8	16	24	32	40	48	56	64	72	80	88	96
9	18	27	36	45	54	63	72	81	90	99	108
10	20	30	40	50	60	70	80	90	100	110	120
11	22	33	44	55	66	77	88	99	110	121	132
12	24	36	48	60	72	84	96	108	120	132	144

Division Table

÷1	÷2	÷3	÷4	÷5
$0 \div 1 = 0$	$0 \div 2 = 0$	$0 \div 3 = 0$	$0 \div 4 = 0$	$0 \div 5 = 0$
$1 \div 1 = 1$	$2 \div 2 = 1$	$3 \div 3 = 1$	$4 \div 4 = 1$	$5 \div 5 = 1$
$2 \div 1 = 2$	$4 \div 2 = 2$	$6 \div 3 = 2$	$8 \div 4 = 2$	$10 \div 5 = 2$
$3 \div 1 = 3$	$6 \div 2 = 3$	$9 \div 3 = 3$	$12 \div 4 = 3$	$15 \div 5 = 3$
$4 \div 1 = 4$	$8 \div 2 = 4$	$12 \div 3 = 4$	$16 \div 4 = 4$	$20 \div 5 = 4$
$5 \div 1 = 5$	$10 \div 2 = 5$	$15 \div 3 = 5$	$20 \div 4 = 5$	$25 \div 5 = 5$
$6 \div 1 = 6$	$12 \div 2 = 6$	$18 \div 3 = 6$	$24 \div 4 = 6$	$30 \div 5 = 6$
$7 \div 1 = 7$	$14 \div 2 = 7$	$21 \div 3 = 7$	$28 \div 4 = 7$	$35 \div 5 = 7$
$8 \div 1 = 8$	$16 \div 2 = 8$	$24 \div 3 = 8$	$32 \div 4 = 8$	$40 \div 5 = 8$
$9 \div 1 = 9$	$18 \div 2 = 9$	$27 \div 3 = 9$	$36 \div 4 = 9$	$45 \div 5 = 9$

÷6	÷7	÷8	÷9	÷10
$0 \div 6 = 0$	$0 \div 7 = 0$	$0 \div 8 = 0$	$0 \div 9 = 0$	$0 \div 10 = 0$
$6 \div 6 = 1$	$7 \div 7 = 1$	$8 \div 8 = 1$	$9 \div 9 = 1$	$10 \div 10 = 1$
$12 \div 6 = 2$	$14 \div 7 = 2$	$16 \div 8 = 2$	$18 \div 9 = 2$	$20 \div 10 = 2$
$18 \div 6 = 3$	$21 \div 7 = 3$	$24 \div 8 = 3$	$27 \div 9 = 3$	$30 \div 10 = 3$
$24 \div 6 = 4$	$28 \div 7 = 4$	$32 \div 8 = 4$	$36 \div 9 = 4$	$40 \div 10 = 4$
$30 \div 6 = 5$	$35 \div 7 = 5$	$40 \div 8 = 5$	$45 \div 9 = 5$	$50 \div 10 = 5$
$36 \div 6 = 6$	$42 \div 7 = 6$	$48 \div 8 = 6$	$54 \div 9 = 6$	$60 \div 10 = 6$
$42 \div 6 = 7$	$49 \div 7 = 7$	$56 \div 8 = 7$	$63 \div 9 = 7$	$70 \div 10 = 7$
$48 \div 6 = 8$	$56 \div 7 = 8$	$64 \div 8 = 8$	$72 \div 9 = 8$	$80 \div 10 = 8$
$54 \div 6 = 9$	$63 \div 7 = 9$	$72 \div 8 = 9$	$81 \div 9 = 9$	$90 \div 10 = 9$

Glossary

A

Absolute value (ab´ sə lüt val´ yü) the distance from zero of a number on a number line (p. 205)

$|-4|$ is read "the absolute value of negative 4."

$|-4| = 4$, 4 units from 0.

$|4| = 4$, 4 units from 0.

Acute (ə kyüt´) an angle less than 90° (p. 360)

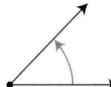

Acute triangle (ə kyüt´ trī´ ang gel) a triangle with three angles less than 90° (p. 370)

Addend (əd´ end) number to be added to another (p. 24)

$4 + 2 = 6$ **The numbers 4 and 2 are addends.**

Addition (ə dish´ ən) the arithmetic operation of combining two or more numbers to find a total (p. 6)

$3 + 5 = 8$

Adjacent angles (ə jā´ snt ang´ gəlz) two angles that have the same vertex and share a common side (p. 360)

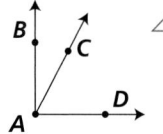

∠CAD is adjacent to ∠BAC.

Algebra (al´ jə brə) the branch of mathematics that uses both letters and numbers to show relations between quantities (p. 24)

Algebraic expression (al´ jə brā´ ik ek spresh´ ən) a mathematical statement that includes at least one operation and variable (p. 38)

$2x + 5$ $m \cdot 3$

Angle (ang´ gel) a figure made up of two sides or rays with a common endpoint (p. 254)

Area (âr´ ē ə) the number of square units inside a closed region (p. 238)

Arithmetic (ə rith´ mə tik) the study of the properties of numbers using four basic operations—addition, subtraction, multiplication, and division (p. 24)

B

Bar graph (bär graf) a way of comparing information using rectangular bars (p. 400)

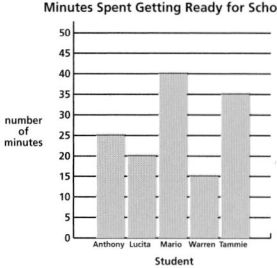

Base (bās) the number being multiplied; a factor (p. 232)

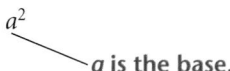

Base 2 (bās tü) a system of counting in powers of 2 (p. 10)

Base 5 (bās fīv) a system of counting in powers of 5 (p. 14)

Base 10 (bās ten) a system of counting based on groups of tens (p. 2)

Binary system (bī′ nər ē sis′ təm) a system of counting that uses only the numerals 0 and 1 (p. 10)

Box-and-whiskers plot (boks and wis′ kərz plot) a way to show the spread of data in a set of numbers (p. 418)

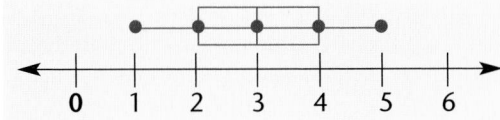

C

Circle graph (sėr′ kəl graf) a way to present information using the parts of a circle (p. 404)

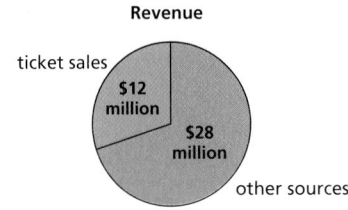

Circumference (sər kum′ fər əns) distance around a circle (p. 56)

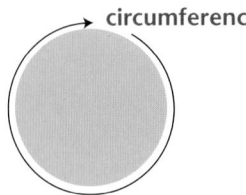

circumference

Common factor (kom′ ən fak′ tər) a number that will divide each of two or more numbers with no remainder (p. 82)

The common factor 9 and 12 is 3.

Compatible numbers (kəm pat′ ə bəl num′ bərs) two numbers that form a basic division fact (p. 34)

$16 \div 2 = 8$ **16 and 2 are compatible numbers.**

Complementary angles (kom plə men′ tər ē ang′ gəlz) two angles whose sum of their measures is 90 degrees (p. 362)

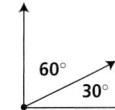 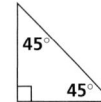

Complex fraction (kəm pleks′ frak′ shən) a fraction in which the numerator, the denominator, or both the numerator and the denominator are fractions (p. 152)

$$\frac{\frac{3}{8}}{5} \qquad \frac{10}{\frac{3}{5}} \qquad \frac{\frac{2}{3}}{\frac{1}{2}}$$

Composite number (kəm poz′ it num′ bər) a whole number that is not a prime number (p. 80)

$2 \cdot 2 \cdot 2 \cdot 2 = 16$ **16 is a composite number.**

Compounding period (kom pound′ ing pir′ ē əd) the amount of time that the interest rate is calculated (p. 192)

Compound interest (kom′ pound in′ tər ist) interest paid on both the original amount of money plus any interest added to date; compound interest is usually computed on deposits placed into savings accounts (p. 192)

Cone (kōn) a solid figure with a circular base connected to a vertex (p. 293)

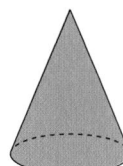

Congruent (kən grü′ ənt) figures that have the same size and shape (p. 372)

Consecutive (kən sek′ yə tiv) following one after the other in order (p. 208)

a	hat	e	let	ī	ice	ȯ	order	ủ	put	sh	she	ə	a	in about
ā	age	ē	equal	o	hot	oi	oil	ü	rule	th	thin		e	in taken
ä	far	ėr	term	ō	open	ou	out	ch	child	ᴙ	then		i	in pencil
â	care	i	it	ȯ	saw	u	cup	ng	long	zh	measure		o	in lemon
													u	in circus

Constant (kon´ stənt) a number in an expression that does not change, such as 2, −6, and $\frac{1}{3}$ in an expression such as $2x - 6y + \frac{1}{3}z$ (p. 142)

Coordinate system (kō ôrd´ n it sis´ təm) a way of using number lines to locate points on a plane or in space (p. 324)

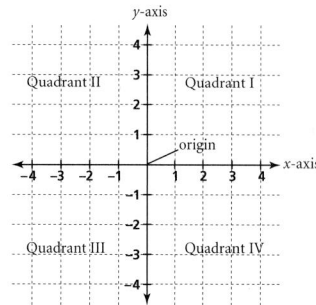

Corresponding angles (kôr ə spon´ ding ang´ gəlz) interior or exterior angles of figures in the same position as those of figures with the same shape (p. 374)

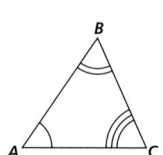 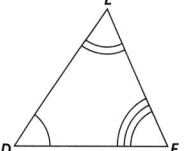

Cross product (krȯs prod´ əkt) the result of multiplying the denominator of one fraction with the numerator of another (p. 170)

If $\frac{a}{b} = \frac{c}{d}$, then the cross products are $a \cdot d$ and $b \cdot c$

Cube (kyüb) a solid with six square faces (p. 240)

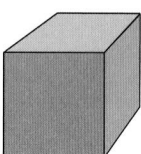

Cylinder (sil´ ən dər) a solid figure with two equal circular bases that are parallel (p. 293)

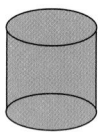

Data (dā´ tə) information given in numbers (p. 400)

Decimal (des´ ə məl) a number that has a decimal point in it (p. 48)

Decimal number (des´ ə məl num´ bər) a number written in base 10 (p. 2)

Decimal point (des´ ə məl point) a period that separates digits representing numbers that are one or more from digits representing numbers that are less than one (p. 48)

Denominator (di nom´ ə nā tər) the number below the fraction bar (p. 62)
$\frac{1}{2}$ 2 is the denominator.

Dependent event (di pen´ dənt i vent´) in a probability experiment, the outcome of one event is affected by the outcome of any other event (p. 423)

Dependent variable (di pen´ dənt vâr´ ē ə bəl) the value of the y variable that depends on the value of x (p. 334)

Diagonal (dī ag´ ə nəl) a line segment connecting two vertices that are not next to each other (p. 378)

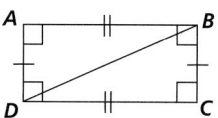

BD is a diagonal of rectangle *ABCD*.

Diameter (dī am´ ə tər) distance across a circle through the center (p. 56)

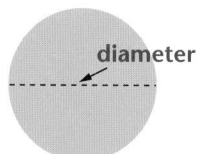

Difference (dif´ ər əns) the result of subtraction (p. 26)
$8 - 2 = 6$ 6 is the difference.

Digit (dig´ it) any one of the symbols 0, 1, 2, 3, 4, 5, 6, 7, 8, or 9 (p. 2)

Dimension (də men´ shən) the measure, such as length, width, or height, of the size of an object (p. 194)

Distributive property (dis trib′ yə tiv prop′ ər tē) numbers within parentheses can be multiplied by the same factor (p. 84)

$$4(2 + 1) = (4 \cdot 2) + (4 \cdot 1)$$

Dividend (div′ ə dend) the number that is divided (p. 32)

$$6 \div 3 = 2 \qquad \textbf{6 is the dividend.}$$

Divisible (də viz′ ə bəl) able to be divided by a whole number with no remainder (p. 76)

Division (də vizh′ ən) the arithmetic operation of finding how many times a number goes into another number (p. 8)

Divisor (də vī′ zər) the number that is used to divide (p. 32)

$$10 \div 5 = 2 \qquad \textbf{5 is the divisor.}$$

Domain (dō mān′) the dependent variables, or set of y-values, of a function (p. 336)

 E

Equality (i kwol′ ə tē) the state of being equal; shown by the equal sign (p. 314)

$$2 \cdot 2 = 4 \cdot 1$$

Equation (i kwā′ zhən) a mathematical sentence stating that two quantities are equal and written as two expressions separated by an equal sign (p. 146)

$$4n + 4n = 8n$$

Equiangular triangle (ē kwē ang′ gyə lər trī′ ang gəl) a triangle with three equal angles, each measuring 60° (p. 370)

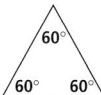

Equilateral triangle (ē kwə lat′ ər əl trī′ ang gəl) a triangle with three equal sides (p. 258)

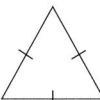

Equivalent (i kwiv′ ə lənt) the same in value (p. 172)

Equivalent fraction (i kwiv′ ə lənt frak′ shən) a fraction that has the same value as another fraction (p. 62)

$$\frac{4}{6} = \frac{2}{3}$$

Estimate (es′ tə māt) a careful guess; a close or nearly correct answer (p. 28)

Evaluate (i val′ yü āt) to find the numerical value of an algebraic expression (p. 40)

Expanded form (ek spand′ əd fôrm) numbers written to show the place value of each digit (p. 4)

Exponent (ek spō′ nənt) number that tells how many times another number is a factor (p. 4, 232)

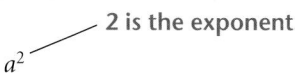

Expression (ek spresh′ ən) a mathematical statement that usually includes numbers, variables, and symbols (p. 36)

$$10 \div 5 = 2 \qquad 3n + 4 = 10$$

Exterior angle (ek stir′ ē ər ang′ gel) an angle formed by extending one side of a polygon at any vertex (p. 367)

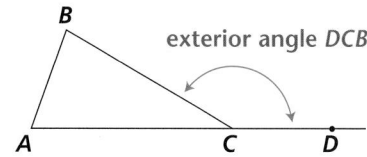

 F

Factor (fak′ tər) the numbers in a multiplication operation (p. 30)

$$4 \cdot 3 = 12 \qquad \textbf{4 and 3 are the factors.}$$

Formula (fôr′ myə lə) a combination of symbols used to state a rule (p. 52)

Fraction (frak′ shən) part of a whole number such as $\frac{1}{2}$ (p. 62)

Frequency (frē′ kwən sē) the number of times an event, value, or characteristic occurs (p. 402)

a	hat	e	let	ī	ice	ȯ	order	u̇	put	sh	she		a	in about
ā	age	ē	equal	o	hot	oi	oil	ü	rule	th	thin	ə	e	in taken
ä	far	ėr	term	ō	open	ou	out	ch	child	ᴛʜ	then		i	in pencil
â	care	i	it	ȯ	saw	u	cup	ng	long	zh	measure		o	in lemon
													u	in circus

Frequency table (frē´ kwən sē tā´ bəl) a chart showing the number of of items or number of times something happened (p. 402)

Frequency Table		
Interval	Tally	Frequency
0–9		0
10–19		0
20–29	ⲖⲖⲦ		6

Function (fungk´ shən) a rule that associates every *x*-value with one and only one *y*-value (p. 320)

Fundamental Law of Fractions (fun də men´ tl lȯ ov frak´ shənz) the value of a fraction does not change if its numerator and its denominator are multiplied by the same number (p. 106)

$$\frac{2}{3} = \frac{2}{3} \cdot \frac{5}{5} = \frac{10}{15}$$

Fundamental principle of counting (fun də men´ tl prin´ sə pəl ov koun´ ting) a general rule that states if one task can be completed *a* different ways, and a second task can be completed *b* different ways, the first task followed by the second task can be completed *a • b* or *ab* different ways (p. 426)

G

Geometry (jē om´ ə trē) the study of points, lines, angles, surfaces, and solids (p. 266)

Graph (graf) a diagram showing how one quantity depends on another (p. 246)

Graphing (graf´ ing) showing on a number line the relationship of a set of numbers (p. 314)

$$x = 3$$

Greatest common divisor (GCD) (grāt´ est kom´ ən də vī´ zər) the largest factor that two or more numbers or terms have in common (p. 82)

16: 1, 2, 4, 8, 16   **The GCD of 16**
20: 1, 2, 4, 5, 10, 20   **and 20 is 4.**

Greatest common factor (GCF) (grāt´ est kom´ ən fak´ tər) the largest factor of two or more numbers or terms (p. 83)

10 = 5 • 2   **The GCF of 10**
15 = 5 • 3   **and 15 is 5.**

H

Heptagon (hep´ tə gon) a seven-sided polygon (p. 271)

Hexagon (hek´ sə gon) a six-sided polygon (p. 270)

Histogram (his´ te gram) a bar graph that displays data in equal number groupings with no spaces between the bars (p. 406)

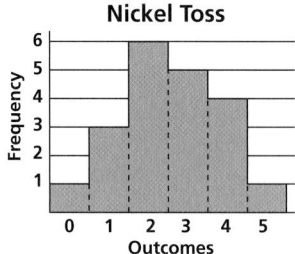

Horizontal (hôr ə zon´ tl) left to right or parallel to the horizon (p. 324)

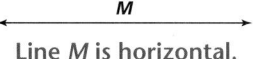

Line *M* is horizontal.

Hypotenuse (hī pot´ n üs) the longest side in a right triangle (p. 254)

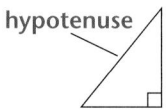

I

Image (im´ ij) reflection of an object (p. 382)

Improper fraction (im prop´ ər frak´ shən) a fraction in which the numerator is greater than or equal to the denominator (p. 102)

$$\frac{2}{2} \qquad \frac{6}{5}$$

Independent event (in di pen´ dənt i vent´) In a probability experiment, the outcome of any event does not affect the outcome of any other event (p. 424)

Independent variable (in di pen´ dənt vâr´ ē ə bəl) the value of *x* that determines the value of *y* (p. 334)

Inequality (in i kwol´ ə tē) two quantities that are not the same; shown by the less than, greater than, and unequal to signs (p. 316)
$$5 > 2 \quad 5 < 7 \quad 5 \neq 4$$

Integer (in´ tə jər) any positive or negative whole number including zero (p. 204)
$$(\ldots -2, -1, 0, 1, 2, \ldots)$$

Interest (in´ tər ist) the amount of money paid or received for the use of money (p. 66)

Interior angle (in tir´ ē ər ang´ gəl) any angle within a polygon (p. 367)

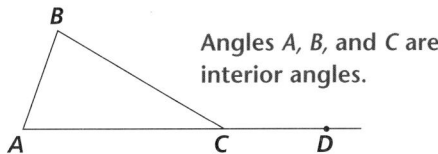

Angles *A*, *B*, and *C* are interior angles.

Intersection (in tər sek´ shən) a point at which two or more lines cross in a figure (p. 358)

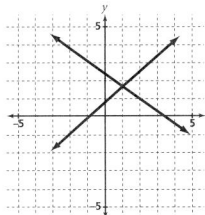

Interval (in´ tər vəl) set of all numbers between two stated numbers (p. 400)

Inverse (in vėrs´) exactly opposite (p. 6)

Inverse operation (in vėrs´ op ə rā´ shən) an operation that undoes another operation (p. 6)

Irrational number (i rash´ ə nəl num´ bər) a real number such as $\sqrt{2}$ that cannot be written in the form $\frac{a}{b}$ in which *a* and *b* are whole numbers and $b \neq 0$ (p. 246)

Irregular polygon (i reg´ yə lər pol´ ē gon) a polygon that is not uniform in shape or size (p. 274)

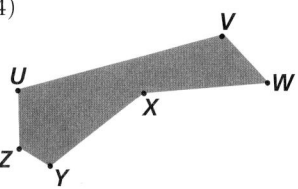

Isosceles triangle (ī sos´ ə lēz trī´ ang gəl) a triangle with two sides of equal length (p. 258)

L

Least common multiple (LCM) (lēst kom´ ən mul´ tə pəl) the smallest number divisible by all numbers in a group (p. 88)

4: 4, 8, *12*, . . .   **The LCM of 4 and 6**
6: 6, *12*, . . .   **is 12.**

Linear equation (lin´ ē ər i kwā´ zhən) an equation whose graph is a straight line (p. 330)

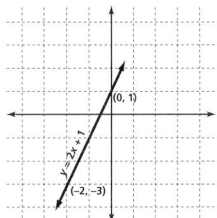

Line of symmetry (līn ov sim´ ə trē) reflection line of an object that leaves the object and the image in the same place (p. 386)

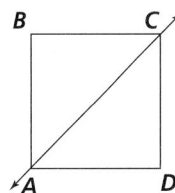

a	hat	e	let	ī	ice	ô	order	ù	put	sh	she		a	in about
ā	age	ē	equal	o	hot	oi	oil	ü	rule	th	thin	ə	e	in taken
ä	far	ėr	term	ō	open	ou	out	ch	child	ᴛʜ	then		i	in pencil
â	care	i	it	ȯ	saw	u	cup	ng	long	zh	measure		o	in lemon
													u	in circus

Lower extreme (lō´ ər ek strēm´) the least value of a set of data (p. 418)

{2, 3, 5, 6, 8, 9, 11}   **2 is the lower extreme.**

Lower quartile (lō´ ər kwȯr´ tīl) the median of scores below the median (p. 418)

{2, 3, 5, 6, 8, 9, 11}   **3 is the lower quartile.**

M

Mean (mēn) the sum of the values in a set of data divided by the number of pieces of data in the set (p. 410)

{2, 3, 5, 6, 8, 9, 11}   **6.3 is the mean.**

Measures of central tendency (mezh´ ərz ov sen´ trəl ten´ dən sē) the mean, median, and mode of a set of data (p. 414)

Median (mē´ dē ən) the middle value in an ordered set of data (p. 412)

{2, 3, 5, 6, 8, 9, 11}   **6 is the median.**

Mixed number (mikst num´ bər) an integer and a proper fraction (p. 102)

$$1\frac{3}{4} \qquad 5\frac{1}{2} \qquad 7\frac{2}{3}$$

Mode (mōd) the value or values that occur most often in a set of data (p. 414)

{2, 3, 5, 2}   **2 is the mode.**

Multiplication (mul tə plə kā´ shən) the arithmetic operation that adds a number a given amount of times (p. 8)

$$3 \cdot 5 = 15 \qquad 5 + 5 + 5 = 15$$

N

Negative integer (neg´ ə tiv in´ tə jər) a whole number less than zero (p. 204)

Numeral (nü´ mər əl) a symbol representing a number (p. 2)

Numerator (nü´ mə rā tər) the number above the fraction bar (p. 62)

$$\frac{1}{2} \qquad \text{1 is the numerator.}$$

Numerical expression (nü mer´ ə kəl ek spresh´ ən) a mathematical sentence that uses operations and numbers (p. 38)

$$3 + 2 \qquad 6 - 4 \qquad 12 \div 3 \qquad 5 \cdot 2$$

O

Obtuse (əb tüs´) an angle with a measure between 90 and 180 degrees (p. 360)

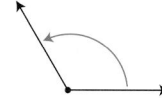

Obtuse triangle (əb tüs´ trī´ ang gəl) a triangle with one angle greater than 90° (p. 370)

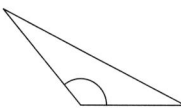

Octagon (ok´ tə gon) an eight-sided polygon (p. 271)

Open statement (ō´ pən stāt´ mənt) a sentence that is neither true nor false (p. 36)

$$6a = 30 \qquad 30 \div n = 5$$

Operation (op ə rā´ shən) addition, subtraction, multiplication, and division (p. 6)

Opposites (op´ ə zits) numbers the same distance from zero but on different sides of zero on the number line (p. 205)

4 and −4 are opposites.

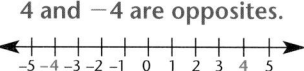

Ordered pair (ȯr´ dərd pâr) two real numbers that locate a point in a plane; the x is always first, the y is always second (p. 324)

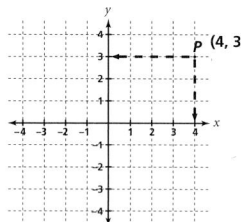

Order of operations (ô r´ dər ov op ə rā´ shəns) rules that describe the order addition, subtraction, multiplication, and division must be performed (p. 138)

Origin (ôr′ ə jin) the point at which the *x*-axis and *y*-axis in the coordinate system intersect (p. 324)

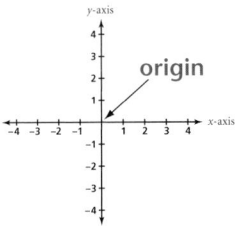

Outcome (out′ kum) a result of a probability experiment (p. 420)

 P

Parallel (par′ ə lel) lines that never meet and are in the same plane (p. 266)

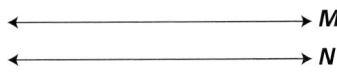

Lines *M* and *N* are parallel.

Parallelogram (par ə lel′ ə gram) a four-sided polygon with two pairs of equal and parallel sides (p. 284)

Pattern (pat′ ərn) a list of numbers, shapes, colors, and so on that repeats in such a way that the next item can be guessed (p. 330)

Pentagon (pen′ tə gon) a five-sided polygon (p. 270)

Percent (pər sent′) part per one hundred; hundredths (p. 66)

Perimeter (pə rim′ ə tər) the distance around the outside of a shape (p. 52)

Perpendicular (pėr pən dik′ yə lər) two intersecting lines forming right angles (p. 282)

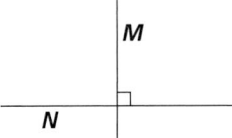

Lines *M* and *N* are perpendicular.

Pi (π) (pī) ratio of the circumference of a circle to its diameter; about 3.14 (p. 56)

Place value (plās val′ yü) worth of a digit based on its position in a number (p. 4)

Polygon (pol′ ē gon) a closed, many-sided figure that is made up of line segments (p. 266)

Positive integer (poz′ ə tiv in′ tə jər) a whole number greater than zero (p. 204)

Power (pou′ ər) the product of multiplying any number by itself once or many times (p. 232)
$$2^1 = 2 \quad 2^2 = 4 \quad 2^3 = 8 \quad 2^4 = 16$$
16 is the fourth power of 2

Power of 2 (pou′ ər ov fīv) the product of 2 multiplied by itself 1 or more times (p. 10)
$$2^1 = 2 \quad 2^2 = 4 \quad 2^3 = 8$$

Power of 5 (pou′ ər ov tü) the product of 5 multiplied by itself 1 or more times (p. 14)
$$5^1 = 5 \quad 5^2 = 25 \quad 5^3 = 125$$

Power of 10 (pou′ ər ov ten) a product of multiplying 10 by itself one or more times (p. 4)
$$10^1 = 10 \qquad 10^2 = 10 \cdot 10 = 100$$
$$10^3 = 10 \cdot 10 \cdot 10 = 1,000$$

Prime factorization (prīm fak tə rə zā′ shən) an expression showing a composite number as a product of its prime factors (p. 88)
$$15 = 3 \cdot 5 \qquad 55 = 5 \cdot 11$$

Prime number (prīm num′ bər) a whole number greater than one that has only 1 and itself as factors (p. 80)
$$7 = 7 \cdot 1$$

a	hat	e	let	ī	ice	ô	order	ů	put	sh	she		a	in about
ā	age	ē	equal	o	hot	oi	oil	ü	rule	th	thin	ə	e	in taken
ä	far	ėr	term	ō	open	ou	out	ch	child	ᴛʜ	then		i	in pencil
â	care	i	it	ó	saw	u	cup	ng	long	zh	measure		o	in lemon
													u	in circus

Prism (priz´ əm) a solid figure with two parallel bases that are polygons of the same shape and size (p. 292)

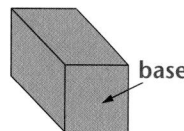

base

Probability (prob ə bil´ ə tē) the chance or likelihood of an event occurring (p. 420)

Product (prod´ əkt) the result of multiplication (p. 30)

$3 \cdot 4 = 12$ **12 is the product.**

Proper fraction (prop´ ər frak´ shən) a fraction in which the numerator is less than the denominator (p. 100)

$\frac{2}{3}$ $\frac{3}{4}$ $\frac{1}{5}$

Proportion (prə pôr´ shən) an equation made up of two equal ratios (p. 170)

$\frac{1}{2} = \frac{2}{4}$

Protractor (prō trak´ tər) a tool used to draw or measure angles (p. 358)

Pyramid (pir´ ə mid) a solid figure with a base that is a polygon and triangular sides (p. 292)

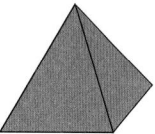

Pythagorean theorem (pə thag ə rē´ ən thē´ ər əm) a formula that states that in a right triangle, the length of the hypotenuse c squared is equal to the length of side a squared plus the length of side b squared (p. 254)

$c^2 = a^2 + b^2$

Q

Quadrant (kwäd´ rənt) one of four regions of a coordinate system bounded by the x-axis and y-axis (p. 324)

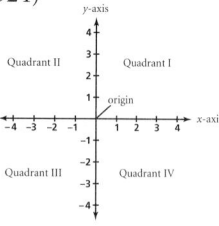

Quadrilateral (kwäd rə lat´ ər əl) a polygon with four sides (p. 267)

Quinary system (kwīnərē sis´ təm) a system of counting that uses only the numerals 0, 1, 2, 3, and 4; also known as base 5 (p. 14)

Quotient (kwō´ shənt) the result of division (p. 32)

$20 \div 5 = 4$ **4 is the quotient.**

R

Radical (rad´ ə kəl) a number that is written with the radical sign ($\sqrt{}$) (p. 248)

Radical sign (rad´ ə kəl sīn) the mathematical symbol ($\sqrt{}$) placed before a number or algebraic expression to indicate that the root should be found (p. 248)

$\sqrt[3]{8}$

Radius (rā´ dē əs) distance from the center of a circle to the edge of the circle (p. 288)

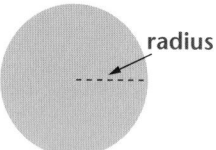

radius

Range (rānj) the dependent variables, or set of y-values, of a function (p. 336); the difference between the greatest and least values in a set of data (p. 416)

$\{2, 3, 5, 6\}$ $6 - 2 = 4$ **4 is the range.**

Ratio (rā´ shē ō) a comparison of two like quantities using a fraction (p. 168)

$\frac{a}{b}$ also $a:b$ or a to b

Rational expression (rash´ ə nəl ek spresh´ ən) an algebraic expression that can be written like a fraction (p. 156)

$\frac{5 + x}{3x}$

Rational number (rash´ ə nəl num´ bər) any number that can be represented by $\frac{a}{b}$ where a and b are integers and $b \neq 0$ (p. 102)

2 $\frac{1}{3}$ -3 $\frac{-2}{5}$

Ray (rā) part of a line—a ray has one endpoint and extends indefinitely in one direction (p. 358)

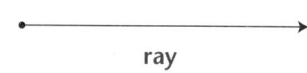

ray

Real number (rē′ əl num′ bər) any number on the number line (p. 204)

Reciprocal (ri sip′ rə kəl) the reciprocal of any non-zero number x is $\frac{1}{x}$, sometimes called the *multiplicative inverse* of that number (p. 128)

$\frac{1}{2}$ and 2 are reciprocals.

Rectangle (rek′ tang gəl) a four-sided polygon with four right angles and the opposite sides equal (p. 267)

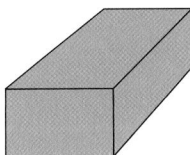

Rectangular prism (rek tang′ gyə lər priz′ əm) a solid figure with parallel faces and bases that are rectangles (p. 294)

Regular polygon (reg′ yə lər pol′ ē gon) a polygon in which each side and each angle has the same measure (p. 270)

Relationship (ri lā′ shən ship) a set of grouped pairs (p. 320)

$n > 16$ shows a relationship

Remainder (ri mān′ dər) amount left over when dividing (p. 32)

Rename (rē nām′) to give a new form that is equal to the original (p. 26)

Repeating decimal (ri pēt′ ing des′ ə məl) a decimal in which one or more digits repeat (p. 64)

$0.3333\ldots = 0.\overline{3}$

Rhombus (rom′ bəs) a four-sided polygon with two pairs of parallel and equal sides (p. 267)

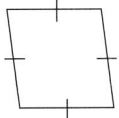

Right angle (rīt ang′ gəl) a 90° angle (p. 254)

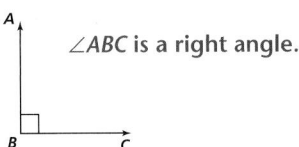

∠*ABC* is a right angle.

Right prism (rīt priz′ əm) prism in which the base and the sides are at right angles (p. 292)

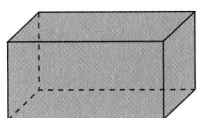

Right triangle (rīt trī′ ang gəl) a three-sided figure, or triangle, with one right, or 90°, angle (p. 254)

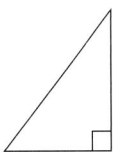

Root (rüt) an equal factor of a number (p. 242)

$\sqrt{25} = 5 \qquad \sqrt[3]{64} = 4$

Root of the equation (rüt ov ŦHə i kwā′ zhən) the number substituted for a variable that makes the equation a true statement (p. 146)

$3 + 6x = 15 \qquad x = 2$

Rotation (rō tā′ shən) transformation in which a geometric figure turns around a center without affecting its size or shape (p. 390)

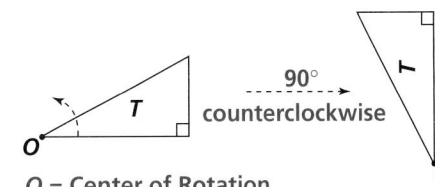

O = Center of Rotation

a	hat	e	let	ī	ice	ô	order	ú	put	sh	she	ə	a in about
ā	age	ē	equal	o	hot	oi	oil	ü	rule	th	thin		e in taken
ä	far	ėr	term	ō	open	ou	out	ch	child	ŦH	then		i in pencil
â	care	i	it	ò	saw	u	cup	ng	long	zh	measure		o in lemon
													u in circus

Scale drawing (skāl drô´ ing) a picture in which the relative sizes have been kept (p. 194)

Scalene triangle (skā lēn´ trī´ ang gəl) a triangle with no equal sides (p. 258)

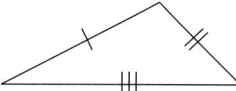

Scatterplot (skat´ ər plot) a graph in which the points plotted show the relationship between two variables (p. 408)

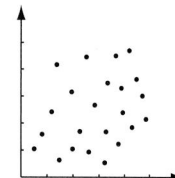

Scientific notation (sī ən tif´ ik nō tā´ shən) a number written as the product of a number between 1 and 10 and a power of 10 (p. 92)
$$5,432 = 5.432 \cdot 10^3$$

Similar (sim´ ə lər) figures that have the same shape but not the same size (p. 374)

Simplest form (sim´ plest fôrm) a fraction in which the only common factor of the numerator and denominator is 1 (p. 82)
$$\frac{1}{2} \qquad \frac{1}{4} \qquad \frac{2}{3}$$

Simplify (sim´ plə fī) combine like terms (p. 62)
$$2a + 3a = 5a$$

Slope (slōp) the measure of the steepness of a line, slope $= \frac{\text{rise}}{\text{run}}$ (p. 342)

Slope-intercept form (slōp in tər sept´ fôrm) the slope-intercept form of a line in which $m =$ slope and $b = y$-intercept is $y = mx + b$ (p. 348)

Solution (sə lü´ shən) the value of a variable that makes an open statement true (p. 314)

Sphere (sfir) a round solid figure in which all points on the surface are at an equal distance from the center (p. 293)

Square (skwâr) a four-sided shape with sides of equal length and four right angles (p. 238)

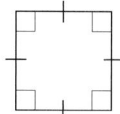

Square pyramid (skwâr pir´ ə mid) a solid figure with a square base and triangular sides (p. 302)

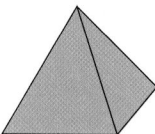

Square root (skwâr rüt) a factor of a power of two (p. 242)
$$\sqrt{16} = 4 \qquad 4^2 = 16$$
The square root of 16 is 4.

Statistics (stə tis´ tiks) numerical facts about people, places, or things (p. 400)

Substitute (sub´ stə tüt) to put a number in place of a variable (p. 40)

Subtraction (səb trak´ shən) the arithmetic operation of taking one number away from another (p. 6)
$$10 - 3 = 7$$

Sum (sum) the result of addition (p. 24)
$$6 + 4 = 10 \qquad \textbf{10 is the sum.}$$

Supplementary angles (sup lə men´ tər ē ang´ gəls) two angles whose sum of their measures is 180 degrees (p. 362)

Tally (tal′ ē) a mark of each count (p. 402)

Terms (tėrms) parts of an expression separated by operation signs such as +, −, •, or ÷ (p. 36)

$3x + 2x + x$ **3x, 2x, and x are terms.**

Tick (tik) a short line used to mark the sides of a triangle (p. 370)

Transformation (tran sfәr mā′ shәn) movement of a geometric figure from one location to another (p. 388)

Translation (tran slā′ shәn) transformation in which a geometric figure slides from one location to another without affecting its size or shape (p. 388)

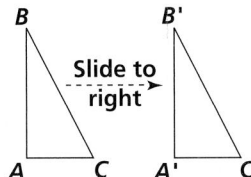

Trapezoid (trap′ ә zoid) a four-sided polygon with one pair of parallel sides and one pair of sides that are not parallel (p. 284)

Triangle (trī′ ang gәl) a closed figure with three sides (p. 254)

Upper extreme (up′ әr ek strēm′) the greatest value of a set of data (p. 418)

{2, 3, 5, 6, 8, 9, 11} **11 is the upper extreme.**

Upper quartile (up′ әr kwȯr′ tīl) the median of scores above the median (p. 418)

{2, 3, 5, 6, 8, 9, 11} **9 is the upper quartile.**

Variable (vâr′ ē ә bәl) a letter that represents an unknown number (p. 38)

$5x$ **x is the variable.**

Vertex (vėr′ teks) a common point opposite the base of a pyramid or cone (p. 292); a common point to both sides of an angle; the plural of vertex is vertices (p. 358)

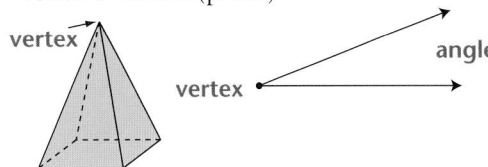

Vertical (vėr′ tә kәl) straight up and down (p. 324)

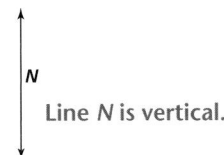

Line *N* is vertical.

Vertical angles (vėr′ tә kәl ang′ gәls) pairs of opposite angles formed by intersecting lines. Vertical angles have the same measure. (p. 360)

Angles *a* and *b* are vertical angles.

Vertical line test (vėr′ tә kәl līn test) a way of determining whether a graph is a function; if a vertical line intersects a graph at more than 1 point, the graph is not a function (p. 334)

Volume (vol′ yәm) the number of cubic units that fills the interior of a solid (p. 240)

a	hat	e	let	ī	ice	ȯ	order	u̇	put	sh	she	ə	a	in about
ā	age	ē	equal	o	hot	oi	oil	ü	rule	th	thin		e	in taken
ä	far	ėr	term	ō	open	ou	out	ch	child	ᴛʜ	then		i	in pencil
â	care	i	it	ȯ	saw	u	cup	ng	long	zh	measure		o	in lemon
													u	in circus

Whole number (hōl num´ bər) a number such as 0, 1, 2, 3, 4, 5, 6, . . . (p. 24)

***x*-axis** (eks´ ak sis) the horizontal, or left-to-right, axis in a coordinate system (p. 324)

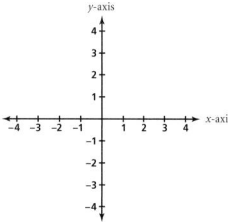

***x*-intercept** (eks´ in tər sept´) the point at which a line crosses or intersects the *x*-axis (p. 348)

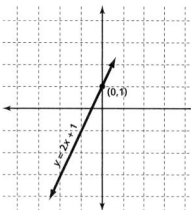

$-\frac{1}{2}$ **is the *x*-intercept.**

***x*-value** (eks val´ yü) the value of a given point on a horizontal number line on a coordinate plane; the first number in an ordered pair of coordinates (p. 408)

***y*-axis** (wī´ ak sis) the vertical, or up-and-down, axis in a coordinate system (p. 324)

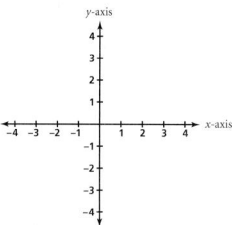

***y*-intercept** (wī´ in tər sept´) the point at which a line crosses or intersects the *y*-axis (p. 348)

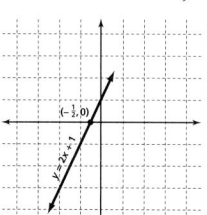

1 is the *y*-intercept.

***y*-value** (wī val´ yü) the value of a given point on a vertical number line on a coordinate plane; the second number in an ordered pair of coordinates (p. 408)

Index

Multiplication
of decimals, 56–57
by powers of 10, 54–55
defined, 8
distributive property of, 84–87
with exponents, 234–35
of fractions and mixed numbers, 126–27
of positive and negative integers, 220–23
of rational expressions, 160–61
of terms with exponents, 234–35
of whole numbers, 8, 30–31

N

Negative integers, 204–07
addition of, 214–15
defined, 204
division of positive and, 224–25
multiplication of positive and, 220–23
subtraction of, 216–19
Number line, 204–07, 314–23
comparing integers, 208–09
Numbers
compatible, 34
composite, 80–81
irrational, 246–49
mixed, 102–05, 113–31
perfect, 94
prime, 80–81
rational, 102–05
real, 204–07
with exponents, 234–37
Number systems
base 2, 10–13
base 5, 14–17
base 10, 2–3
Numeral
defined, 2
Numerator, 100–11
defined, 62
Numerical expression, 38–39
defined, 38

O

Obtuse
angles, 360–61
defined, 360
triangles, 370–71
defined, 370
Octagons
perimeter of, 271

Open statements
defined, 36
Operations
defined, 6
Opposites
defined, 205
Ordered pair
defined, 324
Order of operations, 138–41
defined, 138
Ordering fractions, 112–15
Origin
defined, 324
Outcome, 420–25
defined, 420

P

Parallel
defined, 266
Parallelograms, 376–77
area of, 284–85
defined, 284
Pattern, 42, 330
defined, 330
Pentagon
perimeter of, 270
Percents
and decimals, 66–67, 182–85
defined, 66
finding, 186–89
formulas and, 192–93
and fractions, 178–81
of increase and decrease, 190–91
renaming to decimals, 66–67
Perfect numbers, 94
Perimeter
defined, 52
of equilateral triangle, 270–73
of a hexagon, 270–73
of irregular polygons, 274–77
of a pentagon, 270–73
of polygons, 266–77
of a rectangle, 267–69
of regular polygons, 270–73
of a rhombus, 267–69
of a square, 270–73
of a triangle, 266–69
Perpendicular
defined, 282

Reciprocals, 128–31
   defined, 128
Rectangles
   area of, 278–81
   defined, 267
   perimeter of, 267–69
Rectangular prism
   surface area of, 294
Reflection, 382–87
Regular polygons
   defined, 270
   perimeter of, 270–73
Relationship
   defined, 320
Remainder
   defined, 32
Rename
   defined, 26
   percents to decimals, 66–67
Repeating decimals, 64–65
   defined, 64
Rhombus
   defined, 267
   perimeter of, 267
Right angle, 254–57
   defined, 254
Right prism
   defined, 292
   surface area of, 295
Right triangle, 254–57, 370–71
   defined, 254
Roots, 242–57
   defined, 242
Root of the equation
   defined, 146
Rotation, 390–93
   defined, 390

S

Scale drawings, 194–97
   defined, 194
Scalene triangles, 258–59, 370–71
   defined, 258
Scatterplots, 408–09
   defined, 408
Scientific notation, 92–93
   defined, 92
Similar
   defined, 374
   triangles, 374–75

Simplest form, 110–11
   defined, 82
Simplify
   defined, 62
   rational expressions, 156–59
Slides, 388–89
Slope-intercept form, 348–51
   defined, 348
Slopes, 342–51
   defined, 342
   formula for slope of a line, 344–47
   graphing, 342–47
Solid figures, 292–308
Solutions
   defined, 314
   of equalities, 314–15, 320–21
   of inequalities, 316–19, 322–23
Solving equations,
   by substitution, 146–47
   using addition, 150–51
   using subtraction, 148–49
Spheres
   defined, 293
   volume of, 306–07
Square root, 242–57
   defined, 242
Squares, 238–39
   area of, 238–39
   defined, 238
   perimeter of, 270–73
Statistics
   defined, 400
Substitute
   defined, 40
Subtraction
   of decimals, 52–53
   defined, 6
   of fractions, 124–25
   of positive and negative integers, 216–19
   of rational expressions, 158–59
   of whole numbers, 6, 26–27
Sums
   defined, 24
   estimating, 28–29
Supplementary angles, 362–65
   defined, 362
Surface areas, 294–301
Symmetries, 386–87

Mathematics: Pathways   *Index*   **523**

Photo Credits

Cover, © PunchStock; p. xx, © Nick Koudis/ PhotoDisc; p. 13, © Spencer Grant/PhotoEdit; p. 22, © Photri-Microstock; p. 29, © Charles Krebs/Stone; p. 42, © Mug Shots/Corbis; p. 46, © Steve Cole/PhotoDisc; p. 63, © Michael Newman/PhotoEdit; p. 67, © David Young-Wolff/PhotoEdit; p. 70 © Loubat-Petit/Photo Researchers, Inc.; p. 74, © T. E. Adams/Visuals Unlimited; p. 87, © Bob Daemmrich/Stock Boston; p. 91, © David Madison/Stone; p. 94, © Mark Burnett/Stock Boston; pp. 98 and 115, © David Young-Wolff/PhotoEdit; p. 131, © Ed Bock/Corbis; p. 136, © Corbis; p. 151, © V. C. L./Taxi; p. 159, © Bachmann/ Photo Researchers, Inc., p. 162, © Tim Davis/Photo Researchers, Inc.; p. 166, © Benjamin Shearn/Taxi; p. 177, © Aaron Haupt/Stock Boston; p. 185, ©Will Hart/PhotoEdit; p. 198, © Christopher Bissell/Stone; p. 202, © Fred Bavendam/Minden Pictures; p. 207, © Skjold/ Photri-Microstock; p. 215, © Stuart Williams/ Dembinsky Photo Associates; p. 219, © Francisco Cruz/SuperStock International; p. 223, © Bob Daemmrich/Stock Boston; p. 226, © RO-MA Stock/Index Stock Imagery; p. 230, © Cathy Melloan/PhotoEdit; p. 239, © Myrleen Ferguson Cate/PhotoEdit; p. 252, © Kim Golding/Stone; p. 260, © Roger Smith/Index Stock Imagery; p. 264, © J Silver/SuperStock International; p. 273, © Science VU(c)NGDC/Visuals Unlimited; p. 281, © Bob Daemmrich/Stock Boston; p. 302, © V. C. L./Taxi; p. 305, © Mark Burnett/Stock Boston; p. 312, © Steve Allen/ Brand X Pictures/Alamy.com; pp. 321 and 323, © David Young-Wolff/PhotoEdit; p. 352, © Joaquin Palting/SuperStock International; p. 356, © Craig Aurness/Corbis; pp. 371 and 382, © IFA Bilderteam/eStock Photo; p. 394, © John Wells/Science Photo Library/Photo Researchers, Inc.; p. 398, © Steve Bronstein/Image Bank; p. 401, © Gibson Stock Photography; p. 417, © Carr Clifton/Minden Pictures

Midterm Mastery Test

Chapters 1–7 Midterm Mastery Test

Directions Circle the letter of the correct answer.

1. Evaluate $\frac{4}{x} + x$ when $x = 3$.
   A 12
   B $4\frac{1}{3}$
   C $1\frac{1}{3}$
   D $\frac{7}{3}$

2. What is the greatest common divisor of 49 and 35?
   A 1
   B 49
   C 7
   D 35

3. Find the difference. $\frac{2x}{3} - \frac{x}{2}$
   A $\frac{x}{1}$
   B $\frac{x}{6}$
   C $\frac{x}{3}$
   D $\frac{x}{2}$

4. Find the quotient. $2.4 \div 0.3$
   A 80
   B 0.8
   C 8
   D 0.72

5. Write 4,901 in expanded form using the powers of ten.
   A $(4 \times 10^3) + (9 \times 10^2) + (0 \times 10^1) + (1 \times 1)$
   B $(4 \times 1000) + (9 \times 100) + (0 \times 0) + (1 \times 1)$
   C $(4 \times 10^3) + (9 \times 10^2) + (0 \times 10^1) + (1 \times 0)$
   D $(4 \times 10^3) + (9 \times 10^2) + (0 \times 10^1) + (1 \times 10^0)$

6. Solve for x. $15 - x = 8$
   A 23
   B −15
   C 7
   D −7

7. What is the least common multiple of 30 and 42?
   A 6
   B 120
   C 30
   D 210

8. Change 111_{10} to a base 2 number.
   A 1101111_2
   B 1110000_2
   C 1101110_2
   D 111_2

9. Solve for n in the proportion $\frac{3}{n} = \frac{12}{28}$.
   A $n = 28$
   B $n = 12$
   C $n = 7$
   D $n = 3$

10. Change 629_{10} to a base 5 number.
    A 10204_5
    B 1354_5
    C 100004_5
    D 10004_5

Mathematics: Pathways

Midterm Mastery Test Page 1

Chapters 1–7 Midterm Mastery Test, continued

Directions Solve for x.

11. $x - \frac{5}{12} = \frac{1}{6}$ _____

Directions Name the value of the underlined digit.

12. 7,2<u>3</u>1,584 _____

Directions Rewrite in vertical form and add. Check using the inverse operation.

13. $676 + 3,271 =$ _____

Directions Find the quotient. Check using the inverse operation.

14. $128 \div 4$ _____

Directions Change to a base 10 number.

15. 11010111_2 _____

16. 1000033_5 _____

Directions Find each sum, difference, product, or quotient. If possible, express your answer in simplest form.

17. $8)\overline{120c}$ _____

18. $\frac{3}{5} + \frac{1}{5}$ _____

19. $\frac{3}{4} \div \frac{7}{8}$ _____

20. $34.1 - 7.08$ _____

21. $10.4 \times 1.2y$ _____

22. $1\frac{1}{4} \times \frac{1}{4}$ _____

23. $\frac{3m}{7} \times 1\frac{1}{3}$ _____

24. $\frac{11n}{15} - \frac{3n}{5}$ _____

Directions Write two equivalent fractions for this pair of figures.

25.

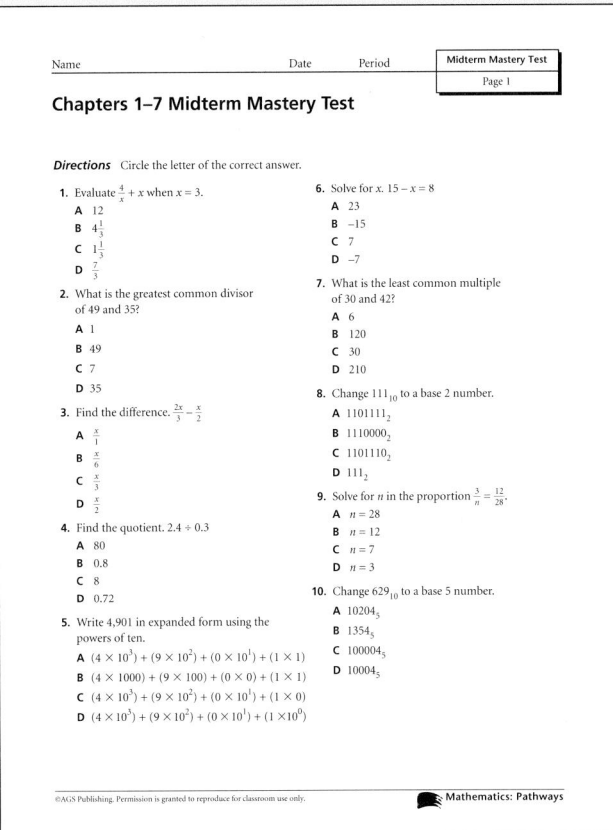

_____

Mathematics: Pathways

Midterm Mastery Test Page 2

Chapters 1–7 Midterm Mastery Test, continued

Directions Estimate each sum, difference, product, or quotient.

26. 49×71 _____

27. $20,308 + 9,895$ _____

28. $5,991 - 1,047$ _____

29. $607 \div 31$ _____

Directions Solve for x. Write your answer in simplest form.

30. $100 = 63 + x$ _____

Directions Round to the indicated place.

31. 3.905 (hundredth) _____

Directions Write the number in scientific notation.

32. 0.000035065 _____

Directions Write an algebraic expression.

33. The product of thirteen and some number. _____

34. Four less than some number. _____

Directions Rename each percent as a decimal or each decimal as a percent.

35. 6% _____

36. 7.41 _____

Directions Factor each expression.

37. $4x + 12y$ _____

38. $cd + de$ _____

Directions Compare. Write > or <.

39. $\frac{5}{8} \square \frac{7}{12}$ _____

Mathematics: Pathways

Midterm Mastery Test Page 3

Chapters 1–7 Midterm Mastery Test, continued

Directions Solve each problem.

40. 25% of 52 is what number? _____

41. 120% of 200 is what number? _____

42. Miguel needs gasoline for his lawnmower. There are two containers in the garage. The smaller container holds 4 gallons. The ratio between the two containers is 1:3. How much gasoline can the larger container hold?

_____

43. An airplane has a speed of 510 mph. The flight is 3 hours long. How many miles did the airplane travel?

_____

44. A map has a scale of $\frac{1}{2}$ in. = 5 miles. Two cities are $6\frac{1}{2}$ in. apart. How far apart are they in miles?

_____

Directions Simplify the complex fraction. Write your answer in simplest form.

45. $\frac{\frac{3}{8}}{\frac{5}{6}}$ _____

Mathematics: Pathways

Midterm Mastery Test Page 4

Final Mastery Test

Chapters 1–13 Final Mastery Test

Directions Circle the letter of the correct answer.

1. Divide $3.2 \div 0.4$.
   - **A** 8
   - **B** 0.8
   - **C** 80
   - **D** 0.08

2. Write 6,025 in expanded form.
   - **A** $(6 \times 10^3) + (0 \times 10^2) + (2 \times 10^1) + (5 \times 10^0)$
   - **B** $(6 \times 1{,}000) + (0 \times 100) + (2 \times 10) + (5 \times 1)$
   - **C** $(6 \times 1{,}000) + (0 \times 0) + (2 \times 10) + (5 \times 1)$
   - **D** $(6 \times 100) + (0 \times 10) + (2 \times 1) + (5 \times 0)$

3. Find the product. $6(-4)$
   - **A** −10
   - **B** 10
   - **C** 24
   - **D** −24

4. Find the sum. $\frac{5}{16} + \frac{3}{16}$ Choose the answer in simplest form.
   - **A** $\frac{8}{16}$
   - **B** $\frac{8}{32}$
   - **C** $\frac{1}{2}$
   - **D** $\frac{1}{4}$

5. Find the product. $\frac{m}{2} \cdot \frac{5}{6}$ Choose the answer in simplest form.
   - **A** $\frac{m}{30}$
   - **B** $\frac{m}{6}$
   - **C** $\frac{5m}{12}$
   - **D** $\frac{m}{2}$

6. Find the square root of 225, and identify it as rational or irrational.
   - **A** 15, irrational
   - **B** 25, rational
   - **C** 15, rational
   - **D** 25, irrational

7. Solve $\frac{5}{8} = \frac{x}{24}$ for x.
   - **A** $x = 15$
   - **B** $x = 8$
   - **C** $x = 24$
   - **D** $x = 5$

8. Round 0.0184 to the thousandths place.
   - **A** 1,840
   - **B** 0.02
   - **C** 0.18
   - **D** 0.018

9. Evaluate the function. Use $x = -2$ and 3 for $f(x) = 3x^2 + x$.
   - **A** 10 and 30
   - **B** −10 and 30
   - **C** 14 and 30
   - **D** −10 and 30

10. Simplify the expression $2(12 - 7) + 3 \cdot 4$ using order of operations.
    - **A** 52
    - **B** 22
    - **C** −72
    - **D** 64

11. Express 25,000 in scientific notation.
    - **A** 250×10^2
    - **B** 2.5×10^3
    - **C** 2510×10
    - **D** 2.51×10^4

12. Two 6-sided number cubes are rolled. What is the probability of getting a 6 on either cube?
    - **A** 1 out of 2 $\left(\frac{1}{2}\right)$
    - **B** 2 out of 6 $\left(\frac{2}{6}\right)$
    - **C** 1 out of 12 $\left(\frac{1}{12}\right)$
    - **D** 2 out of 12 $\left(\frac{2}{12}\right)$

13. 2 is what percent of 25?
    - **A** 8%
    - **B** 12.5%
    - **C** 0.08%
    - **D** 10%

14. Find the product. $(-2)(7)$
    - **A** 14
    - **B** 9
    - **C** −14
    - **D** 5

15. Find the difference. $-3 - (-6)$
    - **A** 3
    - **B** −9
    - **C** 9
    - **D** −3

Mathematics: Pathways

Final Mastery Test Page 1

Chapters 1–13 Final Mastery Test, continued

Directions Solve each problem.

16. Name the value of the underlined digit: 8,9̲00,831 _____

17. Subtract $427 - 318$. Check using the inverse operation. _____

18. Change 105_{10} to a base 2 number. _____

19. Change 105_{10} to a base 5 number. _____

Directions Find each sum, difference, product, or quotient. Whenever possible, express your answer in simplest form.

20. $\frac{2}{3} \div \frac{1}{2}$ _____

21. 6.1×0.23 _____

22. $\frac{3x}{4} - \frac{x}{3}$ _____

23. $1.04 + 130.82$ _____

Directions Estimate each sum, difference, product, or quotient.

24. $10{,}849 - 7{,}091$ _____

25. 81×39 _____

26. $402 \div 81$ _____

27. $2{,}133 + 2{,}985$ _____

Directions Solve each problem.

28. Compare $\frac{3}{4} \,\square\, \frac{5}{7}$. Write >, <, or =. _____

29. Simplify $59 - 20 \cdot 2 + 18 \div 9$ using the order of operations. _____

30. Write the place *and* the value of the underlined digit: $87.\underline{3}$ _____

31. Is 52 a prime or composite number? _____

32. How many three-digit numbers can be formed using the digits 1, 2, and 3? (In any number, a digit may not be used more than once.) _____

33. Factor $18 + 12b$. _____

34. Find the LCM of 36 and 24. _____

35. A ladder is 8 feet tall. The ladder can extend 2 times its original length. How high can the ladder extend? _____

36. Jenny ran a 10-mile race in $1\frac{1}{2}$ hours. On average, how fast did she run? _____

Mathematics: Pathways

Final Mastery Test Page 2

Chapters 1–13 Final Mastery Test, continued

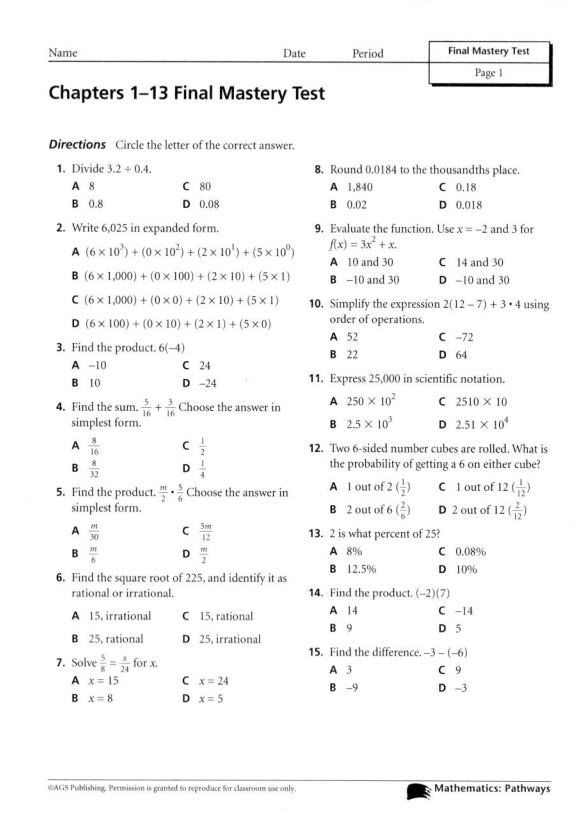

37. An architect creates a scale model of a building. The model is 5 feet tall. The ratio of the height of the model to the height of the real building is 1 foot = 30 feet. How tall is the real building? _____

38. Find the sum of $10 + (-5)$. _____

39. Evaluate $4m + 3m$ when $m = 3$. _____

40. The temperature was $-11°$ F yesterday and $5°$ F today. How much did the temperature increase? _____

Directions Write a fraction in simplest form and a percent to describe the shaded area of the figure.

41. _____

Directions Solve the equation for x.

42. $9 + \sqrt{2x} = 13$ _____

Directions Find the measurements for each figure. Use 3.14 for π.

43. 7.5 m

perimeter = _____
area = _____

44. 12 in.

circumference = _____
area = _____

45. 8 in.

volume = _____

Directions Find the surface area of the following objects. Use $\pi = 3$. Round your answers to the nearest hundredth.

46. _____   10 in.   2 in.

47. _____   17 mm   4 mm   13 mm

48. _____ $1\frac{1}{2}$ mm   9 mm

49. _____   7 ft   4 ft   10 ft

Mathematics: Pathways

Final Mastery Test Page 3

Chapters 1–13 Final Mastery Test, continued

Directions Find the volume of each of the following objects. Use $\pi = 3$. Round your answers to the nearest hundredth.

50. _____   22 mm   4 mm

51. _____   4 ft

Use this coordinate system for problems 52–55.

Directions Identify the quadrant in which each of these points is located.

52. Point N _____

53. Point T _____

Directions Write an ordered pair to describe the location of each point.

54. Point Q _____

55. Point G _____

Directions Determine the range for the function with the given domain.

56. $f(x) = 2x - x^2$ domain: −3, 1, 3, 6, 10   range: _____

Mathematics: Pathways

Final Mastery Test Page 4

Final Mastery Test

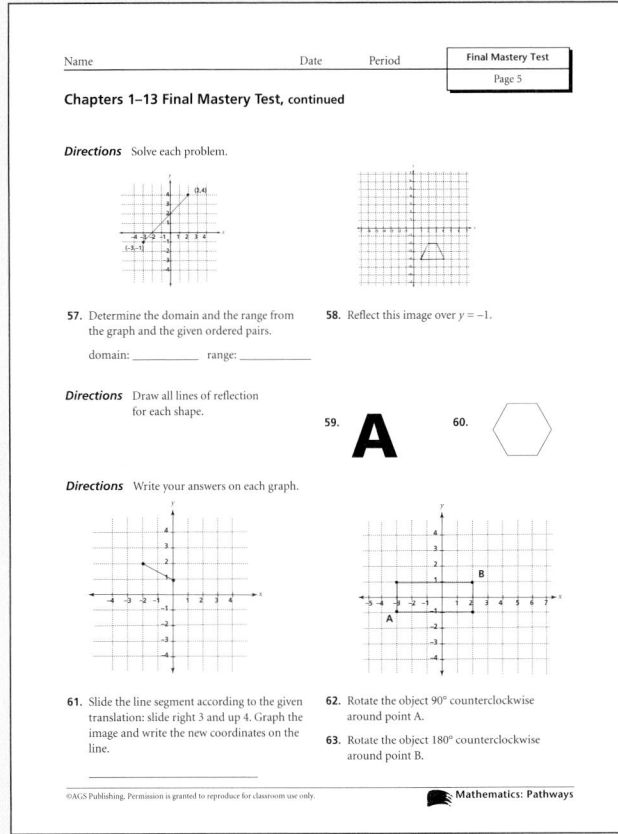

Directions Solve each problem.

57. Determine the domain and the range from the graph and the given ordered pairs.

domain: _____ range: _____

58. Reflect this image over $y = -1$.

Directions Draw all lines of reflection for each shape.

59. A   **60.**

Directions Write your answers on each graph.

61. Slide the line segment according to the given translation: slide right 3 and up 4. Graph the image and write the new coordinates on the line.

_____

62. Rotate the object 90° counterclockwise around point A.

63. Rotate the object 180° counterclockwise around point B.

Mathematics: Pathways

Final Mastery Test Page 5

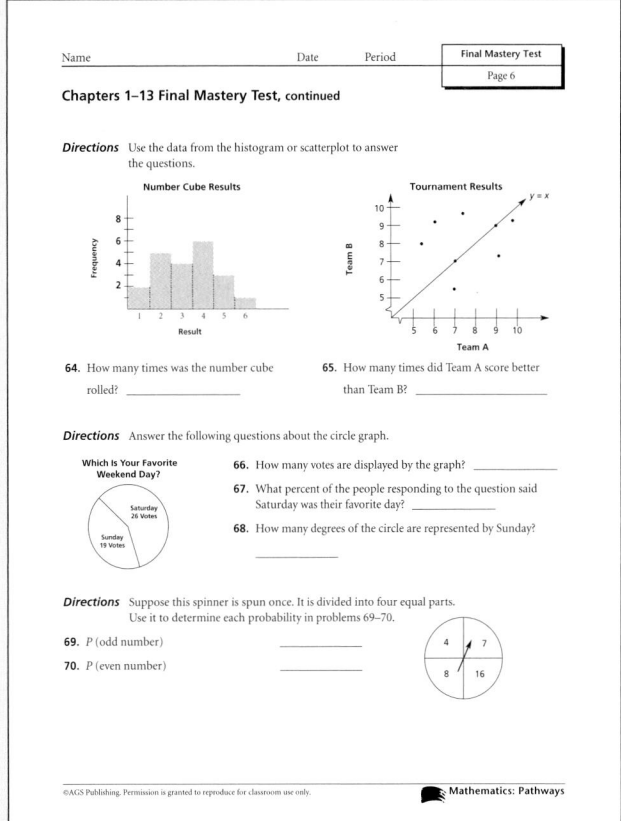

Directions Use the data from the histogram or scatterplot to answer the questions.

Number Cube Results

Tournament Results

64. How many times was the number cube rolled? _____

65. How many times did Team A score better than Team B? _____

Directions Answer the following questions about the circle graph.

Which Is Your Favorite Weekend Day?

Saturday 26 Votes

Sunday 19 Votes

66. How many votes are displayed by the graph? _____

67. What percent of the people responding to the question said Saturday was their favorite day? _____

68. How many degrees of the circle are represented by Sunday? _____

Directions Suppose this spinner is spun once. It is divided into four equal parts. Use it to determine each probability in problems 69–70.

69. P (odd number) _____

70. P (even number) _____

4 7
8 16

Mathematics: Pathways

Final Mastery Test Page 6

The lists below show how items from the Midterm and Final correlate to the chapters in the student edition.

Midterm Mastery Test

Chapter 1: 5, 8, 10, 12, 14–16

Chapter 2: 13, 17, 26–29, 33–34

Chapter 3: 4, 20–21, 31, 35–36

Chapter 4: 2, 7, 32, 37–38

Chapter 5: 18–19, 22–25, 39

Chapter 6: 1, 3, 6, 11, 30, 45

Chapter 7: 9, 40–44

Final Mastery Test

Chapter 1: 2, 16–19

Chapter 2: 24–27

Chapter 3: 1, 8, 21, 23, 30

Chapter 4: 11, 31, 33–34

Chapter 5: 4–5, 20, 22, 28

Chapter 6: 7, 10, 29, 39

Chapter 7: 13, 35–37, 41

Chapter 8: 3, 14–15, 38, 40

Chapter 9: 6, 9, 42–43, 45

Chapter 10: 44, 46–51

Chapter 11: 52–57

Chapter 12: 58–63

Chapter 13: 12, 32, 64–70

Teacher's Resource Library Answer Key

Activities

Activity 1—Counting by Tens

1. 5 groups of ten planes plus 2. **2.** 1 group of ten hearts plus 2.
3. 6 groups of ten checks plus 1. **4.** 9 groups of ten angles plus 9.
5. 2, 2,000 **6.** 3, 10 **7.** 6, 600 **8.** 9, 1,000, 90,000 **9.** 4, 100, 4,000
10. 600 + 1,000 + 40,000 = 41,600 **11.** 200 + 0 + 10,000 = 10,200
12. 800 + 7,000 + 0 = 7,800 **13.** 400 + 4,000 + 40,000 = 44,400
14. 0 + 9,000 + 50,000 = 59,000
15. 300 + 2,000 + 80,000 = 82,300

Activity 2—Choosing a Classroom Calculator

Answers will vary.

Activity 3—Value of Numbers

1. Hundreds **2.** Hundreds **3.** Ten-thousands **4.** Millions
5. Hundred-thousands **6.** 0 **7.** 9,000 **8.** 9,000 **9.** 6 **10.** 10
11. $(9 \times 10,000) + (9 \times 1,000) + (2 \times 100) + (0 \times 10) + (0 \times 1)$
12. $(6 \times 1,000,000) + (7 \times 100,000) + (8 \times 10,000) + (9 \times 1,000) + (5 \times 100) + (2 \times 10) + (2 \times 1)$
13. $(2 \times 1,000) + (2 \times 100) + (2 \times 10) + (0 \times 1)$
14. $(8 \times 100) + (9 \times 10) + (1 \times 1)$
15. $(1 \times 100) + (0 \times 10) + (1 \times 1)$
16. $(4 \times 10^3) + (3 \times 10^2) + (5 \times 10^1) + (7 \times 10^0)$
17. $(8 \times 10^6) + (1 \times 10^5) + (0 \times 10^4) + (2 \times 10^3) + (3 \times 10^2) + (6 \times 10^1) + (4 \times 10^0)$
18. $(2 \times 10^6) + (3 \times 10^5) + (6 \times 10^4) + (5 \times 10^3) + (8 \times 10^2) + (0 \times 10^1) + (1 \times 10^0)$
19. $(2 \times 10^2) + (1 \times 10^1) + (3 \times 10^0)$
20. $(6 \times 10^5) + (4 \times 10^4) + (3 \times 10^3) + (8 \times 10^2) + (2 \times 10^1) + (4 \times 10^0)$

Activity 4—Inverse Operations: Adding and Subtracting

1. 4 + 6

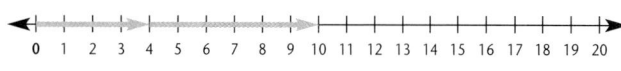

2. 16 − 5

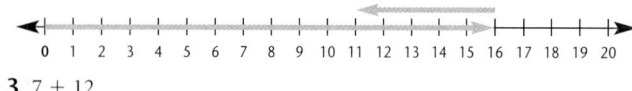

3. 7 + 12

4.
21	39
+ 18	− 21
39	19

5.
77	103
+ 26	− 26
103	77

6.
157	205
+ 48	− 157
205	48

7.
1,255	1,894
+ 639	− 1,255
1,894	639

8.
1,402	1,931
+ 529	− 529
1,931	1,402

9.
17	31
+ 14	− 14
31	17

10.
220	911
+ 691	− 691
911	220

11.
366	802
+ 436	− 366
802	436

12.
455	803
+ 348	− 455
803	348

13.
19
+ 33
52

14.
923
− 216
707

15.
693
− 218
475

16.
206
+ 114
320

17.
1,576
+ 658
2,234

18.
115
− 66
49

19. 68 miles per hour **20.** 2003

Activity 5—Inverse Operations: Multiplying and Dividing

1. 56 **2.** 91 **3.** 294 **4.** 45 **5.** 112 **6.** 57 **7.** 90 **8.** 6 **9.** 32 **10.** 8
11. 27 **12.** 70 **13.** 56 ÷ 8 = 7 **14.** 144 ÷ 4 = 36 **15.** 567 ÷ 63 = 9
16. 16 × 5 = 80 **17.** 62 × 3 = 186 **18.** 6 × 53 = 318 **19.** 78
20. 91 cookies **21.** subtract (−) **22.** add (+) **23.** divide (÷)
24. multiply (×) **25.** divide (÷)

Activity 6—Binary System

1. 1001_2 **2.** 101101_2 **3.** 10110100_2 **4.** 1100001_2 **5.** 1000010_2
6. 10101_2 **7.** 110100_2 **8.** 111111_2 **9.** 10_{10} **10.** 27_{10} **11.** 6_{10} **12.** 59_{10}
13. 123_{10} **14.** 36_{10} **15.** 13_{10} **16.** 1110 **17.** 17 **18.** 6 **19.** 4
20. 111111 **21.** 1011 **22.** 2 **23.** 110111 **24.** 16 **25.** 11111

Activity 7—Quinary System

1. 223_5 **2.** 344_5 **3.** 21_5 **4.** 2001000_5 **5.** 200001_5 **6.** 30130_5 **7.** 18_{10}
8. 111_{10} **9.** 5_{10} **10.** 586_{10} **11.** 763_{10} **12.** $2,251_{10}$ **13.** 42 **14.** 78
15. 1033 **16.** 125 **17.** 332 **18.** 434 **19.** 220 **20.** 201 **21.** 4014
22. 56 **23.** 411 **24.** 344 **25.** 119

Activity 8—Whole Numbers—Adding

1. 133 **2.** 110 **3.** 756 **4.** 453 **5.** 434 **6.** 2,220 **7.** 950 **8.** 1,802
9. 121x **10.** 1,121y **11.** 1,074b **12.** 4,377a **13.** 562b **14.** 1,323x
15. 2,498y **16.** 2,323a **17.** 5,517y **18.** 3,626g **19.** 28 + 63 + 16 = 107 pages **20.** 53 + 37 + 137 = 227 books

Activity 9—Whole Numbers—Subtracting

1. 13 **2.** 111 **3.** 321y **4.** 1,188 **5.** 175y **6.** 448 **7.** 979 **8.** 3,125b
9. 1,099x **10.** 4,789y **11.** 1,136c **12.** 3,714a **13.** 430 **14.** 188
15. 819y **16.** 1,368a **17.** 2,684y **18.** 111b **19.** 781 − 159 = 622
students **20.** 401 − 386 = 15 hours

Activity 10—Sums and Differences—Estimation

1. 40 + 30 = 70 **2.** 70 + 40 = 110 **3.** 300 + 60 = 360 **4.** 700 + 3,000 = 3,700 **5.** 1,000 + 3,000 = 4,000 **6.** 3,000 + 2,000 = 5,000
7. 60 − 30 = 30 **8.** 800 − 400 = 400 **9.** 700 − 400 = 300 **10.** 500 −80 = 420 **11.** 1,000 − 700 = 300 **12.** 3,000 − 2,000 = 1,000
13. 70 + 80 = 150 people **14.** 60 − 40 = 20 boxes **15.** 400 − 80 = 320 jeans

Activity 11—Whole Numbers—Multiplying
1. $17 \cdot 8$ or $(17)(8)$; 136 **2.** $20 \cdot 31$ or 20×31; 620 **3.** $(18)(9b)$ or $18 \times 9b$; $162b$ **4.** $(47)(12x)$ or $47 \cdot 12x$; $564x$ **5.** $(51)(72)$ or 51×72; 3,672 **6.** $31y \cdot 18$ or $31y \times 18$; $558y$ **7.** $8 \cdot 25y$ or $8 \times 25y$; $200y$ **8.** $44 \cdot 17$ or $(44)(17)$; 748 **9.** $(67)(49)$ or 67×49; 3,283 **10.** 1,065 **11.** 1,512 **12.** 1,815x **13.** 2,021a **14.** 2,028 **15.** 493y **16.** 1,701z **17.** 1,050 **18.** 258x **19.** $37 \times 16 = 592$ books **20.** $24 \times 86 = 2{,}064$ videotapes

Activity 12—Whole Numbers—Dividing
1. 9; $9 \times 7 = 63$ **2.** 4; $4 \times 12 = 48$ **3.** $3c$; $3c \times 6 = 18c$ **4.** 3; $3 \times 7 = 21$ **5.** 4; $4 \times 6 = 24$ **6.** $7a$; $7a \times 11 = 77a$ **7.** 9 r3; $9 \times 9 + 3 = 84$ **8.** $13y$; $13y \times 3 = 39y$ **9.** 5 r7; $5 \times 8 + 7 = 47$ **10.** 23 **11.** 65 **12.** 91x **13.** 123 r2 **14.** 250 r3 **15.** 431 r2 **16.** 420x **17.** 362 r3 **18.** 623a **19.** $576 \div 72 = 8$ chairs **20.** $5{,}334 \div 127 = 42$ items

Activity 13—Products and Quotients—Estimating
1. 40×80 **2.** 40×60 **3.** 90×50 **4.** 100×20 **5.** $3{,}000 \times 200$ **6.** $20{,}000 \times 5{,}000$ **7.** $100 \div 5$ **8.** $280 \div 40$ **9.** $800 \div 40$ **10.** $3{,}000 \div 60$ **11.** $2{,}400 \div 80$ **12.** $21{,}000 \div 70$ **13.** $60 \times 10 = 600$ **14.** $20 \times 50 = 1{,}000$ **15.** $30 \times 20 = 600$ **16.** $40 \times 90 = 3{,}600$ **17.** $40 \times 40 = 1{,}600$ **18.** $150 \div 10 = 15$ **19.** $500 \div 50 = 10$ **20.** $1{,}600 \div 80 = 20$ **21.** $9{,}000 \div 60 = 150$ **22.** $12{,}000 \div 40 = 300$ **23.** $40 \times 400 = 16{,}000$; $36 \times 368 = 13{,}248$ **24.** $240 \div 6 = 40$; $234 \div 6 = 39$ **25.** $400 \times 0.60 = \$240$; $386 \times 0.55 = \$212.30$

Activity 14—Operations and Open Statements
1. addition **2.** division **3.** subtraction; multiplication **4.** multiplication; division **5.** multiplication **6.** subtraction; multiplication; division **7.** $8 \cdot 6$; $(8)(6)$ **8.** $\frac{18}{6}$; $18 \div 6$ **9.** $5 \cdot n$; $5n$ **10.** $\frac{40}{x}$; $40 \div x$ **11.** false **12.** false **13.** open **14.** true **15.** true **16.** open **17.** false **18.** open **19.** true **20.** true **21.** false **22.** open **23.** open **24.** open **25.** true **26.** false **27.** open **28.** open **29.** open **30.** true

Activity 15—Using Letters for Numbers
1. k **2.** x **3.** g **4.** y **5.** n **6.** f **7.** m **8.** b **9.** c **10.** a **11.** algebraic **12.** multiplication **13.** numerical **14.** addition; multiplication **15.** numerical **16.** division **17.** algebraic **18.** multiplication; subtraction **19.** algebraic **20.** multiplication; addition **21.** numerical **22.** division; subtraction **23.** numerical **24.** subtraction; addition **25.** $12 + 8 = x$

Activity 16—Replacing Variables with Numbers
1. true **2.** false **3.** false **4.** true **5.** true **6.** 8 **7.** 48 **8.** 24 **9.** 24 **10.** 19 **11.** 0 **12.** 16 **13.** 37 **14.** 2 **15.** 18 **16.** 23 **17.** 9 **18.** $n - 16$ **19.** $24 + n$ **20.** $6n$ **21.** $25 \div n$ **22.** $4n + 12$ **23.** $8n - 17$ **24.** $n \div 6$ **25.** $(n - 8) + 21$

Activity 17—Place Value of Numbers
1. hundredths **2.** tens **3.** tenths **4.** ones **5.** hundreds **6.** ones **7.** thousands **8.** hundredths **9.** hundreds **10.** tenths **11.** tenths **12.** thousandths **13.** ten-thousandths **14.** ten-thousands **15.** hundredths **16.** thousandths **17.** hundreds **18.** thousands **19.** tens **20.** hundredths **21.** 80 **22.** 0.01 **23.** 10,000 **24.** 200 **25.** 4,000 **26.** 0.008 **27.** 100 **28.** 40 **29.** 0.10 **30.** 4

Activity 18—Decimals—Comparing and Rounding
1. false **2.** true **3.** true **4.** true **5.** false **6.** true **7.** false **8.** true **9.** false **10.** false **11.** 18.4 **12.** 196.84 **13.** 0.568 **14.** 15.76 **15.** 65.7 **16.** 432.84 **17.** 83.01 **18.** 2.676 **19.** Tonya **20.** Jan: 5.68; Pat: 6.02

Activity 19—Decimals—Adding and Subtracting
1. 20.835 **2.** 112.975 **3.** 53.091 **4.** 1,017.76 **5.** 180.8078 **6.** 24.637 **7.** 96.039 **8.** 201.26 **9.** 69.0075 **10.** 8.835 **11.** 18.73 **12.** 46.296 **13.** 0.169 **14.** 16.382 **15.** 0.445 **16.** 0.025 **17.** 1.96 **18.** 31.04 **19.** 1,480.25 **20.** $14.93

Activity 20—Multiplying Decimals—Powers of 10
1. 117 **2.** 11,700 **3.** 8.4 **4.** 84 **5.** 840 **6.** 8,400 **7.** 84,000 **8.** 567.2 **9.** 5,672 **10.** 56,720 **11.** 567,200 **12.** 5,672,000 **13.** 39.01 **14.** 390.1 **15.** 3,901 **16.** 39,010 **17.** 390,100 **18.** 2,250 **19.** 22,500 **20.** 225,000 **21.** 2,250,000 **22.** 22,500,000 **23.** 234 **24.** 2,340 **25.** 23,400 **26.** 234,000 **27.** 2,340,000 **28.** $23.90 **29.** $18,790 **30.** 94,172.6

Activity 21—Decimals—Multiplying
1. 152.19 **2.** 177.407 **3.** 0.34163 **4.** 83.961 **5.** 0.01155 **6.** 1,622.9294 **7.** 2,645.7263 **8.** 11.87458 **9.** 99.2592 **10.** 58.90944 **11.** 1,533 **12.** $114.75 **13.** $87.19 **14.** 17.5 **15.** 584.892

Activity 22—Dividing Decimals—Powers of 10
1. 0.732 **2.** 0.000851 **3.** 0.10489 **4.** 0.00624 **5.** 0.2399 **6.** 0.041262 **7.** 0.0057 **8.** 0.2974 **9.** 0.97366 **10.** 0.87121 **11.** 0.68818 **12.** 0.3472 **13.** 0.2129 **14.** 0.000358 **15.** 0.0054784 **16.** 0.71421 **17.** 0.919 **18.** 1.0534 **19.** 0.017687 **20.** 0.0084257 **21.** 0.0954 **22.** 0.085 **23.** $1.67 **24.** 0.857 acres **25.** $18.67

Activity 23—Decimals—Dividing
1. 21.13 **2.** 31.931 **3.** 0.008 **4.** 8.888 **5.** 640.533 **6.** 112.294 **7.** 7.296 **8.** 122.533 **9.** 6,305.833 **10.** 17.973 **11.** true **12.** false **13.** true **14.** false **15.** true **16.** true **17.** false **18.** $1.35 **19.** 27.5 inches **20.** 7

Activity 24—Fractions and Decimals
1. $\frac{9}{500}$ **2.** $2\frac{24}{25}$ **3.** $\frac{9}{25}$ **4.** $1\frac{51}{200}$ **5.** $\frac{43}{125}$ **6.** $9\frac{21}{100}$ **7.** 0.11 **8.** 0.375 **9.** 2.16 **10.** 0.78 **11.** 0.725 **12.** 0.208 **13.** false **14.** false **15.** true **16.** false **17.** true **18.** false **19.** true **20.** false **21.** false **22.** true **23.** The Schneider farm is larger. **24.** $140.63 **25.** $4.60

Activity 25—Writing Repeating Decimals
1. $0.3\overline{6}$ **2.** 0.4375 **3.** 0.875 **4.** $0.3\overline{8}$ **5.** $0.2\overline{4}$ **6.** $0.\overline{23}$ **7.** 0.912 **8.** 0.6429 **9.** $0.7\overline{3}$ **10.** 0.512 **11.** 2°C **12.** −7°C **13.** 27°C **14.** 18°C **15.** 23°C **16.** 17°C **17.** 18°C **18.** 3°C **19.** 8°C **20.** 1°C

Activity 26—Percents to Decimals
1. true **2.** false **3.** false **4.** true **5.** true **6.** false **7.** true **8.** true **9.** true **10.** false **11.** $2.75 **12.** $5,000 **13.** $792.27 **14.** $112 **15.** Angela: $100.80; William: $100.80

Activity 27—Expressions with Decimals
1. false **2.** true **3.** false **4.** false **5.** false **6.** false **7.** false **8.** false **9.** true **10.** false **11.** true **12.** false **13.** 12.57 **14.** 131.9166 **15.** 0.10237 **16.** 746.488 **17.** 62.2 **18.** 6.59 **19.** 199.2 **20.** 1.280772

Activity 28—Rules of Divisibility

1. yes, no, no, no, no, no, no, no **2.** yes, yes, yes, no, yes, yes, yes, no
3. yes, yes, yes, no, yes, yes, yes, no **4.** yes, no, yes, yes, no, yes, no,
yes **5.** yes, yes, no, no, yes, no, no, no **6.** no, yes, no, yes, no, no, no,
no **7.** yes, yes, yes, no, yes, yes, yes, no **8.** yes, no, no, no, no, no, no,
no **9.** yes, yes, yes, yes, yes, yes, yes **10.** yes, yes, yes, no, yes, yes,
no, no **11.** no, yes, no, no, no, no, no, no **12.** no, no, no, yes, no,
no, no, no **13.** yes, no, yes, yes, no, yes, no, yes **14.** yes, no, no, no,
no, no, no, no **15.** no, no, yes, no, no, no, no, no **16.** yes, yes, yes,
no, yes, yes, no, no **17.** yes, no, no, no, no, no, no, yes **18.** yes, yes,
no, no, yes, no, yes, no **19.** no, no, no, no, no, no, no, no
20. yes, no, no, yes, no, no, no, yes

Activity 29—Numbers—Prime and Composite

1. 2 **2.** 3 **3.** 5 **4.** 7 **5.** 11 **6.** 13 **7.** 17 **8.** 19 **9.** 23 **10.** 29 **11.** 31
12. 37 **13.** 41 **14.** 43 **15.** 47 **16.** $2 \times 7 = 14$ **17.** $4 \times 5 = 20$ or $2 \times 10 = 20$ **18.** $9 \times 9 = 81$ or $3 \times 27 = 81$ **19.** $7 \times 9 = 63$
20. $5 \times 3 = 15$ **21.** $2 \times 8 = 16$ or $4 \times 4 = 16$ **22.** $3 \times 7 = 21$
23. $6 \times 6 = 36$ or $4 \times 9 = 36$ or $12 \times 3 = 36$ or $2 \times 18 = 36$
24. $6 \times 7 = 42$ or $14 \times 3 = 42$ **25.** $4 \times 3 = 12$ or $6 \times 2 = 12$

Activity 30—GCD—Greatest Common Divisor

1. no, 8 **2.** no, 4 **3.** no, 11 **4.** yes **5.** no, 14 **6.** yes **7.** no, 13
8. no, 7 **9.** no, 16 **10.** yes **11.** no, 8 **12.** yes **13.** yes **14.** no, 6
15. no, $9x$ **16.** no, $8b$ **17.** yes **18.** no, $2g$ **19.** 6 people **20.** 12 cases

Activity 31—Factoring Expressions

1. 14 **2.** 60 **3.** 88 **4.** $2x + 6$ **5.** $32m + 32$ **6.** $3a + 3b$ **7.** 4 **8.** 2
9. p **10.** d **11.** g **12.** 2 **13.** $3(3c + 1)$ **14.** $4(3y + 5)$ **15.** $6(h + 6)$
16. $14(m + 2k)$ **17.** $10(b + 4n)$ **18.** $y(x + b)$ **19.** $72 **20.** 14 times

Activity 32—LCM—Least Common Multiple

1. 72 **2.** 1,024 **3.** 200 **4.** 1,250 **5.** 576 **6.** 320 **7.** 686 **8.** 1,024
9. 1,080 **10.** 5,184 **11.** 34 **12.** 63 **13.** 456 **14.** 405 **15.** 266
16. 114 **17.** 36 **18.** 672 **19.** 120 stops **20.** number 60

Activity 33—Using Scientific Notation

1. true **2.** true **3.** false, 8.3×10^4 **4.** false, 6.5×10^{-4} **5.** false, 7.8×10^{-3} **6.** true **7.** false, 6.72×10^6 **8.** true **9.** false, 9.37×10^{-2}
10. false, 4.37×10^8 **11.** 2.4×10^4 **12.** 6.06×10^8 **13.** 3.47×10^{-3} **14.** 5.17×10^{11} **15.** 4.38×10^{-4} **16.** 8.4×10^{10} **17.** 9.47×10^{-5} **18.** 3.46×10^{-7} **19.** 5.96×10^6 people **20.** 1.02×10^{-1} cm

Activity 34—Writing Proper Fractions

1. $\frac{11}{16}$ **2.** $\frac{3}{10}$ **3.** $\frac{1}{14}$ **4.** $\frac{7}{12}$ **5.** $\frac{7}{8}$ **6.** $\frac{0}{2}, \frac{1}{2}, \frac{2}{2}$ **7.** $\frac{0}{4}, \frac{1}{4}, \frac{2}{4}, \frac{3}{4}, \frac{4}{4}$ **8.** $\frac{0}{3}, \frac{1}{3}, \frac{2}{3}$
9. $\frac{0}{6}, \frac{1}{6}, \frac{2}{6}, \frac{3}{6}, \frac{4}{6}, \frac{5}{6}, \frac{6}{6}$ **10.** $\frac{0}{7}, \frac{1}{7}, \frac{2}{7}, \frac{3}{7}, \frac{4}{7}, \frac{5}{7}, \frac{6}{7}$ **11.** $\frac{3}{7}$ **12.** $\frac{1}{12}$ **13.** $\frac{3}{7}$
14. $\frac{7}{20}$ **15.** $\frac{10}{13}$

Activity 35—Improper Fractions, Mixed Numbers

1. proper **2.** improper **3.** proper **4.** proper **5.** improper
6. improper **7.** proper **8.** improper **9.** proper **10.** improper
11. 1 **12.** 5 **13.** $3\frac{1}{5}$ **14.** $4\frac{1}{2}$ **15.** $4\frac{1}{6}$ **16.** $10\frac{3}{4}$ **17.** 12 **18.** $5\frac{3}{5}$
19. $6\frac{5}{9}$ **20.** $3\frac{2}{3}$ **21.** $2\frac{4}{5}$ **22.** $33\frac{1}{2}$ **23.** $6\frac{5}{7}$ **24.** $3\frac{3}{4}$ **25.** 9 **26.** $\frac{25}{3}$
27. $\frac{67}{4}$ **28.** $\frac{19}{8}$ **29.** $\frac{32}{9}$ **30.** $\frac{45}{2}$ **31.** $\frac{26}{3}$ **32.** $\frac{75}{8}$ **33.** $\frac{97}{5}$ **34.** $\frac{103}{4}$
35. $\frac{27}{7}$

Activity 36—Using Equivalent Fractions

1. $\frac{3}{4}$ and $\frac{6}{8}$ **2.** $\frac{1}{2}$ and $\frac{4}{8}$ **3.** $\frac{1}{4}$ and $\frac{2}{8}$ For problems **4–12,** sample
answers are given. **4.** $\frac{2}{6}$ and $\frac{3}{9}$ **5.** $\frac{14}{16}$ and $\frac{21}{24}$ **6.** $\frac{4}{10}$ and $\frac{6}{15}$ **7.** $\frac{16}{18}$ and
$\frac{24}{27}$ **8.** $\frac{6}{14}$ and $\frac{9}{21}$ **9.** $\frac{10}{16}$ and $\frac{15}{24}$ **10.** $\frac{2}{4}$ and $\frac{3}{6}$ **11.** $\frac{6}{8}$ and $\frac{9}{12}$ **12.** $\frac{6}{10}$
and $\frac{9}{15}$ **13.** yes **14.** no **15.** yes **16.** no **17.** no **18.** yes **19.** yes
20. no **21.** yes **22.** no **23.** yes **24.** no **25.** no

Activity 37—Writing in Simplest Form

1. 5 **2.** 2 **3.** 3 **4.** 7 **5.** 12 **6.** 9 **7.** 5 **8.** 2 **9.** 12 **10.** 6 **11.** $\frac{3}{8}$
12. $\frac{1}{2}$ **13.** $\frac{1}{3}$ **14.** $\frac{21}{40}$ **15.** $\frac{1}{5}$ **16.** $\frac{6}{7}$ **17.** $\frac{7}{10}$ **18.** $\frac{5}{21}$ **19.** $\frac{7}{11}$ **20.** $\frac{8}{9}$
21. $\frac{1}{2}$ **22.** $\frac{8}{15}$ **23.** yes, it is a multiple of 5 **24.** yes, 5 is a multiple of
20 **25.** yes, 3 is a multiple of 24

Activity 38—Comparing, Ordering Fractions

1. > **2.** > **3.** < **4.** > **5.** > **6.** < **7.** < **8.** < **9.** > **10.** > **11.** >
12. < **13.** < **14.** > **15.** > **16.** $\frac{1}{8}$ $\frac{1}{5}$ **17.** $\frac{1}{2}$ $\frac{5}{14}$ $\frac{2}{7}$ **18.** $\frac{11}{12}$ $\frac{5}{8}$ $\frac{1}{3}$
19. $\frac{9}{10}$ $\frac{3}{5}$ $\frac{1}{2}$ **20.** $\frac{2}{3}$ $\frac{3}{7}$ $\frac{5}{21}$ **21.** $\frac{11}{12}$ $\frac{7}{8}$ $\frac{5}{6}$ **22.** $\frac{9}{15}$ $\frac{2}{3}$ $\frac{4}{5}$ **23.** $\frac{1}{10}$ $\frac{1}{8}$ $\frac{1}{5}$
24. $\frac{5}{12}$ $\frac{1}{2}$ $\frac{5}{6}$ **25.** $\frac{7}{15}$ $\frac{19}{30}$ $\frac{9}{10}$ **26.** $\frac{5}{12}$ $\frac{2}{3}$ $\frac{3}{4}$ **27.** $\frac{3}{10}$ $\frac{3}{8}$ $\frac{3}{4}$ **28.** Ellen
29. Jessica **30.** Quin

Activity 39—Fractions with Like Denominators

1. $1\frac{3}{8}$ **2.** $1\frac{5}{9}$ **3.** $\frac{1}{5}$ **4.** $3\frac{1}{2}$ **5.** $3\frac{1}{6}$ **6.** $12\frac{6}{11}$ **7.** $12\frac{4}{5}$ **8.** $\frac{2x}{5}$ **9.** x
10. $\frac{(x-4)}{10}$ **11.** $\frac{(x+3)}{y}$ **12.** $\frac{8x}{15}$ **13.** $\frac{(4y-3)}{x}$ **14.** $\frac{8x}{9}$ **15.** y **16.** $\frac{1}{2}$
17. $1\frac{1}{5}$ **18.** $\frac{2}{3}$ **19.** 1 **20.** $1\frac{1}{7}$ **21.** $\frac{4}{5}$ **22.** $1\frac{5}{8}$ **23.** $\frac{3}{8}$ **24.** $1\frac{4}{13}$ **25.** $\frac{3x}{4}$
26. $\frac{4y}{5}$ **27.** $\frac{x}{7}$ **28.** $\frac{7y}{8}$ **29.** $\frac{5x}{13}$ **30.** $\frac{x}{2}$

Activity 40—Fractions with Unlike Denominators

1. $1\frac{2}{15}$ **2.** $\frac{3}{16}$ **3.** $1\frac{7}{20}$ **4.** $\frac{1}{5}$ **5.** $\frac{1}{24}$ **6.** $\frac{3}{10}$ **7.** $1\frac{1}{14}$ **8.** $\frac{1}{6}$ **9.** $1\frac{22}{63}$
10. $1\frac{7}{24}$ **11.** $\frac{17}{40}x$ **12.** $\frac{(y+9x)}{xy}$ **13.** $\frac{19x}{24}$ **14.** $\frac{(6y-3x)}{xy}$ **15.** $\frac{4x}{15}$
16. $2\frac{1}{3}$ **17.** $7\frac{8}{9}$ **18.** $8\frac{1}{6}$ **19.** $5\frac{3}{20}$ **20.** $5\frac{3}{16}$ **21.** $17\frac{1}{8}$ **22.** $17\frac{2}{9}$
23. $56\frac{7}{24}$ **24.** $5\frac{1}{24}$ **25.** $17\frac{1}{6}x$ **26.** $6\frac{2}{15}x$ **27.** $55\frac{11}{15}y$ **28.** $3\frac{1}{8}x$
29. $5y$ **30.** $6\frac{3}{16}x$

Activity 41—Subtracting Fractions—Regrouping

1. $1\frac{7}{8}$ **2.** $\frac{1}{2}$ **3.** $2\frac{11}{24}$ **4.** $3\frac{3}{5}$ **5.** $5\frac{1}{2}$ **6.** $5\frac{6}{7}$ **7.** $8\frac{2}{3}$ **8.** $7\frac{3}{4}$ **9.** $29\frac{7}{16}$
10. $2\frac{1}{12}$ **11.** $5\frac{3}{8}$ **12.** $10\frac{23}{24}$ **13.** $1\frac{1}{3}$ **14.** $37\frac{11}{12}$ **15.** $6\frac{11}{12}$ **16.** $7\frac{1}{2}$
17. $5\frac{13}{16}$ **18.** $6\frac{2}{3}$ **19.** $1\frac{1}{6}$ **20.** $1\frac{7}{12}$ **21.** $3\frac{13}{24}$ hours **22.** $2\frac{3}{8}$ miles
23. $50\frac{9}{16}$ or $50.56 **24.** $110 **25.** $6\frac{1}{2}$ or $6.50

Activity 42—Multiplying Fractions, Mixed Numbers

1. $\frac{1}{7}$ **2.** $\frac{3}{7}$ **3.** $\frac{5}{9}$ **4.** $\frac{6}{35}$ **5.** $\frac{5}{14}$ **6.** $\frac{9}{40}$ **7.** $\frac{1}{6}$ **8.** $\frac{2}{3}$ **9.** $\frac{2}{5}$ **10.** $\frac{14}{23}y$ **11.** $\frac{1}{6x}$
12. $\frac{1}{10}y$ **13.** $2\frac{1}{4}$ **14.** $6\frac{3}{5}$ **15.** $4\frac{11}{20}$ **16.** $16\frac{3}{5}$ **17.** $13\frac{1}{7}$ **18.** $9\frac{1}{2}$
19. $10\frac{1}{5}$ **20.** $7\frac{13}{20}$ **21.** $4\frac{3}{4}$ **22.** $2\frac{11}{16}$ **23.** $9\frac{2}{3}$ **24.** $7\frac{1}{3}$ **25.** $8\frac{5}{8}x$
26. $4\frac{1}{8}x$ **27.** $18\frac{9}{16}$ feet **28.** $6\frac{2}{3}$ cups **29.** 15 hours **30.** $4\frac{1}{2}$ gallons

Activity 43—Dividing Fractions, Mixed Numbers

1. $1\frac{1}{4}$ **2.** $1\frac{1}{3}$ **3.** $\frac{4}{7}$ **4.** $\frac{5}{9}$ **5.** $1\frac{5}{27}$ **6.** $\frac{5}{6}$ **7.** $2\frac{4}{5}$ **8.** $\frac{10}{11}$ **9.** $\frac{1}{6}$ **10.** $\frac{2}{3}$
11. $\frac{3b}{4}$ **12.** $2\frac{1}{3}n$ **13.** $1\frac{13}{15}$ **14.** $\frac{2}{3}$ **15.** $\frac{3}{4}$ **16.** $1\frac{8}{11}$ **17.** $\frac{3}{4}$ **18.** 5
19. $\frac{7}{12}$ **20.** $3\frac{1}{11}$ **21.** $\frac{1}{2}$ **22.** $1\frac{1}{10}y$ **23.** $2w$ **24.** $3\frac{1}{8}$ weeks
25. $\frac{3}{7}$ or $0.4287

Activity 44—Order of Operations

1. 38 **2.** 62 **3.** 16 **4.** 40 **5.** 11 **6.** 10 **7.** 33 **8.** 12 **9.** 39 **10.** 0
11. 48 **12.** 8 **13.** 0 **14.** 4 **15.** 12 **16.** 9 **17.** 3 **18.** 1 **19.** 8 **20.** 40
21. 19 **22.** 76 **23.** 29 **24.** $55\frac{1}{3}$ **25.** 114 **26.** 13 **27.** 160 **28.** 44
29. 66 **30.** 5

Activity 45—Substituting Values

1. 11 **2.** 7 **3.** 6 **4.** 59 **5.** 17 **6.** $1\frac{1}{2}$ **7.** 31 **8.** $3\frac{2}{5}$ **9.** $3\frac{19}{30}$ **10.** 10
11. 15 **12.** 1 **13.** 0 **14.** 43 **15.** 13 **16.** 3 **17.** 54 **18.** $6\frac{1}{8}$ **19.** $\frac{9}{16}$
20. 24 **21.** 10 **22.** 1 **23.** 7 **24.** 46 **25.** 18 **26.** $\frac{1}{4}$ **27.** 24 **28.** $5\frac{4}{9}$
29. $\frac{7}{18}$ **30.** 27

Activity 46—Solution by Substitution

1. 3 **2.** 5 **3.** 4 **4.** 1 **5.** 3 **6.** 4 **7.** 9 **8.** 4 **9.** 7 **10.** 8 **11.** 8 **12.** 6
13. 1 **14.** 0 **15.** 2 **16.** 3 **17.** 5 **18.** 10 **19.** 9 **20.** 4 **21.** 3 **22.** 3
23. 7 **24.** 0 **25.** 3 **26.** 8 **27.** 10 **28.** 4 **29.** 2 **30.** 1

Activity 47—Addition Equations

1. 3 **2.** 13 **3.** 19 **4.** 9 **5.** 11 **6.** 8 **7.** 15 **8.** 41 **9.** 13 **10.** 14
11. 10 **12.** 27 **13.** 7 **14.** 18 **15.** 6 **16.** $\frac{1}{2}$ **17.** $\frac{2}{3}$ **18.** $\frac{1}{3}$ **19.** $\frac{1}{4}$
20. $\frac{3}{8}$ **21.** $\frac{3}{10}$ **22.** $\frac{5}{12}$ **23.** $\frac{3}{4}$ **24.** $\frac{2}{5}$ **25.** $\frac{1}{4}$ **26.** $\frac{1}{8}$ **27.** $\frac{3}{16}$ **28.** $\frac{3}{5}$
29. $\frac{6}{7}$ **30.** $\frac{1}{2}$

Activity 48—Subtraction Equations

1. 53 **2.** 62 **3.** 76 **4.** 37 **5.** 67 **6.** 13 **7.** 21 **8.** 100 **9.** 31
10. 66 **11.** 21 **12.** 38 **13.** $\frac{5}{8}$ **14.** $\frac{3}{4}$ **15.** $1\frac{1}{4}$ **16.** $\frac{9}{10}$ **17.** $\frac{7}{12}$
18. $\frac{2}{3}$ **19.** 1 **20.** $\frac{15}{16}$ **21.** $\frac{8}{9}$ **22.** $\frac{1}{3}$ **23.** $\frac{4}{5}$ **24.** 8 million ounces of
gold **25.** 19 million ounces of gold

Activity 49—Simplify Complex Fractions

1. $\frac{3}{5}$ **2.** $1\frac{5}{16}$ **3.** $10\frac{2}{3}$ **4.** $\frac{8}{9}$ **5.** $\frac{5}{6}$ **6.** $\frac{8}{9}$ **7.** $1\frac{3}{10}$ **8.** 8 **9.** $\frac{16}{19}$ **10.** $\frac{1}{9}$
11. $2\frac{1}{2}$ **12.** $1\frac{1}{6}$ **13.** $5\frac{1}{3}$ **14.** $\frac{5}{8}$ **15.** $3\frac{1}{3}$

Activity 50—Simplify by Addition

1. $\frac{3x}{5}$ **2.** $\frac{1}{2y}$ **3.** $\frac{4b}{3}$ or $1\frac{1}{3}b$ **4.** $\frac{1}{2c}$ **5.** $\frac{11h}{15}$ **6.** $1f$ **7.** $\frac{6w}{5}$ or $1\frac{1}{5}w$ **8.** $\frac{3}{2g}$
9. $\frac{5e}{7}$ **10.** $\frac{2n}{3}$ **11.** $\frac{8}{5p}$ **12.** $\frac{5x}{6}$ **13.** $\frac{1}{3z}$ **14.** $\frac{1q}{2}$ **15.** $\frac{7}{11u}$ **16.** $\frac{11d}{6}$ or
$1\frac{5}{6}d$ **17.** $\frac{9s}{10}$ **18.** $1x$ **19.** $\frac{10}{17a}$ **20.** $\frac{5}{4n}$ **21.** $\frac{23}{24x}$ **22.** $\frac{11m}{10}$ or $1\frac{1}{10}m$
23. $\frac{9n}{14}$ **24.** $\frac{25}{16p}$ **25.** $\frac{5h}{6}$ **26.** $\frac{5}{8k}$ **27.** $\frac{5}{9y}$ **28.** $\frac{15t}{16}$ **29.** $\frac{4s}{3}$ or $1\frac{1}{3}s$
30. $\frac{19}{24v}$

Activity 51—Simplify by Subtraction

1. $\frac{1g}{9}$ **2.** $\frac{2c}{5}$ **3.** $\frac{1}{3h}$ **4.** $\frac{3d}{7}$ **5.** $\frac{3}{5i}$ **6.** $\frac{1e}{2}$ **7.** $\frac{1j}{2}$ **8.** $\frac{1}{6f}$ **9.** $\frac{2k}{5}$ **10.** $\frac{3}{5g}$
11. $\frac{7}{10l}$ **12.** $\frac{2h}{3}$ **13.** $\frac{13}{21a}$ **14.** $\frac{1}{6x}$ **15.** $\frac{7b}{24}$ **16.** $\frac{5w}{16}$ **17.** $\frac{1}{2c}$ **18.** $\frac{2}{15d}$
19. $\frac{3w}{20}$ **20.** $\frac{1}{15v}$ **21.** $\frac{1}{6f}$ **22.** $\frac{9g}{16}$ **23.** $\frac{13}{16}$ of the walk **24.** $\frac{5}{16}$ of a
dollar **25.** $\frac{1}{4}$ yards

Activity 52—Multiply Rational Expressions

1. $\frac{1}{5}$ **2.** $\frac{3}{7}$ **3.** $\frac{3}{8}$ **4.** $\frac{8}{13}$ **5.** $\frac{13}{16}$ **6.** $\frac{1}{15}$ **7.** $\frac{1}{2}$ **8.** $\frac{5}{12}$ **9.** $\frac{3}{4}$ **10.** $\frac{2}{35}$ **11.** $\frac{1}{18}$
12. $\frac{1}{4}$ **13.** $\frac{5}{16}$ **14.** $\frac{1}{3}$ **15.** $\frac{7}{13}$ **16.** $\frac{16}{33}$ **17.** $\frac{1}{18}$ **18.** $\frac{3}{8}$ **19.** $\frac{2}{5}$ **20.** $\frac{1}{5}$
21. $\frac{4}{7}$ **22.** $\frac{1}{4}$ **23.** $\frac{1}{5}$ **24.** $\frac{11}{18}$ **25.** $\frac{1}{3}$ **26.** $\frac{3}{40}$ **27.** $\frac{3}{8}$ **28.** $\frac{3}{16}$ of a tank
29. $\frac{1}{8}$ of a bowl **30.** 100 seats

Activity 53—Using Ratios

1. $\frac{2}{1}$ **2.** $\frac{3}{8}$ **3.** $\frac{5}{9}$ **4.** $\frac{8}{17}$ **5.** $\frac{4}{11}$ **6.** $\frac{23}{9}$ **7.** $\frac{16}{5}$ **8.** $\frac{32}{41}$ **9.** $\frac{8}{7}$ **10.** $\frac{7}{12}$; 7 to
12 **11.** $\frac{8}{11}$; 8:11 **12.** $\frac{6}{5}$; 6:5 **13.** $\frac{9}{8}$; 9 to 8 **14.** $\frac{15}{17}$; 15:17 **15.** $\frac{25}{43}$; 25
to 43 **16.** $\frac{6}{8}; \frac{3}{4}$ **17.** $\frac{9}{18}; \frac{1}{2}$ **18.** $\frac{14}{42}; \frac{1}{3}$ **19.** $\frac{18}{27}; \frac{2}{3}$ **20.** $\frac{5}{25}; \frac{1}{5}$ **21.** $\frac{17}{51}; \frac{1}{3}$
22. $\frac{7}{49}; \frac{1}{7}$ **23.** $\frac{16}{64}; \frac{1}{4}$ **24.** 4 goldfish **25.** $\frac{2}{3}$

Activity 54—Using Proportions

1. $\frac{8}{12}$ **2.** $\frac{3}{5}$ **3.** $\frac{4}{16}$ **4.** $\frac{72}{81}$ **5.** $\frac{42}{49}$ **6.** $\frac{30}{45}$ **7.** $\frac{6}{30}$ **8.** $\frac{18}{45}$ **9.** $\frac{2}{3}$ **10.** $\frac{16}{36}$
11. 3 **12.** 30 **13.** 3 **14.** 7 **15.** 36 **16.** 40 **17.** 8 **18.** 49
19. $\frac{5}{1} = \frac{x}{3}$; 15 lemons **20.** $\frac{8}{160} = \frac{x}{1,440}$; 72 burned chips

Activity 55—Ratios, Proportions

1. $13.50 **2.** 70 cans **3.** 40 ringers **4.** 1,968 feet **5.** 240 people
6. 12 toys **7.** 118 girls **8.** $250 **9.** $109 **10.** 170 hot dogs with
mustard

Activity 56—Solving Proportional Relationships

1. 3 miles each day **2.** $3\frac{3}{4}$ lb **3.** $106\frac{2}{3}$ lb; Marie cannot ride the bike.
4. 1 lb:$1\frac{1}{4}$ lb **5.** 56 g **6.** 1 mL:1.42mL **7.** 72 cubic in. **8.** 15:1
9. $\frac{3}{4}$ lb **10.** 5 lb:1 lb

Activity 57—Distance, Rate, and Time Problems

1. r **2.** d **3.** t **4.** r **5.** 240 miles **6.** 44 km/h **7.** 27 miles
8. 190 km/h **9.** 62.5 mph **10.** $2\frac{1}{2}$ hours

Activity 58—Percents, Fractions

1. $\frac{73}{100}$; 73% **2.** $\frac{9}{100}$; 9% **3.** $\frac{24}{100}$; 24% **4.** $\frac{61}{100}$; 61% **5.** $\frac{39}{100}$; 39%
6. $\frac{44}{100}$; 44% **7.** 17% **8.** 54 squares **9.** $\frac{43}{100}$ **10.** 71%

Activity 59—Percents, Decimals

1. 50% **2.** 25% **3.** 40% **4.** 87.5% **5.** 58% **6.** 20% **7.** 37.5%
8. 75% **9.** 55% **10.** 70% **11.** 46% **12.** 91% **13.** 83% **14.** 3%
15. 17% **16.** 5% **17.** 35.7% **18.** 41.3% **19.** 40% **20.** 25%

Activity 60—The Percent of a Number

1. 4 **2.** 12 **3.** 15 **4.** 80 **5.** 104 **6.** 3.6 **7.** 6 **8.** 25.2 **9.** 50
10. 129.2 **11.** 1.5 **12.** 0.15 **13.** 0.015 **14.** 196 people
15. 171 cars

Activity 61—What Percent?

1. 37.5% **2.** 25% **3.** 31.7% **4.** 30% **5.** 20% **6.** 196.77%
7. 771.43% **8.** 138.75% **9.** 29% **10.** 44.44% **11.** 93.36%
12. 96.2% **13.** 31.2% **14.** 32.26% **15.** 14.88%

Activity 62—Percent of Increase, Decrease

1. increase **2.** increase or decrease **3.** decrease **4.** increase
5. increase **6.** increase **7.** 10.55% **8.** 49.66% **9.** 66.67%
10. 34.92%

Activity 63—Percents and Formulas

1. $126.08; $125.46; $0.62 **2.** $998.09; $993.23; $4.86 **3.** $667.15;
$663.90; $3.25 **4.** $2,810.42; $2,796.73; $13.69 **5.** $5,473.76;
$5,447.09; $26.67 **6.** $10,784.67; $10,732.12; $52.55 **7.** $74.92
8. Sara; 26¢ **9.** $15.38 **10.** $13,891.50

Activity 64—Scale Drawings, Models

1. $x = 10\frac{1}{2}$ **2.** $x = 2$ **3.** $x = 9$ **4.** $x = 7$ **5.** $x = 9$ **6.** 5 ft:1 in. **7.** 1 in.:10 miles **8.** 3 in. **9.** 4 ft **10.** $\frac{1}{5}$ in. long

Activity 65—Real Number Line and Integers

1. 8 **2.** 14 **3.** 15 **4.** 23 **5.** 99 **6.** 87 **7.** 7 **8.** 29 **9.** 43 **10.** 12 **11.** 17 **12.** −50 **13.** 62 **14.** 9 **15.** −13 **16.** 51 **17.** −38 **18.** −25 **19.** 47 **20.** −4 **21.** −5 **22.** +3 **23.** −4 **24.** +75 **25.** −85 **26.** −200 **27.** +2,000 **28.** −15 **29.** +10 **30.** −3

Activity 66—Greater Than and Less Than

1. > **2.** < **3.** = **4.** < **5.** > **6.** > **7.** < **8.** > **9.** > **10.** = **11.** < **12.** = **13.** > **14.** < **15.** < **16.** > **17.** = **18.** < **19.** < **20.** > **21.** = **22.** < **23.** > **24.** = **25.** > **26.** < **27.** > **28.** Mandy's house **29.** today **30.** 7 numbers $(−3, −2, −1, 0, 1, 2, 3)$

Activity 67—Odd and Even Integers

1. 198 even **2.** 372 even **3.** 363 odd **4.** 935 odd **5.** 110 even **6.** 672 even **7.** 790 even **8.** 1,067 odd **9.** 286 even **10.** 452 even **11.** 563 odd **12.** 192 even **13.** 916 even **14.** 255 odd **15.** 118 even **16.** 352 even **17.** 630 even **18.** 825 odd **19.** 512 even **20.** 732 even **21.** 504 even **22.** 1,512 even **23.** 399 odd **24.** 1,440 even **25.** 1,484 even **26.** 999 odd **27.** 1,876 even **28.** 1,980 even **29.** 429 odd **30.** 1,161 odd

Activity 68—Positive Integers—Adding

1. 1 **2.** 11 **3.** −1 **4.** 9 **5.** 0 **6.** 6 **7.** −5 **8.** −6 **9.** 8 **10.** 7 **11.** −1 **12.** 12 **13.** −5 **14.** 10 **15.** 12 **16.** 1 **17.** −3 **18.** 2 **19.** −6 **20.** −2 **21.** −133 **22.** 343 **23.** 700 **24.** 1,038 **25.** −515 **26.** 81 **27.** 1,127 **28.** −149 **29.** 1,593 **30.** −37

Activity 69—Negative Integers—Adding

1. 1 **2.** −12 **3.** −2 **4.** −18 **5.** −1 **6.** −4 **7.** 0 **8.** 0 **9.** −5 **10.** −1 **11.** −11 **12.** −16 **13.** 5 **14.** −8 **15.** −9 **16.** −574 **17.** 96 **18.** −1,116 **19.** 62 **20.** −1,461 **21.** 220 **22.** −569 **23.** −1,637 **24.** 271 **25.** −636 **26.** −36 **27.** −675 **28.** 427 **29.** 394 feet **30.** 20 feet

Activity 70—Subtracting Positive, Negative Integers

1. 12 **2.** −13 **3.** 2 **4.** 3 **5.** 4 **6.** −7 **7.** −1 **8.** −9 **9.** −1 **10.** 5 **11.** 12 **12.** −5 **13.** 7 **14.** 2 **15.** 9 **16.** −6 **17.** 17 **18.** −8 **19.** −12 **20.** 16 **21.** 4 **22.** 1 **23.** −6 **24.** −7 **25.** −7 **26.** 15 **27.** −4 **28.** 3 **29.** 4,145 feet **30.** 14,855 feet

Activity 71—Multiplying Positive Integers

1. −45 **2.** 28 **3.** −6 **4.** −21 **5.** −35 **6.** 36 **7.** 0 **8.** −12 **9.** 54 **10.** 8 **11.** −3 **12.** 27 **13.** 30 **14.** −64 **15.** 14 **16.** −36 **17.** −20 **18.** 12 **19.** −32 **20.** 45 **21.** positive **22.** positive **23.** positive **24.** negative **25.** negative **26.** negative **27.** negative **28.** positive **29.** negative **30.** positive

Activity 72—Multiplying Negative Integers

1. negative **2.** positive **3.** negative **4.** positive **5.** positive **6.** negative **7.** negative **8.** positive **9.** negative **10.** positive **11.** negative **12.** positive **13.** negative **14.** positive **15.** positive **16.** negative **17.** positive **18.** negative **19.** positive **20.** negative **21.** positive **22.** negative **23.** positive **24.** positive **25.** negative **26.** negative **27.** positive **28.** negative **29.** $8.00 **30.** $36.00

Activity 73—Dividing Positive, Negative Integers

1. −4 **2.** −4 **3.** 6 **4.** 7 **5.** 5 **6.** −8 **7.** −9 **8.** 8 **9.** −2 **10.** −5 **11.** −8 **12.** 3 **13.** 4 **14.** −4 **15.** positive **16.** negative **17.** negative **18.** positive **19.** zero **20.** negative **21.** negative **22.** negative **23.** negative **24.** positive **25.** positive **26.** negative **27.** positive **28.** positive **29.** 157 children **30.** $21.00

Activity 74—Using Exponents

1. 2 **2.** 3 **3.** n **4.** 1 **5.** 6 **6.** 10 **7.** 4 **8.** 5 **9.** m **10.** 9 **11.** 4 **12.** a **13.** 10 **14.** $(−y)$ **15.** $(−4)$ **16.** 6 **17.** r^2 **18.** $(−10)^2$ **19.** 3^5 **20.** $(−b)^2$ **21.** 7^7 **22.** 5^3 **23.** 2^2 **24.** $(−n)^4$ **25.** c^3 **26.** 10^{10} **27.** $(−2)^4$ **28.** 5^5 **29.** $(−z)^2$ **30.** 8^7

Activity 75—Exponents—Multiplying

1. m^6 **2.** 10^7 **3.** r^4 **4.** 12^9 **5.** n^8 **6.** 6^{14} **7.** q^{15} **8.** 18^9 **9.** 2^{5y} **10.** 100^{10} **11.** false, $4^{3n} \cdot 4^{3n} = 4^{6n}$ **12.** true **13.** true **14.** true **15.** true **16.** false, $a^8 \cdot a^{10} = a^{18}$ **17.** true **18.** true **19.** false, $p^7 \cdot p^2 = p^9$ **20.** false, $5^5 \cdot 5 = 5^6$ **21.** true **22.** true **23.** false, $3^c \cdot 3^c = 3^{2c}$ **24.** true **25.** true **26.** false, $8^{10} \cdot 8^{10} = 8^{20}$ **27.** true **28.** true **29.** true **30.** true

Activity 76—Exponents—Dividing

1. a^2 **2.** 3^7 **3.** 1 **4.** 12^2 **5.** r^2 **6.** 9^4 **7.** q^3 **8.** 8^5 **9.** 2^{11} **10.** 1 **11.** false, $9^{6n} \div 9^{3n} = 9^{3n}$ **12.** true **13.** true **14.** true **15.** true **16.** false, $a^{12} \div a^6 = a^6$ **17.** true **18.** true **19.** true **20.** true **21.** true **22.** false, $6^6 \div 6^6 = 1$ **23.** true **24.** false, $a^7 \div a^4 = a^3$ **25.** false, $15^2 \div 15^2 = 1$ **26.** true **27.** true **28.** true **29.** true **30.** true

Activity 77—Area of Squares

1. Area $= 2^2$ **2.** Area $= 5^2$ **3.** Area $= 1^2$ **4.** Area $= p^2$ **5.** Area $= d^2$ **6.** Area $= h^2$ **7.** 16 sq cm **8.** 81 sq cm **9.** 49 sq cm **10.** 121 sq cm **11.** 196 sq cm **12.** 484 sq cm **13.** 25 sq yd **14.** 100 sq ft **15.** Yes, the scrapbook page has an area of 256 square inches, so the square picture with an area of 169 square inches will easily fit on the page.

Activity 78—Volume of Cubes

1. Volume $= 7^3$ **2.** Volume $= s^3$ **3.** Volume $= k^3$ **4.** 64 cu cm **5.** 27 cu cm **6.** 512 cu cm **7.** 1,000 cu cm **8.** 1,728 cu cm **9.** 5,832 cu cm **10.** 9,261 cu cm **11.** 2,744 cu cm **12.** 35,937 cu cm **13.** 238,328 cu cm **14.** 343 cu cm of wax **15.** 2,197 cu in., 1,331 cu in.; difference of 866 cu in.

Activity 79—Square Root Values

1. 5, 6; 5.20 **2.** 7, 8; 7.21 **3.** 4, 5; 4.36 **4.** 6, 7; 6.08 **5.** 6, 7; 6.63 **6.** 9, 10; 9.54 **7.** 8, 9; 8.54 **8.** 4, 5; 4.58 **9.** 3, 4; 3.61 **10.** 8, 9; 8.12 **11.** 7, 8; 7.75 **12.** 6, 7; 6.16 **13.** 9, 10; 9.11 **14.** 1, 2; 1.41 **15.** 4.58 **16.** 8.19 **17.** 8.72 **18.** 6 **19.** 12 feet **20.** 75 meters

Activity 80—Irrational Numbers, Square Roots

1. rational **2.** irrational **3.** irrational **4.** rational **5.** irrational **6.** rational **7.** irrational **8.** rational **9.** rational **10.** irrational For **11–15**, accept any irrational number within 0.3 of the following numbers. **11.** 2.2 **12.** 3.2 **13.** 7.1 **14.** 7.4 **15.** 10

Activity 81—Irrational Numbers as Decimals

1. irrational **2.** rational **3.** rational **4.** irrational **5.** rational
6. rational **7.** irrational **8.** irrational **9.** rational **10.** irrational
11. irrational **12.** rational **13.** irrational **14.** rational
15. irrational **16.** rational **17.** 20 inches **18.** 30.48 m **19.** 60 cm
20. no, one side of the square tray is $\sqrt{112.4}$, or about 10.6 inches

Activity 82—Equations with Radicals

1. 36 **2.** 11 cm **3.** $5\sqrt{10}$ feet **4.** $2\sqrt{7}$ feet **5.** $2\sqrt{13}$ inches

Activity 83—Pythagorean Theorem

1. 6.40 **2.** 10.95 **3.** 4.90 **4.** 17.2 **5.** 10.82 **6.** 10.95 **7.** 9.17 **8.** 5.83
9. 13.90 inches **10.** 2.83 meters

Activity 84—About Triangles

1. yes **2.** no **3.** no **4.** yes **5.** no **6.** yes, no, no, yes **7.** 5, no, yes, no
8. no, yes, no **9.** 5, yes, no, no **10.** no, no, no

Activity 85—Polygon Perimeters

1. 45 ft **2.** 20.426 mm **3.** $17\frac{1}{4}$ in. **4.** 38.4 m **5.** $6\frac{2}{3}$ yards **6.** 35.06 m
7. 14 cm **8.** 274.2 ft **9.** 2.1 pints or 3 pint cans **10.** 6.7 feet each

Activity 86—Regular Polygon Perimeters

1. 28 mm **2.** 6 in. **3.** 28.1 m **4.** 600 ft **5.** $8\frac{1}{4}$ yd **6.** 29.58 mi
7. 14 sides **8.** 21 sides **9.** 9 sides **10.** 13 sides

Activity 87—Irregular Polygon Perimeters

1. $39\frac{1}{4}$ in. **2.** 47 cm **3.** 73.4 ft **4.** 184.1 m **5.** $20\frac{5}{12}$ km **6.** 117.8 in.
7. 4.4 **8.** $8\frac{1}{3}$ **9.** 321 m **10.** 100 ft

Activity 88—Areas of Rectangles, Squares

1. 15 mm^2 **2.** 44 in.^{2} **3.** 156.8 yd^2 **4.** 57 m^2 **5.** $53\frac{5}{6}$ mi^2
6. $48\frac{1}{10}$ yd^2 **7.** 49 dm^2 **8.** 625 in.^{2} **9.** 37.21 m^2 **10.** 4,173.16 mm^2
11. $84\frac{16}{25}$ ft^2 **12.** $32\frac{1}{9}$ yd^2 **13.** 900 m^2 **14.** 1,049.76 km^2
15. 62.41 ft^2 **16.** 7,056 yd^2 **17.** 13.4689 mi^2 **18.** 845.6464 km^2
19. $4\frac{1}{2}$ boxes **20.** 1,122.3 ft^2; 138.6 ft

Activity 89—Area—Triangles

1. 60 in.^{2} **2.** 126.5 ft^2 **3.** 156 m^2 **4.** 21 km^2 **5.** 18 cm^2 **6.** 210 yd^2
7. 8 m **8.** 6 in. **9.** 10 yd **10.** 24 m **11.** 3 mm **12.** 8 mi **13.** 8 ft
14. 20 in. **15.** 30 cm **16.** 7 mm **17.** 3 yd **18.** 11 ft **19.** 10 ft
20. No, both triangles are 200 ft^2.

Activity 90—Area—Trapezoids and Parallelograms

1. 24 ft^2 **2.** 90 yd^2 **3.** 450 m^2 **4.** 340 in.^{2} **5.** 31.8645 m^2 **6.** 10 cm
7. 17 m **8.** 15 ft **9.** 16 yd **10.** 17 mm **11.** 29 cm **12.** 15.5 mi
13. 4 cm **14.** 42 ft **15.** 219 m

Activity 91—Area—Irregular Polygons

1. 50 units^2 **2.** 175 units^2 **3.** 88 units^2 **4.** 173 units^2 **5.** 425 units^2
6. 350.5 units^2 **7.** 315.5 units^2 **8.** 1,550.5 units^2 **9.** 33 units^2
10. 2,185 units^2

Activity 92—Circumferences, Areas of Circles

1. 12.56 km **2.** 25.12 ft **3.** 18.84 cm **4.** 21.98 mm **5.** 31.4 in.
6. 25.12 yd **7.** 43.96 in. **8.** 50.24 m **9.** 56.52 ft **10.** 62.8 m
11. 50.24 ft^2 **12.** 113.04 cm^2 **13.** 200.96 yd^2 **14.** 28.26 km^2
15. 78.5 in.^{2} **16.** 78.5 m^2 **17.** 153.86 mi^2 **18.** 200.96 ft^2
19. 452.16 in.^{2} **20.** 3.14 m^2 **21.** 15.89625 mi^2 **22.** 154,751.76 yd^2
23. 98.4704 m^2 **24.** 44.15625 ft^2 **25.** 8.0384 in.^{2} **26.** 5,538.96 km^2
27. 572.265 yd^2 **28.** 0.4415625 mm^2 **29.** 1,149,318.5 cm^2
30. 775,608.26 ft^2

Activity 93—Faces, Edges, and Vertices

1. cube, 6 faces, 12 edges, 8 vertices
2. triangular prism, 5 faces, 9 edges, 6 vertices
3. square pyramid, 5 faces, 8 edges, 5 vertices
4. sphere, 0 faces, 0 edges, 0 vertices
5. hexagonal prism, 8 faces, 18 edges, 12 vertices
6. rectangular prism, 6 faces, 12 edges, 8 vertices
7. cylinder, 2 faces, 0 edges, 0 vertices
8. cone, 1 face, 1 edge, 1 vertex
9. square pyramid, 5 faces, 8 edges, 5 vertices
10. (Answers may vary.) house or cube and square pyramid, 9 faces, 16 edges, 9 vertices

Activity 94—Surface Area—Prisms and Cylinders

1. 726 cm^2 **2.** 552 ft^2 **3.** 408 square units **4.** 471 m^2
5. 420 square units **6.** 2,736 cm^2 **7.** 1,860 in.^{2} **8.** 84 mm^2
9. 1,257 m^2 **10.** 1,120 square units

Activity 95—Surface Area—Pyramids and Cones

1. 360 in.^{2} **2.** 84.82 cm^2 **3.** 56 ft^2 **4.** 204.20 m^2 **5.** 300 yd^2
6. 402.12 mm^2 **7.** 260 ft^2 **8.** 508.94 cm^2 **9.** 1,536 mm^2
10. 1,225.22 in.^{2}

Activity 96—Cubes, Prisms, and Pyramids—Volumes

1. 30 ft^3 **2.** 64 m^3 **3.** 21 cm^3 **4.** 1,000 in.^{3} **5.** 108 yd^3 **6.** 42.67 mm^3
7. 32,768 mi^3 **8.** 4.913 in.^{3} **9.** 1,560,896 km^3 **10.** 0.064 mm^3
11. 27,000 cm^3 **12.** 1.728 ft^3 **13.** 300,763 in.^{3} **14.** 35,937 m^3
15. 5,088.448 mm^3 **16.** 1,404,928 ft^3 **17.** 0.857375 dm^3
18. 15,625,000 m^3 **19.** 20 books **20.** 1,300 ft^3

Activity 97—Cylinders, Cones, and Spheres—Volumes

1. 42.39 mm^3 **2.** 226.08 ft^3 **3.** 445.095 in.^{3} **4.** 12.56 yd^3
5. 3.925 cm^3 **6.** 117.75 m^3 **7.** 937.81$\overline{3}$ cm^3 **8.** 7.32$\overline{6}$ ft^3
9. 1,004.8 yd^3 **10.** 76,930 cm^3 **11.** 9.42 m^3 **12.** 52,987.5 mm^3
13. 7,234.56 mm^3 **14.** 904.32 ft^3 **15.** 18,807.03 cm^3 **16.** 3,052,080 yd^3
17. 113,040 ft^3 **18.** 14,130 cm^3 **19.** Cylinder; Its volume is 50.24 cm^3. The volume of the sphere is only 33.49$\overline{3}$ cm^3. **20.** One needs to know the height of the cylinder to compare the volumes.

Activity 98—Equalities—Graphing

1.

2.

3.

4.

5.

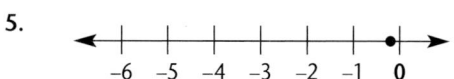

6. $x = 5$ **7.** $x = -2$ **8.** $x = 7$ **9.** $x = -4$ **10.** $x = 3\frac{1}{2}$

Activity 99—Inequalities—Graphing

1.

2.

3.

4.

5.

6. $x < 5$ **7.** $x > -2$ **8.** $x \le 3$ **9.** $x \ge -4$ **10.** $x < 2$

Activity 100—Solutions of Equalities—Graphing

1. $y = -1$ **2.** $c = 7$ **3.** $p = 1$ **4.** $u = 10$ **5.** $h = -8$ **6.** $g = 4$
7. $s = 2$ **8.** $w = 8$ **9.** $x = 8$ **10.** $k = -2$ **11.** $j = -1$ **12.** $d = 0$
13. $v = -3$

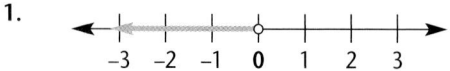

14. $x = 210$

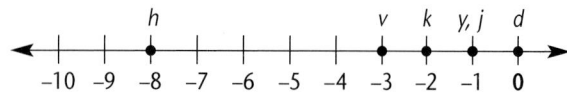

15. $x = 3$

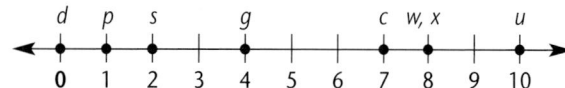

Activity 101—Solutions of Inequalities—Graphing

1. $q \ge 4$

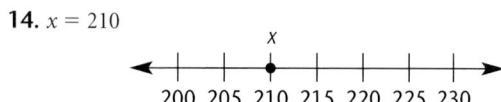

2. $a \le 3$

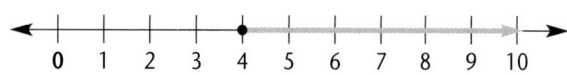

3. $z > 6$

4. $w > -1$

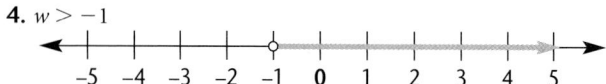

5. $s \ge -3$

6. $x < 10$

7. $e < -6$

8. $d \le 8$

9. $c < 4$

10. $r > -8$

11. $f < -2$

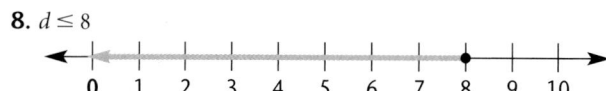

12. $v \ge 3$

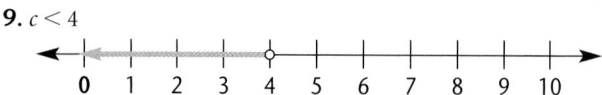

13. $t > -1$

14. $y \ge 217$

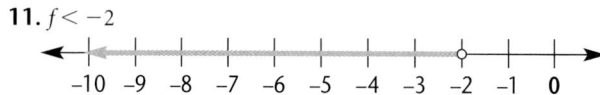

15. $y \ge$ May 25

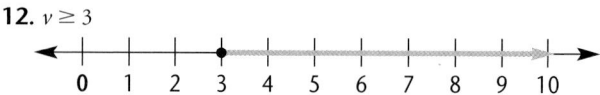

Activity 102—Locating Points—The Coordinate System

1. $(1, 4)$ **2.** $(2, 0)$ **3.** $(-4, -1)$ **4.** $(7, 2)$ **5.** $(-1, 4)$ **6.** $(3, -3)$
7. $(0, 5)$ **8.** $(-5, 2)$ **9.** $(-4, 3)$ **10.** $(0, -6)$ **11.** $(1, 0)$ **12.** $(3, -1)$
13. $(5, -4)$ **14.** $(-4, -6)$ **15.** $(3, 5)$ **16.** Quadrant III
17. Quadrant I **18.** Quadrant IV **19.** Quadrant II **20.** Quadrant
IV **21.** Quadrant III **22.** 10 units **23.** 21 units **24.** 18 units
25. 8 units

Activity 103—Plotting Points—The Coordinate System

1–10.

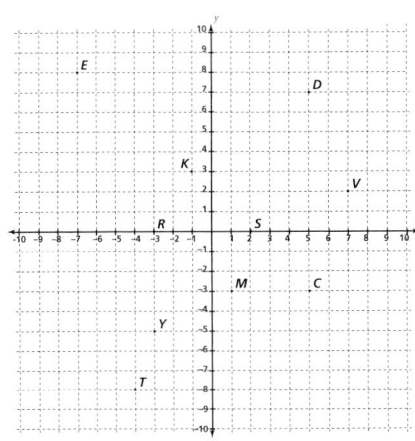

11. Quadrant IV **12.** Quadrant I **13.** Quadrant III **14.** Quadrant IV
15. Quadrant II

Activity 104—The Points of a Line

1.

y = x + 2	
x	y
−2	0
4	6
7	9

2.

y = x − 3	
x	y
−3	−6
0	−3
3	0

3.

y = x − 2	
x	y
−5	−7
1	−1
4	2

4.

y = x + 5	
x	y
−3	2
0	5
4	9

5.

y = x − 4	
x	y
−6	−10
−4	−8
4	0

6.

y = x + 7	
x	y
−4	3
0	7
7	14

7.

y = x + 4	
x	y
−1	3
3	7
7	11

8.

y = x − 5	
x	y
−3	−8
−1	−6
2	−3

9.

y = x − 8	
x	y
−2	−10
0	−8
7	−1

10.

y = x + 3	
x	y
−4	−1
2	5
6	9

11.

y = x + 6	
x	y
−8	−2
−1	5
3	9

12.

y = x − 1	
x	y
−5	−6
0	−1
3	2

13.

y = x − 7	
x	y
−2	−9
0	−7
6	−1

14.

y = x + 1.26	
x	y
−4.82	−3.56
−3.72	−2.46
4.18	5.44

15.

y = x − 58.9	
x	y
−4.9	−63.8
25.4	−33.5
50.7	−8.2

Activity 105—Functions and Lines

1. $-\frac{8}{3}$ or $-2\frac{2}{3}$; B **2.** $\frac{1}{5}$; A **3.** $\frac{7}{6}$ or $1\frac{1}{6}$; A **4.** $-\frac{5}{7}$; B **5.** $-\frac{1}{2}$; B **6.** 15
7. 0 **8.** 215 **9.** 0 **10.** 3 **11.** 8 **12.** 21 **13.** 9 **14.** $8\frac{1}{2}$ or $\frac{17}{2}$ **15.** −4

Activity 106—Finding the Domain and Range

1. 0, 1, 4, 8, 100 **2.** −11, −10, 17, 206, 1,718 **3.** $-6\frac{3}{8}$, −6, $-4\frac{1}{8}$, $-2\frac{1}{4}$, $1\frac{1}{2}$ **4.** 104, 14, −4, −4, 24 **5.** −2, 13, 19, 25, 40 **6.** −19, −5, −3, 3, 15 **7.** −26, −20, −6, 16, 46 **8.** 23, 9, −9, −7, 119 **9.** (−4, 5) (−3, 6) domain: −4, −3 range: 5, 6 **10.** (5, 3) (6, −10) domain: 5, 6 range: 3, −10 **11.** (−123, 18) (47, −190) domain: −123, 47 range: 18, −190 **12.** (2, 3) (3, 7) (4, 11) domain: 2, 3, 4 range: 3, 7, 11 **13.** (−1, 9) (9, 9) (27, 9) (43, 9) domain: −1, 9, 27, 43 range: 9 **14.** domain: $-6 \le x \le 6$ range: $-1 \le y \le 1$ **15.** domain: $-4 \le x \le 7$ range: $-2 \le y \le 4$

Activity 107—Graphing a Line

1. $x = -3, 0, 3; y = 0, 3, 6$

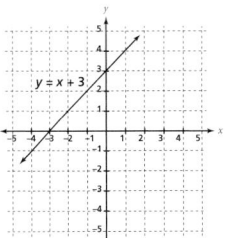

2. $x = 0, 1, 2; y = 1, 0, -1$

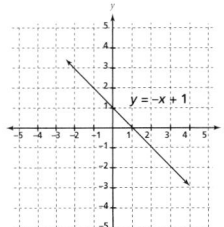

3. $x = -1, 0, 1; y = -4, 0, 4$

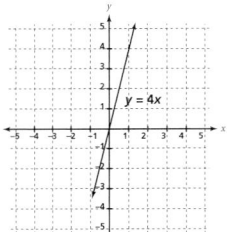

4. $x = 0, 1, 2; y = 1, 3, 5$

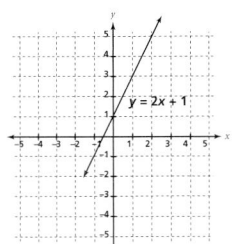

5. $x = -1, 0, 1; y = 0, 3, 6$

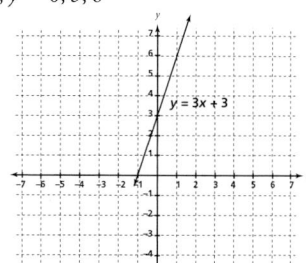

Activity 108—Slope of a Line
1. -40 **2.** 9 **3.** 0.05 **4.** 0.16 **5.** 88 **6.** 1.23 **7.** -25 **8.** -9 **9.** 0.29
10. -0.97 **11.** 23.2 **12.** 1.6 **13.** 0.09 **14.** 90.88 **15.** -32 **16.** 684
17. 5.89 **18.** 0.007 **19.** 0.965 **20.** -1.84

Activity 109—Formula—Slope of a Line
1. $\frac{1}{5}$ **2.** $-\frac{1}{8}$ **3.** 0 **4.** $\frac{6}{5}$ **5.** $-\frac{2}{3}$ **6.** -2 **7.** 2 **8.** $-\frac{2}{3}$ **9.** $-\frac{5}{3}$ **10.** $-\frac{4}{7}$
11. $\frac{5}{3}$ **12.** $-\frac{9}{8}$ **13.** $\frac{1}{2}$ **14.** -1 **15.** $-\frac{4}{5}$ **16.** $-\frac{4}{11}$ **17.** $\frac{9}{8}$ **18.** 2
19. -1 **20.** $\frac{1}{2}$ **21.** 1 **22.** 1 **23.** $\frac{4}{3}$ **24.** Monroe Hill, because
$\frac{180}{640} > \frac{96}{640}$ so $\frac{9}{32} > \frac{3}{20}$ **25.** the second slope because it has a negative
or downward slope, which would be easier to ride a bike on than the
first slope's upward slope

Activity 110—Slope-Intercept Form of a Line
1. $m = 1$, y-intercept $= 3$, x-intercept $= -3$ **2.** $m = 2$, y-intercept
$= -2$, x-intercept $= 1$ **3.** $y = x + 2$ **4.** $y = 3x - 4$ **5.** $y = -x + 5$
6. $y = 5x - 1$ **7.** $y = 2x + 5$ **8.** $y = x - 3$ **9.** $m = 1$, y-intercept $=$
-3, x-intercept $= 3$ **10.** $m = 2$, y-intercept $= 5$, x-intercept $= -\frac{5}{2}$
11. $m = 4$, y-intercept $= 2$, x-intercept $= -\frac{1}{2}$ **12.** $m = -1$,
y-intercept $= -8$, x-intercept $= -8$ **13.** $m = 3$, y-intercept $= -6$,
x-intercept $= 2$ **14.** $m = -2$, y-intercept $= 7$, x-intercept $= \frac{7}{2}$
15. $m = 1$, y-intercept $= 9$, x-intercept $= -9$ **16.** $m = -2$, y-
intercept $= 4$, x-intercept$= 2$ **17.** $m = 3$, y-intercept $= -3$, x-
intercept $= 1$ **18.** $m = 5$, y-intercept $= -1$, x-intercept $= \frac{1}{5}$
19. $m = -1$, y-intercept $= 8$, x-intercept $= 8$ **20.** $m = 2$,
y-intercept $= -9$, x-intercept $= \frac{9}{2}$

Activity 111—Angles, Angle Measures
1. YU and YV **2.** $\angle SYR$ **3.** $\angle QYR$ and $\angle RYQ$ **4.** point Y **5.** $\overline{YV}$
6. $\angle RYQ$, $\angle RYS$, $\angle RYT$, $\angle RYU$, $\angle RYV$, $\angle RYW$, $\angle RYX$ **7.** $\angle 3$
8. $\angle XYV$ **9.** $25°$ **10.** $95°$ **11.** $85°$ **12.** $107°$ **13.** $62°$ **14.** $50°$
15. $36°$

Activity 112—Classifying Angles
1. obtuse **2.** right **3.** obtuse **4.** acute **5.** acute **6.** straight
7. angles f and h **8.** angles e and g; h and f **9.** $125°, 55°$
10. vertical, obtuse **11.** adjacent **12.** vertical, acute **13.** true
14. false **15.** true

Activity 113—Complementary, Supplementary Angles
1. $\angle TVU$ **2.** $\angle WVY$ and $\angle XVY$ **3.** $90°$ **4.** $\angle XVW$ or $\angle ZVT$
5. answers may vary **6.** $80°$ **7.** $25°$ **8.** $40°$ **9.** $48°$ **10.** $53°$ **11.** $65°$
12. $68°$ **13.** $85°$ **14.** $40°$ **15.** $5°$ **16.** $100°$ **17.** $136°$ **18.** $15°$
19. $71°$ **20.** $92°$

Activity 114—Measures of Triangle Angles
1. $55°$ **2.** $90°$ **3.** $40°$ **4.** $65°$ **5.** $45°$ **6.** $65°$ **7.** $60°$ **8.** $65°$ **9.** $70°$
10. $30°$ **11.** $80°$ **12.** $60°$ **13.** $25°$ **14.** $40°$ **15.** $25°$

Activity 115—Triangle Names
1. right scalene **2.** equilateral **3.** acute isosceles **4.** equilateral and
equiangular **5.** obtuse scalene **6.** right isosceles **7.** scalene
8. isosceles acute **9.** right **10.** obtuse

Activity 116—Triangles That Are Congruent
1. SSS **2.** SAS **3.** ASA **4.** Yes, ASA **5.** No, none of the sides are
congruent or there is not enough information to tell.

Activity 117—Triangles That Are Similar
1. yes **2.** no **3.** yes **4.** not enough information **5.** yes
6. not enough information **7.** false **8.** true **9.** false **10.** true

Activity 118—Naming Parallelograms
Note: All figures are quadrilateral.
1. square **2.** trapezoid **3.** trapezoid **4.** parallelogram
5. quadrilateral **6.** rhombus **7.** Tennessee **8.** Vermont or
Connecticut or New Hampshire **9.** Wyoming and Colorado
10. North Dakota or South Dakota

Activity 119—Quadrilaterals—Diagonals
1. $110°$ **2.** no **3.** $90°$ **4.** 6 **5.** yes **6.** $40°$ **7.** $110°$ **8.** They are
congruent. **9.** $59°$ **10.** no

Activity 120—Polygons—Diagonals
1. 5 **2.** 6 **3.** 12 **4.** quadrilateral **5.** octagon **6.** decagon **7.** $540°$
8. $900°$ **9.** $1{,}440°$ **10.** $1{,}980°$ **11.** $2{,}160°$ **12.** $120°$ **13.** $140°$
14. $147.3°$ **15.** $152.3°$ **16.** $154.3°$ **17.** $90°$ **18.** $45°$ **19.** $32.7°$
20. $27.7°$

Activity 121—Points and Their Reflections
1. $A' = (4, -1)$ **2.** $B' = (1, 6)$ **3.** $C' = (-5, 0)$ **4.** $D' = (7, 3)$
5. $E' = (-2, -1)$ **6.** $A' = (-4, 5)$ **7.** $A' = (-3, -2)$ **8.** $H' = (6, 0)$
9. $I' = (-9, 4)$ **10.** $J' = (3, -3)$ **11.** $K' = (-4, 1)$ **12.** $L' = (-5, 3)$
13. $M' = (2, 0)$ **14.** $N' = (7, 4)$ **15.** $O' = (1, 1)$ **16.** $P' = (3, 3)$
17. $Q' = (-4, -5)$ **18.** $R' = (0, -5)$ **19.** $S' = (-3, -2)$
20. $T' = (7, 0)$

Activity 122—Lines of Symmetry
1. Yes **2.** Yes **3.** Yes **4.** No **5.** Yes **6.** Yes **7.** No **8.** No **9.** No
10. Yes **11.** No **12.** Yes **13.** Yes **14.** No **15.** Yes

Activity 123—Slides, Translations
1. $A' = (5, -3)$ **2.** $B' = (3, 2)$ **3.** $C' = (1, -1)$ **4.** $D' = (11, -9)$
5. $E' = (8, 0)$ **6.** $J' = (-2, 1)$ **7.** $K' = (1, 4)$ **8.** $L' = (5, 2)$
9. $M' = (-5, 3)$ **10.** $N' = (4, -3)$ **11.** $A' = (7, 7), B' = (0, 9)$
12. $C' = (-4, -5), D' = (0, -9)$ **13.** $E' = (7, -7), F' = (12, -2)$
14. $G' = (-5, 8), H' = (1, 4)$ **15.** $I' = (1, -3), J' = (8, 4)$

Activity 124—Clockwise and Counterclockwise Rotations
1. new coordinate $P' = (-3, 3)$ **2.** new coordinate $P' = (-2, 0)$
3. new coordinate $P' = (-1, 5)$ **4.** new coordinate $P' = (5, 8)$
5. new coordinate $P' = (-4, 5)$

Activity 125—Reading Bar Graphs
1. Enterprise; Piedmont **2.** Forestdale **3.** Piedmont **4.** Enterprise
5. Forestdale **6.** Enterprise **7.** less than **8.** 15,499; When rounding
to the nearest thousand, 15,499 is the greatest number that rounds to
15,000. **9.** 14,450; When rounding to the nearest thousand, 14,450 is
the least number that rounds to 15,000. **10.** Sample answer: a title, a
horizontal axis with labels, a vertical axis with labels, an interval, data

Activity 126—Reading Frequency Tables

1. Sample answer: Without a title, the data displayed by a frequency graph would not be meaningful. **2.** 10 years **3.** Yes. Sample explanation: Various intervals can be chosen for any frequency graph. **4.** between 20 and 29 years old; Sample explanation: The table does not give an exact age. Instead, it gives a range or interval of ages. **5.** between 70 and 79 years old; Sample explanation: The table does not give an exact age. Instead, it gives a range or interval of ages. **6.** 20 students; The sum of the tally marks in the tally column and the sum of the numbers in the frequency column are 20. **7.** The sums should be identical. **8.** Sample answer: The frequency table contains one or more errors. **9.** Sample answer: The data can be interpreted two ways—by tally or by number. **10.** Sample answer: If the number of tallies to be displayed by a frequency table is great, the table can become physically large.

Activity 127—Reading Circle Graphs

1. 75% **2.** 25% **3.** 15 students **4.** 45 students **5.** 270°; Sample explanation: 75% of 360° is 270°. **6.** 90°; Sample explanation: 25% of 360° is 90°. **7.** Sample answer: The number of degrees representing data that have been rounded may not have a sum of exactly 360°. **8.** Sample answer: The sum of percent data that is rounded to the nearest whole number may not be exactly 100%. **9.** 450 students; 150 students **10.** Sample answer: a title, labels, numerical data

Activity 128—Organizing Data

1. 20 **2.** >121; Because only one person had that score. **3.** 71–80 **4.** 4 **5.** Yes; Because 3 people were in the lowest range of scores (61–70).

Activity 129—Comparing Data

1. 2 **2.** 3 **3.** 4 **4.** no; no **5.** no

Activity 130—Mean Values

1. Sample answer: Find the sum of the data values in the set, then divide by the number of data values. **2.** 12 **3.** 645 **4.** 53.75 **5.** 10 **6.** 539 **7.** 53.9 **8.** Yes; Find the sum of the fractions in the set, then divide by the number of fractions. **9.** Yes. Find the sum of the decimals in the set, then divide by the number of decimals. **10.** zero

Activity 131—Median Values

1. Charmaine; 102 points **2.** Karin; 80 points **3.** an even number **4.** No. The median represents the middle value of the set of data. The actual number of values in the set of data is not relevant. **5.** Sample answer: 102; 99; 93; 93; 92; 90; 90; 88; 86; 85; 85; 83; 81; 80 **6.** 89 **7.** Sample answer: easier because there would have been only one middle value **8.** Sample answer: No; the median of the data set {4, 2, 3} can be found using mental math. **9.** Sample answer: No. Adding the teacher's age simply moves the location of the median up or down one value in a data set in which most of the values are nearly the same. **10.** Answers will vary.

Activity 132—Mode Values

1. 2, 5 **2.** The number of tallies and the number of data values should be identical. **3.** The mode of any set of data is the value or values that occur most often. **4.** Sample answer: {100, 300, 500, 500, 700, 900} **5.** Sample answer: {the set of counting numbers}

Activity 133—Range Values

1. 9 in. **2.** $1\frac{1}{4}$ in. **3.** 1 in. **4.** $\frac{6}{8}$ inch or $\frac{3}{4}$ inch **5.** Answers will vary.

Activity 134—A Box-and-Whiskers Plot

1. 5; 6; 6; 6; 7; 7; 7; 8; 8; 8; 10 **2.** 5 hours **3.** 10 hours **4.** 7 hours **5.** 6 hours **6.** 8 hours **7.** Check students' plots. **8.** Check students' plots. **9.** Check students' plots.

10.

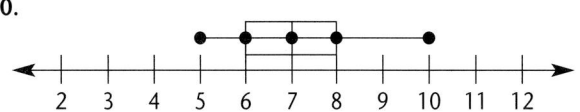

Activity 135—Using the Probability Fraction

1. $\frac{1}{2}$; 50% **2.** $\frac{1}{3}$; $33\frac{1}{3}$% **3.** $\frac{2}{3}$; $66\frac{2}{3}$% **4.** $\frac{6}{6}$ or 1; 100% **5.** $\frac{0}{6}$ or 0; 0% **6.** $\frac{3}{4}$; 75% **7.** $\frac{1}{4}$; 25% **8.** $\frac{1}{4}$; 25% **9.** $\frac{3}{4}$; 75% **10.** $\frac{4}{4}$ or 1; 100%

Activity 136—Dependent, Independent Events

1. $\frac{1}{100}$ **2.** $\frac{1}{4}$ **3.** $\frac{1}{100}$ **4.** $\frac{1}{2,300}$ **5.** $\frac{11}{46}$

Activity 137—Fundamental Principle of Counting

1. 5 ways **2.** 120 ways **3.** 24 ways **4.** 1,000 combinations **5.** 24 combinations

Alternative Activities

Alternative Activity 1—Counting by Tens
1. 6 groups of 10 blocks circled, plus 2 not circled
2. 1 group of 10 diamonds circled, plus 1 not circled
3. 4 groups of 10 angles circled, plus 9 not circled
4. 2, 20,000 **5.** 3, 10 **6.** 6, 600 **7.** 600, 1,000, 10,000, 11,600
8. 800, 7,000, 0, 7,800 **9.** 400, 5,000, 50,000, 55,400
10. 300, 2,000, 80,000, 82,300

Alternative Activity 2—Choosing a Classroom Calculator
Answers will vary.

Alternative Activity 3—Value of Numbers
1. tens **2.** hundreds **3.** ten-thousands **4.** millions **5.** 0 **6.** 9,000
7. 9,000 **8.** 6
9. $(1 \times 10,000) + (2 \times 1,000) + (2 \times 100) + (0 \times 10) + (0 \times 1)$
10. $(6 \times 10,000) + (7 \times 1,000) + (8 \times 100) + (9 \times 10) + (5 \times 1)$
11. $(2 \times 1,000) + (1 \times 100) + (0 \times 10) + (0 \times 1)$
12. $(8 \times 100) + (9 \times 10) + (1 \times 1)$
13. $(4 \times 10^3) + (3 \times 10^2) + (5 \times 10^1) + (7 \times 10^0)$
14. $(2 \times 10^2) + (1 \times 10^1) + (3 \times 10^0)$
15. $(8 \times 10^6) + (4 \times 10^5) + (6 \times 10^4) + (5 \times 10^3) + (8 \times 10^2) + (0 \times 10^1) + (1 \times 10^0)$

Alternative Activity 4—Inverse Operations: Adding and Subtracting
1.

2.
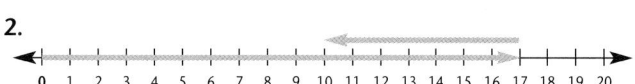

3. 21 40 **4.** 75 101 **5.** 223 920
$+ 19$ $- 21$ $+ 26$ $- 26$ $+ 697$ $- 223$
40 19 101 75 920 697

6. 1,259 1,898 **7.** 218 251 **8.** 707 975
$+ 639$ $- 639$ $+ 33$ $- 33$ $+ 268$ $- 268$
1,898 1,259 251 218 975 707

9. 33 **10.** 923 **11.** 206 **12.** 1,576 **13.** 355
$+ 19$ $- 216$ $+ 114$ $+ 658$ $+ 336$
52 707 320 2,234 691

14. 65 minutes **15.** 31 years old

Alternative Activity 5—Inverse Operations: Multiplying and Dividing
1. 21 **2.** 77 **3.** 45 **4.** 104 **5.** 40 **6.** 6 **7.** 96 **8.** 6 **9.** 50
10. $35 \div 5 = 7$ **11.** $72 \div 36 = 2$ **12.** $40 \times 6 = 240$
13. $3 \times 60 = 180$ **14.** $56 \div 8 = 7$ **15.** 30 bones **16.** multiply $(\times)$
17. divide $(\div)$ **18.** subtract $(-)$ **19.** add $(+)$ **20.** subtract $(-)$

Alternative Activity 6—Binary System
1. 11_2 **2.** 1010_2 **3.** 1100100_2 **4.** 1010111_2 **5.** 10000101_2 **6.** 11111_2
7. 4_{10} **8.** 27_{10} **9.** 2_{10} **10.** 13_{10} **11.** 1_{10} **12.** 1010 **13.** 9 **14.** 8 **15.** 3
16. 110010 **17.** 11001 **18.** 7 **19.** 101 **20.** 1100

Alternative Activity 7—Quinary System
1. 43_5 **2.** 110_5 **3.** 211_5 **4.** 400_5 **5.** 4000_5 **6.** 16_{10} **7.** 110_{10} **8.** 3_{10}
9. 9_{10} **10.** 152_{10} **11.** 134_5 **12.** 75_{10} **13.** 2333_5 **14.** 25_{10} **15.** 330_5
16. 23301_5 **17.** 39 **18.** 390 **19.** 232 **20.** 1311

Alternative Activity 8—Whole Numbers—Adding
1. 133 **2.** 110 **3.** 453 **4.** 756 **5.** 2,220 **6.** $121x$ **7.** $1,121y$ **8.** $1,074b$
9. $4,377a$ **10.** $562b$ **11.** $1,323x$ **12.** $2,498y$ **13.** $2,323a$
14. $28 + 63 + 16 = 107$ pages **15.** $53 + 37 + 137 = 227$ books

Alternative Activity 9—Whole Numbers—Subtracting
1. 13 **2.** 114 **3.** $435y$ **4.** 1,188 **5.** $175y$ **6.** 439 **7.** 979 **8.** $3,125b$
9. $1,099x$ **10.** 350 **11.** 188 **12.** $819y$ **13.** $1,368a$ **14.** $781 - 159 =$
622 students **15.** $401 - 386 = 15$ hours

Alternative Activity 10—Sums and Differences—Estimation
1. $50 + 40 = 90$ **2.** $80 + 50 = 130$ **3.** $400 + 20 = 420$ **4.** $700 +$
$3,000 = 3,700$ **5.** $50 - 40 = 10$ **6.** $800 - 400 = 400$ **7.** $700 - 400$
$= 300$ **8.** $500 - 80 = 420$ **9.** $60 - 40 = 20$ boxes **10.** $400 - 80 =$
320 jeans

Alternative Activity 11—Whole Numbers—Multiplying
1. $19 \cdot 7$ or $(19)(7)$; 133 **2.** $30 \cdot 41$ or 30×41; 1,230 **3.** $(24)(6)$ or
24×6; 144 **4.** $(47)(12x)$ or $47 \cdot 12x$; $564x$ **5.** $(51)(72)$ or 51×72;
3,672 **6.** $31y \cdot 18$ or $31y \times 18$; $558y$ **7.** 1,162 **8.** 1,728 **9.** $1,815x$
10. $2,021a$ **11.** 2,028 **12.** $493y$ **13.** $258x$ **14.** $37 \times 16 = 592$ books
15. $24 \times 86 = 2,064$ videotapes

Alternative Activity 12—Whole Numbers—Dividing
1. 9; $9 \times 8 = 72$ **2.** 3; $3 \times 13 = 39$ **3.** $4c$; $4c \times 8 = 32c$ **4.** 3; 3×7
$= 21$ **5.** $7a$; $7a \times 11 = 77a$ **6.** 9 r3; $9 \times 9 + 3 = 84$ **7.** 23 **8.** 65
9. $91x$ **10.** 123 r2 **11.** 250 r3 **12.** $431b$ **13.** $420x$ **14.** $576 \div 72 =$
8 chairs **15.** $5,334 \div 127 = 42$ items

Alternative Activity 13—Products and Quotients—Estimating
1. 50×60 **2.** 90×20 **3.** 90×50 **4.** 100×20 **5.** $3,000 \times 200$
6. $200 \div 4$ **7.** $280 \div 40$ **8.** $800 \div 40$ **9.** $3,000 \div 60$ **10.** $2,400 \div$
80 **11.** $80 \times 10 = 800$ **12.** $20 \times 50 = 1,000$ **13.** $30 \times 20 = 600$
14. $40 \times 90 = 3,600$ **15.** $40 \times 40 = 1,600$ **16.** $150 \div 10 = 15$
17. $500 \div 50 = 10$ **18.** $1,600 \div 80 = 20$ **19.** $40 \times 400 = 16,000$;
$36 \times 368 = 13,248$ **20.** $240 \div 6 = 40$; $234 \div 6 = 39$

Alternative Activity 14—Operations and Open Statements
1. subtraction **2.** division **3.** addition; multiplication
4. multiplication; division **5.** multiplication **6.** $9 \cdot 5$; $(9)(5)$ **7.** $\frac{18}{6}$;
$18 \div 6$ **8.** $5 \cdot n$; $5n$ **9.** $\frac{40}{x}$; $40 \div x$ **10.** false **11.** false **12.** open
13. true **14.** true **15.** open **16.** false **17.** open **18.** true **19.** true
20. false **21.** open **22.** open **23.** open **24.** true **25.** false

Alternative Activity 15—Using Letters for Numbers
1. p **2.** y **3.** g **4.** y **5.** n **6.** f **7.** m **8.** algebraic **9.** multiplication
10. numerical **11.** addition; multiplication **12.** numerical
13. division **14.** algebraic **15.** multiplication; subtraction
16. algebraic **17.** multiplication; addition **18.** numerical
19. subtraction; addition **20.** $12 + 8 = x$

Alternative Activity 16—Replacing Variables with Numbers
1. true **2.** false **3.** false **4.** true **5.** true **6.** 6 **7.** 48 **8.** 26 **9.** 24
10. 19 **11.** 0 **12.** 16 **13.** 37 **14.** 2 **15.** $n - 25$ **16.** $24 + n$
17. $6n$ **18.** $25 \div n$ **19.** $8n - 17$ **20.** $n \div 6$

Alternative Activity 17—Place Value of Numbers

1. hundredths **2.** tens **3.** tenths **4.** ones **5.** hundreds **6.** ones
7. thousands **8.** hundredths **9.** hundreds **10.** tenths
11. thousandths **12.** ten-thousandths **13.** ten-thousands
14. hundredths **15.** thousandths **16.** hundreds **17.** thousands
18. 30 **19.** 0.01 **20.** 10,000 **21.** 300 **22.** 4,000 **23.** 0.008 **24.** 100
25. 40

Alternative Activity 18—Decimals—Comparing and Rounding

1. false **2.** true **3.** true **4.** true **5.** false **6.** true **7.** false **8.** true
9. 17.3 **10.** 196.84 **11.** 0.568 **12.** 15.76 **13.** 65.7 **14.** 432.84
15. Jan: 5.68; Pat: 6.02

Alternative Activity 19—Decimals—Adding and Subtracting

1. 20.688 **2.** 337.894 **3.** 74.186 **4.** 1,017.76 **5.** 180.8078 **6.** 96.039
7. 8.654 **8.** 623.76 **9.** 46.296 **10.** 0.169 **11.** 16.382 **12.** 0.445
13. 0.025 **14.** 1,480.25 **15.** $14.93

Alternative Activity 20—Multiplying Decimals— Powers of 10

1. 229 **2.** 22,900 **3.** 7.6 **4.** 76 **5.** 760 **6.** 7,600 **7.** 76,000 **8.** 567.2
9. 5,672 **10.** 56,720 **11.** 567,200 **12.** 5,672,000 **13.** 39.01
14. 390.1 **15.** 3,901 **16.** 39,010 **17.** 390,100 **18.** $23.90
19. $18,790 **20.** 94,172.6

Alternative Activity 21—Decimals—Multiplying

1. 190.47 **2.** 277.338 **3.** 0.67482 **4.** 83.961 **5.** 0.01155
6. 1,622.9294 **7.** 2,645.7263 **8.** 1,533 **9.** $114.75 **10.** 17.5

Alternative Activity 22—Dividing Decimals—Powers of 10

1. 0.843 **2.** 0.000642 **3.** 0.10489 **4.** 0.00624 **5.** 0.2399
6. 0.041262 **7.** 0.0057 **8.** 0.2974 **9.** 0.73393 **10.** 0.8741
11. 0.2129 **12.** 0.000358 **13.** 0.0054784 **14.** 0.71421 **15.** 0.919
16. 1.0534 **17.** 0.017687 **18.** 0.0084257 **19.** $1.67 **20.** $18.67

Alternative Activity 23—Decimals—Dividing

1. 2.648 **2.** 21.3 **3.** 0.008 **4.** 8.888 **5.** 640.533 **6.** 112.294 **7.** 7.296
8. false **9.** false **10.** true **11.** true **12.** true **13.** true **14.** $1.35
15. 27.5 inches

Alternative Activity 24—Fractions and Decimals

1. $\frac{11}{500}$ **2.** $3\frac{21}{25}$ **3.** $\frac{9}{25}$ **4.** $1\frac{51}{200}$ **5.** $\frac{43}{125}$ **6.** 0.15 **7.** 0.425 **8.** 2.16
9. 0.78 **10.** 0.725 **11.** false **12.** false **13.** true **14.** false **15.** true
16. false **17.** true **18.** false **19.** The Lee farm is larger. **20.** $4.60

Alternative Activity 25—Writing Repeating Decimals

1. $0.\overline{36}$ **2.** 0.625 **3.** 0.875 **4.** $0.3\overline{8}$ **5.** 0.24 **6.** $0.2\overline{3}$ **7.** 0.912
8. 0.6429 **9.** $0.7\overline{3}$ **10.** 2 °C **11.** −7°C **12.** 27°C **13.** 18°C
14. 23°C **15.** 17°C

Alternative Activity 26—Percents to Decimals

1. true **2.** false **3.** false **4.** true **5.** true **6.** false **7.** true **8.** $2.75
9. $792.27 **10.** $112

Alternative Activity 27—Expressions with Decimals

1. false **2.** true **3.** false **4.** false **5.** false **6.** false **7.** false **8.** false
9. true **10.** 12.57 **11.** 131.9166 **12.** 0.10237 **13.** 746.488 **14.** 62.2
15. 6.59

Alternative Activity 28—Rules of Divisibility

1. yes, no, yes, no, no, yes, no, no **2.** yes, yes, yes, no, yes, yes, yes, no
3. no, no, no, no, no, no, no, no **4.** yes, no, yes, yes, no, yes, no, yes
5. yes, yes, yes, no, yes, no, no, no **6.** no, yes, no, yes, no, no, no, no
7. yes, yes, yes, no, yes, no, yes, no **8.** yes, yes, yes, yes, yes, yes, yes,
yes **9.** yes, yes, yes, no, yes, no, no, no **10.** no, no, no, yes, no, no,
no, no **11.** yes, no, yes, yes, no, yes, no, yes **12.** yes, no, no, no, no,
no, no, no **13.** no, no, no, yes, no, no, no, no **14.** yes, yes, yes, no,
yes, yes, no, no **15.** yes, no, no, yes, no, no, no, yes

Alternative Activity 29—Numbers—Prime and Composite

1. 2 **2.** 3 **3.** 5 **4.** 7 **5.** 11 **6.** 13 **7.** 17 **8.** 19 **9.** 23 **10.** 29 **11.** 31
12. 37 **13.** 41 **14.** 43 **15.** 47 **16.** $3 \times 4 = 12$ or $2 \times 6 = 12$
17. $2 \times 9 = 18$ or $3 \times 6 = 18$ **18.** $8 \times 9 = 72$ or $3 \times 24 = 72$
19. $7 \times 7 = 49$ **20.** $7 \times 5 = 35$

Alternative Activity 30—GCD—Greatest Common Divisor

1. no, 9 **2.** yes **3.** no, 11 **4.** yes **5.** no, 14 **6.** yes **7.** no, 13
8. no, 7 **9.** no, 16 **10.** yes **11.** no, 8 **12.** yes **13.** yes **14.** 6 people
15. 12 cases

Alternative Activity 31—Factoring Expressions

1. 36 **2.** 45 **3.** 120 **4.** $2x + 6$ **5.** $3a + 3b$ **6.** 8 **7.** 2 **8.** d **9.** g
10. $3(3c + 1)$ **11.** $4(3y + 5)$ **12.** $14(m + 2k)$ **13.** $10(b + 4n)$
14. $72 **15.** 14 times

Alternative Activity 32—LCM—Least Common Multiple

1. 64 **2.** 216 **3.** 1,000 **4.** 640 **5.** 576 **6.** 320 **7.** 686 **8.** 9,408
9. 26 **10.** 63 **11.** 456 **12.** 405 **13.** 266 **14.** 114 **15.** 120 stops

Alternative Activity 33—Using Scientific Notation

1. true **2.** true **3.** false, 6.7×10^4 **4.** false, 6.5×10^{-4} **5.** false, 7.8
$\times 10^{-3}$ **6.** true **7.** false, 6.72×10^6 **8.** true **9.** 3.6×10^4
10. 6.06×10^8 **11.** 3.47×10^{-3} **12.** 6.43×10^{-4} **13.** 9.47×10^{-5}
14. 5.96×10^6 people **15.** 1.02×10^{-1} cm

Alternative Activity 34—Writing Proper Fractions

1. $\frac{13}{16}$ **2.** $\frac{7}{10}$ **3.** $\frac{5}{14}$ **4.** $\frac{7}{8}$ **5.** $\frac{0}{2}$ $\frac{1}{2}$ **6.** $\frac{0}{4}$ $\frac{1}{4}$ $\frac{2}{4}$ $\frac{3}{4}$ **7.** $\frac{0}{6}$ $\frac{1}{6}$ $\frac{2}{6}$ $\frac{3}{6}$ $\frac{4}{6}$ $\frac{5}{6}$
8. $\frac{3}{7}$ **9.** $\frac{1}{12}$ **10.** $\frac{3}{7}$

Alternative Activity 35—Improper Fractions, Mixed Numbers

1. proper **2.** improper **3.** proper **4.** proper **5.** improper
6. improper **7.** proper **8.** improper **9.** 1 **10.** 4 **11.** $3\frac{1}{5}$ **12.** $4\frac{1}{2}$
13. $4\frac{1}{6}$ **14.** $10\frac{3}{4}$ **15.** 12 **16.** $5\frac{3}{5}$ **17.** $6\frac{5}{9}$ **18.** $3\frac{2}{3}$ **19.** $2\frac{4}{5}$ **20.** $33\frac{1}{2}$
21. $6\frac{5}{7}$ **22.** $3\frac{3}{4}$ **23.** $\frac{37}{4}$ **24.** $\frac{67}{4}$ **25.** $\frac{19}{8}$ **26.** $\frac{32}{9}$ **27.** $\frac{45}{2}$ **28.** $\frac{26}{3}$
29. $\frac{75}{8}$ **30.** $\frac{97}{5}$

Alternative Activity 36—Using Equivalent Fractions

1. $\frac{2}{3}$ and $\frac{4}{6}$ **2.** $\frac{1}{4}$ and $\frac{4}{16}$ **3.** $\frac{1}{2}$ and $\frac{4}{8}$ For problems **4–12**, sample
answers are given. **4.** $\frac{2}{8}$ and $\frac{4}{16}$ **5.** $\frac{12}{14}$ and $\frac{24}{28}$ **6.** $\frac{4}{10}$ and $\frac{6}{15}$ **7.** $\frac{16}{18}$
and $\frac{24}{27}$ **8.** $\frac{6}{14}$ and $\frac{9}{21}$ **9.** $\frac{10}{16}$ and $\frac{15}{24}$ **10.** $\frac{2}{4}$ and $\frac{3}{6}$ **11.** yes **12.** no
13. yes **14.** no **15.** no **16.** yes **17.** yes **18.** no **19.** yes **20.** no

Alternative Activity 37—Writing in Simplest Form

1. 4 **2.** 3 **3.** 3 **4.** 7 **5.** 13 **6.** 9 **7.** 5 **8.** 2 **9.** $\frac{4}{9}$ **10.** $\frac{1}{3}$ **11.** $\frac{1}{3}$ **12.** $\frac{1}{5}$
13. $\frac{6}{7}$ **14.** $\frac{7}{10}$ **15.** $\frac{5}{21}$ **16.** $\frac{8}{9}$ **17.** $\frac{1}{2}$ **18.** $\frac{8}{15}$ **19.** yes, it is a multiple
of 5 **20.** yes, 3 is a multiple of 24

Alternative Activity 38—Comparing, Ordering Fractions

1. > **2.** < **3.** < **4.** > **5.** > **6.** < **7.** < **8.** < **9.** > **10.** >
11. $\frac{1}{2}$, $\frac{1}{3}$, $\frac{1}{5}$ **12.** $\frac{1}{2}$, $\frac{5}{14}$, $\frac{2}{7}$ **13.** $\frac{9}{10}$, $\frac{3}{5}$, $\frac{1}{2}$ **14.** $\frac{2}{3}$, $\frac{3}{7}$, $\frac{5}{21}$ **15.** $\frac{9}{15}$, $\frac{2}{3}$, $\frac{4}{5}$
16. $\frac{1}{10}$, $\frac{1}{8}$, $\frac{1}{5}$ **17.** $\frac{7}{15}$, $\frac{19}{30}$, $\frac{9}{10}$ **18.** $\frac{5}{12}$, $\frac{2}{3}$, $\frac{3}{4}$ **19.** Ellen **20.** Quin

Alternative Activity 39—Fractions with Like Denominators

1. $\frac{7}{9}$ **2.** $1\frac{3}{13}$ **3.** $\frac{1}{4}$ **4.** $3\frac{1}{2}$ **5.** $3\frac{1}{6}$ **6.** $12\frac{6}{11}$ **7.** $12\frac{4}{5}$ **8.** $\frac{2x}{5}$ **9.** x
10. $\frac{(x-4)}{10}$ **11.** $\frac{(x+3)}{y}$ **12.** $\frac{8x}{15}$ **13.** $\frac{(4y-3)}{x}$ **14.** $\frac{2}{3}$ **15.** $1\frac{1}{5}$ **16.** $\frac{2}{3}$
17. 1 **18.** $1\frac{3}{7}$ **19.** $\frac{4}{5}$ **20.** $1\frac{5}{8}$ **21.** $\frac{3}{8}$ **22.** $1\frac{4}{13}$ **23.** $\frac{3x}{4}$ **24.** $\frac{4y}{5}$ **25.** $\frac{x}{7}$

Alternative Activity 40—Fractions with Unlike Denominators

1. $1\frac{1}{15}$ **2.** $\frac{3}{8}$ **3.** $1\frac{7}{20}$ **4.** $\frac{1}{5}$ **5.** $\frac{1}{24}$ **6.** $\frac{3}{10}$ **7.** $1\frac{1}{14}$ **8.** $\frac{1}{6}$ **9.** $\frac{3}{20}x$
10. $\frac{(y+9x)}{xy}$ **11.** $\frac{19x}{24}$ **12.** $\frac{(6y-3x)}{xy}$ **13.** $2\frac{1}{2}$ **14.** $7\frac{8}{9}$ **15.** $8\frac{5}{6}$ **16.** $5\frac{3}{20}$
17. $5\frac{3}{16}$ **18.** $17\frac{1}{8}$ **19.** $17\frac{2}{9}$ **20.** $56\frac{7}{24}$ **21.** $5\frac{1}{24}$ **22.** $17\frac{1}{6}x$ **23.** $6\frac{2}{15}x$
24. $55\frac{11}{15}y$ **25.** $3\frac{1}{8}x$

Alternative Activity 41—Subtracting Fractions—Regrouping

1. $2\frac{3}{4}$ **2.** $3\frac{3}{4}$ **3.** $2\frac{11}{24}$ **4.** $3\frac{3}{5}$ **5.** $5\frac{1}{2}$ **6.** $5\frac{6}{7}$ **7.** $4\frac{4}{5}$ **8.** $7\frac{3}{4}$ **9.** $29\frac{7}{16}$
10. $2\frac{1}{12}$ **11.** $5\frac{3}{8}$ **12.** $10\frac{23}{24}$ **13.** $1\frac{3}{5}$ **14.** $37\frac{11}{12}$ **15.** $6\frac{11}{12}$ **16.** $7\frac{1}{2}$
17. $3\frac{13}{24}$ hours **18.** $2\frac{3}{8}$ miles **19.** $50\frac{9}{16}$ or \$50.56 **20.** \$110

Alternative Activity 42—Multiplying Fractions, Mixed Numbers

1. $\frac{1}{13}$ **2.** $\frac{1}{3}$ **3.** $\frac{5}{9}$ **4.** $\frac{2}{15}$ **5.** $\frac{5}{14}$ **6.** $\frac{9}{40}$ **7.** $\frac{1}{6}$ **8.** $\frac{2}{3}$ **9.** $\frac{2}{5}$ **10.** $\frac{14}{23}y$
11. $2\frac{3}{4}$ **12.** $6\frac{3}{5}$ **13.** $4\frac{11}{20}$ **14.** $16\frac{3}{5}$ **15.** $8\frac{1}{2}$ **16.** $4\frac{3}{4}$ **17.** $2\frac{11}{16}$ **18.** $9\frac{2}{3}$
19. $18\frac{9}{16}$ feet **20.** $6\frac{2}{3}$ cups

Alternative Activity 43—Dividing Fractions, Mixed Numbers

1. $1\frac{1}{2}$ **2.** $2\frac{1}{3}$ **3.** $\frac{4}{7}$ **4.** $1\frac{2}{3}$ **5.** $1\frac{5}{27}$ **6.** $\frac{5}{6}$ **7.** $1\frac{3}{7}$ **8.** $\frac{10}{11}$ **9.** $\frac{2}{3}$ **10.** $\frac{3b}{4}$
11. $1\frac{5}{9}$ **12.** $\frac{2}{3}$ **13.** $\frac{3}{4}$ **14.** $1\frac{8}{11}$ **15.** $\frac{3}{4}$ **16.** 5 **17.** $\frac{7}{12}$ **18.** $3\frac{1}{11}$
19. $3\frac{1}{8}$ weeks **20.** $\$\frac{3}{7}$ or \$0.4287

Alternative Activity 44—Order of Operations

1. 26 **2.** 34 **3.** 30 **4.** 40 **5.** 10 **6.** 33 **7.** 12 **8.** 27 **9.** 0 **10.** 48
11. 8 **12.** 0 **13.** 12 **14.** 19 **15.** 3 **16.** 8 **17.** 40 **18.** 19 **19.** 76
20. 1 **21.** $55\frac{1}{3}$ **22.** 114 **23.** 13 **24.** 66 **25.** 5

Alternative Activity 45—Substituting Values

1. 12 **2.** 10 **3.** 11 **4.** 49 **5.** 17 **6.** $1\frac{1}{2}$ **7.** 31 **8.** $3\frac{2}{5}$ **9.** 10 **10.** 16
11. 8 **12.** 0 **13.** 43 **14.** 13 **15.** 3 **16.** 54 **17.** $6\frac{1}{8}$ **18.** 17 **19.** 5
20. 7 **21.** 46 **22.** 18 **23.** $\frac{1}{4}$ **24.** $5\frac{4}{9}$ **25.** 27

Alternative Activity 46—Solution by Substitution

1. 5 **2.** 6 **3.** 4 **4.** 1 **5.** 3 **6.** 4 **7.** 12 **8.** 7 **9.** 8 **10.** 8 **11.** 2 **12.** 0
13. 2 **14.** 5 **15.** 10 **16.** 9 **17.** 4 **18.** 3 **19.** 3 **20.** 0 **21.** 4 **22.** 7
23. 10 **24.** 2 **25.** 1

Alternative Activity 47—Addition Equations

1. 7 **2.** 15 **3.** 34 **4.** 9 **5.** 11 **6.** 8 **7.** 15 **8.** 41 **9.** 73 **10.** 14
11. 10 **12.** 7 **13.** 18 **14.** $\frac{1}{2}$ **15.** $\frac{2}{3}$ **16.** $\frac{1}{3}$ **17.** $\frac{1}{4}$ **18.** $\frac{1}{16}$ **19.** $\frac{3}{10}$
20. $\frac{3}{8}$ **21.** $\frac{2}{5}$ **22.** $\frac{1}{4}$ **23.** $\frac{1}{8}$ **24.** $\frac{3}{5}$ **25.** $\frac{6}{7}$

Alternative Activity 48—Subtraction Equations

1. 47 **2.** 19 **3.** 56 **4.** 55 **5.** 67 **6.** 13 **7.** 21 **8.** 100 **9.** 31
10. $\frac{7}{8}$ **11.** $\frac{11}{16}$ **12.** $1\frac{1}{4}$ **13.** $\frac{17}{32}$ **14.** $\frac{7}{12}$ **15.** $\frac{2}{3}$ **16.** $\frac{11}{12}$ **17.** $\frac{8}{9}$ **18.** $\frac{1}{3}$
19. 8 million ounces of gold **20.** 19 million ounces of gold

Alternative Activity 49—Simplify Complex Fractions

1. $\frac{1}{3}$ **2.** $1\frac{7}{8}$ **3.** $16\frac{2}{3}$ **4.** $\frac{6}{7}$ **5.** $1\frac{1}{4}$ **6.** 8 **7.** $\frac{16}{19}$ **8.** $2\frac{1}{2}$ **9.** $5\frac{1}{3}$ **10.** $3\frac{1}{3}$

Alternative Activity 50—Simplify by Addition

1. $\frac{5x}{7}$ **2.** $\frac{1}{2y}$ **3.** $\frac{4b}{3}$ or $1\frac{1}{3}b$ **4.** $\frac{1}{2c}$ **5.** $\frac{9h}{13}$ **6.** $1f$ **7.** $\frac{6w}{5}$ or $1\frac{1}{5}w$ **8.** $\frac{3}{2g}$
9. $\frac{5e}{10}$ **10.** $\frac{n}{2}$ **11.** $\frac{8}{5p}$ **12.** $\frac{5x}{6}$ **13.** $\frac{1}{3z}$ **14.** $\frac{7}{11u}$ **15.** $\frac{11d}{6}$ or $1\frac{5}{6}d$
16. $1x$ **17.** $\frac{10}{17a}$ **18.** $\frac{11}{18x}$ **19.** $\frac{11m}{10}$ or $1\frac{1}{10}m$ **20.** $\frac{9n}{14}$ **21.** $\frac{25}{16p}$
22. $\frac{5h}{6}$ **23.** $\frac{5}{8k}$ **24.** $\frac{5}{9y}$ **25.** $\frac{15t}{16}$

Alternative Activity 51—Simplify by Subtraction

1. $\frac{1y}{11}$ **2.** $\frac{2c}{7}$ **3.** $\frac{1}{3h}$ **4.** $\frac{3d}{7}$ **5.** $\frac{3}{5i}$ **6.** $\frac{1j}{2}$ **7.** $\frac{1}{6f}$ **8.** $\frac{2k}{5}$ **9.** $\frac{3}{5g}$ **10.** $\frac{7}{10l}$
11. $\frac{4}{9a}$ **12.** $\frac{1}{6x}$ **13.** $\frac{7b}{24}$ **14.** $\frac{5w}{15d}$ **15.** $\frac{2}{15d}$ **16.** $\frac{3w}{20}$ **17.** $\frac{1}{15v}$ **18.** $\frac{1}{6f}$
19. $\frac{13}{16}$ of the walk **20.** $\frac{1}{4}$ yards

Alternative Activity 52—Multiply Rational Expressions

1. $\frac{1}{10}$ **2.** $\frac{1}{4}$ **3.** $\frac{3}{8}$ **4.** $\frac{8}{13}$ **5.** $\frac{13}{16}$ **6.** $\frac{1}{15}$ **7.** $\frac{1}{2}$ **8.** $\frac{1}{3}$ **9.** $\frac{3}{4}$ **10.** $\frac{2}{35}$ **11.** $\frac{1}{18}$
12. $\frac{1}{4}$ **13.** $\frac{5}{16}$ **14.** $\frac{1}{3}$ **15.** $\frac{6}{17}$ **16.** $\frac{16}{33}$ **17.** $\frac{1}{32}$ **18.** $\frac{3}{8}$ **19.** $\frac{2}{5}$ **20.** $\frac{1}{5}$
21. $\frac{4}{7}$ **22.** $\frac{1}{3}$ **23.** $\frac{1}{3}$ **24.** $\frac{3}{16}$ of a tank **25.** 100 seats

Alternative Activity 53—Using Ratios

1. $\frac{3}{2}$ **2.** $\frac{4}{7}$ **3.** $\frac{5}{9}$ **4.** $\frac{9}{15}$ **5.** $\frac{4}{11}$ **6.** $\frac{23}{9}$ **7.** $\frac{19}{8}$ **8.** $\frac{32}{41}$ **9.** $\frac{5}{10}$; 5 to 10
10. $\frac{8}{11}$; 8:11 **11.** $\frac{7}{4}$; 7:4 **12.** $\frac{9}{8}$; 9 to 8 **13.** $\frac{6}{12}$; $\frac{1}{2}$ **14.** $\frac{9}{81}$; $\frac{1}{9}$ **15.** $\frac{14}{42}$; $\frac{1}{3}$
16. $\frac{18}{27}$; $\frac{2}{3}$ **17.** $\frac{5}{25}$; $\frac{1}{5}$ **18.** $\frac{17}{51}$; $\frac{1}{3}$ **19.** 4 goldfish **20.** $\frac{2}{3}$

Alternative Activity 54—Using Proportions

1. $\frac{9}{12}$ **2.** $\frac{4}{5}$ **3.** $\frac{4}{16}$ **4.** $\frac{72}{81}$ **5.** $\frac{42}{49}$ **6.** $\frac{30}{45}$ **7.** $\frac{6}{30}$ **8.** 3 **9.** 30 **10.** 3 **11.** 4
12. 30 **13.** 40 **14.** $\frac{5}{1} = \frac{x}{3}$; 15 lemons **15.** $\frac{8}{160} = \frac{x}{1,440}$; 72 burned chips

Alternative Activity 55—Ratios, Proportions

1. \$15.00 **2.** 40 cans **3.** 40 ringers **4.** 1,968 feet **5.** 240 people
6. 12 toys **7.** 162 girls **8.** \$250 **9.** \$126.75 **10.** 170 hot dogs with mustard

Alternative Activity 56—Solving Proportional Relationships

1. 5 times **2.** 4 in. **3.** 1 lb:$1\frac{1}{4}$ lb **4.** 1 mL:1.42 mL **5.** 72 in.³
6. 3 miles each day **7.** 5 lb:1 lb

Alternative Activity 57—Distance, Rate, and Time Problems

1. t **2.** r **3.** t **4.** r **5.** 168 miles **6.** 44 km/h **7.** 24 miles
8. 190 km/h **9.** 62.5 mph **10.** 2.5 hours

Alternative Activity 58—Percents, Fractions

1. $\frac{63}{100}$; 63% **2.** $\frac{47}{100}$; 47% **3.** $\frac{18}{100}$; 18% **4.** $\frac{75}{100}$; 75% **5.** $\frac{39}{100}$; 39%
6. $\frac{44}{100}$; 44% **7.** 23% **8.** 54 squares **9.** $\frac{61}{100}$ **10.** 71%

Alternative Activity 59—Percents, Decimals

1. 33.3% **2.** 30% **3.** 40% **4.** 87.5% **5.** 60% **6.** 37.5% **7.** 75%
8. 55% **9.** 61% **10.** 18% **11.** 99.9% **12.** 7% **13.** 35.7% **14.** 40%
15. 25%

Alternative Activity 60—The Percent of a Number

1. 3 **2.** 9 **3.** 16 **4.** 80 **5.** 104 **6.** 3.2 **7.** 6 **8.** 29.2 **9.** 50 **10.** 129.2
11. 1.7 **12.** 0.17 **13.** 0.017 **14.** 171 cars **15.** 196 people

Alternative Activity 61—What Percent?

1. 37.5% **2.** 25% **3.** 31.7% **4.** 40% **5.** 20% **6.** 771.43%
7. 121.05% **8.** 96.2% **9.** 31.2% **10.** 32.26%

Alternative Activity 62—Percent of Increase, Decrease

1. increase **2.** increase or decrease **3.** decrease **4.** increase
5. increase **6.** increase **7.** 10.55% **8.** 49.66% **9.** 40.1% **10.** 34.92%

Alternative Activity 63—Percents and Formulas

1. $189.11; $188.19; $0.92 **2.** $914.04; $909.59; $4.45 **3.** $803.73;
$799.81; $3.92 **4.** $2,810.42; $2,796.73; $13.69 **5.** $5,473.76;
$5,447.09; $26.67 **6.** $10,784.67; $10,732.12; $52.55 **7.** $74.92
8. Sara; 26¢ **9.** $17.94 **10.** $13,891.50

Alternative Activity 64—Scale Drawings, Models

1. $x = 6$ **2.** $x = 3$ **3.** $x = 10\frac{1}{2}$ **4.** $x = 9$ **5.** 80 in. **6.** 5 ft:1 in.
7. $\frac{1}{5}$ in. long

Alternative Activity 65—Real Number Line and Integers

1. 9 **2.** 21 **3.** 13 **4.** 23 **5.** 99 **6.** 87 **7.** 7 **8.** 29 **9.** 43 **10.** 14
11. 60 **12.** 144 **13.** 9 **14.** −13 **15.** 51 **16.** −38 **17.** −25 **18.** 47
19. −5 **20.** +3 **21.** +75 **22.** −85 **23.** +2,000 **24.** −15 **25.** −3

Alternative Activity 66—Greater Than and Less Than

1. > **2.** < **3.** > **4.** = **5.** > **6.** < **7.** > **8.** > **9.** > **10.** > **11.** >
12. = **13.** < **14.** < **15.** > **16.** > **17.** = **18.** < **19.** = **20.** >
21. < **22.** > **23.** Mandy's house **24.** today **25.** 7 numbers (−3,
−2, −1, 0, 1, 2, 3)

Alternative Activity 67—Odd and Even Integers

1. 248 even **2.** 400 even **3.** 543 odd **4.** 935 odd **5.** 110 even
6. 672 even **7.** 790 even **8.** 1,115 odd **9.** 286 even **10.** 452 even
11. 563 odd **12.** 192 even **13.** 576 even **14.** 1,125 odd **15.** 429 odd
16. 512 even **17.** 732 even **18.** 504 even **19.** 1,512 even **20.** 899
odd **21.** 1,440 even **22.** 1,484 even **23.** 999 odd **24.** 1,876 even
25. 1,980 even

Alternative Activity 68—Positive Integers—Adding

1. 1 **2.** 10 **3.** −1 **4.** 9 **5.** 0 **6.** 6 **7.** −5 **8.** −6 **9.** 8 **10.** 7 **11.** −1
12. 12 **13.** −5 **14.** 10 **15.** 12 **16.** 1 **17.** −3 **18.** −178 **19.** 296
20. 600 **21.** 1,038 **22.** −515 **23.** 81 **24.** 1,127 **25.** −444

Alternative Activity 69—Negative Integers—Adding

1. 1 **2.** −13 **3.** 0 **4.** −18 **5.** −1 **6.** −4 **7.** 0 **8.** 0 **9.** −5 **10.** −1
11. −11 **12.** −16 **13.** −13 **14.** −574 **15.** 324 **16.** −1,116 **17.** 62
18. −1,461 **19.** 220 **20.** −569 **21.** −1,637 **22.** 271 **23.** −636
24. −36 **25.** 20 feet

Alternative Activity 70—Subtracting Positive, Negative Integers

1. 14 **2.** −13 **3.** 3 **4.** 5 **5.** 4 **6.** −7 **7.** −1 **8.** −9 **9.** −1 **10.** 5
11. 11 **12.** −5 **13.** 7 **14.** −10 **15.** 17 **16.** −8 **17.** −12 **18.** 4
19. 1 **20.** −7 **21.** −9 **22.** −4 **23.** 4 **24.** 4,145 feet **25.** 14,855 feet

Alternative Activity 71—Multiplying Positive Integers

1. −48 **2.** 27 **3.** −12 **4.** −18 **5.** −16 **6.** 30 **7.** 0 **8.** −12 **9.** 54
10. 8 **11.** −3 **12.** 27 **13.** 30 **14.** −64 **15.** 14 **16.** positive
17. positive **18.** positive **19.** negative **20.** negative **21.** negative
22. negative **23.** positive **24.** negative **25.** positive

Alternative Activity 72—Multiplying Negative Integers

1. negative **2.** positive **3.** negative **4.** positive **5.** positive
6. negative **7.** negative **8.** positive **9.** negative **10.** positive
11. negative **12.** positive **13.** negative **14.** positive **15.** positive
16. negative **17.** positive **18.** negative **19.** positive **20.** negative
21. positive **22.** negative **23.** positive **24.** $8.00 **25.** $33.00

Alternative Activity 73—Dividing Positive, Negative Integers

1. −3 **2.** −2 **3.** 5 **4.** 7 **5.** 5 **6.** −8 **7.** −9 **8.** 9 **9.** −2 **10.** −5
11. −9 **12.** 3 **13.** positive **14.** negative **15.** negative **16.** positive
17. zero **18.** negative **19.** negative **20.** negative **21.** negative
22. positive **23.** negative **24.** 157 children **25.** $21.00

Alternative Activity 74—Using Exponents

1. 3 **2.** 3 **3.** n **4.** 1 **5.** 5 **6.** 10 **7.** 4 **8.** 5 **9.** x **10.** 8 **11.** 4
12. a **13.** 18 **14.** $(-y)$ **15.** (-4) **16.** h^3 **17.** $(-10)^2$ **18.** 3^5
19. $(-b)^2$ **20.** 7^7 **21.** 5^3 **22.** c^3 **23.** 10^{10} **24.** $(-2)^4$ **25.** 5^5

Alternative Activity 75—Exponents—Multiplying

1. n^7 **2.** 5^{10} **3.** p^6 **4.** 12^9 **5.** n^8 **6.** 6^{14} **7.** q^{15} **8.** 18^9 **9.** 3^{6x}
10. 100^{10} **11.** false, $4^{3n} \cdot 4^{3n} = 4^{6n}$ **12.** false, $10^5 \cdot 10^5 = 10^{10}$
13. true **14.** true **15.** true **16.** false, $a^8 \cdot a^{10} = a^{18}$ **17.** true
18. false, $9^{4n} \cdot 9^{4n} = 9^{8n}$ **19.** false, $p^7 \cdot p^2 = p^9$ **20.** false, $5^5 \cdot 5 = 5^6$
21. true **22.** false, $3^c \cdot 3^c = 3^{2c}$ **23.** true **24.** true
25. false, $8^{10} \cdot 8^{10} = 8^{20}$

Alternative Activity 76—Exponents—Dividing

1. b^4 **2.** 5^6 **3.** 1 **4.** 12^2 **5.** r^2 **6.** 18^2 **7.** q^3 **8.** 8^5 **9.** 2^{11} **10.** 1
11. false, $9^{6n} \div 9^{3n} = 9^{3n}$ **12.** true **13.** false, $24^4 \div 24^2 = 24^2$
14. true **15.** true **16.** false, $a^{12} \div a^6 = a^6$ **17.** true **18.** true
19. true **20.** true **21.** false, $6^4 \div 6^1 = 6^3$ **22.** false, $6^6 \div 6^6 = 1$
23. true **24.** false, $a^7 \div a^4 = a^3$ **25.** false, $15^2 \div 15^2 = 1$

Alternative Activity 77—Area of Squares

1. Area = 3^2 **2.** Area = 6^2 **3.** Area = p^2 **4.** Area = d^2 **5.** 36 sq cm
6. 81 sq cm **7.** 49 sq cm **8.** 484 sq cm **9.** 36 sq yd **10.** 100 sq ft

Alternative Activity 78—Volume of Cubes

1. Volume = 9^3 **2.** Volume = m^3 **3.** 125 cu cm **4.** 27 cu cm **5.** 512
cu cm **6.** 1,331 cu cm **7.** 9,261 cu cm **8.** 2,744 cu cm **9.** 512 cu cm
of wax **10.** 2,197 cu in., 1,331 cu in.; difference of 866 cu in.

Alternative Activity 79—Square Root Values

1. 5, 6; 5.29 **2.** 7, 8; 7.75 **3.** 9, 10; 9.75 **4.** 6, 7; 6.08 **5.** 9, 10; 9.54
6. 4, 5; 4.58 **7.** 3, 4; 3.61 **8.** 5, 6; 5.48 **9.** 7, 8; 7.42 **10.** 6, 7; 6.16
11. 1, 2; 1.41 **12.** 4.69 **13.** 7 **14.** 13 feet **15.** 75 meters

Alternative Activity 80—Irrational Numbers, Square Roots
1. rational 2. irrational 3. irrational 4. rational 5. irrational
6. rational 7. rational For **8–10,** accept any irrational number within 0.3 of the numbers given. 8. 2.2 9. 7.1 10. 10

Alternative Activity 81—Irrational Numbers, Decimals
1. rational 2. irrational 3. rational 4. rational 5. irrational
6. irrational 7. irrational 8. rational 9. irrational 10. irrational
11. rational 12. irrational 13. 20 in. 14. 60 cm 15. No. The square tray is about 10.6 inches wide, and 10.6 > 10.2, so the tray will not fit on the counter.

Alternative Activity 82—Equations with Radicals
1. 25 2. 12 cm 3. $5\sqrt{10}$ ft 4. $2\sqrt{7}$ ft 5. $2\sqrt{13}$ in.

Alternative Activity 83—Pythagorean Theorem
1. 10.63 2. 12 3. 5.29 4. 21.63 5. 10.82 6. 10.95 7. 9.17
8. 5.83 9. 5.83 inches 10. 2.83 meters

Alternative Activity 84—About Triangles
1. no 2. no 3. no 4. yes 5. no 6. yes, no, no, yes 7. 5, no, yes, no
8. no, yes, no 9. 5, yes, no, no 10. no, no, no

Alternative Activity 85—Polygon Perimeters
1. 38 ft 2. 15.636 mm 3. $17\frac{1}{3}$ in. 4. 38.4 m 5. $17\frac{1}{3}$ yards
6. 35.06 m 7. 14 cm 8. 274.2 ft 9. 2.1 pints or 3 pint cans
10. 10.1 feet each

Alternative Activity 86—Regular Polygon Perimeters
1. 42 mm 2. 10 in. 3. 32.15 m 4. 400 ft 5. $8\frac{1}{4}$ yd 6. 29.58 mi
7. 8 sides 8. 21 sides 9. 9 sides 10. 14 sides

Alternative Activity 87—Irregular Polygon Perimeters
1. 44 in. 2. 54.1 cm 3. 85.4 ft 4. 184.1 m 5. $20\frac{5}{12}$ km
6. 117.8 in. 7. 4.4 8. $8\frac{1}{3}$ 9. 321 m 10. 100 ft

Alternative Activity 88—Areas of Rectangles, Squares
1. 63 mm^2 2. 80 in.^{2} 3. 91 m^2 4. $53\frac{5}{6}$ mi^2 5. $56\frac{7}{10}$ yd^2 6. 49 dm^2
7. 625 in.^{2} 8. 67.24 m^2 9. 4,173.16 mm^2 10. 900 m^2
11. 1,049.76 km^2 12. 7,056 yd^2 13. 13.4689 mi^2 14. $3\frac{3}{4}$ boxes
15. 1,122.3 ft^2; 138.6 ft

Alternative Activity 89—Area—Triangles
1. 240 in.^{2} 2. 186 ft^2 3. 261 m^2 4. 21 km^2 5. 18 cm^2 6. 210 yd^2
7. 6 m 8. 6 in. 9. 10 yd 10. 25 km 11. 3 mm 12. 20 mi 13. 20 in.
14. 10 ft 15. No, both triangles are 200 ft^2.

Alternative Activity 90—Area—Trapezoids and Parallelograms
1. 40 ft^2 2. 120 yd^2 3. 720 m^2 4. 80 in.^{2} 5. 31.8645 m^2 6. 10 cm
7. 21 m 8. 15 ft 9. 29 cm 10. 42 ft

Alternative Activity 91—Area—Irregular Polygons
1. 87 units^2 2. 112 units^2 3. 88 units^2 4. 246 units^2 5. 425 units^2
6. 350.5 units^2 7. 315.5 units^2 8. 1,550.5 units^2 9. 33 units^2
10. 2,185 units^2

Alternative Activity 92—Circumferences, Areas of Circles
1. 18.84 km 2. 18.84 ft 3. 12.56 cm 4. 56.52 mm 5. 31.4 in.
6. 25.12 yd 7. 43.96 in. 8. 50.24 m 9. 56.52 ft 10. 12.56 ft^2
11. 314 cm^2 12. 200.96 yd^2 13. 28.26 km^2 14. 78.5 in.^{2} 15. 78.5 m^2
16. 153.86 mi^2 17. 200.96 ft^2 18. 33.16625 mi^2 19. 154,751.76 yd^2
20. 98.4704 m^2 21. 44.15625 ft^2 22. 8.0384 in.^{2} 23. 5,538.96 km^2
24. 572.265 yd^2 25. 0.4415625 mm^2

Alternative Activity 93—Faces, Edges, and Vertices
1. cone, 1 face, 1 edge, 1 vertex
2. cylinder, 2 faces, 0 edges, 0 vertices
3. rectangular prism, 6 faces, 12 edges, 8 vertices
4. square pyramid, 5 faces, 8 edges, 5 vertices
5. sphere, 0 faces, 0 edges, 0 vertices
6. cube, 6 faces, 12 edges, 8 vertices
7. triangular prism, 5 faces, 9 edges, 6 vertices
8. hexagonal prism, 8 faces, 18 edges, 12 vertices

Alternative Activity 94—Surface Area—Prisms and Cylinders
1. 600 m^2 2. 442 cm^2 3. 432 square units 4. 2,548 cm^2
5. 471 m^2 6. 1,000 square units 7. 2,124 m^2 8. 2,008 in.^{2}
9. 108 mm^2 10. 390 square units

Alternative Activity 95—Surface Area—Pyramids and Cones
1. 120 ft^2 2. 402.12 mm^2 3. 1,960 mm^2 4. 898.49 in.^{2} 5. 260 ft^2
6. 204.20 m^2 7. 456 in.^{2} 8. 84.82 cm^2 9. 300 yd^2 10. 226.19 cm^2

Alternative Activity 96—Cubes , Prisms, and Pyramids—Volumes
1. 96 ft^3 2. 216 m^3 3. 48 cm^3 4. 8,000 in.^{3} 5. 108 yd^3 6. 42.67 mm^3
7. 5,832 mi^3 8. 4.913 in.^{3} 9. 1,560,896 km^3 10. 27,000 cm^3
11. 1.728 ft^3 12. 97,336 in.^{3} 13. 35,937 m^3 14. 0.857375 dm^3
15. 2,700 ft^3

Alternative Activity 97—Cylinders, Cones and Spheres—Volumes
1. 538.51 cm^3 2. 1.74 in.^{3} 3. 401.92 in.^{3} 4. 56.52 yd^3 5. 3.925 cm^3
6. 39.25 m^3 7. 937.81$\overline{3}$ cm^3 8. 7.32$\overline{6}$ ft^3 9. 63.585 in.^{3}
10. 4,186.67 mm^3 11. 7,234.56 ft^3 12. 5,572.45$\overline{3}$ cm^3
13. 3,052,080 yd^3 14. 113,040 ft^3 15. Cylinder; Its volume is
50.24 cm^3. The volume of the sphere is only 33.493 cm^3.

Alternative Activity 98—Equalities—Graphing

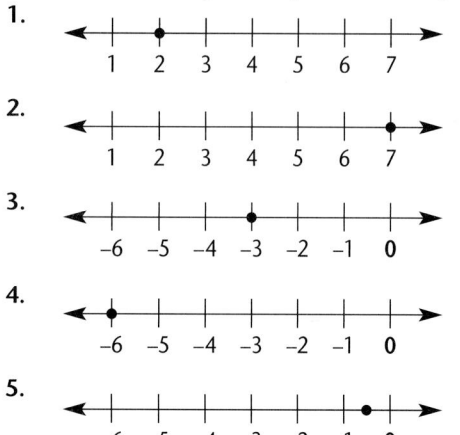

6. $x = 5$ 7. $x = -2$ 8. $x = 7$ 9. $x = -4$ 10. $x = 3\frac{1}{2}$

Alternative Activity 99—Inequalities—Graphing

1.
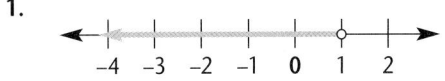

2.
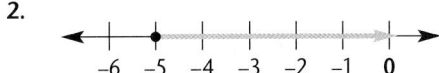

3.

4.
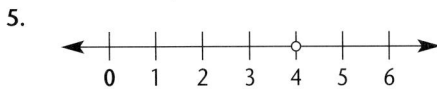

5.
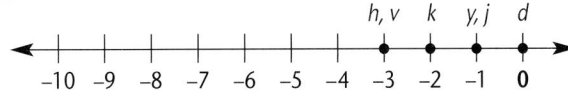

6. $x < 5$ **7.** $x > -2$ **8.** $x \leq 3$ **9.** $x \geq -4$ **10.** $x < 2$

Alternative Activity 100—Solutions of Equalities—Graphing

1. $y = -1$ **2.** $c = 8$ **3.** $p = 1$ **4.** $u = 6$ **5.** $h = -3$ **6.** $g = 4$
7. $s = 2$ **8.** $w = 8$ **9.** $x = 8$ **10.** $k = -2$ **11.** $j = -1$ **12.** $d = 0$
13. $v = -3$

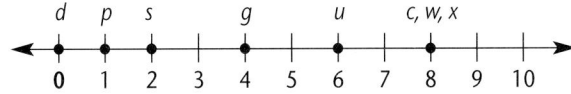

14. $x + 10 = 220$; $x = 210$ points

15. $x + 4 = 7$; $x = 3$ spares

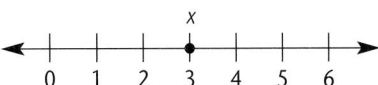

Alternative Activity 101—Solutions of Inequalities—Graphing

1. $q \geq 3$

2. $a \leq 3$

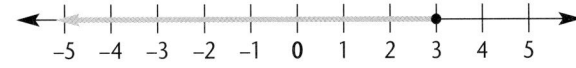

3. $z > 6$

4. $w > -1$

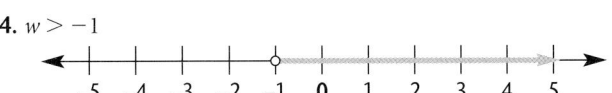

5. $s \geq -3$

6. $x < 10$

7. $e < -6$

8. $d \leq 9$

9. $c < 4$

10. $r > -8$

11. $f < -2$

12. $v \geq 3$

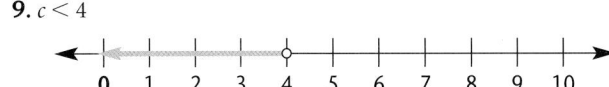

13. $t > 3$

14. $y - 67 \geq 150$; $y \geq 217$

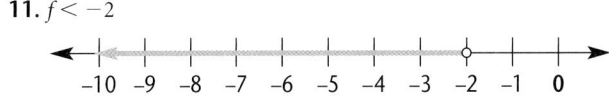

15. $y - 10 \geq$ May 15; $y \geq$ May 25

Alternative Activity 102—Locating Points—The Coordinate System

1. $(5, -4)$ **2.** $(-4, 3)$ **3.** $(3, 5)$ **4.** $(3, -3)$ **5.** $(0, 5)$ **6.** $(7, 2)$
7. $(-1, 4)$ **8.** $(-5, 2)$ **9.** $(2, 0)$ **10.** $(1, 0)$ **11.** $(3, -1)$ **12.** $(1, 4)$
13. $(-4, -6)$ **14.** $(-4, -1)$ **15.** Quadrant III **16.** Quadrant I
17. Quadrant II **18.** Quadrant IV **19.** 10 units **20.** 18 units

Alternative Activity 103—Plotting Points—The Coordinate System

1–10.

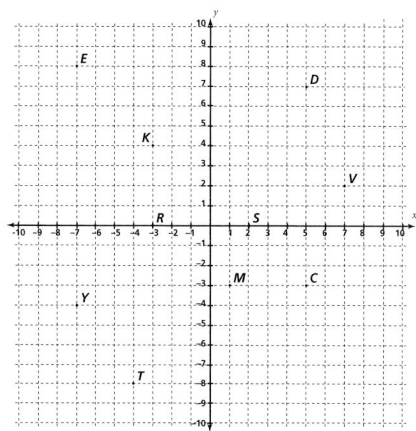

11. Quadrant IV **12.** Quadrant I **13.** Quadrant III **14.** Quadrant IV
15. Quadrant II

Alternative Activity 104—The Points of a Line

1.

y = x + 1	
x	y
−2	−1
4	5
7	8

2.

y = x − 6	
x	y
0	−6
3	−3
6	0

3.

y = x − 6	
x	y
−5	−11
5	−1
8	2

4.

y = x + 8	
x	y
−6	2
0	8
4	12

5.

y = x − 4	
x	y
−6	−10
−4	−8
4	0

6.

y = x + 7	
x	y
−4	3
0	7
7	14

7.

y = x + 4	
x	y
−1	3
3	7
7	11

8.

y = x − 5	
x	y
−3	−8
−1	−6
2	−3

9.

y = x + 1.26	
x	y
−4.82	−3.56
−3.72	−2.46
4.18	5.44

10.

y = x − 58.9	
x	y
−4.9	−63.8
25.4	−33.5
50.7	−8.2

Alternative Activity 105—Functions and Lines

1. $\frac{-5}{7}$, Model B **2.** $\frac{7}{6}$, Model A **3.** $\frac{1}{5}$, Model A **4.** $\frac{-8}{3}$, Model B
5. 15 **6.** 0 **7.** −15 **8.** 0 **9.** 3 **10.** 8

Alternative Activity 106—Finding the Domain and Range

1. 1, 2, 5, 9, 82 **2.** −7, −8, 1, 28, 136 **3.** $-6\frac{3}{8}, -6, -4\frac{1}{8}, -2\frac{1}{4}, 1\frac{1}{2}$
4. 104, 14, −4, −4, 24 **5.** −21, −1, 7, 15, 56 **6.** −19, −5, −3, −1, 9, 17 **7.** 15, −85, −84, −49, 15 **8.** $11\frac{7}{8}, 12, 12\frac{1}{8}, 12\frac{1}{2}, 14\frac{1}{2}$
9. Domain: −7, −2, Range: 6, 5 **10.** Domain: 5, 6, Range: 3, −10
11. Domain: −123, 47, Range: 18, −190 **12.** Domain: 2, 3, 4, Range: 3, 7, 11 **13.** Domain: −1, 9, 27, Range: 9
14. Domain: $-6 \leq x \leq 6$, Range: $-1 \leq y \leq 1$
15. Domain: $-4 \leq x \leq 7$, Range: $-2 \leq y \leq 4$

Alternative Activity 107—Graphing a Line

1. $x = -2, 0, 2; y = 0, 2, 4$

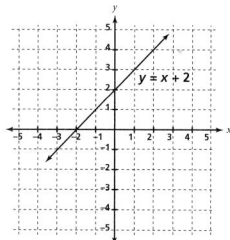

2. $x = 0, 1, 3; y = 3, 2, 0$

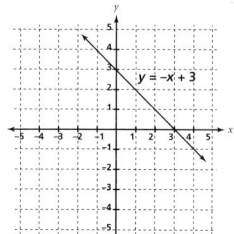

3. $x = -1, 0, 1; y = -4, 0, 4$

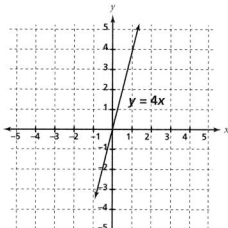

4. $x = 0, 1, 2; y = 1, 3, 5$

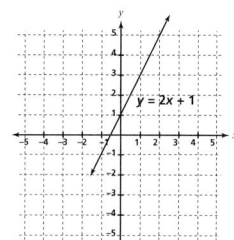

5. $x = -1, 0, 1; y = 0, 3, 6$

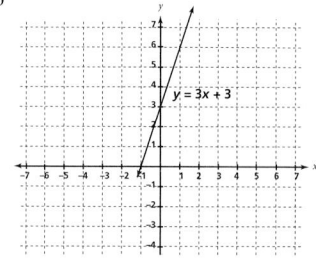

Alternative Activity 108—Slope of a Line

1. −30 **2.** 7 **3.** 0.05 **4.** 0.14 **5.** 88 **6.** 1.23 **7.** −24 **8.** −9 **9.** 0.29
10. −0.97 **11.** 23.2 **12.** 1.6 **13.** 0.09 **14.** 90.88 **15.** −50

Alternative Activity 109—Formula—Slope of a Line
1. $\frac{1}{7}$ 2. $-\frac{1}{3}$ 3. 0 4. $\frac{6}{5}$ 5. $-\frac{2}{3}$ 6. -2 7. 2 8. $-\frac{2}{3}$ 9. $-\frac{5}{3}$ 10. $-\frac{4}{7}$
11. $\frac{5}{3}$ 12. $-\frac{9}{8}$ 13. $\frac{1}{4}$ 14. -1 15. $-\frac{4}{5}$ 16. $-\frac{4}{11}$ 17. $\frac{9}{8}$ 18. 2
19. Monroe Hill, because $\frac{180}{640} > \frac{96}{640}$ so $\frac{9}{32} > \frac{3}{20}$ 20. the second slope because it has a negative or downward slope, which would be easier to ride a bike on than the first slope's upward slope

Alternative Activity 110—Slope-Intercept Form of a Line
1. $m = 1$, y-intercept $= 4$, x-intercept $= -4$ 2. $m = 3$, y-intercept $= -3$, x-intercept $= 1$ 3. $y = x + 2$ 4. $y = 3x - 4$ 5. $y = -x + 5$ 6. $y = 5x - 1$ 7. $y = 2x + 5$ 8. $y = x - 3$ 9. $m = 1$, y-intercept $= -3$, x-intercept $= 3$ 10. $m = 2$, y-intercept $= 5$, x-intercept $= -\frac{5}{2}$ 11. $m = 4$, y-intercept $= 2$, x-intercept $= -\frac{1}{2}$ 12. $m = -1$, y-intercept $= -8$, x-intercept $= -8$ 13. $m = 3$, y-intercept $= -6$, x-intercept $= 2$ 14. $m = -2$, y-intercept $= 7$, x-intercept $= \frac{7}{2}$ 15. $m = 1$, y-intercept $= 9$, x-intercept $= -9$

Alternative Activity 111—Angles, Angle Measures
1. UP and UQ 2. $\angle OUN$ 3. $\angle MUN$ and $\angle NUM$ 4. point U 5. $\overline{UR}$ or $\overline{RU}$ 6. $\angle MUN$, $\angle NUO$, $\angle NUP$, $\angle NUQ$, $\angle NUR$, $\angle NUS$, $\angle NUT$ 7. 25° 8. 95° 9. 62° 10. 36°

Alternative Activity 112—Classifying Angles
1. obtuse 2. acute 3. right 4. straight 5. angles f and h 6. angles e and g; h and f 7. vertical, obtuse 8. adjacent 9. true 10. false

Alternative Activity 113—Complementary, Supplementary Angles
1. $\angle DCE$ 2. $\angle GCF$ and $\angle FCE$ 3. 90° 4. $\angle ACG$ or $\angle BCE$ 5. 80° 6. 25° 7. 48° 8. 53° 9. 68° 10. 85° 11. 5° 12. 100° 13. 15° 14. 71° 15. 92°

Alternative Activity 114—Measures of Triangle Angles
1. 55° 2. 90° 3. 35° 4. 70° 5. 60° 6. 65° 7. 70° 8. 80° 9. 25° 10. 40°

Alternative Activity 115—Triangle Names
1. right isosceles 2. equilateral and equiangular 3. equilateral 4. right scalene 5. acute isosceles 6. obtuse scalene 7. scalene 8. isosceles acute 9. right 10. obtuse

Alternative Activity 116—Triangles That Are Congruent
1. ASA 2. SSS 3. SAS 4. Yes, ASA 5. No, none of the sides are congruent or there is not enough information to tell.

Alternative Activity 117—Triangles That Are Similar
1. no 2. yes 3. not enough information 4. yes 5. not enough information 6. yes 7. false 8. true 9. false 10. true

Alternative Activity 118—Naming Parallelograms
Note: All figures are quadrilateral.
1. trapezoid 2. rhombus 3. quadrilateral 4. trapezoid 5. parallelogram 6. square 7. Tennessee 8. Vermont or Connecticut or New Hampshire 9. Wyoming and Colorado 10. North Dakota or South Dakota

Alternative Activity 119—Quadrilaterals—Diagonals
1. 100° 2. no 3. 90° 4. 4 5. yes 6. 40° 7. 110° 8. They are congruent. 9. 59° 10. no

Alternative Activity 120—Polygons—Diagonals
1. 4 2. 8 3. pentagon 4. decagon 5. 360° 6. 720° 7. 900° 8. 1,260° 9. 1,800° 10. 108° 11. 144° 12. 147.3° 13. 90° 14. 60° 15. 36°

Alternative Activity 121—Points and Their Reflections
1. $(1, -4)$ 2. $(-6, -1)$ 3. $(3, 0)$ 4. $(5, 3)$ 5. $(-2, -1)$ 6. $(-4, 5)$ 7. $(-3, -2)$ 8. $(3, -3)$ 9. $(-4, 1)$ 10. $(-5, 3)$ 11. $(2, 0)$ 12. $(7, 4)$ 13. $(0, -5)$ 14. $(-6, 0)$ 15. $(-4, -5)$

Alternative Activity 122—Lines of Symmetry
1. yes 2. no 3. yes 4. no 5. yes 6. yes 7. yes 8. no 9. yes 10. no

Alternative Activity 123—Slides, Translations
For 1–10, check student graphs. 1. $(3, -5)$ 2. $(9, -11)$ 3. $(1, 0)$ 4. $(6, -2)$ 5. $(-5, 3)$ 6. $(4, -3)$ 7. $(5, 2)$ 8. $A' = (8, 8)$, $B' = (1, 10)$ 9. $C' = (-3, -4)$, $D' = (1, -8)$ 10. $E' = (6, -6)$, $F' = (11, 1)$

Alternative Activity 124—Clockwise and Counterclockwise Rotations
For 1–5, check student graphs. 1. $P' = (3, -4)$ 2. $P' = (6, -1)$ 3. $P' = (3, -3)$ 4. $P' = (4, 0)$ 5. $P' = (-5, -1)$

Alternative Activity 125—Reading Bar Graphs
1. Alabaster; Madison 2. Enterprise 3. Piedmont 4. Enterprise 5. Piedmont 6. Enterprise 7. less than 8. 15,499; When rounding to the nearest thousand, 15,499 is the greatest number that rounds to 15,000. 9. 14,450; When rounding to the nearest thousand, 14,450 is the least number that rounds to 15,000. 10. Sample answer: a title, a horizontal axis with labels, a vertical axis with labels, an interval, data

Alternative Activity 126—Reading Frequency Tables
1. between 20 and 29 years old; Sample explanation: The table does not give an exact age. Instead, it gives a range or interval of ages. 2. between 70 and 79 years old; Sample explanation: The table does not give an exact age. Instead, it gives a range or interval of ages. 3. 26 students; The sum of the tally marks in the tally column and the sum of the numbers in the frequency column are 26. 4. 10 years 5. Yes. Sample explanation: Various intervals can be chosen for any frequency graph. 6. Sample answer: Without a title, the data displayed by a frequency graph would not be meaningful. 7. The sums should be identical. 8. Sample answer: The frequency table contains one or more errors. 9. Sample answer: The data can be interpreted two ways—by tally or by number. 10. Sample answer: If the number of tallies to be displayed by a frequency table is great, the table can become physically large.

Alternative Activity 127—Reading Circle Graphs
1. 70% 2. 30% 3. 15 students 4. 35 students 5. 252°; Sample explanation: 70% of 360° is 252°. 6. 108°; Sample explanation: 30% of 360° is 108°. 7. Sample answer: The number of degrees representing data that have been rounded may not have a sum of exactly 360°. 8. Sample answer: The sum of percent data that is rounded to the nearest whole number may not be exactly 100%. 9. 350 students; 150 students 10. Sample answer: a title, labels, numerical data

Alternative Activity 128—Organizing Data
1. 17 2. 251–300; One person scored within that range. 3. 10 4. 1–50 and 251–300 5. 101–150

Alternative Activity 129—Comparing Data

1. 2 **2.** 5 cm and 11 cm **3.** 1 **4.** Their heights are random because there is no clustering around the line $y = x$. **5.** No.

Alternative Activity 130—Mean Values

1. 8 **2.** 472 **3.** Sample answer: Find the sum of the data values in the set, then divide by the number of data values. **4.** 59 **5.** 6 **6.** 365 **7.** 60.83 **8.** Yes; Find the sum of the fractions in the set, then divide by the number of fractions. **9.** Yes. Find the sum of the decimals in the set, then divide by the number of decimals.
10. zero

Alternative Activity 131—Median Values

1. an odd number **2.** Char; 102 points **3.** Karin; 80 points
4. Sample answer: 80; 81; 83; 85; 85; 86; 88; 90; 90; 99; 102 **5.** No. The median represents the middle value of the set of data. The actual number of values in the set of data is not relevant. **6.** 86
7. Sample answer: easier because there would have been only one middle value **8.** Sample answer: No; the median of the data set {4, 2, 3} can be found using mental math. **9.** Sample answer: No. Adding the teacher's age simply moves the location of the median up or down one value in a data set in which most of the values are nearly the same. **10.** Answers will vary.

Alternative Activity 132—Mode Values

1. 5, 9 **2.** The number of tallies and the number of data values should be identical. **3.** The mode of any set of data is the value or values that occur most often. **4.** Sample answer: {100, 100, 500, 500, 700, 900, 900} **5.** Sample answer: {the set of counting numbers}

Alternative Activity 133—Range Values

1. 7 in. **2.** 1 in. **3.** $\frac{6}{8}$ inch or $\frac{3}{4}$ inch **4.** 1 in. **5.** Answers will vary.

Alternative Activity 134—A Box-and-Whiskers Plot

1. 4; 6; 6; 7; 7; 8; 8; 8; 14 **2.** 4 hours **3.** 14 hours **4.** 7 hours **5.** 6 hours **6.** 8 hours **7.** Check students' plots. **8.** Check students' plots. **9.** Check students' plots.
10.

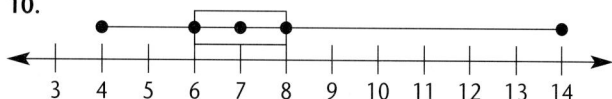

Alternative Activity 135—Using the Probability Fraction

1. $\frac{1}{2}$; 50% **2.** $\frac{1}{2}$; 50% **3.** $\frac{5}{6}$; $83\frac{1}{3}$% **4.** $\frac{6}{6}$ or 1; 100% **5.** $\frac{0}{6}$ or 0; 0%
6. $\frac{3}{4}$; 75% **7.** $\frac{1}{4}$; 25% **8.** $\frac{1}{4}$; 25% **9.** $\frac{3}{4}$; 75% **10.** $\frac{4}{4}$ or 1; 100%

Alternative Activity 136—Dependent, Independent Events

1. $\frac{1}{25}$ **2.** $\frac{1}{4}$ **3.** $\frac{1}{100}$ **4.** $\frac{1}{2,300}$ **5.** $\frac{11}{46}$

Alternative Activity 137—Fundamental Principle of Counting

1. 6 ways **2.** 23 ways **3.** 120 ways **4.** 1,000 combinations
5. 24 combinations

Workbook Activities

Workbook Activity 1—The Base 10 System
1. > 2. > 3. > 4. > 5. > 6. > 7. < 8. 90 9. 600 10. 4,000
11. 50 12. 3,000 13. 400 14. 40,000 15. 200

Workbook Activity 2—Place Value
1. 1,010,000 2. 100,010 3. 100,100 4. 11,000 5. 110 6. 100,001
7. 9 8. 0 9. 999,000 10. 990 11. 300 miles 12. 200 miles
13. 100 miles 14. 100 miles 15. 700 miles

Workbook Activity 3—Addition and Subtraction
1. 544 2. 592 3. 681 4. 860 5. 1,683 6. 719 7. 1,942 8. 301
9. 837 10. 943 11. 111 12. 91 13. 918 14. 201 15. 190
16. 1,182 17. 376 18. 1,001 19. 295 20. 1,006

Workbook Activity 4—Multiplication and Division
Answers may vary. Examples are given.
1. $36 \div 4 = 9$ and $9 \times 4 = 36$
2. $70 \div 7 = 10$ and $10 \times 7 = 70$
3. $41 \times 3 = 123$ and $123 \div 3 = 41$
4. $4 \times 5 = 20$ and $20 \div 5 = 4$
5. $594 \div 6 = 99$ and $6 \times 99 = 594$
6. $56 \div 2 = 28$ and $28 \times 2 = 56$
7. $126 \div 9 = 14$ and $9 \times 14 = 126$
8. $28 \div 7 = 4$ and $4 \times 7 = 128$
9. $100 \times 5 = 500$ and $500 \div 100 = 5$
10. $135 \div 15 = 9$ and $15 \times 9 = 135$
11. $200 \div 10 = 20$ and $10 \times 20 = 200$
12. $12 \div 2 = 6$ and $2 \times 6 = 12$
13. $64 \div 4 = 16$ and $16 \times 4 = 64$
14. $72 \div 9 = 8$ and $8 \times 9 = 72$
15. $123 \div 3 = 41$ and $3 \times 41 = 123$

Workbook Activity 5—The Base 2 System
1. < 2. < 3. < 4. < 5. > 6. < 7. > 8. > 9. > 10. < 11. <
12. < 13. > 14. < 15. <

Workbook Activity 6—The Base 5 System
1. 34_{10} 2. 25_{10} 3. 150_{10} 4. 8_{10} 5. 45_{10} 6. 27_{10} 7. 200_{10} 8. 114_5
9. 100_5 10. 1100_5 11. 13_5 12. 140_5 13. 102_5 14. 1300_5
15. 1000000_5

Workbook Activity 7—Adding Whole Numbers
1. 60 2. 72 3. 336a 4. 1,583x 5. 1,673b 6. 61 7. 180 8. 216x
9. 420 10. 1,382b 11. 784a 12. 1,818 13. 4,547y 14. 5,224
15. 6,382z

Workbook Activity 8—Subtracting Whole Numbers
1. 13 2. 34 3. 53 4. 35y 5. 6c 6. 36 7. 116 8. 115 9. 507b
10. 184c 11. 1,196y 12. 456a 13. 21 14. 55x 15. 144 16. 259c
17. 255y 18. 618b 19. 1,164z 20. 4,537a

Workbook Activity 9—Estimating Sums and Differences
1. 70 2. 100 3. 200 4. 1,000 5. 3,000 6. 400 7. 5,000
8. 500 9. 200 10. 600 11. 8,000 12. 700 13. 6,000 14. 500
15. 9,000 16. $60 + 90 = 150; 151$ 17. $300 + 500 = 800; 776$
18. $700 + 900 = 1,600; 1,606$ 19. $2,000 + 200 = 2,200; 1,804$
20. $4,000 + 500 = 4,500; 4,272$ 21. $70 - 40 = 30; 23$
22. $400 - 300 = 100; 134$ 23. $900 - 400 = 500; 491$
24. $600 - 300 = 300; 343$ 25. $2,000 - 500 = 1,500; 1,504$

Workbook Activity 10—Multiplying Whole Numbers
1. 32 2. 63 3. 81 4. 30a 5. 12b 6. 40y 7. 384 8. 782 9. 595x
10. 728x 11. 783z 12. 152c 13. 2,128y 14. 608z 15. 1,782b

Workbook Activity 11—Dividing Whole Numbers
1. 5 2. 8 3. 9 4. 7 5. 6 6. 3 7. 9 8. 8a 9. 2 10. 3 11. 4
12. 9y 13. 62 14. 74 15. 125 16. 34x 17. 134a 18. 88b
19. 51 r4 20. 182 r1 21. 85 r2 22. 249; $249 \times 18 = 4,482$
23. 91x; $91x \times 27 = 2,457x$ 24. 138 r1; $138 \times 61 = 8,418 + 1 = 8,419$ 25. 134a; $134a \times 43 = 5,762a$

Workbook Activity 12—Basic Operations
1. 121a 2. 10 3. 14x 4. 225 5. 1a 6. 52 7. 32b 8. 763 9. 748a
10. 26 11. 8a 12. 2x 13. 104x 14. 5,130b 15. 35 16. 102,863
17. 84 18. 88,992 19. 11,980 20. 1,842

Workbook Activity 13—Estimating Products and Quotients
1. $60 \times 20; 1,200; 1,512$ 2. $90 \times 40; 3,600; 3,060$ 3. $20 \times 40; 800; 714$ 4. $40 \times 80; 3,200; 3,300$ 5. $60 \times 10; 600; 826$ 6. $30 \times 60; 1,800; 1,760$ 7. $70 \times 60; 4,200; 4,672$ 8. $30 \times 80; 2,400; 2,241$
9. $540 \div 6; 90; 89$ 10. $720 \div 8; 90; 92$ 11. $1,400 \div 20; 70; 60$
12. $3,000 \div 50; 60; 53$ 13. $6,300 \div 70; 90; 85$ 14. $4,800 \div 80; 60; 61$
15. $10,000 \div 50; 200, 237$

Workbook Activity 14—Open Statements
1. addition 2. division 3. multiplication 4. subtraction
5. multiplication; division 6. multiplication 7. division
8. multiplication; subtraction 9. addition; multiplication
10. multiplication; addition; subtraction 11. true 12. true
13. false 14. false 15. open 16. true 17. true 18. open
19. false 20. false 21. open 22. false 23. open 24. true
25. open 26. true 27. false 28. true 29. open 30. true

Workbook Activity 15—Using Letters to Represent Numbers
1. algebraic 2. numerical 3. numerical 4. algebraic 5. numerical
6. algebraic 7. numerical 8. numerical 9. algebraic 10. algebraic
11. x 12. b 13. y 14. k 15. d 16. x 17. y 18. m 19. x 20. d
21. multiplication; subtraction 22. multiplication 23. addition; multiplication 24. multiplication 25. division; subtraction

Workbook Activity 16—Replacing Variables
1. false 2. false 3. true 4. false 5. true 6. false 7. false 8. false
9. true 10. true 11. false 12. false 13. 32 14. 3 15. 3 16. 31
17. 31 18. 6 19. 64 20. 18

Workbook Activity 17—Place Value and Decimals
1. three-tenths 2. eighty-one one-hundredths 3. twelve one-hundredths 4. seventy-seven thousandths 5. three hundred twenty-five thousandths 6. 0.42 7. 0.7 8. 0.02 9. 0.033 10. 0.25

Workbook Activity 18—Comparing and Rounding Decimals
1. 46.9 2. 108.2 3. 17.0 4. 2.1 5. 39.0 6. 199.99 7. 20.06
8. 5.99 9. 77.81 10. 10.78 11. 13.426 12. 0.057 13. 399.113
14. 12.667 15. 251.703 16. > 17. < 18. > 19. > 20. <
21. < 22. < 23. > 24. < 25. <

Workbook Activity 19—Adding and Subtracting Decimals

1. 16.11 cm **2.** 2.78 cm **3.** 48.397 cm **4.** 6.15 cm **5.** 30.691 cm
6. 50.309 cm **7.** 84.239 cm **8.** 5.508 cm **9.** 23.361 cm
10. $20.77 **11.** $0.17 **12.** $573.03 **13.** $83.71 **14.** $0.69
15. $986.89 **16.** $333.12 **17.** $16.78 **18.** 3.173 cm **19.** $181.00
20. 22.257 miles

Workbook Activity 20—Multiplying Decimals by Powers of 10

1. 2.345×10 **2.** 23.45 **3.** 17.425×100 **4.** 1,742.5 **5.** $8.7 \times 10,000$ **6.** 87,000 **7.** $0.0651 \times 100,000$ **8.** 6,510 **9.** 643×100
10. 64,300 **11.** 0.53219×10^3 **12.** 532.19 **13.** 44.22×10^1
14. 442.2 **15.** 1.359×10^4 **16.** 13,590 **17.** 39.71×10^5
18. 3,971,000 **19.** 0.07125×10^2 **20.** 7.125

Workbook Activity 21—Multiplying Decimals

1. 22.608 cm **2.** 9.106 inches **3.** 43.96 cm **4.** 56.8968 cm
5. 17.8038 inches **6.** 1.6642 inches **7.** 201.902 cm **8.** 91.374 inches
9. 41.9818 cm **10.** 11.59602 cm **11.** 30.52 **12.** 36.44 **13.** 16.38
14. 38.624 **15.** 19.88 **16.** 188.7786 **17.** 289.4457 **18.** 0.92988
19. 719.68384 **20.** 299.1417

Workbook Activity 22—Dividing Decimals by Powers of 10

1. 8.242 **2.** 0.08242 **3.** 6.149 **4.** 0.6149 **5.** 0.06149 **6.** 0.006149
7. 0.0267 **8.** 0.00267 **9.** 0.000267 **10.** 0.0000267 **11.** 0.3195
12. 0.03195 **13.** 0.003195 **14.** 0.0003195 **15.** 0.053 **16.** 0.0053
17. 0.00053 **18.** 0.000053 **19.** 18.475 **20.** 1.8475 **21.** 0.18475
22. 0.018475 **23.** 0.708 **24.** 0.0708 **25.** 0.00708 **26.** 0.000708
27. 1.485 **28.** 0.1485 **29.** 0.01485 **30.** 0.001485

Workbook Activity 23—Dividing Decimals

1. 4.69 **2.** 9.855 **3.** 16.32 **4.** 1.57 **5.** 3.19 **6.** 11.98 **7.** 3.79 **8.** 37.19
9. 17.18 **10.** 29.83 **11.** 98.1 **12.** 16.17 **13.** 26.4 **14.** 20.61
15. 19.2 **16.** 607.1 **17.** 871 **18.** 17.33 **19.** 91.28 **20.** 183.4

Workbook Activity 24—Using Decimals

1. $0.28 **2.** 41.3° F **3.** 95 **4.** $32.25 **5.** 1,280.2 m **6.** 55.1 miles
7. $3.69 **8.** $7.01 **9.** $7.68 **10.** 25.5 kilometers

Workbook Activity 25—Decimals and Fractions

1. 10 **2.** 100 **3.** 100 **4.** 10 **5.** 1,000 **6.** $\frac{17}{50}$ **7.** $\frac{6}{25}$ **8.** $\frac{9}{20}$ **9.** $\frac{1}{100}$
10. $\frac{1}{5}$ **11.** $\frac{13}{100}$ **12.** $3\frac{2}{25}$ **13.** $\frac{3}{500}$ **14.** $\frac{9}{25}$ **15.** $7\frac{4}{5}$ **16.** 0.32 **17.** 0.15
18. 1.14 **19.** 0.725 **20.** 0.65 **21.** 3.72 **22.** 0.375 **23.** 7.2 **24.** 0.61
25. 0.64

Workbook Activity 26—Repeating Decimals

1. −4°C **2.** 43°C **3.** 29°C **4.** 20°C **5.** 0°C **6.** 24°C **7.** 6°C
8. 73°C **9.** 11°C **10.** 32°C **11.** $0.\overline{2}$ **12.** $0.5\overline{3}$ **13.** $0.\overline{5}$ **14.** $0.1\overline{6}$
15. $0.2\overline{6}$ **16.** $0.\overline{7}$ **17.** $0.\overline{27}$ **18.** $0.58\overline{3}$ **19.** $0.7\overline{2}$ **20.** $0.\overline{18}$

Workbook Activity 27—Renaming Percents to Decimals

1. 0.18 **2.** 0.94 **3.** 0.003 **4.** 0.0275 **5.** 0.29 **6.** 3.00 **7.** 0.48
8. 0.012 **9.** 0.81 **10.** 0.02 **11.** $1,352.81 **12.** $25.31 **13.** $69.00
14. $640.00 **15.** $203.88

Workbook Activity 28—Evaluating Expressions with Decimals

1. 54.33 **2.** 14.402 **3.** 24 **4.** 87.1199 **5.** 69.18 **6.** $n + \$12.81$; $50.46
7. $4.2l + 5.6m$; 99.4 **8.** $p - \$42.95$; $73.85 **9.** $\$4,503.04 \div n$; $562.88
10. $125.75l$; $2,263.50

Workbook Activity 29—Divisibility Rules

1. true; $15 \div 5 = 3$ **2.** true; $36 \div 4 = 9$ **3.** false; $39 \div 6 = 6$ r3
4. true; $40 \div 8 = 5$ **5.** false; $82 \div 9 = 9$ r1 **6.** false; $46 \div 6 = 7$ r4
7. true; $90 \div 3 = 30$ **8.** true; $85 \div 5 = 17$ **9.** true; $128 \div 4 = 32$
10. false; $374 \div 8 = 46$ r6 **11.** false; $577 \div 2 = 288$ r1 **12.** false;
$634 \div 4 = 158$ r2 **13.** true; $567 \div 9 = 63$ **14.** false; $473 \div 7 = 67$ r4
15. true; $688 \div 8 = 86$

Workbook Activity 30—Prime and Composite Numbers

1. P 3; C 6 **2.** P 17; C 8 **3.** P 31; C 27 **4.** P 5; C 12 **5.** P 13; C 16
6. P 43; C 50 **7.** P 41; C 20 **8.** P 83; C 106 **9.** P 149; C 125
10. P 97; C 221 **11.** P 7; C 12 **12.** P 37; C 20 **13.** P 41; C 38
14. P 89; C 81 **15.** P 67; C 121 **16.** P 79; C 72 **17.** P 691; C 177
18. P 197; C 221 **19.** P 109; C 301 **20.** P 239; C 108 **21.** 2, 9
22. 3, 7 **23.** 3, 5 **24.** 4, 6 **25.** 4, 8 **26.** 5, 7 **27.** 6, 8 **28.** 5, 9
29. 3, 4 **30.** 5, 6

Workbook Activity 31—Greatest Common Divisor

1. 9: 1, 3, 9; 24: 1, 2, 3, 4, 6, 8, 12, 24; GCD: 3 **2.** 14: 1, 2, 7, 14; 28: 1, 2, 4, 7, 14, 28; GCD: 14 **3.** 8: 1, 2, 4, 8; 16: 1, 2, 4, 8, 16; GCD: 8
4. 11: 1, 11; 77: 1, 7, 11, 77; GCD: 11 **5.** 4: 1, 2, 4; 20: 1, 2, 4, 5, 10, 20; GCD: 4 **6.** $3x$: 1, 3, x; 21: 1, 3, 7, 21; GCD: 3 **7.** 8: 1, 2, 4, 8; $48y$: 1, 2, 3, 4, 6, 8, 12, 16, 24, 48, y; GCD: 8 **8.** $12x$: 1, 2, 3, 4, 6, 12, x; $60x$: 1, 2, 3, 4, 5, 6, 10, 12, 15, 20, 30, 60, x; GCD: $12x$ **9.** $7a$: 1, 7, a; $42a$: 1, 2, 3, 6, 7, 14, 21, 42, a; GCD: $7a$ **10.** $6c$: 1, 2, 3, 6, c; $54c$: 1, 2, 3, 6, 9, 18, 27, 54, c; GCD: $6c$

Workbook Activity 32—Factoring

1. 3 **2.** 6 **3.** 8 **4.** 5 **5.** 10 **6.** 6 **7.** 9 **8.** 1 **9.** 25 **10.** 3
11. $6(3x + 2)$ **12.** $2(3y + 4)$ **13.** $3(c + 3)$ **14.** $3(2a + 5)$
15. $2h + 11$ **16.** $9(6b + w)$ **17.** $5(4m + 3k)$ **18.** $4(3n + p)$
19. $9(q + 9c)$ **20.** $b(a + c)$

Workbook Activity 33—Least Common Multiple

1. 8: 2, 4; 2, 2   9: 3, 3 **2.** 9: 3, 3   3 **3.** $2^3 \cdot 3^2$ **4.** 3^3 **5.** 12 **6.** 90
7. 60 **8.** 560 **9.** 140 **10.** 168

Workbook Activity 34—Scientific Notation

1. 5; left; 3.25×10^5 **2.** 4; left; 2.78×10^4 **3.** 8; left; 1.05×10^8
4. 1; right; 6.53×10^{-1} **5.** 2; right; 3.25×10^{-2} **6.** 5; right; 8.17×10^{-5} **7.** 11; left; 6.81×10^{11} **8.** 7; right; 7.83×10^{-7} **9.** 5; right; 1.818×10^{-5} **10.** 10; left; 8.6×10^{10} **11.** 620 **12.** 87,000
13. 387,000,000 **14.** 0.715 **15.** 0.0384

Workbook Activity 35—Proper Fractions

1. $\frac{1}{3}$ **2.** $\frac{3}{8}$ **3.** $\frac{2}{5}$ **4.** $\frac{0}{3}, \frac{1}{3}, \frac{2}{3}$ **5.** $\frac{0}{5}, \frac{1}{5}, \frac{2}{5}, \frac{3}{5}, \frac{4}{5}$ **6.** $\frac{0}{2}, \frac{1}{2}$ **7.** $\frac{11}{15}$ **8.** $\frac{15}{21} = \frac{5}{7}$
9. $\frac{23}{27}$ **10.** $\frac{3}{8}$

Workbook Activity 36—Improper Fractions and Mixed Numbers

1. $2\frac{2}{3}$ **2.** $1\frac{4}{5}$ **3.** 5 **4.** $3\frac{1}{2}$ **5.** $1\frac{3}{8}$ **6.** $3\frac{1}{8}$ **7.** $6\frac{2}{5}$ **8.** $1\frac{1}{11}$ **9.** 6 **10.** $3\frac{1}{5}$
11. $3\frac{3}{4}$ **12.** 1 **13.** $4\frac{1}{2}$ **14.** $1\frac{7}{19}$ **15.** $1\frac{1}{7}$ **16.** $\frac{14}{3}$ **17.** $\frac{21}{8}$ **18.** $\frac{16}{3}$
19. $\frac{20}{11}$ **20.** $\frac{30}{7}$ **21.** $\frac{205}{3}$ **22.** $\frac{25}{2}$ **23.** $\frac{63}{8}$ **24.** $\frac{51}{4}$ **25.** $\frac{15}{2}$ **26.** $\frac{39}{4}$
27. $\frac{67}{2}$ **28.** $\frac{71}{5}$ **29.** $\frac{99}{10}$ **30.** $\frac{94}{5}$

Workbook Activity 37—Equivalent Fractions

For problems **1–10**, sample answers are given. **1.** $\frac{4}{6}$ and $\frac{6}{9}$ **2.** $\frac{6}{8}$ and $\frac{9}{12}$ **3.** $\frac{10}{12}$ and $\frac{15}{18}$ **4.** $\frac{2}{32}$ and $\frac{3}{48}$ **5.** $\frac{4}{10}$ and $\frac{6}{15}$ **6.** $\frac{14}{20}$ and $\frac{21}{30}$ **7.** $\frac{4}{14}$ and $\frac{6}{21}$ **8.** $\frac{10}{18}$ and $\frac{15}{27}$ **9.** $\frac{2}{4}$ and $\frac{3}{6}$ **10.** $\frac{6}{20}$ and $\frac{9}{30}$ **11.** yes **12.** no **13.** no **14.** no **15.** yes **16.** no **17.** yes **18.** no **19.** yes **20.** yes **21.** no **22.** yes **23.** yes **24.** no **25.** no

Workbook Activity 38—Simplest Form

1. 8 **2.** 5 **3.** 2 **4.** 3 **5.** 2 **6.** $\frac{2}{3}$ **7.** $\frac{2}{3}$ **8.** $\frac{13}{15}$ **9.** $\frac{1}{5}$ **10.** $\frac{5}{6}$ **11.** $\frac{4}{5}$ **12.** $\frac{2}{5}$ **13.** $\frac{2}{3}$ **14.** $\frac{9}{10}$ **15.** $\frac{4}{5}$ **16.** $\frac{1}{4}$ **17.** $\frac{7}{12}$ **18.** $\frac{1}{2}$ **19.** $\frac{1}{3}$ **20.** $\frac{3}{4}$ **21.** $\frac{2}{3}$ **22.** $\frac{6}{13}$ **23.** yes, they both are $\frac{3}{4}$ **24.** no, Ashley's total number of animals must be a multiple of 4 **25.** yes, 24 is a multiple of 3

Workbook Activity 39—Comparing and Ordering Fractions

1. > **2.** > **3.** < **4.** > **5.** < **6.** < **7.** > **8.** < **9.** > **10.** < **11.** >
12. $\frac{3}{8}$ $\frac{1}{2}$ $\frac{2}{3}$ **13.** $\frac{1}{4}$ $\frac{1}{3}$ $\frac{1}{2}$ **14.** $\frac{3}{5}$ $\frac{2}{3}$ $\frac{3}{4}$ **15.** $\frac{1}{2}$ $\frac{3}{4}$ $\frac{7}{8}$ **16.** $\frac{3}{16}$ $\frac{2}{3}$ $\frac{7}{8}$
17. $\frac{3}{5}$ $\frac{7}{10}$ $\frac{17}{20}$ **18.** $\frac{1}{4}$ $\frac{9}{32}$ $\frac{5}{16}$ **19.** $\frac{3}{35}$ $\frac{3}{7}$ $\frac{3}{5}$ **20.** $\frac{5}{16}$ $\frac{3}{8}$ $\frac{1}{2}$

Workbook Activity 40—Fractions—Like Denominators

1. $\frac{1}{5}$ **2.** $1\frac{2}{3}$ **3.** $\frac{1}{5}$ **4.** $1\frac{1}{2}$ **5.** $6\frac{1}{6}$ **6.** $2\frac{1}{2}$ **7.** $15\frac{2}{5}$ **8.** $\frac{x}{4}$ **9.** $\frac{3x}{10}$ **10.** $\frac{13}{y}$
11. $\frac{(4+x)}{y}$ **12.** $\frac{x}{2}$ **13.** $\frac{5y}{8}$ **14.** $\frac{(3y+5)}{12}$ **15.** $\frac{14x}{9}$ or $1\frac{5}{9}x$ **16.** $\frac{4}{5}$ **17.** $\frac{3}{4}$
18. $\frac{3}{16}$ **19.** $\frac{9}{11}$ **20.** $1\frac{1}{3}$ **21.** $\frac{1}{3}$ **22.** $\frac{11}{25}$ **23.** $\frac{7x}{8}$ **24.** x **25.** $\frac{7y}{12}$

Workbook Activity 41—Fractions—Unlike Denominators

1. $1\frac{1}{2}$ **2.** $\frac{7}{16}$ **3.** $1\frac{5}{12}$ **4.** $\frac{3}{20}$ **5.** $\frac{4}{9}$ **6.** $\frac{1}{5}$ **7.** $1\frac{11}{24}$ **8.** $\frac{2}{15}$ **9.** $1\frac{7}{16}$ **10.** $1\frac{2}{3}$
11. $\frac{5x}{21}$ **12.** $\frac{(y+4x)}{xy}$ **13.** $\frac{31x}{24}$ or $1\frac{7}{24}x$ **14.** $\frac{13}{16y}$ **15.** $\frac{x}{12}$ **16.** $12\frac{19}{40}$
17. $1\frac{2}{21}$ **18.** $15\frac{1}{10}$ **19.** $8\frac{3}{10}$ **20.** $16\frac{1}{3}$ **21.** $6\frac{3}{32}$ **22.** $1\frac{9}{40}$ **23.** $65\frac{5}{12}$
24. $9\frac{3}{8}x$ **25.** $1\frac{1}{2}x$

Workbook Activity 42—Subtracting Fractions with Regrouping

1. $\frac{17}{24}$ **2.** $4\frac{1}{4}$ **3.** $\frac{13}{30}$ **4.** $1\frac{4}{5}$ **5.** $7\frac{3}{4}$ **6.** $4\frac{4}{7}$ **7.** $14\frac{2}{3}$ **8.** $6\frac{4}{5}$ **9.** $2\frac{5}{8}$ **10.** $2\frac{1}{2}$
11. $8\frac{3}{16}$ **12.** $14\frac{13}{18}$ **13.** $4\frac{5}{12}$ miles **14.** $1\frac{3}{4}$ pounds **15.** $1\frac{7}{12}$ hours

Workbook Activity 43—Multiplying Fractions and Mixed Numbers

1. $\frac{1}{6}$ **2.** $\frac{3}{5}$ **3.** $\frac{1}{4}$ **4.** $\frac{1}{2}$ **5.** $\frac{3}{7}$ **6.** $\frac{1}{4}$ **7.** $\frac{1}{6}$ **8.** $\frac{19}{24}yx$ **9.** $\frac{1}{2}y$ **10.** 3 **11.** $3\frac{1}{4}$
12. $3\frac{4}{5}$ **13.** $9\frac{1}{2}$ **14.** $12\frac{4}{5}$ **15.** $4\frac{7}{8}$ **16.** $9\frac{1}{6}a$ **17.** $12\frac{2}{5}y$ **18.** $4\frac{19}{24}x$
19. $\frac{7}{10}$ of both classes **20.** $37\frac{11}{12}$ ounces

Workbook Activity 44—Dividing Fractions and Mixed Numbers

1. $\frac{3}{4}$ **2.** $\frac{4}{15}$ **3.** $\frac{3}{4}$ **4.** $\frac{5}{8}$ **5.** $1\frac{3}{4}$ **6.** $2\frac{2}{5}$ **7.** $\frac{7}{9}$ **8.** $\frac{3}{2n}$ **9.** $1\frac{1}{2}y$ **10.** $1\frac{1}{2}$
11. $2\frac{13}{20}$ **12.** $1\frac{1}{3}$ **13.** $2\frac{1}{2}$ **14.** $\frac{7}{10}$ **15.** $1\frac{1}{4}$ **16.** $\frac{1}{2}$ **17.** $\frac{1}{3j}$ **18.** $3w$
19. $30\frac{2}{3}$ pieces **20.** $4\frac{3}{4}$ miles per hour

Workbook Activity 45—Using Fractions

1. $\frac{1}{2}=15$; $\frac{1}{3}=10$; $\frac{1}{15}=2$; $\frac{1}{10}=3$ **2.** Dennis **3.** Sam **4.** Ali
5. $7\frac{1}{8}$ blocks **6.** $6\frac{23}{24}$ in. **7.** $8\frac{17}{24}$ miles **8.** $8.75 **9.** yes **10.** 9

Workbook Activity 46—The Order of Operations

1. 1 **2.** 31 **3.** 12 **4.** 48 **5.** 13 **6.** 14 **7.** 1 **8.** 20 **9.** 44 **10.** 5
11. 21 **12.** 2 **13.** 70 **14.** 7 **15.** 12 **16.** 8 **17.** 17 **18.** 22 **19.** 1
20. 101 **21.** 67 **22.** 75 **23.** 4 **24.** 72 **25.** 46 **26.** 90 **27.** 1
28. 60 **29.** 11 **30.** 85

Workbook Activity 47—Evaluating Algebraic Expressions

1. 10 **2.** 3 **3.** 24 **4.** 32 **5.** 16 **6.** 2 **7.** 11 **8.** $3\frac{1}{2}$ **9.** $\frac{7}{12}$ **10.** 6
11. 10 **12.** 4 **13.** 0 **14.** 43 **15.** 13 **16.** $1\frac{1}{3}$ **17.** 12 **18.** $6\frac{1}{7}$
19. $4\frac{16}{21}$ **20.** 42 **21.** 28 **22.** 18 **23.** 2 **24.** 34 **25.** 16 **26.** $2\frac{1}{3}$
27. 20 **28.** $1\frac{1}{10}$ **29.** $5\frac{1}{2}$ **30.** 30

Workbook Activity 48—Equations—Solution by Substitution

1. 3 **2.** 4 **3.** 7 **4.** 10 **5.** 0 **6.** 3 **7.** 5 **8.** 2 **9.** 4 **10.** 7 **11.** 2 **12.** 5
13. 6 **14.** 10 **15.** 1 **16.** 6 **17.** 3 **18.** 2 **19.** 4 **20.** 8 **21.** 7 **22.** 9
23. 10 **24.** 2 **25.** 4

Workbook Activity 49—Solving Addition Equations

1. 6 **2.** 22 **3.** 30 **4.** 17 **5.** 18 **6.** 16 **7.** 20 **8.** 11 **9.** 5 **10.** 13
11. 21 **12.** 23 **13.** $\frac{3}{8}$ **14.** $\frac{3}{16}$ **15.** $\frac{1}{2}$ **16.** $\frac{1}{8}$ **17.** $\frac{3}{5}$ **18.** $\frac{2}{3}$ **19.** $\frac{4}{5}$
20. $\frac{1}{6}$ **21.** $\frac{1}{4}$ **22.** $\frac{3}{4}$ **23.** $\frac{1}{3}$ **24.** $\frac{1}{4}$ **25.** $\frac{2}{3}$

Workbook Activity 50—Solving Subtraction Equations

1. 38 **2.** 15 **3.** 42 **4.** 11 **5.** 50 **6.** 67 **7.** 38 **8.** 72 **9.** 55 **10.** $\frac{1}{2}$
11. $\frac{5}{6}$ **12.** $\frac{2}{3}$ **13.** $\frac{3}{4}$ **14.** $\frac{7}{8}$ **15.** $1\frac{1}{4}$ **16.** $\frac{15}{16}$ **17.** $\frac{9}{10}$ **18.** $\frac{2}{5}$ **19.** 11
million ounces of gold **20.** 321 thousand ounces of gold

Workbook Activity 51—Complex Fractions

1. 2 **2.** $\frac{5}{6}$ **3.** $\frac{8}{15}$ **4.** $7\frac{1}{2}$ **5.** 9 **6.** $1\frac{4}{5}$ **7.** $1\frac{1}{2}$ **8.** $\frac{1}{2}$ **9.** $\frac{8}{9}$ **10.** $\frac{1}{8}$
11. $18\frac{2}{3}$ **12.** $\frac{5}{6}$ **13.** $3\frac{1}{3}$ **14.** $\frac{2}{3}$ **15.** $\frac{4}{7}$ **16.** $1\frac{1}{4}$ **17.** 22 **18.** $\frac{4}{7}$
19. 6 **20.** $\frac{7}{27}$ **21.** $\frac{1}{3}$ **22.** $25\frac{3}{5}$ **23.** $2\frac{6}{25}$ **24.** $\frac{1}{12}$ **25.** 15

Workbook Activity 52—Simplifying by Addition

1. $\frac{3}{5x}$ **2.** $\frac{3c}{4}$ **3.** $\frac{7}{8y}$ **4.** $1\frac{3}{7}b$ **5.** $1\frac{2}{5}z$ **6.** $\frac{5}{8j}$ **7.** $\frac{w}{2}$ **8.** $\frac{3}{2x}$ **9.** d **10.** $\frac{7}{9y}$
11. $1g$ **12.** $\frac{1}{2b}$ **13.** $\frac{6}{5q}$ **14.** $1\frac{1}{2}x$ **15.** $\frac{7}{11p}$ **16.** $\frac{11}{15c}$ **17.** $\frac{13b}{16}$ **18.** $\frac{11y}{12}$
19. $\frac{19}{12j}$ **20.** $\frac{23}{30r}$ **21.** $\frac{9e}{14}$ **22.** $\frac{7}{6k}$ **23.** $\frac{13}{9m}$ **24.** $\frac{5e}{9}$ **25.** $\frac{19}{20v}$

Workbook Activity 53—Simplifying by Subtraction

1. $\frac{1c}{4}$ **2.** $\frac{1}{2d}$ **3.** $\frac{1w}{5}$ **4.** $\frac{1}{2e}$ **5.** $\frac{3}{7h}$ **6.** $\frac{3g}{5}$ **7.** $\frac{2}{3s}$ **8.** $\frac{1b}{3}$ **9.** $\frac{1}{3q}$ **10.** $\frac{2}{5a}$
11. $\frac{2c}{9}$ **12.** $\frac{1p}{16}$ **13.** $\frac{1}{24r}$ **14.** $\frac{7x}{40}$ **15.** $\frac{5s}{16}$ **16.** $\frac{2}{9k}$ **17.** $\frac{3y}{16}$ **18.** $\frac{5}{8}$ of the
time **19.** $\frac{5}{24}$ yards **20.** $\frac{5}{16}$ of the class

Workbook Activity 54—Multiplying Rational Expressions

1. $\frac{3}{5}$ **2.** $\frac{5}{9}$ **3.** $\frac{2}{3}$ **4.** $\frac{3}{4}$ **5.** $\frac{4}{5}$ **6.** $\frac{8}{45}$ **7.** $\frac{1}{2}$ **8.** $\frac{2}{3}$ **9.** $\frac{2}{5}$ **10.** $\frac{2}{27}$ **11.** $\frac{5}{18}$
12. $\frac{1}{12s}$ **13.** $\frac{1}{4}$ **14.** $\frac{14g}{17}$ **15.** $\frac{1}{8}$ **16.** $\frac{8}{11d}$ **17.** $\frac{1}{3m}$ **18.** $\frac{3}{5}$ **19.** $\frac{x}{3}$
20. $\frac{5}{12}$ **21.** $\frac{2b}{9}$ **22.** $\frac{4}{9}$ **23.** $\frac{1}{20}$ of the bar **24.** $\frac{1}{9}$ **25.** 200 miles

Workbook Activity 55—Ratios

1. 8 to 13; 8:13 **2.** $\frac{4}{11}$; 4:11 **3.** $\frac{5}{17}$; 5 to 17 **4.** $\frac{16}{9}$; 16:9 **5.** 12 to 7;
12:7 **6.** $\frac{21}{14}$; 21 to 14 **7.** 11 to 15; 11:15 **8.** $\frac{27}{41}$; 27:41 **9.** $\frac{37}{19}$; 37 to 19
10. $\frac{53}{61}$; 53:61 **11.** $\frac{1}{3}$ **12.** OK **13.** $\frac{3}{4}$ **14.** $\frac{1}{8}$ **15.** OK **16.** $\frac{1}{4}$ **17.** OK
18. $\frac{3}{8}$ **19.** OK **20.** $3\frac{5}{9}$

Workbook Activity 56—Proportions
1. yes **2.** no **3.** no **4.** yes **5.** yes **6.** yes **7.** $(2)(x) = (3)(6)$
8. $(1)(81) = (9)(b)$ **9.** $(6)(42) = (c)(36)$ **10.** $(x)(72) = (12)(30)$
11. $(42)(8) = (48)(t)$ **12.** $(3)(w) = (8)(30)$ **13.** 8 **14.** 9 **15.** 25
16. 18 **17.** 20 **18.** 8 **19.** 12 **20.** 4

Workbook Activity 57—Ratios and Proportions
1. 3, $1.80; 9, x; $5.40 **2.** 1, 18; 6, x; 108 **3.** 2, 84; x, 504; 12 **4.** 2, 9;
x, 63; 14 **5.** 20, $4.40; 3, x; $0.66

Workbook Activity 58—Proportional Relationships
1. 35 in. tall **2.** 195 ft **3.** 60 lb **4.** 1:3 **5.** 4 qt

**Workbook Activity 59—Solving Distance, Rate,
and Time Problems**
1. 2.5 miles **2.** 144 km **3.** 1.5 hours **4.** 82 km/h **5.** 3 hours
6. 9 km **7.** 83 km/h **8.** 0.2 hours **9.** 411 mph **10.** 72 km

Workbook Activity 60—Percents and Fractions
1. $\frac{43}{100}$ **2.** $\frac{86}{100}$ **3.** $\frac{22}{100}$ **4.** $\frac{61}{100}$ **5.** 8 shaded squares **6.** 25 shaded
squares **7.** 87 shaded squares **8.** 43 shaded squares **9.** 92 shaded
squares **10.** 12 shaded squares

Workbook Activity 61—Percents and Decimals
1. $0.63; \frac{63}{100}$ **2.** $0.40; 40\%$ **3.** $10\%; \frac{1}{10}$ **4.** $0.25; \frac{1}{4}$ **5.** $0.51; 51\%$
6. $41\%; \frac{41}{100}$ **7.** $0.55; \frac{11}{20}$ **8.** $67\%; \frac{67}{100}$ **9.** $0.36; 36\%$ **10.** $0.85; 85\%$
11. $50\%; \frac{1}{2}$ **12.** $0.93; \frac{93}{100}$ **13.** $0.42; 42\%$ **14.** $0.35; 35\%$
15. $0.88; \frac{22}{25}$

Workbook Activity 62—More Percents and Decimals
1. 10% **2.** 80% **3.** 50% **4.** 87.5% **5.** 20% **6.** 60% **7.** 25%
8. 68% **9.** 37.5% **10.** 43.75% **11.** 0.10 **12.** 0.80 **13.** 0.50
14. 0.875 **15.** 0.20 **16.** 0.60 **17.** 0.25 **18.** 0.68 **19.** 0.375
20. 0.4375 **21.** $33.3\%; 0.\overline{33}; 90$ **22.** $40\%; 0.40; 256$ **23.** $62.5\%;$
$0.625; 125$ **24.** $30\%; 0.30; 141$ **25.** $75\%; 0.75; 1,200$

Workbook Activity 63—Finding the Percent of a Number
1. 16; 0.75; 12 **2.** 30%; 30; 9 **3.** 55; 0.26; 14.3 **4.** 93%; 70; 65.1
5. 42; 0.77; 32.34 **6.** 8 **7.** 30 **8.** 24.5 **9.** 48 **10.** 20.25 **11.** 6.36
12. 28.08 **13.** 50.4 **14.** 178.4 **15.** 175.5

Workbook Activity 64—Finding the Percent
1. 75 **2.** 20 **3.** 50 **4.** 250 **5.** 400 **6.** 2,000 **7.** 3.78 **8.** 5.46
9. 15.33 **10.** 13.14 **11.** 18.98 **12.** 53.29 **13.** 11.7 **14.** 16.9
15. 47.45 **16.** 10.08 **17.** 14.56 **18.** 40.88 **19.** 14.76 **20.** 21.32
21. 59.86 **22.** 6.66 **23.** 9.62 **24.** 27.01 **25.** 5.04 **26.** 7.28
27. 20.44 **28.** 8.1 **29.** 11.7 **30.** 32.85

Workbook Activity 65—Percent of Increase and Decrease
1. 80; 67% **2.** 20; 24% **3.** 12; 20% **4.** 142; 115% **5.** 104; 49%
6. 6; 7% **7.** 232; 109% **8.** 54; 26% **9.** 20; 24% **10.** 122; 73%
11. 94; 21% **12.** 12; 80% **13.** 76; 22% **14.** 16; 17% **15.** 66; 31%

Workbook Activity 66—Formulas and Percents
1. 0.0375 **2.** 0.0425 **3.** 0.025 **4.** 0.0125 **5.** 0.0333 **6.** 0.0275
7. 0.0550 **8.** 0.0425 **9.** 0.0875 **10.** 1.1249 **11.** 1.0692 **12.** 1.0868
13. 1.0764 **14.** 1.2861 **15.** 1.0506 **16.** $267.81 **17.** $1,928.21
18. $787.35 **19.** $2,297.78 **20.** $9,233.96

Workbook Activity 67—Scale Drawings and Models
1. $x = 7$ **2.** $x = 11$ **3.** $x = 18$ **4.** 1 in. = 25 ft
5. The new room is 6 in. long and $6\frac{1}{2}$ in. wide.

**Workbook Activity 68—The Real Number Line
and Integers**
1. 6 **2.** 4 **3.** 8 **4.** 0 **5.** 11 **6.** 72 **7.** 31 **8.** 25 **9.** 92 **10.** 16 **11.** 6
12. 9 **13.** -15 **14.** 24 **15.** -11 **16.** 52 **17.** -84 **18.** 5 **19.** 42
20. -38 **21.** $+3$ **22.** -10 **23.** -8 **24.** $+5$ **25.** -80 **26.** -55
27. $+300$ **28.** -20 **29.** -5 or $+5$ **30.** $+4$ or -4

Workbook Activity 69—Comparing Integers
1. < **2.** > **3.** < **4.** = **5.** > **6.** > **7.** < **8.** < **9.** > **10.** > **11.** <
12. > **13.** < **14.** < **15.** > **16.** = **17.** < **18.** > **19.** < **20.** >
21. < **22.** = **23.** < **24.** > **25.** = **26.** Tuesday **27.** number line
shows dots at 2 and 5 **28.** $-2, -1, 0, 1, 3$ **29.** Saturday **30.** yes

Workbook Activity 70—Even and Odd Integers
1. 63 odd **2.** 113 odd **3.** 114 even **4.** 240 even **5.** 1,250 even
6. 470 even **7.** 645 odd **8.** 246 even **9.** 275 odd **10.** 248 even
11. 729 odd **12.** 381 odd **13.** 96 even **14.** 3,132 even **15.** 113
odd **16.** 780 even **17.** 483 odd **18.** 1,872 even **19.** 5,248 even
20. 1,536 even **21.** 108 even **22.** 3,233 odd **23.** 1,728 even
24. 2,520 even **25.** 1,380 even **26.** 323 odd **27.** 832 even
28. 1,475 odd **29.** 1,207 odd **30.** 1,656 even

Workbook Activity 71—Adding Positive Integers
1. 0 **2.** 11 **3.** 1 **4.** 0 **5.** 9 **6.** 7 **7.** -6 **8.** 10 **9.** 1 **10.** 15 **11.** -2
12. 11 **13.** 6 **14.** 17 **15.** 2 **16.** 8 **17.** 9 **18.** -2 **19.** 7 **20.** 12
21. 536 **22.** 1,107 **23.** -97 **24.** 1,833 **25.** 862 **26.** -214 **27.** 138
28. 900 **29.** 30 **30.** -93

Workbook Activity 72—Adding Negative Integers
1. -14 **2.** 3 **3.** 3 **4.** -11 **5.** 0 **6.** -13 **7.** -7 **8.** 3 **9.** -14 **10.** 4
11. 4 **12.** -3 **13.** -5 **14.** -16 **15.** $-1,125$ **16.** -60 **17.** 185
18. -651 **19.** 198 **20.** 560 **21.** 250 **22.** -416 **23.** $-1,027$
24. $-1,046$ **25.** 22 **26.** $-1,508$ **27.** 75 **28.** -954
29. 17,881 feet deep **30.** 35,840 feet deep

**Workbook Activity 73—Subtracting Positive and Negative
Integers**
1. -13 **2.** 13 **3.** -17 **4.** 9 **5.** -4 **6.** -11 **7.** 7 **8.** -4 **9.** -17
10. 16 **11.** -12 **12.** 0 **13.** 0 **14.** -14 **15.** 4 **16.** 15 **17.** -12
18. 10 **19.** 20 **20.** -7 **21.** -1 **22.** 2 **23.** -1 **24.** 18 **25.** -15
26. -5 **27.** 2 **28.** 2 **29.** 20,320 feet **30.** 19,340 feet

**Workbook Activity 74—Using Positive and Negative
Integers**
1. 17,563 **2.** 223 **3.** 26,887 **4.** 4,549 **5.** 16,053 **6.** 192° **7.** 76°
8. 265° **9.** 14° **10.** 147°

Workbook Activity 75—Multiplying by Positive Integers
1. -40 **2.** 48 **3.** -42 **4.** 6 **5.** 6 **6.** -7 **7.** 81 **8.** -32 **9.** 48
10. -18 **11.** 20 **12.** -5 **13.** -18 **14.** 3 **15.** -35 **16.** 10
17. -21 **18.** 42 **19.** -36 **20.** 6 **21.** negative **22.** negative
23. positive **24.** positive **25.** negative **26.** positive **27.** negative
28. positive **29.** negative **30.** positive

Workbook Activity 76—Multiplying by Negative Integers
1. positive **2.** negative **3.** negative **4.** positive **5.** negative
6. positive **7.** positive **8.** negative **9.** negative **10.** positive
11. negative **12.** positive **13.** negative **14.** positive **15.** positive
16. negative **17.** positive **18.** negative **19.** positive **20.** positive
21. negative **22.** positive **23.** negative **24.** positive **25.** negative
26. positive **27.** negative **28.** negative **29.** $-24°$F **30.** $-40°$F

Workbook Activity 77—Dividing Positive and Negative Integers
1. 4 **2.** 5 **3.** -7 **4.** -5 **5.** -9 **6.** -4 **7.** -3 **8.** -8 **9.** -2 **10.** 4
11. 4 **12.** 17 **13.** 4 **14.** -8 **15.** -4 **16.** -3 **17.** 7 **18.** 6 **19.** 10
20. 5 **21.** negative **22.** zero **23.** negative **24.** negative
25. negative **26.** positive **27.** positive **28.** negative
29. 22 classrooms **30.** 40 classrooms

Workbook Activity 78—Exponents
1. 10^2 **2.** 4^{10} **3.** $(-6)^3$ **4.** 8^4 **5.** $(-3)^2$ **6.** 2^7 **7.** a^4 **8.** $(-10)^5$
9. $(-b)^{10}$ **10.** 9^9 **11.** 8 **12.** 9 **13.** n **14.** 1 **15.** 3 **16.** 5 **17.** 15
18. 2 **19.** (-5) **20.** $(-n)$ **21.** $(-7)^5$ **22.** 4^2 **23.** 8^4 **24.** $(-c)^3$
25. 12^3

Workbook Activity 79—Multiplying with Exponents
1. 7^6 **2.** 6^3 **3.** $(-m)^{10}$ **4.** 2^7 **5.** n^4 **6.** 14^{11} **7.** a^7 **8.** $(-10)^5$ **9.** 3^{3y}
10. 6^{10} **11.** 2^{6p} **12.** 15^{11} **13.** 3^7 **14.** b^6 **15.** $(-n)^4$ **16.** true
17. false, $5^3 \cdot 5^4 = 5^7$ **18.** true **19.** false, $b^7 \cdot b^2 = b^9$ **20.** true
21. false, $3^4 \cdot 3^2 = 3^6$ **22.** true **23.** true **24.** true **25.** true

Workbook Activity 80—Dividing with Exponents
1. 7^{3n} **2.** 8^6 **3.** 1 **4.** 22^4 **5.** k **6.** 10^2 **7.** $(-y)^3$ **8.** 1 **9.** 7^7 **10.** 10^2
11. $(-6)^{4n}$ **12.** 1 **13.** 30 **14.** d^3 **15.** 17^6 **16.** false, $4^4 \div 4^4 = 1$
17. true **18.** true **19.** true **20.** true **21.** false, $16^4 \div 16^2 = 16^2$
22. true **23.** true **24.** false, $(-j)^7 \div (-j)^2 = (-j)^5$ **25.** true

Workbook Activity 81—Squares
1. Area $= 3^2$ **2.** Area $= x^2$ **3.** Area $= y^2$ **4.** 49 sq cm **5.** 4 sq cm
6. 36 sq cm **7.** Area $= 18^2$ in.$^2 = 324$ sq in. **8.** Area $= 20^2$ ft$^2 =$
400 sq ft **9.** Area $= 40^2$ ft$^2 = 1,600$ sq ft **10.** Area $= 5^2$ ft$^2 = 25$ sq ft

Workbook Activity 82—Cubes
1. Volume $= 4^3$ **2.** Volume $= 6^3$ **3.** Volume $= n^3$ **4.** 343 cu cm
5. 1 cu cm **6.** 729 cu cm **7.** 2,197 cu cm **8.** 42,875 cu cm
9. 512 cu in. **10.** 27 cu ft

Workbook Activity 83—Square Roots
1. 3, 4; 3.87 **2.** 3, 4; 3.46 **3.** 2, 3; 2.83 **4.** 3, 4; 3.32 **5.** 1, 2; 1.73
6. 2, 3; 2.65 **7.** 3, 4; 3.74 **8.** 2, 3; 2.45 **9.** 5 **10.** 6.24

Workbook Activity 84—Irrational Numbers and Square Roots
(Accept any irrational number within 0.3 of the following numbers.)
1. 9.7 **2.** 9.5 **3.** 9.2 **4.** 8.9 **5.** 8.7 **6.** 8.4 **7.** 8.1 **8.** 7.7 **9.** 6.7 **10.** 6.3 **11.** 5.9 **12.** 5.5 **13.** 5 **14.** 4.5 **15.** 3.9

Workbook Activity 85—Irrational Numbers as Decimals
Note: Irrational roots are approximate.
1. 7 **2.** rational **3.** 3.87298… **4.** irrational **5.** 3.31662...
6. irrational **7.** 2.44948… **8.** irrational **9.** 12 **10.** rational **11.** 11
12. rational **13.** 7.07106… **14.** irrational **15.** 3.68403…
16. irrational **17.** 6 **18.** rational **19.** 2.62074… **20.** irrational
21. 13 **22.** rational **23.** 5 **24.** rational **25.** 9

Workbook Activity 86—Radicals in Equations
1. $x = 25$ **2.** $n = 64$ **3.** $k = 1$ **4.** $a = 169$ **5.** $r = 136$
6. $y = 30$ **7.** $m = 256$ **8.** $n = 3$ **9.** $\sqrt{n} + \sqrt{100} = 19, 81$
10. $n^2 = 800, 20\sqrt{2}$ inches

Workbook Activity 87—The Pythagorean Theorem
1. 13 **2.** 9.2 **3.** 6.9 **4.** 13.5 **5.** 11.5

Workbook Activity 88—More About Triangles
1. scalene, yes **2.** isosceles, yes **3.** scalene, no **4.** isosceles, no
5. equilateral, no

Workbook Activity 89—Perimeters of Polygons
1. 12 mm **2.** 20.34 ft **3.** 11 yd **4.** 28.4 in. **5.** 22 ft **6.** 22.57 m
7. 144 yards **8.** 1,792.5 ft **9.** 4 ft each **10.** Yes. $3 \cdot 4.25 = 12.75$
inches, which means she will have enough string.

Workbook Activity 90—Perimeters of Regular Polygons
1. 24 ft **2.** $10\frac{1}{2}$ in. **3.** 6.372 mm **4.** 1,600 dm **5.** $226\frac{1}{3}$ yd
6. 35.9 mi **7.** 13 sides **8.** 17 sides **9.** 23 sides **10.** 7 sides

Workbook Activity 91—Perimeters of Irregular Polygons
1. 25 m **2.** 19.5 ft **3.** 59.72 cm **4.** 194.7 mm **5.** $32\frac{5}{12}$ yd
6. 99.3 in. **7.** $x = 8, P = 54$ **8.** $x = 1\frac{1}{4}, P = 15\frac{1}{2}$ **9.** $x = 9$ yd,
$P = 32 + \sqrt{8}$ or 34.8 yd **10.** $x = 20.1$ m, $P = 123.1$ m

Workbook Activity 92—Areas of Rectangles and Squares
1. 48 ft^2 **2.** 52 m^2 **3.** 124 cm^2 **4.** $28\frac{1}{8}$ yd^2 **5.** 100 mm^2 **6.** 441 ft^2
7. 17.64 cm^2 **8.** $30\frac{1}{4}$ m^2 **9.** 529 m^2 **10.** 44.89 ft^2 **11.** 72.25 cm^2
12. 1,764 in.^{2} **13.** 2.0164 mi^2 **14.** Yes, he has only 384 ft^2 of walls
to paint. **15.** 39 yards

Workbook Activity 93—Areas of Triangles
1. 12 ft^2 **2.** 90 m^2 **3.** 72 km^2 **4.** 6 ft **5.** 8 in. **6.** 3 m **7.** 8 yd
8. 6 km **9.** 22 ft **10.** 8 ft^2

Workbook Activity 94—Areas of Trapezoids and Parallelograms
1. 54 m^2 **2.** 30 in.^{2} **3.** 312 ft^2 **4.** 12 cm **5.** 34.3 ft **6.** 16 m
7. 14 in. **8.** 4 km **9.** 6 mm **10.** 8 yd

Workbook Activity 95—Areas of Irregular Polygons
1. 27 units^2 **2.** 125 units^2 **3.** 87 units^2 **4.** 114 units^2 **5.** 205 units^2

Workbook Activity 96—Working with Areas of Shapes
1. 34.65 in.^{2} **2.** 25 mi^2 **3.** 265.69 yd^2 **4.** $10\frac{9}{16}$ ft^2 **5.** 152.0289 mi^2
6. 4 ft **7.** 6 mm **8.** 6 cm **9.** 10 in. **10.** 20 m **11.** 9 ft **12.** 5 dm
13. 16 in. **14.** 52 mm **15.** 29 mi

Workbook Activity 97—Circumferences and Areas of Circles
1. 25.12 in. **2.** 18.84 ft **3.** 12.56 m **4.** 31.4 mm **5.** 43.96 km
6. 28.26 yd^2 **7.** 78.5 cm^2 **8.** 153.86 ft^2 **9.** 12.56 m^2 **10.** 153.86 in.^{2}
11. 113.04 km^2 **12.** 78.5 mi^2 **13.** 28.26 in.^{2} **14.** 200.96 ft^2
15. 314 m^2 **16.** 1.2265625 yd^2 **17.** 145,146.5 mi^2 **18.** 140.9546 ft^2
19. 70.84625 m^2 **20.** 10.1736 km^2

Workbook Activity 98—Solid Figures
1. triangular prism, 9 edges **2.** rectangular prism, 12 edges
3. triangular pyramid, 4 vertices **4.** cone, 1 vertex
5. hexagonal prism, 8 faces, 18 edges, 12 vertices

Workbook Activity 99—Surface Areas of Prisms and Cylinders

1. 384 **2.** 680 **3.** 360 **4.** 251.32 **5.** 1,200 **6.** 3,174 **7.** 15,700
8. 552 **9.** 468 **10.** 2,035.69

Workbook Activity 100—Surface Areas of Pyramids and Cones

1. 351 **2.** 138.23 **3.** 56 **4.** 207.34 **5.** 900 **6.** 395.83 **7.** 299
8. 395.83 **9.** 1,188 **10.** 339.28

Workbook Activity 101—Volumes of Cubes, Prisms, and Pyramids

1. 216 cm^3 **2.** 72 ft^3 **3.** 8 m^3 **4.** 12,167 mm^3 **5.** 5.832 in.^{3}
6. 2,000,376 ft^3 **7.** 0.729 mi^3 **8.** 125,000 cm^3 **9.** 1.061208 km^3
10. 314,432 dm^3 **11.** 79,507 m^3 **12.** 7,077.888 in.^{3}
13. 8,242,408 ft^3 **14.** 12 books **15.** 20,736 inches^3

Workbook Activity 102—Volumes of Cylinders, Cones, and Spheres

1. 141.3 in.^{3} **2.** 351.68 ft^3 **3.** 628 mm^3 **4.** 56.52 cm^3 **5.** 18.84 yd^3
6. 50.24 cm^3 **7.** 1,102.14 m^3 **8.** 6.28 ft^3 **9.** 718.01$\overline{3}$ cm^3
10. 471 yd^3 **11.** 31.7925 m^3 **12.** 1,798.958$\overline{3}$ mm^3 **13.** 113.04 cm^3
14. 904.32 ft^3 **15.** 57,876.48 mm^3 **16.** 14,130 cm^3 **17.** 7,234.56 ft^3
18. 4,846.59 m^3 **19.** 381.51 inches^3 of water **20.** Cylinder; it is
1,099 in.^{3} and the rectangular box is only 1,080 in.^{3}.

Workbook Activity 103—Graphing Equalities

1.
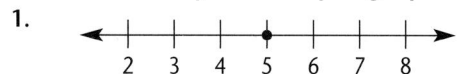

2.

3.

4.

5.

6.

7.

8.

9.

10.

11. $x = 6$ **12.** $x = -1$ **13.** $x = 4$ **14.** $x = -3$ **15.** $x = \frac{1}{2}$

Workbook Activity 104—Graphing Inequalities

1.
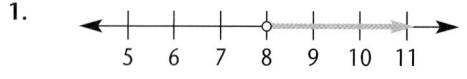

2.

3.

4.

5.

6.

7.

8.

9.

10.

11. $x < 4$ **12.** $x \geq -6$ **13.** $x > 0$ **14.** $x \neq 3$ **15.** $x < -3$

Workbook Activity 105—Graphing Solutions of Equalities
Check students' graphs **1.** $x = 4$ **2.** $c = -1$ **3.** $h = 3$ **4.** $m = -9$
5. $j = -5$ **6.** $s = 6$ **7.** $g = -4$ **8.** $v = 2$ **9.** $d = 8$ **10.** $p = -2$
11. $y = -8$ **12.** $t = 1$ **13.** $a = 0$ **14.** $e = 13$ **15.** $l = 5$
16. $b = -15$ **17.** $n = 2$ **18.** $z = 7$ **19.** $x + 300 = 900; x = 600$
meters **20.** $x - 3 = 6$ feet 8 inches; $x = 6$ feet 11 inches

Workbook Activity 106—Graphing Solutions of Inequalities
Check students' graphs **1.** $x \leq 2$ **2.** $p < 11$ **3.** $d > -4$ **4.** $t > -2$
5. $r \geq 5$ **6.** $e < -7$ **7.** $w \leq 11$ **8.** $q \leq -3$ **9.** $a < 9$ **10.** $b > -2$
11. $x < -10$ **12.** $f \geq -6$ **13.** $s > 3$ **14.** $g \geq 2$ **15.** $n \leq 3$
16. $m \geq 10$ **17.** $k < -1$ **18.** $p > 11$ **19.** $w \leq -3$ **20.** $u > 4$
21. $d < 2$ **22.** $i \geq 5$ **23.** $z \geq 1$ **24.** $x \geq 10 - 6; x \geq 4$
25. $x \geq 10 + 25; x \geq 35$

Workbook Activity 107—The Coordinate System—Locating Points

1. $(1, 1)$ **2.** $(3, 0)$ **3.** $(-3, -1)$ **4.** $(6, 2)$ **5.** $(-1, 2)$ **6.** $(2, -4)$
7. $(0, 7)$ **8.** $(-6, 1)$ **9.** $(-3, 4)$ **10.** $(0, -4)$ **11.** $(4, 0)$ **12.** $(2, -1)$
13. $(5, -3)$ **14.** $(-5, -2)$ **15.** $(2, 5)$ **16.** Quadrant I
17. Quadrant IV **18.** Quadrant II **19.** Quadrant III **20.** Quadrant I

Workbook Activity 108—The Coordinate System— Plotting Points

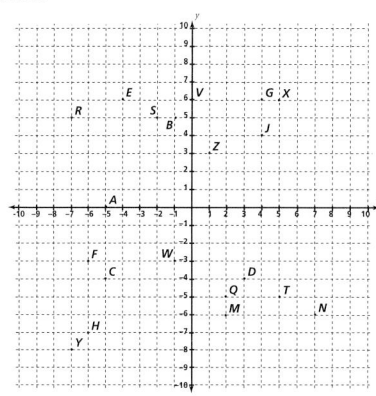

21. Quadrant III **22.** Quadrant IV **23.** Quadrant I **24.** Quadrant II **25.** Quadrant IV

Workbook Activity 109—Determining the Points of a Line

1.

y = x + 5	
x	y
−3	2
2	7
6	11

2.

y = x − 4	
x	y
−2	−6
−1	−5
3	−1

3.

y = x + 7	
x	y
−4	3
0	7
4	11

4.

y = x − 3	
x	y
4	1
0	−3
−2	−5

5.

y = x + 9	
x	y
−3	6
0	9
5	14

6.

y = x + 8	
x	y
−7	1
0	8
2	10

7.

y = x − 2	
x	y
−1	−3
3	1
6	4

8.

y = x + 6	
x	y
−7	−1
−4	2
−1	5

9.

y = x + 25.7	
x	y
−6.9	18.8
−3.4	22.3
8.7	34.4

10.

y = x − 12.3	
x	y
−7.8	−20.1
4.1	−8.2
23.2	10.9

Workbook Activity 110—Tables of Values and Coordinate Systems

Sample answers are given.

1.

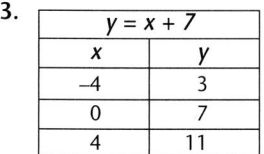

y = x + 1	
x	y
−1	0
0	1
1	2

2.

y = x − 5	
x	y
5	0
3	−2
0	−5

3.

y = x − 7	
x	y
10	3
5	−2
0	−7

4.

y = x − 1	
x	y
0	−1
1	0
3	2

5.

y = x + 2	
x	y
4	6
1	3
−2	0

6.

y = x + 4	
x	y
0	4
1	5
2	6

7. 6 units **8.** 12 units **9.** 7 units **10.** 6 units

Workbook Activity 111—Lines as Functions

1. yes, any single vertical line crosses it only once **2.** no, a vertical line may cross it more than one time **3.** yes, any single vertical line crosses it only once **4.** yes, any single vertical line crosses it only once **5.** no, a vertical line may cross it more than one time.

Workbook Activity 112—Domain and Range of a Function

1. 3, 5, 11, 19, 25 **2.** −1, 0, 8, 125, 512 **3.** $-2\frac{1}{4}$, −2, $-\frac{1}{2}$, $\frac{1}{2}$, $2\frac{1}{2}$ **4.** −4, −4, 6, 24, 50 **5.** −21, −18, −9, −6, 15 **6.** 12, 2, 0, 2, 6 **7.** Domain: $-3 \leq x \leq 5$ Range: $-3 \leq y \leq 4$ **8.** Domain: $-5 \leq x \leq 4$ Range: $-2 \leq y \leq 7$ **9.** Domain: $-4 \leq x \leq 6$ Range: $y = -3$ **10.** Domain: $x = -2$ Range: $-2 \leq y \leq 4$

Workbook Activity 113—Graphing Lines

Sample answers are given.

1. $x = 0, -1, -3; y = 3, 2, 0$

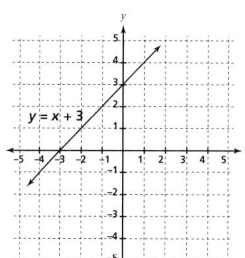

2. $x = 2, 0, -2; y = 8, 4, 0$

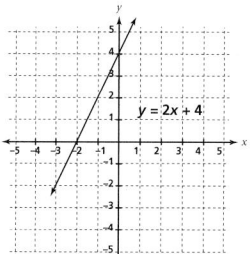

3. $x = 2, 0, 1; y = 1, -1, 0$

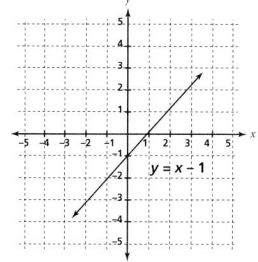

4. $x = 3, 1, 0; y = 9, 3, 0$

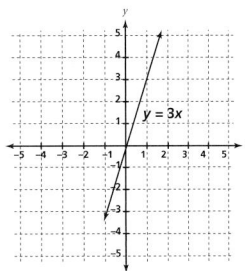

5. $x = 2, 1, 0; y = -2, -1, 0$

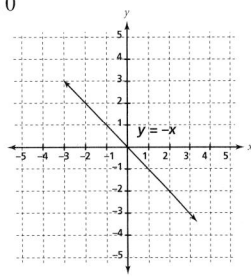

Workbook Activity 114—The Slope of a Line
1. 0.75 **2.** 0.875 **3.** 2.4 **4.** −0.69 **5.** 1.83 **6.** 0.02 **7.** −13 **8.** 2.25
9. 0.93 **10.** 6 **11.** 0.77 **12.** −32 **13.** 4.4 **14.** −0.3 **15.** −25.6

Workbook Activity 115—Formula for the Slope of a Line
1. 3 **2.** 1 **3.** $\frac{1}{2}$ **4.** $\frac{1}{4}$ **5.** −3 **6.** 0 **7.** −4 **8.** $\frac{5}{6}$ **9.** $\frac{5}{7}$ **10.** $\frac{7}{4}$ **11.** $\frac{1}{5}$
12. −2 **13.** $\frac{6}{5}$ **14.** 2 **15.** 2 **16.** $-\frac{1}{4}$ **17.** −2 **18.** the second part,
because $\frac{-100}{400}$ is steeper than $\frac{-80}{400}$ so $\frac{-4}{16}$ is steeper than $\frac{-5}{25}$
19. the first slope, because it is negative so it is downhill
20. Neither; they have the same slope.

Workbook Activity 116—The Slope-Intercept Form of a Line
1. $m = 1$, x-intercept $= -4$, y-intercept $= 4$ **2.** $m = 2$, x-intercept
$= \frac{1}{2}$, y-intercept $= -1$ **3.** $y = 2x + 5$ **4.** $y = x - 8$ **5.** $y = -3x + 3$
6. $y = -2x - 1$ **7.** $y = x - 7$ **8.** $y = -x + \frac{1}{2}$ **9.** $m = 1$, x-intercept
$= 5$, y-intercept $= -5$ **10.** $m = 2$, x-intercept $= -2$, y-intercept $= 4$
11. $m = -3$, x-intercept $= \frac{-1}{3}$, y-intercept $= -1$ **12.** $m = 1$, x-
intercept $= 2$, y-intercept $= -2$ **13.** $m = 4$, x-intercept $= -\frac{1}{4}$, y-
intercept $= 1$ **14.** $m = -1$, x-intercept $= 3$, y-intercept $= 3$
15. $m = -2$, x-intercept $= \frac{5}{2}$, y-intercept $= 5$

Workbook Activity 117—Angles and Angle Measures
1. GF and HF, 10° **2.** GF and IF, 35° **3.** GF and JF, 60° **4.** GF and
KF, 90° **5.** GF and LF, 155° **6.** LF and MF, 25° **7.** KF and MF, 90°
8. JF and MF, 120° **9.** IF and MF, 145° **10.** HF and MF, 170°

Workbook Activity 118—Identifying and Classifying Angles
1. vertical, obtuse **2.** adjacent **3.** obtuse **4.** acute **5.** adjacent
6. vertical, acute **7.** acute **8.** obtuse **9.** 70° **10.** 110°

Workbook Activity 119—Complementary and Supplementary Angles
1. m∠y + 50° = 90° m∠y = 90° − 50° m∠y = 40° **2.** m∠y + 20°
= 90° m∠y = 90° − 20° m∠y = 70° **3.** m∠y + 45° = 90° m∠y
= 90° − 45° m∠y = 45° **4.** m∠y + 30° = 90° m∠y = 90° − 30°
m∠y = 60° **5.** 45° **6.** 135° **7.** 135° **8.** 160° **9.** 20° **10.** 20°

Workbook Activity 120—Angle Measure in a Triangle
1. m∠XYZ + 55° = 180° m∠XYZ = 180° − 55° m∠XYZ = 125°
2. m∠TUV + 90° = 180° m∠TUV = 180° − 90° m∠TUV = 90°
3. m∠1 + 35° = 180° m∠1 = 180° − 35° m∠1 = 145° **4.** 75°; 65°
5. 65°; 65°

Workbook Activity 121—Naming Triangles
1. right **2.** equilateral **3.** scalene **4.** equiangular **5.** isosceles
6. obtuse **7.** right scalene **8.** right isosceles **9.** obtuse
10. acute scalene

Workbook Activity 122—Congruent Triangles
1. yes, SSS **2.** yes, SAS **3.** yes, SAS **4.** yes, ASA **5.** yes, SSS

Workbook Activity 123—Similar Triangles
1. 60° **2.** 4 cm **3.** 60° **4.** 2.7 cm **5.** 50°

Workbook Activity 124—Parallelograms
1. one pair of parallel sides, 4 sides, trapezoid **2.** opposite sides same
length, two pairs of parallel sides, parallelogram **3.** all angles 90°,
opposite sides same length, rectangle **4.** all sides equal length, all
angles 90°, square **5.** four sides, four angles, quadrilateral **6.** one pair
of parallel sides, 4 sides, trapezoid **7.** true **8.** true **9.** false **10.** true

Workbook Activity 125—Quadrilaterals and Diagonals
1. MN = 3 cm; **2.** $3^2 + 3^2 = c^2$; $9 + 9 = c^2$; $18 = c^2$; $c = 4.24$ cm
3. yes **4.** m∠R = 90°; opposite angles in a rectangle are equal
5. ST = 4 cm **6.** SQ = 6.4 cm **7.** RT = 6.4 cm **8.** VW = 3 cm
9. m∠VUX = 90° **10.** yes

Workbook Activity 126—Polygons and Diagonals
1. 128.6° **2.** 51.4° **3.** 900° **4.** 135° **5.** 45°

Workbook Activity 127—Reflections in the Coordinate Plane
1. $A' = (1, -1), B' = (1, -5), C' = (5, -5), D' = (5, -1)$
2. $E' = (-2, 3), F' = (-5, 3), G' = (-5, -4), H' = (-2, -4)$
3. $I' = (-2, -1), J' = (0, -4), K' = (4, -4), L' = (4, -1)$
4. $M' = (-3, -2), N' = (-1, -6), O' = (3, -6), P' = (1, -2)$
5. $Q' = (-1, 1), R' = (-1, 5), S' = (-3, 7), T' = (-5, 5),$
$U' = (-5, 1)$

Workbook Activity 128—Reflections Over Different Lines
1. $A' = (2, 2), B' = (0, 2), C' = (0, -3), D' = (2, -3)$
2. $E' = (-2, 2), F' = (0, 2), G' = (2, 7), H' = (0, 7)$
3. $I' = (-3, -3), J' = (-3, 3), K' = (-5, 2), L' = (-5, -2)$
4. $X' = (4, 4), R' = (4, 6)$
5. $Q' = (-3, -3), R' = (-3, -6), S' = (-1, -6), T' = (-1, -3)$

Workbook Activity 129—Special Reflections: Symmetries
All lines are centered on the letters. **1.** one vertical line
2. one vertical line **3.** one vertical line, one horizontal line
4. one horizontal line **5.** one horizontal line **6.** one vertical line
7. one vertical line, one horizontal line **8.** one horizontal line
9. no lines **10.** one vertical line, one horizontal line

Workbook Activity 130—Slides and Translations
1. (0, 6) **2.** (5, 3) **3.** (−2, 1) **4.** (7, 5) **5.** (−4, 2) **6.** (−7, 0) **7.** (2, 4)
8. (−4, 4) **9.** (17, −1) **10.** (−8, 2) **11.** (−2, 0) **12.** (−10, 4)
13. $(x - 2, y - 3)$ **14.** $(x + 3, y + 6)$ **15.** $(x + 5, y + 7)$

Workbook Activity 131—Rotations

1. rotated image's endpoints: (2, 1), (6, 1), (2, −2)
2. rotated image's endpoints: (−3, 2), (0, −1), (−2, −3)
3. rotated image's endpoints: (−4, −5), (3, −7), (0, −11)
4. rotated image's endpoints: (−3, 1), (1, 3), (0, −7)
5. rotated image's endpoints are (−4, −2), (−1, −4), (−2, −8)

Workbook Activity 132—Bar Graphs

1. Sample answer: Election Results for Class President **2.** Sample answer: Candidate **3.** Sample answer: Number of Votes **4.** Sample answer: 2; Each data value to be displayed by the bar graph is a multiple of 2. **5.** Sample graph shown.

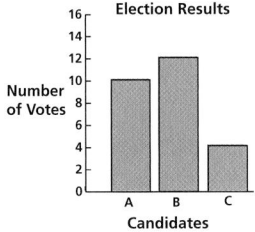

Workbook Activity 133—Frequency Tables

1. The greatest possible sum of 12 is created if each cube has an outcome of 6. **2.** The least possible sum of 2 is created if each cube has an outcome of 1. **3.** 36; Both the sum of the tally column and the sum of the frequency column is 36. **4.** most often: 7; least often: 2 or 12 **5.** The interval is 1. Sample explanation: One is a good interval to use for the data because the table displays 11 different outcomes, and it is not possible to divide 11 evenly, except by 1.

Workbook Activity 134—Circle Graphs

1. $\frac{1}{2}$; 0.5; 180° **2.** $\frac{3}{8}$; 0.375; 135° **3.** $\frac{1}{8}$; 0.125; 45° **4.** Sample answers: The sum of the fractions that represent the graph should be 1; the sum of the decimals that represent the graph should be 1; the sum of the percents that represent the graph should be 100%; the sum of the degrees that represent the graph should be 360°. **5.** 1,000 votes

Workbook Activity 135—Histograms

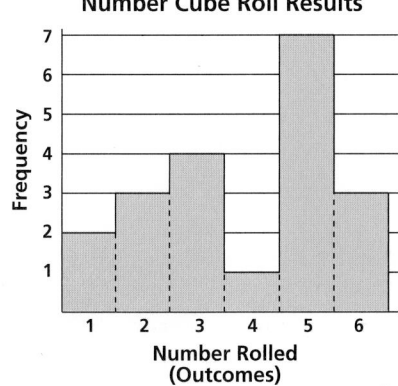

Workbook Activity 136—Scatterplots

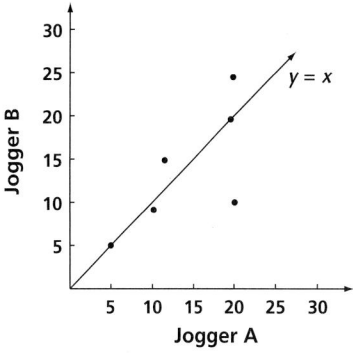

Workbook Activity 137—Mean

1. The labels explain what the data values represent. **2.** 12 **3.** 55.9 **4.** Find the sum of the data values in the set, then divide by the number of data values. **5.** 4.66 inches per month

Workbook Activity 138—Median

1. greatest to least: 57, 57, 56, 55, 55, 55, 54, 54, 52, 52; least to greatest: 52, 52, 54, 54, 55, 55, 55, 56, 57, 57. **2.** even number **3.** If the data set has an odd number of values, the median is the middle value. If the data set has an even number of values, the median is the mean of the two middle values. **4.** 55 **5.** no

Workbook Activity 139—Mode

1. The labels explain what the data values represent. **2.** Six different data values appear in the table; 5, 20, 35, 40, 60, and 70. **3.** Identify the data value or values that occur most often. **4.** 20 **5.** The data have no mode.

Workbook Activity 140—Range

1. Mississippi; 2,340 miles **2.** Kentucky; 259 miles **3.** Subtract the least data value from the greatest. **4.** 2,081 miles **5.** Sample answer: No; if the greatest and least data values can be computed mentally, it is not necessary to order the data.

Workbook Activity 141—Data and Statistics

1. The data show the location and height in feet of famous waterfalls. **2.** 6 **3.** Sample answer: 20; All of the data values are multiples of 20. **4.** Sample answer: The axis should be broken if the chosen interval creates a graph that is physically large. **5.** Sample answer: It would be difficult because a circle graph is based on a whole, and the whole in the waterfall data table is unknown.
6. Sample answer: No; Organizing the data values in a frequency table will not help someone who interprets the data gain a better understanding of the data. **7.** 577 feet **8.** 610 feet **9.** 620 feet **10.** 160 feet

Workbook Activity 142—Box-and-Whiskers Plots

1. greatest to least: 23, 22, 21, 19, 18, 17, 16, 15, 12, 11, 10; least to greatest: 10, 11, 12, 15, 16, 17, 18, 19, 21, 22, 23 **2.** 17 **3.** 12; 21 **4.** 10; 23
5.

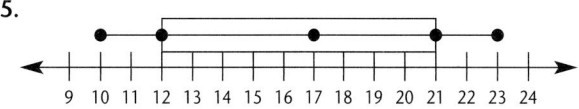

Workbook Activity 143—The Probability Fraction

1. $\frac{1}{12}$ **2.** $\frac{1}{9}$ **3.** $\frac{1}{18}$ **4.** $\frac{1}{36}$ **5.** $\frac{1}{2}$ **6.** $\frac{1}{2}$ **7.** 7 **8.** 2 and 12 **9.** 7; 3 and 11

10. Sample answer: A knowledge of the probability of the likelihood of sums might help you anticipate when an opponent is more likely to land on your properties.

Workbook Activity 144—Dependent and Independent Events

1. dependent **2.** independent **3.** dependent **4.** dependent
5. independent **6.** dependent **7.** dependent **8.** independent
9. dependent **10.** independent

Workbook Activity 145—The Fundamental Principle of Counting

1. 2 ways **2.** 24 numbers **3.** 20 combinations **4.** 12 outcomes
5. 24 different three-digit numbers

1357.
1375.
1573.
1537
1735
1753

321
312
231
213
123
132

Application Activities

Application Activity 1—Binary Number System and Electrical Circuits
1. A 1 must be on the top or bottom of the bracket.
2. A 1 must be before and after the second arrow. **3.** 1 **4.** 3 **5.** 2

Application Activity 2—Using Patterns
1. $n + 9$ **2.** 75 **3.** $n + 8$ **4.** 57 **5.** $n \times 2$ **6.** 512 **7.** $n + 20$ **8.** 159
9. $n + 11$ **10.** 87

Application Activity 3—Converting a Measurement
1. 2 meters **2.** 7 inches **3.** 5 kilometers **4.** 4 gallons
5. 21 centimeters **6.** 2 square meters **7.** 1 meter **8.** 8 liters
9. 10 inches **10.** 1 square meter

Application Activity 4—Finding Perfect Numbers
1. 4,064 **2.** 2,032 **3.** 1,016 **4.** 508 **5.** 254 **6.** 127
7. 1, 2, 4, 8, 16, 32, 64, 127, 254, 508, 1,016, 2,032, 4,064
8. The sum of the factors is 8,128. This is equal to the number being factored. **9.** Each number is doubled. **10.** Each number is doubled.

Application Activity 5—Moving with the Beat
1. 4 **2.** $\frac{1}{8}$ **3.** 2 **4.** $\frac{1}{2}$ **5.** quarter note **6.** eighth note
7. sixteenth note **8.** half note **9.** quarter note **10.** eighth note

Application Activity 6—Converting Measurements
1. 26,400 ft **2.** 5 tons **3.** $\frac{1}{2}$ gal **4.** 3,960 fpm **5.** $\frac{1}{2}$ ft

Application Activity 7—Rates of Change
1. $10.75 an hour **2.** 60 words per minute **3.** Brent: $22\frac{1}{2}$ miles per gallon; Karen: $16\frac{2}{3}$ miles per gallon; Brent **4.** $1.40 per year
5. 15 mph each minute

Application Activity 8—Ice Cold
1. $+500$ ft above the waterline, $-3,500$ ft below the waterline
2. $+160$ ft above the waterline, $-1,440$ ft below the waterline
3. $-4,950$ ft below the waterline
4. 1,000 ft in total height
5. New: $+400$ ft above the waterline, $-2,800$ ft below the waterline
Old: $+320$ ft above the waterline, $-2,880$ ft below the waterline

Application Activity 9—Applying the Pythagorean Theorem
1. 121 **2.** 256 **3.** 15 **4.** 8 **5.** 12 **6.** 17 feet **7.** 13 feet
8. $10^2 + 30^2 = 100 + 900 = 1,000$. The square root of 1,000 is 31.6. This means that in order to plug in the sign, there must be at least 31.6 feet of cord. **9.** 5 feet **10.** 20 feet

Application Activity 10—Dilation
1. a. 600 cubic cm b. 4,800 cubic cm **2.** a. 62.5 cubic in. b. 2 cubic in.
3. a. 360 cubic in. b. 11,111.11 cubic in. c. 18.75 cubic in.
4. a. 949.2 cubic m b. 29,296.29 cubic m c. 49.44 cubic m
5. a. 0.9 cubic mm b. 27.78 cubic mm c. 0.05 cubic mm

Application Activity 11—The Story Line
1. A bird gliding **2.** Ski jumper **3.** Driving a car and then running out of gas **4.** Roller coaster ride **5.** Answers will vary.

Application Activity 12—Plane Cover-Up
1. reflection, translation **2.** rotation, reflection, translation
3. reflection **4.** reflection, translation, rotation **5.** rotation, reflection, translation

Application Activity 13—Tally Up
Projects will vary. Make sure that students address each of the five steps outlined in the lesson by completing the entire Application Activity page.

Everyday Math

Everyday Math 1—Sales Figures

1. 800 **2.** 2,600 **3.** 1,000 **4.** 900 **5.** 1,700 **6.** 7,000 **7.** less than **8.** 3,400 **9.** 5,300 **10.** 500 **11.** 3,100 **12.** 2,200 **13.** 14,500 **14.** greater than **15.** 5H + 1T + 2TT

Everyday Math 2—Plastic Money

1. 102.27 **2.** 3.00 **3.** 35.92 **4.** 407.75 **5.** 323.67 **6.** 3.00 **7.** 231.46 **8.** 55.75 **9.** 163.16 **10.** 155.00 **11.** by subtracting the withdrawal amount from the current balance **12.** deposit on 5/10 **13.** The transaction will be denied. There is not enough money in the account.

Everyday Math 3—Metric Measures

1. 0.28 cm, 2.8 mm **2.** about 20 years old **3.** 1.5 cm; 15 mm **4.** $0.8\overline{3}$ m; $83.\overline{3}$ cm **5.** 180 cm; 1.8 m **6.** 200 weeks (3.8 years); 2,000 weeks (38.5 years)

Everyday Math 4—Light Goes the Distance

1. 3.57×10^7 **2.** 6.81×10^7 **3.** 9.26×10^7 **4.** 1.42×10^8 **5.** 4.82×10^8 **6.** 8.85×10^8 **7.** 1.81×10^9 **8.** 2.81×10^9 **9.** 3.68×10^9 **10.** 4.91×10^7 miles **11.** 244 minutes or 4.1 hours **12.** 9.23×10^8

Everyday Math 5—Survey Says

1. $\frac{3}{10}$ **2.** $\frac{1}{6}$ **3.** $\frac{3}{20}$ **4.** $\frac{5}{9}$ **5.** $\frac{5}{16}$

Everyday Math 6—Order, Order

Answers may vary **1.** $(2 \div 2) \cdot (2 \div 2)$ **2.** $(2 \div 2) + (2 \div 2)$ **3.** $(2 + 2 + 2) \div 2$ **4.** $(2 + 2) + (2 - 2)$ **5.** $2 + 2 + (2 \div 2)$ **6.** $(3 + 3 + 3) \div 3$ **7.** $[(3 \cdot 3) + 3] \div 3$ **8.** $3 + 3 - (3 \div 3)$ **9.** $3 + 3 + 3 - 3$ **10.** $3 + 3 + (3 \div 3)$

Everyday Math 7—Mapping Distances

1. 225 miles **2.** 825 miles **3.** 533.3 km **4.** 813.75 miles **5.** 812.50 miles **6.** 830 miles **7.** Accurate measures are difficult on smaller maps.

Everyday Math 8—Up and Away

1. 15,000 feet **2.** 17,000 feet **3.** 27,000 feet **4.** 12,000 feet **5.** 24,000 feet **6.** entry 3; entry 1 and entry 4

Everyday Math 9—Triangle Two-Step

1. $\sqrt{2^2 + 3^2} = 3.6$ **2.** $\sqrt{2^2 + 5^2} = 5.4$ **3.** $\sqrt{5^2 + 7^2} = 8.6$ **4.** $\sqrt{9^2 + 9^2} = 12.7$ **5.** $\sqrt{5^2 + 7^2} = 8.6$ **6.** $\sqrt{2^2 + 8^2} = 8.2$

Everyday Math 10—Packaging a Volume

1. 64 cubic units; 96 square units **2.** 64 cubic units; 112 square units **3.** 64 cubic units; 136 square units **4.** 64 cubic units, 258 square units

Everyday Math 11—Talk Isn't Cheap

1.

minutes	cost	cost
10	$4.95	$9.95
50	$4.95	$9.95
100	$4.95	$9.95
150	$7.95	$9.95
200	$12.95	$12.45

2. $11.95, 190 minutes; That's where the lines of the graphs intersect.

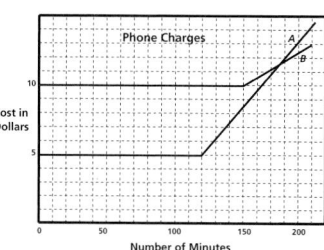

3. less than 190 minutes a month **4.** more than 190 minutes a month

Everyday Math 12—Tangram Teasers

1. five right triangles, a square, and a parallelogram **2.** They're similar; they are the same shape but three different sizes. **3.** Answers will vary. **4.** Answers will vary. **5.** Answers will vary. **6.** Answers will vary.

Everyday Math 13—Data Check

1. true **2.** true **3.** true **4.** true **5.** true **6.** true **7.** true **8.** true **9.** Opinions will vary.

Review of Basic Skills

Review of Basic Skills 1—Place Value of Whole Numbers
1. ones **2.** tens **3.** hundreds **4.** hundreds **5.** tens **6.** ones
7. thousands **8.** hundreds **9.** tens **10.** ones **11.** hundreds
12. thousands **13.** tens **14.** ten-thousands **15.** ten-thousands
16. hundred-thousands **17.** thousands **18.** millions
19. hundred-thousands **20.** hundred-millions

Review of Basic Skills 2—Rounding Whole Numbers
1. 10 **2.** 20 **3.** 190 **4.** 360 **5.** 1,890 **6.** 2,390 **7.** 4,020 **8.** 55,490
9. 63,560 **10.** 100 **11.** 100 **12.** 300 **13.** 600 **14.** 800 **15.** 8,700
16. 13,400 **17.** 64,800 **18.** 416,300 **19.** 1,000 **20.** 5,000 **21.** 9,000
22. 10,000 **23.** 21,000 **24.** 148,000 **25.** 250,000

Review of Basic Skills 3—Adding Whole Numbers
1. 9 **2.** 8 **3.** 19 **4.** 27 **5.** 113 **6.** 1,017 **7.** 36 **8.** 118 **9.** 377
10. 43,888 **11.** 110,682 **12.** 256,818 **13.** 1,050 **14.** 2,107
15. 6,628

Review of Basic Skills 4—Subtracting Whole Numbers
1. 4 **2.** 5 **3.** 10 **4.** 11 **5.** 37 **6.** 141 **7.** 404 **8.** 506 **9.** 309 **10.** 411
11. 736 **12.** 950 **13.** 40,736 **14.** 49,654 **15.** 1,692 **16.** 4,052
17. 873 **18.** 80,033 **19.** 59,960 **20.** 17,785

Review of Basic Skills 5—Multiplying Whole Numbers
1. 2, 4, 6, 8, 10, 12, 14, 16, 18, 20
2. 3, 6, 9, 12, 15, 18, 21, 24, 27, 30
3. 4, 8, 12, 16, 20, 24, 28, 32, 36, 40
4. 5, 10, 15, 20, 25, 30, 35, 40, 45, 50
5. 6, 12, 18, 24, 30, 36, 42, 48, 54, 60
6. 7, 14, 21, 28, 35, 42, 49, 56, 63, 70
7. 8, 16, 24, 32, 40, 48, 56, 64, 72, 80
8. 9, 18, 27, 36, 45, 54, 63, 72, 81, 90
9. 138 **10.** 182 **11.** 315 **12.** 252 **13.** 576 **14.** 1,610 **15.** 1,443
16. 2,997 **17.** 3,087 **18.** 2,163 **19.** 21,298 **20.** 48,020

Review of Basic Skills 6—Multiplying Whole Numbers by Powers of 10
1. 30 **2.** 500 **3.** 7,000 **4.** 60 **5.** 1,400 **6.** 12,000 **7.** 270 **8.** 2,700
9. 27,000 **10.** 430 **11.** 4,300 **12.** 2,670 **13.** 26,700 **14.** 3,490
15. 34,900 **16.** 830 **17.** 8,300 **18.** 83,000 **19.** 5,860 **20.** 58,600
21. 586,000 **22.** 41,840 **23.** 418,400 **24.** 4,184,000 **25.** 41,840,000

Review of Basic Skills 7—Division of Whole Numbers with Zero Remainders
1. 8 **2.** 2 **3.** 4 **4.** 6 **5.** 7 **6.** 7 **7.** 6 **8.** 9 **9.** 9 **10.** 9 **11.** 7 **12.** 6
13. 23 **14.** 53 **15.** 123 **16.** 207 **17.** 47 **18.** 17 **19.** 15 **20.** 57

Review of Basic Skills 8—Division of Whole Numbers with Fractional Remainders
1. $27\frac{3}{14}$ **2.** $15\frac{1}{39}$ **3.** $45\frac{18}{21} = 45\frac{6}{7}$ **4.** $9\frac{7}{71}$ **5.** $24\frac{7}{20}$ **6.** 591.52
7. 423.10 **8.** 2,838.33 **9.** 7,467.47 **10.** 17,082.15

Review of Basic Skills 9—Division of Whole Numbers with Zeros in the Quotient
1. 170 **2.** 304 **3.** 120 **4.** 460 **5.** 360 **6.** 502 **7.** 610 **8.** 6,011
9. 21,100 **10.** 4,300

Review of Basic Skills 10—Numbers with Exponents
1. 9 **2.** 16 **3.** 25 **4.** 36 **5.** 49 **6.** 64 **7.** 81 **8.** 100 **9.** 32 **10.** 625
11. 16 **12.** 27 **13.** 125 **14.** 1,000 **15.** 64 **16.** 121 **17.** 1,000,000
18. 1,000,000 **19.** 2^4 **20.** 3^3 **21.** 9^2 **22.** 7^5 **23.** 92^3 **24.** 10^6 **25.** 4^4
26. 6^3 **27.** 90^5 **28.** 5^8 **29.** 36^4 **30.** 100^5

Review of Basic Skills 11—Using the Order of Operations
1. 6 **2.** 12 **3.** 8 **4.** 23 **5.** 1 **6.** 8 **7.** 5 **8.** 35 **9.** 43 **10.** 15 **11.** 25
12. 159 **13.** 22 **14.** 45 **15.** 0

Review of Basic Skills 12—Finding an Average (Mean)
1. 47.4 **2.** 64.2 **3.** 53.2 **4.** 70.7 **5.** 62.7 **6.** 50.7 **7.** 61.7 **8.** 53.7
9. 68.6 **10.** 51.6 **11.** 103.5 **12.** 54.7 **13.** 95.3 **14.** 42.7 **15.** 41.2

Review of Basic Skills 13—Comparing Fractions
1. < **2.** > **3.** < **4.** < **5.** < **6.** > **7.** < **8.** < **9.** < **10.** > **11.** <
12. < **13.** > **14.** < **15.** < **16.** > **17.** < **18.** < **19.** > **20.** <

Review of Basic Skills 14—Changing Fractions to Higher Terms
1. $\frac{15}{30}$ **2.** $\frac{10}{24}$ **3.** $\frac{9}{21}$ **4.** $\frac{12}{18}$ **5.** $\frac{21}{36}$ **6.** $\frac{27}{39}$ **7.** $\frac{20}{35}$ **8.** $\frac{15}{40}$ **9.** $\frac{30}{35}$ **10.** $\frac{90}{100}$
11. $\frac{9}{33}$ **12.** $\frac{18}{39}$ **13.** $\frac{25}{60}$ **14.** $\frac{18}{45}$ **15.** $\frac{36}{64}$ **16.** $\frac{15}{65}$ **17.** $\frac{15}{51}$ **18.** $\frac{12}{38}$
19. $\frac{30}{550}$ **20.** $\frac{14}{630}$

Review of Basic Skills 15—Renaming Fractions in Simplest Terms
1. $\frac{1}{2}$ **2.** $\frac{1}{23}$ **3.** $\frac{5}{11}$ **4.** $\frac{1}{5}$ **5.** $\frac{1}{3}$ **6.** $\frac{28}{29}$ **7.** $\frac{7}{9}$ **8.** $\frac{1}{9}$ **9.** $\frac{1}{7}$ **10.** $\frac{3}{4}$ **11.** $\frac{1}{5}$
12. $\frac{1}{4}$ **13.** $\frac{1}{2}$ **14.** $\frac{2}{11}$ **15.** $\frac{1}{2}$ **16.** $\frac{1}{4}$ **17.** $\frac{1}{3}$ **18.** $\frac{5}{22}$ **19.** $\frac{5}{26}$ **20.** $\frac{1}{2}$

Review of Basic Skills 16—Renaming Improper Fractions as Mixed Numbers
1. $3\frac{3}{5}$ **2.** 6 **3.** $3\frac{1}{6}$ **4.** $4\frac{2}{3}$ **5.** $5\frac{3}{4}$ **6.** 6 **7.** $7\frac{3}{5}$ **8.** 6 **9.** $5\frac{1}{11}$ **10.** $3\frac{4}{5}$
11. $1\frac{5}{8}$ **12.** $6\frac{7}{8}$ **13.** $4\frac{2}{3}$ **14.** 8 **15.** 30

Review of Basic Skills 17—Renaming Mixed Numbers as Improper Fractions
1. $\frac{17}{5}$ **2.** $\frac{32}{5}$ **3.** $\frac{31}{6}$ **4.** $\frac{86}{12}$ **5.** $\frac{13}{6}$ **6.** $\frac{19}{2}$ **7.** $\frac{37}{9}$ **8.** $\frac{90}{11}$ **9.** $\frac{17}{3}$ **10.** $\frac{25}{3}$
11. $\frac{88}{13}$ **12.** $\frac{50}{3}$ **13.** $\frac{59}{8}$ **14.** $\frac{47}{3}$ **15.** $\frac{191}{14}$ **16.** $\frac{29}{3}$ **17.** $\frac{61}{10}$ **18.** $\frac{62}{3}$ **19.** $\frac{341}{21}$ **20.** $\frac{89}{8}$

Review of Basic Skills 18—Multiplying Fractions
1. $\frac{1}{3}$ **2.** $\frac{1}{2}$ **3.** $\frac{21}{52}$ **4.** $\frac{2}{15}$ **5.** $\frac{3}{7}$ **6.** $\frac{6}{55}$ **7.** $\frac{4}{63}$ **8.** $\frac{5}{44}$ **9.** $\frac{1}{27}$ **10.** $\frac{5}{24}$ **11.** $\frac{1}{22}$
12. $\frac{8}{45}$ **13.** $\frac{1}{14}$ **14.** $\frac{13}{112}$ **15.** $\frac{1}{6}$ **16.** $\frac{5}{104}$ **17.** $\frac{1}{8}$ **18.** $\frac{5}{9}$ **19.** $\frac{1}{2}$ **20.** $\frac{1}{8}$

Review of Basic Skills 19—Multiplying Mixed Numbers
1. $\frac{5}{6}$ **2.** $\frac{3}{5}$ **3.** $\frac{8}{21}$ **4.** $\frac{8}{35}$ **5.** $2\frac{2}{5}$ **6.** $1\frac{2}{15}$ **7.** $1\frac{39}{56}$ **8.** $1\frac{1}{4}$ **9.** 3 **10.** $3\frac{3}{25}$
11. $6\frac{1}{14}$ **12.** $11\frac{11}{35}$ **13.** $6\frac{1}{5}$ **14.** $2\frac{4}{9}$ **15.** $2\frac{41}{56}$ **16.** $17\frac{7}{8}$ **17.** $4\frac{1}{5}$ **18.** $5\frac{5}{8}$
19. 8 **20.** $5\frac{7}{8}$

Review of Basic Skills 20—Dividing Fractions
1. $1\frac{2}{5}$ **2.** $2\frac{1}{2}$ **3.** $2\frac{2}{7}$ **4.** $4\frac{4}{5}$ **5.** $\frac{12}{35}$ **6.** $\frac{3}{4}$ **7.** $\frac{24}{25}$ **8.** $1\frac{1}{9}$ **9.** $2\frac{1}{12}$ **10.** 5
11. $1\frac{3}{5}$ **12.** $\frac{1}{2}$ **13.** $\frac{9}{10}$ **14.** $1\frac{1}{3}$ **15.** $\frac{2}{3}$ **16.** $1\frac{2}{3}$ **17.** $1\frac{7}{48}$ **18.** $\frac{35}{48}$
19. $\frac{7}{10}$ **20.** 2

Review of Basic Skills 21—Dividing Mixed Numbers

1. 3 **2.** $7\frac{1}{3}$ **3.** $2\frac{2}{5}$ **4.** $3\frac{1}{4}$ **5.** $\frac{1}{10}$ **6.** $\frac{26}{45}$ **7.** $2\frac{1}{10}$ **8.** 10 **9.** 7
10. $4\frac{1}{2}$ **11.** 2 **12.** $3\frac{1}{2}$ **13.** 8 **14.** 6 **15.** 7 **16.** $8\frac{1}{3}$ **17.** $4\frac{1}{7}$ **18.** $7\frac{1}{9}$
19. $13\frac{1}{2}$ **20.** $15\frac{4}{5}$

Review of Basic Skills 22—Adding Mixed Numbers
with Like Denominators

1. 3 **2.** $5\frac{1}{2}$ **3.** 8 **4.** 13 **5.** $7\frac{2}{3}$ **6.** $8\frac{1}{4}$ **7.** 10 **8.** $8\frac{1}{2}$ **9.** $8\frac{5}{16}$ **10.** $3\frac{1}{2}$
11. 9' **12.** 4' **13.** 17' **14.** 7' **15.** 12'

Review of Basic Skills 23—Adding Fractions and Mixed
Numbers with Unlike Denominators

1. $\frac{3}{4}$ **2.** $\frac{8}{15}$ **3.** $1\frac{1}{4}$ **4.** $\frac{7}{10}$ **5.** $\frac{11}{12}$ **6.** $\frac{17}{30}$ **7.** $\frac{19}{30}$ **8.** $\frac{3}{4}$ **9.** $\frac{13}{14}$ **10.** $\frac{2}{3}$
11. $3\frac{5}{6}$ **12.** $7\frac{5}{6}$ **13.** $5\frac{1}{4}$ **14.** $5\frac{11}{12}$ **15.** $6\frac{7}{10}$

Review of Basic Skills 24—Subtracting Mixed Numbers
with Like Denominators

1. $\frac{1}{4}$ **2.** $\frac{3}{7}$ **3.** $3\frac{1}{4}$ **4.** $4\frac{1}{4}$ **5.** $1\frac{1}{2}$ **6.** $2\frac{1}{4}$ **7.** $1\frac{1}{6}$ **8.** $2\frac{1}{4}$ **9.** $3\frac{1}{5}$ **10.** $3\frac{1}{2}$
11. $2\frac{1}{8}$ **12.** $\frac{1}{4}$ **13.** $1\frac{1}{8}$ **14.** $2\frac{1}{4}$ **15.** $3\frac{2}{5}$ **16.** 1 **17.** $2\frac{1}{17}$ **18.** $5\frac{11}{39}$
19. $2\frac{1}{5}$ **20.** $2\frac{1}{2}$

Review of Basic Skills 25—Subtracting with Unlike
Denominators

1. $\frac{1}{8}$ **2.** $\frac{1}{4}$ **3.** $1\frac{1}{8}$ **4.** $2\frac{1}{4}$ **5.** $4\frac{7}{20}$ **6.** $1\frac{1}{6}$ **7.** $3\frac{1}{8}$ **8.** $4\frac{1}{8}$ **9.** $3\frac{27}{100}$
10. $1\frac{31}{100}$ **11.** $7\frac{5}{8}$ **12.** $2\frac{1}{2}$ **13.** $4\frac{4}{9}$ **14.** $2\frac{1}{10}$ **15.** 7

Review of Basic Skills 26—Subtracting with Renaming

1. $3\frac{3}{4}$ **2.** $3\frac{1}{4}$ **3.** $7\frac{1}{2}$ **4.** $2\frac{2}{3}$ **5.** $1\frac{1}{3}$ **6.** $2\frac{2}{5}$ **7.** $2\frac{3}{4}$ **8.** $2\frac{4}{7}$ **9.** $4\frac{7}{10}$ **10.** $4\frac{7}{9}$
11. $3\frac{1}{2}$ **12.** $3\frac{2}{3}$ **13.** $4\frac{3}{5}$ **14.** $1\frac{5}{6}$ **15.** $1\frac{7}{8}$

Review of Basic Skills 27—Identifying Place Value with
Decimals

1. tenths **2.** thousandths **3.** ten-thousandths **4.** thousandths
5. hundred-thousandths **6.** millionths **7.** thousandths
8. hundreds **9.** hundredths **10.** hundred-thousandths **11.** >
12. < **13.** < **14.** < **15.** >

Review of Basic Skills 28—Rounding Decimals

1. 2.1, 2.06, 2.063 **2.** 0.1, 0.09, 0.089 **3.** 1.0, 1.04, 1.035
4. 0.2, 0.15, 0.155 **5.** 32.7, 32.70, 32.704 **6.** 7.6, 7.63, 7.630
7. 19.8, 19.81, 19.809 **8.** 34.0, 34.00, 34.004 **9.** 2.1, 2.06, 2.061
10. 139.4, 139.42, 139.418

Review of Basic Skills 29—Adding Decimals

1. $18.03 **2.** $13.73 **3.** $18.20 **4.** $13.42 **5.** $18.64 **6.** $15.78
7. $33.09 **8.** $26.26 **9.** $26.25 **10.** $29.93 **11.** 15.32 **12.** 20.13
13. 12.11 **14.** 31.383 **15.** 64.403 **16.** 18.099 **17.** 11.617
18. 24.098 **19.** 86.0991 **20.** 28.8514

Review of Basic Skills 30—Subtracting Decimals

1. $16.33 **2.** $3.11 **3.** $11.35 **4.** $10.00 **5.** $2.11 **6.** $27.18
7. $8.26 **8.** $8.28 **9.** $13.37 **10.** $5.19 **11.** 5.09 **12.** 0.66
13. 1.09 **14.** 5.29 **15.** 5.79 **16.** 74.51 **17.** 21.81 **18.** 35.13
19. 36.73 **20.** 80.63

Review of Basic Skills 31—Multiplying Decimals

1. 2.8 **2.** 12 **3.** 18.9 **4.** 14.7 **5.** 33.5 **6.** 3.12 **7.** 15.86 **8.** 15.99
9. 8.04 **10.** 58.48 **11.** 3.159 **12.** 17.748 **13.** 7.408 **14.** 26.568
15. 14.094 **16.** 11.993 **17.** 36.036 **18.** 8.838 **19.** 27.434 **20.** 55.188

Review of Basic Skills 32—Scientific Notation

1. $2.9 \cdot 10^3$ **2.** $3.6 \cdot 10^3$ **3.** $8.75 \cdot 10^3$ **4.** $6.32 \cdot 10^3$ **5.** $3.5 \cdot 10^4$
6. $4.6 \cdot 10^4$ **7.** $7.11 \cdot 10^4$ **8.** $4.0 \cdot 10^5$ **9.** $4.0 \cdot 10^6$ **10.** $1.7 \cdot 10^9$
11. $3.8 \cdot 10^{-4}$ **12.** $3.9 \cdot 10^{-1}$ **13.** $4.1 \cdot 10^{-1}$ **14.** $7.2 \cdot 10^{-2}$
15. $7.2 \cdot 10^{-3}$ **16.** $8.1 \cdot 10^{-3}$ **17.** $7.4 \cdot 10^{-4}$ **18.** $1.2 \cdot 10^{-5}$
19. $1.23 \cdot 10^{-3}$ **20.** $2.46 \cdot 10^{-4}$

Review of Basic Skills 33—Dividing Decimals by
Whole Numbers

1. 2.35 **2.** 0.26 **3.** 0.25 **4.** 3.17 **5.** 6.5 **6.** 3.1 **7.** 7.1 **8.** 0.21 **9.** 7.1
10. 2.1 **11.** 3.1 **12.** 3.3 **13.** 20.5 **14.** 9.09 **15.** 6.1 **16.** 1.202
17. 6.1 **18.** 0.51 **19.** 1.02 **20.** 0.5

Review of Basic Skills 34—Dividing Decimals by Decimals

1. 7.2 **2.** 12.3 **3.** 11 **4.** 14.9 **5.** 55.7 **6.** 37.4 **7.** 96.7 **8.** 427
9. 0.002 **10.** 210.5 **11.** 210.5 **12.** 6,460 **13.** 810 **14.** 81 **15.** 8.1
16. 707 **17.** 33 **18.** 6,620 **19.** 532 **20.** 0.98

Review of Basic Skills 35—Rewriting Decimals as Fractions

1. $\frac{14}{100}$ $\frac{7}{50}$ **2.** $\frac{15}{100}$ $\frac{3}{20}$ **3.** $\frac{75}{100}$ $\frac{3}{4}$ **4.** $\frac{36}{100}$ $\frac{9}{25}$ **5.** $\frac{79}{100}$ **6.** $\frac{15}{100}$ $\frac{3}{20}$
7. $\frac{159}{1,000}$ **8.** $\frac{375}{1,000}$ $\frac{3}{8}$ **9.** $\frac{875}{1,000}$ $\frac{7}{8}$ **10.** $\frac{999}{1,000}$ **11.** $\frac{42}{100}$ $\frac{21}{50}$ **12.** $\frac{65}{100}$ $\frac{13}{20}$
13. $\frac{60}{100}$ $\frac{3}{5}$ **14.** $\frac{45}{100}$ $\frac{9}{20}$ **15.** $\frac{50}{100}$ $\frac{1}{2}$ **16.** $\frac{168}{1,000}$ $\frac{21}{125}$ **17.** $\frac{22}{100}$ $\frac{11}{50}$
18. $\frac{98}{100}$ $\frac{49}{50}$ **19.** $\frac{568}{1,000}$ $\frac{71}{125}$ **20.** $\frac{72}{100}$ $\frac{18}{25}$

Review of Basic Skills 36—Renaming Fractions as Decimals

1. 0.1 **2.** 0.2 **3.** 0.5 **4.** 0.12 **5.** 0.18 **6.** 0.35 **7.** 0.36 **8.** 0.006
9. 0.4285714 **10.** 0.7142857 **11.** 0.6666666 **12.** 0.2222222
13. 0.3846153 **14.** 0.117647 **15.** 0.1578947

Community Connections

Community Connection 1—Base Systems
1–3. Answers will vary. Check students' responses.

Community Connection 2—Fund-Raiser
1–5. Answers will vary. Check students' responses.

Community Connection 3—The Better Buy
1–10. Answers will vary. Check students' responses.

Community Connection 4—Sports Figures
1–2. Answers will vary. Check students' responses.

Community Connection 5—A Fractional Market
1–3. Answers will vary. Check students' responses.

Community Connection 6—Voter Registration
1–7. Answers will vary. Check students' responses.

Community Connection 7—A Home Loan
1–7. Answers will vary. Check students' responses.

Community Connection 8—Utility Bills
1–4. Answers will vary. Check students' responses. **5.** Feb.
6. June through September **7.** It is less.

Community Connection 9—Triangle Tally
1–6. Answers will vary. Check students' responses.

Community Connection 10—School Measures Up
1. Answers will vary. **2.** Answers will vary. **3.** Answers will vary.
4. Answers will vary. **5.** Answers will vary. **6.** Answers will vary.
7. Answers will vary.

Community Connection 11—Line Graphs
1–5. Answers will vary.

Community Connection 12—Similar or Congruent
Answers will vary.

Community Connection 13—Number Please
1. $10 \cdot 10 \cdot 10 \cdot 10 \cdot 10 \cdot 10 \cdot 10$ **2.** 10,000,000 **3.** Answers will vary;
The population may be more or less than the number of possible
phone numbers. **4.** $10 \cdot 10 \cdot 10 \cdot 10 \cdot 10 \cdot 10 \cdot 10 \cdot 10 \cdot 10 \cdot 10$ or
$10^{10} = 10,000,000,000$, or 10 billion **5.** nonassigned, toll-free,
toll-free, and specialty businesses **6.** $10 \cdot 10 \cdot 10 = 1000$
7. Answers will vary but may include 611—telephone repair,
411—directory assistance, and 911—police or fire emergency.

Estimation Exercises

Estimation Exercise 1—Estimating Multiplication
Estimates will vary. Sample answers are given.
1. 1,200,000; 1,087,440 **2.** 4,000,000; 4,248,531 **3.** 800,000; 872,712
4. 2,100,000; 2,192,430 **5.** 1,600,000; 1,954,512 **6.** 900,000;
1,075,528 **7.** 4,500,000; 4,232,250 **8.** 5,600,000; 5,520,482 **9.**
8,100,000; 8,270,878 **10.** 1,600,000; 1,819,775

Estimation Exercise 2—Estimating Addition
Common values and estimates will vary. Sample answers are given.
1. 33, 165, 164 **2.** 44, 225, 231 **3.** 135, 540, 536 **4.** 13, 78, 76
5. 31, 310, 324

Estimation Exercise 3—Estimating with Decimals
1. 19.4 **2.** 41.3 **3.** 20.8 **4.** 10.2 **5.** 115.5 **6.** 14 **7.** 1 **8.** 18 **9.** 67
10. 55

Estimation Exercise 4—Estimating Quotients
Compatible numbers may vary. Sample answers are given. **1.** 420 and
7, 60 **2.** 720 and 9, 80 **3.** 3,000 and 30, 100 **4.** 6,400 and 80, 80 **5.**
20,000 and 50, 400 **6.** 36,000 and 60, 600 **7.** 120,000 and 400, 300
8. 49,000 and 70, 700 **9.** 1,800 and 600, 3 **10.** 56,000 and 80, 700

Estimation Exercise 5—Estimating Using Mixed Numbers
1. 9 **2.** 13 **3.** 9 **4.** 49 **5.** 4 **6.** 18 **7.** 129 **8.** 54 **9.** 32 **10.** 25

Estimation Exercise 6—Estimating Solutions for Equations
Answers may vary. Suggested answers are given.
1. $p = 20$ **2.** $b = 30$ **3.** $h = 20$ **4.** $t = 70$ **5.** $q = 70$ **6.** $a = 70$
7. $z = 50$ **8.** $m = 30$ **9.** $y = 90$ **10.** $x = 140$

Estimation Exercise 7—Estimating the Percent of a Number
Answers will vary. Sample estimates are given. **1.** around $3.40
2. around 6 **3.** around 58 **4.** around 270 **5.** around 1,800
6. around 30 **7.** around $7.00 **8.** around 1,100 **9.** around $30.00
10. No. Explanations will vary. $4.00 isn't even 10% of $43.89. Each
person would have to put around $2.00 on the table to come up
with a 14% tip.

Estimation Exercise 8—Estimating Products and Quotients
Answers will vary. Sample answers are given. **1.** $-3,000$ **2.** 350
3. $-24,000$ **4.** 9,000 **5.** 290,000 **6.** 100 **7.** 15 **8.** -5 **9.** 20 **10.** -90

Estimation Exercise 9—Estimating Square Roots
2. 25, 36, more, 5 **3.** 49, 64, more, 7 **4.** 49, 64, less, 8 **5.** 64, 81,
more, 8 **6.** 16, 25, more, 4 **7.** 9, 16, more, 3 **8.** 81, 100, less, 10
9. 16, 25, less, 5 **10.** 36, 49, less, 7

Estimation Exercise 10—Estimating the Perimeter of Polygons
Some answers may vary. Sample answers given. **1.** 120 ft **2.** 480 in.
3. 450 m **4.** 8 km **5.** 90 in.

Estimation Exercise 11—Estimating Slope
1. m is less than -2. **2.** m is greater than 2. **3.** m is greater than 6
4. m is greater than -6. **5.** m is less than 10. **6.** m is less than -8.
7. m is greater than 3. **8.** m is greater than 4. **9.** m is greater than -3.
10. m is greater than 10.

Estimation Exercise 12—Estimating the Measure of Acute Angles
Estimates will vary. Actual measures are given. **1.** 45° **2.** 80° **3.** 15°
4. 50° **5.** 30°

Estimation Exercise 13—Estimating the Mean
1. 7 **2.** 20 **3.** 53 **4.** 125 **5.** 72 **6.** 11.5 **7.** 103.5 **8.** 252.5
9. 84 **10.** 159, 389

Chapter Mastery Tests

Chapter 1 Mastery Test A

1. A **2.** B **3.** D **4.** B **5.** C **6.** D **7.** 7,000,000 **8.** 200 **9.** thousands
10. tens **11.** $(9 \times 10^3) + (1 \times 10^2) + (2 \times 10^1) + (3 \times 10^0)$
12. $(4 \times 10^4) + (5 \times 10^3) + (3 \times 10^2) + (1 \times 10^1) + (1 \times 10^0)$
13. 247_{10} **14.** $3,949_{10}$ **15.** 34_5 **16.** 1221_5 **17.** 9H + 4T + 7TT
18. 1H + 2T + 6TT **19.**

713	781	**20.**	3,204	3,098
+ 68	− 68		− 106	+ 106
781	713		3,098	3,204

21. 101 seconds **22.** 1917 **23.** 100_{10} **24.** 95_{10} **25.** 10100101_2
26. 110101_2 **27.** $30 \times 4 = 120$ **28.** $246 \div 6 = 41$ or $246 \div 41 = 6$
29. 84 books **30.** 9 balloons

Chapter 1 Mastery Test B

1. B **2.** D **3.** B **4.** C **5.** D **6.** D **7.** 30 **8.** 80,000 **9.** hundreds
10. 3 millions **11.** $(2 \times 10^5) + (1 \times 10^4) + (9 \times 10^3) + (3 \times 10^2)$
$+ (8 \times 10^1) + (8 \times 10^0)$ **12.** $(2 \times 10^4) + (9 \times 10^3) + (3 \times 10^2) +$
$(6 \times 10^1) + (5 \times 10^0)$ **13.** $2,382_{10}$
14. $1,934_{10}$ **15.** 10143_5 **16.** 103043_5 **17.** 3H + 5T + 9TT
18. 4H + 8T + 2TT **19.**

834	806	**20.**	2,662	2,909
− 28	+ 28		+ 247	− 247
806	834		2,909	2,662

21. 5:18 **22.** 114 **23.** 15_{10} **24.** 103_{10} **25.** 1010001_2 **26.** 11111010_2
27. $213 \div 71 = 3$ or $213 \div 3 = 71$ **28.** $32 \times 7 = 224$
29. 58 pictures **30.** 7 carrots

Chapter 2 Mastery Test A

1. C **2.** A **3.** D **4.** C **5.** A **6.** 598 **7.** 2,945c **8.** 1,421x **9.** 11,650
10. 859 **11.** 1,126s **12.** 773 **13.** 672 **14.** 97w **15.** 7,520 **16.** 28e
17. 2,945 **18.** 1,632 **19.** 4,800 **20.** 80,000 **21.** 3,000,000 For
problems 22–24, estimates may vary. **22.** 100f **23.** 400 **24.** 3,000
25. $n - 17$ **26.** $4n + 3$ **27.** 600 **28.** 500 **29.** 90 hours
30. 4,384 pages

Chapter 2 Mastery Test B

1. B **2.** C **3.** A **4.** B **5.** C **6.** 609 **7.** 4,964c **8.** 294 **9.** 1,443x
10. 8,030 **11.** 911 **12.** 1,144s **13.** 787 **14.** 15,363 **15.** 71w
16. 7,332 **17.** 60e **18.** 1,995 **19.** 1,360 **20.** 1,800 **21.** 80,000 For
problems 22–24, estimates may vary. **22.** 100f **23.** 350 **24.** 100
25. $x - 20$ **26.** $6x + 8$ **27.** 700 **28.** 200 **29.** 95 hours
30. 6,324 pages

Chapter 3 Mastery Test A

1. A **2.** C **3.** B **4.** A **5.** A **6.** tenths; 0.6 **7.** hundredths; 0.07
8. thousandths; 0.009 **9.** > **10.** < **11.** > **12.** < **13.** 19.3
14. 0.087 **15.** 35.73 **16.** 68.35 **17.** 1.463 **18.** 4.43 **19.** 126.533
20. 37,000 **21.** 15.21 **22.** 18.42 **23.** 0.03 **24.** 841.2 **25.** 0.0002
26. 20 **27.** 0.0241 **28.** 50 **29.** $\frac{7}{20}$ **30.** $\frac{1}{250}$ **31.** 0.2 **32.** 0.082
33. $0.1\overline{8}$ **34.** 0.15 **35.** 0.06 **36.** 3.69 **37.** 9.31 **38.** 15.8 **39.** 1.4
40. 6 feet 0 inches

Chapter 3 Mastery Test B

1. D **2.** A **3.** D **4.** C **5.** A **6.** hundredths; 0.07 **7.** tenths; 0.3
8. tenths; 0.9 **9.** < **10.** < **11.** > **12.** > **13.** 17.2 **14.** 0.078
15. 29.64 **16.** 68.36 **17.** 1.175 **18.** 6.42 **19.** 127.966
20. 3,800,000 **21.** 16.24 **22.** 36.6 **23.** 0.014 **24.** 773.3 **25.** 0.004
26. 23.75 **27.** 0.242 **28.** 120 **29.** $\frac{9}{20}$ **30.** $\frac{1}{200}$ **31.** $0.1\overline{6}$ **32.** 0.086
33. 0.25 **34.** 0.25 **35.** 0.09 **36.** 5.79 **37.** 5.91 **38.** 30.2 **39.** 1.2
40. 6 feet 3.6 inches

Chapter 4 Mastery Test A

1. D **2.** A **3.** D **4.** B **5.** D **6.** true **7.** true **8.** false **9.** false
10. false **11.** true **12.** true **13.** false **14.** true **15.** false **16.** true
17. prime **18.** composite **19.** composite **20.** 6w **21.** 4 **22.** 1
23. 3a **24.** 1 **25.** 3 **26.** 10 **27.** 12d + 12e **28.** 5(3p + 8q)
29. 8(3g + h) **30.** $b(a + c)$ **31.** 80 **32.** 60 **33.** 72 **34.** 180
35. 5.4×10^3 **36.** 2.08×10^5 **37.** 3.1×10^{10} **38.** 7.0×10^{-3}
39. 8.1×10^{-6} **40.** 15 minutes

Chapter 4 Mastery Test B

1. B **2.** A **3.** C **4.** D **5.** B **6.** true **7.** false **8.** true **9.** true **10.** false
11. false **12.** false **13.** true **14.** true **15.** true **16.** false
17. composite **18.** composite **19.** prime **20.** 3w **21.** 6 **22.** 9
23. 6a **24.** 7 **25.** 1 **26.** 25 **27.** 14d + 14e **28.** 35(p + 2q)
29. 7(4g + h) **30.** $c(b + a)$ **31.** 70 **32.** 90 **33.** 63 **34.** 140
35. 6.4×10^3 **36.** 3.08×10^5 **37.** 3.3×10^{10} **38.** 6.0×10^{-3}
39. 7.2×10^{-6} **40.** 5 minutes

Chapter 5 Mastery Test A

1. C **2.** C **3.** A **4.** B **5.** A **6.** $\frac{2}{5}$; $\frac{3}{5}$ **7.** proper **8.** improper
9. proper **10.** 1 **11.** 5 **12.** $\frac{29}{8}$ **13.** $\frac{38}{5}$ **14.** $\frac{33}{32}$ **15.** $\frac{127}{10}$
For problems 16–18, sample answers are given. **16.** $\frac{6}{9}$; $\frac{2}{3}$ **17.** $\frac{6}{8}$; $\frac{9}{12}$
18. $\frac{10}{24}$; $\frac{15}{36}$ **19.** $\frac{1}{3}$ **20.** $\frac{4}{27}$ **21.** $\frac{3}{4}$ **22.** $\frac{1}{6}$ **23.** > **24.** > **25.** <
26. $\frac{1}{2}$ $\frac{5}{8}$ $\frac{3}{4}$ **27.** $\frac{5}{8}$ $\frac{13}{24}$ $\frac{1}{3}$ **28.** $1\frac{1}{7}$ **29.** $\frac{2x}{3}$ **30.** $\frac{3d}{8}$ **31.** $\frac{8}{9}$ **32.** $3\frac{3}{5}$
33. $2\frac{1}{6}$ **34.** $1\frac{1}{54}x$ **35.** $\frac{8}{8}$ or $\frac{1}{1}$

Chapter 5 Mastery Test B

1. A **2.** C **3.** D **4.** A **5.** A **6.** $\frac{4}{5}$; $\frac{1}{5}$ **7.** improper **8.** improper
9. proper **10.** 4 **11.** 1 **12.** $\frac{10}{3}$ **13.** $\frac{32}{5}$ **14.** $\frac{35}{34}$ **15.** $\frac{68}{5}$ For problems
16–18, sample answers are given. **16.** $\frac{3}{9}$; $\frac{1}{3}$ **17.** $\frac{2}{8}$; $\frac{3}{12}$ **18.** $\frac{14}{24}$; $\frac{21}{36}$
19. $\frac{1}{4}$ **20.** $\frac{3}{22}$ **21.** $\frac{3}{5}$ **22.** $\frac{1}{6}$ **23.** < **24.** > **25.** < **26.** $\frac{1}{3}$ $\frac{3}{6}$ $\frac{7}{9}$
27. $\frac{8}{14}$ $\frac{1}{2}$ $\frac{3}{7}$ **28.** 1 **29.** $\frac{1x}{2}$ or $\frac{x}{2}$ **30.** $\frac{7d}{26}$ **31.** $\frac{3}{8}$ **32.** $2\frac{7}{10}$ **33.** $2\frac{1}{12}$
34. $\frac{36x}{17}$ or $2\frac{2}{17}x$ **35.** $\frac{9}{6}$ or $\frac{3}{2}$

Chapter 6 Mastery Test A

1. B **2.** A **3.** B **4.** A **5.** B **6.** 28 **7.** 17 **8.** 6 **9.** 10 **10.** 4 **11.** 1
12. 10 **13.** 19 **14.** true **15.** false **16.** true **17.** false **18.** false
19. $x = 12$ **20.** $x = 15$ **21.** $x = 3\frac{1}{2}$ **22.** $x = 34$ **23.** $x = \frac{3}{10}$
24. $x = 72$ **25.** $\frac{2}{3}$ **26.** 3 **27.** $\frac{1}{50}$ **28.** $\frac{3}{14}$ **29.** $\frac{1}{30}$ **30.** $3\frac{1}{3}$ **31.** $\frac{3}{2a}$
32. $\frac{6b}{5}$ or $1\frac{1}{5}b$ **33.** $\frac{7}{8m}$ **34.** $\frac{9}{20y}$ **35.** $\frac{1}{5}$ **36.** $\frac{9}{32}$ **37.** $\frac{1}{9a}$ **38.** $\frac{9}{20}$
39. $\frac{1}{2}$ **40.** $\frac{9}{20}$

Chapter 6 Mastery Test B

1. A **2.** C **3.** A **4.** A **5.** B **6.** 45 **7.** 17 **8.** 9 **9.** 19 **10.** 5 **11.** 2 **12.** 11 **13.** 17 **14.** false **15.** true **16.** false **17.** false **18.** false **19.** $x = 1$ **20.** $x = 5$ **21.** $x = \frac{1}{4}$ **22.** $x = 30$ **23.** $x = \frac{1}{10}$ **24.** $x = 48$ **25.** 1 **26.** $4\frac{1}{2}$ **27.** $\frac{1}{70}$ **28.** $1\frac{1}{6}$ **29.** $\frac{3}{65}$ **30.** $1\frac{1}{7}$ **31.** $\frac{4}{5a}$ **32.** $\frac{71b}{21}$ or $3\frac{8}{21}b$ **33.** $\frac{7}{8m}$ **34.** $\frac{2}{15y}$ **35.** $\frac{2}{15}$ **36.** $\frac{9}{16}$ **37.** $\frac{1}{12a}$ **38.** $\frac{3}{5}$ **39.** $\frac{9}{16}$ **40.** $\frac{1}{5}$

Chapter 7 Mastery Test A

1. C **2.** C **3.** A **4.** D **5.** $\frac{5}{12}$ **6.** $\frac{3}{5}$ **7.** $\frac{4}{9}$ **8.** $n = 5$ **9.** $a = 8$ **10.** $b = 7$ **11.** $c = 6$ **12.** $z = 20$ **13.** $m = 5$ **14.** $\frac{3}{25}$; 12% **15.** $\frac{27}{50}$; 54% **16.** 24% **17.** 56.25% **18.** 14% **19.** 190% **20.** 0.73 **21.** 1.5 **22.** 9 **23.** 252 **24.** 9 **25.** 0.55 **26.** 50% **27.** 150% **28.** 80% **29.** 160% **30.** increase; 8% **31.** 1.5 times larger **32.** 570 ft **33.** 7 hours **34.** 11.43 mph **35.** 15 ft by 9 ft

Chapter 7 Mastery Test B

1. B **2.** A **3.** C **4.** D **5.** $\frac{3}{7}$ **6.** $\frac{8}{13}$ **7.** $\frac{1}{4}$ **18.** $n = 4$ **9.** $a = 20$ **10.** $z = 9$ **11.** $c = 20$ **12.** $b = 18$ **13.** $m = 3$ **14.** $\frac{1}{5}$, 20% **15.** $\frac{23}{50}$, 46% **16.** 38% **17.** 45% **18.** 17% **19.** 185% **20.** 0.83 **21.** 1.75 **22.** 13.5 **23.** 189 **24.** 3.60 **25.** 0.6 **26.** 33.3% **27.** 50% **28.** 60% **29.** 150% **30.** decreases; 7.7% **31.** 1.75 times larger **32.** 250 ft **33.** $4\frac{1}{2}$ hours **34.** 8 mph **35.** 8 ft by 8 ft

Chapter 8 Mastery Test A

1. B **2.** D **3.** A **4.** D **5.** C **6.** 8 **7.** 14 **8.** 50 **9.** +51 or 51 **10.** −3 **11.** +6 or 6 **12.** −44 **13.** < **14.** > **15.** > **16.** = **17.** 17 **18.** 5 **19.** 16 **20.** −5 **21.** −13 **22.** −12 **23.** 6 **24.** 18 **25.** −11 **26.** 1 **27.** 1 **28.** 24 **29.** −24 **30.** 30 **31.** −4 **32.** 2 **33.** −9 **34.** −8 **35.** −21 **36.** 18 **37.** 2 **38.** toward the bottom; 20 meters **39.** 2,089 feet **40.** increase; 13°F

Chapter 8 Mastery Test B

1. C **2.** B **3.** A **4.** B **5.** D **6.** 7 **7.** 22 **8.** 49 **9.** 49 **10.** 7 **11.** −33 **12.** −4 **13.** > **14.** < **15.** > **16.** > **17.** 19 **18.** 4 **19.** 18 **20.** −7 **21.** −19 **22.** −9 **23.** 4 **24.** 25 **25.** −16 **26.** 2 **27.** 3 **28.** 27 **29.** −20 **30.** 35 **31.** −6 **32.** 3 **33.** −8 **34.** −10 **35.** −35 **36.** 24 **37.** 3 **38.** Toward the surface; 15 meters **39.** 1,995 feet **40.** Increase; 14°F

Chapter 9 Mastery Test A

1. A **2.** C **3.** D **4.** D **5.** C **6.** C **7.** 3^2 **8.** $(-10)^4$ **9.** 3^3 **10.** 8^1 or 8 **11.** 5^6 **12.** 2^3 **13.** 7^4 **14.** 64 **15.** −32 **16.** between 2 and 3 **17.** between 8 and 9 **18.** irrational **19.** irrational **20.** 64 cm² **21.** 225 ft² **22.** 8 in.³ **23.** 125 ft³ **24.** 10 in. **25.** 9.2 cm **26.** 12 feet **27.** 8.49 centimeters **28.** $x = 81 \div 3$ or 27 **29.** 36 **30.** 81

Chapter 9 Mastery Test B

1. C **2.** B **3.** C **4.** D **5.** A **6.** C **7.** 8^2 **8.** $(-b)^3$ **9.** 7^3 **10.** 9^3 **11.** 3^{10} **12.** 5^2 **13.** 6^4 **14.** −512 **15.** 1,024 **16.** 3, 4 **17.** 5, 6 **18.** irrational **19.** rational **20.** 16 m² **21.** 196 ft² **22.** 125 cm³ **23.** 216 ft³ **24.** 10.6 in. **25.** 15 ft **26.** 9 inches **27.** 7.14 inches **28.** 121 **29.** $x = 225 \div 5$ or 45 **30.** 256

Chapter 10 Mastery Test A

1. D **2.** A **3.** B **4.** A **5.** 14 in. **6.** 45 ft **7.** sphere **8.** rectangular prism **9.** triangular prism **10.** 324 in.² **11.** 287 mm² **12.** 352 cm² **13.** 288 in.² **14.** 810 cm³ **15.** 2,143.6 in.³ **16.** 28,260 in.³ **17.** 84.78 in.² **18.** 193.5 ft² **19.** 48.88 m² **20.** 382.5 mm²

Chapter 10 Mastery Test B

1. D **2.** B **3.** B **4.** C **5.** 20 in. **6.** 61 ft **7.** cone **8.** cylinder **9.** hexagonal prism **10.** 234 in.² **11.** 145 mm² **12.** 262 cm² **13.** 468 in.² **14.** 853.3 cm³ **15.** 904.32 in.³ **16.** 33,761.3 in.³ **17.** 267.3 cm³ **18.** 180 ft² **19.** 51.84 m² **20.** 459 mm²

Chapter 11 Mastery Test A

1. B **2.** D **3.** A **4.** B **5.** C **6.** A **7.** $x = 15$ **8.** $x > -3$ **9.** Yes **10.** range: −19, 1, −1, −11, −19 **11.** range: 39, 17, −3, 17, 39 **12.** Quadrant III **13.** Quadrant II **14.** (−2, 0) **15.** (0, −1) **16–17,** check students' graphs. **16.** Point T should be located at (4, 0). **17.** Point Q should be located at (0, 6). **18.** $x = -3, 0, 3$; Check students' graphs; the line should pass through (−3, 0), (0, 3), and (3, 6). **19.** $-5 \le y \le -2$ **20.** domain: $-1 \le x \le 5$ range: $-2 \le y \le 5$

Chapter 11 Mastery Test B

1. B **2.** D **3.** C **4.** B **5.** D **6.** C **7.** $x = 0$ **8.** $x > 4$ **9.** No **10.** range: 4, 0, 4, 9, 16 **11.** range: −24, −6, 4, 4, 0 **12.** I **13.** IV **14.** (7, 2) **15.** (−7, 5) **16–17,** check students' graphs. **16.** Point T should be located at (5, 1) **17.** Point Q should be located at (−3, −6) **18.** $x = -2, -1, 0$; Check students' graphs; the line should pass through (−2, 0), (−1, 3), and (0, 6). **19.** $-2 \le y \le 22$ **20.** domain: $-1 \le x \le 5$ range: $-2 \le y \le 5$

Chapter 12 Mastery Test A

1. A **2.** A **3.** C **4.** 45° **5.** 25° **6.** adjacent; supplementary **7.** vertical; equal **8.** 105° **9.** 75° **10.** 35° **11.** 128° **12.** No; two pairs of corresponding angles are not equal. **13.** quadrilateral; parallelogram **14.** right isosceles triangle **15.** $x = 5.5$ **16.** (2, 4), (0, 4), (0, 5), (−1, 5), (−1, 2), (0, 2), (0, 3), (2, 3) **17.** 4 lines **18.** 1 line **19.** (0, −4), (4, −4), (2, −1) **20.** (0, 0), (0, 5), (−2, 0), (−2, 5)

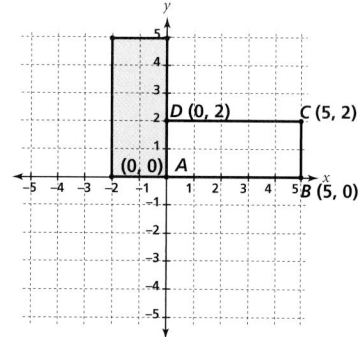

Chapter 12 Mastery Test B

1. B **2.** B **3.** A **4.** 35° **5.** 20° **6.** vertical; equal **7.** adjacent; supplementary **8.** 60° **9.** 120° **10.** $x = 30°$ **11.** $x = 110°$
12. Yes, because both triangles have equal corresponding angles.
13. quadrilateral; parallelogram; rectangle; square **14.** scalene triangle
15. $x = 8.1$ units **16.** $(2, -2), (4, -2), (4, -3), (5, -3), (5, 0), (4, 0),$ $(4, -1), (2, -1)$ **17.** 2 lines **18.** 0 lines **19.** $(-2, 3), (1, 6), (1, 3)$
20. $(2, 2), (-2, 2), (0, -2)$

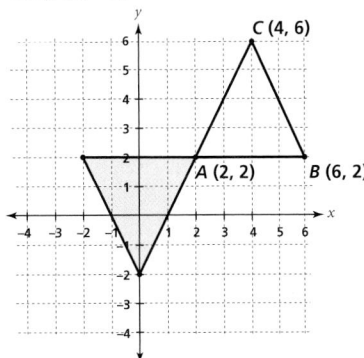

Chapter 13 Mastery Test A

1. A **2.** D **3.** B **4.** B **5.** 4
6. Sample graph:

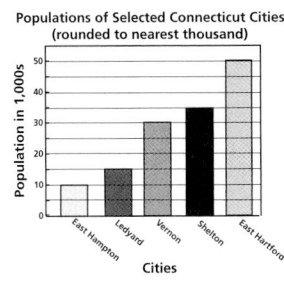

7. 40 votes **8.** 16 votes **9.** 15 **10.** 14.5 or $14\frac{1}{2}$ **11.** 11 **12.** 2, 11
13. 5, 9 **14.** 2 **15.** independent

Chapter 13 Mastery Test B

1. B **2.** D **3.** A **4.** D **5.** 3
6. Sample graph:

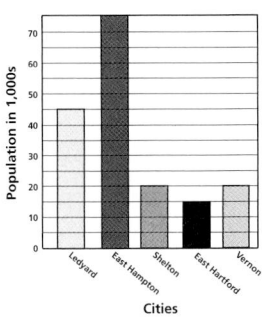

7. Candidate B **8.** 20 **9.** $11.8\overline{3}$ **10.** 13 **11.** 13 **12.** 2, 12 **13.** 7, 11
14. 5 **15.** dependent

Midterm Mastery Test

1. B **2.** C **3.** B **4.** C **5.** D **6.** C **7.** D **8.** A **9.** C **10.** D **11.** $x = \frac{7}{12}$

12. 30,000

13.
$$\begin{array}{r} 3{,}271 \\ +\ \ 676 \\ \hline 3{,}947 \end{array} \qquad \begin{array}{r} 3{,}947 \\ -\ 3{,}271 \\ \hline 676 \end{array} \ \text{or} \ \begin{array}{r} 3{,}947 \\ -\ \ 676 \\ \hline 3{,}271 \end{array}$$
14. $128 \div 4 = 32$
$$\begin{array}{r} 32 \\ \times\ 4 \\ \hline 128 \end{array}$$

15. 215_{10} **16.** $15{,}643_{10}$ **17.** $15c$ **18.** $\frac{4}{5}$ **19.** $\frac{6}{7}$ **20.** 27.02

21. $12.48y$ **22.** $\frac{5}{16}$ **23.** $\frac{4m}{7}$ **24.** $\frac{2n}{15}$ **25.** Sample answer: $\frac{1}{4}; \frac{2}{8}$

26. Sample estimate: 3,500 **27.** Sample estimate: 30,000

28. Sample estimate: 5,000 **29.** Sample estimate: 20 **30.** $x = 37$

31. 3.91 **32.** 3.5065×10^{-5} **33.** $13n$ **34.** $n - 4$ **35.** 0.06 **36.** 741%

37. $4(x + 3y)$ **38.** $d(c + e)$ or $d(e + c)$ **39.** $>$ **40.** 13 **41.** 240

42. 12 gallons **43.** 1,530 miles **44.** 65 miles **45.** $\frac{9}{20}$

Final Mastery Test

1. A **2.** B **3.** D **4.** C **5.** C **6.** C **7.** A **8.** D **9.** A **10.** B **11.** D

12. D **13.** A **14.** C **15.** A **16.** 900,000

17.
$$\begin{array}{r} 427 \\ -\ 318 \\ \hline 109 \end{array} \qquad \begin{array}{r} 318 \\ +\ 109 \\ \hline 427 \end{array} \ \text{or} \ \begin{array}{r} 109 \\ +\ 318 \\ \hline 427 \end{array}$$
18. 1101001_2 **19.** 410_5 **20.** $1\frac{1}{3}$

21. 1.403 **22.** $\frac{5x}{12}$ **23.** 131.86 **24.** Possible estimate: 4,000

25. Possible estimate: 3,200 **26.** Possible estimate: 5 **27.** Possible estimate: 5,000 **28.** $>$ **29.** 21 **30.** tenths; 0.3 **31.** composite

32. 6 **33.** $6(3 + 2b)$ **34.** 72 **35.** 16 ft **36.** $6\frac{2}{3}$ mph **37.** 150 ft

38. 5 **39.** 21 **40.** 16° F **41.** $\frac{1}{2}$, 50% **42.** $x = 8$ **43.** 30 m, 56.25 m²

44. 75.36 in., 452.16 in.² **45.** 512 in.³ **46.** 144 in.² **47.** 682 m²

48. 47.25 mm² **49.** 213.60 ft² or $68 + 20\sqrt{53}$ ft² **50.** 1,056 mm³

51. 256 ft³ **52.** Quadrant III **53.** Quadrant I **54.** $(2, -4)$

55. $(-3, 1)$ **56.** $-15, 1, -3, -24, -80$ **57.** domain: $-3 \le x \le 2$; range: $-1 \le y \le 4$ **58.** $(2, 0)\ (3, 0)\ (4, 2)\ (1, 2)$ **59.** 1 line **60.** 6 lines

61. $(1, 6)\ (3, 5)$ **62.** $(-3, -1)\ (-5, -1)\ (-3, 4)\ (-5, 4)$

63. $(2, 1)\ (2, 3)\ (7, 1)\ (7, 3)$ **64.** 20 times **65.** 3 times **66.** 45 votes

67. 57.8% **68.** 152° **69.** $\frac{1}{4}$ **70.** $\frac{3}{4}$

Teacher Questionnaire

Attention Teachers! As publishers of *Mathematics: Pathways,* we would like your help in making this textbook more valuable to you. Please take a few minutes to fill out this survey. Your feedback will help us to better serve you and your students.

1. What is your position and major area of responsibility? _____

   _____

   _____

2. Briefly describe your setting:

   ____ regular education ____ special education ____ adult basic education

   ____ community college ____ university ____ other _____

3. The enrollment in your classroom includes students with the following (check all that apply):

   ____ at-risk for failure ____ low reading ability ____ behavior problems

   ____ learning disabilities ____ ESL ____ other _____

4. Grade level of your students: _____

5. Racial/ethnic groups represented in your classes (check all that apply):

   ____ African-American ____ Asian ____ Caucasian ____ Hispanic

   ____ Native American ____ Other

6. School Location:

   ____ urban ____ suburban ____ rural ____ other _____

7. What reaction did your students have to the materials? (Include comments about the cover design, lesson format, illustrations, etc.)

   _____

   _____

   _____

8. What features in the student text helped your students the most?

   _____

   _____

   _____

9. What features in the student text helped your students the least? Please include suggestions for changing these to make the text more relevant.

_____

_____

10. How did you use the Teacher's Edition and support materials, and what features did you find to be the most helpful?

_____

_____

11. What activity from the program did your students benefit from the most? Please briefly explain.

_____

_____

_____

12. Optional: Share an activity that you used to teach the materials in your classroom that enhanced the learning and motivation of your students.

_____

_____

_____

Several activities will be selected to be included in future editions. Please include your name, address, and phone number so we may contact you for permission and possible payment to use the material.

Thank you!

▼ fold in thirds and tape shut at the top ▼

BUSINESS REPLY MAIL

FIRST-CLASS MAIL   PERMIT NO.12   CIRCLE PINES MN

POSTAGE WILL BE PAID BY ADDRESSEE

AGS Publishing   ATTN: Marketing Support
4201 WOODLAND ROAD
PO BOX 99
CIRCLE PINES MN 55014-9911

NO POSTAGE
NECESSARY
IF MAILED
IN THE
UNITED STATES

Name: _____
School: _____
Address: _____
City/State/ZIP: _____
Phone: _____